Langenscheidt

Pocket Chinese Dictionary

Chinese – English
English – Chinese

Edited by the
Langenscheidt Editorial Staff

Langenscheidt

New York · Berlin · Munich · Vienna · Zurich

Compiled by LEXUS with

吴乐军 (*Emma Lejun Wu*)
张晨阳 (*Lulu Langtree*)
Jim Weldon
Gaius Moore
Kyoko Galloway

General editor: Peter Terrell

© *2005 Langenscheidt KG, Berlin and Munich*
Printed in Germany

05 06 07 08 09 * 5 4 3 2 1

Preface

Here is a new dictionary of English and Chinese, a tool with some 40,000 references for those who work with the English and Chinese languages at beginner's or intermediate level.

Focusing on modern usage, the dictionary offers coverage of everyday language, including vocabulary from areas such as computers and business.

The Chinese in this dictionary is mainland Chinese, written in simplified characters, with pinyin pronunciation. A short appendix of important Taiwanese equivalents in traditional characters has also been included.

The two sides of this dictionary, the English-Chinese and the Chinese-English, are quite different in structure and purpose. The English-Chinese is designed for productive usage, for self-expression in Chinese. The Chinese-English, which can also be accessed through a specially compiled radical index, is a decoding dictionary, a dictionary to enable the native speaker of English to understand Chinese.

Clarity of presentation has been a major objective. The editors of this book have set out to provide the means to enable you, the user of the dictionary, to get straight to the translation that fits a particular context of use. Is the *mouse* you need for your computer, for example, the same in Chinese as the *mouse* you don't want in the house? Is *flimsy* referring to furniture the same in Chinese as *flimsy* referring to an excuse? The English-Chinese dictionary is rich in sense distinctions like this – and in translation options tied to specific, identified senses.

Grammatical or function words are treated in some detail, on both the English-Chinese and the Chinese-English sides. And a large number of idiomatic phrases are given to show how the two languages correspond in context.

All in all, this is a book full of information, which will, we hope, become a valuable part of your language toolkit.

Contents

How to use the dictionary

To get the most out of your dictionary you should understand how and where to find the information you need. Whether you are writing a text in Chinese or want to understand a text in Chinese, the following pages should help.

1. How and where do I find a word?

1.1 English headwords. The English word list is arranged in alphabetical order.

Sometimes you might want to look up terms made up of two separate words, for example **antivirus program**, or hyphenated words, for example **absent-minded**. These words are treated as though they were a single word and their alphabetical ordering reflects this. Compound words like **bookseller**, **bookstall**, **bookstore** are also listed in alphabetical order.

The only exception to this strict alphabetical ordering is made for English phrasal verbs – words like ♦**go off**, ♦**go out**, ♦**go up**. These are positioned directly after their main verb (in this case **go**), rather than being scattered around in alphabetical positions.

1.2 Chinese headwords. The Chinese word list is arranged in English alphabetical order by being sorted on the romanization system, pinyin. So if you know how a word is pronounced, or how it is written in pinyin, you can look it up straightforwardly.

If, however, you are decoding a Chinese character, and have no idea how it is pronounced or written in pinyin, then you will have to make use of the Radical Index in order to find out the pinyin for the character in question. An explanation of the Radical Index is given on page 14.

1.3 Running heads

If you are looking for an English or a Chinese word you can use the **running heads** printed in bold in the top corner of each page. The running head on the left tells you the *first* headword or compound on the left-hand page and the one on the right tells you the *last* headword or compound on the right-hand page.

2. Swung dashes

2.1 A swung dash (~) replaces the entire headword when the headword is repeated within an entry:

sly jiǎohuá 狡猾; *on the* **~** mìmì 秘密

Here *on the* **~** means *on the sly*.

2.2 When a headword changes form in an entry, for example if it is put in the past tense or in the plural, then the past tense or plural ending is added to the swung dash - but only if the rest of the word doesn't change:

fluster *v/t* shǐ jǐnzhāng 使紧张; *get* **~ed** jǐnzhāng 紧张

fore: *come to the* **~** tuō yǐng ér chū 脱颖而出

But:

horrify: *I was horrified* wǒ bèi xiàhuàile 我被吓坏了

★come back huílái 回来; *it came back to me* wǒ xiǎng qǐláile 我想起来了

2.3 Double or treble headwords are replaced by a single swung dash:

♦**hold on** *(wait,* TELEC*)* děngyíxià 等一下; *now* **~** *a minute!* biézháojí! 别着急！

♦**measure up to:** **~X** dádào X de biāozhǔn 达到 X 的标准

3. What do the different typefaces mean?

3.1 All Chinese and English headwords and the Arabic numerals differentiating between English parts of speech appear in **bold**:

alcoholic 1 *n* xùjiǔ zhě 酗酒者 **2** *adj* hán jiǔjīng 含酒精

3.2 *italics* are used for:

   a) abbreviated grammatical labels: *adj, adv, v/i, v/t* etc
   b) all the indicating words which are the signposts pointing to the correct translation for your needs
   c) explanations

mailbox *(in street)* yóutǒng 邮筒; *(for house, e-mail)* xìnxiāng 信箱

Thai 1 *adj* Tàiguó 泰国 **2** *n* (*person*) Tàiguó rén 泰国人; (*language*) Tàiguó yǔ 泰国语

serve 1 *n* (*in tennis*) fāqiú 发球 **2** *v/t food, meal* duānshang 端上; *customer in store* zhāodài 招待; *one's country, the people* fúwù 服务

水面 **shuǐmiàn** surface (*of water*)

伤感情 **shānggǎnqíng** hurt (*emotionally*)

把 **bǎ** *measure word for knives and chairs*; 一把刀 **yìbǎ dāo** a knife; 一把钳子 **yìbǎ qiánzi** a pair of pliers/pincers ◊ (*marking an object moved for emphasis to the start of a sentence*): 我要把车修了 **wǒ yào bǎ chē xiūle** I'll have the car repaired

3.3 All phrases (examples and idioms) are given in **secondary bold italics**:

剩 **shèng** remain, be left over; 没剩什么 **méishèng shénme** there is nothing left

vent *n* (*for air*) tōngfēng kǒng 通风孔; *give ~ to feelings, emotions* fàxiè 发泄

3.4 The normal typeface is used for the translations.

3.5 If a translation is given in italics, and not in the normal typeface, this means that the translation is more of an *explanation* in the other language and that an explanation has to be given because there is no real equivalent:

stag party hūnqián nánzi jùhuì 婚前男子聚会

阿姨 **āyí** auntie (*used also to address a woman of an age similar to one's parents*)

4. What do the various symbols and abbreviations tell you?

4.1 A solid black lozenge is used to indicate a phrasal verb:

♦**auction off** *v/t* pāimài diào 拍卖掉

4.2 A white lozenge is used to divide up longer entries into more easily digested chunks of related bits of text:

a, an ◊ (*no translation*): *~ bus* gōnggòng qìchē 公共汽车; *I'm ~ student* wǒ shì xuésheng 我是学生 ◊ (*with a measure word*) yī 一; *can I have ~ cup of coffee?* qǐng gěi wǒ yìbēi kāfēi? 请给我一杯咖啡?; *five men and ~ woman* wǔge nánde yíge nǚde 五个男的一个女的 ◊ *(per)*: *$50 ~ time* yícì wǔshí měiyuán 一次五十美元

It is also used, in the Chinese-English dictionary, to split different translations when the part of speech of each translation is different:

白 **bái** white ◊ in vain ◊ family name

冷冻 **lěngdòng** freeze ◊ frozen

4.3 The abbreviation F tells you that the word or phrase is used colloquially rather than in formal contexts. The abbreviation V warns you that a word or phrase is vulgar or taboo. Be careful how you use these words.

4.4 The symbol ⇩ means that a Taiwanese equivalent translation is given in the Taiwanese appendix on pages 669-671.

4.5 A colon before an English or Chinese word or phrase means that usage is restricted to this specific example (at least as far as this dictionary's choice of vocabulary is concerned):

accord: *of one's own ~* zìyuàn 自愿

通缉 **tōngjí**: 被通缉 **bèi tōngjí** wanted

4.6 The letters X and Y are used to indicate insertion points for other words if you are building a complete sentence in Chinese, for example:

grateful gǎnjī 感激; *be ~ to X* duì X xīncún gǎnjī 对 X 心存感激

pelt 1 *v/t*: *~ X with Y* jiāng Y tóuxiàng X 将 Y 投向 X

Suspension points (...) are used in a similar way:

below 1 *prep* zài ... de xiàmian 在 ... 的下面

5. Does the dictionary deal with grammar too?

5.1 All English headwords are given a part of speech label, unless, in normal modern English, the headword is only used as one part of speech and so no confusion or ambiguity is likely. In these cases no part of speech label is needed.

abolish fèichú 废除

lastly zuìhòu 最后

glory *n* róngyù 荣誉

own[1] *v/t* yōngyǒu 拥有

5.2 Chinese headwords are not given part of speech labels. Where their English translations can be of more than one part of speech, then these are separated by a white lozenge. For example:

统计 **tǒngjì** statistics ◊ statistical

挖掘 **wājué** excavate ◊ excavation

5.3 Where a Chinese word has a grammatical function, this is illustrated:

被 **bèi** quilt ◊ (*passive indicator*): 被炒鱿鱼了 **bèi chǎo yóuyú le** be fired; 被淘汰 **bèi táotài** be eliminated

了 **le** (*particle indicating completed action*): 雨停了 **yǔtíngle** it has stopped raining ◊ (*particle indicating change of state*): 头发白了了 **tóufa báile** his hair is going gray; 我买了 **wǒ mǎi le** I'll take it ◊ (*for emphasis*): 你太好了 **nǐ tài hǎo le** that's very kind

6. de 的 with adjectives.

In translations of adjectives the word **de** 的 has been omitted. This should be added if you are using a Chinese adjective (especially one of more than one syllable) attributively before a noun. Usually the noun would also have to have more than one syllable:

faded *color, jeans* tuìsè 退色

faded jeans tuìsède niúzǎikù 退色的牛仔裤

The pronunciation of Chinese

All Chinese characters in this dictionary are accompanied by a romanized script known as pinyin. Not all pinyin letters, or groups of letters, are pronounced as you would normally expect them to be in English. The following is a guide to the pronunciation of pinyin.

Initial consonants

b	more abrupt than English, like p in spare
c	like ts in bets
ch	like ch in church, pronounced with the tip of the tongue curled back
d	more abrupt than English, like t in stare
g	more abrupt than English, like c in scare; always hard as in go or girl
h	like the Scottish pronunciation of loch, with a little friction in the throat
j	like j in jeep, pronounced with the lips spread as in a smile
k	pronounced with a slight puff of air as in cop
p	pronounced with a slight puff of air as in pop
q	like ch in cheap, pronounced with the lips spread as in a smile
r	like r in rung, pronounced with the tip of the tongue curled back
sh	like sh in shirt, pronounced with the tip of the tongue curled back
t	pronounced with a slight puff of air as in top
x	like sh in sheep, pronounced with the lips spread as in a smile
z	like ds in beds
zh	like j in judge, pronounced with the tip of the tongue curled back

Finals

a	as in father
ai	as in aisle
an	as in ran (with the a slightly longer as in ah); but: yan as in yen
ang	as in rang (with the a slightly longer as in ah)
ao	like ow in how
e	as in her
ei	as in eight
en	as in open
eng	like en in open and g

er	like *err* – but with the tongue curled back and the sound coming from the back of the throat
i	(1) as in maga*zi*ne
	(2) after c, ch, r, s, sh, z and zh like the i in b*i*rd
ia	like ya in *ya*rd
ian	similar to *yen*
iang	*i* (as in maga*zi*ne) merged with *ang* (above) – but without lengthening the *a*
iao	as in *yow*l
ie	like ye in *ye*s
in	as in th*in*
ing	as in th*ing*
iong	*i* (as in maga*zi*ne) merged with *ong* (below)
iu	like yo in *yo*ga
o	as in m*o*re
ou	as in d*ou*gh
ong	oong with oo as in s*oo*n
u	(1) as in r*u*le
	(2) after j, q and x like the 'u' sound in French t*u* or German *ü*ber
ua	w followed by *a* (above)
uai	similar to *why*
uan	w followed by *an* (above)
uang	w followed by *ang* (above)
ue	u (above) followed by e as in l*e*t
ui	similar to *way*
un	like uan in tr*uan*t
uo	similar to *war*
ü	as in French t*u* or German *ü*ber
üe	ü followed by e as in g*e*t

Tones

First tone, as in 鸡 **jī** (chicken): a high, level tone with the volume held constant.

Second tone, as in 极 **jí** (extreme, extremely): rises sharply from middle register and increasing in volume, shorter than the first tone; like a surprised 'what?'

Third tone, as in 脊 **jǐ** (ridge): starts low, then falls lower before rising again to a point slightly higher than the starting point; louder at the beginning and end than in the middle; slightly longer than the first tone.

Fourth tone, as in 季 **jì** (season): starts high then drops sharply in pitch and volume; like saying 'right' when agreeing to an instruction.

Abbreviations

adj	adjective	NAUT	nautical
adv	adverb	*pej*	pejorative
ANAT	anatomy	PHOT	photography
BIO	biology	PHYS	physics
BOT	botany	POL	politics
Br	British English	*prep*	preposition
CHEM	chemistry	*pron*	pronoun
COM	commerce,	*prov*	proverbial
	business	PSYCH	psychology
COMPUT	computers,	RAD	radio
	IT term	RAIL	railroad
conj	conjunction	REL	religion
EDU	education	s.o.	someone
ELEC	electricity,	SP	sports
	electronics	sth	something
F	familiar, colloquial	TECH	technology
fig	figurative	TELEC	telecommunications
FIN	financial	THEA	theatre
fml	formal usage	TV	television
GRAM	grammar	V	vulgar
hum	humorous	*v/i*	intransitive verb
interj	interjection	*v/t*	transitive verb
LAW	law	→	see
MATH	mathematics	®	registered
MED	medicine		trademark
MIL	military	⇩	Taiwanese
MOT	motoring		equivalent given in
MUS	music		the appendix

How to find Chinese characters in the Chinese-English dictionary using the Radical Index

How can I look up the meaning of a Chinese character if I don't know how to pronounce it? This is a problem that the Radical Index solves.

There are two sets of tables to be used: the Radical Chart and the Radical Index. The Radical Chart is a means for leading you into the Radical Index; and the Radical Index is a means for leading you to the entry in the Chinese-English dictionary.

1. First you have to identify the radical in the Chinese character which you want to look up. Then look for this radical in the Radical Chart on pages 14-15 and find its radical number.

2. Go to the Radical Index and find the section starting with the number allocated to the radical you have just looked up. This number is printed as a heading.

3. If this is a shortish section, you will be able to see the Chinese character you want without any difficulty. If this is a long section, you can use another device to home in on the character you are looking for.

4. Count the number of strokes in the character you are looking for (not including the strokes in the radical itself). The Chinese characters are listed according to their stroke count. The number to the left of the characters gives you the stroke count (minus the radical strokes) in each block of characters. This narrows down the list of characters you will have to scan through.

5. When you have found the character you are looking for in the Radical Index, you will see its pinyin pronunciation given. You can then go to the Chinese-English dictionary - which is ordered in English alphabetical order according to the pinyin pronunciation - and use this like an ordinary dictionary.

6. Some Chinese characters can be analyzed as having more than one possible radical. When this happens, we have used the radical which has the smallest number of strokes.

7. Some radicals have variants. These are listed after the main radical in both the Radical Chart and the Radical Index.

Radical Chart

1 stroke

1 　丶
2 　一
3 　丨
4 　丿
5 　乙, ⺄, 乛, 亅

2 strokes

6 　亠
7 　冫
8 　冖
9 　讠
10 　二
11 　十
12 　厂
13 　匚
14 　卜
15 　刂
16 　冂
17 　八, 丷
18 　人, 亻, 入
19 　勹
20 　几, 八
21 　几
22 　厶, 又
23 　又, 又
24 　廴
25 　阝 (left)
26 　阝 (right)
27 　卩, 㔾
28 　凵

30 　刀, ⺈
31 　力

3 strokes

32 　氵
33 　忄, 小
34
35 　屮, ⺶
36 　广
37 　门
38 　辶
39 　工
40 　土
41 　士
42 　艹
43 　大
44 　廾
45 　尢
46 　寸
47 　扌
48 　小, ⺌
49 　口
50 　口
51 　巾
52 　山
53 　彳
54 　彡
55 　夕
56 　夂
57 　犭
60 　彐, ⺕, 彑

4 strokes

61 　尸
62 　己, 已
63
64 　弓
65 　女
66 　幺
67 　子
68 　纟
69 　马
　　巛

70 　灬
71 　斗
72 　文
73 　方
74 　火
75 　心
76 　户
77 　礻
78 　王
79 　韦
80 　木
81 　犬
82 　歹
83 　车
84 　戈
85 　比
86 　瓦
87 　止
88 　攴
89 　日
90 　曰
91 　贝

92	见	129	疋，正	163	采	
93	父	130	皮	164	身	
94	牛，牛，牜			165	角	
95	手		**6 strokes**			
96	毛				**8 strokes**	
97	气	131	衣			
98	攵	132	羊，羌，羊	166	青	
99	片	133	米	167	其	
100	斤，⺁	134	耒	168	雨	
101	爪，⺥	135	老	169	齿	
102	月	136	耳	170	金	
103	欠	137	西，覀	171	隹	
104	风	138	页	172	鱼	
105	殳	139	庀			
106	聿，聿，聿	140	虫		**9 strokes**	
107	毋	141	缶			
108	水，水	142	舌	173	音	
		143	竹，⺮	174	革	
	5 strokes	144	白	175	骨	
		145	自	176	食	
109	穴	146	血	177	鬼	
110	立	147	舟			
111	疒	148	羽		**10 strokes**	
112	衤	149	艮，⻏			
113	示	150	糸	178	髟	
114	石					
115	龙		**7 strokes**		**11 strokes**	
116	业					
117	目	151	辛	179	鹿	
118	田	152	言			
119	罒	153	麦		**12 strokes**	
120	皿	154	走			
121	钅	155	赤	180	黑	
122	矢	156	豆	181	鼠	
123	禾	157	酉			
124	白	158	辰		**14 strokes**	
125	瓜	159	里			
126	鸟	160	足	182	鼻	
127	用	161	豸			
128	矛	162	谷			

Radical Index

甲 jiǎ
申 shēn
且 qiě
史 shǐ
央 yāng
凹 āo
出 chū
归 guī

5 师 shī
曳 yè

6 串 chuàn

7 非 fēi
畅 chàng

8 临 lín

4 丿

1 九 jiǔ
乃 nǎi
匕 bǐ

2 千 qiān
川 chuān
么 me
久 jiǔ
及 jí

3 乏 fá
午 wǔ
升 shēng
长 zhǎng,
   cháng
币 bì
反 fǎn
丹 dān
氏 shì

乌 wū

4 乎 hū
生 shēng
失 shī
乐 lè, yuè
丘 qiū

5 丢 diū
年 nián
乒 pāng
杀 shā
后 hòu
向 xiàng
兆 zhào

6 卵 luǎn
希 xī
囱 cōng
系 xì,
   jì

7 乖 guāi

8 拜 bài
垂 chuí
重 zhòng,
   chóng

9 乘 chéng

11 甥 shēng

13 孵 fū
舞 wǔ
睾 gāo

14 靠 kào

5 乙, ⺄, ⺄, ㄥ

乙 yǐ

1 刁 diāo

了 le, liǎo

2 飞 fēi
乞 qǐ
习 xí
也 yě

3 书 shū
以 yǐ
予 yǔ
孔 kǒng

4 电 diàn
民 mín
司 sī

5 买 mǎi

6 乱 luàn

7 乳 rǔ
承 chéng

14 豫 yù

6 亠

1 亡 wáng

2 六 liù

3 市 shì

4 亥 hài
交 jiāo
亦 yì

5 亩 mǔ
弃 qì

6 变 biàn
卒 zú
京 jīng
氓 máng
享 xiǎng
夜 yè

7 哀 āi
　亮 liàng
　亭 tíng
8 高 gāo
　离 lí
　衰 shuāi
　衷 zhōng
9 毫 háo
　率 shuài
　烹 pēng
10 就 jiù
　裹 xiè
12 膏 gāo
　裹 guǒ
　豪 háo
15 赢 yíng

7 冫

4 冰 bīng
　冲 chōng
　次 cì
　决 jué
5 冻 dòng
　况 kuàng
　冷 lěng
　冶 yě
6 净 jìng
8 准 zhǔn
　凋 diāo
　凉 liáng
　凌 líng
9 凑 còu
　减 jiǎn

14 凝 níng

8 冖

2 冗 rǒng
3 写 xiě
4 军 jūn
5 罕 hǎn
7 冠 guàn,
　　　guān

9 讠

2 订 dìng
　讣 fù
　讥 jī
　计 jì
　认 rèn
3 记 jì
　让 ràng
　讨 tǎo
　训 xùn
　讯 xùn
　议 yì
4 访 fǎng
　讽 fěng
　讳 huì
　讲 jiǎng
　诀 jué
　论 lùn
　设 shè
　讼 sòng
　许 xǔ
　讶 yà

5 词 cí
　评 píng
　识 shí
　诉 sù
　译 yì
　诈 zhà
　诊 zhěn
　证 zhèng
　诅 zǔ
　诋 dǐ
6 诧 chà
　诚 chéng
　该 gāi
　诡 guǐ
　话 huà
　诗 shī
　试 shì
　详 xiáng
　询 xún
　诘 jié
　诙 huī
7 诞 dàn
　诲 huì
　说 shuō,
　　　shuì
　诵 sòng
　诬 wū
　误 wù
　诱 yòu
　语 yǔ
8 调 diào,
　　　tiáo
　读 dú
　诽 fěi

课 kè
谅 liàng
诺 nuò
请 qǐng
谁 shuí
谈 tán
谊 yì
诿 wěi
9 谍 dié
谎 huǎng
谜 mí
谋 móu
谓 wèi
谐 xié
谚 yàn
10 谦 qiān
谤 bàng
谢 xiè
谣 yáo
11 谨 jǐn
谬 miù
12 谱 pǔ
13 遣 qiǎn
谵 zhān

10 二

二 èr
1 亏 kuī
2 云 yún
6 些 xiē

11 十

十 shí
2 支 zhī
3 古 gǔ
4 华 huá
协 xié
5 克 kè
6 卓 zhuó
卑 bēi
卖 mài
丧 sāng,
sàng
直 zhí
卒 zú
7 南 nán
8 真 zhēn
索 suǒ
9 啬 sè
10 博 bó
韩 hán
辜 gū

12 厂

厂 chǎng
2 厄 è
历 lì
厅 tīng
3 厉 lì
4 厌 yàn
压 yā
6 厕 cè
7 厚 hòu

厘 lí
8 原 yuán
9 厩 jiù
厢 xiāng
10 厨 chú
厦 xià,
shà
厥 jué
12 斯 sī
14 赝 yàn

13 匚

2 区 qū
巨 jù
匹 pǐ
4 匠 jiàng
5 匣 xiá
医 yī
8 匪 fěi
匿 nì

14 卜

卜 bǔ
3 卡 kǎ, qiǎ
外 wài
处 chù,
chǔ
占 zhàn
4 贞 zhēn
6 卧 wò
卓 zhuó

15 刂

3	刊	kān
4	创	chuàng
	刚	gāng
	划	huá, huà
	列	liè
	刑	xíng
	则	zé
	刘	liú
5	别	bié
	利	lì
	判	pàn
	刨	bào
	删	shān
6	刺	cì
	到	dào
	刮	guā
	刽	guì
	剂	jì
	刻	kè
	刹	chà, shā
	刷	shuā
	制	zhì
7	剑	jiàn
	剃	tì
	削	xiāo, xuē
8	剥	bō, bāo
	剧	jù
	剖	pōu
	剔	tī
9	副	fù

10	割	gē
	剩	shèng

16 冂

2	内	nèi
4	肉	ròu
	同	tóng
	网	wǎng
6	周	zhōu

17 八, 丷

	八	bā
2	分	fēn
	公	gōng
3	兰	lán
	只	zhǐ, zhī
4	并	bìng
	共	gòng
	关	guān
	兴	xīng, xìng
5	兑	duì
	兵	bīng
	弟	dì
6	单	dān, chán
	典	diǎn
	具	jù
	卷	juǎn, juàn
7	兹	zī
	前	qián

	首	shǒu
	差	chà, cī, chā, chāi
8	兼	jiān
9	黄	huáng
	兽	shòu
10	尊	zūn

18 人, 入

	人	rén
	入	rù
1	个	gè
2	仓	cāng
	从	cóng
	介	jiè
	今	jīn
3	丛	cóng
	令	lìng
4	合	hé
	会	huì
	企	qǐ
	全	quán
	伞	sǎn
	众	zhòng
	尬	gà
5	含	hán
	余	yú
6	命	mìng
	舍	shě, shè
10	禽	qín
	舒	shū

19 亻

1 亿 yì
2 仇 chóu
　化 huà
　仅 jǐn
　仆 pū, pú
　仁 rén
　仍 réng
　什 shí,
　　 shén
3 代 dài
　付 fù
　们 men
　他 tā
　仙 xiān
　仪 yí
　仗 zhàng
　仔 zǎi, zǐ
4 传 chuán
　伐 fá
　仿 fǎng
　份 fèn
　伏 fú
　伙 huǒ
　价 jià
　件 jiàn
　伦 lún
　任 rèn
　伤 shāng
　似 sì, shì
　伟 wěi
　伪 wěi
　伍 wǔ

　休 xiū
　仰 yǎng
　伊 yī
　优 yōu
　仲 zhòng
5 伴 bàn
　伯 bó
　但 dàn
　低 dī
　佛 fó
　估 gū
　何 hé
　伶 líng
　你 nǐ
　伸 shēn
　伺 cì
　体 tǐ
　位 wèi
　佣 yòng,
　　 yōng
　佑 yòu
　住 zhù
　作 zuò,
　　 zuō
6 侧 cè
　侈 chǐ
　供 gōng,
　　 gòng
　佳 jiā
　侥 jiǎo,
　　 yáo
　佬 lǎo
　例 lì
　侣 lǚ

　佩 pèi
　侨 qiáo
　使 shǐ
　侍 shì
　侠 xiá
　依 yī
　侦 zhēn
　侄 zhí
　侏 zhū
7 保 bǎo
　便 biàn
　促 cù
　俄 é
　俘 fú
　侯 hóu
　俭 jiǎn
　俊 jùn
　俐 lì
　俩 liǎ,
　　 liǎng
　俏 qiào
　侵 qīn
　俗 sú
　侮 wǔ
　信 xìn
　修 xiū
　俚 lǐ
　俑 yǒng
8 倍 bèi
　倡 chàng
　倒 dǎo,
　　 dào
　俯 fǔ
　候 hòu

健 jiàn	**20 勹**	6 凯 kǎi
借 jiè		凭 píng
俱 jù	1 勺 sháo	9 凰 huáng
倦 juàn	2 勾 gōu	12 凳 dèng
倾 qīng	勿 wù	
倚 yǐ	匀 yún	**23 厶**
债 zhài	3 包 bāo	
值 zhí	匆 cōng	2 允 yǔn
倌 guān	句 jù	3 台 tái
9 偿 cháng	4 匈 xiōng	去 qù
假 jiǎ,	5 甸 diàn	5 县 xiàn
jià	7 匍 pú	6 参 cān
傀 kuǐ	9 够 gòu	7 垒 lěi
偶 ǒu	匐 fú	8 能 néng
偏 piān		
停 tíng	**21 儿**	**24 又, 廴**
偷 tōu		
做 zuò	儿 ér	又 yòu
10 傲 ào	2 允 yǔn	1 叉 chā
傍 bàng	3 兄 xiōng	2 双 shuāng
储 chǔ	4 先 xiān	友 yǒu
傅 fù	充 chōng	劝 quàn
傧 bīn	光 guāng	支 zhī
11 催 cuī	5 克 kè	3 对 duì
傻 shǎ	兑 duì	发 fā, fà
12 僚 liáo	9 兜 dōu	圣 shèng
像 xiàng		4 观 guān
13 僵 jiāng	**22 几, 八**	欢 huān
僻 pì		戏 xì
14 儒 rú	几 jǐ	6 艰 jiān
15 儡 lěi	1 凡 fán	取 qǔ
	2 凤 fèng	受 shòu
	5 壳 ké, qiào	叔 shū
	秃 tū	7 叙 xù

8	难 nán,	陀 tuó
	nàn	阻 zǔ
11	叠 dié	6 降 jiàng,
		xiáng
25 廴		陋 lòu
		陌 mò
4	廷 tíng	限 xiàn
	延 yán	7 除 chú
6	建 jiàn	陡 dǒu
		险 xiǎn
26 卩, 巳		院 yuàn
		陨 yǔn
2	卫 wèi	8 陵 líng
3	印 yìn	陪 péi
	叩 kòu	陶 táo
5	即 jí	陷 xiàn
	却 què	9 隆 lóng
7	卸 xiè	随 suí
8	卿 qīng	隐 yǐn
		10 隘 ài
27 阝 L		隔 gé
		隙 xì
2	队 duì	11 障 zhàng
4	防 fáng	12 隧 suì
	阶 jiē	
	阳 yáng	**28 阝 R**
	阴 yīn	
	阵 zhèn	2 邓 dèng
	阱 jǐng	4 邦 bāng
5	阿 ā, ē	那 nà,
	陈 chén	nèi
	附 fù	邪 xié
	际 jì	5 邻 lín
	陆 lù	邮 yóu

6	郊 jiāo
	郎 láng
	耶 yé, yē
	郁 yù
	郑 zhèng
7	郡 jùn
8	部 bù
	都 dū, dōu
11	鄙 bǐ

29 凵

2	凶 xiōng
6	函 hán
	画 huà

30 刀, 𠂇

	刀 dāo
2	切 qiē
3	召 zhāo,
	zhào
4	负 fù
	色 sè,
	shǎi
	危 wēi
	争 zhēng
5	龟 guī
	免 miǎn
6	券 quàn
	兔 tù
9	剪 jiǎn
	象 xiàng
13	劈 pī

31 力

力 lì
2 办 bàn
  劝 quàn
3 加 jiā
  务 wù
  幼 yòu
4 动 dòng
  劣 liè
5 劫 jié
  励 lì
  男 nán
  助 zhù
6 劲 jìn
  努 nǔ
  势 shì
7 勃 bó
  勉 miǎn
  勋 xūn
  勇 yǒng
9 勘 kān
11 勤 qín

32 氵

2 汉 hàn
  汇 huì
  汁 zhī
3 池 chí
  汗 hàn
  江 jiāng
  汤 tāng
  污 wū

4 沧 cāng
  沉 chén
  泛 fàn
  沟 gōu
  沥 lì
  没 méi,
      mò
  沛 pèi
  汽 qì
  沙 shā
  汰 tài
  汪 wāng
  沃 wò
  汩 gǔ
5 波 bō
  泊 bó, pō
  法 fǎ
  沸 fèi
  河 hé
  沮 jǔ
  泪 lèi
  泌 mì
  沫 mò
  泥 ní
  泞 níng
  泡 pào
  泼 pō
  泣 qì
  浅 qiǎn
  泄 xiè
  泻 xiè
  沿 yán
  泳 yǒng
  油 yóu

  泽 zé
  沾 zhān
  沼 zhǎo
  治 zhì
  注 zhù
  沱 tuó
6 洛 luò
  测 cè
  洞 dòng
  洪 hóng
  浑 hún
  活 huó
  济 jǐ, jì
  浇 jiāo
  洁 jié
  津 jīn
  浓 nóng
  派 pài
  洽 qià
  洒 sǎ
  洼 wā
  洗 xǐ
  洋 yáng
  洲 zhōu
  浊 zhuó
  浏 liú
7 涤 dí
  浮 fú
  海 hǎi
  浩 hào
  涣 huàn
  渐 jiàn
  浸 jìn
  酒 jiǔ

浚 jùn
浪 làng
流 liú
润 rùn
涩 sè
涉 shè
涛 tāo
涕 tì
涂 tú
涡 wō
涎 xián
消 xiāo
涌 yǒng
浴 yù
涨 zhàng,
　　zhǎng
浣 huàn

8 淡 dàn
淀 diàn
涵 hán
涸 hé
混 hún,
　　hùn
淋 lín
清 qīng
深 shēn
渗 shèn
淌 tǎng
淘 táo
添 tiān
淆 xiáo
涯 yá
淹 yān
液 yè

淫 yín
淤 yū
渔 yú
渊 yuān
淇 qí
渎 dú

9 渤 bó
渡 dù
溉 gài
港 gǎng
湖 hú
滑 huá
溅 jiàn
渴 kě
溃 kuì
湿 shī
湍 tuān
湾 wān
温 wēn
游 yóu
渝 yú
渣 zhā
滞 zhì
滋 zī
渲 xuàn
湄 méi

10 滨 bīn
滚 gǔn
滥 làn
漓 lí
溜 liū, liù
滤 lù
满 mǎn
漠 mò

溺 nì, niào
溶 róng
溯 sù
滩 tān
滔 tāo
溪 xī
溢 yì
源 yuán
滓 zǐ
滂 pāng

11 滴 dī
漏 lòu
漫 màn
漂 piāo
漆 qī
漱 shù
演 yǎn
潢 huáng

12 澳 ào
潮 cháo
澈 chè
澄 chéng
潦 liǎo
潜 qián

13 濒 bīn
激 jī
澡 zǎo

15 瀑 bào, pù
17 灌 guàn

33 忄, 小

1 忆 yì
3 忙 máng

3	忏 chàn	惯 guàn		**34 宀**	
4	忱 chén	悸 jì			
	怀 huái	惊 jīng	*2*	宁 níng	
	快 kuài	惧 jù		它 tā	
	忧 yōu	情 qíng	*3*	安 ān	
	忡 chōng	惕 tì		守 shǒu	
	松 sōng	惋 wǎn		宇 yǔ	
	忸 niǔ	惜 xī		宅 zhái	
5	怖 bù	惘 wǎng		字 zì	
	怪 guài	惚 hū	*4*	宏 hóng	
	怜 lián	悴 cuì		牢 láo	
	怕 pà	*9* 惰 duò		宋 sòng	
	怯 qiè	愤 fèn		完 wán	
	性 xìng	慌 huāng		灾 zāi	
	怩 ní	惶 huáng	*5*	宝 bǎo	
6	恫 dòng,	慨 kǎi		宠 chǒng	
	tōng	愧 kuì		定 dìng	
	恨 hèn	惺 xīng		官 guān	
	恒 héng	愉 yú		审 shěn	
	恍 huǎng	愕 è		实 shí	
	恢 huī	*10* 慑 shè		宜 yí	
	恼 nǎo	慎 shèn		宙 zhòu	
	恰 qià	*11* 慷 kāng		宗 zōng	
	恸 tòng	慢 màn	*6*	宫 gōng	
7	悔 huǐ	*12* 懊 ào		客 kè	
	悯 mǐn	懂 dǒng		室 shì	
	悄 qiāo	憎 zēng		宪 xiàn	
	悟 wù	憔 qiáo		宣 xuān	
	悦 yuè	*13* 憾 hàn	*7*	宾 bīn	
	悚 sǒng	懒 lǎn		害 hài	
8	惭 cán	懈 xiè		家 jiā	
	惨 cǎn	*14* 懦 nuò		宽 kuān	
	悼 dào			宵 xiāo	
	惦 diàn			宴 yàn	

宰 zǎi

8 密 mì
寄 jì
寂 jì
宿 sù, xiǔ,
xiù

9 富 fù
寒 hán
寓 yù

10 寞 mò
寝 qǐn
塞 sāi, sài,
sè

11 察 chá
寡 guǎ
蜜 mì
赛 sài
寨 zhài

35 丬

3 壮 zhuàng
妆 zhuāng
4 状 zhuàng
6 将 jiāng

36 广

广 guǎng
3 庆 qìng
庄 zhuāng
4 庇 bì
床 chuáng
库 kù

序 xù
应 yìng,
yīng

5 底 dǐ
店 diàn
废 fèi
府 fǔ
庙 miào
庞 páng

6 庭 tíng
度 dù

7 唐 táng
席 xí
座 zuò

8 康 kāng
廊 láng
麻 má
庸 yōng

10 廓 kuò
廉 lián

11 腐 fǔ

15 鹰 yīng

16 靡 mí, mǐ

37 门

门 mén
1 闩 shuān
2 闪 shǎn
3 闭 bì
闯 chuǎng
问 wèn
4 间 jiān,
jiàn

闷 mēn,
mèn
闰 rùn
闲 xián

5 闹 nào
闸 zhá

6 阀 fá
阁 gé
闻 wén

7 阅 yuè
阄 jiū

8 阐 chǎn
阉 yān

9 阔 kuò
阑 lán

38 辶

2 边 biān
3 达 dá
过 guò
迈 mài
迄 qì
迁 qiān
巡 xún
迅 xùn
迂 yū
4 迟 chí
返 fǎn
还 huán
进 jìn
近 jìn
连 lián
违 wéi

	迎 yíng	8	逮 dǎi	**40 土**	
	远 yuǎn		逻 luó		
	运 yùn	9	遊 yóu		土 tǔ
	这 zhè,		逼 bī	3	场 chǎng
	zhèi		遍 biàn		地 dì
5	迪 dí		道 dào		圾 jī
	迭 dié		遏 è		在 zài
	迫 pò		遗 yí		寺 sì
	述 shù		遇 yù		尘 chén
6	迸 bèng,	10	遣 qiǎn		至 zhì
	bìng		遥 yáo		考 kǎo
	迹 jì		遢 ta	4	坝 bà
	迷 mí		遛 liū		坊 fāng,
	逆 nì	11	遭 zāo		fáng
	适 shì		遮 zhē		坟 fén
	送 sòng	12	遵 zūn		坏 huài
	逃 táo	13	避 bì		坚 jiān
	退 tuì		邀 yāo		均 jūn
	选 xuǎn		邂 xiè		坑 kēng
	逊 xùn	15	邋 lā		块 kuài
	追 zhuī				坍 tān
	逅 hòu	**39 工**			坛 tán
7	递 dì				址 zhǐ
	逗 dòu		工 gōng		坠 zhuì
	逢 féng	2	功 gōng		坐 zuò
	逛 guàng		巧 qiǎo	5	垃 lā
	逝 shì		左 zuǒ		坯 pī
	速 sù	4	攻 gōng		坪 píng
	通 tōng		巫 wū		坡 pō
	透 tòu		贡 gòng		坦 tǎn
	途 tú	6	项 xiàng		坞 wù
	造 zào				幸 xìng
	逐 zhú				垄 lǒng
	逍 xiāo			6	城 chéng

	垫 diàn	*4*	声 shēng		苦 kǔ
	垢 gòu		志 zhì		茅 máo
	垮 kuǎ	*7*	壶 hú		茂 mào
	型 xíng	*9*	喜 xǐ		苗 miáo
7	埃 āi	*10*	鼓 gǔ		苹 píng
	埋 mái	*11*	嘉 jiā		若 ruò
	埔 pǔ	*17*	馨 xīn		苔 tái
8	堵 dǔ				英 yīng
	堆 duī		**42** 艹		茁 zhuó
	堕 duò				茉 mò
	基 jī	*1*	艺 yì	*6*	草 cǎo
	培 péi	*2*	艾 ài, yì		茬 chá
	域 yù		节 jié		茶 chá
9	堡 bǎo	*3*	芒 máng		荡 dàng
	堤 dī		芝 zhī		荒 huāng
	堪 kān	*4*	芭 bā		荤 hūn
	塔 tǎ		苍 cāng		茧 jiǎn
	堰 yàn		芳 fāng		荐 jiàn
10	塑 sù		芬 fēn		荔 lì
	塌 tā		花 huā		茫 máng
	塘 táng		芥 jiè		荣 róng
	填 tián		劳 láo		药 yào
11	境 jìng		芦 lú		荫 yīn
	墙 qiáng		芹 qín		荨 xún
	墅 shù		苏 sū	*7*	荷 hé
	墟 xū		苇 wěi		获 huò
12	增 zēng		芯 xīn		莱 lái
13	壁 bì		芽 yá		莉 lì
17	壤 rǎng	*5*	茄 qié, jiā		莲 lián
			苯 běn		莽 mǎng
	41 士		范 fàn		莫 mò
			苟 gǒu		莓 méi
	士 shì		茎 jīng		莺 yīng
3	吉 jí		苛 kē	*8*	堇 jǐn

菠 bō
菜 cài
菲 fēi
菇 gū
菊 jú
菌 jūn, jùn
菱 líng
萝 luó
萌 méng
菩 pú
萨 sà
萄 táo
萎 wěi
萧 xiāo
营 yíng
著 zhù
萦 yíng
9 葱 cōng
蒂 dì
董 dǒng
葛 gě
蒋 jiǎng
葵 kuí
落 luò, là
募 mù
葡 pú
惹 rě
葬 zàng
10 蓝 lán
蒙 méng
墓 mù
幕 mù
蓬 péng
蒜 suàn

蓄 xù
蒸 zhēng
蓓 bèi
11 蔼 ǎi
蔽 bì
蔓 mán,
màn,
wàn
蔑 miè
摹 mó
慕 mù
蔗 zhè
12 蕉 jiāo
蔬 shū
蕨 jué
蕃 fān
13 薄 bó, bò,
báo
蕾 lěi
薯 shǔ
薪 xīn
14 藏 cáng,
zàng
藉 jí
15 藕 ǒu
藤 téng
16 蘑 mó
藻 zǎo

大 dà
1 太 tài
3 夺 duó

尖 jiān
夸 kuā
5 奔 bēn,
bèn
奋 fèn
奈 nài
奇 qí
6 奖 jiǎng
美 měi
契 qì
牵 qiān
7 套 tào
8 奢 shē
爽 shuǎng
9 奥 ào

3 异 yì
4 弄 lòng,
nòng
11 弊 bì

尤 yóu

寸 cùn
3 寻 xún
导 dǎo
寺 sì
4 寿 shòu

6 封 fēng
  耐 nài
7 辱 rǔ
  射 shè
8 尉 wèi

47 弋

式 shì

48 扌

1 扎 zā, zhā, zhá
2 扒 bā, pá
  打 dǎ
  扑 pū
  扔 rēng
3 扬 yáng
  执 zhí
  扣 kòu
  扩 kuò
  扫 sǎo
  托 tuō
4 抑 yì
  找 zhǎo
  折 zhé
  抓 zhuā
  把 bǎ
  扳 bān
  扮 bàn
  报 bào
  抄 chāo
  扯 chě

抖 dǒu
扼 è
扶 fú
抚 fǔ
护 hù
技 jì
拒 jù
抗 kàng
抠 kōu
拟 nǐ
扭 niǔ
抛 pāo
批 pī
抢 qiǎng
扰 rǎo
抒 shū
投 tóu
5 押 yā
拥 yōng
择 zé
招 zhāo
拙 zhuō
拗 niù, ǎo, ào
拔 bá
拌 bàn
抱 bào
拨 bō
拆 chāi
抽 chōu
担 dān, dàn
抵 dǐ
拐 guǎi

拣 jiǎn
拘 jū
拉 lā
拢 lǒng
抹 mǒ
拇 mǔ
拧 nǐng
拍 pāi
抨 pēng
披 pī
抬 tái
拖 tuō
拓 tuò
6 挣 zhēng
拯 zhěng
指 zhǐ
拽 zhuài, yè
按 àn
持 chí
挡 dǎng
拱 gǒng
挂 guà
挥 huī
挤 jǐ
括 kuò
挪 nuó
拼 pīn
拾 shí
拴 shuān
挑 tiāo
挺 tǐng
挖 wā
挝 wō

7	振 zhèn		推 tuī	12	撰 zhuàn
	捉 zhuō	9	握 wò		撞 zhuàng
	挨 āi, ái		援 yuán		播 bō
	捕 bǔ		揍 zòu		撤 chè
	挫 cuò		插 chā		撑 chēng
	捣 dǎo		搽 chá		撮 cuō
	捍 hàn		搀 chān		撅 juē
	换 huàn		搓 cuō		捻 niǎn
	捡 jiǎn		搭 dā		撬 qiào
	捐 juān		搁 gē		撒 sā, sǎ
	捆 kǔn		搅 jiǎo		撕 sī
	捏 niē		揭 jiē	13	擀 gǎn
	损 sǔn		揩 kāi		操 cāo
	捅 tǒng		揽 lǎn		撼 hàn
	挽 wǎn		搂 lǒu		擂 léi, lèi
8	掩 yǎn		揉 róu		擅 shàn
	掷 zhì		搔 sāo	14	擤 xǐng
	捺 nà		搜 sōu		擦 cā
	措 cuò		提 tí	16	攒 zǎn
	掉 diào	10	携 xié	17	攘 rǎng
	接 jiē		摇 yáo		
	捷 jié		摆 bǎi		**49 小, ⸌**
	据 jù		搬 bān		
	掘 jué		搏 bó		小 xiǎo
	控 kòng		搐 chù	1	少 shǎo,
	掠 lüè		搞 gǎo		shào
	描 miáo		摸 mō	2	尔 ěr
	捻 niǎn		摄 shè	3	当 dāng,
	排 pái		摊 tān		dàng
	捧 pěng		搪 táng	3	尘 chén
	掐 qiā	11	摘 zhāi		尖 jiān
	授 shòu		摧 cuī	4	肖 xiāo,
	探 tàn		撇 piē, piě		xiào
	掏 tāo		摔 shuāi	5	尚 shàng

6	尝 cháng		吹 chuī		呦 yōu
7	党 dǎng		呆 dāi		呸 pēi
8	常 cháng		吨 dūn		和 hé, hè,
	堂 táng		吠 fèi		huò, hú
9	辉 huī		否 fǒu		呜 wū
	掌 zhǎng		告 gào		知 zhī

50 口

	口 kǒu		吼 hǒu	6	哆 duō
2	叭 bā		君 jūn		哈 hā
	叮 dīng		吭 kēng		哄 hǒng
	号 háo,		呕 ǒu		咯 gē
	hào		启 qǐ		咳 ké, hāi
	叫 jiào		吮 shǔn		哪 nǎ, něi
	可 kě		听 tīng		品 pǐn
	另 lìng		吞 tūn		哇 wā
	叹 tàn		吻 wěn		响 xiǎng
	叶 yè		呀 ya		哑 yǎ
	右 yòu		吟 yín		咽 yān,
	叨 dāo		员 yuán		yàn
3	吃 chī		吱 zhī		咬 yǎo
	吊 diào		吝 lìn		哟 yōu
	各 gè	5	哎 āi		咱 zán
	吗 ma		咕 gū		咨 zī
	名 míng		呵 hē		咧 liē, liě
	吐 tǔ		呼 hū		咪 mī
	吸 xī		咀 jǔ		哝 nóng
	吓 xià, hè		咖 kā, gā		虽 suī
	吁 yù, xū		咙 lóng	7	啊 ā, á, a
	吉 jí		鸣 míng		唉 āi, ài
4	吧 ba		呢 ne, ní		哺 bǔ
	吵 chǎo		咆 páo		唇 chún
	呈 chéng		呻 shēn		哥 gē
			味 wèi		哼 hēng
			咒 zhòu		唤 huàn
			呱 guā		哨 shào

7	唆 suō		喧 xuān	14	嚎 háo
	哮 xiào		喻 yù		嚏 tì
	唁 yàn		嗒 dā		嚓 cā
	哲 zhé		喱 lí	15	嚣 xiāo,
	唠 lào		喙 huì		āo
	唧 jī		喔 ō, wol	17	嚼 jiáo,
	哦 ó, ò, é		喜 xǐ		jiào,
8	唱 chàng	10	嗓 sǎng		jué
	啡 fēi		嗜 shì		嚷 rǎng
	唬 hǔ		嗡 wēng		
	哗 huā,		嗅 xiù		
	huá		嘟 dū	**51 口**	
	啃 kěn		嗦 suo		
	啦 la		嗝 gé	2	囚 qiú
	啮 niè		嗳 ài, āi		四 sì
	啪 pā		嗨 hāi,	3	回 huí
	啤 pí		hēi		团 tuán
	商 shāng		嗬 hē		因 yīn
	售 shòu		嗯 ńg, ǹg	4	囤 dún
	唾 tuò	11	嘎 gā		困 kùn
	唯 wéi		嘛 má		围 wéi
	啸 xiào		嗽 sòu		园 yuán
	啄 zhuó		嘘 xū	5	固 gù
	喵 miāo		嘈 cáo		国 guó
	唿 hū	12	嘲 cháo		图 tú
	喋 dié		嘶 sī	7	圃 pǔ
9	喘 chuǎn		嘱 zhǔ		圆 yuán
	喊 hǎn		噜 lū	8	圈 quān
	喝 hē, hè		嘿 hēi		
	喉 hóu		噢 ō	**52 巾**	
	喀 kā	13	器 qì		
	喇 lǎ		噪 zào		巾 jīn
	喷 pēn		嘴 zuǐ	2	布 bù
	喂 wèi		噱 xué, jué		帅 shuài
				3	帆 fān

吊 diào
4 帐 zhàng
5 帚 zhǒu
帖 tiē
6 帮 bāng
带 dài
帝 dì
8 帷 wéi
9 幅 fú
帽 mào
10 幌 huǎng
12 幢 zhuàng

53 山

山 shān
3 岁 suì
屿 yǔ
4 岔 chà
岛 dǎo
岗 gāng
岖 qū
5 岸 àn
岭 lǐng
岩 yán
岳 yuè
6 炭 tàn
峡 xiá
峋 xún
7 峨 é
峰 fēng
峻 jùn
8 崩 bēng
崇 chóng

崎 qí
崖 yá
崭 zhǎn
9 嵌 qiàn
12 嶙 lín
18 巍 wēi

54 彳

3 行 xíng,
háng
4 彻 chè
役 yì
5 彼 bǐ
径 jìng
往 wǎng,
wàng
征 zhēng
6 待 dài
很 hěn
律 lǜ
衍 yǎn
7 徒 tú
8 得 dé, de,
děi
衔 xián
9 街 jiē
循 xún
御 yù
10 微 wēi
12 德 dé
13 衡 héng
14 徽 huī

55 彡

4 形 xíng
杉 shān
5 衫 shān
6 须 xū
8 彩 cǎi
彬 bīn
12 影 yǐng

56 夕

夕 xī
3 多 duō
岁 suì
8 梦 mèng

57 夂

2 冬 dōng
3 各 gè
4 条 tiáo
5 备 bèi
6 复 fù
7 夏 xià
9 惫 bèi

58 犭

2 犯 fàn
4 狂 kuáng
犹 yóu
5 狗 gǒu
狐 hú

狙 jū
狒 fèi
6 狠 hěn
狡 jiǎo
狮 shī
狭 xiá
狱 yù
独 dú
狩 shòu
7 狼 láng
狸 lí
8 猜 cāi
猎 liè
猫 māo
猛 měng
猪 zhū
猕 mí
9 猴 hóu
猾 huá
猩 xīng
猥 wěi
猬 wèi
13 獭 tà

59 饣

2 饥 jī
4 饭 fàn
饮 yǐn
饨 tún
饪 rèn
5 饱 bǎo
饯 jiàn
饰 shì

饲 sì
6 饼 bǐng
饵 ěr
饺 jiǎo
饶 ráo
蚀 shí
7 饿 è
馁 něi
8 馆 guǎn
馄 hún
馅 xiàn
9 馈 kuì
馊 sōu
11 馒 mán

60 彐, ⺕, ⺕

3 寻 xún
4 灵 líng
5 录 lù
帚 zhǒu
8 彗 huì

61 尸

尸 shī
1 尺 chǐ
2 尼 ní
3 尽 jìn
4 层 céng
局 jú
尿 niào
屁 pì
尾 wěi

5 届 jiè
居 jū
屈 qū
屉 tì
6 屏 bǐng,
píng
屎 shǐ
屋 wū
7 屑 xiè
展 zhǎn
8 屠 tú
9 屡 lǚ
属 shǔ
犀 xī
12 履 lǚ

62 己, 已

己 jǐ
已 yǐ
1 巴 bā
3 异 yì
导 dǎo
6 巷 xiàng

63 弓

弓 gōng
1 引 yǐn
3 弛 chí
4 张 zhāng
5 弧 hú
弥 mí
弦 xián

6	弯 wān		妻 qī		**65 幺**	
7	弱 ruò		始 shǐ			
8	弹 tán,		委 wěi		幺 xiāng	
	dàn		姓 xìng		幺 yāo	
9	强 qiáng		妾 qiè	1	幻 huàn	
	粥 zhōu	6	姜 jiāng	6	幽 yōu	
16	疆 jiāng		娇 jiāo			
			姥 lǎo		**66 子**	

64 女

			耍 shuǎ		子 zǐ	
	女 nǚ		娃 wá	2	孕 yùn	
2	奶 nǎi		姨 yí	3	存 cún	
	奴 nú		姻 yīn		孙 sūn	
3	妇 fù		姿 zī	4	孝 xiào	
	好 hǎo,		要 yāo		孜 zī	
	hào	7	娩 miǎn	5	孤 gū	
	奸 jiān		娘 niáng		学 xué	
	妈 mā		娱 yú		孟 mèng	
	如 rú		娴 xián	6	孩 hái	
	她 tā	8	婚 hūn			
	妄 wàng		婪 lán		**67 纟**	
	妃 fēi		婆 pó			
4	妒 dù		婉 wǎn	2	纠 jiū	
	妨 fáng		婴 yīng	3	红 hóng	
	妓 jì		婊 biǎo		级 jí	
	妙 miào	9	媒 méi		纪 jì	
	妥 tuǒ		嫂 sǎo		纫 rèn	
	妖 yāo		婿 xù		纤 xiān,	
	姊 zǐ	10	嫉 jí		qiàn	
	妞 niū		嫁 jià		约 yuē	
5	妹 mèi		媳 xí	4	纯 chún	
	姑 gū		嫌 xián		纺 fǎng	
	姐 jiě	11	嫩 nèn		纷 fēn	
	姆 mǔ	12	嬉 xī		纲 gāng	
		17	孀 shuāng			

纳 nà	绩 jì	驱 qū
纽 niǔ	绿 lù	5 驾 jià
纱 shā	绵 mián	驹 jū
纬 wěi	绳 shéng	驶 shǐ
纹 wén	维 wéi	驼 tuó
纸 zhǐ	绪 xù	驻 zhù
纵 zòng	续 xù	6 骇 hài
5 绊 bàn	缀 zhuì	骄 jiāo
经 jīng	综 zōng	骆 luò
练 liàn	9 编 biān	骂 mà
绍 shào	缔 dì	7 验 yàn
绅 shēn	缎 duàn	8 骑 qí
细 xì	缓 huǎn	9 骗 piàn
线 xiàn	缉 jī	骚 sāo
织 zhī	缆 lǎn	11 骡 luó
终 zhōng	缕 lǚ	14 骤 zhòu
组 zǔ	缅 miǎn	
绉 zhòu	缘 yuán	**69 巛**
6 绑 bǎng	10 缠 chán	
给 gěi, jǐ	缝 féng,	巢 cháo
绘 huì	fèng	
结 jiē	缚 fù	**70 灬**
绝 jué	缤 bīn	
络 luò	11 缩 suō	4 杰 jié
绕 rào	12 缮 shàn	5 点 diǎn
绒 róng	13 缰 jiāng	6 羔 gāo
统 tǒng		烈 liè
7 继 jì	**68 马**	热 rè
绢 juàn		7 焉 yān
绦 tāo	马 mǎ	8 焦 jiāo
绣 xiù	3 驰 chí	然 rán
8 绷 bēng	驯 xùn	煮 zhǔ
绸 chóu	4 驳 bó	9 煎 jiān
绰 chuò	驴 lǘ	照 zhào

10	熬 áo	**74 火**	8	焚 fén
	熙 xī			焰 yàn
	熊 xióng	火 huǒ	9	煌 huáng
	熏 xūn	1 灭 miè		煤 méi
11	熟 shú,	2 灯 dēng		煳 hú
	shóu	灰 huī		煨 wēi,
12	燕 yàn	3 灿 càn		wèi
		灸 jiǔ		煸 biān

71 斗

斗 dòu, dǒu
7 斜 xié

72 文

文 wén
2 齐 qí
6 斋 zhāi
斋 wěn

73 方

方 fāng
4 房 fáng
放 fàng
5 施 shī
6 旅 lǚ
旁 páng
7 旋 xuán, xuàn
族 zú
10 旗 qí

74 火

火 huǒ
1 灭 miè
2 灯 dēng
灰 huī
3 灿 càn
灸 jiǔ
灶 zào
灼 zhuó
4 炒 chǎo
炬 jù
炉 lú
炎 yán
炖 dùn
5 烂 làn
炼 liàn
炮 pào
烁 shuò
烃 tīng
炸 zhà, zhá
炫 xuàn
6 烦 fán
烘 hōng
烬 jìn
烤 kǎo
烧 shāo
烫 tàng
烟 yān
烛 zhú
7 焊 hàn
焕 huàn
烯 xī

8 焚 fén
焰 yàn
9 煌 huáng
煤 méi
煳 hú
煨 wēi, wèi
煸 biān
10 熔 róng
煽 shān, shàn
熄 xī
11 熨 yùn
12 燃 rán
13 爆 zào
15 爆 bào

75 心

心 xīn
1 必 bì
3 忌 jì
忍 rěn
忘 wàng
4 忽 hū
念 niàn
怂 sǒng
态 tài
忠 zhōng
5 怠 dài
急 jí
怒 nù
思 sī
怨 yuàn

怎 zěn
总 zǒng
6 恶 è, wù, ě
恩 ēn
恳 kěn
恐 kǒng
恋 liàn
恕 shù
息 xī
恙 yàng
恣 zì
7 患 huàn
您 nín
悉 xī
悬 xuán
恿 yǒng
悠 yōu
8 悲 bēi
惩 chéng
惠 huì
惑 huò
9 愁 chóu
慈 cí
感 gǎn
想 xiǎng
意 yì
愚 yú
愈 yù
10 愿 yuàn
11 慧 huì
慰 wèi

76 户

户 hù
4 房 fáng
所 suǒ
肩 jiān
戾 lì
5 扁 biǎn
6 扇 shàn
8 雇 gù

77 礻

1 礼 lǐ
3 社 shè
祀 sì
4 视 shì
祈 qí
5 神 shén
祝 zhù
祖 zǔ
祠 cí
6 祥 xiáng
7 祷 dǎo
祸 huò
8 禅 chán
9 福 fú

78 王

王 wáng
1 玉 yù
3 玛 mǎ
4 环 huán

玫 méi
玩 wán
现 xiàn
5 玻 bō
珐 fà
珊 shān
珍 zhēn
玷 diàn
6 班 bān
珠 zhū
7 琅 láng
理 lǐ
球 qiú
琐 suǒ
望 wàng
8 斑 bān
琴 qín
琢 zhuó
9 瑰 guī
瑚 hú
瑞 ruì
瑜 yú
瑕 xiá
10 璃 lí
11 璜 huáng

79 韦

韧 rèn

80 木

木 mù
1 本 běn

术 shù	标 biāo	栓 shuān
2 朵 duǒ	柄 bǐng	桃 táo
机 jī	查 chá	桅 wéi
朴 pǔ	栋 dòng	校 xiào,
权 quán	柑 gān	jiào
朽 xiǔ	架 jià	样 yàng
杂 zá	枯 kū	案 àn
3 材 cái	栏 lán	桩 zhuāng
村 cūn	柳 liǔ	桌 zhuō
杜 dù	某 mǒu	桦 huà
杆 gǎn,	柠 níng	7 梗 gěng
gān	染 rǎn	检 jiǎn
杠 gàng	柔 róu	梨 lí
极 jí	柿 shì	梁 liáng
李 lǐ	树 shù	梅 méi
杏 xìng	相 xiāng	渠 qú
杨 yáng	栅 shān,	梢 shāo
杖 zhàng	zhà	梳 shū
4 杰 jié	柱 zhù	梯 tī
采 cǎi	柚 yòu,	桶 tǒng
板 bǎn	yóu	梧 wú
杯 bēi	栎 yuè, lì	械 xiè
枫 fēng	6 柴 chái	8 棒 bàng
构 gòu	档 dàng	棺 guān
柜 guì	格 gé	棍 gùn
果 guǒ	根 gēn	集 jí
林 lín	桂 guì	椒 jiāo
枪 qiāng	核 hé	棵 kē
枢 shū	桨 jiǎng	椰 liáng
松 sōng	桔 jú	棱 léng,
析 xī	框 kuàng	líng
枕 zhěn	栖 xī, qī1	棉 mián
枝 zhī	桥 qiáo	棚 péng
5 柏 bǎi, bó	桑 sāng	棋 qí

森 sēn
椭 tuǒ
椰 yē
椅 yǐ
植 zhí
椎 zhuī,
　　 chuí
棕 zōng
椋 liáng
9 椽 chuán
概 gài
槐 huái
楞 lèng
楼 lóu
楔 xiē
榆 yú
楂 zhā
榄 lǎn
槌 chuí
栌 lú
桦 jǔ
10 榜 bǎng
槛 jiàn,
　　 kǎn
榴 liú
模 mó, mú
榨 zhà
榛 zhēn
槟 bīng
11 槽 cáo
横 héng
樱 yīng
樟 zhāng
橄 gǎn

12 橙 chéng
橱 chú
橇 qiāo
橡 xiàng
橹 lǔ
橘 jú
13 檬 méng
檐 yán

81 犬

犬 quǎn
6 臭 chòu,
　　 xiù
哭 kū
9 献 xiàn

82 歹

歹 dǎi
2 死 sǐ
5 残 cán
6 殊 shū
殉 xùn
8 殖 zhí
10 殡 bìn

83 车

车 chē
1 轧 yà, zhá
2 轨 guǐ
3 轩 xuān
4 轰 hōng

轮 lún
软 ruǎn
转 zhuàn,
　　 zhuǎn
5 轻 qīng
轴 zhóu
6 轿 jiào
较 jiào,
　　 jiào
7 辅 fǔ
辆 liàng
8 辈 bèi
辊 gǔn
9 毂 gū, gǔ
辐 fú
辑 jí
输 shū
10 辗 zhǎn
12 辙 zhé

84 戈

戈 gē
2 成 chéng
戍 shù
3 戒 jiè
我 wǒ
4 或 huò
5 威 wēi
咸 xián
栽 zali
战 zhàn
6 载 zǎi, zài
7 戚 qī

8	裁 cái	
10	截 jié	
11	戮 lù	
13	戴 dài	
14	戳 chuō	

85 比

	比 bǐ	
2	毕 bì	
6	毙 bì	

86 瓦

	瓦 wǎ	
6	瓷 cí	
	瓶 píng	

87 止

	止 zhǐ	
2	此 cǐ	
3	步 bù	
4	歧 qí	
	武 wǔ	
	肯 kěn	
5	歪 wāi	
6	耻 chǐ	
11	整 zhěng	

88 攴

	敲 qiāo

89 日

	日 rì
1	旦 dàn
2	早 zǎo
3	旱 hàn
	旷 kuàng
	时 shí
4	昂 áng
	昌 chāng
	昏 hūn
	昆 kūn
	明 míng
	旺 wàng
	易 yì
5	春 chūn
	昧 mèi
	是 shì
	显 xiǎn
	星 xīng
	映 yìng
	昭 zhāo
	昨 zuó
	昵 nì
6	晃 huàng, huǎng
	晋 jìn
	晒 shài
	晓 xiǎo
	晕 yūn, yùn
7	晨 chén
	匙 chí, shi

	晚 wǎn
	晤 wù
8	晷 guǐ
	晶 jīng
	景 jǐng
	量 liàng
	晾 liàng
	普 pǔ
	晴 qíng
	暑 shǔ
	晰 xī
	暂 zàn
	智 zhì
	晳 xī
9	暗 àn
	暖 nuǎn
	暇 xiá
10	暧 ài
11	暴 bào
14	曝 bào
16	曦 xī

90 曰

2	曲 qū
4	者 zhě
5	冒 mào
8	替 tì
	曾 céng, zēng
	最 zuì

91 贝

	贝	bèi
3	财	cái
4	败	bài
	贯	guàn
	贬	biǎn
	贩	fàn
	购	gòu
	货	huò
	贫	pín
	贪	tān
	责	zé
	账	zhàng
	质	zhì
	贮	zhù
5	贷	dài
	费	fèi
	贵	guì
	贺	hè
	贱	jiàn
	贸	mào
	贴	tiē
	贻	yí
6	贿	huì
	赂	lù
	赃	zāng
	资	zī
7	赊	shē
	赈	zhèn
8	赐	cì
	赌	dǔ
	赋	fù
	赔	péi

	赏	shǎng
	赎	shú
9	赖	lài
10	赚	zuàn
11	赘	zhuì
12	赞	zàn
	赠	zèng
13	赡	shàn

92 见

	见	jiàn
4	规	guī
	视	shì
5	觉	jué, jiào
	览	lǎn

93 父

	父	fù
2	爷	yé
4	斧	fǔ
	爸	bà
6	爹	diē

94 牛, 牛, 牛

	牛	niú
3	牡	mǔ
4	牧	mù
	物	wù
	牦	máo
5	牲	shēng
	牯	gǔ

6	特	tè
	牺	xī
7	犁	lí
8	犊	dú

95 手

	手	shǒu
6	拿	ná
	挛	luán
	拳	quán
	挚	zhì
8	掰	bāi
11	摩	mó
12	擎	qíng
15	攀	pān

96 毛

	毛	máo
5	毡	zhān
8	毯	tǎn

97 气

	气	qì
4	氛	fēn
5	氟	fú
	氢	qīng
6	氧	yǎng
8	氮	dàn
	氯	lù

98 攵

2 收 shōu
3 改 gǎi
4 放 fàng
5 故 gù
　政 zhèng
6 敌 dí
　效 xiào
　致 zhì
7 敢 gǎn
　教 jiào,
　　jiāo
　救 jiù
　敏 mǐn
　赦 shè
8 敞 chǎng
　敦 duì,
　　dūn
　敬 jìng
　散 sǎn, sàn
9 数 shù,
　　shǔ,
　　shuò
11 敷 fū
　整 zhěng

99 片

　片 piān
4 版 bǎn
8 牌 pái
　牒 dié

100 斤

　斤 jīn
1 斥 chì
4 所 suǒ
　欣 xīn
7 断 duàn
8 斯 sī
9 新 xīn

101 爪, 爫

　爪 zhuǎ,
　　zhǎo
4 爬 pá
　采 cǎi
　斧 fǔ
6 奚 xī
　爱 ài
　舀 yǎo
13 爵 jué

102 月

　月 yuè
2 肌 jī
　肋 lèi
　有 yǒu
3 肠 cháng
　肚 dǔ, dù
　肝 gān
　肛 gāng
　肘 zhǒu
4 肮 āng

肪 fáng
肥 féi
肺 fèi
肤 fū
服 fú
股 gǔ
朋 péng
肾 shèn
胁 xié
育 yù
胀 zhàng
肢 zhī
肿 zhǒng
肩 jiān
肯 kěn
5 胞 bāo
　背 bèi
　胆 dǎn
　胡 hú
　脉 mò
　胖 pàng
　胚 péi
　胜 shèng
　胎 tāi
　胃 wèi
　胧 lóng
　胛 jiǎ
　胫 jìng
6 脆 cuì
　胳 gē
　脊 jǐ
　胶 jiāo
　胯 kuà
　朗 lǎng

	脑 nǎo		腭 è	9	彀 gū, gǔ
	脓 nóng	10	膀 bǎng		毁 huǐ
	脐 qí		膊 bó		殿 diàn
	胸 xiōng		膜 mó		
	胰 yí	11	膝 xī	**106 聿, 聿, 聿**	
	脏 zàng,	12	膨 péng		
	zāng		膳 shàn	4	肃 sù
	脂 zhī	13	臂 bì	7	肆 sì
	胱 guāng		臀 tún		
	胭 yān		臊 sāo	**107 母**	
7	脖 bó				
	脯 fǔ	**103 欠**			母 mǔ
	脚 jiǎo			2	每 měi
	脸 liǎn		欠 qiàn	4	贯 guàn
	脱 tuō	4	欧 ōu		毒 dú
	豚 tún		欣 xīn		
8	朝 cháo,	7	欲 yù	**108 水, 氺**	
	zhāo	8	款 kuǎn		
	腊 là		欺 qī		水 shuǐ
	脾 pí	9	歇 xiē	1	永 yǒng
	腔 qiāng	10	歌 gē	5	泵 bèng
	腆 tiǎn		歉 qiàn		泰 tài
	腕 wàn				泉 quán
	腋 yè	**104 风**		6	浆 jiāng
	腌 yān			10	黎 lí
	腱 jiàn		风 fēng		
	期 qī	8	飓 jù	**109 穴**	
9	腹 fù	11	飘 piāo		
	腻 nì				穴 xuè
	腮 sāi	**105 殳**		2	究 jiū
	腾 téng				穷 qióng
	腿 tuǐ	4	殴 ōu	3	空 kōng,
	腺 xiàn	5	段 duàn		kòng
	腰 yāo	6	殷 yīn		帘 lián

4	穿 chuān	3	疙 gē		痱 fèi	
	窃 qiè		疚 jiù		瘀 yū	
	突 tū		疟 nüè	9	瘩 dá, da	
5	窍 qiào		疡 yáng		瘦 shòu	
	容 róng		疝 shàn		瘟 wēn	
	窄 zhǎi	4	疤 bā	10	瘪 biě, biē	
6	窑 yáo		疮 chuāng		瘤 liú	
	窒 zhì		疯 fēng		瘫 tān	
7	窗 chuāng		疫 yì		瘠 jí	
	窖 jiào		疣 yóu	11	瘸 qué	
	窘 jiǒng	5	病 bìng		瘾 yǐn	
	窝 wō		疾 jí	12	癌 ái	
8	窟 kū		痉 jìng	13	癞 lài	
	窥 kuī		疲 pí		癖 pǐ	
	窦 dòu		疼 téng	16	癫 diān	

110 立

立 lì
1 产 chǎn
4 亲 qīn
竖 shù
5 竞 jìng
站 zhàn
6 竟 jìng
章 zhāng
7 童 tóng
9 端 duān
竭 jié

疹 zhěn
症 zhèng
疸 da, dǎn
疱 pào
痂 jiā
6 疵 cī
痕 hén
痊 quán
痒 yǎng
痔 zhì
7 痘 dòu
痪 huàn
痢 lì
痛 tòng
痣 zhì
痫 xián
8 痹 bì
痴 chī
痰 tán

112 衤

2 补 bǔ
初 chū
3 衬 chèn
衩 chǎ
5 被 bèi
袍 páo
袒 tǎn
袜 wà
袖 xiù
7 裤 kù
裙 qún
裕 yù
8 褂 guà
裸 luǒ
裱 biǎo
9 褐 hè

111 疒

2 疗 liáo
疖 jiē

褪 tuì
褛 lǚ
10 褥 rù
褴 lán
11 褶 zhě
13 襟 jīn

113 示

示 shì
5 祟 suì
6 祭 jì
票 piào
8 禁 jìn, jīn

114 石

石 shí
3 矿 kuàng
码 mǎ
4 砍 kǎn
砂 shā
研 yán
砚 yàn
砖 zhuān
5 础 chǔ
砾 lì
砰 pēng
破 pò
砸 zá
6 硅 guī
硕 shuò
7 硫 liú
确 què

硬 yìng
8 碍 ài
碑 bēi
碘 diǎn
碉 diāo
碌 lù
碰 pèng
碎 suì
碗 wǎn
9 磁 cí
磋 cuō
碟 dié
碳 tàn
10 磅 bàng
磕 kē
碾 niǎn
11 磺 huáng
磨 mó
12 礁 jiāo

115 龙

龙 lóng
6 聋 lóng
龛 kān
袭 xí

116 业

业 yè
7 凿 záo

117 目

目 mù
2 盯 dīng
3 盲 máng
4 盾 dùn
看 kàn,
kān
眉 méi
盼 pàn
省 shěng,
xǐng
眨 zhǎ
盹 dǔn
5 眠 mián
眩 xuàn
6 眼 yǎn
7 睑 jiǎn
8 督 dū
睫 jié
睛 jīng
瞄 miáo
睦 mù
睡 shuì
10 瞒 mán
瞎 xiā
瞌 kē
11 瞥 piē
12 瞪 dèng
瞧 qiáo
瞬 shùn
瞳 tóng

118 田

	田	tián
	由	yóu
4	界	jiè
	畏	wèi
5	留	liú
	畜	xù, chù
6	累	lèi, lěi
	略	lüè
7	畴	chóu
	番	fān
8	畸	jī

119 ⽹

3	罗	luó
4	罚	fá
5	罢	bà
8	署	shǔ
	罩	zhào
	置	zhì
	罪	zuì

120 皿

	皿	mǐn
4	盆	pén
	盈	yíng
5	盎	àng
	监	jiān
	盐	yán
	益	yì
6	盗	dào

	盒	hé
	盔	kuī
	盘	pán
	盛	shèng, chéng
	盖	gài
7	尴	gān
8	盟	méng
11	盥	guàn

121 钅

2	钉	dìng
	针	zhēn
3	钓	diào
4	钞	chāo
	钝	dùn
	钙	gài
	钢	gāng
	钩	gōu
	钮	niǔ
	钦	qīn
	钥	yào
	钟	zhōng
5	铂	bó
	铃	líng
	铆	mǎo
	铅	qiān
	钱	qián
	钳	qián
	铁	tiě
	铀	yóu
	钻	zuān, zuàn

6	铲	chǎn
	铬	gè
	铰	jiǎo
	铝	lǚ
	铭	míng
	铜	tóng
	银	yín
	铐	kǎo
7	锄	chú
	锋	fēng
	锅	guō
	链	liàn
	铺	pù
	锐	ruì
	锁	suǒ
	销	xiāo
	锌	xīn
	锈	xiù
	铸	zhù
	锉	cuò
8	锤	chuí
	错	cuò
	锭	dìng
	键	jiàn
	锦	jǐn
	锯	jù
	锣	luó
	锚	máo
	锡	xī
	锥	zhuī
9	镀	dù
	锻	duàn
	锹	qiāo
10	镑	bàng

镊 niè
镍 niè
镇 zhèn
11 镜 jìng
13 镰 lián
镯 zhuó
15 镳 biāo
17 镶 xiāng

122 矢

4 矩 jǔ
6 矫 jiǎo
7 短 duǎn
8 矮 ǎi
9 疑 yí

123 禾

2 私 sī
秀 xiù
3 秆 gǎn
季 jì
4 科 kē
秒 miǎo
秋 qiū
香 xiāng
种 zhòng,
zhǒng
5 称 chēng,
chèng,
chèn
秤 chèng
积 jī

秘 mì, bì
秦 qín
秩 zhì
租 zū
6 秽 huì
移 yí
7 程 chéng
稍 shāo
税 shuì
稀 xī
8 稠 chóu
稚 zhì
9 稳 wěn
10 稻 dào
稿 gǎo
稽 jī
稼 jià
11 穆 mù
12 黏 nián
穗 suì

124 白

白 bái
2 皂 zào
3 的 de, dì,
dí
4 皇 huáng

125 瓜

瓜 guā
11 瓢 piáo

126 鸟

鸟 niǎo
2 鸡 jī
3 鸢 yuān
4 鸥 ōu
鸦 yā
5 鸵 tuó
鸭 yā
鸫 dōng
6 鸽 gē
7 鹅 é
8 鹊 què
鹉 wǔ
11 鹦 yīng
12 鹫 jiù
13 鹭 lù
17 鹳 guàn

127 用

用 yòng
甩 shuǎi

128 矛

矛 máo

129 疋, ⺪

6 蛋 dàn
7 疏 shū
8 楚 chǔ
9 疑 yí

130 皮

皮 pí
5 皱 zhòu

131 衣

衣 yī
5 袋 dài
6 裂 liè
　裝 zhuāng
7 裔 yì

132 羊, 丷, 𦍌

羊 yáng
3 养 yǎng
4 羞 xiū
5 着 zháo,
　　zhe,
　　zhāo,
　　zhuó
6 善 shàn
　羡 xiàn
7 群 qún
11 羹 gēng

133 米

米 mǐ
3 类 lèi
4 粉 fěn
　料 liào
5 粗 cū

粒 lì
粘 zhān,
　nián
6 粪 fèn
7 粮 liáng
8 粹 cuì
　精 jīng
9 糊 hú, hù,
　　hū
10 糙 cāo
　糕 gāo
　糖 táng
11 糟 zāo
12 糨 jiàng
14 糯 nuò

134 耒

4 耙 pá
　耕 gēng
　耗 hào

135 老

老 lǎo

136 耳

耳 ěr
4 耽 dān
　耸 sǒng
5 聊 liáo
　职 zhí
6 联 lián

7 聘 pìn
8 聚 jù
9 聪 cōng

137 西, 覀

西 xī
4 栗 lì
6 粟 sù
12 覆 fù

138 页

页 yè
2 顶 dǐng
　顷 qǐng
3 顺 shùn
4 顿 dùn
　顾 gù
　颂 sòng
　顽 wán
　预 yù
5 颈 gěng,
　　jǐng
　领 lǐng
　颅 lú
6 颊 jiá
　颌 hé
7 频 pín
　颓 tuí
　颐 yí
　颖 yǐng
8 颗 kē
9 额 é

题 tí
颜 yán
10 颠 diān
13 颤 chàn,
   zhàn
17 颧 quán

139 虍

2 虎 hǔ
  虏 lǔ
3 虐 nüè
4 虑 lù
  虔 qián
5 虚 xū

140 虫

  虫 chóng
2 虱 shī
3 虹 hóng
  蚂 mǎ
  虾 xiā
  蚁 yǐ
  蚤 zǎo
4 蚕 cán
  蚊 wén
  蚋 ruì
  蚝 háo
  蚪 dǒu
  蚓 yǐn
5 蛆 qū
  蛇 shé
  蚱 zhà

蚯 qiū
6 蛤 gé, há
  蛮 mán
  蛙 wā
  蜒 yán
  蛛 zhū
  蜓 yán
  蛞 kuò
  蛴 qí
7 蜂 fēng
  蜕 tuì
  蜗 wō
  蜃 shèn
  蜇 zhē
  蜊 li
8 蝉 chán
  蜡 là
  蝇 yíng
  蜘 zhī
  蜻 qīng
  蜥 xī
  蜚 fēi
  蜴 yì
  蜷 quán
  蜿 wān
  螂 láng
  蜢 měng
9 蝶 dié
  蝴 hú
  蝗 huáng
  蝠 fú
  蝌 kē
  蝓 yú
  蝙 biān

10 融 róng
   螯 áo
   蟆 ma
   螃 páng
11 螺 luó
   螫 shì, zhē
   螬 cáo
   蟑 zhāng
   蟀 shuài
13 蟹 xiè
   蟒 měng
14 蠕 rú
15 蠢 chǔn

141 缶

3 缸 gāng
4 缺 quē
8 罂 yīng
17 罐 guàn

142 舌

  舌 shé
5 甜 tián
7 辞 cí
8 舔 tiǎn

143 竹, ⺮

  竹 zhú
3 竿 gān
4 笆 bā
  笔 bǐ

笋 sǔn	篱 lí	舷 xián
笑 xiào	篷 péng	6 艇 tǐng
5 笨 bèn	篝 golu	
笛 dí	11 簇 cù	**148 羽**
第 dì	簧 huáng	
符 fú	12 簿 bù	羽 yǔ
笺 jiān	13 簸 bó, bò	4 翅 chì
笼 lǒng	14 籍 jí	翁 wēng
笤 tiáo		6 翘 qiào
6 策 cè	**144 臼**	翔 xiáng
答 dá		10 翱 áo
等 děng	臼 jiù	11 翼 yì
筏 fá	7 舅 jiù	12 翻 fān
筋 jīn		14 耀 yào
筐 kuāng	**145 自**	
筛 shāi		**149 艮, 艮**
筒 tǒng	自 zì	
筑 zhù		既 jì
筝 zhēng	**146 血**	
7 筹 chóu		**150 糸**
简 jiǎn	血 xuè,	
筷 kuài	xiě	4 紧 jǐn
签 qiān	5 衅 xìn	素 sù
8 箔 bó		6 絮 xù
箍 gū	**147 舟**	紫 zǐ
管 guǎn		11 繁 fán
箕 jī	舟 zhōu	
算 suàn	4 般 bān	**151 辛**
9 箭 jiàn	舱 cāng	
篓 lǒu	航 háng	辛 xīn
篇 piān	舰 jiàn	6 辟 pì
箱 xiāng	5 舶 bó	7 辣 là
10 篡 cuàn	船 chuán	9 辨 biàn
篮 lán	舵 duò	辩 biàn

10 辮 biàn
12 瓣 bàn

152 言

言 yán
6 誉 yù
7 誓 shì
12 警 jǐng

153 麦

麦 mài

154 走

走 zǒu
3 赶 gǎn
起 qǐ
5 超 chāo
趋 qū
越 yuè
8 趣 qù
趟 tāng

155 赤

赤 chì
7 赫 hè

156 豆

豆 dòu
5 登 dēng

8 豌 wān

157 酉

3 配 pèi
酌 zhuó
4 酗 xù
酝 yùn
5 酣 hān
酥 sū
6 酬 chóu
酱 jiàng
酷 kù
酪 lào
酯 zhǐ
7 酸 suān
酵 xiào, jiào
酿 niàng
8 醇 chún
醋 cù
醉 zuì
9 醒 xǐng

158 辰

辰 chén

159 里

里 lǐ
4 野 yě

160 足

足 zú
2 趴 pā
4 距 jù
跄 qiàng
跃 yuè
趾 zhǐ
5 跋 bá
跌 diē
践 jiàn
跑 pǎo
跚 shān
跛 bǒ
6 跺 duò
跟 gēn
跪 guì
跨 kuà
路 lù
跳 tiào
跷 qiāo
跤 jiāo
7 踉 liàng
8 踩 cǎi
踏 tà
踢 tī
踪 zōng
踝 huái
9 蹄 tí
踱 duó
10 蹈 dǎo
蹋 tà
蹒 pán
11 蹦 bèng

12 蹲 dūn
蹼 pǔ
13 躁 zào

161 豸

3 豹 bào
5 貂 diāo
7 貌 mào

162 谷

谷 gǔ

163 采

释 shì

164 身

身 shēn
3 躬 gōng
4 躯 qū
6 躲 duǒ
8 躺 tǎng

165 角

角 jiǎo,
jué
6 触 chù
解 jiě,
xiè

166 青

青 qīng
6 静 jìng

167 其

其 qí

168 雨

雨 yǔ
3 雪 xuě
4 雳 lì
5 雾 wù
雹 báo
雷 léi
零 líng
6 需 xū
霆 tíng
7 霉 méi
震 zhèn
8 霍 huò
霓 ní
9 霜 shuāng
霞 xiá
13 霸 bà
露 lù, lòu
霹 pī

169 齿

齿 chǐ
5 龄 líng

6 龈 yín
9 龋 qǔ

170 金

金 jīn
5 鉴 jiàn

171 隹

2 隼 sǔn
3 雀 què
4 雄 xióng
雅 yǎ
5 雏 chú
6 雌 cí
8 雕 diāo

172 鱼

鱼 yú
鱿 yóu
4 鲁 lǔ
5 稣 sū
6 鲜 xiān
7 鲤 lǐ
鲨 shā
8 鲸 jīng
鲱 fēi
9 鳄 è
10 鳍 qí
鳏 guān
11 鳕 xuě
鳗 mán

12 鳞 lín
鳟 zūn

173 音

音 yīn
4 韵 yùn

174 革

革 gé
2 勒 lè
4 靶 bǎ
靴 xuē
6 鞍 ān
鞋 xié
鞑 dá
7 鞘 qiào
8 鞠 jū
9 鞭 biān

175 骨

骨 gū
4 骰 tóu
5 骷 kū
6 骸 hái
9 髅 lóu
12 髓 suǐ

176 食

食 shí
7 餐 cān

177 鬼

鬼 guǐ
4 魂 hún
魁 kuí
5 魅 mèi
11 魔 mó

178 髟

4 髦 máo
6 髻 jì
8 鬃 zōng
鬈 quán
10 鬓 bìn

179 鹿

鹿 lù
2 麂 jǐ
8 麓 lù

180 黑

黑 hēi
3 墨 mò
4 默 mò
5 黝 yǒu

181 鼠

鼠 shǔ

182 鼻

鼻 bí
3 鼾 hān

A

啊 ā (*surprise, wonderment*) oh

啊 à (*realization*) ah

阿尔巴尼亚 Ā'ěrbāníyà Albania ◊ Albanian

阿富汗 Āfùhàn Afghanistan ◊ Afghan

阿根廷 Āgēntíng Argentina ◊ Argentinian

哀 āi sorrow; mourning

唉 āi alas

挨 āi be next to

唉 āi (*when someone calls your name*): 小王？－唉，什么事儿？ *xiǎo Wáng? – āi, shénme shìr?* Wang? – yes, what's up?

哎 āi (*dissatisfaction*): 哎，你怎么没告诉我呢？ *āi, nǐ zěnme méi gàosù wǒ ne?* well, why didn't you tell me then?

挨 ái undergo, suffer; endure

癌 ái cancer

矮 ǎi short *person*; low

嗳 ǎi (*disagreement*): 嗳，说哪儿去了 *ǎi, shuō nǎr qù le* hey, don't be silly

爱 ài love; like; be in the habit of; 做爱 *zuò'ài* make love; 有爱心 *yǒu àixīn* caring; 爱发脾气 *ài fā píqì* short-tempered

嗳 ài (*annoyance*): 嗳，我怎就忘不了她呢？ *ài, wǒ zěn jiù wàngbùliǎo tā ne?* why can't I just forget her?

碍 ài block; hinder; obstruct

爱称 àichēng diminutive, short form of a name

挨打 áidǎ get a beating

哀悼 āidào mourn; grieve

哀悼者 āidào zhě mourner

挨饿 ái'è starve

爱尔兰 Ài'ěrlán Ireland ◊ Irish

爱抚 àifǔ caress; fondle; pet

爱管事 ài guǎnshì bossy

爱国 àiguó patriotic

爱国者 àiguó zhě patriot

爱国主义 àiguó zhǔyì patriotism

哀号 āiháo howl

爱好 àihào enjoy ◊ hobby

爱护 àihù cherish; take care of

埃及 Āijí Egypt ◊ Egyptian

挨脚 áijiǎo get caught in the rain

挨近 āijìn approach

暧昧 àimèi ambiguous; dubious; 和 … 有暧昧关系 *hé … yǒu àimèi guānxì* have an affair with …

埃面子 àimiànzi be determined to save face

爱慕 àimù affection; worship ◊ be attached to; be attracted to

矮胖 ǎipàng tubby

爱情 àiqíng love

爱情生活 àiqíng shēnghuó lovelife

哀求 āiqiú implore

爱人 àirén husband; wife

哀伤 āishāng plaintive

爱上 àishàng fall in love with

唉声叹气 āishēng-tànqì sigh

哎呀 āiya! wow!; 哎呀，我的天啊！ *āiya, wǒde tiān'a!* good heavens!; 哎呀，糟了！ *āiya, zāole!* oh, no!

唉哟 āiyō! ouch!

哀乐 āiyuè lament MUS

挨着 āizhe be next to

挨着 áizhe linger; put off; procrastinate

癌症 áizhèng cancer

矮壮 ǎizhuàng stocky, thickset

矮子 ǎizi short person; dwarf

艾滋病 àizībìng Aids

阿拉伯 Ālābó Arabia ◊ Arab(ic)

阿弥陀佛 Āmítuófó Amitabha Buddha

安 ān peace ◊ peaceful ◊ fit; install, set up ◊ how (*rhetorical questions*)

鞍 ān saddle

按 àn press, push; click on ◊

according to

岸 **àn** shore

案 **àn** (legal) case; record; file

暗 **àn** dark; dim; secret

案板 **ànbǎn** worktop; workbench

暗淡 **àndàn** dim, gloomy; bleak; black; 使暗淡 **shǐ àndàn** dim the headlights

安定 **āndìng** calm ◊ secure

安放 **ānfàng** position

安抚 **ānfǔ** conciliatory ◊ pacify

昂贵 **ángguì** expensive

盎司 **àngsī** ounce

肮脏 **āngzāng** dirty; filthy

安好 **ānhǎo** be installed, be up

安家 **ānjiā** settle down; set up home

案件 **ànjiàn** case LAW

暗礁 **ànjiāo** reef; hidden danger

按揭贷款 **ànjiē dàikuǎn** mortgage

安静 **ānjìng** calm ◊ peacefully ◊ calm down; shut up ◊ silent, quiet; placid ◊ in silence

按扣 **ànkòu** snap fastener, press stud

按喇叭 **àn lǎba** honk the horn

安乐死 **ānlèsǐ** euthanasia

安乐椅 **ānlèyǐ** easy chair

按铃 **ànlíng** ring (the bell)

安眠药 **ānmiányào** sleeping pill

按摩 **ànmó** massage

按摩技师 **ànmójìshī** chiropractor

按摩小姐 **ànmó xiǎojie** masseuse

按摩院 **ànmóyuàn** massage parlor

按摩浴缸 **ànmó yùgāng** whirlpool, jacuzzi

按钮 **ànniǔ** button (on machine)

安排 **ānpái** arrange, fix; arrange for; lay out; allocate; order ◊ arrangement

安全 **ānquán** safe ◊ safely ◊ safety; security; 处于安全状态 **chǔyú ānquán zhuàngtài** be safe

安全出口 **ānquán chūkǒu** fire escape

安全带 **ānquándài** seat belt

安全岛 **ānquándǎo** traffic island

安全感 **ānquángǎn** sense of security

安全检查 **ānquán jiǎnchá** security check

安全装置 **ānquán zhuāngzhì** safeguard

暗杀 **ànshā** assassinate ◊ assassination

岸上 **ànshang** on shore

暗杀者 **ànshā zhě** assassin

按时 **ànshí** on time

暗示 **ànshì** hint; implication ◊ imply, insinuate; point to, indicate

安慰 **ānwèi** comfort; console; soothe ◊ comfort; compensation; consolation

安心 **ānxīn** reassured

安葬 **ānzàng** bury the dead

按照 **ànzhào** according to

暗指 **ànzhǐ** imply

按住 **ànzhù** pin; hold down

安装 **ānzhuāng** fit, install ◊ installation

鞍子 **ānzi** saddle

案子 **ànzi** case

凹 **āo** concave; sunken

螯 **áo** pincers

熬 **áo** endure; boil

傲 **ào** arrogant; obstinate

凹槽 **āochū** dent; recess (in wall)

澳大利亚 **Àodàlāxīyà** Australasia ◊ Australasian

澳大利亚 **Àodàlìyà** Australia ◊ Australian

奥地利 **Àodìlì** Austria ◊ Austrian

懊悔 **àohuǐ** remorse; regret

奥林匹克运动会 **Àolínpǐkè Yùndònghuì** Olympic Games

傲慢 **àomàn** arrogance ◊ arrogant, haughty

澳门 **Àomén** Macao ◊ Macanese

奥秘 **àomì** great mystery

懊丧 **àosàng** depressed; morose

凹凸不平 **āotū bùpíng** lumpy

螯虾 **áoxiā** lobster

凹陷 **āoxiàn** dip; hollow ◊ sunken cheeks ◊ cave in

翱翔 **áoxiáng** hover; soar

熬夜 **áoyè** stay up late; burn the midnight oil

奥运会 **Àoyùnhuì** Olympics

阿司匹林 **āsīpǐlín** aspirin

阿姨 **āyí** auntie (used also to address a woman of one's parents' age)

B

八 **bā** eight

疤 **bā** scar

拔 **bá** pull out, extract

靶 **bǎ** target

把 **bǎ** *measure word for knives and chairs;* 一把刀 **yìbǎ dāo** a knife; 一把钳子 **yìbǎ qiánzi** a pair of pliers / pincers ◊ *(marking an object moved for emphasis to the start of a sentence):* 我要把车修了 **wǒ yào bǎ chē xiūle** I'll have the car repaired

爸 **bà** dad, pop

霸 **bà** tyrant, despot

坝 **bà** dam

罢 **bà** stop, cease

把 **bà** handle

吧 **ba** *(to make suggestions):* 走吧 **zǒu ba** let's go ◊ *(in tag questions)* is he?; isn't he?; are you?; aren't you? etc; 你很忙吧 **nǐ hěn máng ba** you're very busy, aren't you?

爸爸 **bàba** dad, pop

靶场 **bǎchǎng** shooting range

拔出 **báchū** extract, pull out ◊ extraction

拔出插头 **báchū chātóu** unplug

霸道 **bàdào** domineering

罢工 **bàgōng** strike *(of workers)*

罢工者 **bàgōng zhě** striker

拔河 **báhé** tug of war

白 **bái** white ◊ in vain ◊ family name

百 **bǎi** hundred

柏 **bǎi** cypress

摆 **bǎi** place; lay

败 **bài** be defeated; defeat; fail

拜 **bài** congratulate

拜拜 **báibái** bye-bye

白班儿 **báibānr** day shift

百倍 **bǎibèi** hundredfold

摆布 **bǎibù** manipulate ◊ manipulation; 任由 X 摆布 **rènyóu X bǎibù** be at X's mercy

白菜 **báicài** Chinese cabbage

白痴 **báichī** idiot

摆翅 **bǎichì** flutter *(of wings)*

摆动 **bǎidòng** swing; wag; wiggle

白饭 **báifàn** boiled rice

摆放 **bǎifàng** set out *goods*

拜访 **bàifǎng** call on, visit ◊ visit

白费力 **bái fèilì** waste one's time, go to a lot of trouble for nothing

百分比 **bǎifēnbǐ** percentage

百分之 **bǎifēnzhī** percent; 百分之百 **bǎifēnzhī bǎi** one hundred percent

白宫 **Báigōng** White House

百和花 **bǎihéhuā** lily

白喉 **báihóu** diphtheria

白桦 **báihuà** birch

败坏 **bàihuài** spoil

百花齐放 **Bǎihuāqífàng** Hundred Flowers Movement

白灰 **báihuī** lime

百货商店 **bǎihuò shāngdiàn** department store

摆架子 **bǎi jiàzi** put on airs; behave snobbishly

白酒 **báijiǔ** clear grain spirit

白开水 **báikāishuǐ** boiled water

百科词典 **bǎikē cídiǎn** encyclopedia; dictionary

百科全书 **bǎikēquán shū** encyclopedia

白兰地 **báilándì** brandy; cognac

白领工人 **báilǐng gōngrén** white-collar worker

败露 **bàilù** emerge

拜年 **bàinián** pay a New Year's visit; wish a happy New Year; 给李先生拜年 **gěi Lǐ xiānsheng bàinián** wish Mr Li a happy New Year

摆弄 **bǎinòng** fiddle with; fool around with; toy with; twiddle

白葡萄酒 **bái pútaojiǔ** white wine

白人 **báirén** white *person*

百日咳 **bǎirìké** whooping cough

白日梦 **báirìmèng** daydream

白肉 **báiròu** white meat; boiled pork fat

白色 **báisè** white

白手起家的人 **báishǒuqǐjiāde rén** self-made man

白糖 **báitáng** white sugar

白天 **báitiān** daytime, day ◊ in the daytime

白涂料 **bái túliào** whitewash

摆脱 **bǎituō** get rid of; free oneself from

拜托 **bàituō** request; 拜托！ **bàituō!** do me a favor!

百万 **bǎiwàn** million

百万富翁 **bǎiwànfùwēng** millionaire

摆碗筷 **bǎi wǎnkuài** set the table

白皙 **báixī** fair *complexion*

掰下 **bāixià** break off

败兴者 **bàixìng zhě** spoilsport

白血病 **báixuèbìng** leukemia

百叶帘 **bǎiyè lián** venetian blind

白银 **báiyín** silver

柏油 **bǎiyóu** asphalt, tar

白字 **báizì** typo in Chinese characters

拔尖儿 **bájiānr** excellent

八角 **bājiǎo** star anise

巴基斯坦 **Bājīsītǎn** Pakistan ◊ Pakistani

芭蕾舞 **bāléiwǔ** ballet

芭蕾舞演员 **bāléiwǔ yǎnyuán** ballet dancer

拔毛 **bámáo** pluck

把门人 **bǎmén rén** bouncer, doorman

班 **bān** class; shift (*at work*) ◊ *measure word for bus, train etc*; 下一班飞机 **xià yì bān fēijī** the next flight

搬 **bān** move; shove; dislodge

斑 **bān** stain; spot; stripe ◊ striped

扳 **bān** turn; pull

板 **bǎn** board; sheet (*of metal, glass*)

版 **bǎn** edition; page (*of newspaper*)

半 **bàn** half; 十点半 **shídiǎnbàn** half past ten

瓣 **bàn** petal; segment

拌 **bàn** stir; mix; 拌色拉 **bàn sèlā** dress a salad

绊 **bàn** stumble, trip

扮 **bàn** get dressed up as; play the role of

办 **bàn** do; manage; deal with; 办签证 **bàn qiānzhèng** apply for a visa

版本 **bǎnběn** edition; version

半场 **bànchǎng** half time

伴唱 **bànchàng** backing (*singers*)

伴唱组 **bànchàng zǔ** backing group

搬出 **bānchū** move out

班船 **bānchuán** liner (*ship*)

版次 **bǎncì** impression (*of a book*)

绊倒 **bàndǎo** knock over; trip; stumble

半岛 **bàndǎo** peninsula

办到 **bàndào** manage to do

半导体 **bàndǎotǐ** semiconductor

板凳 **bǎndèng** stool

斑点 **bāndiǎn** spot

办法 **bànfǎ** method; means; way; way out; solution

邦 **bāng** nation; state

帮 **bāng** help ◊ gang; 帮 X 个忙 **bāng X ge máng** do X a favor

绑 **bǎng** bind

磅 **bàng** pound (*weight, sterling*)

棒 **bàng** stick; club ◊ great; excellent

榜 **bǎng** official announcement

棒棒冰 **bàngbàngbīng** Popsicle®

棒棒糖 **bàngbàng táng** sucker, lollipop

绷带 **bǎng bēngdài** bandage

半个小时 **bànge xiǎoshí** half an hour

半个月 **bàngeyuè** two weeks

绑架 **bǎngjià** kidnap ◊ kidnaping

邦交 **bāngjiāo** diplomatic relations

绑架者 **bǎngjià zhě** kidnaper

棒极了 **bàngjíle** fantastic, superb

帮忙 **bāngmáng** help

办公楼 **bàngōnglóu** office (*building*)

办公室 **bàngōngshì** office (*room*)

办公时间 **bàngōng shíjiān** office hours

绑票 **bǎngpiào** hold to ransom

棒球 **bàngqiú** baseball

棒球场 **bàngqiú chǎng** ballpark

棒球棍 **bàngqiú gùn** baseball bat

棒球帽 **bàngqiú mào** baseball cap

棒球运动员 **bàngqiú yùndòngyuán** baseball player

帮手 **bāngshǒu** helper

帮头 **bāngtóu** godfather (*in mafia*)

傍晚 **bàngwǎn** toward evening ◊ dusk

绑鞋带 **bǎng xiédài** do up one's shoelaces

帮凶 **bāngxiōng** accessory; accomplice

榜样 **bǎngyàng** role model; 树立好榜样 **shùlì hǎo bǎngyàng** set a good example

帮助 **bāngzhù** help, assist ◊ help, assistance

绑住 **bǎngzhù** lash down; tie up

棒子 **bàngzi** stick; pole

版画 **bǎnhuà** engraving; print

扳机 **bānjī** trigger

班级 **bānjí** school class; grade

搬家 **bānjiā** move, move house

绊脚 **bànjiǎo** stumble

绊脚石 **bànjiǎoshí** obstacle

搬进 **bānjìn** move in

半径 **bànjìng** radius

半决赛 **bànjuésài** semifinal

板栗 **bǎnlì** Chinese chestnut

办理 **bànlǐ** handle, take care of

伴侣 **bànlǚ** companion; company

斑马 **bānmǎ** zebra

伴娘 **bànniáng** bridesmaid

般配 **bānpèi** complement; 他们很般配 **tāmén hěn bānpèi** they complement each other

半票 **bànpiào** half-price ticket

搬迁 **bānqiān** relocate

搬迁公司 **bānqiān gōngsī** movers

半球 **bànqiú** hemisphere

版权 **bǎnquán** copyright

伴儿 **bànr** companionship

办事处 **bànshì chù** office, bureau

扳手 **bānshǒu** wrench (*tool*)

伴随 **bànsuí** pursue; accompany; follow

半天 **bántiān** half a day; a long time

版图 **bǎntú** territory

半途 **bàntú** halfway

板岩 **bǎnyán** slate

扮演 **bànyǎn** play, portray ◊ portrayal; 扮演哈姆莱特 **bànyǎn Hāmǔláitè** as Hamlet

半夜 **bànyè** midnight; 半夜三更 **bànyè sāngēng** in the middle of the night

半圆形 **bànyuánxíng** semicircle ◊ semicircular

搬运 **bānyùn** carry; handle

拌匀 **bànyún** toss; mix

搬运工（人）**bānyùn gōng(rén)** porter; stevedore; laborer

斑疹伤寒 **bānzhěn shānghán** typhus

板子 **bǎnzi** board; plate

搬走 **bānzǒu** move away

伴奏 **bànzòu** accompaniment, backing ◊ accompany MUS

伴奏组 **bànzòu zǔ** backing group

包 **bāo** bag; pack ◊ bundle; wrap; assure; hire; 包春卷 **bāo chūnjuǎn** wrap a spring roll; 一包香烟 **yìbāo xiāngyān** a pack of cigarettes; 把 ... 包起来 **bǎ ... bāo qǐlái** bundle up

剥 **bāo** peel

雹 **báo** hail

薄 **báo** thin

宝 **bǎo** treasure ◊ precious

保 **bǎo** protect; keep; guarantee

饱 **bǎo** full

堡 **bǎo** castle

豹 **bào** leopard

报 **bào** newspaper; report

暴 **bào** sudden; violent

爆 **bào** explode; blow up

抱 **bào** take in one's arms; hug

刨 **bào** plane (*tool*)

保安 **bǎo'ān** ensure public safety

报案 **bào'àn** report a case

保安部 **bǎo'ānbù** security

保安部队 **bǎo'ān bùduì** security forces

保安人员 **bǎo'ān rényuán** security guard

包办 **bāobàn** cater for

包办旅行 **bāobàn lǚxíng** package deal, package tour

雹暴 **báobào** hailstorm

宝贝 **bǎobèi** treasure; darling

包庇 **bāobì** harbor

保镳 **bǎobiāo** bodyguard

保持 **bǎochí** hold, maintain, keep, stay ◊ preservation; 保持沉默 **bǎochí chénmò** stay silent; 保持距离 **bǎochí jùlí** keep one's distance; 保持冷静 **bǎochí lěngjìng** keep one's cool; 与 X 保持联络 **yǔ X bǎochí liánluò** keep in contact with X

报仇 **bàochóu** take revenge

报酬 **bàochóu** reward; remuneration

保存 **bǎocún** conserve, preserve; embalm

报答 **bàodá** repay

保单 **bǎodān** warranty (card)

报道 **bàodào** cover; report, report on; present oneself ◊ coverage; report, story

暴跌 **bàodiē** drop; crash

暴动 **bàodòng** outbreak of violence

爆发 **bàofā** break out; erupt ◊ outbreak; eruption

暴发户 **bàofāhù** nouveau riche

报贩 **bàofàn** newsvendor

报废 **bàofèi** scrap

暴风雪 **bàofēngxuě** snowstorm

暴风雨 **bàofēngyǔ** rainstorm

报复 **bàofù** pay back fig; retaliate ◊ retaliation; revenge ◊ vindictive; 报复 X **bàofù X** get even with X

报告 **bàogào** report news; report, account ◊ presentation

饱嗝儿 **bǎogér** belch

保管 **bǎoguǎn** take care of ◊ storeman ◊ certainly

报关 **bàoguān** customs declaration

曝光 **bàoguāng** exposure; 曝光不足 **bàoguāng bù zú** underexposed

宝贵 **bǎoguì** precious; valuable

包裹 **bāoguǒ** package; parcel

包含 **bāohán** comprise; incorporate; include

饱和 **bǎohé** saturation

保护 **bǎohù** conservation; protection ◊ preserve; protect; safeguard ◊ shelter; shield

保护地区 **bǎohù dìqū** reservation (special area)

保护费 **bǎohùfèi** protection money

包机 **bāojī** charter flight

报价 **bàojià** quotation ◊ quote price

保健 **bǎojiàn** health care

报警 **bàojǐng** raise the alarm

饱经沧桑 **bǎo jīng cāngsāng** checkered career

饱经风霜 **bǎo jīng fēngshuāng** weather-beaten

报警器 **bàojǐngqì** siren

暴君 **bàojūn** despot, tyrant

剥壳 **bāoké** shell

包括 **bāokuò** consist of; count, include; take in ◊ including

暴力 **bàolì** violence ◊ violent

爆裂 **bàoliè** burst

保龄球 **bǎolíng qiú** bowling; bowl; 打保龄球 **dǎ bǎolíng qiú** bowl; go bowling

保龄球道 **bǎolíng qiú dào** bowling alley

保留 **bǎoliú** keep, hang on to; hold; reserve ◊ reservation

暴露 **bàolù** reveal; expose ◊ skimpy

暴乱 **bàoluàn** disorder, unrest, riot

暴露自己 **bàolù zìjǐ** give oneself away

保密 **bǎomì** keep secret; conceal ◊ secrecy ◊ secret

爆米花 **bàomǐhuā** puffed rice; popcorn

暴民 **bàomín** mob

报名 **bàomíng** register; enrol; sign up

报名参军 **bàomíng cānjūn** enlist

保姆 **bǎomǔ** nanny; housekeeper

报幕 **bàomù** announce a program

暴怒 **bàonù** fury

暴虐 **bàonüè** oppressive; tyrannical ◊ tyranny

爆破 **bàopò** blow up; pop, burst

抱歉 **bàoqiàn** be sorry, regret

宝石 **bǎoshí** precious stone, jewel

保释 **bǎoshì** bail ◊ bail out LAW

报失 **bàoshī** report a loss

保释金 **bǎoshì jīn** bail

保守 **bǎoshǒu** conservative; straight

保守承诺 **bǎoshǒu chéngnuò** keep a promise

报税 **bàoshuì** make a tax declaration

宝塔 **bǎotǎ** pagoda

报摊儿 **bàotānr** newsstand

暴跳如雷 **bàotiào rúléi** go on the rampage

包围 **bāowéi** encircle; mob; lay siege to; surround; 被 X 包围 **bèi X bāowéi** be surrounded by X

保卫 **bǎowèi** defend ◊ defense

保温瓶 **bǎowēn píng** vacuum flask, thermos flask

保险 **bǎoxiǎn** insurance; safety ◊ safe ◊ be bound to

保险单 **bǎoxiǎndān** insurance policy

保险费 **bǎoxiǎnfèi** premium

保险杠 **bǎoxiǎn gàng** bumper

保险公司 **bǎoxiǎn gōngsī** insurance company

保险柜 **bǎoxiǎnguì** safe (*for valuables*)

保险金额 **bǎoxiǎn jīn'é** sum insured

保险丝 **bǎoxiǎnsī** fuse

保险丝盒 **bǎoxiǎnsī hé** fusebox

保险丝线 **bǎoxiǎnsī xiàn** fuse wire

保鲜纸 **bǎoxiān zhǐ** clingfilm

报销 **bàoxiāo** claim expenses

报销帐户 **bàoxiāo zhànghù** expense account

暴行 **bàoxíng** atrocity; brutality; outrage

保修期 **bǎoxiūqī** warranty period

保养 **bǎoyǎng** maintain ◊ maintenance

报应 **bàoyìng** just deserts; 他会得 到报应 **tā huì dédào bàoyìng** he'll get his comeuppance

保佑 **bǎoyòu** bless

暴雨 **bàoyǔ** torrential rain

抱怨 **bàoyuàn** grumble, moan

暴躁 **bàozào** cranky, bad-tempered; fiery; hot-headed

爆炸 **bàozhà** blast, explosion ◊ explode, go off; blow (*of tire*); detonate

保障 **bǎozhàng** guarantee; security

保证 **bǎozhèng** assurance; security, guarantee ◊ ensure, guarantee; pledge; promise; 我向你保证 **wǒ xiàng nǐ bǎozhèng** you have my word

暴政 **bàozhèng** tyranny

保证期 **bǎozhèngqī** guarantee period

报纸 **bàozhǐ** newspaper

保质 **bǎozhì** keep (*of food*)

保重 **bǎozhòng** look after oneself; 保重！ **bǎozhòng!** take care (of yourself)!

保住 **bǎozhù** keep

包装 **bāozhuāng** pack; package ◊ packaging

包装材料 **bāozhuāng cáiliào** packaging

包装纸 **bāozhuāngzhǐ** wrapping paper

刨子 **bàozi** plane (*tool*)

包租 **bāozū** charter

拔起 **báqǐ** pull up

跋涉 **báshè** trudge; wade

八十 **bāshí** eighty

巴士 **bāshì** bus

把手 **bǎshou** handle

把握 **bǎwò** grasp; seize; certainty

巴西 **Bāxī** Brazil ◊ Brazilian

靶心 **bǎxīn** bull's-eye

八月 **bāyuè** August ◊ in August

巴掌 **bāzhang** palm of the hand

八字胡 **bāzì hú** mustache

BB机 **BB jī** bleeper, pager

杯 **bēi** cup; glass; 一杯茶 **yìbēi chá** a cup of tea

悲 **bēi** sad; mournful

背 **bēi** carry on one's back

卑 **bēi** low; inferior; humble

碑 **bēi** monument; gravestone

北 **běi** north ◊ northern; northerly

倍 **bèi** -fold; 价格长三倍 **jiàgé zhǎng sānbèi** treble the price; X

比 Y 大 … 倍 **X bǐ Y dà … bèi** X outnumbers Y by … times

辈 **bèi** generation; lifetime

背 **bèi** back ◊ recite; memorize

贝 **bèi** shellfish

备 **bèi** have; be equipped with; prepare

被 **bèi** quilt ◊ (passive indicator) 被炒鱿鱼了 **bèi chǎo yóuyú le** be fired; 被淘汰 **bèi táotài** be eliminated

悲哀 **bēi'āi** mournful; sad; distressed

背包 **bèibāo** pack; backpack, rucksack

卑鄙 **bēibǐ** cowardly; mean, nasty; sordid

卑鄙交易 **bēibǐ jiāoyì** sharp practice

卑鄙行为 **bēibǐ xíngwéi** dirty trick

北部 **běibù** north; X 北部 **X běibù** north of X

被捕 **bèibǔ** be under arrest

悲惨 **bēicǎn** tragic; miserable ◊ misery

北朝鲜 **Běi Cháoxiǎn** North Korea ◊ North Korean

被单 **bèidān** sheet

被动 **bèidòng** passive; 被动形式 **bèidòng xíngshì** in the passive

被动语态 **bèidòng yǔtài** passive

北方 **běifāng** north ◊ northern

北方人 **běifāng rén** northerner

被告 **bèigào** accused, defendant; defense

被告席 **bèigào xí** dock (in court)

卑躬屈膝 **bēigōng qūqī** slimy

悲观 **bēiguān** pessimistic; dim ◊ pessimism

悲观者 **bēiguān zhě** pessimist

悲后 **bēihòu** behind ◊ behind one's back

北极 **Běijí** Arctic; North Pole

卑贱 **bēijiàn** humble, lowly

备件 **bèijiàn** spare part

北京 **Běijīng** Beijing, Peking

背景 **bèijīng** setting, background; 以 … 为背景 **yǐ … wéi bèijīng** set in, located in

北京烤鸭 **Běijīng kǎoyā** Peking

duck

背景音乐 **bèijīng yīnyuè** piped music

背景资料 **bèijīng zīliào** background information

北极熊 **běijíxióng** polar bear

悲剧 **bēijù** tragedy

贝壳 **bèiké** shell

蓓蕾 **bèilěi** bud

贝类 **bèilèi** shellfish

卑劣 **bēiliè** contemptible; shoddy

北美洲 **Běi Měizhōu** North America ◊ North American

背面 **bèimiàn** back

背叛 **bèipàn** betray; break away ◊ betrayal

被迫 **bèipò** forced

被褥 **bèirù** quilt

悲伤 **bēishāng** sad ◊ grief

背书 **bèishū** endorse

背诵 **bèisòng** recite

被套 **bèitào** quilt cover

悲痛 **bēitòng** grief; mourning ◊ grieve

悲痛欲绝 **bēitòngyùjué** prostrate with grief

备忘录 **bèiwànglù** memo

碑文 **bēiwén** inscription

背向 **bèixiàng** back onto

背心 **bèixīn** undershirt; vest; T-shirt

背阴 **bèiyīn** in the shade

备用 **bèiyòng** spare

备用车轮 **bèiyòng chēlún** spare wheel

备用磁盘 **bèiyòng cípán** backup disk

备用轮胎 **bèiyòng lúntāi** spare tire

备有 **bèiyǒu** stock

北约 **Běiyuē** NATO

北越 **Běiyuè** North Vietnam ◊ North Vietnamese

倍增 **bèizēng** double

背着 **bēizhe** carry, hump

备注 **bèizhù** remarks; notes

杯子 **bēizi** cup; glass

被子 **bèizi** cover; quilt

奔 **bēn** run fast

本 **běn** copy ◊ root, origin; originally ◊ this ◊ measure word for *books*; 四本书 **sìběn shū** four books

笨 **bèn** stupid, dumb; clumsy

奔波 **bēnbō** rush around; juggle *fig*

奔驰 **bēnchí** dash, speed

笨蛋 **bèndàn** idiot; ass(hole)

本地 **běndì** local; native

本地人 **běndì rén** local (person)

绷 **bēng** tack; tighten; bounce

崩 **bēng** collapse; burst

泵 **bèng** pump

蹦 **bèng** leap; skip; jump

蹦蹦车 **bèngbèngchē** motor rickshaw

绷床 **bēngchuáng** trampoline

绷带 **bēngdài** bandage

进发 **bèngfā** outburst

绷紧 **bēngjǐn** tense up

崩溃 **bēngkuì** breakdown, collapse ◊ crumble; give way

绷绳 **bēngshéng** string

绷索 **bēngsuǒ** tightrope

崩塌 **bēngtā** collapse

本国 **běnguó** native

本国语 **běnguó yǔ** native language

本来 **běnlái** actual ◊ actually; to begin with, originally

本领 **běnlǐng** ability

本能 **běnnéng** instinct ◊ instinctive

奔跑 **bēnpǎo** sprint

本钱 **běnqián** capital

本人 **běnrén** personal ◊ personally, oneself

本身 **běnshēn** itself; in itself

笨手笨脚 **bènshǒu bènjiǎo** clumsy

本性 **běnxìng** nature, character

本质 **běnzhì** nature ◊ fundamental

笨重 **bènzhòng** cumbersome

笨拙 **bènzhuō** clumsy; awkward ◊ clumsiness

逼 **bī** force

鼻 **bí** nose

比 **bǐ** compare; compete with; 我比不过 **wǒ bǐ bú guò** I can't rival that; X 比 Y 好 **X bǐ Y hǎo** X is better than Y; 他比我高 **tā bǐ wǒ gāo** he's taller than me

鄙 **bǐ** lowly; mean; my humble

笔 **bǐ** writing implement ◊ *measure word for sums of money*; 一大笔钱 **yí dà bǐ qián** a large sum of money

必 **bì** must

毕 **bì** finish

币 **bì** money; currency

避 **bì** avoid; prevent

壁 **bì** wall

臂 **bì** arm

闭 **bì** close; shut

边 **biān** side; rim

边…边… **biān … biān …**: 我们边喝/吃边谈 **wǒmen biānhē/chī biān tán** let's talk over a drink/meal; 边听边写 **biān tīng biān xiě** listen and take notes

编 **biān** weave; organize; edit; write; make up 编辫子 **biān biànzi** plait

鞭 **biān** whip

扁 **biǎn** flat

贬 **biǎn** devalue

变 **biàn** change; change into, become; 变老 **biànlǎo** get old

辨 **biàn** differentiate

辩 **biàn** discuss; argue

辫 **biàn** plait

便 **biàn** convenient ◊ defecate; shit; urinate; piss ◊ then

便秘 **biànbì** constipation

辨别 **biànbié** differentiate; distinguish

辩驳 **biànbó** dispute; refute

遍布 **biànbù** widespread

变成 **biànchéng** become

编程序 **biān chéngxù** program

辨出 **biànchū** discern

鞭打 **biāndǎ** whip, flog, lash ◊ whipping

扁担 **biǎndan** yoke, shoulder pole

便当 **biàndāng** lunch box

变得 **biànde** become, go

贬低 **biǎndī** belittle, run down

变动 **biàndòng** alteration; swing, upheaval

扁豆 **biǎndòu** scarlet runner

编队 **biānduì** formation

蝙蝠 **biānfú** bat

便服 **biànfú** casual wear; civilian clothes

编号 **biānhào** number ◊ serial number

辩护 **biànhù** plead; defend ◊ defense; 为 X 辩护 **wèi X biànhù** defend X LAW; stick up for X

变化 **biànhuà** change, switch; variation ◊ vary

变化无常 **biànhuà wúcháng** fickle, volatile

辩护律师 **biànhù lǜshī** defense lawyer

辩护人 **biànhù rén** defense lawyer

辩护证人 **biànhù zhèngrén** defense witness

编辑 **biānjí** edit ◊ editor ◊ editorial; 体育／政治栏编辑 **tǐyù／zhèngzhì lán biānjí** sports／political editor

便笺 **biànjiān** pad (for writing)

边疆 **biānjiāng** frontier

编辑部 **biānjíbù** editorial department

边界 **biānjiè** border; boundary

边境 **biānjìng** border; frontier

遍及世界 **biànjí shìjiè** worldwide

便利 **biànlì** convenient

变量 **biànliàng** variable

编列 **biānliè** list

辩论 **biànlùn** debate

便秘 **biànmì** constipated ◊ constipation

鞭炮 **biānpào** firework; firecracker

便盆 **biànpén** chamber pot; potty (for baby)

变迁 **biànqiān** change

辨认 **biànrèn** make out, spot

辨认出 **biànrèn chū** recognize

变速杆 **biànsùgǎn** gear lever, gear shift

变速器 **biànsùqì** gearbox; transmission

变态 **biàntài** abnormal; kinky ◊ metamorphosis

变态心理 **biàntài xīnlǐ** perversion

扁桃腺 **biǎntáoxiàn** tonsil

扁桃腺炎 **biǎntáoxiàn yán** tonsillitis

便条 **biàntiáo** note; compliments slip

便条本 **biàntiáo běn** notepad

便条纸 **biàntiáo zhǐ** notepaper

变通 **biàntōng** flexible

编舞 **biān wǔ** choreography; choreographer

边线 **biānxiàn** touchline; sideline; foul line

边线外 **biānxiàn wài** touch

便鞋 **biànxié** cloth shoes; slippers

变形 **biànxíng** buckle (change shape)

变压器 **biànyāqì** transformer

贬义 **biǎnyì** derogatory, disparaging

贬抑 **biǎnyì** pejorative

便衣 **biànyī** plain clothes; civilian clothes

变音 **biànyīn** inflection

边缘 **biānyuán** edge, border; brim; fringe; periphery; surround ◊ outlying

编造 **biānzào** make up, concoct

编织 **biānzhī** knit; weave ◊ knitting; weaving

编制 **biānzhì** compile

贬值 **biǎnzhí** depreciate; devalue ◊ depreciation; devaluation

变质 **biànzhì** spoil; deteriorate

编织物 **biānzhīwù** knitting

便装 **biànzhuāng** civilian dress

鞭子 **biānzi** whip

辫子 **biànzi** braid, plait

标 **biāo** mark, sign

表 **biǎo** table; form; meter; watch; surface; outside ◊ show, express

表达 **biǎodá** convey, express; formulate; show; 表达能力强 **biǎodá nénglì qiáng** articulate; 表达意见 **biǎodá yìjiàn** have one's say

表达法 **biǎodáfǎ** expression

表带 **biǎodài** watch strap

表弟 **biǎodì** cousin (younger male on mother's side)

标点 **biāodiǎn** punctuation

标点符号 **biāodiǎn fúhào** punctuation mark

表哥 **biǎogē** cousin (elder male)

表格 **biǎogé** form; table;

spreadsheet

裱糊 **biǎohú** paper

标记 **biāojì** sign; symbol

表姐 **biǎojiě** cousin (*elder female on mother's side*)

表决 **biǎojué** decide by vote

表决通过 **biǎojué tōngguò** pass, approve

表露 **biǎolù** show, display

表妹 **biǎomèi** cousin (*younger female on mother's side*)

表面 **biǎomiàn** surface; 表面上 **biāomiàn shang** on the surface

标明 **biāomíng** mark

表明 **biǎomíng** indicate

表皮 **biǎopí** cuticle ◊ superficial

标签 **biāoqiān** label; nametag; sticker

标枪 **biāoqiāng** javelin

表情 **biǎoqíng** expression

表示 **biǎoshì** give, convey; show; express; mean ◊ display; expression; gesture

标题 **biāotí** heading; headline

标题点 **biāotídiǎn** bullet point

表现 **biǎoxiàn** show; behave ◊ performance; behavior

表兄 **biǎoxiōng** cousin (*elder male on mother's side*)

表演 **biǎoyǎn** act; perform; play; stage ◊ acting; performance; exhibition

表扬 **biǎoyáng** praise; pay a compliment

表演者 **biǎoyǎn zhě** entertainer; performer

标语 **biāoyǔ** slogan

标语牌 **biāoyǔpái** placard

标志 **biāozhì** mark; logo

标准 **biāozhǔn** standard; criterion

标准杆数 **biāozhǔn gānshù** par

婊子 **biǎozi** prostitute; whore

臂膀 **bìbǎng** arm

必备 **bìbèi** precondition, prerequisite

弊病 **bìbìng** disadvantage; mistake; defect

必不可少 **bùbù kěshǎo** necessary; vital

壁橱 **bìchú** cabinet

彼此 **bǐcǐ** each other

必定 **bìdìng** must; be sure to ◊ for sure; definitely

弊端 **bìduān** corrupt practices

别 **bié** other ◊ don't ◊ leave; part; 还要别的吗？ **hái yào biéde ma?** anything else?; 别的东西 **biéde dōngxi** something else; 别动！ **biédòng!** don't move!

瘪 **biě** shriveled; shrunken; flat tire

别处 **biéchù** elsewhere

别具一格 **biéjùyìgé** unique

别离 **biélí** leave; part from

别人 **biérén** someone else; other people; 别人都去 **biérén dōu qù** everyone else is going

别墅 **biéshù** villa

别针 **biézhēn** safety pin

比分 **bǐfēn** score; goal; 比分是多少？ **bǐfēn shì duōshǎo?** what's the score?

庇护 **bìhù** asylum; refuge; shelter

笔画 **bǐhuà** stroke (*in writing*)

壁画 **bìhuà** fresco; mural

避讳 **bìhuì** taboo

笔迹 **bǐjì** handwriting

笔记 **bǐjì** write down ◊ notes

比价 **bǐjià** price ratio ◊ compare prices

比较 **bǐjiào** compare ◊ comparison ◊ comparative ◊ comparatively; relatively; rather; 比较便宜 **bǐjiào piányi** cheaper ◊ it costs less

比较级 **bǐjiào jí** comparative (form)

笔记本 **bǐjìběn** notebook; notebook computer

毕竟 **bìjìng** after all

比基尼 **bǐjīní** bikini

避开 **bìkāi** dodge, evade; ward off; keep out; make oneself scarce

鼻孔 **bíkǒng** nostril

壁垒 **bìlěi** rampart

避雷导线 **bìléi dǎoxiàn** lightning conductor

比例 **bǐlì** proportion; scale

鼻梁 **bíliáng** bridge (*of nose*)

比例绘图 **bǐlì huìtú** scale drawing

比利时 **Bǐlìshí** Belgium ◊ Belgian

壁炉台 **bìlútái** mantelpiece, mantelshelf

壁炉 **bìlú** fireplace; hearth

比率 **bǐlǜ** rate

闭路电视 **bìlù diànshì** closed-circuit television

笔帽 **bǐmào** cap (of pen)

避免 **bìmiǎn** avoid, avert; keep off

笔名 **bǐmíng** pen name

闭幕式 **bìmùshì** closing ceremony

宾 **bīn** guest

避难所 **bìnànsuǒ** haven; sanctuary; refuge

彬彬有礼 **bīnbīn yǒu lǐ** well-mannered

冰 **bīng** ice

兵 **bīng** soldier

柄 **bǐng** stem

饼 **bǐng** round, flat cake; pancake

病 **bìng** illness ◊ sick

并 **bìng** combine; merge ◊ and ◊ (negative intensifier): 我并不在意 **wǒ bìng bú zàiyì** I really don't mind

冰雹 **bīngbáo** hail

冰场 **bīngchǎng** ice rink

冰川 **bīngchuān** glacier

冰灯 **bīngdēng** ice-lantern

冰点 **bīngdiǎn** freezing point

冰冻 **bīngdòng** freeze

病毒 **bìngdú** virus, bug ◊ viral

病房 **bìngfáng** hospital room

并发症 **bìngfā zhèng** complications MED

冰封 **bīngfēng** frozen

饼干 **bǐnggān** cookie; cracker

冰激凌 **bīngjīlíng** ice cream

冰棍儿 **bīnggùnr** Popsicle®

病假 **bìngjià** sick leave

并肩 **bìngjiān** side by side

病菌 **bìngjūn** germ

冰咖啡 **bīngkāfēi** iced coffee

冰块 **bīngkuài** ice cube

冰冷 **bīnglěng** ice-cold

兵力 **bīnglì** troops; armed forces; military strength

病例 **bìnglì** case MED

冰凉 **bīngliáng** frozen

病理学 **bìnglǐxué** pathology

病理学家 **bìnglǐxuéjiā** pathologist

兵马俑 **bīngmǎyǒng** terracotta army

并排 **bìngpái** side by side

并且 **bìngqiě** and; besides

冰淇淋 **bīngqílín** ice cream

冰淇淋店 **bīngqílín diàn** ice cream parlor

冰球 **bīngqiú** (ice) hockey

病人 **bìngrén** patient; sick person

病弱 **bìngruò** invalid ◊ sickly

冰山 **bīngshān** iceberg

病史 **bìngshǐ** case history, medical history

病态 **bìngtài** morbid; pathological; sick society

冰糖 **bīngtáng** candy sugar

病痛 **bìngtòng** pain; ailment

宾馆 **bīnguǎn** hotel; guest house

冰箱 **bīngxiāng** refrigerator, icebox; freezer

冰鞋 **bīngxié** ice-skate

兵役义务 **bīngyì yìwù** military service

病友 **bìngyǒu** friend made in the hospital; fellow patient

冰镇 **bīngzhèn** chilled

病症晚期 **bìngzhèng wǎnqī** terminally ill

冰柱 **bīngzhù** icicle

屏住呼吸 **bǐngzhù hūxī** hold one's breath

滨海区 **bīnhǎiqū** coastal region

殡仪馆 **bìnyíguǎn** funeral home

濒于 **bīnyú** be on the verge of

逼迫 **bīpò** push, pressure

壁球 **bìqiú** squash (game)

必然 **bìrán** inevitably

必然性 **bìrán xìng** certainty, inevitability

比如 **bǐrú** for example

比萨 **bǐsà** pizza

比赛 **bǐsài** competition; contest; match; 我和你比赛 **wǒ hé nǐ bǐsài** I'll race you; 与X比赛 **yǔ X bǐsài** compete against X

比赛场地 **bǐsài chǎngdì** arena

比赛项目 **bǐsài xiàngmù** event

闭上 **bìshàng** close ◊ closed

毕生 **bìshēng** lifetime ◊ all one's life

鄙视 **bǐshì** despise; scorn

匕首 **bǐshǒu** dagger

必死 **bìsǐ** mortal

壁毯 **bìtǎn** tapestry

鼻涕 **bíti** snot

笔芯 **bǐxīn** pencil lead; pen refill

必修 **bìxiū** compulsory *course*

必须 **bìxū** must, have (got) to ◊ obligatory

必需 **bìxū** necessary

必需品 **bìxū pǐn** necessity

必须要 **bìxū yào** call for

必要 **bìyào** essential, necessary

必要时 **bìyàoshí** if necessary, at a pinch

必要性 **bìyào xìng** necessity ◊ must

毕业 **bìyè** graduate ◊ graduation

毕业生 **bìyèshēng** graduate

鼻音 **bíyīn** twang

笔友 **bǐyǒu** penfriend, penpal

比喻 **bǐyù** analogy ◊ figurative

避孕 **bìyùn** birth control; contraception

避孕器 **bìyùn qì** contraceptive

避孕套 **bìyùn tào** condom

避孕药 **bìyùn yào** contraceptive (pill), the pill

逼真 **bīzhēn** true to life

笔直 **bǐzhí** straight; upright

币值 **bìzhí** currency value

壁纸 **bìzhǐ** (wall)paper

币制 **bìzhì** monetary system

鼻子 **bízi** nose

闭嘴 **bìzuǐ** be quiet; 闭嘴！ **bìzuǐ!** be quiet!, shut up!

拨 **bō** dial *telephone number*

播 **bō** sow seed; broadcast

波 **bō** wave

剥 **bō** peel

铂 **bó** platinum

伯 **bó** uncle (*father's elder brother*)

脖 **bó** neck

博 **bó** extensive; broad

驳 **bó** refute

跛 **bǒ** lame

博爱 **bó'ài** universal love; fraternity

薄饼 **bóbǐng** pancake

伯伯 **bóbo** uncle (*father's elder brother*); *used to address a man older than one's father*

菠菜 **bōcài** spinach

波长 **bōcháng** wavelength

驳斥 **bóchì** refute; disprove

拨出 **bōchū** set aside, earmark

驳船 **bóchuán** barge

驳倒 **bódǎo** refute; outargue

波动 **bōdòng** fluctuate ◊ fluctuation

搏动 **bódòng** pulsate

搏斗 **bódòu** fight, battle

波段 **bōduàn** frequency RAD

剥夺 X 的 Y **bōduó Xde Y** strip X of Y

播放 **bōfàng** transmission ◊ transmit

波状 **bōfú** wavy

伯父 **bófù** uncle (*father's elder brother*)

脖颈儿 **bógěngr** (nape of) neck

剥光衣服 **bōguāng yīfu** strip, undress

渤海湾 **Bóhǎi Wān** Bohai Gulf

拨号 **bōhào** dial

拨号盘 **bōhào pán** dial

拨号音 **bōhàoyīn** dial tone

薄荷 **bòhe** mint; peppermint

薄荷糖 **bòhetáng** peppermint candy

簸箕 **bòji** dustpan

拨款 **bōkuǎn** fund ◊ grant

波兰 **Bōlán** Poland ◊ Polish

波浪 **bōlàng** wave

拨浪鼓 **bōlànggǔ** rattle (*toy*)

博览会 **bólǎnhuì** trade fair

玻璃 **bōli** glass

玻璃杯 **bōlibēi** glass (*for drinking*)

玻璃纤维 **bōli xiānwéi** fiberglass

玻璃纸 **bōlizhǐ** cellophane

菠萝 **bōluó** pineapple

剥落 **bōluò** flake off, peel

勃鲁斯歌手 **bólǔsī gēshǒu** blues singer

勃鲁斯音乐 **bólǔsī yīnyuè** blues

勃起 **bóqǐ** erection ◊ erect

勃然大怒 **bórán dànù** fly into a rage

薄弱 **bóruò** weak; vulnerable

薄纱 **bóshā** gauze

博士 **bóshì** doctor; doctorate, PhD

播送 **bōsòng** on the air

波涛 **bōtāo** wave

薄雾 **bówù** haze, mist

博物馆 **bówùguǎn** museum

薄雾笼罩 **bówù lǒngzhào** misty

博物学家 **bówù xuéjiā** naturalist

跛行 **bǒxíng** limp

剥削 **bōxuē** exploit ◊ exploitation; rip-off

博学 **bóxué** well-read

播音 **bōyīn** broadcast ◊ broadcasting

播音员 **bōyīn yuán** radio announcer; broadcaster

播种 **bōzhǒng** sow *seeds*

驳船 **bózhuán** barge *(boat)*

脖子 **bózi** neck

补 **bǔ** darn; patch up; 补车票 **bǔ chēpiào** buy a ticket after boarding

捕 **bǔ** catch

部 **bù** department, ministry; unit

不 **bù** no; non …, un …, in …; not ◊ won't ◊ *(in questions)*: 疼不疼？ **téng bùténg?** does it hurt?; 疼不？ **téng bù?** does it hurt?

步 **bù** pace, step

部 **bù** unit

布 **bù** material, cloth

簿 **bù** book; exercise book; notebook

不安 **bù'ān** uneasy ◊ disquiet; 令人不安 **lìngrén bù'ān** disturbing, worrying; uneasy

不安分 **bù ānfèn** restless

不安全 **bù ānquán** insecure; unsafe

不安全感 **bù ānquángǎn** insecurity

不必 **búbì** unnecessary ◊ needn't

不变 **búbiàn** always, invariably ◊ unswerving

不便 **búbiàn** inconvenient

步兵 **bùbīng** infantry; infantry soldier

不必要 **bú bìyào** unnecessary

不测事件 **bùcè shìjiàn** contingency

补偿 **bǔcháng** compensate for; make up for; reimburse ◊ recompense

不超过 **bù chāoguò** within; no more than

不成比例 **bù chéng bǐlì** disproportionate

不称职 **bú chènzhí** incompetent ◊ incompetence

补充 **bǔchōng** add to ◊ additional; incidental ◊ addition

不纯 **bùchún** impure

不辞辛苦 **bùcí xīnkǔ** spare no effort

不错 **búcuò** not bad; excellent

不大 **búdà** small

不大可能 **bú dà kěnéng** improbable, unlikely

不丹 **Bùdān** Bhutan ◊ Bhutanese

不当 **búdàng** unsuitable

不到 **bú dào** under, less than

捕到 **bǔdào** catch

不道德 **bú dàodé** immoral ◊ immorality

布道坛 **bùdàotán** pulpit

不得不 **bùdébù** have to, be compelled to

不得了 **bùdéliǎo** fantastic ◊ extremely ◊ no way out; 好得不得了 **hǎo dé bùdéliǎo** absolutely fantastic, out of this world; 多得不得了 **duōde bùdéliǎo** a hell of a lot

不得人心 **bùdé rénxīn** unpopular

不得入内 **bùdé rùnèi** no trespassing

补丁 **bǔdīng** darn; patch

布丁 **bùdīng** pudding

不定冠词 **búdìng guàncí** indefinite article

不定式 **búdìngshì** infinitive

不动 **búdòng** motionless

不动产 **búdòngchǎn** real estate

不动产商 **búdòngchǎn shāng** developer; real estate agent

不动产中间商 **búdòng chǎn zhōngjiān shāng** real estate agent

不断 **búduàn** constant, continual

不对 **bú duì** be wrong ◊ incorrect

部队 **bùduì** corps, unit; forces

不对劲儿 **bú duì jìnr** shifty; strange

步伐 **bùfá** step

不方便 **bù fāngbiàn** inconvenient ◊ inconvenience

部分 **bùfen** part, bit; component;

piece, section; patch; proportion ◊ partly

补付 **bǔfù** pay extra; pay later

不服 **bùfú** disobey

不符 **bùfú** not agree with; not comply with

不服从 **bù fúcóng** disobedience ◊ insubordinate

不服管 **bù fúguǎn** rebellious

不负责任 **búfùzérèn** irresponsible

不干涉 **bùgānshè** hands-off ◊ non-intervention

不干预 **bù gānyù** noninterference, nonintervention

布告 **bùgào** bulletin; announcement

布告板 **bùgào bǎn** bulletin board

不给 **bù gěi** withhold

不共戴天 **búgòng dàitiān** mortal enemy

不够 **búgòu** insufficient; 不够好 **búgòuhǎo** not good enough

不顾 **búgù** regardless of, irrespective of

不关你的事！**bùguān nǐde shì!** mind your own business!

不管 **bùguǎn** 我才不管呢！**wǒ cái bùguǎn ne!** I don't give a damn!; for all I care; 不管什么 **bùguǎn shénme** no matter what, whatever; 不管他们多大 **bùguǎn tāmen duō dà** however big they are; 不管她说什么 **bùguǎn tā shuō shénme** no matter what she says

不顾后果 **búgù hòuguǒ** reckless

不规范 **bùguīfàn** irregular

不规矩 **bù guījù** unruly

不规律 **bùguīlǜ** irregular

不规则 **bùguīzé** irregular

补过 **bǔguò** make amends

不过 **búguò** however

不寒而栗 **bùhán'érlì** shake with fear

不含铅 **bù hán qiān** lead-free

不好 **bùhǎo** bad ◊ badly

不合法 **bù héfǎ** illegal, wrongful

不合格 **bù hégé** unqualified

不合逻辑 **bù hé luójí** illogical

不合群 **bù héqún** unsociable

不合适 **bù héshì** unsuitable

不和谐 **bù héxié** discord

步话机 **bùhuàjī** walkie-talkie

捕获 **bǔhuò** capture; catch

捕获物 **bǔhuò wù** catch (of fish)

不活跃 **bù huóyuè** inactive

簿记 **bùjì** bookkeeping

部件 **bùjiàn** unit

不间断 **bù jiānduàn** uninterrupted

不讲道德 **bù jiǎng dàodé** unscrupulous

不坚定 **bù jiāngù** unstable

不健康 **bú jiànkāng** unfit; unhealthy; sickly

不结盟 **bù jiéméng** nonaligned

不结实 **bù jiēshí** flimsy

不及格 **bù jígé** flunk

不仅 **bùjǐn** not only

捕鲸 **bǔjīng** whaling

布景 **bùjǐng** scenes, set THEA

不景气 **bù jǐngqì** recession; depression ◊ unhealthy economy

不经心 **bù jīngxīn** inattentive

补救 **bǔjiù** remedy

不久 **bùjiǔ** before long, soon

不久之后 **bùjiǔ zhīhòu** soon after

布局 **bùjú** layout

不拘礼节 **bùjū lǐjié** offhand

不拘束 **bùjūshù** irrepressible

不拘形式 **bùjū xíngshì** free and easy

不可避免 **bùkě bìmiǎn** inevitable, unavoidable ◊ inevitably

不可分割 **bùkě fēngē** indivisible; inseparable

不可否认 **bùkě fǒurèn** undeniable

不可救药 **bùkě jiùyào** incorrigible

不可靠 **bù kěkào** unreliable

不可理解 **bùkě lǐjiě** incomprehensible

不可能 **bù kěnéng** impossible ◊ that can't be right; that's out of the question

不客气 **bú kèqi** impolite ◊ you're welcome

不可饶恕 **bùkě ráoshù**

unforgivable

不可思议 **bùkě sīyì** unthinkable; uncanny ◊ mysteriously

不可挽回 **bùkě wǎnhuí** irretrievable

不可信 **bù kěxìn** questionable

不可原谅 **bùkě yuánliàng** inexcusable

不可战胜 **bùkě zhànshèng** unbeatable

不快 **búkuài** unhappy; 令人不快 **lìngrén búkuài** miserable; unsavory; disagreeable

不愧于 **bú kuìyú** live up to; be worthy of

不老实 **bù lǎoshi** deceitful

布雷区 **bùléiqū** minefield

不理 **bùlǐ** brush aside; ignore

不利 **búlì** detrimental; disadvantageous; unfavorable; 对 … 不利 **duì … búlì** to the detriment of

不连贯 **bù liánguàn** incoherent

布料 **bùliào** cloth, fabric, material

不了解 **bù liǎojiě** be out of touch

不礼貌 **bù lǐmào** impolite, disrespectful

不领情 **bù lǐngqíng** ungrateful

不利之处 **bùlì zhīchù** disadvantage

不漏水 **búlòushuǐ** watertight

不论 **búlùn** no matter

部落 **bùluò** tribe

不落俗套 **búluò sútào** unconventional

布满 **bùmǎn** be full of; be bristling with

不满 **bùmǎn** discontent, dissatisfied; disgruntled; resentful ◊ displeasure; dissatisfaction; resentment ◊ resent

不满意 **bù mǎnyì** discontented; dissatisfied

部门 **bùmén** department; division; sector

不免 **bùmiǎn** unavoidable

不免一死 **bùmiǎnyìsǐ** mortal ◊ mortality

不明朗 **bù mínglǎng** noncommittal, vague ◊ vaguely

不能 **bùnéng** not be able to; be

unable; can't; mustn't; shouldn't; cannot be …

不能消化 **bùnéng xiāohuà** indigestible

不能抑制 **bùnéng yìzhì** irrepressible

不偏不倚 **bù piānbùyǐ** detachment, objectivity

不偏袒 **bù piāntǎn** unbiased

不偏心 **bù piānxīn** dispassionate

补票 **bǔpiào** buy a ticket after boarding

补票费 **bǔpiàofèi** excess fare

不平常 **bù píngcháng** extraordinary; unusual

不平等 **bù píngděng** unequal ◊ inequality

不平衡 **bù pínghéng** unbalanced, lop-sided

不恰当 **bú qiàdàng** improper; undeserved; unfortunate

不清楚 **bù qīngchu** unclear

不请自到 **bùqǐngzìdào** come uninvited, gatecrash

不确定 **bú quèdìng** indefinite; uncertain ◊ uncertainty

不然 **bùrán** otherwise; not so

不然的话 **bùrán dehuà** otherwise

不让步 **bú ràngbù** uncompromising

不容置疑 **bùróng zhìyí** indisputable ◊ indisputably

哺乳 **bǔrǔ** breastfeed

不如 **bùrú** not as good as … ◊ be better to …

哺乳动物 **bǔrǔ dòngwù** mammal

不少 **bùshǎo** quite a lot (of)

不慎 **búshèn** careless

不是 **búshì** not; no

捕食 **bǔshí** prey on

不适当 **búshì dàng** unduly ◊ inappropriate; inadequate

不适合 **bú shìhé** unfit; unsuitable; inappropriate

不实际 **bù shíjì** impractical

不适用 **bú shìyòng** inapplicable

部首 **bùshǒu** radical (of Chinese character)

不受欢迎 **bú shòu huānyíng** unpopular; undesirable

捕兽机关 **bǔshòu jīguān** trap

不守秩序 **bù shǒu zhìxù** disorderly

不受重视 **bú shòu zhòngshì** neglected

不舒服 **bùshūfu** unwell, poorly; uncomfortable

不熟练 **bù shúliàn** inept; unskilled

不顺眼 **bú shùnyǎn** eyesore

不舒适 **bù shūshì** uncomfortable

不熟悉 **bù shúxī** unfamiliar; 不熟悉 X **bù shúxī X** be unfamiliar with X

不太可能 **bú tài kěnéng** unlikely

补贴 **bǔtiē** allowance, grant

不通 **bùtōng** impassable

不同 **bùtóng** different; distinct; varied; various ◊ differ ◊ otherwise, differently

不同寻常 **bùtóng xúncháng** unusual

不同意 **bù tóngyì** disagree

不同意见 **bù tóngyì yìjiàn** disagreement

不透明 **bù tòumíng** opaque

不褪色 **bù tuìsè** colorfast

不完美 **bù wánměi** imperfect

不完全 **bù wánquán** partial

不完整 **bù wánzhěng** incomplete

部位 **bùwèi** position

不卫生 **bú wèishēng** unhygienic, insanitary

不像 **búxiàng** unlike

不祥 **bùxiáng** ominous

不相符 **bù xiāngfú** incompatible ◊ incompatibility

不相干 **bù xiānggān** irrelevant

不相关 **bù xiāngguān** unrelated

不现实 **bú xiànshí** impractical; unrealistic

不显眼 **bù xiǎnyǎn** inconspicuous

不显著 **bù xiǎnzhù** dim

不小心 **bùxiǎoxīn** careless ◊ by accident

不懈 **búxiè** relentless

不谢 **búxiè** that's alright (*when somebody says thank you*)

不协调 **bùxiétiáo** clash; discord ◊ incongruous

不幸 **búxìng** poor; ill-fated;

unfortunate, unlucky; tragic; regrettable ◊ regrettably ◊ misfortune

不行 **bùxíng** it's not allowed; that's out ◊ impossible

步行 **bùxíng** walk; hike ◊ on foot

不幸的是 **búxìng de shì** unfortunately

不醒人事 **bù xǐng rénshì** unconscious; 打得 X 不醒人事 **dǎde X bù xǐng rénshì** knock X unconscious

不幸事故 **búxìng shìgù** mishap

不信任 **búxìnrèn** mistrust

不朽 **bùxiǔ** immortal ◊ immortality

不锈钢 **búxiùgāng** stainless steel

不炫耀 **bú xuànyào** unpretentious

不许 **bùxǔ** not allowed; 不许动！ **bùxǔdòng!** don't make a move!

不寻常 **bù xúncháng** uncommon

补牙 **bǔyá** filling (*in tooth*)

不言而喻 **bù yán ér yù** self-evident

不厌其烦 **búyànqífán** thorough

不要 **búyào** not want; don't; 我不要，谢谢 **wǒ búyào, xièxiè** not for me, thanks

不要脸 **bú yào liǎn** shameless

不宜食用/饮用 **bùyí shíyòng / yǐnyòng** be unfit to eat / drink

不一样 **bù yíyàng** it varies

不遗余力 **búyíyúlì** be unstinting in one's efforts

不一致 **bù yízhì** inconsistent; uneven, patchy ◊ clash

不用 **búyòng**: 不用，我来吧 **búyòng, wǒ lái ba** no, I'll do it; 不用，谢谢 **búyòng, xièxie** no thank you; 不用客气 **búyòngkèqi** don't mention it; 不用了！ **búyòngle!** don't bother!

不由自主 **bù yóu zìzhǔ** compulsive; stray

捕鱼 **bǔyú** fish; fishing

哺育 **bǔyù** feed; bring up

不育 **búyù** sterile

不愿 **búyuàn** be unwilling

不愿意 **bú yuànyì** disinclined

不在 **búzài** be away; be out

不赞成 **bú zànchéng** disapprove (of)

不早了 **bù zǎo le** get on ◊ it's getting late

不怎么样 **bù zěnme** not very, not particularly

不怎么样 **bù zěnme yàng** lousy ◊ not really; not much

不粘 **bùzhān** nonstick

部长 **bùzhǎng** minister POL; secretary ◊ ministerial

不扎实 **bù zhāshí** shaky

不真诚 **bù zhēnchéng** insincere

不正常 **bú zhèngcháng** abnormal

不整洁 **bù zhěngjié** unkempt

不整齐 **bù zhěngqí** disheveled

不正确 **bú zhèngquè** incorrect ◊ incorrectly

不真实 **bù zhēnshí** unreal; untrue

不只 **bùzhǐ** not only

布置 **bùzhì** arrange; fit out ◊ arrangement

不知害臊 **bùzhī hàisào** it's a disgrace

不知所措 **bù zhī suǒ cuò** in a daze, dazed ◊ overwhelm; paralyze *fig*; be at a loss

不值一读 **bùzhí yìdú** unreadable

不值一顾 **bùzhí yígù** beneath contempt

不知怎的 **bùzhī zěnde** somehow

不忠 **bù zhōng** disloyal; unfaithful; treacherous ◊ disloyalty; infidelity

不重要 **bú zhòngyào** unimportant

不中意 **bù zhòngyì** not appealing

不中用 **bù zhōngyòng** useless

步骤 **bùzhòu** procedure

补助 **bǔzhù** subsidy

不准 **bùzhǔn** forbid ◊ not allowed; not accurate

不准停车 **bùzhǔn tíngchē** no stopping

捕捉 **bǔzhuō** catch

簿子 **bùzi** notebook

不自然 **bú zìrán** labored, stilted; self-conscious

不自在 **bú zìzài** discomfort; 我跟他在一起感到不自在 **wǒ gēn tā zài yìqǐ gǎndào bú zìzài** I feel uncomfortable with him

不足 **bùzú** inadequate; unsatisfactory

不尊重 **bù zūnzhòng** disrespect

不足为奇 **bùzú wéiqí** unsurprising

不足信 **bù zúxìn** flimsy *excuse*

C

擦 cā dab

擦 cā mop, wipe

擦掉 cādiào erase; rub off; wipe away; wipe off

擦干 cāgān (wipe) dry

擦光剂 cāguāngjì polish

猜 cāi guess

才 cái talent ◊ only; only if; 他昨天才到 tā zuótiān cái dào he only arrived yesterday; 你说了他们才能做 nǐ shuōle tāmen cáinéngzuò they won't do anything until you say so

裁 cái cut *paper, cloth*

材 cái timber; material

财 cái assets; wealth

采 cǎi pick; mine

踩 cǎi step; trample on; tread on; 踩刹车 cǎi shāchē apply the brake(s)

彩 cǎi color

菜 cài dish; vegetable; (non-staple) food

彩笔 cǎibǐ highlighter; marker

猜测 cāicè guess; conjecture; speculation ◊ speculate

彩色照片 cǎicè zhàopiàn color photograph

财产 cáichǎn possession; property

菜单 càidān menu

菜刀 càidāo kitchen knife

彩电 cǎidiàn color TV

裁定 cáidìng convict ◊ conviction; sentencing; 裁定 X 无罪／有罪 cáidìng X wúzuì／yǒuzuì find X innocent／guilty

采访 cǎifǎng interview

采访者 cǎifǎng zhě interviewer

裁缝 cáifeng dressmaker; tailor

财富 cáifù treasure; wealth

采购 cǎigòu purchase ◊ purchaser ◊ purchasing

采购员 cǎigòu yuán buyer, purchaser

彩虹 cǎihóng rainbow

才华 cáihuá brilliance; intelligence

菜花 càihuā cauliflower

采集 cǎijí collect

裁减 cáijiǎn reduce

裁决 cáijué judgment; ruling; verdict

裁军 cáijūn disarm ◊ disarmament

采矿 cǎikuàng mining

材料 cáiliào materials

采纳 cǎinà adopt ◊ adoption

才能 cáinéng ability

菜农 càinóng truck farmer

彩排 cǎipái dress rehearsal

裁判（员）cáipàn (yuán) umpire; referee; judge

裁判院 cáipàn yuàn tribunal

彩票 cǎipiào lottery ticket; raffle ticket

菜谱 càipǔ recipe

彩色 cǎisè color

彩色电视 cǎisè diànshì color television

彩色胶卷 cǎisè jiāojuǎn color film

采石场 cǎishíchǎng quarry (*for mining*)

踩踏板 cǎi tàbǎn pedal

财务 cáiwù finance ◊ financial

财务部 Cáiwù Bù Treasury Department

财务处 cáiwùchù accounts (department)

财务软件 cáiwù ruǎnjiàn accounting software

猜想 cāixiǎng guess

采用 cǎiyòng use

菜油 càiyóu rapeseed oil; vegetable oil

踩油门儿 cǎi yóuménr put one's foot down, accelerate; rev up

裁员 cáiyuán cut back, downsize ◊ layoff

财源 cáiyuán means
菜园 càiyuán vegetable garden
财政 cáizhèng finance ◊ fiscal
财政年度 cáizhèng niándù fiscal year
才智 cáizhì wisdom
擦净 cājìng mop up
擦亮 cāliàng polish
餐 cān meal
惭 cán ashamed
蚕 cán silkworm
惨 cǎn tragic; brutal; disastrous
惨案 cǎn'àn massacre
惨败 cǎnbài massacre; thrashing
残暴 cánbào cruel
餐车 cānchē restaurant car
蚕豆 cándòu broad bean
残废 cánfèi disabled, crippled
残废者 cánfèi zhě disabled person
舱 cāng ship's cabin; aircraft cabin; module
仓 cāng storehouse
苍 cāng dark green; blue; grey
藏 cáng hide
苍白 cāngbái pale; wan
仓促 cāngcù hasty
舱口 cāngkǒu hatch (on ship)
仓库 cāngkù depot, warehouse; storehouse; stockroom, store
苍鹭 cānglù heron
藏匿 cángnì hide ◊ secretion
仓鼠 cāngshǔ hamster
参观 cānguān tour
餐馆 cānguǎn restaurant
参观者 cānguān zhě visitor
苍蝇 cāngying fly (insect)
残骸 cánhái remains; wreck; wreckage; debris
残迹 cánjì remnant
残疾 cánjí disabled, handicapped ◊ disability, physical handicap
参加 cānjiā attend; compete; enter, go in for, take part in; sit exam; participate; join; join in ◊ participation; 参加考试 cānjiā kǎoshì sit an exam
蚕茧 cánjiǎn silk cocoon
参加者 cānjiā zhě entrant, participant; entry; turnout
餐巾 cānjīn napkin

残疾人士 cánjí rénshì disabled person, cripple
餐具 cānjù tableware
餐具垫 cānjù diàn place mat
餐具柜 cānjùguì sideboard
参军 cānjūn enlist
参考 cānkǎo refer to ◊ reference
参考书 cānkǎo shū reference book
参考书目 cānkǎo shūmù bibliography
残酷 cánkù cut-throat competition; savage; sick sense of humor, cruel
惭愧 cánkuì ashamed
灿烂 cànlàn radiant; brilliant; magnificent
残缺 cánquē incomplete
残忍 cánrěn brutal, cruel, ferocious ◊ brutally; in cold blood ◊ cruelty
参赛 cānsài play SP; participate (in match, contest)
参赛表 cānsàibiǎo entry form
参赛者 cānsài zhě participant; contestant
餐室 cānshì dining room
餐厅 cāntīng dining hall; restaurant
惨痛 cántòng painful
参议员 cānyìyuán senator
参议院 cānyìyuàn senate
参与 cānyù participate in; be a party to
残余 cányú remainder; remains
残渣 cánzhā residue
餐桌 cānzhuō dining table
餐座 cānzuò booth
操 cāo hold, grasp; do; speak
槽 cáo trough; tank; groove
草 cǎo grass; straw
操 cào ∨ fuck
草地 cǎodì lawn
草稿 cǎogǎo (rough) draft
操劳 cāoláo work hard; struggle
操练 cāoliàn drill MIL
草帽 cǎomào straw hat
草莓 cǎoméi strawberry
草皮 cǎopí turf
草坪 cǎopíng lawn; meadow; green space
草率 cǎoshuài careless, sloppy;

hasty

草图 cǎotú outline; sketch

操心 cāoxīn worry

槽牙 cáoyá molar

草药 cǎoyào herbal medicine

草原 cǎoyuán grasslands

嘈杂 cáozá noisy

操纵 cāozòng operate; control; manipulate; rig

操纵装置 cāozòng zhuāngzhì controls

操作 cāozuò operate ◊ operation

操作手则 cāozuò fāngfǎ mode

操作手则 cāozuò shǒuzé operating instructions

操作系统 cāozuò xìtǒng operating system

操作者 cāozuò zhě operator

擦伤 cāshāng graze, scrape

擦洗 cāxǐ scrub

擦油 cāyóu put cream on

擦子 cāzi grater

册 cè volume; (exercise) book

测 cè measure

侧 cè lateral, side

策 cè strategy

测定 cèdìng gauge

测航 cèháng navigate

策划 cèhuà intrigue

测量 cèliáng measure ◊ measurement

策略 cèlüè tactics; strategy

侧面 cèmiàn side; profile

策谋 cèmóu contrive

参差不齐 cēncī bùqí jagged

层 céng coat, layer; coating; story (of building); tier

曾 céng ever; once; formerly; 我曾喜欢过他 wǒ céng xǐhuānguò tā I used to like him

曾经 céngjīng ever; once, formerly

厕所 cèsuǒ toilet, bathroom

测验 cèyàn test

侧翼 cèyì flank

插 chā insert; stick in

差 chā difference MATH

叉 chā fork

茶 chá tea

搽 chá rub in

查 chá check; test; 查地图 chá

dìtú consult a map

察 chá inspect; examine

差 chà poor quality; inferior ◊ badly ◊ lack; be short of; 差五分九点 chà wǔfēn jiǔdiǎn five (minutes) of nine; 差一刻五点 chà yíkè wǔdiǎn a quarter of 5

茶包 chábāo teabag

茶杯 chábēi teacup

茶杯碟 chábēidié saucer

差别 chābié difference; 没什么差别 méi shénme chābié it doesn't make any difference, it doesn't change anything

查查 cháchá check

叉车 chāchē forklift (truck)

茶匙 cháchí teaspoon

查出 cháchū dig up

差错 chācuò mistake; discrepancy

茶袋 chádài teabag

茶点 chádiǎn refreshments, tea and snacks

差额 chā'é balance, remainder

搽粉 cháfěn powder

茶馆 cháguǎn tea house

查号台 cháhàotái information TELEC

茶壶 cháhú teapot

插花 chāhuā arrangement

插话 chāhuà interrupt; 我插不上话 wǒ chābúshàng huà I couldn't get a word in edgewise

拆 chāi tear open; take apart; dismantle; demolish

柴 chái firewood

拆除 chāichú demolish

拆掉 chāidiào tear down

拆毁 chāihuǐ demolish ◊ demolition

拆开 chāikāi take to pieces; unravel; dismantle

差使 chāishǐ errand

拆下 chāixià unfix

拆卸 chāixiè dismantle

柴油 cháiyóu diesel

茶几 chájī coffee table

茶巾 chájīn tea cloth

差劲 chàjìn disappointing; bad; useless

差距 chājù gap; difference; distance

茶具 **chájù** tea service, tea set

察觉 **chájué** detect, discern

岔开 **chàkāi** diverge; sidetrack

察看 **chákàn** check on; look up

查明 **chámíng** determine; make sure

禅 **Chán** Zen

缠 **chán** wind round; bind; wrap; 硬缠着 X **yìng chánzhe X** impose oneself on X

蝉 **chán** cicada

产 **chǎn** give birth to; produce ◊ product; property

阐 **chǎn** explain

铲 **chǎn** shovel

颤 **chàn** tremble

颤动 **chàndòng** pulsate

颤抖 **chàndǒu** quaver; shake; shiver

产房 **chǎnfáng** labor ward

长 **cháng** long ◊ length

尝 **cháng** taste; 尝一尝 **chángyīcháng** have a taste

偿 **cháng** repay; compensate for; fulfil

常 **cháng** frequent

肠 **cháng** intestines

场 **cháng** place; space; course; court SP; field SP; round; scene; meeting place

厂 **chǎng** factory; plant

敞 **chǎng** spacious; open

唱 **chàng** sing

畅 **chàng** smooth; unimpeded

长白山 **Chángbáishān** Changbai mountain

长柄勺 **cháng bǐngsháo** ladle

常常 **chángcháng** frequently, often

长城 **Chángchéng** the Great Wall

长处 **chángchu** advantage; strength

常春藤 **chángchūnténg** ivy

长笛 **chángdí** flute

场地 **chǎngdì** site

长度 **chángdù** length

长短 **chángduǎn** length

唱反调 **chàng fǎndiào** dissent from

长方形 **chángfāng xíng** rectangle ◊ rectangular

偿付 **chángfù** settlement, payment

唱歌 **chànggē** sing (a song)

常规 **chángguī** customary; standard; routine ◊ custom, practice; rut; 常规上 ... **chángguī shàng ...** it is customary to ...

长号 **chánghào** trombone

偿还 **chánghuán** pay back; settle

唱机 **chàngjī** record player

长江 **Chángjiāng** Yangtze River

场景 **chángjǐng** scene

长颈鹿 **chángjǐnglù** giraffe

长久 **chángjiǔ** long; long-time ◊ forever, always

敞开 **chǎngkāi** open

敞开天窗说亮话 **chǎngkāi tiānchuāng shuō liànghuà** get down to basics

常客 **chángkè** regular

厂矿企业 **chǎngkuàng qǐyè** industrial enterprises

场面 **chángmiàn** scene

长年 **chángnián** all year round

长袍 **chángpáo** gown

长跑 **chángpǎo** long-distance running

敞篷货车 **chǎngpéng huòchē** wagon

唱片 **chàngpiàn** album, record

长篇大论 **chángpiān dàlùn** monolog

唱片架 **chàngpiàn jià** record rack

长波 **chángpō** long wave

长期 **chángqī** the long term ◊ long-term ◊ permanently

常青 **chángqīng** evergreen

偿清 **chángqīng** pay off

长沙发 **cháng shāfā** couch

厂商 **chǎngshāng** commercial and industrial enterprises; factories and stores; manufacturer

长舌 **chángshé** gossip

昌盛 **chāngshèng** flourish; do well ◊ flourishing

常识 **chángshí** general knowledge

尝试 **chángshì** attempt; try; taste

常识 **chángshí** common sense

长寿 **chángshòu** long life

场所 **chǎngsuǒ** place

畅所欲言 **chàngsuǒyùyán** vocal

长条 **chángtiáo** strip

畅通 **chàngtōng** unobstructed

长统袜 **chángtǒngwà** stocking

长途 **chángtú** long distance

长途电话 **chángtú diànhuà** long-distance call

长途汽车 **chángtú qìchē** (long-distance) bus

肠胃 **chángwèi** intestines and stomach; guts

畅销 **chàngxiāo** in demand; selling well

畅销书 **chàngxiāo shū** best-seller

长袖 **chángxiù** long-sleeved

长袖运动服 **chángxiù yùndòngfú** tracksuit

肠炎 **chángyán** enteritis

长椅 **chángyǐ** bench

常用 **chángyòng** in common use; everyday

长于 **chángyú** be good at

长远 **chángyuǎn** long-range; long-term

厂长 **chǎngzhǎng** director of a factory

长征 **Chángzhēng** Long March

肠子 **chángzi** intestine

产后 **chǎnhòu** postnatal

忏悔 **chànhuǐ** repent; confess ◊ confession; penitence

搀假 **chānjiǎ** adulterate

产假 **chǎnjià** maternity leave

缠结 **chánjié** snarl

产科病房 **chǎnkē bìngfáng** maternity ward

产科医师 **chǎnkē yīshī** obstetrician

产量 **chǎnliàng** production; capacity; output; yield; turnover ◊ turn over

阐明 **chǎnmíng** explain; interpret

产品 **chǎnpǐn** produce ◊ product

铲平 **chǎnpíng** bulldoze, demolish

产前 **chǎnqián** antenatal

缠绕 **chánrào** wrap; wind; curl

缠人 **chánrén** clingy

产生 **chǎnshēng** produce; emerge; generate; give rise to

阐述 **chǎnshù** explain

铲子 **chǎnzi** shovel; spade

禅宗佛教 **Chánzōng Fójiào** Zen Buddhism

抄 **chāo** copy; transcribe; plagiarize

钞 **chāo** bank bill

超 **chāo** exceed; surpass; transcend ◊ super; ultra; extra

巢 **cháo** nest

潮 **cháo** tide ◊ damp

嘲 **cháo** ridicule; mock

朝 **cháo** toward; facing ◊ court; dynasty

炒 **chǎo** cook; stir-fry

吵 **chǎo** make a noise; quarrel

炒菜 **chǎo cài** cook ◊ stir-fried dish

炒菜锅 **chǎocàiguō** wok

超车 **chāochē** pass, overtake

超出 **chāochū** exceed ◊ beyond; 超出我的能力范围 **chāochū wǒde nénglì fànwéi** it's beyond me

朝代 **cháodài** dynasty

超短裙 **chāoduǎnqún** mini, miniskirt

炒饭 **chǎofàn** fried rice ◊ fry rice

超过 **chāoguò** exceed; outgrow; overtake, pass ◊ over

吵架 **chǎojià** argue ◊ argument

超级大国 **chāojí dàguó** superpower

超级市场 **chāojí shìchǎng** supermarket

潮流 **cháoliú** trend

炒面 **chǎomiàn** fried noodles ◊ fry noodles

吵闹 **chǎonào** carry on, make a fuss ◊ noise; scene

嘲弄 **cháonòng** jeer; mockery

钞票 **chāopiào** bank bill

超声波 **chāoshēngbō** ultrasound

朝圣者 **cháoshèng zhě** pilgrim

朝圣之行 **cháoshèng zhī xíng** pilgrimage

超时 **chāoshí** overrun

潮湿 **cháoshī** moist; damp

潮水 **cháoshuǐ** tide

超速 **chāosù** overdrive ◊ speed ◊ speeding

超文本 **chāowénběn** hypertext

抄袭 **chāoxí** copy

朝鲜 **Cháoxiān** Korea

朝向 **cháoxiàng** look onto, face

嘲笑 **cháoxiào** laugh at, poke fun at; taunt ◊ taunt

抄写 **chāoxiě** copy; transcribe

巢穴 **cháoxué** den; lair

超音速 **chāoyīnsù** supersonic

炒鱿鱼 **chǎo yóuyú** dismiss, fire; 被炒鱿鱼了 **bèi chǎo yóuyú le** be fired

超载 **chāozài** overload

超支 **chāozhī** overdraft ◊ overdraw; overspend; 超支八百美元 **chāozhī bābǎi měiyuán** be $800 overdrawn

超重 **chāozhòng** overload ◊ overweight

超重的行李 **chāozhòngde xíngli** excess baggage

超自然 **cháozìrán** supernatural

吵嘴 **chǎozuǐ** quarrel

查票员 **chápiào yuán** (ticket) inspector

插入 **chārù** insert; slot in ◊ insertion; 把 X 插入 Y **bǎ X chārù Y** insert X into Y

茶室 **cháshì** tearoom

插手 **chāshǒu** involvement

插头 **chātóu** pin; plug ELEC

插图 **chātú** illustration

查问 **cháwèn** questioning

插销 **chāxiāo** bolt

查询 **cháxún** enquire

茶叶 **cháyè** tea; tea leaves

差异 **chāyì** gap

诧异 **chàyì** amazed

搽用 **cháyòng** put on

查阅 **cháyuè** look up; consult

叉子 **chāzi** cross; fork

查字典 **chá zìdiǎn** look up; consult a dictionary

插嘴 **chāzuǐ** butt in, chip in

插座 **chāzuò** socket

车 **chē** vehicle; car; bus

扯 **chě** pull; bear; tell lies; talk nonsense

撤 **chè** pull back; withdraw

彻 **chè** thorough; penetrating

车把 **chēbǎ** handlebars

车床 **chēchuáng** lathe

车次 **chēcì** train number; bus number

扯蛋 **chědàn** talk nonsense

彻底 **chèdǐ** exhaustive, thorough; outright; resounding; radical; solid *support* ◊ radically; right, completely; soundly

彻底变革 **chèdǐ biàngé** revolutionize

彻底击垮 **chèdǐ jīkuǎ** undermine

车顶架 **chēdǐng jià** roof rack

车队 **chēduì** convoy, fleet (of vehicles)

撤回 **chèhuí** withdraw

车祸 **chēhuò** traffic accident

车架横梁 **chējià héngliáng** crossbar

车间 **chējiān** workshop

车库 **chēkù** garage

撤离 **chèlí** evacuate; move out; pull out

车辆 **chēliàng** vehicle

车龙 **chēlóng** traffic jam

车轮 **chēlún** wheel

沉 **chén** sink

晨 **chén** morning

陈 **chén** old; stale ◊ lay out; display

衬 **chèn** line *coat etc*

陈词滥调 **chéncí làndiào** platitude

衬垫 **chèndiàn** lining

沉淀物 **chéndiànwù** sediment

陈腐 **chénfǔ** conventional; hackneyed

撑 **chēng** support; hold up

称 **chēng** call; say; weigh; 称 … 的重量 **chēng … de zhòngliàng** weigh

乘 **chéng** by ◊ multiply; 二乘四 **èr chéng sì** 2 by 4

橙 **chéng** orange (*color, fruit*)

成 **chéng** achieve; become; succeed; mature

诚 **chéng** honest; sincere

城 **chéng** city; wall

呈 **chéng** submit

程 **chéng** rule; pattern

惩 **chéng** punish

澄 **chéng** clear

承 **chéng** hold; carry; undertake

秤 **chèng** scales

承包 **chéngbāo** commission;

contract

城堡 **chéngbǎo** castle; fortress

呈报 **chéngbào** declare

承包人 **chéngbāo rén** contractor

成本 **chéngběn** cost

成本加运费 **chéngběn jiā yùnfèi** cost and freight

成本价格 **chéngběn jiàgé** cost price

成比例 **chéng bǐlì** proportional

乘车 **chèngchē** ride

惩处 **chéngchǔ** punish; penalize

承担 **chéngdān** bear; undertake; 承担责任 **chéngdān zérèn** be held responsible; take responsibility

成单行 **chéngdānháng** in single file

呈递 **chéngdì** submit; hand in; hand over

程度 **chéngdù** degree, extent; measure; 在一定程度上 **zài yídìng chéngdùshang** to a certain extent; in a way

成堆 **chéngduī** in piles; loads of

承兑 **chéngduì** cash; accept *check*

惩罚 **chéngfá** discipline; penalty; punishment ◊ punish

成分 **chéngfèn** component; ingredient

撑杆跳 **chēnggān tiào** vault

撑竿跳高 **chēnggān tiàogāo** polevault

成功 **chénggōng** do well, succeed, prosper ◊ success ◊ successful; fruitful ◊ successfully; 取得成功 **qǔdé chénggōng** work out, succeed

成果 **chéngguǒ** achievement; success

称号 **chēnghào** title; designation

称呼 **chēnghu** form of address ◊ address

乘机 **chéngjī** fly (*in plane*)

成绩 **chéngjì** achievement; results

成见 **chéngjiàn** prejudice; stereotype

呈交 **chéngjiāo** put in, submit

成交! **chéngjiāo!** it's a deal!

成吉思汗 **Chéngjísīhàn** Genghis Khan

成就 **chéngjiù** achievement

撑开 **chēngkāi** open *umbrella*

乘客 **chéngkè** passenger

诚恳 **chéngkěn** sincere

乘客座位 **chéngkè zuòwèi** passenger seat

成立 **chénglì** establish, set up ◊ foundation

成名 **chéngmíng** make a name for oneself

成年 **chéngnián** come of age ◊ adult ◊ F all year

承诺 **chéngnuò** promise; commit; pledge

尘垢 **chéngòu** grime

澄清 **chéngqīng** clarify; acquit, clear; unravel; settle (*of liquid*)

成人 **chéngrén** adult

承认 **chéngrèn** acknowledge, recognize; admit, confess; concede ◊ admission; recognition

成人片 **chéngrén piān** adult film

橙色 **chéngsè** orange (*color*)

诚实 **chéngshí** honest, truthful ◊ honesty; integrity

城市 **chéngshì** city ◊ civic

城市化 **chéngshìhuà** urbanization

成熟 **chéngshóu** ripen

承受 **chéngshòu** bear, carry; 承受压力 **chéngshòu yālì** be under pressure

成熟 **chéngshú** full-grown; grown-up; ripe; mature ◊ maturity ◊ mature; ripen

成套 **chéngtào** complete set; 成套用品 **chéngtào yòngpǐn** complete set of equipment

成为 **chéngwéi** become; turn into

呈文 **chéngwén** submission; petition

乘务员 **chéngwùyuán** conductor; ticket collector; steward; stewardess

呈现 **chéngxiàn** arise; materialize

成效 **chéngxiào** effect

称心如意 **chènxīn rúyì** desirable

程序 **chéngxù** program; procedure; system; order

程序表 **chéngxùbiǎo** schedule

程序员 **chéngxùyuán** programmer

诚意 **chéngyì** honesty; sincerity

成瘾者 **chéngyǐn zhě** addict

盛有 **chéngyǒu** hold

乘游艇 **chéng yóutǐng** yachting

成员 **chéngyuán** member

成员人数 **chéngyuán rénshù** membership

成员证 **chéngyuánzhèng** membership card

成员资格 **chéngyuán zīgé** membership

称赞 **chēngzàn** praise

成长 **chéngzhǎng** grow ◊ growth

诚挚 **chéngzhì** sincere ◊ sincerely

称职 **chèngzhí** competent

橙汁 **chéngzhī** orange juice; orangeade

称重量 **chēng zhòngliàng** weigh

撑柱 **chēngzhù** stilts (*under house*)

沉着冷静 **chéngzhuó lěngjìng** imperturbable

橙子 **chéngzi** orange (*fruit*)

橙子酱 **chéngzijiàng** marmalade

沉积 **chénjī** deposit

沉浸 **chénjìn** immerse oneself in

陈旧 **chénjiù** outmoded

衬里 **chènlǐ** lining; 安衬里 **ān chènlǐ** line (*with material*)

衬料 **chènliào** lining; padding

陈列 **chénliè** display ◊ be on display

陈列柜 **chénlièguì** display cabinet

沉闷 **chénmèn** dreary; close, oppressive *weather*; dejected; reserved *character*

沉没 **chénmò** sink, go under

沉默 **chénmò** silent ◊ silence

沉默寡言 **chénmò guǎyán** silent; taciturn

沉溺 **chénnì** addiction

衬裙 **chènqún** underskirt

衬衫 **chènshān** shirt; blouse

陈述 **chénshù** set out

沉思 **chénsī** thoughtful, pensive ◊ muse

沉痛 **chéntòng** deeply distressed

尘土 **chéntǔ** dust

晨曦 **chénxī** daybreak

称心 **chènxīn** be satisfied with

沉重 **chénzhòng** heavy; serious; oppressive *weather*

沉着 **chénzhuó** level-headed, composed; self-possessed

车子 **chēzi** bicycle; car

车牌 **chēpái** license plate

车牌号码 **chēpái hàomǎ** license number

车皮 **chēpí** freight car

车票 **chēpiào** ticket

车身 **chēshēn** bodywork

车胎 **chētāi** tire

车胎爆炸 **chētāi bàozhà** blow-out

车条 **chētiáo** spoke

撤退 **chètuì** retreat; withdraw ◊ withdrawal

车厢 **chēxiāng** car (*of train*)

撤销 **chèxiāo** undo COMPUT; withdraw; cancel; get rid of ◊ withdrawal

车站 **chēzhàn** bus stop; bus station; station

车辙 **chēzhé** rut

吃 **chī** eat; take; live on; absorb; suffer; bear; 吃点儿饭怎么样？ **chī diǎnr fàn zěnmeyàng?** what about some dinner?; 吃早餐 **chī zǎocān** have breakfast

池 **chí** pool; pond

迟 **chí** late

持 **chí** hold; grasp; keep; maintain; manage

匙 **chí** spoon

尺 **chǐ** Chinese foot; rule; ruler

耻 **chǐ** shame; disgrace

齿 **chǐ** tooth

赤 **chì** red; bare

翅 **chì** wing; shark's fin

斥 **chì** scold

翅膀 **chìbǎng** wing

吃饱了 **chī bǎo le** full up

持不同政见者 **chí bùtóng zhèngjiàn zhě** dissident

吃不消 **chībùxiāo** unbearable

吃草 **chīcǎo** graze

吃醋 **chīcù** be jealous

尺寸 **chǐcùn** dimension; measurement

迟到 **chídào** be late

赤道 **chìdào** equator

吃的 **chīde** food

尺度 **chǐdù** measure; standard; rule

迟钝 **chídùn** clumsy, awkward; stupid; backward; numb

吃饭 **chīfàn** eat, have a meal

吃个饱 **chīgebǎo** eat one's fill

齿冠 **chǐguàn** crown (*on tooth*)

吃光 **chīguāng** eat up; scoff

吃好 **chīhǎo** enjoy!

迟缓 **chíhuǎn** slow; hesitant

持家 **chíjiā** keep house, run a home

赤脚 **chìjiǎo** barefoot

赤脚医生 **chìjiǎo yīshēng** barefoot doctor

吃惊 **chījīng** be amazed; be surprised; 令人吃惊 **lìngrén chījīng** staggering

持久 **chíjiǔ** enduring

吃苦 **chīkǔ** bear hardships; suffer

吃亏 **chīkuī** be at a disadvantage ◊ disadvantaged

吃力 **chīlì** with difficulty ◊ punishing

齿轮 **chǐlún** gear

赤裸裸 **chì luǒluo** in the nude

持枪歹徒 **chíqiāng dǎitú** gunman

耻辱 **chǐrǔ** dishonor; disgrace; shame

池塘 **chítáng** pond

赤陶 **chìtáo** terracotta

持械抢劫 **chíxiè qiǎngjié** armed robbery

持续 **chíxù** continue; last; endure

持续不断 **chíxù búduàn** persistent

持续观察 **chíxù guānchá** monitor

吃药 **chīyào** take medicine

齿龈 **chǐyín** gum

持异议 **chí yìyì** dissent

持有 **chíyǒu** possess, hold ◊ possession

迟于 **chíyú** past; later than

迟早 **chízǎo** sooner or later

斥责 **chìzé** rebuke, reprimand

吃住 **chīzhù** board and lodging

尺子 **chǐzi** ruler (*for measuring*)

赤子 **chìzǐ** newborn child

赤字 **chìzì** shortfall, deficit

充 **chōng** full

冲 **chōng** push forward; charge; attack; flush; rinse

虫 **chóng** insect

重 **chóng** repeat; double ◊ again ◊ layer

宠爱 **chǒng'ài** dote on

崇拜 **chóngbài** worship

崇拜者 **chóngbài zhě** admirer; worshipper

重播 **chóngbō** repeat (broadcast)

冲刺 **chōngcì** spurt (*in race*)

充当 **chōngdāng** serve as

充电 **chōngdiàn** charge; recharge

冲掉 **chōngdiào** flush away

重迭 **chóngdié** overlap

冲动 **chōngdòng** impulse; 凭一时的冲动 **píng yìshíde chōngdòng** on the spur of the moment

宠儿 **chǒng'ér** pet, favorite

重放 **chóngfàng** replay

充分 **chōngfèn** full; ample; sufficient

冲锋 **chōngfēng** charge (*of troops*)

重逢 **chóngféng** meet again

冲锋枪 **chōngfēngqiāng** submachine gun

重复 **chóngfù** repetition; duplicate; action replay ◊ repeat; echo ◊ repetitive; 我是不是重复了？ **wǒ shìbúshì chóngfù le?** am I repeating myself?

崇高 **chónggāo** lofty; exalted

虫害 **chónghài** plague of insects

宠坏 **chǒnghuài** spoil ◊ spoilt

重婚 **chónghūn** bigamy

冲昏了头 **chōnghūn le tóu** get carried away

重获 **chónghuò** regain

冲击 **chōngjī** lunge at; lash; charge

重建 **chóngjiàn** rebuild

崇敬 **chóngjìng** revere

冲浪板 **chōnglàngbǎn** surfboard

冲浪运动 **chōnglàng yùndòng** surfing

冲浪者 **chōnglàng zhě** surfer

充满 **chōngmǎn** fill up ◊ be full of

充满怨恨 **chōngmǎn yuànhèn** bitter

充气 **chōngqì** inflate ◊ pneumatic

充任 **chōngrèn** occupy; hold the post of

重赛 **chóngsài** replay

重申 **chóngshēn** echo *views*; reiterate

重审 **chóngshěn** reopen

充实 **chōngshí** beef up ◊ full *life*

冲突 **chōngtū** clash; conflict

重温 **chóngwēn** brush up

宠物 **chǒngwù** pet (*animal*)

冲洗 **chōngxǐ** develop *photograph*; flush ◊ development

重现 **chóngxiàn** reappear

重写 **chóngxiě** rewrite

重新 **chóngxīn** again

重新安排 **chóngxīn ānpái** reorganize, rearrange ◊ reorganization

重新出现 **chóngxīn chūxiàn** resurface

重新发展 **chóngxīn fāzhǎn** redevelop

重新开始 **chóngxīn kāishǐ** go back to the drawing board; renew ◊ renewal; fresh start

重新开张 **chóngxīn kāizhāng** reopen

重新考虑 **chóngxīn kǎolù** reconsider

重新命名 **chóngxīn mìngmíng** rename

重新评价 **chóngxīn píngjià** revaluation

重新武装 **chóngxīn wǔzhuāng** rearm

重新装修 **chóngxīn zhuāngxiū** redecorate

充血 **chōngxuè** congestion; MED hyperemia

虫牙 **chóngyá** decayed tooth

重阳节 **Chóngyángjié** Double Ninth Festival

重印 **chóngyìn** reprint

重影 **chóngyǐng** double

充裕 **chōngyù** abundant

虫子 **chóngzi** insect; worm

充足 **chōngzú** ample; sufficient ◊ sufficiently

重组 **chóngzǔ** shake-up ◊ reshuffle; reorganize

抽 **chōu** pull out; draw

稠 **chóu** thick; dense

筹 **chóu** plan; prepare

酬 **chóu** reward; remuneration

愁 **chóu** worry

仇 **chóu** enemy; hatred

丑 **chǒu** ugly

臭 **chòu** stinking

酬报 **chóubào** reward; payment

筹备 **chóubèi** arrange

抽不开身 **chōu bù kāi shēn** tied up, busy

抽出 **chōuchū** pull out, draw

抽搐 **chōuchù** convulsion; twitch

仇敌 **chóudí** enemy

丑恶 **chǒu'è** repulsive, revolting

仇恨 **chóuhèn** hatred; enmity

筹划 **chóuhuà** map out

筹集 **chóují** raise *money*

抽奖 **chōujiǎng** raffle

丑角 **chǒujiǎo** comedian; clown

抽筋 **chōujīn** cramp

酬金 **chóujīn** fee

丑角 **chǒujué** clown

抽开 **chōukāi** pull away

抽空 **chōukòng** take time; devote time

丑陋 **chǒulòu** ugly, hideous

筹码 **chóumǎ** chip, counter

臭骂一顿 **chòumà yídùn** bawl out

愁闷 **chóumèn** worried; down

稠密 **chóumì** thick; dense

稠密度 **chóumì dù** density

臭名远扬 **chòumíng yuǎnyáng** infamous

臭名昭著 **chòumíng zhāozhù** infamous

抽泣 **chōuqì** sob

臭气 **chòuqì** stink

抽税 **chōushuì** tax; levy a tax

抽丝 **chōusī** run (*in pantyhose*)

抽屉 **chōutì** drawer

臭味儿 **chòuwèir** stink

丑闻 **chǒuwén** scandal

抽吸 **chōuxī** suction

抽象 **chōuxiàng** abstract

抽烟 **chōuyān** smoke

抽样 **chōuyàng** sampling

臭氧 **chòuyǎng** ozone

臭氧层 **chòuyǎng céng** ozone

layer

抽油烟机 **chōuyóu yānjī** hood (*over cooker*)

出 **chū** out ◊ go out; come out; give out; publish; produce; happen

初 **chū** beginning ◊ first

橱 **chú** cupboard

除 **chú** eliminate; remove; except; divide MATH; 除 … 外 **chú … wài** apart from …

锄 **chú** hoe

雏 **chú** young *bird*

储 **chú** store up

处 **chú** get along with; manage; be situated in

穿 **chuān** wear; pierce; penetrate; 穿衣服 **chuān yīfu** get dressed, dress; 穿黄色衣服 **chuān huángsè yīfu** dressed in yellow; 我穿不上裤子 **wǒ chuān bú shàng kùzǐ** I can't get these pants on

传 **chuán** pass on; spread; infect; transmit; call

船 **chuán** boat, ship, vessel; 在船上 **zài chuánshàng** be aboard

喘 **chuǎn** breathe heavily; 喘不过气来 **chuǎn bū guò qì lái** breathless, out of breath

串 **chuàn** string together ◊ bunch; kebab ◊ *measure word for strings, bunches of things*; 一串项链 **yíchuàn xiàngliàn** a necklace

传播 **chuánbō** spread

船舶 **chuánbó** shipping

喘不过气 **chuǎn bū guò qì** breathlessness

船舱 **chuáncāng** cabin

船厂 **chuánchǎng** dockyard

传达 **chuándá** pass on; transmit ◊ janitor; 请传达给我 **qǐng chuándá gěi wǒ** please keep me informed

穿戴 **chuāndài** wear; dress

传单 **chuándān** flyer (*leaflet*)

传导 **chuándǎo** conduct ELEC

传道 **chuándào** preach

传道人 **chuándào rén** preacher

传达器 **chuándáqì** transmitter

传递 **chuándì** pass on; convey

传动 **chuándòng** transmission

疮 **chuāng** sore

窗 **chuāng** window

床 **chuáng** bed

创 **chuàng** start; initiate

窗板 **chuāngbǎn** shutter

创办 **chuàngbàn** found, start

创办人 **chuàngbàn rén** promoter

窗玻璃 **chuāng bōlí** windowpane

床单 **chuángdān** sheet

床垫 **chuángdiàn** mattress

窗户 **chuānghu** window

创建 **chuàngjiàn** found, establish

创建人 **chuàngjiàn rén** founder

创可贴 **chuàngkětiē** adhesive plaster

窗口 **chuāngkǒu** hatch; window; contact

创立 **chuànglì** found, establish

窗帘 **chuānglián** curtain; drapes

床铺 **chuángpù** bunk

闯入 **chuǎngrù** burst into a room

创伤性 **chuàngshāng xìng** traumatic

床上用品 **chuángshàng yòngpǐn** bedclothes, linen

创始人 **chuàngshǐ rén** founder; originator

窗台 **chuāngtái** windowsill

床头 **chuángtóu** bedstead

穿过 **chuānguò** cross ◊ through

创新 **chuàngxīn** create ◊ revolutionary *new ideas*

创业 **chuàngyè** enterprise; 有创业才能 **yǒu chuàngyè cáinéng** entrepreneurial

创业园 **chuàngyèyuán** venture park

创造 **chuàngzào** create

创造者 **chuàngzào zhě** creator

床罩 **chuángzhào** bedspread

创作 **chuàngzuò** create; compose ◊ creation

传呼 **chuánhū** page

传唤 **chuánhuàn** subpoena; summon to court

传话 **chuánhuà** pass on a message

传呼机 **chuánhūjī** pager

传教 **chuánjiào** do missionary work

传教士 **chuánjiàoshì** missionary

穿孔 **chuān kǒng** puncture

窗框 **chuānkuàng** sash

船篷 **chuánpéng** awning

传票 **chuánpiào** subpoena; summons

船票 **chuánpiào** ticket (*for ship*)

传奇 **chuánqí** legend

喘气 **chuánqì** gasp (for breath); pant

传球 **chuánqiú** pass (the ball)

传染 **chuánrǎn** infect ◊ contagious

传染性 **chúanrǎn xìng** catching; infectious

船首 **chuánshǒu** prow

传授 **chuánshòu** teach

传说 **chuánshuō** legend ◊ legend has it; it is said

传送 **chuánsòng** carry (*of sound*)

传送带 **chuánsòng dài** conveyor belt

穿梭 **chuānsuō** shuttle

穿梭业务 **chuānsuō yèwù** shuttle service

穿梭营运 **chuānsuō yíngyùn** shuttlebus

船台 **chuántái** berth

传统 **chuántǒng** tradition ◊ traditional ◊ traditionally

穿透 **chuāntòu** penetrate

船头 **chuántóu** bow (*of ship*)

船桅 **chuánwéi** mast

船尾电动机 **chuánwěi diàndòngjī** outboard motor

传闻 **chuánwén** hearsay; rumor ◊ it is said

船屋 **chuánwū** houseboat

船坞 **chuánwù** dock

喘息 **chuánxī** gasp, pant; puff

传下来 **chuánxiàlái** hand down

船舷 **chuánxián** side of a ship

传销 **chuánxiāo** pyramid selling

传下去 **chuánxiàqù** hand on

传讯 **chuánxùn** summons

船员 **chuányuán** sailor

传阅 **chuányuè** circulate

船长 **chuánzhǎng** captain, skipper

传真 **chuánzhēn** fax; 用传真传 *yòng chuánzhēn chuán* fax, send by fax; 把X传真给Y *bǎ X chuánzhēn gěi Y* fax X to Y

传真机 **chuánzhēnjī** fax machine

船主 **chuánzhǔ** shipowner

穿着 **chuānzhuó** clothing; 穿着单薄 *chuānzhuó dānbó* scantily clad

椽子 **chuánzi** rafter

出版 **chūbǎn** publish; come out

出版公司 **chūbǎn gōngsī** publishing company

出版社 **chūbǎnshè** publisher

出版物 **chūbǎnwù** publication

出版业 **chūbǎnyè** publishing

储备 **chǔbèi** store; reserve ◊ stock up on; stockpile

储备金 **chǔbèi jīn** reserves FIN

储备物资 **chǔbèi wùzī** stockpile

除冰 **chúbīng** de-ice

除冰器 **chúbīng qì** de-icer

储藏 **chǔcáng** store; deposit

除草剂 **chúcǎojì** weedkiller

出差错 **chū chācuò** slip up

出差 **chūchāi** go on a business trip

出产 **chūchǎn** yield; produce

出场 **chūchǎng** entrance

出丑 **chūchǒu** make a spectacle of oneself; 别当众让我出丑 *bié dāngzhòng ràng wǒ chūchǒu* don't show me up in public

橱窗 **chúchuāng** display window; store window ◊ in the window

初次 **chūcì** the first time

储存 **chǔcún** put aside, put by; save; bank ◊ stock; store; reserves

出错 **chūcuò** make a mistake; stumble over

处得来 **chùdélái** get on, be friendly

触电 **chùdiàn** shock

除掉 **chúdiào** eliminate

出尔反尔 **chū'ěr fǎněr** backpedal; contradict oneself

出发 **chūfā** departure ◊ leave; set off

除法 **chúfǎ** division

触发 **chùfā** trigger off

出发点 **chūfā diǎn** starting point

厨房 **chúfáng** kitchen

处方 **chǔfāng** prescribe ◊ prescription

除非 **chúfēi** only if; unless

橱柜 **chúguì** compartment

出国 chūguó go abroad

出汗 chūhàn sweat, perspire

出航 chūháng outgoing *flight*

储户 chǔhù depositor

出乎意料 chūhū yìliào unexpected ◊ strangely enough

吹 chuī blow

垂 chuí hang down; droop

锤 chuí hammer

吹风器 chuīfēngqì hairdrier

吹干 chuīgān blow-dry

吹鼓手 chuīgǔshǒu *band that plays at weddings and funerals*

吹口 chuīkǒu mouthpiece

吹口哨 chuī kǒushào whistle

垂柳 chuíliǔ weeping willow

吹灭 chuīmiè blow out *candle*

吹牛 chuīniú boast, talk big

吹牛拍马 chuīniú pāimǎ suck up; brown nose; be obsequious

吹气 chuīqì blow

吹哨 chuīshào blow

垂死 chuísǐ dying

垂下 chuíxià hang

垂涎 chuíxián lick one's lips; 令人垂涎 lìngrén chuíxián mouthwatering

吹嘘 chuīxū show off, brag

垂直 chuízhí perpendicular; vertical

垂直上移 chuízhí shàngyí scroll up

垂直下移 chuízhí xiàyí scroll down

锤子 chuízi hammer

初级 chūjí elementary

雏鸡 chújī baby chicken

出家 chūjiā become a monk / nun

出价 chūjià bid

触角 chùjiǎo antenna, feeler

出家人 Chūjiā rén Buddhist monk / nun

出借 chūjiè lend; loan

初级阶段 chūjí jiēduàn infancy

出境 chūjìng leave the country

处境 chǔjìng position

初级小学 chūjí xiǎoxué lower elementary school

处决 chǔjué execute, put to death

触觉 chùjué touch

出口 chūkǒu exit; export; outlet ◊ export

出口处 chūkǒuchù exit

出口商 chūkǒushāng exporter

出口物 chūkǒuwù exports

出来 chūlái come out; get out; be out ◊ out

畜栏 chùlán corral

除了 chúle apart from, besides, except; all but; besides; excluding; 除了 X 以外 chúle X yǐwài except for X; 除了 X 之外 chúle X zhīwài in addition to X

处理 chǔlǐ attend to; take care of; deal with; process *data*; treat ◊ disposal (*of waste*); treatment, processing

处理不当 chǔlǐ búdàng mishandle

处理器 chǔlǐqì processor

出路 chūlù exit, way out

出卖 chūmài sell; betray, sell out

出毛病 chū máobìng break down ◊ broken

除毛剂 chúmáojì hair remover

出名 chūmíng well-known ◊ become famous

触摸 chùmò feel; touch

春 chūn spring

纯 chún pure; neat, straight *drink*; net *price*; solid *gold*

唇 chún lip

蠢 chǔn stupid

处男 chǔ'nán virgin (*male*)

出纳员 chū'nàyuán cashier; teller

蠢材 chǔncái clown

纯粹 chúncuì pure; unspoilt

唇读 chúndú lipread

纯度 chúndù purity

春分 Chūnfēn Spring equinox

唇膏 chúngāo lipstick

春季 chūnjì spring, springtime

春节 Chūnjié Chinese New Year, Spring Festival

纯洁 chúnjié innocent; pure; honest

纯净 chúnjìng clean

春卷 chūnjuǎn spring roll

纯利润 chún lìrùn net profit

纯巧克力 chún qiǎokèlì plain chocolate

蠢人 chǔnrén fool

纯熟 **chúnshú** proficient; skillful

春天 **chūntiān** spring

处女 **chǔnǚ** virgin (*female*)

纯正 **chúnzhèng** pure

纯种 **chúnzhǒng** pedigree, thoroughbred

戳 **chuō** jab; prick

绰号 **chuòhào** nickname

出钱 **chūqián** chip in; fork out

出勤 **chūqín** attendance

出去 **chūqù** go out; 出去！ **chūqù!** get out!

除去 **chúqù** drop; remove; obliterate; strip

出去吃 **chūqù chī** eat out

出去一会儿 **chūqù yíhuìr** step out, go out

出让 **chūràng** part with; sell; lease out

出人意外 **chūrényìwài** surprisingly

出入境口 **chūrùjìng kǒu** terminal

出身 **chūshēn** family background

出神 **chūshén** fascinated ◊ space out

出生 **chūshēng** be born; 孩子什么时候出生 **háizi shénme shíhòu chūshēng?** when is the baby due?

畜生 **chùshēng** beast; brute

出声 **chūshēng** aloud; 别出声！ **bié chūshēng!** just be quiet!, hush!

出生地 **chūshēng dì** birthplace

出生率 **chūshēng lǜ** birthrate

出生年份 **chūshēng niánfèn** year of birth

出生日期 **chūshēng rìqī** date of birth

出生证 **chūshēng zhèng** birth certificate

出神儿 **chūshénr** go into a trance; space out

出示 **chūshì** show

出事 **chūshì** go wrong; have an accident

厨师 **chúshī** chef; cook

出事故 **chū shìgù** crash COMPUT

出售 **chūshòu** put up for sale

触手 **chùshǒu** tentacle

储水池 **chǔshuǐ chí** tank (*for water etc*)

出庭 **chūtíng** appearance (*in court*)

锄头 **chútou** pickaxe; hoe

出席 **chūxí** be present; attend

除夕 **Chúxī** Chinese New Year's Eve

出现 **chūxiàn** appear; emerge

出血 **chūxiě** hemorrhage

除臭剂 **chúxiù jì** deodorant

除锈剂 **chúxiùjì** rust remover

储蓄 **chǔxù** save; deposit ◊ savings

初选 **chūxuǎn** primary

出血 **chūxuè** bleed

初学者 **chūxué zhě** beginner

储蓄银行 **chǔxū yínháng** savings bank

储蓄帐户 **chǔxù zhànghù** savings account

初一 **Chūyī** (Chinese) New Year's Day; Grade 1 in Junior High

出游 **chūyóu** outing, trip

出狱 **chūyù** get out of prison

处于 **chǔyú** be (*in a situation*); 处于困境 **chǔyú kùnjìng** be stranded

出院 **chūyuàn** discharge

出证 **chūzhèng** give evidence

出众 **chūzhòng** excel, shine

初中 **chūzhōng** junior high school

出皱褶 **chū zhòuzhě** wrinkle

出租 **chūzū** rent ◊ for rent

出租车 **chūzūchē** taxi, cab

出租车司机 **chūzūchē sījī** taxidriver, cab driver

出租车停车处 **chūzūchē tíngchēchù** taxi rank, cab stand

出租车站 **chūzūchē zhàn** taxi rank, cab stand

出租汽车 **chūzū qìchē** cab, taxi

出租汽车司机 **chūzū qìchē sījī** cab driver, taxi driver

磁 **cí** magnetism; china; ceramic

瓷 **cí** porcelain; china

词 **cí** term; word

慈 **cí** kind

雌 **cí** female

辞 **cí** word

祠 **cí** ancestral temple

此 **cǐ** this

刺 **cì** prick (*pain*); prickle, spine;

thorn; splinter ◊ stab

次 cì time

刺鼻 cìbí pungent

辞别 cíbié say goodbye ◊ farewell

磁带 cídài cassette; tape

磁带驱动器 cídài qūdòngqì tape drive

词典 cídiǎn dictionary

刺耳 cì'ěr ear-piercing; shrill; grating

词根 cígēn root (of word)

刺骨 cìgǔ piercing

此后 cǐhòu after this; henceforth

伺候 cìhou attend to; wait on; serve

词汇 cíhuì vocabulary

词汇表 cíhuì biǎo vocabulary; glossary

刺激 cìjī stimulate; irritate

此刻 cǐkè at present, right now

此路不通 cǐ lù bù tōng dead end

磁盘 cípán disk

磁盘带机 cípán dàijī disk drive

瓷漆 cíqī enamel

瓷器 cíqì porcelain; china

瓷器厂 cíqìchǎng porcelain factory

慈善 císhàn benevolent; charitable

慈善机构 císhàng jīgòu charity (organization)

慈善家 císhànjiā philanthropist

磁石 císhí magnet

次数 cìshù number of times; frequency

刺探 cìtàn pry into

祠堂 cítáng ancestral temple

刺痛 cìtòng smart

刺透 cìtòu pierce

辞退 cítuì dismiss, fire

此外 cǐwài besides; also

词尾 cíwěi ending (of word)

刺猬 cìwei hedgehog

慈祥 cíxiáng kind; loving

雌性 cíxìng female

词性 cíxìng part of speech

磁性 cíxìng magnetism ◊ magnetic

雌性动植物 cíxìng dòngzhíwù female

刺绣 cìxiù embroider ◊ embroidery

刺绣品 cìxiùpǐn embroidery

次序 cìxù order

次序颠倒 cìxù diāndǎo out of order

次要 cìyào minor, secondary; peripheral

赐予 cìyǔ bestow

词藻华丽 cízǎo huálì flowery

辞职 cízhí quit; resign ◊ resignation

此致 cǐzhì yours truly; best regards

瓷砖 cízhuān tile

葱 cōng scallion; green onion; Chinese onion

匆 cōng hasty; urgent

丛 cóng bushes

从 cóng from; 从十八世纪起 **cóng shíbā shìjì qǐ** from the 18th century; 从他来中国以后 **cóng tā lái Zhōngguó yǐhòu** ... ever since he came to China ... ; 我从没去过北京 **wǒ cóng méi qùguò Běijīng** I've never been to Beijing; 从 ... 以来 **cóng ... yǐlái** since ...; 从明天开始 **cóng míngtiān kāishǐ** (starting) from tomorrow; 从五月一日起生效 **cóng wǔyuè yīrì qǐ shēngxiào** effective May 1; 从现在开始 **cóng xiànzài kāishǐ** from now on; 从星期一到星期三 **cóng xīngqīyī dào xīngqīsān** from Monday to Wednesday; 从 Y 中减去 X **cóng Y zhōng jiǎnqù X** deduct X from Y

从不 cóng bù never

从 ... 下来 **cóng ... xiàlái** get off

从此 cóngcǐ from now on; henceforth

匆匆 cōngcōng hurried

从句 cóngjù clause

从来 cónglái ever

从来不 cónglái bù never; 她从来不工作 **tā cónglái bù gōngzuò** she never does a stroke

从来没 cónglái méi (has) never; 他从来没去过那儿 **tā cónglái méi qùguò nàr** he has never been there

丛林 cónglín jungle

匆忙 **cōngmáng** hasty ◊ in a hurry; 匆忙做 … **cōngmáng zuò** … do … in a rush; 匆忙写 **cōngmáng xiě** dash off

聪敏 **cōngmǐn** smart

聪明 **cōngmíng** intelligent, bright, clever ◊ intelligence

从前 **cóngqián** earlier; in the past; once upon a time

从容 **cóngróng** calm; leisurely

从事 **cóngshì** engage in; deal with

从事间谍活动 **cóngshì jiàndié huódòng** spy

从头到尾 **cóngtóu dàowěi** from beginning to end; from top to toe; through

头头至尾 **cóngtóu zhìwěi** overall

从中 **cóngzhōng** from among; between; out of

从中获利 **cóngzhōng huòlì** cash in on

凑合 **còuhe** rough it; make the best of ◊ so-so, average

凑巧 **còuqiǎo** luckily; by chance

粗 **cū** thick; coarse; rough

醋 **cù** vinegar

促 **cù** urge

篡改 **cuàngǎi** fiddle, falsify

粗暴 **cūbào** rough; gruff; 粗暴地对待 **cūbàode duìdài** manhandle

粗笨 **cūbèn** crude; awkward

粗糙 **cūcāo** coarse; rough

促成 **cùchéng** contribute to; shape

促动 **cùdòng** motivate

粗话 **cūhuà** bad language

催 **cuī** rush; drive; urge

摧 **cuī** break; destroy

脆 **cuì** fragile; brittle; crisp

催促 **cuīcù** hurry up; press for

催化转化器 **cuīhuà zhuǎnhuà qì** catalytic converter

摧毁 **cuīhuǐ** destroy; devastate

摧毁性 **cuīhuǐ xìng** devastating

催泪气 **cuīlèi qì** tear gas

催眠疗法 **cuīmián liáofǎ** hypnotherapy

催眠曲 **cuīmián qǔ** lullaby

催眠术 **cuīmiánshù** hypnosis

脆弱 **cuìruò** weak; frail

催账单 **cuīzhàng dān** reminder

促进 **cùjìn** advance, further; stimulate ◊ boost

醋栗 **cùlì** gooseberry

粗鲁 **cūlǔ** crude, vulgar; ignorant; fresh, impertinent; rude; 他待她很粗鲁 **tā dài tā hěn cūlǔ** he was very unpleasant to her

粗略 **cūlüè** rough; cursory

粗面 **cūmiàn** matt

村 **cūn** village

存 **cún** exist; survive; store; save

寸 **cùn** Chinese inch

存储 **cúnchǔ** deposit

存储力 **cúnchǔlì** memory COMPUT

存储器 **cúnchǔqì** memory chip

存储容量 **cúnchǔ róngliàng** storage capacity COMPUT

存放 **cúnfàng** keep, store; check (in checkroom)

存放行李处 **cúnfàng xínglì chù** baggage check

存根 **cúngēn** stub

存活 **cúnhuó** survive

存货 **cúnhuò** stock

存款 **cúnkuǎn** savings ◊ deposit

村里人 **cūnlǐ rén** villager

存盘 **cúnpán** save; saving

存入 **cúnrù** pay in; deposit; 存入帐户 **cúnrù zhànghù** credit an amount to an account

村舍 **cūnshè** cottage

存为 **cúnwéi** save as COMPUT

存在 **cúnzài** exist ◊ existence

存折 **cúnzhé** bank book

村庄 **cūnzhuāng** village

错 **cuò** wrong ◊ mistake; fault; 是你的/我的错 **nǐde/wǒde cuò** it's your/my fault; 不错 **bú cuò** not bad; excellent; 错了 **cuòle** that's wrong; you're wrong

撮 **cuō** group, clump

搓 **cuō** rub; twist

挫 **cuò** foil, thwart

锉 **cuò** file

挫败 **cuòbài** foil, thwart

措词 **cuòcí** phrase ◊ wording

锉刀 **cuòdāo** file (for wood, nails)

错过 **cuòguò** miss

错觉 **cuòjué** misconception; illusion

错开 **cuòkāi** stagger

磋商 **cuōshāng** consult

挫伤 **cuòshāng** bruise

措施 **cuòshī** step, measure

错视 **cuòshì** optical illusion

错误 **cuòwù** error, mistake ◊ wrong; false ◊ wrongly; 犯错误 **fàn cuòwù** make a mistake; go wrong; 使 … 犯错误 **shǐ … fàn cuòwù** trip up; 错误地 **cuòwùde** by mistake

错印 **cuòyìn** misprint

挫折 **cuòzhé** setback; failure; rebuff

错综复杂 **cuòzōng-fùzá** complicated

粗砂 **cūshā** grit

粗石 **cūshí** rubble

促使 **cùshǐ** impel; spur; cause to happen

粗饲料 **cū sìliào** roughage

粗俗 **cūsú** coarse, vulgar; gross; tasteless

粗体 **cūtǐ** bold

粗心 **cūxīn** careless, slipshod; thoughtless

粗心大意 **cūxīn dàyì** negligent

簇叶丛生 **cùyè cóngshēng** overgrown

粗硬 **cūyìng** coarse

促孕药 **cùyùnyào** fertility drug

粗壮 **cūzhuàng** stocky

答 **dā** reply, answer

搭 **dā** pitch; put up; take

打 **dá** dozen

达 **dá** arrive at, reach

答 **dá** reply, answer

打 **dǎ** hit, beat; play; make; do; get ◊ beating

大 **dà** big, large; great

答案 **dá'àn** answer

打败 **dǎbài** thrash; defeat ◊ thrashing; defeat; 被打败 **bèi dǎbài** get a thrashing

大白菜 **dàbáicài** Chinese cabbage

打扮 **dǎbàn** dress up; put on make-up; get dolled up ◊ style; dress; make-up

打包 **dǎbāo** package; pack; bale

大杯 **dàbēi** mug

大便 **dàbiàn** defecate; shit F ◊ feces; shit F

搭便车 **dā biànchē** ride, lift ◊ hitch a ride; get a lift

大鼻子 **dà bízi** *pej* Westerner; Caucasian (*literally*: big nose)

大伯子 **dàbózi** brother-in-law (*husband's older brother*)

大步 **dàbù** stride

打补丁 **dǎ bǔdīng** patch

大不列颠 **Dà Bùlièdiān** Great Britain ◊ British

打不碎的 **dǎ bú suì** unbreakable

大步走 **dàbù zǒu** stride

打草图 **dǎ cǎotú** outline

大草原 **dàcǎoyuán** prairie

大吵大闹 **dàchǎo dà'nào** make a scene

搭车 **dāchē** thumb a ride; take a cab

搭乘 **dāchéng** fly

达成交易 **dáchéng jiāoyì** clinch a deal

达成协议 **dáchéng xiéyì** reach agreement on

大吃 **dàchī** big eater; food freak ◊ tuck away; gorge oneself

大吃大喝 **dàchīdàhē** eat, drink and be merry

大吃一惊 **dàchīyìjīng** stun; be flabbergasted

大锤 **dàchuí** sledge hammer

大吹大擂 **dàchuī dàléi** hype

大葱 **dàcōngī** leek; Chinese onion

大错 **dàcuò** blunder; big mistake

大胆 **dàdǎn** bold, daring

大胆地说 **dàdǎn de shuō** speak out

搭档 **dādàng** partner

搭档关系 **dādàng guānxi** partnership

达到 **dádào** come to; reach, attain; accomplish

大道 **dàdào** avenue; main road

达到顶峰 **dádào dǐngfēng** peak

打电话 **dǎ diànhuà** call, phone; make a call ◊ (tele)phone; 给 X 打电话 **gěi X dǎ diànhuà** give X a call

打电话给 **dǎ diànhuà gěi** call

打电话来 **dǎ diànhuà lái** call in

大调 **dàdiào** major MUS

大跌 **dàdiē** plummet

打动 **dǎdòng** touch, move

大豆 **dàdòu** soybean

打赌 **dǎdǔ** bet

打断 **dǎduàn** interrupt

打盹儿 **dǎdǔnr** doze; have a nap

大多数 **dà duōshù** bulk, majority; most

大都市 **dà dūshì** metropolis ◊ metropolitan

大肚子 **dà dùzi** paunch ◊ pregnant

打发 **dǎfa** idle away

大发雷霆 **dà fā léitíng** fly off the handle

大方 **dàfang** generous; liberal ◊ generosity

大方的举动 **dàfang de jùdòng**

sporting gesture

大发脾气 **dàfā píqì** blow up, get really angry

大风 **dàfēng** gale

答复 **dáfù** answer; respond ◊ answer; response

大概 **dàgài** about, roughly ◊ rough, approximate

大纲 **dàgāng** syllabus

大钢琴 **dàgāngqín** grand piano

打嗝 **dǎgé** belch, burp

大哥 **dàgē** eldest brother; *a term of address for a man of similar age to oneself*

大哥大 **dàgēdà** cell phone

嗝儿 **dágér** hiccup ◊ have the hiccups

大公无私 **dàgōng wúsī** selfless

搭钩 **dāgōu** buckle

打勾 **dǎgōu** check ◊ check(mark), tick

打鼓 **dǎgǔ** beat a drum; play drums

大褂 **dàguà** gown

达观 **dáguān** resilient

达官贵人 **dáguān guìrén** dignitary

打官司 **dǎ guānsī** sue; 和 X 打官司 **hé X dǎ guānsī** take X to court

大规模 **dàguīmó** wholesale, indiscriminate; large-scale

大姑姐 **dàgūjiě** sister-in-law (*husband's elder sister*)

大海 **dàhǎi** sea

打鼾 **dǎ hān** snore

大喊 **dàhǎn** call, call out; shout, shout out

大汗淋漓 **dàhàn línlí** covered in sweat

打哈欠 **dǎ hāqian** yawn

打呵欠 **dǎ hēqian** yawn

打滑 **dǎhuá** skid

大黄蜂 **dàhuángfēng** hornet

大会 **dàhuì** convention

打昏 **dǎhūn** stun

打火机 **dǎhuǒjī** (cigarette) lighter

打火钥匙 **dǎhuǒ yàoshi** ignition key

呆 **dāi** slow-witted; dull; blank ◊ F stay

待 **dāi** wait

带 **dài** bring; take ◊ belt; area; 我能带个朋友来吗？ **wǒ néng dàige péngyǒu láima?** can I bring a friend?

代 **dài** replace ◊ era; generation

袋 **dài** bag; pack

戴 **dài** put on; wear

贷 **dài** loan ◊ borrow, lend

待 **dài** await, wait for

呆板 **dāibǎn** mechanical ◊ mechanically

代表 **dàibiǎo** represent ◊ representative

代表大会 **dàibiǎo dàhuì** congress

代表人 **dàibiǎo rén** representative

代表团 **dàibiǎotuán** delegation

代表我/他 **dàibiǎo wǒ/tā** on my/his behalf

逮捕 **dàibǔ** arrest

代词 **dàicí** pronoun

贷方 **dàifāng** credit

大夫 **dàifu** doctor, physician

怠工 **dàigōng** go-slow

代沟 **dàigōu** generation gap

待会 X **dāihuir** in a minute

代价 **dàijià** cost

代价惨重 **dàijià cǎnzhòng** costly

带菌者 **dàijùn zhě** carrier (*of disease*)

贷款 **dàikuǎn** loan

带来 **dàilái** bring; bring about

代理 **dàilǐ** represent; act for

代理处 **dàilǐ chù** agency

代理 **dàilǐ** lead; guide

带领 **dàilǐng** lead; guide

代理权 **dàilǐ quán** proxy

代理人 **dàilǐ rén** agent; representative

代理商 **dàilǐ shāng** rep, representative; agent

怠慢 **dàimàn** snub

代母 **dàimǔ** surrogate mother; godmother

带球 **dàiqiú** dribble SP

戴上帽子 **dàishang màozi** put one's hat on

待售 **dàishòu** for sale

代替 **dàitì** stand in for; substitute

代替人 **dàitìrén** replacement

歹徒 **dǎitú** mobster, gangster

带血 **dàixuè** bloody, blood-stained

呆一会儿 **dāi yíhuìr** stick around

代用品 **dàiyòngpǐn** makeshift

待遇 **dàiyù** perk; package; treatment

呆在 **dāizài** stay, remain; 呆在家里 **dāi zài jiālǐ** stay at home; 呆在一起 **dāi zài yìqǐ** stay together, stick together

带着 **dàizhe** carry; leave on

呆滞 **dāizhì** glazed *expression*

带状疱疹 **dàizhuàng pàozhěn** shingles

带子 **dàizi** belt; tape; strip

袋子 **dàizi** bag

打击 **dǎjī** blow ◊ hit; deal a blow to

打架 **dǎjià** fight

大家 **dàjiā** everyone; all of us

大剪刀 **dàjiǎndāo** shears

打搅 **dǎjiǎo** bother, disturb; 请勿打搅 **qǐngwù dǎjiǎo** please do not disturb

大叫 **dàjiào** shout, bawl, yell

打交道 **dǎ jiāodào** have dealings with

大教堂 **dà jiàotáng** cathedral

打结 **dǎjié** knot, tie

大姐 **dàjiě** eldest sister

大惊小怪 **dàjīng xiǎoguài** fuss

大祭司 **dà jìsī** high priest

搭救 **dājiù** save, rescue

打击乐 **dǎjīyuè** percussion

打击乐器 **dǎjī yuèqì** percussion instrument

大咀大嚼 **dàjǔdàjué** munch

打开 **dǎkāi** open; turn on; switch on ◊ wide-open

打开包裹 **dǎkāi bāoguǒ** unpack

打瞌睡 **dǎ kēshuì** doze off; snooze

打孔 **dǎ kǒng** punch *hole* ◊ perforated

打孔机 **dǎkǒngjī** punch (*tool*)

大口袋 **dà kǒudài** sack

大块 **dàkuài** chunk

打烂 **dǎlàn** break down

打雷 **dǎléi** thunder

打量 **dǎliang** look over; size up

大梁 **dàliáng** girder

大量 **dàliàng** generous; great; heavy; plentiful ◊ wealth of; loads of

大量买进 **dàliàng mǎijìn** buy up

大量生产 **dàliàng shēngchǎn** mass-produce ◊ mass-production

打猎 **dǎliè** hunt

打临时工 **dǎ línshígōng** (work as a) temp

大理石 **dàlǐshí** marble

大陆 **dàlù** continent, mainland; mainland China

大路 **dàlù** main road

打乱 **dǎluàn** disrupt; screw up

大麻 **dàmá** hemp; marijuana

大马哈鱼 **dàmǎhāyú** salmon

大麦 **dàmài** barley

大门 **dàmén** (entrance) door; gate

打磨机 **dǎmójī** sander

大模型 **dàmóxíng** mock-up

大牧场 **dà mùchǎng** ranch

单 **dān** simple; only; single; odd *number* ◊ list; sheet; bill

担 **dān** carry on one's shoulder; undertake

丹 **dān** red

胆 **dǎn** gall bladder; courage, guts

蛋 **dàn** egg

氮 **dàn** nitrogen

淡 **dàn** faint; weak; bland *taste*; pale *color*; light; 淡粉 **dànfěn** pale pink

诞 **dàn** birth

但 **dàn** but; only

旦 **dàn** dawn

担 **dàn** burden

弹 **dàn** bullet; bomb; pellet

大男人主义者 **dà nánrén zhǔyì zhě** chauvinist

大男子气 **dànánziqì** macho

大闹一场 **dànào yìchǎng** kick up a stink

蛋白 **dànbái** white (*of egg*)

蛋白质 **dànbáizhì** protein

担保 **dānbǎo** guarantee; vouch for; sponsor ◊ sponsorship

担保人 **dānbǎo rén** guarantor; sponsor

单薄 **dānbó** scanty

蛋炒饭 **dànchǎofàn** egg fried rice

诞辰 **dànchén** birthday

单程 **dānchéng** one-way

单程票 **dānchéng piào** one-way ticket

单纯 **dānchún** simple; pure; alone

单词 **dāncí** word

单打 **dāndǎ** singles (*in tennis*)

弹道导弹 **dàndào dǎodàn** ballistic missile

单调 **dāndiào** monotonous; dull; drab

单调乏味 **dāndiào fáwèi** monotonous

单独 **dāndú** alone; independently of; in isolation

单方面 **dān fāngmiàn** unilateral

当 **dāng** work as; equal; should ◊ when; just at; 当 … 的时候 *dāng … de shíhòu* when …; 把 X 当成 Y *bǎ X dāngchéng Y* confuse X with Y

党 **dǎng** party

挡 **dǎng** block, obstruct ◊ gear

档 **dǎng** shelf; file

荡 **dàng** shake; swing

当 **dàng** right; proper ◊ pawn; equal; treat as; think

胆敢 **dǎngǎn** dare

档案 **dàng'àn** file; records; archives

档案室 **dàng'ànshì** archives

档案箱 **dàng'ànxiāng** file cabinet

蛋糕 **dàngāo** cake

当场 **dāngchǎng** immediately, on the spot; 当场抓获 *dāngchǎng zhuāhuò* caught in the very act

当代 **dāngdài** contemporary ◊ the present era

党代会 **dǎngdàihuì** party conference

当地 **dāngdì** local

当地人 **dāngdì rén** native; local

当地时间 **dāngdì shíjiān** local time

当地特产 **dāngdì tèchǎn** local produce

耽搁 **dāngé** detain, hold up

挡风玻璃 **dǎngfēng bōlí** windshield

当今 **dāngjīn** nowadays

当局 **dāngjú** the authorities

挡路 **dǎnglù** be in the way

当铺 **dàngpù** pawnshop

当前 **dāngqián** present

荡秋千 **dàng qiūqiān** swing; rock

当权 **dāngquán** ruling

当权派 **dāngquánpài** the Establishment

当权者 **dāngquán zhě** the authorities; decision-maker

当然 **dāngrán** of course, naturally; 当然可以 *dāngrán kěyǐ* by all means

当时 **dāngshí** at that time; then

当天 **dàngtiān** on the same day

胆固醇 **dǎngùchún** cholesterol

党委 **dǎngwěi** party committee

当心 **dāngxīn** be careful

当演员 **dāng yǎnyuán** go on the stage

党员 **dǎngyuán** party member

当中 **dāngzhōng** in the middle

当众 **dāngzhòng** in public, publicly

党中央 **Dǎng-Zhōngyāng** Communist Party Central Committee

挡住 **dǎngzhù** block out

淡化 **dànhuà** play down

蛋黄 **dànhuáng** yolk

单簧管 **dānhuángguǎn** clarinet

淡季 **dànjì** low season, off-season

担架 **dānjià** stretcher

单价 **dānjià** unit cost; unit price

单脚跳 **dānjiǎotiào** hop

胆结石 **dǎnjiéshí** gallstone

蛋壳 **dànké** eggshell

胆量 **dǎnliàng** guts, nerve

丹麦 **Dānmài** Denmark ◊ Danish

胆囊 **dǎnnáng** gall bladder

单排扣 **dānpáikòu** single-breasted

单枪匹马 **dānqiāng pīmǎ** single-handed

胆怯 **dǎnqiè** cowardly

单亲 **dānqīn** single parent

单亲家庭 **dānqīn jiātíng** single parent family

单曲唱片 **dānqǔ chàngpiàn** single (*record*)

单人 **dānrén** solo

担任 **dānrèn** take on; act as

单人床 **dānrénchuáng** single bed

单人房间 **dānrén fángjiān** single room

单人沙发 **dānrén shāfā** armchair

单色 dānsè plain, self-colored

淡色 dànsè tint

单身 dānshēn single, unmarried

诞生 dànshēng be born ◊ birth

单身汉 dānshēn hàn bachelor

单身母亲 dānshēn mǔqīn single mother

单身女子 dānshēn nǚzǐ single woman

但是 dànshì but; nevertheless

单数 dānshù singular

淡水 dànshuǐ fresh water

单体 dāntǐ module

单体设计 dāntǐ shèjì modular

弹头 dàntóu warhead

大怒 dànù be fuming

淡忘 dànwàng gradually forget

单位 dānwèi unit; work unit

耽误 dānwù delay, hold up

胆小 dǎnxiǎo cowardice ◊ cowardly

胆小鬼 dǎnxiǎo guǐ coward

担心 dānxīn be afraid of; worry ◊ apprehensive; worried; 令人担心 lìngrén dānxīn worrying

单行道 dānxíng dào one-way street

弹药 dànyào ammunition

单一 dānyī isolated

担忧 dānyōu worry, concern; disturb, trouble ◊ worried ◊ worry

单元 dānyuán unit

但愿 dànyuàn hopefully

单张 dānzhāng leaflet

胆汁 dǎnzhī bile

胆子 dǎnzi courage

担子 dànzi burden

胆子大 dǎnzi dà brave

胆子小 dǎnzi xiǎo cowardly

刀 dāo knife

岛 dǎo island

捣 dǎo pound; thresh; attack

导 dǎo guide; lead; conduct

倒 dǎo fall; fall down; trip over; close down ◊ change; exchange

道 dào way; road; path; Tao ◊ say

倒 dào empty; pour; tip over; rewind; reverse ◊ upside-down ◊ however; actually; maybe

到 dào arrive; reach ◊ to; up to; 到时间了 dào shíjiān le time is up;

到我那儿去 dào wǒ nàr qù go to my place

盗 dào steal ◊ thief

悼 dào mourn

稻 dào paddy; rice

盗版 dàobǎn pirate ◊ pirate copy

倒闭 dàobì go bankrupt, go bust

倒彩 dàocǎi catcall; boo

稻草人 dàocǎorén scarecrow

到场 dàochǎng appear

倒车 dàochē back, reverse car

倒出 dàochū pour out

到处 dàochù everywhere

悼词 dàocí lament

到此为止 dàocǐ wéizhǐ as yet

到达 dàodá arrival; arrivals ◊ arrive; come in; come to; get in; get to; reach ◊ in, arrived

导弹 dǎodàn (guided) missile

捣蛋 dǎodàn get up to mischief

倒档 dàodǎng reverse gear

道德 dàodé morals, ethics

道德高尚 dàodé gāoshàng virtuous

道德经 Dàodéjīng Tao Te Ching

到底 dàodǐ ever; at last; after all ◊ to the end

祷告 dǎogào prayer; 道高一尺，魔高一丈 dàogāo yìchǐ, mógāo yízhàng prov magic works better than doctrine

稻谷 dàogǔ rice (as crop)

倒光 dàoguāng drain

导火线 dǎohuǒ xiàn fuse; catalyst

到家 dàojiā get in; get home

道家 Dàojiā Taoism, Taoist philosophy

道教 Dàojiào Taoism, Taoist religion

倒酒 dàojiǔ pour wine

道具 dàojù prop

倒空 dàokōng empty

到来 dàolái arrive, show up ◊ appearance

道理 dàolǐ sense; reason; principle; truth

道路 dàolù road

捣乱 dǎoluàn cause trouble; create unrest

捣乱分子 dǎoluàn fènzǐ

undesirable element

捣乱者 **dǎoluàn zhě** troublemaker

倒霉 **dǎoméi** have bad luck ◊ unfortunate

悼念 **dàoniàn** mourn

到期 **dàoqī** become due; mature; expire; be up

道歉 **dàoqiàn** apologize ◊ apology

盗窃 **dàoqiè** steal; burglarize ◊ break-in, burglary

道士 **Dàoshì** Taoist priest

倒数第二 **dàoshǔ dì'er** penultimate

倒数数 **dào shǔshù** countdown

倒塌 **dǎotā** collapse, cave in

倒台 **dǎotái** fall

稻田 **dàotián** paddy field, ricefield

倒下 **dǎoxià** fall down; collapse

导线 **dǎoxiàn** (electrical) wire; cable

倒叙 **dàoxù** flashback

导演 **dǎoyǎn** direct *play, movie* ◊ direction ◊ director

盗用 **dàoyòng** embezzle ◊ embezzlement

导游 **dǎoyóu** courier; guide

导游旅游 **dǎoyóu lǚyóu** guided tour

岛屿 **dǎoyǔ** island

岛屿人 **dǎoyǔ rén** islander

导致 **dǎozhì** result in; set off

倒置 **dàozhì** invert

稻子 **dàozi** paddy

大炮 **dàpào** artillery; cannon

打喷嚏 **dǎ pēntì** sneeze

打屁股 **dǎ pìgu** spank

打平局 **dǎ píngjú** draw (*in match*)

大皮箱 **dà píxiāng** trunk

打破 **dǎpò** break; 打破沉默 **dǎpò chénmò** break the ice

打破纪录 **dǎpò jìlù** record-breaking

大气 **dàqì** atmosphere

大气外层 **dàqì wàicéng** upper atmosphere

大气污染 **dàqì wūrǎn** atmospheric pollution

打圈 **dǎquān** circle

大群 **dàqún** swarm; crowd

打扰 **dǎrǎo** disturb; trespass on

打入 **dǎrù** infiltrate; penetrate

打扫 **dǎsǎo** sweep; clean

大扫除 **dà sǎochú** spring-cleaning

打扫干净 **dǎsǎo gānjìng** clean out

大厦 **dàshà** high-rise building

打闪 **dǎshǎn** flash (*of lightning*)

打伤 **dǎshāng** wound

大赦 **dàshè** amnesty

大声 **dàshēng** in a loud voice

大声点 **dàshēng diǎn** speak up

大声呼喊 **dàshēng hūhǎn** give a cry; shout

大声说出 **dàshēng shuōchū** cry out

大声笑 **dàshēng xiào** roar with laughter

大使 **dàshǐ** ambassador

大使馆 **dàshǐguǎn** embassy

大手大脚的人 **dàshǒu dàjiǎo** wasteful; extravagant; 大手大脚地花钱 **dàshǒu dàjiǎo di huāqián** splash out

打手势 **dǎ shǒushì** gesticulate

大蒜 **dàsuàn** garlic

打碎 **dǎsuì** shatter; break ◊ broken, bust

大体来说 **dàtǐ láishuō** broadly speaking

打听 **dǎtīng** pry; inquire about; make enquiries; 向 X 打听 Y **xiàng X dǎtīng Y** ask X about Y

大厅 **dàtīng** hall

大提琴 **dà tíqín** cello

大体上 **dàtǐshang** in general

打通 **dǎtōng** (*on telephone*) get through

大头针 **dàtóuzhēn** pin

大腿 **dàtuǐ** thigh

打退堂鼓 **dǎ tuìtánggǔ** back off; get cold feet, chicken out

大屠杀 **dà túshā** carnage; massacre

大为 **dàwéi** great achievement; greatly; 使大为吃惊 **shǐ dàwéi chījīng** amaze; 大为惊讶 **dàwéi jīngyà** marvel at

大乌鸦 **dà wūyā** raven

大虾 **dàxiā** shrimp

大象 **dàxiàng** elephant

大小 **dàxiǎo** size

打消疑虑 **dǎxiāo yílǜ** reassure

大写 **dàxiě** print (in block letters) ◊ capitalization; full form of Chinese numeral

大写字母 **dàxiě zìmǔ** capital letter(s)

)大型 **dàxíng** large-scale

大猩猩 **dàxīngxing** gorilla

大型衣柜 **dàxíng yīguì** walk-in closet

大型游艇 **dàxíng yóutǐng** cruise liner

大修 **dàxiū** overhaul

大西洋 **Dàxīyáng** Atlantic

大学 **dàxué** university

大学毕业后 **dàxué bìyèhòu** postgraduate

大削减 **dà xuējiǎn** slash, cut

大学生 **dàxué shēng** (college) student; undergraduate

大烟囱 **dà yāncōng** stack

打哑语 **dǎ yǎyǔ** mime

大衣 **dàyī** overcoat

大意 **dàyì** gist

大意 **dàyì** careless

打印 **dǎyìn** print, run off

答应 **dāyìng** reply; agree

打印机 **dǎyìnjī** printer

打印文本 **dǎyìn wénběn** hard copy

大雨 **dàyǔ** deluge; 大雨倾盆 **dàyǔ qīngpén** it's pouring (with rain)

大约 **dàyuē** approximate ◊ approximately, around, in the region of ◊ thereabouts

大跃进 **Dàyuèjìn** Great Leap Forward

大运河 **Dàyùnhé** Grand Canal

大斋节 **Dàzhāijié** Lent

大帐篷 **dàzhàngpéng** marquee

打招呼 **dǎ zhāohu** greet

打折扣 **dǎ zhékòu** discount

大致 **dàzhì** more or less

打中 **dǎzhòng** hit *target*

大众 **dàzhòng** the masses

大众传媒 **dàzhòng chuánméi** mass media

大众化 **dàzhònghuà** popularize

打字 **dǎzì** type

大字标题 **dàzì biāotí** headline

打字机 **dǎzì jī** typewriter

打字员 **dǎzìyuán** typist

大宗 **dàzōng** block

大走财运 **dàzǒucáiyùn** make a killing

打坐 **dǎzuò** meditate ◊ meditation

大作 **dàzuò** great work, masterpiece

的 **de** of; 书的名字 **shūde míngzi** the title of the book ◊ (*makes adjectives attributive*): 漂亮的姑娘 **piàoliangde gūniang** a beautiful girl ◊ (*introducing relative clause*): 我喜欢的宾馆 **wǒ xǐhuande bīnguǎn** the hotel which I prefer

得 **de** (*before a qualifying word*): 好得多 / 容易得多 **hǎo de duō / róngyì de duō** a lot better / a lot easier ◊ (*when result of an action is expressed*): 看得见 **kàn de jiàn** be able to see

地 **de** (*to form adverbs*): 高兴地 **gāoxìngde** happily

得 **dé** get, obtain

德 **dé** morals; virtue

得不偿失 **dé bùchángshī** the loss outweighs the gain; 做 X 得不偿失 **zuò X dé bùchángshī** it doesn't pay to do X

得到 **dédào** get, obtain; reach *decision*

得到...的风声 **dédào ... de fēngshēng** get wind of ...

得到消息 **dédào xiāoxi** hear from; get news of

得分 **défēn** score

得分运动员 **défēn yùndòngyuán** scorer

得感冒 **dé gǎnmào** catch (a) cold

德国 **Déguó** Germany ◊ German

得过且过 **déguòqiěguò** muddle along

得啦, 得啦 **déla, déla** now, now!

得了 **déle** alright, that's enough!

得了吧 **déleba** will you stop that!

得了 … 病 **déle … bìng** be sickening for

得力助手 **délì zhùshǒu** righthand man

灯 **dēng** light; lamp

登 **dēng** climb

等 **děng** wait; grade, class; 你 等着 吧 ！ **nǐ děngzhe ba!** just you wait!; 让 X 等 **ràng X děng** keep X waiting; 我们 等 他 准备 好 **wǒmen děng tā zhǔnbèihǎo** we'll wait until he's ready

凳 **dèng** stool

登场 **dēngchǎng** appear ◊ appearance (*in movie*)

等待 **děngdài** wait; wait for ◊ waiting

等等 **děngděng** and so on, etc ◊ hang on

登高 **dēnggāo** climb a mountain

登广告 **dēng guǎnggào** advertise

登广告者 **dēng guǎnggào zhě** advertiser

等候 **děnghòu** wait

等候室 **děnghòushì** waiting room

等候者名单 **děnghòuzhě míngdān** waiting list

登记 **dēngjì** check in; register; book ◊ registration

等级 **děngjí** class; classification; grade; rank

等价 **děngjià** of equivalent value

登记簿 **dēngjì bù** register

登机卡 **dēngjī kǎ** boarding card

登机口 **dēngjīkǒu** gate (*at airport*)

登记人 **dēngjì rén** registrar

等级制度 **děngjí zhìdù** hierarchy

灯笼 **dēnglong** lantern

灯泡 **dēngpào** light bulb

登山 **dēngshān** mountaineering

登山者 **dēngshān zhě** mountaineer, climber

等式 **děngshì** equation

灯塔 **dēngtǎ** lighthouse

等同 **děngtóng** equal

等退票 **děng tuìpiào** on standby

等退票旅客 **děng tuìpiào lǚkè** standby passenger

邓小平 **Dèng Xiǎopíng** Deng Xiaoping

邓小平理论 **Dèng Xiǎopíng lǐlùn** Deng Xiaoping theory

灯芯绒 **dēngxīnróng** corduroy

灯芯绒裤 **dēngxīnróng kù** cords

等一下 **děngyíxià** hold on; wait a moment

等于 **děngyú** equal; correspond to

灯罩 **dēngzhào** (lamp)shade

凳子 **dèngzi** stool

得体 **détǐ** proper; tactful

得知 **dézhī** become aware of

得罪 **dézuì** insult; offend

滴 **dī** drop; blob ◊ drip; trickle

堤 **dī** dike

低 **dī** low; junior

笛 **dí** bamboo flute

敌 **dí** enemy

底 **dǐ** bottom

递 **dì** pass

帝 **dì** emperor

弟 **dì** younger brother

第 **dì** *used to create ordinal numbers*

递 **dì** hand over, deliver

地 **dì** the earth; ground

堤岸 **dī'àn** embankment

点 **diǎn** dot; (decimal) point; point; drop; spot ◊ dip; dunk ◊ a little, some ◊ o'clock 好 / 容易 点 儿 了 吗 ？ **hǎo / róngyì diǎnr le ma?** is that any better / easier?; 几 点 了 ？ **jǐdiǎnle?** what's the time?

碘 **diǎn** iodine

电 **diàn** electric(al) ◊ electricity

垫 **diàn** cushion; mat

店 **diàn** store; shop

电报 **diànbào** telegram

颠簸 **diānbǒ** jolt ◊ bumpy

点菜 **diǎncài** order (*in restaurant*)

电唱机 **diànchàngjī** record player

电唱盘 **diànchàng pán** turntable

电车 **diànchē** streetcar

垫衬 **diànchèn** pad

电池 **diànchí** battery

典当 **diǎndàng** pawn

颠倒 **diāndǎo** reverse; 把 X 上下 颠倒 过来 **bǎ X shàngxià diāndǎo guòlái** turn X upside down

颠倒黑白 **diāndǎo hēibái** topsy-turvy

电灯 **diàndēng** electric light

电灯泡 **diàndēng pào** light bulb
点滴 **diǎndī** drip MED
电动机 **diàndòng jī** dynamo
典范 **diǎnfàn** characterize ◊ example; model
电饭锅 **diànfànguō** rice cooker
淀粉 **diànfěn** starch; cornstarch
颠覆分子 **diānfù fènzǐ** subversive
电工 **diàngōng** electrician
佃户 **diànhù** tenant
电话 **diànhuà** telephone; 打个电话 **dǎ ge diànhuà** make a telephone call
电话簿 **diànhuà bù** phone book
电话磁卡 **diànhuà cíkǎ** phonecard
电话费 **diànhuà fèi** toll TELEC
电话号码 **diànhuà hàomǎ** telephone number
电话机 **diànhuàjī** telephone
电话交换台 **diànhuà jiāohuàntái** switchboard
电话亭 **diànhuà tíng** phone booth
电话线 **diànhuà xiàn** telephone line
点火 **diǎnhuǒ** light *fire*
点击 **diǎnjī** click COMPUT
电级 **diànjí** electrode
电缆 **diànlǎn** electricity cable
电缆塔 **diànlǎntǎ** pylon
典礼 **diǎnlǐ** ceremony ◊ ceremonial
垫料 **diànliào** pad; padding; upholstery
电流 **diànliú** electric current
电炉 **diànlú** hotplate; electric stove
点名 **diǎnmíng** roll call
电脑 **diànnǎo** computer
电脑化 **diànnǎo huà** computerize
电脑空间 **diànnǎo kōngjiān** cyberspace
电脑控制 **diànnǎo kòngzhì** computer-controlled
电脑使用 **diànnǎo shǐyòng** computing
惦念 **diànniàn** worry; worry about
电脑站 **diànnǎo zhàn** computer terminal
垫片 **diànpiàn** gasket; washer

电气 **diànqì** electricity
电器 **diànqì** electrical appliance
点燃 **diǎnrán** ignite
电热水器 **diàn rèshuǐqì** immersion heater
电热毯 **diànrètǎn** electric blanket
电扇 **diànshàn** electric fan
电视 **diànshì** television; 电视上 **diànshì shang** on TV
电视会议 **diànshì huìyì** video conference
电视机 **diànshì jī** television set
电视节目 **diànshì jiémù** television program
电视摄影室 **diànshì shèyǐng shì** television studio
电视遊戏 **diànshì yóuxì** video game
电死 **diànsǐ** electrocute
电台 **diàntái** station RAD, TV
电梯 **diàntī** elevator
电筒 **diàntǒng** flashlight
点头 **diǎntóu** nod
玷污 **diànwū** taint; cast a slur on
癫痫 **diànxián** epileptic
点线 **diǎnxiàn** dotted line
电线 **diànxiàn** cable; wire; power line
癫痫发作 **diānxián fāzuò** epileptic fit
电线杆 **diànxiàn gān** telegraph pole
癫痫症 **diānxiánzhèng** epilepsy
点心 **diǎnxin** dim sum
电信 **diànxìn** telecommunications
典型 **diǎnxíng** characteristic; classic; representative; typical ◊ typically; 典型美国人 **diǎnxíng měiguórén** typically American
电压 **diànyā** voltage
点烟 **diǎnyān** light up *cigarette*
电椅 **diànyǐ** electric chair
电影 **diànyǐng** movie, motion picture
电影剧本 **diànyǐng jùběn** screenplay
电影迷 **diànyǐng mí** movie buff
电影明星 **diànyǐng míngxīng** movie star
电影院 **diànyǐng yuàn** movie theater

电影预告片 **diànyǐng yùgào piàn** trailer

店员 **diànyuán** sales clerk

电源电缆 **diànyuán diànlǎn** power cable

点钟 **diǎnzhōng** o'clock; 五点钟 **wǔdiǎnzhōng** five o'clock

店主 **diànzhǔ** landlord; shopkeeper

点缀 **diǎnzhuì** decorate; jazz up

点子 **diǎnzi** pointer; 出点子 **chū diǎnzi** give advice

电子 **diànzǐ** electron ◊ electronic

垫子 **diànzi** cushion; padding

电子表 **diànzǐbiǎo** quartz watch

电子数据处理 **diànzǐ shùjù chǔlǐ** electronic data processing, EDP

电子信箱 **diànzǐ xìnxiāng** e-mail address

电子学 **diànzǐxué** electronics

电子邮件 **diànzǐ yóujiàn** e-mail; 打电子邮件 **dǎ diànzǐ yóujiàn** e-mail, send an e-mail

电子遊戏 **diànzǐ yóuxì** computer game

凋 **diāo** wither

雕 **diāo** carve; engrave

刁 **diāo** wily

调 **diāo** move, transfer

吊 **diào** hang; suspend

钓 **diào** fish with hook and line

掉 **diào** come out (of stain) ◊ (getting rid of): 吃掉 **chī diào** eat up; 擦掉 **cā diào** wipe off; 卖掉 **mài diào** sell off; 掉了 **diàole** come away (of button etc)

碉堡 **diāobǎo** fortress

调查 **diàochá** look into, check out; investigate; poll; survey ◊ investigation

调查方法 **diàochá fāngfǎ** line of inquiry

吊床 **diàochuáng** hammock

钓到 **diàodào** catch fish

吊灯 **diàodēng** chandelier

钓竿 **diàogān** fishing rod

调换 **diàohuàn** exchange

吊架 **diàojià** trapeze

雕刻 **diāokè** carve; engrave

雕刻（塑）**diāokè (sù)** sculpture

雕刻（塑）家 **diāokè (sù) jiā** sculptor

吊裤带 **diàokùdài** suspenders

掉落 **diàoluò** fall out

刁难 **diāonàn** give a hard time; create difficulties; be obstructive

貂皮 **diāopí** mink

貂皮大衣 **diāopí dàyī** mink (coat)

吊桥 **diàoqiáo** suspension bridge

掉色 **diàoshǎi** fade

吊死 **diàosǐ** hang

雕塑 **diàosù** sculpture

吊索运输车 **diàosuǒ yùnshūchē** ski lift

调头 **diàotóu** turn around

吊袜带 **diàowàdài** garter

凋谢 **diāoxiè** wither

吊唁 **diàoyàn** offer condolences

钓鱼 **diàoyú** go fishing

钓鱼杆 **diàoyúgān** fishing rod

掉转 **diàozhuǎn** steer; turn

第八 **dì bā** eighth

地板 **dìbǎn** floor; floorboard

第八十 **dì bāshí** eightieth

底部 **dǐbù** base; bottom

地产 **dìchǎn** estate

低潮 **dīcháo** low tide

底朝上 **dǐ cháo shàng** upside down

低沉 **dīchén** low; deep; oppressive

滴答 **dīdā** tick (of clock)

抵达 **dǐdá** arrive at

地带 **dìdài** zone; area

抵挡 **dǐdǎng** resist; repel

地道 **dìdào** authentic; idiomatic

低地 **dīdì** lowlands

弟弟 **dìdi** younger brother

地点 **dìdiǎn** place; spot; location

低调 **dīdiào** low key

敌对 **díduì** hostile

跌 **diē** fall; stumble

爹 **diē** dad, pop

叠 **dié** stack, pile

蝶 **dié** butterfly

跌倒 **diēdǎo** fall over

爹爹 **diēdie** dad, pop

喋喋不休 **diédié bùxiū** chatter

跌跌撞撞 **diēdie zhuàngzhuàng** stagger

跌价 diējià price drop

跌落 diēluò drop

第二 dì'èr second; 第二大 dì'èr dà second biggest; 第二好 dì'èr hǎo second best

第二点 dì'èrdiǎn secondly

第二十 dì'èrshí twentieth

第二天 dì'èr tiān the day after

蝶泳 diéyǒng butterfly stroke

碟子 diézi dish

提防 dīfáng be on one's guard against

地方 dìfāng place ◊ local

地方政府 dìfāng zhèngfǔ local government

低峰时间 dīfēng shíjiān off-peak

滴干 dīgān drip-dry

低估 dīgū underestimate; undervalue

帝国 dìguó empire

帝国主义 dìguó zhǔyì imperialism

诋毁 dǐhuǐ slur

低级 dījí low; crude

地基 dìjī foundations

地极 dìjí pole ◊ polar

递交 dìjiāo hand over; deliver

地窖 dìjiào cellar; vaults

缔结 dìjié conclude contract

第九 dì jiǔ ninth

第九十 dì jiǔshí ninetieth

低卡路里 dī kǎlùlǐ low-calorie

抵抗 dǐkàng resist ◊ resistance

地雷 dìléi (land) mine

地理 dìlǐ geography

低廉 dīlián knockdown price

低领口 dī lǐngkǒu low-cut

第六 dìliù sixth

第六十 dì liùshí sixtieth

地理学 dìlǐxué geography

低落 dīluò subdued

弟妹 dìmèi sister-in-law (younger brother's wife); younger brothers and sisters

地面 dìmiàn ground; bottom

地面控制 dìmiàn kòngzhì ground control

低能 dīnéng ineffectual; mentally handicapped

低能儿 dīnéng'ér imbecile

叮 dīng sting; stab

钉 dīng nail; staple

丁 dīng cube

盯 dīng stare

顶 dǐng top; crest ◊ replace; cope with; push up ◊ very ◊ measure word for hats: 一顶草帽 yīdǐng cǎomào a straw hat

锭 dìng ingot

定 dìng set, fix; 那就定了！nà jiù dìng le! that settles it!

订 dìng order; subscribe

钉 dìng nail

定菜单 dìng càidān order (in restaurant)

定餐 dìngcān set meal

顶层公寓 dǐngcéng gōngyù penthouse

顶层楼座 dǐngcéng lóuzuò gallery

订单 dìngdān order (for goods); order form

叮当声 dīngdāng shēng tinkle; clink

顶点 dǐngdiǎn summit; culmination

定额 dìng'é quota; target

定发胶 dìng fàjiāo lacquer

顶峰 dǐngfēng high point, peak

顶风 dǐngfēng against the wind ◊ headwind

定购 dìnggòu order

定冠词 dìngguàncí definite article

订户 dìnghù customer; subscriber

订婚 dìnghūn engaged ◊ get engaged ◊ engagement

订婚戒指 dìnghūn jièzhǐ engagement ring

订货 dìnghuò order goods

定价 dìngjià price goods; set a price

定计划 dìng jìhuà plan

定金 dìngjīn deposit; down payment

订机票 dìng jīpiào book a flight

定居 dìngjū settle (down)

钉牢 dìngláo fix

定量 dìngliàng quota

定量供应 dìngliàng gōngyìng ration

顶楼 dǐnglóu garret

定论 **dìnglùn** verdict

钉帽 **dīngmào** head (*of nail*)

定名 **dìngmíng** entitled *book*

定期 **dìngqī** regular ◊ periodically ◊ set a date

定期航班 **dìngqī hángbān** scheduled flight

盯梢 **dīngshāo** tail, shadow

定时器 **dìngshíqì** timer; time switch

定时炸弹 **dìngshí zhàdàn** time bomb

订书钉 **dìngshūdīng** staple

订书机 **dìngshūjī** stapler

定位 **dìngwèi** location

丁香 **dīngxiāng** lilac

定向发射 **dìngxiàng fāshè** beam

丁香花 **dīngxiāng huā** lilac

定义 **dìngyì** definition

订阅 **dìngyuè** subscribe to *publication*

订阅者 **dìngyuè zhě** subscriber (*to publication*)

盯着 **dīngzhe** stare at; 盯着 X 的眼睛 *dīngzhe X de yǎnjīng* look X straight in the eye

顶针 **dǐngzhēn** thimble

顶住 **dǐngzhù** resist

订桌 **dìngzhuō** book a table

钉子 **dīngzi** brush-off; snub; nail; 钉钉子 *dīng dīngzi* hammer in a nail

定罪 **dìngzuì** conviction (*criminal*) ◊ convict

定做 **dìngzuò** made-to-measure; tailor-made

底盘 **dǐpán** chassis

地皮 **dìpí** plot of land to build on

底片 **dǐpiàn** negative (*photographic*)

地平线 **dìpíngxiàn** horizon

第七 **dì qī** seventh

第七十 **dì qīshí** seventieth

地球 **dìqiú** earth; world; globe

地球居民 **dìqiú jūmín** terrestrial

地球仪 **dìqiúyí** globe

低气压区 **dī qìyā qū** low (*in weather*)

地区 **dìqū** area; neighborhood;

region ◊ regional

的确 **díquè** indeed; undeniably

敌人 **dírén** enemy

第三 **dìsān** third ◊ thirdly

第三方保险 **dìsān fāng bǎoxiǎn** third-party *or* liability insurance

第三个 **dìsān gè** third

第三十 **dìsānshí** thirtieth

第三世界 **Dìsān Shìjiè** Third World

第三者 **dìsānzhě** third party

低声 **dīshēng** softly

低声说 **dīshēng shuō** whisper; mutter

第十 **dìshí** tenth

地势 **dìshì** terrain

第十八 **dì shíbā** eighteenth

第十二 **dì shí'èr** twelfth

第十六 **dì shíliù** sixteenth

第十七 **dì shíqī** seventeenth

第十三 **dì shísān** thirteenth

第十四 **dì shísì** fourteenth

第十五 **dì shíwǔ** fifteenth

第十一 **dì shíyī** eleventh

滴水 **dīshuǐ** drain

第四 **dìsì** fourth

迪斯科 **dísīkē** disco

第四十 **dìsìshí** fortieth

递送 **dìsòng** deliver

地毯 **dìtǎn** carpet

地铁 **dìtiě** subway

迪厅 **dítīng** disco

低头 **dītóu** bow; duck *head*

地图 **dìtú** map

地图册 **dìtúcè** atlas

丢 **diū** lose; throw away

丢掉 **diūdiào** throw away

丢脸 **diūliǎn** lose face ◊ humiliating

丢弃 **diūqì** dump

丢失 **diūshī** lose

丢下 X 不管 **diūxià X bùguǎn** leave X unattended

低微 **dīwēi** humble

地位 **dìwèi** position, standing, status

地位低 **dìwèi dī** junior

地位低下 **dìwèi dīxià** underprivileged

第五 **dìwǔ** fifth

第五十 **dì wǔshí** fiftieth

低下 **dīxià** menial
地下 **dīxià** underground
地线 **dìxiàn** ground ELEC
抵消 **dǐxiāo** offset
地下室 **dìxiàshì** basement
地下通道 **dìxià tōngdào** underpass
地形 **dìxíng** geography; terrain
抵押 **dǐyā** mortgage
低压地区 **dīyā dìqū** low-pressure area
低压区 **dīyā qū** depression (*meteorological*)
敌意 **díyì** animosity, antagonism, hostility
第一 **dìyī** first; leading
第一百 **dì yìbǎi** hundredth
第一次 **dìyícì** the first time
第一个 **dìyígè** first
第一流 **dìyìliú** ace; first-class
低音提琴 **dīyīn tíqín** double-bass
低音乐器 **dīyīn yuèqì** bass
第一千个 **dì yì qiān gè** thousandth
第一手 **dìyīshǒu** at first hand
低于 **dīyú** below, beneath
低语 **dīyǔ** murmur
地狱 **dìyù** hell
低噪音 **dī zàoyīn** quiet
地震 **dìzhèn** earthquake
地震学 **dìzhènxué** seismology
地支 **dìzhī** earthly branches (*in Chinese calendar*)
抵制 **dǐzhì** resist; boycott
地址 **dìzhǐ** address
地质 **dìzhì** geology ◊ geological
低脂肪 **dīzhīfáng** low-fat
地质学 **dìzhìxué** geology
地质学者 **dìzhìxué zhě** geologist
地主 **dìzhǔ** land owner
笛子 **dízi** flute
底座 **dǐzuò** base
东 **dōng** east
鸫 **dōng** robin
冬 **dōng** winter
懂 **dǒng** understand; know
洞 **dòng** hole; cave
动 **dòng** move; 别як来动去! *bié dònglái dòngqù!* keep still!
冻 **dòng** freeze; 我冻坏了 *wǒ dònghuài le* I'm frozen

栋 **dòng** *measure word for houses*; 一栋房屋 *yídòng fángwū* a house
东北 **dōngběi** northeast
东部 **dōngbù** eastern
洞察 **dòngchá** insight
洞察力 **dòngchálì** perception
动产 **dòngchǎn** moveable assets
冻疮 **dòngchuāng** chilblain
动词 **dòngcí** verb
动荡不定 **dòngdàng búdìng** unstable
东道主 **dōngdàozhǔ** host
东方 **dōngfāng** east; the East; Orient ◊ eastern; oriental; Oriental
东方人 **dōngfāng rén** Oriental
冬菇 **dōnggū** dried winter mushroom
东海 **Dōnghǎi** East China Sea
懂行 **dǒngháng** expert
恫吓 **dònghè** threaten; intimidate
动画片 **dònghuà piàn** animated cartoon
动画片摄制 **dònghuà piàn shèzhì** animation
动机 **dòngjī** motive
冻僵 **dòngjiāng** numb with cold, frozen stiff
冻结 **dòngjié** freeze
冬季运动 **dōngjì yùndòng** winter sports
东拉西扯 **dōnglā xīchě** ramble (*in speaking*) ◊ rambling
动力 **dònglì** driving force; dynamism; momentum; incentive; stimulus; motivation
动乱 **dòngluàn** turmoil; unrest; upheaval
动脉 **dòngmài** artery
冬眠 **dōngmián** hibernation ◊ hibernate
东南 **dōngnán** southeast, southeastern
东南部 **dōngnán bù** southeast
东南亚 **Dōngnán Yà** Southeast Asia ◊ Southeast Asian
鸫鸟 **dōngniǎo** thrush
冬青 **dōngqīng** holly
动人 **dòngrén** moving
冻伤 **dòngshāng** frostbite ◊ frostbitten

东山再起 dōngshān zàiqǐ make a comeback

动身 dòngshēn set off

懂事 dǒngshì understanding; sensible

董事 dǒngshì board member; director

董事会 dǒngshì huì board of directors

董事会会议 dǒngshìhuì huìyì board meeting

董事长 dǒngshìzhǎng chairman of the board

动手 dòngshǒu get to work

动手动脚 dòngshǒu dòngjiǎo touch up; make a pass; get fresh

动手术 dòng shǒushù operate MED

冻死 dòngsǐ freeze to death; 我冻死了 wǒ dòngsǐle I'm freezing

冬天 dōngtiān winter

动物 dòngwù animal

动物学 dòngwù xué zoology ◊ zoological

动物园 dòngwù yuán zoo

东西 dōngxi thing

洞穴 dòngxuè cave

动摇 dòngyáo waver

动作 dòngzuò movement

都 dōu all; both ◊ even

陡 dǒu steep ◊ suddenly

抖 dǒu tremble; shake

豆 dòu bean

斗 dòu fight; struggle

逗 dòu tease; amuse ◊ funny

豆瓣酱 dòubànjiàng black bean sauce

兜捕 dōubǔ round up ◊ round-up

斗橱 dǒuchú bureau; chest of drawers

逗点 dòudiǎn comma

抖动 dǒudòng shake

兜风 dōufēng drive

豆腐 dòufu tofu, bean curd

逗号 dòuhào comma

豆浆 dòujiāng soy milk

逗留 dòuliú stay; stop over; linger

抖落 dǒuluò shake off

逗弄 dòunòng tease

斗殴 dòu ōu brawl

斗篷 dǒupeng cape

豆芽 dòuyá beansprouts

窦炎 dòuyán sinusitis

豆油 dòuyóu soy bean oil

斗争 dòuzhēng battle; struggle; fight for

都 dū city; capital

督 dū supervise

读 dú read; 他在读大学 tā zài dú dàxué he is at university

毒 dú poison; narcotics ◊ poisonous; toxic

独 dú only; alone

肚 dǔ tripe

堵 dǔ block

赌 dǔ gamble

肚 dù belly; stomach

度 dù degree ◊ spend, pass time

渡 dù cross water; ferry

妒 dù envy

端 duān end; extremity ◊ carry

短 duǎn short

段 duàn section; paragraph

缎 duàn satin

断 duàn break

短波 duǎnbō short wave

短处 duǎnchù shortcoming

断定 duàndìng conclude; decide

短棍 duǎngùn baton

断绝 duànjué break off

断绝关系 duànjué guānxi drop; 与X断绝关系 yǔ X duànjué guānxi finish with X, drop X

端口 duānkǒu port COMPUT

短裤 duǎnkù shorts

锻炼 duànliàn exercise ◊ gymnastics; workout

断裂 duànliè snap, break

短路 duǎnlù short circuit

断路开关 duànlù kāiguān circuit breaker

段落 duànluò paragraph

短跑 duǎnpǎo sprint

短跑运动员 duǎnpǎo yùndòng yuán sprinter

短篇小说 duǎnpiān xiǎoshuō short story

短期 duǎnqī short term

短缺 duǎnquē shortage

断然 duànrán point blank

端上 duānshang serve

断头 duàntóu break

短袜 duǎnwà sock

短文 duǎnwén essay

端午节 Duānwǔjié Dragon Boat Festival

断线 duànxiàn cut off *telephone*

短袖 duǎnxiù short-sleeved

断言 duànyán maintain, argue; affirm

短暂 duǎnzàn momentary, fleeting, short-lived

锻造 duànzào forge

缎子 duànzi satin

赌博 dǔbó bet; gamble ◊ gambling

独裁 dúcái dictatorial

独裁者 dúcái zhě dictator

赌场 dǔchǎng casino

独唱曲 dúchàng qǔ solo

独唱演员 dúchàng yǎnyuán soloist

堵车 dǔchē traffic jam

都城 dūchéng capital

渡船 dùchuán ferry

独创力 dúchuànglì originality

督促 dūcù urge; press

读错 dúcuò misread

嘟嘟声 dūdū shēng beep

读给 X 听 dúgěi X tīng read to X

度过 dùguò pass, spend *time*

毒害 dúhài poison

堆 duī heap, pile, mound ◊ pile up, stack

兑 duì exchange

对 duì correct; right ◊ against; toward; facing; opposite; with regard to; for; to ◊ pair ◊ face; 对啊! duì a! that's right!; 对了! duìle! that's it!, that's right!; X 对 Y **X duì Y** X against Y; X versus Y

队 duì team; line

对半 duìbàn fifty-fifty

对比 duìbǐ compare

对不起 duìbùqǐ sorry; I'm sorry; pardon me

对称 duìchèn symmetrical ◊ symmetry

堆成堆 duīchéngduī pile up

对待 duìdài treat ◊ treatment; 认真对待 X **rènzhēn duìdài X** take X seriously

对等 duìděng corresponding

对方 duìfāng opposite side

对付 duìfu handle; 对付 X **duìfu X** have X to reckon with

对话 duìhuà dialog

兑换 duìhuàn exchange

兑换率 duìhuànlǜ exchange rate

堆积 duījī pile up, heap up

对讲机 duìjiǎngjī intercom

对接处 duì jiē chù dock (*of spaceship*)

对抗 duìkàng opposite ◊ defiance

对立 duìlì oppose ◊ contrast ◊ contrary; 与 X 对立 **yǔ X duìlì** be at odds with X

对面 duìmiàn opposite; 邮局在银行的对面 **yóujú zài yínháng de duìmiàn** the post office is opposite the bank

对手 duìshǒu opponent, adversary

对外贸易 duìwài màoyì foreign trade

队伍 duìwǔ troops; ranks

兑现 duìxiàn cash *check*

对象 duìxiàng target; boyfriend; girlfriend

对象市场 duìxiàng shìchǎng target market

对象组 duìxiàng zǔ target group

队长 duìzhǎng captain (*of team*)

对照 duìzhào contrast

对折 duìzhé double

对质 duìzhì confront

对准 duìzhǔn point

妒忌 dùjì jealous ◊ jealousy; envy; 妒忌 … **dùjì …** be jealous of …

独家 dújiā exclusive

度假 dùjià spend one's vacation

度假胜地 dùjià shèngdì resort

镀金材料 dùjīn cáiliào gilt

赌纪人 dǔjì rén bookmaker, bookie

独立 dúlì independence ◊ independent ◊ independently

度量衡 dùliánghéng system of measurement

独立日 Dúlìrì Independence Day

独立生活 dúlì shēnghuó fend for oneself

独轮车 dúlún chē barrow

独木舟 dúmù zhōu canoe

蹲 dūn squat, crouch

吨 **dūn** ton

钝 **dùn** blunt; dull

炖 **dùn** braise; simmer; stew

盾 **dùn** shield

顿 **dùn** *measure word for meals;* 一顿饭 **yídùn fàn** a meal

敦促 **dūncù** call on, urge; press

独女 **dúnǚ** only daughter

钝吻鳄 **dùnwěn'è** alligator

多 **duō** a lot of; many; much; more ◊ however; 比…多 **bǐ … duō** above, more than; 好得多 **hǎo dé duō** much better; 好 / 容易多了 **hǎo/róngyì duōle** so much better / easier; 多滑稽 / 悲哀! **duō huájī/bēiāi!** how funny / sad!; 你 / 他多大年纪了? **nǐ/tā duōdà niánjì le?** how old are you / is he?; 要多长时间? **yào duōcháng shíjiān?** how long does it take?; 多经常? **duō jīngcháng?** how often?

夺 **duó** take by force

朵 **duǒ** *measure word for flowers, clouds;* 一朵花 **yīduǒ huā** a flower

躲 **duǒ** hide; dodge

跺 **duò** chop

舵 **duò** helm; rudder

堕 **duò** fall; sink

跺 **duò** stamp *foot*

多半儿 **duōbànr** in all likelihood ◊ the majority

躲避 **duǒbì** dodge; elude

多变 **duōbiàn** variable

多病 **duōbìng** sickly

踱步 **duóbù** pace up and down

多才多艺 **duōcái duōyì** versatile ◊ versatility

躲藏 **duǒcáng** hide; 躲藏起来 **duǒcáng qǐlái** go into hiding; 躲藏着 **duǒcángzhe** be in hiding

躲藏处 **duǒcángchù** hiding place

多草 **duōcǎo** grassy

多产 **duōchǎn** productive; prolific

多尘土 **duō chéntǔ** dusty

多愁善感 **duōchóu shàngǎn** corny

多刺 **duōcì** prickly

多次 **duōcì** time and again

夺得 **duódé** snatch

多风 **duōfēng** windy

多个 **duōgè** multiple

多功能 **duō gōngnéng** versatile ◊ versatility

多关系户 **duō guànxì hù** be well-connected

多国 **duōguó** multinational

多花 **duōhuā** flowery

夺回 **duóhuí** recapture

跺脚 **duòjiǎo** stamp one's feet

多久 **duōjiǔ** how long; 多久之前? **duōjiǔ zhīqián?** how long ago?

多亏 **duōkuī** fortunately

堕落 **duòluò** degenerate; 使堕落 **shǐ duòluò** corrupt

多毛 **duōmáo** hairy

多么 **duōme** how; what; 多么蓝的天啊! **duōme lán de tiān a!** what a blue sky!

多媒体 **duōméitǐ** multimedia

夺取 **duóqǔ** conquer; overcome

堕入 **duòrù** sink into

多沙 **duōshā** sandy

多山 **duōshān** mountainous

多少 **duōshǎo** much; many ◊ how much; how many; 你需要多少? **nǐ xūyào duōshao?** how many do you need?; 多少钱? **duōshao qián?** how much is it?

多石 **duōshí** stony

多数 **duōshù** majority ◊ most; 占多数 **zhàn duōshù** be in the majority

多水 **duōshuǐ** watery

哆嗦 **duōsuo** quake

堕胎 **duòtāi** abortion ◊ have an abortion

多雾 **duōwù** foggy

多险 **duōxiǎn** perilous

多香料 **duō xiāngliào** spicy

多谢 **duōxiè** thanks very much

多雪 **duōxuě** snowy

多烟 **duōyān** smoky

多样化 **duōyàng huà** diverse ◊ diversity; variety

多岩石 **duō yánshí** rocky

多疑 **duōyí** paranoid

多用途 **duō yòngtú** all-purpose

多于 **duōyú** excess ◊ in excess of, more than

多余 **duōyú** spare; redundant, superfluous

多雨 **duōyǔ** rainy

多云 **duōyún** overcast

多汁 **duōzhī** juicy

多种经营 **duōzhǒng jīngyíng** diversification ◊ diversify

多皱纹 **duō zhòuwén** rugged

毒品 **dúpǐn** drugs, narcotics

毒品贩子 **dúpǐn fànzi** pusher

肚脐 **dùqí** navel

堵塞 **dǔsāi** block, block up ◊ blockage; congestion ◊ congested

堵塞 **dǔsè** block; jam ◊ blocked

独身 **dúshēn** single

都市 **dūshì** metropolis

读数 **dúshù** reading

毒死 **dúsǐ** poison

杜松子酒 **dùsōngzǐjiǔ** gin

独特 **dútè** unique

独特性 **dútèxìng** peculiarity

赌徒 **dǔtú** gambler

读物 **dúwù** reading material

妒羡 **dùxiàn** envy

毒药 **dúyào** poison

毒液 **dúyè** venom

镀银 **dùyín** silver-plated

独一无二 **dúyīwú'èr** unique

独有 **dúyǒu** exclusive

独占 **dúzhàn** monopoly

读者 **dúzhě** reader

赌咒 **dùzhòu** swear; take an oath

赌注 **dùzhù** bet; stake

堵住 **dǔzhù** block in; clog up; 堵住了 **dǔzhùle** stuck fast

杜撰 **dùzhuàn** make up; invent

独自 **dúzì** alone; by itself; by myself; single-handed; 她独自 **tā dúzì** by herself

肚子 **dùzi** stomach; abdomen; belly

独子 **dúzǐ** only son

肚子疼 **dùzi téng** stomach-ache

独自一人 **dúzì yīrén** solitude

独奏曲 **dúzòu qǔ** solo

独奏演员 **dúzòu yǎnyuán** soloist

E

额 é forehead; volume (*of business*)

鹅 é goose

蛾 é moth

恶 è evil

腭 è palate

饿 è hunger ◊ hungry; 我饿了 *wǒ è le* I'm hungry

恶霸 èbà bully; despot

恶臭 èchòu stench

恶毒 èdú malevolent; savage; vicious

恶棍 ègùn gangster; ruffian

恶化 èhuà deteriorate

饿坏了 èhuàile ravenous

恶劣 èliè foul, nasty; vile

俄罗斯 Éluósī Russia ◊ Russian

恶梦 èmèng nightmare

恶魔 èmó devil; demon

恩 ēn favor; kindness

而 ér and; but

儿 ér child; son

耳 ěr ear

二 èr two

耳背 ěrbèi hard of hearing

而不是 ér búshì instead of

二冲程 èrchōngchéng two-stroke

二档 èrdàng second gear

二等 èrděng second class

耳朵 ěrduǒ ear

儿歌 érgē nursery rhyme

耳垢 ěrgòu (ear)wax

耳光 ěrguāng clip around the ear

而后 érhòu then

耳环 ěrhuán earring

耳机 ěrjī headphones, earphones

二进制 èrjìn zhì binary

二进制位 èrjìn zhì wèi bit COMPUT

儿科学 érkēxué pediatrics

儿科学家 érkēxuéjiā pediatrician

二流 èrliú second-rate

二年级 èrniánjí sophomore

而且 érqiě moreover; plus

二十 èrshí twenty

二十分之一 èrshífēnzhīyī twentieth

二手 èrshǒu secondhand

儿童 értóng children

耳痛 ěrtòng earache

儿童节 Értóng Jié Children's Day

二头肌 èrtóu jī biceps

儿媳妇 érxífu daughter-in-law

耳语 ěryǔ whisper

二月 èryuè February

儿子 érzi son

扼杀 èshā strangle, throttle

饿死 èsǐ starve to death; 我饿死了 *wǒ èsǐ le* I'm starving

扼死 èsǐ strangle

额外 éwài additional, extra

额外品 éwài pǐn bonus

恶习 èxí vice

恶心 ěxīn nausea ◊ revolting ◊ feel nauseous; 我感到恶心 *wǒ gǎndào ěxīn* I feel nauseous; 使恶心 *shǐ ěxīn* nauseate

恶性 èxìng malignant; virulent

恶意 èyì ill will; malice, spite ◊ malicious, spiteful

俄语 Éyǔ Russian (*language*)

鳄鱼 èyú crocodile

恶运、厄运 èyùn jinx

遏制 èzhì bottle up

蛾子 ézi moth

恶作剧 èzuòjù mischief; practical joke, prank

F

发 **fā** send out; give out; issue; emit

阀 **fá** valve

罚 **fá** punish

乏 **fá** lack ◊ exhausted

筏 **fá** raft

法 **fǎ** law; method

发 **fà** hair

发表 **fābiǎo** publish; issue

发表意见 **fābiǎo yìjiàn** comment; express an opinion

发财 **fācái** make a fortune; get rich

发愁 **fāchóu** worry; be anxious

发出 **fāchū** send off, dispatch; give off; issue

发错 **fācuò** mispronounce

发达 **fādá** developed ◊ develop

发大财 **fā dàcái** hit the jackpot

发达国家 **fādá guójiā** developed country

发呆 **fādāi** be in a daze

发电 **fādiàn** generate electricity

法典 **fǎdiǎn** code; statutes

发电机 **fādiànjī** generator

发电站 **fādiànzhàn** power station

法定 **fǎdìng** legal; statutory; 未到法定年龄 **wèidào fǎdìng niánlíng** below the legal age

发动 **fādòng** start; launch; mobilize

发动机 **fādòngjī** motor

发抖 **fādǒu** shake; shudder; tremble

发奋 **fāfèn** make an effort

发疯 **fāfēng** go crazy; 使 X 发疯 **shǐ X fāfēng** drive X mad

法官 **fǎguān** judge; 法官判定 … **fǎguān pàndìng …** the judge ruled that …

发光 **fāguāng** glow; shine

发光二极管 **fāguāng èrjí guǎn** LED, light-emitting diode

法规 **fǎguī** law; act; legislation

法国 **Fǎguó** France ◊ French

发慌 **fāhuāng** feel nervous

发挥 **fāhuī** summon up

发昏 **fāhūn** dazed

发火 **fāhuǒ** erupt; get angry

发货 **fāhuò** send goods

法家 **fǎjiā** legalism (*philosophy*)

法家 **fǎjiā** legalist

发夹 **fàjiá** hairpin

发奖 **fājiǎng** award prizes

发酵 **fājiào** ferment ◊ fermentation

罚金 **fájīn** fine

发掘 **fājué** find, uncover, unearth

罚款 **fákuǎn** fine

发狂 **fākuáng** go crazy

发困 **fākùn** drowsy

珐琅质 **fàlángzhì** enamel

法兰绒 **fǎlánróng** washcloth

发牢骚 **fā láosāo** grumble, complain, bitch; 爱发牢骚的人 **ài fā láosao de rén** grumbler

乏力 **fálì** weak

发亮 **fāliàng** shiny

法令 **fǎlìng** law; statute; court order

法律 **fǎlǜ** law ◊ legal

法轮功 **fǎlúngōng** Falungong sect

发麻 **fāmá** pins and needles ◊ get pins and needles; go numb

发霉 **fāméi** go moldy

发明 **fāmíng** invent ◊ invention

发明者 **fāmíng zhě** inventor

翻 **fān** overturn; roll over

帆 **fān** sail

烦 **fán** annoyed

反 **fǎn** anti-; counter- ◊ reverse; inside-out; 穿反了 **chuānfǎnle** back to front

返 **fǎn** return

饭 **fàn** (cooked) rice; food; meal

犯 **fàn** commit *crime, blunder*

帆板 **fānbǎn** sailboard; windsurfer

翻版 **fānbǎn** reprint

帆板运动 **fānbǎn yùndòng**

windsurfing

帆板运动员 fānbǎn yùndòngyuán windsurfer

反驳 fǎnbó contradict; counter; retort

帆布 fānbù canvas

帆布篷 fānbùpéng tarpaulin; awning

帆布鞋 fānbùxié sneakers

饭菜 fàncài food

反常 fǎncháng unnatural; warped;

反常现象 fǎncháng xiànxiàng freak

范畴 fànchóu category

翻船 fānchuán capsize

帆船 fānchuán junk; sailboat

饭店 fàndiàn hotel; restaurant

贩毒 fàndú drug dealing; drug trafficking ◊ push

反对 fǎnduì oppose; be against; take exception to; object; protest ◊ opposition; objection; 我抽烟你不反对吗？ *wǒ chōuyān nǐ bù fǎnduì ma?* do you mind if I smoke?

反毒警 fǎndú jǐng narcotics agent

贩毒者 fàndú zhě drug dealer

犯法 fànfǎ break the law

反复 fǎnfù repeated

反复无常 fǎnfù wúcháng unpredictable; unstable; volatile

方 fāng square; to the power of MATH

房 fáng house; room

防 fáng prevent

妨 fáng hinder; obstruct

纺 fǎng spin

访 fǎng visit

仿 fǎng copy; imitate

放 fàng place, put, set; put on; release; 放在一边 *fàngzài yìbiān* put aside; 放风筝 *fàng fēngzhēng* fly a kite

犯病 fànbìng relapse MED

妨碍 fáng'ài hinder; obstruct

反感 fǎngǎn aversion; antipathy; dislike; revulsion; 使反感 *shǐ fǎngǎn* disgust

方案 fāng'àn plan; program

方便 fāngbiàn convenience ◊ convenient; 在你方便的时候

zài nǐ fāngbiàn de shíhòu at your convenience

方便面 fāngbiànmiàn instant noodles

方便食品 fāngbiàn shípǐn convenience food

防波堤 fángbōdī jetty

放长 fàngcháng let down *pants etc*

防虫药 fángchóngyào insect repellent

放大 fàngdà amplify; enlarge; magnify

放大镜 fàngdàjìng magnifying glass

防弹 fángdàn bullet-proof

放荡 fàngdàng debauchery ◊ debauched, dissolute; loose

放荡女子 fàngdàng nǚzǐ slut

放大器 fàngdàqì amplifier

房地产 fángdìchǎn property; real estate

房地产开发人 fángdìchǎn kāifárén property developer

房东 fángdōng landlord; landlady

方法 fāngfǎ method, means, way

防腐剂 fángfǔjì preservative

方格 fānggé check (*pattern*); box (*on form*)

放过 fàngguò let off; pass up

防护 fánghù protect

防滑 fánghuá nonskid

防滑链 fáng huá liàn snow chains

放回 fànghuí put back; return; replace

放回原处 fànghuí yuánchù put back

防火 fánghuǒ fire prevention

放火 fànghuǒ set fire to

放假 fàngjià be on leave; have a day off; have a vacation; 放假一星期 *fàngjià yìxīngqī* take a week off

房间 fángjiān room

放进去 fàngjìnqù put in; get in

放开 fàngkāi open up; let go of

房客 fángkè lodger; tenant

方块儿 fāngkuàir diamond

放慢 fàngmàn slacken off

方面 fāngmiàn aspect; side; 在这方面 *zài zhè fāngmiàn* in this respect

防抹舌 **fángmǒshé** tab

放屁 **fàngpì** fart; break wind

放弃 **fàngqì** abandon; give up; jettison

防窃警报器 **fángqiè jǐngbào qì** burglar alarm

放晴 **fàngqíng** clear up (*of weather*)

防热 **fángrè** heat-resistant

放任 **fàngrèn** permissive

防晒膏 **fángshàigāo** sun block

放哨 **fàngshào** keep watch

放射 **fàngshè** radiate

放射尘 **fàngshèchén** fallout

放射疗法 **fàngshè liáofǎ** radiotherapy

放声大哭 **fàngshēng dàkū** burst into tears

放射性 **fàngshè xìng** radioactive ◊ radioactivity

方式 **fāngshì** way; manner; mode; approach; pattern

防守 **fángshǒu** defense

防水 **fángshuǐ** waterproof

放肆 **fàngsì** impertinent; audacious; presumptuous

放松 **fàngsōng** ease; relieve; lighten up; relax; unwind ◊ relaxed, easy ◊ relaxation

方糖 **fāngtáng** sugar cubes

反光 **fǎn'guāng** reflect

泛光灯 **fàn'guāngdēng** floodlight

反光镜 **fǎn'guāngjìng** mirror

犯规 **fàn'guī** break the rules; foul SP

翻滚 **fān'gǔn** roll

翻过来 **fān guòlái** turn over; overturn

方位 **fāng'wèi** directions

防卫 **fángwèi** defend; protect

访问 **fǎngwèn** pay a visit

放下 **fàngxià** put down, lay down; lower

芳香 **fāngxiāng** bouquet; fragrance

方向 **fāngxiàng** direction

方向盘 **fāngxiàng pán** steering wheel

方向指示器 **fāngxiàng zhǐshìqì** indicator

仿效者 **fǎngxiào zhě** imitator

放心 **fàngxīn** put one's mind at rest; rest assured

防锈 **fángxiù** rustproof

方言 **fāngyán** dialect

放映 **fàngyìng** screen *movie*

放映机 **fàngyìngjī** projector

防雨 **fángyǔ** showerproof

防御 **fángyù** defend ◊ defensive ◊ defense

仿造 **fǎngzào** copy ◊ imitation

放债者 **fàngzhài zhě** money-lender

仿照 **fǎngzhào** copy; imitate

方针 **fāngzhēn** policy; guideline

防止 **fángzhǐ** guard against; prevent

纺织 **fǎngzhī** textile

仿制 **fǎngzhì** fake

纺织品 **fǎngzhīpǐn** textiles

防撞头盔 **fángzhuàng tóukuī** crash helmet

房子 **fángzi** house; building

放纵 **fàngzòng** indulgence ◊ indulge; pamper

房租 **fángzū** rent

返回 **fǎnhuí** return; turn back; 顺原路返回 **shùn yuánlù fǎnhuí** retrace

反击 **fǎnjī** counter; hit back ◊ counter-attack

反间谍活动 **fǎn jiàndié huódòng** counterespionage

烦交 **fánjiāo** c/o, care of

反诘问 **fǎn jiéwèn** cross-examine

翻筋斗 **fān jīndǒu** somersault

反抗 **fǎnkàng** revolt

饭筐 **fànkuāng** hamper

反馈信息 **fǎnkuì xìnxī** feedback

泛滥 **fànlàn** overflow; flood

烦劳… **fánláo …** would you mind …?

翻了三番 **fānle sān fān** treble

翻领 **fānlǐng** lapel

贩卖 **fànmài** traffic in; peddle

繁忙 **fánmáng** busy

反面 **fǎnmiàn** reverse (side); opposite

烦恼 **fánnǎo** annoyance ◊ vexed; 令人烦恼 **lìngrén fánnǎo** annoying

反叛 **fǎnpàn** rebellion; mutiny

反叛军队 **fǎnpàn jūnduì** rebel troops

反叛者 **fǎnpàn zhě** rebel

翻篇儿 **fān piānr** turn over *page*; turn the page

翻起 **fānqǐ** turn up; turn over

蕃茄 **fānqié** tomato

番茄酱 **fānqiéjiàng** tomato ketchup

烦扰 **fánrǎo** bother, plague

烦人 **fánrén** irritating; troublesome ◊ nuisance

繁荣 **fánróng** boom ◊ flourishing, thriving; prosperous ◊ promote; develop

反射 **fǎnshè** reflect, mirror ◊ reflection

翻身 **fānshēn** turn over, roll over; toss and turn

反手击球 **fǎnshǒu jīqiú** backhand SP

繁体字 **fántǐzì** traditional Chinese characters

发怒 **fānù** flare up; be in a rage; get angry

饭碗 **fànwǎn** rice bowl

范围 **fànwéi** range; scope; 在一定范围内 **zài yídìng fànwéi nèi** within specific limits

反问 **fǎnwèn** rhetorical question

翻下 **fānxià** turn down

反响 **fǎnxiǎng** echo; repercussion

反省 **fǎnxǐng** reflect, think ◊ reflection, consideration

翻寻 **fānxún** rummage around

翻译 **fānyì** translate; interpret ◊ translation; interpretation; translator; interpreter; 翻译成英语 **fānyì chéng Yīngyǔ** translate into English

翻一番 **fānyìfān** double

反应 **fǎnyìng** react ◊ reaction

反应堆 **fǎnyìng duī** reactor

反应能力 **fǎnyìng nénglì** reflex

反右运动 **Fǎnyòu Yùndòng** Anti-rightists Campaign

犯有罪恶 **fànyǒu zuì'è** sin, commit a sin

繁育 **fányù** fertility ◊ breed; reproduce

翻阅 **fānyuè** leaf through

烦躁 **fánzào** fret ◊ irritable ◊ irritation

烦躁不安 **fánzào bù'ān** fidget

反证 **fǎnzhèng** disprove

反正 **fǎnzhèng** in any case; anyway

繁殖 **fánzhí** breed; reproduce ◊ reproduction; reproductive

反之亦然 **fǎnzhī yìrán** vice versa

翻转 **fānzhuàn** overturn

犯罪 **fànzuì** commit a crime

犯罪率 **fànzuì lǜ** crime rate

反作用 **fǎnzuòyòng** reaction; counteraction

发牌 **fāpái** deal; deal the cards

发牌者 **fāpái zhě** dealer (*cards*)

发胖 **fāpàng** put on weight

发票 **fāpiào** receipt; invoice

发脾气 **fā píqì** huff; tantrum ◊ be in a huff; be in a temper; lose one's temper, get angry 爱发脾气 **ài fā píqì** short-tempered

发起 **fāqǐ** mount *campaign*; originate; initiate; launch; sponsor

发卡 **fāqiǎ** barrette; hairpin

发起人 **fāqǐ rén** creator; originator; sponsor

发球 **fāqiú** serve SP

罚球 **fáqiú** penalty SP

发球得分 **fāqiú défēn** ace (*in tennis*)

罚球区 **fáqiúqū** penalty area

发球人 **fāqiúrén** server (*in tennis*)

法人 **fǎrén** legal person; legal entity

发热器 **fārèqì** heater

发烧 **fāshāo** have a fever

发射 **fāshè** launch; blast off

发生 **fāshēng** happen, occur; take place

发生冲突 **fāshēng chōngtū** clash

发生的事情 **fāshēng de shìqíng** goings-on

发生关系 **fāshēng guānxì** have a relationship (*sexual*)

发生故障 **fāshēng gùzhàng** malfunction

发射上天 **fāshè shàngtiān** blast off

发射台 **fāshè tái** launch pad

发誓 **fāshì** swear; vow; pledge

发式 **fàshì** hairdo

发条 **fātiáo** clockwork

法庭 **fǎtíng** (law) court

乏味 **fáwèi** tasteless; bland; boring

发微光 **fāwēiguāng** glimmer

发现 **fāxiàn** discover; find; realize; notice ◊ discovery

发泄 **fāxiè** give vent to; release

发薪 **fāxīn** pay wages; pay salary

发信 **fāxìn** send off a letter

发行 **fāxíng** issue; publish; launch; release; distribute; put on sale

发型 **fāxíng** hairstyle

发薪日 **fāxīnrì** payday

法西斯 **fǎxīsī** fascist

法西斯主义 **fǎxīsī zhǔyì** fascism

法西斯主义者 **fǎxīsī zhǔyì zhě** fascist

法学 **fǎxué** law

发芽 **fāyá** sprout; germinate

发言 **fāyán** speak

发炎 **fāyán** inflammation ◊ become inflamed

发痒 **fāyǎng** itch; tickle; 使发痒 **shǐ fāyǎng** tickle

发扬 **fāyáng** develop; make the most of

发炎膏 **fāyángāo** inflammation

发言人 **fāyán rén** spokesman; spokeswoman; spokesperson

法衣 **fǎyī** robe

发音 **fāyīn** pronounce ◊ pronunciation

发音错误 **fāyīn cuòwù** mispronunciation

发育 **fāyù** grow ◊ growth

法语 **Fǎyǔ** French (*language*)

发源 **fāyuán** spring; rise; originate

法院 **fǎyuàn** court; courthouse

发展 **fāzhǎn** develop, build up; grow ◊ development; growth

发展中国家 **fāzhǎn zhōng guójiā** developing country

发作 **fāzuò** bout; seizure

非本意 **fēiběnyì** involuntary

飞 **fēi** fly

非 **fēi** not

肥 **féi** fat; fatty; fertile ◊ fertilizer

费 **fèi** cost; fee ◊ cost; spend; expend

肺 **fèi** lung

吠 **fèi** bark (*of dog*)

废 **fèi** useless

沸 **fèi** boil

非 ... 非 ... **fēi ... fēi ...** neither ... nor ...

非 ... 即 ... **fēi ... jí ...** either ... or ...

肺癌 **fèi'ái** lung cancer

诽谤 **fěibàng** libel; slander ◊ defamation ◊ defamatory

诽谤活动 **fěibàng huódòng** smear campaign

非暴力 **fēi bàolì** nonviolence ◊ nonviolent

飞奔 **fēibēn** dash; run quickly

非常 **fēicháng** extraordinary ◊ extremely, very; 非常感谢 **fēicháng gǎnxiè** thanks very much

非常规 **fēi chángguī** nonstandard

废除 **fèichú** abolish, do away with; repeal, revoke; undo

肥大 **féidà** bulky

飞到 **fēidào** fly in; fly to

废掉 **fèidiào** scrap

飞碟 **fēidié** flying saucer

非法 **fēifǎ** illegal; 非法麻醉品 **fēifǎ mázuì pǐn** illegal drugs

非凡 **fēifán** remarkable; phenomenal ◊ remarkably

非法侵入 **fēifǎ qīnrù** trespass (on)

非法侵入者 **fēifǎ qīnrù zhě** trespasser

狒狒 **fèifèi** baboon

飞过 **fēiguò** whizz by

废话 **fèihuà** nonsense; gibberish

飞回 **fēihuí** fly back

飞机 **fēijī** airplane

飞溅 **fēijiàn** splash

飞机场 **fēijīchǎng** airport

费解 **fèijiě** inexplicable; puzzling

飞机库 **fēijīkù** hangar

费劲 **fèijìn** strenuous

废金属 **fèijīnshǔ** scrap metal

飞机失事 **fēijī shīshì** plane crash

飞快 **fēikuài** lightning fast; quick as a flash

费力 **fèilì** effort; exertion; hard work ◊ laborious; strenuous; exhausting

肥料 **féiliào** fertilizer; manure

废料堆 **fèiliàoduī** scrap heap

菲律宾 **Fēilǜbīn** the Philippines

肥胖 **féipàng** plump; chubby; stout

肥胖症 **féipàngzhèng** obesity

飞跑 **fēipǎo** rush, fly; gallop

废品 **fèipǐn** trash, junk; waste product

废品站 **fèipǐnzhàn** junkyard

废气 **fèiqì** exhaust; fumes

废弃 **fèiqì** abandon ◊ disused; waste

非人造 **fēi rénzào** natural, non-artificial

飞逝 **fēishì** fly past (of time)

费事 **fèishì** painful

飞速 **fēisù** very fast; meteoric

沸腾 **fèiténg** boil

飞脱 **fēituō** fly off (of hat etc)

肥沃 **féiwò** fertile ◊ fertility

废物 **fèiwù** waste

飞行 **fēixíng** flight; flying ◊ fly

飞行甲板 **fēixíng jiǎbǎn** flight deck

飞行记录仪 **fēixíng jìlùyí** flight recorder

飞行路线 **fēixíng lùxiàn** flight path

飞行时间 **fēixíng shíjiān** flight time

飞行员 **fēixíngyuán** pilot

飞行中 **fēixíngzhōng** in-flight

废墟 **fèixū** ruins; wasteland

肺炎 **fèiyán** pneumonia

沸溢 **fèiyì** boil over

费用 **fèiyong** charge; fee; costs; expenses

鲱鱼 **fēiyú** herring

飞跃 **fēiyuè** leap; become popular; take off

肥皂 **féizào** soap

肥皂剧 **féizào jù** soap opera

非正式 **fēi zhèngshì** informal; unofficial ◊ unofficially

非正义 **fēizhèngyì** injustice ◊ unjust

废纸 **fèizhǐ** wastepaper; scrap paper

废纸篓 **fèizhǐlǒu** wastepaper basket

非洲 **Fēizhōu** Africa ◊ African

痱子 **fèizi** prickly heat

飞走 **fēizǒu** fly away

分 **fēn** divide; split; share ◊ cent; minute fraction ◊ measure word for time, money, length

坟 **fén** grave

焚 **fén** burn

粉 **fěn** powder ◊ pink

份 **fèn** portion; share; part; copy ◊ measure word for newspapers, documents; 一份报纸 **yífèn bàozhǐ** a newspaper; 一份饭 **yífèn fàn** a helping of food

粪 **fèn** excrement; dung

分包合同 **fēnbāo hétong** subcontract

分包人 **fēnbāo rén** subcontractor

分贝 **fēnbèi** decibel

粉笔 **fěnbǐ** chalk

粪便 **fènbiàn** dung

分别 **fēnbié** separate ◊ separately; respectively

分不开 **fēnbùkāi** inseparable

分岔 **fēnchà** branch off

分岔处 **fēnchàchù** fork

分成两半 **fēnchéng liǎngbàn** halve

分成四份 **fēnchéng sìfèn** quarter

粉刺 **fěncì** acne; pimples

分店 **fēndiàn** branch

奋斗 **fèndòu** strive, struggle

份额 **fèn'é** share

分发 **fēnfā** give out; distribute ◊ distribution

分房 **fēnfáng** allocate accommodation

粪肥 **fènféi** manure

封 **fēng** seal; board up ◊ measure word for letters; 三封信 **sānfēng xìn** three letters

锋 **fēng** edge; front (weather)

疯 **fēng** mad

枫 **fēng** maple

风 **fēng** wind; style; tendency

丰 **fēng** abundant

蜂 **fēng** bee

峰 **fēng** summit; peak

缝 **féng** sew; stitch

缝 **fèng** crack; seam; part (in hair)

凤 **fèng** phoenix

风暴 **fēngbào** storm

风暴警报 **fēngbào jǐngbào** storm warning

封闭 **fēngbì** seal; close up

风车 **fēngchē** windmill

奉承 **fèngchéng** flatter; suck up to ◊ flattery

讽刺 **fěngcì** mock, deride, ridicule ◊ ironic(al); satirical ◊ irony; satire

讽刺画 **fěngcì huà** cartoon; caricature

讽刺者 **fěngcì zhě** satirist

分割 **fēn'gē** division; split

分隔 **fēn'gé** isolate

分给 **fēn'gěi** distribute

蜂房 **fēngfáng** hive

丰富 **fēngfù** abundance ◊ abundant ◊ enrich; 丰富多彩的活动 **fēngfù duōcǎi de huódòng** a variety of things to do

风干 **fēnggān** seasoned *wood*

风格 **fēnggé** method; style; format

风寒 **fēnghán** cold

缝合 **fénghé** sew up

风和日丽 **fēnghé rìlì** *a gentle breeze and glorious sunshine*

凤凰 **fènghuáng** phoenix

风景 **fēngjǐng** view; landscape

风景画 **fēngjǐng huà** landscape (*painting*)

疯狂 **fēngkuáng** insane, crazy ◊ insanity ◊ insanely

锋利 **fēnglì** sharp

风凉话 **fēngliánghuà** wisecrack

风流 **fēngliú** romantic; unrestrained; admirable

风流人物 **fēngliú rénwù** influential person; moldbreaker; romantic hero; great man

风流韵事 **fēngliú yùnshì** love affair; romance

丰满 **fēngmǎn** busty; plump; rounded

风帽 **fēngmào** hood

蜂蜜 **fēngmì** honey

封面 **fēngmiàn** (front) cover

蜂鸣器 **fēngmíng qì** buzzer

分公司 **fēn gōngsī** branch (*of company*)

奉陪 **fèngpéi** *fml* accompany; 我有急事，不能奉陪 **wǒ yǒu**

jíshì, bù néng fèngpéi I'm sorry, I can't make it due to a prior engagement

风琴 **fēngqín** organ MUS

奉劝 **fèngquàn** *fml* advise

疯人 **fēngrén** madman

缝纫 **féngrèn** sew ◊ sewing

缝纫机 **féngrènjī** sewing machine

缝上 **féngshang** sew on

风扇皮带 **fēngshàn pídài** fan belt

丰盛 **fēngshèng** rich; copious; 丰盛可口 **fēngshèng kěkǒu** magnificent *meal*

风湿 **fēngshī** rheumatism

丰收 **fēngshōu** good harvest

封锁 **fēngsuǒ** blockade ◊ cordon off; seal off

风俗习惯 **fēngsú xíguàn** traditions, customs

风头主义者 **fēngtóu zhǔyì zhě** exhibitionist

蜂王 **fēngwáng** queen bee

风味 **fēngwèi** savor

缝隙 **fèngxì** crack

风险 **fēngxiǎn** risk; 有风险 **yǒu fēngxiǎn** adventurous; risky

蜂箱 **fēngxiāng** beehive

风行一时 **fēngxíng yìshí** all the rage

风信子 **fēngxìnzǐ** hyacinth

风雪大衣 **fēngxuě dàyī** parka

蜂拥 **fēngyōng** swarm

缝针 **féngzhēn** stitches

风筝 **fēngzheng** kite

疯子 **fēngzi** lunatic

风钻 **fēngzuàn** pneumatic drill

分行 **fēnháng** branch (*of bank, company*)

分号 **fēnhào** semicolon

粉红 **fěnhóng** pink

焚化炉 **fénhuàlú** incinerator

分机 **fēnjī** extension

分解 **fēnjiě** break up

分居 **fēnjū** separate; live apart

分开 **fēnkāi** break; part; separate; detach; 把 X 与 Y 分开 **bǎ X yǔ Y fēnkāi** separate X from Y

愤慨 **fènkǎi** indignant ◊ indignation

芬兰 **Fēnlán** Finland ◊ Finnish

分类 **fēnlèi** break down; classify;

group ◊ breakdown; classification; 给 ... 分类 **gěi ... fēnlèi** grade

分类广告 **fēnlèi guǎnggào** classified advertisement

分离 **fēnlí** separate ◊ separation

分裂 **fēnliè** division; partition; breach; rift; split ◊ divide; splinter

分裂人格 **fēnliè rén‌gé** split personality

分流术 **fēnliú shù** bypass

分泌 **fēnmì** secrete ◊ secretion

分娩 **fēnmiǎn** childbirth; labor; delivery; 在分娩中 **zài fēnmiǎn zhōng** in labor

分泌物 **fēnmìwù** secretion

粉末 **fěnmò** powder

坟墓 **fénmù** grave; tomb

愤怒 **fènnù** anger ◊ angry

分配 **fēnpèi** allot; assign; allocate; distribute ◊ distribution

分批 **fēnpī** in groups; partially

分歧 **fēnqí** difference; gulf

分期付款 **fēnqī fùkuǎn** pay in installments ◊ installment plan

分散 **fēnsàn** scattered

分散注意力 **fēnsàn zhìyì lì** distract

焚烧 **fénshāo** burn

粉饰 **fěnshì** gloss over

愤世嫉俗 **fènshì jísú** cynical ◊ cynicism

愤世嫉俗者 **fènshì jísú zhě** cynic

分手 **fēnshǒu** split up; break up ◊ breakup; separation ◊ separated

分数 **fēnshù** fraction; mark

粉刷 **fěnshuā** paintwork ◊ whitewash

粉刷工 **fěnshuāgōng** painter

粉丝 **fěnsī** Chinese vermicelli, rice noodles

粉碎 **fěnsuì** shatter; pulverize

分析 **fēnxī** analysis ◊ analyze

分享 **fēnxiǎng** share

分心 **fēnxīn** distract; 使 X 分心 **shǐ X fēnxīn** drive X to distraction

分着 **fēnzhe** separately

分钟 **fēnzhōng** minute

分子 **fēnzǐ** numerator MATH; molecule ◊ molecular

分组 **fēnzǔ** divide into groups

佛 **Fó** Buddha

佛教 **Fójiào** Buddhism ◊ Buddhist

佛教徒 **Fójiào tú** Buddhist

否 **fǒu** no; not

否定 **fǒudìng** negative ◊ negate; deny; repudiate; 给予否定的回答 **jǐyú fǒudìngde huídá** answer in the negative

否决 **fǒujué** overrule; throw out; veto

否决权 **fǒujué quán** veto

否认 **fǒurèn** denial ◊ deny; disclaim; 否认自己和 X 有关系 **fǒurèn zìjǐ hé X yǒu guānxi** dissociate oneself from X

否则 **fǒuzé** or else; otherwise

佛爷 **Fóye** Buddha

夫 **fū** husband; man

敷 **fū** apply

孵 **fū** hatch; incubate

肤 **fū** skin

扶 **fú** hold up; support

福 **fú** luck; happiness; fortune

辐 **fú** spoke

幅 **fú** *measure word for paintings, cloth*; 一幅画 **yìfú huà** a picture

浮 **fú** float

服 **fú** take *medicine*

斧 **fǔ** ax

腐 **fǔ** rotten; stale

抚 **fǔ** stroke

附 **fù** attach; enclose

副 **fù** vice-; deputy; assistant ◊ pack (*of cards*)

付 **fù** pay

父 **fù** father

富 **fù** rich, wealthy

复 **fù** again ◊ duplicate ◊ reply

腹 **fù** abdomen; stomach

负 **fù** negative; minus ◊ bear

妇 **fù** wife; woman

腐败 **fǔbài** corrupt

副本 **fùběn** copy

辅币 **fǔbì** token

浮标 **fúbiāo** buoy

副标题 **fùbiāotí** subheading

服兵役 **fú bīngyì** do military service

敷布 **fūbù** compress

腹部 **fùbù** stomach ◊ abdominal

复查 **fùchá** doublecheck

副产品 **fù chǎnpǐn** by-product

扶车 **fúchē** walker

俯冲 **fúchōng** dive

孵出 **fūchū** hatch out

付出 **fùchū** pay out; stump up; put in *time*; donate ◊ donation; 付出的款项 **fùchūde kuǎnxiàng** payment

副词 **fùcí** adverb

服从 **fúcóng** obey; comply ◊ obedience ◊ obedient; 服从命令 **fúcóng mìnglìng** obey orders

附带 **fùdài** incidental; supplementary ◊ incidentally

附带条件 **fùdài tiáojiàn** proviso

负担 **fùdān** load; burden

辅导 **fǔdǎo** counsel; tutor ◊ counseling; tuition

辅导课 **fǔdǎokè** tutorial

副导演 **fù dǎoyǎn** assistant director

辅导员 **fǔdǎo yuán** counselor; tutor

负电 **fùdiàn** negative ELEC

浮雕 **fúdiāo** relief (*in sculpture*)

浮动 **fúdòng** float

复发 **fùfā** relapse

复方药 **fùfāngyào** mixture (*medicine made from a combination of compounds*)

夫妇 **fūfù** (married) couple

覆盖 **fùgài** cover

讣告 **fùgào** obituary

副歌 **fùgē** refrain MUS

浮垢 **fúgòu** scum

腹股沟 **fùgǔgōu** groin

敷裹 **fūguǒ** dress

符号 **fúhào** symbol

符合 **fúhé** agreement ◊ accordingly ◊ tally (with); conform (to) ◊ compatible; 符合标准 **fúhé biāozhǔn** be up to standard

复合 **fùhé** overlap

负荷 **fùhé** load; 负荷过重 **fùhé guòzhòng** overload

符合性 **fúhé xìng** compatibility

孵化器 **fūhuàqì** incubator

付回款 **fùhuíkuǎn** repayment

复活 **fùhuó** resurrection

复活节 **Fùhuójié** Easter

伏击 **fújī** ambush

附加 **fùjiā** add ◊ additional

附加费 **fùjiāfèi** extra charge; supplement; surcharge

附件 **fùjiàn** accessory; add-on; enclosure; attachment (*to e-mail*) ◊ enclose (*in letter*); attach

复件 **fùjiàn** duplicate

副教授 **fù jiàoshòu** associate professor

副驾驶员 **fù jiàshǐ yuán** co-pilot

附加物 **fùjiāwù** frill; extra; insert

附近 **fùjìn** close by ◊ neighboring; 他住在附近 **tā zhù zài fùjìn** he lives around here

副经理 **fù jīnglǐ** assistant manager

妇科医生 **fùkē yīshēng** gynecologist

付款 **fùkuǎn** pay ◊ payment

付款人 **fùkuǎn rén** payer

付款台 **fùkuǎn tái** cash desk

腐烂 **fǔlàn** decay; perish; rot ◊ rotten

富丽 **fùlì** palatial

敷料 **fūliào** dressing MED

福利 **fúlì** welfare

福利工作 **fúlì gōngzuò** welfare work

福利国家 **fúlì guójiā** welfare state

福利救济 **fúlì jiùjì** welfare

俘房 **fúlǔ** capture ◊ prisoner; captive; 俘房 X **fúlǔ X** take X prisoner

附录 **fùlù** appendix

负面 **fùmiàn** unfavorable, negative

覆灭 **fùmiè** demise; downfall

抚摸 **fǔmō** stroke; caress

抚摩 **fǔmó** stroke; caress

父母 **fùmǔ** parents ◊ parental

妇女 **fùnǚ** woman

夫妻 **fūqī** married couple

福气 **fúqi** luck; happiness

肤浅 **fūqiǎn** superficial; sketchy

付钱 **fùqián** pay

父亲 **fùqīn** father

付清 **fùqīng** pay off *debt*

父亲身分 **fùqīn shēnfèn** paternity

夫人 **fūrén** Mrs; wife

富人 **fùrén** the rich; rich person

附入 **fùrù** enclose; add

服丧 **fúsāng** mourning; 在服丧 **zài fúsāng** in mourning

肤色 **fūsè** skin color

负伤 **fùshāng** injured

敷设 **fūshè** lay *cable*

辐射 **fúshè** radiate ◊ radiation

服侍 **fúshì** attend to

服饰 **fúshì** clothes and accessories; get-up

腐蚀 **fǔshí** corrode ◊ corrosion

俯视 **fǔshì** overlook

扶手 **fúshǒu** armrest; handrail; banister; balustrade

副手 **fùshǒu** mate

扶手椅 **fúshǒu yǐ** armchair

复数 **fùshù** plural

复述 **fùshù** relate; repeat

负数 **fùshù** negative (number)

附属公司 **fùshǔ gōngsī** subsidiary (company)

复数形式 **fùshù xíngshì** plural

伏特 **fútè** volt

伏特加 **fútèjiā** vodka

伏天 **fútiān** dog days

服贴 **fútiē** obedient; manageable

斧头 **fǔtóu** ax

浮凸 **fútú** emboss

富翁 **fùwēng** rich man

俯卧撑 **fǔ wòchēng** push-up

服务 **fúwù** serve ◊ service

服务费 **fúwùfèi** service charge

服务行业 **fúwù hángyè** service industry; service sector

服务器 **fúwùqì** server COMPUT

服务区 **fúwùqū** service area

服务台 **fúwùtái** reception

服务员 **fúwù yuán** attendant; maid; clerk; waiter; waitress

复习 **fùxí** review; revise

父系 **fùxì** paternal

复写 **fùxiě** copy; duplicate

腹泻 **fùxiè** diarrhea

复习课程 **fùxí kèchéng** refresher course

附信 **fùxìn** covering letter

复兴 **fùxīng** revival ◊ revive

敷衍 **fūyǎn** stall; hold off ◊ perfunctory

抚养 **fǔyǎng** raise

抚养费 **fúyǎngfèi** maintenance (*money*)

扶养权 **fúyǎng quán** custody

副业 **fùyè** sideline

附议 **fùyì** second *motion*

福音 **fúyīn** gospel

辅音 **fǔyīn** consonant

复印 **fùyìn** copy; photocopy; duplicate

复映 **fùyìng** rerun

复印机 **fùyìn jī** copier

复印件 **fùyìn jiàn** copy

浮油 **fúyóu** (oil) slick

富有 **fùyǒu** wealthy; rich in; with a lot of ◊ be rich in; have plenty of

富有表情 **fùyǒu biǎoqíng** expressive

富裕 **fùyù** affluent, well-off

赋予权利 **fùyù quánlì** entitled; empowered

复杂 **fùzá** complex, complicated; intricate; involved; mixed *feelings*

负载 **fùzài** load ELEC

负责 **fùzé** answer for; take care of; be in charge of; accept responsibility for ◊ responsible; liable; conscientious

负责人 **fùzé ren** person in charge

负责任 **fù zérèn** be held accountable ◊ responsible

付账 **fùzhàng** pay the bill

复职 **fùzhí** be reinstated

复制 **fùzhì** copy; duplicate; clone; 复制一份档案 **fùzhì yífèn dàng'an** make a copy of a file

复制品 **fùzhì pǐn** copy; replica; reproduction

复制钥匙 **fùzhì yàoshi** duplicate key

负重 **fùzhòng** burden

符咒 **fúzhòu** magic spell

辅助 **fǔzhù** auxiliary

服装 **fúzhuāng** dress; clothing; garment; costume; uniform

副主管 **fù zhǔguǎn** assistant director

副总管 **fù zǒngguǎn** deputy leader

副总统 **fù zǒngtǒng** vice president

富足 **fùzú** plenty

服罪 **fúzuì** plead guilty

副作用 **fùzuòyòng** side effect

G

嘎嘎声 **gāgā shēng** rattle

该 **gāi** be supposed to; should; be next; 我该做什么？ *wǒ gāi zuò shénme?* what should I do?; 该你了 *gāi nǐ le* it's your turn; over to you

改 **gǎi** change; correct

盖 **gài** cover ◊ top; lid; 盖好被子 *gàihǎo bèizi* tuck in

钙 **gài** calcium

改编 **gǎibiān** adapt; arrange; reorganize ◊ adaptation; arrangement

改变 **gǎibiàn** change, alter; transform; vary ◊ shift; transformation; change; 改变话题 *gǎibiàn huàtí* change the subject

改编本 **gǎibiān běn** version; adaptation

改革 **gǎigé** reform

改换 **gǎihuàn** switch; change

改建 **gǎijiàn** convert

改进 **gǎijìn** improve; upgrade ◊ development; improvement

概况 **gàikuàng** survey; overview

概括 **gàikuò** generalization ◊ generalize; sum up; summarize

概括性 **gàikuò xìng** broad; general

盖了帽了 **gàilemàole** terrific, awesome

概念 **gàiniàn** concept

改期 **gǎiqī** be postponed; be rescheduled

改日 **gǎirì** sometime; another day

改善 **gǎishàn** improve

概述 **gàishù** sum up ◊ summary

该死 **gāisǐ** damn

改天 **gǎitiān** another day; another time

改线 **gǎixiàn** diversion ◊ divert

改小 **gǎixiǎo** take in, make narrower

改写 **gǎixiě** rewrite; transliterate; paraphrase

改邪归正 **gǎixiéguīzhèng** rehabilitate; go straight

概要 **gàiyào** outline; overview

改用 **gǎiyòng** adapt

盖章 **gàizhāng** stamp; seal

改正 **gǎizhèng** amend; correct

盖住 **gàizhù** cover up

改装 **gǎizhuāng** do up; make over

盖子 **gàizi** lid; cap

改组 **gǎizǔ** reorganization ◊ reorganize

咖喱 **gālí** curry

干 **gān** dry; dried; empty ◊ dry; empty ◊ in vain

肝 **gān** liver

杆 **gān** pole

竿 **gān** rod

甘 **gān** sweet

敢 **gǎn** dare; 你敢！*nǐgǎn!* how dare you!

赶 **gǎn** drive out; banish; rush; catch up with; hurry; 赶时髦 *gǎn shímáo* keep up with the latest fashions

秆 **gǎn** stalk; straw

擀 **gǎn** roll out

感 **gǎn** feel; sense

干 **gàn** do ◊ stem; trunk; 你今晚干什么？*nǐ jīnwǎn gàn shénme?* what are you doing tonight?; 干吧 *gàn ba* go ahead

干爸 **gànbà** godfather

干杯 **gānbēi** cheers!; 为 ... 干杯 *wèi ... gānbēi* toast; propose a toast to

干部 **gànbu** cadre; official

干草 **gāncǎo** hay

甘草 **gāncǎo** licorice

甘草栗子 **gāncǎo lìzi** water chestnut

赶超 **gǎnchāo** emulate; surpass

赶出 **gǎnchū** drive out; flush out

感到 gǎndào feel; 感到无聊 gǎndào wúliáo feel bored

赶掉 gǎndiào chase away

干掉 gàndiào kill, eliminate ◊ murder, elimination

感动 gǎndòng affect; move, touch ◊ moved, touched

干豆腐 gāndòufu dried bean curd

干儿子 gān érzi godson

感恩 gǎn'ēn gratitude

感恩节 Gǎn'ēn Jié Thanksgiving Day

钢 gāng steel

缸 gāng earthenware vessel; vat; jar

刚 gāng just

港 gǎng harbor, port

杠 gàng lever

尴尬 gān'gà embarrassed; awkward ◊ feel awkward ◊ embarrassment; 令人尴尬 lìngrén gāngà embarrassing

钢笔 gāngbǐ fountain pen

港币 gǎngbì Hong Kong dollar

刚才 gāngcái just now

杠杆 gànggǎn lever

刚刚 gānggang (only) just; 我刚刚看到了她 wǒ gānggang kàndào tā I've just seen her

杠杆力量 gànggǎn lìliàng leverage

刚好 gānghǎo just right; exact ◊ exactly

钢筋混凝土 gāngjīn hùnníng tǔ reinforced concrete

港口 gǎngkǒu port, harbor

肛门 gāngmén anus

钢琴 gāngqín piano

钢琴家 gāngqínjiā pianist

岗哨 gǎngshào guard; lookout

港市 gǎngshì port (city)

钢丝绳 gāngsī shéng cable; high wire; tight-rope

钢铁厂 gāngtiěchǎng ironworks

港湾 gǎngwān harbor; bay

岗位 gǎngwèi guard

港务局 gǎngwùjú port authorities

缸子 gāngzi beaker; mug; bowl

干旱 gānhàn drought

干涸 gānhé dry out; dry up

感激 gǎnjī appreciation ◊ appreciate; feel grateful; be thankful ◊ thankfully

赶集 gǎnjí go to market

赶紧 gǎnjǐn hurry

干净 gānjìng clean

柑桔 gānjú tangerine

感觉 gǎnjué feeling; sensation; sense ◊ feel; experience; 我感觉累了 gǎnjué lèi le I feel tired

干枯 gānkū dry up ◊ dried up

甘苦 gānkǔ ups and downs

赶快 gǎnkuài hurry ◊ quickly

橄榄 gǎnlǎn olive

橄榄球 gǎnlǎn qiú rugby; football

橄榄油 gǎnlǎn yóu olive oil

干酪 gānlào cheese

干裂 gānliè dry and cracked; chapped

赶拢 gǎnlǒng round up

干妈 gānmā godmother

感冒 gǎnmào cold; flu ◊ catch a cold; 我感冒了 wǒ gǎnmàole I have a cold

甘美 gānměi luscious

擀面杖 gǎnmiànzhàng rolling pin

干女儿 gān nǚ'er goddaughter

赶跑 gǎnpǎo chase off; see off

感情 gǎnqíng expression; feeling; emotion; 我对他有很多矛盾的感情 wǒ duì tā yǒu hěn máodùnde gǎnqíng I have mixed feelings about him

感染 gǎnrǎn contract, pick up; infect; influence; affect; become infected ◊ infected; infectious; septic

干扰 gānrǎo disturbance; interference ◊ interfere with; jam

感人 gǎnrén moving, touching

赶上 gǎnshàng catch; catch up

干涉 gànshè interfere; intervene; meddle ◊ interference

感叹 gǎntàn exclamation

感叹号 gǎntànhào exclamation point

干洗 gānxǐ dryclean ◊ drycleaning

干线 gànxiàn arterial road

干洗店 gānxǐ diàn dry cleaner

感谢 gǎnxiè thanks ◊ thank; say

thanks; be grateful

甘心 **gānxīn** willingly ◊ resign oneself to

感性 **gǎnxìng** sensory

感兴趣 **gǎn xìngqù** be interested

甘心情愿 **gānxīn qíngyuàn** willingly

甘心于 **gānxīn yú** reconcile oneself to

干洗衣物 **gānxǐ yīwù** drycleaning

肝炎 **gānyán** hepatitis

干预 **gānyù** poke one's nose into

敢于 **gǎnyú** dare

肝藏 **gānzàng** liver

干燥 **gānzào** dry

甘蔗 **gānzhe** sugar cane

感知 **gǎnzhī** feel

赶制 **gǎnzhì** run up *clothes*

感知能力 **gǎnzhī nénglì** perception

杆子 **gǎnzi** post (*wooden*)

赶走 **gǎnzǒu** chase away; banish ◊ family name

高 **gāo** big; tall; high ◊ top (*gear*)

比高 **bǐ … gāo** above; higher/taller than

膏 **gāo** ointment; cream

糕 **gāo** cake

搞 **gǎo** do; make

高傲 **gāo'ào** lofty

高保真电器 **gāo bǎozhēn diànqì** hi-fi

告别 **gàobié** say goodbye; 向死者告别 **xiàng sǐzhě gàobié** pay one's last respects

告别会 **gàobié huì** leaving party

高超 **gāochāo** masterly

高潮 **gāocháo** climax; high tide

高大 **gāodà** enormous; massive

高等 **gāoděng** higher; advanced; elite

高等教育 **gāoděng jiàoyù** higher education

糕点 **gāodiǎn** bread; cakes and pastries

高调 **gāodiào** highbrow

高顶帽 **gāodǐngmào** top hat

高度 **gāodù** height; altitude

高尔夫俱乐部 **gāo'ěrfū jùlèbù** golf club (*organization*)

高尔夫（球） **gāo'ěrfū(qiú)** golf

高尔夫球场 **gāo'ěrfū qiúchǎng** golf course

高尔夫球棍 **gāo'ěrfū qiúgùn** golf club (*stick*)

告发 **gàofā** inform; inform on; 向警方告发 X **xiàng jǐngfāng gàofā X** report X to the police

告发人 **gàofā rén** informer

高峰 **gāofēng** peak; summit

高峰时间 **gāofēng shíjiān** peak hours; rush hour

高跟 **gāogēn** high-heeled

高跟鞋 **gāogēn xié** high heels; high-heeled shoes

高贵 **gāoguì** noble

搞鬼 **gǎoguǐ** cheat; play tricks; cause trouble

高呼 **gāohū** chant

搞坏 **gǎohuài** mess up, ruin

高级 **gāojí** high-class; high-level; select; upmarket; senior; top

稿件 **gāojiàn** manuscript; article

高脚椅 **gāojiǎoyǐ** highchair

高架铁路 **gāojià tiělù** elevated railroad

高阶层 **gāo jiēcéng** high-level

高级法庭 **gāojí fǎtíng** Supreme Court

高空跳水 **gāokōng tiàoshuǐ** high diving

高粱 **gāoliáng** sorghum

高楼大厦 **gāolóu dàshà** high-rise buildings

高炉 **gāolú** blast furnace

搞乱 **gǎoluàn** confuse; mix up; mess up

告密 **gàomì** sneak; inform on

高明 **gāomíng** masterly

高能 **gāonéng** high-energy; high-power

高能汽车 **gāonéng qìchē** performance car

高能转向 **gāonéng zhuǎnxiàng** power steering

高频 **gāopín** high-frequency

高人一等 **gāorén yìděng** patronizing; superior; 他觉得自己高人一等 **tā juéde zìjǐ gāorén** he feels superior to others

高尚 **gāoshàng** noble

高烧 **gāoshāo** high fever

高耸于 **gāosǒng yú** dominate

高速 **gāosù** high-speed

告诉 **gàosu** tell; say; 别告诉妈妈 **bié gàosu māma** don't tell Mom

高速公路 **gāosù gōnglù** freeway; expressway

高速缓存 **gāosù huǎncún** cache COMPUT

高速火车 **gāosù huǒchē** high-speed train

睾丸 **gāowán** testicles

高效率 **gāo xiàolǜ** efficient; streamlined

高效益 **gāo xiàoyì** businesslike; highly efficient

高兴 **gāoxìng** happy; pleased, glad, delighted ◊ happily; 见到你真高兴! **jiàndào nǐ zhēn gāoxìng!** great to see you!

高新技术 **gāoxīn jìshù** high tech

高血压 **gāoxuèyā** hypertension, high blood pressure

高压 **gāoyā** high pressure; high-tension

高雅 **gāoyǎ** elegance ◊ elegant

羔羊 **gāoyáng** lamb

膏药 **gāoyao** plaster MED

高要求 **gāo yāoqiú** demanding ◊ tall order

高音 **gāoyīn** soprano

高音调 **gāoyīndiào** high-pitched

高原 **gāoyuán** plateau

搞运动 **gǎo yùndòng** campaign

搞糟 **gǎozāo** bungle; mess up

高涨 **gāozhǎng** upturn

告知 **gàozhī** inform

告终 **gàozhōng** culminate

稿子 **gǎozi** copy

嘎吱作声 **gāzhī zuòshēng** crunch

搁 **gē** put; add; put aside; deposit; 搁在 ... 上 **gē zài ... shàng** rest on, lean on

割 **gē** cut; mow

哥 **gē** elder brother

歌 **gē** song

鸽 **gē** dove; pigeon

格 **gé** grid; grating; square (*in board game*)

革 **gé** leather

嗝 **gé** hiccups

隔 **gé** cut off; separate

铬 **gè** chrome, chromium

个 **gè** general purpose measure word; 两个问题 **liǎnggè wèntí** two questions; 一个人 **yīgè rén** a person

各 **gè** each; every; various

隔壁 **gébì** adjoining ◊ next door ◊ next-door neighbor

个别 **gèbié** individual

戈壁滩 **Gēbìtān** Gobi Desert

胳膊 **gēbo** arm

胳膊肘儿 **gēbozhǒur** elbow

割草机 **gēcǎo jī** lawn mower

歌唱家 **gēchàng jiā** vocalist

歌唱团 **gēchàng tuán** vocal group

各处 **gèchù** everywhere

歌词 **gēcí** lyrics

疙瘩 **gēda** boil; pimple; lump; knot

格调 **gédiào** style

格斗 **gédòu** struggle

隔断 **géduàn** separate

哥哥 **gēge** elder brother

格格不入 **gégébùrù** go against the grain

咯咯地笑 **gēgē de xiào** giggle; gurgle; chuckle

给 **gěi** give; administer ◊ for; to; for the attention of

给以荣誉 **gěiyǐ róngyù** honor

歌剧 **gējù** opera

隔绝 **géjué** cut off; isolate

歌剧院 **gējù yuàn** opera house

隔开 **gékāi** partition off

蛤蜊 **gélí** clam

隔离 **gélí** isolate; segregate ◊ isolation; segregation; quarantine

隔帘 **gélián** screen

隔离间 **gélíjiān** isolation ward

格林威治标准时间 **Gélínwēizhì Biāozhǔn Shíjiān** Greenwich Mean Time

阁楼 **gélóu** attic; loft

哥们儿 **gēmenr** pal, buddy

革命 **gémìng** revolution ◊ revolutionary

革命家 **gémìng jiā** revolutionary

隔膜 **gémó** diaphragm

根 **gēn** root

跟 **gēn** follow ◊ with ◊ and ◊ heel

根本 **gēnběn** ultimate; underlying ◊ at all; fundamentally ◊ base; foundation; 他们根本不像 **tāmen gēnběn búxiàng** they're not at all alike

根除 **gēnchú** eradicate

耕 **gēng** plow

更 **gēng** change ◊ watch (*2 hour period*)

梗 **gěng** stalk

更 **gèng** more; even more; 更好 **gèng hǎo** better; 我更喜欢她了 **wǒ gèng xǐhuān tā le** I like her better

耕地 **gēngdì** plow ◊ arable land

更多 **gèngduō** more

更改 **gēnggǎi** alter ◊ alteration; 更改线路 **gēnggǎi xiànlù** reroute

更换 **gēnghuàn** exchange

更坏 **gènghuài** worse

耕牛 **gēngniú** (draft) ox

更新 **gēngxīn** renew; replace; upgrade

更衣室 **gēngyī shì** cubicle

耕种 **gēngzhòng** till; cultivate

耕作 **gēngzuò** cultivate ◊ cultivation

根基 **gēnjī** roots

根据 **gēnjù** basis ◊ according to; 根据具体环境来考虑 X **gēnjù jùtǐ huánjìng lái kǎolù** X look at X in context

根据地 **gēnjùdì** stronghold

跟上 **gēnshàng** keep up

根深蒂固 **gēnshēndìgù** entrenched

跟随 **gēnsuí** follow; string along

根源 **gēnyuán** origin; source ◊ originate

跟着 **gēnzhe** follow

跟踪 **gēnzōng** stalk; trace; trail

跟踪会议 **gēnzōng huìyì** follow-up meeting

跟踪者 **gēnzōng zhě** stalker

跟踪追捕 **gēnzōng zhuībǔ** track down

歌曲 **gēqǔ** song

个儿 **gèr** height

隔热 **gérè** insulate ◊ insulation

隔热垫 **gérèdiàn** mat

个人 **gèrén** individual ◊ personal ◊ privately

个人电脑 **gèrén diànnǎo** personal computer

个人卫生 **gèrén wèishēng** personal hygiene

个人主义者 **gèrénzhǔyì zhě** individualist

哥儿们 **gērmen** buddy, pal

各色各样 **gèsè gèyàng** all kinds; a choice

格式 **géshì** layout

各式各样 **gèshì gèyàng** assortment

格式设定 **géshì shèdìng** format

歌手 **gēshǒu** singer

个体 **gètǐ** freelance; self-employed

个体户 **gètǐhù** privately owned small business; freelancer

个体遗传性征 **gètǐ yíchuán xìngzhēng** genetic fingerprint

格外 **géwài** particularly; extra

割腕 **gēwàn** slash one's wrists

歌舞表演 **gēwǔ biǎoyǎn** song and dance performance; cabaret

歌舞剧 **gēwǔjù** musical

革新 **géxīn** innovation ◊ innovative

个性 **gèxìng** personality; character; 他很有个性 **tā hěn yǒu gèxìng** he's a real character

革新者 **géxīn zhě** innovator

隔音 **géyīn** soundproof

胳肢 **gēzhi** tickle

革制品 **gézhìpǐn** leather goods

各种各样 **gèzhǒng gèyàng** mixed, varied; miscellaneous; 各种各样的人 **gèzhǒng gèyàngde rén** all kinds of people

鸽子 **gēzi** dove; pigeon

格子 **gézi** checked ◊ grille

各自 **gèzì** respective ◊ individually; each; 各自付款 **gèzì fùkuǎn** go Dutch

弓 **gōng** bow

工 **gōng** work; worker

攻 **gōng** attack

功 **gōng** merit; service

供 **gōng** supply; provide

恭 **gōng** respectful

公 **gōng** public; male
宫 **gōng** palace
拱 **gŏng** arch
共 **gòng** common; joint; mutual ◊ together; altogether
公安局 **Gōng'ān jú** Public Security Bureau
公布 **gōngbù** announce; declare; release
共产党 **Gòngchǎndǎng** Communist Party
共产党员 **Gòngchǎndǎng yuán** Communist Party member
工厂 **gōngchǎng** factory
共产主义 **gòngchǎn zhǔyì** communism ◊ communist
工程 **gōngchéng** construction; engineering
工程师 **gōngchéngshī** engineer
共处 **gòngchǔ** coexist ◊ coexistence
供词 **gòngcí** confession
共存 **gòngcún** coexist ◊ coexistence
公道 **gōngdào** justice
工地 **gōngdì** building site
宫殿 **gōngdiàn** palace
拱顶 **gŏngdĭng** vault
攻读 **gōngdú** study
公愤 **gōngfèn** outrage
功夫 **gōngfu** kung-fu
公告牌 **gōnggào pái** bulletin board
公共 **gōnggòng** public
公共汽车 **gōnggòng qìchē** bus
公共汽车总站 **gōnggòng qìchē zŏngzhàn** bus station
公关 **gōngguān** public relations
公害 **gōnghài** environmental damage
公函 **gōnghán** official letter
恭贺 **gōnghè** congratulate
共和国 **gònghé guó** republic
共和主义 **gònghé zhǔyì** republicanism ◊ republican
共和主义者 **gònghé zhǔyì zhě** republican
工会 **gōnghuì** labor union
工会发言人 **gōnghuì fāyánrén** shop steward
公鸡 **gōngjī** rooster

攻击 **gōngjí** attack, assault; go for ◊ offensive
供给 **gōngjĭ** supply
弓箭 **gōngjiàn** bow and arrow
弓箭手 **gōngjiàn shŏu** archer
共计 **gòngjì** amount to, add up to
公斤 **gōngjīn** kilogram
恭敬 **gōngjìng** respect
工具 **gōngjù** tool; implement
公爵 **gōngjué** duke
工具格 **gōngjùgé** toolbar COMPUT
公开 **gōngkāi** public; open
功劳 **gōngláo** merit; service
公里 **gōnglĭ** kilometer
公路 **gōnglù** highway; road
公路赛车 **gōnglù sàichē** rally MOT
公路支线 **gōnglù zhīxiàn** access road
公猫 **gōngmāo** tomcat
拱门 **gŏngmén** archway
公民 **gōngmín** citizen ◊ civic; civil
公民权 **gōngmín quán** civil rights
公民投票 **gōngmín tóupiào** referendum
公墓 **gōngmù** graveyard, cemetery
功能 **gōngnéng** function
公鸟 **gōngniăo** cock (*male bird*)
公牛 **gōngniú** bull
供暖 **gōngnuăn** heating
公公 **gōnggōng** father-in-law (*husband's father*)
贡品 **gòngpĭn** tribute
公平 **gōngpíng** fair, just; balanced ◊ justice
公婆 **gōngpó** in-laws (*husband's parents*)
供求 **gōngqiú** supply and demand
公顷 **gōngqĭng** hectare
工人 **gōngrén** worker; workman
供认 **gòngrèn** confess ◊ confession
工人阶级 **gōngrén jiējí** working class
工伤 **gōngshāng** industrial accident
工商管理学硕士 **gōngshāng guănlĭxué shuòshì** MBA, master of business administration
公社 **gōngshè** commune

公升 gōngshēng liter

公式 gōngshì formula

供水 gōngshuǐ water supply

公司 gōngsī company; business; firm ◊ incorporated

公司车 gōngsī chē company car

公司法 gōngsī fǎ company law

公司形象 gōngsī xíngxiàng corporate image

公诉人 gōngsùrén (public) prosecutor

共同 gòngtóng collective; common; joint; shared; 和 X 有共同之处 hé X yǒu gòngtóng zhīchù have something in common with X

共同体 gòngtóngtǐ community

恭维 gōngwei compliment; flatter

公文 gōngwén document

公文包 gōngwén bāo briefcase

公物 gōngwù public property

公务员 gōngwùyuán civil servant

攻下 gōngxià capture

贡献 gòngxiàn contribute; devote ◊ contribution

恭喜 gōngxǐ congratulations

恭喜发财 gōngxǐ fācái wishing you prosperity (a New Year greeting)

公学 gōngxué public school

公羊 gōngyáng ram (male sheep)

供养 gōngyǎng keep, maintain, provide for

工业 gōngyè industry ◊ industrial

工业废料 gōngyè fèiliào industrial waste

工业化 gōngyèhuà industrialize

工业行动 gōngyè xíngdòng industrial action

工艺 gōngyì craft; technology

工艺美术 gōngyì měishù arts and crafts

供应 gōngyìng supply, provide ◊ provision

供应品 gōngyìngpǐn supplies

供应商 gōngyìngshāng supplier

供应与需求 gōngyìng yǔ xūqiú supply and demand

公用 gōngyòng communal; public

公用电话 gōngyòng diànhuà pay phone

公用实业 gōngyòng shíyè public utilities

共有者 gòngyǒu zhě part owner

公寓 gōngyù apartment

公园 gōngyuán park

公寓大厦 gōngyù dàshà apartment block

公约 gōngyuē pact; convention

公正 gōngzhèng fair, just; impartial ◊ fairly, justly ◊ fairness

公证 gōngzhèng authenticate; witness

公证人 gōngzhèng rén notary

公制 gōngzhì metric system

供职 gōngzhí serve; hold office

公职人员 gōngzhí rényuán official

公众 gōngzhòng public

公众交通运输工具 gōngzhòng jiāotōng yùnshū gōngjù public transportation

公主 gōngzhǔ princess

工资 gōngzī wage; salary

工资袋 gōngzīdài pay envelope

工作 gōngzuò work; job; business; employment ◊ work; 她很会工作 tā hěn huì gōngzuò she's a good worker; 工作的满足感 gōngzuò de mǎnzúgǎn job satisfaction

工作狂 gōngzuòkuáng workaholic

工作量 gōngzuòliàng workload

工作期间 gōngzuò qījiān work hours

工作日 gōngzuòrì work day

工作室 gōngzuòshì studio

工作台 gōngzuò tái workbench

工作许可 gōngzuò xǔkě work permit

工作站 gōngzuòzhàn work station

沟 gōu trench; ditch; channel

钩 gōu hook; jack (playing cards) ◊ crochet

狗 gǒu dog

购 gòu buy

够 gòu sufficient; enough; 够朋友 gòu péngyǒu true friend; 够大 gòudà quite big; big enough; 够

了 **gòule** that's enough; stop that!; 我受够了 **wǒ shòugòu le** I've had enough; 五十美元够了吗？**wǔshí měiyuán gòule ma?** will $50 be enough?

构成 **gòuchéng** comprise, constitute

狗狗 **gǒugǒu** doggie

篝火 **gōuhuǒ** fire

构架 **gòujià** structure ◊ structural

勾结 **gōujié** collaborate

勾结者 **gōujié zhě** collaborator

购买 **gòumǎi** purchase

狗屁 **gǒu pì!**∨ bullshit!

狗屎不如 **gǒushǐ bùrú**∨ dirtier than dog shit; lowest of the low

沟通 **gōutōng** communicate ◊ communication

狗窝 **gǒuwō** kennel

购物 **gòuwù** shopping ◊ do one's shopping

购物人 **gòuwùrén** shopper

购物中心 **gòuwù zhōngxīn** (shopping) mall

勾销 **gōuxiāo** write off *debt*

勾引 **gōuyǐn** pick up; seduce

构造 **gòuzào** construction; design

钩针 **gōuzhēn** crochet hook

钩子 **gōuzi** hook

姑 **gū** aunt (*father's sister*); sister-in-law (*husband's sister*)

箍 **gū** hoop

估 **gū** estimate

孤 **gū** orphaned; lonely

鼓 **gǔ** drum

股 **gǔ** share, stock ◊ *measure word for smells, wind*; 一股风 **yìgǔ fēng** a gust of wind; 一股味 **yìgǔ wèi** a smell

古 **gǔ** ancient; antiquated

骨 **gǔ** bone

谷 **gǔ** valley; grain

雇 **gù** take on; employ; 他被雇作… **tā bèi gù zuò** … he's employed as a

顾 **gù** look around

故 **gù** therefore

固 **gù** solid; firm

瓜 **guā** melon

刮 **guā** scrape; shave

挂 **guà** hang; drape

刮擦 **guācā** scrape

刮掉 **guādiào** shave off; scrape off

挂断 **guàduàn** hang up TELEC

刮风 **guāfēng** blow

寡妇 **guǎfù** widow

挂钩 **guàgōu** hook, peg

呱呱叫 **guāguājiào** great

呱呱叫声 **guāguā jiàoshēng** croak; quack

挂号 **guàhào** register

挂号信 **guàhào xìn** registered letter; 寄挂号信 **jì guàhào xìn** send a letter registered

乖 **guāi** good; well-behaved

拐 **guǎi** turn; 向右拐 **xiàng yòu guǎi** turn to the right

怪 **guài** strange

拐棍 **guǎigùn** crook; walking stick

拐角 **guǎijiǎo** turning

乖戾 **guāilì** surly

乖僻 **guāipì** morose

拐骗 **guǎipiàn** kidnap

怪人 **guàirén** freak, weirdo; crank; nerd

拐弯 **guǎiwān** turn off; turn; corner; twist

拐弯抹角 **guǎiwān mòjiǎo** beat around the bush

怪物 **guàiwu** monster

怪相 **guàixiàng** grimace

怪异 **guàiyì** weird ◊ peculiarity

拐杖 **guǎizhàng** walking stick

呱啦呱啦 **guālā guālā** yap, yak

刮脸 **guāliǎn** shave, have a shave

关 **guān** close, shut; turn off; 他们已经关了 **tāmen yǐjīng guānle** they were shut

官 **guān** official

棺 **guān** casket, coffin

鳏 **guān** widower ◊ widowed

观 **guān** look at; observe

管 **guǎn** manage; control; concern oneself with; bother ◊ tube; pipe; 不要管 **bùyào guǎn** take no notice of

罐 **guàn** jar; pitcher

冠 **guàn** hat; crown

灌 **guàn** pour into

鹳 **guàn** stork

惯 **guàn** used to; accustomed

关隘 **guān'ài** pass

关闭 **guānbì** close (down), shut (down); wind up ◊ closure ◊ closed

棺材 **gūancai** casket, coffin

观测 **guāncè** observe

观察 **guānchá** keep an eye on; monitor ◊ observation

惯常 **guàncháng** habitual

观察员 **guānchá yuán** observer

罐车 **guànchē** tanker (*truck*)

贯彻 **guànchè** implement; carry out

贯穿 **guànchuān** throughout

冠词 **guàncí** article

管道 **guǎndào** pipeline; tube; pipe

管道装置 **guǎndào zhuāngzhi** plumbing

观点 **guāndiǎn** point; point of view; view; slant

关掉 **guāndiào** turn off; be off

官方 **guānfāng** formal; official ◊ officially

鳏夫 **guānfū** widower

官服 **guānfú** robe

光 **guāng** light; brightness; glory; finished; gone; bare; naked ◊ only

广 **guǎng** wide; broad; extensive

逛 **guàng** wander; stroll; 逛商店 **guàng shāngdiàn** walk around the stores

灌溉 **guàngài** irrigate ◊ irrigation

灌溉渠 **guàngài qú** irrigation canal

光笔 **guāngbǐ** light pen

光标 **guāngbiāo** cursor

广播 **guǎngbō** broadcast

广播电台 **guǎngbō diàntái** radio station

光彩 **guāngcǎi** brilliance

广场 **guǎngchǎng** square; place

光导纤维 **guāngdǎo xiānwéi** fiber optics

光点 **guāngdiǎn** blip

光碟 **guāngdié** disc

广东 **Guǎngdōng** Canton ◊ Cantonese

广东话 **Guǎngdōnghuà** Cantonese

广度 **guǎngdù** width; breadth

广而言之 **guǎng ér yán zhī** in general

广泛 **guǎngfàn** wide, extensive ◊ widely

广告 **guǎnggào** advertisement

广告公司 **guǎnggào gōngsī** advertising agency

广告牌 **guǎnggào pái** billboard

广告业 **guǎnggào yè** advertising (industry)

光顾 **guānggù** patronize

光滑 **guānghuá** smooth; glossy

光滑面 **guānghuámiàn** glaze

光环 **guānghuán** halo

光辉 **guānghuī** glow

光辉灿烂 **guānghuī cànlàn** splendor

光脚 **guāngjiǎo** be barefoot

光洁 **guāngjié** clear

广阔 **guǎngkuò** wide; great; enormous

光芒四射 **guāngmáng sìshè** radiate

光面 **guāngmiàn** glossy

光明 **guāngmíng** bright; rosy

光年 **guāngnián** light year

光盘 **guāngpán** CD-ROM; CD

光驱 **guāngqū** CD-ROM drive

光圈 **guāngquān** aperture

光荣 **guāngróng** honor; glory ◊ honorable; glorious

光天化日 **guāngtiān huàrì** in broad daylight

光秃秃 **guāng tūtū** bare; bald

观光 **guānguāng** look around; go sightseeing

观光客 **guānguāngkè** sightseer; tourist

观光旅游 **guānguāng lǚyóu** sightseeing tour

光纤 **guāng xiān** fiber optics

光线 **guāngxiàn** light; ray

光学 **guāngxué** optics

光泽 **guāngzé** shine; luster

光着头 **guāngzhe tóu** bare-headed

关怀 **guānhuái** show sympathy for; show concern for

关机 **guānjī** shut down COMPUT

管家 **guǎnjiā** housekeeper; butler ◊ run a household

关键 **guānjiàn** key, crucial, vital ◊ key; crux; bolt (*of door*)

关键钮 guān jiànniǔ off switch

关节 guānjié joint

关节炎 guānjié yán arthritis

关进 guānjìn put away

冠军 guànjūn champion; championship

观看 guānkàn watch

官吏 guānlì mandarin

管理 guǎnlǐ control; manage; administer; operate; run ◊ administration; management

关联 guānlián relevance

官僚 guānliáo bureaucrat ◊ bureaucratic

官僚程序 guānliáo chéngxù red tape

官僚制度 guānliáo zhìdù bureaucracy

官僚主义 guānliáo zhǔyì bureaucracy

惯例 guànlì custom; habit

管理人员 guǎnlǐ rényuán administrator; management team

管理学 guǎnlǐxué management studies

管理员 guǎnlǐyuán superintendent

关门 guānmén close store etc; close down; close the door ◊ closed

关门时间 guānmén shíjiān closing time

灌木 guànmù bush; shrub

灌木丛 guànmùcóng shrubbery; undergrowth

官能 guānnéng sense

关卡 guānqiǎ checkpoint

灌输 guànshū indoctrinate

关税 guānshuì customs duty, tariff

罐头 guàntou can (for drinks etc)

观望点 guānwàng diǎn vantage point

关系 guānxi connection, relation; relationship; 没关系 méi guānxi it doesn't matter; 外交关系 wàijiāo guānxì diplomatic relations; 与 X 关系好 yǔ X guānxì hǎo be on good terms with X

管弦乐 guǎnxiányuè orchestral music

管弦乐队 guǎnxián yuèduì orchestra

关小 guānxiǎo turn down volume

关系到 guānxì dào apply to, affect

关心 guānxīn concern; care; consideration ◊ be concerned about; care about

冠心病 guànxīnbìng coronary disease

惯性 guànxìng inertia

盥洗室 guànxǐshì washroom

关押 guānyā lock up

惯用 guànyòng commonly use; 惯用法 guànyòngfǎ common usage; habitual; 惯用左手 guànyòng zuǒshǒu left-handed

关于 guānyú with reference to, regarding; about

官员 guānyuán official

管乐器 guǎnyuèqì wind instrument

馆长 guǎnzhǎng curator

管制措施 guǎnzhì cuòshī controls, restrictions

观众 guānzhòng audience; crowd; spectators; viewers

罐装 guànzhuāng can ◊ canned

冠状动脉 guànzhuàng dòngmài coronary artery

冠状动脉血栓 guànzhuàng dòngmài xuèshuān coronary thrombosis

管子 guǎnzi pipe; tube

馆子 guǎnzi restaurant

管嘴 guǎnzuǐ jet

刮水器 guāshuǐqì windshield wiper

挂锁 guàsuǒ padlock

挂毯 guàtǎn tapestry; wall hanging

挂衣钩 guàyīgōu coat hook

瓜子 guāzǐ melon seed

古巴 Gǔbā Cuba ◊ Cuban

古板 gǔbǎn straitlaced, stuffy

鼓吹 gǔchuī advocate

鼓槌 gǔchuí drumstick

古代 gǔdài antiquity; ancient times; ancient China ◊ ancient

孤单 gūdān alone; solitary

古典 **gǔdiǎn** classic; classical

古典音乐 **gǔdiǎn yīnyuè** classical music

固定 **gùdìng** fasten; fix ◊ fixed; 把 X 固定在 Y 上 **bǎ X gùdìng zài Y shang** fasten X onto Y; 用针固定 **yòng zhēn gùdìng** pin

固定装置 **gùdìng zhuāngzhì** fixture

股东 **gǔdōng** stockholder, shareholder

古董 **gǔdǒng** antique

股东公司 **gǔdōng gōngsī** holding company

古董商 **gǔdǒng shāng** antique dealer

孤独 **gūdú** lonely; solitary

孤独感 **gūdú gǎn** loneliness

孤儿 **gū'er** orphan

孤儿院 **gū'er yuàn** orphanage

股份 **gǔfèn** stock, share

股份公司 **gǔfèn gōngsī** joint-stock company

股份有限公司 **gǔfèn yǒuxiàn gōngsī** corporation

姑父 **gūfu** uncle (*father's sister's husband*)

辜负 **gūfù** disappoint

毂盖 **gǔgài** hubcap

故宫 **Gùgōng** *the former imperial palace in Beijing*; the Forbidden City

姑姑 **gūgu** auntie (*father's sister*)

古怪 **gǔguài** funny; odd; eccentric; 古怪的人 **gǔguài de rén** eccentric; weirdo

汩汩地流 **gǔgǔ de liú** gurgle

鼓鼓囊囊 **gǔgǔ nāngnang** bulging

固化 **gùhuà** solidify

骨灰 **gǔhuī** ashes (*after cremation*)

骨灰盒 **gǔhuīhé** urn (*for ashes*)

硅 **guī** silicon

归 **guī** return; belong to

龟 **guī** turtle; tortoise

鬼 **guǐ** ghost

轨 **guǐ** rail; track

贵 **guì** expensive; noble

桂 **guì** cassia; laurel; osmanthus

柜 **guì** cupboard

跪 **guì** kneel

鬼把戏 **guǐbǎxì** gimmick

贵宾 **guìbīn** guest of honor

归并 **guībìng** merge; 把 … 归并在一起 **bǎ … guībìng zài yìqǐ** lump together

轨道 **guǐdào** track; orbit; 绕轨道运行 **rào guǐdào yùnxíng** orbit

鬼地方 **guǐdìfāng** horrible place; dump

规定 **guīdìng** stipulate ◊ stipulation; regulation; rule; 违约罚款的规定 **wéiyuē fákuǎn de guīdìng** penalty clause; 规定的任期 **guīdìng de rènqī** stint; period of office

规范 **guīfàn** rules; standard

归附者 **guīfù zhě** convert

规格 **guīgé** specifications

归根结底 **guīgēn jiédǐ** boil down to

归功于 **guīgōng yú** owing to; thanks to

鬼鬼祟祟 **guǐguǐ suìsuì** shifty-looking; sneaky

规划 **guīhuà** plan ◊ planning

归还 **guīhuán** give back; return

归家 **guījiā** homecoming

诡计多端 **guǐjì duōduān** scheming

规矩点! **guījǔ diǎn!** behave (yourself)!

归类 **guīlèi** classify

规模 **guīmó** scale

桂皮 **guìpí** cinnamon

硅片 **guīpiàn** silicon chip

归属 **guīshǔ** belong to

柜台 **guìtái** counter, bar

归途 **guītú** way back

跪下 **guìxià** kneel

规则 **guīzé** rule; regulations

诡诈 **guǐzhà** underhand

规章 **guīzhāng** regulation

贵重 **guìzhòng** valuable

贵重物品 **guìzhòng wùpǐn** valuables

柜子 **guìzi** cabinet; cupboard

刽子手 **guìzishǒu** executioner

贵族 **guìzú** nobility

估计 **gūjì** calculate; estimate; assess; put the cost at ◊ estimate; valuation

古迹 **gǔjì** antiquities; historical

sites

顾及 gùjí take into account; consider

估价 gūjià appraise; value

骨节嶙峋 gǔjié línxún gnarled

故居 gùjū former residence

顾客 gùkè client, customer; consumer

顾客关系 gùkè guānxi customer relations

古老 gǔlǎo ancient

谷类 gǔlèi cereal

孤立 gūlì isolate; separate ◊ isolated

鼓励 gǔlì encourage; urge on ◊ encouragement; 鼓励的话 gǔlìde huà pep talk

谷粒 gǔlì grain

估量 gūliáng size up, weigh up; assess; estimate

孤零零 gū línglíng solitary; all alone

孤立无援 gūlì wúyuán defenseless

顾虑 gùlǜ misgivings, scruples

鼓膜 gǔmó eardrum

滚 gǔn roll ◊ get lost!

棍 gùn rod

滚出去！gǔnchūqù! get out!

滚蛋！gǔndàn! get lost!

滚动 gǔndòng roll

姑娘 gūniang girl

牯牛 gǔniú bull

滚开！gǔnkāi! ∨ fuck off!

咕哝 gūnong mumble, mutter

滚烫 gǔntàng piping hot

滚珠轴承 gǔnzhū zhóuchéng ball bearing

棍子 gùnzi stick; rod

锅 guō pot, pan; wok

国 guó state; country

果 guǒ fruit; result

裹 guǒ wrap

过 guò across; over ◊ pass; cross; spend; 走过 zǒuguò walk past ◊ (*past indicator*): 我去过中国 wǒ qùguo Zhōngguó I've been to China; 我吃过了 wǒ chīguò le I have eaten

锅铲 guōchǎn spatula

过程 guòchéng process

过错 guòcuò error; mistake

过道 guòdào corridor

过得快乐 guòde kuàilè enjoy oneself

过得去 guòdequ tolerable; acceptable ◊ be able to get by; be able to get through

过低评价 guòdī píngjià underrate

果冻 guǒdòng jelly

过度 guòdù excess ◊ excessive; undue; 过度感光 guòdù gǎnguāng overexpose

过渡 guòdù transition ◊ transitional

果断 guǒduàn decisive

过度紧张 guòdù jǐnzhāng hypertension

国防部 Guófáng Bù Department of Defense

国防部长 Guófáng Bùzhǎng Defense Secretary

国防开支 guófáng kāizhī defense budget

过分 guòfèn excessive; unreasonable ◊ unduly; 他太过分了 tā tài guòfènle he's gone too far; he's too much

果脯 guǒfǔ candied fruit

过高 guògāo exorbitant; extortionate; too high

过高估计 guògāo gūjì overestimate ◊ overrated

过高要价 guògāo yàojià overcharge

国歌 guógē national anthem

国会 guóhuì Congress ◊ Congressional

国会议员 guóhuì yìyuán Congressman, member of Congress

过火 guòhuǒ exaggerated; overdone ◊ exaggerate

国籍 guójí citizenship; nationality

国际 guójì international ◊ internationally

国家 guójiā country; nation; state ◊ national

国家队 guójiāduì national team

国家公园 guójiā gōngyuán national park

果酱 guǒjiàng jam; conserve

国际比赛 guójì bǐsài international (match)

过节 guòjié celebrate a festival

国际法庭 Guójì Fǎtíng International Court of Justice

国际货币基金 Guójì Huòbì Jījīn International Monetary Fund

国际劳动节 Guójì Láodòngjié International Labor Day

过境 guòjìng be in transit (*between countries*)

过境签证 guòjìng qiānzhèng transit visa

国际收支差额 guójì shōuzhī chā'é (international) balance of payments

过来 guòlái step in; come over ◊ across

国立 guólì national; state-run

过量 guòliàng overdose

锅炉 guōlú boiler

过滤 guòlǜ filter; strain; 过滤式咖啡壶 *guòlǜshì kāfēihú* percolator

过滤器 guòlǜ qì filter; strainer

过路人 guòlùrén passer-by

过滤嘴香烟 guòlǜzuǐ xiāngyān filter-tipped cigarette

国民 guómín national

过敏 guòmǐn allergy ◊ hypersensitive

国民党 Guómíndǎng Kuomintang, KMT, Nationalist Party

国民生产总值 guómín shēngchǎn zǒngzhí GNP, gross national product

国内 guónèi domestic; internal; 在国内 *zài guónèi* at home (*in country*)

国内航班 guónèi hángbān domestic flight

国内贸易 guónèi màoyì internal trade

国内生产总值 guónèi shēngchǎn zǒngzhí GDP, gross domestic product

国内外 guónèiwài at home and abroad

过年 guònián celebrate Chinese New Year

果皮 guǒpí peel (*of fruit*)

国旗 guóqí national flag

过期 guòqī out of date

国庆节 Guóqìngjié National Day

过去 guòqù past ◊ go by; 那都已经过去了 *nà dōu yǐjīng guòqù le* that's all past now; 在过去 *zài guòqù* in the past

过去分词 guòqù fēncí past participle

过去时 guòqùshí past tense

果然如此 guǒrán rúcǐ sure enough

果肉 guǒròu flesh (*of fruit*); pulp

过山车 guò shān chē roller coaster

过剩 guòshèng surplus

果实 guǒshí fruit

过时 guòshí out of date; dated; old-fashioned; out of fashion; stale *news*

果树 guǒshù fruit tree

过堂风 guòtáng fēng draft

国外 guówài abroad ◊ foreign

国王 guówáng king

国务访问 guówù fǎngwèn state visit

国务卿 Guówùqīng Secretary of State

国务院 Guówùyuàn Department of State, State Department

果馅饼 guǒxiànbǐng flan

果馅儿饼 guǒxiànr bǐng tart

国宴 guóyàn state banquet

过夜 guòyè stay the night, spend the night

过一会儿 guò yíhuìr by and by, soon

国营 guóyíng state-owned; state-run

国有化 guóyǒu huà nationalize

过于 guòyú excessively; too

果园 guǒyuán orchard

过早 guòzǎo untimely

国债 guózhài national debt

果汁 guǒzhī fruit juice

骨盆 gǔpén pelvis

孤僻 gūpì withdrawn; autistic

股票 gǔpiào stock, share

股票交易所 gǔpiào jiāoyìsuǒ

stock exchange

股票经纪人 **gǔpiào jīngjì rén** stockbroker

股票市场 **gǔpiào shìchǎng** stock market; 股票市场暴跌 **gǔpiào shìchǎng bàodiē** stockmarket crash

鼓起 **gǔqǐ** drum up; rouse

鼓起劲儿来！ **gǔ qǐ jìnr lái!** cheer up!

鼓起勇气 **gǔqǐ yǒngqì** pluck up courage

故事 **gùshi** story; tale; narrative; joke

鼓手 **gǔshǒu** drummer

固守 **gùshǒu** cling to

骨髓 **gǔsuǐ** bone marrow

固体 **gùtǐ** solid

骨头 **gǔtou** bone

顾问 **gùwèn** adviser; consultant

鼓舞 **gǔwǔ** encourage; 令人鼓舞 **lìngrén gǔwǔ** encouraging

股息 **gǔxī** dividend

故乡 **gùxiāng** home town; homeland

古雅小巧 **gǔyǎ xiǎoqiǎo** quaint

故意 **gùyì** deliberate; willful ◊ deliberately, on purpose

雇佣 **gùyōng** employ

雇佣兵 **gùyōngbīng** mercenary

固有 **gùyǒu** inherent

雇员 **gùyuán** employee; staff

鼓掌 **gǔzhǎng** applaud ◊ applause

故障 **gùzhàng** breakdown; defect; bug COMPUT

骨折 **gǔzhé** break, fracture ◊ broken

固执 **gùzhí** persistent, dogged; inflexible; stubborn; willful

雇主 **gùzhǔ** employer

孤注一掷 **gūzhù yízhì** desperate ◊ desperation; 孤注一掷之举 **gūzhù yízhì zhījǔ** an act of desperation

故作姿态 **gùzuò zītài** put on an act, put on airs

H

哈 **hā** exhale ◊ ha-ha

嗨，咳 **hāi** (*regret*): 嗨，我怎么给忘了呢? *hāi, wǒ zěnme gěi wàng le?* oh no, how come I forgot it?

还 **hái** still; as well as; yet; quite; even more; also; 还有什么? *háiyǒu shénme?* anything else?; 你还要吗? *ní háiyào ma?* do you still want it?

海 **hǎi** sea

害 **hài** harm

海岸 **hǎi'àn** coast

海岸线 **hǎi'àn xiàn** coastline

海拔 **hǎibá** altitude; elevation; height above sea level

海报 **hǎibào** poster, bill

海豹 **hǎibào** seal (*animal*)

海边 **hǎibiān** seaside

海滨 **hǎibīn** seaside

海滨砂石 **hǎibīn shāshí** shingle

海滨胜地 **hǎibīn shèngdì** seaside resort

害虫 **hàichóng** pest; vermin

害处 **hàichu** damage; harm

海带 **hǎidài** kelp, (edible) seaweed

海胆 **hǎidǎn** sea urchin

海港 **hǎigǎng** seaport

海关 **hǎiguān** customs

海关官员 **hǎiguān guānyuán** customs officer

还好 **háihǎo** alright, not bad

海军 **hǎijūn** navy ◊ naval

海军基地 **hǎijūn jīdì** naval base

海军兰 **hǎijūn lán** navy blue

海军强国 **hǎijūn qiángguó** sea power

海军上将 **hǎijūn shàngjiàng** admiral

海里 **hǎilǐ** nautical mile

海陆兵 **hǎilùbīng** marine MIL

海洛因 **hǎiluòyīn** heroin

海绵 **hǎimián** sponge; foam rubber

海南岛 **Hǎinán Dǎo** Hainan Island

害鸟 **hàiniǎo** pest (*bird*)

海鸥 **hǎi'ōu** seagull

害怕 **hàipà** be afraid, be frightened; be afraid of, dread

海平面 **hǎipíngmiàn** sea level

骇人听闻 **hài rén tīngwén** hideous; shocking

海上 **hǎishàng** maritime; seafaring

还是 **háishi** or

海市蜃楼 **hǎishì shènlóu** mirage

害兽 **hàishòu** pest

海难 **hǎinàn** shipwreck; 遇海难 *yù hǎinàn* be shipwrecked

海损 **hǎisǔn** maritime damage

海滩 **hǎitān** beach

海豚 **hǎitún** dolphin

海外 **hǎiwài** overseas

海湾 **hǎiwān** gulf; inlet

海味 **hǎiwèi** seafood

海峡 **hǎixiá** channel; strait

海星 **hǎixīng** starfish

害羞 **hàixiū** shy

海洋 **hǎiyáng** ocean ◊ marine

海员 **hǎiyuán** sailor

海运 **hǎiyùn** ship; shipping

海蜇 **hǎizhé** jellyfish

孩子 **háizi** child

孩子气 **háiziqì** infantile

哈喇 **hāla** rancid

蛤蟆 **háma** toad

寒 **hán** cold

含 **hán** contain; suck

函 **hán** letter

喊 **hǎn** shout

汉 **Hàn** Han

汗 **hàn** sweat

旱 **hàn** dryness

焊 **hàn** weld

汉堡包 **hànbǎobāo** hamburger, beefburger

旱冰鞋 **hànbīng xié** roller skate;

四轮旱冰鞋 **sìlún hànbīng xié** in-line skate, rollerblade®

汉朝 **Hàncháo** Han Dynasty

行 **háng** line; row; trade; profession

航班 **hángbān** flight

航班号 **hángbān hào** flight number

航标 **hángbiāo** buoy

航程 **hángchéng** voyage

行道 **hángdào** lane (on freeway)

航海 **hánghǎi** voyage ◊ nautical ◊ navigate

航海家 **hánghǎi jiā** navigator

航海图 **hánghǎi tú** chart

行话 **hánghuà** jargon, slang

行家 **hángjia** expert; connoisseur

航空 **hángkōng** aviation ◊ aeronautical ◊ by air

航空公司 **hángkōng gōngsī** airline

航空母舰 **hángkōng mǔjiàn** aircraft carrier

航空摄影 **hángkōng shèyǐng** aerial photography

航空图 **hángkōng tú** chart

航空信件 **hángkōng xìnjiàn** air letter, airmail

航空邮件 **hángkōng yóujiàn** air letter, airmail

行列 **hángliè** procession

航天 **hángtiān** space flight

航天飞机 **hángtiān fēijī** space shuttle

航线 **hángxiàn** airline; flight route

航向 **hángxiàng** course

航行 **hángxíng** cruise

航行学 **hángxíng xué** navigation

行业 **hángyè** trade; profession

含糊 **hánhú** ambiguous

含糊不清 **hánhu bùqīng** unclear; mumble

含糊地说 **hánhude shuō** mumble

含糊其辞 **hánhu qící** oblique; coy

旱季 **hànjì** dry season

罕见 **hǎnjiàn** rare

喊叫 **hǎnjiào** call; cry; cry out ◊ shouting

喊叫声 **hǎnjiào shēng** yell; scream

焊接 **hànjiē** weld; solder

焊接工人 **hànjiē gōngrén** welder

含酒精 **hán jiǔjīng** alcoholic

寒冷 (刺骨) **hánlěng (cìgǔ)** icy cold, bitterly cold

含量 **hánliàng** content

汗淋淋 **hànlínlín** sweaty

寒流 **hánliú** stream of cold air

含氯氟烃 **hánlù fútīng** chlorofluorocarbon, CFC

汗沫儿 **hànmòr** sweat; lather

汗衫 **hànshān** T-shirt

鼾声 **hānshēng** snoring

喊声 **hǎnshēng** shout

函授 **hánshòu** correspondence course

寒暑表 **hánshǔbiāo** thermometer

酣睡 **hānshuì** sound sleep

汗水 **hànshuǐ** sweat, perspiration

寒酸 **hánsuān** shabby

捍卫 **hànwèi** defend ◊ defense

捍卫者 **hànwèi zhě** champion

含蓄 **hánxù** reserve ◊ implicit

汉学 **hànxué** sinology

汉学家 **hànxuéjiā** sinologist

含药物 **hán yàowù** medicated

含义 **hányì** meaning

汉语 **Hànyǔ** Chinese

旱灾 **hànzāi** drought

汉藏 **Hànzàng** Sino-Tibetan

汉字 **Hànzì** Chinese character

汉族 **Hànzú** the Han people

蚝 **háo** oyster

毫 **háo** milli- ◊ in the least

好 **hǎo** good; fine ◊ well; quite; very; 比 … 好 **bǐ … hǎo** better than; 太好了！ **tàihǎole!** great!

耗 **hào** use; consume

号 **hào** number

好 **hào** like

好吧 **hǎoba** very well, ok

毫不犹豫 **háobù yóuyù** like a shot, without the least hesitation

好吵闹 **hào chǎonào** rowdy

号称 **hàochēng** be called

好吃 **hǎochī** delicious; good to eat

好处 **hǎochù** advantage, benefit; compensation; 对你有好处 **duì nǐ yǒu hǎochù** it's to your advantage; it's good for you

耗费 **hàofèi** spend; use

好感 **hǎogǎn** fondness; affection

豪华 **háohuá** luxury ◊ luxurious; de luxe; plush; 豪华的生活方式 **háohuáde shēnghuó fāngshì** high life

嚎叫 **háojiào** howl

浩劫 **hàojié** havoc

好极了 **hǎojíle** excellent, very good

耗尽 **hàojìn** run down; use up; run out

好竞争 **hào jìngzhēng** competitive

好看 **hǎokàn** good-looking

毫克 **háokè** milligram

好客 **hàokè** hospitable; 好客的主人 **hàokè de zhǔrén** a congenial host

好了，好了! **hǎole, hǎole!** there, there!

号码 **hàomǎ** number; size

毫米 **háomǐ** millimeter

好奇 **hàoqí** curious, inquisitive ◊ curiously

好强 **hàoqiáng** ambitious

好球 **hǎoqiú** strike (in baseball)

好奇心 **hàoqí xīn** curiosity; 引起好奇心 **yǐnqǐ hàoqí xīn** intrigue

好听 **hǎotīng** melodious; nice-sounding

好哇 **hǎowa** hurray

毫无 **háowú** not in the least; 毫无用处 **háowú yòngchù** no use at all

毫无顾忌 **háowú gùjì** regardless

好象 **hǎoxiàng** seem; resemble; look like ◊ apparently ◊ as if, as though

好笑 **hǎoxiào** amusing, funny; jovial

好心 **hǎoxīn** kind-hearted, sweet

好学 **hàoxué** academic, studious

好意 **hǎoyì** kindness

耗用 **hàoyòng** consume, use

蚝油 **háoyóu** oyster sauce

号召 **hàozhào** call; call on

豪猪 **háozhū** porcupine

好转 **hǎozhuǎn** get better, improve ◊ improvement, upturn

哈萨克斯坦 **Hāsàkèsītǎn** Kazakhstan ◊ Kazakh

哈腰 **hāyāo** stoop; bow

喝 **hē** drink

和 **hé** and; along with ◊ harmonious; mild ◊ sum; peace; 和 ... 一起 **hé ... yìqǐ** with

盒 **hé** case; box; container

颌 **hé** jaw

何 **hé** who; what; which; why; how

核 **hé** core, center; pip, pit

河 **hé** river

荷 **hé** lotus

合 **hé** join; fit; suit; 合你口味儿 **hé nǐ kǒuwèir** to your liking

褐 **hè** brown

贺 **hè** congratulate

和蔼可亲 **hé'ǎi kěqīn** amiable

河岸 **hé'àn** river bank

荷包蛋 **hébao dàn** fried egg

合抱双臂 **hébào shuāngbì** fold one's arms

河边 **hébiān** riverside

合并 **hébìng** merge, amalgamate ◊ merger

合不来 **hébùlái** not get on; be incompatible

喝采 **hècǎi** applaud; cheer; cheer on

合唱 **héchàng** sing in chorus ◊ choir

合成 **héchéng** synthesis

合成代谢激素 **héchéng dàixiè jīsù** anabolic steroid

河床 **héchuáng** riverbed

喝倒彩 **hè dàocǎi** boo

合得来 **hédelái** get on well; be compatible

合调 **hédiào** in tune

核对 **héduì** check

荷尔蒙 **hé'ěrméng** hormone

合法 **héfǎ** legal; legitimate; lawful

核反应堆 **hé fǎnyìng duī** nuclear reactor

合法性 **héfǎ xìng** legality

核废物 **hé fèiwù** nuclear waste

和服 **héfú** kimono

合格 **hégé** qualified; eligible; competent

合格会计师 **hégé kuàijì shī** certified public accountant

喝光 **hēguāng** drink up

和好 **héhǎo** make it up; be reconciled

和乎 **héhu** conform with; 和乎语法 **héhu yǔfǎ** grammatical

荷花 **héhuā** lotus (flower)

和缓 **héhuǎn** gentle, mild

合伙 **héhuǒ** team up; form a partnership; 合伙攻击 **héhuǒ gōngjī** gang up on; 合伙经营 **héhuǒ jīngyíng** partnership COM

合伙人 **héhuǒ rén** partner

嘿 **hēi** (appreciation): 嘿, 这可不错 **hēi, zhè kě búcuò** hey, this isn't bad at all

黑 **hēi** black; dark

黑暗 **hēi'àn** blackness; dark, darkness

黑白片 **hēibái piàn** black and white movie

黑板 **hēibǎn** blackboard

黑板擦 **hēibǎncā** blackboard eraser

黑板架 **hēibǎnjià** (blackboard) easel

黑客 **hēikè** hacker

黑麦 **hēimài** rye

黑莓 **hēiméi** blackberry

黑名单 **hēi míngdān** blacklist

黑啤酒 **hēi píjiǔ** dark beer

黑钱 **hēiqián** slush fund

黑人 **hēirén** black (person)

黑色 **hēisè** black (color)

黑社会 **hēi shèhuì** underworld

黑市 **hēishì** black market

黑市经济 **hēishì jīngjì** black economy

黑手党 **Hēishǒudǎng** Mafia

黑桃 **hēitáo** spades (in cards)

黑线鳕 **hēixiàn xuě** haddock

黑匣子 **hēi xiázi** black box

黑猩猩 **hēi xīngxing** chimpanzee

黑眼镜 **hēi yǎnjìng** dark glasses

核计 **héjì** calculate

合计 **héjì** add up

和解 **héjiě** make up

合金 **héjīn** alloy

喝酒 **héjiǔ** drink; drinking; 我不喝酒 **wǒ bù héjiǔ** I don't drink

河口 **hékǒu** rivermouth

河口湾 **hékǒu wān** estuary

荷兰 **Hélán** Holland, the

Netherlands ◊ Dutch

合礼 **hélǐ** kosher

合理 **hélǐ** rational, reasonable; sensible, sound ◊ reasonably, rationally

核裂变 **hé lièbiàn** nuclear fission

合理化 **hélǐ huà** rationalize ◊ rationalization

河流 **héliú** river

合理性 **hélǐ xìng** rationality

河马 **hémǎ** hippopotamus

褐煤 **hèméi** brown coal

和睦 **hémù** harmony

痕 **hén** mark; trace; scar

很 **hěn** very; quite

狠 **hěn** hard-hearted

恨 **hèn** hate ◊ hatred

很棒 **hěnbàng** great

狠毒 **hěndú** malicious; venomous

核能 **hénéng** nuclear power, nuclear energy

核能站 **hénéng zhàn** nuclear power station

横 **héng** horizontal

哼唱 **hēngchàng** hum

横冲直撞 **héngchōng zhízhuàng** rampage

横渡 **héngdù** crossing NAUT

横幅 **héngfú** banner, streamer

横杆 **hénggān** crossbar (of high jump)

横贯 **héngguàn** cross

横跨 **héngkuà** span

横跨大西洋 **héngkuà Dàxīyáng** transatlantic

横梁 **héngliáng** beam

衡量 **héngliáng** consider; weigh up

衡量标准 **héngliáng biāozhuǐ** yardstick

横木 **héngmù** crossbar (of goal)

横排 **héngpái** landscape print

恒温器 **héngwēn qì** thermostat

恒温育婴箱 **héngwēn yùyīng xiāng** incubator

横向 **héngxiàng** thwart

恒心 **héngxīn** stamina; persistence

痕迹 **hénjì** evidence; trail; traces

狠揍 **hěnzòu** beat up

和平 **hépíng** peace

和平队 **Hépíngduì** Peace Corps

和平主义 **hépíng zhǔyì** pacifism

和平主义者 **hépíng zhǔyì zhě** pacifist

和气 **héqi** polite; friendly; peaceable

呵欠 **hēqiàn** yawn

合群 **héqún** sociable ◊ fit in

和善 **héshàn** friendly

和尚 **héshàng** Buddhist monk

合身 **héshēn** fit

和声 **héshēng** harmony

核实 **héshí** verification ◊ verify

合适 **héshì** suitable, appropriate; right; convenient ◊ fit; 合适的位置 **héshìde wèizhi** niche

合算 **hésuàn** profitable

喝汤 **hētāng** drink soup

核桃 **hétáo** walnut

合同 **hétóng** contract ◊ contractual

合为一体 **hé wéi yītǐ** merge

核武器 **hé wǔqì** nuclear weapons

贺喜 **hèxǐ** congratulate

和谐 **héxié** harmonious

核心 **héxīn** core; kernel

贺信 **hèxìn** letter of congratulation

合意 **héyì** please; appeal to

合意男士 **héyì nánshì** eligible bachelor

合影 **héyǐng** group photo

合用 **héyòng** double up, share

和约 **héyuē** peace treaty

盒子 **hézi** box

合资企业 **hézī qǐyè** joint venture

合组 **hézǔ** consortium

喝醉 **hēzuì** get drunk

喝醉了 **hēzuìle** drunk; drunken

合作 **hézuò** cooperate, collaborate ◊ cooperation, collaboration ◊ cooperative

合作社 **hézuò shè** cooperative

合作者 **hézuò zhě** collaborator

轰 **hōng** chuck out, drive away

红 **hóng** red

虹 **hóng** rainbow

洪 **hóng** big ◊ flood

哄 **hǒng** coax

红宝石 **hóng bǎoshí** ruby

红茶 **hóngchá** black tea

红肠面包 **hóngcháng miànbāo** hot dog

宏大 **hóngdà** great

红灯 **hóngdēng** red light

红灯区 **hóngdēng qū** red light district

轰的一声 **hōngde yīshēng** bang

轰动 **hōngdòng** cause a sensation ◊ sensation ◊ sensational

红光满面 **hóngguāng mǎnmiàn** radiant

轰击 **hōngjī** shoot at; bombard

红军 **Hóngjūn** Red Army

烘烤 **hōngkǎo** toast

洪亮 **hóngliàng** sonorous

红绿灯 **hónglǜdēng** traffic light

轰鸣 **hōngmíng** roar

轰鸣声 **hōngmíng shēng** roar

虹膜 **hóngmó** iris (of eye)

哄骗 **hǒngpiàn** deceive; swindle

红润 **hóngrùn** glow ◊ rosy; ruddy

红色 **hóngsè** red

红色中国 **Hóngsè Zhōngguó** Red China

红十字 **Hóngshízì** Red Cross

红薯 **hóngshǔ** sweet potato

洪水 **hóngshuǐ** flood

洪水泛滥 **hóngshuǐ fànlàn** flooding

红桃 **hóngtáo** hearts (in cards)

红外线 **hóngwàixiàn** infra-red rays

宏伟 **hóngwěi** grandiose

红卫兵 **Hóngwèibīng** Red Guard

轰炸 **hōngzhà** bomb

轰炸机 **hōngzhà jī** bomber (plane)

轰炸警告 **hōngzhà jǐnggào** bomb scare

猴 **hóu** monkey

喉 **hóu** throat

吼 **hǒu** roar

后 **hòu** back; rear; behind

厚 **hòu** thick

候 **hòu** wait

厚板 **hòubǎn** slab

后背 **hòubèi** back

后备 **hòubèi** back up ◊ backup

后部 **hòubù** back

候车场 **hòuchē chǎng** cab rank, cab stand

候车室 **hòuchē shì** waiting room

后代 **hòudài** offspring; posterity

后跟 **hòugēn** heel

后果 **hòuguǒ** consequence; effect

后花园 **hòu huāyuán** backyard

后悔 **hòuhuǐ** regret; repent; be sorry

吼叫 **hǒujiào** bellow

吼叫声 **hǒujiào shēng** bellow

喉结 **hóujié** Adam's apple

候机室 **hòujī shì** departure lounge

后来 **hòulái** after; afterward; later; later on; subsequently

喉咙 **hóulóng** throat

后门 **hòumén** backdoor

后面 **hòumian** behind, in back

候鸟 **hòuniǎo** bird of passage

后勤学 **hòuqín xué** logistics

喉舌 **hóushé** mouthpiece, spokesperson

吼声 **hǒushēng** bellow

后视镜 **hòushì jìng** rear-view mirror

后天 **hòutiān** the day after tomorrow

后退 **hòutuì** back away; back off; back up (*in car*); stand back ◊ retrograde

后卫 **hòuwèi** back SP

候选人 **hòuxuǎn rén** candidate

后续 **hòuxù** follow up

喉炎 **hóuyán** laryngitis

厚颜无耻 **hòuyán wúchǐ** outrageous; impertinent

后腰 **hòuyāo** small of the back

后裔 **hòuyì** descendant

后院 **hòuyuàn** backyard

后者 **hòuzhě** latter

猴子 **hóuzi** monkey

呼 **hū** beep

忽 **hū** overlook ◊ suddenly

壶 **hú** jug; kettle; pot

湖 **hú** lake

核 **hú** pit (*in fruit*)

胡 **hú** mustache; beard

糊 **hú** stick

煳 **hú** burnt

虎 **hǔ** tiger

糊 **hú** mush

户 **hù** door; household; bank account

护 **hù** protect

互 **hù** mutual

花 **huā** flower; blossom ◊ spend; cost; 他们花了五百美金 **tāmen huāle wǔbǎi měijīn** it cost them $500

划 **huá** row; paddle; strike *match*

滑 **huá** slide; slip ◊ slippery, icy

华 **huá** glory; China

画 **huà** draw; paint; portray ◊ drawing; painting

话 **huà** talk; words; remark

化 **huà** change; melt; dissolve ◊ (*to make adjectives and nouns into verbs*) -ize; 大众化 **dàzhònghuà** popularize; 简化 **jiǎnhuà** simplify

画 **huà** stroke (*in character*); picture ◊ paint

花瓣 **huābàn** petal

滑板 **huábǎn** skateboard

画报 **huàbào** magazine

画笔 **huàbǐ** paintbrush

花边 **huābiān** lace

哗变 **huábiàn** mutiny

滑冰 **huábīng** skate ◊ skating

化冰 **huàbīng** defrost

滑冰场 **huábīng chǎng** ice rink

滑冰人 **huábīng rén** skater

划船 **huáchuán** row; paddle

花点 **huādiǎn** spotted

划掉 **huádiào** delete; strike out

化冻 **huà** thaw

花朵 **huāduǒ** bloom

华而不实 **huá ér bùshí** ornate

华尔街 **Huá'ěrjiē** Wall Street

华尔兹 **huá'ěrzī** waltz

花费 **huāfèi** spend ◊ expenditure

化肥 **huàféi** artificial fertilizer

花粉 **huāfěn** pollen

划分 **huàfēn** divide; 划分轻重缓急 **huàfēn qīngzhòng huǎnjí** prioritize

花粉计数 **huāfěn jìshù** pollen count

花粉热 **huāfěn rè** hay fever

花岗石 **huāgāng shí** granite

花岗岩 **huāgāng yán** granite

化工 **huàgōng** chemical industry

滑旱冰 **huá hànbīng** skate

化合 **huàhé** combine

划痕 **huáhén** cut; score ◊ scratch

化合物 huàhé wù compound
CHEM

画画 huàhua draw

花花公子 huāhuā gōngzǐ playboy

花环 huāhuán garland

怀 huái bosom ◊ cherish; 怀好意 huái hǎoyì mean well

踝 huái ankle

坏 huài bad

坏处 huàichu disadvantage

坏蛋 huàidàn gangster; villain

怀旧 huáijiù nostalgia ◊ nostalgic ◊ reminisce

怀念 huáiniàn long for

坏人 huàirén rogue

坏事 huàishì evil; evil thing

槐树 huáishù scholar tree

怀疑 huáiyí doubt; suspect; question ◊ suspicion ◊ skeptical

怀疑论者 huáiyílùn zhě skeptic

怀疑态度 huáiyí tàidù skepticism

怀有 huáiyǒu harbor grudge etc; 怀有恶意 huáiyǒu èyì spiteful; 怀有希望 huáiyǒu xīwàng expectant

怀孕 huáiyùn conceive; expect ◊ pregnant ◊ pregnancy; conception

怀着 huáizhe carry (of pregnant woman)

滑稽 huájī comical ◊ funnily; 滑稽的模仿 huájī de mófǎng (comic) impression; 滑稽短剧 huájī duǎnjù (comedy) sketch

画家 huàjiā artist, painter

花椒 huājiāo Sichuan pepper

花轿 huājiào bridal palanquin

滑稽可笑 huájī kěxiào very funny, hysterical

哗啦 huālā crash; clatter; crackle

滑来滑去 huálái huáqù slither

画廊 huàláng art gallery

哗啦声 huālā shēng crash; clatter; crackle

花蕾 huālěi bud

华丽的词藻 huálìde cízǎo rhetoric

滑轮 huálún pulley

画面 huàmiàn image

化名 huàmíng pseudonym

欢 huān happy

还 huán return, give back; 将X还给Y jiāng X huángěi Y give X back to Y

环 huán ring; circle

缓 huǎn slow; leisurely ◊ postpone, put off

换 huàn change; swap; switch; 换衣服 huàn yīfu change clothes; 用X换Y yòng X huàn Y exchange X for Y

患 huàn worry; catch disease

唤 huàn shout

幻 huàn unreal; magic

换班 huànbān change shifts

环保 huánbǎo environmental protection

患病 huànbìng be ill

欢畅 huānchàng cheerful

缓冲器 huǎnchōng qì buffer COMPUT

换档键 huàndǎng jiàn shift key

幻灯 huàndēng slide show

幻灯片 huàndēng piàn slide; transparency

荒 huāng desolate

慌 huāng nervous; 别慌 biéhuāng don't panic

黄 huáng yellow

皇 huáng emperor ◊ imperial

晃 huǎng dazzle

谎 huǎng lie

晃 huàng swing; wave

蝗虫 huángchóng locust

荒诞 huāngdàn absurd; grotesque

黄疸 huángdǎn jaundice

黄道带 huángdào dài zodiac

黄道十二宫图 huángdào shí'èr gōngtú signs of the zodiac

荒地 huāngdì wasteland; heath

皇帝 huángdì emperor ◊ imperial

黄帝 Huángdì Yellow Emperor

晃动 huàngdòng shake; waggle

黄豆 huángdòu soybean

荒废 huāngfèi lie fallow

黄蜂 huángfēng wasp

皇宫 huánggōng imperial palace

黄瓜 huángguā cucumber

黄海 Huánghǎi Yellow Sea

黄河 Huánghé Yellow River

皇后 huánghòu empress; queen

恍惚 huǎnghū trance

谎话 **huǎnghuà** lie

黄昏 **huánghūn** dusk, twilight

皇家 **huángjiā** royal family ◊ royal

黄金 **huángjīn** gold

黄金时间 **huángjīn shíjiān** prime time

荒凉 **huāngliáng** bleak; deserted; desolate; stark

慌忙 **huāngmáng** hurried

荒谬 **huāngmiù** preposterous, ridiculous ◊ ridiculously

荒漠 **huāngmò** barren

荒僻 **huāngpì** remote, out-of-the-way

黄色 **huángsè** yellow ◊ pornographic

黄色电影 **huángsè diànyǐng** blue movie

黄色杂志 **huángsè zázhì** pornographic magazine

黄色作品 **huángsè zuòpǐn** pornography

荒疏 **huāngshū** lose the knack

荒唐 **huāngtáng** ludicrous, absurd ◊ absurdity

黄铜 **huángtóng** brass

环顾 **huángù** look around

荒无人烟 **huāng wú rényān** uninhabited

荒野 **huāngyě** the bush; the wilds

黄油 **huángyóu** butter

荒原 **huāngyuán** wilderness

慌张 **huāngzhāng** nervous

幌子 **huǎngzi** front

皇族 **huángzú** royalty

缓和 **huǎnhé** lighten; soften; tone down ◊ détente; respite

欢呼 **huānhū** cheer ◊ cheering

还击 **huánjī** hit back

环礁湖 **huánjiāo hú** lagoon

缓解 **huǎnjiě** relax; alleviate; ease off; smooth over

环境 **huánjìng** environment; surroundings; setting

环境保护 **huánjìng bǎohù** environmental protection

环境保护论者 **huánjìng bǎohùlùn zhě** environmentalist

环境卫生部门 **huánjìng wèishēng bùmén** sanitation department

环境污染 **huánjìng wūrǎn** environmental pollution

欢聚 **huānjù** social gathering, get-together

欢快 **huānkuài** bright ◊ brightness

欢乐 **huānlè** happy; cheerful; convivial ◊ merriment

还礼 **huánlǐ** return the salute, salute back

缓慢 **huǎnmàn** slow; leisurely; tardy; 缓慢进行 **huǎnmàn jìnxíng** plod along, plod on

幻灭 **huànmiè** disillusionment

化脓 **huànóng** fester

唤起 **huànqǐ** evoke; arouse; call up

还钱 **huánqián** pay back

换钱 **huànqián** change money

欢庆 **huānqìng** festivities

还清 **huánqīng** pay off

换取 **huànqǔ** exchange; 用来换取 **yònglái huànqǔ** in exchange for

焕然一新 **huànrán yìxīn** renew; take on a new look

环绕 **huánrào** surround, encircle

涣散 **huànsàn** loose; limp

换算 **huànsuàn** convert

换算表 **huànsuàn biǎo** conversion table

欢喜 **huānxǐ** rapturous

幻象 **huànxiàng** illusion; fantasy

幻想 **huànxiǎng** illusion; 使幻想破灭 **shǐ huànxiǎng pòmiè** disillusion

欢笑 **huānxiào** mirth

欢欣 **huānxīn** jubilation

缓刑 **huǎnxíng** reprieve ◊ probation

唤醒 **huànxǐng** wake; rouse

唤醒电话 **huànxǐng diànhuà** wake-up call

缓刑监督官 **huǎnxíng jiāndūguān** probation officer

浣熊 **huànxióng** raccoon

还押 **huányā** be on remand

欢迎 **huānyíng** welcome ◊ reception; 受欢迎 **shòu huānyíng** be popular; go down well

患有 **huànyǒu** be suffering from

花盆 **huāpén** flowerpot

花瓶 huāpíng vase

花钱 huāqián spend

华侨 Huáqiáo overseas Chinese

划清界线 huàqīng jièxiàn delimit

花圈 huāquān wreath

花色俱全 huāsè jùquán assortment

花色牌 huāsè pái suit (*in cards*)

花商 huāshāng florist

花哨 huāshao flashy, gaudy

化身 huàshēn embodiment

花生 huāshēng peanut

华盛顿 Huáshèngdùn Washington

花生酱 huāshēng jiàng peanut butter

华氏 huáshì Fahrenheit

化石 huàshí fossil

划时代 huàshídài epoch-making

花时间 huā shíjiān time-consuming

花束 huāshù bouquet

滑水 huáshuǐ waterskiing

划算 huásuàn pay off; be worthwhile ◊ cost-effective

花坛 huātán flowerbed

滑梯 huátī slide

话题 huàtí topic of conversation

划艇 huátǐng rowboat

话务员 huàwù yuán telephonist; switchboard operator

化纤 huàxiān synthetic fiber

划线标出 huàxiàn biāochū mark out

滑翔 huáxiáng glide

滑翔机 huáxiáng jī glider

滑翔运动 huáxiáng yùndòng gliding

滑翔者 huáxiáng zhě glider (*person*)

滑行 huáxíng glide; slide; coast; taxi (*of airplane*)

滑行运动 huáxíng yùndòng gliding; sliding; coasting; taxiing

滑雪 huáxuě ski ◊ skiing

化学 huàxué chemistry ◊ chemical

滑雪道 huáxuě dào ski run

化学家 huàxué jiā chemist

化学疗法 huàxué liáofǎ chemotherapy

化学战 huàxué zhàn chemical warfare

滑雪杖 huáxuě zhàng ski pole

滑雪者 huáxuě zhě skier

化学制品 huàxué zhìpǐn chemical

花样滑冰 huāyàng huábīng figure skating

化验室 huàyàn shì laboratory

华裔 Huáyì person of Chinese descent

花园 huāyuán garden

画展 huàzhǎn exhibition of paintings

花招 huāzhāo trick

化妆 huàzhuāng put on make-up

化妆品 huàzhuāng pǐn make-up; cosmetics

化装室 huàzhuāng shì dressing room

化妆晚会 huàzhuāng wǎnhuì fancy-dress party

划子 huázi rowboat

护板 hùbǎn shield

湖滨 húbīn shore, lakeside

胡茬子 húchází stubble

胡扯 húchě rave

呼出 hūchū breathe; breathe out

护创膏 hùchuàng gāo sticking plaster

蝴蝶 húdié butterfly

蝴蝶结 húdié jié bow (*knot*)

忽动忽停 hūdòng hūtíng jerky

护发剂 hùfà jì conditioner

煳饭 húfàn burnt rice

胡蜂 húfēng wasp

护封 hùfēng jacket (*of book*)

呼喊 hūhǎn call

呼唤 hūhuàn call; bleep

互换 hùhuàn exchange

互惠 hùhuì bilateral; reciprocal

灰 huī ash; dust

挥 huī wave

回 huí return; go back

悔 huǐ regret

毁 huǐ damage

会 huì be able to; meet ◊ meeting; 你会说法语吗？ **nǐ huì shuō Fǎyǔ ma?** can you speak French?; 我说过我会去 **wǒ shuōguò wǒ huì qù** I said that I could go; 会用

电脑 **huìyòng diànnǎo** computer literate

喙 **huì** beak; snout

汇 **huì** converge

绘 **huì** paint; draw

灰暗 **huī'àn** dark; somber

回报 **huíbào** return *favor, invitation*

汇报 **huìbào** report card

回避 **huíbì** evade; duck

会场 **huìchǎng** meeting place

回车健 **huíchē jiàn** return key COMPUT

灰尘 **huīchén** dust

回程 **huíchéng** return journey

回程飞机 **huíchéng fēijī** return flight

回答 **huídá** answer, reply

回荡 **huídàng** echo

回到 **huídào** return, get back

回电话 **huí diànhuà**; 他能给我回电话吗? **tā néng gěi wǒ huí diànhuà ma?** can he call me back?

挥动 **huīdòng** swing; wield, brandish

汇兑 **huìduì** transfer *money*

挥发 **huīfā** evaporate

回放 **huífàng** playback

会费 **huìfèi** membership fee

恢复 **huīfù** recover; restore; return; bring back; resume ◊ recovery; 他恢复得很好 **tā huīfù de hěnhǎo** he has made a good recovery

恢复元气 **huīfù yuánqì** recuperate

恢复知觉 **huīfù zhījué** regain consciousness

回顾 **huígù** look back ◊ retrospective

惠顾 **huìgù** custom, patronage

回归线 **huíguī xiàn** tropic

回国 **huíguó** go home (*to one's own country*)

回合 **huíhé** round (*in boxing*)

汇合 **huìhé** join

会合 **huìhé** meet; convene; link up

悔恨 **huǐhèn** regret

绘画 **huìhuà** paint ◊ painting; picture

毁坏 **huǐhuài** destroy; ruin, wreck; mangle

辉煌 **huīhuáng** brilliant; glorious

挥霍 **huīhuò** wasteful; extravagant; lavish ◊ squander

回家 **huíjiā** go home

会见 **huìjiàn** meeting

灰浆 **huījiāng** mortar

回教 **Huíjiào** Islam

灰烬 **huījìn** ash

回扣 **huíkòu** bribe, kickback

汇款单 **huìkuǎn dān** money order

回来 **huílái** come back

贿赂 **huìlù** bribe ◊ bribery

汇率 **huìlǜ** exchange rate

会面 **huìmiàn** meet

毁灭 **huǐmiè** wreck; obliterate

灰泥 **huīní** plaster

汇票 **huìpiào** bill of exchange

会签 **huìqiān** countersign

回球 **huíqiú** return (*in tennis*)

回去 **huíqù** go back, return

毁容 **huǐróng** disfigure

灰色 **huīsè** gray

灰色跑犬 **huīsè pǎoquǎn** grayhound

声声 **huíshēng** echo

挥手 **huīshǒu** wave

回收 **huíshōu** recycle ◊ recycling

会谈 **huìtán** have a conversation

回头 **huítóu** turn back

回头生意 **huítóu shēngyì** repeat business

绘图 **huìtú** drawing

绘图人 **huìtú rén** illustrator

绘图仪 **huìtú yí** plotter COMPUT

绘图员 **huìtú yuán** draftsman

挥舞 **huīwǔ** wave

污物 **huìwù** filth

会晤 **huìwù** meet with

回响 **huíxiǎng** reverberate

回想 **huíxiǎng** think back

诙谐 **huīxié** humorous

灰心 **huīxīn** discouraged; frustrated; frustrating ◊ frustratingly

回信 **huíxìn** reply, write back ◊ (letter of) reply

彗星 **huìxīng** comet

回形针 **huíxíngzhēn** paper clip

会演 **huìyǎn** festival

回忆 **huíyì** recollect ◊ recollection; 引起 X 的回忆 **yǐnqǐ X de huíyì** jog X's memory

会议 **huìyì** convention, conference; congress; meeting

回忆录 **huíyìlù** memoirs

会议室 **huìyì shì** board room; meeting room

会议中心 **huìyì zhōngxīn** convention center

徽章 **huīzhāng** button, badge, pin

绘制 **huìzhì** draw

回转 **huízhuǎn** turn around

回嘴 **huízuǐ** answer back

护甲 **hùjiǎ** armor

胡椒 **hújiāo** pepper

胡椒薄荷 **hújiāo bòhé** peppermint

胡椒粉 **hújiāofěn** (ground) pepper

呼叫机 **hūjiào jī** bleeper

呼救 **hūjiù** emergency call

户口 **hùkǒu** household registration

狐狸 **húli** fox

护理 **hùlǐ** nurse ◊ nursing

护林员 **hùlínyuán** forest ranger

护理人员 **hùlǐ rényuán** nursing staff

胡乱 **húluàn** carelessly; 胡乱摆弄 **húluàn bǎinòng** fiddle around with

忽略 **hūlüè** neglect ◊ overlook, ignore

胡萝卜 **húluóbo** carrot

呼噜声 **hūlushēng** grunt; purr

护目镜 **hùmùjìng** goggles

荤 **hūn** meat or fish

昏 **hūn** dark ◊ swoon

婚 **hūn** marriage ◊ marry

混 **hùn** mix

昏暗 **hūn'an** dark; dim; obscure; dingy

胡闹 **húnào** make trouble; fool around

混蛋 **húndàn** bastard; pig

昏倒 **hūndǎo** faint

混合 **hùnhé** mix; combine; mingle; blend

混合物 **hùnhéwù** mix; mixture

昏厥 **hūnjué** fit MED ◊ pass out

婚礼 **hūnlǐ** marriage; wedding

婚礼蛋糕 **hūnlǐ dàngāo** wedding cake

婚礼日 **hūnlǐrì** wedding day

混乱 **hùnluàn** chaos; muddle ◊ chaotic; turbulent; 我的思维一片混乱 **wǒde sīwéi yípiàn hùnluàn** my mind is in a whirl

昏迷 **hūnmí** black out ◊ blackout; coma ◊ unconscious

混凝土 **hùnníngtǔ** concrete

糊弄 **hùnong** mess around

婚前 **hūnqián** premarital

婚纱 **hūnshā** wedding dress

浑身 **húnshēn** the entire body ◊ all over; 我浑身都疼 **wǒ húnshēn dōu téng** it hurts all over

馄饨 **húntun** won ton (type of dumpling)

婚外 **hūnwài** extramarital

混淆 **hùnxiáo** confuse ◊ confusion

混血儿 **hùnxuè'ér** half-caste

婚姻 **hūnyīn** marriage ◊ marital

婚姻顾问 **hūnyīn gùwèn** marriage counselor

婚约 **hūnyuē** engagement

浑浊 **húnzhuó** cloudy; muddy

或 **huò** or

活 **huó** live ◊ alive ◊ work; 你有活儿干了 **nǐ yǒu huór gànle** you'll have a job, it won't be easy

伙 **huǒ** partner; bunch (of people)

火 **huǒ** fire

货 **huò** stock; goods

祸 **huò** accident

获 **huò** achieve

火把 **huǒbǎ** torch

伙伴 **huǒbàn** buddy

货板 **huòbǎn** pallet

活板门 **huóbǎnmén** trapdoor

货币 **huòbì** currency ◊ monetary

货舱 **huòcāng** hold

火柴 **huǒchái** match

火柴盒 **huǒcháihé** matchbox

货车 **huòchē** truck; freight car

火车 **huǒchē** train

火车头 **huǒchētóu** locomotive

货车厢 **huòchēxiāng** freight car

火车站 **huǒchē zhàn** train station

货船 **huòchuán** freighter

货到付款 huòdào fùkuǎn collect on delivery

获得 huòdé acquire, get; achieve; capture; 获得成功 huòdé chénggōng achieve success; make it

活动 huódòng activity; pastime; pursuit ◊ move ◊ mobile

活动扳手 huódòng bānshǒu monkey wrench

活动边 huódòngbiān flap (of table)

活动过度 huódòng guòdù hyperactive

活动家 huódòngjiā campaigner

活动住房 huódòng zhùfáng mobile home

火锅 huǒguō hot pot

火红 huǒhóng lurid; fiery

火花 huǒhuā spark

火化 huǒhuà cremate ◊ cremation

火化场 huǒhuà chǎng crematorium

火花塞 huǒhuāsāi spark plug

火鸡 huǒjī turkey

货价 huòjià cost (of goods)

火箭 huǒjiàn rocket

获奖 huòjiǎng prizewinning ◊ win a prize

获奖者 huòjiǎng zhě prizewinner

火警 huǒjǐng fire alarm

火炬 huǒjù torch

活力 huólì vigor; vitality; spirit

霍乱 huòluàn cholera

货品 huòpǐn merchandise

活泼 huópo animated; brisk; lively; sprightly; vivacious

活泼有力 huópo yǒulì frisky

获取 huòqǔ extract

活塞 huósāi piston

火山 huǒshān volcano

火山口 huǒshān kǒu crater

获胜 huòshèng win ◊ winning ◊ winner

祸首 huòshǒu instigator; culprit; ringleader

货摊 huòtān booth

火腿 huǒtuǐ ham

货物 huòwù goods; cargo, freight; consignment, shipment

获悉 huòxī discover

火星 huǒxīng spark

活性洗涤剂 huóxìng xǐdí jì biological detergent

或许 huòxǔ perhaps

火焰 huǒyàn flame

活页夹 huóyè jiá binder (for papers)

活跃 huóyuè active; effervescent; vivid

货运列车 huòyùn lièchē freight train

货运站 huòyùnzhàn freight depot

活着 huózhe alive; living ◊ live

或者 huòzhě or; alternatively; 或者 … 或者 huòzhě … huòzhě either … or

获知 huòzhī find out

虎皮鹦鹉 hǔpí yīngwǔ budgerigar

糊墙纸 húqiángzhǐ wallpaper

忽然 hūrán suddenly

呼声 hūshēng clamor

忽视 hūshì neglect; disregard

护士 hùshì nurse

胡刷 húshuā shaving brush

胡说 húshuō nonsense

胡说八道 húshuō bādào nonsense

胡同 hútòng alley, lane

户头 hùtóu account

糊涂 hútu confused; 令人糊涂 lìngrén hútú confusing

护卫 hùwèi escort

互为补充 hùwéi bǔchōng complementary

呼吸 hūxī breath; breathing ◊ breathe

互相 hùxiāng reciprocal; mutual ◊ mutually; each other; one another

互相传 hùxiāng chuán pass around

弧形 húxíng arched

呼吁 hūyù appeal

护照 hùzhào passport

护照检查处 hùzhào jiǎncháchù passport control

互撞 hùzhuàng collision

胡子 húzi beard; mustache; whiskers; sideburns

胡子楂 húzi chá bristles

J

击 jī attack; strike; knock ◊ blow

鸡 jī chicken

基 jī base; foundation

机 jī machine; airplane; opportunity

奇 jī odd *number*

即 jí namely; promptly

吉 jí lucky; auspicious

集 jí collect ◊ episode

及 jí and ◊ reach

极 jí extreme ◊ extremely

级 jí level; grade; 我们是同级的 **wǒmen shì tóngjí de** we were in the same year

急 jí impatient; in a hurry; urgent

脊 jí ridge

几 jǐ some; a few; several; how many?; 几百美元 **jǐbǎi měiyuán** a few hundred dollars; 几张票 **jǐzhāng piào** a few tickets

系 jì fasten; tie; buckle

迹 jì mark; trace

计 jì calculate; count

技 jì skill

妓 jì prostitute

寄 jì send; mail

季 jì season

既 jì already ◊ since

记 jì remember; 记笔记 **jì bǐjì** take notes; 记不得 **jìbudé** I don't remember; 记不住 **jìbuzhù** I can't remember

忌 jì envy

纪 jì record

继 jì continue

系 jì button up; tie up

既 … 又 … **jì … yòu …** both … and …

加 jiā add ◊ plus

夹 jiā clip ◊ squeeze

家 jiā home; family; 在家 **zài jiā** at home

痂 jiā scab

佳 jiā very good; fine; beautiful

颊 jiá cheek

假 jiǎ false, fake; bogus; 假钞票 **jiǎchāopiào** counterfeit bill

甲 jiǎ first; armor; nail; A; *unspecified person or thing in lists etc*

架 jià shelf; rack; frame

价 jià price

假 jià vacation

驾 jià drive

加班 jiābān work overtime

甲板 jiǎbǎn deck

假扮 jiǎbàn impersonate

夹板 jiā bǎn jiá splint

加倍 jiābèi double

加标点 jiā biāodiǎn punctuate

加冰 jiābīng iced

夹层 jiácéng compartment

家常闲话 jiācháng xiánhuà chitchat; gossip

甲虫 jiǎchóng beetle

家畜 jiāchù domestic animal

假定 jiǎdìng assume

加法 jiāfǎ addition MATH

假发 jiǎfà wig

价格 jiàgé price; cost

价格战 jiàgézhàn price war

加工 jiāgōng process; embellish

加固 jiāgù fasten; secure

加号 jiāhào plus sign

家伙 jiāhuo guy, fellow

嘉奖 jiājiǎng praise

佳节 jiājié celebration; festival

嫁接 jiājiē graft BOT

夹紧 jiājǐn clamp

家具 jiājù furniture; 一件家具 **yíjiàn jiājù** a piece of furniture; 一套家具 **yítào jiājù** suite

加剧 jiājù intensify

家具罩 jiājù zhào dust cover

家具装饰材料 jiājù zhuāngshì cáiliào upholstery

茄克 jiākè jacket; coat

架空 jiàkōng overhead

加快 jiākuài accelerate, speed up

加宽 jiākuān widen

假面具 **jiǎ miànjù** disguise

价目表 **jiàmùbiǎo** tariff

煎 **jiān** shallow fry

尖 **jiān** tip, point ◊ pointed; sharp; acute

肩 **jiān** shoulder

监 **jiān** prison ◊ supervise

坚 **jiān** solid; firm

艰 **jiān** difficult

奸 **jiān** traitor; adultery ◊ wicked; evil; cunning

剪 **jiān** cut; clip; 把头发剪了 **bǎ tóufa jiǎn le** get one's hair cut

减 **jiǎn** reduce; take away, subtract ◊ minus

简 **jiǎn** uncomplicated, straightforward, simple

检 **jiǎn** inspect, check

捡 **jiǎn** collect, pick up

键 **jiàn** key

见 **jiàn** see; meet

溅 **jiàn** splash; splatter

剑 **jiàn** sword

腱 **jiàn** tendon

渐 **jiàn** gradually

舰 **jiàn** warship

箭 **jiàn** arrow

件 **jiàn** *measure word for items, matters, clothing, furniture*; 三件行李 **sānjiàn xíngli** three pieces of baggage; 一件 **yíjiàn** an article, an item; 一件上衣 **yíjiàn duǎnshàngyī** a jacket

建 **jiàn** build; put up

健 **jiàn** healthy

加拿大 **Jiānádà** Canada ◊ Canadian

肩膀 **jiānbǎng** shoulder

简报 **jiǎnbào** briefing; clipping

简便机场 **jiǎnbiàn jīchǎng** landing strip

鉴别 **jiànbié** identify; differentiate

兼并 **jiānbìng** take over ◊ takeover

剑柄 **jiànbǐng** hilt

兼并投标 **jiānbìng tóubiāo** takeover bid

剪裁 **jiǎncái** cut to size; cut out

剪草钳 **jiǎncǎo qián** clippers

检测 **jiǎncè** detect ◊ detection

检查 **jiǎnchá** check; examine; inspect ◊ examination; inspection;

检查 … 的拼写 **jiǎnchá … de pīnxiě** do a spellcheck on …

检察 **jiǎnchá** prosecute

检察官 **jiǎncháguān** prosecuting attorney

减产 **jiǎnchǎn** wind down production

检查员 **jiǎncháyuán** inspector

简称 **jiǎnchēng** abbreviation

建成 **jiànchéng** construct; be up; be built

坚持 **jiānchí** maintain; insist; hold; adhere; stand by, stick to ◊ insistent; 坚持自己的立场 **jiānchí zìjǐ de lìchǎng** stand one's ground; assert oneself

坚持不懈 **jiānchí búxiè** persistence, perseverance

剪出 **jiǎnchū** cut out

肩带 **jiāndài** shoulder strap; sash

煎蛋 **jiāndàn** fried egg

简单 **jiǎndān** simple; straightforward; humble ◊ briefly; simply ◊ simplicity

煎蛋卷 **jiān dànjuǎn** omelet

剪刀 **jiǎndāo** scissors

剪掉 **jiǎndiào** cut off

间谍 **jiàndié** spy

间谍活动 **jiàndié huódòng** espionage

坚定 **jiāndìng** firm; determined; confirmed; stalwart, staunch ◊ be firm, put one's foot down

鉴定 **jiàndìng** survey; assess

鉴定人 **jiàndìng rén** surveyor

监督 **jiāndū** supervise; monitor

尖端 **jiānduān** point (*of knife etc*)

简短 **jiǎnduǎn** brief

尖端产品 **jiānduān chǎnpǐn** top-quality product

舰队 **jiànduì** fleet

简而言之 **jiǎn ér yánzhī** in short

减肥 **jiǎnféi** slim, diet; lose weight

减肥食品 **jiǎnféi shípǐn** diet

姜 **jiāng** ginger (*spice*)

将 **jiāng** take; will; 将东西装入 **jiāng dōngxi zhuāngrù** pack; 将头发分开 **jiāng tóufà fēnkāi** part one's hair; 将 … 归档 **jiāng … guīdàng** file away; 他将去旅行 **tā jiāng qù lǚxíng** he's going to travel around

僵 jiāng stiff

缰 jiāng rein

桨 jiāng paddle; oar

讲 jiǎng speak; talk; tell; 讲电话 *jiǎng diànhuà* be on the telephone

奖 jiǎng award; prize

降 jiàng lower; sink

酱 jiàng paste; sauce

奖杯 jiǎngbēi trophy

讲道 jiǎngdào sermon

讲道德 jiǎngdàodé moral

降低 jiàngdī decline; die down; lower; reduce; 使降低 *shǐ jiàngdī* bring down

降低标价 jiàngdī biāojià mark down

降低等级 jiàngdī děngjí downgrade

间隔 jiàngé interval; distance

浆果 jiāngguǒ berry

糨糊 jiànghú paste

讲话 jiǎnghuà speak; deliver a speech

姜黄色 jiānghuángsè red; ginger

讲价 jiǎngjià haggle; bargain

降价 jiàngjià get cheaper, drop in price; drop (its) prices

讲解 jiǎngjiě explain

蒋介石 Jiǎng Jièshí Chiang Kai-shek

将近 jiāngjìn almost

奖金 jiǎngjīn bonus

将就 jiāngjiù make do with

讲究 jiǎngjiu fussy, particular ◊ be particular about

讲究细节 jiǎngjiu xìjié finicky

僵局 jiāngjú deadlock, impasse; stalemate

将军 jiāngjūn general ◊ check (*in chess*)

讲课 jiǎngkè give a lecture

将来 jiānglái in the future; 不远 的将来 *bùyuǎnde jiānglái* in the near future

将来时 jiāngláishí future tense

讲理 jiǎnglǐ reason with ◊ reasonable

奖励 jiǎnglì award; reward

降临 jiànglín onset ◊ strike

降落 jiàngluò land

降落伞 jiàngluòsǎn parachute

奖品 jiǎngpǐn prize

奖赏 jiǎngshǎng prize

缰绳 jiāngsheng lead, leash; rein

讲师 jiǎngshī lecturer

讲实际 jiǎng shíjì hardheaded

讲述 jiǎngshù tell

将死 jiāngsǐ checkmate

讲台 jiǎngtái rostrum

坚固 jiāngù strong, solid; resistant; robust

兼顾 jiāngù combine; do both ... and ...; 兼顾 X 和 Y *jiāngù X hé Y* combine X with Y

见怪 jiànguài take badly; mind; take offense

监管人 jiānguǎn rén prison guard

坚果 jiānguǒ nut

坚果钳 jiānguǒ qián nutcrackers

坚果味儿 jiānguǒ wèir nutty *taste*

降温 jiàngwēn drop in temperature

讲习班 jiǎngxíbān workshop, seminar

奖学金 jiǎngxuéjīn scholarship

讲演 jiǎngyǎn lecture

讲演厅 jiǎngyǎn tīng lecture hall

将要 jiāngyào about to

僵硬 jiāngyìng stiff

酱油 jiàngyóu soy sauce

疆域 jiāngyù territory

降雨量 jiàngyǔ liàng rainfall

奖章 jiǎngzhāng medal

奖章获得者 jiǎngzhang huòdé zhě medalist

降职 jiàngzhí downgrade

讲座 jiǎngzuò course; lecture

减号 jiǎnhào minus sign

简化 jiǎnhuà simplify

减缓 jiǎnhuǎn drop; ease off; slacken off

监护人 jiānhùrén guardian

剪辑 jiǎnjí clip; cutting; editing ◊ edit ◊

减价 jiǎnjià reduce the price; 减价 二十美元 *jiǎnjià èrshí měiyuán* knock $20 off

肩胛骨 jiānjiǎgǔ shoulder blade

渐渐 jiànjiàn gradually

尖叫 jiānjiào scream, shriek; yelp

建交 jiànjiāo establish diplomatic

relations

尖叫声 **jiānjiàoshēng** scream, screech

剪接 **jiǎnjiē** edit

简洁 **jiǎnjié** concise; lean

简介 **jiǎnjiè** blurb

间接 **jiànjiē** indirect ◊ indirectly

监禁 **jiānjìn** imprison; confine ◊ imprisonment; confinement

坚决 **jiānjué** determined, resolute; decided; strong; 坚决要求 **jiānjué yāoqiú** insist on

键卡 **jiànkǎ** keycard

健康 **jiànkāng** fit; healthy ◊ fitness; health; well-being, welfare ◊ be well

健康保险 **jiànkāng bǎoxiǎn** health insurance

健康检查 **jiànkāng jiǎnchá** checkup

健康食品 **jiànkāng shípǐn** health food

健康食品店 **jiànkāng shípǐndiàn** health food store

健康证书 **jiànkāng zhèngshū** medical certificate

尖刻 **jiānkè** cutting; bitter; harsh

艰苦 **jiānkǔ** difficult; strenuous

尖利 **jiānlì** sharp; piercing

建立 **jiànlì** establish, set up, found

建立桥梁 **jiànlì qiáoliáng** bridge gap

尖利声 **jiānlìshēng** screech

简陋 **jiǎnlòu** primitive, crude; humble

溅落 **jiànluò** splash down

减慢 **jiǎnmàn** slow down

健美锻炼 **jiànměi duànliàn** bodybuilding

见面 **jiànmiàn** meet

简明 **jiǎnmíng** concise

艰难 **jiānnán** difficult ◊ difficulty; hardship

艰难行走 **jiānnán xíngzǒu** plod

键盘 **jiànpán** keyboard

剪票 **jiǎnpiào** punch a ticket

简朴 **jiǎnpǔ** austere

柬埔寨 **Jiǎnpǔzhài** Cambodia ◊ Cambodian

拣起 **jiǎnqǐ** pick up

坚强 **jiānqiáng** strong; tough;

forceful

剪切 **jiǎnqiē** cut

减轻 **jiǎnqīng** alleviate; relieve; lighten; ease; soften; 减轻的情节 **jiǎnqīngde qíngjié** mitigating circumstances

减去 **jiǎnqù** minus ◊ subtract

尖儿 **jiānr** ace (in cards)

坚韧 **jiānrèn** tough; tenacious

键入 **jiànrù** key in, enter COMPUT

尖锐 **jiānruì** incisive; penetrating; pointed; sharp; shrill

尖锐刺耳 **jiānruì cì'ěr** strident

尖锐而深刻 **jiānruì ér shēnkè** searching

减弱 **jiǎnruò** die down; subside; moderate; shrink; wane ◊ muted

减色 **jiǎnsè** detract from

减少 **jiǎnshǎo** reduce; cut down; decline; dwindle ◊ reduction; 使减少 **shǐ jiǎnshǎo** diminish; deaden

建设 **jiànshè** build; construct; develop ◊ construction; development

健身 **jiànshēn** keep fit

尖声说出 **jiānshēng shuōchū** shriek

健身俱乐部 **jiànshēn jùlèbù** health club

健身中心 **jiànshēn zhōngxīn** fitness center

建设性 **jiànshè xìng** constructive

坚实 **jiānshí** solid

监视 **jiānshì** oversee; watch

见识 **jiànshí** experience; common sense

监视器 **jiānshìqì** monitor COMPUT

减速 **jiǎnsù** decelerate, slow down

尖酸刻薄 **jiānsuān kèbó** sour

尖塔 **jiāntǎ** spire, steeple

健谈 **jiàntán** talkative, chatty

剪贴板 **jiǎntiē bǎn** clipboard COMPUT

剪贴簿 **jiǎntiēbù** scrapbook

监听 **jiāntīng** listen to; listen in on; tap; bug

坚挺 **jiāntǐng** strong currency

简体字 **jiǎntǐzì** simplified characters

箭头 **jiàntóu** arrow; arrowhead

健忘 **jiànwàng** forgetful;

scatterbrained

奸污 **jiānwū** rape

见习 **jiànxí** become familiar with one's work; train

间隙 **jiànxì** gap

尖笑 **jiānxiào** smirk

尖啸 **jiānxiào** wail

减小 **jiǎnxiǎo** taper

见效 **jiànxiào** effective

尖啸声 **jiānxiàoshēng** wail

间歇 **jiànxiē** interval; lull

艰辛 **jiānxīn** suffering; hardship

减刑 **jiǎnxíng** commute a sentence

饯行 **jiànxíng** have a farewell meal

尖牙 **jiānyá** fang

检验 **jiǎnyàn** test

简要 **jiǎnyào** succinct

检疫 **jiǎnyì** quarantine

建议 **jiànyì** suggest, proposition ◊ suggestion, proposition; 一项建议 *yíxiàng jiànyì* a piece of advice; a proposal

坚硬 **jiānyìng** rigid; hard

监狱 **jiānyù** prison, jail; penitentiary

鉴于 **jiànyú** in view of

检阅 **jiǎnyuè** review *troops*

建造 **jiànzào** build, construct ◊ building, construction (*activity*); 在建造中 *zài jiànzào zhōng* under construction

见证人 **jiànzhèng rén** witness

减震器 **jiǎnzhènqì** shock absorber

减震装置 **jiǎnzhèn zhuāngzhì** suspension

兼职 **jiānzhí** moonlight

简直 **jiǎnzhí** simply; utterly; 简直是最好的 *jiǎnzhí shì zuìhǎode* it is simply the best; 简直了 *jiǎnzhí le!* amazing!

剪纸 **jiǎnzhǐ** paper cut

建筑 **jiànzhù** building; construction; architecture

健壮 **jiànzhuàng** robust

建筑工地 **jiànzhù gōngdì** construction site

建筑工人 **jiànzhù gōngrén** construction worker

建筑公司 **jiànzhù gōngsī** construction company

建筑区 **jiànzhù qū** built-up area

建筑师 **jiànzhù shī** architect

建筑物 **jiànzhùwù** structure

建筑学 **jiànzhù xué** architecture

建筑业 **jiànzhù yè** construction industry

尖子 **jiānzi** top

剪子 **jiǎnzi** scissors

胶 **jiāo** glue

教 **jiāo** teach

礁 **jiāo** reef

浇 **jiāo** pour; water

交 **jiāo** hand over; cross; 把X交给Y *bǎ X jiāogěi Y* send X to Y; 交朋友 *jiāo péngyǒu* make friends; 与X交朋友 *yǔ X jiāo péngyǒu* make friends with X

郊 **jiāo** suburbs

焦 **jiāo** burnt

嚼 **jiáo** chew

脚 **jiǎo** foot; bottom

角 **jiǎo** corner; horn; jiao (*Chinese money*)

搅 **jiǎo** stir

叫 **jiào** call; be called; summon; ask; draw, lead; 叫X帮忙 *jiào X bāngmáng* enlist the help of X; 叫X进去 *jià X jìnqù* send in X

较 **jiào** relatively

教 **jiào** teach ◊ religion

轿 **jiào** palanquin, sedan chair

校 **jiào** check; proofread

骄傲 **jiāo'ào** proud

骄傲自大 **jiāo'ào zìdà** arrogant

搅拌 **jiǎobàn** stir; whisk

搅拌器 **jiǎobànqì** mixer

脚背 **jiǎobèi** instep

脚本 **jiǎoběn** script

教鞭 **jiàobiān** pointer

胶布 **jiāobù** adhesive tape

脚步 **jiǎobù** footstep

叫菜 **jiàocài** order *food*

窖藏 **jiàocáng** hoard

交叉 **jiāochā** cross, intersect

交叉道 **jiāochādào** interchange

交叉路口 **jiāochā lùkǒu** junction

交叉双腿 **jiāochā shuāngtuǐ** cross one's legs

轿车 **jiàochē** car

交出 **jiāochū** give in, hand in, surrender

搅打 **jiǎodǎ** whip

胶带 jiāodài adhesive tape

搅蛋器 jiǎodànqì egg whisk

教导 jiàodǎo civilize; educate; instruct ◊ instruction

脚灯 jiǎodēng footlights

焦点 jiāodiǎn focus; 在焦点上 **zài jiāodiǎn shang** be in focus

脚底板 jiǎodǐ bǎn sole

搅动 jiǎodòng stir; move

角度 jiǎodù angle

交锋 jiāofēng cross swords; fight

焦干 jiāogān parched; very dry

娇惯 jiāoguàn spoil (indulge)

叫喊 jiàohǎn shout, yell

搅和 jiǎohe blend in

胶合板 jiāohébǎn plywood

搅和机 jiǎohéjī blender

脚后跟 jiǎohòugēn heel

狡猾 jiǎohuá crafty; cunning; devious; sly

交换 jiāohuàn exchange, swap; barter; trade; 交换意见 **jiāohuàn yìjiàn** confer

教皇 jiàohuáng pope

教诲 jiàohuì explain; instruct ◊ explanation; instruction

交货 jiāohuò deliver goods

搅和 jiǎohuo mix

交货付款 jiāohuò fùkuǎn collect on delivery

交互式 jiāohùshì interactive

焦急 jiāojí anxious ◊ anxiety; 焦急等待 **jiāojí děngdài** be anxious for

交界 jiāojiè border (on)

铰接车 jiāojiēchē semi trailer

绞尽脑汁 jiǎojìn nǎozhī rack one's brains

焦距 jiāojù focal length

教具 jiàojù teaching aid

胶卷 jiāojuǎn film (for camera)

教科书 jiàokē shū textbook

交口称赞 jiāokǒu chēngzàn rave review

教练 jiàoliàn coach

较量 jiàoliàng compete; compare

教练员 jiàoliàn yuán trainer

交流 jiāoliú exchange; flow

交流电 jiāoliúdiàn alternating current

交流量 jiāoliú liàng traffic

角楼 jiǎolóu turret

焦虑 jiāolǜ agitation

焦虑不安 jiāolǜ bù'ān agitated

脚轮 jiǎolún caster

角落 jiǎoluò corner

角膜 jiǎomó cornea

酵母 jiàomǔ yeast

胶囊 jiāonáng capsule (of medicine)

娇嫩 jiāonèn tender; sensitive

教派 jiàopài denomination REL

交配 jiāopèi mate

脚蹼 jiǎopǔ flipper

娇气 jiāoqì squeamish; fragile

娇气包 jiāoqìbāo wimp

角球 jiǎoqiú corner (kick)

郊区 jiāoqū suburbs; outskirts ◊ suburban

教区牧师 jiàoqū mùshī vicar

教区牧师住所 jiàoqū mùshī zhùsuǒ vicarage

绞肉机 jiǎoròujī meat grinder

矫揉造作 jiǎoróu zàozuò affected

娇生惯养 jiāoshēng guànyǎng coddle

礁石 jiāoshí reef

教师 jiàoshī teacher

教室 jiàoshì classroom

教师培训 jiàoshī péixùn teacher training

教授 jiàoshòu professor

脚手架 jiǎoshǒujià scaffolding

教授职位 jiàoshòu zhíwèi chair (at university)

教书 jiào shū teach

浇水筒 jiāoshuǐtǒng watering can

教唆 jiàosuō instigate

脚踏车 jiǎotàchē bicycle

交谈 jiāotán talk, converse

焦炭 jiāotàn coke

教堂 jiàotáng church

教堂集会 jiàotáng jíhuì congregation

脚踏实地 jiǎotà shídì down-to-earth

交替 jiāotì alternate

教条 jiàotiáo doctrine; dogma

教条主义 jiàotiáo zhǔyì dogmatism ◊ dogmatic

交通 jiāotōng traffic

绞痛 jiǎotòng colic

交通标志 jiāotōng biāozhì traffic sign

交通部 Jiāotōng Bù Department of Transportation

交通岛 jiāotōng dǎo traffic island

交通堵塞 jiāotōng dǔsè traffic jam; gridlock

交通费用 jiāotōng fèiyòng travel expenses

交通工具 jiāotōng gōngjù means of transportation

交通警 jiāotōng jǐng traffic cop; traffic police

焦头烂额 jiāotóulàn'é stressed out

脚腕 jiǎowàn ankle

交往 jiāowǎng mingle; mix with; contact ◊ dealings; contract; association

交响乐 jiāoxiǎngyuè symphony

娇小 jiāoxiǎo petite

胶鞋 jiāoxié sneakers

矫形 jiǎoxíng orthopedic ◊ orthopedics

侥幸 jiǎoxìng lucky; 他侥幸得以逃生 tā jiǎoxìng déyǐ táoshēng he's lucky to be alive

叫醒 jiàoxǐng wake

绞刑架 jiǎoxíngjià gallows

矫形外科 jiǎoxíng wàikē orthopedics; orthopedic surgery

教学 jiàoxué teaching

教训 jiàoxun lesson; moral; 教训 X jiàoxun X teach X a lesson

教养 jiàoyǎng upbringing; manners; breeding ◊ bring up; train

校样 jiàoyàng proof (of book)

交易 jiāoyì deal; transaction ◊ transact

交易会 jiāoyìhuì trade fair

脚印 jiǎoyìn footprint

交易所 jiāoyìsuǒ exchange

郊游 jiāoyóu excursion

教育 jiàoyù education ◊ educational ◊ educate

教员 jiàoyuán teacher

教员室 jiàoyuán shì staffroom

教育学 jiàoyùxué (the study of) education

焦躁 jiāozào harassed

交战 jiāozhàn (military) engagement ◊ fight ◊ belligerent

矫正 jiǎozhèng correct; adjust

校正 jiàozhèng correct ◊ correction

脚指 jiǎozhǐ toe

浇铸 jiāozhù cast; mold

脚注 jiǎozhù footer; footnote

骄子 jiāozǐ very talented person; whizzkid

饺子 jiǎozi Chinese dumpling

叫做 jiàozuò be called

家谱 jiāpǔ family tree

假期 jiàqī vacation; leave

加强 jiāqiáng intensify; reinforce; strengthen

家禽 jiāqín poultry (birds)

家禽肉 jiāqínròu poultry (meat)

加燃料 jiā ránliào refuel

加热 jiārè heat up

家人 jiārén family members

加热器 jiārèqì stove

假日 jiàrì (public) holiday

加入 jiārù add; join; 加入国籍 jiārù guójí become naturalized; 加入交易 jiārù jiāoyì come in on a deal

加上 jiāshàng add on ◊ plus; 加上一层 jiāshàng yìcéng cover, coat

假设 jiǎshè suppose ◊ assuming ◊ hypothesis ◊ hypothetical

加深 jiāshēn deepen

夹生 jiāshēng half-done

假释 jiǎshì parole; 获得假释 huòdé jiǎshì be on parole

驾驶 jiàshǐ drive; steer; fly; sail ◊ driving; driver; 左/右座驾驶 zuǒ/yòu zuò jiàshǐ left-/right-hand drive

驾驶船 jiàshǐchuán sail a boat

驾驶教练 jiàshǐ jiàoliàn driving instructor

驾驶机构 jiàshǐ jīgòu steering

驾驶室 jiàshǐ shì cab (of truck)

驾驶台 jiàshǐ tái bridge

驾驶学校 jiàshǐ xuéxiào driving school

驾驶学员 jiàshǐ xuéyuán beginner driver

驾驶员 jiàshǐ yuán driver

驾驶执照 jiàshǐ zhízhào driver's license

家属 jiāshǔ family members; household

加速 jiāsù accelerate; speed up ◊ acceleration

家庭 jiātíng family ◊ domestic

家庭妇女 jiātíng fùnǚ housewife

家庭录像 jiātíng lùxiàng home movie

家庭医生 jiātíng yīshēng family doctor

家庭主妇 jiātíng zhǔfù housewife

家庭作业 jiātíng zuòyè homework

家兔 jiātù rabbit

家务 jiāwù housework; chores

家务管理 jiāwù guǎnlǐ housekeeping

家务开消 jiāwù kāixiāo housekeeping (money)

家乡 jiāxiāng home; home town

假想 jiǎxiǎng imaginary, make-believe

加楔儿 jiāxiēr shove in

假惺惺 jiǎxīngxīng hypocritical ◊ hypocritically

假牙 jiǎyá dentures, false teeth

家用电脑 jiāyòng diànnǎo home computer

家用器械 jiāyòng qìxiè (household) appliance

加油 jiāyóu fill up; refuel; oil; come on!; go!

加油站 jiāyóuzhàn gas station

家喻户晓 jiāyù hùxiǎo household name

加载 jiāzài upload COMPUT

家长 jiāzhǎng head of household; parent

家长主义 jiāzhǎng zhǔyì paternalism

家长作风 jiāzhǎng zuòfēng paternalistic

假正经 jiǎzhèngjing prude ◊ prudish

假肢 jiǎzhī artificial limb

价值 jiàzhí value; worth; 价值上升／下降 jiàzhí shàngshēng／xiàjiàng rise／fall in value

jiàzhí kǎoshì driving test 驾驶

考试

加重 jiāzhòng become heavier; deepen

假装 jiǎzhuāng pretend; (play)act; make believe; put on ◊ masquerade

甲状腺 jiǎzhuàngxiàn thyroid gland

假珠宝 jiǎ zhūbǎo costume jewelry

夹竹桃 jiāzhútáo oleander

夹子 jiāzi clip; clamp; clasp

架子 jiàzi stand; frame; shelf; airs

家族 jiāzú clan

鸡巴 jībā ∨ prick

击败 jībài beat, defeat; overpower

基本 jīběn basic, fundamental; main; essential ◊ foundation ◊ basically

基本利率 jīběn lìlǜ base rate

基本上 jīběnshang basically; essentially

基本原理 jīběn yuánlǐ basic principles

基本知识 jīběn zhīshi basic knowledge

级别 jíbié rank; level

级别条纹 jíbié tiáowén stripe (indicating rank)

疾病 jíbìng disease; illness; sickness

既不 ... 也不 ... jìbù ... yěbù ... neither ... nor ...

机场 jīchǎng airport; airfield

继承 jìchéng inherit; 剥夺继承权 bōduó jìchéng quán disinherit

计程表 jìchéngbiǎo meter; taxi meter

计程车 jìchéngchē taxi

计程车司机 jìchéngchē sījī taxi driver

集成电路 jíchéng diànlù integrated circuit

继承人 jìchéngrén heir

急冲 jíchōng dash

基础 jīchǔ basis; foundation; 以 ... 为基础 yǐ ... wéi jīchǔ base on; be based on

挤出 jǐchū squeeze out

基础工作 jīchǔ gōngzuò

groundwork

基础结构 **jīchǔ jiégòu** infrastructure

击打 **jīdǎ** beat; hit; punch

即达 **jídá** incoming

极大 **jídà** enormous

鸡蛋 **jīdàn** egg

鸡蛋杯 **jīdànbēi** eggcup

击倒 **jīdǎo** knock out; flatten ◊ knockout

记得 **jìde** remember

基地 **jīdì** base

激动 **jīdòng** excite; inflame ◊ feverish; impassioned

机动 **jīdòng** flexible

机动车 **jīdòngchē** motor vehicle

激动人心 **jīdòng rénxīn** stirring

基督 **Jīdū** Christ ◊ Christian

嫉妒 **jídù** jealousy ◊ be jealous; envy; be envious

极度 **jídù** extreme; utmost ◊ extremely

忌妒 **jìdu** envy ◊ envious

季度 **jìdù** quarter; quarterly

极端 **jíduān** drastic; extreme; unbelievable ◊ exceedingly

极端主义者 **jíduānzhǔyì zhě** extremist

基督教 **Jīdūjiào** Christianity ◊ Christian

基督徒 **Jīdū tú** Christian

饥饿 **jī'è** starvation; hunger ◊ hungry

街 **jiē** street

接 **jiē** contact; join; call for, collect; pick up; fetch; catch

结 **jiē** bear *fruit*

揭 **jiē** take off *lid*

阶 **jiē** steps; stairs

结 **jié** knot

节 **jié** festival; knot; verse ◊ *measure word for sections, lengths*; 一节竹子 **yìjié zhúzi** a length of bamboo

解 **jiě** untie

姐 **jiě** older sister

借 **jiè** borrow; lend ◊ loan; 借个手，行吗？ **jiè gè shǒu, xíng ma?** can you lend me a hand?; 借给 X Y **jiègěi X Y** lend X to Y

戒 **jiè** cut out; give up

界 **jiè** border; limit

结巴 **jiēba** stammer; stutter

接班人 **jiēbān rén** successor

戒备 **jièbèi** vigilance ◊ vigilant

结冰 **jiébīng** freeze; ice up

阶层 **jiēcéng** (social) class

截查 **jiéchá** intercept

结肠 **jiécháng** bowels; colon

劫车 **jiéchē** hijack a car

劫车者 **jiéchē zhě** carjacker

劫持 **jiéchí** hijack; abduct

接触 **jiēchù** contact ◊ touch

杰出 **jiéchū** brilliant, outstanding; eminent

解除 **jiěchú** take away

戒除 **jièchú** remove; get rid off; kick *habit*; 解除武装 **jiěchú wǔzhuāng** disarm ◊ disarmament

揭穿 **jiēchuān** expose ◊ exposure

介词 **jiècí** preposition

结余 **jiéyú** balance FIN

解答 **jiědá** solution; answer; reply

接待 **jiēdài** greet; receive

接待处 **jiēdài chù** reception (area)

接待员 **jiēdài yuán** receptionist; desk clerk

街道 **jiēdào** street

街灯 **jiēdēng** streetlight

解冻 **jiědòng** defrost; thaw

戒毒 **jièdú** withdrawal (*from drugs*)

街段 **jiēduàn** block

阶段 **jiēduàn** phase, stage

截短 **jiéduǎn** cut short, curtail

解毒药 **jiědúyào** antidote

揭发 **jiēfā** uncover; discover

解放 **jiěfàng** liberate ◊ emancipated ◊ liberation; emancipation; the 1949 Communist victory in China

借方 **jièfāng** debit ◊ debtor

解放军 **Jiěfàngjūn** People's Liberation Army, PLA; PLA soldier

姐夫 **jiěfu** brother-in-law (*elder sister's husband*)

结构 **jiégòu** structure

解雇 **jiěgù** dismiss, sack; lay off ◊ dismissal

接管 **jiēguǎn** take charge, take over

结果 **jiéguǒ** result, outcome ◊ end

up; put away

结核病 jiéhébìng tuberculosis, TB

结合器 jiéhé qì adapter

结婚 jiéhūn marry; get married; 跟 X 结婚 **gēn X jiéhūn** get married to X

结婚公告 jiéhūn gōnggào banns

结婚戒指 jiéhūn jièzhǐ wedding ring

结婚礼服 jiéhūn lǐfú wedding gown

结婚证书 jiéhūn zhèngshū marriage certificate

结婚周年 jiéhūn zhōunián wedding anniversary

劫机 jiéjī hijack a plane

阶级 jiējí (social) class; 阶级斗争 **jiējí dòuzhēng** class warfare

截击 jiéjī intercept *missile*

节俭 jiéjiǎn economic ◊ economically

街角 jiējiǎo street corner

结交 jiéjiāo associate with

姐姐 jiějie older sister

结结巴巴 jiējie bābā broken *English etc*

接近 jiējìn near ◊ access ◊ verge on

竭尽 jiéjìn exhaust; use up; 竭尽 所能 **jiéjìn suǒnéng** do one's utmost

洁净 jiéjìng clean; pure

捷径 jiéjìng short cut

解救 jiéjiù extricate

戒酒 jiéjiǔ give up alcohol; be on the wagon

劫机者 jiéjī zhě hijacker

结局 jiéjú outcome; ending

借据 jièjù IOU

解决 jiéjué solve; settle *dispute*; sort out *problem* ◊ fix; settlement

解开 jiékāi undo; loosen; unfasten; 解开纽扣 **jiékāi niǔkòu** unbutton

捷克 Jiékè Czech

捷克共和国 Jiékè Gònghéguó Czech Republic

借口 jièkǒu excuse; pretext

结块 jiékuài clot (*of blood*)

解缆 jiělǎn cast off

接连不断 jiēlián búduàn successive; 接连五天 **jiēlián wǔ**

tiān 5 days in a row

接力赛 jiēlì sài relay (race)

节流阀 jiéliú fá throttle (*on motorbike etc*)

揭露 jiēlù expose; reveal

节录 jiélù excerpt

睫毛 jiémáo eyelash

睫毛膏 jiémáogāo mascara

姐妹 jiěmèi sisters; 同父异母姐 妹 **tóngfù yìmǔ jiěmèi**, 同母异父 姐妹 **tóngmǔ yìfù jiěmèi** stepsister

界面 jièmiàn interface

解密码 jiě mìmǎ decipher

芥末 jièmò mustard

结膜炎 jiémó yán conjunctivitis

揭幕 jiēmù unveil

节目 jiémù program; show; 今晚 有什么节目？ **jīnwǎn yǒu shén-me jiémù?** what's on tonight?

节目表 jiémù biǎo listings magazine

节目单 jiémùdān program

接纳 jiēnà admit

节能 jiénéng save energy ◊ energy-saving

节拍 jiépāi rhythm; beat

解剖 jiěpōu dissect ◊ dissection; anatomy

揭起 jiēqǐ take up

截球 jiéqiú tackle SP

接球者 jiēqiú zhě receiver SP

接壤 jiērǎng border (on)

截然相反 jiérán xiāngfǎn contrasting; diametrically opposed

节日 jiérì festival; (public) holiday

吉尔吉斯 Jíěrjísī Kyrgyzstan ◊ Kirg(h)iz

介入 jièrù intervene ◊ intervention; 他不想介入 **tā bùxiǎng jièrù** he won't have anything to do with it

街上 jiēshang in the street

介绍 jièshào introduce ◊ introduction; profile; 我来介绍 一下 … **wǒ lái jièshào yíxià …** may I introduce …?; 向 X 介绍 Y **xiàng X jièshào Y** brief X on Y

介绍信 jièshào xìn testimonial

节省 jiéshěng economize on;

save; stint on ◊ economy; saving ◊ economical

节省时间 **jiéshěng shíjiān** timesaving

结实 **jiēshí** sturdy; firm

解释 **jiěshì** explain; account for; interpret; rationalize ◊ explanation

接收 **jiēshōu** receive

接手 **jiēshǒu** take over ◊ catcher SP

接受 **jiēshòu** accept; take; receive; admit ◊ acceptance; 接受手术治疗 **jiēshòu shǒushù zhìliáo** undergo surgery; 我接受你的提议 **wǒ jiēshòu nǐde tíyì** I'll take you up on your offer; 接受 X 的意见 **jiēshòu X de yìjiàn** take X's advice

接收力 **jiēshōu lì** reception (for TV etc)

接收人 **jiēshōu rén** recipient

结束 **jiēshù** end, finish, conclude; put an end to

结算 **jiésuàn** balance the books; settle bill

结算单 **jiésuàn dān** (bank) statement

阶梯 **jiētī** step; stairs

接替 **jiētī** replace; relieve

解体 **jiětǐ** disintegrate

接通 **jiētōng** connect; put through

接通电源 **jiētōng diànyuán** plug in

解脱开 **jiětuō kāi** disentangle

结网 **jiéwǎng** spin web

结尾 **jiéwěi** conclusion, end

接吻 **jiēwěn** kiss

接下来 **jiēxiàlái** succeeding

界限 **jièxiàn** border; parameter

接线生 **jiēxiàn shēng** operator

戒严令 **jièyánlìng** martial law

解压缩 **jiě yāsuō** unzip COMPUT

介意 **jièyì** mind, object; object to; 我抽烟你介意吗？**wǒ chōuyān nǐ jièyì ma?** would you mind if I smoked?

解疑屏幕 **jiěyí píngmù** help screen

借用 **jièyòng** borrow ◊ on loan

节育 **jiéyù** birth control

节约 **jiéyuē** economize; save ◊

thrift ◊ thrifty; cost-conscious

解约 **jiěyuē** cancel a contract

节约行动 **jiéyuē xíngdòng** economy drive

结扎 **jiēzā** sterilize

结账 **jiézhàng** checkout ◊ check out; settle an account; pay the bill

结账时间 **jiézhàng shíjiān** checkout time

接着 **jiēzhe** following

节肢 **jiézhī** amputate

节制 **jiézhì** moderation, restraint

戒指 **jièzhǐ** ring (on finger)

接种 **jiēzhòng** vaccinate; inoculate ◊ vaccination; inoculation; 接种 X 疫苗 **jiēzhòng X yìmiáo** be vaccinated against X

接种疫苗 **jiēzhòng yìmiáo** vaccinate

接住 **jiēzhù** catch

疖子 **jiēzi** boil

节奏 **jiézòu** rhythm; beat

杰作 **jiézuò** masterpiece

激发 **jīfā** arouse; work up

记分 **jìfēn** (keep the) score

讥讽 **jīfěng** sarcasm ◊ sarcastic

季风 **jìfēng** monsoon

季风雨季 **jìfēng yǔjì** monsoon season

记分员 **jìfēnyuán** scorer

继父 **jìfù** stepfather

挤干 **jǐgān** squeeze dry

及格 **jígé** pass (in exam)

几个 **jǐge** a few, several; how many?

及格分 **jígéfēn** pass mark

技工 **jìgōng** mechanic; skilled worker

机构 **jīgòu** organization; institution; structure; mechanism

籍贯 **jíguàn** home; birthplace

激光 **jīguāng** laser

激光唱片 **jīguāng chàngpiàn** compact disc

激光打印机 **jīguāng dǎyìn jī** laser printer

激光光束 **jīguāng guāngshù** laser beam

极好 **jí hǎo** fabulous, swell, marvelous

记号 **jìhao** mark, sign

集合 **jíhé** meet; assemble;

combine; pool ◊ set MATH

记恨 jìhèn bear a grudge

几何学 jǐhéxué geometric ◊ geometrical

几乎 jǐhū almost

激化 jīhuà intensify; increase

计划 jìhuà plan; project; figure on; structure ◊ planning; program; project

计划表 jìhuàbiǎo schedule

极坏 jíhuài rotten

饥荒 jīhuāng famine

计划生育 jìhuà shēngyù family planning; birth control; one child policy

击毁 jīhuǐ destroy

机会 jīhuì opportunity, chance

集会 jíhuì meeting; assembly; rally; function

积极 jījí active; dynamic; positive; energetic

击剑 jījiàn fencing

即将 jíjiāng about to; on the brink of ◊ soon

即将来临 jíjiāng láilín upcoming

计件工作 jìjiàn gōngzuò piecework

寄件人 jìjiànrén sender

集结 jíjié mass

季节 jìjié season

积极分子 jījí fènzi activist; militant

唧唧叫 jījī jiào chirp

基金 jījīn fund

激进 jījìn radical

挤紧 jǐjǐn squeeze up

挤 jǐ jìn jam, squeeze

机警 jījǐng on the ball; alert

寂静 jìjìng quiet

基金会 jījīnhuì foundation

激进主义 jījìn zhǔyì radicalism

激进主义者 jījìn zhǔyì zhě radical

急救 jíjiù first aid

急救箱 jíjiùxiāng first-aid box, first-aid kit

积极性 jījíxìng initiative; dynamism; activity

积累 jīlèi build-up ◊ build up, mount up

急剧 jíjù rapid; abrupt

即刻 jíkè immediate, instantaneous ◊ immediately; instantly; momentarily

疾苦 jíkǔ suffering

系牢 jìláo do up

积累 jīlěi accumulate; pile up

激励 jīlì boost; spur; stimulation;

激励 ... 前进 jīlì ... qiánjìn spur on

吉利 jílì fortunate; favorable; lucky

剂量 jìliàng dose

脊梁骨 jǐliáng gǔ backbone; spine

计量器 jìliángqì gauge

激烈 jīliè intense; fierce; heated

机灵 jīling smart; sharp; nimble

急流 jíliú rapids; torrent

纪录 jìlù record; note ◊ minutes; log; 纪录保持者 jìlù bǎochí zhě record holder

纪律 jìlù discipline

击落 jīluò shoot down

纪录片 jìlù piān documentary

记录 X jìlù X keep track of X

挤满 jǐmǎn be full of

急忙 jímáng hurried; in a hurry

机密 jīmì classified; confidential; top secret

机敏 jīmǐn quickwitted

寂寞 jìmò lonely

计谋 jìmóu trick

继母 jìmǔ stepmother

金 jīn gold; golden

津 jīn ford; ferry crossing

巾 jīn cloth

今 jīn now; today; the present

筋 jīn tendon

斤 jīn jin (500 grams)

紧 jǐn tight; tense; taut

锦 jǐn brocade

仅 jǐn only

尽 jǐn furthest; 尽里面 jǐn lǐmiàn back; very back; furthest back

尽 jìn exhaust; try one's best ◊ exhausted; finished ◊ to the limit

近 jìn close, near

进 jìn go in; enter; 请进 ! qǐngjìn! come in!

禁 jìn prohibit

劲 jìn strength; energy

浸 jìn soak

缉拿 jīná manhunt

挤奶 jǐnǎi milk

金边儿股票 **jīnbiānr gǔpiào** gilts

锦标旗 **jǐnbiāoqí** pennant

锦标赛 **jǐnbiāo sài** championship; tournament

进步 **jìnbù** advance; progress ◊ progressive

惊呆 **jīngdāi** bowl over, amaze

禁不住 **jīnbúzhù** can't help; 我禁不住笑了 **wǒ jīnbúzhù xiàole** I couldn't help laughing

进餐时间 **jìncān shíjiān** mealtime

进程 **jìnchéng** proceedings; course; process

紧凑 **jǐncòu** tight *timing*; compact; terse

禁得住 **jīndezhù** withstand

禁地 **jìndì** restricted area

筋斗 **jīndǒu** somersault

金额 **jīn'é** amount

技能 **jìnéng** technique; skills; knowhow

金发 **jīnfà** blond hair

谨防 **jǐnfáng** be wary of

劲风 **jìnfēng** high wind

茎 **jīng** stem

鲸 **jīng** whale

京 **jīng** capital city

惊 **jīng** alarm; surprise

精 **jīng** essence; spirit; seed; semen ◊ refined; excellent

晶 **jīng** crystal

经 **jīng** warp; longitude ◊ experience

井 **jǐng** well (*for water*)

警 **jǐng** warn ◊ alarm; police

景 **jǐng** landscape; scenery

颈 **jǐng** neck; throat

净 **jìng** clean; net

境 **jìng** border

镜 **jìng** mirror

静 **jìng** quiet

敬 **jìng** respect ◊ respectful

径 **jìng** path; diameter

紧盖器 **jǐn'gàiqì** fastener

金刚石 **jīngāngshí** diamond

警报 **jǐngbào** alarm; alert

胫部 **jìngbù** shin

精彩 **jīngcǎi** wonderful

警察 **jǐngchá** police; police oficer

警察国家 **jǐngchá guójiā** police state

警察纠捕队 **jǐngchá jiūbǔ duì** vice squad

警察局 **jǐngchájú** police station, station house

经常 **jīngcháng** often ◊ frequent; habitual

精打细算 **jīngdǎ xìsuàn** be on a budget

境地 **jìngdì** situation; position

静电 **jìngdiàn** static electricity

经典作品 **jīngdiǎn zuòpǐn** classic

经度 **jīngdù** longitude

精读课 **jīngdúkè** intensive course

惊愕 **jīng'è** stupefied

警方 **jǐngfāng** police

警告 **jǐnggào** warn ◊ warning

胫骨 **jìnggǔ** shin; shinbone

警官 **jǐngguān** police officer

警棍 **jǐnggùn** nightstick

经过 **jīngguò** pass by; pass ◊ past; by; via; through

精华 **jīnghuá** essence; goodness

净化 **jìnghuà** purify

惊慌 **jīnghuāng** alarmed ◊ get alarmed

惊惶失措 **jīnghuāng shīcuò** panic-stricken

静火山 **jìng huǒshān** dormant volcano

经济 **jīngjì** economy ◊ economic; economical

竞技 **jìngjì** athletics; sports

精简 **jīngjiǎn** abridge

惊叫 **jīngjiào** exclaim

经济舱 **jīngjìcāng** economy class

警戒 **jǐngjiè** warn

警戒线 **jǐngjiè xiàn** cordon

经济紧缩 **jīngjì jǐnsuō** austerity

井井有条 **jǐngjǐng yǒutiáo** in good trim; in order

经济气候 **jīngjì qìhòu** economic climate

经济情况 **jīngjì qíngkuàng** economics; financial circumstances

经纪人 **jīngjì rén** broker; middleman

经济上 **jīngjì shang** economically; in financial terms

经济特区 **jīngjì tèqū** special economic zone, SEZ

经济学 **jīngjìxué** economics

(subject)

经济学家 jīngjìxuéjiā economist

京剧 Jīngjù Peking Opera

警觉 jǐngjué alert

惊恐 jīngkǒng consternation; scare

净空高度 jìngkōng gāodù headroom

镜框 jìngkuàng frame (of picture, glasses)

境况 jìngkuàng circumstances

经理 jīnglǐ manager

经历 jīnglì experience; background ◊ go through

精力 jīnglì energy; drive

敬礼 jìnglǐ salute

精力充沛 jīnglì chōngpèi dynamic; vigorous; inexhaustible ◊ nervous energy

痉挛 jìngluán cramp

静脉 jìngmài vein

静脉内 jìngmàinèi intravenous

静脉曲张 jìngmài qūzhāng varicose vein

精美 jīngměi exquisite, beautiful

精密 jīngmì precise; accurate; sophisticated, complex

精明 jīngmíng clever; ingenious; calculating; shrewd ◊ ingenuity

进攻 jìngōng advance MIL; charge

惊跑 jīngpǎo stampede

敬佩 jìngpèi respect

精辟 jīngpì profound

惊奇 jīngqí amazement, surprise; wonder ◊ be amazed

精确 jīngquè precise; rigorous ◊ precisely ◊ precision

井然 jǐngrán neat; proper

惊人 jīngrén amazing, mind-boggling, breathtaking ◊ phenomenally

竞赛 jìngsài race; racing ◊ run

径赛 jìngsài track event; athletics meeting

景色 jǐngsè scenery

精神 jīngshen vigor; energy ◊ lively; vigorous; smart

精神 jīngshén soul; spirit; mind; essence ◊ mental; 精神好 / 坏 **jīngshén hǎo / huài** be in good / poor spirits

精神崩溃 jīngshén bēngkuì nervous breakdown

精神变态者 jīngshén biàntài zhě psychopath

精神病 jīngshénbìng mental illness ◊ psychiatric

精神病学 jīngshénbìngxué psychiatry

精神病院 jīngshénbìngyuàn mental hospital

精神错乱 jīngshén cuòluàn demented

精神分裂 jīngshén fēnliè schizophrenic

精神分裂症 jīngshén fēnlièzhèng schizophrenia

精神分裂症患者 jīngshén fēnlièzhèng huàn zhě schizophrenic

精神分析 jīngshén fēnxī psychoanalysis

精神分析学家 jīngshén fēnxīxuéjiā psychoanalyst

精神恍惚 jīngshén huǎnghū dreamy

精神科医生 jīngshénkē yīshēng psychiatrist

精神虐待 jīngshén nüèdài mental cruelty

精神失常 jīngshén shīcháng madness ◊ mentally disturbed

紧身套衫 jǐnshēn tàoshān sweater

经受 jīngshòu undergo; suffer

景泰蓝 jǐngtàilán cloisonné

惊叹 jīngtàn exclaim; admire; marvel at; 令人惊叹 **lìngrén jīngtàn** amazing; shattering

晶体 jīngtǐ crystal

警惕 jǐngtì alert ◊ watchful ◊ warily

惊跳 jīngtiào jump

晶体管 jīngtǐguǎn transistor

晶体管收音机 jīngtǐguǎn shōuyīnjī transistor radio

精通 jīngtōng be expert at; master ◊ impeccable; proficient ◊ mastery

精通世故 jīngtōng shìgù sophisticated

镜头 jìngtóu shot; scene;

photograph; lens

镜头盖 jìngtóu gài lens cover

尽管 jǐnguǎn although; despite, in spite of

尽管如此 jǐnguǎn rúcǐ all the same, nevertheless

警卫 jǐngwèi guard

紧握 jǐnwò clasp

精细 jīngxì meticulous; refined

惊吓 jīngxià fright ◊ frighten, scare; startle

惊险电影 jīngxiǎn diànyǐng thriller (movie)

惊险小说 jīngxiǎn xiǎoshuō thriller (novel)

经销 jīngxiāo distribute ◊ distribution

经销商 jīngxiāo shāng distributor

精心 jīngxīn carefully; nicely

精心制作 jīngxīn zhìzuò elaborate

精选 jīngxuǎn choice

竞选 jìngxuǎn run (for election)

竞选活动 jìngxuǎn huódòng election campaign

竞选人 jìngxuǎn rén contender

竞选总统 jìngxuǎn zǒngtǒng run for President

惊讶 jīngyà astonishment ◊ be astonished

经验 jīngyàn experience

敬仰 jìngyǎng admire; worship

精液 jīngyè sperm; semen

惊异 jīngyì stunned, amazed

敬意 jìngyì respect; deference; 表示敬意 biǎoshì jìngyì deferential; 令人惊异 lìngrén jìngyì stunning

精英 jīngyīng elite

经营 jīngyíng manage; operate; run ◊ running; trade; operations ◊ managerial

经营顾问 jīngyíng gùwèn management consultant

经由 jīngyóu by way of

鲸鱼 jīngyú whale

竞争 jìngzhēng compete; contend for ◊ competition; contest; rivalry

竞争对手 jìngzhēng duìshǒu competitor

竞争力很强 jìngzhēnglì competitive

竞争者 jìngzhēng zhě contender; rival; contestant

精致 jīngzhì delicate; fancy; exquisite ◊ delicacy

径直 jìngzhí straight

晶质玻璃 jīngzhì bōlí crystal

警钟 jǐngzhōng alarm

净重 jìngzhòng net weight

精子 jīngzǐ sperm

镜子 jìngzi mirror; glasses, specs

精子库 jīngzǐ kù sperm bank

今后 jīnhòu in future

进化 jìnhuà evolve ◊ evolution

金婚纪念 jīnhūn jìniàn golden wedding anniversary

纪念 jìniàn commemorate, mark ◊ memorial; 作为对X的纪念 zuòwéi duì X de jìniàn in memory of X

纪念碑 jìniànbēi memorial; monument

纪念品 jìniàn pǐn souvenir; memento

紧急 jǐnjí urgent; imperative ◊ urgency

晋级 jìnjí promotion

近郊 jìnjiāo environs

紧急出口 jǐnjí chūkǒu emergency exit

紧接着 jǐnjiēzhe in the wake of

仅仅 jǐnjǐn only; merely; barely; solely

紧急情况 jǐnjí qíngkuàng emergency

近几天 jìnjǐtiān the past few days

禁酒 jìnjiǔ dry

紧急着陆 jǐnjí zháoluò emergency landing

紧急状态 jǐnjí zhuàngtài state of emergency

尽可能 jìn kěnéng as far as possible; 尽可能最好 … jìn kěnéng zuìhǎo … the best possible …

进口 jìnkǒu import

进口商 jìnkǒushāng importer

金库 Jīnkù National Treasury

尽快 jìnkuài as soon as possible

近况如何？ jìnkuàng rúhé? how are things?

近来 jìnlái recent ◊ recently

尽力 jìnlì endeavor

尽量 jìnliàng as well as one can

尽量利用 jìnliàng lìyòng make the most of

尽力而为 jìnlì érwéi do one's best

尽力解决 jìnlì jiějué grapple with

紧邻 jǐnlín the immediate neighborhood

禁令 jìnlìng ban

浸满水 jìnmǎnshuǐ waterlogged

今年 jīnnián this year

金牌 jīnpái gold medal

浸泡 jìnpào soak; immerse ◊ infusion

筋疲力尽 jīnpí lìjìn exhaust; drain ◊ exhausted; shattered

紧迫 jǐnpò extremely urgent

谨启 jǐnqǐ yours sincerely

金枪鱼 jīnqiāng yú tuna

近亲繁殖 jìnqīn fánzhí inbreeding

进去 jìnqu go in

禁区 jìnqū no-go area

进取心 jìnqǔ xīn enterprise, initiative

金融 jīnróng finance ◊ financial

金融家 jīnróng jiā financier

金融市场 jīnróng shìchǎng money market

进入 jìnrù enter; get in ◊ entrance; entry

金色 jīnsè golden

紧身 jǐnshēn tight-fitting; skin-tight

谨慎 jǐnshèn careful, cautious; discreet ◊ caution; tact, delicacy

晋升 jìnshēng promote

紧身套衫 jǐnshēn tàoshān sweater; sweatshirt

紧身胸衣 jǐnshēn xiōngyī bodice

紧身衣 jǐnshēn yī body suit; leotard

近视 jìnshi shortsighted ◊ myopia

浸湿 jìnshī soak

禁食 jìnshí fast (not eating)

近视眼 jìnshìyǎn shortsighted ◊ myopia

金首饰商 jīnshǒushìshāng goldsmith

金属 jīnshǔ metal

金属器具 jīnshǔ qìjù hardware

金属丝 jīnshǔsī wire

金属网 jīnshǔwǎng wire netting

近似 jìnsì almost; roughly ◊ border on

金丝雀 jīnsīquè canary

紧缩开支 jǐnsuō kāizhī economize

今天 jīntiān today; 今天几号？jīntiān jǐhào? what's the date today?; 今天上午 jīntiān shàngwǔ this morning; 今天晚上 jīntiān wǎnshang this evening; 今天下午 jīntiān xiàwǔ this afternoon; 今天星期几？jīntiān xīngqī jǐ? what day is it today?; 今天早晨 jīntiān zǎochén this morning

津贴 jīntiē subsidy; allowance

尽头 jìntóu end

劲头 jìntóu enthusiasm

浸透 jìntòu soak (through), saturate

进退两难 jìntuì liǎngnán dilemma

激怒 jīnù incense, infuriate; provoke ◊ enraged

妓女 jìnǚ prostitute

继女 jìnǚ stepdaughter

今晚 jīnwǎn tonight

紧握 jǐnwò clutch; grip

进行 jìnxíng carry out; execute; progress, move on; 在进行中 zài jìnxíngzhōng be under way

进修 jìnxiū continue one's education

紧要 jǐnyào critical

紧要关头 jǐnyào guāntóu tension

襟翼 jīnyì flap

进一步 jìnyíbù a step further; further

金银丝 jīnyín sī tinsel

禁用 jìnyòng heavy-duty; long-lasting; hard-wearing

金鱼 jīnyú goldfish

禁运 jìnyùn embargo

尽早 jìnzǎo as early as possible

进站 jìn zhàn pull in, arrive

进展 jìnzhàn proceed, progress

紧张 jǐnzhāng nervous; tense; uptight; stressed ◊ get nervous;

get flustered; tense up ◊ nervousness; tension; 别紧张 *bié jǐnzhāng* take it easy!

紧张感 jǐnzhānggǎn suspense

紧张慌乱 jǐnzhāng huāngluàn be in a flap

禁止 jìnzhǐ ban, forbid, prohibit ◊ ban, prohibition; 禁止 X 做 Y *jìnzhǐ X zuò Y* forbid X to do Y

禁止入内 jìnzhǐ rùnèi no admittance; off limits

禁止停车 jìnzhǐ tíngchē no parking

禁止吸烟 jìnzhǐ xīyān no smoking

窘况 jiǒngkuàng predicament

窘迫 jiǒngpò poverty-stricken; in a predicament

麂皮 jǐpí chamois (leather)

鸡皮疙瘩 jīpí gēda gooseflesh; 他使我浑身起鸡皮疙瘩 *tā shǐwǒ húnshēn qǐ jīpí gēda* he gives me the creeps

祭品 jìpǐn sacrifice

击破 jīpò strike down; fell

急迫 jípò urgent

吉普车 jípǔchē jeep

吉普赛人 jípǔsài rén gipsy

激起 jīqǐ prompt; cause; excite; work up

机器 jīqì machine; machinery

极其 jíqí extremely

记起 jìqǐ recall; remember

机枪 jīqiāng machine gun

技巧 jìqiǎo skill; knack

急切 jíqiè eager

激情 jīqíng passion

机器人 jīqìrén robot

击球 jīqiú bat; strike *ball* ◊ batting

击球员 jīqiú yuán batter

寄去 jìqù send in, mail in

极权主义 jíquán zhǔyì totalitarian

既然 jìrán since

既然这样 jìrán zhèyàng in that case

急人 jírén frightening; worrying

继任 jìrèn succeed (*to office etc*)

继任人 jìrènrén successor

鸡肉 jīròu chicken (*meat*)

肌肉 jīròu muscle

肌肉发达 jīròu fādá muscular

机身 jīshēn fuselage

寄生虫 jìshēngchóng parasite; sponger, freeloader

及时 jíshí prompt; timely ◊ promptly; in time

即时 jíshí immediately

即使 jíshí even if

疾驶 jíshí speed

集市 jíshì market

几时 jǐshí when; what time

集市广场 jíshì guǎngchǎng market place

计时钟 jìshízhōng time clock (*in factory*)

棘手 jíshǒu tricky

奇数 jīshù odd number

技术 jìshù skill; technique; technology ◊ technological

计数 jìshù count

技术娴熟 jìshù xiánshú workmanlike

技术性 jìshù xìng technical

技术员 jìshùyuán technician

祭祀 jìsì sacrifice

激素 jīsù steroids

计算 jìsuàn calculate; count; budget for; allow

计算出 jìsuànchù figure out

计算机 jìsuànjī computer; calculator

计算结果 jìsuàn jiēguǒ calculation

计算机科学 jìsuànjī kēxué computer science

计算机科学家 jìsuànjī kēxué jiā computer scientist

计算器 jìsuàn qì calculator

寄宿生 jìsù shēng boarder (*at school*)

急速行驶 jísù xíngshí zoom, race

寄宿学校 jìsù xuéxiào boarding school

吉他 jítā guitar

祭坛 jìtán altar

集体 jítǐ collective

几天 jǐtiān a few days, a couple of days

集体精神 jítǐ jīngshén team spirit

集体抛售 jítǐ pāoshòu raid FIN

集体协定 jítǐ xiédìng collective

bargaining

集团 jítuán group; bloc ◊ corporate

鸡腿 jītuǐ drumstick (*chicken leg*)

击退 jītuì repel

阄儿 jiū 抓阄儿 *zhuǎjiūr* draw lots

酒 jiǔ alcoholic drink; liquor

九 jiǔ nine

久 jiǔ a long time

舅 jiù uncle (*mother's brother*); brother-in-law (*wife's brother*)

旧 jiù old; obsolete; former; threadbare

就 jiù right; directly; just; only; regarding; 就我而言 *jiù wǒ ér yán* as far as I'm concerned

救 jiù save; rescue

酒吧 jiǔbā bar

旧病复发 jiùbìng fùfā relapse ◊ have a relapse

韭菜 jiǔcài Chinese chives

纠察 jiūchá picket

纠察队 jiūchádùi picket

纠缠 jiūchán badger, pester

纠察线 jiūcháxiàn picket line

旧城区 jiùchéngqū inner city

臼齿 jiùchǐ molar

韭葱 jiǔcōng leek

酒店 jiǔdiàn bar; wineshop; restaurant

酒店伙计 jiǔdiàn huǒjì bartender

纠纷 jiūfēn dispute; quarrel

纠葛 jiūgé dispute; involvement

酒鬼 jiǔguǐ drunk; alcoholic

酒后开车 jiǔhòu kāichē drunk driving

救护车 jiùhùchē ambulance

旧货 jiùhuò second-hand goods

救急 jiùjí urgent

究竟 jiūjìng actually; at the end of the day; 你究竟在干什么? *nǐ jiūjìng zài gàn shénme?* what the hell are you doing?

酒精 jiǔjīng alcohol

酒精饮料 jiǔjīng yǐnliào liquor

舅舅 jiùjiu uncle (*mother's brother*)

救济院 jiùjìyuàn hospice

旧历 jiùlì Chinese lunar calendar

九龙 Jiǔlóng Kowloon

救命 jiùmìng save s.o.'s life ◊ help!

就寝 jiùqǐn go to bed

救球 jiùqiú save SP

救生 jiùshēng life-saving

救生圈 jiùshēng quān life belt

救生艇 jiùshēng tǐng lifeboat

救生衣 jiùshēng yī life jacket

救生员 jiùshēng yuán lifeguard

九十 jiǔshí ninety

就是 jiùshi exactly!

就事论事 jiùshìlùnshì *prov* call a spade a spade

就是说 jiùshìshuō that is to say

救世主 jiùshìzhǔ savior

灸术 jiǔshù moxibustion

九死一生 jiǔsǐyìshēng have a narrow escape

酒窝 jiǔwō dimple

酒席 jiǔxí banquet

就医 jiùyī go to the doctor

久远 jiǔyuǎn remote *ancestor*

九月 jiǔyuè September

纠正 jiūzhèng correct

纠正错误 jiūzhèng cuòwù put things right

就职 jiùzhí inauguration ◊ inaugural

就职仪式 jiùzhí yíshì induction ceremony

酒钻 jiǔzuàn corkscrew

就座 jiùzuò take a seat

就座勿动 jiùzuò wùdòng please remain seated

极为 jíwéi extremely

即位 jíwèi succeed ◊ succession

鸡尾酒 jīwěijiǔ cocktail

极微小 jíwēixiǎo microscopic

极限 jíxiàn limit; frontier

吉祥 jíxiáng lucky

挤向 jǐxiàng crowd

迹象 jìxiàng mark; pointer, sign

集线器 jíxiànqì hub COMPUT

讥笑 jīxiào scoff; laugh at

极小 jíxiǎo tiny; remote *possibility*

机械 jīxiè machinery; mechanism ◊ mechanical ◊ mechanically

机械化 jīxièhuà mechanize

机械装置 jīxiè zhuāngzhì mechanism

畸形 jīxíng freak; monstrosity ◊ misshapen; monstrous

疾行 jíxíng race; run

即兴 jíxìng improvise

急性 jíxìng acute *illness*

记性 jìxìng memory

鸡心领 jīxīn lǐng V-neck

继兄弟 jìxiōngdì stepbrother

积蓄 jīxù save up; keep ◊ savings

急需 jíxū be in urgent need of

继续 jìxù continue; go on; keep on; carry on; conduct

积雪 jīxuě snowy

积压 jīyā backlog

挤压 jǐyā press

鸡眼 jīyǎn corn (*on foot*)

给养 jǐyǎng provisions

技艺 jìyì skill; art; craft; workmanship

记忆 jìyì remember ◊ memory; recollection

记忆力 jìyìlì memory; 记忆力好 / 坏 jìyìlì hǎo / huài have a good / bad memory

基因 jīyīn gene

集邮 jíyóu stamp collecting

极右主义 jíyòu zhǔyì right-wing extremism

给予 jǐyǔ render; provide; give *answer*

基于 jīyú because of; on the basis of

机遇 jīyù chance; stroke of luck

积怨 jīyuàn rancor

纪元 jìyuán era, epoch

妓院 jìyuàn brothel

给予优先 jǐyǔ yōuxiān prioritize

记载 jìzǎi record

及早 jízǎo early; premature

急躁 jízào on edge

激增 jīzēng sudden increase; surge; explosion (*in population*)

机长 jīzhǎng captain (*of aircraft*)

记账 jìzhàng bookkeeping ◊ do the books; charge

记账人 jìzhàng rén bookkeeper

记者 jìzhě reporter; journalist

急诊医生 jízhěn yīshēng emergency doctor

记者招待会 jìzhě zhāodàihuì press conference

机制 jīzhì machine

机智 jīzhì tact; wit ◊ witty; resourceful

机智幽默 jīzhì yōumò wit

集中 jízhōng assemble; collect;

centralize; concentrate ◊ cluster; focus (*of attention*)

集中精力 jízhōng jīnglì concentrate

脊柱 jǐzhù spine; spinal column ◊ spinal

记住 jìzhù remember; memorize; 记住锁门 jìzhù suǒmén remember to lock the door

系住 jìzhù tie up

集装箱 jízhuāng xiāng container

集装箱船 jízhuāng xiāng chuán container ship

急转弯 jízhuǎnwān hairpin curve

脊椎 jǐzhuī vertebra; 有脊椎 yǒu jǐzhuī vertebrate

基准 jīzhǔn benchmark

髻子 jìzi bun (*in hair*)

继子 jìzǐ stepson

机组人员 jīzǔ rén yuán air crew

基座 jīzuò pedestal

拘 jū restrict

驹 jū foal

居 jū live; reside; occupy ◊ house; residence; 居要位 jū yàowèi have priority

局 jú department; office; game; set; situation

举 jǔ raise; hold up; elect ◊ act; deed

剧 jù drama; play; theater

锯 jù saw

聚 jù assemble; get together

巨 jù giant, huge

具 jù tool, utensil

句 jù sentence

据 jù according to; 据我所知 jù wǒ suǒzhī as far as I know, to the best of my knowledge

捐 juān donate; contribute

卷 juǎn roll; reel; coil ◊ curly, frizzy; 把 X 卷成球 bǎ X juǎn chéngqiú roll X into a ball

卷 juàn volume

圈 juàn pen; enclosure

卷尺 juǎnchǐ tape measure

卷发 juǎnfà curly hair

卷发卷 juǎnfà juǎn roller; tongs (*for hair*)

绢纺 juànfǎng silk spinning

卷角 juǎnjiǎo dog-eared

捐款 juānkuǎn donation;

捐款人 **juānkuǎn rén** contributor; donor

卷盘 **juǎnpán** spool

卷起来 **juǎn qǐlái** roll up; coil up

卷入 **juǎnrù** involvement; 卷入 X **juǎnrù X** get involved with X

捐献 **juānxiàn** contribute; donate ◊ contribution; donation

捐献者 **juānxiàn zhě** donor

卷心菜 **juǎnxīn cài** cabbage

捐赠 **juānzèng** donate; contribute

举办 **jǔbàn** organize; hold

具备 **jùbèi** own; have

剧本 **jùběn** (stage) play

聚苯乙烯 **jùběnyǐxī** polystyrene

剧变 **jùbiàn** upheaval

局部 **júbù** partial ◊ partially

剧场 **jùchǎng** theater

局促不安 **júcù bù'ān** feel ill at ease; squirm

举措 **jǔcuò** move

巨大 **jùdà** enormous, immense, vast; astronomical

锯掉 **jùdiào** saw off

蕨 **jué** fern

觉 **jué** sense; feel ◊ feeling

角 **jué** role

决 **jué** decide

掘 **jué** dig

绝 **jué** cut off ◊ absolute

绝版 **juébǎn** out of print

决不 **juébù** on no account, under no circumstances

决策者 **juécè zhě** mastermind; decision maker

觉察 **juéchá** perceive

觉得 **juéde** feel; think; 我觉得很冷 **wǒ juéde hěnlěng** I feel cold; 你觉得怎么样？ **nǐ juéde zěn-meyàng?** what do you make of it?

决定 **juédìng** decide, make up one's mind ◊ decision; resolution; 你来决定 **nǐ lái juédìng** you decide, it's up to you

决定性 **juédìng xìng** decisive, conclusive ◊ decidedly

决断力 **juéduànlì** judgment

绝对 **juéduì** absolute; total ◊ definitely, absolutely; 绝对不行！ **juéduì bùxíng!** no way!,

certainly not!

倔强 **juéjiàng** disobedient

绝交 **juéjiāo** sever relations; 我与 X绝交 **wǒ yǔ X juéjiāo** I'm through with X

绝经期 **juéjīngqī** menopause

绝密 **juémì** top secret

绝妙 **juémiào** sensational, tremendous; magic

掘起 **juéqǐ** dig up

诀窍 **juéqiào** knack

决赛 **juésài** decider; final SP; 参加决赛者 **cānjiā juésài zhě** finalist

角色 **juésè** part, role

绝食 **juéshí** hunger strike

爵士音乐 **juéshì yīnyuè** jazz

爵士乐队 **juéshì yuèduì** jazz band

决算 **juésuàn** balance (sheet)

掘土机 **juétǔjī** excavator

绝望 **juéwàng** despair

决心 **juéxīn** determination; resolution

决选 **juéxuǎn** shortlist

决议 **juéyì** decision; resolution

绝缘 **juéyuán** insulation

绝缘材料 **juéyuán cáiliào** insulation

绝缘胶布 **juéyuán jiāobù** friction tape

绝种 **juézhǒng** extinct ◊ extinction

撅嘴 **juēzuǐ** pout

句法 **jùfǎ** syntax

飓风 **jùfēng** hurricane

拒服兵役者 **jù fú bīngyì zhě** conscientious objector

鞠躬 **jūgōng** bow

聚光灯 **jùguāng dēng** spotlight

句号 **jùhào** period, full stop

聚合 **jùhé** meet (of committee)

菊花 **júhuā** chrysanthemum

聚会 **jùhuì** gathering; get-together

聚集 **jùjí** assemble; gather; congregate

聚焦于 **jùjiāo yú** focus on

拘谨 **jūjǐn** stiff; uptight; reserved

拘禁 **jūjìn** lock up

狙击手 **jūjīshǒu** sniper

拒绝 **jùjué** refusal; denial; rejection ◊ refuse; deny; reject; 拒绝参加 **jùjué cānjiā** boycott; refuse to take part in

锯开 jùkāi saw

俱乐部 jùlèbù club

距离 jùlí distance ◊ apart

剧烈 jùliè fierce; energetic; 剧烈的头痛 jùliè de tóutòng splitting headache

拘留 jūliú detain; intern ◊ detention; 被拘留 bèi jūliú in custody

居留 jūliú stay; reside

居留证 jūliúzhèng residence permit

聚氯乙烯 jùlǜyǐxī PVC

局面 júmiàn situation

居民 jūmín inhabitant; resident

锯末 jùmò sawdust

军 jūn army

均 jūn same; equal ◊ all; both

君 jūn king; gentleman ◊ you fml

郡 jùn county; prefecture (in old China)

军备 jūnbèi armament

均等 jūnděng equal ◊ equality

军队 jūnduì army; the military; the services; troops

军阀 jūnfá warlord

军官 jūnguān officer MIL

均衡 jūnhéng balance; equalize (pressure etc)

均衡饮食 jūnhéng yǐnshí balanced diet

军火 jūnhuǒ ammunition

军舰 jūnjiàn warship

军警 jūnjǐng military police

峻岭 jùnlǐng high mountains

军旗 jūnqí colors MIL

军人 jūnrén serviceman; soldier

军事 jūnshì military

军事法庭 jūnshì fǎtíng court martial

军事学院 jūnshì xuéyuàn military academy

军事装备 jūnshì zhuāngbèi military installation

军衔 jūnxián rank

均匀 jūnyún even, regular ◊ evenly

君主 jūnzhǔ monarch

君子 jūnzǐ gentleman

举起 jǔqǐ lift; put up; 举起手来！jǔqǐshǒulái! hands up!

巨人 jùrén giant

沮丧 jǔsàng dejected; depressed; downcast; frustrated; 令人沮丧 lìngrén jǔsàng dismal

居士 jūshì hermit

居首位 jū shǒuwèi take the lead

拘束 jūshù awkward; constrained; unnatural; 别拘束 bié jūshù make yourself at home

据说 … jùshuō … it is said that …; they say …; be supposed to …; 据说他在香港 jù shuō tā zài Xiānggǎng he is reported to be in Hong Kong; 据说这首诗是 … 所作 jùshuō zhèi shǒu shī shì … suǒzuò the poem has been attributed to …

具体 jùtǐ concrete; specific

具体细致 jùtǐ xìzhì in minute detail

巨头 jùtóu tycoon

据为己有 jùwéi jǐyǒu pocket

据悉 … jùxī … it has emerged that …

局限 júxiàn limit; confine ◊ limitation

举行 jǔxíng stage; organize; hold

句型 jùxíng sentence pattern

举行罢工 jǔxíng bàgōng go on strike

聚乙烯 jùyǐxī polyethylene

具有 jùyǒu own; have; 具有想象力 jùyǒu xiǎngxiànglì imaginative

剧院 jùyuàn theater; opera house

剧增 jùzēng increase suddenly

举止 jǔzhǐ conduct, behavior

举止不当 jǔzhǐbúdàng misbehave

举止粗鲁 jǔzhǐ cūlǔ ill-mannered

聚酯纤维 jùzhǐxiánwéi polyester

举重 jǔzhòng weightlifting

举重运动员 jǔzhòng yùndòngyuán weightlifter

居住 jūzhù live

居住者 jūzhù zhě occupant

橘子 júzi mandarin orange

句子 jùzi sentence GRAM

锯子 jùzi saw

剧作家 jùzuò jiā dramatist, playwright

K

卡 **kǎ** card

喀嚓声 **kāchāshēng** snap, click

卡车 **kǎchē** truck

卡车司机 **kǎchē sījī** truck driver, teamster

咖啡 **kāfēi** coffee

咖啡店 **kāfēi diàn** coffee shop

咖啡馆 **kāfēiguǎn** café

咖啡壶 **kāfēi hú** coffee pot

咖啡机 **kāfēi jī** coffee maker

咖啡因 **kāfēiyīn** caffeine

开 **kāi** open; turn on; start; drive; boil; write *check* ◊ (*away*): 离开 *líkāi* leave; 走开 *zǒukāi* go away; 开户 *kāi hù* open a bank account

揩 **kāi** wipe

开本 **kāiběn** format

开采 **kāicǎi** mine; mine for

开叉 **kāichà** slit

开车 **kāichē** drive (a car)

开除 **kāichú** expel; discharge ◊ expulsion

开创 **kāichuàng** initiate ◊ initiation

开大 **kāidà** turn up *volume*

开刀 **kāidāo** operate; perform surgery

开灯 **kāidēng** turn the light on

开动 **kāidòng** work (*of machine*)

开端 **kāiduān** start, beginning

开发 **kāifā** develop

开放政策 **kāifàng zhèngcè** open-door policy

开区 **kāifāqū** development area

开关 **kāiguān** switch

揩汗 **kāihàn** wipe away perspiration

开花 **kāihuā** bloom, blossom

开会 **kāihuì** hold a meeting; 他在开会 *tā zài kāihuì* he's in a meeting

开机 **kāijī** boot up

开奖 **kāijiǎng** draw; lottery result

开襟毛衣 **kāijīn máoyī** cardigan

开扣 **kāikòu** fly (*on pants*)

开阔 **kāikuò** extensive

开朗 **kāilǎng** open; clear; outgoing; cheerful

开门 **kāimén** open the door

开明 **kāimíng** enlighten ◊ progressive; enlightened

开幕 **kāimù** open; inaugurate; raise the curtain

开枪 **kāiqiāng** fire a gun

开球 **kāiqiú** kickoff ◊ kick off

开始 **kāishǐ** begin, start ◊ beginning ◊ initially

开始曲 **kāishǐqǔ** signature tune

开水 **kāishuǐ** boiled water

开庭 **kāitíng** sitting; hearing

开头 **kāitóu** start

开拓 **kāituò** pioneering; 开拓殖民地 *kāituò zhímíndì* colonize

开玩笑 **kāi wánxiào** joke; kid ◊ joking; 别开玩笑了! *bié kāi wánxiào le!* you can't be serious!, you must be joking!

开胃 **kāiwèi** appetizing

开胃酒 **kāiwèi jiǔ** aperitif

开胃品 **kāiwèi pǐn** appetizer

开小差 **kāi xiǎochāi** desert ◊ desertion

开心 **kāixīn** have a good time; 玩儿得很开心 *wánr de hěn kāixīn* it was great fun

凯旋 **kǎixuán** triumph

开演 **kāiyǎn** be on (*of program*)

开药方 **kāi yàofāng** prescribe

开业 **kāiyè** start a business

开账单 **kāi zhàngdān** bill, invoice

开着 **kāizhe** open

开支 **kāizhī** budget; expenditure; expenses

开走 **kāizǒu** drive

卡拉 OK **kǎlā OK** karaoke

卡路里 **kǎlùlǐ** calorie

刊 **kān** publication

砍 **kǎn** chop

看 **kàn** look at; see; watch; read; visit ◊ look, glance; 看电视 **kàn diànshì** watch television; 看天气吧 **kàn tiānqì ba** it depends on the weather; 我看是这样 **wǒ kàn shì zhèyàng** I suppose so; 我能看一下吗? **wǒ néng kàn yíxià ma?** can I have a look?

看病 **kànbìng** see a doctor

看不起 **kànbùqǐ** look down on, despise

刊出 **kānchū** publish

看穿 **kànchuān** see through

看待 **kàndài** view

砍刀 **kǎndāo** chopper

砍倒 **kǎndǎo** chop down

看得见 **kàndejiàn** be visible; show

砍掉 **kǎndiào** lop off

砍伐 **kǎnfá** fell *trees*

看法 **kànfǎ** view; belief; idea

康 **kāng** healthy

抗 **kàng** resist; fight

抗病毒程序 **kàng bìngdú chéngxù** antivirus program

康采恩 **kāngcǎi'ēn** group (of companies); concern

康复 **kāngfù** get well again; recuperate

抗菌 **kàngjūn** antiseptic

抗菌剂 **kàngjūnjì** antiseptic

抗菌素 **kàngjūnsù** antibiotic

慷慨 **kāngkǎi** generous; liberal; magnanimous

康乃馨 **kāngnǎixīn** carnation

抗热 **kàngrè** heatproof, heat-resistant

抗日战争 **Kàngrì Zhànzhēng** Anti-Japanese War

抗体 **kàngtǐ** antibody

看管 **kānguǎn** guard; look after

看管人 **kānguǎn rén** caretaker

抗议 **kàngyì** protest

看护 **kānhù** look after; nurse

看见 **kànjiàn** see; catch sight of, catch a glimpse of

看来 **kànlái** seemingly, it appears that ...; 在我看来 **zài wǒ kànlái** in my opinion

看门人 **kānmén rén** doorman; janitor

看起来 **kànqǐlái** seem, appear to be

看上去 **kànshàngqu** seemingly

看守 **kānshǒu** guard, lookout

勘探 **kāntàn** prospect for

看望 **kànwàng** visit

刊物 **kānwù** publication; periodical

看作 **kànzuò** regard as, look on as; 把 X 看作 Y **bǎ X kànzuò Y** regard X as Y

烤 **kǎo** barbecue; broil; roast; bake ◊ barbecued; broiled; roast; baked; 烤牛肉 **kǎo niúròu** roast beef; barbecued beef; 烤猪肉 **kǎo zhūròu** roast pork; barbecued pork

考 **kǎo** examine, test *student*; take *exam*; 考驾照 **kǎo jiàzhào** take one's driving test

靠 **kào** lean against; be near; rely on; 靠 ... 生活 **kào ... shēnghuó** live on, subsist on

靠岸 **kào'àn** dock

靠背 **kàobèi** back (of chair)

靠不住 **kàobuzhù** unreliable; deceptive; dubious; shady

考察 **kǎochá** inspect; explore

考查 **kǎochá** examine

靠窗座位 **kàochuāng zuòwei** window seat

靠垫 **kàodiàn** cushion

考古学 **kǎogǔ xué** archeology

考古学家 **kǎogǔ xué jiā** archeologist

靠近 **kàojìn** by, near

靠拢 **kàolǒng** move closer; close up

烤炉 **kǎolú** oven

考虑 **kǎolǜ** consider; think over ◊ consideration, thought

考虑不周 **kǎolǜ bùzhōu** inconsiderate

考虑到 **kǎolǜ dào** allow for, take account of; make allowances

考虑周到 **kǎolǜ zhōudào** discreet

烤面包 **kǎo miànbāo** toast

烤肉 **kǎoròu** roast; barbecue

考试 **kǎoshì** exam

考试卷 **kǎoshìjuàn** exam paper

烤土豆 **kǎo tǔdòu** baked potato

烤箱 **kǎoxiāng** oven

考验 **kǎoyàn** test

靠着 **kàozhe** lean on; rely on

卡片 **kǎpiàn** card

卡片目录 **kǎpiàn mùlù** card index

卡片钥匙 **kǎpiàn yàoshí** card key

卡通片 **kǎtōng piàn** cartoon

棵 **kē** *measure word for trees*; 一棵树 **yīkē shù** a tree

颗 **kē** *measure word for small round things*; 三颗米 **sānkē mǐ** three grains of rice

科 **kē** department

咳 **ké** cough

壳 **ké** shell

渴 **kě** thirst ◊ thirsty

可 **kě** can; may ◊ -able; 可变 **kěbiàn** changeable; variable

刻 **kè** carve ◊ quarter of an hour; 五点一刻 **wǔdiǎn yīkè** quarter after 5

课 **kè** class; lesson; subject

克 **kè** gram

客 **kè** guest

可爱 **kě'ài** delightful; lovable; cute

刻板 **kèbǎn** rigid

可悲 **kěbēi** pathetic

课本 **kèběn** textbook

可鄙 **kěbǐ** pitiful

可变 **kěbiàn** changeable; variable

可辨认出 **kě biànrèn chū** discernible

刻薄 **kèbó** scathing; unkind, hurtful

客车 **kèchē** passenger train

课程 **kèchéng** course; curriculum

课程表 **kèchéngbiǎo** schedule

可耻 **kěchǐ** dishonorable

可充气 **kě chōngqì** inflatable

客店 **kèdiàn** guest house; inn

可调换 **kě diàohuàn** transferable

蝌蚪 **kēdǒu** tadpole

刻度 **kèdù** scale

客房 **kèfáng** guest room; spare room

克服 **kèfú** overcome, surmount

可观 **kěguān** substantial

客观 **kèguān** objective

可贵 **kěguì** valuable; praiseworthy

刻痕 **kèhén** nick; cut

科幻 **kēhuàn** science fiction

科技 **kējì** science and technology

可敬 **kějìng** worthy; venerable

可靠 **kěkào** reliable; responsible; trustworthy

可靠性 **kěkào xìng** reliability

可卡因 **kěkǎyīn** cocaine

苛刻 **kēkè** demanding; severe

可可 **kěkě** cocoa

可口 **kěkǒu** tasty

可口可乐 **Kěkǒu Kělè** Coca Cola®

刻苦 **kèkǔ** hard-working

克拉 **kèlā** carat

可怜 **kělián** pitiful; pitiable

客满 **kèmǎn** fully booked ◊ no vacancies

科目 **kēmù** subject

啃 **kěn** chew; gnaw; nibble

肯 **kěn** be willing to

肯定 **kěndìng** confirm; be sure about ◊ sure, certain, definite; positive GRAM ◊ certainly, definitely; 你能不能肯定? **nǐ néngbùnéng kěndìng?** are you definite about that?; 他们现在肯定到了 **tāmen xiànzài kěndìng dàole** they must have arrived by now

可能 **kěnéng** possibility; chance ◊ possible; likely, probable ◊ possibly; maybe; 可能会下雨 **kěnéng huì xiàyǔ** it may rain

可能性 **kěnéng xìng** possibility; liability; likelihood; probability; prospect ◊ must

坑 **kēng** ditch; pit

坑道 **kēngdào** gallery; tunnel

坑害 **kēnghài** set up; frame

坑洼 **kēngwā** pothole

恳切请求 **kěnqiè qǐngqiú** appeal for

恳求 **kěnqiú** implore; plead for ◊ plea

可怕 **kěpà** terrible; terrifying; horrifying; formidable

客气 **kèqi** polite; friendly; 别客气 **biékèqì** you're welcome

苟求 **kèqiú** pushy

可取 **kěqǔ** advisable

客人 **kèrén** visitor; guest

可溶 **kěróng** soluble

可食用 **kě shíyòng** edible

瞌睡 **kēshuì** sleepy ◊ snooze

咳嗽 **késou** cough

可塑 **kěsù** pliable

课堂 **kètáng** classroom; lecture room

课题 **kètí** subject, topic

客厅 **kètīng** living room

磕头 **kētóu** kowtow

渴望 **kěwàng** crave; yearn for, long for ◊ craving; longing ◊ eager; wistful

可恶 **kěwù** horrible, repulsive

可惜 **kěxī** what a shame ◊ unfortunately

可笑 **kěxiào** funny, amusing; ridiculous

可信 **kěxìn** trusted; credible; reliable

可行 **kěxíng** workable; feasible

可行性研究 **kěxíngxìng yánjiū** feasibility study

信任性 **kěxìn xìng** credibility

科学 **kēxué** science ◊ scientific

科学家 **kēxuéjiā** scientist

可疑 **kěyí** suspicious

可以 **kěyǐ** can; may ◊ OK ◊ -able ◊ not bad; 可以吗? – 可以 **kěyǐma? – kěyǐ** can I/he? – ok, you/he can; 可以喝 **kěyǐ hē** drinkable; 还可以 **hái kěyǐ** not bad; 我觉得可以 **wǒ juédé kěyǐ** that's OK *or* fine by me

可以忍受 **kěyǐ rěnshòu** tolerable, bearable

可以容忍 **kěyǐ róngrěn** acceptable

可以想象 **kěyǐ xiǎngxiàng** imaginable, conceivable

可再用 **kě zài yòng** reusable, recyclable

可争论 **kě zhēnglùn** debatable ◊ arguably

克制 **kèzhì** control oneself

空 **kōng** empty; bare; vacant ◊ sky; air

恐 **kǒng** be afraid; fear

孔 **kǒng** hole

空 **kòng** spare time; leisure time

控 **kòng** control

空白 **kòngbái** gap; hole; empty space; margin ◊ blank

恐怖 **kǒngbù** terror; horror ◊ scary

恐怖电影 **kǒngbù diànyǐng** horror movie

恐怖分子 **kǒngbù fènzi** terrorist

恐怖机构 **kǒngbù jīgòu** terrorist organization

恐怖症 **kǒngbùzhèng** phobia

恐怖主义 **kǒngbù zhǔyì** terrorism

空档 **kōngdǎng** neutral

空洞 **kōngdòng** empty; meaningless

空洞无物 **kōngdòng wúwù** wishy-washy

空额 **kòng'é** opening (*at work*)

空腹 **kōngfù** empty stomach

控告 **kònggào** indict; charge; sue ◊ charge; 被控告 **bèi kònggào** ... be accused of ...

空隔键 **kònggé jiàn** space-bar

控股权益 **kònggǔ quányì** controlling interest

恐吓 **kǒnghè** terrify; terrorize

恐慌 **kǒnghuāng** panic

空间 **kōngjiān** space; room; void

空姐 **kōngjiě** air hostess

恐惧 **kǒngjù** fear; terror

空军 **kōngjūn** air force

空军基地 **kōngjūn jīdì** airbase

空旷 **kōngkuàng** open *countryside*

恐龙 **kǒnglóng** dinosaur

空落落 **kōng luòluo** stark *decor, room*

恐怕 **kǒngpà** I'm afraid (*regret*)

空气 **kōngqì** air

空前 **kōngqián** unprecedented

空气动力 **kōngqì dònglì** aerodynamic

空气污染 **kōngqì wūrǎn** air pollution

孔雀 **kǒngquè** peacock

空缺 **kòngquē** opening

空儿 **kòngr** parking space

空手道 **kōngshǒudào** karate

控诉 **kòngsù** bring charges

空谈 **kōngtán** empty talk; 他 只 是 空 谈 **tā zhǐshì kōngtán** he's all talk

空调 **kōngtiáo** air-conditioning

空头支票 **kōngtóu zhīpiào** blank check

空位 **kòngwèi** blank; space

空隙 **kòngxì** opening; gap

空闲 **kòngxián** leisure; leisure time ◊ unoccupied; at a loose end

空想 **kōngxiǎng** daydream; utopian fantasy

空心 **kōngxīn** hollow

空虚 **kōngxū** empty; meaningless ◊ emptiness; void

空域 **kōngyù** airspace

空余 **kòngyú** free *room, table*

空运 **kōngyùn** air transport

空晕病 **kōngyūnbìng** airsickness

空余时间 **kòngyú shíjiān** leisure time

空着 **kōngzhe** empty; unoccupied *room*

控制 **kòngzhì** control; regulate; dominate ◊ control; domination; 我们无法控制的因素 **wǒmén wúfǎ kòngzhì de yīnsù** circumstances beyond our control

控制键 **kòngzhìjiàn** control key

控制盘 **kòngzhì pán** control panel

控制中心 **kòngzhì zhōngxīn** control center

空中交通 **kōngzhōng jiāotōng** air traffic

空中交通控制 **kōngzhōng jiāotōng kòngzhì** air-traffic control

空中交通控制人员 **kōngzhōng jiāotōng kòngzhì rényuán** air-traffic controller

空中小姐 **kōngzhōng xiǎojie** air hostess

空转 **kōngzhuàn** idling; in neutral

孔子 **Kǒngzǐ** Confucius

口 **kǒu** mouth

扣 **kòu** button up

口才 **kǒucái** eloquence

口吃 **kǒuchī** stutter; speech impediment

口齿不清 **kǒuchǐ bùqīng** inarticulate

扣除 **kòuchú** deduct; subtract ◊ deduction

口袋 **kǒudài** pocket

口服避孕药 **kǒufú bìyùnyào** contraceptive pill

口供 **kǒugōng** statement (*to police*)

口号 **kǒuhào** slogan

口红 **kǒuhóng** lipstick

叩击 **kòujī** rap; knock on

口径 **kǒujìng** caliber (*of gun*)

叩声 **kòujī shēng** rap; knock

口技艺人 **kǒujì yìrén** ventriloquist

口渴 **kǒukě** thirsty

扣子 **kòu kòuzi** button up

口令 **kǒulìng** password

抠门儿 **kōuménr** stingy; tight-fisted

口腔卫生 **kǒuqiāng wèishēng** oral hygiene

口琴 **kǒuqín** mouth organ

扣球 **kòuqiú** smash (*in tennis*)

扣人心弦 **kòu rén xīnxián** gripping

口哨声 **kǒushàoshēng** whistle (*sound*)

口授 **kǒushòu** dictate ◊ dictation

口水 **kǒushuǐ** saliva

口试 **kǒutóu** oral exam

口头 **kǒutóu** oral

口吐狂言 **kǒutù kuángyán** rant and rave

口香糖 **kǒuxiāng táng** chewing gum

扣押 **kòuyā** seize; impound ◊ seizure

扣眼儿 **kòuyǎnr** buttonhole

口译 **kǒuyì** interpret ◊ interpretation

口音 **kǒuyīn** accent

口淫 **kǒuyín** oral sex; blow job

口译者 **kǒuyì zhě** interpreter

口语 **kǒuyǔ** colloquial language ◊ colloquial; conversational

口子 **kǒuzi** tear; slit

扣子 **kòuzi** button

哭 **kū** cry

枯 **kū** dried up; parched

苦 **kǔ** bitter ◊ bitterness

酷 **kù** cool, great

库 **kù** storehouse; warehouse

裤 **kù** pants

夸 **kuā** praise; exaggerate

跨 **kuà** step; step across

胯 **kuà** hip

夸大 **kuādà** exaggerate

垮掉 **kuǎdiào** crack up; have a breakdown

酷爱 **kù'ài** go in for; enjoy

块 **kuài** piece; block; dollar; yuan; lump (*of sugar*); pane (*of glass*) ◊ *measure word for money, pieces*; 五块钱 **wǔkuài qián** five yuan; 一块派／面包 **yīkuài pài／miànbāo** a piece of pie/bread

快 **kuài** quick; rapid; sharp ◊ quickly; soon; 他快五十了 **tā kuài wǔshí le** he's getting on for 50

酷爱 **kù'ài** be in love with *job, hobby*

快餐 **kuàicān** fast food; quick snack

快餐店 **kuàicāndiàn** fast food restaurant

快车 **kuàichē** fast train

快吃 **kuàichī** eat quickly; bolt

快点儿！ **kuàidiǎnr!** hurry up!; come on!

快感 **kuàigǎn** pleasurable feeling; thrill

快活 **kuàihuó** cheerful

会计 **kuàijì** accounting ◊ accountant; bookkeeper

快捷键 **kuàijiéjiàn** hot key

快进 **kuàijìn** fast forward

快乐 **kuàilè** joy; pleasure; bliss ◊ happy; 使人快乐 **shǐrén kuàilè** entertain

快门儿 **kuàiménr** shutter PHOT

快速 **kuàisù** fast; rapid; express ◊ velocity; rapidity

快艇 **kuàitǐng** speedboat

筷子 **kuàizi** chopsticks

快走 **kuàizǒu** hurry

夸奖 **kuājiǎng** praise

垮了 **kuǎle** break down; have a breakdown; be exhausted

宽 **kuān** broad; 十米宽 **shímǐkuān** 10m across

款 **kuǎn** sum of money; article (*of law, act*)

宽敞 **kuānchang** spacious

宽大 **kuāndà** spacious; lenient

款待 **kuǎndài** treat; 用 Y 款待 X **yòng Y kuǎndài X** treat X to Y

宽度 **kuāndù** width

筐 **kuāng** basket

狂 **kuáng** crazy

框 **kuāng** frame

矿 **kuàng** mine

旷 **kuàng** spacious

狂暴 **kuángbào** turbulent; ferocious ◊ turbulence; ferocity; rage

矿藏 **kuàngcáng** mineral resources

矿层 **kuàngcéng** seam (*of ore*)

旷工 **kuànggōng** skip work ◊ absence (from work) ◊ absent

矿工 **kuànggōng** miner

狂欢 **kuánghuān** live it up

狂欢节 **kuánghuānjié** carnival

框架 **kuàngjià** outline; framework

矿井 **kuàngjǐng** mine shaft

旷课 **kuàngkè** play hookey ◊ absence (from school) ◊ absent

矿坑 **kuàngkēng** mine; pit

况且 **kuàngqiě** furthermore

狂犬病 **kuángquǎn bìng** rabies

矿泉水 **kuàngquánshuǐ** mineral water

狂热 **kuángrè** craze, fad ◊ fanatical; feverish

狂人 **kuángrén** madman, maniac

狂热者 **kuángrè zhě** fanatic

矿山 **kuàngshān** mine

矿石 **kuàngshí** ore

狂妄 **kuángwàng** arrogant; presumptuous

矿物 **kuàngwù** mineral

狂喜 **kuángxǐ** joy; rejoicing ◊ exult; rejoice ◊ overjoyed

狂笑 **kuángxiào** guffaw; howl with laughter ◊ guffaw, howl; hysterics

矿业 **kuàngyè** mining

狂饮 **kuángyǐn** bender (*drinking*)

宽宏大量 **kuānhóng dàliàng** generous

宽厚 **kuānhòu** lenient; soft

宽阔 **kuānkuò** wide *street, field*

宽容 **kuānróng** tolerant; lenient;

forbearing; broad *smile* ◊ tolerance ◊ condone

宽容度 **kuānróng dù** freedom; latitude

款式 **kuǎnshì** cut (*of clothes, hair*)

宽恕 **kuānshù** forgive

宽松 **kuānsōng** loose; baggy

宽松裤 **kuānsōng kù** slacks

宽慰 **kuānwèi** relief ◊ be relieved

垮台 **kuǎtái** downfall; fall; 使 … 垮台 *shǐ … kuǎtái* bring down

夸脱 **kuātuō** quart

跨越 **kuàyuè** cross; pass; exceed

夸张 **kuāzhāng** exaggerate; overdo ◊ ostentatious

裤衩 **kùchǎ** underpants; panties

库存 **kùcún** stock

裤兜 **kùdōu** pants pocket

苦干 **kǔgàn** toil

亏 **kuī** lose

盔 **kuī** helmet

窥察 **kuīchá** snoop around

葵花 **kuíhuā** sunflower

窥孔 **kuīkǒng** peephole

傀儡 **kuǐlěi** puppet

傀儡政府 **kuǐlěi zhèngfǔ** puppet government

亏损 **kuīsǔn** deficit; loss ◊ make a loss

魁梧 **kuíwú** burly ◊ great hunk

溃疡 **kuìyáng** ulcer

骷髅 **kūlóu** skeleton

捆 **kǔn** bundle

困 **kùn** tired

苦难 **kǔnàn** difficulty; suffering

苦难的经历 **kǔnànde jīnglì** ordeal

苦恼 **kǔnǎng** distress; mental suffering

苦恼 **kǔnǎo** vexed; worried ◊

worry; trouble; grief

哭闹纠缠 **kūnào jiūchán** whine

昆虫 **kūnchóng** insect; bug

困乏 **kùnfá** weary; 使人困乏 *shǐrén kùnfá* wearing

困惑 **kùnhuò** confused; perplexed ◊ perplexity; 使 … 困惑 *shǐ … kùnhuò* puzzle, perplex

困境 **kùnjìng** mess, jam; plight

困倦 **kùnjuàn** sleepy

困难 **kùnnan** difficulty; trouble; complication

困扰 **kùnrǎo** nagging; niggling

捆住 **kǔnzhù** tie down; make fast

扩 **kuò** expand

阔 **kuò** wide; rich

括 **kuò** include

扩充 **kuòchōng** branch out

扩大 **kuòda** expand; enlarge; extend ◊ expansion; enlargement; extension

括号 **kuòhào** brackets; parentheses

扩建 **kuòjiàn** extension (*on house*)

扩军 **kuòjūn** arm; build up the army

阔气 **kuòqi** wealthy

蛞蝓 **kuòyú** slug (*animal*)

扩张 **kuòzhāng** dilate (*of pupils*)

哭泣 **kūqì** weep

酷热 **kùrè** sweltering, very hot

哭诉 **kūsù** moan

枯萎 **kūwěi** droop; wilt ◊ wilting; drooping

裤线 **kùxiàn** crease (*in pants*)

苦笑 **kǔxiào** wry smile

苦心 **kǔxīn** pains; 费苦心 *fèi kǔxīn* take pains

枯燥 **kūzào** boring

枯燥无味 **kūzào wúwèi** bland

裤子 **kùzi** pants

L

拉 **lā** pull; draw; drag
辣 **là** hot, spicy
蜡 **là** wax
喇叭 **lǎba** trumpet; horn; loudspeaker; 按喇叭 **àn lǎba** hoot; sound one's horn
喇叭状 **lǎbazhuàng** flare (*in dress*)
拉丁美洲 **Lādīng Měizhōu** Latin America
拉丁字母 **Lādīng zìmǔ** Roman alphabet
拉肚子 **lādùzi** diarrhea
拉关系 **lā guānxi** pull strings
拉过来 **lā guòlái** draw up *chair*
拉环 **lāhuán** ring-pull
来 **lái** come ◊ (*toward speaker*): 拿进来 **nájìn lai** bring in; 过来 **guòlai** come over
来迟 **láichí** belated
来到 **láidào** come along, turn up; arrive
癞蛤蟆 **làiháma** toad
来回 **láihuí** back and forth; there and back; to and fro
来回票 **láihuí piào** round trip ticket
来历 **láilì** origin
来临 **láilín** approach; come; fall (*of night*)
来世 **láishì** afterlife
来往 **láiwǎng** contact; dealings
来由 **láiyóu** reason; cause
来源 **láiyuán** source
来自 **láizì** come from; originate in, stem from
垃圾 **lājī** garbage, trash; litter
辣椒 **làjiāo** chili pepper
拉紧 **lājǐn** pull tight
拉近 **lājìn** zoom in on
垃圾桶 **lājītǒng** trashcan
垃圾箱 **lājīxiāng** garbage can
垃圾站 **lājī zhàn** garbage dump
拉开 **lākāi** draw back, pull back; pull apart, separate

拉开拉链 **lākāi lāliàn** unzip
啦啦队 **lālā duì** cheerleaders
拉力 **lālì** tension
拉链 **lāliàn** fastener, zipper; 拉链拉上 **lā lāliàn** zip up
喇嘛 **lǎma** lama
拉门 **lāmén** sliding door
拉面 **lāmiàn** hand-pulled noodles
栏 **lán** railing; hurdle; column (*of text*)
兰 **lán** orchid
拦 **lán** block; obstruct
蓝 **lán** blue
篮 **lán** basket
懒 **lǎn** lazy
缆 **lǎn** cable; rope
烂 **làn** decayed; rotten
滥 **làn** excessive
蓝宝石 **lánbǎoshí** sapphire
缆车 **lǎnchē** cable car
蓝调 **lándiào** blues
懒惰 **lǎnduò** laziness, indolence ◊ lazy, indolent
狼 **láng** wolf
浪 **làng** wave
栏杆 **lángān** barrier; railings
浪潮 **làngcháo** tide; wave
朗读 **lǎngdú** read aloud
浪费 **làngfèi** waste
浪花 **lànghuā** seaspray; foam
浪漫 **làngmàn** romantic ◊ romance
朗诵 **lǎngsòng** read out
榔头 **lángtou** hammer
浪头 **làngtóu** trend; wave; 赶浪头 **gǎn làngtóu** jump on the bandwagon
狼吞虎咽 **lángtūn hǔyàn** devour, wolf down ◊ voracious
懒觉 **lǎnjué** idle, lazy
懒汉 **lǎnhàn** bum; hobo
拦河坝 **lánhébà** dam
兰花 **lánhuā** orchid

拦截 lánjié intercept *ball*

蓝领工人 lánlǐng gōngrén blue-collar worker

褴褛 lánlǚ ragged

烂泥 lànní mud

篮球 lánqiú basketball

懒散 lǎnsǎn laze around ◊ lethargic

蓝色 lánsè blue

蓝图 lántú blueprint

阑尾 lánwěi appendix

阑尾炎 lánwěiyán appendicitis

懒洋洋 lǎnyāngyāng unenthusiastic; listless

蓝眼睛 lányǎnjing blue eyes ◊ blue-eyed

滥用 lànyòng misuse; abuse

拦住 lánzhù hold back; stop; accost

篮子 lánzi basket

牢 láo pen; prison ◊ solid; sturdy

劳 láo work

老 lǎo old ◊ F very, dead; always; 他老迟到 **tā lǎo chídào** he's always late; 老了 **lǎo le** get on, grow old; pass away

老板 lǎobǎn owner (of a business); proprietor; boss; landlord

老板娘 lǎobǎnniáng landlady; proprietress

老成练达 lǎochéng liàndá worldly; sophisticated

唠叨 láodao go on; go on at

唠叨不停 láodao bùtíng nag

劳动 láodòng work; labor

劳动节 Láodòngjié Labor Day

劳动力 láodònglì manpower, workers; workforce

劳动日 láodòngrì working day

劳动者 láodòng zhě laborer

牢房 láofáng prison cell

牢固 láogù solid; sturdy; durable

老虎 lǎohǔ tiger

老虎机 lǎohǔjī slot machine; gambling machine

老虎钳 lǎohǔqián pliers; pincers

劳驾 láojià excuse me; would you mind; 劳驾帮帮忙 **láojià bāngbang máng** could you help me?

老家 lǎojiā home

姥姥 lǎolao grandma

劳累 láolèi tire ◊ tired

老练 lǎoliàn diplomacy, tact ◊ diplomatic; veteran

老年 lǎonián geriatric ◊ old age

老年病学 lǎonián bìngxué geriatrics

老气 lǎoqì old-fashioned *clothes*

老前辈 lǎoqiánbèi senior citizen; senior

老人 lǎorén old person; senior citizen

老人院 lǎorényuàn old people's home, nursing home

牢骚 láosao complaint

老实 lǎoshí honest

老师 lǎoshī teacher

老式 lǎoshì old-fashioned *equipment*

老是 lǎoshì always

老鼠 lǎoshǔ rat; mouse

劳损 láosǔn strain

老外 lǎowài foreigner; layman

老挝 Lǎowō Laos ◊ Laotian

老兄 lǎoxiōng pal, buddy

老早 lǎozǎo long ago

老子 Lǎozǐ Lao-tzu (*Taoist sage*)

劳资纠纷 láozī jiūfēn industrial dispute

拉票 lāpiào canvass POL

拉平 lāpíng even out; smooth out; 拉平比分 **lāpíng bǐfēn** even the score; 和 … 拉平 **hé … lāpíng** draw level with

拉萨 Lāsà Lhasa

拉伤 lāshāng pull, strain

拉舌 lāshé tab

拉屎 lāshǐ shit

拉手 lāshǒu doorknob

邋遢 lāta messy *person*; scruffy; slovenly

拉下 lāxià pull down; lower

蜡烛 làzhú candle

了 le (*particle indicating completed action*): 雨停了 **yǔtíngle** it has stopped raining ◊ (*particle indicating change of state*): 头发白了 **tóufa báile** his hair is going gray; 我买了 **wǒ mǎi le** I'll take it ◊ (*for emphasis*): 你太好了 **nǐ**

tài hǎo le that's very kind

勒 lè rein in; check

乐 lè joy; happiness

乐观 **lèguān** optimistic; hopeful; positive ◊ optimism

乐观者 **lèguān zhě** optimist

雷 léi thunder

累 léi accumulate

泪 lèi tear

累 lèi tired

类 lèi sort, type, kind

肋 lèi side (*of body*)

肋部 **lèibù** flank; side (*of body*)

雷达 **léidá** radar

雷锋叔叔 **Léi Fēng shūshu** do-gooder

肋骨 **lèigǔ** rib

累积 **lèijī** accumulate

雷鸣 **léimíng** thunder

类似 **lèisì** similar; comparable ◊ likeness

累死了 **lèi sǐ le** dead tired

类型 **lèixíng** type

雷雨 **léiyǔ** thunderstorm

雷阵雨 **léizhènyǔ** thundery shower

累赘 **léizhuì** cumbersome

勒令停职 **lèlìng tíngzhí** suspend

冷 lěng cold

棱 léng edge

冷冰冰 **lěng bīngbīng** cold; icy

冷藏 **lěngcáng** chill; refrigerate ◊ refrigeration

冷淡 **lěngdàn** chilly; indifferent; impassive; frigid

冷冻 **lěngdòng** freeze ◊ frozen

冷冻室 **lěngdòngshì** freezer

冷冻食品 **lěngdòng shípǐn** frozen food

冷静 **lěngjìng** calm, collected

冷酷 **lěngkù** in cold blood ◊ cold-blooded; heartless

冷气 **lěngqì** chill (*in air*)

冷门 **lěngmén** outsider

冷面 **lěngmiàn** cold noodles

冷漠 **lěngmò** cool; remote, unfriendly; unconcerned; apathetic

冷凝 **lěngníng** condense ◊ condensation

冷盘 **lěngpán** cold cuts

冷却 **lěngquè** cool ◊ cooling

冷杉 **lěngshān** fir

冷烫 **lěngtàng** cold wave (*in hairdressing*)

冷笑 **lěngxiào** sneer

冷血 **lěngxuè** cold-blooded

冷饮 **lěngyǐn** cold drinks

棱锥体 **léngzhuītǐ** pyramid

乐趣 **lèqù** amusement; enjoyment; fun; pleasure

勒索 **lèsuǒ** extort; blackmail ◊ extortion; blackmail

乐意 **lèyì** with pleasure; willingly

乐于 **lèyú** willing; 乐于助人 **lèyú zhùrén** obliging

乐园 **lèyuán** paradise; amusement park

狸 lí beaver

梨 lí pear

犁 lí plow

离 lí leave ◊ from; 离这儿很远 **lí zhèr hěn yuǎn** it's far from here; 离圣诞节还有六星期 **lí Shèngdànjié háiyǒu liù xīngqī** Christmas is still six weeks away

礼 lǐ rite; ritual; etiquette

李 lǐ plum

里 lǐ in; inside ◊ neighborhood; *measure of distance, approx. one third of a mile*

理 lǐ reason ◊ pay attention to; put in order, sort

粒 lì grain, speck; particle

力 lì strength; power

立 lì stand

利 lì sharp ◊ profit; benefit

例 lì example

历 lì experience; calendar

俩 liǎ both; two; 他们俩儿 **tāmen liǎ** the two of them, both of them

帘 lián curtain; blind

联 lián join; unite with

连 lián link; connect ◊ even; 连 ... 也不 **lián ... yěbù** not even

莲 lián lotus

脸 liǎn face

恋 liàn love

炼 liàn refine

练 liàn practise; train

链 liàn chain

恋爱 **liàn'ài** love

联邦 **liánbāng** federation; union

联邦调查局 **Liánbāng Diàochájú** FBI, Federal Bureau of Investigation

联邦制 **liánbāngzhì** federal

连播 **liánbō** serialize

脸蛋儿 **liǎndànr** face

镰刀 **liándāo** sickle

凉 **liáng** cool; cold

良 **liáng** good

粮 **liáng** grain

量 **liáng** measure; 量体温 **liáng tǐwēn** take sb's temperature

两 **liǎng** two; 两盘磁带 **liǎngpán cídài** two cassettes

量 **liàng** capacity; quantity; volume

谅 **liàng** forgive

亮 **liàng** bright; light; clear

辆 **liàng** *measure word for vehicles*; 一辆小汽车 **yíliàng xiǎoqìchē** a car

炼钢厂 **liàngāngchǎng** steelworks

两倍 **liǎngbèi** double

两边 **liǎngbiān** bilateral

粮仓 **liángcāng** barn

两重 **liǎngchóng** double; dual

量出 **liángchū** measure out

两次 **liǎngcì** twice

亮度 **liàngdù** lightness; brightness

晾干 **liànggān** air-dry

谅解 **liàngjiě** understand; forgive

两极分化 **liǎngjí fēnhuà** polarize; split

量具 **liángjù** measuring instrument

凉开水 **liáng kāishuǐ** cold boiled water

凉快 **liángkuai** pleasantly cool

两面派 **liǎngmiànpài** two-faced

椋鸟 **liángniǎo** starling

两栖 **liǎngqī** amphibious

跟跄 **liàngqiàng** stagger; sway

俩儿 **liǎngr** two; both

粮食 **liángshi** grain; cereal

良师益友 **liángshī yìyǒu** mentor

凉爽 **liángshuǎng** cool; crisp; fresh ◊ freshness

凉台 **liángtái** balcony

连贯 **liánguàn** coherent; lucid

连贯性 **liánguàn xìng** continuity

两位数 **liǎngwèi shù** double figures

凉鞋 **liángxié** sandal

良心 **liángxīn** conscience

良性 **liángxìng** benign

联合 **liánhé** unite; form an alliance ◊ alliance; union ◊ concerted

联合国 **Liánhéguó** United Nations

联合企业 **liánhé qǐyè** cartel

联合收割机 **liánhé shōugējī** combine harvester

联合王国 **Liánhé Wángguó** United Kingdom

脸红 **liǎnhóng** blush

连环漫画 **liánhuán mànhuà** comic strip

连环碰撞 **liánhuán pèngzhuàng** pile-up, crash

恋家 **liànjiā** homeloving

廉价出售 **liánjià chūshòu** be on sale

离岸价格 **lí'àn jiàgé** FOB, free on board

连接 **liánjiē** join, connect; link

联接 **liánjiē** link; connect

联结 **liánjié** bond

连接处 **liánjiēchù** joint

联结处 **liánjiéchù** join

连接词 **liánjiēcí** conjunction GRAM

连接器 **liánjiē qì** connector COMPUT

连襟儿 **liánjīnr** brother-in-law

连裤袜 **liánkùwà** pantyhose

连累 **liánlěi** get ... involved

联络 **liánluò** contact, get in touch with ◊ liaison

联络网 **liánluò wǎng** network

联盟 **liánméng** coalition; league; union; alliance

连绵 **liánmián** continuous; 连绵一百英里 **liánmián yìbǎi yīnglǐ** it stretches for 100 miles

怜悯 **liánmǐn** sympathize with

脸盆 **liǎnpén** washbasin

莲蓬头 **liánpengtóu** shower head

脸皮厚 **liǎnpí hòu** thick-skinned; insensitive; shameless

连日 **liánrì** lasting for days

炼乳 **liànrǔ** condensed milk

联赛 liánsài league SP
脸色 liǎnsè color (in cheeks)
脸色苍白 liǎnsè cāngbái pallor
连锁店 liánsuǒ diàn chain store
连锁反应 liánsuǒ fǎnyìng chain reaction
链条 liàntiáo chain
连体双胞胎 liántǐ shuāngbāotāi Siamese twins
连同 liántóng in conjunction with
联系 liánxì contact; connect ◊ connection; 将 X 与 Y 联系起来 jiāng X yǔ Y liánxì qǐlái relate X to Y; 我们保持联系 wǒmen bǎochí liánxì we keep in touch
练习 liànxí practice; training; exercise
练习本 liànxíběn exercise book
联系电话 liánxì diànhuà contact number
连续 liánxù continuous; uninterrupted; consecutive; 连续两天 liánxù liǎngtiān for two days running
连续不断 liánxù búduàn continuous ◊ persistently
连衣裤 liányīkù dungarees
连衣裙 liányīqún dress
联运 liányùn connection (train etc)
帘子 liánzi curtain
连字号 liánzìhào hyphen
聊 liáo chat
疗 liáo treat ◊ treatment
了 liǎo finish, end ◊ understand; 对 X 了如指掌 duì X liǎo rú zhǐzhǎng have X at one's fingertips ◊ (completed action): 吃不了 chī liǎo eat up ◊ (ability): 我去不了 wǒ qù bu liǎo I can't go; 我办得了 wǒ bàn de liǎo I can manage it
料 liào material, fabric
了不起 liǎobùqǐ terrific, fantastic
潦草 liáocǎo careless; messy; 潦草的字迹 liáocǎode zìjì scrawl, scribble
疗程 liáochéng course of treatment
疗法 liáofǎ cure; remedy; therapy
了结 liǎojié deal with; settle
了解 liǎojiě understand; 据了解

他们在加拿大 jù liáojiě tāmen zài Jiānádà they are understood to be in Canada
料理 liàolǐ take care of
聊天 liáotiān chat
料想 liàoxiǎng suppose
疗养 liáoyǎng convalesce
疗养地 liáoyǎngdì health resort
疗养期 liáoyǎng qī convalescence
疗养院 liáoyǎngyuàn sanatorium
篱笆 líba fence
离别 líbié separation ◊ separate; part from (of people)
利比亚 Lìbǐyà Libya ◊ Libyan
立场 lìchǎng standpoint; point of view
里程 lǐchéng mileage
里程碑 lǐchéngbēi milestone
里程表 lǐchéng biǎo odometer
里道 lǐdào inside lane (of road)
列 liè list ◊ column, row ◊ measure word for trains; 一列火车 yīliè huǒchē a train
裂 liè crack; split
烈 liè intense
劣 liè inferior; poor
猎 liè hunt
列车 lièchē train
列车长 lièchē zhǎng conductor (on train)
裂缝 lièfèng crack; crevice; gap; slit, opening
裂痕 lièhén crack
烈酒 lièjiǔ hard liquor
列举 lièjǔ enumerate
裂开 lièkāi disintegrate; split; damage; gape ◊ gaping hole
裂口 lièkǒu tear (in cloth, paper); burst; chip (in cup); split
列宁 Lièníng Lenin
猎枪 lièqiāng shotgun
猎区 lièqū hunting ground
猎取 lièqǔ hunt; prey on
猎犬 lièquǎn hunting dog; retriever
猎人 lièrén hunter
列入计划 lièrù jìhuà schedule
烈士 lièshì martyr
猎手 lièshǒu hunter
猎物 lièwù prey
烈性 lièxìng strong drink

劣质 **lièzhì** inferior; shoddy; trashy

咧嘴 **liězuǐ** grin

理发 **lǐfà** haircut; hairdressing ◊ style hair

立法 **lìfǎ** legislate ◊ legislation ◊ legislative

立法过程 **lìfǎ guòchéng** legislation

立法机构 **lìfǎ jīgòu** legislature

立方 **lìfāng** cubic

立方米 **lìfāngmǐ** cubic meter

立方形 **lìfāng xíng** cube

理发师 **lǐfàshī** hairdresser

理发厅 **lǐfàtīng** hairdressing salon; barber shop

礼服 **lǐfú** formal wear; tuxedo

利害 **lìhai** severe; tough; formidable

离合器 **líhéqì** clutch

离婚 **líhūn** divorce; get divorced ◊ divorced

里脊 **lǐjǐ** fillet

痢疾 **lìji** dysentery

立即 **lìjí** immediate ◊ immediately

理解 **lǐjiě** understand; view, perceive ◊ comprehension; understanding

离开 **líkāi** leave, depart; go away; quit; 我们明天离开 **wǒmen míngtiān líkāi** we're off tomorrow

立刻 **lìkè** immediately; in no time

力量 **lìliàng** power; strength; force; might

理疗 **lǐliáo** physiotherapy

理疗医生 **lǐliáo yīshēng** physiotherapist

利率 **lìlǜ** interest rate

理论 **lǐlùn** theory ◊ theoretical

利落 **lìluò** clear and concise; snappy

礼貌 **lǐmào** courtesy; politeness ◊ courteously; 有/没有礼貌 **yǒu/méiyǒu lǐmào** have good/bad manners

厘米 **límǐ** centimeter

里面 **lǐmiàn** inside

黎明 **límíng** daybreak

林 **lín** wood; forest

淋 **lín** drip; soak

临 **lín** overlook ◊ be about to

邻 **lín** neighbor; neighborhood

淋巴结 **línbājié** lymph gland

临床 **línchuáng** clinical

铃 **líng** bell

零 **líng** zero; nil; 零下十度 **língxià shídù** 10 degrees below zero; 从零开始 **cóng líng kāishǐ** start from scratch

陵 **líng** mound; tomb

灵 **líng** spirit; soul

领 **líng** neck; collar ◊ claim; withdraw *money*

另 **lìng** other; in addition

令 **lìng** order

领班 **língbān** foreman

灵车 **língchē** hearse

凌晨 **língchén** early morning

领带 **língdài** necktie

领导 **língdǎo** leader; head; boss ◊ lead; 在他的领导下 **zài tāde língdǎo xià** under his leadership

领导技巧 **língdǎo jìqiǎo** leadership skills

领导人 **língdǎo rén** leader; manager

零度 **língdù** zero degrees

领队 **língduì** bandleader

灵感 **línggǎn** inspiration; brainwave

领海 **línghǎi** territorial waters

领会 **línghuì** grasp; comprehend; digest *information*

灵魂 **línghún** soul; spirit; 灵魂转世 **línghún zhuǎnshì** reincarnation

灵活 **línghuó** flexible; agile

零下 **língxià** below zero

灵机 **língjī** inspiration; 灵机一动 **língjīyídòng** have a flash of inspiration

零件 **língjiàn** (spare) part

领结 **língjié** bow tie

领口 **língkǒu** neckline

铃兰 **línglán** lily of the valley

伶俐 **línglì** quick; nimble; apt

领路 **línglù** navigation

凌乱 **língluàn** untidy; messy

灵敏 **língmǐn** sharp; quick *mind*

陵墓 **língmù** mausoleum

零钱 **língqián** loose change, coins

灵巧 **língqiǎo** deft; quick

令人 **lìngrén** (*causing a person to*

feel something): 令人恶心 **lìngrén ěxin** disgusting, revolting; 令人愉快 **lìngrén yúkuài** enjoyable; 令人失望 **lìngrén shīwàng** disappointing

零散 **língsǎn** sporadic

零食 **língshí** snacks; nibbles; candy

领事 **língshì** consul

领事馆 **língshì guǎn** consulate

零售 **língshòu** retail

零售价 **língshòu jià** retail price

零售商 **língshòu shāng** retailer

零碎 **língsuì** incomplete; fragmented

领头 **língtóu** lead *race, procession*

领土 **língtǔ** territory ◊ territorial

另外 **lìngwài** other ◊ in addition; apart from that

另外收费 **lìngwài shōufèi** be extra

领先 **língxiān** be in the lead; be ahead of ◊ in front; leading ◊ lead (*in race*)

零星 **língxīng** scattered

菱形 **língxíng** diamond; lozenge

另行通知 **lìngxíng tōngzhī** until further notice

领袖 **língxiù** leader

领养 **língyǎng** adopt ◊ adoption

另一个 **lìng yígè** another

另一件事 **lìng yījiàn shì** another matter; a different ball game

零用钱 **língyòng qián** allowance

零用现金 **língyòng xiànjīn** petty cash

领域 **língyù** territory; field; preserve; sphere; 戏剧领域 **xìjù língyù** the world of the theater

领子 **língzi** collar

临海 **línhǎi** coastal

林火 **línhuǒ** forest fire

临街店铺 **línjiē diànpù** storefront

邻近 **línjìn** adjacent

临近 **línjìn** approach ◊ proximity

邻居 **línjū** neighbor

鳞片 **línpiàn** scale (*on fish*)

吝啬 **lìnsè** miserly, tight-fisted

吝啬鬼 **lìnsèguǐ** miser

临时 **línshí** provisional; temporary; casual

临时担任 **línshí dānrèn** act as,

fill in as

临时工 **línshígōng** temp

林荫道 **línyīndào** avenue

淋浴 **línyù** take a shower ◊ shower

淋浴帘 **línyùlián** shower curtain

礼炮 **lǐpào** salute

礼品 **lǐpǐn** gift, present

离奇 **líqí** strange; uncanny

离弃 **líqì** abandon

力气 **lìqì** strength (*physical*)

沥青 **lìqīng** asphalt

里圈跑道 **lǐquān pǎodào** inside lane SP

例如 **lìrú** for instance, e.g.

利润 **lìrùn** profit

利润率 **lìrùnlǜ** profit margin

理事 **lǐshì** director; trustee

砾石 **lìshí** gravel

历史 **lìshǐ** history

历史性 **lìshǐxìng** historic; historical

历史学家 **lìshǐ xuéjiā** historian

理所当然 **lǐsuǒ dāngrán** naturally; of course

礼堂 **lǐtáng** (ceremonial) hall; church

离题 **lítí** beside the point

立体声装置 **lìtǐshēng zhuāngzhì** stereo system

留 **liú** stay; keep; let grow *hair*; 你留着吧 **nǐ liúzhe ba** please keep it, I insist

流 **liú** flow, run

硫 **liú** sulfur

柳 **liǔ** willow

六 **liù** six

遛 **liù** walk; 遛狗 **liùgǒu** walk the dog

溜冰场 **liūbīng chǎng** ice rink

流鼻涕 **liú bítì** runny nose

流鼻血 **liú bíxuè** nosebleed

流产 **liúchǎn** miscarriage

流畅 **liúchàng** smooth; fluent

流程图 **liúchéngtú** flowchart

流传 **liúchuán** spread; circulate

溜出去 **liūchūqù** slip out

流弹 **liúdàn** stray bullet

流荡 **liúdàng** drift

流动 **liúdòng** flow

流动工人 **liúdòng gōngrén** migrant worker

流动基金 liúdòng jījīn cash flow

流放 liúfàng exile

流感 liúgǎn flu

刘海 liúhǎi bangs; fringe

留话 liúhuà leave a message

硫磺 liúhuáng sulfur

流口水 liú kǒushuǐ dribble; slobber

浏览 liúlǎn skim; browse; flick through

流浪汉 liúlànghàn drifter; hobo

浏览器 liúlǎn qì browser COMPUT

流泪 liúlèi shed tears

流利 liúlì fluent ◊ fluency; 他讲一口流利的汉语 tā jiǎng yīkǒu liúlìde Hànyǔ he speaks fluent Chinese

流氓 liúmáng hoodlum; hooligan

留念 liúniàn keep as a memento

流沙 liúshā quicksand

留神 liúshén look out; pay attention

流逝 liúshì slip away; elapse; pass

六十 liùshí sixty

柳树 liùshù willow

流水 liúshuǐ running water

六四 Liùsì Tiananmen Square (incident)

流苏 liúsū tassel

流体 liútǐ fluid

流亡 liúwáng exile

留下 liúxià bequeath; leave

流线型 liúxiànxíng streamlined

留心 liúxīn be alert, be observant; listen to, heed

流星 liúxīng meteor; falling star

流行 liúxíng in fashion, fashionable; popular; pop

流行病 liúxíngbìng epidemic

流行歌曲 liúxíng gēqǔ pop song; hit

流行款式 liúxíng kuǎnshì style, fashion

流行性 liúxíngxìng epidemic

流行性感冒 liúxíngxìng gǎnmào influenza

流行音乐 liúxíng yīnyuè pop music

留学 liúxué study abroad

流血 liúxuè bleed ◊ bleeding; bloodshed

留言 liúyán leave a message

流言蜚语 liúyán fēiyǔ gossip; scandal

六月 liùyuè June

流走 liúzǒu drain, flow away

例外 lìwài exception

礼物 lǐwù gift

利息 lìxī interest

离线 líxiàn go off-line

理想 lǐxiǎng ideal

理想化 lǐxiǎnghuà idealistic

理性 lǐxìng reason; sense

利息率 lìxīlǜ interest rate

力学 lìxué mechanics

离异 líyì break up (of couple)

礼仪 lǐyí protocol; etiquette; ceremony

利益 lìyì interest; advantage; benefit

利用 lìyòng use; exploit; take advantage of

理由 lǐyóu reason; cause; grounds

鲤鱼 lǐyú carp

俚语 lǐyǔ slang

力争 lìzhēng strive for

例证 lìzhèng illustration; example

理智 lǐzhì reason (faculty)

荔枝 lìzhī lychee

李子 lǐzi plum

里子 lǐzi lining

例子 lìzi example; case; instance

栗子 lìzi chestnut

粒子 lìzǐ particle PHYS

栗子树 lìzi shù chestnut tree

笼 lóng cage

聋 lóng deaf ◊ deafness

龙 lóng dragon

隆冬季节 lóngdōng jìjié in the depths of winter

垄断 lǒngduàn monopolize ◊ monopoly

龙骨 lónggǔ keel

龙卷风 lóngjuǎn fēng tornado; whirlwind

隆隆声 lónglong shēng boom; peal (of thunder)

笼统 lóngtǒng sweeping statement

龙头 lóngtóu faucet

龙虾 lóngxiā lobster

聋哑 lóngyǎ deaf-and-dumb

笼罩 lǒngzhào descend (of mood,

darkness)

隆重 lóngzhòng festive

笼子 lóngzi cage

楼 lóu building; story, floor

搂 lǒu hug, embrace

漏 lòu seep; drip; leak ◊ leaky

楼层 lóucéng floor, story

漏出 lòuchū escape, leak; seep

漏洞 lòudòng leak; loophole

漏斗 lòudǒu funnel

楼房 lóufáng building

露面 lòumiàn turn up; put in an appearance

漏气 lòuqì leak out (*of air, gas*)

楼上 lóushàng upstairs

楼梯 lóutī stairs, staircase

楼厅 lóutīng balcony

楼下 lóuxià downstairs

炉 lú oven

橹 lǔ paddle

鹿 lù deer

路 lù road; way; possibility; 五路有轨电车 wǔlù yǒuguǐdiànchē streetcar line 5

露 lù dew ◊ reveal

录 lù record

驴 lǘ donkey

铝 lǚ aluminum

缕 lǚ strand, lock

氯 lǜ chlorine

滤 lǜ filter, strain

率 lǜ level, amount, rate (*of pay*)

绿 lǜ green

卵 luǎn (human) egg

乱 luàn chaotic, in a mess ◊ chaos

卵巢 luǎncháo ovary

乱砍 luànkǎn slash

乱伦 luànlún incest

乱蓬蓬 luàn péngpeng ragged

乱七八糟 luànqī bāzāo in a mess, in confusion, topsy-turvy

卵石 luǎnshí pebble

乱弹 luàntán strum

乱涂 luàntú daub

乱写 luànxiě scrawl, scribble

绿宝石 lǜbǎoshí emerald

路边 lùbiān roadside

路标 lùbiāo roadsign; signpost; landmark

铝箔 lǚbó aluminum foil

绿茶 lǜchá green tea

旅程 lǚchéng itinerary

露出 lùchū expose, reveal

屡次 lǚcì over and over again

路堤 lùdī embankment

陆地 lùdì land, shore, dry land; mainland ◊ terrestrial

旅店 lǚdiàn hostel; inn

掠夺 lüèduó loot

掠夺者 lüèduó zhě looter

掠过 lüèguò skim *surface*

略过 lüèguò skip, omit

略微 lüèwēi hint, trace

滤干 lǜgān strain; drain

路过 lùguò pass by

绿化 lǜhuà put plants / trees in, plant up

鹿角 lùjiǎo antlers

路径 lùjìng path

旅客 lǚkè passenger

履历 lǚlì résumé

陆路 lùlù track; overland route

鲁莽 lǔmǎng rash, impetuous

路面 lùmiàn pavement, road surface

轮 lún wheel; round (*of drinks*)

论 lùn discuss

轮齿 lúnchǐ cog

轮船 lúnchuán steamer; ship

论点 lùndiǎn thesis

伦敦 Lúndūn London

轮毂 lúngǔ hub (*of wheel*)

轮换 lúnhuàn alternate

论据 lùnjù argument; reasoning

轮廓 lúnkuò contour, outline; silhouette

轮流 lúnliú alternate ◊ alternately; 轮流做 lúnliú zuò do in rotation, take turns in doing

伦理学 lúnlǐxué ethics

轮盘赌 lúnpán dǔ roulette

轮胎 lúntāi tire

论文 lùnwén thesis, dissertation, treatise; paper

轮椅 lúnyǐ wheelchair

论语 Lúnyǔ Analects of Confucius

轮缘 lúnyuán rim (*of wheel*)

轮值表 lúnzhí biǎo rota

轮轴 lúnzhóu axle

轮子 lúnzi wheel

落 luò fall; sink; land (*of ball etc*); set (*of sun*)

锣 **luó** gong

骡 **luó** mule

裸 **luǒ** naked, bare

萝卜 **luóbo** turnip; radish

落地窗 **luòdìchuāng** French doors

落地灯 **luòdìdēng** floor lamp

落后 **luòhòu** backward ◊ be behind, trail; lose the lead; 在 X 方面落后 **zài X fāngmiàn luòhòu** be behind with X

落花生 **luòhuāshēng** groundnut

逻辑 **luójí** logic ◊ logical

落空 **luòkōng** fall through, fail

罗马数字 **Luómǎ shùzì** Roman numerals

螺母 **luómǔ** nut (for bolt)

罗盘仪 **luópán yí** compass

落泊 **luòpò** comedown

罗圈腿 **luóquān tuǐ** bandy

络腮胡子 **luòsāi húzi** full beard

螺栓 **luóshuān** bolt

落水 **luòshuǐ** fall into the water; 有人落水！**yǒurén luòshuǐ!** man overboard!

螺丝 **luósī** screw

螺丝刀 **luósīdāo** screwdriver

螺丝钉 **luósīdīng** screw

裸体 **luǒtǐ** naked, nude

裸体画 **luǒtǐ huà** nude

裸体主义者 **luǒtǐ zhǔyì zhě** nudist

骆驼 **luòtuo** camel

螺纹 **luówén** thread (of screw)

落下 **luòxià** go down, sink

裸胸 **luǒxiōng** topless

螺旋 **luóxuán** spiral

螺旋桨 **luóxuánjiǎng** propeller

录取 **lùqǔ** admit, take in

鹿肉 **lùròu** venison

绿色 **lǜsè** green

律师 **lǜshī** attorney, lawyer

露水 **lùshuǐ** dew

露宿街头 **lùsù jiētóu** sleep rough

芦笋 **lúsǔn** asparagus

露天 **lùtiān** open-air ◊ in the open air

旅途 **lǚtú** ride, drive; travels

芦苇 **lúwěi** reed

路线 **lùxiàn** route; way

录像 **lùxiàng** video; video recording

录像带 **lùxiàng dài** video cassette; videotape

录像机 **lùxiàng jī** video recorder, VCR

履行 **lǚxíng** fulfill ◊ fulfillment

旅行 **lǚxíng** travel; get around ◊ journey, trip; traveling

旅行包 **lǚxíngbāo** travel bag

旅行保险 **lǚxíng bǎoxiǎn** travel insurance

旅行袋 **lǚxíng dài** travel bag

旅行社 **lǚxíng shè** travel agency

旅行推销员 **lǚxíng tuīxiāo yuán** commercial traveler

旅行者 **lǚxíng zhě** traveler

旅行支票 **lǚxíng zhīpiào** traveler's check

陆续 **lùxù** one after the other

录音 **lùyīn** (tape) recording ◊ (tape) record ◊ audio

录音电话 **lùyīn diànhuà** answerphone

露营 **lùyíng** camp ◊ camping

录音机 **lùyīnjī** cassette player; cassette recorder; tape recorder

录音室 **lùyīn shì** recording studio

录音座 **lùyīnzuò** tape deck

旅游 **lǚyóu** tour ◊ tourism; tour

旅游公司 **lǚyóu gōngsī** tour operator

旅游业 **lǚyóu yè** tourism

旅游者 **lǚyóu zhě** tourist

旅游指南 **lǚyóu zhǐnán** guidebook

路障 **lùzhàng** barricade; roadblock

绿洲 **lǜzhōu** oasis

炉子 **lúzi** stove; furnace

M

妈 mā mom, ma
抹 mā wipe
麻 má hemp
马 mǎ horse; 老马识途 lǎo mǎ shí tú prov the old horse knows the way
码 mǎ yard
骂 mà curse, swear
吗 ma (question indicator): 你认识他吗? nǐ rènshi tā ma? do you know him?

马表 mǎbiǎo stopwatch
抹布 mābù cloth; dish cloth
马车 mǎchē cart
马达 mǎdá motor, engine
马大哈 mǎdàhā disaster area fig
妈的! māde! ∨ shit!
麻烦 máfán bother, trouble; 太麻烦你了 tài máfán nǐle you needn't have bothered
吗啡 mǎfēi morphine
马夫 mǎfū groom (for horse)
马虎 mǎhū careless, sloppy
埋 mái bury; 埋头于工作 máitóu yú gōngzuò bury oneself in work
买 mǎi buy
麦 mài wheat
迈 mài step
脉 mài blood vessel
卖 mài sell
脉搏 màibó pulse
迈步 màibù stride
买不到 mǎi bú dào unobtainable
埋藏 máicáng bury
买单 mǎidān pay the bill
买东西 mǎi dōngxi shop
卖方 màifāng seller
埋伏 máifú ambush
卖高价票 mài gāojià piào scalper
买家 mǎijiā buyer
麦克风 màikèfēng microphone
买卖 mǎimài buying and selling; business; 做 X 的买卖 zuò X de

卖买 mǎimài trade in X
麦片 màipiàn rolled oats
卖俏 màiqiào flirt
卖肉的 màiròu de butcher
麦乳精 màirǔjīng malted milk
卖艺 màiyì work as a performer
卖淫 màiyín prostitute oneself
买主 mǎizhǔ purchaser; customer
卖主 màizhǔ seller, vendor
麦子 màizi wheat
麻将 májiàng mah-jong
马厩 mǎjiù stable
马克 mǎkè mark (currency)
马克思 Mǎkèsī Marx
马克思主义 Mǎkèsīzhǔyì Marxism ◊ Marxist
马克思主义者 Mǎkèsīzhǔyì zhě Marxist
马来西亚 Mǎláixīyà Malaysia ◊ Malaysian
马来语 Mǎlái yǔ Malay (language)
马拉松 mǎlāsōng marathon
马力 mǎlì horsepower
马列主义 Mǎlièzhǔyì Marxism-Leninism
马列主义者 Mǎlièzhǔyì zhě Marxist-Leninist
马笼头 mǎ lóngtóu bridle
马路 mǎlù street
妈妈 māma mom, ma
马马虎虎 mǎma hǔhū so-so, average, mediocre
麻木 mámù numb
蛮 mán quite; very
鳗 mán eel
瞒 mán conceal; keep secret
满 mǎn full
慢 màn slow
漫 màn overflow
漫步 mànbù ramble; saunter; wander ◊ rambling
满不在乎 mǎn bù zàihu not care at all

漫步者 **mànbù zhě** rambler

漫长 **màncháng** lengthy

慢动作 **màndòngzuò** slow motion

盲 **máng** blind

忙 **máng** busy ◊ be in a rush; 忙什么? **máng shénme?** what's the big rush?

盲点 **mángdiǎn** blind spot

芒果 **mángguǒ** mango

忙碌 **mánglù** busy; hectic; on the go ◊ bustle around; be busy; rush, scramble

盲目 **mángmù** blind; wild, crazy *scheme*

茫然 **mángrán** blank, vacant *look*

盲人 **mángrén** blind person; the blind

盲文 **mángwén** braille

蛮横 **mánhèng** harden *attitude* ◊ insolent

漫画 **mànhuà** comic

漫画书 **mànhuà shū** comic book

慢跑 **mànpǎo** jog ◊ jogging

满身 **mǎn shēn** the whole body; all over

蔓生植物 **mànshēng zhíwù** climbing plant

漫谈 **màntán** ramble ◊ rambling, incoherent

馒头 **mántou** steamed bun

漫无目的 **màn wú mùdì** aimless

慢性 **mànxìng** chronic

蔓延 **mànyán** spread (*of fire, disease, belief*); sprawl (*of city*); be overrun with ◊ contagious *fear, laughter*; sprawling; 四处蔓延 **sìchù mànyán** run wild

满意 **mǎnyì** satisfied; 令人满意 **lìngrén mǎnyì** fulfilling; satisfactory

漫游 **mànyóu** roam, wander around

满员 **mǎnyuán** full; booked up; packed

满月 **mǎnyuè** full moon

满洲 **Mǎnzhōu** Manchuria

慢走 **mànzǒu** goodbye, so long

满足 **mǎnzú** satisfy *needs, desires* ◊ satisfied, content, contented ◊ contentment; fulfillment; satisfaction

满族 **Mǎnzú** Manchu

猫 **māo** cat

锚 **máo** anchor

毛 **máo** hair; bristles; wool; mao (*Chinese money*)

矛 **máo** spear; javelin

铆 **mǎo** rivet

冒 **mào** emit, give off

毛笔 **máobǐ** writing brush

毛病 **máobìng** fault, defect; 车有点毛病 **chē yǒu diǎn máobìng** there is something wrong with the car

毛虫 **máochóng** caterpillar

冒充 **màochōng** impersonate, pose as

铆钉 **mǎodīng** rivet

矛盾 **máodùn** contradiction ◊ contradictory

冒犯 **màofàn** offend, insult

毛纺厂 **máofǎngchǎng** textile mill

毛骨悚然 **máogǔ sǒngrán** terrifying, hair-raising

冒号 **màohào** colon GRAM

铆接 **mǎojiē** rivet

毛巾 **máojīn** towel; washcloth

毛巾架 **máojīn jià** towel rail

毛孔 **máokǒng** pore

毛毛雨 **máomao yǔ** drizzle

猫咪 **māomī** puss, pussycat

牦牛 **máoniú** yak

毛皮 **máopí** coat, fur

茅舍 **máoshè** hovel

帽舌 **màoshé** visor

茂盛 **màoshèng** rampant; flourishing; luxuriant

冒失 **màoshī** presumptuous

毛毯 **máotǎn** blanket

猫头鹰 **māotóuyīng** owl

毛线 **máoxiàn** knitting wool

冒险 **màoxiǎn** adventure; venture, undertaking ◊ take a risk; venture into ◊ dangerous, risky; bold, audacious

冒险家 **màoxiǎnjiā** adventurer

帽檐 **màoyán** brim (*of hat*)

毛衣 **máoyī** sweater

贸易 **màoyì** trade, commerce

贸易差额 **màoyì chā'é** balance

of trade

贸易关系 **màoyì guānxi** trade
relations

毛泽东 **Máo Zédōng** Mao Tse-
tung, Mao Zedong

毛泽东思想 **Máo Zédōng
sīxiǎng** Mao Zedong thought

毛毡 **máozhān** felt

毛主席 **Máo Zhǔxí** Chairman
Mao

毛主席像章 **Máo Zhǔxí
xiàngzhāng** Mao badge

毛主席语录 **Máo Zhǔxí Yǔlù**
Little Red Book

帽子 **màozi** cap; hat

麻雀 **máquè** sparrow

骂人 **màrén** curse, swear

骂人话 **màrénhuà** swearword

马赛克 **mǎsàikè** mosaic

马上 **mǎshàng** immediately, right
now, straight away

马蹄 **mǎtí** hoof

马蹄铁 **mǎtítiě** horseshoe

马桶 **mǎtǒng** lavatory

码头 **mǎtóu** dock; wharf; port

马尾辫 **mǎwěibiàn** pigtail

马尾发 **mǎwěifà** ponytail

马戏团 **mǎxìtuán** circus

蚂蚁 **mǎyǐ** ant

麻油 **máyóu** sesame oil

马掌 **mǎzhǎng** horseshoe

麻疹 **mázhěn** measles

麻醉 **mázuì** anesthetize; drug ◊
anesthesia; anesthetic; drug ◊
high, stoned

麻醉剂 **mázuìjì** anesthetic;
narcotic

麻醉品 **mázuìpǐn** narcotic; drug

麻醉师 **mázuì shī** anesthetist

煤 **méi** coal

霉 **méi** mold, mildew

没 **méi** not ◊ have not; 我没钱 **wǒ
méi qián** I've got no money; 我没
看过这本书 **wǒ méi kànguo zhè
běn shū** I haven't read this book;
没多少 **méi duōshǎo** nothing
much ◊ (in questions): 你去没
去？ **nǐ qù méi qù?** did you go or
not?

梅 **méi** plum

眉 **méi** eyebrow

每 **měi** every; each; per

美 **měi** beautiful, pretty, lovely

妹 **mèi** younger sister

美餐 **měicān** good meal

每次 **měicì** each time

美德 **měidé** morality

没的比 **méidebǐ** there's no
comparison

梅毒 **méidú** syphilis

妹夫 **mèifū** brother-in-law
(younger sister's husband)

没赶上 **méigǎnshàng** miss

每隔 **měigé** alternate

每个 **měigè** each

每个人 **měigè rén** everyone

每隔一天 **měigéyìtiān** every
other day

湄公河 **Méigōnghé** Mekong
River

没工作 **méi gōngzuò** jobless

美观 **měiguān** esthetic

没关系 **méi guānxi** it doesn't
matter, never mind; it's a
pleasure, you're welcome

玫瑰 **méigui** rose

美国 **Měiguó** America, USA ◊
American

美国人 **Měiguó rén** American

没骨气 **méi gǔqì** spineless

美好 **měihǎo** wonderful; good

美化 **měihuà** make more
attractive; brighten up

没化妆 **méi huàzhuāng** unmade-
up, without make-up

媒介 **méijiè** medium; means

没经验 **méi jīngyàn**
inexperienced

没开 **méikāi** be off (of TV,
machine, light)

煤矿 **méikuàng** coal-mine

美丽 **měilì** beautiful, lovely ◊
beauty

魅力 **mèilì** attraction, magnetism;
charm; glamor

美利坚合众国 **Měilìjiān
Hézhòngguó** United States of
America

没礼貌 **méilǐmào** have no
manners

眉毛 **méimao** eyebrow

美貌 **měimào** looks

妹妹 **mèimèi** younger sister

没门儿！ **méiménr!** no way!

美妙 **měimiào** wonderful

每年 **měinián** yearly ◊ per annum

美女 **měinǚ** pin-up; pretty girl

煤气 **méiqì** coal gas

没前途 **méi qiántú** have no future ◊ hopeless, useless; 没前途的工作 **méi qiántú de gōngzuò** dead-end job

煤气灶 **méiqìzào** gas stove

没人 **méirén** nobody

每日 **měirì** daily

美容 **měiróng** cosmetic

美容家 **měiróng jiā** beautician

美容洗液 **měiróng xǐyè** face lotion

美容院 **měiróng yuàn** beauty parlor

美食 **měishí** delicacy

没事儿 **méi shìr** it's alright; 我没事儿 **wǒ méi shìr** I'm alright

美术片 **měishùpiàn** animation

每天 **měitiān** daily, everyday ◊ every day

媒体渲染 **méitǐ xuànrǎn** media hype

没完 **méiwán** never-ending

每晚 **měiwǎn** every evening

没完没了 **méiwán méiliǎo** on and on, endlessly; 没完没了地要 X 去做 Y **méiwán méiliǎo de yào X qù zuò Y** go on and on at X to do Y

没完全准备好 **méi wánquán zhǔnbèi hǎo** not quite ready

美味 **měiwèi** delicacy

没味儿 **méiwèir** tasteless

没问题 **méi wèntí** certainly, no problem

每小时 **měi xiǎoshí** hourly; 每小时一百五十公里 **měi xiǎoshí yībǎi wǔshí gōnglǐ** at 150 km/h

没兴趣 **méi xìngqu** uninterested; uninteresting

没修面 **méi xiūmiàn** unshaven

美学 **měixué** esthetics

没牙 **méiyá** toothless

没一个 **méi yīgè** none

没用 **méiyòng** useless ◊ it's no use; 试也没用 **shì yě méiyòng** it's useless trying

没用的东西 **méiyòng de dōngxi** bum

没用的人 **méiyòng de rén** good-for-nothing

煤油 **méiyóu** paraffin; kerosene

没有 **méiyǒu** without ◊ no ◊ not ◊ there is/are not; 没有多少 **méiyǒu duōshao** not much; not many; 没有咖啡／茶了 **méiyǒu kāfēi/chá le** there's no coffee/tea left; 没有钱 **méiyǒu qián** have no money ◊ (in questions): 你去了没有？ **nǐ qùle méiyou?** did you go or not?

没有结果 **méiyǒu jiéguǒ** unproductive

没有察觉到 **méiyǒu juéchádào** be unaware of

没有什么 **méiyǒu shénme** nothing

没有时间 **méiyǒu shíjiān** have no time; be booked up

没有图案 **méiyǒu tú'àn** plain, unadorned

没有问题 **méiyǒu wèntí** no problem; without a hitch

没有希望 **méiyǒu xīwàng** hopeless

没有音乐天赋 **méiyǒu yīnyuè tiānfù** unmusical

美元 **měiyuán** US dollar

每月 **měiyuè** monthly

没粘住 **méi zhānzhù** come unstuck

没治了 **méizhìle** amazing

美洲 **Měizhōu** (continent of) America

美洲鹫 **měizhōu jiù** vulture

美洲山核桃 **měizhōu shānhétáo** pecan

每周一次 **měizhōu yīcì** weekly

闷 **mēn** stuffy, airless

门 **mén** door

闷 **mèn** bored; 闷死了 **mènsǐle** be bored to death

门把手 **mén bǎshǒu** doorknob

门垫 **méndiàn** doormat

蒙 **méng** cover

猛 **měng** fierce

梦 **mèng** dream

蒙蔽 **méngbì** deceive ◊ deception, deceit

蠓虫 **měngchóng** midge, gnat

蒙古 **Měnggǔ** Mongolia ◊ Mongolian

猛击 **měngjī** bang; blow ◊ blaze away

孟加拉 **Mèngjiālā** Bangladesh ◊ Bangladeshi

梦见 **mèngjian** dream about

猛拉 **měnglā** jerk, wrench

猛烈 **měngliè** fierce, violent; passionate ◊ with a vengeance

朦朦胧胧 **méngméng lónglóng** misty *color*

蒙蒙细雨 **méngméng xìyǔ** drizzle

蒙骗 **mēngpiàn** cheat, deceive

猛扑 **měngpū** pounce, swoop

猛抬物价 **měngtái wùjià** bump up *prices*

猛推 **měngtuī** thrust, force

梦想 **mèngxiǎng** dream, fantasize

梦想家 **mèngxiǎng jiā** dreamer

萌芽 **méngyá** shoot, sprout

梦游者 **mèngyóu zhě** sleep walker

猛增 **měngzēng** jump, soar

猛掷 **měngzhì** hurl

蒙住眼睛 **méngzhù yǎnjīng** blindfold

孟子 **Mèngzǐ** Mencius

门阶 **ménjiē** doorstep

门槛 **ménkǎn** threshold

门口 **ménkǒu** gateway

门廊 **ménláng** porch, stoop

门铃 **ménlíng** doorbell

闷闷不乐 **mènmèn búlè** sullen

门牌号 **ménpáihào** house number

门票 **ménpiào** entrance ticket

闷热 **mènrè** clammy, sultry

闷人 **mènrén** bore

门闩 **ménshuān** bolt; latch

闷死 **mēnsǐ** suffocate

门厅 **méntīng** lobby

门卫 **ménwèi** porter, doorman

门诊部 **ménzhěnbù** outpatient department

门诊治疗 **ménzhěn zhìliáo** outpatient treatment

闷住 **mēnzhù** smother

门柱 **ménzhù** goalpost

迷 **mí** lost ◊ fan; 足球迷 **zúqiúmí** soccer fan

谜 **mí** mystery; riddle

米 **mǐ** rice; meter

密 **mì** thick; close

秘 **mì** secret

蜜 **mì** honey

棉 **mián** cotton

眠 **mián** sleep

免 **miǎn** avoid; prohibit

面 **miàn** face; side; flour; noodle

面包 **miànbāo** bread

面包店 **miànbāo diàn** bakery

面包渣 **miànbāo zhā** breadcrumbs

棉布 **miánbù** cotton

面部 **miànbù** face; 面部拉皮手术 **miànbù lāpí shǒushù** facelift

免除 **miǎnchú** immune ◊ be exempt from; 免除 X 的 Y **miǎnchú X de Y** excuse X from Y

面的 **miàndī** cab, taxi

缅甸 **Miǎndiàn** Burma ◊ Burmese

面的司机 **miàndī sījī** cab driver

面对 **miànduì** confront, stand up to; face (toward)

面对面 **miàn duì miàn** face to face

面额 **miàn'é** denomination (*of money*)

免费 **miǎnfèi** free, free of charge; 免费入场 **miǎnfèi rùchǎng** admission free

免费样品 **miǎnfèi yàngpǐn** free sample

面粉 **miànfěn** (wheat) flour

面糊 **miànhú** batter

棉花 **miánhua** cotton

棉花糖 **miánhuā táng** cotton candy; marshmallow

面积 **miànjī** area; proportions

面颊 **miànjiá** cheek

面具 **miànjù** mask

面孔 **miànkǒng** face

勉励 **miǎnlì** encourage

面貌 **miànmào** face; appearance

面前 **miànqián** in front of; 在 X 面前 **zài X miànqián** in the presence of X

勉强 miǎnqiǎng manage with difficulty ◊ reluctant, grudging, forced ◊ reluctantly; 勉强及格 *miǎnqiǎng jígé* scrape through; 勉强维持生活 *miǎnqiǎng wéichí shēnghuó* scrape a living

面色 miànsè complexion

面纱 miànshā veil

面食 miànshí pasta; pastry

面试 miànshì (job) interview

面熟 miànshú seem familiar

免税 miǎnshuì tax-free; duty-free

免税商店 miǎnshuì shāngdiàn duty-free store

免税物品 miǎnshuì wùpǐn duty-free goods

缅腆 miǎntiǎn shy; timid; retiring ◊ shyness; timidity

面条 miàntiáo noodle

面团 miàntuán dough

绵羊 miányáng sheep

免疫 miǎnyì immune ◊ immunity

免疫性 miǎnyìxìng immune ◊ immunity

免疫系统 miǎnyì xìtǒng immune system

免职 miǎnzhí oust

免租 miǎnzū rent-free

免罪 miǎnzuì redeem *sinner*

喵 miāo miaow

苗 miáo young plant

秒 miǎo second

庙 miào temple; temple market

妙 miào wonderful; 妙极了！ *miàojíle!* fantastic!

秒表 miǎobiǎo stopwatch

妙不可言 miàobùkěyán magical, enchanting

描绘 miáohuì portray, represent; describe

庙会 miàohuì carnival

苗圃 miáopǔ nursery (*for plants*)

描述 miáoshù describe; depict, portray ◊ description; portrayal

苗条 miáotiáo slim, slight; trim

描写 miáoxiě describe ◊ description; portrayal

妙语 miàoyǔ punch line

庙宇 miàoyǔ temple

妙语 miàoyǔ witticism

秒针 miǎozhēn second hand

瞄准 miáozhǔn aim ◊ be aimed at

弥补 míbǔ catch up on; make up for; recoup; rectify ◊ compensation

灭 miè extinguish, put out

灭火 mièhuǒ put out a fire

灭火器 mièhuǒqì fire extinguisher

灭绝 mièjué die out; wipe out, eradicate, exterminate

灭亡 mièwáng decline, disappearance ◊ go under, be ruined

米粉 mǐfěn rice noodles; vermicelli

密封 mìfēng airtight ◊ seal

蜜蜂 mìfēng bee

迷宫 mígōng maze

猕猴桃 míhóutáo kiwi fruit

迷惑 míhuò mystify; mislead; confuse ◊ disoriented

密集 mìjí dense *crowd* ◊ swarm

米酒 mǐjiǔ rice wine

秘诀 mìjué formula

迷恋 míliàn be infatuated with, be nuts about

迷路 mílù lose one's way; 我迷路了 *wǒ mílù le* I'm lost

密码 mìmǎ code; combination; PIN; 通路密码 *tōnglù mìmǎ* access code

秘密 mìmì secret ◊ covert, undercover

靡靡之音 mǐmǐ zhī yīn schmaltzy music; schmaltzy song

密谋 mìmóu conspire, plot

民 mín people; folk

民兵 mínbīng militia

名 míng name

鸣 míng ring, chime; toll; cry (*of birds, animals*)

明 míng bright; light

命 mìng life

敏感 mǐngǎn sensitive; touchy; acute *sense* ◊ sensitivity; 对冷／热敏感 *duì lěng／rè mǐngǎn* be sensitive to the cold／heat

敏感性 mǐngǎnxìng sensitivity

明白 míngbái understand ◊ clear

名册 míngcè roll, list

明朝 Míngcháo Ming Dynasty

明晨 **míngchén** tomorrow morning

名称 **míngchēng** name; designation

名词 **míngcí** noun

名次 **míngcì** place, position

民歌 **míngē** folk song

民歌手 **míngēshǒu** folk singer

明亮 **míngliàng** bright; light, brilliant ◊ brightness

明了 **míngliǎo** lucid

命令 **mìnglìng** command, order

命令式 **mìnglìng shì** dictatorial

鸣锣令 **míngluó lìng** gong; bell

命名 **mìngmíng** name

明年 **míngnián** next year

名牌 **míngpái** well-known brand

名牌服装 **míngpái fúzhuāng** designer clothes

名牌商品 **míngpái shāngpǐn** brand name

名片 **míngpiàn** business card, visiting card

明确 **míngquè** define ◊ definite; pronounced; explicit

明确指出 **míngquè zhǐchū** pinpoint

名人 **míngrén** prominent figure; celebrity

名声 **míngshēng** reputation; 有好 / 坏名声 **yǒuhǎo / huài míngshēng** have a good / bad reputation

名胜 **míngshèng** scenic spot

明天 **míngtiān** tomorrow; 明天上午 **míngtiān shàngwǔ** tomorrow morning (*between 10am and noon*); 明天早晨 **míngtiān zǎochén** tomorrow morning (*before 10am*)

铭文 **míngwén** inscription

明显 **míngxiǎn** clear, obvious; transparent

明星 **míngxīng** star

明信片 **míngxìnpiàn** postcard

名义上 **míngyì shàng** nominal

名誉 **míngyù** fame; reputation

命运 **mìngyùn** fate

明智 **míngzhì** wise; sensible

名字 **míngzi** name; given name; 你叫什么名字? **nǐ jiào shénme míngzi?** what's your name?

民航 **mínháng** civil aviation

民间 **mínjiān** civil; folk

民间舞 **mínjiānwǔ** folk dance

敏捷 **mǐnjié** quick, rapid; nimble; sharp, smart

民谣 **mínyáo** ballad

民意测验 **mínyì cèyàn** poll, survey

民意调查 **mínyì diàochá** poll, survey

民营企业 **mínyíng qǐyè** private sector

民乐 **mínyuè** folk music

民众 **mínzhòng** the people; the public

民主 **mínzhǔ** democracy ◊ democratic

民主党 **Mínzhǔ Dǎng** Democratic Party

民主主义者 **mínzhǔ zhǔyì zhě** democrat

民族 **mínzú** people; ethnic group; race; nation; nationality

民族主义 **mínzú zhǔyì** nationalism

密切 **mìqiè** intimate, close

迷人 **mírén** fascinating; charming; enchanting

弥撒 **mísa** mass REL

米色 **mǐsè** cream (*color*)

秘书 **mìshū** secretary ◊ secretarial

迷途知返 **mítú zhīfǎn** straighten out

迷惘 **míwǎng** be mixed up

迷信 **míxìn** superstition ◊ superstitious

密友 **mìyǒu** crony, pal

谜语 **míyǔ** riddle

蜜月 **mìyuè** honeymoon

迷住 **mízhù** enthrall, bewitch; 被 X 迷住 **bèi X mízhù** be hooked on X

摸 **mō** touch, feel; grope

膜 **mó** membrane

磨 **mó** grind; sharpen

魔 **mó** demon

抹 **mǒ** spread *butter etc*

磨 **mò** grind (down)

末 **mò** end

墨 **mò** ink

没 **mò** sink

殁 mò perish, meet one's end

末班车 mòbānchē last bus; last train

漠不关心 mò bù guānxīn indifference ◊ indifferent; nonchalant

摸不着头脑 mōbùzháo tóunǎo be baffled

摩擦 mócā friction ◊ rub

末代皇帝 Mòdài Huángdì Last Emperor

磨掉 módiào rub off (of paint etc)

抹掉 mǒdiào erase, wipe

魔法 mófǎ magic ◊ magical

模范 mófàn example, model ◊ exemplary

模仿 mófǎng imitate, mimic; forge ◊ imitation, impersonation

磨坊 mòfáng mill

蘑菇 mógū mushroom

磨光 móguāng polish

魔鬼 móguǐ devil; demon

模糊 móhu vague; indistinct; fuzzy, hazy; misty ◊ blur ◊ mist over

墨家 Mòjiā Mohism ◊ Mohist

墨镜 mòjìng sunglasses

魔力 mólì magic

茉莉 mòlì jasmine

茉莉花茶 mòlìhuāchá jasmine tea

莫名其妙 mò míng qí miào mysterious

模拟 mónǐ analog

摹拟 mónǐ mock, simulated, imitation ◊ simulate

末期 mòqī final stage; 十九／二十世纪末期 shíjiǔ／èrshí shìjì mòqī the late 19th／20th century

默契 mòqì chemistry (between people)

磨砂玻璃 móshā bōlí frosted glass

陌生 mòshēng strange, unfamiliar; alien

陌生人 mòshēng rén stranger

模式 móshì model, pattern

没收 mòshōu confiscate

墨守成规者 mòshǒu chéngguī zhě stick-in-the-mud

魔术 móshù conjuring tricks, magic

墨水 mòshuǐ ink

魔术师 móshùshī magician, conjurer

莫斯科 Mòsīkē Moscow

磨碎 mósuì grate

磨损 mósǔn wear; abrasion ◊ wear away, wear out ◊ worn

摸索 mōsuǒ grope

模特儿 mótèr (fashion) model

摩天大楼 mótiān dàlóu skyscraper

摩托 mótuō motor, engine

摩托车 mótuōchē motorcycle

谋 móu scheme

某 mǒu certain; some; 某处 mǒuchù somewhere; 某人 mǒurén a certain person, someone

谋杀 móushā murder

谋生 móushēng living ◊ earn one's living

末尾 mòwěi end

墨西哥 Mòxīgē Mexico ◊ Mexican

模型 móxíng model; prototype; cast, mold

磨牙 móyá molar

墨鱼 mòyú cuttlefish

某种 mǒuzhǒng certain, particular

母 mǔ mother; female (of animal or bird)

幕 mù curtain; act (of play)

木 mù wood

墓 mù grave

目 mù eye

牧 mù tend livestock

母爱 mǔ'ài motherly love

母斑 mǔbān birthmark

母板 mǔbǎn motherboard

木板 mùbǎn plank

墓碑 mùbēi tombstone, gravestone

目标 mùbiāo aim, objective; goal; target

木材 mùcái lumber, wood

牧草 mùcǎo graze

木柴 mùchái firewood

牧场 mùchǎng pasture

牧场主 mùchǎng zhǔ rancher

牡丹 mǔdān peony

目瞪口呆 mùdèng kǒudāi stupefied, astonished

墓地 mùdì graveyard, cemetery

目的 mùdì purpose, aim, end

目的地 mùdìdì destination

木耳 mù'ěr wood-ear mushroom

木筏 mùfá raft

木工 mùgōng carpenter; joiner

木工活 mùgōnghuó woodwork (*activity*)

母狗 mǔgǒu bitch (*dog*)

目光 mùguāng look

木棍 mùgùn stick; club

幕后 mùhòu behind the scenes

幕后策划 mùhòu cèhuà mastermind, organize

母鸡 mǔjī hen

目击 mùjī witness

幕间 mùjiān interlude

木匠 mùjiàng carpenter

幕间休息 mùjiān xiúxī intermission

目击者 mùjīzhě eyewitness

募捐 mùjuān collect donations

募捐者 mùjuān zhě fundraiser

木刻 mùkè wood carving

母鹿 mǔlù doe

目录 mùlù catalog; directory; list; table of contents

暮 mù evening

母马 mǔmǎ mare

牡马 mǔmǎ stallion

牧民 mùmín herdsman

母牛 mǔniú cow

木偶 mù'ǒu puppet

木偶戏 mù'ǒuxì puppet show

木排 mùpái raft

目前 mùqián at present, currently

母亲 mǔqīn mother

母亲节 Mǔqīnjié Mother's Day

暮色降临 mùsè jiànglín get dark

牧师 mùshī priest, minister, clergyman, pastor

穆斯林 Mùsīlín Muslim

木炭 mùtàn charcoal

木纹 mùwén grain

木屋 mùwū log cabin

木屑 mùxiè chip (*of wood*)

母性 mǔxìng maternity ◊ motherly

母羊 mǔyáng ewe

牧羊犬 mùyángquǎn sheepdog

牧羊人 mùyáng rén shepherd

母语 mǔyǔ mother tongue

拇指 mǔzhǐ thumb

木制 mùzhì wooden

木制管乐器 mùzhì guānyuèqì woodwind instrument

墓志铭 mùzhìmíng epitaph

木制品 mùzhìpǐn woodwork (*object*)

目中无人 mùzhōng wúrén snooty

母猪 mǔzhū sow (*pig*)

木柱 mùzhù pin, skittle

模子 múzi mold

N

拿 **ná** carry (*in hand*); hold; fetch; collect; take, remove

哪 **nǎ** which; 哪一个？ *nǎ yīgè?* which one?

那 **nà** that; those ◊ then; 那不行 *nà bùxíng* that's not right, that's not allowed; 那两人 *nà liǎngrén* those two people; 那是什么？ *nà shì shénme?* what is that?; 那又怎么样？ *nà yòu zěnmeyàng?* so what?

拿不准 **ná bùzhǔn** be doubtful

拿出 **náchū** produce, take out

纳粹 **Nàcuì** Nazi

拿掉 **nádiào** get off, remove

拿动 **nádòng** manage

哪个 **nǎge** which; which one; who; 哪个是你的？ *nǎge shì nǐde?* which one is yours?; 哪个都行 *nǎge dōuxíng* either

那个 **nàge** that, that one

奶 **nǎi** milk

耐穿 **nàichuān** sturdy, hardwearing

耐久 **nàijiǔ** durable

奶酪 **nǎilào** cheese

耐力 **nàilì** stamina, endurance

奶奶 **nǎinai** grandma (*paternal*)

奶瓶 **nǎipíng** baby's bottle

耐心 **nàixīn** patience; 耐心点儿！ *nàixīn diǎnr!* just be patient!

耐用 **nàiyòng** hardwearing ◊ wear, last

奶油 **nǎiyóu** cream

奶子 **nǎizi** tit, boob

奶嘴 **nǎizuǐ** pacifier; nipple

拿来 **nálái** bring

哪里 **nǎli** where, whereabouts

那里 **nàli** there

那么 **nàme** such a ◊ (so) that ◊ then, therefore; 那么大／贵 *nàme dà/guì* that big/expensive; 那么多？ *nàme duō?* as much as that?

南 **nán** south ◊ southern; southerly

难 **nán** difficult, hard

男 **nán** man ◊ male

难 **nàn** disaster

男扮女装 **nánbàn nǚzhuāng** in drag ◊ transvestite

南边 **nánbiān** south; the south side; 在X的南边 *zài X de nánbiān* to the south of X

男傧相 **nánbīnxiàng** best man

南部 **nánbù** south

男厕 **náncè** men's room, washroom

难道 … ？ **nándào …?** can it be that …?; 你难道没看见？ *nǐ nándào méi kànjiàn?* can't you see?

男低音 **nán dīyīn** bass

难度 **nándù** difficulty, hardness

南方 **nánfāng** south

南非 **Nánfēi** South Africa ◊ South African

南风 **nánfēng** southerly wind

男服务员 **nán fúwùyuán** waiter

男高音 **nán gāoyīn** tenor

南瓜 **nánguā** squash, pumpkin

难怪！ **nánguài!** no wonder!

难过 **nánguò** upset; sad, unhappy; sorry; 令人难过 *lìngrén nánguò* upsetting

囊肿 **nángzhǒng** cyst

男孩 **nánhái** boy

南海 **Nánhǎi** South China Sea

南韩 **Nánhán** South Korea ◊ South Korean

男护士 **nán hùshi** male nurse

南极 **Nánjí** South Pole ◊ Antarctic

男妓 **nánjì** male prostitute

难解 **nánjiě** obscure, difficult

难接近 **nán jiējìn** inaccessible

难堪 **nánkān** embarrassed; 使X难堪 *shǐ X nánkān* embarrass X, put X on the spot

难看 **nánkàn** ugly

难理解 **nán lǐjiě** unintelligible

南美 **Nánměi** South America ◊ South American

难免 **nánmiǎn** inevitable; inescapable

难民 **nànmín** refugee

男模特儿 **nán mótèr** male model

男朋友 **nán péngyou** boyfriend

男仆从 **nán púcóng** valet

男人 **nánrén** man, male

南沙群岛 **Nánshā Qúndǎo** Spratley Islands

男士护肤液 **nánshì hùfū yè** aftershave

难受 **nánshòu** feel ill-at-ease

难忘 **nánwàng** unforgettable

难为情 **nánwéiqíng** ashamed, embarrassed

难闻 **nánwén** foul-smelling

男性 **nánxìng** masculine, male

南亚 **Nányà** South Asia ◊ South Asian

难以 **nányǐ** *difficult to*

难以表述 **nányǐ biǎoshù** inexpressible

难以察觉 **nányǐ chájué** imperceptible

难以对付 **nányǐ duìfu** awkward, obstreperous

难以估量 **nányǐ gūliàng** inestimable

难以解答 **nányǐ jiědá** baffling

难以接近 **nányǐ jiējìn** unapproachable

难以描述 **nányǐ miáoshù** indefinable

难以扑捉 **nányǐ pūzhuō** elusive

难以确定 **nányǐ quèdìng** be in doubt

难以忍受 **nányǐ rěnshòu** unbearable

难以容忍 **nányǐ róngrěn** trying

难以想象 **nányǐ xiǎngxiàng** unimaginable

难以形容 **nányǐ xíngróng** indescribable

难以预料 **nányǐ yùliào** it is doubtful whether

难以置信 **nányǐ zhìxìn** unbelievable

男用卫生间 **nányòng**

wèishēngjiān washroom, men's room

难住 **nánzhù** baffle, stump

男子汉气 **nánzǐhànqì** manhood; manliness

男子气 **nánzǐqì** masculine

男子气概 **nánzi qìgài** virility; machismo

脑 **nǎo** brain

闹 **nào** noisy ◊ make a noise; beef, bellyache

闹别扭 **nào bièniu** fall out, argue

闹鬼 **nàoguǐ** haunted

恼火 **nǎohuǒ** mad, sore ◊ be mad, be sore

闹剧 **nàojù** farce

脑门儿 **nǎoménr** forehead, brow

脑膜炎 **nǎomóyán** meningitis

恼怒 **nǎonù** annoyed, pissed

恼人 **nǎorén** annoying

闹事 **nàoshì** make a scene; riot

闹事者 **nàoshì zhě** rioter

脑髓 **nǎosuǐ** brain

脑外科医生 **nǎo wàikē yīshēng** brain surgeon

脑震荡 **nǎozhèndàng** concussion

闹着玩儿 **nàozhe wánr** playful; joking; 不是闹着玩儿的 **búshì nàozhe wánr de** it's no joke

闹钟 **nàozhōng** alarm clock

脑子 **nǎozi** brains, intelligence

拿起 **náqǐ** pick up

哪儿 **nǎr** where; 我哪儿都找不着 **wǒ nǎr dōu zhǎobùzháo** I can't find it anywhere

那儿 **nàr** there; 他在那儿！ **tā zài nàr!** there he is!

拿上去 **ná shàngqù** take up, fetch up

那时 **nàshí** then

那时候 **nàshíhòu** in those days

拿手好菜 **náshǒu hǎocài** specialty

纳税人 **nàshuì rén** taxpayer

那天 **nàtiān** the other day

哪些 **nǎxiē** which; which ones; who

那些 **nàxiē** those

捺着性子 **nàzhe xìngzi** keep one's temper

拿走 **názǒu** take away, remove

呢 **ne** (*in questions*):你呢？ *nǐ ne?* and you? ◊ (*emphasis*):他还没来呢！ *ta hái méi lái ne!* he still hasn't come!

哪 **něi** which

内 **nèi** inside ◊ inner; internal

那 **nèi** that; those

内部 **nèibù** inside, interior ◊ internal; inward; inner ◊ internally

内部人 **nèibùrén** insider

内部消息 **nèibù xiāoxi** inside information

内部装修 **nèibù zhuāngxiū** interior decoration

内存 **nèicún** RAM, random access memory

内弟 **nèidì** brother-in-law (*wife's younger brother*)

内地 **nèidì** interior; inland

内阁 **nèigé** cabinet POL

内含 **nèihán** built-in

内涵 **nèihán** hidden

内疚 **nèijiù** guilt; guilty conscience ◊ guilty; 我一直感到内疚 *wǒ yīzhí gǎndào nèijiù* it has been on my conscience

内科医生 **nèikē yīshēng** internist

内裤 **nèikù** underpants, panties

内陆 **nèilù** interior, inland

内蒙古 **Nèiménggǔ** Inner Mongolia ◊ Inner Mongolian

内蒙古大草原 **Nèiménggǔ Dà Cǎo Yuán** Inner Mongolian Grasslands

内幕交易 **nèimù jiāoyì** insider trading

内燃机 **nèiránjī** internal combustion engine

内容 **nèiróng** content; contents

内胎 **nèitāi** inner tube

内向 **nèixiàng** reserved; introverted

内斜视 **nèi xiéshì** cross-eyed

内心 **nèixīn** privately, inwardly

内兄 **nèixiōng** brother-in-law (*wife's older brother*)

内衣 **nèiyī** underwear

内脏 **nèizàng** guts; giblets

内战 **nèizhàn** civil war

内政 **nèizhèng** domestic policy; domestic affairs

内政部 **Nèizhèng Bù** Department of the Interior

内装 **nèizhuāng** built-in

嫩 **nèn** tender

能 **néng** can, be able to ◊ energy; 你能帮我吗？ *nǐ néng bāng wǒ ma?* can you help me?

能干 **nénggàn** capable

能够 **nénggòu** be able to

能见度 **néngjiàn dù** visibility

能力 **néngli** ability, capacity; competence; faculty (*hearing, vision etc*)

能量 **néngliàng** power, energy; 能量爆发 **néngliàng bàofā** in a burst of energy

能量单位 **néngliàng dānwèi** power unit

能耐梗 **néngnàigěng** wise guy

能胜任 **néngshèngrèn** be equal to

能生育 **néng shēngyù** fertile

能手 **néngshǒu** expert

能养活 **néng yǎnghuó** viable *life form*

能源 **néngyuán** energy (*gas etc*)

嫩鸡 **nènjī** broiler (*chicken*)

嫩芽 **nènyá** shoot BOT

嗯 **ńg** (*questioning*): 嗯，你说什么？ *ńg, nǐ shuō shénme?* huh?, what did you say?

嗯 **ǹg** (*promising*): 嗯！就这么办吧 *ǹg! jiù zhème bàn ba* ok, it's a deal!

泥 **ní** mud

你 **nǐ** you *sg* ◊ your *sg*

拟 **nǐ** draft, draw up

溺爱 **nì'ài** mollycoddle

年 **nián** year ◊ annual

粘 **nián** sticky ◊ stick

念 **niàn** think of; read (out loud); study

黏稠度 **niánchóu dù** consistency, texture

年初 **niánchū** start of the year

年底 **niándǐ** end of the year

年度 **niándù** year ◊ annual

粘附 **niánfù** adhere to

娘 **niáng** mother; woman

酿 niàng ferment; brew

娘家姓 niángjiāxìng maiden name

酿酒厂 niàngjiǔchǎng distillery; winery

娘儿们 niángrmen broad, chick

酿造 niàngzào brew

酿造厂 niàngzào chǎng brewery

酿造者 niàngzào zhě brewer

黏糊糊 nián hūhu sticky, clammy

年级 niánjí grade, class EDU

年纪 niánjì age

粘结 niánjié bond, stick

年龄 niánlíng age; 年龄为 niánlíng wéi at the age of

碾灭 niǎnmiè stub out

粘膜 niánmó mucous membrane

年青 niánqīng young

碾碎 niǎnsuì grind

捻碎 niǎnsuì scrunch up

念头 niàntou thought, idea

粘土 niántǔ clay

粘液 niányè mucus

年长 niánzhǎng senior; elder; eldest

年长者 niánzhǎngzhě elder

粘住 niánzhù stick, glue, adhere

撵走 niǎnzǒu throw out, expel

鸟 niǎo bird

尿 niào urine, piss

尿布 niàobù diaper

鸟类保护区 niǎo lèibǎohù qū bird sanctuary

鸟笼 niǎolóng birdcage

尿片 niàopiàn diaper

鸟嘴 niǎozuǐ bill, beak

尼泊尔 Níbó'ěr Nepal ◊ Nepalese

昵称 nìchēng pet name

你的 nǐde your sg ◊ yours sg; 你的朋友 nǐde péngyǒu a friend of yours

拟订 nǐdìng draft, draw up

捏 niē pinch; 一捏 yìniē a pinch (of salt etc)

镍 niè nickel

啮合 nièhé engage, become operative

捏造 niēzào invent

镊子 nièzi tweezers

逆风 nìfēng headwind

尼姑 nígū Buddhist nun

你好 nǐ hǎo hello, hi; 你好吗？nǐ hǎo ma? how do you do?; how are you?

霓虹灯 níhóng dēng neon light

霓虹灯管 níhóng dēngguǎn neon strip

泥浆 níjiāng slime

尼龙 nílóng nylon

你们 nǐmen you pl ◊ your pl

你们的 nǐmende your pl ◊ yours pl

匿名 nìmíng anonymous

您 nín you polite ◊ your polite

您的 nínde your polite ◊ yours polite

宁 níng peaceful

拧 níng twist; pinch

凝 níng condense; congeal

拧出 níngchū wring out

拧干 nínggān wring dry

凝固 nínggù freeze; congeal

凝结 níngjié set; coagulate; curdle

宁静 níngjìng peace, tranquility ◊ serene; tranquil, quiet, peaceful

拧开 níngkāi unscrew lid

柠檬 níngméng lemon

柠檬茶 níngméng chá lemon tea

柠檬汽水 níngméng qìshuǐ carbonated lemonade

柠檬水 níngméng shuǐ lemonade

柠檬汁儿 níngméng zhīr lemon juice

凝视 níngshì gaze; peer; gaze at ◊ stare; gaze

宁愿 nìngyuàn would rather

泥泞 níníng muddy

泥石流 níshí liú landslide

逆时针 nì shízhēn counterclockwise

妞 niū chick, babe

牛 niú cattle; cow; bull; ox

扭 niǔ twist

扭打 niǔdǎ scuffle; fight

扭动 niǔdòng squirm, wriggle, writhe; wiggle

牛犊 niúdú calf

牛奶 niúnǎi (cow's) milk

牛奶场 niúnǎichǎng dairy

牛奶加工 niúnǎi jiāgōng dairy

忸怩 niǔní bashful
牛排 niǔpái steak
牛皮纸 niúpí zhǐ brown paper
扭曲 niǔqū screw up, contort ◊ gnarled
牛肉 niúròu beef
牛肉面 niúròumiàn beef noodles
扭伤 niǔshāng sprain, wrench
纽约 Niǔyuē New York
牛仔 niúzǎi cowboy
牛仔布 niúzǎi bù denim
牛仔裤 niúzǎikù jeans
扭转 niǔzhuǎn deflect; turn around
扭转方向 niǔzhuǎn fāngxiàng deflect
泥瓦工 níwǎgōng bricklayer
泥瓦匠 níwǎ jiàng bricklayer; mason
你自己 nǐ zìjǐ yourself
脓 nóng pus
浓 nóng thick; strong tea etc
农 nóng agriculture, farming; farmer; peasant ◊ agricultural
弄 nòng do; make; obtain
脓包 nóngbāo pimple
农场 nóngchǎng farm
农场工人 nóngchǎng gōngrén farmworker
弄出 nòngchū get out, extract
农村 nóngcūn village; countryside ◊ rural
弄错 nòngcuò be mistaken
弄掉 nòngdiào shift, get rid of
浓度 nóngdù depth (of color); level
弄短 nòngduǎn shorten
弄翻 nòngfān upset, spill
农夫 nóngfū farmer
浓厚 nónghòu dense, thick; strong
农户 nónghù farm
弄坏 nònghuài break; wear out; spoil
弄糊涂 nòng hútu muddle
浓烈 nóngliè strong
弄乱 nòngluàn mess up; be in a mess; ruffle hair
浓密 nóngmì bushy
农民 nóngmín farmer; peasant
弄明白 nòng míngbái work out
弄清 nòngqīng make clear

农舍 nóngshè farmhouse
弄湿 nòng shī dampen, moisten
弄死 nòngsǐ kill
弄碎 nòngsuì crumble stock cube
浓缩 nóngsuō concentrated
农田 nóngtián field
浓烟 nóngyān smoke
农业 nóngyè agriculture ◊ agricultural
弄脏 nòngzāng dirty, soil; smudge
弄糟 nòngzāo screw up; spoil
弄直 nòngzhí straighten
脓肿 nóngzhǒng abscess
奴 nú slave
女 nǚ female; feminine
暖 nuǎn warm
暖房 nuǎnfáng hothouse; greenhouse; conservatory
暖和 nuǎnhuo warm, snug
暖瓶 nuǎnpíng flask
暖气 nuǎnqì heating; central heating; radiator
女厕 nǚcè ladies room
女厕所 nǚcèsuǒ ladies room, powder room
女店主 nǚ diànzhǔ landlady
虐待 nüèdài ill-treat, abuse ◊ ill-treatment, abuse
疟疾 nüèji malaria
女儿 nǚ'ér daughter
女服务员 nǚ fúwùyuán waitress; (chamber)maid
女孩 nǚhái girl
怒号 nùháo howl; roar
怒吼 nùhǒu howl; roar; bellow
女皇 nǚhuáng empress
女继承人 nǚ jìchéng rén heiress
女警察 nǚ jǐngchá policewoman
奴隶 núlì slave
努力 nǔlì effort, attempt; endeavor ◊ laborious; struggle; work hard
努力不懈 nǔlì búxiè plug away, persevere
怒目而视 nùmù ér shì glare at
女牧师 nǚ mùshī woman priest
挪 nuó slide
挪动 nuódòng move, shift; stir (in sleep)
懦夫 nuòfū coward ◊ cowardly
糯米 nuòmì glutinous rice

挪威 **Nuówēi** Norway ◊ Norwegian

诺言 **nuòyán** promise, word

女朋友 **nǚ péngyou** girlfriend (*of boy*)

女仆 **nǚpú** maid

女权 **nǚquán** women's rights

女权主义 **nǚquán zhǔyì** feminism

女权主义者 **nǚquán zhǔyì zhě** feminist

女人 **nǚrén** woman; female

女人气 **nǚrénqì** effeminate

怒容 **nùróng** scowl

女神 **nǚshén** goddess

女生 **nǚshēng** female student

怒视 **nùshì** scowl

女士 **nǚshì** lady ◊ ma'am ◊ Ms; Miss

女同性恋者 **nǚtóng xìngliàn zhě** lesbian

女王 **nǚwáng** queen

女巫 **nǚwū** witch

女性 **nǚxìng** female

女性朋友 **nǚxìng péngyou** girlfriend (*of girl*)

女婿 **nǚxù** son-in-law

女招待 **nǚzhāodài** hostess (*in bar*)

女主人 **nǚzhǔ rén** mistress (*employer, owner*); hostess

O

噢，喔 ō (*understanding*): 噢，我明白了 *ō, wǒ míngbái le* oh, I see

哦 ó (*doubt*): 哦，你确定吗？*ó, nǐ quèdìng ma?* really? are you sure?

鸥 ōu gull

偶 ǒu mate

藕 ǒu lotus root

殴打 ōudǎ assault, attack

偶尔 ǒu'ěr every now and then, occasionally ◊ occasional

欧化 ōuhuà westernize

偶然 ǒurán chance ◊ by chance; occasionally; 偶然发现 *ǒurán fāxiàn* happen across

偶然性 ǒuránxìng haphazard

偶数 ǒushù even *number*

呕吐 ǒutù bring up, throw up ◊ vomiting; vomit

偶像 ǒuxiàng heart throb, idol

欧元 ōuyuán euro

欧洲 Ōuzhōu Europe ◊ European

P

趴 **pā** lie on one's stomach

爬 **pá** climb; crawl

耙 **pá** rake

怕 **pà** fear

啪嗒声 **pādāshēng** patter

拍 **pāi** take *photograph*; shoot *film*; beat, pound; clap; pat

牌 **pái** plate; brand; card

排 **pái** line, row; tier; cluster; platoon ◊ rank (*in order*); discharge, expel; 排成长龙 **páichéng chánglóng** be backed up (*of traffic*)

派 **pài** group; pie

排版 **páibǎn** typeset

陪伴 **péibàn** companionship

派别 **pàibié** group; faction; sect

排斥 **páichì** exclude, bar; push away

排出 **páichū** discharge

排出的废气 **páichūde fèiqì** exhaust fumes

排除 **páichú** eliminate; cut out; exclude; rule out ◊ removal

排除故障 **páichú gùzhàng** troubleshooting

派出所 **pàichūsuǒ** police station

排除在外 **páichú zàiwài** exclude; ignore

拍打 **pāidǎ** buffet; patter; smack

排队 **páiduì** stand in line

排房 **páifáng** row house

排放 **páifàng** emission

排干 **páigān** drain *liquid*

排骨 **páigǔ** chop; spare ribs

排挤 **páijǐ** displace

迫击炮 **pǎijīpào** mortar

排练 **páiliàn** rehearse ◊ rehearsal

排列 **páiliè** sort COMPUT

拍卖 **pāimài** auction

拍卖掉 **pāimài diào** auction off

拍马屁 **pāi mǎpì** brown-nose

排尿 **páiniào** urinate, pass water

拍拍 **pāipāi** pat *dog etc*

派遣 **pàiqiǎn** send

排气管 **páiqìguǎn** exhaust (pipe)

排球 **páiqiú** volleyball

排去 **páiqù** drain away; drain off

派人去找 **pàirén qùzhǎo** send for

拍摄 **pāishè** film, shoot; photograph

拍摄场地 **pāishè chǎngdì** (film) set

派生 **pàishēng** derivative

拍手 **pāishǒu** clap, applaud

排水 **páishuǐ** drainage

排水工程 **páishuǐ gōngchéng** sewerage

排水沟 **páishuǐgōu** gutter

排水管 **páishuǐ guǎn** drainpipe

派往 **pàiwǎng** post; transfer

排演 **páiyǎn** rehearse ◊ rehearsal

拍照 **pāizhào** photograph

牌照 **páizhào** vehicle registration

拍子 **pāizi** bat; racket; club; stick

牌子 **páizi** sign; nameplate; brand, make

攀 **pān** climb

盘 **pán** dish; plate; set (*in tennis*) ◊ *measure word for cassettes, CDs*

判 **pàn** judge

叛 **pàn** betray

盼 **pàn** hope for; expect

攀登 **pāndēng** climb; scramble

盘点 **pándiǎn** take stock ◊ stocktaking

判断 **pànduàn** judge; make a judgment

判断能力 **pànduàn nénglì** discretion, judgment

旁 **páng** side

胖 **pàng** fat

旁边 **pángbiān** side; 在 X 的旁边 **zài X de pángbiān** next to X, beside X

庞大 **pángdà** enormous

判给 **pàngěi** award

旁观 **pángguān** look on, watch

膀胱 **pángguāng** bladder

旁观者 **pángguān zhě** bystander, onlooker

胖乎乎 **pànghūhū** plump

庞然大物 **pángrán dàwù** monster

旁听 **pángtīng** listen in; audit *course*

滂沱 **pāngtuó** pouring; 大雨滂沱 **dàyǔ pāngtuó** pouring with rain

叛国罪 **pànguó zuì** treason

螃蟹 **pángxiè** crab

胖子 **pàngzi** fat person, fatso

判决 **pànjué** pass judgment ◊ judgment, verdict

叛乱 **pànluàn** mutiny

叛逆 **pànnì** rebel

蹒跚 **pánshān** hobble; lurch; totter

叛徒 **pàntú** traitor

盼望 **pànwàng** long for

盘问 **pánwèn** question, quiz

判刑 **pànxíng** sentence; pass sentence; 判死刑 **pàn sǐxíng** condemn to death

盘旋 **pánxuán** twist, wind; circle

攀缘 **pānyuán** climb

盘子 **pánzi** plate

抛 **pāo** throw

跑 **pǎo** run; run away

泡 **pào** bubble ◊ soak, steep; brew, infuse (*of tea*)

炮 **pào** cannon; gun

炮兵 **pàobīng** artillery

跑步 **pǎobù** run, jog

泡菜 **pàocài** pickles

泡茶 **pàochá** make tea

跑车 **pǎochē** sports car

刨出 **páochū** dig out; dig up

炮弹 **pàodàn** shell MIL

跑道 **pǎodào** runway; racetrack; lane

跑掉 **pǎodiào** run off; run away

炮火 **pàohuǒ** gunfire; shelling

炮击 **pàojī** shell MIL

跑马 **pǎomǎ** the races

跑马道 **pǎomǎ dào** racecourse

抛锚 **pāomáo** break down; stall (*of vehicle*); anchor (*of ship*)

泡沫 **pàomò** foam, froth; suds; lather

泡沫橡胶 **pàomò xiàngjiāo** foam rubber

泡泡糖 **pàopao táng** bubble gum

抛起 **pāoqǐ** throw up *ball*

抛弃 **pāoqì** abandon; leave; discard; ditch ◊ desertion

跑气 **pǎoqì** flat *beer*

跑腿 **pǎotuǐ** run errands

咆哮 **páoxiào** growl; roar

疱疹 **pàozhěn** herpes; 嘴边疱疹 **zuǐbiān pàozhěn** cold sore

扒手 **páshǒu** pickpocket

爬行 **páxíng** creep; crawl

爬行动物 **páxíng dòngwù** reptile

耙子 **pázi** rake

呸 **pēi** (*scorn*): 呸！谁要你的臭钱！**pēi! shéi yào nǐde chòuqián!** bah!, who needs your damn money!

陪 **péi** accompany, go with; escort

赔 **péi** pay compensation

配 **pèi** match, go together; 配钥匙 **pèi yàoshi** copy a key

陪伴 **péibàn** accompany

赔本 **péiběn** make a loss

赔偿 **péicháng** compensate ◊ compensation; damages

佩服 **pèifú** admire

配合 **pèihé** cooperate ◊ teamwork

配给 **pèijǐ** ration; 少量配给 **shǎoliàng pèijǐ** dole out

配给量 **pèijǐ liàng** ration

赔礼 **péilǐ** apologize

配偶 **pèi'ǒu** spouse

赔钱 **péiqián** be out of pocket

陪审团 **péishěntuán** jury

陪审员 **péishěnyuán** juror

胚胎 **pēitāi** embryo

陪同 **péitóng** escort; accompany

陪同者 **péitóngzhě** escort; companion; accompanist

培训 **péixùn** train; groom, prepare ◊ training

培训课程 **péixùn kèchéng** training course

培养 **péiyǎng** raise; develop; train; cultivate *plants*

配音 **pèiyīn** dub *movie*

配乐 **pèiyuè** soundtrack, score

培植 **péizhí** breeding ◊ cultivate *plants*

喷 pēn spray; spurt

盆 pén bowl; plant pot; 一盆花 **yīpén huā** a potted plant

喷出 pēnchū spout, spurt

盆地 péndì basin (*geographical*)

喷发胶 pēnfà jiāo hair spray

砰 pēng thump

烹 pēng cook

棚 péng shed; stall, pen

碰 pèng touch; knock; push; bump into; meet; 别碰! **bié pèng!** hands off!

碰杯 pèngbēi clink glasses

篷车 péngchē trailer

碰钉子 pèng dīngzi get the brushoff

捧腹大笑 pěngfù dàxiào crack up, laugh

抨击 pēngjī hit out at, criticize, attack

碰见 pèngjiàn bump into, meet

蓬乱 péngluàn unkempt, dishevelled; tousled

碰碰车 pèngpèngchē bumper car, dodgem®

捧起 pěngqǐ scoop up

碰巧 pèngqiǎo by chance, coincidentally; 如果你碰巧见到他 **rúguǒ nǐ pèngqiǎo jiàndào tā** if you happen to see him

烹饪书 pēngrèn shū cookbook

碰伤 pèngshāng bruise (*of fruit*)

蓬松 péngsōng fluffy

烹调 pēngtiáo cook ◊ cookery ◊ culinary

碰头 pèngtóu meet

棚屋 péngwū hut

朋友 péngyou friend

膨胀 péngzhàng expand; bulge; inflate *economy* ◊ expansion ◊ swollen; puffy

碰撞 pèngzhuàng collide

棚子 péngzi shack

喷壶 pēnhú watering can

盆景 pénjǐng bonsai

喷沫 pēnmò aerosol

喷墨 (打印机) pēnmò (dǎyìnjī) inkjet (printer)

喷漆 pēnqī spray paint

喷枪 pēnqiāng spraygun

喷气发动机 pēnqì fādòngjī jet engine

喷气式 pēnqìshì jet

喷气式飞机 pēnqìshì fēijī jet plane

喷泉 pēnquán fountain

喷射 pēnshè squirt; spurt

喷嚏 pēntì sneeze

喷雾器 pēnwù qì spray

喷嘴 pēnzuǐ nozzle

劈 pī split *logs etc*

批 pī batch

披 pī put on; drape

脾 pí spleen

皮 pí skin; hide; leather; shell

癖 pǐ addiction; obsession

匹 pǐ *measure word for horses*; 四匹马 **sìpǐ mǎ** four horses

屁 pì fart; ass, butt

偏 piān leaning to one side; partial; 偏大/小 **piāndà/xiǎo** on the big/small side

篇 piān piece of writing ◊ *measure word for paper, books etc*; 一篇文章 **yìpiān wénzhāng** an article

骗 piàn cheat, deceive, con

片 piàn slice (*of bread etc*); stretch (*of land etc*) ◊ *measure word for slices, flat things*; 两片安眠药 **liǎngpiàn ānmiányào** two sleeping pills

偏爱 piān'ài favorite ◊ be partial to; have a soft spot for ◊ preference

偏差 piānchā difference; deviation

偏高 piāngāo sharp MUS

偏激 piānjī extreme *views*

骗计 piànjì swindle

偏见 piānjiàn prejudice; bias

骗局 piànjú deception; fraud; con; racket

片刻 piànkè moment

偏离 piānlí deviate; differ ◊ departure

片面 piànmiàn biased

篇名 piānmíng title (*of novel etc*)

偏僻 piānpì remote

偏偏 piānpiān of all people; just; 他偏偏不做 **tā piānpiān bú zuò** he just won't do it

骗取 piànqǔ defraud

偏袒 **piāntǎn** bias (*in favor of*) ◊ biased

偏头痛 **piāntóutòng** migraine

偏向 **piānxiàng** take sides

偏心 **piānxīn** prejudiced

便宜 **piányi** cheap; inexpensive

便宜货 **piányi huò** buy; bargain

片语 **piànyǔ** phrase

篇章 **piānzhāng** chapter

骗子 **piànzi** cheat; fraud; crook; con man

飘 **piāo** drift

瓢 **piáo** ladle

票 **piào** ticket

漂白剂 **piǎobái jì** bleach

漂泊 **piāobó** drift

瓢虫 **piáochóng** ladybug

飘荡 **piāodàng** drift; float

飘动 **piāodòng** flutter (*of flag*)

票贩子 **piàofànzi** scalper

漂浮 **piāofú** float; drift ◊ afloat

票价 **piàojià** fare

漂亮 **piàoliang** pretty, beautiful, lovely

漂亮的一举 **piàoliàng de yījǔ** coup, feat

票面价值 **piàomiàn jiàzhí** face value

瓢泼大雨 **piáopō dàyǔ** cloudburst

票券 **piàoquàn** voucher

漂洗 **piǎoxǐ** rinse

飘扬 **piāoyáng** flutter; flap; blow; fly (*of flag*)

皮包骨 **píbāogǔ** skinny

皮惫 **píbèi** exhausted

皮带 **pídài** leather belt

皮蛋 **pídàn** preserved egg

匹敌 **pídí** equal; evenly matched; 与 X 匹敌 **yǔ X pídí** match X

屁兜儿 **pìdōur** hip pocket

撇号 **piěhào** apostrophe

瞥见 **piējiàn** glimpse; catch a glimpse of; peek

撇去 **piēqù** skim *milk*

批发 **pīfā** wholesale

疲乏 **pífá** tired

批发商 **pīfāshāng** wholesaler

皮肤 **pífū** skin

批改 **pīgǎi** mark EDU

皮革 **pígé** leather

皮革制品 **pígé zhìpǐn** leather goods

屁股 **pìgu** bottom, butt

癖好 **pǐhào** mania, passion

披肩 **pījiān** shawl

僻静处 **pìjìngchù** hideaway

否极泰来 **pǐjítàilái** *prov* good luck comes after a lot of misfortune

啤酒 **píjiǔ** beer

啤酒厂 **píjiǔchǎng** brewery

啤酒花 **píjiǔhuā** hops

疲倦 **píjuàn** tire ◊ tiredness; fatigue ◊ tired; run-down; 令人疲倦 **lìngrén píjuàn** exhausting; 使... 疲倦 **shǐ ... píjuàn** wear out

劈开 **pīkāi** split

疲劳 **píláo** exhausting; 疲劳不堪 **píláo bùkān** totally exhausted

劈雳 **pīlì** crash (*of thunder*)

皮毛 **pímáo** fur, coat; skin; fleece

拼 **pīn** put together; spell

频 **pín** frequency

贫 **pín** poor

品 **pǐn** item, article

品尝 **pǐncháng** savor; taste, sample

拼凑 **pīncòu** piece together; pad *speech etc*

频道 **píndào** channel (*TV etc*)

品德 **pǐndé** virtue

频繁 **pínfán** frequently

瓶 **píng** bottle; jar

平 **píng** even, level; peaceful; safe; 二平 **èrpíng** two all

评 **píng** criticize

凭 **píng** rely on; lean on

平安 **píng'ān** safe ◊ safely; 平安到达 **píng'ān dàodá** arrive safe and sound; 平安无恙 **píng'ān wúyàng** unharmed

平常 **píngcháng** usually, normally ◊ common; conventional

平淡 **píngdàn** bland; tame; uneventful; flat *tone of voice*

平等 **píngděng** equal ◊ equality

平等主义 **píngděngzhǔyì** egalitarian

平底 **píngdǐ** flat *shoes*

平底锅 **píngdǐguō** frying pan; pan

平底雪橇 **píngdǐ xuěqiāo** toboggan

平凡 **píngfán** usual; normal

平方 **píngfāng** square MATH

平方根 **píngfāng gēn** square root

平放着 **píng fàngzhe** lie (of object)

平分 **píngfēn** share out

屏风 **píngfēng** partition, screen

平分球 **píngfēnqiú** equalizer SP

评估 **pínggū** evaluate, assess; take stock ◊ evaluation

苹果 **píngguǒ** apple

苹果酒 **píngguǒ jiǔ** cider

苹果派 **píngguǒ pài** apple pie

苹果汁儿 **píngguǒ zhīr** apple sauce

平衡 **pínghéng** balance; equilibrium ◊ balance; stabilize ◊ balanced

平衡力 **pínghéng lì** counterbalance

评价 **píngjià** assess, evaluate

平静 **píngjìng** quiet; calm; peaceful

平静下来 **píngjìng xiàlái** calm down

平局 **píngjú** draw, tie; deuce (in tennis)

凭据 **píngjù** evidence

平均 **píngjūn** average; 平均来说 **píngjūn láishuō** on average

平均水准 **píngjūn shuǐzhǔn** average; 高于／低于平均水准 **gāoyú／dīyú píngjūn shuǐzhǔn** above／below average

凭空 **píngkōng** unfounded, baseless

凭空想出 **píngkōng xiǎngchū** dream up

平乱警察 **píngluàn jǐngchá** riot police

评论 **pínglùn** review, write-up; commentary ◊ review; remark, comment

评论家 **pínglùn jiā** critic; commentator; reviewer

平面 **píngmiàn** plane ◊ level; graphic

平面交叉 **píngmiàn jiāochā** grade crossing

平面图 **píngmiàntú** ground plan

平民 **píngmín** civilian

屏幕 **píngmù** screen COMPUT

屏幕保护器 **píngmù bǎohùqì** screen saver

兵乓球 **pīngpāngqiú** table tennis; ping-pong

瓶塞 **píngsāi** cork; stopper

平时 **píngshí** ordinarily; usually

平台 **píngtái** patio

平坦 **píngtǎn** flat, level

平头 **píngtóu** crew cut

评委 **píngwěi** judge (in competition)

平稳 **píngwěn** smooth; steady

平息 **píngxī** cool down; die down; subside; appease

平行 **píngxíng** parallel

平行线 **píngxíngxiàn** parallel line

平胸 **píngxiōng** flat-chested

平易近人 **píngyì jìnrén** approachable

平庸 **píngyōng** commonplace; mediocre ◊ mediocrity

平庸的人 **píngyōngde rén** mediocrity

评语 **píngyǔ** comment; assessment

平原 **píngyuán** plain, prairie

平直 **píngzhí** straight; lank

平装书 **píngzhuāng shū** paperback, pocketbook

瓶装水 **píngzhuāng shuǐ** bottled water

瓶子 **píngzi** bottle

贫瘠 **pínjí** barren

聘金 **pìnjīn** retainer

贫困 **pínkùn** poor, deprived; destitute; impoverished ◊ poverty

贫困不堪 **pínkùn bùkān** poverty-stricken

频率 **pínlǜ** frequency

拼命 **pīnmìng** all out, like mad

贫民窟 **pínmínkū** slum

品牌 **pǐnpái** kind, variety; brand

拼盘 **pīnpán** cold platter

贫穷 **pínqióng** poor

品脱 **pǐntuō** pint

拼图游戏 **pīntú yóuxì** jigsaw (puzzle)

品位 **pǐnwèi** taste

拼写 **pīnxiě** spell

品行 **pǐnxíng** conduct, behavior

贫血 **pínxuè** anemia ◊ anemic

拼音 pīnyīn pinyin

聘用 pìnyòng hire, take on

品种 pǐnzhǒng breed

批评 pīpíng criticize ◊ criticism

脾气 píqi temperament; temper;

脾气好 *píqi hǎo* good-natured;

脾气坏 *píqi huài* bad-tempered, ill-natured

皮箱 píxiāng suitcase

皮鞋 píxié leather shoes

癖性 pǐxìng idiosyncrasy

屁眼儿 pìyǎnr asshole

皮衣 píyī leather garment; leather clothing

皮疹 pízhěn rash MED

批准 pīzhǔn approve, pass ◊ approval, sanction

坡 pō slope

泼 pō splash

婆 pó old woman

破 pò break ◊ broken

迫 pò force; press ◊ pressing

破冰船 pòbīngchuán icebreaker

迫不及待 pòbù jídài pressing, urgent ◊ can't wait

破产 pòchǎn bankrupt ◊ go bankrupt; go into liquidation; be in receivership ◊ bankruptcy

坡道 pōdào ramp

坡顶 pōdǐng brow (*of hill*)

泼妇 pōfù bitch; dragon (*woman*)

迫害 pòhài persecute ◊ persecution

破坏 pòhuài ruin; destroy; sabotage; corrupt COMPUT ◊ destruction; disruption; sabotage

破坏公共财产行为 pòhuài gōnggòng cáichǎn xíngwéi vandalism

破坏公共财产者 pòhuài gōnggòng cáichǎn zhě vandal

破坏性 pòhuài xìng destructive; disruptive

迫降 pòjiàng forced landing

迫近 pòjìn close in; be imminent ◊ imminent

破旧 pòjiù beat-up; worn-out; run-down; seedy

破烂 pòlàn ragged, tattered ◊ trash, crap

破牢 pòláo break out, escape

破裂 pòliè rupture; burst ◊ rupture; bust-up ◊ broken; in ruins; cracked

破门而入 pòmén ér rù break in

破灭 pòmiè dash, shatter *hopes*

婆婆 pópó mother-in-law (*of woman*)

破破烂烂 pòpo lànlan in tatters

迫切 pòqiè pressing

迫切需要 pòqiè xūyào cry out for

破伤风 pòshāngfēng tetanus

迫使 pòshǐ force

破碎 pòsuì break, smash ◊ broken

剖 pōu cut open; dissect; analyze

剖腹产 pōufùchǎn cesarean

剖面 pōumiàn profile; section

破晓 pòxiǎo daybreak, dawn

破译 pòyì crack, solve

迫在眉睫 pò zài méijié impending

破折号 pòzhé hào dash (*in punctuation*)

铺 pū spread; unfold; pave

谱 pǔ musical notation

普遍 pǔbiàn general, widespread; universal

普遍存在 pǔbiàn cúnzài pervasive

瀑布 pùbù waterfall

铺床 pūchuáng make the bed

仆从 púcóng henchman

扑动 pūdòng flutter (*of heart*)

扑粉 pūfěn powder

匍匐植物 púfú zhíwù creeper

曝光 pùguāng expose ◊ exposure

普及 pǔjí generalize; popularize ◊ widespread; universal

扑克 pūkè poker; playing cards

扑克牌 pūkèpái poker; playing cards

铺路石板 pūlù shíbǎn paving stone

扑灭 pūmiè extinguish

谱曲 pǔqǔ compose

仆人 púrén servant

菩萨 Púsà Bodhisattva; Buddha

铺设 pūshè pave; lay

朴素 pǔsù modest; plain, simple ◊ modesty

葡萄 pútao grape; vine

葡萄干 pútáo gān raisin

葡萄酒 **pútaojiǔ** wine

葡萄糖 **pútaotáng** glucose

葡萄牙 **Pútaoyá** Portugal ◊ Portuguese

葡萄柚 **pútaoyòu** grapefruit

葡萄柚汁 **pútaoyòu zhī** grapefruit juice

葡萄园 **pútáo yuán** vineyard

扑通 **pūtōng** splash (*noise*)

普通 **pǔtōng** ordinary; common, standard; plain *features etc*

普通股 **pǔtōnggǔ** equity

普通话 **Pǔtōnghuà** Mandarin, Putonghua

普通邮件 **pǔtōng yóujiàn** surface mail

铺位 **pùwèi** berth

普选 **pǔxuǎn** general election

溥仪 **Pǔ Yí** Pu Yi (*last Emperor of China*)

Q

漆 qī paint
妻 qī wife
七 qī seven
期 qī period; issue, edition
欺 qī cheat, deceive
鳍 qí fin
旗 qí flag
骑 qí ride; pedal
齐 qí even; neat
其 qí his; her; its
启 qǐ open; start; enlighten
起 qǐ get up; 起风了 **qǐ fēng le** it's getting windy ◊ (*ability*): 买得起 **mǎi de qǐ** be able to afford
器 qì device; utensil; meter
汽 qì vapor; steam
气 qì air; gas; 胃肠中的气 **wèicháng zhōng de qì** wind, flatulence
迄 qì until; by
掐 qiā nip
卡 qiǎ jam; choke
恰当 qiàdàng proper, correct; appropriate; applicable
恰到好处 qiàdào hǎochù to perfection
恰好 qiàhǎo just; in the nick of time
亲爱 qī'ài darling
千 qiān thousand
铅 qiān lead (*metal*)
牵 qiān pull; lead
签 qiān sign
迁 qiān move
前 qián before; in front of; ex-, former; 两天前 **liǎngtiān qián** 2 days ago; 前一个星期 **qián yīgè xīngqī** the week before
潜 qián dive; submerge ◊ hidden
钱 qián money; 我欠你多少？ **wǒ qiàn nǐ duōshǎo?** how much do I owe you?
浅 qiǎn shallow; light
欠 qiàn owe ◊ due, owed

钱包 qiánbāo wallet, billfold; purse
谦卑 qiānbēi humble
前辈 qiánbèi senior; elder
铅笔 qiānbǐ pencil
前臂 qiánbì forearm
浅薄 qiǎnbó shallow, superficial
前部 qiánbù foreground; 在X的前部 **zài X de qiánbù** at the front of X
潜藏 qiáncáng lurk
浅尝 qiǎncháng foretaste
虔诚 qiánchéng devout; pious; ardent
嵌齿轮 qiàn chǐlún cogwheel
前灯 qiándēng headlight
签订 qiāndìng sign; conclude *contract*
前额 qián'é forehead, brow
签发 qiānfā issue
前锋 qiánfēng forward SP
千分之一 qiānfēnzhīyī thousandth
前夫 qiánfū ex(-husband)
潜伏 qiánfú latent; potential
枪 qiāng gun
强 qiáng strong
墙 qiáng wall
抢 qiǎng rob; snatch, nab
强暴 qiángbào violent ◊ violently ◊ rape
墙报 qiángbào wall news-sheet
枪毙 qiāngbì shoot dead
墙壁 qiángbì wall
强大 qiángdà powerful
强盗 qiángdào robber; bandit
强调 qiángdiào emphasize, stress; accentuate
强度 qiángdù strength, force
抢购 qiǎnggòu snap up, buy
强化 qiánghuà intensive
强奸 qiángjiān rape
强奸犯 qiángjiān fàn rapist
抢劫 qiǎngjié rob; hold up ◊

robbery; holdup; raid; 我被抢劫了 **wǒ bèi qiǎngjié le** I've been robbed

抢劫犯 **qiǎngjié fàn** robber; raider

强劲 **qiángjìn** strong; virile

抢救 **qiǎngjiù** rescue; recover; save; salvage

跄踉 **qiàngliàng** stumble

强烈 **qiángliè** strong; fierce; keen ◊ intensity

谦恭 **qiāngōng** humility

钳工 **qiángōng** fitter

强迫 **qiǎngpò** coerce; compel; put pressure on

枪伤 **qiāngshāng** gunshot wound

牵挂 **qiānguà** worry about

抢先报道 **qiǎngxiān bàodào** scoop

强硬路线者 **qiángyìng lùxiàn zhě** hardliner

强有力 **qiángyǒulì** powerful

枪支 **qiāngzhī** firearm

墙纸 **qiángzhǐ** wallpaper

强制 **qiángzhì** force ◊ mandatory

强壮 **qiángzhuàng** strong; sound; hardy

前后颠倒 **qiánhòu diāndǎo** back to front

千斤顶 **qiānjīndǐng** jack MOT

前景 **qiánjǐng** view; prospects

迁就 **qiānjiù** accommodate

迁居 **qiānjū** move house ◊ move; migration

千克 **qiānkè** kilogram

潜力 **qiánlì** potential

牵连 **qiānlián** involve; 与 X 有牵连 **yǔ X yǒu qiānlián** be mixed up in X

前门 **qiánmén** front door

千米 **qiānmǐ** kilometer

前面 **qiánmian** front; in front; ahead; 在 X 的前面 **zài X de qiánmian** in front of X

签名 **qiānmíng** sign ◊ signature

前排 **qiánpái** front row

前妻 **qiánqī** ex(-wife)

牵强 **qiānqiáng** farfetched

欠缺 **qiànquē** go without; lack

前任者 **qiánrèn zhě** predecessor

潜入 **qiánrù** submerge

遣散 **qiǎnsàn** discharge

浅色 **qiǎnsè** light-colored; fair *hair*

牵涉 **qiānshè** entail

歉收 **qiànshōu** crop failure

签署 **qiānshǔ** sign

潜水 **qiánshuǐ** dive ◊ diving

潜水艇 **qiánshuǐtǐng** submarine

潜水员 **qiánshuǐyuán** diver

前所未闻 **qián suǒ wèi wén** unheard-of

潜逃车 **qiántáochē** getaway car

前提 **qiántí** prerequisite; condition

前天 **qiántiān** the day before yesterday

潜艇 **qiántǐng** submarine

前途 **qiántú** future; prospects

欠妥 **qiàntuǒ** inappropriate

前途未卜 **qiántú wèibǔ** journey into the unknown

前夕 **qiánxī** eve

前线 **qiánxiàn** front, frontline

前行 **qiánxíng** proceed

潜行 **qiánxíng** prowl

谦虚 **qiānxū** modest, unassuming

谦逊 **qiānxùn** modest, unassuming ◊ modesty

前言 **qiányán** foreword; preface

迁移 **qiānyí** move; migrate; transfer

潜意识 **qiányìshí** subconscious

签约方 **qiānyuēfāng** signatory

潜在 **qiánzài** potential

谴责 **qiǎnzé** condemn; accuse ◊ condemnation; accusation

欠债 **qiànzhài** be in debt; 欠 X 债 **qiàn X zhài** be indebted to X

千兆字节 **qiānzhào zìjié** gigabyte

前者 **qiánzhě** the former

签证 **qiānzhèng** visa

牵制 **qiānzhì** diversion

钳制 **qiánzhì** clamp down on; 钳制新闻 **qiánzhì xīnwén** muzzle the press

前缀 **qiánzhuì** prefix

签字 **qiānzì** sign *check etc*

钳子 **qiánzi** forceps; pliers; tongs

千字节 **qiānzìjié** kilobyte

前奏 **qiánzòu** overture; prelude

敲 **qiāo** knock

锹 **qiāo** spade

211 qiēsuì

桥 qiáo bridge
瞧 qiáo look
巧 qiǎo skillful; coincidental
鞘 qiào sheath (*for knife*)
瞧不起 qiáobuqǐ look down on
憔悴 qiáocuì gaunt, haggard
敲打 qiāodǎ beat; drum
巧合 qiǎohé coincide ◊ coincidence
侨居 qiáojū live abroad
撬开 qiàokāi lever open
巧克力 qiǎokèlì chocolate
巧克力蛋糕 qiǎokèlì dàngāo chocolate cake
翘棱 qiáoleng warp
巧妙 qiǎomiào clever; neat; subtle
巧妙地安排 qiǎomiàode ānpái engineer, arrange
巧妙的手法 qiǎomiàode shǒufǎ sleight of hand
桥牌 qiáopái bridge (*cards*)
俏皮话 qiàopí huà quip
悄悄 qiāoqiao stealthy
跷跷板 qiāoqiāobǎn seesaw
悄然去逝 qiāorán qùshì slip away
敲响 qiāoxiǎng strike
敲诈 qiāozhà blackmail
敲钟 qiāozhōng ring
敲竹杠 qiāo zhúgàng cheat, rip off
恰恰 qiàqià exactly
恰如其分 qiàrú qífèn apt; applicable; accurate
洽商 qiàshāng negotiate
洽谈 qiàtán discuss; negotiate
卡住 qiǎzhù jam; lodge; be jammed; seize up
起博器 qǐbóqì pacemaker MED
器材 qìcái equipment
蛴螬 qícáo grub (*of insect*)
起草 qǐcǎo draw up
起草稿 qǐ cǎogǎo draft
起草人 qǐcǎo rén draftsman
汽车 qìchē automobile
汽车道 qìchē dào driveway
汽车旅馆 qìchē lǚguǎn motel
汽车喇叭 qìchē lǎba (car) horn
启程 qǐchéng leave
启程时间 qǐchéng shíjiān departure time

汽车棚 qìchēpéng car port
汽车修理站 qìchē xiūlǐzhàn garage
汽车业 qìchē yè automobile industry
汽车站 qìchē zhàn depot, bus station
气冲冲 qìchōngchōng furious
起初 qǐchū at first
汽船 qìchuán motorboat
气喘 qìchuǎn gasp ◊ asthma; 气喘吁吁 qìchuǎn xūxū be out of breath
起床 qǐchuáng get up; get out of bed; 起床走动 qǐchuáng zǒudòng be up and about
其次 qícì secondly
期待 qīdài expect; look forward to
脐带 qídài umbilical cord
期待以久 qīdài yǐjiǔ overdue; long-awaited
祈祷 qídǎo pray; wish for
启迪 qǐdí enlighten
起点 qǐdiǎn starting point
气垫船 qìdiànchuán hovercraft
启动 qǐdòng boot up
起动装置 qǐdòng zhuāngzhì starter motor; trigger; record button
切 qiē cut; carve *meat*
妾 qiè concubine
窃 qiè steal
企鹅 qǐ'é penguin
怯场 qièchǎng stage fright
切成薄片 qiēchéng báopiàn slice
切成丁 qiēchéng dīng dice
切成小条 qiēchéng xiǎotiáo shred
切除 qiēchú remove; cut out
切断 qiēduàn cut off, disconnect; sever
切合实际 qièhé shíjì realistic
切开 qiēkāi incision
切口 qiēkǒu cut
切片面包 qiēpiàn miànbāo sliced bread
窃窃私语 qièqiè sīyǔ whisper
切实可行 qièshí kěxíng viable, feasible
切碎 qiēsuì chop, mince

切碎机 qiēsuìjī (document) shredder

窃听 qiètīng eavesdrop; tap

窃听器 qiètīng qì bug; 装窃听器 zhuāng qiètīng qì bug; tap; wire up

茄子 qiézi eggplant

起反作用 qǐ fǎn zuòyòng counterproductive

启发性 qǐfāxìng illuminating

起飞 qǐfēi take off ◊ takeoff

起飞时间 qǐfēi shíjiān flight time

气氛 qìfēn atmosphere, mood; tone

气愤 qìfèn outraged

欺负 qīfu bully, pick on

起伏 qǐfú swell (of sea)

乞丐 qǐgài beggar

汽缸 qìgāng cylinder (of engine)

漆革 qīgé patent leather

气功 qìgōng qigong (Chinese system of breath control)

奇怪 qíguài strange, odd

器官 qìguān organ

妻管严 qīguǎnyán henpecked

气管炎 qìguǎn yán bronchitis

旗鼓相当 qígǔ xiāngdāng meet one's match

启航 qǐháng sail, depart

漆黑 qīhēi pitch black

起哄 qǐhòng jeer

气候 qìhòu climate

汽化 qìhuà vaporize

汽化器 qìhuàqì carburetor

期货 qīhuò futures

期货市场 qīhuò shìchǎng futures market

奇迹 qíjī miracle ◊ miraculous

期间 qījiān duration; 夏季期间 xiàjì qījiān through the summer; 在 X 期间 zài X qījiān during X

奇迹般 qíjìbān miraculous

迄今 qìjīn yet, so far

骑警 qíjǐng mounted police

汽酒 qìjiǔ sparkling wine

器具 qìjù device, gadget

起居室 qǐjū shì lounge

期刊 qīkān periodical; magazine

起来 qǐlái rise, stand up ◊ (start of action): 唱起来 chàng qǐlai start singing

起立 qǐlì stand, rise

气轮机 qìlún jī turbine

起落架 qǐluòjià undercarriage

起落装置 qǐluò zhuāngzhì landing gear

骑马 qímǎ ride (a horse) ◊ riding ◊ on horseback

起码 qǐmǎ at least

期满 qīmǎn expire ◊ expiry

起锚 qǐmáo weigh anchor

骑马人 qímǎ rén rider

妻妹 qīmèi sister-in-law (wife's younger sister)

奇妙 qímiào wonderful

器皿 qìmǐn vessel; container

起名 qǐmíng name, call

骑摩托车的人 qí mótuōchē de rén motorcyclist

亲 qīn kiss ◊ intimate ◊ relatives

侵 qīn invade

禽 qín bird; fowl

勤 qín hardworking

亲爱 qīn'ài dear; darling; 亲爱的王丽 qīn'àide Wáng Lì Dear Wang Li

亲爱的 qīn'àide darling, honey

亲笔签名 qīnbǐ qiānmíng autograph

芹菜 qíncài celery

秦朝 Qín Cháo Qin Dynasty

气馁 qìněi demoralized; 令人气馁 lìngrén qìněi unnerving; 使 … 气馁 shǐ … qìněi daunt

侵犯 qīnfàn encroach; breach; intrude ◊ intrusion

侵犯行为 qīnfàn xíngwéi aggression

侵犯者 qīnfàn zhě intruder

勤奋 qínfèn diligent, hard-working, industrious

氢 qīng hydrogen

轻 qīng light ◊ lightness

青 qīng green; blue; black; young

清 qīng clear; pure

倾 qīng incline

情 qíng feeling

晴 qíng sunny; clear

请 qǐng please ◊ ask; invite; 我可以请你吃顿饭吗? wǒ kěyǐ qǐng nǐ chī dùn fàn ma? can I invite you for a meal?; 请勿吸

烟！ *qǐng wù xīyān!* no smoking, please!；请勿打搅 *qǐngwù dǎjiǎo* please do not disturb

庆 qìng celebrate

清白 qīngbái pure; clear; flawless

情报 qíngbào intelligence; information; news

情报局 qíngbàojú intelligence service

轻便 qīngbiàn handy

请便 qǐngbiàn please yourself

轻搽 qīngcā dab

清仓大拍卖 qīngcāng dà pāimài clearance sale

清偿 qīngcháng settle; pay off ◊ settlement

清朝 Qīng Cháo Qing Dynasty

清澈 qīngché clear *water, eyes*

清晨 qīngchén early morning

清楚 qīngchu clear ◊ understand (clearly); 我没讲清楚 *wǒ méi jiǎng qīngchu* I didn't make myself clear

清除 qīngchú clear *road, table*; clean up, purge

轻触 qīngchù brush, touch

清除堵塞 qīngchú dǔsè unblock

青春 qīngchūn youth

青春年代 qīngchūn niándài youth

青春期 qīngchūn qī adolescent ◊ adolescence; puberty

清单 qīngdān checklist

氢弹 qīngdàn hydrogen bomb

清淡 qīngdàn mild; weak; plain; simple; slack *period*

清淡色 qīngdànsè pastel

倾倒 qīngdǎo tip over; overturn

倾倒 qīngdào dump

轻而薄 qīng'érbó flimsy

轻浮 qīngfú flighty

情妇 qíngfù mistress (*lover*)

情感 qínggǎn emotion; passion ◊ emotional

请假 qǐngjià ask for leave

请教 qǐngjiào ask for advice

清教徒 qīngjiàotú puritan

清教徒式 qīngjiàotúshì puritanical

清洁 qīngjié cleanse ◊ clean, sanitary

清节 qíngjié plot

清洁工 qīngjié gōng cleaner

清洁剂 qīngjié jì cleanser

清洁女工 qīngjié nǚgōng cleaning woman

情景 qíngjǐng scene, sight

情景喜剧 qíngjǐng xǐjù sitcom

请客 qǐngkè invite guests; pay

轻快 qīngkuài brisk; springy

情况 qíngkuàng circumstances, situation; scenario; 在这种情况 下 *zài zhèzhǒng qíngkuàng xià* under the circumstances

晴朗 qínglǎng bright, fine, sunny; clear

清理 qīnglǐ clear out

清凉 qīngliáng refreshing

轻量级 qīngliàng jí lightweight

情侣 qínglǚ couple

青绿色 qīnglùsè turquoise

青霉素 qīngméisù penicillin

轻描淡写 qīngmiáo dànxiě downplay

轻蔑 qīngmiè contempt ◊ contemptuous; 用轻蔑的口吻 谈 X *yòng qīngmiède kǒuwěn tán X* pour scorn on X

清明节 Qīngmíngjié Tomb Sweeping Day

青年 qīngnián youth

青年旅社 qīngnián lǚshè youth hostel

青年人 qīngnián rén young people; young person

青年招待所 qīngnián zhāodài suǒ youth hostel

轻拍 qīngpāi pat

倾盆大雨 qīngpén dàyǔ downpour, cloudburst ◊ be pouring

清漆 qīngqī varnish

轻敲 qīngqiāo tap

轻轻 qīngqīng lightly

轻轻移动 qīngqīng yídòng prowl

轻轻走 qīngqīng zǒu pad

请求 qǐngqiú ask; plead

情人 qíngrén lover

情人节 Qíngrénjié Valentine's Day

清嗓子 qīng sǎngzi clear one's throat

青少年 qīngshàonián teenager; youngster; young people ◊ teenage

轻视 qīngshì despise; scorn; put down, belittle

情书 qíngshū love letter

轻率 qīngshuài impetuous; indiscreet ◊ indiscretion

清爽 qīngshuǎng refreshing

轻松 qīngsōng relaxed

倾诉 qīngsù pour out

清算 qīngsuàn liquidation

青苔 qīngtái moss

轻弹 qīngtán flick

晴天霹雳 qíngtiān pīlì like a bolt from the blue

请帖 qīngtiě invitation (card)

倾听 qīngtīng listen

蜻蜓 qīngtíng dragonfly

青铜 qīngtóng bronze

轻推 qīngtuī nudge

青蛙 qīngwā frog

请问 qīngwèn excuse me; may I ask?; 请问几点了？ qǐngwèn jǐdiǎnle? excuse me, what time is it?; 请问贵姓？ qǐngwèn guìxìng? may I ask your name?

清晰 qīngxī vivid

清洗 qīngxǐ rinse; flush

倾向 qīngxiàng tendency; current; trend; disposition; 有 X 的倾向 yǒu X de qīngxiàng be subject to X

倾向于 qīngxiàng yú incline toward; tend toward

轻笑 qīngxiào chuckle

清晰度 qīngxīdù clarity; resolution

倾斜 qīngxié slope; tilt; lurch; dip ◊ slanting

轻信 qīngxìn credulous

清醒 qīngxǐng awake; conscious; sober

轻型小货车 qīngxíng xiǎohuòchē pick-up (truck)

清新悦目 qīngxīn yuèmù refreshing

轻信者 qīngxìn zhě sucker

情绪 qíngxù mood; spirits ◊ sentimental; 情绪低落 qíngxù dīluò be down; 情绪好／坏

情绪好／坏 qíngxù hǎo／huài be in a good／ bad mood; 情绪稳定 qíngxù wěndìng well-balanced

轻摇 qīngyáo rock

轻音乐 qīngyīnyuè light music

情愿 qíngyuàn prefer; 我情愿在这儿住 wǒ qíngyuàn zài zhèr zhù I'd prefer to stay here

请愿书 qǐngyuàn shū petition

晴雨表 qíngyǔ biǎo barometer; indicator

青藏高原 Qīngzàng Gāoyuán Tibetan Plateau

请找 … ？ qīngzhǎo …? can I talk to …?

清真寺 qīngzhēnsì mosque

庆祝 qìngzhù celebrate

庆祝会 qìngzhù huì celebration, party

庆祝活动 qìngzhù huódòng celebration, party

亲自动手 qīnzì dòngshǒu hands-on

轻罪 qīngzuì misdemeanor

亲和性 qīnhéxìng friendly

亲近 qīnjìn familiar ◊ affinity; 和 X 亲近 hé X qīnjìn be close to X

寝具 qīnjù bedding

勤快 qínkuai hardworking

勤劳 qínláo hardworking

侵略 qīnlüè invade ◊ invasion; aggression

亲密 qīnmì close; intimate ◊ intimacy

勤勉 qínmiǎn hard-working

亲昵 qīnnì (sexually) intimate ◊ intimacy

钦佩 qīnpèi admire ◊ admiration; 令人钦佩 lìngrén qīnpèi admirable

亲戚 qīnqi relatives

亲切 qīnqiè kind; familiar; genial

侵入 qīnrù intrude

身身 qīnshēn bodily; firsthand

亲生父母 qīnshēng fùmǔ biological parents

侵蚀 qīnshí erode ◊ erosion

秦始皇 Qínshǐhuáng First Emperor of China

亲手 qīnshǒu in person; with one's own hands

亲属 qīnshǔ relation

侵吞 qīntūn embezzle; misappropriate

亲吻 qīnwěn kiss

侵袭 qīnxí affect MED; strike

勤杂工 qínzá gōng (hospital) orderly

侵占 qīnzhàn encroach on; overrun

亲自 qīnzì in person; personally

穷 qióng poor

穷困潦倒 qióngkùn liáodǎo down-and-out

穷人 qióngrén the poor; poor person

穷乡僻壤 qióngxiāng pìrǎng hick town ◊ out in the boonies

穷凶极恶 qióngxiōng jí'è enormity

棋盘 qípán board; chessboard

旗袍 qípáo qipao, cheongsam (high-necked Chinese dress with side slits)

起泡 qǐpào carbonated

气泡 qìpào bubble

起泡沫 qǐ pàomò frothy

漆皮 qīpí patent leather

欺骗 qīpiàn deceive; delude; doublecross; trick ◊ deceit; deception; fraud; hoax; trickery

欺骗性 qīpiànxìng fraudulent

漆器 qīqì lacquerware

乞求 qǐqiú bum; cadge; 跟 Y 乞求 X gēn Y qǐqiú X cadge X from Y

气球 qìqiú balloon

崎岖 qíqū rugged

齐全 qíquán complete

弃权 qìquán abstain ◊ abstention

骑上 qíshàng mount

祈神赐福 qíshén cìfú blessing

七十 qīshí seventy

骑师 qíshī jockey

祈使 qíshǐ imperative

歧视 qíshì discriminate against ◊ discrimination

启示 qǐshì message

漆刷 qīshuā paintbrush

汽水 qìshuǐ carbonated mineral water; carbonated drink

起水疱 qǐ shuǐpào blister

起诉 qǐsù sue; bring an action against, prosecute ◊ prosecution

其他 qítā other (of people)

其它 qítā other (of things)

其他的 qítāde the others (people)

其它的 qítāde the others (things)

奇谈 qítán yarn, story

乞讨 qǐtǎo beg

奇特 qítè original; unique; strange; curious

奇特服装 qítè fúzhuāng fancy dress

气体 qìtǐ gas

汽艇 qìtǐng motor boat

企图 qǐtú try, attempt

起推进作用 qǐ tuījin zuòyòng propellant

秋 qiū fall, autumn

球 qiú ball

求 qiú implore, beseech

囚 qiú imprison ◊ prisoner

囚车 qiúchē patrol wagon

球队 qiúduì team (for ball game)

囚犯 qiúfàn prisoner; convict

秋分 qiūfēn autumn equinox

球杆 qiúgān cue (for pool); club (for golf)

球棍 qiúgùn bat

求婚 qiúhūn propose ◊ proposal

球茎 qiújīng bulb

求救 qiújiù call for help

求救信号 qiújiù xìnhào distress signal

丘陵 qiūlíng hill

球拍 qiúpāi bat; racket

秋千 qiūqiān swing

球体 qiútǐ sphere

秋天 qiūtiān fall, autumn

蚯蚓 qiūyǐn earthworm

球员 qiúyuán soccer player; player

丘疹 qiūzhěn spot

球座 qiúzuò tee

期望 qīwàng hope for; expect ◊ prospect; expectation

气味 qìwèi smell, odor

气温 qìwēn temperature

栖息 qīxī perch

期限 qīxiàn deadline; time limit

气象 qìxiàng weather

气象学 qìxiàngxué meteorology ◊ meteorological

气象学家 **qìxiàngxuéjiā** meteorologist

气象预报员 **qìxiàng yùbàoyuán** weatherman

栖息处 **qīxīchù** perch

栖息地 **qīxīdì** habitat

器械 **qìxiè** apparatus; appliance

气压 **qìyā** air pressure

气压表 **qìyā biǎo** barometer

企业 **qìyè** enterprise

企业家 **qìyèjiā** entrepreneur

起义 **qǐyì** uprising

奇异的事物 **qíyìde shìwù** marvel

汽油 **qìyóu** gasoline, gas

汽油泵 **qìyóubèng** gas pump

其余 **qíyú** the remainder, the rest

起于 **qǐyú** result from

起源 **qǐyuán** be derived from; stem from ◊ origin, beginning

七月 **qīyuè** July

契约 **qìyuē** contract; deed

气质 **qìzhì** charisma

其中 **qízhōng** among; among which; of which

起重机 **qǐzhòng jī** crane; hoist

妻子 **qīzi** wife

妻姊 **qīzǐ** sister-in-law (*wife's elder sister*)

旗子 **qízi** flag

棋子 **qízǐ** man, piece (*in chess etc*)

骑自行车 **qí zìxíngchē** cycle, ride ◊ cycling

骑自行车的人 **qí zìxíngchē de rén** cyclist

区 **qū** district; zone

蛆 **qū** maggot

曲 **qū** curved

取 **qǔ** take; fetch; get

曲 **qǔ** tune; song; music

去以 **qù** go; 去 X 的火车 **qù X de huǒchē** a train for X; 到 X 去有多远？**dào X qù yǒu duōyuǎn?** how far is it to X?; 去你的！**qùnǐde!** go to hell!

圈 **quān** ring, circle; lap; circuit; loop

拳 **quán** fist ◊ punch

泉 **quán** spring; stream

权 **quán** right; power; authority

全 **quán** whole; entire

犬 **quǎn** dog

劝 **quàn** persuade

全部 **quánbù** all; entire

全部付清 **quánbù fùqīng** pay up; pay in full

全部湿透 **quánbù shītòu** dripping (wet)

全长 **quáncháng** full-length

劝导 **quàndǎo** teach; advise; instruct

鬈发 **quánfà** curl; curly hair

蜷伏 **quánfú** snuggle down

劝告 **quàngào** advise, counsel

颧骨 **quángǔ** cheekbone

全国人大 **Quánguó Réndà** National People's Congress, NPC

权衡 **quánhéng** weigh up

拳击 **quánjī** box ◊ boxing; fight

全集 **quánjí** collected

拳击比赛 **quánjī bǐsài** boxing match

拳击场 **quánjī chǎng** ring

全景 **quánjǐng** panorama ◊ panoramic

拳击手 **quánjī shǒu** boxer, fighter

权力 **quánlì** power, authority

权利 **quánlì** right

全面 **quánmiàn** comprehensive; overall; all-round

全民所有制 **quánmín suǒyǒuzhì** national property; property of the people

全能者 **Quánnéng zhě** the Almighty

全球 **quánqiú** global

全球经济 **quánqiú jīngjì** global economy

全球气温升高 **quánqiú qìwēn shēnggāo** global warming

全球市场 **quánqiú shìchǎng** global market

拳曲 **quánqū** curl (up) ◊ curly

全权 **quánquán** power of attorney; full powers

全权代表 **quánquán dàibiǎo** authorized representative

全人类 **quánrénlèi** all humankind

全日 **quánrì** full-time

全日制 **quánrìzhì** full-time

全盛期 **quánshèngqī** heyday

全神贯注于 quánshén guànzhù yú engrossed in

全世界 quánshìjiè worldwide

全食宿 quán shísù full board

泉水 quánshuǐ spring water

劝说 quànshuō persuade; persuasion

蜷缩 quánsuō writhe; double up; curl up; cower; 蜷缩在一起 quánsuō zài yìqǐ huddle together

圈套 quāntào trap; snare; noose; 设圈套 shè quāntào trap; set up

全体 quántǐ all; whole ◊ totality; 全体选民 quántǐ xuǎnmín electorate

拳头 quántou fist

权威 quánwēi authority

权威性 quánwēi xìng classic; definitive; authoritative

全心全意 quánxīn quányì wholehearted

全息图 quánxītú hologram

痊愈 quányù recuperate; convalesce

劝止 quànzhǐ dissuade

圈子 quānzi circle

劝阻 quànzǔ advise against; 劝阻 X 不要去做 Y quànzǔ X bùyào qù zuò Y dissuade X from doing Y

区别 qūbié distinguish, discriminate between ◊ distinction; 区别好坏 qūbié hǎohuài know right from wrong

驱车离开 qūchē líkāi drive away; drive off

龋齿 qǔchǐ cavity

驱虫剂 qūchóng jì repellent

驱除 qūchú remove; drive out; boot out

取出 qǔchū take out, extract

驱除出境 qūchú chūjìng deport ◊ deportation

驱除舰 qūchú jiàn destroyer

驱除令 qūchú lìng deportation order

取代 qǔdài substitution; 用 X 取代 Y yòng X qǔdài Y substitute X for Y

渠道 qúdào drain

取得 qǔdé gain; achieve; acquire, obtain

曲调 qǔdiào tune

去掉 qùdiào remove; get rid of

驱动 qūdòng drive; 四轮驱动 sìlún qūdòng all-wheel drive

驱动器 qūdòngqì disk drive

缺 quē lack; miss

瘸 qué lame

雀 què sparrow

雀斑 quèbān freckle

缺点 quēdiǎn disadvantage; weakness, shortcoming

确定 quèdìng confirm, make certain; be sure

确定不变 quèdìng búbiàn fixed

缺乏 quēfá absence; deficiency; shortage ◊ lack; be short of

缺口 quēkǒu niche

缺钱 quēqián hard up

确切 quèqiè exact

确认 quèrèn confirm

缺少 quēshǎo lack

确实 quèshí really; actually

缺席 quēxí absent ◊ absence

缺陷 quēxiàn defect; downside

确信 quèxìn be convinced ◊ certainty, conviction; 使 … 确信 shǐ … quèxìn assure

确证 quèzhèng validate

瘸子 quézi cripple

区分 qūfēn differentiate between; tell the difference between; 区分 X 和 Y qūfēn X hé Y distinguish between X and Y

屈服 qūfú give in; succumb; knuckle under

驱赶 qūgǎn repel; chase away; dispel

躯干 qūgàn trunk

去骨 qùgǔ bone

去国 qùguó zhě exile

区号 qūhào area code

取回 qǔhuí pick up

曲解 qūjiě misinterpret ◊ misinterpretation

曲径 qūjìng maze

取景器 qǔjǐng qì viewfinder

取决于 qǔjuéyú depend on

取款机 qǔkuǎn jī ATM, cash machine

取乐 qǔlè have fun

群 **qún** group; crowd; flock; cluster;
一群人 **yīqún rén** a crowd of
people

裙 **qún** skirt

区内电话 **qūnèi diànhuà** local
call

去年 **qùnián** last year

取暖 **qǔnuǎn** warm up

取暖器 **qǔnuǎn qì** radiator

群众 **qúnzhòng** the masses

裙子 **qúnzi** skirt

曲奇 **qǔqí** cookie

驱散 **qūsàn** break up; disperse

趋势 **qūshì** tendency, trend

去世 **qùshì** pass away, die ◊
demise

躯体 **qūtǐ** body

去污剂 **qùwū jì** stain remover

去下 **qǔxià** take down; take off

曲线 **qūxiàn** curve

趋向 **qūxiàng** trend

取消 **qǔxiāo** cancel; revoke ◊
cancellation

取笑 **qǔxiào** deride; mock, send
up ◊ derision; banter

区域 **qūyù** region, area

取悦 **qǔyuè** ingratiate oneself with

曲折 **qūzhé** twist

曲折行进 **qūzhé xíngjìn** zigzag

取之不尽 **qǔ zhī bù jìn**
inexhaustible

曲轴 **qūzhóu** crankshaft

驱逐 **qūzhú** expel; deport; kick
out ◊ expulsion

屈尊 **qūzūn** deign to

R

燃 **rán** burn; ignite

染 **rǎn** color; dye

然而 **rán'ér** but, however; nonetheless; though

染发 **rǎnfà** dye one's hair

让 **ràng** let, allow; give way; make, cause; 让他进来 **ràng tā jìnlái** let him come in; 让我走！**ràng wǒ zǒu!** let me go!; 让人听懂 **ràng ren tīng dǒng** get through, make oneself understood; 让X等 **ràng X děng** keep X waiting

让步 **ràngbù** give way, capitulate; relent ◊ concession

让路 **rànglù** yield, give way

嚷嚷 **rāngrang** yell

让位 **ràngwèi** step down

然后 **ránhòu** then; next; afterward

燃料 **ránliào** fuel

染料 **rǎnliào** dye

染色 **rǎnsè** color; dye; stain; tint

染色剂 **rǎnsè jì** (wood) stain

染上 **rǎnshàng** catch

燃烧 **ránshāo** burn ◊ combustion

燃烧弹 **ránshāodàn** incendiary device

绕 **rào** around

绕道 **ráodào** go around; detour

绕道行驶 **ràodào xíngshǐ** detour

绕杆 **ràogān** turnstile

绕过 **ràoguò** bypass

扰乱 **rǎoluàn** disrupt ◊ disruption

扰频 **rǎopín** scramble

饶舌者 **ráoshé zhě** chatterbox

绕行 **ràoxíng** round

惹 **rě** start; cause; provoke; 惹麻烦 **rě máfan** cause trouble; play up; 惹人喜爱 **rě rén xǐ'ài** sweet, cute

热 **rè** hot; warm ◊ heat ◊ warm up

热爱 **rè'ài** love passionately

热忱 **rèchén** enthusiastic; hearty

热诚 **rèchéng** fervent

热带 **rèdài** tropics ◊ tropical

热带地区 **rèdài dìqū** tropics

热带雨林 **rèdài yǔlín** tropical rain forest

热点 **rèdiǎn** hot spot

热浪 **rèlàng** heatwave

热恋 **rèliàn** have a crush on ◊ madly in love; passionate

热烈 **rèliè** enthusiastic; heated *discussion*; wild *applause*

热门 **rèmén** popular; sought-after; blue chip

人 **rén** person; human being; people; man ◊ *used to form nationality words*: 法国人 **Fǎguó rén** Frenchman; Frenchwoman; the French

忍 **rěn** endure

认 **rèn** recognize; 认不出来了 **rèn bù chūlái le** beyond recognition

刃 **rèn** blade

任 **rèn** task; mission; term ◊ take responsibility

惹恼 **rěnǎo** exasperate

热闹 **rènao** exciting; lively ◊ hustle and bustle

忍不住 **rěnbúzhù**: 我忍不住 **wǒ rěnbúzhù** I can't help it

人称代词 **rénchēng dàicí** personal pronoun

认出 **rènchū** recognize, know; pick out

仁慈 **réncí** clemency; humanity; mercy; philanthropy ◊ kind; merciful; philanthropic

韧带 **rèndài** ligament

人道 **réndào** humane ◊ humanity

人道主义者 **réndào zhǔyì zhě** humanitarian

认得 **rènde** recognize

认定 **rèndìng** be sure of; identify

扔 **rēng** throw; throw away; drop; dump

仍 **réng** still; yet

扔掉 rēngdiào get rid of, dispose of; throw away ◊ disposal

人格 réngé personality

人工 réngōng man-made, artificial

人工呼吸器 réngōng hūxī qì respirator

人工流产 réngōng liúchǎn abortion

人工智能 réngōng zhìnéng artificial intelligence

仍然 réngrán still; 她可能仍然会来 tā kěnéng réngrán huìlái she might still come

扔下 rēngxià leave behind; 扔下X不管 rēngxià X bùguǎn turn one's back on X

任何 rènhé any; whatever; whichever

任何东西 rènhé dōngxi anything

任何人 rènhé rén anybody

人际罕至 rénjì hǎnzhì secluded

认可 rènkě acknowledgement

人口 rénkǒu population; 人口密集 rénkǒu mìjí densely populated

人类 rénlèi human race, man, mankind ◊ human

人类丧失免疫力病毒 rénlèi sàngshī miǎnyìlì bìngdú HIV

人类资源 rénlèi zīyuán human resources

人力 rénlì labor; manpower

人力车 rénlìchē rickshaw

人们 rénmen people, folk

人民 rénmín the people

人民币 rénmínbì renminbi, RMB

人民大会堂 Rénmín Dàhuìtáng Great Hall of the People

人民代表大会 Rénmín Dàibiǎo Dàhuì People's Congress

任命 rènmìng appointment; nomination ◊ appoint; designate

人民公社 Rénmín Gōngshè People's Commune

人民解放军 Rénmín Jiěfàngjūn People's Liberation Army

人民日报 Rénmín Rìbào People's Daily

忍耐 rěnnài endure

忍耐力 rěnnàilì endurance

任期 rènqī term of office

人权 rénquán human rights

人群 rénqún crowd, throng

人参 rénshēn ginseng

人生 rénshēng (human) life

认生 rènshēng be afraid of strangers

认识 rènshi know; get to know; recognize; 很高兴认识你 hěn gāoxìng rènshí nǐ pleased to meet you; 她认识汉字 tā rènshí Hànzì she can read Chinese characters

人事部 rénshìbù personnel (department)

人事部主任 rénshìbù zhǔrèn personnel manager

人世间 rénshìjiān the world ◊ earthly

忍受 rěnshòu accept; put up with, bear

人寿保险 rénshòu bǎoxiǎn life insurance

人体模型 réntǐ móxíng mannequin, dummy (for clothes)

认同 rèntóng approve of

惹怒 rěnù irritate

认为 rènwéi consider; believe; think; feel; 我不认为如此 wǒ bú rènwéi rúcǐ I don't think so; 认为有能力做 rènwéi yǒu nénglì zuò feel up to

人物 rénwù figure, personality; character (in book)

任务 rènwù assignment, mission; job, task

任务钮 rènwùniǔ task button

人性 rénxìng human ◊ humanity

任性 rènxìng headstrong

人行道 rénxíngdào sidewalk

人行横道 rénxíng héngdào (pedestrian) crosswalk

人烟稀少 rényān xīshǎo sparsely populated

任意 rènyì arbitrary

任意而为 rènyì ér wéi indiscriminate

任一个 rèn yígè either; any

任意球 rènyì qiú free kick

人员 rényuán personnel, staff

人造 rénzào artificial, man-made, synthetic

人造黄油 **rénzào huángyóu** margarine

人造卫星 **rénzào wèixīng** satellite

忍着 **rěnzhe** stifle, repress

认真 **rènzhēn** serious; earnest; conscientious ◊ in earnest; religiously

人质 **rénzhì** hostage; 被扣作人质 **bèi kòuzuò rénzhì** be taken hostage

人种 **rénzhǒng** race

认罪书 **rènzuì shū** confession

热切 **rèqiè** eager

热起来 **rèqǐlái** warm up

热情 **rèqíng** enthusiastic; warm; passionate ◊ warmth; enthusiasm; zest; passion

热气球 **rè qìqiú** balloon

热水袋 **rèshuǐdài** hot-water bottle

热水瓶 **rèshuǐpíng** vacuum flask

热死了 **rèsǐle** scorching hot

热腾腾 **rè téngténg** red-hot

热心 **rèxīn** enthusiastic; warm-hearted ◊ eagerness; zeal

热心肠 **rèxīncháng** warmhearted

热衷于 **rèzhōng yú** be wild about; 热衷于做X **rèzhōng yú zuò X** be eager to do X

热中者 **rèzhōngzhě** enthusiast

日 **rì** sun; day

日报 **rìbào** daily paper

日本 **Rìběn** Japan ◊ Japanese

日本人 **Rìběn rén** Japanese

日常 **rìcháng** everyday; daily

日出 **rìchū** sunrise

日光 **rìguāng** daylight

日光灯 **rìguāngdēng** fluorescent light

日晷 **rìguǐ** sundial

日记 **rìjì** diary; journal

日间服 **rìjiānfú** day wear

日历 **rìlì** calendar

日落 **rìluò** sunset

日期 **rìqī** date

日晒肤色 **rì shài fūsè** tan

日蚀 **rìshí** eclipse

日语 **Rìyǔ** Japanese (*language*)

日元 **rìyuán** yen FIN

日志 **rìzhì** logbook

绒 **róng** down (*feathers*)

容 **róng** contain; tolerate ◊ face

溶 **róng** dissolve

荣 **róng** honor

融 **róng** melt; meld; merge; 融为一体 **róng wéi yìtǐ** integrate

冗长 **rǒngcháng** lengthy

融和 **rónghé** blend in

熔合 **rónghé** fusion

融化 **rónghuà** melt; thaw ◊ molten

熔化 **rónghuà** smelt

熔毁 **rónghuǐ** melt down

容积 **róngjī** volume

溶解 **róngjiě** dissolve

容积量 **róngjī liàng** cubic capacity

容量 **róngliàng** volume; capacity

熔流 **róngliú** torrent

熔炉 **rónglú** melting pot

绒毛 **róngmáo** down (*on bird*)

容貌 **róngmào** feature

绒面革 **róngmiàngé** suede

容纳 **róngnà** hold, contain

容器 **róngqì** container

融洽 **róngqià** peaceable; 与X关系融洽 **yǔ X guānxì róngqià** be friendly with X

容忍 **róngrěn** tolerate, stand for

荣幸 **róngxìng** privilege ◊ privileged

容许 **róngxǔ** permit, allow; tolerate

溶液 **róngyè** solution

容易 **róngyì** easy; effortless ◊ ease

容易饱人 **róngyì bǎorén** filling

容易上口 **róngyì shàngkǒu** catchy

荣誉 **róngyù** glory; honor; kudos

柔 **róu** soft; gentle

揉 **róu** knead; rub

鞣 **róu** tan

肉 **ròu** meat

柔道 **róudào** judo

肉店 **ròudiàn** butcher shop

肉冠 **ròuguàn** crest

肉桂 **ròuguì** cinnamon

柔和 **róuhé** soft; mild; subdued; mellow

肉麻 **ròumá** nauseating

肉末 **ròumò** ground meat

柔懦情调 **róunuò qíngdiào**

sentimentality

柔懦情感 **róunuò qínggǎn** sentiment

软软 **róuruǎn** soft; supple

肉体 **ròutǐ** flesh

肉丸子 **ròuwánzi** meatball

肉馅 **ròuxiàn** mincemeat

肉眼 **ròuyǎn** naked eye

肉欲 **ròuyù** lust; sensuality

肉汁 **ròuzhī** gravy

如 **rú** like; as; if

乳 **rǔ** breast; milk; gel

辱 **rǔ** disgrace

入 **rù** enter

乳癌 **rǔ'ái** breast cancer

软 **ruǎn** soft; tender ◊ tenderness

软磁盘 **ruǎn cípán** diskette

软膏 **ruǎngāo** ointment; balm

软骨 **ruǎngǔ** gristle

软管 **ruǎnguǎn** hose

软件 **ruǎnjiàn** software

软木 **ruǎnmù** cork (*wood*)

软木塞 **ruǎnmùsāi** cork (*stopper*)

软盘 **ruǎnpán** floppy disk

软驱 **ruǎnqū** floppy drive

软弱 **ruǎnruò** weak

软卧 **ruǎnwò** soft sleeper (*on train*); first-class sleeping car

软性饮料 **ruǎnxìng yǐnliào** soft drink

软座 **ruǎnzuò** soft seat

入场费 **rùchǎngfèi** entrance fee

如此 **rúcǐ** thus, in this way; 我希望如此 **wǒ xīwàng rúcǐ** I hope so

入店行窃 **rùdiàn xíngqiè** shoplifter

蠕动 **rúdòng** squirm, writhe

乳房 **rǔfáng** breast

如果 **rúguǒ** if

如画 **rúhuà** picturesque

蚋 **ruì** gnat

锐 **ruì** sharp

锐不可当 **ruì bù kě dāng** inexorable; irresistible

瑞典 **Ruìdiǎn** Sweden ◊ Swedish

锐利 **ruìlì** piercing

瑞士 **Ruìshì** Switzerland ◊ Swiss

儒家 **Rújiā** Confucianism

如今 **rújīn** nowadays; at present, currently

入境 **rùjìng** enter *country*

入境签证 **rùjìng qiānzhèng** entry visa

入口 **rùkǒu** way in, entrance; inlet

辱骂 **rǔmà** abuse

入迷 **rùmí** be fascinated; be spellbound

润 **rùn** moist ◊ profit

润肤膏 **rùnfūgāo** moisturizer

润肤霜 **rùnfūshuāng** moisturizer

润喉糖 **rùnhóu táng** throat lozenges

润滑 **rùnhuá** lubricate ◊ lubrication

润滑剂 **rùnhuá jì** lubricant

润滑油箱 **rùnhuá yóuxiāng** sump

闰年 **rùnnián** leap year

润色 **rùnsè** polish

弱 **ruò** weak

若 **ruò** if ◊ like

弱点 **ruòdiǎn** weakness

若干 **ruògān** some; a number

弱小 **ruòxiǎo** puny

弱者 **ruòzhě** weakling

入神 **rùshén** be engrossed; be entranced

入室抢劫 **rùshì qiǎngjié** housebreaking

乳霜 **rǔshuāng** cream

入睡 **rùshuì** fall asleep

如同 **rútóng** just like; 如同往常 **rútóng wǎngcháng** as usual

乳头 **rǔtóu** nipple; teat

如下 **rúxià** the following ◊ as follows; see below

入乡随俗 **rùxiāngsuísú** *prov* when in Rome …

乳牙 **rǔyá** milk tooth

如意 **rúyì** hunky-dory

如愿 **rúyuàn** as planned; as hoped

乳罩 **rǔzhào** brassiere

乳制品 **rǔzhì pǐn** dairy products

乳猪 **rǔzhū** sucking pig

S

撒 **sǎ** scatter; sprinkle

洒 **sǎ** sprinkle; spill

撒旦 **Sādàn** Satan

撒谎 **sāhuǎng** fib, lie

塞 **sāi** cram; jam; plug; squeeze in; stick in; 把 X 塞入 Y 手中 *bǎ X sāirù Y shǒu zhōng* thrust X into Y's hands

腮 **sāi** cheek

赛 **sài** competition; race

赛车 **sàichē** racing car

赛车运动员 **sàichē yùndòngyuán** racing driver

塞进 **sāijìn** tuck

赛马 **sàimǎ** horse race

赛跑 **sàipǎo** race (*on foot*)

赛跑者 **sàipǎo zhě** runner

腮腺炎 **sāixiànyán** mumps

塞住 **sāizhù** clog up; 塞住 … 的嘴 *sāizhù … de zuǐ* gag

塞子 **sāizi** plug, stopper

萨克斯管 **sàkèsīguǎn** saxophone

三 **sān** three

伞 **sǎn** umbrella

散 **sǎn** scattered; loose

散 **sàn** spread; distribute; disseminate

三八妇女节 **Sānbā Fùnǚjié** Women's Day

三胞胎 **sānbāotāi** triplets

三倍 **sānbèi** treble

伞兵 **sǎnbīng** paratrooper

散步 **sànbù** stroll ◊ take a stroll

散布 **sànbù** spread

三重唱 **sān chóng chàng** trio

三等仓 **sānděngcāng** third-class cabin

散发 **sànfā** distribute

丧 **sāng** mourning; 穿丧服 *chuān sāngfú* wear mourning

桑 **sāng** mulberry

丧 **sàng** lose

丧礼 **sānglǐ** funeral service

丧命 **sàngmìng** die

桑拿浴 **sāngnáyù** sauna

丧失 **sàngshī** loss ◊ forfeit; 使丧失名誉 *shǐ sàngshī míngyù* discredit

丧失志气 **sàngshī zhìqì** demoralized

桑树 **sāngshù** mulberry tree

三国 **Sānguó** Three Kingdoms

嗓音 **sǎngyīn** voice ◊ vocal

嗓子 **sǎngzi** throat

撒尿 **sāniào** pee, piss

三脚架 **sānjiǎojià** tripod

三角裤 **sānjiǎo kù** briefs

三角形 **sānjiǎo xíng** triangle ◊ triangular

伞菌 **sǎnjūn** toadstool

散开 **sànkāi** scatter

三轮车 **sānlúnchē** tricycle; pedicab

三明治 **sānmíngzhì** sandwich

三色堇 **sānsèjǐn** pansy

三十 **sānshí** thirty

散文 **sǎnwén** prose

三峡 **Sānxiá** Three Gorges

三心二意 **sānxīn èryì** half-hearted

三月 **sānyuè** March

搔 **sāo** scratch

扫 **sǎo** sweep; drag

扫除 **sǎochú** root out

搔动 **sāodòng** commotion

扫雷艇 **sǎoléi tǐng** minesweeper

扫拢 **sǎolǒng** sweep up

骚乱 **sāoluàn** commotion; turmoil; trouble; disturbances

扫描 **sǎomiáo** scan

扫描器 **sǎomiáoqì** scanner MED

扫描仪 **sǎomiáoyí** scanner COMPUT

扫灭 **sǎomiè** mow down

骚扰 **sāorǎo** harass; molest ◊ harassment

扫射 **sǎoshè** burst (of gunfire)

扫视 **sǎoshì** glance; glance at; scan

扫兴 **sǎoxìng** be disappointed

搔痒 **sāoyǎng** scratch, have a scratch

扫帚 **sàozhou** broom

嫂子 **sǎozi** sister-in-law (*older brother's wife*)

撒手 **sāshǒu** release one's grip, let go; back out

撒种 **sǎzhǒng** sow *seeds*

涩 **sè** sharp, tart; tight

色 **sè** color

色彩 **sècǎi** color, tone

色彩设计 **sècǎi shèjì** color scheme

色度 **sèdù** shade

色鬼 **sèguǐ** womanizer

色拉 **sèlā** salad

色狼 **sèláng** wolf, womanizer

色盲 **sèmáng** color-blind

森林 **sēnlín** forest

森林学 **sēnlínxué** forestry

色情 **sèqíng** pornographic; erotic

色情作品 **sèqíng zuòpǐn** pornography

刹 **shā** brake

沙 **shā** sand

鲨 **shā** shark

杀 **shā** kill, slay

砂 **shā** sand

纱 **shā** thread, yarn

傻 **shǎ** dumb, dim; brainless; silly

纱布 **shābù** gauze

刹车 **shāchē** brake; skid ◊ brakes

刹车灯 **shāchē dēng** stoplight

刹车踏板 **shāchē tàbǎn** brake pedal

杀虫剂 **shāchóngjì** pesticide; insecticide

沙袋 **shādài** sandbag

沙丁鱼 **shādīngyú** sardine

沙发 **shāfā** sofa

沙发床 **shāfā chuáng** sofa bed

傻瓜 **shǎguā** idiot, moron

杀害 **shāhài** kill; murder

筛 **shāi** sift

晒 **shài** put out in the sun ◊ too sunny

晒斑 **shàibān** sunburn

晒黑 **shài hēi** tan ◊ tanned

晒伤 **shàishāng** burn ◊ sunburnt

晒太阳 **shài tàiyáng** sunbathe; bask

筛子 **shāizi** sieve

色子 **shǎizi** dice

砂浆 **shājiāng** mortar

沙坑 **shākēng** sandpit

砂砾 **shālì** grit

沙龙 **shālóng** salon

杀戮 **shālù** slaughter

沙漠 **shāmò** desert

山 **shān** mountain; mount

闪 **shǎn** flash

疝 **shàn** hernia

扇 **shàn** fan ◊ *measure word for doors and windows*; 两扇窗 **liǎngshàn chuāng** two windows; 给自己扇风 **gěi zìjǐ shānfēng** fan oneself

善 **shàn** good; kind-hearted

刹那 **shànà** instant

擅长 **shàncháng** be good at, excel at

删除 **shānchú** delete; erase; take out ◊ deletion

闪电 **shǎndiàn** lightning; flash of lightning

闪电般 **shǎndiànbān** in a flash

山车 **shāndichē** mountain bike

山顶 **shāndǐng** peak, summit

煽动 **shāndòng** incite; rouse; stir up; 煽动 X 做 Y **shāndòng X zuò Y** incite X to do Y

闪动 **shǎndòng** flicker

山东半岛 **Shāndōng Bàndǎo** Shandong Peninsula

煽动者 **shàndòng zhě** agitator

山峰 **shānfēng** peak, summit

伤 **shāng** hurt; strain ◊ wound

商 **shāng** business; quotient ◊ commercial

赏 **shǎng** reward

上 **shàng** on; at the top; up ◊ get on, board; 上车 **shàng chē** get on the bus/train; 在屋顶上 **zài wūdǐng shang** up on the roof

删改 **shāngǎi** censor

上岸 **shàng'àn** go ashore

伤疤 **shāngbā** scar

上班 **shàngbān** go to work; be at work; 我坐公车去上班 **wǒ zuò gōngchē qù shàngbān** I go to work by bus

上臂 **shàngbì** upper arm

上标 **shāngbiāo** brand name; trademark

商标概念 **shāngbiāo gàiniàn** brand image

上部 **shàngbù** top part, upper part

上菜 **shàng cài** serve (the food)

上层 **shàngcéng** upper

上层社会 **shàngcéng shèhuì** upper class

上场 **shāngchǎng** department store; bazaar

上场 **shàngchǎng** enter (of actors)

上车 **shàngchē** get on a train / bus / bicycle

上船 **shàngchuán** go aboard (a ship)

上床 **shàngchuáng** go to bed, turn in; 和 … 上床 **hé … shàngchuáng** go to bed with …

上等货 **shàngděnghuò** top-quality goods

上等阶层 **shàngděng jiēcéng** upper classes

上帝 **Shàngdì** God

商店 **shāngdiàn** shop; store

上吊 **shàngdiào** hang oneself

上定 **shāngdìng** agree; arrange

上发条 **shàng fātiáo** wind up

上飞机 **shàng fēijī** board a plane

伤风 **shāngfēng** catch a cold

伤感情 **shānggǎnqíng** hurt (emotionally)

伤害 **shānghài** wound; injury; bruise ◊ injure

上海 **Shànghǎi** Shanghai

伤寒 **shānghán** typhoid (fever)

商会 **shānghuì** chamber of commerce

上火车 **shàng huǒchē** board a train

上机 **shàngjī** log on

上级 **shàngjí** boss; superior

上交 **shàngjiāo** hand over

伤口 **shāngkǒu** wound; injury; cut

上来 **shànglái** board

商量 **shāngliang** discuss

上流 **shàngliú** high-class

上流社会 **shàngliú shèhuì** high society

上面 **shàngmian** top ◊ at the top ◊ up ◊ upper

伤脑筋 **shāng nǎojīn** annoying; frustrating

上年纪 **shàng niánjì** elderly, getting on in years; 他上了了年纪 **tā shàngle niánjì** he's getting on

上牌 **shàngpái** register

商品 **shāngpǐn** commodity; goods

商品陈列室 **shāngpǐn chénlièshì** showroom

商品券 **shāngpǐn quàn** token

商品特色 **shāngpǐn tèsè** selling point

上坡 **shàngpō** uphill

上去 **shàngqù** come up; go up ◊ up

商人 **shāngrén** businessman; dealer; merchant; trader

伤人感情 **shāngrén gǎnqíng** cutting

上色 **shàngshǎi** brown (in cooking)

上身 **shàngshēn** upper body

上升 **shàngshēng** rise; climb

赏识 **shǎngshí** have great respect for

上市 **shàngshì** on the market ◊ launch

上述 **shàngshù** above-mentioned

上水 **shàngshuǐ** upstream

上司 **shàngsi** boss, chief

上诉 **shàngsù** appeal

商谈 **shāngtán** discuss, kick around

商讨 **shāngtǎo** discuss

上调 **shàngtiáo** push up

山谷 **shāngǔ** valley

闪光 **shǎnguāng** glisten

闪光灯 **shǎnguāngdēng** flash; flashlight

闪光指示灯 **shǎnguāng zhǐshìdēng** flasher MOT

闪光装置 **shǎnguāng zhuāngzhì** flare

上网 **shàngwǎng** log on; go on-line ◊ on-line

伤亡人士 **shāngwáng rénshì** casualties

上午 **shàngwǔ** morning ◊ in the morning; 上午好 **shàngwǔ hǎo** good morning

商务舱 **shāngwù cāng** business class

上相 **shàngxiàng** photogenic

上校 **shàngxiào** colonel

上下文 **shàngxià wén** context

伤心 **shāngxīn** sad; brokenhearted; heartrending ◊ distress;

令人伤心 **lìngrén shāngxīn** upsetting; depressing; disheartening

伤心事 **shāngxīn shì** sorrow

上学 **shàngxué** go to school

上演 **shàngyǎn** perform, put on

商业 **shāngyè** business; commerce ◊ commercial

上夜班 **shàng yèbān** work nights

商业化 **shāngyè huà** commercialize

商业会议 **shāngyè huìyì** business meeting

商业秘密 **shāngyè mìmì** trade secret

商业午餐 **shāngyè wǔcān** business lunch

商业信用书 **shāngyè xìnyòng shū** letter of credit

商业学 **shāngyè xué** business studies

商业学校 **shāngyè xuéxiào** business school

上衣 **shàngyī** top (clothing)

上一次 **shàng yīcì** last ◊ last time

上瘾 **shàngyǐn** be addicted to

上映 **shàngyìng** show

上游 **shàngyóu** upper reaches of a river

伤员 **shāngyuán** casualty

上闸 **shàngzhá** put the brakes on

上涨 **shàngzhǎng** rise; go up

珊瑚 **shānhú** coral

闪回 **shǎnhuí** flashback

山脊 **shānjǐ** ridge

闪开 **shǎnkāi** dodge

闪亮 **shǎnliàng** flash

善良 **shànliáng** generous; kind

山麓小丘 **shānlù xiǎoqiū** foothills

山脉 **shānmài** mountain range

山猫 **shānmāo** lynx

山毛榉 **shānmáo jǔ** beech

山坡 **shānpō** hill; hillside

山穷水尽 **shānqióng shuǐjìn** be at the end of one's tether

山区 **shānqū** mountainous area

删去 **shānqù** delete

山雀 **shānquè** tit (bird)

闪闪发光 **shǎnshǎn fāguāng** glitter

闪烁 **shǎnshuò** flash; glint; blink ◊ gleam

膳宿 **shànsù** board with

山头 **shāntóu** mountain top

善行 **shànxíng** goodness

山羊 **shānyáng** goat

赡养 **shànyǎng** support

赡养费 **shànyǎng fèi** alimony

闪耀 **shǎnyào** sparkle; twinkle; glare

善意 **shànyì** goodwill

善于 **shànyú** be good at

山楂 **shānzhā** haw (berry)

擅自 **shànzì** unauthorized

扇子 **shànzi** fan

擅自占地者 **shànzì zhàndì zhě** squatter

擅自占用 **shànzì zhànyòng** squat

烧 **shāo** burn; fry

稍 **shāo** slightly; 稍醉 **shāo zuì** slightly drunk, tipsy

勺 **sháo** spoon; 两勺糖 **liǎng sháo táng** two spoonfuls of sugar

少 **shǎo** few; less ◊ lack, be without; 少吃 / 说 **shǎo chī / shuō** eat / talk less

哨 **shào** whistle

少 **shào** young

哨兵 **shàobīng** sentry

少不得 **shǎobude** essential, indispensable

烧断 **shāoduàn** blow (of fuse)

烧毁 **shāohuǐ** burn down

烧焦 **shāojiāo** burn; singe ◊ charred

烧开 **shāokāi** boil

少量 **shǎoliàng** small amount ◊ meager

少男 **shàonán** teenage boy

少年 **shàonián** young person (in early teens)

少年犯 **shàoniánfàn** juvenile

delinquent

少年犯罪 **shàonián fànzuì** juvenile delinquency

少女 **shàonǚ** teenage girl

烧伤 **shāoshāng** burn

少数 **shǎoshù** few ◊ minority

少数几个 **shǎoshù jǐgè** few

少数民族 **shǎoshù mínzú** ethnic minority

稍微 **shāowēi** a little; some ◊ slightly; marginally

少校 **shàoxiào** major MIL

稍许 **shāoxǔ** a little

少许 **shǎoxǔ** a little

少有 **shǎoyǒu** infrequent

少于 ... **shǎoyú** ... fewer than ...

烧着 **shāozhe** burn; catch fire

哨子 **shàozi** whistle

杀气腾腾 **shāqì téngténg** murderous

沙丘 **shāqiū** (sand) dune

杀人犯 **shārénfàn** murderer

沙色 **shāsè** sandy *color*

沙沙声 **shāshāshēng** rustle

杀死 **shāsǐ** kill

沙滩 **shātān** sandy beach

砂糖 **shātáng** granulated sugar

沙特阿拉伯 **Shātè'Ālābó** Saudi (Arabia) ◊ Saudi

纱线 **shāxiàn** yarn, thread

傻笑 **shǎxiào** giggle; titter

沙哑 **shāyǎ** rough; husky *voice*

沙岩 **shāyán** sandstone

鲨鱼 **shāyú** shark

砂纸 **shāzhǐ** sandpaper

砂质土壤 **shāzhì tǔrǎng** sandy soil

傻子 **shǎzi** dope, idiot

蛇 **shé** snake

舌 **shé** tongue

社 **shè** society

设 **shè** set up, establish

射 **shè** shoot

设备 **shèbèi** equipment

设备齐全 **shèbèi qíquán** self-contained

射程 **shèchéng** range

奢侈 **shēchǐ** extravagant; luxurious; magnificent ◊ extravagance

社工 **shègōng** social worker

社会 **shèhuì** society ◊ social

社会工作 **shèhuì gōngzuò** social work

社会习俗 **shèhuì xísú** convention

社会学 **shèhuì xué** sociology

社会渣滓 **shèhuì zhāzǐ** the dregs of society

社会主义 **shèhuì zhǔyì** socialism ◊ socialist

社会主义者 **shèhuì zhǔyì zhě** socialist

谁 **shéi** who; 谁是第一个？ **shéi shì dìyīgè?** who's first please?

谁的 **shéide** whose

射击 **shèjī** fire, shoot ◊ gunshot

涉及 **shèjí** involve; concern ◊ reference

设计 **shèjì** design; plan; create

社交 **shèjiāo** social interaction ◊ socialize

社交礼节 **shèjiāo lǐjié** social niceties

射击声 **shèjīshēng** shot

设计师 **shèjì shī** designer

设计失误 **shèjì shīwù** design fault

设计图 **shèjìtú** plan; design

设计学院 **shèjì xuéyuàn** design school

设计者 **shèjì zhě** creator

设立 **shèlì** set up, establish

社论 **shèlùn** editorial

射落 **shèluò** bring down

蛇麻草 **shémácǎo** hop (*plant*)

赦免 **shèmiǎn** pardon; amnesty ◊ absolve

深 **shēn** deep ◊ dearly *love*; 深绿／蓝 **shēn lǜ／lán** dark green／blue

身 **shēn** body

伸 **shēn** stretch; 伸长脖子 **shēncháng bózi** crane one's neck

神 **shén** god; deity ◊ divine; spiritual

肾 **shèn** kidney

渗 **shèn** seep; leak

深奥 **shēn'ào** deep; mysterious; baffling

申辩 **shēnbiàn** defend oneself

身材 **shēncái** build; figure

审查 **shěnchá** check; examine;

review
审查制度 **shěnchá zhìdù** censorship
深沉 **shēnchén** deep
申斥 **shēnchì** reprimand
伸出 **shēnchū** jut out, stick out; hold out
渗出 **shēnchū** ooze
深度 **shēndù** depth
身分 **shēnfen** identity; status
身份的象征 **shēnfènde xiàngzhēng** status symbol
身分证 **shēnfenzhèng** identity card
身分证明 **shēnfen zhèngmíng** identification
生 **shēng** give birth to; grow; live ◊ raw; unripe; ... 有点儿生了 ... *yǒudiǎnr shēng le* ... is a little rusty
升 **shēng** rise; hoist ◊ liter
声 **shēng** sound
绳 **shéng** cord; rope
省 **shěng** province ◊ provincial
盛 **shèng** height ◊ flourishing, prosperous
剩 **shèng** remain, be left over; 没剩什么 *méishèng shénme* there is nothing left
胜 **shèng** win ◊ victory
圣 **shèng** saint; sage
身高 **shēngāo** height
声辩 **shēngbiàn** protest
生病 **shēngbìng** fall ill, be taken ill ◊ sick
声部 **shēngbù** part
生菜叶 **shēngcài yè** lettuce
生产 **shēngchǎn** produce; output ◊ childbirth; production
生产耗资 **shēngchǎn chéngběn** production costs
生产力 **shēngchǎnlì** productivity
生产能力 **shēngchǎn nénglì** production capacity
生产线 **shēngchǎn xiàn** production line
生产者 **shēngchǎn zhě** manufacturer
声称 **shēngchēng** claim; profess
生成 **shēngchéng** generate
牲畜 **shēngchù** stock; livestock

生存 **shēngcún** exist; live ◊ existence; being
声带 **shēngdài** vocal cords
圣诞节 **Shèngdàn Jié** Christmas; Christmas Day
圣诞卡 **Shèngdàn kǎ** Christmas card
圣诞快乐！**Shèngdàn kuàilè!** Merry Christmas!
圣诞老人 **Shèngdàn Lǎorén** Santa Claus
圣诞礼物 **Shèngdàn lǐwù** Christmas present
圣诞树 **Shèngdàn shù** Christmas tree
圣诞夜 **Shèngdàn Yè** Christmas Eve
圣地 **shèngdì** sanctuary
声调 **shēngdiào** tone of voice; ring
省掉 **shěngdiào** spare
生动 **shēngdòng** vivid; graphic; lifelike
升高 **shēnggāo** raise
胜过 **shèngguò** outdo; eclipse
生孩子 **shēng háizi** give birth
省会 **shěnghuì** provincial capital
生活 **shēnghuó** live ◊ life
生活水平 **shēnghuó shuǐpíng** standard of living
生活方式 **shēnghuò fāngshì** way of life
生活费用 **shēnghuó fèiyòng** cost of living
生活史 **shēnghuó shǐ** life history
生活水准 **shēnghuó shuǐzhǔn** standard of living
升级 **shēngjí** escalation
生计 **shēngjì** livelihood; keep
圣经 **Shèngjīng** the Bible
声卡 **shēngkǎ** sound card
盛开 **shèngkāi** in full bloom
牲口 **shēngkou** livestock
生来 **shēnglái** genetically ◊ inborn; 他生来如此 *tā shēnglái rúcǐ* it's in his genes
胜利 **shènglì** victory, win ◊ victorious; 胜利的喜悦 *shènglì de xǐyuè* triumph
圣灵 **Shènglíng** Holy Spirit
胜利者 **shènglì zhě** victor

省略 **shěnglüè** leave out, omit

生闷气 **shēng mènqì** sulk; brood ◊ sulky

生面团 **shēngmiàn tuán** dough

声明 **shēngmíng** declare; state ◊ declaration; statement

生命 **shēngmìng** life

声名 **shēngmíng** reputation

声名败坏 **shēngmíng bàihuài** disreputable

声名狼籍 **shēngmíng lángjí** notorious

申明缘由 **shēnmíng yuányóu** justify *text*

盛年 **shèngnián** prime of one's life

生啤酒 **shēng píjiǔ** draft (beer)

举起 **shēngqǐ** hoist

升起 **shēngqǐ** rise; be up (*of sun*)

生气 **shēngqì** annoy; be annoyed; get worked up; 令人生气 **lìngrén shēngqì** infuriating; 使 X 生气 **shǐ X shēngqì** make X angry; 跟 X 生气 **gēn X shēngqì** be angry with X

生气勃勃 **shēngqì bóbo** spirited; energetic

升起来 **shēng qǐlái** come up

省却 **shěngquè** dispense with

圣人 **shèngrén** saint; sage

胜任 **shèngrèn** be equal to, be able to manage; 我觉得自己不能胜任 **wǒ juédé zìjǐ bùnéng shèngrèn** I don't feel up to it

生日 **shēngrì** birthday; 生日快乐！ **shēngrì kuàilè!** happy birthday!

升入 **shēngrù** soar (*of rocket*)

生手 **shēngshǒu** greenhorn

生疏 **shēngshū** rusty *subject*

声嘶力竭 **shēngsī lìjié** strident

生态 **shēngtài** ecology ◊ ecological

生态平衡 **shēngtài pínghéng** ecological balance

生态系统 **shēngtài xìtǒng** ecosystem

生态学 **shēngtàixué** ecology

生态学家 **shēngtài xuéjiā** ecologist

圣坛 **shèngtán** altar

生铁 **shēngtiě** cast iron

圣徒 **shèngtú** saint

深谷 **shēngǔ** ravine

声望 **shēngwàng** popularity; reputation; standing

生物 **shēngwù** being; organism ◊ biological

生物工艺学 **shēngwù gōngyì xué** biotechnology

生物学 **shēngwù xué** biology

生息 **shēngxī** yield

剩下 **shèngxià** be left, remain; 有五个剩下 **yǒu wǔge shèngxià** there were five to spare

盛夏 **shèngxià** height of summer

声响 **shēngxiǎng** sound

圣像 **shèngxiàng** icon

生效 **shēngxiào** take effect; come into force; 使 … 生效 **shǐ … shēngxiào** validate

生肖 **shēngxiào** the twelve animals of the Chinese horoscope

盛行 **shèngxíng** prevailing

生锈 **shēngxiù** rust ◊ rusty

生涯 **shēngyá** career

盛宴 **shèngyàn** feast; spread

生意 **shēngyi** business; trade

声音 **shēngyīn** sound; noise; voice

生硬 **shēngyìng** abrupt, brusque; brisk

生意兴隆 **shēngyì xīnglóng** busy

生育 **shēngyù** bear *child*

声誉 **shēngyù** reputation; renown; fame

剩余 **shèngyú** surplus; remainder, rest ◊ be over, be left

声誉不好 **shēngyù bùhǎo** disreputable

剩余收入 **shèngyú shōurù** disposable income

生长 **shēngzhǎng** grow

升值 **shēngzhí** revalue

生殖 **shēngzhí** reproduce

生殖器 **shēngzhíqì** genitals

绳子 **shéngzi** cord

审核 **shěnhé** audit

深红色 **shēnhóng sè** dark red; crimson

深厚 **shēnhòu** deep, profound

神话 **shénhuà** myth

神话故事 **shénhuà gùshì** fairy tale

神话学 shénhuà xué mythology

深呼吸 shēn hūxī breathe deeply

审计 shěnjì audit

伸脚空间 shēnjiǎo kōngjiān leg room

肾结石 shènjiéshí kidney stone

神经 shénjīng ◊ screwed up

神经崩溃 shénjīng bēngkuì nervous breakdown

神经病 shénjīng bìng mental illness ◊ crazy

神经病学家 shénjīngbìng xuéjiā neurologist

神经过敏 shénjīng guòmǐn neurotic

神经机能病 shénjīng jīnéng bìng neurosis

神经性 shénjīng xìng nervous

神经质 shénjīng zhì neurotic

审计师 shěnjì shī auditor

伸开四肢 shēnkāi sìzhī sprawl

神龛 shénkān shrine

深刻 shēnkè deep; 给人以深刻印象 gěi rén yǐ shēnkè yìnxiàng impressive, which makes a deep impression

伸懒腰 shēn lǎnyāo stretch

渗漏 shènlòu leak; drip; seep out

什么 shénme what ◊ anything; 什么事? shénme shì? what is it?; 那是什么? nà shì shénme? what is that?; 我没听见什么 wǒ méi tīngjiàn shénme I didn't hear anything; 什么时候还给我? shénme shíhou huángěi wǒ? when can I have it back?; 什么也不缺 shénme yě bùquē want for nothing

神秘 shénmì mysterious; occult

申明 shēnmíng declare, profess; protest

深明真相 shēnmíng zhēnxiàng penetrating

审判 shěnpàn try ◊ trial

审判室 shěnpàn shì courtroom

神奇 shénqí supernatural

深切 shēnqiè profound

申请 shēnqǐng apply for; put in for ◊ application

申请表格 shēnqǐng biǎogé application form

申请人 shēnqǐng rén applicant; claimant

深入 shēnrù deep ◊ in depth

渗入 shènrù sink in

深深 shēnshēn profoundly; head over heels; 深深地爱上 X shēnshen de àishàng X fall madly in love with X

审慎 shěnshèn prudent; scrupulous ◊ prudence

神圣 shénshèng holy, sacred ◊ sanctity

绅士 shēnshì gentleman

审视 shěnshì survey

身势语 shēnshì yǔ body language

伸手 shēnshǒu stretch

深思 shēnsī ponder

申诉 shēnsù lodge a complaint ◊ complaint

伸缩 shēnsuō flexible; stretchy

身体 shēntǐ body ◊ physical; 身体不好 shēntǐ bùhǎo be in poor health

身体上 shēntǐ shang physically

神童 shéntóng (infant) prodigy

身为人父 shēnwéi rénfù fatherhood

审问 shěnwèn question

审问者 shěnwèn zhě interrogator

身陷困境 shēnxiàn kùnjìng deep trouble

神学 shénxué theology

审讯 shěnxùn examine; hear ◊ hearing; inquest

深夜 shēnyè in the dead of night

呻吟 shēnyín groan; moan

深渊 shēnyuān abyss

深远 shēnyuǎn far-reaching

深造 shēnzào continue one's education

伸展 shēnzhǎn stretch; extend; spread

伸展四肢 shēnzhǎn sìzhī stretch

甚至 shènzhì even; to the extent that

神志不清 shénzhì bùqīng stupor ◊ in a stupor

神志清醒 shénzhì qīngxǐng lucid ◊ lucidity

神职人员 **shénzhí rényuán** clergy

神志正常 **shénzhì zhèngcháng** sane ◊ sanity

慎重 **shènzhòng** careful

舍弃 **shěqì** abandon

赊欠 **shēqiàn** credit FIN

社区 **shèqū** community

设施 **shèshī** facilities

摄氏 **shèshì** Celsius; centigrade; 摄氏十度 **shèshì shídù** 10 degrees centigrade

射手 **shèshǒu** marksman

舌舔 **shétiǎn** lick

舌头 **shétou** tongue

社团 **shètuán** society, organization

设想 **shèxiǎng** conceive of; visualize ◊ assumption

摄像机 **shèxiàng jī** video camera; camcorder

摄影 **shèyǐng** photography

摄影棚 **shèyǐng péng** studio

摄影师 **shèyǐng shī** photographer; cameraman

摄远镜头 **shèyuǎn jìngtóu** telephoto lens

设置 **shèzhì** locate

射中 **shèzhòng** shoot

诗 **shī** poem; verse; poetry

湿 **shī** wet; damp

师 **shī** master

狮 **shī** lion

失 **shī** lose

施 **shī** carry out

尸 **shī** corpse

十 **shí** ten

实 **shí** real; solid

识 **shí** know; recognize

石 **shí** stone

时 **shí** time; hour; 十八岁时 **shíbāsuì shí** at the age of 18; 午夜时 **wǔyèshí** at midnight

食 **shí** food ◊ eat

屎 **shǐ** feces, shit

史 **shǐ** history

使 **shǐ** cause; make; 使 … 吃亏 **shǐ … chīkuī** put at a disadvantage; 使 … 不高兴 **shǐ … bù gāoxìng** displease; 使 … 尴尬 **shǐ … gāngà** embarrass

始 **shǐ** begin, start

事 **shì** matter, affair

是 **shì** be ◊ yes; 是，我知道 **shì, wǒ zhīdào** yes, I know

室 **shì** room

市 **shì** city; market

式 **shì** type; style

试 **shì** try; 试做 X **shì zuò X** have a try at X

示 **shì** show; indicate

视 **shì** see; watch; 视 … 而定 **shì … érdìng** conditional on …

誓 **shì** vow

势 **shì** power

氏 **shì** family name

十八 **shíbā** eighteen

失败 **shībài** fail; lose ◊ failure; defeat

失败者 **shībài zhě** loser

失败主义 **shībài zhǔyì** defeatism ◊ defeatist

饰板 **shìbǎn** plaque

施暴虐 **shī bàonüè** tyrannize

饰边 **shìbiān** frill; fringe

事变 **shìbiàn** incident

识别 **shíbié** recognize; distinguish

士兵 **shìbīng** soldier; private; the ranks

时差 **shíchā** time difference

视察 **shìchá** inspect ◊ inspection

时差反应 **shíchā fǎnyìng** jetlag

失常 **shīcháng** unbalanced; abnormal

时常 **shícháng** frequently, often

市场 **shìchǎng** market; marketplace

市场调查 **shìchǎng diàochá** market survey

市场经济 **shìchǎng jīngjì** market economy

市场力量 **shìchǎng lìliàng** market forces

市场占有率 **shìchǎng zhànyǒulǜ** market share

市场主导 **shìchǎng zhǔdǎo** market leader

试车 **shìchē** test drive; trial run

世仇 **shìchóu** feud

驶出 **shǐchū** pull out (of train, ship)

试穿 **shìchuān** try on

视窗 **shíchuāng** window

时代 **shídài** age, era; generation

实弹 **shídàn** live ammunition

适当 **shìdàng** proper, appropriate, suitable ◊ properly; duly

食道 **shídào** gullet

使得 **shǐde** so; so that ◊ make; cause

是的 **shìde** yes; that's right

实得工资 **shídé gōngzī** take-home pay

湿度 **shīdù** humidity

适度 **shìdù** moderate ◊ mildly; moderately; in moderation

十二 **shí'èr** twelve, dozen

视而不见 **shì'ér bùjiàn** blind to

十二分之一 **shí'èr fēn zhīyī** twelfth

十二月 **shí'èryuè** December

示范 **shìfàn** demonstrate ◊ demonstration, demo

示范碟 **shìfàn dié** demo disk

释放 **shìfàng** release, free

施肥 **shīféi** fertilize

是否 **shìfǒu** whether or not

师傅 **shīfu** master

石膏 **shígāo** plaster

石膏绷带 **shígāo bēngdài** plaster cast

诗歌 **shīgē** poem; poetry

施工工地 **shīgōng gōngdì** construction site

石工技巧 **shígōng jìqiǎo** masonry (skill)

尸骨 **shīgǔ** skeleton

事故 **shìgù** accident; crash; 在事故中丧生 **zài shìgù zhōng sàngshēng** be killed in an accident

使馆 **shǐguǎn** embassy

试管 **shìguǎn** test tube

试管婴儿 **shìguǎn yīng'ér** test-tube baby

嗜好 **shìhào** hobby; addiction; 有吸毒嗜好 **yǒu xīdú shìhào** be on drugs

适合 **shìhé** suit; fit; be in accordance with; 适合于 X **shìhé yú X** be cut out for X

事后 **shìhòu** subsequent ◊ subsequently, afterward

石灰 **shíhuī** lime

失火 **shīhuǒ** fire ◊ catch fire

实际 **shíjì** real, actual; practical; substantive

世纪 **shìjì** century

时间 **shíjiān** time; while; interlude; 请再给我一些时间？ **qǐng zài gěi wǒ yìxiē shíjiān?** can I have more time?; 时间自会定论 **shíjiān zì huì dìnglùn** time will tell

实践 **shíjiàn** practice

事件 **shìjiàn** event, happening; incident; business

时间安排 **shíjiān ānpái** timing

时间表 **shíjiān biǎo** timetable

时刻表 **shíkè biǎo** schedule

时间段 **shíjiānduàn** sitting

时间范围 **shíjiān fànwéi** timescale

时间间隔 **shíjiān jiāngé** time-lag

时间顺序 **shíjiān shùnxù** chronological

市郊 **shìjiāo** suburbs

施加压力 **shījiā yālì** put pressure on

世界 **shìjiè** world

世界大战 **shìjiè dàzhàn** world war

世界地图 **shìjiè dìtú** map of the world; atlas

世界观 **shìjièguān** world view

世界冠军 **shìjiè guànjūn** world champion

世界记录 **shìjiè jìlù** world record

世界强国 **shìjiè qiángguó** world power

世界性 **shìjiè xìng** cosmopolitan

世界著名 **shìjiè zhùmíng** world-famous

什锦 **shíjǐn** mixed; miscellaneous

试镜 **shìjìng** screen test

实际上 **shíjì shàng** actually, in fact; in practice

十几岁 **shíjǐ suì** be in one's teens

十九 **shíjiǔ** nineteen

诗句 **shījù** verse

视觉 **shìjué** vision ◊ visual; 视觉上来说 **shìjué shàng láishuō** visually

势均力敌 **shìjūn lìdí** evenly matched

时刻 **shíkè** moment ◊ constantly

时刻表 **shíkèbiǎo** schedule

蚀刻术 **shíkèshù** etching

石窟 **shíkū** grotto

实况 **shíkuàng** live

实况转播 **shíkuàng zhuǎnbō** live transmission

湿冷 **shīlěng** cold and damp

失利 **shīlì** lose out

实力 **shílì** strength

势力 **shìlì** strength, power

视力 **shìlì** sight, eyesight, vision

势利 **shìlì** snobbish

失恋 **shīliàn** be jilted

势力范围 **shìlì fànwéi** sphere of influence

失灵 **shīlíng** out of order; dead ◊ malfunction; jam ◊ be down

石榴 **shíliu** pomegranate

十六 **shíliù** sixteen

势利眼 **shìlìyǎn** snob

时髦 **shímáo** fashionable

失眠 **shīmián** insomnia

市民 **shìmín** city dweller

失明 **shīmíng** go blind

使命 **shǐmìng** mission; vocation

室内 **shìnèi** indoors; inside

室内设计 **shìnèi shèjì** interior design

室内设计者 **shìnèi shèjì zhě** interior designer

十年 **shínián** decade

施虐狂 **shīnüèkuáng** sadism

失陪 **shīpéi** please excuse me

食品 **shípǐn** food

视频 **shìpín** video COMPUT

食品杂货业 **shípǐn záhuò yè** grocery business

识破 **shípò** see through

食谱 **shípǔ** recipe; cookbook

十七 **shíqī** seventeen

时期 **shíqī** term; period

拾起 **shíqǐ** lift, pick up

士气 **shìqì** morale

史前 **shǐqián** prehistoric

事情 **shìqíng** issue; matter

失去 **shīqù** lose; 失去控制 **shīqù kòngzhì** lose control; 失去知觉 **shīqù zhījué** lose consciousness

时区 **shíqū** time zone

拾取 **shíqǔ** pick up

市区 **shìqū** city area

湿热 **shīrè** humid

诗人 **shīrén** poet; 抒情诗人 **shūqíng shīrén** lyric poet

使人 **shǐrén** causative: 使人困乏 **shǐrén kùnfá** wearing, tiring; 使人兴奋 **shǐrén xīngfèn** exciting

食肉动物 **shíròu dòngwù** carnivore; predator

湿软 **shīruǎn** swampy

湿润 **shīrùn** moisture ◊ moist; soggy

失散 **shīsàn** stray

十三 **shísān** thirteen

时尚 **shíshàng** fashion

失身 **shīshēn** lose one's virginity

失声 **shīshēng** let out a cry

失势 **shīshì** fall from power

失事 **shīshì** have an accident

实施 **shíshī** implement; execute ◊ execution

实时 **shíshí** real time

时事 **shíshì** current affairs, current events

史诗 **shǐshī** epic

试试 **shìshi** try; 让我试试 **ràng wǒ shìshi** can I have a try?

事实 **shìshí** fact; truth

适时 **shìshí** well-timed

逝世 **shìshì** pass away

实事求是 **shíshì qiúshì** practical; down-to-earth

事实上 **shìshí shang** indeed, as a matter of fact

时事讨论节目 **shíshì tǎolùn jiémù** current affairs program

尸首分离 **shīshǒu fēnlí** decapitate

十四 **shísì** fourteen

时速 **shísù** speed

世俗 **shìsú** worldly; secular

失算 **shīsuàn** miscalculate

时态 **shítài** tense

食堂 **shítáng** cafeteria; canteen

食糖 **shítáng** sugar

尸体 **shītǐ** corpse, cadaver

失调 **shītiáo** disorder

视听 **shìtīng** audiovisual

湿透 **shītòu** soaked ◊ be wet through

石头 **shítou** stone

试图 **shìtú** attempt

室外 **shìwài** outdoors; outside ◊ outdoor

世外桃源 **shìwài táoyuán** oasis *fig*

失望 **shīwàng** be disappointed ◊ disappointment ◊ disappointed; 令人失望 **lìngrén shīwàng** disappointing ◊ dismay; 使 ... 失望 **shǐ ... shīwàng** disappoint; 让 X 失望 **ràng X shīwàng** let X down

视网膜 **shìwǎngmó** retina

示威 **shìwēi** demonstration, protest ◊ demonstrate

示威游行 **shìwēi yóuxíng** demonstration

示威者 **shìwēi zhě** demonstrator, protester

失误 **shīwù** mistake, error

十五 **shíwǔ** fifteen

食物 **shíwù** food; diet

事务 **shìwù** concern; affair

食物搅拌器 **shíwù jiǎobànqì** food mixer

史无前例 **shǐ wú qiánlì** unprecedented

事物 **shìwù** thing

失物招领处 **shīwù zhāolǐng chù** lost-and-found (office)

食物中毒 **shíwù zhòngdú** food poisoning

实习 **shíxí** work as an intern ◊ internship

世袭 **shìxí** hereditary; inherited

实现 **shíxiàn** fulfill; realize; come true ◊ realization

事先 **shìxiān** beforehand ◊ prior

事先形成 **shìxiān xíngchéng** preconceived

实习护士 **shíxí hùshi** student nurse

实习教师 **shíxí jiàoshī** student teacher

时新 **shíxīn** fashionable, stylish

实行 **shíxíng** implement, carry out

失信 **shīxìn** go back on one's word, break one's promise

实习期 **shíxí qī** trial period

实习生 **shíxí shēng** trainee

失修 **shīxiū** in a state of disrepair; run-down; derelict

世袭遗产 **shìxí yíchǎn** heritage

实验 **shíyàn** experiment

誓言 **shìyán** oath, vow

试演 **shìyǎn** audition

试验 **shìyàn** test; experiment; trial; 试验 X **shìyàn X** have X on trial; test X

试验方案 **shìyàn fāng'àn** pilot scheme

试样 **shìyàng** sample

式样 **shìyàng** style; type

试验期 **shìyàn qī** trial period

试验区 **shìyàn qū** pilot plant

使眼色 **shǐ yǎnsè** wink

实验室 **shíyàn shì** lab, laboratory

实验室技师 **shíyàn shì jìshī** laboratory technician

失业 **shīyè** unemployed, out of work ◊ unemployment

视野 **shìyě** vision; outlook; 使视野开阔 **shǐ shìyě kāikuò** broaden one's mind; 在 X 视野之内 **zài X shìyě zhī nèi** within sight of X

事业 **shìyè** undertaking; career

实业家 **shíyèjiā** industrialist

失业者 **shīyè zhě** the unemployed

诗意 **shīyì** poetic

十一 **shíyī** eleven

十亿 **shíyì** billion

适宜 **shìyí** appropriate, suitable

释义 **shìyì** paraphrase

示意 **shìyì** sign, signal; 他示意我前行 **tā shìyì wǒ qiánxíng** he motioned me forward

石英 **shíyīng** quartz

适应 **shìyìng** adapt; acclimate, acclimatize; adjust

侍应生 **shìyìng shēng** busboy

石英钟 **shíyīng zhōng** quartz clock

十一月 **shíyīyuè** November

食用 **shíyòng** consume

实用 **shíyòng** practical; useful

使用 **shǐyòng** apply, use, employ; access

适用 **shìyòng** applicable ◊ apply

试用 **shìyòng** probation ◊ try out

试用期 **shìyòng qī** probation period

使用时间 **shǐyòng shíjiān** access time

使用说明书 **shǐyòng shuōmíng shū** instruction manual

实用主义 **shíyòng zhǔyì** pragmatism

石油 **shíyóu** oil; petroleum

食油 **shíyóu** cooking oil

石油公司 **shíyóu gōngsī** oil company

石油化学产品 **shíyóu huàxué chǎnpǐn** petrochemical

石油输出国组织 **Shíyóu Shūchūguó Zǔzhī** OPEC, Organization of Petroleum Exporting Countries

食欲 **shíyù** appetite

十月 **shíyuè** October

誓约 **shìyuē** vow

适于 **shìyú**: 适于居住 **shìyú jūzhù** habitable, inhabitable; 适于青年 **shìyú qīngnián** youthful *fashion, music*; 适于远航 **shìyú yuǎnháng** seagoing

实在 **shízài** real ◊ really

施展 **shīzhǎn** unfold, develop; display

市长 **shìzhǎng** mayor

使者 **shǐzhě** envoy

侍者 **shìzhě** bellhop

湿疹 **shīzhěn** eczema

市镇 **shìzhèn** urban

实证 **shízhèng** testament

市政 **shìzhèng** municipal

市政厅 **shìzhèng tīng** city hall

食指 **shízhǐ** forefinger, index finger

实质 **shízhì** essence; substance

实质上 **shízhì shang** substantially

始终 **shǐzhōng** from start to finish

始终不渝 **shǐzhōng bù yú** consistent ◊ consistently

市中心 **shì zhōngxīn** down-town ◊ city center

施主 **shīzhǔ** benefactor

时装 **shízhuāng** fashion

时装表演 **shízhuāng biǎoyǎn** fashion show

时装商店 **shízhuāng shāngdiàn** boutique

时装设计师 **shízhuāng shèjìshī** fashion designer

时装展览 **shízhuāng zhǎnlǎn** collection

狮子 **shīzi** lion

虱子 **shīzi** louse

师资 **shīzī** teachers

柿子 **shìzi** persimmon

十字架 **shízìjià** cross, crucifix

十字路口 **shízì lùkǒu** crossroads; intersection

狮子舞 **shīziwǔ** lion dance

失踪 **shīzōng** missing ◊ disappearance

十足 **shízú** absolute, complete; downright

氏族 **shìzú** family, kin; clan

失足跌倒 **shīzú diēdǎo** lose one's footing

收 **shōu** receive; accept

熟 **shóu** ripe; cooked; familiar ◊ ripeness ◊ soundly

手 **shǒu** hand

守 **shǒu** keep watch; guard; abide by

首 **shǒu** head ◊ first

瘦 **shòu** thin; lean

兽 **shòu** beast; animal

受 **shòu** receive; accept; 不受诱惑 **búshòu yòuhuò** resist temptation; 受感染 **shòu gǎnrǎn** go septic

授 **shòu** give; teach

售 **shòu** sell

售报亭 **shòubào tíng** newsstand

手臂 **shǒubì** arm

手边 **shǒubiān** within reach

手表 **shǒubiǎo** wristwatch

守财奴 **shǒucái nú** miser

收藏 **shōucáng** tuck away

收藏家 **shōucáng jiā** collector

收藏品 **shōucáng pǐn** collection

手册 **shǒucè** handbook

首倡 **shǒuchàng** pioneer

收成 **shōucheng** crop, harvest

首次公演 **shǒucì gōngyǎn** première

手袋 **shǒudài** purse

收到 **shōudào** receive, get

手电筒 **shǒudiàntǒng** flashlight

首都 **shǒudū** capital

收短 **shōuduǎn** take up *dress etc*

手段 **shǒuduàn** means

守法 shǒufǎ comply with the law

收费 shōufèi charge

收费处 shōufèi chù toll booth

收费公路 shōufèi gōnglù toll road

手风琴 shǒufēng qín accordion

手稿 shǒugǎo manuscript

收割 shōugē reap

手工 shǒugōng manual ◊ handiwork

手工业 shǒugōngyè craft; handicraft

手工业者 shǒugōngyè zhě craftsman

手工艺 shǒugōngyì handicraft

手工艺者 shǒugōngyì zhě craftsman

手工制作 shǒugōng zhìzuò handmade

收购 shōugòu purchase ◊ purchasing

守规矩 shǒu guīju behave (oneself)

受过教育 shòuguò jiàoyù educated

受害 shòuhài sustain damage; suffer an injury

受害者 shòuhài zhě victim

首航 shǒuháng maiden voyage

守候 shǒuhòu watch for

售后服务 shòuhòu fúwù after-sales service

守护 shǒuhù look after, watch

受欢迎 shòu huānyíng popular; welcome; well-received

收回 shōuhuí repossess; reclaim; retract

受贿 shòuhuì corruption

收获 shōuhuò harvest

售货亭 shòuhuò tíng kiosk

售货员 shòuhuò yuán sales clerk

收集 shōují collect

售价 shòujià retail price

收件人 shōujiàn rén addressee

手巾 shǒujīn towel

受惊 shòujīng panic

受精 shòujīng be fertilized; 使 ... 受精 shǐ ... shòujīng fertilize

受惊吓 shòujīngxià petrified

守旧 shǒujiù provincial

熟记 shóujì know by heart

收据 shōujù receipt

手绢 shǒujuàn handkerchief

收看 shōukàn view; tune in; tune in to

手铐 shǒukào handcuffs

受苦 shòukǔ suffer

收款人 shōukuǎn rén recipient; payee

收款台 shōukuǎn tái till, cash register

受冷遇 shòu lěngyù get the cold shoulder; be in the doghouse

受连累 shòu liánlèi incriminate oneself

狩猎 shòuliè hunt

首领 shǒulǐng leader

收留 shōuliú take in

手榴弹 shǒuliúdàn grenade

收买 shōumǎi purchase; buy off, bribe

守门人 shǒumén rén doorman; super

守门员 shǒumén yuán goalkeeper

寿命 shòumìng life, lifetime

受虐狂 shòunüèkuáng masochism

受虐狂者 shòunüèkuáng zhě masochist

受骗 shòupiàn be deceived; 易受骗 yì shòupiàn gullible

售票处 shòupiào chù box office, ticket office

售票机 shòupiào jī ticket machine

收票员 shōupiào yuán ticket collector

售票员 shòupiào yuán booking clerk, ticket seller

收瓶处 shōupíng chù bottle bank

手枪 shǒuqiāng handgun; pistol

收起来 shōuqǐlái put away

授权 shòuquán authorize; warrant; delegate ◊ mandate; power of attorney

兽群 shòuqún herd

熟人 shóurén acquaintance; friend

收入 shōurù income; revenue

受伤 shòu shāng wounded; 腿受

伤 **tuǐ shòu shāng** wounded in the leg

受伤害 **shòu shānghài** injured

受伤者 **shòu shāng zhě** the injured

受伤至残 **shòu shāng zhì cán** cripple

受审 **shòushěn** on trial

收拾 **shōushi** clear away; clear up, tidy up; pack up

首饰 **shǒushi** jewelry

守时 **shǒushí** be punctual ◊ punctuality

手势 **shǒushì** gesture

熟食店 **shóushí diàn** delicatessen, deli

收拾干净 **shōushí gānjìng** clean up

手势语言 **shǒushì yǔyán** sign language

手术 **shǒushù** surgery; operation;

做手术 **zuò shǒushù** have an operation

手术刀 **shǒushù dāo** scalpel

手术室 **shǒushù shì** operating room

收缩 **shōusuō** contract, shrink

手套 **shǒutào** glove

手提包 **shǒutí bāo** bag; purse

手提电话 **shǒutí diànhuà** cell phone

收听 **shōutīng** tune in; tune in to

手提式 **shǒutíshì** portable

手提行李 **shǒutí xínglǐ** hand baggage

手提衣箱 **shǒutí yīxiāng** suitcase

手推车 **shǒutuīchē** wheelbarrow

受托集团 **shòutuō jítuán** trust
FIN

手腕 **shǒuwàn** wrist

售完为止 **shòuwán wéizhǐ** subject to availability

守卫 **shǒuwèi** guard

守卫队员 **shǒuwèi duìyuán** defense player

守卫者 **shǒuwèi zhě** guard, watchman

首先 **shǒuxiān** firstly, to begin with, in the first place

首相 **shǒuxiàng** prime minister

受限制 **shòu xiànzhì** restricted

手写 **shǒuxiě** handwritten ◊ write by hand

收信人 **shōuxìn rén** addressee; receiver

首席小提琴演奏者 **shǒuxí xiǎo tíqín yǎnzòu zhě** concertmaster

手续 **shǒuxù** formality; procedure

授勋 **shòuxūn** decorate

首演 **shǒuyǎn** début

收养 **shōuyǎng** adopt

手摇风琴 **shǒuyáo fēngqín** barrel organ

收益 **shōuyì** return, yield

兽医 **shòuyī** veterinary surgeon

受益 **shòuyì** benefit

手淫 **shǒuyín** masturbate

手印 **shǒuyìn** fingerprint

收音机 **shōuyīnjī** radio; 收音机里 **shōuyīnjī lǐ** on the radio

手艺人 **shǒuyì rén** craftsman; artisan

授予 **shòuyǔ** grant; present; confer

受约束 **shòu yuēshù** be bound, be committed; 受约束去做 X **shòu yuēshù qùzuò X** be bound to do X

受灾地区 **shòuzāi dìqū** disaster area

守则 **shǒuzé** rules

手轧 **shǒuzhá** parking brake

手掌 **shǒuzhǎng** palm

手杖 **shǒuzhàng** walking stick

手指 **shǒuzhǐ** finger

手指甲 **shǒuzhǐjiǎ** fingernail

收支平衡 **shōuzhī pínghéng** balance ◊ break even

受重伤 **shòu zhòngshāng** seriously injured

手爪子 **shǒuzhuǎzi** paw

手镯 **shǒuzhuó** bracelet

手足之情 **shǒuzú zhī qíng** fraternal love

书 **shū** book

梳 **shū** comb

输 **shū** lose

叔 **shū** uncle

熟 **shú** cooked; ripe; familiar ◊ ripeness ◊ soundly

赎 **shú** redeem

数 **shǔ** count

鼠 **shǔ** mouse; rat

暑 **shǔ** summer heat

属 **shǔ** belong to; 我属龙 **wǒ shǔ lóng** I was born in the year of the dragon

数 **shù** number

树 **shù** tree

竖 **shù** vertical

术 **shù** skill; art

述 **shù** tell, narrate

束 **shù** bundle, bunch, sheaf; 一束玫瑰 **yīshù méigui** a bunch of roses

刷 **shuā** clean ◊ brush

刷掉 **shuādiào** brush off

耍滑头 **shuǎ huátóu** try to be clever; 跟 X 耍滑头 **gēn X shuǎ huátóu** get smart with X

摔 **shuāi** fall; drop; throw down

帅 **shuài** handsome; snazzy

衰败 **shuāibài** go to seed

摔倒 **shuāidǎo** fall, fall down

甩干 **shuǎigān** spin-dry

甩干机 **shuǎigān jī** (spin-)dryer, (tumble-)dryer

摔跤 **shuāijiāo** fall; slip; wrestle

摔跤比赛 **shuāijiāo bǐsài** wrestling match

摔跤运动 **shuāijiāo yùndòng** wrestling

摔跤运动员 **shuāijiāo yùndòng yuán** wrestler

衰老 **shuāilǎo** senile

衰老状态 **shuāilǎo zhuàngtài** senility

衰落 **shuāiluò** go downhill, deteriorate

衰弱 **shuāiruò** weak ◊ waste away

衰退 **shuāituì** decay; decline

率直 **shuàizhí** plain; blunt

刷净 **shuājìng** scour

刷卡 **shuākǎ** smartcard

闩 **shuān** bolt ◊ catch (on door)

拴 **shuān** tie up, tether; 把 X 拴在 Y 上 **bǎ X shuān zài Y shàng** hitch X to Y; chain X to Y

双 **shuāng** both; even; double; dual; twin ◊ measure word for pairs; 一双袜子 **yìshuāng wàzi** a pair of socks

霜 **shuāng** frost

双胞胎 **shuāng bāo tāi** twins

双倍 **shuāngbèi** double

双边 **shuāngbiān** bilateral

双层玻璃 **shuāngcéng bōli** double glazing

双层床 **shuāngcéng chuáng** bunk beds

双重 **shuāngchóng** double

双打 **shuāngdǎ** doubles SP

霜冻 **shuāngdòng** frost

双方 **shuāngfāng** both sides

媚妇 **shuāngfù** widow

双关语 **shuāngguānyǔ** pun

双击 **shuāngjī** double click

爽快 **shuǎngkuài** refreshed; invigorating

双排扣式 **shuāngpái kòushì** double-breasted

双人床 **shuāngrén chuáng** double bed

双人房 **shuāngrén fáng** double (room)

爽身粉 **shuǎngshēnfěn** talcum powder

双数 **shuāngshù** even number

双下巴 **shuāngxiàbā** double chin

双向交通 **shuāngxiàng jiāotōng** two-way traffic

双性 **shuāngxìng** bisexual

双语 **shuāngyǔ** bilingual

栓剂 **shuānjì** suppository

栓牢 **shuānláo** attach

耍弄 **shuǎnòng** kick around

栓塞 **shuānsè** embolism

栓住 **shuānzhù** bolt; hitch

耍小聪明 **shuǎ xiǎo cōngmíng** smart, cute

刷牙 **shuāyá** brush one's teeth

刷子 **shuāzi** brush

书包 **shūbāo** schoolbag

鼠标 **shǔbiāo** mouse COMPUT

鼠标垫 **shǔbiāodiàn** mouse mat

数不清 **shǔbuqīng** innumerable; incalculable, countless

蔬菜 **shūcài** vegetable

蔬菜农场 **shūcài nóngchǎng** truck farm

蔬菜水果商 **shūcài shuǐguǒ shāng** greengrocer

输出 **shūchū** output; export

书呆子 **shūdāizi** bookworm;

pedant

竖笛 shùdí recorder MUS

书店 shūdiàn bookstore

输掉 shūdiào lose

数额 shù'é amount, sum

书法 shūfǎ calligraphy

书房 shūfáng study, den

竖放 shùfàng stand

舒服 shūfu comfortable ◊ well

束缚 shùfù tie; bind

树干 shùgàn trunk

疏忽 shūhū oversight

谁 shuí who

水 shuǐ water

睡 shuì sleep; 我睡不着 **wǒ shuìbùzháo** I couldn't get to sleep; 睡个懒觉 **shuìgè lǎnjiào** sleep late

税 shuì tax; duty; tariff

水坝 shuǐbà dam

水边 shuǐbiān waterside

水彩 shuǐcǎi watercolor

水彩画 shuǐcǎihuà watercolor (*painting*)

水池 shuǐchí pond; basin

睡袋 shuìdài sleeping bag

水电站 shuǐdiànzhàn hydroelectric power plant

水痘 shuǐdòu chicken pox

睡房 shuìfáng bedroom

水肺 shuǐfèi air tank, aqualung

水管 shuǐguǎn water pipe

水果 shuǐguǒ fruit

水果色拉 shuǐguǒ sèlā fruit salad

睡过头 shuì guòtóu oversleep

水花 shuǐhuā spray

睡觉 shuìjiào sleep; go to bed; 我需要好好睡一觉 **wǒ xūyào háohǎo shuìyíjiào** I need a good sleep; 和 ... 睡觉 **hé ... shuìjiào** sleep with ...

水晶 shuǐjīng crystal

水坑 shuǐkēng puddle

水库 shuǐkù reservoir

睡裤 shuìkù pajama pants

睡懒觉 shuì lǎnjiào sleep late

水冷却 shuǐlěngquè water-cooling

水力发电 shuǐlì fādiàn hydroelectric

水龙头 shuǐlóngtóu faucet

水路 shuǐlù waterway

水面 shuǐmiàn surface (*of water*)

睡眠 shuìmián sleep

水墨画 shuǐmòhuà ink wash painting

水泥 shuǐní cement

水牛 shuǐniú water buffalo

水暖工 shuǐnuǎngōng plumber

水疱 shuǐpào blister

水平 shuǐpíng standard, level; horizontal

水平面 shuǐpíngmiàn water level; level surface

水栖 shuǐqī aquatic, water-dwelling

水上运动 shuǐshàng yùndòng watersports

水手 shuǐshǒu sailor, seaman

税收 shuìshōu tax revenue

水手领 shuǐshǒu lǐng crew neck

水獭 shuǐtǎ otter

水桶 shuǐtǒng pail, bucket

水位 shuǐwèi water level

税务调查员 shuìwù diàocháyuán tax inspector

税务局 shuìwùjú tax office

水箱 shuǐxiāng cistern

睡醒 shuìxǐng wake up

睡眼惺忪 shuìyǎn xīngsōng bleary-eyed

睡衣 shuìyī nightdress; pajamas; pajama jacket

睡衣裤 shuìyīkù pajamas; pajama pants

水银 shuǐyín mercury, quicksilver

水翼艇 shuǐyìtǐng hydrofoil

水域 shuǐyù waters; area of water

睡着 shuìzháo fall asleep

水准仪 shuǐzhǔn yí spirit level

水准 shuǐzhǔn standard, level

水族馆 shuǐzú guǎn aquarium

书脊 shūjǐ spine

书籍 shūjí books

书架 shūjià bookcase

暑假 shǔjià summer vacation

树胶 shùjiāo gum

赎金 shújīn ransom

数据 shùjù data

数据保护 shùjù bǎohù data protection

数据储存 **shùjù chǔcún** data storage

数据处理 **shùjù chǔlǐ** data processing

数据俘获 **shùjù fúhuò** data capture

数据库 **shùjù kù** database

疏浚 **shūjùn** dredge

数据载体 **shùjù zàitǐ** data carrier

熟客 **shúkè** regular visitor

漱口 **shùkǒu** gargle

漱口剂 **shùkǒujì** mouthwash

树篱 **shùlí** hedge

熟练 **shúliàn** skillful; proficient; practised ◊ proficiency

数量 **shùliàng** amount

熟练技巧 **shúliàn jìqiǎo** dexterity

树林 **shùlín** wood

数落 **shǔluò** tell off, chew out

书面 **shūmiàn** written ◊ in writing; 以书面形式 **yǐ shūmiàn xíngshì** in writing

数目 **shùmù** number, numeral; sum

吮 **shǔn** suck

顺便 **shùnbiàn** in passing

顺便过访 **shùnbiàn guòfǎng** stop by

顺便看望 **shùnbiàn kànwàng** look in on

顺便来访 **shùnbiàn láifǎng** drop in

顺便问一下 **shùnbiàn wènyīxià** by the way, incidentally

顺从 **shùncóng** obey; submit ◊ obedient; submissive; docile

顺从的人 **shùncóng de rén** conformist

顺风 **shùnfēng** tail wind

枢纽 **shūniǔ** hub; center

瞬间 **shùnjiān** moment, instant ◊ momentarily

顺口溜 **shùnkǒuliū** jingle

顺利 **shùnlì** smooth ◊ smoothly

顺势疗法 **shùnshì liáofǎ** homeopathy

顺时针 **shùn shízhēn** clockwise

吮吸 **shǔnxī** suck; 吮吸拇指 **shǔnxī mǔzhǐ** suck one's thumb

顺心 **shùnxīn** satisfactory

顺序 **shùnxù** sequence

说 **shuō** talk; speak; say; 你说呢？ **nǐ shuō ne?** what do you think?; 你说什么？ **nǐ shuō shénme?** pardon me? what did you say?; 那就是说 **nà jiùshì shuō** that is to say; 说吧 **shuō ba** go ahead; 说正经的 **shuō zhèngjing de** seriously, joking apart; 我在说正经的 **wǒ zài shuō zhèngjing de** I'm serious

说唱音乐 **shuōchàng yīnyuè** rap MUS

说定 **shuōdìng** agree on; arrange; 说定了 **shuōdìngle** and that's flat; that's settled

说法 **shuōfǎ** way of saying something; version

说服 **shuōfú** persuade, convince; 说服X做Y **shuōfú X zuò Y** persuade X to do Y, talk X into doing Y

说话 **shuōhuà** speak

说话方式 **shuōhuà fāngshì** speech, way of speaking

说话能力 **shuōhuà nénglì** speech, ability to speak

说谎话 **shuō huǎnghuà** lie

说谎者 **shuōhuǎng zhě** liar

说教 **shuōjiào** preach

说明 **shuōmíng** explain ◊ explanation; caption

说明书 **shuōmíng shū** instruction manual

硕士 **shuòshì** master's (degree)

说说而已 **shuōshuo ér yǐ** all talk and no action

说笑话 **shuō xiàohuà** joke; crack a joke

说真的 **shuōzhēnde** honestly; 说真的吗？ **shuōzhènde ma?** seriously?

说正事 **shuō zhèngshì** get to the point

竖排 **shùpái** portrait *print*

书皮 **shūpí** dust cover

树皮 **shùpí** bark

薯片 **shǔpiàn** (potato) chips

鼠拼 **shǔpīn** rat race

述评 **shùpíng** comment ◊ commentary

竖起 **shùqǐ** erect, put up ◊ erection

书签 **shūqiān** bookmark

竖起耳朵 **shùqǐ ěrduo** prick up one's ears

竖琴 **shùqín** harp

熟人 **shúrén** acquaintance; friend

输入 **shūrù** input; import

输入端口 **shūrù duānkǒu** input port

疏散 **shūsàn** disperse; decentralize

书商 **shūshāng** bookseller

树梢 **shùshāo** tree top

舒适 **shūshì** cozy; comfortable

熟食 **shúshí** cooked meal

竖式(钢琴) **shùshì (gāngqín)** upright (piano)

叔叔 **shūshu** uncle (*father's younger brother*); *also used to address non-related men*

数数 **shǔshù** count

熟睡 **shúshuì** fast asleep

输送 **shūsòng** transport; convey; inject *fuel*

书摊 **shūtān** bookstall

薯条 **shǔtiáo** (French) fries

熟透 **shútòu** well-done, cooked through

鼠尾草 **shǔwěicǎo** sage

梳洗 **shūxǐ** clean up, freshen up

熟悉 **shúxī** know; be familiar with

书写体 **shūxiětǐ** script

书写体系 **shūxiě tǐxì** writing

书信往来 **shūxìn wǎnglái** correspondence

输血 **shūxuè** (blood) transfusion

数学 **shùxué** mathematical ◊ mathematical

数学家 **shùxué jiā** mathematician

输液 **shūyè** infusion

树液 **shùyè** sap

鼠疫 **shǔyì** plague

属于 **shǔyú** belong; belong to; 我不属于这里 **wǒ bù shǔyú zhèlǐ** I don't belong here

术语 **shùyǔ** terminology; term

疏远 **shūyuǎn** drift apart; alienate; distance oneself ◊ estranged

疏于练习 **shūyú liànxí** be out of practice

输者 **shūzhě** loser

树枝 **shùzhī** branch

树脂 **shùzhī** resin

树桩 **shùzhuāng** stump

梳妆台 **shūzhuāng tái** dressing table, dresser

书桌 **shūzhuō** desk

梳子 **shūzi** hairbrush; comb

数字 **shùzì** number, digit, figure ◊ digital; 四位数字 **sìwèi shùzì** four digit number

嘶 **sī** neigh

撕 **sī** tear (up)

思 **sī** think; consider

私 **sī** private

丝 **sī** silk

死 **sǐ** die ◊ death ◊ dead; 死于癌症 **sǐyú áizhèng** die of cancer

寺 **sì** Buddhist temple

四 **sì** four

似 **sì** resemble, be like; seem

饲 **sì** feed, fodder

四胞胎 **sì bāotāi** quadruplets

私奔 **sībēn** elope

四边形 **sìbiān xíng** quadrangle; rectangle

死不开口 **sǐ bù kāikǒu** clam up

死产 **sǐchǎn** be stillborn

撕成碎片 **sīchéng suìpiàn** shred

四重唱 **sì chōngchàng** quartet

四重奏 **sì chóngzòu** quartet

丝绸 **sīchóu** silk

丝绸之路 **Sīchóu zhī lù** Silk Road

四川 **Sìchuān** Sichuan, Szechuan

四川盆地 **Sìchuān Péndì** Sichuan Basin

四次 **sìcì** four times

丝带 **sīdài** ribbon

斯大林 **Sīdàlín** Stalin

死定了 **sǐdìngle** doomed

司法 **sīfǎ** justice ◊ judicial

四方形 **sìfāng xíng** square

四方院 **sìfāng yuàn** quadrangle

司法权 **sīfǎquán** jurisdiction

似非而是 **sìfēi'érshì** paradoxical ◊ paradoxically

四分音符 **sì fēn yīnfú** quarternote

四分之三 sì fēn zhī sān three-quarters

四分之一 sì fēn zhī yī quarter

丝瓜 sīguā loofah

丝毫 sīháo shred, vestige

似乎 sìhū looks like; seems ◊ apparently; 她似乎是 … *tā sìhū shì* … she comes across as …

撕毁 sīhuǐ tear up

厮混 sīhùn play around, be unfaithful; 与 X 厮混 *yǔ X sīhùn* get mixed up with X

死胡同 sǐ hútòng dead end, blind alley

司机 sījī driver; motorist; chauffeur

四季豆 sìjìdòu green bean

撕开 sīkāi slit; rip open

思考 sīkǎo contemplate, think about

司库 sīkù treasurer

私利 sīlì self-interest

饲料 sìliào fodder

撕裂 sīliè rip

司炉 sīlú stoker, boilerman

思路 sīlù line of thought

思念 sīniàn long for, pine for

死气沉沉 sǐqì chénchén dead *place* ◊ dull, boring

私人 sīrén private, personal; intimate

死人 sǐrén the dead; dead person

四人帮 Sìrénbāng Gang of Four

私人财产 sīrén cáichǎn private property

私人教师 sīrén jiàoshī (private) tutor

私人空间 sīrén kōngjiān privacy

私人助理 sīrén zhùlǐ personal assistant

丝绒 sīróng velvet

私生 sīshēng illegitimate

私生活 sīshēnghuó private life

私生子 sīshēngzǐ illegitimate child, bastard

死尸 sǐshī corpse

四十 sìshí forty

撕碎 sīsuì tear to pieces

私通 sītōng adultery ◊ commit adultery

死亡 sǐwáng death; fatality

死亡率 sǐwáng lǜ mortality, death rate

死亡总数 sǐwáng zǒngshù death toll

私下 sīxià in private, privately

撕下 sīxià tear out; tear off

思想 sīxiǎng thought; thinking; idea; ideology

死刑 sǐxíng capital punishment, death penalty; execution

私刑处死 sīxíng chùsǐ lynch

四星级 sìxīngjí four-star

嘶哑 sīyǎ hoarse

饲养 sìyǎng breed ◊ breeding

饲养员 sìyǎng yuán breeder

司仪 sīyí marshal; master of ceremonies

肆意破坏 sìyì pòhuài vandalize

私语 sīyǔ whisper

寺院 sìyuàn temple

四月 sìyuè April

死者 sǐzhě the deceased

丝织 sīzhī silk

四肢 sìzhī limbs

丝织品 sīzhīpǐn silk goods

四周 sìzhōu all around

四足动物 sìzú dòngwù quadruped

松 sōng pine ◊ loose ◊ loosely; 松一口气 *sōng yìkǒu qì* heave a sigh of relief

送 sòng deliver; give; accompany, escort; 我送你到门口 *wǒ sòng nǐ dào ménkǒu* I'll see you to the door

送别 sòngbié see off

送别宴会 sòngbié yànhuì farewell party

宋朝 Sòng Cháo Song Dynasty

松弛 sōngchí slack; flabby ◊ slacken; 松弛的肌肉 *sōngchíde jīròu* flab

宋词 Sòngcí Song Dynasty lyric poetry

松动 sōngdong loose ◊ work loose; loosen up

颂歌 sònggē carol

送回 sònghuí send back

送回国 sòng huíguó repatriate

送货 sònghuò delivery

送货车 sònghuò chē delivery

van

送货单 **sònghuò dān** delivery note

送货日期 **sònghuò rìqī** delivery date

耸肩 **sǒngjiān** shrug; 他耸了耸肩就走了 **tā sǒnglesǒng jiān jiù zǒule** he gave a shrug and left

松紧带 **sōngjǐndài** elastic

松开 **sōngkāi** release

松垮 **sōngkuǎ** lax

耸立 **sǒnglì** tower; rise

送礼 **sònglǐ** offer a present; give a bribe

松木 **sōngmù** pine (wood)

耸人听闻 **sǒngrén tīngwén** lurid

松软 **sōngruǎn** floppy; fluffy

松手 **sōngshǒu** let go

松鼠 **sōngshǔ** squirrel

松树 **sōngshù** pine (tree)

送送 **sòngsòng** see out, see to the door

松塔 **sōngtǎ** (pine) cone

松香 **sōngxiāng** resin

松懈 **sōngxiè** relax

送行 **sòngxíng** see off

怂恿 **sǒngyǒng** egg on

馊 **sōu** sour

搜捕 **sōubǔ** search

搜查 **sōuchá** search; frisk

搜查证 **sōucházhèng** search warrant

搜集 **sōují** gather; save

搜索 **sōusuǒ** search; scour; scan

搜索队 **sōusuǒduì** search party

搜寻 **sōuxún** search ◊ hunt for; scour; comb; surf (the Net)

酥 **sū** crisp

俗 **sú** vulgar; common

宿 **sù** stay overnight

塑 **sù** mold; sculpt

素 **sù** plain; white ◊ vegetarian food

速 **sù** fast

酸 **suān** acid ◊ acidic; sour; aching; sore

算 **suàn** count, include

蒜 **suàn** garlic

酸橙 **suānchéng** lime

酸辣汤 **suānlàtāng** hot and sour soup

算命 **suànmìng** tell s.o.'s fortune; tell fortunes

算命者 **suànmìng zhě** fortune-teller

酸奶 **suānnǎi** yogurt

算盘 **suànpan** abacus

算术 **suànshù** arithmetic; sum

酸味 **suānwèi** acidity; sourness

酸雨 **suānyǔ** acid rain

算帐 **suànzhàng** settle accounts; settle scores; 跟 X 算旧帐 **gēn X suàn jiùzhàng** have an old score to settle with X

酥饼 **sūbǐng** flaky pastry

俗不可耐 **sú bù kě nài** garish

素菜 **sùcài** vegetarian dish

速成课 **sùchéng kè** crash course

酥脆 **sūcuì** crispy; crunchy

苏打 **sūdá** soda

速冻 **sùdòng** quick-freeze ◊ quick-frozen

速度 **sùdù** speed, pace, rate; tempo; 速度每小时一百五十英里 **sùdù měi xiǎoshí yībǎi wǔshí yīnglǐ** at a speed of 150 mph

速度极限 **sùdù jíxiàn** speed limit

苏格兰 **Sūgélán** Scotland ◊ Scottish

虽 **suī** although

髓 **suí** pith

随 **suí** follow; 随你的便! **suí nǐde biàn!** suit yourself!

穗 **suì** ear (of corn)

碎 **suì** shatter ◊ shattered

岁 **suì** year; years old; 她五岁了 **tā wǔsuì le** she's five years old

随便 **suíbiàn** arbitrary; casual ◊ at random; at will; 随便拿 **suíbiàn ná** take as much as you want; help yourself; 随便你 **suíbiàn nǐ** if you like; suit yourself

随便看看 **suíbiàn kànkan** browse

随从人员 **suícóng rényuán** entourage

穗带 **suìdài** braid

隧道 **suìdào** tunnel

随和 **suíhé** easy-going

随后 **suíhòu** afterward,

subsequently ◊ subsequent

随机 **suíjī** random

随机抽样 **suíjī chōuyàng** random sample

碎块 **suìkuài** fragment

碎裂 **suìliè** break up; crumble

碎片 **suìpiàn** piece; flake; shred; splinter; fragment

虽然 **suīrán** although, while

碎肉 **suìròu** ground meat

随身听 **suíshēntīng** Walkman®, personal stereo

随时 **suíshí** at any time

碎石 **suìshí** gravel

随意 **suíyì** as one likes; 你要吃什么？－随意 **nǐ yào chī shénme? – suíyì** what would you like to eat? – anything will be fine

速记 **sùjì** shorthand ◊ take shorthand

肃静！**sùjìng!** silence!

诉苦 **sùkǔ** complain

苏联 **Sūlián** Soviet Union

塑料 **sùliào** plastic

塑料袋 **sùliào dài** plastic bag

素描簿 **sùmiáo bò** sketchbook

宿命 **sùmìng** predestination

塑膜 **sùmó** shrink-wrapping

塑膜包装 **sùmó bāozhuāng** shrink-wrap ◊ shrink-wrapping

孙 **sūn** grandson

损 **sǔn** lose; damage

笋 **sǔn** bamboo shoot

损害 **sǔnhài** harm, damage; impair

损耗 **sǔnhào** wear (and tear)

损坏 **sǔnhuài** break; damage

损坏表面 **sǔnhuài biǎomiàn** deface

孙女 **sūnnǚ** granddaughter (*son's daughter*)

损伤 **sǔnshāng** damage; mutilate; 未受损伤 **wèi shòu sǔnshāng** uninjured; unscathed; undamaged

损失 **sǔnshī** damage; loss; toll

损失惨重 **sǔnshī cǎnzhòng** disastrous

孙中山 **Sūn Zhōngshān** Sun Yat-sen

孙子 **sūnzi** grandson (*son's son*)

锁 **suǒ** lock; 锁在里面 **suǒ zài lǐmiàn** lock in; 锁在外面 **suǒ zài wàimiàn** lock out

缩 **suō** shrink, contract; retract

索 **suǒ** rope

所 **suǒ** what, that which; 据我所知 **jù wǒ suǒ zhī** according to what I know ◊ *measure word for institutions*; 一所学校 **yì suǒ xuéxiào** a school

索道 **suǒdào** cable railroad

所得税 **suǒdéshuì** income tax

缩短 **suōduǎn** shorten; 缩短会议 **suōduǎn huìyì** cut a meeting short

缩格书写 **suōgé shūxiě** indent *text*

锁骨 **suǒgǔ** collarbone

缩回 **suōhuí** draw back

缩减 **suōjiǎn** decrease; cut back

锁匠 **suǒjiàng** locksmith

缩进 **suōjìn** retract

缩进排印 **suōjìn páiyìn** indent (*in text*)

锁孔 **suǒkǒng** keyhole

索赔 **suǒpéi** claim

锁起来 **suǒ qǐlái** lock away

索取 **suǒqǔ** claim

索取单 **suǒqǔ dān** coupon

琐事 **suǒshì** triviality, trifle

所述 **suǒshù** above-mentioned

缩水 **suōshuǐ** shrink

琐碎事 **suǒsuì shì** odds and ends; trivia; minor details

所谈 **suǒtán** in question

所谓 **suǒwèi** alleged; so-called

缩微胶卷 **suōwēi jiāojuǎn** microfilm

缩小 **suōxiǎo** reduce, make smaller

缩写 **suōxiě** abbreviate ◊ abbreviation

所以 **suǒyǐ** therefore; so; consequently

索引 **suǒyǐn** index

索引卡 **suǒyǐn kǎ** index card

所有 **suǒyǒu** own ◊ all; 他把所有的东西都吃了 **tā bǎ suǒyǒude dōngxi dōu chī le** he ate all of it

所有权 **suǒyǒu quán** ownership; title

所有物 **suǒyǒu wù** belongings, possessions, stuff, things

所在地 **suǒzàidì** seat; site
锁住 **suǒzhù** immobilize
俗气 **súqi** tacky
肃清 **sùqīng** mop up MIL
速溶咖啡 **sùróng kāfēi** instant coffee
宿舍 **sùshè** hostel; boarding house; dormitory
素食 **sùshí** vegetarian
素食者 **sùshí zhě** vegetarian
素食主义 **sùshí zhǔyì** vegan
素食主义者 **sùshí zhǔyì zhě** vegan
诉讼 **sùsòng** lawsuit

诉讼细节 **sùsòng xìjié** legal technicality
俗套 **sútào** corny
俗套情节 **sútào qíngjié** hokum
塑像 **sùxiàng** statue
苏醒 **sūxǐng** come around, come to ◊ revival; 使 .. 苏醒 **shǐ ... sūxǐng** revive
俗艳 **súyàn** loud *color*
宿营地 **sùyíngdì** quarters
酥油 **sūyóu** butter; cream
塑造 **sùzào** form, shape
素质 **sùzhì** constitution, make-up; qualities

T

他 tā he; him ◊ his
她 tā she; her
它 tā it ◊ its
塔 tǎ tower
獭 tǎ otter
踏 tà step, tread
踏板 tàbǎn pedal; treadle
踏板车 tàbǎnchē scooter
塌鼻 tābí snub-nosed
她的 tāde her ◊ hers
他的 tāde his
它的 tāde its
塌方 tāfāng landslide
胎 tāi embryo; fetus
苔 tái moss
台 tái platform; terrace; Taiwan
太 tài too; very 太多饭 tài duō fàn too much rice; 太大 tài dà too big
台北 Táiběi Taipei
台布 táibù tablecloth
台词 táicí speech
态度 tàidù attitude, manner
胎儿 tāi'ér embryo; fetus
太妃糖 tàifēi táng toffee
台风 táifēng typhoon
泰国 Tàiguó Thailand ◊ Thai
太极拳 tàijíquán tai chi
太空 tàikōng (outer) space
太空舱 tàikōng cāng (space) capsule
胎面 tāimiàn tread
太平间 tàipíngjiān mortuary
太平洋 Tàipíngyáng Pacific Ocean
太平洋岸 Tàipíngyáng àn Pacific Rim
太平洋岸国家 Tàipíngyáng àn guójiā Pacific Rim countries
台球 táiqiú snooker; billiards
泰然自若 tàirán zìruò poised
泰山 Tàishān Mount Tai
台式机 táishìjī desk top computer
太太 tàitai Mrs ◊ wife
台湾 Táiwān Taiwan ◊ Taiwanese

台湾海峡 Táiwān Hǎixiá Taiwan Straits
台湾话 Táiwān huà Taiwanese
台湾人 Táiwān rén Taiwanese
太阳 tàiyáng sun
太阳电池板 tàiyáng diànchí bǎn solar panel
太阳镜 tàiyáng jìng sunglasses
太阳能 tàiyáng néng solar energy
太阳穴 tàiyáng xuè temple
踏脚石 tàjiǎo shí stepping stone
塔吉克 Tǎjíkè Tajikistan ◊ Tajiki
他妈的 tāmāde √ damn, fuck ◊ fucking; 去他妈的! qù tāmāde! fuck!; fuck him/that!
他们 tāmen they; them ◊ their
她们 tāmen they; them ◊ their (female only)
她们的 tāmende ◊ theirs (female only)
他们的 tāménde their ◊ theirs
他们自己 tāmen zìjǐ themselves
摊 tān pool
贪 tān covet
瘫 tān paralyzed
坛 tán bed (of flowers)
谈 tán talk; 我会和他谈 wǒ huì hé tā tán I'll talk to him about it
痰 tán spit, spittle
弹 tán play string instrument; 弹钢琴 tán gāngqín play the piano; 弹吉他 tán jítā play the guitar
叹 tàn sigh
碳 tàn carbon
炭 tàn charcoal
坦白 tǎnbái confess ◊ frankly ◊ open; 坦白告诉我 tǎnbái gàosù wǒ give it to me straight
炭笔 tànbǐ charcoal (for drawing)
探测 tàncè probe
探测器 tàncè qì detector
探查 tànchá probe
摊贩 tānfàn street trader

探访者 tànfǎng zhě caller, visitor

汤 tāng soup; stock; broth

糖 táng sugar; candy

躺 tǎng lie

淌 tǎng run (of nose etc)

烫 tàng hot

唐朝 Táng Cháo Tang Dynasty

汤匙 tāngchí spoon; soup spoon

搪瓷 tángcí enamel

糖醋 tángcù sweet and sour

堂弟 tángdì cousin (younger male on father's side)

探戈舞 tàngé wǔ tango

烫发 tàngfà have a perm ◊ perm

糖粉 tángfěn confectioners' sugar

糖罐 tángguàn sugar bowl

糖果 tángguǒ candy

糖浆 tángjiāng molasses, syrup

烫焦 tàngjiāo scorch; singe

堂姐 tángjiě cousin (older female on father's side)

糖精 tángjīng saccharin

淌流 tāngliú run (of nose)

堂妹 tángmèi cousin (younger female on father's side)

汤面 tāngmian noodle soup

糖尿病 tángniàobìng diabetes ◊ diabetic

唐人街 tángrénjiē Chinatown

唐三彩 tángsāncǎi Tang ceramics glazed in three colors

搪塞 tángsè stonewall, stall

烫伤 tàngshāng scald

唐诗 Tángshī Tang poetry

糖霜 tángshuāng frosting

蹚水 tāngshuǐ wade; paddle

唐突草率 tángtū cǎoshuài curt

汤碗 tāngwǎn soup bowl

躺下 tǎngxià lie down

堂兄 tángxiōng cousin (older male on father's side)

躺椅 tǎngyǐ deck chair; lounger

谈话 tánhuà talk

谈话节目 tánhuà jiémù talk show

瘫痪 tānhuàn paralysis ◊ paralyze; 使…瘫痪 shǐ … tānhuàn immobilize

弹簧 tánhuáng spring

坍毁 tānhuǐ dilapidated

弹回来 tán huílái rebound

摊开 tānkāi open; unfold; spread

坦克 tǎnkè tank MIL

贪婪 tānlán greedy; acquisitive

谈恋爱 tán liàn'ài date

摊凉 tānliáng cool (down)

谈判 tánpàn negotiate ◊ negotiations

谈判员 tánpàn yuán negotiator

弹起 tánqǐ bounce

叹气 tànqì sigh

弹射 tánshè eject

贪食 tānshí gluttony ◊ gluttonous

贪食者 tānshí zhě glutton

坦率 tǎnshuài frank, open, candid ◊ candor

碳水化合物 tànshuǐ huàhéwù carbohydrate

探索 tànsuǒ exploration ◊ seek

探索性 tànsuǒ xìng exploratory

探索者 tànsuǒ zhě explorer

坍塌 tāntā give way

探讨 tàntǎo explore

弹跳 tántiào bounce

探听 tàntīng investigate; nose around

探望时间 tànwàng shíjiān visiting hours

贪污 tānwū embezzle ◊ embezzlement

叹息 tànxī sigh

探险 tànxiǎn expedition

贪心 tānxīn greed

弹性 tánxìng elasticity

探照灯 tànzhàodēng searchlight

摊子 tānzi stall, stand, booth

毯子 tǎnzi blanket, rug

弹奏 tánzòu play

逃 táo flee; escape

桃 táo peach

讨 tǎo discuss

套 tào set; suit; suite ◊ measure word for rooms, furniture, clothes; 一套家具 yītào jiāju a suite of furniture

逃避 táobì escape, elude; shirk ◊ evasion

逃兵 táobīng deserter

绦虫 tāochóng tapeworm

掏出 tāochū get out; cough up money

陶瓷 táocí ceramics

逃犯 **táofàn** fugitive

套服 **tàofú** suit

陶工 **táogōng** potter

讨好 **tǎohǎo** flatter ◊ flattering

讨价还价 **tǎojià huánjià** bargain, haggle

套间 **tàojiān** suite (of rooms)

掏空 **tāokōng** empty

讨论 **tǎolùn** discuss, talk over; debate ◊ discussion

讨论会 **tǎolùn huì** conference

逃跑 **táopǎo** run away, flee ◊ flight; getaway

陶器 **táoqì** ceramics, pottery, earthenware

淘气 **táoqì** naughty

掏钱 **tāoqián** cough up, pay

淘气包 **táoqìbāo** rogue; brat

陶器作坊 **táoqì zuòfang** pottery (place)

讨人喜欢 **tǎorén xǐhuān** endearing

淘汰 **táotài** eliminate; weed out ◊ elimination

淘汰赛 **táotàisài** knockout competition

滔滔不绝 **tāotao bùjué** torrent (of words)

逃脱 **táotuō** escape; 逃脱处分 **táotuō chǔfèn** get off, escape punishment

逃学 **táoxué** play hookey

讨厌 **tǎoyàn** disgusting; tiresome ◊ detest, loathe ◊ what a nuisance!; 令人讨厌 **lìngrén tǎoyàn** rotten trick; unsavory; bitchy

讨厌鬼 **tǎoyànguǐ** pest, so-and-so; creep

套装 **tàozhuāng** outfit

桃子 **táozi** peach

套子 **tàozi** housing; case

逃走 **táozǒu** flee, run away

逃罪 **táozuì** get away with

陶醉 **táozuì** intoxicated; high

她自己 **tā zìjǐ** herself

他自己 **tā zìjǐ** himself

它自己 **tā zìjǐ** itself

特 **tè** special

特别 **tèbié** special, specific, particular, ◊ specially, specifically, particularly

特别工作组 **tèbié gōngzuòzǔ** task force

特产 **tèchǎn** specialty

特大 **tèdà** king-size(d)

特大号 **tè dàhào** outsize

特等包厢 **tèděng bāoxiāng** dress circle

特地 **tèdì** expressly

特点 **tèdiǎn** characteristic, peculiarity

特工人员 **tègōng rényuán** secret agent

特护（部）**tèhù (bù)** intensive care (unit)

特技 **tèjì** trick; stunt

特快 **tèkuài** express

特免 **tèmiǎn** immunity, exemption

疼 **téng** pain, hurt ◊ sore; 疼不疼？**téng bùténg?** is it sore?, does it hurt?

腾出 **téngchū** vacate

藤条 **téngtiáo** wicker

疼痛 **téngtòng** hurt, pain ◊ painful

藤椅 **téngyǐ** wicker chair

特权 **tèquán** privilege

特色 **tèsè** feature, characteristic

特殊 **tèshū** special, particular; exceptional; 特殊情况 **tèshū qíngkuàng** one-off, exception; special circumstances

特务 **tèwu** secret agent

特务机关 **tèwù jīguān** secret service

特写镜头 **tèxiě jìngtóu** close-up

特性 **tèxìng** quality, trait

特有 **tèyǒu** distinctive; peculiar to

特征 **tèzhēng** attribute, characteristic

特种 **tèzhǒng** special ◊ special type

特种饮食 **tèzhǒng yǐnshí** special diet

踢 **tī** kick; 踢足球 **tī zúqiú** play soccer

梯 **tī** ladder; steps

蹄 **tí** hoof

题 **tí** subject, theme

提 **tí** carry; lift; raise; 不提X的事 **bù tí X de shì** keep quiet about X

体 **tǐ** body

剃 **tì** shave

替 **tì** replace; substitute ◊ in behalf of; 替我问她好 **tì wǒ wèn tā hǎo** remember me to her

天 **tiān** sky; heaven; day; 天晚了 **tiānwǎn le** it's getting late

添 **tiān** add

甜 **tián** sweet

填 **tián** fill out, fill in

田 **tián** field

舔 **tián** lick; lap up

天安门广场 **Tiān'ānmén Guǎngchǎng** Tiananmen Square

填表 **tiánbiǎo** fill out a form

天才 **tiāncái** talent; genius ◊ ingenious

甜菜 **tiáncài** sugar beet

填充 **tiánchōng** stuff *turkey etc*

天窗 **tiānchuāng** skylight

田地 **tiándì** field; farmland

天鹅 **tiān'é** swan

天鹅绒 **tiān'éróng** velvet

天份 **tiānfèn** gift, talent; flair

天赋 **tiānfù** gift, talent

天沟 **tiāngōu** gutter

天黑 **tiānhēi** dark; 天黑以后 **tiānhēi yǐhòu** after dark

天花 **tiānhuā** smallpox

天花板 **tiānhuābǎn** ceiling

添加 **tiānjiā** add

添加剂 **tiānjiā jì** additive

田径 **tiánjìng** track and field; athletics

天空 **tiānkōng** sky

填料 **tiánliào** stuffing

填满 **tiánmǎn** fill up; fill in

天哪！ **tiānna!** good heavens! oh God!

甜品 **tiánpǐn** dessert

天平 **tiānpíng** scales

天气 **tiānqì** weather; 天气很冷 **tiānqì hěnlěng** it's cold; 天气晴朗 **tiānqì qínglǎng** it's sunny

天气预报 **tiānqì yùbào** weather forecast

天然 **tiānrán** natural ◊ naturally

天然气 **tiānrán qì** natural gas

田赛 **tiánsài** field events

天生 **tiānshēng** innate ◊ naturally; 天生的 ... **tiānshēngde ...** be a natural ...

天使 **tiānshǐ** angel

甜食 **tiánshí** confectionery

田鼠 **tiánshǔ** vole

天坛 **Tiāntán** Temple of Heaven

天堂 **tiāntáng** heaven; paradise

天体 **tiāntǐ** heavenly body

天体运行轨道 **tiāntǐ yùnxíng guǐdào** orbit

甜味剂 **tiánwèijì** sweetener

天文 **tiānwén** astronomy

天文台 **tiānwén tái** observatory

天文学 **tiānwén xué** astronomy

天文学家 **tiānwén xuéjiā** astronomer

天线 **tiānxiàn** aerial, antenna

天线塔 **tiānxiàntǎ** (radio) mast

填写 **tiánxiě** fill out, fill in, complete

天性 **tiānxìng** disposition, nature

填鸭式灌输 **tiānyā shì guànshū** spoonfeed

天衣无缝 **tiān yī wú fèng** perfect

田园式 **tiányuánshì** idyllic

甜玉米 **tián yùmǐ** sweetcorn

天真 **tiānzhēn** naive; childlike

天真无邪 **tiānzhēn wúxié** childlike; innocent

天主教 **Tiānzhǔjiào** (Roman) Catholic

天主教徒 **Tiānzhǔjiào tú** (Roman) Catholic

天资 **tiānzī** aptitude

挑 **tiāo** choose, pick

条 **tiáo** strip; item ◊ *measure word for long thin things*; 一条裤子 **yìtiáo kùzi** a pair of pants; 一条香烟 **yìtiáo xiāngyān** a carton of cigarettes; 一条新闻 **yìtiáo xīnwén** a bit of news

调 **tiáo** adjust

挑 **tiǎo** push; provoke

跳 **tiào** jump, leap; hop; skip

跳板 **tiàobǎn** springboard; gangway

挑拨 **tiǎobō** provoke

挑出 **tiāochū** single out

挑刺儿 **tiāocìr** be critical ◊ critical

挑动 **tiǎodòng** stir up

跳动 **tiàodòng** beat, throb

挑逗 **tiǎodòu** provoke ◊ provocative; 挑斗 Y 去做 Y **tiǎodòu X qù zuò Y** dare X to do Y

挑逗嗯哨 **tiǎodòu hūshào** wolf whistle

跳高 **tiàogāo** high jump

调羹 **tiáogēng** spoon

调合 **tiáohé** set *alarm clock etc*

挑拣 **tiāojiǎn** be selective ◊ selective

条件 **tiáojiàn** condition, term, requirement, stipulation ◊ conditional

条件反射 **tiáojiàn fǎnshè** conditioning

调节 **tiáojié** adjust

调解 **tiáojiě** mediate; reconcile ◊ mediation; reconciliation

调解人 **tiáojiě rén** mediator; troubleshooter

条款 **tiáokuǎn** clause; provision

跳栏 **tiàolán** hurdle; hurdles

跳栏运动员 **tiàolán yùndòng yuán** hurdler

调料 **tiáoliào** spice; herb; condiment; ingredient

调配饮料 **tiáopèi yǐnliào** mixer (*drink*)

调皮 **tiáopí** naughty; rude

调皮鬼 **tiáopíguǐ** little monkey, scamp

跳棋 **tiàoqí** Chinese checkers

调情 **tiáoqíng** flirt; 向 X 调情 **xiàng X tiáoqíng** make a pass at X

调情者 **tiáoqíng zhě** flirt (*person*)

跳棋盘 **tiàoqí pán** checkerboard

跳伞 **tiàosǎn** parachute; bail out

挑三拣四 **tiāosān jiǎnsì** choosey, discriminating

跳伞者 **tiàosǎn zhě** parachutist

调色剂 **tiáosè jì** toner

跳绳 **tiàoshéng** jump rope

跳水 **tiàoshuǐ** dive; diving

跳水板 **tiàoshuǐ bǎn** diving board

跳水者 **tiàoshuǐ zhě** diver

挑剔 **tiāoti** fussy, particular, choosey, picky; 挑剔食物的人 **tiāoti shíwù de rén** fussy eater

挑挑拣拣 **tiāotiāo jiǎnjiǎn** pick and choose ◊ picky, choosey

调停 **tiáotíng** arbitrate, intercede

调味 **tiáowèi** season; 给 X 调味 **gěi X tiáowèi** flavor X

调味品 **tiáowèipǐn** flavoring, seasoning

调味汁儿 **tiáowèi zhīr** dressing

条纹 **tiáowén** streak; stripe

跳舞 **tiàowǔ** dance

调谐 **tiáoxié** tune up

调谐器 **tiáoxié qì** tuner

挑衅 **tiāoxìn** provoke ◊ provocation ◊ provocative

条形码 **tiáoxíng mǎ** bar code

挑选 **tiāoxuǎn** choose, select

调音 **tiáoyīn** tune up

跳远 **tiàoyuǎn** long jump

条约 **tiáoyuē** treaty, pact

跳跃 **tiàoyuè** jump, bound, spring

跳蚤 **tiàozao** flea

跳蚤市场 **tiàozao shìchǎng** flea market

挑战 **tiǎozhàn** challenge; 挑战 X 做 Y **tiǎozhàn X zuò Y** challenge X to Y

挑战者 **tiǎozhàn zhě** challenger

调整 **tiáozhěng** adjust

调制 **tiáozhì** concoct

调制解调器 **tiáozhì jiětiáoqì** modem

调制品 **tiáozhì pǐn** concoction

笤帚 **tiáozhǒu** broom

体操 **tǐcāo** gymnastics

体操家 **tǐcāojiā** gymnast

提倡 **tíchàng** advocate

提出 **tíchū** bring up, broach, raise; advance; 提出辞职通知 **tíchū cízhí tōngzhī** hand in one's notice

提词 **tící** prompt

题词 **tící** dedication ◊ dedicate

替代 **tìdài** replace; deputize for

替代演员 **tìdài yǎnyuán** double (*of actor*)

提到 **tídào** mention, touch on, refer to

剃刀 **tìdāo** shaver

踢踏舞 **tīdá wǔ** tap dance

贴 **tiē** stick; 贴壁纸 **tiē bìzhǐ** wallpaper

铁 **tiě** iron

贴边 **tiēbiān** hem; seam; edge

贴标签 **tiē biāoqiān** label

铁饼 **tiěbǐng** discus

铁饭碗 **tiě fànwǎn** iron rice bowl, job for life

铁轨 **tiěguǐ** rail

铁匠 tiějiàng blacksmith

铁路 tiělù railroad

贴签 tiēqiān sticky label

铁锹 tiěqiāo shovel, spade

贴身 tiēshēn skin-tight ◊ cling

贴邮票 tiē yóupiào stamp

体罚 tǐfá corporal punishment

提高 tígāo raise, elevate; increase; improve ◊ rise

提高 ... 等级 tígāo ... děngjí upgrade

提高标价 tígāo biāojià mark up

提高价值 tígāo jiàzhí appreciate FIN

提高效率 tígāo xiàolǜ streamline

体格 tǐgé physique; 体格健美 **tǐgé jiànměi** athletic

体格检查 tǐgé jiǎnchá physical, medical check-up

提供 tígōng supply, provide, furnish; offer; 提供资金 **tígōng zījīn** finance

提供信息 tígōng xìxī inform ◊ informative

提供消息人 tígōng xiāoxī rén informant

剃光 tiguāng shaven

屉柜 tì guì chest of drawers

替换 tìhuàn substitute, replace; 替换队员 **tìhuàn duìyuán** make a substitution

替换衣服 tìhuàn yīfu change one's clothes

剃胡子 tì húzi shave

梯级 tījí stair; rung

提及 tíjí mention

体积 tǐjī volume

替件 tìjiàn replacement part

提款 tíkuǎn withdraw ◊ withdrawal

提炼 tíliàn refine

提炼厂 tíliàn chǎng refinery

体面 tǐmiàn face; dignity ◊ respectable

提名 tímíng nominate ◊ nomination

题目 tímù topic

体内 tǐnèi internally

厅 tīng hall; auditorium

听 tīng listen; listen to; obey; 我听你之便 **wǒ tīng nǐ zhī biàn** I am at your disposal; 听电话 **tīng**

diànhuà answer the telephone

停 tíng stop; 停了 **tíngle** come to a stop

亭 tíng pavilion

挺 tǐng very, quite; 挺好 **tǐng hǎo** very good, terrific

停泊 tíngbó moor

停泊区 tíngbó qū moorings

听不见 tīngbújiàn inaudible

停车 tíngchē park ◊ parking

停车标志 tíngchē biāozhì stop sign

停车场 tíngchē chǎng parking lot; 室内停车场 **shìnèi tíngchē chǎng** parking garage

停车处 tíngchē chù parking place

听从 tīngcóng obey; respond

听到 tīngdào hear; hear about

听得见 tīngde jiàn audible

停电 tíngdiàn power cut, blackout

停顿 tíngdùn pause; disruption ◊ be at a standstill; 使停顿 **shǐ tíngdùn** disrupt

停放 tíngfàng park MOT

听话 tīnghuà listen; obey ◊ obedient

停火 tínghuǒ cease-fire

听见 tīngjiàn hear

听距 tīngjù within hearing

挺括 tǐngkuò crisp

听力 tīnglì hearing; comprehension

听起来 tīngqǐlái sound; 听起来很有趣 **tīngqǐlái hěn yǒuqù** that sounds interesting

听清楚 tīng qīngchu hear, catch

听其自然 tīngqí zìrán resign oneself to

听取意见 tīngqǔ yìjiàn canvass

挺身而出 tǐngshēn ér chū come forward

停尸房 tíngshīfáng morgue

听说 ... tīngshuō ... people say ..., they say that ...

听天由命 tīngtiān yóumìng resigned

听筒 tīngtǒng receiver TELEC

停歇 tíngxiē rest

停业 tíngyè shut down, fold, cease trading

听诊 **tīngzhěn** sound MED
听诊器 **tīngzhěnqì** stethoscope
停职 **tíngzhí** suspension (*from duty*)
停止 **tíngzhǐ** stop, halt; let up
停滞 **tíngzhì** stagnant
挺直 **tǐngzhí** straighten up
停滞不前 **tíngzhì bù qián** come to a halt
停止生产 **tíngzhǐ shēngchǎn** discontinue
听众 **tīngzhòng** audience; listeners
停住 **tíngzhù** stop
亭子 **tíngzi** kiosk; pavilion
提起 **tíqǐ** pull up
提前 **tíqián** early, in advance
提起公诉 **tíqǐ gōngsù** prosecute
提取 **tíqǔ** withdraw; extract
体弱 **tǐruò** infirm; weak ◊ infirmity; 体弱的人 **tǐruò de rén** weakling
提神 **tíshén** freshen up; refresh oneself
提升 **tíshēng** promote
替身演员 **tìshēn yǎnyuán** stuntman
提示 **tíshì** point out; hint ◊ cue
提示符 **tíshìfú** prompt
梯田 **tītián** terraced field, terrace
体贴 **tǐtiē** nice; considerate
剃头匠 **tìtóu jiàng** barber
提问 **tíwèn** ask
体温 **tǐwēn** (body) temperature
体温过低 **tǐwēn guòdī** hypothermia
题献 **tíxiàn** dedicate
体现 **tǐxiàn** embody
提心吊胆 **tíxīn diàodǎn** be on tenterhooks
提醒 **tíxǐng** remind; 提醒 X 做 Y **tíxǐng X zuò Y** remind X to do Y
体臭 **tǐxiù** BO, body odor
剃须刀 **tìxū dāo** razor
剃须刀刀片 **tìxū dāo dāopiàn** razor blade
剃须膏 **tìxūgāo** shaving soap
体验 **tǐyàn** experience
提议 **tíyì** suggest, propose ◊ proposal, motion
体育 **tǐyù** sport

体育版 **tǐyù bǎn** sports page
体育场 **tǐyù chǎng** stadium
体育馆 **tǐyù guǎn** gymnasium
体育记者 **tǐyù jìzhě** sports journalist
体育新闻 **tǐyù xīnwén** sports news
体育运动 **tǐyù yùndòng** sport ◊ sporting
体质 **tǐzhì** physique; constitution
体制 **tǐzhì** system
体重 **tǐzhòng** (body) weight
梯子 **tīzi** ladder
替罪羊 **tìzuìyáng** scapegoat
通 **tōng** through; 通了 **tōngle** you're through TELEC
铜 **tóng** copper
童 **tóng** child
瞳 **tóng** pupil
同 **tóng** same; similar; with; and
桶 **tǒng** barrel, drum; tub; pail
捅 **tǒng** poke, prod
统 **tǒng** unite
痛 **tòng** pain, hurt; ache ◊ sore, aching; 痛不痛? **tòng bútòng?** does it hurt?
同伴 **tóngbàn** partner
铜版画 **tóngbǎnhuà** copperplate
同胞 **tóngbāo** fellow citizen; fellow countryman
同步 **tóngbù** same speed; 使 … 同步 **shǐ … tóngbù** synchronize
统舱 **tǒngcāng** lower deck
通常 **tōngcháng** usual, normal ◊ usually, normally
通常开支 **tōngcháng kāizhī** overhead FIN
痛打 **tòngdǎ** thrashing, hiding ◊ lay into
同代人 **tóngdài rén** contemporary
通道 **tōngdào** passage; aisle
同等 **tóngděng** equal ◊ equally; 同等价值 **tóngděng jiàzhí** of equal value
同等人 **tóngděngrén** peer
通风 **tōngfēng** air; ventilate ◊ airy; drafty ◊ ventilation
通风报信 **tōngfēng bàoxìn** tip off
通风井 **tōngfēng jǐng** ventilation shaft

通风孔 tōngfēng kǒng vent

通风设备 tōngfēng shèbèi ventilator

同感 tónggǎn sympathy

通告 tōnggào notice

通关 tōngguān customs clearance

铜管乐队 tóngguǎn yuèduì brass band

通过 tōngguò pass, get by ◊ via, through; 通过考试 *tōngguò kǎoshì* pass an exam; 通过他安排 *tōngguò tā ānpái* arranged through him

童话 tónghuà fairy tale

通货膨胀 tōnghuò péngzhàng inflation

通货再膨胀 tōnghuò zài péngzhàng reflation

通缉 tōngjí: 被通缉 *bèi tōngjí* wanted

统计 tǒngjì statistics ◊ statistical

同届 tóngjiè contemporary

统计学 tǒngjì xué statistics; 从统计学角度来说 *cóng tǒngjìxué jiǎodù láishuō* statistically

统计资料 tǒngjì zīliào statistics

同居 tóngjū cohabit; 和 X 同居 *hé X tóngjū* live with X

瞳孔 tóngkǒng pupil

痛哭 tòngkū bawl, wail

恸哭 tòngkū bawl, wail

痛苦 tòngkǔ suffering; misery; distress; discomfort; 令人痛苦 *lìngrén tòngkǔ* painful; distressing

痛快一番 tòngkuài yīfān go (out) on a spree

恸哭声 tòngkūshēng wail

通力合作 tōnglì hézuò pull together

同卵双胎 tóngluǎn shuāngtāi identical twins

同盟 tóngméng alliance, confederation

同盟者 tóngméng zhě ally

同名人 tóngmíng rén namesake

童年 tóngnián childhood

同年 tóngnián same year ◊ of the same age

铜牌 tóngpái bronze medal

通气 tōngqì ventilate, air

痛切 tòngqiè poignant

通气管 tōngqìguǎn snorkel

同情 tóngqíng pity; sympathize with; empathize with; commiserate ◊ compassion

通情达理 tōngqíng dálǐ understanding

同情心 tóngqíngxīn sympathy

同时 tóngshí at the same time, simultaneously, together; in the meantime ◊ simultaneous

同事 tóngshì colleague, associate

痛惜 tòngxī deplore

通向 tōngxiàng give onto

通宵 tōngxiāo throughout the night

通晓 tōngxiǎo familiarity

通泄药 tōngxiè yào laxative

通信 tōngxìn correspond

通行费 tōngxíng fèi toll

同性恋 tóngxìngliàn homosexual ◊ homosexuality

同性恋者 tóngxìngliàn zhě homosexual; lesbian

通行权 tōngxíng quán right of way

同形异义词 tóngxíng yìyì cí homograph

通行证 tōngxíngzhèng pass

通信联络 tōngxìn liánluò correspondence

通信员 tōngxìn yuán messenger

通信者 tōngxìn zhě correspondent

同学 tóngxué classmate; fellow student

通讯录 tōngxùn lù address book

通讯社 tōngxùn shè news agency

通讯卫星 tōngxùn wèixīng communications satellite

通讯业 tōngxùn yè communications

通讯员 tōngxùn yuán correspondent

同样 tóngyàng same

童谣 tóngyáo nursery rhyme

同意 tóngyì agree, concur; consent; grant ◊ agreement; approval; 我同意这个想法 *wǒ tóngyì zhègè xiǎngfǎ* I am for the idea

统一 **tǒngyī** unite; unify ◊ unified; uniform ◊ uniformly ◊ unity; unification

同义词 **tóngyìcí** synonym

统一收费率 **tǒngyī shōufèilǜ** flat rate

同意资助 **tóngyì zīzhù** underwrite FIN

同狱犯人 **tóngyù fànrén** inmate

通知 **tōngzhī** inform, notify; report ◊ circular; notice

同志 **tóngzhì** comrade

统治 **tǒngzhì** reign; rule

统治者 **tǒngzhì zhě** ruler

童装 **tóngzhuāng** children's clothes

偷 **tōu** take, steal

头 **tóu** head

投 **tóu** hurl, fling, throw; pitch

透 **tòu** pass through

投案 **tóu'àn** give oneself up

头版 **tóubǎn** front page

头版新闻 **tóubǎn xīnwén** front page news

投标 **tóubiāo** tender

偷捕 **tōubǔ** poach

头朝下 **tóu cháoxià** head over heels

投弹手 **tóudàn shǒu** bomber (terrorist)

头等 **tóuděng** first class

头等大事 **tóuděng dàshì** a matter of paramount importance ◊ be paramount

投递 **tóudì** deliver ◊ delivery

头顶 **tóudǐng** top of the head

头顶上 **tóudǐng shàng** overhead

头顶的 **tóudǐngde** head-on

偷东西 **tōu dōngxi** steal

头发 **tóufa** hair; 做头发 **zuò tóufà** have one's hair done

头发花白 **tóufa huābái** gray-haired

投稿 **tóugǎo** contribute ◊ contribution

投稿人 **tóugǎo rén** contributor

头昏脑胀 **tóuhūn nǎozhàng** dizzy, giddy

投机活动 **tóujī huódòng** venture

投机买卖 **tóujī mǎimài** speculation

头巾 **tóujīn** (head)scarf

透镜 **tòujìng** lens

投机商 **tóujī shāng** speculator FIN

偷看一眼 **tōukàn yīyǎn** sneak a glance at

头靠 **tóukào** headrest

头盔 **tóukuī** helmet

头懒 **tóulǎn** laze around; goof off

头栏 **tóulán** header

投篮 **tóulán** shoot (at the basket)

头颅 **tóulú** skull

头路 **tóulù** part (in hair)

透露 **tòulù** leak out; disclose, divulge ◊ disclosure; 未透露 **wèi tòulù** untold

头颅骨 **tóulúgǔ** skull

透露真相 **tòulù zhēnxiàng** revealing

透明 **tòumíng** see-through, transparent

头目 **tóumù** ringleader

偷拿 **tōuná** sneak, steal

头脑 **tóunǎo** mind; chief

头脑简单 **tóunǎo jiǎndān** simple(-minded)

头脑冷静 **tóunǎo lěngjìng** level-headed; 头脑敏锐的人 **tóunǎo mǐnruì de rén** clear thinker

头盘 **tóupán** starter (of meal)

头皮 **tóupí** scalp

投票 **tóupiào** vote ◊ voting; ballot

投票间 **tóupiào jiān** voting booth

投票决定 **tóupiào juédìng** ballot; vote on

投票箱 **tóupiào xiāng** ballot box

投票站 **tóupiàozhàn** polling booth

头屑 **tóupíxiè** dandruff

投弃 **tóuqì** jettison

偷窃 **tōuqiè** steal ◊ larceny, theft

投球 **tóuqiú** pitch

投入 **tóurù** put in, insert; plunge into; inject ◊ input; injection

透入 **tòurù** penetrate

头上空间 **tóushang kōngjiān** headroom

投手 **tóushǒu** pitcher

投手场地 **tóushǒu chǎngdì** mound

偷税 **tōushuì** evade taxes

透水汽 **tòu shuǐqì** porous

投诉 **tóusù** complain; make a fuss ◊ complaint

头条新闻 **tóutiáo xīnwén** headline news

偷听 **tōutīng** overhear; eavesdrop

头痛 **tóutòng** headache

偷偷 **tōutōu** furtive; 偷偷溜进房间 **tōutōu liūjìn fángjiān** sneak into the room

头衔 **tóuxián** title

投降 **tóuxiáng** yield, surrender ◊ submission

投影器 **tóuyǐng qì** projector

头晕 **tóuyūn** dizzy, giddy ◊ feel dizzy

投掷 **tóuzhì** throw

透支 **tòuzhī** advance

头重脚轻 **tóuzhòng jiǎoqīng** top-heavy

骰子 **tóuzi** dice

投资 **tóuzī** invest ◊ investment

投资者 **tóuzī zhě** investor

偷走 **tōuzǒu** snatch; make off with

突 **tū** suddenly

秃 **tū** bald

图 **tú** picture; diagram

涂 **tú** apply

屠 **tú** kill

途 **tú** path; road; way

徒 **tú** follower; disciple

土 **tǔ** earth; land

吐 **tǔ** spit

吐 **tù** vomit; 我要吐 **wǒ yào tù** I'm going to throw up

兔 **tù** rabbit; hare

图案 **tú'àn** pattern; design

团 **tuán** round ◊ gather ◊ group; society; mass; wad; expedition; regiment

团结 **tuánjié** unite ◊ united; 团结在 X 的周围 **tuánjié zài X de zhōuwéi** rally around X

团结一致 **tuánjié yīzhì** solidarity

团聚 **tuánjù** reunion ◊ reunite

湍流 **tuānliú** turbulence

团体 **tuántǐ** group

团圆 **tuányuán** reunion; get-together

团子 **tuánzi** dumpling

图板 **túbǎn** drawing board

突变 **tūbiàn** sudden change

图标 **túbiāo** icon

图表 **túbiāo** chart; graph

徒步旅行 **túbù lǚxíng** backpack

徒步旅行者 **túbù lǚxíng zhě** hiker; walker; backpacker

涂层 **túcéng** coat

突出 **tūchū** stick out, project ◊ prominent; imposing; glaring; outstanding, excellent; 突出的椎间盘 **tūchūde zhuījiānpán** slipped disc

吐出 **tǔchū** spit (out); 吐出心里的话 **tǔchū xīnlǐ de huà** get ... off one's chest

凸窗 **tūchuāng** bay window

土地 **tǔdì** land; soil

秃顶 **tūdǐng** bald; 他开始秃顶了 **tā kāishǐ tūdǐng le** he's going bald

图钉 **túdīng** thumbtack

土豆 **tǔdòu** potato

土豆泥 **tǔdòuní** mashed potatoes

土耳其 **Tǔ'ěrqí** Turkey ◊ Turkish

突发奇想 **tūfā qíxiǎng** whim

土匪 **tǔfěi** bandit

屠夫 **túfū** butcher

涂改液 **túgǎiyè** whiteout (for text)

图画 **túhuà** picture; drawing; painting

图画书 **túhuàshū** picture book

推 **tuī** push; jolt

腿 **tuǐ** leg

退 **tuì** move backward; retreat; retire

退步 **tuìbù** go backward; fall behind

推测 **tuīcè** suspect; assume; presume; guess

退场 **tuìchǎng** exit; walk out

退潮 **tuìcháo** ebb tide

推迟 **tuīchí** postpone, put off, defer; delay

推出 **tuīchū** bring out

退出 **tuìchū** withdraw, pull out, stand down, drop out; exit, quit

推辞 **tuīcí** decline

退掉 **tuìdiào** take back; 退掉 X **tuìdiào X** take X back to the store

推定 **tuīdìng** presumption

推动 **tuīdòng** push forward; promote; boost; budge

推动力 **tuīdòng lì** impetus

推断 **tuīduàn** conclude ◊ conclusion; 由 Y 推断出 X **yóu Y tuīduàn chū X** conclude X from Y

腿肚子 **tuǐdùzi** calf (*of leg*)

推翻 **tuīfān** overthrow, topple, overturn

颓废 **tuífèi** decadent

退格 **tuìgé** backspace (key)

推合门 **tuīhémén** swing-door

退化 **tuìhuà** degenerate into

退还 **tuìhuán** return, send back

推挤 **tuījǐ** jostle

推荐 **tuījiàn** recommend ◊ recommendation; reference; 推荐 X 任某个职位 **tuījiàn X rèn mǒugè zhíwèi** recommend X for a post

推荐人 **tuījiàn rén** referee

推进 **tuījìn** propel

推开 **tuīkāi** push away

退款 **tuìkuǎn** refund

推理 **tuīlǐ** deduce

推论 **tuīlùn** deduction

退落 **tuìluò** ebb

蜕皮 **tuìpí** peel; shed its skin

退去 **tuìqù** subside

退让 **tuìràng** retreat

褪色 **tuìsè** faded

退烧 **tuìshāo** subside (*of fever*)

退缩 **tuìsuō** flinch; wince

推土机 **tuītǔ jī** bulldozer

退位 **tuìwèi** abdicate

推诿责任 **tuīwěi zérèn** pass the buck

退伍 **tuìwǔ** discharge

退伍军人 **tuìwǔ jūnrén** veteran

推想 **tuīxiǎng** gather, understand

推销 **tuīxiāo** market, sell; plug ◊ marketing

推销员 **tuīxiāo yuán** salesman

推行 **tuīxíng** implement; pursue

退休 **tuìxiū** retire ◊ retired ◊ retirement

退休金 **tuìxiū jīn** pension

退休老人 **tuìxiū lǎorén** senior citizen

退休年龄 **tuìxiū niánlíng** retirement age

退休者 **tuìxiū zhě** retired person; pensioner

退学学生 **tuìxué xuéshēng** dropout

推移 **tuīyí** pass, go by ◊ passage (*of time*)

退职金 **tuìzhí jīn** gratuity (*on retirement*)

推子 **tuīzi** clippers

突击 **tūjī** rush

途经 **tújīng** by way of, via ◊ pass through

途径 **tújìng** way, path; gateway

土块 **tǔkuài** clump

凸块儿 **tūkuàir** bump

徒劳 **túláo** thankless ◊ in vain

图利 **túlì** mercenary

涂料 **túliào** paint; 上涂料 **shàng túliào** paint

吐露 **tùlù** confide

涂满 **túmǎn** be plastered with

涂抹 **túmǒ** smear

图谋 **túmóu** scheme

土木工程师 **tǔmù gōngchéngshī** civil engineer

吞 **tūn** swallow

吞并 **tūnbìng** annex

臀部 **túnbù** buttocks; rump; hip

臀部牛排 **túnbù niúpái** rumpsteak

吞饵 **tūn'ěr** bite (*of fish*)

囤积 **túnjī** hoard

吞没 **tūnmò** engulf

吞食 **tūnshí** devour

豚鼠 **túnshǔ** guinea pig

吞吞吐吐 **tūntun tǔtǔ** cagey

吞下 **tūnxià** down; keep down food

吞咽 **tūnyàn** gulp

脱 **tuō** remove, get off; take down

拖 **tuō** drag; pull

托 **tuō** entrust

妥 **tuǒ** appropriate

拖把 **tuōbǎ** mop

驼背 **tuóbèi** hunchback; hump

拖布 **tuōbù** mop

拖长 **tuōcháng** drag out, spin out

拖车 **tuōchē** trailer; wrecker

拖船 **tuōchuán** tug

拖地 **tuōdì** mop

脱掉 **tuōdiào** slip off

拖动 **tuōdòng** drag

托儿所 **tuō'érsuǒ** day-nursery, crèche

驼峰 **tuófēng** hump

脱光衣服 **tuōguāng yīfu** strip

脱轨 **tuōguǐ** be derailed

托架 **tuōjià** bracket (*for shelf*)

脱缰 **tuōjiāng** bolt

脱节 **tuōjié** disjointed

脱臼 **tuōjiù** dislocation

拖拉 **tuōlā** trail

拖拉机 **tuōlājī** tractor

拖缆 **tuōlǎn** towrope

脱离 **tuōlí** break away ◊ out of

脱粒 **tuōlì** thresh

脱离关系 **tuōlí guānxì** disown

脱离危险 **tuōlí wēixiǎn** out of danger

驼鹿 **tuólù** moose, elk

脱落 **tuōluò** come off; fall out; peel; shed

陀螺 **tuóluó** (spinning) top

唾沫 **tuòmo** spittle

鸵鸟 **tuóniǎo** ostrich

拖盘 **tuōpán** tray

拖欠 **tuōqiàn** be in arrears

拖欠款 **tuōqiàn kuǎn** arrears

脱去衣服 **tuōqù yīfu** strip

脱色 **tuōsè** lose its color, fade; 使脱色 **shǐ tuōsè** bleach

脱水 **tuōshuǐ** dehydrated

拖网鱼船 **tuōwǎng yúchuán** trawler

托位 **tuōwèi** dislocate

拖鞋 **tuōxié** slippers; flip-flops; mules

妥协 **tuǒxié** compromise

拖延 **tuōyán** stall

脱氧核糖核酸 **tuōyǎng hétáng hésuān** DNA, deoxyribonucleic acid

托曳 **tuōyè** haul; pull

唾液 **tuòyè** saliva

脱衣服 **tuō yīfu** undress, get undressed

脱颖而出 **tuō yǐng ér chū** come to the fore

椭圆 **tuǒyuán** oval; ellipse

托运 **tuōyùn** ship, send

托运公司 **tuōyùn gōngsī** freight company, freight forwarder

脱脂棉 **tuōzhīmián** absorbent cotton

脱脂乳 **tuōzhīrǔ** skimmed milk

拖走 **tuōzǒu** tow away

涂片 **túpiàn** smear

突破 **tūpò** breakthrough; penetration

土丘 **tǔqiū** mound

突然 **tūrán** suddenly ◊ abrupt, sudden; 突然跌落 **tūrán diēluò** plunge; 突然袭击 **tūrán xíjī** raid; pounce

土壤 **tǔrǎng** soil

土人 **tǔrén** native

屠杀 **túshā** massacre; slaughter

徒手格斗 **túshǒu gédòu** unarmed combat

图书馆 **túshūguǎn** library

图书馆员 **túshūguǎn yuán** librarian

吐痰 **tǔtán** spit

突袭 **tūxí** raid

图形 **túxíng** figure; graphic

徒刑 **túxíng** prison sentence

图形卡 **túxíngkǎ** graphics card

图形控制器 **túxíng kòngzhì qì** graphics controller

图形学 **túxíngxué** graphics

凸印 **tūyìn** emboss

涂油漆 **tú yóuqī** paint

屠宰 **túzǎi** slaughter

屠宰场 **túzǎichǎng** slaughterhouse

突增 **tūzēng** jump

图章 **túzhāng** chop, stamp, seal

途中 **túzhōng** en route

土著 **tǔzhù** native

兔子 **tùzi** rabbit; hare

T字形拐杖 **T zì xíng guǎizhàng** crutch

UW

U 形弯 **U xíngwān** U-turn

挖 **wā** dig

蛙 **wā** frog

瓦 **wǎ** roof tile

袜 **wà** socks; stockings

挖鼻孔 **wā bíkǒng** pick one's nose

挖出 **wāchū** dredge up

歪 **wāi** leaning, slanting; crooked

外 **wài** outside ◊ external; foreign;
outward ◊ externally; outwardly

外币 **wàibì** foreign currency

外边 **wàibiān** outside; offside

外表 **wàibiǎo** appearance;
exterior; façade; veneer ◊
outward

外部 **wàibù** outside, exterior ◊
outer; external

外出 **wàichū** go out

外出旅程 **wàichū lǚchéng**
outward journey

外公 **wàigōng** grandfather
(*maternal*)

外观 **wàiguān** exterior;
appearance; look

外国 **wàiguó** foreign country ◊
abroad ◊ foreign

外国人 **wàiguó rén** foreigner

外行 **wàiháng** layman; layperson

外号 **wàihào** nickname

外汇 **wàihuì** foreign currency,
foreign exchange

外交 **wàijiāo** diplomacy ◊
diplomatic

外交部 **Wàijiàobù** Department of
State, Ministry of Foreign Affairs

外交部长 **Wàijiàobù Zhǎng**
Secretary of State, Foreign
Minister

外交官 **wàijiāo guān** diplomat

外交免疫力 **wàijiāo miǎnyì lì**
diplomatic immunity

外交事物 **wàijiāo shìwù** foreign
affairs

外交政策 **wàijiāo zhèngcè**
foreign policy

外景 **wàijǐng** on location

外科 **wàikē** surgical

外壳 **wàiké** hull; husk

外科医师 **wàikē yīshī** surgeon

外来语 **wàiláiyǔ** foreign word;
loan word

外贸 **wàimào** foreign trade

外面 **wàimiàn** outside ◊ external

外婆 **wàipó** grandmother
(*maternal*)

歪曲 **wāiqū** distort, misrepresent;
对正义的歪曲 **duì zhèngyì de
wāiqū** travesty of justice

外甥 **wàisheng** nephew (*sister's
son*)

外甥女 **wàishengnǚ** niece (*sister's
daughter*)

外孙女 **wàisūnnǚ** granddaughter
(*daughter's daughter*)

外孙子 **wàisūnzi** grandson
(*daughter's son*)

外围装置 **wàiwéi zhuāngzhì**
peripheral

外星人 **wàixīng rén** alien

外衣 **wàiyī** coat

外语 **wàiyǔ** foreign language

曾外孙 **wàizēngsūn** great-
grandson (*daughter's grandson*)

外祖父 **wàizǔfù** grandfather
(*maternal*)

外祖父母 **wàizǔfùmǔ** grand
parents (*maternal*)

外祖母 **wàizǔmǔ** grandmother
(*maternal*)

瓦解 **wǎjiě** disintegrate

挖掘 **wājué** excavate ◊ excavation

挖掘机 **wājuéjī** excavator

挖空 **wākōng** excavate; dig

挖苦 **wākǔ** dry

瓦楞铁 **wǎléngtiě** corrugated iron

瓦楞纸板 **wǎléng zhǐbǎn**
corrugated cardboard

瓦砾 **wǎlì** rubble

湾 **wān** bay

弯 **wān** bend ◊ bent

完 **wán** finish ◊ finished, over; complete; 她还没完呢 **tā hái méiwán ne** she still hasn't finished; 完了 **wánle** be through, be finished; 完了! **wánle!** that's it!; there you are!

玩 **wán** play

碗 **wǎn** bowl

晚 **wǎn** late ◊ evening; night; 天晚了 **tiānwǎn le** it's getting late

万 **wàn** ten thousand

晚安 **wǎn'ān** good night

晚报 **wǎnbào** evening paper

完毕 **wánbì** finished

晚餐 **wǎncān** dinner

完成 **wánchéng** complete; accomplish ◊ completion

完成式 **wánchéngshì** perfect tense

碗橱 **wǎnchú** cupboard

晚点 **wǎndiǎn** delayed

碗碟柜 **wǎndié guì** dresser

豌豆 **wāndòu** pea

晚饭 **wǎnfàn** supper

王 **wáng** king

网 **wǎng** net; network; web; grid; Internet; 一网鱼 **yìwǎngyú** a haul of fish

往 **wǎng** to; toward ◊ past

忘 **wàng** forget

望 **wàng** look ahead; expect

旺 **wàng** prosperous

网吧 **wǎngbā** Internet café

挽歌 **wǎngē** lament

忘恩负义 **wàng'ēn fùyì** ingratitude

往返 **wǎngfǎn** there and back

王国 **wángguó** kingdom

王后 **wánghòu** queen (*monarch's wife*)

旺火煸炒 **wànghuǒ biānchǎo** stir-fry

忘记 **wàngjì** forget

旺季 **wàngjì** high season

往来 **wǎnglái** contact; dealings; relations

网络 **wǎngluò** network; Internet

网络服务 **wǎngluò fúwù** on-line service

完工 **wángōng** complete

王牌 **wángpái** trump card

网球 **wǎngqiú** tennis; tennis ball

网球场 **wǎngqiú chǎng** tennis court

网球拍 **wǎngqiú pāi** tennis racket

网球手 **wǎngqiú shǒu** tennis player

网球网 **wǎngqiú wǎng** net (*in tennis*)

忘却 **wàngquè** forget; get over *lover etc*

网上 **wǎngshang** on-line COMPUT

往事 **wǎngshì** the past

顽固 **wángù** obstinate, stubborn; set ◊ obstinacy

汪汪叫 **wāngwang jiào** yap; bark

王位 **wángwèi** throne

往下 **wǎngxià** downward

妄想 **wàngxiǎng** delusion

妄想狂 **wàngxiǎng kuáng** paranoia

网眼 **wǎngyǎn** mesh

望远镜 **wàngyuǎn jìng** telescope; binoculars

网址 **wǎngzhǐ** web site; web page

王子 **wángzǐ** prince

妄自尊大的人 **wàngzì zūndà de rén** squirt

完好无损 **wánhǎo wúsǔn** sound, in good repair

晚会 **wǎnhuì** party; (evening) function

玩忽职守 **wánhū zhíshǒu** misconduct; negligence; malpractice

完结 **wánjié** be over

万金油 **wànjīnyóu** balm

挽救 **wǎnjiù** retrieve

玩具 **wánjù** toy

万里长城 **Wànlǐ Chángchéng** Great Wall of China

晚礼服 **wǎnlǐfú** evening dress

完美 **wánměi** perfect, flawless; beautiful ◊ perfection

完美主义者 **wánměi zhǔyì zhě** perfectionist

万能钥匙 **wànnéng yàoshi** master key, skeleton key

顽皮 **wánpí** mischievous

晚期 **wǎnqī** terminal ◊ terminally

顽强 **wánqiáng** stubborn; tenacious

弯曲 **wānqū** bend ◊ crooked ◊ curve; 使弯曲 **shǐ wānqū** warp

完全 **wánquán** complete; total ◊ completely, fully; 完全一样 **wánquán yīyàng** exactly the same

玩儿 **wánr** play; party; 玩儿开心点儿 **wánr kāixīn diǎnr** have a good time

完善 **wánshàn** perfect

晚上 **wǎnshang** evening; 晚上十一点 **wǎnshàng shíyī diǎn** 11 o'clock at night; 晚上好！**wǎnshang hǎo!** good evening!

弯身 **wānshēn** bend; double up

玩世不恭 **wán shì bù gōng** cynically

玩耍 **wánshuǎ** enjoy oneself

玩童 **wántóng** urchin

弯弯曲曲 **wānwan qūqu** twisty

万无一失 **wàn wú yì shī** unerring

惋惜 **wǎnxī** pity; 令人惋惜 **lìngrén wǎnxī** lamentable

玩笑 **wánxiào** joke

万幸 **wànxìng** fortunate

蜿蜒 **wānyán** wind ◊ winding; 蜿蜒前进 **wānyán xíngjìn** wriggle

晚宴服 **wǎnyànfu** evening wear

弯腰 **wānyāo** bend down, stoop

弯腰曲背 **wānyāo qūbèi** stoop

万一… **wànyī …** in case …

玩意儿 **wányìr** trinket

玩杂耍 **wán záshuǎ** juggle

玩杂耍的人 **wán záshuǎ de rén** juggler

完整 **wánzhěng** complete; thorough ◊ completely

婉转地叫 **wǎnzhuǎn de jiào** warble

晚走 **wǎnzǒu** stay behind

蛙人 **wārén** frogman

瓦特 **wǎtè** watt

娃娃 **wáwa** doll

挖心 **wāxīn** core

蛙泳 **wāyǒng** breaststroke

袜子 **wàzi** socks; stockings

煨 **wēi** poach

微 **wēi** small; micro-

危 **wēi** danger

违 **wéi** break; transgress; violate

围 **wéi** encircle; surround; besiege; 用栅栏围起 **yòng zhàlán wéiqǐ** fence in

唯 **wéi** only

为 **wéi** be ◊ as ◊ achievement

伪 **wéi** false

伟 **wěi** great

尾 **wěi** tail; end

喂 **wèi** hello TELEC; hey! ◊ feed *animals etc*

位 **wèi** position

为 **wèi** for; 为 … 干杯 **wèi … gānbēi** toast, propose a toast to; 为 … 辩护 **wèi … biànhù** stick up for

未 **wèi** not yet; not; 未成文 **wèi chéngwén** unwritten

味 **wèi** taste

畏 **wèi** fear

胃 **wèi** stomach

卫 **wèi** guard

尾巴 **wěiba** tail

违背 **wéibèi** violate; disobey; go against ◊ violation

卫兵 **wèibīng** guard

微波 **wēibō** microwave

微薄 **wēibó** sparse; scanty ◊ scantily; sparsely; 微薄的工资 **wēibóde gōngzī** pittance

微波炉 **wēibōlú** microwave (oven)

微不足道 **wēi bù zú dào** paltry; derisory

未曾 **wèicéng** never

围场 **wéichǎng** pound (*for strays*)

未成年 **wèi chéngnián** juvenile; underage

未成年人 **wèichéngnián rén** minor, juvenile

维持 **wéichí** maintain; get by; hold out

维持生活 **wéichí shēnghuó** manage

微处理机 **wēichǔlǐjī** microprocessor

未出生 **wèi chūshēng** unborn

为此 **wèicǐ** for this reason

伟大 **wěidà** great ◊ greatness

味道 **wèidao** taste, flavor

尾灯 **wěidēng** tail light

微电子学 **wēidiànzǐ xué**

microelectronics

纬度 wěidù latitude

纬度线 wěidùxiàn parallel

巍峨 wēi'é lofty

违法 wéifǎ illicit, illegal ◊ illegally

违法者 wéifǎ zhě criminal; lawbreaker

违犯 wéifàn break, contravene

违犯 wéifàn violate, breach ◊ violation

违反合同 wéifǎn hétóng breach of contract

违反交通法规 wéifǎn jiāotōng fǎguī traffic violation

微风 wēifēng breeze

未付 wèifù nonpayment ◊ outstanding

威佛饼干 wēifú bǐnggān wafer

桅杆 wéigān mast

微光 wēiguāng gleam, glimmer

微观世界 wēiguān shìjiè microcosm

危害 wēihài damage

威吓 wēihè intimidate

维护 wéihù defend, stand up for; uphold; preserve ◊ maintenance

未婚 wèihūn unmarried

未婚夫 wèihūnfū fiancé

未婚妻 wèihūnqī fiancée

维护 wéihù protect, look after

危机 wēijī crisis

危急 wēijí critical; desperate ◊ critically

危及 wēijí endanger

未解决 wèi jiějué unsettled

围巾 wéijīn scarf

味精 wèijīng monosodium glutamate

未经加工 wèijīng jiāgōng raw, unprocessed

微晶片 wēijīngpiàn microchip

伪君子 wěijūnzǐ hypocrite

违抗 wéikàng defy ◊ in defiance of

胃口 wèikǒu appetite

围困 wéikùn besiege ◊ siege

未来 wèilái future

未来式 wèiláishì future tense ◊ futuristic

慰劳金 wèiláojīn golden handshake

为了 wèile for; in order to; because of; 为了我 wèile wǒ for my sake

微量 wēiliàng trace

帷幕 wéimù curtain

喂奶 wèinǎi breast-feed

为难 wéinán uncomfortable; distressed; 使为难 shǐ wéinán disconcert

味浓 wèinóng strong

委派 wěipài posting

围棋 wéiqí Go

委屈 wěiqu injustice

围裙 wéiqún apron

围绕 wéirǎo surround; revolve around ◊ around

委任 wěirèn appoint

微弱 wēiruò feeble

伪善 wěishàn hypocrisy

未删节 wèi shānjié full-length

伪善言词 wěishàn yáncí cant

危慑 wēishè deter

卫生 wèishēng hygienic, sanitary ◊ hygiene

卫生带 wèishēngdài sanitary napkin

卫生间 wèishēngjiān rest room

卫生间用品 wèishēngjiān yòngpǐn toiletries

卫生巾 wèishēngjīn sanitary napkin

卫生设备 wèishēng shèbèi sanitation

维生素 wéishēngsù vitamin

卫生纸 wèishēngzhǐ toilet paper

为什么 wèishénme? why?; what for?; 为什么不？ wèishénme bù? why not?

危慑因素 wēishè yīnsù deterrent

威士忌 wēishìjì whiskey

卫戍部队 wèishù bùduì garrison

畏缩 wèisuō recoil; shrink from; shy away

维他命 wéitāmìng vitamin

维他命药片 wéitāmìng yàopiàn vitamin pill

胃痛 wèitòng stomach ache

委托 wěituō commission; 把 Y 委托给 X bǎ Y wěituōgěi X entrust Y to X

未完待续 **wèiwán dàixù** to be continued

威望 **wēiwàng** prestige

委婉说法 **wěiwǎn shuōfǎ** euphemism

微温 **wēiwēn** lukewarm, tepid

唯物论 **wéiwùlùn** materialistic

唯物主义 **wéiwù zhǔyì** materialism

唯物主义者 **wéiwù zhǔyì zhě** materialist

危险 **wēixiǎn** danger, hazard, peril ◊ dangerous, unsafe; 处于危险境地 **chǔyú wēixiǎn jìngdì** be in jeopardy

危险人物 **wēixiǎn rénwù** security risk

危险者 **wēixiǎn zhě** menace

微小 **wēixiǎo** tiny, minute, minuscule

微笑 **wēixiào** smile; 对 ... 微笑 **duì ... wēixiào** smile at

威胁 **wēixié** threat; menace; intimidation ◊ threaten, intimidate ◊ menacing

猥亵 **wěixiè** obscene, filthy

微型 **wēixíng** pocket

卫星 **wèixīng** satellite

微型电视 **wēixíng diànshì** portable TV

卫星电视 **wèixīng diànshì** satellite TV

卫星电视盘 **wèixīng diànshì pán** satellite dish

唯心论 **wéixīn lùn** spiritualism

维修 **wéixiū** maintain; service; repair

威严 **wēiyán** majestic

喂养 **wèiyǎng** feed

偎依 **wēiyī** nestle, snuggle; cling

唯一 **wéiyī** sole, only, single ◊ solely

位于 **wèiyú** be situated; lie

委员会 **wěiyuánhuì** commission; committee

未预见到 **wèi yùjiàn dào** unforeseen

伪造 **wěizào** counterfeit, forge; falsify

伪造品 **wěizào pǐn** forgery

伪造人 **wěizào rén** forger

违章停车罚款单 **wéizhāng tíngchē fákuǎndān** parking ticket

位置 **wèizhi** location, position; locality, situation

未知 **wèizhī** unknown

未支付 **wèi zhīfù** unsettled

围住 **wéizhù** enclose

伪装 **wěizhuāng** disguise; camouflage ◊ dress up ◊ phoney; 伪装为 X **wěizhuāng wéi X** masquerade as X

位子 **wèizi** seat, place

围嘴 **wéizuǐ** bib

温 **wēn** warm

闻 **wén** smell, sniff

文 **wén** writing; language; literature; culture

蚊 **wén** mosquito

吻 **wěn** kiss

稳 **wěn** stable; steady

问 **wèn** ask; question, query

闻出 **wénchū** smell

问答比赛 **wèndá bǐsài** quiz

问答卷 **wèndá juàn** questionnaire

稳定 **wěndìng** stable ◊ stability ◊ stabilize

温度 **wēndù** temperature

温度表 **wēndùbiǎo** thermometer

温度计 **wēndùjì** thermometer

稳而有力 **wěn ér yǒulì** firm

翁 **wēng** old man

嗡鸣声 **wēngmíng shēng** drone, droning noise

稳固 **wěngù** rigid

嗡嗡作响 **wēngwēng zuòxiǎng** hum; buzz

问好 **wènhǎo** ask after; send greetings; 向她问好 **xiàng tā wènhǎo** give her my love; send her my best wishes

问号 **wènhào** question mark

温和 **wēnhé** mild; moderate; mellow ◊ mildness

温和派 **wēnhépài** moderate POL

问候 **wènhòu** send one's regards; say hello; ask after; 代我向 X 问候 **dài wǒ xiàng X wènhòu** give my regards to X

文化 **wénhuà** culture ◊ cultural

文化冲击 wénhuà chōngjī culture shock

文化大革命 Wénhuà Dàgémìng Cultural Revolution

文件 wénjiàn document; papers; documentation; file

文件管理程序 wénjiàn guǎnlǐ chéngxù file manager

文件夹 wénjiàn jiá folder

文具 wénjù stationery

文具商店 wénjù shāngdiàn stationery store

文科硕士 wénkē shuòshì Master of Arts

文科学位 wénkē xuéwèi arts degree

文盲 wénmáng illiterate

文明 wénmíng civilization; culture

闻名 wénmíng famous

温暖 wēnnuǎn warm

文凭 wénpíng qualification; diploma; certificate

文乞 wénqǐ hack

文人 wénrén egghead

温柔 wēnróu gentle, soft; tender

纹身 wénshēn tattoo

温室 wēnshì greenhouse, hothouse

温室气体 wēnshì qìtǐ greenhouse gas

温室效应 wēnshì xiàoyìng greenhouse effect

文书工作 wénshū gōngzuò paperwork

温顺 wēnshùn meek

问题 wèntí problem; question; matter; 是钱的问题 shì qián de wèntí it's a question of money

温习 wēnxí brush up; revise

蚊香 wénxiāng mosquito coil

问心有愧 wèn xīn yǒu kuì have a guilty conscience

文学 wénxué literature ◊ literary

问讯 wènxùn ask; inquire

问讯处 wènxùn chù information office

问讯台 wènxùn tái information desk

文雅 wényǎ refined; cultivated; elegant

瘟疫 wēnyì epidemic, plague

文艺 wényì art and literature

文章 wénzhāng article

蚊帐 wénzhàng mosquito net

稳重 wěnzhòng sedate; sober

稳住 wěnzhù steady

蚊子 wénzi mosquito

文字 wénzì writing; text

文字处理 wénzì chǔlǐ word processing

文字处理机 wénzì chǔlǐjī word processor

窝 wō nest; socket ◊ measure word for broods, hives of bees etc; 一窝蜜蜂 yìwō mìfēng a hive of bees

我 wǒ I; me ◊ my; 我是 … wǒ shì … TELEC it's … here

卧 wò lie down

握 wò hold; grasp

卧病在床 wò bìng zài chuáng be confined to one's bed

卧车 wòchē sleeping car

卧床不起 wò chuáng bù qǐ bedridden

卧倒 wòdǎo lie flat; drop to the ground

我的 wǒde my; mine

我的天啊！wǒde tiān'a! (oh) dear!, dear me!

握紧 wòjǐn clench

涡轮机 wōlúnjī turbine

我们 wǒmen we; us ◊ our; 我们别吵了 wǒmen bié chǎole let's not argue; 我们走吧 wǒmen zǒu ba let's go

我们的 wǒmende our ◊ ours

我们自己 wǒmen zìjǐ ourselves

蜗牛 wōniú snail

窝棚 wōpeng shed; hovel

卧铺 wòpù place to sleep, bunk (on train)

卧室 wòshì bedroom

握手 wòshǒu handshake ◊ shake hands

我自己 wǒ zìjǐ myself

污 wū dirt

乌 wū black ◊ crow

屋 wū house

无 wú nothing ◊ not; no

五 wǔ five

武 wǔ military

午 wǔ midday

舞 wǔ dance

雾 wù fog; mist

误 wù mistake

勿 wù do not

物 wù thing

五百 wǔbǎi five hundred

舞伴 wǔbàn (dance) partner

无比 wúbǐ incomparable

务必 wùbì must; 务必保证做完 X wùbì bǎozhèng zuòwán X see to it that X gets done

五彩 wǔcǎi colorful; 五彩缤纷 wǔcǎi bīnfēn a blaze of color

午餐 wǔcān lunch

午餐时间 wǔcān shíjiān lunchtime

无常 wúcháng erratic

无偿 wúcháng unpaid

舞场 wǔchǎng dance floor; dance hall

无偿债能力 wú chángzhài nénglì insolvent

无产阶级 wúchán jiējí proletariat

无耻 wúchǐ outrageous; shameless

无处 wúchù nowhere

无带 wúdài strapless

舞蹈 wǔdǎo dancing

误导 wùdǎo misguided

舞蹈编导 wǔdǎo biāndǎo choreographer

舞蹈家 wǔdǎo jiā dancer

舞蹈演员 wǔdǎo yǎnyuán dancer

无敌 wúdí invincible

污点 wūdiǎn mark; blot; flaw

屋顶 wūdǐng roof

无动于衷 wú dòng yúzhōng indifferent; untouched; aloof; unconcerned

无端 wúduān unfounded; unprovoked

无法 wúfǎ unable to

无法超越 wúfǎ chāoyuè insurmountable

无法和解 wúfǎ héjiě irreconcilable

无法解释 wúfǎ jiěshì unaccountable

无法抗拒 wúfǎ kàngjù

irresistible

无法理解 wúfǎ lǐjiě be out of one's depth

无法弥补 wúfǎ míbǔ irreparable

午饭 wǔfàn lunch

无法区别 wúfǎ qūbié indistinguishable

无法挽回 wúfǎ wǎnhuí irrecoverable

无法慰藉 wúfǎ wèijiè inconsolable

无法想象 wúfǎ xiǎngxiàng inconceivable

无法形容 wúfǎ xíngróng indescribable

无风险 wúfēngxiǎn safe

无根据 wúgēnjù groundless, baseless, unfounded

污垢 wūgòu dirt

无辜 wúgū innocent ◊ innocently

无关紧要 wúguān jǐnyào immaterial

乌龟 wūguī tortoise; turtle

无轨电车 wúguǐ diànchē streetcar

无故障 wú gùzhàng trouble-free

无害 wúhài harmless

无核 wúhé nuclear-free

无花果 wúhuāguǒ fig

雾化器 wùhuà qì atomizer

污秽 wūhuì grubby

污秽 wūhuì squalor

舞会 wǔhuì dance; ball; prom

误会 wùhuì misunderstand; misconstrue ◊ misunderstanding

屋脊 wūjǐ ridge (of roof)

污迹 wūjī smudge, smear; 产生污迹 chǎnshēng wūjī stain

无机 wújī inorganic

无家 wújiā homeless

无价 wújià invaluable; priceless

无家的人 wújiāde rén the homeless

无家具设备 wú jiājù shèbèi unfurnished

物件 wùjiàn article, item

误将 X 认作 Y wùjiāng X rènzuò Y mistake X for Y

五角大楼 Wǔjiǎo Dàlóu the Pentagon

物价上涨 wùjià shàngzhǎng

inflationary

无价值 **wú jiàzhí** insignificant; worthless

误解 **wùjiě** misunderstand; misread ◊ misunderstanding, misconception; 使人误解 **shǐrén wùjiě** misleading

无戒心 **wú jièxīn** unsuspecting

无节制 **wú jiézhì** immoderate

无计划性 **wú jìhuà xìng** arbitrary

无精打采 **wújīng dǎcǎi** listless

五金商店 **wǔjīn shāngdiàn** hardware store

无脊椎动物 **wú jízhuī dòngwù** invertebrate

无拘束 **wú jūshù** unrestrained

无咖啡因 **wú kāfēiyīn** decaffeinated

无可奉告 **wúkě fènggào** no comment

无可奈何 **wúkě nàihé** helpless ◊ helplessly ◊ resignation ◊ it can't be helped

无可争辩 **wúkě zhēngbiàn** undisputed ◊ unquestionably

无可指责 **wúkě zhǐzé** beyond reproach, irreproachable

无可指摘 **wúkě zhǐzhāi** irreproachable

无愧 **wúkuì** worthy

无赖 **wúlài** scoundrel; scrounger

无礼 **wúlǐ** rudeness, impertinence ◊ impertinent; saucy

无力 **wúlì** feeble

武力 **wǔlì** force

物理 **wùlǐ** physics

无聊 **wúliáo** boredom; monotony ◊ boring; uninteresting

无力量 **wúlìliàng** powerless

无领长袖衫 **wúlǐng chángxiùshān** sweatshirt

无理性 **wúlǐxìng** irrational

物理学家 **wùlǐ xuéjiā** physicist

无理由 **wú lǐyóu** uncalled-for

乌龙茶 **wūlóngchá** oolong tea

无论哪个 **wúlùn nǎgè** whichever

无论哪里 **wúlùn nǎlǐ** wherever

无论如何 **wúlùn rúhé** still, in any case; no matter what

无论什么时候 **wúlùn shénme shíhòu** whenever

无论是谁 **wúlùn shì shéi** whoever

无毛 **wúmáo** hairless

雾蒙蒙 **wùméngméng** hazy

污蔑 **wūmiè** smear; slander; libel

诬蔑 **wūmiè** smear; slander; libel

无名 **wúmíng** obscure; nameless

无名指 **wúmíngzhǐ** ring finger

无内胎 **wú nèitāi** tubeless

无能 **wúnéng** incompetent; incapable; unable ◊ inability

无能为力 … **wú néng wéilì** … be powerless to …

五年计划 **Wǔnián Jìhuà** Five Year Plan

误判 **wùpàn** miscarriage of justice

无偏见 **wú piānjiàn** detached

物品 **wùpǐn** object; item

武器 **wǔqì** arms, armaments; weapon

雾气 **wùqì** mist, haze

无铅 **wúqiān** unleaded

无情 **wúqíng** ruthless; callous ◊ ruthlessly; callously ◊ ruthlessness; 无情的力量 **wúqíngde lìliàng** brute force

无亲戚关系 **wú qīnqī guānxi** unrelated

无穷 **wúqióng** infinity

舞曲 **wǔqǔ** dance music

无权 **wúquán** unauthorized

污染 **wūrǎn** contaminate; pollute; infect ◊ contamination; pollution ◊ tainted

污染物质 **wūrǎn wùzhì** pollutant

无人操纵 **wúrén cāozòng** unmanned

无人承担 **wúrén chéngdān** unoccupied *post*

无人住 **wúrén zhù** unoccupied *building*

侮辱 **wǔrǔ** insult, slight

物色 **wùsè** hunt

物色人才的人 **wùsè réncái de rén** headhunter

无声 **wúshēng** silent; mute ◊ silently

无生命 **wú shēngmìng** inanimate; lifeless

无生气 **wú shēngqì** be in the doldrums

无生殖能力 **wú shēngzhí nénglì** infertility

无神论者 **wú shén lùn zhě** atheist

五十 **wǔshí** fifty

武士 **wǔshì** warrior

务实 **wùshí** pragmatic

无数 **wúshù** countless, innumerable

武术 **wǔshù** martial arts

污水 **wūshuǐ** sewage

午睡 **wǔshuì** afternoon nap

污水管 **wūshuǐ guǎn** sewer

无私 **wúsī** selfless, unselfish

五四运动 **Wǔsì yùndòng** May 4th movement

误算 **wùsuàn** miscalculate ◊ miscalculation

无所谓 **wúsuǒwèi** indifferent ◊ all the same

勿踏草坪 **wùtà cǎopíng** keep off the grass

舞台 **wǔtái** stage, platform

舞台布景 **wǔtái bùjǐng** scenery THEA

无特殊技能 **wú tèshū jìnéng** unskilled

物体 **wùtǐ** object

无条件 **wú tiáojiàn** unconditional

舞厅 **wǔtīng** ballroom; dancehall

无痛 **wútòng** painless

无头脑 **wútóunǎo** mindless

乌托邦 **wūtuōbāng** utopia

勿忘我 **wùwàngwǒ** forget-me-not

无畏 **wúwèi** fearless, intrepid

无味 **wúwèi** tasteless, insipid; dull

无危险 **wúwēixiǎn** safe

污物 **wūwù** sewage

污物处理场 **wūwù chǔlǐ chǎng** sewage plant

无武器 **wú wǔqì** unarmed

无限 **wúxiàn** infinite, unlimited, boundless; untold

无线 **wúxiàn** cordless, wireless

无线电 **wúxiàn diàn** radio, wireless

无线电话 **wúxiàn diànhuà** cordless phone; radio telephone

无线电视 **wúxiàn diànshì** terrestrial TV

无限制 **wúxiànzhì** unlimited, limitless; indefinite ◊ indefinitely

无效 **wúxiào** invalid, null and void; futile; 使无效 **shǐ wúxiào** neutralize; annul

无效率 **wúxiàolǜ** inefficient

无懈可击 **wúxiè kějī** impeccable

无心 **wúxīn** unintentionally

五星红旗 **wǔxīng hóngqí** Chinese national flag

五星级饭店 **wǔxīngjí fàndiàn** five-star hotel

污朽 **wūxiǔ** stale

无袖 **wúxiù** sleeveless

午休 **wǔxiū** lunch break, lunch hour

乌鸦 **wūyā** crow; raven

呜咽 **wūyān** sob

屋檐 **wūyán** eaves

呜咽 **wūyè** whimper

午夜 **wǔyè** midnight

呜咽声 **wūyèshēng** whimper

午夜时 **wǔyèshí** at midnight

无疑 **wúyí** no doubt, undoubtedly, doubtless; easily

无意 **wúyìde** unintentional ◊ unintentionally

五一节 **Wǔyī Jié** May Day

无意识 **wúyìshí** unconscious ◊ unconsciously

无异议 **wú yìyì** unquestioning

无意义 **wú yìyì** senseless, pointless; meaningless

无用 **wúyòng** useless

无忧虑 **wú yōulǜ** secure *feeling*

无忧无虑 **wúyōu wúlù** carefree, happy-go-lucky

远视见 **wú yuǎnjiàn** short-sighted

无缘无故 **wúyuán wúgù** for no reason

五月 **wǔyuè** May

无与伦比 **wú yǔ lúnbǐ** unique

乌云 **wūyún** dark clouds

无增长 **wú zēngzhǎng** zero growth

无债务 **wú zhàiwù** solvent

无障碍 **wú zhàng'ài** open

无政府状态 **wú zhèngfǔ zhuàngtài** anarchy

无知 **wúzhī** ignorance ◊ ignorant

物质 **wùzhì** matter, substance,

material

无止境 **wú zhǐjìng** endless, unending, infinite ◊ endlessly, infinitely

无中止 **wú zhōngzhǐ** without a break

无主 **wúzhǔ** unattended

无助 **wúzhù** helpless

武装 **wǔzhuāng** arms, weapons ◊ arm ◊ armed

武装力量 **wǔzhuāng lìliàng** armed forces

物主代词 **wùzhǔ dàicí** possessive pronoun

无资格 **wú zīgé** ineligible

无子女 **wú zǐnǚ** childless

无罪 **wúzuì** innocent ◊ innocence

无足轻重 **wúzú qīngzhòng** insignificant, of little importance

无组织 **wú zǔzhī** disorganized

X

X光照片 **X guāng zhàopiān** X-ray

膝 **xī** knee

吸 **xī** inhale; smoke; suck

稀 **xī** rare; sparse; thin

锡 **xī** tin

西 **xī** west ◊ western

溪 **xī** stream

熄 **xī** extinguish

席 **xí** mat; seat; place; feast

袭 **xí** attack

习 **xí** learn; study; practise

洗 **xǐ** wash, clean; shuffle *cards*; develop *photographs*

喜 **xǐ** pleasure, joy

系 **xì** system; department; faculty ◊ tie

细 **xì** fine; thin

戏 **xì** play

瞎 **xiā** blind

虾 **xiā** shrimp

峡 **xiá** strait

狭 **xiá** narrow

下 **xià** down, downward; below; under; next ◊ get off; come down (*of rain etc*); lay eggs; 下个星期／下个月 *xiàgè xīngqī / xiàgè yuè* next week / next month

吓 **xià** scare; 吓了 **X** 一跳 *xià le X yítiào* give X a scare

夏 **xià** summer

下巴 **xiàba** chin

下班 **xiàbān** finish work; go off duty

下边 **xiàbiān** beneath

下车 **xiàchē** get off; get out

下沉 **xiàchén** sink; settle

下船 **xiàchuán** disembark

下垂 **xiàchuí** droop, sag

瑕疵 **xiácī** flaw, blemish

下次 **xiàcì** next time

吓呆 **xiàdāi** petrify

下等 **xiàděng** third-rate

下等场所 **xiàděng chǎngsuǒ**

dive (*bar etc*)

下跌 **xiàdiē** plunge

下定义 **xià dìngyì** define

下毒 **xiàdú** drug

下赌注 **xià dǔzhù** bet on; stake

下飞机 **xià fēijī** disembark (*from plane*)

下岗 **xiàgǎng** unemployed; laid off (*from state enterprise*) ◊ unemployment

下岗工人 **xiàgǎng gōngrén** the unemployed (*from state enterprise*)

峡谷 **xiágǔ** canyon; gorge; glen

吓唬 **xiàhu** browbeat

喜爱 **xǐ'ài** like; love ◊ beloved; fond ◊ favor; fondness

下机 **xiàjī** log off

下级 **xiàjí** subordinate

夏季 **xiàjì** summer

下降 **xiàjiàng** decrease; decline; descend; sink ◊ descent; drop; fall ◊ downward

下降趋势 **xiàjiàng qūshì** downturn

下决心 **xià juéxīn** decide; make up one's mind ◊ determined

下来 **xiàlái** come down, descend ◊ descent

夏令时 **xiàlìngshí** summer time; daylight saving time

下流 **xiàliú** indecent; profane; sleazy; smutty

下流坯 **xiàliúpī** swine (*person*)

下落不明 **xiàluò bùmíng** be missing

下毛毛雨 **xià máomao yǔ** drizzle

下面 **xiàmian** underneath; below

先 **xiān** first, beforehand

仙 **xiān** fairy; immortal

鲜 **xiān** fresh

弦 **xián** chord; string

咸 **xián** salty; savory

闲 **xián** idle ◊ leisure

嫌 **xián** dislike ◊ suspicion

显 **xiǎn** show; be obvious

线 **xiàn** line; thread; cord; 一线希望 **yíxiàn xīwàng** glimmer of hope

县 **xiàn** county

馅 **xiàn** filling

腺 **xiàn** gland

现 **xiàn** appear ◊ current, present

献 **xiàn** give; present

陷 **xiàn** trap; pitfall; snare

限 **xiàn** limit

瞎闹 **xiānào** mess around, waste time

现场 **xiànchǎng** on the spot ◊ scene of the crime

现场示范 **xiànchǎng shìfàn** reconstruct *crime*

现场直播 **xiànchǎng zhíbō** live broadcast

现成 **xiànchéng** ready-made; off the peg

县城 **xiànchéng** county town

舷窗 **xiánchuāng** porthole

现存 **xiàncún** existing; in existence; in stock, available

现代 **xiàndài** modern; contemporary ◊ modern times

现代化 **xiàndàihuà** modernize ◊ modernization

显得 **xiǎndé** appear, seem

限定 **xiàndìng** limit

限度 **xiàndù** limit

显而易见 **xiǎn ér yìjiàn** inevitable

宪法 **xiànfǎ** constitution ◊ constitutional

箱 **xiāng** box; crate; case

香 **xiāng** incense; perfume ◊ fragrant, aromatic, nice-smelling; tasty

相 **xiāng** each other

乡 **xiāng** countryside; hometown

详 **xiáng** details

响 **xiǎng** sound ◊ loud

想 **xiǎng** think; want; 好好想想！ **hǎohao xiǎngxiang!** think hard!; 我也是这么想的 **wǒ yě shì zhème xiǎng de** I think so too; 你想去看电影吗？ **nǐ xiǎng qù kàn diànyǐng ma?** would you like to go to the movies?; 想得开 **xiǎng de kāi** try to look on the bright side of things

享 **xiǎng** enjoy

项 **xiàng** item

相 **xiàng** appearance

向 **xiàng** to; toward; 他向我走过来 **tā xiàng wǒ zǒuguòlái** he came up to me; 向 … 眨眼 **xiàng … zhǎyǎn** wink at; 向 X 挥手 **xiàng X huīshǒu** wave to X

象 **xiàng** elephant ◊ look like, resemble

像 **xiàng** look like, resemble

乡巴佬 **xiāngbālǎo** redneck

镶板 **xiāngbǎn** panel; section

向北 **xiàngběi** north ◊ northward

象鼻 **xiàngbí** (elephant's) trunk

相比 **xiāngbǐ** compare; 与 X 相比 **yǔ X xiāngbǐ** compared with X, next to X

镶边 **xiāngbiān** edge

香槟酒 **xiāngbīn jiǔ** champagne

香草 **xiāngcǎo** vanilla

相册 **xiàngcè** photo album

香肠 **xiāngcháng** sausage

镶齿冠 **xiāng chǐguàn** crown *tooth*

相处 **xiāngchǔ** mix, socialize; 他和人相处不好 **tā hé rén xiāngchù bùhǎo** he doesn't relate to people

想出 **xiǎngchū** think up

相当 **xiāngdāng** quite, considerably ◊ parallel, match; 相当大 **xiāngdāng dà** quite big; sizeable; 相当多 **xiāngdāng duō** quite a few, a lot

相当于 **xiāngdāngyú** equivalent ◊ be equivalent to; be tantamount to ◊ as much as

想到 **xiǎngdào** think of

向导 **xiàngdǎo** guide

想得开 **xiǎngdekāi** light-hearted

向东 **xiàngdōng** eastward, east

相对 **xiāngduì** relative ◊ relatively

想法 **xiǎngfa** thought, idea

相反 **xiāngfǎn** opposite, reverse; 与 … 相反 **yǔ … xiāngfǎn** contrary to …, as opposed to …

相反方向 **xiāngfǎn fāngxiàng** opposite direction

相符 **xiāngfú** correspond, match

香港 **Xiānggǎng** Hong Kong

香港回归 **Xiānggǎng huíguī** Hong Kong handover

相关 **xiāngguān** related

向后 **xiànghòu** backward

相互 **xiānghù** mutual

相互对立 **xiānghù duìlì** contradictory

相互关联 **xiānghù guānlián** interrelated

相互依赖 **xiānghù yīlài** interdependent

相互作用 **xiānghù zuòyòng** interaction

想家 **xiǎngjiā** be homesick

香蕉 **xiāngjiāo** banana

橡胶 **xiàngjiāo** rubber

相接 **xiāngjiē** interface

相近 **xiāngjìn** close

香精 **xiāngjīng** scent, perfume

镶框 **xiāngkuàng** frame

项链 **xiàngliàn** necklace

香料 **xiāngliào** spice

相貌 **xiàngmào** features (*facial*)

项目 **xiàngmù** item; project; entry (*in diary etc*)

橡木 **xiàngmù** oak (*wood*)

向南 **xiàng nán** southward

向内 **xiàngnèi** inward

想念 **xiǎngniàn** miss

相配 **xiāngpèi** match, complement

橡皮 **xiàngpí** rubber; eraser

相片 **xiàngpiàn** photo

橡皮筋 **xiàngpíjīn** elastic band

橡皮奶头 **xiàngpí nǎitóu** pacifier

香气 **xiāngqì** smell, fragrance, aroma

想起 **xiǎngqǐ** remember; think of; 使 X 想起 Y *shǐ X xiǎngqǐ Y* remind X of Y

象棋 **xiàngqí** chess

镶嵌 **xiāngqiàn** inlay; paneling ◊ set *jewel*

向前 **xiàngqián** forward, onward

想起来 **xiǎng qǐlái** think of; come up with

详情 **xiángqíng** details

项圈 **xiàngquān** collar

向日葵 **xiàngrìkuí** sunflower

相容 **xiāngróng** compatible

香山 **Xiāngshān** Fragrant Hills

向上 **xiàngshàng** up, upward

响声 **xiǎngshēng** sound

相识 **xiāngshí** know each other

享受 **xiǎngshòu** enjoy

详述 **xiángshù** discuss; expand on

橡树 **xiàngshù** oak tree

香水 **xiāngshuǐ** perfume

乡思 **xiāngsī** homesickness

相似 **xiāngsì** alike, similar ◊ be alike ◊ similarity

相似处 **xiāngsì chù** resemblance

相似之处 **xiāngsì zhī chù** parallel ◊ similarity

相同 **xiāngtóng** equal; equivalent ◊ equally

闲逛 **xiánguàng** wander, stroll

向外 **xiàngwài** outward

向往 **xiàngwǎng** yearning

香味 **xiāngwèi** perfume, scent, aroma

响尾蛇 **xiǎngwěishé** rattlesnake

详细 **xiángxì** detailed, full ◊ in detail, fully; minutely

向西 **xiàngxī** west ◊ westward

乡下 **xiāngxià** country (*as opposed to town*)

向下 **xiàngxià** down ◊ downward; underneath

乡下佬 **xiāngxiàlǎo** pej hick

想象 **xiǎngxiàng** imagine; envisage ◊ imagination; 我能想象出来 *wǒ néng xiǎngxiàng chūlái* I can just imagine it

想象力 **xiǎngxiànglì** imagination

乡下人 **xiāngxià rén** pej hillbilly

相信 **xiāngxìn** believe; believe in; trust

象牙 **xiàngyá** ivory; tusk

香烟 **xiāngyān** cigarette

象样 **xiàngyàng** respectable

想要 **xiǎngyào** wish

香油 **xiāngyóu** sesame oil

享有 **xiǎngyǒu** enjoy; 享有特权 *xiǎngyǒu tèquán* privileged

相遇 **xiāngyù** meet

香皂 **xiāngzào** toilet soap

象征 **xiàngzhēng** symbol, emblem, token ◊ symbolize

相撞 **xiāngzhuàng** collide; knock together

箱子 **xiāngzi** box; chest; crate;

case; trunk

陷害 xiànhài frame, stitch up

显赫 xiǎnhè influential

鲜红 xiānhóng scarlet

先后顺序 xiānhòu shùnxù order, sequence; 事情发生的先后顺序 *shìqíng fāshēng de xiānhòu shùnxù* the sequence of events

鲜花 xiānhuā fresh flowers

针活 xiānhuózhēni sewing

献祭 xiànjì sacrifice

先见之明 xiānjiàn zhī míng foresight

线接头 xiàn jiētóu terminal

先进 xiānjìn advance ◊ advanced; progressive

现金 xiànjīn cash

现今 xiànjīn nowadays

现金出纳机 xiànjīn chūnà jī cash register

现金短缺 xiànjīn duǎnquē short of cash

陷阱 xiànjǐng pitfall; trap

现金折扣 xiànjīn zhékòu cash discount

现金支付 xiànjīn zhīfù cash down

先决条件 xiānjué tiáojiàn qualification

现款定金 xiànkuǎn dìngjīn cash in advance

先例 xiānlì precedent

闲聊 xiánliáo chatter; gossip

显露 xiǎnlòu be out (of secret)

显露 xiǎnlù manifest itself

线路 xiànlù circuit; line; wiring

线路板 xiànlù bǎn circuit board

线路图 xiànlù tú road map

鲜美 xiānměi delicious; succulent

鲜明 xiānmíng stark

羡慕 xiànmù envy; 令 X 羡慕 *lìng X xiànmù* be the envy of X

仙女 xiānnǚ fairy

险情指示灯 xiǎnqíng zhǐshìdēng hazard lights

先驱 xiānqū pioneer, forerunner

线圈 xiànquān coil

显然 xiǎnrán obvious ◊ apparently, evidently

闲人免进！xiánrén miǎnjìn! keep out!

仙人掌 xiānrénzhǎng cactus

陷入 xiànrù become entangled in; 陷入困境 *xiànrù kùnjìng* be in a fix; 陷入圈套 *xiànrù quāntào* be trapped

先生 xiānsheng mister; sir; teacher; husband

献身于 xiànshēn yú dedicate oneself to

显示 xiǎnshì display, show

现实 xiànshí practical; realistic ◊ reality

现世 xiànshì earthly

显示器 xiǎnshìqì indicator; monitor

现实主义 xiànshí zhǔyì realism

现实主义者 xiànshí zhǔyì zhě realist

咸水 xiánshuǐ salt water

线索 xiànsuǒ clue; thread

献题 xiàntí dedication (in book)

先天性 xiāntiān xìng congenital

线条 xiàntiáo line

纤维 xiānwéi fiber

显微镜 xiǎnwēijìng microscope

纤维素 xiānwéisù cellulose

嫌恶 xiánwù distaste

纤细 xiānxì slender

闲暇 xiánxiá leisure, spare time

显现 xiǎnxiàn unfold; show up, reveal

现象 xiànxiàng phenomenon

现行 xiànxíng going, current

献血 xiànxuè donate blood

献血者 xiànxuè zhě blood donor

险崖 xiǎnyá crag

鲜艳 xiānyàn bright; vivid; colorful ◊ brightly

先验 xiānyàn transcendental

显眼 xiǎnyǎn conspicuous ◊ stand out ◊ conspicuously

嫌疑 xiányí suspicion

嫌疑犯 xiányífàn suspect

献殷勤 xiàn yīnqín make advances

现有 xiànyǒu available; in existence

先于 xiānyú precede

陷于 xiànyú get into; 陷于困境 *xiànyú kùnjìng* get into difficulties

弦乐器 xiányuè qì stringed instrument

弦乐器演奏者 xiányuè qì yǎnzòu zhě string player; strings

现在 xiànzài now, at the moment; 现在不行 xiànzài bùxíng not now

现在看来 xiànzài kànlái in retrospect

现在时 xiànzàishí present tense

闲着 xiánzhe twiddle one's thumbs

闲置 xiánzhì idle *machinery*

限制 xiànzhì restriction ◊ restrict; qualify *remark*; 限制 X xiànzhì X draw the line at X

线轴 xiànzhóu spool

显著 xiǎnzhù outstanding; prominent; striking, marked

仙子 xiānzǐ fairy; immortal

现做的饭 xiànzuòde fàn cooked meal

削 xiāo peel, skin; cut, trim; 用刀削净 yòng dāo xiāojìng scrape

消 xiāo disappear

小 xiǎo small, little; young; 她比我小十岁 tā bǐ wǒ xiǎo shísuì she is ten years my junior; 从小 cóng xiǎo from childhood

晓 xiǎo dawn ◊ know

笑 xiào laugh

效 xiào effect

孝 xiào filial

校 xiào school

小报 xiǎobào tabloid

小便 xiǎobiàn urine; pee ◊ urinate; pee

笑柄 xiàobǐng butt, target; 变成笑柄 biànchéng xiàobǐng become a laughing stock

小病 xiǎobìng indisposed

小部分 xiǎobùfen fraction

小菜 xiǎocài side dish

小菜一碟 xiǎocài yìdié small amount

小册子 xiǎo cèzi booklet, brochure, pamphlet

消沉 xiāochén dismal

小吃 xiǎochī snack

小吃店 xiǎochīdiàn snack bar

小丑 xiǎochǒu clown

消除 xiāochú eliminate, get rid of, delete ◊ elimination, deletion

小船 xiǎochuán boat; launch; dinghy

哮喘 xiàochuǎn asthma

小袋 xiǎodài pouch

小刀 xiǎodāo pocketknife

小调 xiǎodiào minor MUS; D 小调 D xiǎodiào in D minor

消毒 xiāodú sterilize, disinfect ◊ sterile

小段儿 xiǎoduànr bit, length

消毒剂 xiāodú jì disinfectant

小儿麻痹症 xiǎo'ér mábìzhèng polio

效仿 xiàofǎng imitate; 效仿 X xiàofǎng X follow in X's footsteps

消防车 xiāofáng chē fire truck

消防队 xiāofáng duì fire department

消防队员 xiāofáng duìyuán fireman, firefighter

消防龙头 xiāofáng lóngtóu hydrant, fireplug

消费 xiāofèi consume ◊ expense; consumption

小费 xiǎofèi tip

消费品 xiāofèi pǐn consumer goods

消费者 xiāofèi zhě consumer

消费者社会 xiāofèi zhě shèhuì consumer society

小公共 xiǎo gōnggòng public minibus

小狗 xiǎogǒu puppy

小姑 xiǎogū sister-in-law (*husband's younger sister*)

效果 xiàoguǒ effect; 效果不佳 xiàoguǒ bùjiā ineffective

小孩 xiǎohái child, kid

消耗 xiāohào use; consume ◊ consumption

消耗量 xiāohào liàng consumption (*quantity used*)

小河 xiǎohé stream, creek

消化 xiāohuà digest ◊ digestion; 消化不良 xiāohuà bùliáng indigestion

笑话 xiàohua joke, crack

小黄瓜 xiǎohuángguā gherkin

消化系统 xiāohuà xìtǒng

digestive system

销货点 **xiāohuò diǎn** point of sale

小伙子 **xiǎo huǒzi** lad, youth

消极 **xiāojí** negative; destructive

小鸡 **xiǎojī** chick

削价 **xiāojià** cut-price

削减 **xiāojiǎn** cut, ax ◊ cutback

小轿车 **xiǎo jiàochē** sedan, saloon

小教堂 **xiǎo jiàotáng** chapel

小姐 **xiǎojie** Miss ◊ young woman;
王小姐 ***Wáng xiǎojiě*** Miss Wang

小径 **xiǎojìng** track, trail

宵禁令 **xiāojìn lìng** curfew

小孔 **xiǎokǒng** puncture, hole

小块儿 **xiǎokuàir** bit

效力 **xiàolì** effect

小礼服 **xiǎo lǐfú** dinner jacket

销路 **xiāolù** sales; circulation

小路 **xiǎolù** path; back road

效率 **xiàolǜ** efficiency

小旅馆 **xiǎo lǚguǎn** inn

小萝卜 **xiǎoluóbo** radish

小马 **xiǎomǎ** pony

小麦 **xiǎomài** wheat

小猫 **xiǎomāo** kitten

小米 **xiǎomǐ** millet

消灭 **xiāomiè** destroy, exterminate, eradicate; 消灭有害动物 ***xiāomiè yǒuhài dòngwù*** pest control

消磨时间 **xiāomó shíjiān** pass the time

酵母 **xiàomǔ** yeast

小牛 **xiǎoniú** calf

小牛肉 **xiǎo niúròu** veal

小跑 **xiǎopǎo** trot

小朋友 **xiǎo péngyǒu** children

削皮 **xiāopí** peel, pare

小气 **xiǎoqì** mean; mean-spirited

消遣 **xiāoqiǎn** amuse oneself ◊ pastime

削铅笔刀 **xiāo qiānbǐ dāo** pencil sharpener

小汽车 **xiǎo qìchē** automobile

小圈子 **xiǎo quānzi** in-group

小人书 **xiǎorén shū** picture book

笑容满面 **xiàoróng mǎnmiàn** beam, smile

削弱 **xiāoruò** diminish

消散 **xiāosàn** lift, clear

小山坡 **xiǎoshānpō** hill

小声 **xiǎoshēng** quiet

笑声 **xiàoshēng** laugh ◊ laughter

消失 **xiāoshī** disappear; go away; pass ◊ disappearance

小时 **xiǎoshí** hour

小事 **xiǎoshì** trivial matter

消瘦 **xiāoshòu** emaciated

销售 **xiāoshòu** sell, market ◊ sales, marketing

销售点 **xiāoshòu diǎn** (sales) outlet

销售额 **xiāoshòu'é** sales figures

销售会议 **xiāoshòu huìyì** sales meeting

小数 **xiǎoshù** decimal

书包 **xiǎoshūbāo** schoolbag, satchel

小数点 **xiǎoshù diǎn** decimal point

小睡 **xiǎoshuì** grab some sleep; snooze

孝顺 **xiàoshùn** be devoted to

小说 **xiǎoshuō** novel; fiction

小说家 **xiǎoshuō jiā** novelist

小梳妆盒 **xiǎo shūzhuāng hé** vanity case

小叔子 **xiǎoshūzi** brother-in-law (*husband's younger brother*)

小淘气 **xiǎo táoqì** bully; rascal

萧条 **xiāotiáo** depression (*economic*) ◊ depressed

小题大做 **xiǎotí dàzuò** make a fuss

小艇 **xiǎotǐng** motor launch

小提琴 **xiǎo tíqín** violin, fiddle

小提琴家 **xiǎo tíqín jiā** violinist

小桶 **xiǎotǒng** keg

小偷 **xiǎotōu** thief; burglar

小偷小摸 **xiǎotōu xiǎomō** pilfering

小团 **xiǎotuán** pellet

消退 **xiāotuì** fade

小屋 **xiǎowū** hut

消息 **xiāoxi** news

小息 **xiāoxī** coffee break

小虾 **xiǎoxiā** shrimp

小巷 **xiǎoxiàng** lane; side street

肖像 **xiàoxiàng** portrait

消息灵通 **xiāoxī língtōng** be in the know

小心 xiǎoxīn be careful ◊ carefully; 要 很 小 心 **yào hěn xiǎoxīn** it requires great care

笑星 xiàoxīng joker

小型公共汽车 xiǎoxíng gōnggòng qìchē minibus

小型客车 xiǎoxíng kèchē compact MOT

小型摩托车 xiǎoxíng mótuōchē motorscooter

小心谨慎 xiǎoxīn jǐnshèn guarded ◊ gingerly

小心轻放 xiǎoxīn qīngfàng (handle) with care

小学 xiǎoxué elementary school

小学老师 xiǎoxué lǎoshī elementary teacher

小学生 xiǎoxuéshēng schoolchild

小阳春 xiǎoyángchūn Indian summer

逍遥法外 xiāoyáo fǎwài get off scot-free ◊ at large

消音器 xiāoyīn qì silencer

校友 xiàoyǒu schoolmate

校园 xiàoyuán campus

校长 xiàozhǎng principal, head teacher

小折刀 xiǎo zhédāo pocketknife

小装置 xiǎozhuāngzhí gadget

小字 xiǎozì small print

小卒 xiǎozú pawn

小组 xiǎozǔ panel

小组委员会 xiǎozǔ wěiyuánhuì subcommittee

吓跑 xiàpǎo scare away

下坡 xiàpō downhill

下坡滑雪 xiàpō huáxuě downhill skiing

下去 xiàqù go down; continue; 谈 下去 **tán xiàqù** talk on, continue talking

吓人 xiàrén frightening; 吓人一 跳 **xiàrényìtiào** jump, give a jump

下士 xiàshì corporal MIL

下属 xiàshǔ subordinate

下述 xiàshù following

下水 xiàshuǐ launch ◊ downstream

下水道 xiàshuǐ dào drains, drainage

下水系统 xiàshuǐ xìtǒng sanitation

下塌 xiàtà stay

下台 xiàtái step down ◊ downfall

夏天 xiàtiān summer ◊ in the summer

下网 xiàwǎng log off ◊ offline

下午 xiàwǔ afternoon; 下午场 **xiàwǔ chǎng** matinée, afternoon show

下午好 xiàwǔ hǎo good afternoon

下陷 xiàxiàn sink, drop; subside

狭小 xiáxiǎo poky

下雨 xià xiǎoyǔ it's spitting (with rain)

下斜 xiàxié descend (of road)

下雪 xiàxuě snow

侠义 xiáyì chivalrous

狭隘 xiáyì narrow views etc

下一步 xià yībù next

下一个 xià yīgè next; 谁是下一 个? **shuí shì xià yīgè?** who's next?

下意识 xiàyìshí subconscious

下雨 xiàyǔ rain; 下雨了 **xiàyǔ le** it's raining

瑕瑜互见 xiáyú hùjiàn patchy

下载 xiàzài download

狭窄 xiázhǎi narrow; confined

瞎子 xiāzi blind person

西班牙 Xībānyá Spain ◊ Spanish

细胞 xìbāo cell

西北部 xīběi bù northwest

稀薄 xībó thin

西部 xībù west; western

西部片 xībùpiān western (movie)

西餐 xīcān western cuisine

细察 xìchá scrutinize ◊ scrutiny

细长 xìcháng narrow; slim

洗车处 xǐchē chù car wash

洗车服务 xǐchē fúwù valet service (for cars)

吸尘 xīchén vacuum

吸尘器 xīchén qì vacuum cleaner

洗涤 xǐdí clean, wash; erase tape

洗涤槽 xǐdícáo sink

洗涤剂 xǐdí jì detergent

吸毒成瘾 xīdú chéngyǐn be hooked on drugs

吸毒者 xīdú zhě drug addict

歇 xiē rest

斜 **xié** slanting, oblique; diagonal

鞋 **xié** shoe; footwear

携 **xié** carry; hold

邪 **xié** evil

写 **xiě** write

谢 **xiè** thank

卸 **xiè** unload

泄 **xiè** release

蟹 **xiè** crab

斜槽 **xiécáo** chute

写出 **xiěchū** write out

鞋带 **xiédài** shoelace; strap

携带 **xiédài** take (along)

懈怠 **xièdài** slack, lax

携带式电脑 **xiédài shì diànnǎo** laptop

鞋底 **xiédǐ** sole

鞋店 **xiédiàn** shoestore

鞋钉 **xiédīng** spike (*on shoe*)

协定 **xiédìng** agreement

亵渎 **xièdú** blaspheme

邪恶 **xié'è** evil, wicked; spiteful

鞋跟 **xiégēn** heel

邂逅 **xièhòu** encounter

协会 **xiéhuì** association, institute

卸货 **xièhuò** unload

鞋匠 **xiéjiàng** shoemaker, cobbler

谢绝 **xièjué** decline, refuse

斜靠 **xiékào** prop, lean

泄漏 **xièlòu** break; leak out; give away ◊ leak, disclosure

泄露 **xièlòu** disclose, reveal ◊ disclosure, revelation

泄密 **xièmì** reveal a secret

泄密者 **xièmì zhě** telltale

斜坡 **xiépō** slope, gradient

胁迫 **xiépò** blackmail

协商 **xiéshāng** negotiate ◊ negotiation

写生 **xiěshēng** sketch

邪视 **xiéshì** leer

斜视 **xiéshì** squint; look sideways

鞋刷 **xiéshuā** shoe brush

歇斯底里 **xiēsīdǐlǐ** hysteria; hysterical; 歇斯底里的发作 **xiēsīdǐlǐde fāzuò** hysterics

斜体 **xiétǐ** italic

谢天谢地！ **xiètiān xièdì!** thank goodness!

协调 **xiétiáo** harmony;

coordination ◊ coordinate ◊ matching; 和 … 不协调 **hé … bù xiétiáo** clash with

写下 **xiěxià** write down; put down; enter

卸下 **xièxià** unload

斜线 **xiéxiàn** oblique, slash

谢谢 **xièxie** thank you, thanks

写信 **xiěxìn** write a letter

斜眼 **xiéyǎn** squint

泻药 **xièyào** laxative

斜倚 **xiéyǐ** recline

协议 **xiéyì** agreement, understanding; pact

鞋油 **xiéyóu** shoe cream, shoe polish

斜着 **xiézhe** sideways

楔子 **xiēzi** wedge

写字夹板 **xiězì jiábǎn** clipboard

协奏曲 **xiézòu qǔ** concerto

写作 **xiězuò** write (*as author*) ◊ writing (*career*)

洗发剂 **xǐfà jì** shampoo

洗发精 **xǐfà jīng** shampoo

稀饭 **xīfàn** rice porridge, congee

西方 **xīfāng** western; westerly

西方国家 **Xīfāng guójiā** the West ◊ Western

西方化 **Xīfānghuà** Westernized

西方人 **Xīfāngrén** Westerner

细分 **xìfēn** subdivide

西风 **xīfēng** westerly

西服 **xīfú** suit

媳妇 **xífù** daughter-in-law

膝盖骨 **xīgàigǔ** kneecap

吸干 **xīgān** blot

细高跟鞋 **xìgāogēnxié** stilettos

西瓜 **xīguā** watermelon

吸管 **xīguǎn** (drinking) straw

习惯 **xíguàn** custom; habit ◊ be accustomed to; 不习惯 X **bù xíguàn X** be unused to X

希罕 **xīhan** rare ◊ rarity

喜好 **xǐhào** like; love

西红柿 **xīhóngshì** tomato

西湖 **Xīhú** West Lake

喜欢 **xǐhuan** like, be fond of; enjoy; take to; relish

熄火 **xīhuǒ** stall (*of engine*)

袭击 **xíjī** attack; strike

洗剂 **xǐjì** lotion

洗劫 xǐjié ransack

细节 xìjié detail

洗洁精 xǐjié jīng dishwashing liquid

喜剧 xǐjù comedy

戏剧 xìjù drama, play ◊ dramatic, theatrical

戏剧家 xìjù jiā dramatist, playwright

细菌 xìjūn germ, bacterium

细菌战争 xìjūn zhànzhēng germ warfare

戏剧性 xìjù xìng dramatic, exciting

喜剧演员 xǐjù yǎnyuán comedian

希腊 Xīlà Greece ◊ Greek

细浪 xìlàng ripple

西兰花 xīlánhuā broccoli

洗礼 xǐlǐ baptize, christen ◊ baptism

细粒 xìlì granule

系列 xìliè series; range

奚落 xīluò ridicule

喜马拉雅山 Xīmǎlāyǎshān Himalayas

西面 xīmiàn west

熄灭 xīmiè put out; quench; go out

心 xīn heart; mind; center

新 xīn new; unused; 我是新来的 wǒ shì xīnlái de I'm new to the job

锌 xīn zinc

辛 xīn bitter; hard

欣 xīn enjoy; appreciate

信 xìn faith; letter ◊ believe, trust; 他信佛 tā xìn Fó he's a Buddhist

西南 xīnán southwest ◊ southwestern

西南部 xīnán bù southwest

洗脑 xǐnǎo brainwash ◊ brainwashing

新兵 xīnbīng recruit

心不在焉 xīnbúzàiyān preoccupied; absent-minded

新潮 xīncháo trendy

新陈代谢 xīnchén dàixiè metabolism

信贷限额 xìndài xiàn'é credit limit

心烦 xīnfán frustrated; annoyed

新方向 xīn fāngxiàng new departure, new direction

心烦意乱 xīnfán yìluàn get ruffled

新发展 xīn fāzhǎn new departure, new development

信封 xìnfēng envelope

信服 xìnfú believe; 令人信服 lìngrén xìnfú compelling, convincing

星 xīng star

兴 xīng rise

行 xíng go ◊ expedition ◊ you're on!, ok; 星期五行吗？ xīngqī wǔ xíngma? are you ok for Friday?; 行了！ xíngle! enough!, that will do!

形 xíng shape, form

刑 xíng punishment

醒 xǐng awake ◊ rouse

擤 xǐng blow one's nose

杏 xìng apricot

性 xìng nature; character; gender; sex ◊ -ility; 可能性 kěnéngxìng possibility; 灵活性 línghuóxìng flexibility

姓 xìng surname, family name

兴 xìng spirit

幸 xìng lucky, fortunate

性爱 xìng'ài passion

性变态 xìngbiàntài pervert

性别 xìngbié gender, sex

性病 xìngbìng venereal disease

擤鼻涕 xǐng bítì blow one's nose

形成 xíngchéng form; come into existence ◊ formation

行程 xíngchéng trip

性传播疾病 xìng chuánbō jíbìng sexually transmitted disease

幸存 xìngcún survive ◊ survival

幸存者 xìngcún zhě survivor

行动 xíngdòng act ◊ action

幸而 xìng'ér mercifully

刑法 xíngfǎ criminal law, penal law

兴奋 xīngfèn excited ◊ excitement ◊ get excited; 令人兴奋 lìngrén xīngfèn exciting

兴奋 xìngfèn delight; drama, excitement

兴奋剂 xīngfèn jì stimulant

幸福 **xìngfú** happy ◊ happiness

性感 **xìnggǎn** sexy; sultry; sensual

兴高采烈 **xìnggāo cǎiliè** elated, exuberant ◊ elation

性格 **xìnggé** character, nature

性格外向的人 **xìnggé wàixiàng de rén** extrovert

星号 **xīnghào** asterisk

型号 **xínghào** model

猩红热 **xīnghóngrè** scarlet fever

性急 **xìngjí** impatient; petulant ◊ impatiently

性交 **xìngjiāo** sexual intercourse ◊ have sex; 与X性交 **yǔ X xìngjiāo** have sex with X

行经 **xíngjīng** menstruate

行经期 **xíngjīngqī** menstruation

醒酒 **xǐngjiǔ** sober up

行军 **xíngjūn** march

行军床 **xíngjūn chuáng** cot

幸亏 **xìngkuī** fortunately

醒来 **xǐnglái** wake up

行李 **xíngli** luggage, baggage

行李车 **xíngli chē** baggage car; baggage cart

行李传送带 **xíngli chuánsòngdài** (baggage) carousel

行李存放处 **xíngli cúnfàng chù** (baggage) checkroom

行李架 **xíngli jià** luggage rack

行李领取处 **xíngli lǐngqǔ chù** baggage reclaim

行李箱 **xíngli xiāng** trunk (of car)

兴隆 **xīnglóng** brisk

性能 **xìngnéng** performance; efficiency

星期 **xīngqī** week

行乞 **xíngqǐ** beg, panhandle

星期二 **xīngqī'èr** Tuesday

星期六 **xīngqīliù** Saturday

性情 **xìngqíng** temperament

星期日 **xīngqīrì** Sunday

星期三 **xīngqīsān** Wednesday

星期四 **xīngqīsì** Thursday

星期天 **xīngqītiān** Sunday

星期五 **xīngqīwǔ** Friday

星期一 **xīngqīyī** Monday

兴趣 **xìngqù** interest; 引起X的兴趣 **yǐnqǐ X de xìngqù** interest X

行人 **xíngrén** pedestrian

杏仁 **xìngrén** almond

人行道 **xíngrén dào** sidewalk

行人区 **xíngrén qū** pedestrian precinct

形容 **xíngróng** describe; 把X形容成Y **bǎ X xíngróng chéng Y** describe X as Y

形容词 **xíngróngcí** adjective

性骚扰 **xìng sāorǎo** sexual harassment

行善者 **xíngshàn zhě** benefactor

兴盛 **xīngshèng** prosperity

行驶 **xíngshǐ** drive; go; travel; journey

行使 **xíngshǐ** exercise

刑事 **xíngshì** criminal; 有刑事记录 **yǒu xíngshì jìlù** have a criminal record

形势 **xíngshì** situation

形式 **xíngshì** form GRAM; formal; 这只是一种形式 **zhè zhǐshì yīzhǒng xíngshì** it's just a formality

形式上 **xíngshì shàng** formality

形体 **xíngtǐ** figure

星条旗 **Xīngtiáo qí** Stars and Stripes

新贵 **xīnguì** upstart

兴旺 **xīngwàng** flourish ◊ flourishing, prosperous

兴旺的企业 **xīngwàng de qǐyè** going concern

行为 **xíngwéi** behavior; deed; 行为的标准 **xíngwéide biāozhǔn** morals, standards of behavior; 行为规矩 **xíngwéi guījù** well-behaved

醒悟 **xǐngwù** awaken; realize; see things as they are

星象 **xīngxiàng** horoscope

形象 **xíngxiàng** image

形象包装 **xíngxiàng bāozhuāng** packaging, marketing

行销地区 **xíngxiāo dìqū** market

猩猩 **xīngxing** ape

行星 **xíngxīng** planet

行刑人 **xíngxíng rén** executioner

形形色色 **xíngxíng sèsè** varied, diverse

行凶抢劫 **xíngxióng qiǎngjié** mug ◊ mugging

行凶抢劫者 xíngxiōng qiǎngjié zhě mugger

性欲 xìngyù sexual desire, lust

性欲高潮 xìngyù gāocháo orgasm

幸运 xìngyùn fortunate ◊ fortunately ◊ good fortune; lucky break

辛灾乐祸 xìngzāi-lèhuò malicious delight

星占 xīngzhàn horoscope

行政 xíngzhèng administration ◊ administrative

行政机关 xíngzhèng jīguān civil service

行政系统 xíngzhèng xìtǒng bureaucracy

性质 xìngzhì quality; character

形状 xíngzhuàng form, shape

行走 xíngzǒu parade

辛亥革命 Xīnhài Gémìng 1911 Revolution

信号 xìnhào signal

新婚人 xīnhūn rén newlyweds

犀牛 xīniú rhinoceros

心悸 xīnjì palpitations

信笺 xìnjiān writing paper

信件 xìnjiàn letter; correspondence

新教 Xīnjiào Protestant

信教 xìnjiào devout

新教徒 Xīnjiàotú Protestant

新加坡 Xīnjiāpō Singapore ◊ Singaporean

新界 Xīnjiè New Territories

心肌梗塞 xīnjī gěngsè heart attack

薪金 xīnjīn pay

薪金支票 xīnjīn zhīpiào paycheck

心口灼热 xīnkǒu zhuórè heartburn

辛苦 xīnkǔ arduous, strenuous

欣快感 xīnkuàigǎn euphoria

辛辣 xīnlà sharp *taste*

信赖 xìnlài trust; rely on

新郎 xīnláng bridegroom

心理 xīnlǐ psychological ◊ psychologically, mentally

心理疾病 xīnlǐ jíbìng mental illness ◊ mentally ill

心灵感应 xīnlíng gǎnyìng telepathy ◊ telepathic

心理失调 xīnlǐ shītiáo maladjusted

心力衰竭 xīnlì shuāijié heart failure

心理学 xīnlǐ xué psychology ◊ psychological ◊ psychologically

心理学家 xīnlǐ xuéjiā psychologist

心理状态 xīnlǐ zhuàngtài mentality

心满意足 xīnmǎn yìzú contented, happy

新年 Xīnnián New Year (*Western*); 新年快乐 **Xīnnián kuàilè** Happy New Year

信念 xìnniàn conviction, belief

新娘 xīnniáng bride

芯片 xīnpiàn chip COMPUT

新起点 xīn qǐdiǎn new departure

心情 xīnqíng mood, frame of mind; 心情好 **xīnqínghǎo** good-humored

心儿 xīnr core

欣然 xīnrán readily; 欣然接受 **xīnrán jiēshòu** lap up, readily accept

新任 xīnrèn incoming, newly appointed

信任 xìnrèn trust ◊ confidence ◊ trusting

欣赏 xīnshǎng appreciate ◊ appreciation

心上人 xīnshàng rén sweetheart

心神不定 xīnshén bùdìng distraught

新生 xīnshēng newborn ◊ freshman

新式 xīnshì up-to-date

信使 xìnshǐ courier

新手 xīnshǒu beginner; rookie

薪水 xīnshuǐ salary

薪水级别 xīnshuǐ jíbié salary scale

薪水名册 xīnshuǐ míngcè payroll (*staff*)

薪水总额 xīnshuǐ zǒng'é payroll (*money*)

心算 xīnsuàn mental arithmetic

心碎 xīnsuì broken-hearted; 令人

心碎 **lìngrén xīnsuì** heartbreaking

心跳 xīntiào heartbeat

信条 xìntiáo creed

信徒 xìntú believer

喜怒无常 xǐnù wúcháng moody

新闻 xīnwén news

新闻报导 xīnwén bàodǎo news; news report

新闻播音员 xīnwén bōyīn yuán newsreader

新闻工作者 xīnwén gōngzuò zhě journalist

新闻广播 xīnwén guǎngbō newscast

新闻广播员 xīnwén guǎngbō yuán newscaster; anchor man

新闻界 xīnwénjiè the press

新闻写作 xīnwén xiězuò journalism (writing)

新闻业 xīnwényè journalism (career)

新闻自由 xīnwén zìyǒu freedom of the press

欣喜 xīnxǐ jubilant

信息 xìnxī information

新鲜 xīnxiān fresh ◊ freshness

信箱 xìnxiāng mailbox

信息技术 xìnxī jìshù information technology, IT

新西兰 Xīnxīlán New Zealand

信心 xìnxīn confidence

心胸宽阔 xīnxiōng kuānkuò broad-minded

心胸狭窄 xīnxiōng xiázǎi narrow-minded

欣喜若狂 xīnxǐ ruò kuáng rapture ◊ ecstatic

信息学 xìnxī xué information science

新芽 xīnyá sprout

信仰 xìnyǎng belief, faith

新颖 xīnyǐng novelty, freshness

新颖事物 xīnyǐng shìwù novelty

信以为真 xìn yǐwéi zhēn fall for

信用 xìnyòng credit FIN

信用卡 xìnyòng kǎ credit card

信誉 xìnyù credibility

新月 xīnyuè new moon

信誉卓著 xìnyù zhuōzhù creditworthy

心脏 xīnzàng heart ◊ cardiac

心脏病 xīnzàng bìng heart disease

心脏停跳 xīnzàng tíngtiào cardiac arrest

心脏移植 xīnzàng yízhí heart transplant

心照不宣 xīnzhào bù xuān knowing; tacit ◊ knowingly

信纸 xìnzhǐ writing paper

胸 xiōng chest; bust

兄 xiōng elder brother

凶 xiōng fierce; terrible; evil

熊 xióng bear

雄 xióng male

雄辩 xióngbiàn eloquent ◊ eloquently

兄弟 xiōngdì brothers

兄弟般 xiōngdì ban fraternal ◊ like brothers

兄弟姐妹 xiōngdì jiěmèi brothers and sisters

熊蜂 xióngfēng bumblebee

凶狠 xiōnghěn vicious

雄驹 xióngjū colt

熊猫 xióngmāo panda

凶猛 xiōngměng fierce

胸腔 xiōngqiāng thorax

凶杀 xiōngshā murder

凶手 xiōngshǒu murderer, killer

雄伟 xióngwěi imposing; majestic ◊ majestically

雄心勃勃 xióngxīn bóbo ambitious

雄性 xióngxìng male

熊熊燃烧 xióngxiong ránshāo blaze

匈牙利 Xiōngyálì Hungary ◊ Hungarian

胸罩 xiōngzhào brassière

胸针 xiōngzhēn brooch

锡箔 xīpó tinfoil

锡铅合金 xīqiān héjīn pewter

系起来 xì qǐlái tie up hair

喜鹊 xǐque magpie

吸入 xīrù breathe in, inhale

吸入器 xīrù qì inhaler

稀少 xīshǎo rare ◊ rarity

细审 xìshěn sift through

牺牲 xīshēng sacrifice

细绳 xìshéng string

系绳 xìshéng tether

牺牲品 xīshēng pǐn victim

稀释 xīshì dilute, water down

吸收 xīshōu absorb

洗手间 xǐshǒu jiān bathroom

稀疏 xīshū sparse

蟋蟀 xīshuài cricket

嬉水 xīshuǐ splash

习俗 xísú custom

细条纹 xìtiáowén pinstripe

系统 xìtǒng system; set-up ◊ systematic

系统崩溃 xìtǒng bēngkuì system crash

系统分析者 xìtǒng fēnxī zhě systems analyst

羞 xiū shame; embarrass

修 xiū repair; 把车修了 **bǎ chē xiūle** get the car fixed

休 xiū stop; rest; 休病假 **xiū bìngjià** be on sick leave

锈 xiù rust

嗅 xiù smell, sniff

袖 xiù sleeve

秀 xiù beautiful

修补 xiūbǔ mend; darn; reinforce

羞耻 xiūchǐ disgrace, shame

羞答答 xiū dádá coy

修道士 xiūdàoshì monastic

修道院 xiūdàoyuàn convent; monastery

修订 xiūdìng update

修复 xiūfù restore, recondition ◊ restoration

修改 xiūgǎi correct, amend; modify ◊ correction, amendment; modification; 他们要修改法律 **tāmēn yào xiūgǎi fǎlǜ** they are going to change the law

休会 xiūhuì adjourn

休假 xiūjià vacation; recess ◊ take a vacation; take leave; 休假一天 **xiūjià yītiān** take a day off

修剪 xiūjiǎn crop; prune

修剪指甲 xiūjiǎn zhǐjiǎ manicure

嗅觉 xiùjué sense of smell

休克 xiūkè shock; 处于休克状态 **chǔyú xiūkè zhuàngtài** be in shock

袖口 xiùkǒu cuff

袖口链扣 xiùkǒu liànkòu cuff link

羞愧 xiūkuì ashamed

修理 xiūlǐ repair, fix

秀丽 xiùlì beautiful; dainty

修理车间 xiūlǐ chējiān workshop; garage

修理工 xiūlǐ gōng repairman

休眠 xiūmián dormant

修女 xiūnǚ nun

羞怯 xiūqiè shy; sheepish

羞辱 xiūrǔ humiliate ◊ humiliation

修缮 xiūshàn renovate, do up

修饰 xiūshì touch up

袖手旁观 xiùshǒu pángguān stand by

休息 xiūxi rest, take a break ◊ recess; 休息吧! **xiūxiba!** let's call it a day!

休息一下 xiūxi yīxià take a break

休息日 xiūxīrì holiday

休养 xiūyǎng recuperate, recover

休养疗法 xiūyǎng liáofǎ rest cure

休战 xiūzhàn truce

袖珍 xiùzhēn compact; midget

袖珍本 xiùzhēn běn pocketbook, paperback

修正 xiūzhèng revise, correct ◊ revision

修正主义 xiūzhèng zhǔyì revisionism ◊ revisionist

袖珍型 xiùzhēn xíng miniature

休止 xiūzhǐ cessation

袖子 xiùzi sleeve

洗碗布 xǐwǎn bù dishcloth

希望 xīwàng hope; wish; 希望如此 **xīwàng rúcǐ** I hope so

洗碗工 xǐwǎn gōng dishwasher (person)

洗碗机 xǐwǎn jī dishwasher (machine)

洗碗水 xǐwǎn shuǐ dishwater

席位 xíwèi seat POL

细微 xìwēi fine distinction

细心 xìxīn careful; considerate

熙熙攘攘 xīxī rǎngrang busy, crowded

信息学家 xìxī xuéjiā information scientist

吸烟 xīyān smoke; have a smoke ◊ smoking; 请勿吸烟 **qǐngwù**

xīyān please refrain from smoking

吸烟车厢 **xīyān chēxiāng** smoking compartment

吸烟者 **xīyān zhě** smoker

西药 **xīyào** Western medicine (*drugs etc*)

西医 **xīyī** Western medicine (*science*)

蜥蜴 **xīyì** lizard

洗衣店 **xǐyī diàn** laundry (*place*)

洗衣粉 **xǐyī fěn** soap powder, detergent

洗衣服 **xǐyīfu** get one's laundry done; do the washing

洗衣服务 **xǐyī fúwù** valet service (*for clothes*)

洗衣机 **xǐyī jī** washing machine

吸引 **xīyǐn** attract, draw; fascinate, charm; tempt

吸引力 **xīyǐn lì** attraction; appeal

习以为常 **xí yǐ wéi cháng** usual ◊ used to

洗一洗 **xǐyīxǐ** have a wash, wash up

稀有 **xīyǒu** rare

喜悦 **xǐyuè** happy

西藏 **Xīzàng** Tibet ◊ Tibetan

洗澡 **xǐzǎo** bathe; shower ◊ bathing

洗澡间 **xǐzǎo jiān** bathroom

锡纸 **xīzhǐ** tinfoil

细枝 **xìzhī** twig

西装 **xīzhuāng** suit

戏装 **xìzhuāng** costume (*actor's*)

西装上衣 **xīzhuāng shàngyī** coat (*of a suit*)

席子 **xízi** mat

须 **xū** must ◊ whiskers

需 **xū** need

虚 **xū** empty ◊ void

许 **xǔ** promise; permit

叙 **xù** narrate

序 **xù** order, sequence

续 **xù** continue

宣 **xuān** declare

旋 **xuán** rotate; spin, whirl

悬 **xuán** hang, suspend

选 **xuǎn** choose, pick; elect; highlight COMPUT; 他们选他当总统 **tāmén xuǎn tā dāng zǒngtǒng** they voted him

President

选拔 **xuǎnbá** selection

选拔赛 **xuǎnbásài** qualifier, qualifying game

宣布 **xuānbù** announce, declare, proclaim ◊ declaration

宣布无罪 **xuānbù wúzuì** exonerate

选出 **xuǎnchū** elected

宣传 **xuānchuán** promotion, publicity, propaganda ◊ promote, publicize, plug

宣传家 **xuānchuán jiā** publicist; spin doctor

悬垂 **xuánchuí** dangle

选词 **xuǎncí** word

悬而未决 **xuán ér wèi jué** be pending ◊ undecided

旋风 **xuànfēng** whirlwind

宣告 **xuāngào** announce ◊ announcement

悬挂 **xuánguà** suspend, hang

喧哗 **xuānhuá** din, racket ◊ noisy

喧哗声 **xūanhuá shēng** noise

选举 **xuǎnjǔ** election ◊ elect

选举权 **xuǎnjǔ quán** right to vote; 有选举权 **yǒu xuǎnjǔ quán** have the vote

选举日 **xuǎnjǔ rì** election day

选举投票 **xuǎnjǔ tóupiào** vote, go to the polls

选举制度 **xuǎnjǔ zhìdù** electoral system

旋律 **xuánlù** melody

选民 **xuǎnmín** elector, voter

眩目 **xuànmù** blinding

眩目电闪 **xuánmù diànshǎn** bolt of lightning

喧闹 **xuānnào** racket, tumult ◊ noisy, rowdy; tumultuous ◊ blare out

喧闹声 **xuānnào shēng** din

悬念 **xuánniàn** suspense

宣判 **xuānpàn** pass judgment; 宣判无罪 **xuānpàn wúzuì** acquit; 宣判有罪 **xuānpàn yǒuzuì** convict

选票 **xuǎnpiào** vote

轩然大波 **xuānrán dàbō** fuss, stink

选入 **xuǎnrù** vote in

悬赏 **xuánshǎng** offer a reward

宣誓 **xuānshì** swear an oath

选手 **xuǎnshǒu** competitor

悬殊 **xuánshū** disparity

旋涡 **xuánwō** whirlpool

喧嚣 **xuānxiāo** uproar, hullabaloo

悬崖 **xuányá** cliff, bluff

宣言 **xuānyán** manifest

宣扬 **xuānyáng** advertising

炫耀 **xuànyào** show off; parade, flaunt ◊ pretentious

眩晕 **xuànyùn** giddiness, vertigo

选择 **xuǎnzé** choice, option ◊ choose, select

选择过程 **xuǎnzé guòchéng** selection process

宣战 **xuānzhàn** declare war ◊ declaration of war

旋转 **xuánzhuǎn** revolve; rotate; spin; whirl ◊ revolution, rotation

旋转门 **xuánzhuǎn mén** revolving door

旋转木马 **xuánzhuǎn mùmǎ** carousel

旋转炮塔 **xuánzhuǎn pàotǎ** turret (*of tank*)

絮叨 **xùdao** harp on about

蓄电池 **xù diànchí** storage battery

许多 **xǔduō** many; much; a lot of

靴 **xuē** boot

学 **xué** study; learn

穴 **xué** hole; cave

雪 **xuě** snow

血 **xuè** blood

雪白 **xuěbái** snow-white

雪崩 **xuěbēng** avalanche

雪堆 **xuěduī** snowdrift

血管 **xuèguǎn** blood vessel

雪花 **xuěhuā** snowflake

学会 **xuéhuì** learn ◊ academy

血迹 **xuèjì** bloodstain

雪茄 **xuějiā** cigar

削减 **xuējiǎn** cut, trim; whittle

血库 **xuèkù** blood bank

血块 **xuèkuài** blood clot

雪型 **xuělí** snowplow

雪莲 **xuělián** snowdrop

雪利酒 **xuělì jiǔ** sherry

血淋淋 **xuè línlínlín** bloody

学年 **xuénián** academic year

学期 **xuéqī** semester, term

雪橇 **xuěqiāo** bobsleigh, bobsled; sled, sleigh

血亲 **xuèqīn** blood relative

雪球 **xuěqiú** snowball

血球 **xuèqiú** corpuscle

雪人 **xuěrén** snowman

削弱 **xuēruò** impaired ◊ weaken

学生 **xuésheng** student

学生时代 **xuésheng shídài** school days

学术 **xuéshù** academic

血栓形成 **xuěshuān xíngchéng** thrombosis

学术成就 **xuéshù chéngjiù** scholarship (*work*)

学说 **xuéshuō** doctrine

血统 **xuètǒng** breed; pedigree

噱头 **xuétóu** patter, spiel; publicity stunt

学徒 **xuétú** apprentice, novice

学位 **xuéwèi** (university) degree

穴位 **xuéwèi** acupuncture point

学问 **xuéwen** knowledge

雪屋 **xuěwū** igloo

学习 **xuéxí** study; learn ◊ studying; learning; 学习驾驶 **xuéxí jiàshǐ** learn to drive; 学习曲线 **xuéxí qūxiàn** learning curve

学校 **xuéxiào** school

学校假期 **xuéxiào jiàqī** school vacation

血型 **xuèxíng** blood group

血压 **xuèyā** blood pressure

血液 **xuèyè** bloodstream

血液循环 **xuèyè xúnhuán** circulation

血液样本 **xuèyè yàngběn** blood sample

学员 **xuéyuán** cadet

学院 **xuéyuàn** college; academy; school

学者 **xuézhě** scholar

血肿 **xuèzhǒng** hematoma

血中毒 **xuè zhòngdú** blood poisoning

靴子 **xuēzi** boot

虚构 **xūgòu** make up ◊ fictitious

虚构情节 **xūgòu qíngjié** embroider, embellish *story*

虚话 xūhuà myth, fiction

续集 xùjí sequel, continuation

虚假 xūjiǎ hollow, meaningless ◊ pretense

许久 xǔjiǔ a long time

酗酒 xùjiǔ drink, booze

酗酒者 xùjiǔ zhě alcoholic

许可 xǔkě permission, authority ◊ license, permit

许可证 xǔkě zhèng permit, warrant

畜牧 xùmù raise livestock

序幕 xùmù prolog

熏 xūn smoke

询 xún inquire

寻 xún seek

巡 xún patrol, cruise

驯 xún tame

训 xùn instruct, train

迅 xùn fast, rapid

巡边员 xúnbiān yuán linesman

训斥 xùnchì reprimand

殉道者 xùndào zhě martyr

驯服 xùnfú tame, docile

巡官 xúnguān inspector (of police)

驯化 xùnhuà domesticate

循环 xúnhuán circulate ◊ circulation; cycle

巡回 xúnhuí round (of doctor etc)

虚拟现实 xūnǐ xiànshí virtual reality

巡警 xúnjǐng patrolman

训练 xùnliàn train ◊ training

训练班 xùnliàn bān training course

训练有素 xùnliàn yǒusù skillful; polished

巡逻 xúnluó patrol

巡逻车 xúnluó chē patrol car

巡逻队 xúnluó duì patrol

荨麻 xúnmá nettle

训兽者 xùnshòu zhě trainer (of dog)

迅速 xùnsù swift, speedy; express ◊ speedily, swiftly; 他们沿路迅速前进 tāmen yánlù xùnsù qiánjìn they pelted along the road

迅速上升 xùnsù shàngshēng shoot up (of prices)

迅速增长 xùnsù zēngzhǎng mushroom, spread

许诺 xǔnuò promise

询问 xúnwèn inquire; interrogate ◊ inquiry; interrogation

勋章 xūnzhāng medal; decoration

寻找 xúnzhǎo search for, look for, seek

需求 xūqiú demand

序曲 xùqǔ overture

虚荣 xūróng vanity

虚弱 xūruò weak, frail, feeble ◊ frailty, weakness

叙事体 xùshì tǐ narrative

叙事者 xùshì zhě narrator

叙述 xùshù relate, narrate, tell ◊ narration, account, story

虚伪 xūwěi hypocrisy; insincerity ◊ hypocritical

虚线 xūxiàn perforated line

虚心 xūxīn open-minded

嘘嘘声 xūxu shēng boo

序言 xùyán introduction

需要 xūyào need, require; cost; take; entail ◊ requirement, need; 有需要 yǒu xūyào in demand

蓄意 xùyì systematically

虚张声势 xūzhāng shēngshì bravado, bluff

Y

压 **yā** press, crush ◊ pressure
鸭 **yā** duck
鸦 **yā** crow
押 **yā** mortgage; pawn
呀 **yā** (*being at loss*): 呀，这怎么办呢？ **yā, zhè zěnme bàn ne?** oh god, what am I going to do?
牙 **yá** tooth
哑 **yǎ** dumb, mute
亚 **yà** inferior; second best
牙斑 **yábān** plaque
牙齿 **yáchǐ** tooth ◊ dental
牙齿检查 **yáchǐ jiǎnchá** dental checkup
压低 **yādī** keep down *voice etc*
牙膏 **yágāo** toothpaste
雅观 **yǎguān** graceful; refined
押金 **yājīn** deposit, security
亚军 **yàjūn** runner-up
牙科 **yákē** dentistry ◊ dental
哑口无言 **yǎkǒu wúyán** speechless
压力 **yālì** pressure; stress
哑铃 **yǎlíng** dumbbell
亚麻布 **yàmá bù** linen
腌 **yān** salt; pickle; cure
烟 **yān** smoke
淹 **yān** drown
言 **yán** word; words; talking; speech
盐 **yán** salt
严 **yán** tight; rigorous
颜 **yán** face; color
研 **yán** grind; research
岩 **yán** cliff; rock
延 **yán** extend
沿 **yán** along
演 **yǎn** perform
眼 **yǎn** eye
堰 **yàn** weir
咽 **yàn** swallow
宴 **yàn** banquet, feast
燕 **yàn** swallow (*bird*)
厌 **yàn** hate; dislike
砚 **yàn** inkstone

验 **yàn** test, check
掩蔽 **yǎnbì** cover, shelter
掩蔽物 **yǎnbì wù** shelter, screen
演播室 **yǎnbō shì** (TV) studio
掩藏 **yǎncáng** hide; disguise *fear etc*
烟草 **yāncǎo** tobacco
檐槽 **yáncáo** gutter
延长 **yáncháng** extend, lengthen; prolong ◊ lengthy, protracted
延迟 **yánchí** delay
演出 **yǎnchū** perform ◊ performance
烟囱 **yāncōng** chimney; ship's funnel
烟蒂 **yāndì** cigarette butt
烟斗 **yāndǒu** pipe (*for smoking*)
厌烦 **yànfán** be fed up
羊 **yáng** sheep
洋 **yáng** ocean
阳 **yáng** yang; sun
杨 **yáng** poplar
扬 **yáng** raise
痒 **yǎng** itch
养 **yǎng** keep, rear *animals*
氧 **yǎng** oxygen
仰 **yǎng** look up
样 **yàng** style; type; sample; model
掩盖 **yǎngài** cover, cover up; mask
掩盖真相 **yǎngài zhēnxiàng** coverup
洋白菜 **yángbái cài** cabbage (*Northern China*)
样本 **yàngběn** sample, specimen
养病 **yǎngbìng** convalesce
养蚕业 **yǎngcányè** silkworm breeding
养成 **yǎngchéng** pick up *habit*; 养成习惯 **yǎngchéng ... xíguàn** take to, make a habit of
洋葱 **yángcōng** onion
阉割 **yāngē** neuter; castrate
严格 **yángé** rigorous, strict ◊ rigor, strictness

扬帆驾驶 yángfān jiàshǐ sailing

养父母 yǎngfùmǔ foster parents

羊倌 yángguān shepherd

阳光 yángguāng sunshine

阳光充足 yángguāng chōngzú sunny

洋鬼子 yáng guǐzi *pej* foreign devil, damn foreigner

氧化物 yǎnghuà wù oxide

养老金 yǎnglǎo jīn pension

养老院 yǎnglǎo yuàn old people's home

羊毛 yángmáo wool

羊毛衣物 yángmáo yīwù woolen clothing

阉公牛 yān gōngniú steer (*animal*)

羊皮 yángpí sheepskin

样品 yàngpǐn specimen, sample

氧气 yǎngqì oxygen

羊绒 yángróng cashmere

羊肉 yángròu mutton

阳伞 yángsǎn sunshade, parasol

养神 yǎngshén relax

扬声器 yángshēng qì loudspeaker

样式 yàngshì pattern

杨树 yángshù poplar tree

阳台 yángtái balcony; patio; terrace

验关 yànguān customs inspection

验光 yànguāng eye test

言过其实 yán guò qí shí exaggeration

仰望 yǎngwàng look up

阳萎 yángwěi impotence ◊ impotent

仰卧 yǎngwò lie on one's back

阳性 yángxìng positive *test result*

洋洋大作 yángyáng dàzuò blockbuster

仰泳 yǎngyǒng backstroke

养育 yǎngyù bring up

养鱼缸 yǎngyúgāng aquarium

严寒 yánhán frosty

烟盒 yānhé cigarette case

咽喉 yānhóu gullet; larynx

掩护 yǎnhù camouflage

延缓 yánhuǎn postpone, delay

宴会 yànhuì dinner party; banquet

烟灰缸 yānhuī gāng ashtray

烟火 yānhuǒ fireworks

烟火表演 yānhuǒ biǎoyǎn firework display

眼睑 yǎnjiǎn eyelid

演讲 yǎnjiǎng lecture, talk

演讲者 yǎnjiǎng zhě speaker

岩礁 yánjiāo ledge (*on rock face*)

眼睫毛 yǎn jiémáo eyelash

严谨 yánjǐn tight

严禁 yánjìn forbidden

眼睛 yǎnjīng eye

眼镜 yǎnjìng glasses

眼睛疲劳 yǎnjīng píláo eye strain

研究 yánjiū study, research

研究课题 yánjiū kètí research project

研究生 yánjiū shēng postgraduate

研究员 yánjiú yuán researcher

厌倦 yànjuàn be tired of, be sick of

严峻 yánjùn forbidding; somber

眼科医生 yǎnkē yīshēng ophthalmologist

严酷 yánkù stark, grim

眼泪 yǎnlèi teardrop

眼泪汪汪 yǎnlèi wāngwang tearful

严厉 yánlì severe ◊ severely

颜料 yánliào paint

严厉盘问 yánlì pánwèn interrogate, grill

严厉批评 yánlì pīpíng criticize, pan

言论自由 yánlùn zìyóu free speech

燕麦片 yànmài piàn oatmeal; oats

淹没 yānmò flood; submerge; deluge; drown out; 淹没堤岸 yānmò tí'àn flood its banks

赝品 yànpǐn fake

延期 yánqī postpone; extend ◊ postponement; extension

眼球 yǎnqiú eyeball

烟圈儿 yānquānr wisp of smoke

颜色 yánsè color; coloring

延伸 yánshēn stretch, extend

岩石 yánshí rock

掩饰 yǎnshì cover up; 替 X 掩饰 tì X yǎnshì cuòwù quēdiǎn cover up for X

验尸 yànshī autopsy

厌食 yànshí be anorexic

验尸官 yànshī guān coroner

厌食症 yànshí zhèng anorexia

演说家 yànshuō jiā orator; speaker

淹死 yānsǐ drown

严肃 yánsù serious; stern; sober; solemn ◊ severity

研讨会 yántǎo huì seminar

燕尾服 yànwěifú tail coat

烟雾 yānwù smog

延误 yánwù delay, holdup

厌恶 yànwù hate; have an aversion to; 令人厌恶 lìngrén yànwù distasteful; sickening; repulsive

演习 yǎnxí exercise, drill, maneuver

演戏 yǎnxì put on a play; perform

眼下 yǎnxià at present

咽峡炎 yānxiá yán angina

延续 yánxù continue, last

验血 yànxuè blood test

眼药水 yǎnyàoshuǐ eyedrops

演义界 yǎnyìjiè show business

眼影膏 yǎnyǐnggāo eyeshadow

谚语 yànyǔ saying, proverb

演员 yǎnyuán actor; actress

演员表 yǎnyuán biǎo cast

言语 yányǔ speech

言语矫治师 yányǔ jiǎozhì shī speech therapist

言语缺陷 yányǔ quēxiàn speech defect

沿着 yánzhe follow, go along; stick to *path etc* ◊ down, along; 他们沿着街跑 tāmen yánzhe jiē pǎo they ran up the street

验证 yànzhèng identification ◊ test; verify

胭脂 yānzhǐ blusher

严重 yánzhòng severe, grave; serious; drastic ◊ gravity, seriousness

燕子 yànzi swallow (*bird*)

演奏 yǎnzòu perform, play *music* ◊ rendition, playing, performance

演奏会 yǎnzòu huì recital

演奏者 yǎnzòu zhě player, musician

烟嘴 yānzuǐ tip (*of cigarette*)

要 yāo demand

腰 yāo waist

妖 yāo monster; ghost

邀 yāo invite

幺 yāo one (*in phone numbers*)

窑 yáo kiln

摇 yáo shake

遥 yáo far away, distant

咬 yǎo bite

舀 yǎo scoop

药 yào drug, medicine; medication

要 yào want; need; must; will ◊ if; 你要什么都行 nǐ yào shénme dōu xíng you can have whatever you want; 天也许要下雨 tiān yěxǔ yào xiàyǔ it might rain; 我要和你谈话 wǒ yào hé nǐ táihuà I need to talk to you

摇摆 yáobǎi roll, sway; swing; toss ◊ unsteady

腰包 yāobāo fanny pack

腰部 yāobù waist

药草 yàocǎo herb

药草茶 yàocǎo chá herbal tea

舀出 yǎochū scoop up

腰带 yāodài belt; girdle

要道 yàodào main street

要点 yàodiǎn key point; core, nub

药店 yàodiàn pharmacy, drugstore

摇动 yáodòng wave; shake; flap

要饭 yàofàn beg

药方 yàofāng prescription

药房 yàofáng dispensary; pharmacy, drugstore

妖怪 yāoguài monster; ghost

摇滚乐 yáogǔn yuè rock music, rock and roll

摇滚乐歌星 yáogǔn yuè gēxīng rock star

摇晃 yáohuang rock; tremble; wobble ◊ shaky

咬紧 yǎojǐn clench

要紧 yàojǐn important, vital ◊ matter

药剂师 yàojì shī druggist, pharmacist

遥控 yáokòng remote control

摇篮 yáolán cradle

摇橹 yáolǔ paddle

幼苗 yòumiáo seedling

药片 yàopiàn tablet

药品 yàopǐn medicine

药签 **yàoqiān** swab

邀请 **yāoqǐng** invite ◊ invitation

要求 **yāoqiú** request, ask for; demand, require ◊ demand; call

要人 **yàorén** VIP

要塞 **yàosài** fort

摇上 **yáoshàng** wind up *window*

钥匙 **yàoshi** key

要是 **yàoshì** if

钥匙圈 **yàoshiquān** keyring

药水 **yàoshuǐ** tonic

腰疼 **yāoténg** lumbago

腰痛 **yāotòng** lumbago

摇头 **yáotóu** shake one's head

摇头丸儿 **yáotóuwánr** ecstasy (*drug*)

药丸 **yàowán** pill

腰围 **yāowéi** waistline

药物 **yàowù** drug

谣言 **yáoyán** rumor

耀眼 **yàoyǎn** dazzle ◊ dazzling

摇摇欲坠 **yáoyao yùzhuì** ramshackle

摇椅 **yáoyǐ** rocking chair

遥远 **yáoyuǎn** far away

腰子 **yāozi** kidney

鸦片 **yāpiàn** opium

鸦片战争 **Yāpiàn Zhànzhēng** Opium War

压迫 **yāpò** oppress

牙签 **yáqiān** toothpick

牙刷 **yáshuā** toothbrush

压缩 **yāsuō** compress; condense, shorten; zip up COMPUT

压缩空气 **yāsuō kōngqì** compressed air

压缩驱动器 **yāsuō qūdòngqì** zip drive

牙套 **yátào** (dental) brace

牙疼 **yáténg** toothache

牙痛 **yátòng** toothache

牙医 **yáyī** dentist

压抑 **yāyì** inhibit; repress; muffle ◊ inhibited; pent-up ◊ inhibition

压印 **yāyìn** imprint (*of credit card*)

牙龈 **yáyín** gum

压韵 **yāyùn** rhyme; 以 … 压韵 **yǐ … yāyùn** rhyme with …

压制 **yāzhì** suppress, clamp down on; silence ◊ repressive

雅致 **yǎzhì** gracious, elegant

亚洲 **Yàzhōu** Asia ◊ Asian

亚洲人 **Yàzhōu rén** Asian

椰 **yē** coconut

爷 **yé** grandpa, grandfather (*paternal*)

也 **yě** too, also, as well; 她也是 **tā yě shì** so is she; 一点也不奇怪 **yìdiǎn yě bù qíguài** not in the least surprised

野 **yě** wild

液 **yè** liquid

夜 **yè** night

页 **yè** page

叶 **yè** leaf

业 **yè** business; industry

夜班 **yèbān** night shift

夜班服务员 **yèbān fúwùyuán** night porter

野餐 **yěcān** picnic

野地 **yědì** wilderness

野鸡 **yějī** unregistered, unlicensed; worthless; mickey-mouse

夜间 **yèjiān** at night; 夜间飞行 **yèjiān fēixíng** night flight; 夜间旅行 **yèjiān lǚxíng** travel by night

液晶体显示器 **yèjīngtǐ xiǎnshìqì** LCD, liquid crystal display

冶炼厂 **yěliàn chǎng** iron and steel works

叶轮机 **yèlún jī** steam turbine

页码 **yèmǎ** page number

野蛮 **yěmán** inhuman

野牛 **yěniú** buffalo

叶片 **yèpiàn** blade (*of grass*)

野人 **yěrén** savage

野生 **yěshēng** wild

野生动物保护区 **yěshēng dòngwù bǎohù qū** animal sanctuary

夜生活 **yè shēnghuó** nightlife

野生鸟兽 **yěshēng niǎoshòu** wildlife

夜市 **yèshì** night market

野兽 **yěshòu** wild beast

耶稣 **Yēsū** Jesus

液体 **yètǐ** liquid

野兔 **yětù** hare

夜晚 **yèwǎn** night

腋窝 **yèwō** armpit

夜校 **yèxiào** evening classes; night

school

野心 yěxīn ambition; greed

野性 yěxìng savage; wild

也许 yěxǔ may, might ◊ perhaps, possibly, maybe; 我也许迟到 **wǒ yěxǔ chídào** I might be late

液压 yèyā hydraulic

野丫头 yěyātóu tomboy

爷爷 yéye grandpa, grandfather (*paternal*)

夜莺 yèyīng nightingale

野营车 yěyíng chē camper (*vehicle*)

野营者 yěyíng zhě camper (*person*)

业余 yèyú amateur

业余爱好者 yèyú àihào zhě amateur

业余时间 yèyú shíjiān spare time

野猪 yězhū wild boar

业主 yèzhǔ proprietor

液状 yèzhuàng liquid

椰子 yēzi coconut

叶子 yèzi leaf; foliage

椰子奶 yēzi nǎi coconut milk

椰子树 yēzi shù coconut palm

夜总会 yèzǒnghuì nightclub; nightspot

一 yī one

衣 yī clothes; item of clothing

依 yī depend on ◊ according to; 依我看 **yī wǒ kàn** as far as I can see

医 yī medicine; doctor

姨 yí aunt (*mother's sister*)

遗 yí lose; leave behind

仪 yí ceremony, rite

移 yí move

疑 yí doubt, suspect

椅 yǐ chair

倚 yǐ lean on; depend on

已 yǐ already

以 yǐ by; according to; 以 X 为目标 **yǐ X wéi mùbiāo** with a view to X; 以 X 著名 **yǐ X zhùmíng** be famous for X

意 yì thought, idea; intention; meaning

溢 yì overflow

抑 yì suppress

易 yì easy ◊ change; exchange

义 yì justice

议 yì discuss

亿 yì hundred million

艺 yì art; craft

译 yì translate

异 yì different; strange; foreign

议案 yì'àn bill POL

一百 yìbǎi one hundred

一百周年 yìbǎi zhōunián centenary, centennial

一般 yìbān ordinary, usual; mediocre ◊ usually, generally

一半 yíbàn half

一帮 yìbāng gang

易饱 yìbǎo stodgy

贻贝 yíbèi mussel

一辈子 yī bèizi one's whole life, a lifetime

一笔 yìbǐ brushstroke

一边 yìbiān aside

易变 yìbiàn unsettled

一边倒 yìbiān dǎo one-sided

易辨认 yìbiànrèn legible

仪表 yíbiǎo dial; dashboard

疑病症患者 yíbìngzhèng huàn zhě hypochondriac

易剥落 yì bōluò flaky

一波三折 yìbō sānzhé stormy *relationship*

一步 yíbù move (*in chess*)

一部分 yíbùfen part; portion; fragment

一层 yìcéng blanket (*of snow etc*)

易察觉 yì chájué visible

遗产 yíchǎn estate; legacy

异常 yìcháng exceptional; unusual ◊ exceptionally; unusually

一尘不染 yìchén bùrǎn spotless

议程 yìchéng agenda

一成不变 yì chéng búbiàn be very set in one's ways

易冲动 yì chōngdòng impulsive

溢出 yìchū overflow, run over; slop

遗传 yíchuán genetic; hereditary ◊ heredity ◊ pass on

遗传工程 yíchuán gōngchéng genetic engineering

遗传学 yíchuán xué genetics

遗传学家 yíchuán xuéjiā geneticist

一触即发 yíchù jífā simmer (with

rage)

易处理 **yì chǔlǐ** manageable

一次 **yīcì** once

依次 **yīcì** in turn

以此 **yǐcì** for this reason; consequently; hence; thereby

一次性 **yīcìxìng** disposable ◊ one-off

依从 **yīcóng** obey

意大利 **Yìdàlì** Italy ◊ Italian

一旦 **yídàn** ever; once

一当 **yīdāng** as soon as

一道来 **yīdàolái** come along, come too

胰岛素 **yídǎosù** insulin

一大早 **yīdàzǎo** at daybreak

一点 **yīdiǎn** a bit, a little; 一点水 **yīdiǎn shuǐ** a little water; 一点也不奇怪 **yīdiǎn yě bù qíguài** not in the least surprised; 好一点 **hǎo yīdiǎn** a little better; 一点一点 **yīdiǎn yīdiǎn** little by little, bit by bit

疑点 **yídiǎn** question mark

一点点 **yīdiǎndian** a little bit, not a lot ◊ vague *taste*; 我所知道的那一点点 **wǒ suǒ zhīdào de nà yīdiǎndian** the little I know

一点儿 **yìdiǎnr** a bit, a little

一定 **yídìng** definite, certain, sure ◊ definitely; certainly, surely

移动 **yídòng** move; shift; remove ◊ removal; cell phone; 缓慢移动 **huǎnmàn yídòng** edge, move slowly

一动不动 **yídòng búdòng** stand still

移动电话 **yídòng diànhuà** cellular phone

移动性 **yídòng xìng** mobility

易读 **yìdú** readable

一段 **yíduàn** length; passage, extract; period

一段时间 **yíduàn shíjiān** session; spell ◊ for a while

一对 **yíduì** couple; duo

一方 **yìfāng** side, team

已废弃 **yǐ fèiqì** obsolete

一份 **yífèn** helping; share

衣服 **yīfu** clothes, clothing

遗腹 **yífù** posthumous

姨父 **yífù** uncle (*mother's sister's husband*)

衣服架 **yīfújià** clothes hanger

一个 **yīgè** one ◊ single; 一个面包 **yīgè miànbāo** a loaf of bread; 一个挨着一个 **yīgè āizhe yīgè** side by side

一共 **yīgòng** altogether; 一共三个 **yígòng sān gè** three in all

义工 **yìgōng** volunteer

衣钩 **yīgōu** coat hook

一贯 **yīguàn** consistent

衣柜 **yīguì** closet

异国 **yìguó** foreign country

一国两制 **yīguó liǎngzhì** one country, two systems

遗憾 **yíhàn** sad ◊ regret; 遗憾 **yíhàn …** it's a pity that …; 令人遗憾 **lìngrén yíhàn** deplorable ◊ sadly

颐和园 **Yíhéyuán** Summer Palace

以后 **yǐhòu** later, afterward; in future; 从那以后 **cóng nà yǐhòu** ever since

易坏 **yìhuài** perishable

议会 **yìhuì** council; assembly; parliament ◊ parliamentary

一会儿 **yíhuìr** a while; 我再等一会儿 **wǒ zài děng yíhuìr** I'll wait a while longer; 一会见！ **yíhuìr jiàn!** see you later!

已婚 **yǐhūn** married

一伙人 **yīhuǒ rén** crowd, set

异乎寻常 **yì hū xúncháng** uncanny

遗迹 **yíjì** vestige

以及 **yǐjí** and

衣架 **yījià** coathanger

意见 **yìjiàn** opinion; suggestion; complaint; 你有什么意见？ **nǐ yǒu shénme yìjiàn?** what's your opinion?

意见分歧 **yìjiàn fēnqí** dissension

意见相左 **yìjiàn xiāngzuǒ** disagree, differ

移交 **yíjiāo** hand over

异教徒 **yìjiàotú** heathen

易激动 **yì jīdòng** temperamental

已经 **yǐjīng** already; 已经晚了 **yǐjīng wǎn le** it's getting late

易经 **Yìjīng** I-Ching, Book of

Changes
一经要求 **yījīng yāoqiú** on request
以旧换新 **yǐ jiù huàn xīn** trade in
依据 **yījù** basis; grounds
移居 **yíjū** immigrate
移居国外 **yíjū guówài** emigrate ◊ emigration
移开 **yíkāi** move away
一开始 **yīkāishǐ** from the start
一开头 **yīkāitóu** from the outset
依靠 **yīkào** rely on ◊ reliance; 依靠 X 去做 Y **yīkào X qùzuò Y** rely on X to do Y; 依靠自己 **yīkào zìjǐ** self-reliant
倚靠 **yǐkào** lean against
一刻钟 **yīkèzhōng** quarter of an hour
一口 **yīkǒu** bite, mouthful
一口气地说 **yìkǒuqìde shuō** rattle off *poem, list of names*
依赖 **yīlài** depend on ◊ dependent ◊ dependence, dependency
伊拉克 **Yīlākè** Iraq ◊ Iraqi
一览表 **yīlánbiǎo** list
伊朗 **Yīlǎng** Iran ◊ Iranian
依恋 **yīliàn** be attached to, be fond of
一连串 **yīliánchuàn** stream, string, succession
医疗 **yīliáo** medical; therapeutic ◊ (medical) care
医疗保险 **yīliáo bǎoxiǎn** health insurance
一流 **yīliú** first-class, first-rate
遗留 **yíliú** leave behind; bequeath
一楼 **yīlóu** first floor, ground floor *Br*
遗漏 **yílòu** omit ◊ omission
一律 **yīlǜ** without exception
疑虑重重 **yílǜ chóngchong** tormented by doubt
一路平安 **yīlù píng'ān** have a good journey
译码 **yìmǎ** decode
衣帽间 **yīmào jiān** checkroom (*for coats*)
疫苗 **yìmiáo** vaccine
移民 **yímín** immigrate; emigrate ◊ immigrant; emigrant; immigration; emigration

移民局 **Yímínjú** Department of Immigration
一模一样 **yìmú yíyàng** identical
音 **yīn** sound; tone
因 **yīn** because ◊ reason
阴 **yīn** yin; shade; private parts ◊ overcast; 天阴了 **tiānyīnle** cloud over
银 **yín** silver
淫 **yín** lewd
瘾 **yǐn** addiction; 有 X 的瘾 **yǒu X de yǐn** be addicted to X
引 **yǐn** draw, attract
隐 **yǐn** hide
饮 **yǐn** drink
印 **yìn** print ◊ stamp
疑难 **yínàn** problematic
阴暗 **yīn'àn** gloomy; dark ◊ gloom
引爆装置 **yǐnbào zhuāngzhì** detonator, igniter
音标 **yīnbiāo** phonetics
隐藏 **yǐncáng** hide, conceal; bury ◊ hidden
阴沉 **yīnchén** threatening, overcast, dull
印出 **yìnchū** print out
印戳 **yìnchuō** stamp
因此 **yīncǐ** so; therefore; consequently; thus
阴道 **yīndào** vagina ◊ vaginal
引导 **yǐndǎo** lead, guide; educate; direct
印第安人 **Yìndì'ān rén** Indian (*Native American*)
音调 **yīndiào** note; pitch; tone; 调准音调 **tiáo zhǔn yīndiào** tune
音调悦耳 **yīndiào yuè'ěr** tuneful
引渡 **yǐndù** extradite ◊ extradition
印度 **Yìndù** India ◊ Indian
引渡公约 **yǐndù gōngyuē** extradition treaty
印度尼西亚 **Yìndùníxīyà** Indonesia ◊ Indonesian
印度人 **Yìndùrén** Indian
印度洋 **Yìndùyáng** Indian Ocean
印度支那 **Yìndùzhīnà** Indochina ◊ Indochinese
音符 **yīnfú** note
鹰 **yīng** eagle
应 **yīng** should, ought to
婴 **yīng** infant, baby

樱 **yīng** cherry
营 **yíng** camp
赢 **yíng** win; beat
迎 **yíng** welcome; meet
影 **yǐng** shadow; image
硬 **yìng** hard
应 **yìng** respond, reply; deal with; adapt to
英镑 **yīngbàng** (pound) sterling
硬邦邦 **yìng bāngbang** solid; stiff
硬币 **yìngbì** coin
迎宾员 **yíngbīn yuán** usher
应承 **yìngchéng** promise
硬扯入 **yìngchě rù** drag in; mention
英尺 **yīngchǐ** foot
英寸 **yīngcùn** inch
应得 **yìngdé** deserve; earn ◊ well-earned
赢得 **yíngdé** gain, earn; win
营地 **yíngdì** campsite
硬度 **yìngdù** hardness
婴儿 **yīng'ér** baby, infant
婴儿车 **yīng'ér chē** baby carriage, buggy
婴儿期 **yīng'ér qī** infancy, babyhood
营房 **yíngfáng** quarters, barracks
应付 **yìngfù** manage, cope; cope with
应该 **yīnggāi** should, ought to
英格兰 **Yīnggélán** England
英国 **Yīngguó** United Kingdom; Britain; England ◊ British; English; Brit
迎合 **yínghe** cater for
樱花树 **yīnghuā shù** cherry tree
营火 **yínghuǒ** bonfire
影集 **yǐngjí** photo album
硬挤 **yìngjǐ** hustle, hurry along
硬件 **yìngjiàn** hardware COMPUT
迎接 **yíngjiē** greet, welcome
应接不暇 **yìngjiē bùxiá** be swamped with
英俊 **yīngjùn** handsome, cute (male)
应考人 **yìngkǎo rén** (exam) candidate
盈亏平衡点 **yíngkuī pínghéng diǎn** break-even point
硬拉 **yìnglā** drag

英里 **yīnglǐ** mile
盈利 **yínglì** profit; surplus
英明 **yīngmíng** brilliant; wise
英亩 **yīngmǔ** acre
因公 **yīngōng** on business
硬盘 **yìngpán** hard disk
硬皮书 **yìngpíshū** hardback
萦绕于心 **yíngrào yú xīn** haunting
影射 **yǐngshè** allude to
应试者 **yìngshì zhě** interviewee
应受指摘 **yìngshòu zhǐzhāi** reprehensible
硬刷子 **yìngshuāzi** scrubbing brush
罂粟 **yīngsù** poppy
鹰隼 **yīngsǔn** hawk
樱桃 **yīngtáo** cherry (fruit)
硬通货 **yìngtōnghuò** hard currency
硬卧 **yìngwò** hard sleeper (on train)
鹦鹉 **yīngwǔ** parrot
影响 **yǐngxiǎng** influence; impact ◊ influence; affect
影响力 **yǐngxiǎnglì** influence; impact
硬行推销 **yìngxíng tuīxiāo** hard sell
英雄 **yīngxióng** hero
营养 **yíngyǎng** nourishment; nutrition
营养不良 **yíngyǎng bùliáng** malnutrition
营养搭配好 **yíngyǎng dāpèihǎo** well-balanced diet
营养品 **yíngyǎng pǐn** nutrient
硬要 **yìngyào** impose (oneself)
营业经理 **yíngyè jīnglǐ** sales manager
营业时间 **yíngyè shíjiān** business hours
影印 **yǐngyìn** photocopy
影印本 **yǐngyìn běn** photocopy
影印机 **yǐngyìn jī** photocopier
英勇 **yīngyǒng** heroic
应用 **yìngyòng** use; apply ◊ applied
英勇事迹 **yīngyǒng shìjì** exploit, deed
英语 **Yīngyǔ** English (language)

应征 **yìngzhēng** join the army
应征入伍者 **yìngzhēng rùwǔ zhě** draftee
硬纸板 **yìng zhǐbǎn** cardboard
应支付 **yīng zhīfù** payable, due
影子 **yǐngzi** shadow
硬座 **yìngzuò** hard seat (*on train*)
银行 **yínháng** bank FIN
银行贷款 **yínháng dàikuǎn** bank loan
银行家 **yínháng jiā** banker
银行结存 **yínháng jiécún** bank balance
银行结单 **yínháng jiédān** bank statement
银行经理 **yínháng jīnglǐ** bank manager
银行利率 **yínháng lìlǜ** bank rate
银行信用卡 **yínháng xìnyòng kǎ** banker's card
银行帐户 **yínháng zhànghù** bank account
引号 **yǐnhào** quotation mark
淫秽 **yínhuì** obscene; bawdy
银婚 **yínhūn** silver wedding (anniversary)
阴间 **yīnjiān** underworld (*in mythology*)
音阶 **yīnjiē** scale MUS
音节 **yīnjié** syllable
引进 **yǐnjìn** introduce, bring in ◊ introduction
阴茎 **yīnjīng** penis
饮酒者 **yǐnjiǔ zhě** drinker
隐居处 **yǐnjū chù** retreat
阴凉 **yīnliáng** shady
音量 **yīnliàng** volume (*of radio etc*)
阴凉处 **yīnliáng chù** in the shade
音量调控 **yīnliàng tiáokòng** volume control
饮料 **yǐnliào** drink
引路 **yǐnlù** lead the way
淫乱 **yínluàn** indecent, obscene
隐瞒 **yǐnmán** conceal, cover up; disguise
阴毛 **yīnmáo** pubic hair
隐没 **yǐnmò** go in
阴谋 **yīnmóu** conspiracy, plot
阴谋者 **yīnmóu zhě** plotter
银幕 **yínmù** screen
银牌 **yínpái** silver medal

引起 **yǐnqǐ** cause; produce; inspire; arouse; 引起 X 的注意 **yǐnqǐ X de zhùyì** catch X's eye
姻亲 **yīnqīn** in-laws
引擎 **yǐnqíng** engine
引人反感 **yǐn rén fǎngǎn** obnoxious
引人入胜 **yǐn rén rù shèng** compelling
引人注目 **yǐn rén zhùmù** stand out; attract attention ◊ spectacular; striking
阴森森 **yīn sēnsēn** spooky
隐士 **yǐnshì** recluse
印刷 **yìnshuā** print
印刷厂 **yìnshuā chǎng** printing works, press
印刷机 **yìnshuā jī** printing press
印刷品 **yìnshuā pǐn** printed matter
印刷商 **yìnshuā shāng** printer
印刷字体 **yìnshuā zìtǐ** print
饮水 **yǐnshuǐ** water *animals*
因素 **yīnsù** ingredient, factor
因特网 **yīntèwǎng** Internet
阴天 **yīntiān** cloudy
引退 **yǐntuì** resign, step down
易怒 **yìnù** fiery; irritable; snappy
因为 **yīnwèi** because, since ◊ on account of
淫猥 **yínwěi** lewd
引文 **yǐnwén** quotation, quote
阴险 **yīnxiǎn** devious; insidious ◊ deviously; insidiously
音箱 **yīnxiāng** speaker (*of sound system*)
音响 **yīnxiǎng** acoustics; stereo
印象 **yìnxiàng** impression
印象深刻 **yìnxiàng shēnkè** impressive
阴性 **yīnxìng** feminine GRAM; negative *test results*
隐形眼镜 **yǐnxíng yǎnjìng** contact lens
音译 **yīnyì** transliterate
引用 **yǐnyòng** quote
饮用水 **yǐnyòng shuǐ** drinking water
引诱 **yǐnyòu** seduce ◊ seduction
音域 **yīnyù** (vocal) range

音乐 yīnyuè music ◊ musical
音乐会 yīnyuè huì concert
音乐家 yīnyuè jiā musician
音乐片 yīnyuè piān musical (*movie*)
音乐学院 yīnyuè xuéyuàn conservatory, music school
印章 yìnzhāng stamp, seal (*on document*)
引证 yǐnzhèng cite
银制 yínzhì silver
银质 yínzhì silver
印子 yìnzi imprint, impression
一瞥 yìpiē glance, glimpse
一起 yìqǐ together; along; 和 … 一起 *hé … yìqǐ* with
仪器 yíqì apparatus; instrument
遗弃 yíqì jilt; walk out on
以前 yǐqián before; formerly, previously ◊ former, past; 以前干过吗? *yǐqián gàn guò ma?* have you done this before?; 他不再和以前一样了 *tā búzài hé yǐqián yíyàng le* he's not the same any more
一千 yìqiān one thousand
千年 yìqiānnián millennium
一切 yíqiè everything; all; 一切包括在内 *yíqiè bāokuò zàinèi* inclusive
一期付款 yìqī fùkuǎn installment
意气消沉 yìqì xiāochén despondent
一群 yìqún flock
意趣相投 yìqù xiāngtóu be on the same wavelength
易燃 yìrán combustible, inflammable
易燃烧 yì ránshāo flammable
一日游 yìrìyóu daytrip
以色列 Yǐsèliè Israel ◊ Israeli
医生 yīshēng doctor
一生 yìshēng one's whole life, a lifetime
一声不吭 yìshēng būkēng stay silent
一时 yìshí a while, a moment
遗失 yíshī lose; mislay
仪式 yíshì ceremony; ritual
意识 yìshí awareness, consciousness; 意识不到 … *yìshí búdào*

… be oblivious of; 意识到 *yìshí dào* be aware of, realize; 我现在才意识到 … *wǒ xiànzài cái yìshí dào* … I realize now that …
意识形态 yìshí xíngtài ideology ◊ ideological
艺术 yìshù art ◊ artistic
艺术家 yìshù jiā artist
艺术界 yìshù jiè the arts
艺术品 yìshù pǐn work of art
意思 yìsi meaning, sense; interest; 你什么意思? *nǐ shénme yìsi?* what are you driving at?
一丝不苟 yìsī bùgǒu scrupulous
一丝不挂 yìsī búguà stark naked
伊斯兰教 Yīsīlánjiào Islam ◊ Islamic
遗俗 yísú relic
易碎 yìsuì fragile; brittle
遗体 yítǐ remains
一天 yìtiān one day
意图 yìtú intention
一团 yìtuán jumble
一团糟 yìtuánzāo be a mess ◊ tangle
意外 yìwài accidental; unexpected ◊ by chance; unexpectedly
意外发现 yìwài fāxiàn stumble across
遗忘 yíwàng oblivion ◊ leave behind
意味 yìwèi signify ◊ significance
意味深长 yìwèi shēncháng meaningful
疑问 yíwèn doubt; query; interrogative GRAM
译文 yìwén translation
一文不名 yìwén bùmíng penniless
衣物 yīwù laundry, washing ◊ wardrobe, clothes
遗物 yíwù relic
义务 yìwù obligation, duty ◊ voluntary *work*
义务教育 yìwù jiàoyù compulsory education
一无所有 yìwú suǒyǒu zilch
以下 yǐxià under; following; 十岁以下 *shí suì yǐxià* under ten years of age; 读以下说明 *dú yǐxià shuōmíng* read the following

instructions

异想天开! **yìxiǎng tiānkāi!** it boggles the mind!

一向 **yíxiàng** always; till now, so far; 一向准时 *yíxiàng zhǔnshì* have a good record for punctuality

一小袋 **yìxiǎodài** sachet

一小口 **yìxiǎokǒu** sip

一小片 **yìxiǎopiàn** morsel

一下子 **yíxiàzi** all at once; in one shot

一些 **yìxiē** some, a few

一系列 **yíxìliè** succession, series

疑心 **yíxīn** suspicion; 对 X 有疑心 *duì X yǒu yíxīn* be suspicious of X

异性爱 **yìxìng'ài** heterosexual

易兴奋 **yìxīngfèn** excitable

医学 **yīxué** medicine ◊ medical

以牙还牙 **yǐyá huányá** an eye for an eye; tit for tat

一眼 **yìyǎn** peek

一样 **yíyàng** just as; just the same; 和 … 一样高 *hé … yíyàng gāo* as high as …; 看起来一样 *kànqǐlái yíyàng* look the same

一氧化碳 **yīyǎng huàtàn** carbon monoxide

一言为定 **yī yán wéi dìng** it's a deal

一言以蔽之 **yìyán yǐ bìzhī** in a nutshell

一一 **yīyī** one by one

意义 **yìyì** meaning, sense; point, purpose

异议 **yìyì** objection

一饮而尽 **yìyǐn ěr jìn** gulp down

易于 … **yìyú …** be apt to …

医院 **yīyuàn** hospital, infirmary

议员 **yìyuán** representative; congressman

译员 **yìyuán** interpreter

意愿 **yìyuàn** wish; inclination

一月 **yīyuè** January

依仗 **yīzhàng** count on

译者 **yìzhě** translator

一针 **yìzhēn** stitch

一直 **yìzhí** all the time, all along

遗植 **yízhí** transplant; graft

遗址 **yízhǐ** ruin

一致 **yízhì** uniform, identical; unanimous ◊ uniformly; unanimously

意指 **yìzhǐ** mean

抑制 **yìzhì** check, restrain; refrain

意志 **yìzhì** will, willpower

意志力 **yìzhìlì** willpower

一致同意 **yízhì tóngyì** unanimous

一致性 **yízhì xìng** consistency; correspondence

一致意见 **yízhì yìjiàn** consensus

以至于 **yǐzhìyú** so that

遗嘱 **yízhǔ** legacy; will

衣着 **yīzhuó** clothes; 衣着不整 *yīzhuó bùzhěng* sloppily dressed; 衣着整洁 *yīzhuó zhěngjié* well-dressed

椅子 **yǐzi** chair

易醉 **yìzuì** heady *drink, wine etc*

异族通婚 **yìzú tōnghūn** mixed marriage

拥 **yōng** embrace; crowd

永 **yǒng** for ever

涌 **yǒng** surge

勇 **yǒng** brave

用 **yòng** use; apply ◊ with; 用早餐 *yòng zǎocān* have breakfast; 用电子邮件寄 *yòng diànzǐ yóujiàn jì* send by e-mail

拥抱 **yōngbào** cuddle; embrace; hug

用餐 **yòngcān** dine

涌出 **yǒngchū** gush, pour

用处 **yòngchù** usefulness

用错 **yòngcuò** misuse

用法 **yòngfǎ** directions; usage

用费 **yòngfèi** expenses

勇敢 **yǒnggǎn** brave, courageous, valiant ◊ bravely ◊ bravery

用光 **yòngguāng** use up, run out of

永恒 **yǒnghéng** eternal ◊ eternity

拥护 **yōnghù** welcome

用户 **yònghù** user; consumer

用坏 **yònghuài** wear out ◊ wear

用户友好 **yònghù yǒuhǎo** user-friendly

拥护者 **yōnghù zhě** supporter, sympathizer

拥挤 **yōngjǐ** crowd; jostle ◊ crowded, packed

拥挤的人群 **yōngjǐ de rénqún** crush

涌进 **yǒngjìn** surge forward

佣金 **yòngjīn** commission

用尽 **yòngjìn** exhaust, use up

永久 **yǒngjiǔ** permanent, everlasting

用具 **yòngjù** equipment, gear, tackle; utensil

用力 **yònglì** vigorous ◊ exert oneself; 用力打开 **yònglì dǎkāi** force door; 用力举起 **yònglì jǔqǐ** heave

用量 **yòngliàng** dose, dosage

勇气 **yǒngqì** courage, nerve; spirit

佣人 **yōngrén** servant

勇士 **yǒngshì** tough guy

用途 **yòngtú** use, purpose

用过 **yòngguò** used

用完 **yòngwán** run out; run out of; use up

勇往直前 **yǒng wǎng zhí qián** carry on undaunted

拥有 **yōngyǒu** own; keep

拥有者 **yōngyǒu zhě** owner

永远 **yǒngyuǎn** for ever, eternally; 他永远不会厌倦 **ta yǒngyuǎn búhuì yànjuàn** he never tires of it

忧 **yōu** worry ◊ worried

优 **yōu** excellent, very good

幽 **yōu** secluded; peaceful

油 **yōu** oil; fat; grease

铀 **yóu** uranium

疣 **yóu** wart

游 **yóu** travel; float; swim

由 **yóu** from; 由此发生 … **yóucǐ fāshēng** … it follows from this that …; 由 … 主演 **yóu … zhǔyǎn** feature; 由 … 组成 **yóu … zǔchéng** be comprised of …

邮寄 **yóu** mail; 把 X 邮给 Y **bǎ X yóu gěi Y** send X to Y

有 **yǒu** have, have got; there is; there are ◊ (*forming adjectival constructions*): 有空调 **yǒu kōngtiáo** air-conditioned; 有经验 **yǒu jīngyàn** experienced

友 **yǒu** friend

右 **yòu** right ◊ on the right

又 **yòu** again

幼 **yòu** child ◊ young

诱 **yòu** seduce, lure; guide; lead

呦，呦！ **yōu, yōu!** well, well!

又 … 又 … **yòu … yòu …** both …

and …

幽暗 **yōu'àn** dark

有帮助 **yǒu bāngzhù** helpful

有边握 **yǒu bǎwò** safely ◊ self-assured

油泵 **yóubèng** gas pump

右边 **yòubiān** right-hand

有别于 **yǒubiéyú** differ from

幽闭恐怖症 **yōubì kǒngbù zhèng** claustrophobia

有病 **yǒubìng** ill

有必要时 **yǒu bìyào shí** as necessary

油布 **yóubù** tarpaulin

又不 **yòubù** nor

油菜 **yóucài** rape; rapeseed oil, canola

有才华 **yǒu cáihuá** brilliant

有才能 **yǒu cáinéng** accomplished

有偿雇佣 **yǒucháng gùyōng** paid employment

有成效 **yǒu chéngxiào** productive

幼虫 **yòuchóng** larva

忧愁 **yōuchóu** sad; gloomy ◊ sadness

有臭味 **yǒu chòuwèi** smell ◊ smelly

油船 **yóuchuán** (oil) tanker

邮戳 **yóuchuō** postmark

虚弱 **yóu chùtòng** tender

由此 **yóucǐ** from this

有刺铁丝网 **yǒucì tiěsī wǎng** barbed wire

优待 **yōudài** favor, special treatment

邮递 **yóudì** mail delivery

优点 **yōudiǎn** merit, strength

有点 **yǒudiǎn** a bit, a little

有颠覆性 **yǒu diānfù xìng** subversive

有点儿 **yǒudiǎnr** a bit, a little; 有点儿难过 **yǒudiǎnr nánguò** a bit sad, kind of sad

邮递员 **yóudì yuán** mailman

有毒 **yǒudú** poisonous, toxic

有毒瘾者 **yǒu dúyǐn zhě** junkie

诱饵 **yòu'ěr** bait; decoy

幼儿 **yòu'ér** small child, infant

幼儿学校 **yòu'ér xuéxiào**

kindergarten

幼儿圆 **yòu'éryuán** kindergarten

幼儿园老师 **yòu'éryuán lǎoshī** kindergarten teacher

有感染力 **yǒu gǎnrǎn lì** catching

有根据 **yǒu gēnjù** valid

有关 **yǒuguān** concerned, relevant, pertinent ◊ concerning, re

有关系 **yǒu guānxì** connect

有轨电车 **yǒuguǐ diànchē** streetcar

有规律 **yǒu guīlǜ** regular, steady ◊ regularly

有害 **yǒuhài** harmful; mischievous

有害元素 **yǒuhài yuánsù** harmful substance

友好 **yǒuhǎo** friendly, neighborly; kind ◊ goodwill

黝黑 **yǒuhēi** swarthy

油画 **yóuhuà** oil painting

油画布 **yóuhuà bù** canvas

有怀疑 **yǒu huáiyí** dubious

油灰 **yóuhuī** putty

邮汇 **yóuhuì** money order

诱惑 **yòuhuò** lure, entice ◊ alluring ◊ temptation

有活力 **yǒu huólì** perky, cheerful

邮寄 **yóujì** send

有机 **yǒujī** organic ◊ organically

又及 **yòují** PS, postscript

邮件 **yóujiàn** mail

有价证券 **yǒujià zhèngquàn** bond, security

有价值 **yǒu jiàzhí** valuable

游击队 **yóujīduì** guerrilla

有结余 **yǒu jiéyú** in the black

有技能 **yǒu jìnéng** skilled

幽静 **yōujìng** sleepy *town*

油井 **yóujǐng** oil rig, oil well

有经验 **yǒu jīngyàn** experienced, seasoned

有竞争力 **yǒu jìngzhēng lì** competitive

有进取心 **yǒu jìnqǔxīn** enterprising, go-ahead

有技巧 **yǒu jìqiǎo** professional

邮寄 **yóujì** mail, send

邮寄人 **yóujì rén** sender

邮局 **yóujú** post office

游客 **yóukè** visitor

有可能 **yǒu kěnéng** possibly;

potentially ◊ be liable to

有空 **yǒu kōng** have time; be available; 有空吗？ **yǒu kōng ma?** can you spare the time?; 有空时 **yǒu kōng shí** at your leisure

有愧 **yǒukuì** guilt

有困难 **yǒu kùnnán** in need

由来 **yóulái** origin

游览 **yóulǎn** visit; tour; go sightseeing; 游览全中国 **yóulǎn quán Zhōngguó** travel all over China

游廊 **yóuláng** veranda

有了 **yǒule** pregnant ◊ be expecting

游乐场 **yóulè chǎng** amusement park

游乐园 **yóulè yuán** amusement park

有理 **yǒulǐ** reasonable; rational; in the right

有利 **yǒulì** advantageous; favorable

有立法权 **yǒu lìfǎ quán** legislative

有礼貌 **yǒu lǐmào** respectful, polite, courteous, civil ◊ respectfully

幽灵 **yōulíng** vision

有利润 **yǒu lìrùn** be profitable, pay ◊ remunerative

有理由 **yǒu lǐyóu** justifiable

忧虑 **yōulǜ** worry, care ◊ worried; distracted

有逻辑 **yǒu luójí** logical

有毛病 **yǒu máobìng** faulty

优美 **yōuměi** lovely; graceful; dainty ◊ grace

有魅力 **yǒu mèilì** glamorous; attractive; magnetic

霉味儿 **yǒu méiwèir** musty

有没有 … ？ **yǒuméiyǒu …?** is there …?; are there …?

油门 **yóumén** accelerator

右面 **yòumiàn** right-hand side

游民 **yóumín** hobo

有名生 **yǒu míngshēng** reputable

幽默 **yōumò** humor

幽默感 **yōumò gǎn** sense of

humor

柚木 yòumù teak

有耐心 yǒu nàixīn patient

有那么点儿 ... yǒu nàme diǎnr ... sort of ...

有男性 yǒu nánxìng virile

有男子气 yǒu nánzǐqì manly

有能力 yǒu nénglì able ◊ be capable of

油腻 yóunì greasy, oily; rich, heavy

幼年童子军 yòunián tóngzǐjūn Brownie

有粘性 yǒu niánxìng adhesive

有泥浆 yǒu níjiāng slimy

右派 yòupài right; right-winger

邮票 yóupiào stamp

右撇子 yòu piě zi right-handed

有蹼的脚 yǒu pǔ de jiǎo webbed feet

尤其 yóuqí especially, in particular

有钱 yǒuqián rich

有前途 yǒu qiántú promising

有气泡 yǒu qìpào effervescent

有趣 yǒuqù fun, amusing, entertaining; interesting

有权威性 yǒu quánwēi xìng authoritative

有缺陷 yǒu quēxiàn defective

有人 yǒurén someone, somebody ◊ occupied; 有人敲门 yǒurén qiāomén there's someone at the door

诱人 yòurén seductive, tantalizing

友善 yǒushàn amicable

忧伤 yōushāng sorrow

有生命危险 yǒu shēngmìng wēixiǎn life-threatening

优势 yōushì superiority

有事 yǒu shì have on; 你今晚有事吗？ nǐ jīnwǎn yǒushì ma? do you have anything on for tonight?

有时 yǒushí sometimes, now and again

优势和劣势 yōushì hé lièshì the pros and cons

有施虐狂 yǒu shīnüèkuáng sadistic

有失体面 yǒushī tǐmiàn disgraceful

有失体统 yǒu shī tǐtǒng offensive

有诗意 yǒu shīyì poetic

有适应力 yǒu shìyìng lì adaptable

有售 yǒushòu be on sale

幼兽 yòushòu cub

游手好闲 yóushǒu hàoxián loaf around

又瘦又高 yòushòu yòugāo lanky

有说服力 yǒu shuōfúlì forceful, persuasive

有锁柜 yǒu suǒguì locker

油台 yóutái drilling rig

犹太 Yóutài Jewish

犹太人 Yóutài rén Jew

有弹性 yǒu tánxìng springy, elastic; supple

有特异功能 yǒu tèyì gōngnéng psychic

油田 yóutián oil field

有天才 yǒu tiāncái talented

有天赋 yǒu tiānfù gifted

有条不紊 yǒutiáo bùwěn methodical ◊ methodically

有条件 yǒu tiáojiàn conditional

有条理 yǒu tiáolǐ systematic, methodical ◊ systematically

有条纹 yǒu tiáowén striped

有挑战性 yǒu tiǎozhàn xìng challenging

游艇 yóutǐng yacht

游艇驾驶员 yóutǐng jiàshǐ yuán yachtsman

游艇停泊港 yóutǐng tíngbó gǎng marina

邮筒 yóutǒng mailbox

有同情心 yǒu tóngqíng xīn compassionate

有投票权者 yǒu tóupiào quán zhě voter

有图案 yǒu tú'àn patterned

有威望 yǒu wēiwàng prestigious

有威胁性 yǒu wēixié xìng threatening

有文化 yǒu wénhuà be literate

游戏 yóuxì play; game

优先 yōuxiān preferential, priority ◊ take precedence, take priority

悠闲 yōuxián laidback

有限 yǒuxiàn limited

右舷 yòuxián starboard

有线电视 yǒuxiàn diànshì cable

TV

有限度 **yǒu xiàndù** qualified

邮箱 **yóuxiāng** mailbox

有香味 **yǒu xiāngwèi** fragrant

有想像力 **yǒu xiǎngxiàng lì** imaginative

有象征性 **yǒu xiàngzhēng xìng** symbolic

优先权 **yōuxiān quán** priority; 有优先权 **yǒu yōuxiān quán** have priority

优先行驶权 **yōuxiān xíngshǐ quán** right of way

有嫌疑 **yǒu xiányí** alleged

有效 **yǒuxiào** valid; effective

幼小动物 **yòuxiǎo dòngwù** pup

有效率 **yǒu xiàolǜ** efficient ◊ efficiently

游戏场 **yóuxì chǎng** playground

有些 **yǒuxiē** some; 有些人说 ... **yǒuxiē rén shuō ...** some people say that ...

忧心忡忡 **yōuxīn chóngchóng** careworn, sad

游行 **yóuxíng** march, parade

有兴趣 **yǒu xìngqù** interested

有兴致 **yǒu xìngzhì** be in the mood for

有信心 **yǒu xìnxīn** assured

有吸收能力 **yǒu xīshōu nénglì** absorbent

优秀 **yōuxiù** excellent ◊ excellence

有修养 **yǒu xiūyǎng** cultivated, cultured; cultural

有希望 **yǒu xīwàng** hopeful

有吸引力 **yǒu xīyǐn lì** attractive; charming; seductive

优雅 **yōuyǎ** graceful ◊ lightness ◊ beautifully

油烟 **yóuyān** soot

有眼力 **yǒu yǎnlì** discerning, discriminating

有烟嘴 **yǒu yānzuǐ** tipped *cigarettes*

有药性 **yǒu yàoxìng** medicinal

有益 **yǒuyì** beneficial; useful; advantageous; expedient

友谊 **yǒuyì** friendship

有意 **yǒuyì** intend ◊ intentional, conscious ◊ intentionally, deliberately; 我有意移民 **wǒ**

有意移民 **yǒuyì yímín** I'm thinking about emigrating; 有意为 X 准备 **yǒuyì wèi X zhǔnbèi** be meant for X

右翼 **yòuyì** right wing

又一次 **yòu yīcì** once again, once more

又一个 **yòu yígè** another

有益健康 **yǒuyì jiànkāng** healthy

有影响 **yǒu yǐngxiǎng** influential

有营养 **yǒu yíngyǎng** nourishing, nutritious

友谊商店 **Yǒuyì Shāngdiàn** Friendship Store

友谊市 **yǒuyì shì** twin town

有艺术性 **yǒu yìshù xìng** artistic

有意思 **yǒu yìsi** interesting, intriguing; significant

有一天 **yǒu yītiān** one day

有意误导 X **yǒuyì wùdǎo X** string X along

有疑心 **yǒu yíxīn** suspicious

有意义 **yǒu yìyì** meaningful

游泳 **yóuyǒng** swim ◊ swimming

有用 **yǒuyòng** useful

游泳池 **yóuyǒng chí** swimming pool; 室外游泳池 **shìwài yóuyǒng chí** open-air swimming pool

游泳裤 **yóuyǒng kù** swimsuit

游泳衣 **yóuyǒng yī** swimsuit

游泳者 **yóuyǒng zhě** swimmer

忧郁 **yōuyù** gloom ◊ glum; melancholy, depressed

鱿鱼 **yóuyú** squid

由于 **yóuyú** with; through ◊ because of, due to

犹豫 **yóuyù** hesitate ◊ hesitation ◊ tentative; 犹豫不决 **yóuyù bù jué** be indecisive; 犹豫不定 **yóuyù búdìng** be indecisive; 对 X 犹豫不定 **duì X yóuyù búdìng** be undecided about X

优越 **yōuyuè** superior

有余额 **yǒu yú'é** be in credit

忧郁症 **yōuyù zhèng** depression

油炸 **yóuzhá** (deep-)fry

有战斗性 **yǒu zhàndòu xìng** militant

有朝一日 **yǒuzhāo yīrì** someday

悠着点儿! **yōu zhe diǎnr!** steady on!

有哲理 **yǒu zhélǐ** philosophical

邮政 **yóuzhèng** mail

邮政编码 **yóuzhèng biānmǎ** zip code

邮政信箱 **yóuzhèng xìnxiāng** P.O. Box

有争议 **yǒu zhēngyì** controversial

优质 **yōuzhì** high-grade

幼稚 **yòuzhì** childish, juvenile; naive ◊ childishness; child

油脂 **yóuzhī** oil; grease; fat

有志向 **yǒu zhìxiàng** ambitious

有秩序 **yǒu zhìxù** orderly

邮资 **yóuzī** postage

柚子 **yòuzi** pomelo

有资格 **yǒuzīgé** entitled

有罪 **yǒuzuì** guilt ◊ guilty

油嘴滑舌 **yóuzuǐ huáshé** glib

有尊严 **yǒu zūnyán** dignified

右座方向盘 **yòuzuò fāngxiàngpán** right-hand drive

鱼 **yú** fish

于 **yú** to; at; in; from

愚 **yú** stupid

渔 **yú** fishing

与 **yǔ** and; with; 与 … 有关系 **yǔ … yǒuguānxì** in connection with …; 与 X 不同 **yǔ X bùtóng** different from X; 与 X 断绝关系 **yǔ X duànjué guānxi** finish with X

雨 **yǔ** rain; 下着雨呢 **xià zhe yǔ ne** it's raining

语 **yǔ** language ◊ *used to form language names*; 西藏语 **Xīzàng yǔ** Tibetan

羽 **yǔ** feather

玉 **yù** jade

郁 **yù** luxuriant

遇 **yù** meet, encounter

浴 **yù** bath

欲 **yù** desire

愈 **yù** over, more than; 愈快愈好 **yù kuài yù hǎo** the faster the better

预 **yù** beforehand

圆 **yuán** round ◊ circle

元 **yuán** yuan (*Chinese money*)

园 **yuán** garden

原 **yuán** original

远 **yuán** far; distant; 三英里远 **sān yīnglǐ yuǎn** it's three miles off

愿 **yuàn** wish

院 **yuàn** institute

渊博 **yuānbó** vast; high-powered

原材料 **yuán cáiliào** raw materials

元朝 **Yuán Cháo** Yuan Dynasty

远程 **yuǎnchéng** long-range

远处 **yuǎnchù** distant place; 在远处 **zài yuǎnchù** in the distance

元旦 **Yuándàn** New Year's Day

园丁 **yuándīng** gardener

圆顶 **yuándǐng** dome

原定 **yuándìng** default COMPUT

远东 **Yuǎndōng** Far East

缘分 **yuánfèn** destiny

原告 **yuángào** claimant, plaintiff

原告方 **yuángàofāng** prosecution

怨恨 **yuànhèn** grudge

圆滑 **yuánhuá** slick, smooth

元件 **yuánjiàn** unit

远见 **yuǎnjiàn** vision, far-sightedness

援救 **yuánjiù** rescue

援救队 **yuánjiù duì** rescue party

远距离 **yuǎn jùlí** long-distance

援军 **yuánjūn** reinforcements

原来 **yuánlái** original ◊ originally; actually; 原来你在这儿 **yuánlái nǐ zài zhèr** there you are (*finding somebody*)

原谅 **yuánliàng** forgive, excuse, pardon ◊ forgiveness; 请原谅 **qǐng yuánliàng** I beg your pardon

原料 **yuánliào** raw material; ingredient

圆领衫 **yuánlǐng shān** T-shirt

园林师 **yuánlínshī** gardener

圆明园 **Yuánmíngyuán** Old Summer Palace

圆木 **yuánmù** log

圆盘 **yuánpán** disk

圆圈 **yuánquān** circle, ring

原始 **yuánshǐ** primitive

远视 **yuǎnshì** long-sighted, far-sighted

元素 **yuánsù** element CHEM

源头 **yuántóu** source

愿望 **yuànwàng** wish, desire

鸢尾属植物 **yuānwěishǔ zhíwù** iris (*flower*)

原文 **yuánwén** original text

原先 **yuánxiān** originally

元宵节 **Yuánxiāojié** Lantern

Festival

圆形 **yuánxíng** circular, round

园艺 **yuányì** gardening; horticulture

愿意 **yuànyì** willing, ready ◊ willingness, readiness ◊ want

原因 **yuányīn** cause, reason

元音 **yuányīn** vowel

原油 **yuányóu** crude oil

远于 **yuǎnyú** beyond

远远 **yuǎnyuǎn** much, way; 远远不如 **yuǎnyuǎn bùrú** not be a patch on

源源不断 **yuányuán búduàn** inexhaustible ◊ stream

原则 **yuánzé** principle; 原则上 **yuánzé shang** in principle

院长 **yuànzhǎng** dean

圆周 **yuánzhōu** circumference

援助 **yuánzhù** aid

圆柱 **yuánzhù** column

援助 **yuánzhù** support, help

圆珠笔 **yuánzhūbǐ** ballpoint pen

圆锥体 **yuánzhuī tǐ** cone

圆柱体 **yuánzhù tǐ** cylinder

原子 **yuánzǐ** atom ◊ atomic, nuclear

院子 **yuànzi** yard; courtyard

原子弹 **yuánzǐ dàn** atom bomb

原子废物 **yuánzǐ fèiwù** atomic waste

原子核 **yuánzǐ hé** nuclear

原子核物理 **yuánzǐ hé wùlǐ** nuclear physics

原子能 **yuánzǐ néng** atomic energy

远足 **yuǎnzú** excursion; hike

原作 **yuánzuò** original

原作品 **yuán zuòpǐn** original

欲罢不能 **yùbà bùnéng** compulsive

预报 **yùbào** forecast

预备 **yùbèi** prepare

预备队员 **yùbèi duìyuán** reserve SP

预备性 **yùbèi xìng** preliminary

预测 **yùcè** forecast, projection

鱼叉 **yúchā** harpoon

鱼船 **yúchuán** fishing boat

愚蠢 **yúchǔn** stupid, foolish, idiotic ◊ stupidity, folly

鱼刺 **yúcì** fishbone

遇到 **yùdào** encounter, meet, run into

雨点儿 **yǔdiǎnr** raindrop

预定 **yùdìng** book, reserve ◊ booking, reservation; 预定房间 **yùdìng fángjiān** book a room

约 **yuē** arrange

月 **yuè** month

阅 **yuè** read

越 **yuè** surpass, exceed; 越 … 越 … **yuè … yuè …** the more … the more …; 越快越好 **yuèkuài yuèhǎo** the sooner the better

乐 **yuè** music

阅兵 **yuèbīng** parade

月饼 **yuèbǐng** mooncake

约定 **yuēdìng** agree; arrange to meet

阅读 **yuèdú** read ◊ reading; 阅读学习 **yuèdú xuéxí** read up on

阅读材料 **yuèdú cáiliào** reading matter

乐队 **yuèduì** band; orchestra

悦耳 **yuè'ěr** pleasant-sounding; musical, melodious

越发(多)**yuèfā(duō)** more and more

岳父 **yuèfù** father-in-law (*wife's father*)

月光 **yuèguāng** moonlight

月桂 **yuèguì** laurel

越过 **yuèguò** exceed, pass; get over

约会 **yuēhuì** appointment; engagement; date, rendez-vous ◊ ask out

约会对象 **yuēhuì duìxiàng** date (*person*)

月经 **yuèjīng** period; menstruation

月经带 **yuèjīng dài** sanitary napkin

月经栓 **yuèjīng shuān** tampon

月刊 **yuèkān** monthly (*publication*)

越来越 **yuè lái yuè** increasingly; 越来越多的学生 **yuè lái yuè duō de xuéshēng** more and more students; 越来越快 **yuè lái yuè kuài** faster and faster

阅览室 **yuèlǎnshì** reading room

阅历 **yuèlì** experience; 她阅历挺

深 **tā yuèlì tīngshēn** she has been around

月亮 yuèliàng moon ◊ lunar

岳母 yuèmǔ mother-in-law (*of man*)

越南 Yuènán Vietnam ◊ Vietnamese

月票 yuèpiào monthly ticket

乐谱 yuèpǔ music, score

乐器 yuèqì musical instrument

月蚀 yuèshí lunar eclipse

约束 yuēshù restrain; curb; bind; restrict ◊ restriction

约束力 yuēshù lì binding force

越位 yuèwèi offside; 未 越 位 **wèi yuèwèi** onside

月牙形 yuèyá xíng crescent

越野 yuèyě cross-country; 越野赛 **yuèyě sài** cross-country race

乐音 yuèyīn tone

乐章 yuèzhāng movement MUS

语法 yǔfǎ grammar

鱼贩 yúfàn fishmonger

预防 yùfáng prevent ◊ prevention ◊ precautionary

预防措施 yùfáng cuòshī precaution, preventive measure

预防性 yùfáng xìng preventive

渔夫 yúfū fisherman

预付 yùfù advance (payment) ◊ pay in advance

鱼竿 yúgān fishing pole

预感 yùgǎn hunch; premonition

浴缸 yùgāng bathtub, tub

鱼肝油 yúgān yóu cod-liver oil

预告 yùgào forecast, predict

鱼钩 yúgōu fishhook

宇航 yǔháng space travel

宇航服 yǔháng fú spacesuit

宇航工业 yǔháng gōngyè aerospace industry

宇航员 yǔháng yuán astronaut

愈合 yùhé heal

迂回 yūhuí detour

迂回行进 yūhuí xíngjìn weave

与会者 yǔhuì zhě conventioneer

欲火中烧 yùhuǒ zhōngshāo smolder

淤积 yūjī deposit

雨季 yǔjì rainy season, the rains

郁积 yùjī smolder

预计 yùjì estimate; plan; 预计到 达时间 **yùjì dàodá shíjiān** estimated time of arrival

预见 yùjiàn foresee

遇见 yùjian meet

雨夹雪 yǔjiáxuě sleet

余烬 yújìn embers

浴巾 yùjīn bath towel

郁金香 yùjīnxiāng tulip

愉快 yúkuài happy, joyful; 令人 愉快 **lìngrén yúkuài** nice; enjoyable, pleasant

娱乐 yúlè entertainment, amusement; pleasure; recreation

娱乐活动 yúlè huódòng amusements

娱乐园 yúlè yuán amusement park

娱乐中心 yúlè zhōngxīn leisure center; arcade

预料 yùliào anticipate, expect; foretell ◊ anticipation

雨林 yǔlín rain forest

羽毛 yǔmáo feather; plume

浴帽 yùmào shower cap

羽毛球 yǔmáo qiú badminton; shuttlecock

玉米 yùmǐ corn

玉米花 yùmǐhuā popcorn

渔民 yúmín fisherman

预谋 yùmóu premeditated

榆木 yúmù elm

云 yún cloud

允 yǔn permit

熨 yùn iron ◊ ironing; 熨衣服 **yùn yīfu** do the ironing

韵 yùn rhyme

晕 yùn dizzy, giddy

运 yùn transport

孕 yùn pregnant

遇难 yùnàn be killed (in an accident); 遇难船只 **yùnàn chuánzhī** the doomed ship

匀称 yúnchèn regular; shapely

匀出 yúnchū spare

晕船 yùnchuán seasick ◊ get seasick

运动 yùndòng move; movement; campaign; sport; exercise; 作运 动 **zuò yùndòng** take exercise

运动场 yùndòng chǎng playing field

运动会 yùndòng huì meet SP

运动上衣 yùndòng shàngyī sportscoat

运动室 yùndòng shì gym, gymnasium

运动鞋 yùndòng xié sports shoes

运动衣 yùndòng yī jogging suit

运动员 yùndòng yuán sportsman; sportswoman; athlete; player

熨斗 yùndǒu iron

云耳 yún'ěr cloud ear (*mushroom*)

运费 yùnfèi freight

孕妇 yùnfù pregnant woman

孕妇服装 yùnfù fúzhuāng maternity dress

运河 yùnhé canal

与你无关！yǔ nǐ wúguān! that's none of your business!, mind your own business!

晕机 yùnjī airsick ◊ airsickness

酝酿 yùnniàng brew

愚弄 yúnòng tease

孕期 yùnqī pregnancy

运气 yùnqì fortune; luck

云雀 yúnquè lark

运输 yùnshū transport; transportation

运输公司 yùnshū gōngsī shipping company; carrier

运输机 yùnshūjī freighter (*plane*)

运输终点站 yùnshū zhōngdiǎn-zhàn terminal (*for containers*)

运送 yùnsòng ship; shipping

陨星 yùnxīng meteorite

运行 yùnxíng move

允许 yǔnxǔ allow, permit

晕眩 yùnxuàn light-headed

熨衣板 yùnyībǎn ironing board

运用 yùnyòng use; apply

运转 yùnzhuǎn operate; run; function; revolve; 这东西怎么运转？zhèi dōngxi zěnme yùnzhuǎn? how does this thing work?

浴盆 yùpén bathtub

语气 yǔqì tone

预期寿命 yùqī shòumìng life expectancy

羽绒 yǔróng eiderdown

雨伞 yǔsǎn umbrella

瘀伤 yúshāng bruise

于是 yúshì then; consequently

预示 yùshì usher in

浴室 yùshì bathroom

遇事不慌 yùshì bùhuāng presence of mind

与世隔绝 yǔshì géjué seclusion

余数 yúshù remainder

雨水道 yǔshuǐ dào storm drain

预算 yùsuàn calculate ◊ budget

鱼网 yúwǎng fishing net

欲望 yùwàng appetite; desire; longing

余味儿 yúwèir aftertaste

余下 yúxià the rest, remainder

预先 yùxiān in advance; 预先计划／考虑 yùxiān jìhuà／kǎolǜ plan／think ahead; 四个星期的预先通知 sìge xīngqī de yùxiān tōngzhī four weeks' notice

雨靴 yǔxuē rain boot

语言 yǔyán language ◊ linguistic

预言 yùyán prophecy; prediction ◊ predict

语言学 yǔyán xué linguistics

语言学家 yǔyán xuéjiā linguist

语言障碍 yǔyán zhàng'ài language barrier

渔业 yúyè fishing industry

雨衣 yǔyī raincoat

羽衣 yǔyī plumage

浴衣 yùyī bathrobe

寓意 yùyì moral

郁郁不乐 yùyù búlè mope

预约 yùyuē arrange; reserve ◊ advance reservation

预展 yùzhǎn preview

预兆 yùzhào omen, sign ◊ ominous

预支 yùzhī get money in advance

预制 yùzhì prefabricated

雨中 yǔzhōng in the rain

与众不同 yǔzhòng bùtóng odd one out ◊ differently ◊ distinguished, dignified

宇宙 yǔzhòu universe

宇宙飞船 yǔzhòu fēichuán spaceship, spacecraft

宇宙空间站 yǔzhòu kōngjiān zhàn space station

鱼子酱 yúzǐ jiàng caviar

Z

砸 **zá** crack *nut*

杂 **zá** mixed, assorted; miscellaneous

杂草 **zácǎo** weed

杂费 **záfèi** incidental expenses

杂货 **záhuò** groceries

杂货店 **záhuò diàn** grocery store

杂货商 **záhuò shāng** grocer

灾 **zāi** disaster

栽 **zāi** plant; fall; 他栽倒在床上 **tā zāidǎo zài chuáng shàng** he sank onto the bed

再 **zài** again; further; 再来点儿茶吗？**zài láidiǎnr chá ma?** some more tea?; 再走两英里 **zài zǒu liǎng yīnglǐ** two miles further (on)

在 **zài** at; in; on; 在盒子里 **zài hézi lǐ** in the box; 在华盛顿／中国 **zài Huáshèngdùn／Zhōngguó** in Washington／China ◊ *(continuous tense)*: 在服丧 **zài fúsāng** be mourning ◊ *(with sense of be)*: be at; be in; be on; 我在火车上 **wǒ zài huǒchē shang** I'm on the train

在 … 背后 **zài … bèihòu** behind

在 … 的对面 **zài … de duìmiàn** opposite

在 … 的中心 **zài … de zhōngxīn** in the center of

在 … 底下 **zài … dǐxià** underneath

在 … 附近 **zài … fùjìn** in the vicinity of

在 … 后面 **zài … hòumiàn** behind

在 … 里 **zài … lǐ** inside

在 … 里面 **zài … lǐmiàn** within

在 … 旁 **zài … páng** beside

在 … 旁边 **zài … pángbiān** beside

在 … 期间 **zài … qījiān** during

在 … 上 **zài … shàng** on, aboard

在 … 上方 **zài … shàngfāng** over

在 … 上面 **zài … shàngmian** on; above

在 … 时期 **zài … shíqī** while

在 … 条件下 **zài … tiáojiàn xià** on the understanding that

在 … 同时 **zài … tóngshí** during

在 … 下面 **zài … xiàmiàn** beneath, under

在 … 以前 **zài … yǐqián** prior to

在 … 以外 **zài … yǐwài** outside

在 … 之列 **zài … zhī liè** rank among

在 … 之间 **zài … zhījiān** between

在 … 之内 **zài … zhīnèi** within

在 … 之前 **zài … zhīqián** before

在 … 之上 **zài … zhīshàng** on top of

在 … 之中 **zài … zhīzhōng** among(st)

在 … 中 **zài … zhōng** in the middle of

在 … 最上 **zài … zuìshàng** at the top of

在岸上 **zài ànshàng** ashore

再版 **zàibǎn** reprint

在保 **zàibǎo** on bail

在场 **zàichǎng** presence ◊ be present

再次 **zàicì** again

在此日期前使用 **zàicǐ rìqī qián shǐyòng** best before date

再发 **zàifā** recurrent

灾害 **zāihài** disaster

在行 **zàiháng** knowledgeable

在乎 **zàihu** mind, care; 我不在乎咱们做什么 **wǒ bú zàihu zánmen zuò shénme** I don't mind what we do

再婚 **zàihūn** remarry

灾祸 **zāihuò** catastrophe, disaster

再见 **zàijiàn** goodbye, see you

再来 **zàilái** call back, come back again

再来一个 **zàilái yígè** encore

灾难 **zāinàn** disaster, catastrophe

栽培 **zāipéi** cultivation

再说 zàishuō besides

在逃 zàitáo be at large; 在逃罪犯 zàitáo zuìfàn criminal on the run

再体验 zài tǐyàn relive

再现 zàixiàn reproduce

灾星 zāixīng jinx

再一次 zàiyícì once more

再一个 zài yígè another

再用 zàiyòng reuse

载有 zàiyǒu carry

在于 zàiyú rest with

再装满 zài zhuāngmǎn refill

杂技 zájì acrobatics

杂交 zájiāo hybrid

杂技演员 zájì yǎnyuán acrobat

砸烂 zálàn total, write off

杂乱 záluàn disorder ◊ disorderly ◊ be a mess

杂乱无章 záluàn wú zhāng disorder; mess ◊ messy; chaotic

砸门 zámén hammer at the door

暂 zàn temporary

赞成 zànchéng approve, agree with ◊ favorable, agreeable ◊ approval

脏 zāng dirty

葬 zàng bury

葬礼 zànglǐ funeral; burial

脏乱 zāngluàn mess

赃物 zāngwù loot

脏物 zāngwù dirt

暂缓 zànhuǎn wait

赞美 zànměi praise; compliment ◊ complimentary

赞美诗 zànměishī hymn

咱们 zánmen we; us; 咱们快走吧 zánmen kuài zǒu ba let's get out of here

攒钱 zǎnqián save money; 为 … 攒钱 wèi … zǎnqián save up for

赞赏 zànshǎng appreciate

暂时 zànshí temporary ◊ temporarily

暂停 zàntíng pause ◊ time out

赞同 zàntóng agree with; approve

暂行 zànxíng provisional, temporary ◊ temporarily

赞许 zànxǔ applaud ◊ consent

赞扬 zànyáng credit; praise; applause

赞誉 zànyù praise

赞助 zànzhù support; patronage; sponsorship

赞助人 zànzhùrén patron; backer

糟 zāo bad, terrible ◊ damn!

遭 zāo meet, encounter

凿 záo chisel

枣 zǎo Chinese date

早 zǎo morning ◊ early; beforehand; 早在一九三五年 zǎo zài yījiǔ sānwǔ nián back in 1935

灶 zào stove; hearth

噪 zào noise

早餐 zǎocān breakfast

早产 zǎochǎn premature birth

早晨 zǎochén morning ◊ in the morning; 早晨好 zǎochén hǎo good morning

造成 zàochéng form; create; 造成困难 zàochéng kùnnán pose a problem

造船厂 zàochuán chǎng shipyard

遭到 zāodào meet with; 遭到炮火袭击 zāodào pàohuǒ xíjī come under shellfire

造反 zàofǎn revolt

糟糕 zāogāo bad, terrible, awful, horrible ◊ badly, terribly ◊ damn!

早就 zǎojiù for a long time; a long time ago

澡盆 zǎopén bath

早期 zǎoqī early (farther back in time)

早日康复! zǎorì kāngfù! get well soon!

早上 zǎoshang in the morning; 早上好 zǎoshang hǎo good morning

早市 zǎo shì early-morning market

遭受 zāoshòu suffer

早熟 zǎoshú precocious

糟蹋 zāotà murder

糟透 zāotòu abysmal, atrocious; 糟透了! zāotòule! it stinks!, it's awful!

灶头 zàotóu burner

造物主 Zàowù zhǔ the Creator

噪音 **zàoyīn** noise

凿子 **záozi** chisel

枣子 **zǎozi** Chinese date

杂耍 **záshuǎ** vaudeville

杂项 **záxiàng** sundries

杂志 **zázhì** magazine, journal

杂种狗 **zázhǒng gǒu** mongrel

责 **zé** duty, responsibility

责备 **zébèi** blame; reproach; reprimand

责怪 **zéguài** blame ◊ accusation

责骂 **zémà** scold

怎 **zěn** how; why

憎 **zēng** hate

增 **zēng** add; increase

赠 **zèng** give; present

增大 **zēngdà** increase; heighten

增多 **zēngduō** increase; multiply

憎恨 **zēnghèn** hate ◊ hatred

增加 **zēngjiā** increase, boost ◊ raise; 增加体重 **zēngjiā tǐzhòng** put on weight

增进 **zēngjìn** promote

增刊 **zēngkān** supplement

赠品 **zèngpǐn** freebie

增强 **zēngqiáng** strengthen, reinforce

赠券 **zèngquàn** coupon

增湿器 **zēngshī qì** humidifier

赠送 **zèngsòng** give; present ◊ complimentary; 把Y赠送给X **bǎ Y zèngsònggěi X** present Y to X

曾孙 **zēngsūn** great-grandson (*son's grandson*)

曾外祖父 **zēngwài zǔfù** great-grandfather (*maternal*)

曾外祖母 **zēngwài zǔmǔ** great-grandmother (*maternal*)

增长 **zēngzhǎng** grow, expand; increase ◊ growth, expansion

增值 **zēngzhí** increase in value

曾祖父 **zēngzǔfù** great-grandfather (*paternal*)

曾祖母 **zēngzǔmǔ** great-grandmother (*paternal*)

怎么 **zěnme** how; how come; 我不知该怎么办 **wǒ bùzhī gāi zěnmebàn** I don't know what to do; 怎么了？ **zěnmele?** what's wrong?, what's the matter?

怎样 **zěnyàng** how

责任 **zérèn** responsibility, duty; blame

诘问 **zéwèn** heckle

闸 **zhá** lock; sluice

眨 **zhǎ** wink; blink

炸 **zhà** blow up, explode

榨 **zhà** squeeze

榨出 **zhàchū** extract; squeeze out ◊ extraction

炸弹 **zhàdàn** bomb

炸弹攻击 **zhàdàn gōngjī** bomb attack

轧辊 **zhágǔn** roller

诈呼 **zhàhu** bluff

摘 **zhāi** pick, pluck

窄 **zhǎi** narrow

债 **zhài** debt

摘除 **zhāichú** pluck

宅第 **zháidì** mansion

债卷 **zhàijuàn** bond

摘录 **zhāilù** extract, excerpt

债券 **zhàiquàn** promissory note; bond

债权人 **zhàiquán rén** creditor

债务 **zhàiwù** debt

窄小 **zhǎixiǎo** cramped

摘要 **zhāiyào** précis

债主 **zhàizhǔ** creditor

栅栏 **zhàlán** fence; railings; bars

蚱蜢 **zhàměng** grasshopper

沾 **zhān** dip

粘 **zhān** stick, glue

毡 **zhān** felt

展 **zhǎn** develop; open up

占 **zhàn** occupy; take; constitute, make up

站 **zhàn** stand ◊ stop; station; 站直了！ **zhànzhíle!** stand up straight!

战 **zhàn** fight ◊ battle; war

站不住脚 **zhàn búzhù jiǎo** lame excuse

战场 **zhànchǎng** battlefield, battleground

展出 **zhǎnchū** exhibit, display

站点 **zhàndiǎn** web site

战斗 **zhàndòu** combat; fight

战斗机 **zhàndòu jī** warplane, fighter

战俘 **zhànfú** prisoner of war

章 **zhāng** chapter

张 **zhāng** sheet ◊ *measure word for*

flat things; 一张纸 **yìzhāng zhǐ** piece of paper

掌 **zhǎng** palm

涨 **zhǎng** rise

长 **zhǎng** grow ◊ head; 家长 **jiāzhǎng** head of a family

胀 **zhàng** bloated

帐 **zhàng** account

障碍 **zhàng'ài** obstacle, hurdle, stumbling block; barrier

障碍物 **zhàng'ài wù** obstacle; obstruction, barrier, cordon

涨潮 **zhǎngcháo** incoming tide ◊ come in (*of tide*)

章程 **zhāngchéng** rules; statutes

长大 **zhǎngdà** grow up; develop

账单 **zhàngdān** check, bill; invoice

丈夫 **zhàngfu** husband

长高 **zhǎnggāo** shoot up (*of children*)

掌管 **zhǎngguǎn** preside over

掌击 **zhǎngjī** smack; slap; cuff

撞击 **zhàngjī** smash

涨价 **zhǎngjià** price rise

张开 **zhāngkāi** open, unfold

张口 **zhāngkǒu** gape

蟑螂 **zhāngláng** cockroach

长满青苔 **zhǎngmǎn qīngtái** mossy

长满树木 **zhǎngmǎn shùmù** wooded

帐目 **zhàngmù** accounts; books; account

樟脑 **zhāngnǎo** camphor

长女 **zhǎngnǚ** firstborn (daughter)

长胖 **zhǎngpàng** fill out, get fatter

帐篷 **zhàngpeng** tent

掌声 **zhǎngshēng** applause

张贴 **zhāngtiē** put up, post; pin up

战国时期 **Zhànguó Shíqī** Warring States (Period)

掌握 **zhǎngwò** grasp; master; control

章鱼 **zhāngyú** octopus

长子 **zhǎngzǐ** firstborn (son)

粘合剂 **zhānhéjì** adhesive

战后 **zhànhòu** postwar

粘糊糊 **zhānhúhú** sticky

展开 **zhǎnkāi** unfold, unwind; unroll; lay out

粘扣 **Zhānkòu** Velcro®

展览 **zhǎnlǎn** display, exhibit

展览橱窗 **zhǎnlǎn chúchuāng** display cabinet

展览会 **zhǎnlǎnhuì** exhibition

站立 **zhànlì** stand

沾料 **zhānliào** dip (*food*)

站立空间 **zhànlì kōngjiān** standing room

占领 **zhànlǐng** capture; occupy ◊ occupation

战略 **zhànlüè** strategy ◊ strategic

展品 **zhǎnpǐn** exhibit

战前 **zhànqián** prewar

站起来 **zhàn qǐlái** stand up, get up; jump to one's feet; 他腾地站起来 **tā téngde zhàn qǐlái** he scrambled to his feet

占去 **zhànqù** take up *space, time*

占少数 **zhàn shǎoshù** be in the minority

战胜 **zhànshèng** conquer ◊ victorious; 战胜 X **zhànshèng X** win a victory over X

展示 **zhǎnshì** show; show off; model

战时 **zhànshí** wartime

战士 **zhànshì** soldier; warrior; fighter

战术 **zhànshù** tactics ◊ tactical

站台 **zhàntái** platform; 第十站台 **dì shí zhàntái** track 10

粘贴 **zhāntiē** paste, stick; adhere

毡头笔 **zhāntóubǐ** felt-tip (pen)

展望 **zhǎnwàng** outlook

谵妄 **zhānwàng** delirious

站位 **zhànwèi** standing room

沾污 **zhānwū** stain

占线 **zhànxiàn** busy ◊ the line is busy

战线 **zhànxiàn** front; battle line

占线声 **zhànxiàn shēng** busy signal

崭新 **zhǎnxīn** brand-new

占星术 **zhànxīng shù** astrology

占星者 **zhànxīng zhě** astrologer

暂休 **zhànxiū** adjourn

战役 **zhànyì** battle

占用 zhànyòng occupy; encroach on

占有 zhànyǒu own, have; take

占优势 zhàn yōushì dominant; predominant ◊ predominate

占有者 zhànyǒuzhě owner

沾沾自喜 zhānzhān zìxǐ gloat

粘着 zhānzhe cling to

站着 zhànzhe stand

战争 zhànzhēng war; warfare; conflict; hostilities

站住 zhànzhù stop

辗转 zhǎnzhuǎn toss and turn

辗转反侧 zhǎnzhuǎn fǎncè toss and turn

招 zhāo beckon

朝 zhāo morning

着 zháo ignite

找 zhǎo look for; ask for

罩 zhào cover

召 zhào convene; summon

照 zhào photograph; license ◊ shine; light up ◊ according to; 照 X 光 zhào X guāng take an X-ray; 照我看来 zhào wǒ kànlái in my estimation

找出 zhǎochū locate, dig out; work out solution

找挶 zhǎocuò find fault with

招待 zhāodài entertain; serve customer; 热情招待 rèqíng zhāodài hospitality

招待会 zhāodài huì reception

招待所 zhāodàisuǒ guesthouse

找到 zhǎodào find

找工作 zhǎo gōngzuò be job hunting

照顾 zhàogù look after; tend ◊ care

照管 zhàoguǎn look after

照顾不周 zhàogù bùzhōu neglect

召唤 zhāohuàn call out; beckon

召回 zhāohuí recall

找回 zhǎohuí recover, get back ◊ recovery

招魂术者 zhāohúnshù zhě spiritualist

着火 zháohuǒ be on fire ◊ alight, ablaze

着急 zháojí worry; be anxious

召集 zhàojí call, convene; summon

召开 zhàokāi convene; hold

照看 zhàokàn mind, watch, keep an eye on

照亮 zhàoliàng light up

照料 zhàoliào look after; coddle

着陆 zháolù touch down (of plane) ◊ touchdown

着迷 zháomí captivate, entrance ◊ obsession ◊ entranced; 使着迷 shǐ zháomí fascinate; 对 X 着迷 duì X zháomí be mad about X

照明 zhàomíng illuminate, light ◊ lighting

召募 zhāomù enlist

招牌 zhāopai sign

照片 zhàopiàn photograph

招聘 zhāopìn recruit ◊ recruitment

找钱 zhǎoqián change ◊ 等一下，我给你找钱 děng yíxià, wǒ gěi nǐ zhǎoqián just a minute, I'll give you the change

朝气蓬勃 zhāoqì péngbó youthful

招认 zhāorèn confess

着色 zháosè tinted

招收 zhāoshōu intake (of college etc)

招手 zhāoshǒu wave; beckon

朝霞 zhāoxiá dawn

照相 zhàoxiàng take a photo

照像机 zhàoxiàng jī camera

照耀 zhàoyào shine

罩衣 zhàoyī coveralls

照一照 zhàoyīzhào shine

沼泽 zhǎozé swamp, marsh, bog

招致 zhāozhì incur; 招致麻烦 zhāozhì máfán get into trouble

兆字节 zhàozìjié megabyte

榨取 zhàqǔ bleed; drain; overburden

炸薯片 zhá shǔpiàn potato chip

炸薯条 zhá shǔtiáo fried potatoes

扎眼 zhāyǎn pierce

眨眼 zhǎyǎn blink; wink

炸药 zhàyào dynamite; gunpowder; explosive

沾沾自喜 zhāzhan zìxǐ

complacent

渣子 **zhāzi** crumb; dregs; scum (*people*)

螫 **zhē** sting

遮 **zhē** cover

折 **zhé** break; fold

褶 **zhě** fold; pleat; tuck

这 **zhè** this; these; the; 这是谁的？ **zhè shì shéide?** whose is this?

着 **zhe** (*continuing action*): 他抱着孩子 **tā bàozhe háizi** he's holding a baby ◊ (*imperative*): 听着！ **tīngzhe!** listen!

遮蔽 **zhēbì** shade; screen; blot out

螫刺 **zhēcì** sting

这次 **zhècì** this time

折叠 **zhédié** fold ◊ folding *chair etc*, collapsible

折叠椅 **zhédiéyǐ** folding chair

折断 **zhéduàn** break; break off; fracture

这个 **zhège** this ◊ this one

折合 **zhéhé** convert *unit of measurement*

这里 **zhèlǐ** here

这么 **zhème** such; so; this; 这么大 **zhème dà** this big; 这么快 **zhème kuài** so quick

折磨 **zhémó** torment, torture

榛 **zhēn** hazel

针 **zhēn** needle; hand (*of clock*)

真 **zhēn** real, true

侦 **zhēn** detect

珍 **zhēn** valuable ◊ value

疹 **zhěn** rash; blotch

枕 **zhěn** pillow

镇 **zhèn** town

震 **zhèn** tremble, shake; quake; shock

阵 **zhèn** *measure word for smoke or dust*; 一阵烟／尘土 **yízhèn yān／chéntǔ** a cloud of smoke／dust

珍爱 **zhēn'ài** fond *memory*

珍宝 **zhēnbǎo** treasure; gem

针鼻儿 **zhēnbír** eye of a needle

侦察 **zhēnchá** reconnoiter ◊ reconnaissance

震颤 **zhènchàn** throb; tremble; twitch

真诚 **zhēnchéng** sincere ◊ sincerely ◊ sincerity

针刺 **zhēncì** acupuncture

震荡 **zhèndàng** concussion

真的 **zhēnde** really, actually; 真的吗？ **zhēnde ma?** really?

真地 **zhēnde** truly

阵地 **zhèndì** position MIL

镇定 **zhèndìng** calm, composed

镇定自若 **zhèndìng zìruò** unflappable

震动 **zhèndòng** shudder; vibrate ◊ vibration; tremor

振动 **zhèndòng** vibrate ◊ vibration

针对 **zhēnduì** be aimed at

振奋 **zhènfèn** feel inspired; 令人振奋 **lìngrén zhènfèn** rousing

阵风 **zhènfēng** gust of wind

振奋人心 **zhènfèn rénxīn** stimulating

蒸 **zhēng** steam

征 **zhēng** journey ◊ summon; levy *taxes*

争 **zhēng** struggle; contend

整 **zhěng** complete, total; all; 三点整 **sāndiǎn zhěng** at 3 o'clock sharp

挣 **zhèng** earn; struggle

正 **zhèng** positive; plus; upright; just

证 **zhèng** evidence

政 **zhèng** politics ◊ political

争辩 **zhēngbiàn** dispute; 与X争辩 **yǔ X zhēngbiàn** take issue with X

政变 **zhèngbiàn** coup

征兵 **zhēngbīng** draft MIL

政策 **zhèngcè** policy

政策准则 **zhèngcè zhǔnzé** component, aspect (*of policy*)

正常 **zhèngcháng** normal; regular ◊ normally ◊ normality; 一切正常 **yíqiè zhèngcháng** the situation is under control

正常化 **zhèngcháng huà** normalize

争吵 **zhèngchǎo** squabble, quarrel

证词 **zhèngcí** testimony

正当 **zhèngdāng** proper; legitimate; right

正当理由 **zhèngdāng lǐyóu** justification

挣得 **zhèngde** earn

正点 **zhèngdiǎn** on schedule

争斗 **zhēngdòu** fight, struggle

整顿 **zhěngdùn** regulation; arrangement

争夺 **zhēngduó** dispute; compete for/against ◊ contest

争夺者 **zhēngduó zhě** contender

蒸发 **zhēngfā** evaporate; steam

正方形 **zhèngfāng xíng** square

征服 **zhēngfu** conquer, overcome ◊ conquest

政府 **zhèngfǔ** government

政府机构 **zhèngfǔ jīgòu** public sector

征服者 **zhēngfú zhě** conqueror

整 **zhěng** complete; whole; 两点整 **liǎngdiǎn zhěng** at two o'clock prompt

整个 **zhěnggè** whole, entire

正规来说 **zhènggguī láishuō** officially, strictly (speaking)

蒸锅 **zhēngguō** steamer (*for cooking*)

正好 **zhènghǎo** just right

正极 **zhèngjí** positive ELEC

证件 **zhèngjiàn** papers, ID

整洁 **zhěngjié** neat, tidy

整洁漂亮 **zhěngjié piàoliàng** smart, neat, spruce

拯救 **zhěngjiù** save ◊ salvation; redemption

证据 **zhèngjù** evidence; proof

整理 **zhěnglǐ** order, arrange; sort out; clear up

整理行装 **zhěnglǐ xíngzhuāng** pack, do one's packing

争论 **zhēnglùn** argue, contend; dispute ◊ argument; controversy

正门 **zhèngmén** front entrance

正面 **zhèngmiàn** front; façade; 正面还是反面? **zhèngmiàn háishi fǎnmiàn?** heads or tails?

正面看台 **zhèngmiàn kàntái** grandstand

证明 **zhèngmíng** certify; prove;

verify ◊ certificate; confirmation; verification

征募 **zhēngmù** recruit

正派 **zhèngpài** decent; law-abiding; straight ◊ decency

整批 **zhěngpī** in bulk

正片 **zhèngpiān** feature movie

蒸汽 **zhēngqì** steam

整齐 **zhěngqí** neat, tidy; shipshape

挣钱 **zhèngqián** earn money

蒸汽电熨斗 **zhēngqì diàn yùndǒu** steam iron

蒸汽机车 **zhēngqì jīchē** steam locomotive

蒸汽浴 **zhēngqì yù** steam bath

争取 **zhēngqǔ** fight for

政权 **zhèngquán** regime

证券 **zhèngquàn** securities

证券市场 **zhèngquàn shìchǎng** stock market; securities market

正确 **zhèngquè** correct, right ◊ correctly; properly; 大致正确 **dàzhì zhèngquè** approximately right

正确性 **zhèngquè xìng** validity

证人 **zhèngrén** witness

证人席 **zhèngrén xí** witness stand

整容外科 **zhěngróng wàikē** cosmetic surgery

整容外科医生 **zhěngróng wàikē yīshēng** plastic surgeon

正如我言 **zhèngrú wǒ yán** like I said

证实 **zhèngshí** confirm; corroborate; back up ◊ confirmation

证实 **zhèngshí** confirm

正式 **zhèngshì** formal; official ◊ formally; officially

征收 **zhēngshōu** impose, levy, collect

整数 **zhěngshù** in round figures

证书 **zhèngshù** certificate; qualification

征税 **zhēngshuì** taxation

整肃 **zhěngsù** purge

整体 **zhěngtǐ** whole; 我们必须作为一个整体一起工作 **wǒmen bìxū zuòwéi yígè zhěngtǐ yìqǐ gōngzuò** we must work together as a unit

政务会委员 zhèngwùhuì wěiyuán councilor

正相反 zhèng xiāngfǎn on the contrary

整形外科 zhěngxíng wàikē plastic surgery

整形外科医生 zhěngxíng wàikē yīshēng plastic surgeon

整修 zhěngxiū renovate ◊ renovation

正要… zhèngyào … be on the point of; 我正要离开，这时… *wǒ zhèngyào líkāi, zhèishí* … I was just about to leave when …

争议 zhēngyì conflict

正义 zhèngyì just ◊ justice

正在 zhèngzài currently in the process of

正在流行 zhèngzài liúxíng in vogue

证章 zhèngzhāng badge

征兆 zhēngzhào symptom

争执 zhēngzhí disagreement, dispute

正直 zhèngzhí be right ◊ upright, decent

政治 zhèngzhì politics ◊ political; 政治信仰 *zhèngzhì xìnyǎng* political beliefs

政治犯 zhèngzhì fàn political detainee

政治家 zhèngzhì jiā politician; statesman

政治局 Zhèngzhìjú Politbureau

郑重 zhèngzhòng solemn, binding

正中要害 zhèngzhòng yàohài hit the bull's eye

症状 zhèngzhuàng symptom MED; 戒毒时的症状 *jièdú shí de zhèngzhuàng* withdrawal symptoms

正准备… zhèng zhǔnbèi … be about to …

正字法 zhèngzìfǎ orthography

震撼 zhènhàn shake

赈济 zhènjì charity

针脚 zhēnjiǎo stitch

贞洁 zhēnjié chaste ◊ virginity

震惊 zhènjīng shock; 令人震惊 *lìngrén zhènjīng* shocking; appalling

镇静 zhènjìng calm, collected, composed ◊ composure

镇静剂 zhènjìng jì tranquilizer

镇静药 zhènjìng yào sedative

针灸 zhēnjiǔ acupuncture

真空 zhēnkōng vacuum

真空包装 zhēnkōng bāozhuāng vacuum-packed

真空吸尘器 zhēnkōng xīchén qì vacuum cleaner

真理 zhēnlǐ truth

珍品 zhēnpǐn gem

真品 zhēnpǐn genuine

侦破 zhēnpò solve, crack

真实 zhēnshí real; true ◊ really, actually

珍视 zhēnshì prize, value; 不够珍视 X *bú gòu zhēnshì X* take X for granted, not appreciate X

真是的！zhēnshide! really! (*expressing exasperation etc*)

真实性 zhēnshí xìng authenticity

诊所 zhěnsuǒ clinic

侦探 zhēntàn detective

侦探片 zhēntàn piān crime movie

侦探小说 zhēntàn xiǎoshuō detective novel

枕套 zhěntào pillowcase, pillowslip

镇痛 zhèntòng pain-killing, analgesic

针头 zhēntóu needle (*for injection*)

枕头 zhěntou pillow

珍惜 zhēnxī cherish, treasure

针线 zhēnxiàn needlework; needle and thread; notions

真相 zhēnxiàng fact; truth

针线活儿 zhēnxiàn huór needlework

镇压 zhènyā repress, suppress ◊ repression, suppression

针叶树 zhēnyè shù conifer

阵雨 zhènyǔ shower (*of rain*)

真正 zhēnzhèng authentic, real ◊ really

镇政府 zhèn zhèngfǔ town council

针织品 zhēnzhī pǐn knitwear

针织衣服 zhēnzhī yīfú knitwear

震中 **zhènzhōng** epicenter

珍珠 **zhēnzhū** pearl

珍珠母 **zhēnzhūmǔ** mother-of-pearl

榛子 **zhēnzi** hazelnut

折篷车 **zhépéng chē** convertible

折起来 **zhé qǐlái** fold up *chair etc*

这儿 **zhèr** here

折算 **zhésuàn** conversion

折梯 **zhétī** step ladder

这些 **zhèxiē** these

哲学 **zhéxué** philosophy

哲学家 **zhéxué jiā** philosopher

遮掩 **zhēyǎn** hush up

这样 **zhèyàng** like this, this way; so; such; 我认为是这样 **wǒ rènwéi shì zhèyàng** I think so

遮阳帽 **zhēyángmào** baseball cap

折页 **zhéyè** hinge

遮阴 **zhēyīn** shade ◊ shady

之 **zhī** *fml (possessive indicator)*: 东方之珠 **dōngfāng zhī zhū** the pearl of the east

只 **zhī** *measure word for birds, animals, boats*; 两只老虎 **liǎngzhī lǎohǔ** two tigers

汁 **zhī** juice

支 **zhī** *measure word for pens, pencils, cigarettes and long cylindrical things*

织 **zhī** weave; knit

知 **zhī** know

脂 **zhī** fat; grease

直 **zhí** straight

职 **zhí** employment; job

植 **zhí** plant

值 **zhí** value ◊ be worth

执 **zhí** hold

只 **zhǐ** only

纸 **zhǐ** paper

指 **zhǐ** finger ◊ point to

止 **zhǐ** stop

痣 **zhǐ** mole *(on skin)*

掷 **zhì** toss, throw; 掷色子 **zhì shǎizi** throw dice

治 **zhì** control

志 **zhì** will, willpower

至 **zhì** to; up to ◊ reach; 十至十五人 **shí zhì shíwǔ rén** from 10 to 15 people; 星期一至五 **xīngqī yī zhì wǔ** Monday through Friday

致 **zhì** send; cause

制 **zhì** make, manufacture

智 **zhì** wisdom

质 **zhì** substance

致癌 **zhì'ái** carcinogenic

致癌物 **zhì'ái wù** carcinogen

值班 **zhíbān** be on duty

纸板 **zhǐbǎn** cardboard

纸板盒 **zhǐbǎn hé** cardboard box

纸板火柴 **zhǐbǎn huǒchái** book of matches

纸杯子 **zhǐ bēizi** paper cup

直奔 **zhíbēn** make a beeline for

纸币 **zhǐbì** (bank)bill

掷币 **zhìbì** toss a coin

支部 **zhībù** branch, chapter

只不过 **zhǐbúguò** mere ◊ merely

织布机 **zhībùjī** loom

制裁 **zhìcái** crack down on ◊ crackdown; sanction, penalty

致残 **zhìcán** maim

支撑 **zhīcheng** support, hold up; sustain

支撑起 **zhīchēngqǐ** prop up

支撑住 **zhīchēngzhù** hold out, manage

支持 **zhīchí** hold, keep in place; support; back up, endorse ◊ backing; endorsement ◊ supportive; 我支持你 **wǒ zhīchí nǐ** I'm on your side

支持者 **zhīchí zhě** follower, supporter

支出 **zhīchū** pay ◊ expenditure

指出 **zhǐchū** point out

痔疮 **zhìchuāng** piles MED

直达 **zhídá** direct, nonstop *flight etc*

纸袋 **zhǐdài** paper bag

值当 **zhídàng** be good value

知道 **zhīdào** know

直到 **zhídào** until ◊ pending; 直到七月才能完成 **zhídào qīyuè cái néng wánchéng** it won't be finished until July

指导 **zhǐdǎo** guide; instruct; coach ◊ directions; instructions; guidance; directory

指导员 **zhǐdǎo yuán** instructor

指导者 **zhǐdǎo zhě** supervisor

值得 **zhíde** deserve, merit; be

worthwhile ◊ desirable; recommended; 值得信任 **zhíde xìnrèn** trustworthy

质地 zhìdì texture

支点 zhīdiǎn pivot

指定 zhīdìng specify; designate; be meant for, be aimed at; 指定教材 **zhǐdìng jiàocái** set book

制定 zhìdìng enact, institute

指定集合点 zhǐdìng jíhé diǎn rendez-vous; assembly point

制动 zhìdòng brake

制动信号灯 zhìdòng xìnhào dēng brake light

制度 zhìdù system

只读存储器 zhǐdú cúnchǔ qì ROM, read-only memory

只读档案 zhǐdú dǎng'àn read-only file

至多 zhìduō at (the) most

脂肪 zhīfáng fat; 含脂肪多 **hán zhīfáng duo** fatty

支付 zhīfù pay; 支付手段 **zhīfù shǒuduàn** means of payment

制服 zhìfú uniform

至高点 zhìgāodiǎn summit, peak (of powers etc)

趾高气扬 zhìgāo qìyáng swagger

至高无上 zhìgāo wúshàng supreme

吱嘎声 zhīgā shēng squeak; creak

制革 zhìgé tan leather

职工 zhígōng workforce, staff

直观 zhíguān visual

直观教具 zhíguān jiàojù visual aid

直观显示部件 zhíguān xiǎnshì bùjiàn VDU, visual display unit

至关重要 zhìguān zhòngyào of prime importance

直航飞机 zhíháng fēijī through flight

治好 zhìhǎo cure

纸盒 zhǐhé carton

之后 zhīhòu after

指挥 zhǐhuī conduct ◊ bandmaster

智慧 zhìhuì wisdom; intelligence

指挥调度台 zhǐhuī diàodù tái control tower

指挥官 zhǐhuī guān commander

指挥家 zhǐhuī jiā conductor

指挥台 zhǐhuī tái podium

支架 zhījià upright; support, prop

指甲 zhǐjiǎ fingernail

指甲锉 zhǐjiǎ cuò nail file

指甲刀 zhǐjiǎ dāo nail clippers

指甲剪 zhǐjiǎ jiǎn nail scissors

指尖 zhǐjiān fingertip

纸浆 zhǐjiāng paper pulp

直角 zhíjiǎo right-angle; 成直角 **chéng zhíjiǎo** at right-angles to

指甲油 zhǐjiǎ yóu nail polish

指甲油去除剂 zhǐjiǎ yóu qùchú jì nail polish remover

枝节 zhījié detail

直接 zhíjiē direct ◊ directly, straight

直截了当 zhíjié liǎodàng straightforward, direct ◊ straight out, bluntly

掷界外球 zhì jiè wài qiú throw-in (in soccer)

织锦 zhījǐn tapestry

纸巾 zhǐjīn tissue

至今 zhìjīn until now, up to now

直径 zhíjìng diameter

致敬 zhìjìng salute

纸卷 zhǐjuǎn scroll

知觉 zhījué consciousness; feeling MED; 失去/恢复知觉 **shīqù/huīfù zhījué** lose/regain consciousness

直觉 zhíjué intuition

止渴 zhǐkě quench one's thirst

止咳糖 zhǐké táng lozenge

止咳糖浆 zhǐké tángjiāng cough medicine, cough syrup

指控 zhǐkòng accuse; charge ◊ allegation

直立 zhílì erect, upright

治理 zhìlǐ administration ◊ administer, govern

致力 zhìlì dedication

智力 zhìlì intellect; intelligence ◊ intellectual

质量 zhìliàng quality

质量管理 zhìliàng guǎnlǐ quality control

质量控制 zhìliàng kòngzhì quality control

治疗 zhìliáo treatment, therapy ◊

treat

治疗学家 **zhìliáo xuéjiā** therapist

智力迟钝 **zhìlì chídùn** retarded

支离破碎 **zhīlí pòsuì** fragmentary

支流 **zhīliú** tributary

直流电 **zhíliúdiàn** direct current

智力游戏 **zhìlì yóuxì** puzzle

支路 **zhīlù** side road

指路 **zhǐlù** navigate (*in car*)

指路人 **zhǐlùrén** navigator (*in car*)

芝麻 **zhīma** sesame

芝麻油 **zhīma yóu** sesame oil

殖民地 **zhímíndì** colony ◊ colonial

知名 **zhīmíng** famous; prominent

指明 **zhǐmíng** point out

致命 **zhìmìng** lethal, fatal ◊ fatally

殖民者 **zhímín zhě** settler

指南 **zhǐnán** guidebook; manual

指南针 **zhǐnán zhēn** compass

执拗 **zhíniù** stubborn

侄女 **zhínǚ** niece (*brother's daughter*)

纸牌 **zhǐpái** playing card

制片人 **zhìpiàn rén** film-maker; producer

支票 **zhīpiào** check FIN

支票本 **zhīpiào běn** checkbook

支票帐户 **zhīpiào zhànghù** checking account

质朴 **zhìpǔ** unsophisticated

志气 **zhìqì** ambition

之前 **zhīqián** before

支气管炎 **zhīqìguǎn yán** bronchitis

智穷计尽 **zhìqióng jìjìn** be at one's wits' end

支取 **zhīqǔ** withdraw

智商 **zhìshāng** IQ

至少 **zhìshǎo** at least

智胜 **zhìshèng** outwit

直升飞机 **zhíshēng fēijī** helicopter

知识 **zhīshi** knowledge; learning

指示 **zhǐshì** indicate, signal; instruct ◊ indication; directions; 指示 X 做 Y **zhǐshì X zuò Y** instruct X to do Y

只是 **zhǐshì** just, only; except that

知识分子 **zhīshí fènzǐ** intellectual

指示牌 **zhǐshì pái** road sign

直率 **zhíshuài** blunt, direct ◊ bluntly

直爽 **zhíshuǎng** direct

直说 **zhíshuō** speak one's mind

制陶术 **zhìtáoshù** pottery

直通火车 **zhítōng huǒchē** through train

止痛片 **zhǐtòng piàn** painkiller

制图 **zhìtú** draw charts; make maps

指望 **zhǐwàng** bank on ◊ expectations

职位 **zhíwèi** office, position, post

质问 **zhìwèn** question, challenge

植物 **zhíwù** plant ◊ botanical

职务 **zhíwù** duties; job

植物学 **zhíwù xué** botany

知悉 **zhīxī** knowingly

窒息 **zhìxī** suffocate ◊ suffocation; 令人窒息 **lìngrén zhìxī** stifling

支线 **zhīxiàn** branch line

直线 **zhíxiàn** straight line

纸箱 **zhǐxiāng** carton, box, pack

指向 **zhǐxiàng** direct; point at

志向 **zhìxiàng** ambition

致谢 **zhìxiè** give one's thanks

窒息而死 **zhìxī ér sǐ** suffocate

执行 **zhíxíng** carry out, execute

直系亲属 **zhíxì qīnshǔ** immediate family

秩序 **zhìxù** order, orderliness

止血 **zhǐxuè** stop bleeding ◊ styptic

智牙 **zhìyá** wisdom tooth

直言不讳 **zhíyán búhuì** outspoken; blunt

只要 **zhǐyào** provided that; so long as

制药 **zhìyào** pharmaceutical

制药公司 **zhìyào gōngsī** pharmaceutical company

职业 **zhíyè** business; profession; occupation ◊ vocational; occupational; professional

职业介绍所 **zhíyè jièshàosuǒ** employment agency

职业人员 **zhíyè rényuán** professional

职业杀手 **zhíyè shāshǒu** hitman

质疑 **zhìyí** challenge; 对 X 有质疑 **duì X yǒu zhìyí** feel

直译 **zhíyì** literal translation
致意 **zhìyì** greeting
指引 **zhǐyǐn** guide, show, direct
执意做 **zhíyì zuò** persist in
只有 **zhǐyǒu** only if; nothing but;
  只有几个 **zhǐyǒu jǐge** just a
  couple; 只有最好的 **zhǐyǒu**
  zuìhǎo de nothing but the best
至于 **zhìyú** as for
治愈 **zhìyù** heal, cure
职员 **zhíyuán** employee;
  personnel
志愿 **zhìyuàn** voluntary ◊
  volunteer
志愿者 **zhìyuàn zhě** volunteer
置于两侧 **zhìyú liǎngcè** flank
制造 **zhìzào** manufacture,
  produce ◊ manufacturing
制造厂家 **zhìzào chǎngjiā**
  producer
制造商 **zhìzào shāng**
  manufacturer
制造者 **zhìzào zhě** maker
指责 **zhǐzé** rebuke, reproach ◊
  disapproval ◊ reproachful
执照 **zhízhào** license
执照号码 **zhízhào hàomǎ**
  license number
指针 **zhǐzhēn** needle (*on dial*);
  hand (*on clock*)
执政 **zhízhèng** in power
直着走 **zhízhe zǒu** straight ahead
  ◊ carry straight on
纸制 **zhǐzhì** paper
制止 **zhìzhǐ** prevent; deter; stem;
  block
吱吱声 **zhīzhi shēng** squeak (*of*
  mouse); twitter (*of birds*)
蜘蛛 **zhīzhū** spider
支柱 **zhīzhù** support
止住 **zhǐzhù** halt
蜘蛛网 **zhīzhūwǎng** spider's web,
  cobweb
侄子 **zhízi** nephew (*brother's son*)
知足 **zhīzú** undemanding, modest
制作 **zhìzuò** make, produce ◊
  production
钟 **zhōng** clock; bell; o'clock
中 **zhōng** middle; medium; China ◊

be in the process of
忠 **zhōng** loyal; faithful
终 **zhōng** end
种 **zhǒng** species; race; sort, kind;
  两种 **liǎngzhǒng** two kinds of
肿 **zhǒng** swell ◊ swollen
重 **zhòng** heavy
种 **zhòng** plant
中 **zhòng** hit
众 **zhòng** crowd
钟表匠 **zhōngbiǎo jiàng**
  watchmaker
中波 **zhōngbō** medium wave
中部 **zhōngbù** central ◊ central
  part
仲裁 **zhòngcái** arbitrate ◊
  arbitration
中餐 **zhōngcān** Chinese food
中产阶级 **zhōngchǎn jiējí**
  middle-class ◊ the middle classes
忠诚 **zhōngchéng** faithful
重大 **zhòngdà** serious, weighty
中等 **zhōngděng** medium;
  average, middling
中等教育 **zhōngděng jiàoyù**
  secondary education
终点 **zhōngdiǎn** finish, end
重点 **zhòngdiǎn** stress; key point;
  emphasis; 把重点转移到 **bǎ**
  zhòngdiǎn zhuǎnyídào shift the
  emphasis onto
终点线 **zhōngdiǎnxiàn** finishing
  line
终点站 **zhōngdiǎn zhàn** terminus
中东 **Zhōngdōng** Middle East
仲冬 **zhòngdōng** midwinter
重读 **zhòngdú** stress, emphasize
中毒 **zhòngdú** poisoning
中断 **zhōngduàn** interrupt; break
  off ◊ interruption
终端产品 **zhōngduān chǎnpǐn**
  end product
终端用户 **zhōngduān yònghù**
  end-user
众多 **zhòngduō** mass, large
  amount
中耳炎 **zhōng'ěr yán** middle ear
  infection
中饭 **zhōngfàn** lunch
中风 **zhòngfēng** stroke MED
重负 **zhòngfù** strain, stress

忠告 **zhōnggào** advise, recommend

中共 **Zhōnggòng** Chinese Communist Party

重工业 **zhònggōngyè** heavy industry

中共中央委员会 **Zhōnggòng Zhōngyāng Wěiyuánhuì** Central Committee of the Chinese Communist Party

中国 **Zhōngguó** China ◊ Chinese

中国大陆 **Zhōngguó Dàlù** Mainland China

中国国际旅行社 **Zhōngguó Guójì Lǚxíngshè** China International Travel Service, CITS

中国话 **Zhōngguó huà** Chinese (*language*)

中国旅行社 **Zhōngguó Lǚxíngshè** China Travel Service, CTS

中国民航 **Zhōngguó Mínháng** Civil Aviation Administration of China, CAAC

中国人 **Zhōngguó rén** Chinese

中国日报 **Zhōngguó Rìbào** China Daily

中国象棋 **Zhōngguó xiàngqí** Chinese chess

中国银行 **Zhōngguó Yínháng** Bank of China

中国制造 **Zhōngguó zhìzào** made in China

中号 **zhōnghào** medium ◊ medium-sized

中和 **zhōnghé** counteract; neutralize

中华民国 **Zhōnghuá Mínguó** Republic of China, ROC

中华人民共和国 **Zhōnghuá Rénmín Gònghéguó** People's Republic of China, PRC

中级 **zhōngjí** intermediate

重击 **zhòngjī** thump, whack; hammer on

中间 **zhōngjiān** middle ◊ halfway

中间对齐 **zhōngjiān duìqí** center *text*

中兼分子 **zhōngjiān fènzi** hard core POL

中间楼层 **zhōngjiān lóucéng** mezzanine

中间名 **zhōngjiān míng** middle name

中间派 **zhōngjiān pài** center POL

中间人 **zhōngjiān rén** go-between

终究 **zhōngjiū** finally

中肯 **zhòngkěn** apt ◊ aptly

中空 **zhōngkōng** hollow

肿块 **zhǒngkuài** lump, swelling

种类 **zhǒnglèi** kind, type, variety; species

中立 **zhōnglì** disinterested; neutral

重力 **zhònglì** gravity PHYS

重量 **zhòngliàng** weight

中量级 **zhōngliàng jí** middleweight SP

重量级 **zhòngliàng jí** heavyweight SP

中立地位 **zhōnglì dìwèi** neutrality

肿瘤 **zhǒngliú** tumor

钟楼 **zhōnglóu** belfry

钟面 **zhōngmiàn** dial, face (*of clock*)

中年 **zhōngnián** middle age ◊ middle-aged

中篇小说 **zhōngpiān xiǎoshuō** novella

钟情 **zhōngqíng** loving

中秋节 **Zhōngqiūjié** Mid-Autumn Festival, Moon Festival

中人 **zhōngrén** intermediary

中日战争 **Zhōngrì Zhànzhēng** Sino-Japanese war

中山服 **zhōngshānfú** Mao jacket

终身 **zhōngshēn** lifelong; for life

终身伴侣 **zhōngshēn bànlǚ** life partner

钟声 **zhōngshēng** ring (*of bell*)

忠实 **zhōngshí** devoted

中式 **zhōngshì** Chinese-style

中士 **zhōngshì** sergeant

重视 **zhòngshì** value, attach importance to

中世纪 **Zhōngshìjì** Middle Ages ◊ medieval

重事轻说 **zhòngshì qīngshuō** understatement

忠实于 zhōngshí yú be devoted to

中暑 zhòngshǔ heatstroke; 他中暑了 tā zhòngshǔ le he has had too much sun

众所周知 zhòng suǒ zhōu zhī well-known

重听 zhòngtīng hard of hearing

中途 zhōngtú midway

中途停留 zhōngtú tíngliú stop over ◊ stopover

中途退出 zhōngtú tuìchū abort COMPUT

中途退学 zhōngtú tuìxué drop out (of school)

中尉 zhōngwèi lieutenant

中文 Zhōngwén Chinese (language)

中午 zhōngwǔ midday

仲夏 zhòngxià midsummer

中小学教师 zhōngxiǎoxué jiàoshī schoolteacher

中小学女教师 zhōngxiǎoxué nǚ jiàoshī schoolmistress

中小学女生 zhōngxiǎoxué nǚ shēng schoolgirl

中小学男教师 zhōngxiǎoxué nán jiàoshī schoolmaster

中小学男生 zhōngxiǎoxué nánshēng schoolboy

中小学生 zhōngxiǎoxué xuéshēng schoolchild

中心 zhōngxīn center; heart

忠心 zhōngxīn loyal ◊ loyalty

衷心 zhōngxīn sincere; warm

中学 zhōngxué middle school; junior high school

中学生 zhōngxuéshēng middle school student; junior high school student

中央 zhōngyāng central ◊ middle

中央处理机 zhōngyāng chùlǐ jī CPU, central processing unit

中央电视台 Zhōngyāng Diànshìtái China Central Television, CCTV

中央情报局 Zhōngyāng Qíngbào Jú CIA, Central Intelligence Agency

中药 zhōngyào Chinese medicine

重要 zhòngyào important, significant

重要性 zhòngyào xìng importance, significance

中医 zhōngyī Chinese medicine; Chinese doctor

重音 zhòngyīn accent, emphasis

众议员 zhòngyì yuán representative

众议院 Zhòngyì yuàn House of Representatives

终于 zhōngyú finally, eventually, in the end

忠于 zhōngyú stand by, be loyal to

肿胀 zhǒngzhàng swell up ◊ swollen ◊ swelling

忠贞 zhōngzhēn fidelity

终止 zhōngzhǐ terminate ◊ termination

中止 zhōngzhǐ cease, discontinue

中指 zhōngzhǐ middle finger

终止 zhōngzhǐ end, finish

种植 zhòngzhí grow, cultivate; plant

终止日期 zhōngzhǐ rìqī expiry date

种植园 zhòngzhí yuán plantation

种子 zhǒngzi seed, pip

种子选手 zhǒngzi xuǎnshǒu seed (in tennis)

种族 zhǒngzú race, people ◊ ethnic, racial

种族隔离 zhǒngzú gélí racial segregation

重罪 zhòngzuì felony

种族平等 zhǒngzú píngděng racial equality

种族歧视 zhǒngzú qíshì racism ◊ racist

种族歧视者 zhǒngzú qíshì zhě racist

种族社区 zhǒngzú shèqū ethnic group

粥 zhōu rice porridge, congee

洲 zhōu continent

州 zhōu prefecture; state

周 zhōu week; circle

轴 zhóu shaft; axle

肘 zhǒu elbow

皱 zhòu crease, wrinkle

轴承 zhóuchéng bearing TECH

周到 **zhōudao** considerate; tactful

周恩来 **Zhōu Ēnlái** Zhou Enlai, Chou En-lai

周刊 **zhōukān** weekly magazine

咒骂 **zhòumà** curse, swear; 咒骂 X **zhòumà X** swear at X

皱眉 **zhòuméi** frown

周末 **zhōumò** weekend ◊ on the weekend

周年 **zhōunián** anniversary

周年大会 **zhōunián dàhuì** annual general meeting

周期 **zhōuqī** cycle; period

周期性 **zhōuqī xìng** periodic; cyclical

骤然下跌 **zhòurán xiàdiē** decline, slump

周围 **zhōuwéi** around ◊ surrounding ◊ surroundings

皱纹 **zhòuwén** crease, wrinkle

绉纹纸 **zhòuwén zhǐ** crepe paper

骤增 **zhòuzēng** bulge, sudden increase

州长 **zhōuzhǎng** governor

猪 **zhū** hog, pig

珠 **zhū** pearl; bead

逐 **zhú** follow

竹 **zhú** bamboo

煮 **zhǔ** boil

主 **zhǔ** main ◊ master, lord

住 **zhù** live, reside; stop ◊ (showing result): 记住 **jì zhù** remember; 抓住 **zhuā zhù** catch

柱 **zhù** pillar

祝 **zhù** wish; 祝 X 走运 **zhù X zǒuyùn** wish X well; 祝你走运！ **zhù nǐ zǒuyùn!** good luck!; 祝你健康！ **zhù nǐ jiànkāng!** your health!

助 **zhù** help

抓 **zhuā** grasp; scratch

爪 **zhuǎ** claw

拽 **zhuài** pull, tow

抓阄儿 **zhuājiūr** draw lots

抓牢 **zhuā láo** tighten one's grip on

专 **zhuān** special

砖 **zhuān** brick; tile

转 **zhuǎn** turn; move, transfer ◊ turning

转 **zhuàn** turn; revolve

传 **zhuàn** biography

转变 **zhuǎnbiàn** shift, change direction ◊ swing; changeover

转播 **zhuǎnbō** relay signal

专长 **zhuāncháng** prowess; specialty

转车 **zhuǎnchē** change (trains/buses)

转达 **zhuǎndá** communicate, pass on

转达问候 **zhuǎndá wènhòu** send one's regards

赚的钱 **zhuànde qián** earnings

转递 **zhuǎndì** forward letter

转动 **zhuǎndòng** turn

转动 **zhuǎndòng** turn; revolve; swing

桩 **zhuāng** stake, peg

装 **zhuāng** pack; install ◊ clothing; 装胶卷 **zhuāng jiāojuǎn** load camera

庄 **zhuāng** village

撞 **zhuàng** hit; bang, bump, strike

壮 **zhuàng** strong

幢 **zhuàng** measure word for buildings; 一幢楼房 **yízhuàng lóufáng** an apartment block

转告 **zhuǎngào** relay message

撰稿人 **zhuàngǎorén** scriptwriter

装扮 **zhuāngbàn** disguise oneself, dress up; 装扮成 **zhuāngbàn chéng** disguise oneself as, dress up as

装备 **zhuāngbèi** equipment ◊ equip; furnish

装玻璃工人 **zhuāng bōlí de gōngren** glazier

装车 **zhuāng chē** load vehicle

壮大 **zhuàngdà** healthy

装弹药 **zhuāng dànyào** load gun

撞倒 **zhuàngdǎo** run over, knock down; 司机把车撞到 **sījī bǎ chē zhuàngdào …** the driver smashed into …

装钉 **zhuāngdīng** binding

撞翻 **zhuàngfān** knock over

壮观 **zhuàngguān** grand; spectacular ◊ splendor; spectacle

装潢 **zhuānghuáng** décor; decoration

装潢工人 **zhuānghuáng**

gōngrén decorator

撞毁 **zhuànghuǐ** crash *car*

撞击 **zhuàngjī** knock, hit ◊ blow; impact

庄稼 **zhuāngjia** crops

装甲车 **zhuāngjiǎ chē** armored vehicle

撞见 **zhuàngjiàn** bump into; happen to see; 撞见 X 做 Y **zhuàngjiàn X zuò Y** catch X doing Y

状况 **zhuàngkuàng** state, condition

壮丽 **zhuànglì** magnificence

装满 **zhuāngmǎn** fill up; top up ◊ full

装配 **zhuāngpèi** set up

装配厂 **zhuāngpèi chǎng** assembly plant

装配工 **zhuāngpèi gōng** fitter

装配线 **zhuāngpèi xiàn** assembly line

装腔作势 **zhuāngqiāng zuòshì** pose, pretense

装软件 **zhuāng ruǎnjiàn** load COMPUT

装入口袋 **zhuāngrù kǒudài** pack, bag up

装饰 **zhuāngshì** decorate, adorn ◊ decoration, embellishment ◊ decorative, ornamental

装饰物 **zhuāngshì wù** ornament

装饰性 **zhuāngshì xìng** cosmetic, superficial

撞碎 **zhuàngsuì** smash, crash

状态 **zhuàngtài** condition, state; 处于交战状态 **chǔyú jiāozhàn zhuàngtài** be at war; 处于戒备状态 **chǔyú jièbèi zhuàngtài** be on the alert

装卸工 **zhuāngxiè gōng** stevedore

装修 **zhuāngxiū** decorate *room etc*

庄严 **zhuāngyán** dignified

装有 **zhuāngyǒu** be supplied with

装载 **zhuāngzài** load

装置 **zhuāngzhì** fittings

庄重 **zhuāngzhòng** grave, solemn

装作 **zhuāngzuò** pretend; pose as

转航 **zhuǎnháng** tack (*of yacht*)

专横 **zhuānhèng** high-handed

转化 **zhuǎnhuà** convert

转换 **zhuǎnhuàn** change

转机 **zhuǎnjī** transfer (*of passengers*)

传记 **zhuànjì** biography

专家 **zhuānjiā** expert, specialist

专家建议 **zhuānjiā jiànyì** expert advice

转机厅 **zhuǎnjī tīng** transit lounge

专科医生 **zhuānkē yīshēng** specialist (doctor)

专栏 **zhuānlán** column

专栏作家 **zhuānlán zuòjiā** columnist

专利 **zhuānlì** patent

转脸 **zhuǎnliǎn** turn away, look away

专门 **zhuānmén** special; 专门从事 **zhuānmén cóngshì** specialize; specialize in

专门知识 **zhuānmén zhīshi** expertise

转晴 **zhuǎnqíng** brighten up, clear up

转让 **zhuǎnràng** entrust; transfer; 把 X 转让给 Y **bǎ X zhuǎnràng gěi Y** make X over to Y

转让契据 **zhuǎnràng qìjù** bill of sale

专人 **zhuānrén** by hand

转入地下 **zhuǎnrù dìxià** go underground POL

转身 **zhuǎnshēn** turn around, spin around

砖石结构 **zhuānshí jiégòu** masonry

转手 **zhuǎnshǒu** change hands

专题 **zhuāntí** article, feature

砖头 **zhuāntóu** brick

转弯 **zhuǎnwān** turn the corner

转弯处 **zhuǎnwān chù** curve; corner, bend

转向 **zhuǎnxiàng** change direction; turn around; move on ◊ change of direction; U-turn

专心 **zhuānxīn** concentrate ◊ concentration; devotion

专心致志 **zhuānxīn zhìzhì** single-minded

专业 **zhuānyè** professional ◊

subject, field; area of expertise

专业知识 **zhuānyè zhīshi** specialized knowledge

专业人士 **zhuānyè rénshì** professional (*lawyer etc*)

转移 **zhuǎnyí** transfer, move; avert

转运商 **zhuǎnyùn shāng** forwarding agent

转折点 **zhuǎnzhé diǎn** turning point

专政 **zhuānzhèng** dictatorship

转租 **zhuǎnzū** sublet

抓取 **zhuāqǔ** snatch

抓住 **zhuāzhù** grab, grasp; grip; scratch

爪子 **zhuǎzi** claw; paw

主板 **zhǔbǎn** mainboard COMPUT

珠宝 **zhūbǎo** jewel; jewelry

珠宝商 **zhūbǎo shāng** jeweler

逐步 **zhúbù** progressively, steadily; step by step; 逐步引进 **zhúbù yǐnjìn** phase in; 逐步中止 **zhúbù zhōngzhǐ** phase out

逐步发展 **zhúbù fāzhǎn** progressive

逐步升级 **zhúbù shēngjí** escalate

贮藏 **zhùcáng** storage

注册 **zhùcè** enroll ◊ enrolment

助产士 **zhùchǎnshì** midwife

主持 **zhǔchí** present; host; front; chair; preside; 主持会议 **zhǔchí huìyì** chair a meeting; 主持婚礼 **zhǔchí hūnlǐ** conduct a wedding

主持人 **zhǔchí rén** host (*of TV program*)

逐出 **zhúchū** eject, evict

住处 **zhùchù** place (where one lives)

贮存 **zhùcún** store

贮存空间 **zhùcún kōngjiān** storage space

主导 **zhǔdǎo** dominant

主祷文 **Zhǔdǎo Wén** Lord's Prayer

驻地 **zhùdì** resident; garrison

筑堤坝 **zhùdībà** dam

注定 **zhùdìng** condemn, doom; 注定失败 **zhùdìng shībài** doomed to failure

主动 **zhǔdòng** initiative ◊ active

GRAM; 主动做 X **zhǔdòng zuò X** do X on one's own initiative

主动表示 **zhǔdòng biǎoshì** make overtures to

住房 **zhùfáng** housing

住房条件 **zhùfáng tiáojiàn** housing conditions

祝福 **zhùfú** bless ◊ blessing

逐个 **zhúgè** one by one

主观 **zhǔguān** subjective

主管 **zhǔguǎn** supervisor, boss ◊ be in charge of, oversee

主管人员 **zhǔguǎn rényuán** executive; management

主观愿望 **zhǔguān yuànwàng** wishful thinking

煮过火儿 **zhǔ guòhuǒr** overcook

祝好 **zhùhǎo** best wishes, congratulations ◊ congratulate

祝贺 **zhùhè** congratulate; 祝贺 ... **zhùhè** ... congratulations on ...

追 **zhuī** chase, pursue

追赶 **zhuīgǎn** chase, pursue

追赶者 **zhuīgǎn zhě** pursuer

坠毁 **zhuìhuǐ** crash

追究 **zhuījiū** get down to

追求 **zhuīqiú** seek, pursue

追溯 **zhuīsù** date back to; backdate ◊ retroactive

追随者 **zhuīsuí zhě** follower, supporter

追逐 **zhuīzhú** pursue ◊ pursuit

逐渐 **zhújiàn** gradual ◊ gradually; 逐渐减少 **zhújiàn jiǎnshǎo** taper off, decline; 逐渐习惯 **zhújiàn xíguàn** get accustomed to; 逐渐形成 **zhújiàn xíngchéng** evolve

珠江 **Zhūjiāng** Pearl River

珠江三角洲 **Zhūjiāng Sānjiǎozhōu** Pearl River Delta

主教 **zhǔjiào** bishop

助教 **zhùjiào** teaching assistant

主机体 **zhǔjītǐ** mainframe

猪圈 **zhūjuàn** pigpen

主角 **zhǔjué** leading role

主考人 **zhǔkǎo rén** examiner

助理研究员 **zhùlǐ yánjiū yuán** research assistant

注满 **zhùmǎn** fill

著名 **zhùmíng** famous, distinguished; 以 X 著名 **yǐ X**

zhùmíng be famous for X

注明日期 **zhùmíng rìqī** date *letter etc*

珠穆朗玛峰 **Zhūmùlǎngmǎfēng** Mount Everest

准 **zhǔn** allow ◊ accurate

准备 **zhǔnbèi** plan; prepare; fix ◊ preparation; 把 X 准备好 **bǎ X zhǔnbèi hǎo** get X ready

准备工作 **zhǔnbèi gōngzuò** preparations

准备就绪 **zhǔnbèi jiùxù** readiness

准备练习 **zhǔnbèi liànxí** warm up

准确 **zhǔnquè** accurate; precise

准确性 **zhǔnquè xìng** accuracy

准时 **zhǔnshí** punctual ◊ punctually

准许 **zhǔnxǔ** approve; 准许 X 做 Y **zhǔnxǔ X zuò Y** permit X to do Y

准予 **zhǔnyǔ** grant

准予进入 **zhǔnyǔ jìnrù** entrance, admission

准则 **zhǔnzé** principle; norm; standard

捉 **zhuō** hold; catch

桌 **zhuō** table

啄 **zhuó** peck

桌布 **zhuōbù** tablecloth

捉到 **zhuōdào** capture

拙劣 **zhuōliè** badly

着陆 **zhuólù** land (*of aircraft*) ◊ landing

桌面排版 **zhuōmiàn páibǎn** desktop publishing, DTP

捉迷藏 **zhuōmícáng** hide-and-seek

啄木鸟 **zhuómùniǎo** woodpecker

捉弄 **zhuōnòng** take in, take for a ride

酌情 **zhuóqíng** use one's discretion; 由你酌情处理 **yóu nǐ zhuóqíng chǔlǐ** deal with it at your discretion

啄食 **zhuóshí** peck at one's food

着手 **zhuóshǒu** initiate; start work

着想 **zhuóxiǎng** consider, show consideration for

卓有成效 **zhuō yǒu chéngxiào** effective; successful

卓越 **zhuóyuè** outstanding; remarkable; notable ◊ remarkably

捉住 **zhuōzhù** catch, capture

茁壮生长 **zhuózhuàng shēngzhǎng** thrive

桌子 **zhuōzi** table

猪皮 **zhūpí** pigskin

主权 **zhǔquán** sovereign, independent ◊ sovereignty, independence

主人 **zhǔrén** host; master, owner

猪肉 **zhūròu** pork

侏儒 **zhūrú** dwarf

注射 **zhùshè** inject ◊ injection, shot

注射器 **zhùshè qì** syringe

主食 **zhǔshí** staple; staple diet

注视 **zhùshì** gaze ◊ gaze at

注释 **zhùshì** note; gloss

助手 **zhùshǒu** assistant, helper

主诉 **zhǔsù** complain of MED

竹笋 **zhúsǔn** bamboo shoots

住所 **zhùsuǒ** residence; accommodations

烛台 **zhútái** candlestick

主题 **zhǔtí** subject, topic, theme ◊ topical

铸铁 **zhùtiě** cast iron

主题歌 **zhǔtí gē** theme song

助听器 **zhùtīng qì** hearing aid

主卧室 **zhǔwòshì** master bedroom

主席 **zhǔxí** chair; chairman; chairwoman; chairperson

主修 **zhǔxiū** major in, specialize in

助学金 **zhùxuéjīn** grant (*for studies*)

主演 **zhǔyǎn** star

主要 **zhǔyào** main, major; chief ◊ mainly, primarily; mostly

主页 **zhǔyè** homepage

主意 **zhǔyì** idea; 好主意 **hǎo zhǔyì** good idea; inspiration

注意 **zhùyì** notice; pay attention to; 注意到 X **zhùyì dào X** take note of X; 引起 X 的注意 **yǐnqǐ X de zhùyì** catch X's eye

注意力 **zhùyìlì** attention

注意形象 **zhùyì xíngxiàng**

image-conscious

猪油 **zhūyóu** lard

主语 **zhǔyǔ** subject GRAM

住院 **zhùyuàn** go into the hospital

住院病人 **zhùyuàn bìngrén** in-patient

铸造 **zhùzào** cast

铸造厂 **zhùzào chǎng** foundry

驻扎 **zhùzhā** place, station *guard etc*; 驻扎在 **zhùzhā zài** be stationed at

住宅区 **zhùzhái qū** residential area

主张 **zhǔzhāng** cause; position ◊ advocate, stand up for; represent

注重 **zhùzhòng** attach importance to

珠子 **zhūzi** bead; pearl

竹子 **zhúzi** bamboo

柱子 **zhùzi** pillar

住嘴! **zhùzuǐ!** shut up!

资 **zī** money, funds

紫 **zǐ** purple

子 **zǐ** son; child; seed

字 **zì** word; character; handwriting

自 **zì** self ◊ from

自卑感 **zìbēi gǎn** inferiority complex

资本 **zīběn** capital

资本家 **zīběn jiā** capitalist (*businessman*)

资本支出 **zīběn zhīchū** capital expenditure

资本主义 **zīběn zhǔyì** capitalism ◊ capitalist

资本主义者 **zīběn zhǔyì zhě** capitalist

滋补 **zībǔ** nutritious

资产 **zīchǎn** asset FIN

资产阶级 **zīchǎn jiējí** bourgeoisie

自从 **zìcóng** since; 自从你走以后 **zìcóng nǐ zǒu yǐhòu** since you left

自大 **zìdà** big-headed

子弹 **zǐdàn** bullet; cartridge; pellet

子弟 **zǐdì** disciple

字典 **zìdiǎn** dictionary

自动 **zìdòng** automatic ◊ automatically; by itself

自动点唱机 **zìdòng diǎnchàngjī** jukebox

自动扶梯 **zìdòng fútī** escalator

自动化 **zìdòng huà** automation

自动驾驶仪 **zìdòng jiàshǐ yí** autopilot

自动售货机 **zìdòng shòuhuò jī** vending machine

自发 **zìfā** spontaneous

自负 **zìfù** pompous; arrogant; vain, conceited ◊ conceit

兹附上 **zīfùshàng** please find enclosed

自高自大 **zìgāo zìdà** conceited; ostentatious

资格 **zīgé** qualification; 取得资格 **qǔde zīgé** qualify; 取消资格 **qǔxiāo zīgé** disqualify; 我不够资格来决定 **wǒ bùgòu zīgé lái juédìng** I am not qualified to judge

子宫 **zǐgōng** uterus, womb

子宫切除术 **zǐgōng qiēchúshù** hysterectomy

子宫托 **zǐgōng tuō** diaphragm

自豪 **zìháo** pride ◊ proud ◊ proudly; 以 … 为自豪 **yǐ … wéi zìháo** be proud of

自己 **zìjǐ** self; oneself ◊ own ◊ by oneself; 自己做 X **zìjǐ zuò X** do X by oneself; 我自己的公寓 / 车 **wǒ zìjǐde gōngyù / chē** a car / an apartment of my own

字迹 **zìjì** writing

字节 **zìjié** byte

资金 **zījīn** capital, money

紫禁城 **Zǐjìnchéng** Forbidden City

自己一个人 **zìjǐ yīgè rén** alone

自觉 **zìjué** conscious

自控 **zìkòng** control oneself

自来水 **zìláishuǐ** running water

自来水笔 **zìláishuǐ bǐ** fountain pen

资料保密 **zīliào bǎomì** data protection

紫罗兰 **zǐ luólán** violet (*plant*)

紫罗兰色 **zǐ luólán sè** violet (*color*)

自满 **zìmǎn** complacent, smug ◊ complacency, smugness

字面 **zìmiàn** literal ◊ literally

自鸣得意 **zìmíng déyì** self-satisfied

字母 zìmǔ letter (of alphabet); 依字母顺序 yī zìmǔ shùnxù alphabetical order

字幕 zìmù subtitle

字母表 zìmǔbiǎo alphabet

自欺 zìqī delude oneself

子儿 zǐr piece (in chess etc)

自然 zìrán nature ◊ natural ◊ naturally, of course

自然保护区 zìrán bǎohùqū nature reserve

自然环境 zìrán huánjìng the environment

自然界 zìrán jiè natural

自然科学 zìrán kēxué natural science

自然科学家 zìrán kēxué jiā natural scientist

自然灾害 zìrán zāihài natural disaster

紫色 zǐsè purple

自杀 zìshā suicide ◊ commit suicide

滋生地 zīshēng dì breeding ground

姿势 zīshì position; posture; 摆姿势 bǎi zīshì pose

字首 zìshǒu monogram ◊ monogrammed

自首 zìshǒu turn in (to police)

自私 zìsī selfish

自私自利 zìsī-zìlì selfish

字体 zìtǐ font; typeface

紫外 zǐwài ultraviolet

滋味 zīwèi flavor, taste

自卫 zìwèi self-defense

自我 zìwǒ self; ego; 以自我为中心 yǐ zìwǒ wéi zhōngxīn egocentric

自我表达 zìwǒ biǎodá self-expression ◊ express oneself

自我控制 zìwǒ kòngzhì self-control

自我批评 zìwǒ pīpíng self-criticism

自我约束 zìwǒ yuēshù self-discipline

仔细 zìxì careful, thorough ◊ closely; 仔细察看 zìxì chákàn study, examine; investigate; 仔细

检查 zìxì jiǎnchá check, go over; 仔细彻底 zìxì chèdǐ scrupulous; 仔细考虑 zìxì kǎolǜ deliberate; mull over

自相矛盾 zìxiāng máodùn paradox

自信 zìxìn confident; self-confident; assertive ◊ self-confidence

自行车 zìxíngchē bicycle

自行车架 zìxíngchē jià parking rack (for bicycle)

自信心 zìxìnxīn self-confidence

自选 zìxuǎn self-service ◊ optional

自学 zìxué self-study

咨询 zīxún advice; consultancy

咨询公司 zīxún gōngsī consultancy

恣意 zìyì wanton

自以为是 zì yǐwéi shì self-righteous

自由 zìyóu freedom, liberty ◊ free; liberal POL; 自由放荡 zìyóu fàngdàng run wild

自由女神像 Zìyóu Nǚshén Xiàng Statue of Liberty

自由市场经济 zìyóu shìchǎng jīngjì free market economy

自由泳 zìyóuyǒng crawl, freestyle

资源 zīyuán resource

自愿 zìyuàn of one's own accord; voluntary ◊ voluntarily

自治 zìzhì autonomy

自制 zìzhì homemade ◊ self-possession

自制力 zìzhì lì self control

自治区 zìzhì qū autonomous region

资助 zīzhù subsidize; back; stake

自传 zìzhuàn autobiography

自助餐 zìzhù cān buffet, self-service meal

自助餐馆 zìzhù cānguǎn self-service restaurant

自助式 zìzhù shì self-service

孜孜不倦 zīzī bùjuàn tireless

自尊 zìzūn self-esteem; pride, self-respect ◊ proud

自尊心 zìzūn xīn self-respect

鬃 zōng mane

踪 **zōng** footprint

总 **zǒng** total; general; main; gross FIN ◊ always

纵 **zòng** vertical

总部 **zǒngbù** head office

总裁 **zǒngcái** president

总的 **zǒngde** general, overall; 总的看来 **zǒngde kànlái** on the whole

总额 **zǒng'é** lump sum

总共 **zǒnggòng** altogether; 总共七十美元 **zǒnggòng qīshí měiyuán** that comes to $70 altogether

总公司 **zǒnggōngsī** parent company

综合 **zōnghé** comprehensive; 综合报道 **zōnghé bàodào** news round-up

纵横交错 **zònghéng jiāocuò** checkered

棕褐色 **zōnghè sè** tan (color)

综合性 **zōnghé xìng** full, comprehensive

纵火 **zònghuǒ** arson

踪迹 **zōngjī** track, trace

总机 **zǒngjī** telephone exchange

宗教 **zōngjiào** religion ◊ religious

总计 **zǒngjì** total

总结 **zǒngjié** summary

总经理 **zǒng jīnglǐ** CEO, chief executive officer, managing director

总计为 **zǒngjìwéi** add up to

总理 **zǒnglǐ** premier, prime minister

棕榈树 **zōnglǘshù** palm tree

棕色 **zōngsè** brown

纵深 **zòngshēn** deep

总是 **zǒngshì** always

棕树 **zōngshù** palm tree

总数 **zǒngshù** total; sum

总司令 **zǒngsīlìng** commander-in-chief

总体 **zǒngtǐ** overall

总统 **zǒngtǒng** president ◊ presidential

总统竞选 **zǒngtǒng jìngxuǎn** presidential campaign

总统职位 **zǒngtǒng zhíwèi** presidency

总帐 **zǒngzhàng** ledger

总之 **zǒngzhī** anyhow, in any case; to sum up, briefly

总指挥部 **zǒng zhǐhuībù** headquarters

走 **zǒu** walk; go; move; leave; run; navigate COMPUT; 走吧 **zǒuba** let's go; 走了 **zǒule** walk away; walk out; go ◊ gone 我得走了 **wǒ děi zǒule** I must be going

揍 **zòu** beat up; punch, sock

奏 **zòu** play musical instrument

走调 **zǒudiào** out of tune

走动 **zǒudòng** get around; move around

走狗 **zǒugǒu** pej running dog; yesman

走过 **zǒuguò** tread; walk past

走过来 **zǒu guòlai** approach

走后门儿 **zǒu hòuménr** go through the back door

走火 **zǒuhuǒ** go off (of gun)

走近 **zǒujìn** draw near

走进 **zǒujìn** enter

走开 **zǒukāi** buzz off; walk away

走廊 **zǒuláng** corridor; passageway; hall

走路 **zǒulù** walk, go on foot ◊ walking

走慢 **zǒumàn** lose time (of watch)

走散 **zǒusàn** wander off

走神 **zǒushén** wander (of attention)

走失 **zǒushī** stray

走私 **zǒusī** smuggle ◊ smuggling

走私者 **zǒusī zhě** smuggler

走投无路 **zǒutóu wúlù** desperate

走味儿 **zǒuwèir** stale

奏效 **zòuxiào** work, succeed

走走 **zǒuzou** walk, walk around

走嘴 **zǒuzuǐ** slip of the tongue

租 **zū** rent; hire; lease

卒 **zú** pawn (in chess)

足 **zú** foot ◊ enough

组 **zǔ** group; team; crew

祖 **zǔ** ancestor ◊ ancestral

阻 **zǔ** block; stop

阻碍 **zǔ'ài** hinder, impede, frustrate ◊ setback

钻 **zuàn** drill

钻孔 **zuānkǒng** bore a hole

钻石 **zuànshí** diamond

钻头 **zuàntóu** drill

组成 **zǔchéng** make up, comprise

组成成分 **zǔchéng chéngfèn** composition, make-up

租出 **zūchū** lease out

阻挡 **zǔdǎng** obstruct; keep, detain ◊ tackle SP

阻冻剂 **zǔdòngjì** antifreeze

组分 **zǔfèn** constituent, component

阻风门 **zǔfēngmén** choke MOT

祖父 **zǔfù** grandfather (*paternal*)

祖父母 **zǔfùmǔ** grandparents (*paternal*)

足够 **zúgòu** enough, sufficient, ample ◊ amply; 足够多了 **zúgòu duō le** that's plenty

祖国 **zǔguó** native country, homeland

组合 **zǔhé** combination ◊ group

组合成一体 **zǔhéchéng yìtǐ** put together, assemble

组合装置 **zǔhé zhuāngzhì** system COMPUT

嘴 **zuǐ** mouth; spout

醉 **zuì** drunk

最 **zuì** most; 最漂亮 **zuì piàoliàng** the most beautiful; 最大 **zuìdà** the biggest; the eldest

罪 **zuì** crime

最初 **zuìchū** first; original; initial

嘴唇 **zuǐchún** lip

最底 **zuìdǐ** bottom ◊ minimum; lowest

最低工资 **zuìdī gōngzī** minimum wage

最顶 **zuìdǐng** top, uppermost

最多 **zuìduō** maximum; most ◊ at most

罪恶 **zuì'è** sin

罪犯 **zuìfàn** criminal; culprit; offender

最高 **zuìgāo** highest; topmost; tallest

最高档 **zuì gāodàng** top gear

最高级会议 **zuì gāojí huìyì** summit meeting

最高权威 **zuìgāo quánwēi** supremacy

最高限度 **zuìgāo xiàndù** ceiling, limit

最高一层 **zuìgāo yīcéng** top floor

最高音部 **zuì gāoyīn bù** treble MUS

醉鬼 **zuìguǐ** drunk

最好 **zuìhǎo** best; 你最好征得同意 **nǐ zuìhào zhēngdé tóngyì** you'd best ask permission

最后 **zuìhòu** last, final; ultimate ◊ finally, lastly; in the end; 最后关头 **zuìhòu guāntóu** at the eleventh hour; 作为最后一招 **zuòwéi zuìhòu yīzhāo** as a last resort

最后较量 **zuìhòu jiàoliàng** showdown

最后结果 **zuìhòu jiéguǒ** upshot

最后面 **zuìhòumiàn** the very back; bottom (*of garden etc*)

最后期限 **zuìhòu qīxiàn** deadline

最后通牒 **zuìhòu tōngdié** ultimatum

最坏 **zuìhuài** worst ◊ the worst

最佳 **zuìjiā** best, optimum

最近 **zuìjìn** recent; closest ◊ recently; the other day; in the near future, soon; 最近的公共汽车站 **zuìjìnde gōnggòng qìchē zhàn** the nearest bus stop; 最近在忙些什么? **zuìjìn zài mángxiē shénme?** what are you up to these days?

最酒会 **zuìjiǔhuì** cocktail party

最快速度 **zuìkuài sùdù** top speed

最轻微 **zuì qīngwēi** least, slightest

罪人 **zuìrén** sinner; offender

最少 **zuìshǎo** least; minimum

最深 **zuìshēn** innermost; deepest

最适宜 **zuì shìyí** optimum, most suitable

最小 **zuìxiǎo** least, smallest

最喜欢 **zuì xǐhuan** favorite; pet

最新 **zuìxīn** latest; newest; 最新版本 **zuìxīn bǎnběn** latest edition

罪行 **zuìxíng** crime; offense

最优良 **zuì yōuliáng** state-of-the-art

最优秀 **zuì yōuxiù** top (*of class etc*)

罪有应得 **zuì yǒu yīngdé** it serves you/him right

最远 **zuìyuǎn** furthest, farthest

最糟 **zuìzāo** worst

最终 **zuìzhōng** eventual; final, ultimate ◊ eventually; in due course; ultimately, finally

最终结果 **zuìzhōng jiéguǒ** end result

最重要 **zuì zhòngyào** most important, central, paramount ◊ above all

租金 **zūjīn** rent, rental

阻力 **zǔlì** resistance

祖母 **zǔmǔ** grandmother (*paternal*)

祖母绿 **zǔmǔlǜ** emerald green

尊 **zūn** respect

遵 **zūn** follow, abide by

遵从 **zūncóng** follow, comply with ◊ compliance

尊敬 **zūnjìng** respect ◊ honored, esteemed; 尊敬的先生 **zūnjìngde xiānsheng** Dear Sir

遵守 **zūnshǒu** abide by, comply with ◊ observance; 遵守规章 **zūnshǒu guīzhāng** conform, obey the rules

遵循 **zūnxún** follow, keep to

尊严 **zūnyán** dignity

鳟鱼 **zūnyú** trout

尊重 **zūnzhòng** respect; honor

昨 **zuó** yesterday

左 **zuǒ** left

坐 **zuò** sit; sit down; catch, get *bus etc*; go by *car etc*

作 **zuò** make, do; be

做 **zuò** do; make; perform, carry out; have *operation*; 为X做好事 **wèi X zuò hǎoshì** do X a good turn; 做吧! **zuò ba!** go on, do it!

座 **zuò** seat ◊ stand, support ◊ *measure word for mountains and buildings*; 一座山 **yī zuò shān** a mountain

作伴 **zuòbàn** keep ... company

坐班房 **zuò bānfáng** be behind bars

作弊 **zuòbì** cheat; fix, rig

左边 **zuǒbian** left, left-hand side ◊ left-hand

左边驾驶车 **zuǒbiān jiàshǐ chē** left-hand drive

左侧 **zuǒcè** left ◊ to the left

坐舱 **zuòcāng** cabin, cockpit

坐车 **zuòchē** go by car; go by train

做出 **zuòchū** arrive at *decision etc*

坐船 **zuòchuán** go by boat

做出反应 **zuòchū fǎnyìng** respond, react

作出牺牲 **zuòchū xīshēng** make sacrifices

作饭 **zuòfàn** cook

作坊 **zuōfang** workshop

作翻译 **zuò fānyì** interpret; translate

作废 **zuòfèi** expire, become invalid

坐飞机 **zuò fēijī** travel by plane, fly

做工好 **zuògōnghǎo** well-made

作广告 **zuò guǎnggào** publicize; advertize

坐骨神经痛 **zuògǔ shénjīng tòng** sciatica

坐火车 **zuò huǒchē** go by train

作家 **zuòjiā** author, writer

作料 **zuóliào** seasoning

左轮手枪 **zuǒlún shǒuqiāng** revolver

坐落 **zuòluò** be situated

做梦 **zuòmèng** dream; 做梦也想不到 **zuòmèng yě xiǎng bú dào** undreamt-of

琢磨 **zuómo** ponder

作呕 **zuò'ǒu** feel nauseous; 令人作呕 **lìngrén zuò'ǒu** nauseating, disgusting

左派 **zuǒpài** the left POL

作品 **zuòpǐn** work (*book*, *painting etc*); production (*play etc*); composition MUS

作评委 **zuò píngwěi** judge *competition*

坐骑 **zuòqí** mount

坐起来 **zuòqǐlái** sit up (*in bed*)

作曲家 **zuòqǔ jiā** composer

左手 **zuǒshǒu** left-hand

做手势 **zuò shǒushì** gesticulate

昨天 **zuótiān** yesterday

昨天晚上 **zuótiān wǎnshang** last night

昨晚 **zuówǎn** last night

做完 **zuòwán** finish doing

作为 **zuòwéi** as; by way of; 作为 常规 **zuòwéi chángguī** as a matter of course; 作为秘密 **zuòwéi mìmì** in confidence

座位 **zuòwèi** place, seat

作伪证 **zuò wěizhèng** perjury ◊ perjure oneself

作文 **zuòwén** composition, essay

坐卧两用床 **zuòwò liǎngyòng chuáng** couchette

坐下 **zuòxia** sit down

左舷 **zuǒxián** port(side) NAUT

作业 **zuòyè** job, task; homework, assignment

左翼 **zuǒyì** left-wing

作用 **zuòyòng** function

作用力 **zuòyòng lì** strain

座右铭 **zuòyòumíng** motto

作者 **zuòzhě** author, writer

作证 **zuòzhèng** testify, give evidence

坐直 **zuòzhí** sit up straight

做作 **zuòzuò** theatrical, exaggerated; artificial, insincere ◊ exaggerate

租契 **zūqì** lease

足球 **zúqiú** soccer

组曲 **zǔqǔ** suite MUS

阻塞 **zǔsāi** obstruct, block ◊ traffic jam

祖先 **zǔxiān** ancestor; ancestry

足音 **zúyīn** sound of footsteps

租用 **zūyòng** lease

租用车 **zūyòng chē** rental car

租约 **zūyuē** rental agreement

族长 **zúzhǎng** (tribal) chief

组织 **zǔzhī** organization ◊ organize, put together ◊ tissue ANAT

阻止 **zǔzhǐ** stop, prevent, block; 阻 止 X 做 Y **zǔzhǐ X zuò Y** prevent X from doing Y

足智多谋 **zúzhì duōmóu** resourceful

组织者 **zǔzhī zhě** organizer

诅咒 **zǔzhòu** curse

组装 **zǔzhuāng** assemble, put together ◊ assembly

组装件 **zǔzhuāngjiàn** (assembly) kit

a, an ◊ (*no translation*): *a bus* gōnggòng qìchē 公共汽车; *I'm a student* wǒ shì xuésheng 我是学生 ◊ (*with a measure word*): *can I have a cup of coffee?* qǐng gěi wǒ yìbēi kāfēi? 请给我一杯咖啡?; *five men and a woman* wǔge nánde yíge nǚde 五个男的一个女的 ◊ (*per*): *$50 a time* yícì wǔshí měiyuán 一次五十美元

abandon *object, person* pāoqì 抛弃; *car* líqì 离弃; *plan* fàngqì 放弃

abbreviate suōxiě 缩写

abbreviation suōxiě 缩写

abdicate *v/i* tuìwèi 退位

abdomen dùzi 肚子

abdominal fùbù 腹部

abduct jiéchí 劫持

♦ **abide by** zūnshǒu 遵守

ability nénglì 能力

ablaze zháohuǒ 着火

able (*skillful*) yǒu nénglì 有能力; *be ~ to* nénggòu 能够; *I wasn't ~ to see / hear* wǒ dāngshí bùnéng kàn/tīng 我当时不能看/听

abnormal bú zhèngcháng 不正常

aboard 1 *prep* zài ... shàng 在 ... 上 **2** *adv*: ~ (*on ship*) zài chuán shàng 在船上; (*on plane*) zài fēijī shàng 在飞机上; *go ~* (*on ship*) shàng chuán 上船; (*on plane*) shàng fēijī 上飞机

abolish fèichú 废除

abort *v/t mission, rocket launch* shǐ zhōngtú shībài 使中途失败; COMPUT *program* zhōngtú tuìchū 中途退出

abortion réngōng liúchǎn 人工流产; *have an* ~ zuò rénliú 做人流

about 1 *prep* (*concerning*) guānyú ... 关于 ...; *what's it* ~? (*book, film*) jiǎng shénmede? 讲什么的?; (*complaint*) shénme shì? 什么事? **2** *adv* (*roughly*) dàyuē 大

约; ~ *50* dàyuē wǔshí 大约五十; *be ~ to ...* zhèng zhǔnbèi ... 正准备 ...

above 1 *prep* (*higher than*) bǐ ... gāo 比 ... 高; (*more than*) bǐ ... duō 比 ... 多; ~ *all* zuì zhòngyào 最重要 **2** *adv* zài shàngtóu 在上头; *on the floor* ~ lóushàng 楼上

above-mentioned suǒshù 所述

abrasion mósǔn 磨损

abrasive *personality* cūbào 粗暴

abridge jīngjiǎn 精简

abroad *live* guówài 国外; *go* ~ chūguó 出国

abrupt *departure* tūrán 突然; *manner* shēngyìng 生硬

abscess nóngzhǒng 脓肿

absence (*of person*) quēxí 缺席; (*from school*) kuàngkè 旷课; (*from work*) kuànggōng 旷工; (*lack*) quēfá 缺乏

absent *adj* quēxí 缺席; (*from school*) kuàngkè 旷课; (*from work*) kuànggōng 旷工

absent-minded xīnbù zàiyān 心不在焉

absolute *power* juéduì 绝对; *idiot* shízú 十足

absolutely (*completely*) wánquán 完全; ~ *not!* bù kěnéng! 不可能!; *do you agree?* – ~! nǐ tóngyì ma? – tóngyì 你同意吗? – 同意

absolve shèmiǎn 赦免

absorb xīshōu 吸收; ~*ed in ...* quánshén guànzhùyú ... 全神贯注于 ...

absorbent yǒu xīshōu nénglì 有吸收能力

absorbent cotton tuōzhīmián 脱脂棉

abstain (*from voting*) qìquán 弃权

abstention (*in voting*) qìquán 弃权

abstract *adj* chōuxiàng 抽象

absurd huāngtáng 荒唐

absurdity huāngtáng 荒唐
abundance fēngfù 丰富
abundant fēngfù 丰富
abuse[1] *n* (*insults*) rǔmà 辱骂; (*of child*) nüèdài 虐待; (*of thing*) lànyòng 滥用
abuse[2] *v/t* (*physically*) nüèdài 虐待; (*verbally*) rǔmà 辱骂
abusive *language* yǒu nüèdài xìng 有虐待性; *become* ~ kāishǐ chòumà 开始臭骂
abysmal (*very bad*) zāotòu 糟透
abyss shēnyuān 深渊
academic 1 *n* xuézhě 学者 **2** *adj* xuéshù 学术; *person* hàoxué 好学; *~ year* xuénián 学年
academy xuéyuàn 学院
accelerate 1 *v/i* jiāsù 加速 **2** *v/t production* jiākuài 加快
acceleration (*of car*) jiāsù 加速
accelerator yóumén 油门
accent (*when speaking*) kǒuyīn 口音; (*emphasis*) zhòngyīn 重音
accentuate qiángdiào 强调
accept *v/t offer, suggestion, present* jiēshòu 接受; *behavior, conditions* rěnshòu 忍受 **2** *v/i* jiēshòu 接受
acceptable kěyǐ róngrěn 可以容忍
acceptance jiēshòu 接受
access 1 *n* (*to a building*) rùkǒu 入口; (*to secrets*) jiējìn 接近; (*to one's children*) jiējìn de quánlì 接近的权利; *have ~ to computer* shǐyòng quán 使用权; *child* jiēchù quán 有接触权 **2** *v/t also* COMPUT shǐyòng 使用
access code COMPUT tōnglù mìmǎ 通路密码
accessible nénggòu jiējìn 能够接近
accessory (*for wearing*) yīshì fùjiàn 衣饰附件; COMPUT fùjiàn 附件; LAW bāngxiōng 帮凶
access road gōnglù zhīxiàn 公路支线
access time COMPUT shǐyòng shíjiān 使用时间
accident (*involving injury or death*) shìgù 事故; (*something not done on purpose*) bùxiǎoxīn 不小心; *by*

~ bùxiǎoxīn 不小心
accidental yìwài 意外
acclimate, acclimatize *v/t* shìyìng 适应
accommodate gěi ... tígōng zhùsuǒ 给 ... 提供住所; *special requirements* qiānjiù 迁就
accommodations zhùsuǒ 住所
accompaniment MUS bànzòu 伴奏
accompany péitóng 陪同; MUS bànzòu 伴奏
accomplice bāngxiōng 帮凶
accomplish *task* wánchéng 完成; *goal* dádào 达到
accomplished yǒu cáinéng 有才能
accord: *of one's own* ~ zìyuàn 自愿
accordance: *in* ~ *with* gēnjù 根据
according: ~ *to* gēnjù 根据
accordingly (*consequently*) yīncǐ 因此; (*appropriately*) fúhé 符合
account *n* (*financial*) zhàngmù 帐目; (*report, description*) xùshù 叙述; *give an ~ of* xùshù 叙述; *on no ~* juébù 决不; *on ~ of* yīnwèi 因为; *take ... into ~, take ~ of ...* kǎolǜ dào ... 考虑到 ...
♦**account for** (*explain*) jiěshì 解释; (*make up, constitute*) gòngjì dá 共计达
accountability zérèn 责任
accountable: *be held* ~ fù zérèn 负责任
accountant kuàijì 会计
accounting software cáiwù ruǎnjiàn 财务软件
accounts zhàngmù 帐目
accumulate *v/t & v/i* lěijī 累积
accuracy zhǔnquè xìng 准确性
accurate zhǔnquè 准确
accusation zéguài 责怪; (*public*) qiānzé 谴责
accuse zhǐkòng 指控; (*publicly*) qiānzé 谴责; *he ~d me of lying* tā zhǐkòng wǒ sāhuǎng 他指控我撒谎; *be ~d of ...* LAW bèi kònggào ... 被控告 ...
accused: *the* ~ LAW bèigào 被告
accustom: *get ~ed to* zhújiàn

xíguàn 逐渐习惯; *be ~ed to* xíguàn 习惯

ace (*in cards*)⇩ jiānr 尖儿; (*in tennis: shot*) fāqiú défēn 发球得分; (*pilot, designer etc*) dìyīliú 第一流

ache *n & v/i* tòng 痛

achieve huòdé chéngjiù 获得成就

achievement (*of ambition*) huòdé 获得; (*thing achieved*) chéngjiù 成就

acid *n* suān 酸

acid rain suānyǔ 酸雨

acid test *fig* guānjiàn de kǎoyàn 关键的考验

acknowledge chéngrèn 承认

acknowledg(e)ment rènkě 认可

acoustics yīnxiǎng 音响

acquaint: *be ~ed with* rènshi 认识

acquaintance (*person*) shúrén 熟人

acquire *skill, knowledge* huòdé 获得; *property* qǔdé 取得

acquisitive tānlán 贪婪

acquit LAW xuānpàn wúzuì 宣判无罪

acre yīngmǔ 英亩

acrobat zájì yǎnyuán 杂技演员

acrobatics zájì 杂技

across 1 *prep* (*on other side of:* *Atlantic etc*) zài … de lìngyībiān 在 … 的另一边; (*of the street, table etc*) zài … de duìmiàn 在 … 的对面; *the post office is ~ the road from the bank* yóujú zài yínháng de duìmiàn 邮局在银行的对面 ◊ (*to other side of: Atlantic etc*) héngguò 横过; (*of street etc*) guò 过; *he walked ~ America* tā héngguò Měiguó 他横过美国 2 *adv* (*to other side*) guòlái 过来; *10 yards ~* shí mǎ kuān 十码宽

act 1 *v/i* THEA biǎoyǎn 表演; (*pretend*) jiǎzhuāng 假装; *~ as* línshí dānrèn 临时担任 2 *n* (*deed*) xíngdòng 行动; (*of play*) mù 幕; (*in vaudeville*) jiémù 节目; (*pretense*) jiǎzhuāng 假装; (*law*) fǎguī 法规

acting 1 *n* (*profession*) biǎoyǎn yè 表演业; (*performance*) biǎoyǎn 表演 2 *adj* (*temporary*) dàilǐ 代理

action xíngdòng 行动; *out of ~* (*not functioning*) shīlíng 失灵; *take ~* cǎiqǔ xíngdòng 采取行动; *bring an ~ against* LAW qǐsù 起诉

action replay TV chóngfù 重复

active huóyuè 活跃; *party member* jījí 积极; GRAM zhǔdòng 主动

activist POL jījí fènzǐ 积极分子

activity huódòng 活动

actor yǎnyuán 演员

actress nǚyǎnyuán 女演员

actual shíjì 实际

actually (*in fact, to tell the truth*) shíjì shàng 实际上; (*surprise*) zhēnde 真的; *~ I do know him* (*stressing converse*) shíjìshàng wǒ rènshi tā de 实际上我认识他的

acupuncture zhēnjiǔ 针灸

acute *pain* jùliè 剧烈; *sense* mǐngǎn 敏感

ad guǎnggào 广告

adapt 1 *v/t* (*for TV, movies*) gǎibiān 改编; *machine* gǎiyòng 改用 2 *v/i* (*of person*) shìyìng 适应

adaptable *person, plant* yǒu shìyìng lì 有适应力; *vehicle etc* kě gǎiyòng 可改用

adaptation (*of play etc*) gǎibiān 改编

adapter (*electric*) jiēhé qì 接合器

add 1 *v/t* MATH, *sugar, salt etc* jiā 加; (*say, comment*) shuō 说 2 *v/i* (*of person*) suàn suànshù 算算术
♦ **add on** *15% etc* jiāshàng 加上
♦ **add up** 1 *v/t* jiāqǐlái 加起来 2 *v/i* *fig* héli 合理

addict *n* chéngyǐn zhě 成瘾者

addicted: *be ~ to X* yǒu X de yǐn 有X的瘾

addiction (*to drugs*) yǐn 瘾; (*to TV, chocolate etc*) chénní 沉溺

addictive: *be ~* (*of drugs, TV, chocolate etc*) chéngyǐn 成瘾

addition MATH jiāfǎ 加法; (*to list, company etc*) bǔchōng 补充; *in ~* lìngwài 另外; *in ~ to X* chúle X zhīwài 除了X之外

additional fùjiā 附加

additive tiānjiā jì 添加剂

add-on fùjiàn 附件

address 1 *n* dìzhǐ 地址; *form of ~* chēnghu 称呼 **2** *v/t letter* xiě dìzhǐ 写地址; *audience* jiǎnghuà 讲话; *person* chēnghu 称呼

address book tōngxùn lù 通讯录

addressee shōuxìn rén 收信人

adequate chōngfēn 充分; (*satisfactory*) jǐn gòu mǎnyì 仅够满意

adhere jiānchí 坚持

♦ **adhere to** *surface* niánfù 粘附; *rules* zūnshǒu 遵守

adhesive yǒu niánxìng 有粘性

adhesive plaster ⇩ chuàngkětiē 创可贴

adhesive tape jiāobù 胶布

adjacent línjìn 邻近

adjective xíngróngcí 形容词

adjoining gébì 隔壁

adjourn *v/i* (*of court*) zànxiū 暂休; (*of meeting*) xiūhuì 休会

adjust *v/t* tiáozhěng 调整

adjustable kě tiáozhěng 可调整

administer *medicine* gěi 给; *company* guǎnlǐ 管理; *country* zhìlǐ 治理

administration xíngzhèng 行政; (*of company*) guǎnlǐ 管理; (*of country*) zhìlǐ 治理; (*government*) zhèngfǔ 政府

administrative xíngzhèng 行政

administrator guǎnlǐ rényuán 管理人员

admirable lìngrén qīnpèi 令人钦佩

admiral hǎijūn shàngjiàng 海军上将

admiration qīnpèi 钦佩

admire qīnpèi 钦佩

admirer chóngbài zhě 崇拜者

admissible kě yǔnxǔ 可允许

admission (*confession*) chéngrèn 承认; *~ free* miǎnfèi rùchǎng 免费入场

admit (*to a hospital, organization, school*) jiēnà 接纳; (*confess*) chéngrèn 承认; (*accept*) jiēshòu 接受

admittance: *no ~* jìnzhǐ rùnèi 禁止入内

adolescence qīngchūn qī 青春期

adolescent 1 *n* qīngshàonián 青少年 **2** *adj* qīngchūn qī 青春期

adopt *child* lǐngyǎng 领养; *plan* cǎinà 采纳

adoption (*of child*) lǐngyǎng 领养; (*of plan*) cǎinà 采纳

adorable kě'ài 可爱

adore hěn xǐhuān 很喜欢

adult 1 *n* chéngrén 成人 **2** *adj* chéngrén 成人; *~ film* chéngrén piàn 成人片

adultery sītōng 私通

advance 1 *n* (*money*) tòuzhī 透支; (*in science etc*) jìnzhǎn 进展; MIL jìngōng 进攻; *in ~* yùfù 预付; (*of time*) tíqián 提前; (*get money*) yùzhī 预支; *make ~s* (*progress*) jìnbù 进步; (*sexually*) xiàn yīnqín 献殷勤 **2** *v/i* MIL jìngōng 进攻; (*make progress*) jìnbù 进步 **3** *v/t theory* tíchū 提出; *sum of money* yùfù 预付; *human knowledge, a cause* cùjìn 促进

advance booking yùyuē 预约

advanced *country* xiānjìn 先进; *level* gāoděng 高等; *learner* gāojí 高级

advance payment yùfù 预付

advantage hǎochù 好处; *it's to your ~* duì nǐ yǒu hǎochù 对你有好处; *take ~ of opportunity* lìyòng 利用

advantageous yǒulì 有利

adventure màoxiǎn 冒险

adventurous *person* xǐhuān màoxiǎn 喜欢冒险; *investment, policy* yǒu fēngxiǎn 有风险

adverb fùcí 副词

adversary duìshǒu 对手

advertise *v/t & v/i* dēng guǎnggào 登广告

advertisement guǎnggào 广告

advertiser dēng guǎnggào zhě 登广告者

advertising xuānyáng 宣扬; (*industry*) guǎnggào yè 广告业

advertising agency guǎnggào gōngsī 广告公司

advice zīxún 咨询; **take X's ~** jiēshòu X de yìjiàn 接受X的意见

advisable kěqǔ 可取

advise person quàngào 劝告; caution etc zhōnggào 忠告; **~ X to ...** jiànyì X zuò ... 建议X做 ...

adviser gùwèn 顾问

aerial tiānxiàn 天线

aerial photography hángkōngshèyǐng 航空摄影

aerobics ⇩zēng yǎng jiànshēn fǎ 增氧健身法

aerodynamic kōngqì dònglì 空气动力

aeronautical hángkōng 航空

aerosol pēnmò 喷沫

aerospace industry yǔháng gōngyè 宇航工业

affair (matter) shì ér 事儿; (business) shìwù 事务; (love) liàn'ài 恋爱; **foreign ~s** wàijiāo shìwù 外交事务; **have an ~ with** yǔ ... tōngjiān 与 ... 通奸

affect (influence, concern) yǐngxiǎng 影响; MED qīnxí 侵袭

affection àimù 爱慕

affectionate yǒu àimù xīn 有爱慕心

affinity qīnjìn 亲近

affirmative: **answer in the ~** rènkě de huídá 认可的回答

affluent fùyù 富裕; **~ society** fánróng de shèhuì 繁荣的社会

afford (financially) fùdān de qǐ 负担得起

Afghan 1 adj Āfùhàn 阿富汗 **2** n (person) Āfùhàn rén 阿富汗人

Afghanistan Āfùhàn 阿富汗

afloat boat piāofú 漂浮

afraid: **be ~** hàipà 害怕; **be ~ of** hàipà 害怕; of upsetting s.o. etc dānxīn 担心; **I'm ~** (expressing regret) kǒngpà 恐怕; **I'm ~ so** fēicháng bàoqiàn, zhèshì zhēnde 非常抱歉, 这是真的; **I'm ~ not** fēicháng bàoqiàn, bùshì zhèyàng 非常抱歉, 不是这样

Africa Fēizhōu 非洲

African 1 adj Fēizhōu 非洲 **2** n Fēizhōu rén 非洲人

after 1 prep (in order, position, time) zhīhòu 之后; **~ all** bìjìng 毕竟; **~ that** zài nà zhīhòu 在那之后; **it's ten ~ two** liǎngdiǎn shífēn 两点 10 **2** adv (afterward) hòulái 后来; **the day ~** dì'èrtiān 第二天

afternoon xiàwǔ 下午; **in the ~** zài xiàwǔ 在下午; **this ~** jīntiān xiàwǔ 今天下午; **good ~** ⇩xiàwǔ hǎo 下午好

after sales service shòuhòu fúwù 售后服务

aftershave nánshì hùfū yè 男士护肤液

aftertaste yúwèir 余味儿

afterward hòulái 后来

again zài 再

against lean kào 靠; **X ~ Y** SP X duì Y X对Y; **I'm ~ the idea** wǒ fǎnduì zhège zhǔyì 我反对这个主意; **what do you have ~ her?** nǐ duì tā yǒu shénme yìjiàn? 你对她有什么意见?; **~ the law** wéifǎ 违法

age 1 n (of person, object) niánjì 年纪; (era) shídài 时代; **at the ~ of** niánlíng wéi ... 年龄为 ...; **under ~** wèidào fǎdìng niánlíng 未到法定年龄; **she's five years of ~** tā wǔsuì le 她五岁了 **2** v/i biànlǎo 变老

agency dàilǐ chù 代理处

agenda yìchéng 议程; **on the ~** zài yìchéng shàng 在议程上

agent dàilǐ rén 代理人

aggravate (worsen) shǐ èhuà 使恶化

aggression qīnfàn xíngwéi 侵犯行为

aggressive hào xúnxìn 好寻衅; (dynamic) jījí 积极

agile línghuó 灵活

agitated jiāolù bù'ān 焦虑不安

agitation jiāolù 焦虑

agitator shàndòng zhě 煽动者

ago: **2 days ~** liǎngtiān qián 两天前; **long ~** hěnjiǔ yǐqián 很久以前; **how long ~?** duōjiǔ zhīqián? 多久之前?

agonizing nánshòu 难受

agony jídù tòngkǔ 极度痛苦

agree 1 v/i (of people, figures, accounts) tóngyì 同意; **I ~** wǒ

tóngyì 我同意; *I don't* ~ wǒ bù
tóngyì 我不同意; *it doesn't* ~
with me (of food) bú shìhé wǒ 不
适合我 **2** *v/t price* shāngdìng 商
定; ~ *that something should be
done* zànchéng yīnggāi cǎiqǔ
xíngdòng 赞成应该采取行动
agreeable *(pleasant)* lìngrén
yúkuài 令人愉快; *(in agreement)*
zànchéng 赞成
agreement *(consent)* tóngyì 同意;
(contract) xiéyì 协议; *reach* ~ *on*
dáchéng xiéyì 达成协议
agricultural nóngyè 农业
agriculture nóngyè 农业
ahead: *be* ~ *of* lǐngxiān 领先;
plan / think ~ yùxiān jìhuà / kǎolǜ
预先计划 / 考虑
aid n & *v/t* yuánzhù 援助
Aids àizībìng 艾滋病
ailing *economy* xiāotiáo 萧条
aim 1 n *(in shooting)* miáozhǔn 瞄
准; *(objective)* mùbiāo 目标 **2** *v/i
(in shooting)* miáozhǔn 瞄准; ~ *at
doing X*, ~ *to do X* zhìlìyú zuò X
致力于做 X **3** *v/t*: *be ~ed at (of
remark etc)* zhēnduì 针对; *(of
guns)* miáozhǔn 瞄准
air 1 n kōngqì 空气; *by* ~ *travel* zuò
fēijī 坐飞机; *send mail* hángkōng
航空; *in the open* ~ zài shìwài 在
室外; *on the* ~ RAD, TV bōsòng 播
送 **2** *v/t room* shǐ tōngfēng 使通
风; *fig: views* fābiǎo 发表
airbase kōngjūn jīdì 空军基地;
air-conditioned yǒu kōngtiáo 有
空调; **air-conditioning** ⇩
kōngtiáo 空调; **aircraft** fēijī 飞
机; **aircraft carrier** hángkōng
mǔjiàn 航空母舰; **air cylinder**
shuǐfèi 水肺; **airfield** jīchǎng 机
场; **air force** kōngjūn 空军; **air
hostess** kōngjiě 空姐; **air letter**
hángkōng xìnjiàn 航空信件;
airline hángkōng gōngsī 航空公
司; **airmail**: *by* ~ jì hángkōng 寄
航空; **airplane** fēijī 飞机; **air
pollution** kōngqì wūrǎn 空气污
染; **airport** jīchǎng 机场; **airsick**:
get ~ yǒu kōngyūnbìng 有空晕
病; **airspace** kōngyù 空域;

terminal jīchǎng zhōngduān 机
场终端; **airtight** *container* mìfēng
密封; **air traffic** kōngzhōng
jiāotōng 空中交通; **air-traffic
control** kōngzhōng jiāotōng
kòngzhì 空中交通控制; **air-
traffic controller** kōngzhōng
jiāotōng kòngzhì rényuán 空中交
通控制人员
airy *room* tōngfēng 通风; *attitude*
kōngxiǎng 空想
aisle tōngdào 通道
aisle seat kào tōngdào zuòwèi 靠
通道座位
alarm 1 n jǐngzhōng 警钟; *raise
the* ~ bàojǐng 报警 **2** *v/t* shǐ
kǒnghuāng 使恐慌
alarm clock nàozhōng 闹钟
Albania Ā'ěrbāníyà 阿尔巴尼亚
Albanian 1 *adj* Ā'ěrbāníyà 阿尔巴
尼亚 **2** n *(person)* Ā'ěrbāníyà rén
阿尔巴尼亚人; *(language)*
Ā'ěrbāníyà yǔ 阿尔巴尼亚语
album *(for photographs)* yǐngjí 影
集; *(record)* chàngpiān 唱片
alcohol jiǔ 酒
alcoholic 1 n xùjiǔ zhě 酗酒者
2 *adj* hán jiǔjīng 含酒精
alert 1 n *(signal)* jǐngbào 警报; *be
on the* ~ chùyú jièbèi zhuàngtài
处于戒备状态 **2** *v/t* shǐ jǐngjué
使警觉 **3** *adj* líuxīn 留心
alibi n búzài fànzuì xiànchǎng de
shēnbiàn 不在犯罪现场的申
辩
alien 1 n *(foreigner)* wàiguó rén 外
国人; *(from space)* wàixīng rén 外
星人 **2** *adj* mòshēng 陌生; *be ~
to X (not in keeping with a person's
character)* yǔ X běnxìng bùfú 与 X
本性不符
alienate shūyuǎn 疏远
alight *adj* zháohuǒ 着火
alike 1 *adj*: *be* ~ xiāngsì 相似 **2** *adv*
xiāngsì 相似; *old and young* ~
lǎoshào yīyàng 老少一样
alimony shànyǎng fèi 赡养费
alive: *be* ~ huózhe 活着
all 1 *adj* dōu 都; *we* ~ *agree* wǒmen
dōu tóngyì 我们都同意; ~ *Chi-
nese cities* Zhōngguó suǒyǒude

chéngshì 中国所有的城市
2 *pron*: **~ of us** / **them** wǒ / tāmen
dōu 我 / 他们都; **he ate ~ of it** tā
dōu chī le 他都吃了; **that's ~,
thanks** jiù zhèxiē, xièxie 就这
些, 谢谢; **for ~ I care** wǒ cái
bùguǎn ne 我才不管呢; **for ~ I
know** jù wǒ suǒzhī 据我所知; **~
at once** yíxiàzi 一下子; **~ but**
(*nearly*) jīhū 几乎; **~ the better**
gènghǎole 更好了; **~ the time**
yìzhí 一直; **they're not at ~ alike**
tāmen gēnběn búxiàng 他们根本
不像; **not at ~!** yìdiǎnr yě bù! 一
点儿也不! ; **two ~** (*in score*)
èrpíng 二平

allegation zhǐkòng 指控
alleged *culprit* yǒu xiányí 有嫌疑;
reason suǒwèi 所谓
allergic: **be ~ to ...** duì ... guòmǐn
对 ... 过敏
allergy guòmǐn 过敏
alleviate jiǎnqīng 减轻
alley hútòng 胡同
alliance tóngméng 同盟
alligator dùnwěn'è 钝吻鳄
allocate ānpái 安排
allot fēnpèi 分配
allow (*permit*) yǔnxǔ 允许;
(*calculate for*) jìsuàn 计算; **it's not
~ed** bùxíng 不行; **~ X to ...** yǔnxǔ
X ... 允许 X ...
♦ **allow for** kǎolǜ dào 考虑到
allowance (*money*) jīntiē 津贴;
(*pocket money*) língyòng qián 零
用钱; **make ~s** (*for thing, weather
etc*) kǎolǜ dào 考虑到; (*for
person*) yuánliàng 原谅
alloy héjīn 合金
all-purpose duō yòngtú 多用途;
all-round quánmiàn 全面; **all-
time**: **be at an ~ low** kōngqián
wèiyǒu de dī 空前未有的低
♦ **allude to** yǐngshè 影射
alluring yòuhuò 诱惑
all-wheel drive sìlún qūdòng 四轮
驱动
ally *n* tóngméng zhě 同盟者
almond xìngrén 杏仁
almost jīhū 几乎
alone dāndú 单独

along 1 *prep*: **walk ~ this path**
yánzhe zhètiáo xiǎolù zǒu 沿着
这条小路走 **2** *adv* yìqǐ 一起; **~
with** hé 和; **all ~** (*all the time*) yìzhí
一直
aloud chūshēngdi 出声地
alphabet zìmǔ biǎo 字母表
alphabetical order yī zìmǔ
shùnxù 依字母顺序
already yǐjīng 已经
alright: **that's ~** (*doesn't matter*) méi
guānxi 没关系; (*when somebody
says thank you*) búxiè 不谢; (*is
quite good*) búcuò 不错; **I'm ~** (*not
hurt*) wǒ méi shìr 我没事儿;
(*have got enough*) gòule 够了; **~,
that's enough!** déle 得了; **can I?
– ~** kěyǐ ma? – kěyǐ 可以吗? –
可以
also yě 也
altar shèngtán 圣坛
alter *v/t* gǎibiàn 改变
alteration gēnggǎi 更改
alternate 1 *v/i* jiāotì 交替 **2** *adj*
měigé 每隔
alternating current jiāoliúdiàn 交
流电
alternative 1 *n* xuǎnzé 选择 **2** *adj*
lìngyī kě xuǎnzé 另一可选择;
lifestyle, music etc bùtóng zhǒng 不
同种
alternatively huòzhě 或者
although jīnguǎn 尽管
altitude (*of plane*) gāodù 高度; (*of
mountain, city*) hǎibá 海拔
alt key COMPUT Alt jiàn Alt 键
altogether (*completely*) wánquán
完全; (*in all*) yígòng 一共
altruistic lìrén 利人
aluminum lǚ 铝
always zǒngshì 总是; **it's ~ raining
here** zhè zhòngshì xià yǔ 这儿总
是下雨
a.m. (*in the morning*) zǎochén 早晨
amalgamate *v/i* (*of companies*)
hébìng 合并
amateur *n* (*unskilled*) yèyú àihào
zhě 业余爱好者; SP yèyú 业余
amaze shǐ dàwéi chījīng 使大为
吃惊
amazement jīngqí 惊奇

amazing (*surprising*) jīngrén 惊人; (*very good*) méizhìle 没治了

ambassador dàshǐ 大使

amber: *at* ~ huáng 黄

ambiguous hánhú 含糊

ambition zhìxiàng 志向; *pej* yěxīn 野心

ambitious yǒu zhìxiàng 有志向; *plan* xióngxīn bóbó 雄心勃勃

ambulance jiùhùchē 救护车

ambush 1 *n* fújí 伏击 2 *v/t* máifú 埋伏

amend gǎizhèng 改正

amendment xiūgǎi 修改

amends: *make* ~ bǔguò 补过

amenities biànlì shèshī 便利设施

America Měiguó 美国

American 1 *adj* Měiguó 美国 2 *n* Měiguó rén 美国人

amiable héǎi kěqīn 和蔼可亲

amicable yǒushàn 友善

ammunition jūnhuǒ 军火; *fig* jìngōng shǒuduàn 进攻手段

amnesty n shèmiǎn 赦免

among(st) zài ... zhīzhōng 在 ... 之中

amount shùliàng 数量; (*sum of money*) jīn'é 金额

♦ amount to děngyú 等于

ample chōngzú 充足

amplifier fàngdàqì 放大器

amplify *sound* fàngdà 放大

amputate jiézhī 节肢

amuse (*make laugh etc*) dòuxiào 逗笑; (*entertain*) gěi ... tígōng yúlè 给 ... 提供娱乐

amusement (*merriment*) lèqù 乐趣; (*entertainment*) yúlè 娱乐; ~s (*games*) yúlè huódòng 娱乐活动; *to our great* ~ lìng wǒmén hěn gāoxìng 令我们很高兴

amusement arcade yúlè zhōngxīn 娱乐中心

amusement park yúlè yuán 娱乐园

amusing yǒuqù 有趣

anabolic steroid héchéng dàixiè jīsù 合成代谢激素

Analects of Confucius Lúnyǔ 论语

analog COMPUT mónǐ 模拟

analogy bǐyù 比喻

analysis fēnxī 分析; (*psychoanalysis*) jīngshén fēnxī 精神分析

analyze fēnxī 分析

anarchy wúzhèngfǔ zhuàngtài 无政府状态

anatomy jiěpōu 解剖

ancestor zǔxiān 祖先

anchor NAUT 1 *n* máo 锚 2 *v/i* pāomáo 抛锚

anchor man TV xīnwén guǎngbō yuán 新闻广播员

ancient *adj* gǔlǎo 古老

and ◊ (*joining nouns*) hé 和; *you* ~ *me* nǐ hé wǒ 你和我 ◊ (*joining adjectives*) yòu ... yòu ... 又 ... 又 ...; *tall* ~ *thin* yòu gāo yòu shòu 又高又瘦 ◊ (~ *then*) ránhòu 然后; *he checked in* ~ *went to his room* tā dēngjì le ránhòu qùle tāde fángjiān 他登记了然后去了他的房间 ◊ (*two actions at the same time*) biān ... biān ..., yìbiān ... yìbiān ...; *she was laughing* ~ *crying* tā yìbiān xiào yìbiān kū 她一边笑一边哭; *they were eating* ~ *drinking* tāmen biān chī biān hē 他们边吃边喝 ◊ (*when listing things, not translated*): *two beers* ~ *a coffee* liǎngge píjiǔ yíge kāfēi 两个啤酒一个咖啡 ◊: *faster* ~ *faster* yuèlái yuè kuài 越来越快

anemia pínxuè 贫血

anemic: *be* ~ pínxuè 贫血

anesthetic *n* mázuì 麻醉

anesthetist mázuì shī 麻醉师

anger 1 *n* fènnù 愤怒 2 *v/t* shǐ fènnù 使愤怒

angina yānxiá yán 咽峡炎

angle *n* jiǎodù 角度

angry fènnù 愤怒; *be* ~ *with X* duì X shēngqì 对 X 生气

anguish jídù tòngkǔ 极度痛苦

animal dòngwù 动物

animated huópo 活泼

animated cartoon dònghuà piān 动画片

animation (*liveliness*) huópo 活泼; (*cinematic*) dònghuà piān shèzhì 动画片摄制

animosity díyì 敌意

ankle ⇩jiǎowàn 脚腕

annex **1** n (building) kuòjiàn bùfèn 扩建部分 **2** v/t state tūnbìng 吞并

anniversary (wedding ~) zhōunián 周年

announce xuānbù 宣布

announcement xuāngào 宣告

announcer TV, RAD bōyīn yuán 播音员

annoy shǐ fánnǎo 使烦恼; **be ~ed** shēngqì 生气

annoyance (anger) fán nǎo 烦恼; (sth annoying) fánnǎo 烦恼

annoying nǎorén 恼人

annual adj (once a year) nián 年; (of a year) niándù 年度

annul marriage shǐ wúxiào 使无效

anonymous nìmíng 匿名

anorexia yànshí zhèng 厌食症

anorexic be ~ yànshí 厌食

another adj & pron (different) lìng yīge 另一个; (additional) yòu yīge 又一个; (referring to something that hasn't yet happened) zài yīge 再一个; **can I have ~ ...?** wǒ kěyǐ zài lái yīge ... ma? 我可以再来一个 ... 吗?; **one ~** hùxiāng 互相

answer **1** n (to letter, person) dáfù 答复; (to problem, question) dá'àn 答案 **2** v/t letter, person dáfù 答复; question huídá 回答; **~ the door** kāimén 开门; **~ the telephone** tīng diànhuà 听电话

♦ **answer back 1** v/t person huízuǐ 回嘴 **2** v/i huízuǐ 回嘴

♦ **answer for** fùzé 负责

answerphone ⇩lùyīn diànhuà lùyīn diànhuà 录音电话

ant mǎyǐ 蚂蚁

antagonism díyì 敌意

Antarctic Nánjí 南极

antenatal chǎnqián 产前

antenna (of insect) chùjiǎo 触角; (for TV) tiānxiàn 天线

antibiotic kàngjūnsù 抗菌素

antibody kàngtǐ 抗体

anticipate yùliào 预料

anticipation yùliào 预料

antidote jiědúyào 解毒药

antifreeze zǔdòngjì 阻冻剂

Anti-Japanese War Kàng Rì Zhànzhēng 抗日战争

antipathy fǎngǎn 反感

antiquated chénjiù 陈旧

antique n gǔdǒng 古董

antique dealer gǔdǒng shāng 古董商

Anti-rightists Campaign Fǎnyòu Yùndòng 反右运动

antiseptic **1** adj kàngjūn 抗菌 **2** n kàngjūnjì 抗菌剂

antisocial bù héqún 不和群

antivirus program COMPUT kàng bìngdú chéngxù 抗病毒程序

anxiety jiāojí 焦急

anxious jiāojí 焦急; (eager) rèxīn 热心; **be ~ for ...** (for news etc) jiāojí děngdài ... 焦急等待 ...

any **1** adj: **are there ~ diskettes / glasses?** yǒuméiyǒu cípán / bēizi? 有没有磁盘 / 杯子?; **is there ~ bread / improvement?** yǒuméiyǒu miànbāo / jìnbù? 有没有面包 / 进步?; **there aren't ~ diskettes / glasses** méiyǒu cípán / bēizi méiyǒu cípán / bēizi 没有磁盘 / 杯子; **there isn't ~ bread / improvement** méiyǒu miànbāo / jìnbù 没有面包 / 进步; **have you ~ idea at all?** nǐ dàodǐ míng bù míngbái? 你到底明不明白?; **take ~ one you like** suí nǐ ná náyīge 随你拿哪一个 **2** pron: **do you have ~?** nǐ yǒu méiyǒu? 你有没有?; **there isn't / aren't ~ left** méi shèng de le 没剩的了; **~ of them could be guilty** tāmen zhīzhōng rèn yīge dōu kěnéng yǒuzuì 他们之中任一个都可能有罪 **3** adv: **is that ~ better / easier?** hǎo / róngyì diǎnr le ma? 好 / 容易点儿了吗?; **I don't like it ~ more** wǒ bù xīhuānle 我不喜欢了

anybody (emphatic) rènhé rén 任何人; **~ can do that** rènhé rén dōu kěyǐ zuò 任何人都可以做 ◊ (with negatives): **there wasn't ~ there** méirén zài nàr 没人在那儿 ◊ (in questions, conditionals) shéi; *if ~ can help* rúguǒ shéi néng bāngmáng 如果谁能帮忙

anyhow (*summarizing*) zǒngzhī 总之; (*in any way*) wúlùn yòng hézhǒng fāngfǎ 无论用何种方法; (*at least*) zhìshǎo 至少

anyone → **anybody**

anything shénme 什么; *I didn't hear* ~ wǒ méi tīngjiàn shénme 我没听见什么; *~ but* yìdiǎnr yě bù 一点儿也不; *~ else?* háiyǒu shénme? 还有什么？

anyway → **anyhow**

anywhere wúlùn nǎli 无论哪里; *I can't find it* ~ wǒ nǎr dōu zhǎobùzháo 我哪儿都找不着

apart (*in distance*) jùlí 距离; (*of people*) fēnjū 分居; *~ from* (*excepting*) chúle 除了; (*in addition to*) cǐwà 此外

apartment gōngyù 公寓

apartment block gōngyù dàshà 公寓大厦

apathetic lěngmò 冷漠

ape *n* xīngxing 猩猩

aperture PHOT guāngquān 光圈

apologize dàoqiàn 道歉

apology dàoqiàn 道歉

apostrophe GRAM piěhào 撇号

appall shǐ zhènjīng 使震惊

appalling lìngrén zhènjīng 令人震惊; *language* cūlǔ 粗鲁

apparatus qìxiè 器械

apparent míngxiǎn 明显; *become ~ that* .... kāishǐ biànde míngxiǎn ... 开始变得明显

apparently hǎoxiàng 好象

appeal 1 *n* (*charm*) xīyǐn lì 吸引力; (*for funds etc*) hūyù 呼吁; LAW shàngsù 上诉 2 *v/i* LAW shàngsù 上诉

♦ **appeal for** kěnqiè qǐngqiú 恳切请求

♦ **appeal to** (*be attractive to*) duì ... yǒu xīyǐnlì 对 ... 有吸引力

appear chūxiàn 出现; (*in film etc*) dēngchǎng 登场; (*of new product*) chūxiàn 出现; (*arrive*) dàochǎng 到场; (*look, seem*) xiǎndé 显得; *it ~s that* ... kànlái ... 看来 ...

appearance (*arrival*) dàolái 到来; (*in film etc*) dēngchǎng 登场; (*in court*) chūtíng 出庭; (*look*) wàibiǎo 外表; *put in an ~* lòumiàn 露面

appendicitis lánwěiyán 阑尾炎

appendix MED lánwěi 阑尾; (*of book etc*) fùlù 附录

appetite wèikǒu 胃口; *fig* yùwàng 欲望

appetizer (*food*) kāiwèi pǐn 开胃品; (*drink*) kāiwèi jiǔ 开胃酒

appetizing kāiwèi 开胃

applaud 1 *v/i* gǔzhǎng gǔzhǎng 鼓掌 2 *v/t* hècǎi 喝采; *fig* zànxǔ 赞许

applause gǔzhǎng gǔzhǎng 鼓掌; (*praise*) zànyáng 赞扬

apple píngguǒ 苹果

apple pie píngguǒ pài 苹果派

apple sauce píngguǒ zhīr 苹果汁儿

appliance qìxiè 器械; (*household*) jiāyòng qìxiè 家用器械

applicable *ruling* shìyòng 适用

applicant shēnqǐng zhě 申请者

application (*for job, passport, visa, university etc*) shēnqǐng 申请

application form (*for passport, visa, university*) shēnqǐng biǎogé 申请表格

apply 1 *v/t* shìyòng 使用; *ointment* cáyòng 搽用 2 *v/i* (*of rule, law*) shìyòng 适用

♦ **apply for** *job, passport, university* shēnqǐng 申请

♦ **apply to** (*contact*) xiàng ... shēnqǐng 向 ... 申请; (*affect*) guānxì dào 关系到

appoint (*to position*) rènmìng 任命

appointment (*to position*) rènmìng 任命; (*meeting*) yuēhuì 约会

appointments diary yuēhuì rìjìběn 约会日记本

appreciate 1 *v/t* (*value*) xīnshǎng 欣赏; (*be grateful for*) gǎnjī gǎnjī 感激; (*acknowledge*) yìshí dào 意识到; *thanks, I ~ it* fēicháng gǎnxiè 非常感谢 2 *v/i* FIN tígāo jiàzhí 提高价值

appreciation (*of kindness etc*) gǎnjī 感激; (*of music etc*) xīnshǎng 欣赏

apprehensive dānxīn 担心

apprentice xuétú 学徒

approach 1 n línjìn 临近; (offer, proposal) tíyì 提议; (to problem) fāngshì 方式 **2** v/t (get near to) línjìn 临近; (contact) liánxì 联系; problem chǔlǐ 处理

approachable person píngyì jìnrén 平易近人

appropriate adj qiàdàng 恰当

approval tóngyì 同意

approve 1 v/i zànchéng 赞成 **2** v/t pīzhǔn 批准

♦**approve of** rèntóng 认同

approximate adj dàyuē 大约

approximately dàyuē 大约

APR (= **annual percentage rate**) niánlǜ 年率

apricot xìng 杏

April sìyuè 四月

apt pupil línglì 伶俐; remark qiàrú qífèn 恰如其分; **be ~ to ...** yìyú ... 易于...

aptitude tiānzī 天资

aquarium (large) shuǐzú guǎn 水族馆; (small, at home) yǎngyúgāng 养鱼缸

aquatic (water-dwelling) shuǐqī 水栖; sports (in water) shuǐzhōng 水中; (on water) shuǐshàng 水上; (under water) shuǐxià 水下

Arab 1 adj Ālābó 阿拉伯 **2** n Ālābó rén 阿拉伯人

Arabic 1 adj Ālābó 阿拉伯 **2** n Ālābó yǔ 阿拉伯语

arable gēngzhòng 耕种

arbitrary rènyì 任意; remark suíbiàn 随便; attack wú jìhuà xìng 无计划性

arbitrate v/i (in public affair) zhòngcái 仲裁; (in private) tiáotíng 调停

arbitration (in public affair) zhòngcái 仲裁; (in private) tiáotíng 调停

arch n gǒng 拱

archeologist kǎogǔ xué jiā 考古学家

archeology kǎogǔ xué 考古学

archer gōngjiàn shǒu 弓箭手

architect jiànzhù shī 建筑师

architecture jiànzhù xué 建筑学

archives dǎng'àn 档案

archway gǒngmén 拱门

Arctic Běijí 北极

ardent qiánchéng 虔诚

area (region) dìqū 地区; (of activity, job, study etc) fànwéi 范围; (square metres etc) miànjī 面积

area code TELEC qūhào 区号

arena SP bǐsài chǎng 比赛场

Argentina Āgēntíng 阿根廷

Argentinian 1 adj Āgēntíng 阿根廷 **2** n Āgēntíng rén 阿根廷人

arguably kě zhēnglùn 可争论

argue 1 v/i (quarrel) chǎojià 吵架; (reason) zhēnglùn 争论 **2** v/t: **~ that** jiānchí 坚持

argument (quarrel) chǎojià 吵架; (reasoning) zhēnglùn 争论

argumentative ài chǎojià 爱吵架

arid land pínjí 贫瘠

arise (of situation, problem) chéngxiàn 呈现

arithmetic suànshù 算术

arm[1] n (of person) shǒubì 手臂; (of chair) fúshǒu 扶手

arm[2] v/t wǔzhuāng 武装

armaments wǔqì 武器

armchair fúshǒu yǐ 扶手椅

armed wǔzhuāng 武装

armed forces wǔzhuāng lìliàng 武装力量

armed robbery chíxiè qiǎngjié 持械抢劫

armor hùjiǎ 护甲

armored vehicle zhuāngjiǎ chē 装甲车

armpit yèwō 腋窝

arms (weapons) wǔqì 武器

army jūnduì 军队

aroma xiāngwèir 香味儿

around 1 prep (in circle) wéirǎo 围绕; (approximately) dàyuē 大约; **it's ~ the corner** zài guǎijiǎo nàr 在拐角那儿; **we walked ~ the garden** wǒmen zài huāyuán lǐ sànbù 我们在花园里散步了; **they all stood ~ him** tāmen dōu zhàn zài tāde zhōuwéi 他们都站在他的周围 **2** adv (in the area) zài zhèr 在这儿; (encircling)

arouse

zhōuwéi 周围; *he lives ~ here* tā zhùzài fùjìn 他住在附近; *walk ~* zǒuzou 走走; *be ~ (somewhere near)* zài fùjìn 在附近; *there are a lot of people ~* yǒu hěnduō rén 有很多人~; *she has been ~ (has traveled, is experienced)* tā yuèlì tīngshēn 她阅历挺深

arouse *interest, suspicion* yǐnqǐ 引起; *strong feelings* huànxíng 唤醒; *(sexually)* jīfā 激发

arrange *(put in order)* zhěnglǐ 整理; *furniture* bùzhì 布置; *flowers* chā 插; *music* gǎibiān 改编; *meeting, party, time, place etc* ānpái 安排; *I've ~d to meet her* wǒ ānpái hé tā jiànmiàn le 我安排和她见面了

♦ **arrange for** ānpái 安排

arrangement *(plan)* ānpái 安排; *(agreement)* xiéyì 协议; *(layout: of furniture etc)* bùzhì 布置; *(of flowers)* chāhuā 插花; *(of music)* gǎibiān 改编

arrears tuōqiàn kuǎn 拖欠款; *be in ~ (of person)* tuōqiàn 拖欠

arrest 1 *n* dàibǔ 逮捕; *be under ~* bèibǔ 被捕 **2** *v/t* dàibǔ 逮捕

arrival dàodá 到达; *~s (at airport)* dàodá 到达

arrive dàodá 到达

♦ **arrive at** *place* dídá dǐdá 抵达; *decision etc* zuòchū 做出

arrogance àomàn 傲慢

arrogant jiāo'ào zìdà 骄傲自大

arrow jiàntóu 箭头

arson zònghuǒ 纵火

art yìshù 艺术; *the ~s* yìshù jiè 艺术界; *~s degree* wénkē xuéwèi 文科学位

art gallery huàláng 画廊

arterial road gànxiàn 干线

artery MED dòngmài 动脉

arthritis guānjié yán 关节炎

article *(item)* wùjiàn 物件; *(in newspaper)* wénzhāng 文章; *(section of law etc)* kuǎn 款; GRAM guāncí 冠词

articulate *adj person* biǎodá nénglì qiáng 表达能力强; *essay* biǎodá de qīngchǔ yǒulì 表达得清楚有力

力

artificial rénzào 人造; *(not sincere)* zuòzuò 做作

artificial intelligence réngōng zhìnéng 人工智能

artillery dàpào 大炮

artisan shǒuyì rén 手艺人

artist *(painter)* huàjiā 画家; *(artistic person)* yìshù jiā 艺术家

artistic *person* yǒu yìshù xìng 有艺术性; *skills* yìshù 艺术

as 1 *conj* ◊ *(while, when)* dāng ... de shíhou 当...的时候; *~ I was about to leave, the phone rang again* dāng wǒ yào zǒu de shíhou, diànhuà yòu xiǎng le 当我要走的时候，电话又响了; *I saw him ~ I was cycling along* wǒ qí chēzi de shíhou kànjiàn le tā 我骑车子的时候看见了他 ◊ *(because)* yīnwéi 因为; *I didn't go ~ I wasn't feeling well* wǒ méi qù yīnwéi wǒ bú tài shūfu 我没去因为我不太舒服 ◊ *(like)* xiàng 像; *~ I said* xiàng wǒ shuōde 像我说的; *~ if* hǎoxiàng 好像; *~ usual* rútóng wǎngcháng 如同往常; *~ necessary* yǒu bìyào shí 有必要时 **2** *adv*: *~ high / pretty ~ ...* hé ... yíyàng gāo / piàoliang 和 ... 一样高 / 漂亮; *~ much ~ that?* nàme duō? 那么多？ **3** *prep* zuòwéi 作为; *~ a child / schoolgirl* zuòwéi háizi / nǚ xuésheng 作为孩子 / 女学生; *work ~ a teacher / translator* dāng lǎoshī / fānyì 当老师 / 翻译; *~ for* zhìyú 至于; *~ Hamlet* bànyǎn Hāmǔléitè 扮演哈姆莱特

asap (= *as soon as possible*) jìnkuài 尽快

ash huī 灰; *~es* huī 灰; *(after cremation)* gǔhuī 骨灰

ashamed xiūkuì 羞愧; *be ~ of* wèi ... diūliǎn 为 ... 丢脸; *you should be ~ of yourself* nǐ bù hàisào 你不害臊

ash can lājī xiāng 垃圾箱

ashore zài ànshàng 在岸上; *go ~* shàng'àn 上岸

ashtray yānhuī gāng 烟灰缸

Asia Yàzhōu 亚洲

Asian 1 adj Yàzhōu 亚洲 2 n Yàzhōu rén 亚洲人

aside yībiān 一边; ~ from chúle 除了

ask 1 v/t person wèn 问; (invite) jiào 叫; question tíwèn 提问; favor qǐngqiú 请求; can I ~ you something? kěyǐ wèn nǐ xiē shì ma? 可以问你些事吗？; X for ... gēn X yào ... 跟 X 要...; X to ... yào X ... 要 X...; X about Y xiàng X dǎtīng Y 向 X 打听 Y 2 v/i wèn 问

♦ask after person wènhòu 问候

♦ask for yāoqiú 要求; person zhǎo 找

♦ask out (for a drink, night out) yuēhuì 约会

asking price yàojià 要价

asleep: be (fast) ~ shúshuì 熟睡; fall ~ shuìzháo le 睡着了

asparagus lúsǔn 芦笋

aspect fāngmiàn 方面

aspirin āsīpílín 阿司匹林

ass¹ (idiot) bèndàn 笨蛋

ass² ∨ (buttocks) pìgu 屁股; (sex) xìng xìng 性

assassin ànshā zhě 暗杀者

assassinate ànshā 暗杀

assassination ànshā 暗杀

assault 1 n gōngjī 攻击; (physical) ōudǎ 殴打; (verbal) wēixié 威胁 2 v/t (physically) ōudǎ 殴打; (verbally) wēixié 威胁

assemble 1 v/t parts zǔzhuāng 组装 2 v/i (of people) jízhōng 集中

assembly (of parts) zǔzhuāng 组装; POL yìhuì 议会

assembly line zhuāngpèi xiàn 装配线

assembly plant zhuāngpèi chǎng 装配厂

assent v/i tóngyì 同意

assert: ~ oneself jiānchí zìjǐde lìchǎng 坚持自己的立场

assertive person zìxìn 自信

assess situation pínggū 评估; value gūjià 估价

asset FIN zīchǎn 资产; fig bǎobèi 宝贝

asshole ∨ pìyǎnr 屁眼儿; (idiot) bèndàn 笨蛋

assign person, thing fēnpèi 分配

assignment (task, study) rènwù 任务

assimilate v/t information xīshōu 吸收; person into group jiēshòu 接受

assist bāngzhù 帮助

assistance bāngzhù 帮助

assistant zhùshǒu 助手

assistant director fù zhǔguǎn 副主管; (of movie) fù dǎoyǎn 副导演

assistant manager fù jīnglǐ 副经理

associate 1 v/t: X with Y X hé Y liánxiǎng zài yīqǐ X 和 Y 联想在一起 2 v/i: ~ with jiē_jiāo 结交 3 n tóngshì 同事

associate professor fù jiàoshòu 副教授

association xiéhuì 协会; in ~ with yǔ ... hézuò 与 ... 合作

assortment (of food) huāsè jùquán 花色俱全; (of people) gèshì gèyàng 各式各样

assume (suppose) xiǎngxiàng 想象; (for the sake of argument) jiǎdìng 假定

assumption shèxiǎng 设想

assurance bǎozhèng 保证; (confidence) xìnxīn 信心

assure (reassure) shǐ quèxìn 使确信

assured (confident) yǒu xìnxīn 有信心

asterisk xīnghào 星号

asthma xiàochuǎn 哮喘

astonish shǐ jīngyà 使惊讶; be ~ed jīngyà 惊讶

astonishing lìngrén jīngyà 令人惊讶

astonishment jīngyà 惊讶

astrologer zhànxīng zhě 占星者

astrology zhànxīng shù 占星术

astronaut yǔháng yuán 宇航员

astronomer tiānwén xuéjiā 天文学家

astronomical price etc jùdà 巨大

astronomy tiānwén xué 天文学

asylum (*mental*) jīngshén bìngyuàn 精神病院; (*political*) bìhù 庇护

at (*with places*) zài 在; ~ *the cleaner's* zài gānxǐdiàn lǐ 在干洗店里; ~ *Joe's* zài Qiáo jiā lǐ 在乔家里; ~ *the door* zài ménkǒu 在门口; ~ *10 dollars* biāojià shí měiyuán 标价十美元; ~ *the age of 18* shíbāsuì shí 十八岁时; ~ *5 o'clock* wǔ diǎnzhōng 五点钟; *be good/bad* ~ *X* shàncháng/bū shàncháng yú X 擅长/不擅长于 X

atheist wú shén lùn zhě 无神论者

athlete yùndòng yuán 运动员

athletic tǐgé jiànměi 体格健美

athletics tiánjìng yùndòng 田径运动

Atlantic Dàxīyáng 大西洋

atlas dìtú jí 地图集

ATM (= *automated teller machine*) qǔkuǎn jī 取款机

atmosphere (*of earth*) dàqì 大气; (*ambiance*) qìfēn 气氛

atmospheric pollution dàqì wūrǎn 大气污染

atom yuánzǐ 原子

atom bomb yuánzǐ dàn 原子弹

atomic yuánzǐ 原子

atomic energy yuánzǐ néng 原子能

atomic waste yuánzǐ fèiwù 原子废物

atomizer wùhuà qì 雾化器

atrocious zāotòu 糟透

atrocity bàoxíng 暴行

attach shuānláo 栓牢; ~ *importance to* zhùzhòng 注重; *be ~ed to* (*fond of: thing*) yīlài 依恋; (*person*) àimù 爱慕

attachment (*to e-mail*) fùjiàn 附件

attack 1 *n* (*physical*) ōudǎ 殴打; MIL xíjī 袭击; (*verbal*) pēngjī 抨击 **2** *v/t* (*physically*) ōudǎ 殴打; MIL xíjī 袭击; (*verbally*) pēngjī 抨击

attempt 1 *n* chángshì 尝试 **2** *v/t* shìtú 试图

attend cānjiā 参加

♦**attend to** chǔlǐ 处理; *customer* fúshì 服侍

attendance chūqín 出勤

attendant (*in museum*) fúwù yuán 服务员

attention zhùyìlì 注意力; *bring to the* ~ *of* ... shì ... zhùyì 使 ... 注意; *your/please* qǐng zhùyì 请注意; *pay* ~ zhùyì 注意

attentive *listener* rèxīn 热心

attic gélóu 阁楼

attitude tàidù 态度

attn (= *for the attention of*) gěi 给

attorney lùshī 律师; *power of* ~ shòuquán 授权

attract *person, attention* xīyǐn 吸引; *be ~ed to X* (*person*) àimù X 爱慕 X

attraction xīyǐn lì 吸引力; (*romantic*) mèilì 魅力

attractive yǒu xīyǐn lì 有吸引力

attribute[1] *v/t*: ~ *X to* ... bǎ X guīyīn yú ... 把 X 归因于 ...; *the poem has been ~d to* ... jùshuō zhèi shǒu shī wéi ... suǒzuò 据说这首诗是 ... 所作

attribute[2] *n* tèzhēng 特征

auction *n & v/t* pāimài 拍卖

♦**auction off** pāimài diào 拍卖掉

audacious *plan* màoxiǎn 冒险

audacity fàngsì 放肆

audible tīngdéjiàn 听得见

audience (*of concert etc*) tīngzhòng 听众; (*in theater, at show, TV*) guānzhòng 观众

audio *adj* lùyīn 录音

audiovisual shìtīng 视听

audit 1 *n* shěnjì 审计 **2** *v/t* shěnhé 审核; *course* pángtīng 旁听

audition *n & v/i* shìyǎn 试演

auditor shěnjì shī 审计师

auditorium (*of theater etc*) tīng 厅

August bāyuè 八月

aunt (*own, paternal*) gū gū 姑姑; (*own, maternal*) yí yí 姨姨; (*somebody else's*) āyí 阿姨

austere jiǎnpǔ 简朴

austerity (*economic*) jīngjì jǐnsuō 经济紧缩

Australasia Àodàlāxīyà 澳大利西亚

Australia Àodàlìyà 澳大利亚

Australian 1 *adj* Àodàlìyà 澳大利亚 **2** *n* Àodàlìyà rén 澳大利亚人

Austria Àodìlì 奥地利

Austrian 1 *adj* Àodìlì 奥地利 **2** *n* Àodìlì rén 奥地利人

authentic *antique* zhēnzhèng 真正; *accent* dìdào 地道

authenticity zhēnshí xìng 真实性

author zuòzhě 作者

authoritative *person, manner* ài xià mìnglìng 爱下命令; *source of information* yǒu quánwēi xìng 有权威性

authority quánwēi 权威; *(permission)* xǔkě 许可; *be an ~ on ...* shì ... de quánwēi 是 ... 的权威; *the authorities* dāngquán zhě 当权者

authorize shòuquán 授权; *be ~d to ...* shòuquán ... 授权 ...

autistic gūpì 孤僻

auto *n* qìchē 汽车

autobiography zìzhuàn 自传

autograph qīnbǐ qiānmíng 亲笔签名

automate shǐ zìdònghuà 使自动化

automatic 1 *adj* zìdòng 自动 **2** *n* *(car, gun etc)* zìdòng 自动

automatically zìdòng 自动

automation zìdòng huà 自动化

automobile xiǎo qìchē 小汽车

automobile industry qìchē yè 汽车业

autonomous region zìzhìqū 自治区

autonomy zìzhì 自治

autopilot zìdòng jiàshǐ yí 自动驾驶仪

autopsy yànshī 验尸

auxiliary *adj* fúzhù 辅助

available *facility, service, book, information* kě dédào 可得到; *person* yǒukōng 有空

avalanche xuěbēng 雪崩

avenue dàdào 大道; *fig* lù 路

average 1 *adj* píngjūn 平均; *(ordinary)* pǔtōng 普通; *(of mediocre quality)* mǎmǎ hūhū 马马虎虎 **2** *n* píngjūn shuǐzhǔn 平均水准; *above / below ~* gāoyú /

dīyú píngjūn shuǐzhǔn 高于 / 低于平均水准; *on ~* píngjūn láishuō 平均来说 **3** *v/t* píngjūn 平均

♦**average out** *v/t* suàn píngjūn shù 算平均数

♦**average out at** píngjūn shì 平均是

aversion: have an ~ to yànwù 厌恶

avert *one's eyes* zhuǎnyí 转移; *crisis* bìmiǎn 避免

aviary niǎoshè 鸟舍

aviation hángkōng 航空

avid rèxīn 热心

avoid bìmiǎn 避免

awake *adj* xǐng 醒; *it's keeping me ~* ràng wǒ shuìbùzháo 让我睡不着

award 1 *n (prize)* jiǎnglì 奖励 **2** *v/t* jiǎnglì 奖励; *damages* pàngěi 判给

aware: be ~ of X zhīdào X 知道 X; *become ~ of X* dézhī X 得知 X

awareness yìshí 意识

away: be ~ *(traveling, sick etc)* búzài 不在; *walk / run ~* zǒu / pǎo kāi 走 / 跑开; *look ~* búkàn 不看; *it's 2 miles ~* liǎng yīnglǐ yuǎn 两英里远; *Christmas is still six weeks ~* lí shèngdànjié háiyǒu liù xīngqī 离圣诞节还有六星期; *take X ~ from Y (something from somebody)* cóng Y nàlǐ názǒu X 从 Y 那里拿走 X; *put X ~* bǎ X fànghǎo 把 X 放好

away game *SP* kèfāng bǐsài 客方比赛

awesome F *(terrific)* ⇩ gàilemàole 盖了帽了

awful zāogāo 糟糕

awkward *(clumsy)* bènzhuō 笨拙; *(difficult)* nányǐ duìfù 难以对付; *(embarrassing)* gāngà 尴尬; *feel ~* gāngà 尴尬

awning chuánpéng 船篷

ax 1 *n* fǔ 斧 **2** *v/t project, budget, jobs etc* xiāojiǎn 削减

axle lúnzhóu 轮轴

B

BA (= *Bachelor of Arts*) wén xuéshì 文学士

baby n yīng'ér 婴儿

baby carriage yīng'ér chē 婴儿车; **baby-sit** kānháizi 看孩子; **baby-sitter** línshí bǎomǔ 临时保姆

bachelor dānshēn hàn 单身汉

back 1 n (*of person*) hòubèi 后背; (*of car, bus*) hòubù 后部; (*of paper, jacket, house, book*) bèimiàn 背面; (*of drawer*) jǐn lǐmiàn 尽里面; (*of chair*) kàobèi 靠背; SP hòuwèi 后卫; *in* ~ zài hòumian 在后面; *in the* ~ *of the car* zài qìchē hòuzuò 在汽车后座; *at the* ~ *of the bus* zài gōnggòng qìchē hòuzuò 在公共汽车后座; ~ *to front* qiánhòu diāndǎo 前后颠倒; *at the* ~ *of beyond* zài huāngwú rényán de dìfang 在荒无人烟的地方 **2** adj hòu 后; ~ *road* xiǎolù 小路 **3** adv: *please move / stand* ~ qǐng hòutuì 请后退 **2** *meters* ~ *from the edge* lí biānyuán liǎngmǐ 离边缘两米; ~ *in 1935* zǎozài yījiǔ sānwǔ nián 早在一九三五年; *give X* ~ *to Y* jiāng X huángěi Y 将 X 还给 Y; *she'll be* ~ *tomorrow* tā míngtiān huílái 她明天回来; *when are you coming* ~? nǐ shénme shíhou huílái? 你什么时候回来？; *take X* ~ *to the store* (*because unsatisfactory*) tuìdiào X 退掉 X; *they wrote / phoned* ~ tāmen huíxìn / dǎhuí diànhuà le 他们回信 / 打回电话了; *he hit me* ~ tā huíshǒu dǎwǒ 他回手打我 **4** v/t (*support*) zhīchí 支持; *car* dǎochē 倒车; *horse* xià dǔzhù 下赌注 **5** v/i (*of driver*) dǎochē 倒车

◆**back away** hòutuì 后退

◆**back down** fàngqì 放弃

◆**back off** hòutuì 后退; (*from danger*) dǎ tuìtánggǔ 打退堂鼓

◆**back onto** bèixiàng 背向

◆**back out** (*of commitment*) sāshǒu 撒手

◆**back up 1** v/t (*support*) zhīchí 支持; *claim, argument* zhèngshí 证实; *file* hòubèi 后备; *be backed up* (*of traffic*) páichéng chánglóng 排成长龙 **2** v/i (*in car*) hòutuì 后退

back burner: *put ... on the* ~ bǎ ... fàngzài yībiān 把 ... 放在一边

backdate zhuīsù 追溯

backdoor hòumén 后门

backer zànzhù rén 赞助人

backfire v/i fig chǎnshēng shì yǔ yuàn wéi de jiéguǒ 产生事与愿违的结果; **background** bèijǐng 背景; (*of person*) jīnglì jīnglì 经历; (*of situation*) bèijǐng zīliào 背景资料; **backhand** n (*in tennis*) fǎnshǒu jīqiú 反手击球

backing (*support*) zhīchí 支持; (*musicians*) bànzòu 伴奏; (*singers*) bànchàng 伴唱

backing group bànzòu zǔ 伴奏组; (*singers*) bànchàng zǔ 伴唱组

backlash qiángliè fǎnyìng 强烈反应; **backlog** jīyā jīyā 积压; **backpack 1** n bēibāo 背包 **2** v/i túbù lǚxíng 徒步旅行; **backpacker** túbù lǚxíng zhě 徒步旅行者; **backpedal** fig chū'ěr fǎněr 出尔反尔; **backspace** (*key*) tuìgé 退格; **backstairs** hòu lóutī 后楼梯; **backstroke** SP yǎngyǒng 仰泳

backup also COMPUT hòubèi 后备; *take a* ~ COMPUT zuò bèiyòng cípán 做备用磁盘

backup disk COMPUT bèiyòng cípán 备用磁盘

backward 1 adj child chídùn 迟钝

society luòhòu 落后; *glance* xiànghòu 向后 **2** *adv* xiànghòu 向后

backyard hòu huāyuán 后花园; *fig* hòuyuàn 后院

bacon xūn xiánròu 熏咸肉

bacteria xìjūn 细菌

bad bùhǎo 不好; *weather, conditions* èliè 恶劣; *cold, headache etc* jùliè 剧烈; *mistake, accident* yánzhòng 严重; *(rotten)* huài 坏; *it's not ~* hái kěyǐ 还可以; *that's really too ~ (shame)* tài yíhàn le 太遗憾了; *feel ~ about (guilty)* gǎndào qiànjiù and huānxīn 感到歉疚和欢心; *be ~ at* bù zhuāncháng yú 不专长于; *Friday's ~, how about Thursday?* xīngqīwǔ bù héshì, xīngqīsì zěnme yàng? 星期五不合适,星期四怎么样?

bad debt wúfǎ shōuhuí de huàizhàng 无法收回的坏账

bad language cūhuà 粗话

badge zhèngzhāng 证章

badger *v/t* jiūchán 纠缠

badly *behave* bùhǎo 不好; *injured, damaged* yánzhòng 严重; *perform* chà 差; *he ~ needs a haircut / rest* tā jíxū jiǎn tóufa / xiūxi 他急需剪头发 / 休息; *he is ~ off (poor)* tā hěn qióng 他很穷

badminton yǔmáo qiú 羽毛球

baffle shǐ kùnhuò 使困惑; *be ~d* mōbùzháo tóunǎo 摸不着头脑

baffling *mystery* nányǐ jiědá 难以解答; *software etc* shēn'ào 深奥

bag *(plastic, paper)* dàizi 带子; *(for school, traveling)* bāo 包; *(purse)* shǒutí bāo 手提包

baggage xínglǐ 行李

baggage car RAIL xínglǐ chē 行李车; **baggage cart** xínglǐ chē 行李车; **baggage check** cúnfàng xínglǐ chù 存放行李处; **baggage reclaim** xínglǐ lǐngqǔ chù 行李领取处

baggy kuānsōng 宽松

bail *n* LAW bǎoshì 保释; *(money)* bǎoshì jīn 保释金; *on ~* zàibǎo 在保

♦ **bail out 1** *v/t* LAW bǎoshì 保释;

fig bāngzhù dùguò nánguān 帮助渡过难关 **2** *v/i (of airplane)* tiàosǎn 跳伞

bait *n* yòu'ěr 诱饵

bake *v/t* kǎo 烤

baked potato kǎo tǔdòu 烤土豆

baker miànbāo shīfu 面包师傅

bakery miànbāo diàn 面包店

balance 1 *n* pínghéng 平衡; *(remainder)* chā'é 差额; *(of bank account)* jiécún 结存 **2** *v/t* pínghéng 平衡; *~ the books* jiésuàn 结算 **3** *v/i* pínghéng 平衡; *(of accounts)* shōuzhī pínghéng 收支平衡

balanced *(fair)* gōngpíng 公平; *personality* pínghéng 平衡; *~ diet* jūnhéng yǐnshí 均衡饮食

balance of payments shōuzhī chā'é 国际收支差额

balance of trade màoyì chā'é 贸易差额

balance sheet juésuàn biǎo 决算表

balcony *(of house)* yángtái 阳台; *(in theater)* lóutīng 楼厅

bald *man* tūdǐng 秃顶; *he's going ~* tā kāishǐ tūdǐng le 他开始秃顶了

ball qiú 球; *on the ~* jījǐng 机警; *play ~ fig* hézuò 合作; *the ~'s in his court* lúndào tā zuòchū fǎnyìng 轮到他作出反应

ball bearing gǔnzhū zhóuchéng 滚珠轴承

ballerina bāléiwǔ nǚ yǎnyuán 芭蕾舞女演员

ballet bāléiwǔ 芭蕾舞

ballet dancer bāléiwǔ yǎnyuán 芭蕾舞演员

ball game *(baseball game)* qiúsài 球赛; *that's a different ~* nà shì lìng yījiàn shì 那是另一件事

ballistic missile dàndào dǎodàn 弹道导弹

balloon *(child's)* qìqiú 气球; *(for flight)* rè qìqiú 热气球

ballot 1 *n* tóupiào 投票 **2** *v/t members* tóupiào juédìng 投票决定

ballot box tóupiào xiāng 投票箱

ballpark (*baseball*) bàngqiú chǎng 棒球场;*be in the right ~* fig dàzhì zhèngquè 大致正确

ballpark figure dàzhì zhèngquè de shùmù 大致正确的数目

ballpoint (*pen*) ⇩ yuánzhū bǐ 圆珠笔

balls V dàn 蛋;(*courage*) yǒngqì 勇气

bamboo zhúzi 竹子

bamboo shoots zhúsǔn 竹笋

ban **1** *n* jìnlìng 禁令 **2** *v/t* jìnzhǐ 禁止

banana xiāngjiāo 香蕉

band (*musical group*) yuèduì 乐队

bandage **1** *n* bēngdài 绷带 **2** *v/t* bǎng bēngdài 绑绷带

Band-Aid® ⇩ chuàngkětiē 创可贴

bandit tǔfěi 土匪

bandwagon: *jump on the ~* gǎn làngtóu 赶浪头

bandy *legs* luóquān tuǐ 罗圈腿

bang **1** *n* (*noise*) hōngde yīshēng 轰的一声;(*blow*) měngjī 猛击 **2** *v/t door* shuāi 摔;(*hit*) zhuàng 撞 **3** *v/i* fāchū pēngde yīxiǎng 发出砰的一响

Bangladesh Mèngjiālā 孟加拉

Bangladeshi **1** *adj* Mèngjiālā 孟加拉 **2** *n* (*person*) Mèngjiālā rén 孟加拉人

banjo bānzhuō qín 班卓琴

bank¹ (*of river*) hé'àn 河岸

bank² **1** *n* FIN yínháng 银行 **2** *v/i:* *~ with* yòng … yínháng 用 … 银行 **3** *v/t money* chǔcún 储存

◆**bank on** zhǐwàng 指望;*don't ~ it* bié nàme kěndìng 别那么肯定

bank account yínháng zhànghù 银行帐户;**bank balance** yínháng jiécún 银行结存;**bank bill** chāopiào 钞票

banker yínháng jiā 银行家

banker's card yínháng xìnyòng kǎ 银行信用卡

banker's order chángqī wěituō shū 长期委托书

bank loan yínháng dàikuǎn 银行贷款;**bank manager** yínháng jīnglǐ 银行经理;**Bank of China** Zhōngguó Yínháng 中国银行;

bank rate yínháng lìlǜ 银行利率;**bankroll** *v/t* tígōng zījīn 提供资金

bankrupt **1** *adj* pòchǎn 破产;*go ~* pòchǎn 破产 **2** *v/t* pòchǎn 破产

bankruptcy pòchǎn 破产

bank statement yínháng jiédān 银行结单

banner héngfú 横幅

banns jiéhūn gōnggào 结婚公告

banquet yànhuì 宴会

banter *n* qǔxiào 取笑

baptism xǐlǐ 洗礼

baptize xǐlǐ 洗礼

bar¹ (*iron, chocolate*) tiáo 条;(*for drinks*) jiǔbā 酒吧;(*counter*) guìtái 柜台;*a ~ of soap* yīkuài féizào 一块肥皂;*be behind ~s* (*in prison*) zuò bānfáng 坐班房

bar² *v/t* jìnzhǐ 禁止

bar³ *prep* (*except*) chúle 除了

barbecue ⇩ **1** *n* shāokǎo huì 烧烤会;(*equipment*) kǎojià 烤架 **2** *v/t* kǎo kǎo 烤烤

barbed wire yǒucì tiěsī 有刺铁丝

barber tìtóu jiàng 剃头匠

bar code tiáoxíng mǎ 条形码

bare *adj* (*naked*) guāng 光;(*empty:* *room*) kōng 空;*mountainside, floor* guāng tūtu 光秃秃

barefoot: *be ~* guāngjiǎo 光脚

barefoot doctor chìjiǎo yīshēng 赤脚医生

bare-headed guāngzhe tóu 光着头

barely jǐnjǐn 仅仅

bargain **1** *n* (*deal*) jiāoyì 交易;(*good buy*) piányí huò 便宜货;*it's a ~!* (*deal*) zhēn piányí! 真便宜! **2** *v/i* tǎojià huánjià 讨价还价

◆**bargain for** (*expect*) yùliào 预料

barge *n* NAUT bóchuán 驳船

bark¹ **1** *n* (*of dog*) fèi 吠 **2** *v/i* fèi 吠

bark² (*of tree*) shùpí 树皮

barley dàmài 大麦

barn liángcāng 粮仓

barometer qìyā biǎo 气压表;fig qíngyǔ biǎo 晴雨表

barracks MIL yíngfáng 营房

barrel (*container*) tǒng 桶

barren *land* huāngmò 荒漠

barricade *n* lùzhàng 路障

barrier lángān 栏杆; *(cultural)* zhàng'ài 障碍; *language* ~ yǔyán zhàng'ài 语言障碍

bar tender jiǔdiàn huǒjì 酒店伙计

barter **1** *n* yìhuò màoyì 易货贸易 **2** *v/t* jiāohuàn 交换

base **1** *n (bottom end)* dǐbù 底部; *(underneath)* dǐzuò 底座; *(center, MIL)* jīdì 基地 **2** *v/t* yǐ ... wéi jīchǔ yǐ ... 为基础; ~ **X on Y** yǐ Y wéi X de jīchǔ yǐ Y 为 X 的基础; *be* ~**d in** *(in city, country)* yǐ ... wéi jīdì yǐ ... 为基地

baseball *(ball)* bàngqiú 棒球; *(game)* bàngqiú yùndòng 棒球运动

baseball bat bàngqiú gùn 棒球棍; baseball cap bàngqiú mào 棒球帽; baseball player bàngqiú yùndòngyuán 棒球运动员

basement *(of house)* dìxiàshì 地下室; *(of store)* dǐcéng 底层

base rate FIN jīběn lìlù 基本利率

basic *(rudimentary)* jīběn 基本; *(fundamental)* zhǔyào 主要

basically dàzhì shuōlái 大致说来

basics: *the* ~ jīběn yuánlǐ 基本原理; *get down to* ~ chǎngkāi tiānchuāng shuō liànghuà 敞开天窗说亮话

basin *(for washing)* shuǐchí 水池; *(geographical)* péndì 盆地

basis jīchǔ 基础; *(of argument)* gēnjù 根据

bask shài tàiyáng 晒太阳

basket lánzi 篮子; *(in basketball)* wǎng 网

basketball lánqiú 篮球

bass **1** *n (part)* nán dīyīn 男低音; *(singer)* nán dīyīn gēshǒu 男低音歌手; *(instrument)* dīyīn yuèqì 低音乐器 **2** *adj* nán dīyīn 男低音

bastard sīshēngzǐ 私生子; F húndàn 混蛋; *poor* ~ / *stupid* ~ kělián chóng / chǔndàn 可怜虫 / 蠢蛋

bat[1] **1** *n (for baseball)* qiúgùn 球棍;

(for table tennis) qiúpāi 球拍 **2** *v/i (in baseball)* jíqiú 击球

bat[2]: *he didn't* ~ *an eyelid* tā wúdòng yúzhōng 他无动于衷

bat[3] *(animal)* biānfú 蝙蝠

batch *n* pī 批

bath zǎopén 澡盆; *have a* ~, *take a* ~ xǐzǎo 洗澡

bathe *v/i (have a bath)* xǐzǎo 洗澡

bath mat dìjīn 地巾; bathrobe yùyī 浴衣; bathroom *(for bath)* xǐzǎo jiān 洗澡间; *(for washing hands)* xǐshǒu jiān 洗手间; *(toilet)* cèsuǒ / xǐshǒu jiān 厕所 / 洗手间

bath towel yùjīn 浴巾; bathtub yùgāng 浴缸

batter *n* miànhú 面糊; *(in baseball)* jíqiú yuán 击球员

battery diànchí 电池; MOT xù diànchí 蓄电池

battle **1** *n* zhànyì 战役; *fig* dòuzhēng 斗争 **2** *v/i (against illness etc)* bódòu 搏斗

battlefield, battleground zhànchǎng 战场

bawdy yínhuì 淫秽

bawl *(shout)* dàjiào 大叫; *(weep)* tòngkū 痛哭

♦ bawl out *v/t* F chòumà yīdùn 臭骂一顿

bay *(inlet)* wān 湾

bay window tūchuāng 凸窗

be ◊ shì 是; *it's me* shì wǒ shì wǒ; *how much is I are ... ?* ... duōshǎo qián? ... 多少钱？; *there is, there are* yǒu 有; ~ *careful* xiǎoxīn 小心; *don't* ~ *sad* bié shāngxīn 别伤心 ◊ *(not translated)*: *was she there?* tā zài nàr ma? 她在那儿吗？; *I'm happy* wǒ gāoxìng 我高兴; *this book is intereresting* zhè běn shū hěn yǒuqù 这本书很有趣 ◊: *has the mailman been?* yóudìyuán láiguò le ma? 邮递员来过了吗？; *I've never been to Beijing* wǒ cóngméi qùguò Běijīng 我从没去过北京; *I've been here for hours* wǒ láile hěnjiǔ le 我来了很久了 ◊ *(tags)*: *that's right, isn't it?* shìde, duìbùduì? 是的, 对不

对？; **she's Chinese, isn't she?** tā shì Zhōngguó rén, shìba? 她是中国人，是吧？ ◊ *(auxiliary)*: **I am thinking** wǒ zài xiǎng 我在想; **he was running** tā zài pǎobù 他在跑步; **you're ~ing silly** nǐ fànshǎ ne 你犯傻呢 ◊ *(obligation)*: **you are to do what I tell you** nǐ yào zhào wǒ shuōde qùzuò 你要照我说的去做; **I was to tell you this** wǒ běnlái gāi gàosu nǐ wǒ 我本来该告诉你; **you were not to tell anyone** nǐ bù yīnggāi gàosu rènhé rén 你不应该告诉任何人 ◊ *(passive)*: **he was killed** tā bèi shā sǐ le 他被杀死了; **they have been sold** tāmen yǐjīng bèi màidiào le 他们已经被卖掉了

♦ **be in for** surprise, trouble etc huì dédào 会得到

beach hǎitān 海滩

beachwear hǎibīn fúzhuāng 海滨服装

beads zhūzi 珠子

beak huì 喙

beaker wúbǐng jiǔbēi 无柄酒杯

be-all: **the ~ and end-all** liǎobuqǐ 了不起

beam 1 n *(in ceiling etc)* héngliáng 横梁 **2** v/i *(smile)* xiàoróng mǎnmiàn 笑容满面 **3** v/t *(transmit)* dìngxiàng fāshè 定向发射

bean curd dòufu 豆腐

beans dòu 豆; **be full of ~** jīnglì chōngpèi 精力充沛

beansprouts dòuyá 豆芽

bear[1] *(animal)* xióng 熊

bear[2] **1** v/t weight chéngshòu 承受; costs chéngdān 承担; *(tolerate)* rěnshòu 忍受; child shēngyù 生育 **2** v/i: **bring pressure to ~ on** shījiā yālì 施加压力

♦ **bear out** *(confirm)* zhèngshí 证实

bearable kě róngrěn 可容忍

beard húzi 胡子

bearing *(in machine)* zhóuchéng 轴承; **that has no ~ on the case** nà hé zhège ànjiàn méi shénme guānxi 那和这个案件没什么关系

bear market FIN dànshì 淡市

beast chùshēng 畜生

beat 1 n *(of heart)* tiàodòng 跳动; *(of music)* jiézòu 节奏 **2** v/i *(of heart)* tiàodòng 跳动; *(of rain)* qiāodǎ 敲打; **~ about the bush** guǎiwān mòjiǎo 拐弯抹角 **3** v/t *(in competition)* jībài 击败; *(hit)* dǎ 打; *(pound)* pāi pāi 拍拍; **~ it!** F gǔnkāi! 滚开！; **it ~s me** F wǒ bū míngbái 我不明白

♦ **beat up** hěnzòu 狠揍

beaten: **off the ~ track** xiǎn yǒurén shèzú 鲜有人涉足

beating *(physical)* dǎ 打

beat-up F pòjiù 破旧

beautician měiróng jiā 美容家

beautiful woman, house, day měilì 美丽; meal fēngshèng kěkǒu 丰盛可口; vacation wánměi 完美; story, movie dòngrén 动人; **thanks, that's just ~!** xièxie, wǒ gòule! 谢谢，我够了！

beautifully cooked, done gānghǎo 刚好; simple yōuyǎ 优雅

beauty *(of woman, sunset)* měilì 美丽

beauty parlor měiróng yuàn 美容院

♦ **beaver away** nǔlì gōngzuò 努力工作

because yīnwèi 因为; **~ it was too expensive** yīnwèi tàiguì 因为太贵; **~ of** yóuyú 由于

beckon v/i zhāohuàn 召唤

become biànchéng 变成; **what's ~ of her?** tā jiūjìng zěnmeyàng? 她究竟怎么样？

bed chuáng 床; *(of flowers)* tán tǎn 坛; *(of sea, river)* chuáng 床; **go to ~** shuìjiào 睡觉; **he's still in ~** tā háiméi qǐchuáng ne 他还没起床呢; **go to ~ with** hé ... shàngchuáng 和 ... 上床

bedclothes chuángshàng yòngpǐn 床上用品

bedding qǐnjù 寝具

bedridden wòchuáng bùqǐ 卧床不起; **bedroom** shuìfáng 睡房; **bedspread** chuángzhào 床罩; **bedtime** jiùqǐn shíjiān 就寝时间

bee mìfēng 蜜蜂

beech shānmáo jǔ 山毛榉

beef 1 n niúròu 牛肉; F (complaint) láosāo 牢骚 2 v/i F (complain) nào nào 闹

◆beef up chōngshí 充实

beefburger hànbǎo bāo 汉堡包

beef noodles niúròumiàn 牛肉面

beehive fēngxiāng 蜂箱

beeline: make a ~ for zhíbēn 直奔

beep 1 n dūdu shēng 嘟嘟声 2 v/i fāchū dūdu shēng 发出嘟嘟声 3 v/t (call on pager) hū hū 呼呼

beeper kuòjī 扩机

beer píjiǔ 啤酒

beetle jiǎchóng 甲虫

before 1 prep (time, space, order) zhīqián 之前 2 adv yǐqián 以前; the week/day ~ qián yīgè xīngqī/tiān 前一个星期/天 3 conj zhīqián 之前

beforehand shìxiān 事先

beg 1 v/i yàofàn 要饭 2 v/t: ~ X to ... kěnqiú X qùzuò ... 恳求X去做 ...

beggar qǐgài 乞丐

begin 1 v/i kāishǐ 开始; to ~ with (at first) běnlái 本来; (in the first place) shǒuxiān 首先 2 v/t kāishǐ 开始

beginner chūxué zhě 初学者

beginner driver jiàshǐ xuéyuán 驾驶学员

beginning kāishǐ 开始; (origin) qǐyuán 起源

behalf: on or in ~ of dàibiǎo 代表; on my/his ~ dàibiǎo wǒ/tā 代表我/他

behave v/i biǎoxiàn 表现; ~ (oneself) shǒu guījǔ 守规矩; ~ (yourself)! guījǔ diǎn! 规矩点!

behavior xíngwéi 行为

behind 1 prep (in position) zài ... hòumian ... 后面; (in progress, in order) luòhòu 落后; be ~ ... (responsible for) zài ... bèihòu zài ... 背后; (support) zhīchí 支持 2 adv (at the back) zài hòumian 在后面; leave, stay liúxià 留下; be ~ with X zài X fāngmiàn luòhòu 在X方面落后

Beijing Běijīng 北京

being (existence) shēngcún 生存; (creature) shēngwù 生物

belated láichí 来迟

belch n & v/i dǎgé 打嗝

Belgian 1 adj Bǐlìshí 比利时 2 n Bǐlìshí rén 比利时人

Belgium Bǐlìshí 比利时

belief (trust) xìnrèn 信任; (religion) xìnyǎng 信仰; (opinion) kànfǎ 看法

believe xiāngxìn 相信

◆believe in xiāngxìn 相信; ghosts xìn 信; a person xìnrèn 信任

believer (also fig) xìntú 信徒

bell (in church, school) zhōng 钟; (on bike, door) líng 铃

bellhop shìzhě 侍者

belligerent adj jiāozhàn zhōng 交战中

bellow 1 n hǒushēng 吼声; (of bull) hǒujiào shēng 吼叫声 2 v/i nùhǒu 怒吼; (of bull) hǒujiào 吼叫

belly (of person, animal) dùzi 肚子; (fat stomach) pàng dùzi 胖肚子

bellyache v/i F bàoyuàn 抱怨

belong v/i shǔyú 属于; where does this ~? zhè yīnggāi fàngzài nǎli? 这应该放在哪里? I don't ~ here wǒ bù shǔyú zhèli 我不属于这里

◆belong to shǔyú 属于; club, organization shì ... chéngyuán shì ... 成员

belongings suǒyǒu wù 所有物

beloved adj xǐ'ài 喜爱

below 1 prep zài ... de xiàmian 在 ... 的下面; (in amount, rate, level) dīyú 低于 2 adv zài xiàmian 在下面; (in text) zài xiàwén zhōng 在下文中; see ~ rúxià 如下; 10 degrees ~ língxià shídù líng xià shídù 零下十度

belt yāodài 腰带; tighten one's ~ fig jiéyuē 节约

bench (seat) chángyǐ 长椅; (work~) gōngzuò tái 工作台

benchmark jīzhǔn 基准

bend 1 n wānqū 弯曲 2 v/t wān 弯 3 v/i wān 弯; (of person) wānshēn 弯身

♦ **bend down** wānyāo 弯腰

bender ⊦ kuángyǐn 狂饮

beneath 1 *prep* zài … xiàmiàn 在 … 下面; (*in status, value*) dīyú 低于 **2** *adv* xiàbiān 下边

benefactor shīzhǔ 施主

beneficial yǒuyì 有益

benefit 1 *n* hǎochù 好处 **2** *v/t* yǒuyì yú 有益于 **3** *v/i* shòuyì 受益

benevolent císhàn 慈善

benign cíxiáng 慈祥; MED liángxìng 良性

bequeath yíliú 遗留; *fig* liúxià 留下

bereaved 1 *adj* sàngshī qīnrén 丧失亲人 **2** *n*: **the ~** sàngshī qīnrén de rénmen 丧失亲人的人们

berry jiāngguǒ 浆果

berserk: *go ~* fāfēng 发疯

berth (*for sleeping*) pùwèi 铺位; (*for ship*) chuántái 船台; *give X a wide ~* bìkāi X 避开 X

beside zài … pángbiān 在 … 旁边; *be ~ oneself with rage / grief* kuángnù / jí bēishāng 狂怒 / 极悲伤; *that's ~ the point* nàshì wúguān de 那是无关的

besides 1 *adv* zàishuō 再说 **2** *prep* (*apart from*) chúle 除了

best 1 *adj* zuìhǎo 最好 **2** *adv* zuìhǎo 最好; *it would be ~ if …* zuìhǎo … zuìhǎo …; *I like her ~* wǒ zuì xǐhuān tā 我最喜欢她 **3** *n*: *do one's ~* jìnlì érwéi 尽力而为; *the ~* (*thing*) zuìhǎo 最好; (*person*) zuìjiā 最佳; *make the ~ of* còuhe 凑和; *all the ~!* zhù yīqiè shùnlì! 祝一切顺利！

best before date zàicǐ rìqí zhīqián shǐyòng 在此日期之前使用; **best man** (*at wedding*) nán bīnxiàng 男傧相; **best-seller** chàngxiāo shū 畅销书

bet 1 *n* dǔzhùzuì 赌注 **2** *v/i* dǔbó 赌博; (*reckon*) dǎdǔ 打赌; *you ~!* dāngrán le! 当然了！

betray bèipàn 背叛

betrayal bèipàn 背叛

better 1 *adj* gènghǎo 更好; *get ~* gǎijìn 改进; (*in health*) hǎozhuǎn 好转; *he's ~* (*in health*) tā hǎoduǎn le 他好点儿了 **2** *adv* gènghǎo 更好; *you'd ~ ask permission* nǐ zuìhǎo zhēngdé tóngyì 你最好征得同意; *I'd really ~ not* wǒ háishí bùyào le 我还是不要了; *all the ~ for us* duì wǒmen yǒu hǎochù 对我们有好处; *I like her ~* wǒ gèng xǐhuān tā le 我更喜欢她了

better off *adj* fùyù 富裕

between *prep* zài … zhījiān 在 … 之间; *~ you and me* nǐwǒ sīxià shuōshuo 你我私下说说

beverage *fml* yǐnliào 饮料

beware: *~ of* xiǎoxīn 小心

bewilder shǐ hútu 使糊涂

beyond 1 *prep* (*in space*) yuǎnyú 远于; (*in degree, extent*) chāochū 超出; *~ recognition* rèn bù chūlái le 认不出来了; *it's ~ me* (*don't understand*) wǒ bù míngbái 我不明白; (*can't do it*) chāochū wǒde nénglì fànwéi 超出我的能力范围 **2** *adv* gèngyuǎn 更远

Bhutan Bùdān 不丹

Bhutanese 1 *adj* Bùdān 不丹 **2** *n* (*person*) Bùdān rén 不丹人

bias *n* (*against*) piānjiàn 偏见; (*in favor of*) piāntǎn 偏袒

bias(s)ed (*against*) piānjiàn 偏见; (*in favor of*) piāntǎn 偏袒

bib (*for baby*) wéizuǐ 围嘴

Bible shèngjīng 圣经

bibliography cānkǎo shūmù 参考书目

biceps èrtóu jī 二头肌

bicker zhēngchǎo 争吵

bicycle *n* ⇩ zìxíng chē 自行车

bid 1 *n* (*at auction*) chūjià 出价; (*attempt*) qǐtú 企图 **2** *v/i* (*at auction*) chūjià 出价

biennial *adj* liǎngnián yīcì 两年一次

big 1 *adj* dà 大; (*tall*) gāo 高; *my ~ brother / sister* wǒ gēge / jiějie 我哥哥 / 姐姐; *~ name* chūmíng 出名; *~ talk* chuīniú 吹牛

bigamy chónghūn 重婚

big-headed zìdà 自大

bike 1 *n* zìxíng chē 自行车 **2** *v/i* qí

zìxíng chē 骑自行车

bikini bǐjīní 比基尼

bilingual shuāngyǔ 双语

bill 1 n zhàngdān 账单; (money) chāopiào 钞票; POL yì'àn 议案; (poster) hǎibào 海报 2 v/t (invoice) kāi zhàngdān 开账单

billboard guǎnggào pái 广告牌

billfold qiánbāo 钱包

billiards táiqiú 台球

billion shíyì 十亿

bill of exchange huìpiào 汇票

bill of sale zhuǎnràng qìjù 转让契据

bin (for storage) xiāngzi 箱子

binary èrjìn zhì 二进制

bind v/t (connect) liánjiē 连接; (tie) bǎng 绑; (oblige) yuēshù 约束

binder (for papers) huóyè jiā 活页夹

binding 1 adj agreement, promise yǒu yuēshù lì 有约束力 2 n (of book) zhuāngdìng 装钉

binoculars wàngyuǎn jìng 望远镜

biodegradable néng jìnxíng shēngwù jiàngjiě 能进行生物降解

biography zhuànjì 传记

biological shēngwù shēng wù; ~ parents qīnshēng fùmǔ 亲生父母; ~ detergent huóxìng xǐdí jì 活性洗涤剂

biology shēngwù xué 生物学

biotechnology shēngwù gōngyì xué 生物工艺学

bird niǎo 鸟

bird of prey měngqín 猛禽

bird sanctuary niǎolèi bǎohù qū 鸟类保护区

birth (of child) chūshēng 出生; (labor) fēnmiǎn 分娩; fig (of country) dànshēng 诞生; give ~ to child shēng háizi 生孩子; date of ~ chūshēng rìqī 出生日期

birth certificate chūshēng zhèng 出生证; birth control bìyùn 避孕; birthday shēngrì 生日; happy ~! shēngrì kuàilè! 生日快乐！; birthplace chūshēng dì 出生地; birthrate chūshēng lǜ 出生率

biscuit bǐnggān 饼干

bisexual 1 adj shuāngxìng 双性 2 n shuāngxìng rén 双性人

bishop zhǔjiào 主教

bit n (piece) xiǎokuàir 小块儿; (length) xiǎoduànr 小段儿; (part) bùfen 部分; COMPUT èrjìn zhì wèi 二进制位; a ~ (a little) yǒudiǎnr 有点儿; (of time) yíhuìr 一会儿; a ~ of (a little) yìdiǎn 一点; a ~ of news / advice yìtiáo xīnwén / yígè gàojiè 一条新闻 / 一个告诫; ~ by ~ yìdiǎn yìdiǎn 一点一点; I'll be there in a ~ (in a little while) wǒ yīhuìr huìdào 我一会儿会到

bitch 1 n (dog) mǔgǒu 母狗; F (woman) pōfù 泼妇 2 v/t F (complain) fā láosāo 发牢骚

bitchy F person, remark lìngrén tǎoyàn 令人讨厌

bite 1 n (of dog, snake) yǎo 咬; (of mosquito, flea, spider) dīng 叮; (of food) yìkǒu 一口; get a ~ (of angler) yú tūnèr 鱼吞饵; let's have a ~ (to eat) wǒmen chī diǎnr dōngxi ba 我们吃点儿东西吧 2 v/t (of dog, snake) yǎo 咬; (of mosquito, flea, spider) dīng 叮 3 v/i yǎo 咬; (of mosquito, flea) dīng 叮; (of fish) tūněr 吞饵

bitter taste kǔ 苦; person chōngmǎn yuànhèn 充满怨恨; weather hánlěng 寒冷; argument jīliè 激烈

bitterly: ~ cold hánlěng 寒冷

black 1 adj hēi 黑; coffee etc wúnǎi 无奶; fig àndàn 暗淡 2 n (color) hēisè 黑色; (person) hēirén 黑人; in the ~ FIN yǒu jiéyú 有结余

♦ black out v/i hūnmí 昏迷

black bean sauce dòubànjiàng 豆瓣酱; blackberry hēiméi 黑莓; blackbird shānniǎo 山鸟; blackboard hēibǎn 黑板; black box hēi xiázi 黑匣子; black economy hēishì jīngjì 黑市经济

blacken person's name fěibàng 诽谤

black eye qīngzhǒng yǎnkuàng 青肿眼眶; black ice hēibīng 黑冰; blacklist 1 n hēi míngdān 黑名单 2 v/t shàng hēi míngdān 上黑名单; blackmail 1 n xiépò 胁迫;

emotional ~ gǎnqíng qiāozhà 感情敲诈 2 v/t xiépò 胁迫;

blackmailer lèsuǒ zhě 勒索者;

black market hēishì 黑市

blackness hēi'àn 黑暗

blackout ELEC tíngdiàn 停电; MED hūnmí 昏迷; **blacksmith** tiějiàng 铁匠; **black tea** hóngchá 红茶

bladder pángguāng 膀胱

blade (*of knife, sword*) rèn 刃; (*of helicopter*) jiāngyè 浆叶; (*of grass*) yèpiàn 叶片

blame 1 n zébèi 责备; (*responsibility*) zérèn 责任 2 v/t zéguài 责怪; ~ **X for Y** yīnwèi Y zébèi X 因为 Y 责备 X

bland *smile* píngdàn 平淡; *answer* kūzào wúwèi 枯燥无味; *food* dàn 淡

blank 1 adj page, tape kòngbái 空白; *look* mángrán 茫然 **2** n (*empty space*) kòngwèi 空位; *my mind's a* ~ wǒ tóunǎo yīpiàn kòngbái 我头脑一片空白

blank check kōngtóu zhīpiào 空头支票

blanket n tǎnzi 毯子; *a* ~ *of* fig yīcéng 一层

blare v/i xuānnào 喧闹

♦**blare out 1** v/i xuānnào 喧闹 **2** v/t dàshēng fāchū 大声发出

blaspheme v/i xièdú 亵渎

blast 1 n (*explosion*) bàozhà 爆炸; (*gust*) yīgǔ 一股 **2** v/t yòng zhàyào zhà 用炸药炸; ~! gāisǐ! 该死!

♦**blast off** (*of rocket*) fāshè shàngtiān 发射上天

blast furnace gāolú 高炉

blast-off fāshè 发射

blatant míngxiǎn 明显

blaze 1 n (*fire*) huǒyàn 火焰; *a* ~ *of color* wǔcǎi bīnfēn 五彩缤纷 **2** v/i (*of fire*) xióngxióng ránshāo 熊熊燃烧

♦**blaze away** (*with gun*) měngjī 猛击

blazer nánshì biàn shàngzhuāng 男式便上装

bleach 1 n piǎobái jì 漂白剂 **2** v/t *hair* shǐ tuōsè 使脱色

bleak *countryside* huāngliáng 荒凉;

weather hánlěng cìgǔ 寒冷刺骨; *future* àndàn 暗淡

bleary-eyed shuìyǎn xīngsōng 睡眼惺忪

bleat v/i (*of sheep*) miēmie jiào 咩咩叫

bleed 1 v/i liúxuè 流血 **2** v/t fig zhàqǔ 榨取

bleeding n liúxuè 流血

bleep 1 n BB shēng BB 声 **2** v/i fāchū BB shēng 发出 BB 声 **3** v/t (*call on pager*) hūhuàn 呼唤

bleeper hūjiào jī 呼叫机

blemish 1 n xiácī 瑕疵 **2** v/t *reputation* pòhuài 破坏

blend 1 n & v/i hùnhé 混合

♦**blend in 1** v/i rónghé 融和 **2** v/t (*in cooking*) jiǎohé 搅和

blender (*machine*) jiǎohéjī 搅和机

bless zhùfú 祝福; ~ **you** (*in response to sneeze*) no equivalent; *be* ~*ed with* yǒuxìng dédào 有幸得到

blessing REL qíshén cìfú 祈神赐福; fig (*approval*) zànchéng 赞成

blind 1 adj mángmù 盲目; *corner* kànbùjiàn lìngyītóu de guǎijiǎo 看不见另一头的拐角; ~ *to* shì'ér bùjiàn 视而不见 **2** n: *the* ~ mángrén bìngrén 盲人 **3** v/t shǐshīmíng 使失明; fig shǐ shīqù pànduàn lì 使失去判断力

blind alley sǐ hútong 死胡同

blindfold 1 n, & adv méngzhù yǎnjīng 蒙住眼睛

blinding xuànmù 眩目

blind spot (*in road*) mángdiǎn 盲点; fig wúzhī 无知

blink v/i (*of person*) zhǎyǎn 眨眼; (*of light*) shǎnshuò 闪烁

blip (*on radar screen*) guāngdiǎn 光点; fig zànshí quēxiàn 暂时缺陷

bliss kuàilè 快乐

blister 1 n shuǐpào 水疱 **2** v/i (*of skin*) shuǐpào qǐ shuǐpào 起水疱; (*of paint*) qǐ qìpào 起气泡

blizzard bàofēngxuě 暴风雪

bloated zhàngzhàng 胀胀

blob (*of liquid*) dī 滴

bloc POL jítuán 集团

block 1 n kuài 块; (*in town*) jiēduàn

街段; (of shares) dàzōng 大宗;
(blockage) zhàng'ài wù 障碍物
2 v/t dǔsè 堵塞
♦block in (with vehicle) dǔzhù 堵
住
♦block out light dǎngzhù 挡住
♦block up v/t sink etc dǔsāi 堵塞
blockade n & v/t fēngsuǒ 封锁
blockage dǔsāi 堵塞
blockbuster yángyang dàzuò 洋
洋大作
block letters dàxiě zìmǔ 大写字
母
blond adj jīnfà 金发
blonde n (woman) jīnfà nǚláng 金
发女郎
blood xuèyè 血液; in cold ~
cánrěn 残忍
blood bank xuèkù 血库; blood
donor ⇩ xiànxuè zhě 献血者;
blood group xuèxíng 血型
bloodless coup wú liúxuè 无流血
blood poisoning xuè zhòngdú 血
中毒; blood pressure xuèyā 血
压; blood relation, blood relative xuèqīn 血亲; blood sample
xuèyè yàngběn 血液样本;
bloodshed liúxuè 流血; blood-
shot bùmǎn xuèsī 布满血丝;
bloodstain xuèjī 血迹; bloodstream xuè liú 血流; blood test
yànxuè 验血; blood transfusion
shūxuè 输血; blood vessel
xuèguǎn 血管
bloody hands etc dàixuè 带血;
battle xuè línlín 血淋淋
bloody mary hóng mǎlì hùnhé jiǔ
红玛丽混合酒
bloom 1 n huāduǒ 花朵; in full ~
shèngkāi 盛开 2 v/i kāihuā 开花;
fig xīngwàng 兴旺
blossom 1 n huā 花 2 v/i kāihuā 开
花; fig fāzhǎn 发展
blot 1 n mòshuǐ zì 墨水渍; fig
wūdiǎn 污点 2 v/t paper xīgān 吸
干; (wipe dry) cāgān 擦干
♦blot out (hide from view) zhēbì 遮
蔽; memory mǒmiè 抹灭
blotch zhěn 疹
blouse chènshān 衬衫
blow[1] n jī 击; (setback) zǔ'ài 阻碍

blow[2] 1 v/t (of wind) chuī 吹; whistle
chuīshào 吹哨; (spend) làngfèi 浪
费; opportunity shīqù 失去; ~
one's nose xǐng bítì 擤鼻涕 2 v/i
(of wind) guāfēng 刮风; (of
whistle) chuīshào 吹哨; (of person)
chuīqì 吹气; (of fuse) shāoduàn
烧断; (of tire) bàozhà 爆炸
♦blow off v/t & v/i chuīdiào 吹掉
♦blow out v/t & v/i (of candle)
chuīmiè 吹灭
♦blow over 1 v/t chuīdǎo 吹倒
2 v/i chuīdǎo 吹倒; (calm down)
píngxī 平息; (of argument) bèi
dànwàng 被淡忘
♦blow up 1 v/t (with explosives) zhà
zhà 炸; balloon chōngqì 充气;
photograph fàngdà 放大 2 v/i zhà
zhà 炸; (become angry) dàfā píqì 大发
脾气
blow-dry v/t chuīgān 吹干; blow
job √ kǒuyín 口淫; blow-out (of
tire) chētāi bàozhà 车胎爆炸; F
(big meal) měicān 美餐; blow-up
(of photo) fàngdà xiàngpiān 放大
相片
blue 1 adj lánsè 蓝色; ~ movie
huángsè diànyǐng 黄色电影 2 n
lánsè 蓝色
blueberry lán jiāngguǒ 蓝浆果;
blue chip rénmén 热门; blue-
collar worker lánlíng gōngrén 蓝
领工人; blueprint (also fig) lántú
蓝图
blues MUS bólǔsī yīnyuè 勃鲁斯
音乐; have the ~ jǔsàng 沮丧
blues singer bólǔsī gēshǒu 勃鲁
斯歌手
bluff 1 n (deception) xūzhāng
shēngshì 虚张声势 2 v/i zhàhu
诈呼
blunder 1 n dàcuò 大错 2 v/i fàn
dà cuòwù 犯大错误
blunt adj dùn 钝; person zhíshuài
直率
bluntly speak tǎnbái 坦白
blur n & v/t móhu 模糊
blurb (on book) jiǎnjiè 简介
♦blurt out bùshèn shuōchū 不慎
说出
blush 1 n hóngsè 红色 2 v/i

liǎnhóng 脸红

blusher (*cosmetic*) yānzhī 胭脂

BO (*body odor*) tǐxiù 体臭

board 1 *n* bǎn bǎn; (*for game*) qípán 棋盘; (*for notices*) pái pái; ~ (*of directors*) dǒngshì huì 董事会; **on** ~ (*plane*) zài fēijī shàng 在飞机上; (*train*) zài huǒchē shàng 在火车上; (*boat*) zài chuán shàng 在船上; **take on** ~ (*comments etc*) kǎolù 考虑; (*fully realize truth of*) yìshídào zhēnxiàng 意识到真相; **across the** ~ quánmiàn 全面 **2** *v/t airplane etc* shàng 上 **3** *v/i* (*of passengers*) shànglái 上来

♦**board up** fēng 封

♦**board with** shànsù 膳宿

board and lodging chīzhù 吃住

boarder jì shànsù zhě 寄膳宿者; EDU jùsù shēng 寄宿生

board game qípán yóuxì 棋盘游戏

boarding card dēngjī kǎ 登机卡; **boarding house** sùshè 宿舍; **boarding pass** dēngjī kǎ 登机卡; **boarding school** jìsù xuéxiào 寄宿学校

board meeting dǒngshìhuì huìyì 董事会会议; **board room** huìyì shì 会议室; **boardwalk** hǎibīn rénxíngdào 海滨人行道

boast *n* & *v/i* chuīniú 吹牛

boat chuán 船; (*small, for leisure*) xiǎochuán 小船; **go by** ~ zuòchuán 坐船

bob¹ (*haircut*) duǎnfà 短发

bob² *v/i* (*of boat etc*) piāolái piāoqù 漂来漂去

♦**bob up** tūrán chūxiàn 突然出现

bobsleigh, bobsled xuěqiāo 雪橇

bodice jǐnshēn xiōngyī 紧身胸衣

bodily 1 *adj* shēntǐ 身体 **2** *adv eject* qīnshēn 亲身

body shēntǐ 身体; (*dead*) shītǐ 尸体; ~ **of water** shuǐtǐ 水体; ~ (*suit*) (*undergarment*) jǐnshēn yī 紧身衣

bodyguard bǎobiāo 保镖; **body language** shēntǐ yǔ 身势语; **body odor** tǐxiù 体臭; **body shop** MOT chēshēn xiūlǐ chǎng 车

身修理厂; **bodywork** MOT chēshēn 车身

boggle: **it ~s the mind!** yìxiǎng tiānkāi! 异想天开！

bogus jiǎ 假

Bohai Gulf Bóhǎi Wān 渤海湾

boil¹ (*swelling*) jiēzi 疖子

boil² **1** *v/t liquid, egg, vegetables* zhǔ 煮 **2** *v/i* kāi 开

♦**boil down to** guīgēn jiédǐ 归根结底

♦**boil over** (*of milk etc*) fèiyì 沸溢

boiled rice báifàn 白饭

boiled water kāishuǐ 开水

boiler guōlú 锅炉

boisterous xuānnào 喧闹

bold 1 *adj* dàdǎn 大胆 **2** *n* (*print*) cūtǐ 粗体; **in** ~ yòng cūtǐ 用粗体

bolster *v/t confidence* zēngqiáng 增强

bolt 1 *n* luóshuān 螺栓; (*on door*) chāxiāo 插销; (*of lightning*) xuánmù diànshǎn 眩目电闪; **like a ~ from the blue** qíngtiān pīlì 晴天霹雳 **2** *adv*: ~ **upright** bǐzhí 笔直 **3** *v/t* (*fix with bolts*) shuānzhù 栓住; (*close*) shuān 闩 **4** *v/i* (*run off*) tuōjiāng 脱缰; (*of prisoner*) táopǎo 逃跑

bomb 1 *n* zhàdàn 炸弹 **2** *v/t* hōngzhà 轰炸

bombard: ~ **with questions** liánzhǔpào sìdì tíchū wèntí 连珠炮似地提出问题

bomb attack zhàdàn gōngjī 炸弹攻击

bomber (*airplane*) hōngzhà jī 轰炸机; (*terrorist*) tóudàn shǒu 投弹手

bomber jacket duǎn jiákè 短夹克

bomb scare hōngzhà jǐnggào 轰炸警告

bond 1 *n* (*tie*) liánjié 联结; FIN zhàijuàn 债券 **2** *v/i* (*of glue*) niánjié 粘结

bone 1 *n* gútou 骨头 **2** *v/t meat, fish* qùgǔ 去骨

bonfire yínghuǒ 营火

bonsai pénjǐng 盆景

bonus (*money*) jiǎngjīn 奖金; (*something extra*) éwài pǐn 额外品

bottleneck

boo 1 *n* xūxu shēng 嘘嘘声 **2** *v/t actor, speaker* hè dàocǎi 喝倒彩 **3** *v/i* fāchū xūxu shēng 发出嘘嘘声

book 1 *n* shū 书; **~ of matches** zhǐbǎn huǒchái 纸板火柴 **2** *v/t* (*reserve*) yùdìng 预定; (*of policeman*) dēngjì 登记 **3** *v/i* (*reserve*) yùdìng 预定

bookcase shūjià 书架

booked up kèmǎn 客满; *person* méiyǒu shíjiān 没有时间

bookie F dǔjì rén 赌纪人

booking (*reservation*) yùdìng 预定

booking clerk shòupiào yuán 售票员

bookkeeper jìzhàng rén 记账人

bookkeeping jìzhàng 记账

booklet xiǎo cèzi 小册子

bookmaker dǔjì rén 赌纪人

Book of Changes Yìjīng 易经

books (*accounts*) zhàngmù 帐目; **do the ~** jìzhàng 记账

bookseller shūshāng 书商; **bookstall** shūtān 书摊; **bookstore** shūdiàn 书店

boom¹ *n & v/i* (*in business*) fánróng 繁荣

boom² *n* (*noise*) lónglong shēng 隆隆声

boonies F: *out in the ~* qióngxiāng pìrǎng 穷乡僻壤

boost 1 *n* (*to sales, confidence*) jīlì 激励; (*to economy*) cùjìn 促进 **2** *v/t production, sales* zēngjiā 增加; *prices* tígāo 提高; *confidence, morale* zēngqiáng 增强

boot *n* xuēzi 靴子

♦**boot out** F qūchú 驱除

♦**boot up** COMPUT qǐdòng 启动

booth (*at market, fair*) huòtān 货摊; (*at exhibition*) tānzi 摊子; (*in restaurant*) cānzuò 餐座

booze *n* F jiǔ 酒

booze-up Br F kuánghē 狂喝

border 1 *n* (*between countries*) biānjiè 边界; (*edge*) biānyuán 边缘 **2** *v/t country, river* jiāojiè 交界

♦**border on** *country* jiāojiè 交界; (*be almost*) jìnsì 近似

borderline: *a ~ case of ...* liǎngkě

xíngxíng ... 两可性形 ...

bore¹ *v/t hole* zuānkǒng 钻孔

bore² **1** *n* (*person*) mènrén 闷人; *it's such a ~* tài méijìnr le 太没劲儿了 **2** *v/t* shǐ yànfán 使厌烦

bored: *be ~* mèn 闷; *I'm ~* wǒ hěn mèn 我很闷

boredom wúliáo 无聊

boring fáwèir 乏味儿

born: *be ~* chūshēng 出生; *where were you ~?* nǐ zài nǎr chūshēng? 你在哪儿出生?; *be a ~ ...* tiānshēngde ... 天生的 ...

borrow jiè 借

boss shàngjí 上级

♦**boss around** chāilái qiǎnqù 拆来遣去

bossy ài guǎnshì 爱管事

botanical zhíwù 植物

botany zhíwù xué 植物学

botch *v/t* gǎode yītuán zāo 搞得一团糟

both 1 *adj & pron* liǎnggè 两个; *I know ~* (*of the*) *brothers* liǎng xiōngdì wǒ dōu rènshi 两兄弟我都认识; **~** (*of the*) *brothers were there* liǎng xiōngdì dōu zài nàr 两兄弟都在那儿; **~ of them** (*things*) nà liǎnggè 那两个; (*people*) nà liǎngrén 那两人 **3** *adv*: **~ ... and ...** yòu ... yòu ... 又 ... 又 ...; *is it business or pleasure?* – – gōngzuò háishì yúlè? – liǎngyàng dōuyǒu 工作还是娱乐? – 两样都有

bother 1 *n* máfan 麻烦; *it's no ~* méi wèntí 没问题 **2** *v/t* (*disturb*) máfan 麻烦; *person working* dǎjiǎo 打搅; (*worry*) shǐdānxīn 使担心 **3** *v/i* guǎn 管; *don't ~* (*you needn't do it*) búyòngle 不用了; *you needn't have ~ed* tài máfan nǐle 太麻烦你了

bottle 1 *n* píngzi 瓶子; (*for baby*) nǎipíng 奶瓶 **2** *v/t* zhuāngpíng 装瓶

♦**bottle up** *feelings* èzhì 遏制

bottle bank shōupíng chù 收瓶处

bottled water píngzhuāng shuǐ 瓶装水

bottleneck *n* (*in road, production*)

zǔsāi diǎn 阻塞点

bottle-opener kāipíng qì 开瓶器

bottom 1 adj zuìdī 最低 **2** n (on the inside) dǐbù 底部; (of hill) jiǎo 脚; (of pile) zuìdǐ 最底; (underside) dǐmiàn 底面; (of street) jìndǐ chù 最底处; (of garden) zuì hòumiàn 最后面; (buttocks) pìgu 屁股; **at the ~ of the screen** zài píngmù zuìdǐ chù 在屏幕最底处

♦**bottom out** dá zuìdī diǎn 达最低点

bottom line fig (financial outcome) lìrùn zhī lì 利润; (the real issue) zhēnzhèng wèntí 真正问题

boulder dà shítou 大石头

bounce 1 v/t ball tánqǐ 弹起 **2** v/i (of ball) tánqǐ 弹起; (on sofa etc) tántiào 弹跳; (of rain etc) sìxià fēijiàn 四下飞溅; (of check) bèi jù fù tuìhuí 被拒付退回

bouncer bǎmén rén 把门人

bound¹: be ~ to do X (sure to) kěndìng zuò X 肯定做 X; (obliged to) shòu yuēshù qùzuò X 受约束去做 X

bound²: be ~ for (of ship) shǐwǎng 驶往

bound³ n & v/i (jump) tiàoyuè 跳跃

boundary biānjiè 边界

boundless wúxiàn 无限

bouquet (flowers) huāshù 花束; (of wine) fāngxiāng 芳香

bourbon bōpáng wēishìjì jiǔ 波旁威士忌酒

bout MED fāzuò 发作; (in boxing) jiàoliàng 较量

boutique shízhuāng shāngdiàn 时装商店

bow¹ 1 n (as greeting) jūgōng 鞠躬 **2** v/i jūgōng 鞠躬 **3** v/t head dītóu 低头

bow² (knot) húdié jié 蝴蝶结; MUS gōng 弓

bow³ (of ship) chuántóu 船头

bowels jiécháng 结肠

bowl¹ (large container) pén 盆; (small container for rice) wǎn 碗

bowl² 1 n (ball) bǎolíng qiú 保龄球 **2** v/i (in bowling) dǎ bǎolíng qiú 打保龄球

♦**bowl over** fig jīngdāi 惊呆

bowling bǎolíng qiú 保龄球

bowling alley bǎolíng qiú dào 保龄球道

bow tie lǐngjié 领结

box¹ n (container) hézi 盒子; (on form) fānggé 方格

box² v/i quánjí 拳击

boxer quánjí shǒu 拳击手

boxing quánjí 拳击

boxing match quánjí bǐsài 拳击比赛

box office shòupiào chù 售票处

boy nánháir 男孩儿; (son) érzi 儿子

boycott dǐzhì 抵制

boyfriend nán péngyou 男朋友

boyish xiàng nánhái yíyàng 象男孩一样

boyscout tóngzǐ jūnduì yuán 童子军队员

brace (on teeth) yátào 牙套

bracelet shǒuzhuó 手镯

bracket (for shelf) tuōjià 托架; (in text) kuòhào 括号

brag v/i chuīniú 吹牛

braid n (in hair) biànzi 辫子; (trimming) suìdài 穗带

braille mángwén 盲文

brain nǎo 脑

brainless F shǎ 傻

brains (intelligence) nǎozi 脑子

brainstorm (brilliant idea) línggǎn 灵感; **brainstorming** jítǐ zìyóu tǎolùn 集体自由讨论; **brain surgeon** nǎo wàikē yīshēng 脑外科医生; **brainwash** xǐnǎo 洗脑; **brainwashing** xǐnǎo 洗脑; **brainwave** (brilliant idea) línggǎn 灵感

brainy F cōngmíng 聪明

braise dùn chǎo 炖炒

brake n & v/i shāchē 刹车

brake light zhìdòng xìnhào dēng 制动信号灯

brake pedal shāchē tàbǎn 刹车踏板

branch n (of tree) shùzhī 树枝; (of bank) fēnháng 分行; (of company) fēn gōngsī 分公司; (of chain store) fēndiàn 分店

♦ branch off (of road) fēnchà 分岔

♦ branch out kuòchōng 扩充

brand 1 n páizi 牌子 2 v/t: **be ~ed a liar** bèi qiǎnzé wéi piànzi 被谴责为骗子

brand image shāngbiāo gàiniàn 商标概念

brandish huīdòng 挥动

brand leader míngpáir 名牌儿; brand loyalty míngpái zhōngyú gǎn 名牌忠于感; brand name (famous) míngpái shāngpǐn 名牌商品; (name of a brand) shāngbiāo 商标

brand-new zhǎnxīn 崭新

brandy báilándì 白兰地

brass huángtóng 黄铜

brass band tóngguǎn yuèduì 铜管乐队

brassière xiōngzhào 胸罩

brat pej táoqìbāo 淘气包

bravado xūzhāng shēngshì 虚张声势

brave adj yǒnggǎn 勇敢

bravery yǒnggǎn 勇敢

brawl n & v/i dǒu ōu 斗殴

brawny qiángzhuàng 强壮

Brazil Bāxī 巴西

Brazilian 1 adj Bāxī 巴西 2 n Bāxī rén 巴西人

breach (violation) wéifàn 违犯; (in party) fēnliè 分裂

breach of contract LAW wéifǎn hétóng 违反合同

bread n miànbāo 面包

breadcrumbs miànbāo zhā 面包渣

breadth kuāndù 宽度; (of knowledge) guǎngdù 广度

breadwinner yǎngjiā huókǒu de rén 养家活口的人

break 1 n (in bone) gǔzhé 骨折; (in wire etc) duàntóu chù 断头处; (rest) xiūxi 休息; (in relationship) fēnkāi 分开; **give X a ~** (opportunity) gěi X jīhuì 给 X 机会; **take a ~** xiūxi yīxià 休息一下; **without a ~** work, travel wú zhōngzhǐ 无中止 2 v/t machine, device, toy sǔnhuài 损坏; stick, arm, leg zhéduàn 折断; china, glass, egg shí pòsuì 使破

碎; rules, law, promise wéifàn 违反; news bàogào 报告; record dǎpò 打破 3 v/i (of machine, device, toy) sǔnhuài 损坏; (of china, glass, egg) pòsuì 破碎; (of stick) zhéduàn 折断; (of news) xièlòu 泄漏; (of storm) tūrán dàzuò 突然大作; (of boy's voice) biànshēng 变声

♦ break away v/i (escape) táopǎo 逃跑; (from family) líkāi 离开; (from organization) bèipàn 背叛; (from tradition) tuōlí 脱离

♦ break down 1 v/i (of vehicle, machine) chū máobìng 出毛病; (of talks) pòliè 破裂; (in tears) kòngzhì bùzhù 控制不住; (mentally) kuǎle 垮了 2 v/t door dǎlàn 打烂; figures fēnlèi 分类

♦ break even COM shōuzhī pínghéng 收支平衡

♦ break in (interrupt) chāzuǐ 插嘴; (of burglar) pòmén ér rù 破门而入

♦ break off 1 v/t bāixià 掰下; branch zhéduàn 折断; relationship duànjué 断绝; **they've broken it off** tāmen fēnshǒu le 他们分手了 2 v/i (stop talking) zhōngduàn 中断

♦ break out (start up, of disease) bàofā 爆发; (of prisoners) pòláo 破牢; **he broke out in a rash** tā fā hóngzhěn 他发红疹

♦ break up 1 v/t (into component parts) fēnjiě 分解; fight qūsàn 驱散 2 v/i (of ice) suìliè 碎裂; (of couple) líyì 离异; (of band, meeting) fēnshǒu 分手

breakable kě dǎpò 可打破

breakage pòsùn wù 破损物

breakdown (of vehicle, machine) gùzhàng 故障; (of talks) pòliè 破裂; (nervous) ~ bēngkuì 崩溃; (of figures) fēnlèi 分类

break-even point yíngkuī pínghéng diǎn 盈亏平衡点

breakfast n zǎocān 早餐; **have ~** chī zǎocān 吃早餐

break-in dàoqiè 盗窃

breakthrough tūpò 突破

breakup (of marriage, partnership) fēnshǒu 分手

breast (of woman) rǔfáng 乳房

breastfeed v/t bǔrǔ 哺乳

breaststroke wāyǒng 蛙泳

breath hūxī 呼吸; **be out of ~** chuǎn bū guò qì lái chuǎn bu guò qì lái 喘不过气来; **take a deep ~** shēn hūxī 深呼吸

Breathalyzer®, breath analyzer hūqì yànzuì qì 呼气验醉器

breathe 1 v/i hūxī 呼吸 **2** v/t (inhale) xīqì 吸气; (exhale) hūchū 呼出

♦**breathe in** v/t & v/i xīrù 吸入

♦**breathe out** v/t & v/i hūchū 呼出

breathing hūxī 呼吸

breathless chuǎn bū guò qì lái 喘不过气来

breathlessness chuǎn bū guò qì lái 喘不过气

breathtaking jīngrén 惊人

breed 1 n pǐnzhǒng 品种 **2** v/t fánzhí 繁殖; fig yùnniàng 酝酿 **3** v/i (of animals) fánzhí 繁殖

breeder (of animals) sìyǎng yuán 饲养员

breeding (of animals) sìyǎng 饲养

breeding ground fig zīshēng dì 滋生地

breeze wēifēng 微风

brew 1 v/t beer niàngzào 酿造; tea pào pāo 泡泡 **2** v/i (of storm, trouble) yùnniàng 酝酿

brewer niàngzào zhě 酿造者

brewery niàngzào chǎng 酿造厂

bribe n & v/t huìlù 贿赂

bribery huìlù 贿赂

brick zhuāntóu 砖头

bricklayer níwǎ jiàng 泥瓦匠

bride xīnniáng 新娘

bridegroom xīnláng 新郎

bridesmaid bànniáng bàn niáng 伴娘

bridge¹ **1** n qiáo 桥; (of nose) bíliáng 鼻梁; (of ship) jiàshǐ tái 驾驶台 **2** v/t gap jiànlì qiáoliáng 建立桥梁

bridge² (card game) qiáopái 桥牌

brief¹ adj jiǎnduǎn 简短

brief² **1** n (mission) rènwù 任务 **2** v/t: **~ X on Y** xiàng X jièshào Y 向 X 介绍 Y

briefcase gōngwén bāo 公文包

briefing jiǎnbào 简报

briefly (for a short period of time) yīhuìr 一会儿; (in a few words) jiǎndān 简单; (to sum up) zǒngzhī 总之

briefs (for women) duǎn nèikù 短内裤; (for men) sānjiǎo kù 三角裤

bright color xiānyàn 鲜艳; light qiánglìe 强烈; future guāngmíng 光明; smile huānkuài 欢快; (sunny) qínglǎng 晴朗; room míngliàng 明亮; (intelligent) cōngmíng 聪明

♦**brighten up 1** v/t shǐ míngliàng 使明亮; (make more lively) shǐ huóyuè 使活跃 **2** v/i (of weather) zhuǎnqíng 转晴; (of face, person) gāoxìng qǐlái 高兴起来

brightly smile huānkuài 欢快; shine míngliàng 明亮; colored xiānyàn 鲜艳

brightness (of weather) míngliàng 明亮; (of smile) huānkuài 欢快; (intelligence) cōngmíng 聪明

brilliance (of person) cáihuá 才华; (of color) guāngcǎi 光彩

brilliant sunshine etc míngliàng 明亮; (very good) jiéchū 杰出; (very intelligent) yǒu cáihuá 有才华; idea yīngmíng 英明

brim (of container) biānyuán 边缘; (of hat) màoyán 帽檐

brimful mǎn 满

bring object (not immediate) dàilái 带来; object (more immediate) nálái 拿来; person dài 带; peace, happiness, misery dàilái 带来; **~ it here, will you?** nádào zhèrlái, xíngma? 拿到这儿来，行吗?; **can I ~ a friend?** wǒ néng dàigè péngyǒu láima? 我能带个朋友来吗?

♦**bring about** dàilái 带来

♦**bring around** (from a faint) huífù zhījué 恢复知觉; (persuade) shuōfú 说服

♦**bring back** (return) huán 还; (reintroduce) huīfù 恢复; memories shǐ huíyì qǐ 使回忆起; (cause to come back) lìng ... huílái 令 ... 回来

♦**bring down** fence, tree shǐ dǎoxià 使倒下; government shǐ kuǎtái 使垮台; bird, airplane shèluò 射落; rates, inflation, price shǐ jiàngdī 降低

♦**bring in** interest, income zhèng jìn 挣; legislation yǐnjìn 引进; verdict xuānbù 宣布; (involve) shǐ jièrù 使介入

♦**bring out** (produce: book) chūbǎn 出版; video, CD, new product tuīchū 推出

♦**bring to** (from a faint) huīfù zhījué 恢复知觉

♦**bring up** child yǎngyù 养育; subject tíchū 提出; (vomit) ǒutù 呕吐

brink qiàobì biānyuán 峭壁边缘; **on the ~** fig jíjiāng 即将

brisk person huópo 活泼; voice shēngyìng 生硬; walk qīngkuài 轻快; trade xīnglóng 兴隆

bristles (on chin) húzi chá 胡子楂; (of brush) máo 毛

bristling be ~ with (of person) húnshēn dùshì 浑身都是; (of street) bùmǎn 布满

Britain Yīngguó 英国; (formal use) Dà Bùlièdiān 大不列颠

British 1 adj Yīngguó 英国; (formal use) Dà Bùlièdiān 大不列颠 **2** n: **the ~** Yīngguó rén 英国人; (formal use) Dà Bùlièdiān rén 大不列颠人

Briton Yīngguó rén 英国人; (formal use) Dà Bùlièdiān rén 大不列颠人

brittle yìsuì 易碎

broach subject tíchū 提出

broad 1 adj street, shoulders, hips kuān 宽; smile kuānróng 宽容; (general) gàikuò xìng 概括性; **in ~ daylight** guāngtiān huàrì 光天化日 **2** n F (woman) niángrmen 娘儿们

broadcast n & v/t guǎngbō 广播

broadcaster bōyīn yuán 播音员

broadcasting bōyīn 播音

broaden 1 v/i biànkuān 变宽 **2** v/t

shǐ kuòdà 使扩大; **~ the mind** shǐ shìyě kāikuò 使视野开阔

broadjump tiàoyuǎn 跳远

broadly: **~ speaking** dàtǐ láishuō 大体来说

broadminded xīnxiōng kuānkuò 心胸宽阔

broccoli xīlánhuā 西兰花

brochure xiǎo cèzi 小册子

broil v/t kǎo 烤

broiler n (on stove) kǎopán 烤盘; (chicken) nènjī 嫩鸡

broke F (temporarily) méiyǒu yígè zǐr 没有一个子儿; (long term) bùmíng yīwén 不名一文; **go ~** (go bankrupt) pòchǎn 破产

broken adj chū máobìng 出毛病; glass, window pòsuì 破碎; neck, arm gǔzhé 骨折; home, marriage pòliè 破裂; English jiéjiē bābā 结结巴巴

broken-hearted xīnsuì 心碎

broker jīngjì rén 经纪人

bronchitis qìguǎn yán 气管炎

bronze n (metal) qīngtóng 青铜; (~ medal) tóngpái 铜牌

brooch xiōngzhēn 胸针

brood v/i (of person) shēng mènqì 生闷气

broom tiáozhǒu 笤帚

broth (soup) tāng 汤; (stock) liàotāng 料汤

brothel jìyuàn 妓院

brother (own, elder) gēge 哥哥; (own, younger) dìdi 弟弟; (somebody else's, elder or younger) xiōngdì 兄弟; **they're ~s** tāmen shì xiōngdì 他们是兄弟; **~s and sisters** xiōngdì jiěmèi 兄弟姐妹

brother-in-law (elder sister's husband) jiěfu 姐夫; (younger sister's husband) mèifu 妹夫; (husband's younger brother) xiǎoshūzi 小叔子; (husband's older brother) dàbózi 大伯子; (wife's older brother) nèixiōng 内兄; (wife's younger brother) nèidì 内弟; **they're brothers-in-law** tāmen shì liánjīnr 他们是连襟

brotherly xiōngdì bān 兄弟般

brow (forehead) nǎoménr 脑门儿;

(of hill) pōdǐng 坡顶
browbeat xiàhu 吓唬
brown 1 n zōngsè 棕色 2 adj
zōngsè 棕色; (tanned) shàihēile 晒
黑了 3 v/t & v/i (in cooking)
shàngshǎi 上色
brownbag: ~ it zìdài wǔfàn
shàngbān 自带午饭上班
Brownie yòunián tóngzǐjūn 幼年
童子军
brownie (cake) xiǎo qiǎokèlì
dàngāo 小巧克力蛋糕
brown-nose v/t F pāi mǎpì 拍马
屁
browse (in store) suíbiàn kànkan
随便看看; ~ through a book
suíbiàn fānyuè běnshū 随便翻阅
本书
browser COMPUT liúlǎn qì 浏览器
bruise 1 n cuòshāng 挫伤 2 v/t
person dǎqīng 打青; fruit
pèngshāng 碰伤; (emotionally)
shānghài 伤害 3 v/i (of person)
yúshāng 瘀伤; (of fruit)
pèngshāng 碰伤
bruising adj fig yǒu shānghài xìng
有伤害性
brunch zǎowǔcān 早午餐
brunette zōngfà nǚzǐ 棕发女子
brunt: bear the ~ of ... ...
shǒudāng qíchōng . . . 首当其冲
brush 1 n shuā 刷; (conflict) xiǎo
chōngtū 小冲突 2 v/t shuā 刷;
(touch lightly) qīngchù 轻触;
(move away) chúqù 除去
♦ brush against cājí 擦及
♦ brush aside bùlǐ 不理
♦ brush off shuǎdiào 刷掉;
criticism bùtīng 不听
♦ brush up chóngwēn 重温
brushoff F dīngzi 钉子; get the ~
pèng dīngzi 碰钉子
brusque shēngyìng 生硬
Brussels sprouts qiúyá gānlán 球
芽甘蓝
brutal cánrěn 残忍
brutality bàoxíng 暴行
brutally cánrěn dìjí 残忍地; be ~ frank
chèdǐdi tǎnbái 彻底地坦白
brute chùshēng 畜生
brute force wúqíngde lìliàng 无情

的力量
bubble n qìpào 气泡
bubble gum pàopao táng 泡泡糖
buck[1] F (dollar) kuài 块
buck[2] v/i (of horse) měngrán
gōngbèi yuèqǐ 猛然弓背跃起
buck[3]: pass the ~ tuīwěi zérèn 推
诿责任
bucket shuǐtǒng 水桶
buckle[1] 1 n dàgōu 搭钩 2 v/t belt jì
系
buckle[2] v/i (of wood, metal)
biànxíng 变形
bud n BOT huālěi 花蕾
Buddha Fó 佛
Buddhism Fójiào 佛教
Buddhist 1 n Fójiào tú 佛徒;
he's a ~ tā xìn Fó 他信佛 2 adj
Fójiào 佛教
Buddhist temple sì 寺
buddy F huǒbàn 伙伴; (form of
address) gērmen 哥儿们
budge 1 v/t tuīdòng 推动; (make
reconsider) shǐ gǎibiàn zhǔyì 使改
变主意 2 v/i yídòng 移动;
(change one's mind) gǎibiàn zhǔyì
改变主意
budgerigar hǔpí yīngwǔ 虎皮鹦
鹉
budget 1 n yùsuàn 预算; (of a
family) kāizhī 开支 2 v/i zuò
yùsuàn 作预算
♦ budget for jìsuàn 计算
buff[1] adj color tǔhuángsè 土黄色
buff[2]: a movie / jazz ~ yīgè
diànyǐng / juéshì yuè mí 一个电
影 / 爵士乐迷
buffalo yěniú 野牛; water ~
shuǐniú 水牛
buffer RAIL fángzhuàng shān 防撞
栅; COMPUT huǎnchōng qì 缓冲
器; fig huǎnhé zuòyòng 缓和作
用
buffet[1] (meal) zìzhù cān 自助餐
buffet[2] v/t (of wind) pāidǎ 拍打
bug 1 n (insect) kūnchóng 昆虫;
(virus) bìngdú bìngmáo 病毒;
(spying device) qiètīng qì 窃听器; COMPUT
gùzhàng 故障 2 v/t telephones,
room zhuāng qiètīng qì 装窃听

器; F (*annoy*) shǐ nǎonù 使恼怒

buggy (*for baby*) yīng'ér chē 婴儿车

build 1 n (*of person*) shēncái 身材 **2** v/t jiànzào 建造

♦ **build up 1** v/t strength zēngqiáng 增强; *relationship* fāzhǎn 发展; *collection* zhújiàn zàochéng 逐渐造成 **2** v/i zhújiàn jījù 逐渐积聚

builder (*person*) jiànzhù gōngrén 建筑工人; (*company*) jiànzhù gōngsī 建筑公司

building jiànzhù 建筑; (*activity*) jiànzào 建造

building site jiànzhù gōngdì 建筑工地

building trade jiànzhù yè 建筑业

build-up (*accumulation*) jījù jījù 积聚; (*publicity*) yúlùn zhǔnbèi 舆论准备

built-in nèizhuāng 内装; *flash* nèihán nèi cóng 内含

built-up area jiànzhù qū 建筑区

bulb BOT qiújīng 球茎; (*light ~*) diàndēng pào 电灯泡

bulge 1 n (*sudden increase*) zhòuzēng 骤增 **2** v/i (*of pocket*) gǔgu nāngnang 鼓鼓囊囊; (*of wall, eyes*) péngzhàng 膨胀

bulk dà duōshù 大多数; *in ~* zhěngpī 整批

bulky *parcel* tǐjī dà 体积大; *sweater* féidà 肥大

bull (*animal*) gōngniú 公牛

bulldoze (*demolish*) chǎnpíng 铲平; *~ X into Y* fig xiépò X zuò Y 胁迫 X 作 Y

bulldozer tuītǔ jī 推土机

bullet zǐdàn 子弹

bulletin bùgào 布告

bulletin board (*on wall*) bùgào bǎn 布告板; COMPUT gōnggào pái 公告牌

bullet point (*in printing*) biāotídiǎn 标题点

bullet-proof fángdàn 防弹

bull market FIN shàngzhǎng hángqíng 上涨行情

bull's-eye bǎxīn 靶心; *hit the ~* zhèngzhòng yàohài 正中要害

bullshit n & v/i V húshuō bādào 胡说八道

bully 1 n èbà 恶霸; (*child*) xiǎotáoqì 小淘气 **2** v/t qīfu 欺负

bum 1 n (*tramp*) lǎnhàn 懒汉; (*worthless person*) méiyòng de dōngxi 没用的东西 **2** adj (*useless*) sōu 馊 **3** v/t *cigarette etc* qǐqiú 乞求

♦ **bum around** F (*travel*) piāobó liúlàng 漂泊流浪; (*be lazy*) fànfan lǎn 犯犯懒

bumblebee xióngfēng 熊蜂

bump 1 n (*swelling*) zhǒngkuài'r 肿块儿; (*in road*) tūkuài'r 凸块儿; *get a ~ on the head* tóushàng zhǒng le yīkuài'r 头上肿了一块儿 **2** v/t zhuàng 撞

♦ **bump into** *table* zhuàng 撞; (*meet*) pèngjiàn 碰见

♦ **bump off** F (*murder*) gǎodiào 搞掉

♦ **bump up** F *prices* měngtái wùjià 猛抬物价

bumper 1 n MOT bǎoxiǎn gàng 保险杠 **2** adj *harvest* fēngshèng 丰盛; (*extremely good*) jíhǎo 极好

bumpy diānbǒ 颠簸

bun (*hairstyle*) jìzi 髻子; (*for eating*) xiǎoyuán miànbāo 小圆面包

bunch (*of people*) huǒ 伙; (*of keys*) chuàn 串; *a ~ of flowers* yīshù huā 一束花; *a ~ of grapes* yīchuàn pútáo 一串葡萄; *thanks a ~* (*ironic*) duō xièle! 多谢了！

bundle (*of clothes*) bāo bǎo 包; (*of wood*) kǔn 捆

♦ **bundle up** v/t bǎ ... bāo qǐlái bǎ ... 包起来; (*dress warmly*) chuānde nuǎnhuó 穿得暖和

bungle v/t gǎozāo 搞糟

bunk n chuángpù 床铺

bunk beds shuāngcéng chuáng 双层床

buoy n hángbiāo 航标

buoyant fig yúkuài 愉快; *economy* fánróng 繁荣

burden 1 n fùzhòng 负重; fig fùdān 负担 **2** v/t: *~ X with Y* yòng Y lái fánnǎo X 用 Y 来烦恼 X

bureau (*chest of drawers*) dǒuchú 斗橱; (*office*) bànshì chù 办事处

bureaucracy (*red tape*) guānliáo zhǔyì 官僚主义; (*system*) xíngzhèng xìtǒng 行政系统

bureaucrat guānliáo 官僚

bureaucratic guānliáo 官僚

burger hànbǎobāo 汉堡包

burglar xiǎotōu 小偷

burglar alarm ⇩ fángqiè jǐngbào qì 防窃警报器

burglarize dàoqiè 盗窃

burglary dàoqiè 盗窃

burial zànglǐ 葬礼

burly kuíwú 魁梧

Burma Miǎndiàn 缅甸

Burmese 1 *adj* Miǎndiàn 缅甸 **2** *n* (*person*) Miǎndiàn rén 缅甸人; (*language*) Miǎndiàn yǔ 缅甸语

burn 1 *n* shāoshāng 烧伤 **2** *v/t* shāo 烧; *toast, meat* shāojiāo 烧焦; (*of sun*) shàishāng 晒伤; (*consume*) shāo 烧 **3** *v/i* shāozháo 烧着; (*of house*) shāohuǐ 烧毁; (*of toast*) shāojiāo 烧焦; (*get sunburnt*) shàishāng 晒伤

◆**burn down** *v/t & v/i* shāohuǐ 烧毁

◆**burn out**: *burn oneself out* shǐ zìjǐ jīngpí lìjìn 使自己筋疲力尽; *a burned-out car* shāohuǐ de chē 烧毁的车

burner (*on cooker*) zàotóu 灶头

burp *n, v/i & v/t* dǎgé 打嗝

burst 1 *n* (*in water pipe*) lièkǒu 裂口; (*of gunfire*) shàoshè 扫射; *a ~ of energy* néngliàng bàofā 能量爆发 **2** *adj tire* bàoliè 爆裂 **3** *v/t balloon* bàoliè 爆裂 **4** *v/i* (*of balloon, tire*) bàoliè 爆裂; *~ into a room* chuǎngrù 闯入; *~ into tears* tūrán dàkū 突然大哭; *~ out laughing* tūrán dàxiào 突然大笑

bury máizàng 埋葬; (*conceal*) yǐncáng 隐藏; *be buried under …* (*covered by*) máizài … zhīxià 埋在 … 之下; *~ oneself in work* máitóu yú gōngzuò 埋头于工作

bus 1 *n* gōnggòng qìchē 公共汽车; (*long distance*) chángtú qìchē 长途汽车 **2** *v/t* yòng gōnggòng qìchē zǎisòng 用公共汽车载送

busboy shìyìng shēng 侍应生

bush (*plant*) guànmù 灌木; (*land*) huāngyě 荒野

bushed F (*tired*) píláo bùkān 疲劳不堪

bushy *beard* nóngmì 浓密

business (*trade*) shēngyì 生意; (*company*) gōngsī 公司; (*work*) gōngzuò 工作; (*sector*) zhíyè 职业; (*affair, matter*) shìjiàn 事件; (*as subject of study*) shāngyè 商业; *on ~* yīngōng 因公; *that's none of your ~!, mind your own ~!* yǔ nǐ wúguān! 与你无关!

business card míngpiàn 名片

business class shāngwù cāng 商务舱; **business hours** yíngyè shíjiān 营业时间; **businesslike** gāo xiàoyì 高效益; **business lunch** shāngyè wǔcān 商业午餐; **businessman** shāngrén 商人; **business meeting** shāngyè huìyì 商业会议; **business school** shāngyè xuéxiào 商业学校; **business studies** shāngyè xué 商业学; **business trip** chūchāi 出差; **businesswoman** nǚshāngrén 女商人

bus station gōnggòng qìchē zǒngzhàn 公共汽车总站

bus stop chēzhàn 车站

bust[1] *n* (*of woman*) xiōngpú 胸脯

bust[2] F **1** *adj* (*broken*) dǎsuì 打碎; *go ~* pòchǎn 破产 **2** *v/t* dǎsuì 打碎

◆**bustle around** mánglù 忙碌

bust-up F pòliè 破裂

busty fēngmǎn 丰满

busy 1 *adj* máng 忙; *street* yǒu shēngqì 有生气; *store, restaurant*: (*making money*) shēngyì xīnglóng 生意兴隆; (*full of people*) xīxī rǎngrang 熙熙攘攘; TELEC zhànxiàn 占线; *be ~ doing X* mángzhe zuò X 忙着作 X **2** *v/t*: *~ oneself with* zìjǐ mángyú 自己忙于

busybody ài guǎn xiánshì de rén 爱管闲事的人

busy signal zhànxiàn shēng 占线声

but 1 *conj* dànshì 但是; *~ that's*

not fair! shízài tàibù gōngpíng le! 实在太不公平了！；***it's not me ~ my father you want*** nǐ yào zhǎode shì wǒ bàba ér būshì wǒ 你要找的是我爸爸而不是我；**~ then** (*again*) dàn lìngyī fāngmiàn 但另一方面 **2** *prep*: ***all ~ him*** chúle tā zhīwài suǒyǒu rén 除了他之外所有人；***the last ~ one*** dàoshù dièr gè 倒数第二个；***the next ~ one*** jiēzhe dièr 接着第二；***~ for you*** méiyǒu nǐ 没有你；***nothing ~ the best*** zhǐyǒu zuìhǎo de 只有最好的

butcher màiròu de 卖肉的；(*murderer*) túfū 屠夫

butt 1 *n* (*of cigarette*) yāndì 烟蒂；(*of joke*) xiàobǐng 笑柄；F (*buttocks*) pìgu 屁股 **2** *v/t* yòng tóu zhuàng 用头撞；(*of goat, bull*) yòng tóu dǐng 用头顶

♦**butt in** chāzuǐ 插嘴

butter 1 *n* huángyóu 黄油 **2** *v/t* mǒ huángyóu 抹黄油

♦**butter up** F fèngchéng 奉承

butterfly (*insect*) húdié 蝴蝶

buttocks túnbù 臀部

button 1 *n* kòuzi 扣子；(*on machine*) ànniǔ 按钮；(*badge*) huīzhāng 徽章 **2** *v/t* kòu kòuzi 扣扣子

buttonhole 1 *n* (*in suit*) kòuyǎnr 扣眼儿 **2** *v/t* qiángliú jiāotán 强留交谈

buxom fēngmǎn 丰满

buy 1 *n* piányí huò 便宜货 **2** *v/t* mǎi 买；***can I ~ you a drink?*** wǒ néng gěinǐ mǎi bēi yǐnliào ma? 我能给你买杯饮料吗？；***$50 doesn't ~ much*** wǔshí měiyuán mǎibùliǎo shénme 五十美元买不了什么

♦**buy off** (*bribe*) shōumǎi 收买

♦**buy out** COM mǎixià quánbù gǔfèn 买下全部股份

♦**buy up** dàliàng mǎijìn 大量买进

buyer mǎijiā 买家；(*for department store etc*) cǎigòu yuán 采购员

buzz 1 *n* zàoyīn 噪音；F (*thrill*) xìngfèn gǎn 兴奋感 **2** *v/i* (*of insect*) fāchū wēngwēng shēng 发出嗡嗡声；(*with buzzer*) àn fēngmíng qì 按蜂鸣器 **3** *v/t* (*with buzzer*) àn fēngmíng qì jiào 按蜂鸣器叫

♦**buzz off** F zǒukāi 走开

buzzer fēngmíng qì 蜂鸣器

by 1 *prep* (*agency*) bèi 被；(*near, next to*) kàojìn 靠近；(*no later than*) bù chíyú 不迟于；(*past*) jīngguò 经过；(*mode of transport*) chéng 乘；***side - side*** yīgè āizhe yīgè 一个挨着一个；***- day / night*** zài báitiān / wǎnshàng 在白天 / 晚上；***~ bus / train*** chéng gōnggòng qìchē / huǒchē 乘公共汽车 / 火车；***~ the hour / ton*** yī xiǎoshí / dūn jìsuàn 以小时 / 吨计算；***~ my watch*** ànzhào 按照；***a play - ...*** yóu ... xiěde jùzuò 由 ... 写的剧作；***~ oneself*** zìjǐ 自己；***~ a couple of minutes*** yǐ jǐ fēnzhōng zhīchā 以几分钟之差；***2 - 4*** (*measurement*) èr chéng sì 二乘四；***- this time tomorrow*** míngtiān zhège shíhòu 明天这个时候 **2** *adv*: ***- and ~*** (*soon*) guò yīhuìr 过一会儿

bye(-bye) zàijiàn 再见

bygone: ***let ~s be ~s*** guòqùde shì ràngtā guòqù ba 过去的事让它过去吧

bypass 1 *n* (*road*) pánglù 旁路；MED fēnliú shù 分流术 **2** *v/t* ràoguò 绕过

by-product fù chǎnpǐn 副产品

bystander pángguān zhě 旁观者

byte zìjié 字节

byword: ***be a ~ for ...*** chéngwéi ... de dàihào 成为 ... 的代号

C

CAAC (= *Civil Aviation Administration of China*) Zhōngguó Mínháng 中国民航

cab (*taxi*) chūzū qìchē 出租汽车; (*van-type ~*) miàndī 面的; (*in Taiwan*) jìchéngchē 计程车; (*of truck*) jiàshǐ shì 驾驶室

cab driver chūzū qìchē sījī 出租汽车司机; (*of van-type cab*) miàndī sījī 面的司机; (*in Taiwan*) jìchéngchē sījī 计程车司机

cabaret gēwǔ biǎoyǎn 歌舞表演

cabbage (*in northern China*) yángbái cài 洋白菜; (*in southern China*) juǎnxīn cài 卷心菜

cabin (*of plane*) zuòcāng 座舱; (*of ship*) chuáncāng 船舱

cabin crew jīzǔ rényuán 机组人员

cabinet (*cupboard*) guìzi 柜子; (*display ~*) chénlièguì 陈列柜; POL nèigé 内阁

cable (*of electrical appliance, telephone*) diànxiàn 电线; (*for securing*) gāngsī shéng 钢丝绳; ~ (*TV*) yǒuxiàn diànshì 有线电视

cable car lǎnchē 缆车

cab stand chūzūchē zhàn 出租车站

cache COMPUT gāosù huǎncún 高速缓存

cactus xiānrénzhǎng 仙人掌

cadaver shītǐ 尸体

CAD-CAM jìsuànjī fǔzhù shèjì hé zhìzào 计算机辅助设计和制造

caddie 1 *n* (*in golf*) qiútóng 球童 2 *v/i*: ~ *for* ... dāng ... de qiútóng 当 ... 的球童

cadet xuéyuán 学员

cadge: ~ *X from Y* gēn Y qǐqiú X 跟 Y 乞求 X

cadre gànbù 干部

café xiǎo fànguǎnr 小饭馆

cafeteria shítáng 食堂

caffeine kāfēiyīn 咖啡因

cage lóng 笼

cagey tūntun tǔtu 吞吞吐吐

cahoots: *be in ~ with* ... gēn ... tónghuǒ 跟 ... 同伙

cake 1 *n* dàngāo 蛋糕; *be a piece of ~ fig* hěn róngyì 很容易 2 *v/i* (*of mud, blood*) jiékuàir 结块儿

calcium gài 钙

calculate (*work out*) gūjì 估计; (*in arithmetic*) jìsuàn 计算

calculating jīngmíng 精明

calculation jìsuàn jiéguǒ 计算结果

calculator jìsuàn qì 计算器

calendar rìlì 日历

calf[1] (*young cow*) xiǎoniú 小牛

calf[2] (*of leg*) tuǐdùzi 腿肚子

caliber (*of gun*) kǒujìng 口径; *a man of his ~* xiàng tā nàyàng yǒu nénglì de rén 像他那样有能力的人

call 1 *n* (*phone ~*) diànhuà 电话; (*shout*) hǎnjiào 喊叫; (*demand*) yāoqiú 要求; *there's a ~ for you* yǒu nǐde diànhuà 有你的电话; *give X a call* gěi X dǎ diànhuà 给 X 打电话 2 *v/t* (*on phone*) dǎ diànhuà gěi 打电话给; (*summon*) jiào 叫; *meeting* zhàojí 召集; (*by court*) chuán 传; (*describe as*) shuōchéng shì 说成是; (*shout*) dàhǎn 大喊; *what have they ~ed the baby?* tāmen gěi háizi qǐ shénme míngzi? 他们给孩子起什么名字？; ~ *the manager* zhǎo jīnglǐ lái 找经理来; *but we ~ him Old Li* dàn wǒmen jiào tā Lǎo Lǐ 但我们叫他老李; ~ *X names* mà X 骂 X 3 *v/i* (*on phone*) dǎ diànhuà 打电话; (*shout*) hūhǎn 呼喊; (*visit*) lái lái 来

♦ *call at* (*stop at*) qù 去; (*of train*) zài ... tíngchē 在 ... 停车

♦**call back 1** *v/t* (*on phone*) huí diànhuà 回电话; *call X back* (*summon*) jiào X huíqù 叫 X 回去 **2** *v/i* (*on phone*) zài dǎ diànhuà 再打电话; (*make another visit*) zàilái 再来

♦**call for** *person* jiē jiē; *goods* qùná qù ná; (*demand*) yāoqiú 要求; (*require*) bìxū yào 必须要

♦**call in 1** *v/t expert* qǐng qǐng; *call X in* (*summon by person in authority*) jiào X jìnqù 叫 X 进去 **2** *v/i* (*phone*) dǎ diànhuà lái 打电话来; ~ *sick* dǎ diànhuà qǐng bìngjià 打电话请病假

♦**call off** (*cancel*) qǔxiāo 取消

♦**call on** (*urge*) dūncù 敦促; (*visit*) bàifǎng 拜访

♦**call out** (*shout*) dàhǎn 大喊; (*summon*) zhāohuàn 召唤

♦**call up** *v/t* (*on phone*) dǎ diànhuà gěi 打电话给; COMPUT dǎkāi 打开

caller (*on phone*) dǎ diànhuà zhě 打电话者; (*visitor*) tànfǎng zhě 探访者

call girl jìnǚ 妓女

calligraphy shūfǎ 书法

callous wúqíng 无情

calm 1 *adj sea, weather* píngjìng 平静; *person* lěngjìng 冷静 **2** *n* (*of countryside*) ānjìng 安静; (*of person*) lěngjìng 冷静

♦**calm down 1** *v/t*: *calm X down* shǐ X lěngjìng xiàlái 使 X 冷静下来 **2** *v/i* (*of sea, weather, person*) píngjìng xiàlái 平静下来

calorie kǎlùlǐ 卡路里

Cambodia Jiǎnpǔzhài 柬埔寨

Cambodian 1 *adj* Jiǎnpǔzhài 柬埔寨 **2** *n* (*person*) Jiǎnpǔzhài rén 柬埔寨人

camcorder shèxiàn jī 摄像机

camera zhàoxiàng jī 照像机

cameraman shèyǐng shī 摄影师

camouflage 1 *n* wěizhuāng 伪装 **2** *v/t* yǎnhù 掩护

camp 1 *n* yíngdì 营地 **2** *v/i* lùyíng 露营

campaign 1 *n* yùndòng 运动; *presidential* ~ zǒngtǒng jìngxuǎn 总统竞选 **2** *v/i* gǎo yùndòng 搞运动

campaigner (*person*) yěyíng zhě 野营者; (*vehicle*) yěyíng chē 野营车

camper (*person*) yěyíng zhě 野营者; (*vehicle*) yěyíng chē 野营车

camping lùyíng 露营

campsite yíngdì 营地

campus xiàoyuán 校园

can[1] ◊ (*ability*) néng néng; *I* ~'*t* wǒ bùnéng 我不能; ~'*t you see?* nǐ nándào méi kànjiàn ? 你难道没看见 ?; *I* ~'*t see* wǒ kànbújiàn 我看不见; ~ *you hear me?* nǐ tīngde jiàn wǒ ma? 你听得见我吗 ?; ~ *he call me back?* tā néng gěi wǒ huí diànhuà ma? 他能给我回电话吗 ?; *as fast as you* ~ yuèkuài yuèhǎo 越快越好; *as well as you* ~ jìnliàng ba 尽量吧; *you* ~'*t be serious!* bié kāi wánxiào le! 别开玩笑了 !; ~ *I help you?* wǒ néng bāng nǐ máng ma? 我能帮你忙吗?; ~ *you help me?* nǐ néng bāng wǒ ma? 你能帮我吗 ?; ~ *I have a beer/ coffee?* qǐng lái bēi píjiǔ/kāfēi? 请来杯啤酒/咖啡 ?; *that* ~'*t be right* bù kěnéng 不可能 ◊ (*with skills*) huì 会; ~ *you speak French?* nǐ huì shuō Fǎyǔ ma? 你会说法语吗 ? ◊ (*permission*) kěyǐ 可以; ~ *I take this one?* wǒ kěyǐ ná zhège ma? 我可以拿这个吗 ?

can[2] *n* (*for drinks etc*) guàntóu 罐头 **2** *v/t* (*put in* ~) guànzhuāng 罐装

Canada Jiānádà 加拿大

Canadian 1 *adj* Jiānádà 加拿大 **2** *n* Jiānádà rén 加拿大人

canal (*waterway*) yùnhé 运河

canary (*bird*) jīnsīquè 金丝雀

cancel qǔxiāo 取消

cancellation qǔxiāo 取消

cancer áizhèng 癌症

c & f (= *cost and freight*) chéngběn jiā yùnfèi 成本加运费

c & i (= *cost and insurance*) chéngběn jiā bǎoxiǎn fèi 成本加保险费

candid tǎnshuài 坦率

candidacy hòuxuǎn 候选

candidate (*for position*) hòuxuǎn rén 候选人; (*in exam*) yìngkǎo rén 应考人

candle làzhú 蜡烛

candlestick zhútái 烛台

candor tǎnshuài 坦率

candy táng 糖

cannabis dàmá 大麻

canned *fruit, tomatoes* guànzhuāng 罐装; ~ *laughter* (*recorded*) yùlù xiàoshēng 预录笑声

cannibalize *old car etc* chāijiàn 拆件

cannot → **can**¹

canoe dúmù zhōu 独木舟

can opener kāiguàn qì 开罐器

cant wěishàn yáncí 伪善言词

can't → **can**¹

canteen (*in factory*) shítáng 食堂

Canton Guǎngdōng 广东

Cantonese **1** *adj* Guǎngdōng 广东 **2** *n* Guǎngdōng rén 广东人; (*language*) Guǎngdōnghuà 广东话

canvas (*for painting*) yóuhuà bù 油画布; (*material*) fānbù 帆布

canvass **1** *v/t* (*seek opinion of*) tīngqǔ yìjiàn 听取意见 **2** *v/i* POL lāpiào 拉票

canyon xiágǔ 峡谷

cap (*hat*) màozi 帽子; (*of bottle, lens*) gàizi 盖子; (*of pen*) bǐmào 笔帽

capability (*of person*) nénglì 能力; (*of military*) lìliàng 力量

capable nénggàn 能干; *be ~ of* yǒu nénglì 有能力

capacity (*of container, building*) róngliàng 容量; (*of elevator*) fùhè liàng 负荷量; (*of car engine*) róngliàng 容量; (*of factory*) chǎnliàng 产量; (*ability*) nénglì 能力; *in my ~ as ...* yǐwǒ ... de shēnfèn 以我 ... 的身份

capital *n* (*of country*) shǒudū 首都; (*capital letter*) dàxiě zìmǔ 大写字母; (*money*) zījīn 资金

capital expenditure zīběn zhīchū 资本支出; capital gains tax zīběn shōuyì shuì 资本收益税; capital growth zīběn

chéngzhǎng 资本成长

capitalism zīběn zhǔyì 资本主义

capitalist **1** *adj* zīběn zhǔyì 资本主义 **2** *n* (*believer*) zīběn zhǔyì zhě 资本主义者; (*businessman*) zīběn jiā 资本家

capital letter dàxiě zìmǔ 大写字母

capital punishment sǐxíng 死刑

capitulate ràngbù 让步

capsize **1** *v/i* fānchuán 翻船 **2** *v/t* shǐ fānchuán 使翻船

capsule (*of medicine*) jiāonáng jiāo náng 胶囊; (*space* ~) tàikōng cāng 太空舱

captain *n* (*of ship*) chuánzhǎng 船长; (*of aircraft*) jīzhǎng 机长; (*of team*) duìzhǎng 队长

caption *n* (*to photo*) shuōmíng 说明

captivate zháomí 着迷

captive fúlǔ 俘虏

captivity bèi guān qǐlái 被关起来

capture **1** *n* (*of city*) zhànlǐng 占领; (*of criminal*) zhuōdào 捉到; (*of animal*) bǔhuò 捕获 **2** *v/t person*, zhuōdào 捉到; *animal* bǔhuò 捕获; *city, building* gōngxià 攻下; (*win: market share*) huòdé 获得; (*portray: mood*) miáohuì 描绘; ~ *the moment* zhuāzhù nàyī chànà 抓住那一刹那

car chē 车; (*of train*) chēxiāng 车厢; *by* ~ zuòchē 坐车

carafe píng 瓶

carat kèlā 克拉

carbohydrate tànshuǐ huàhéwù 碳水化合物

carbonated *drink* qǐpào 起泡

carbon monoxide yīyǎng huàtàn 一氧化碳

carburetor, carburetor qìhuàqì 汽化器

carcinogen zhì'ái wù 致癌物

carcinogenic zhì'ái 致癌

card (*to mark special occasion*) kǎpiàn 卡片; (*post~*) míngxìnpiàn 明信片儿; (*business* ~) míngpiàn 名片儿; (*playing*) zhǐpái 纸牌

cardboard yìng zhǐbǎn 硬纸板

cardiac xīnzàng 心脏

cardiac arrest xīnzàng tíngtiào 心脏停跳

cardigan kāijīn máoyī 开襟毛衣

card index kǎpiàn mùlù 卡片目录

card key kǎpiàn yàoshí 卡片钥匙

care 1 n (of baby, pet, elderly, sick) zhàogù 照顾; (medical ~) yīliáo 医疗; (worry) yōulǜ 忧虑; *~ of* (on envelope) fánjiāo 烦交; *take ~* (be cautious) xiǎoxīn 小心; *take ~ (of yourself)!* (goodbye) bǎozhòng! 保重！; *take ~ of* baby, dog zhàogù 照顾; tool, house, garden àihù 爱护; (deal with) chǔlǐ 处理; project fùzé 负责; *~ of the check* fùzhàng 付账; (handle) with *~* (on label) xiǎoxīn qīngfàng 小心轻放 **2** v/i guānxīn 关心; *if you really ~d* (were concerned) yàoshì nǐ zhēnde guānxīn dehuà 要是你真的关心的话; *I don't ~!* wǒbú zàihu! 我不在乎！; *I couldn't ~ less* wǒ yìdiǎn yě bú zàihū 我一点也不在乎

♦**care about** guānxīn 关心

♦**care for** (look after) zhàogù 照顾; (like, be fond of) xǐhuān 喜欢; *would you ~ ...?* nǐ yào ... ma? 你要 ... 吗？

career (profession) shìyè 事业; (path through life) jīnglì 经历

carefree wúyōu wúlǜ 无忧无虑

careful (cautious) jǐnshèn 谨慎; (thorough) zǐxì 仔细; person xìxīn 细心; (be) *~!* xiǎoxīn! 小心！

carefully (with caution) xiǎoxīn 小心; worded etc jīngxīn 精心

careless person cūxīn 粗心; work cǎoshuài 草率; *you are so ~!* nǐ tài dàyì le! 你太大意了！

caress n & v/t àifǔ 爱抚

caretaker kānguǎn rén 看管人

carewrn yōuxīn chōngchong 忧心忡忡

cargo huòwù 货物

caricature n (picture) fēngcì huà 讽刺画; (in writing) fēngcì wénzhāng 讽刺文章

caring adj yǒu àixīn 有爱心

carnage dà túshā 大屠杀

carnation kāngnǎixīn 康乃馨

carnival miàohuì 庙会

carol n sònggē 颂歌

carousel (at airport) xínglǐ chuánsòngdài 行李传送带; (at fairground) xuánzhuǎn mùmǎ 旋转木马

carp (fish) lǐyú 鲤鱼

carpenter mùjiàng 木匠

carpet dìtǎn 地毯

carpool n héhuǒ yòngchē 合伙用车; **car port** qìchēpéng 汽车棚; **car rental** chūzū qìchē gōngsī 出租汽车公司

carrier (company) yùnshū gōngsī 运输公司; (of disease) dàijùn zhě 带菌者

carrot húluóbo 胡萝卜

carry 1 v/t (in hand) ná 拿; (on back) bēi 背; (hold in front) bàozhe 抱; (move: goods) bānyùn 搬运; (have on one's person) dàizhe 带着; (of pregnant woman) huáizhe 怀着; disease dài ... dejùn mén ... 的菌; (of ship, plane, bus etc) zàiyǒu 载有; proposal tōngguò 通过; *get carried away* chōnghūn le tóu 冲昏了头 **2** v/i (of sound) chuánsòng 传送

♦**carry on 1** (continue) jiēzhe zuò 接着做; (talking) diédiébùxiū 喋喋不休; (make a fuss) chǎonào 吵闹 **2** v/t (conduct) jìxù jìxù 继续

♦**carry on with** (have an affair with) hé ... yǒu àimèi guānxī 和 ... 有暧昧关系

♦**carry out** survey etc jìnxíng 进行; orders etc zhíxíng 执行

car seat (for child) háitóng qìchē zuòyǐ 孩童汽车座椅

cart (horsedrawn) mǎchē 马车; (for baggage) xínglǐ chē 行李车

cartel liánhé qǐyè 联合企业

carton (for storage, transport) zhǐxiāng 纸箱; (for milk, eggs etc) zhǐhé 纸盒; *a ~ of cigarettes* yītiáo xiāngyān 一条香烟

cartoon (in newspaper, magazine) fēngcì huà 讽刺画; (on TV, film) kǎtōng piàn 卡通片

cartridge (for gun) zǐdàn 子弹

carve *meat* qiē 切; *wood* kè 刻

carving (*figure*) diāokè pǐn 雕刻
品

car wash xǐchēchù 洗车处

case[1] (*container*) hé 盒; (*of Scotch,
wine*) xiāng 箱; (*suitcase*) píxiāng
皮箱

case[2] n (*instance*) lìzi 例子;
(*argument*) gēnjù 根据; (*for police,
attorney*) ànjiàn 案件; MED bìnglì
病例; *in ~ ...* wànyī ... 万一 ...; *in
any ~* zǒngzhī 总之; *in that ~*
jìrán zhèyàng 既然这样

case history MED bìngshǐ 病史

cash 1 n xiànjīn 现金; *short of ~*
xiànjīn duǎnquē 现金短缺; *~
down* xiànjīn zhīfù 现金支付; *
pay (in) ~* fù xiànjīn 付现金; *~ in
advance* xiànkuǎn dìngjīn 现款
定金; *~ on delivery* jiāohuò
fùkuǎn 交货付款 2 v/t check
duìxiàn 兑现
♦ cash in on cóngzhōng huòlì 从
中获利

cash cow jīnkù 金库; cash desk
fùkuǎn tái 付款台; cash dis-
count xiànjīn zhékòu 现金折扣;
cash flow liúdòng jījīn 流动基
金

cashier n (*in store etc*) chūnà yuán
出纳员

cash machine qǔkuǎn jī 取款机

cashmere adj yángróng 羊绒

cash register xiànjīn chūnà jī 现
金出纳机

casino dǔchǎng 赌场

casket (*coffin*) guāncai 棺材

cassette cídài 磁带

cassette player lùyīnjī 录音机

cassette recorder lùyīnjī 录音机

cast 1 n (*of play*) yǎnyuán biǎo yǎn
yuán biǎo; (*mold*) móxíng 模型 2 v/t
metal jiāozhù 浇铸; *play* fēnpèi
juésè 分配角色; *~ X as ...* actor
fēnpèi X bànyǎn ... 分配 X 扮演
...; *~ doubt on* lìngrén huáiyí 令
人怀疑
♦ cast off v/i (*of ship*) jiělǎn 解缆

caste zhǒngxìng 种姓

caster (*on chair etc*) jiǎolún 脚轮

cast iron n shēngtiě 生铁

cast-iron adj shēngtiě 生铁

castle chéngbǎo 城堡

castrate yāngē 阉割

casual (*chance, offhand, not formal*)
suíbiàn 随便; (*not permanent*)
línshí 临时

casualty shāngwáng rénshì 伤亡
人士

casual wear biànfú 便服

cat māo 猫

catalog n mùlù 目录

catalyst fig dǎohuǒ xiàn 导火线

catalytic converter cuīhuà
zhuǎnhuà qì 催化转化器

catastrophe zāinàn 灾难

catch 1 n jiē 接; (*of fish*) bǔhuò wù
捕获物; (*locking device*) shuān
闩; (*problem*) wèntí 问题 2 v/t ball
jiēzhù 接住; *escaped prisoner*
zhuōzhù 捉住; (*get on: bus, train*)
zuò 坐; (*not miss: bus, train*)
gǎnshàng 赶上; *fish with rod*
diàodào 钓到; *fish with net* bǔdào
捕到; (*in order to speak to*)
zhǎodào 找到; (*hear*) tīng
qīngchǔ 听清楚; *illness* rǎnshàng
染上; *~ (a) cold* dé gǎnmào 得感
冒; *~ X's eye*
yǐnqǐ X de zhùyì 引起 X 的注意;
~ sight of, ~ a glimpse of kànjiàn
看见; *~ X doing Y* zhuàngjiàn X
zuò Y 撞见 X 做 Y
♦ catch on (*become popular*) shòu
huānyíng 受欢迎; (*understand*)
lǐjiě 理解
♦ catch up v/i gǎnshàng 赶上
♦ catch up on míbǔ 弥补

catch-22 *it's a ~ situation* jìntuì
liǎngnán 进退两难

catcher (*in baseball*) jiēshǒu 接手

catching *disease* chuánrǎn xìng 传
染性; *fear, panic* yǒu gǎnrǎn lì 有
感染力

catchy *tune* róngyì shàngkǒu 容易
上口

category fànchóu 范畴
♦ cater for (*meet the needs of*)
yínghé 迎合; (*provide food for*)
bāobàn 包办

caterer jiǔxí chéngbàn rén 酒席
承办人

caterpillar máochóng 毛虫

cathedral dà jiàotáng 大教堂

Catholic **1** *adj* Tiānzhǔjiào 天主教
    2 *n* Tiānzhǔ jiàotú 天主教徒

catsup fānqié jiàng 蕃茄酱

cattle niú 牛

catty èdú 恶毒

cauliflower càihuā 菜花

cause **1** *n* (*reason*) yuányīn 原因; (*grounds*)
    lǐyóu 理由; (*aim of movement,
    charity etc*) zhǔzhāng 主张 **2** *v/t*
    yǐnqǐ 引起

caution **1** *n* (*carefulness*) jǐnshèn 谨
    慎; ~ *is advised* jǐnshèn yīxiē 谨
    慎一些 **2** *v/t* (*warn*) jǐnggào 警告

cautious jǐnshèn 谨慎

cave dòng 洞

♦ cave in (*of roof*) dǎotā 倒塌

caviar yúzǐ jiàng 鱼子酱

cavity (*in tooth*) qǔchǐ 龋齿

cc (= *carbon copy*) **1** *n* fùběn 副本
    2 *v/t* fùběn gěi 副本给

CCTV (= *China Central Television*)
    Zhōngyāng Diànshìtái 中央电视
    台

CD (*compact disc*) guānpán 光盘

CD-ROM guāngpán 光盘

CD-ROM drive guāngqū 光驱

cease *v/t* & *v/i* zhōngzhǐ 中止

cease-fire tínghuǒ 停火

ceiling (*of room*) tiānhuābǎn 天花
    板; (*limit*) zuìgāo xiàngdù 最高限
    度

celebrate **1** *v/i* qìngzhù 庆祝 **2** *v/t*
    qìngzhù 庆祝; (*observe*) guò 过

celebrated zhùmíng 著名

celebration qìngzhù huì 庆祝会

celebrity míngrén 名人

celery qíncài 芹菜

cell (*for prisoner*) láofáng 牢房;
    BIO xìbāo 细胞; COMPUT dānyuán
    单元

cellar dìjiào 地窖

cello dà tíqín 大提琴

cellophane bōli zhǐ 玻璃纸

cell(ular) phone ⇩ shǒutí diànhuà
    手提电话

Celsius shèshì 摄氏

cement **1** *n* shuǐní 水泥 **2** *v/t* yòng
    shuǐní hú 用水泥糊; *friendship*
    jiāqiáng 加强

cemetery mùdì 墓地

censor *v/t* shān'gǎi 删改

censorship shēnchá zhìdù 审查制
    度

cent fēn 分

centenary, centennial yìbǎi
    zhōunián 一百周年

center **1** *n* zhōngxīn 中心; POL
    zhōngjiān pài 中间派; *in the ~ of
    ...* zài ... de zhōngxīn 在 ... 的中
    心 **2** *v/t* fàngzài zhōngyāng 放在
    中央; *text* zhōngjiān duìqí 中间
    对齐

♦ center on jízhōng yú 集中于

centigrade shèshì 摄氏; *10 de-
    grees ~* shèshì shídù 摄氏十度

centimeter límǐ 厘米

central zhōngbù 中部; *location,
    apartment* zhōngyāng 中央; (*main*)
    zhǔyào 主要; *be ~ to X* shì X de
    zhōngxīn yàodiǎn 是 X 的中心要
    点

Central Committee of the
    Chinese Communist Party
    Zhōnggòng Zhōngyāng
    Wěiyuánhuì 中共中央委员会

central heating nuǎnqì 暖气

centralize *decision making* jízhōng
    集中

central processing unit
    zhōngyāng chǔlǐ jī 中央处理机

central locking MOT zhōngyāng
    suǒchē 中央锁车

century shìjì 世纪

CEO (= *Chief Executive Officer*)
    zǒng jīnglǐ 总经理

ceramic cí 瓷

ceramics (*objects*) táocí 陶瓷

cereal (*grain*) gǔlèi 谷类

ceremonial **1** *adj* diǎnlǐ 典礼 **2** *n*
    diǎnlǐ 典礼

ceremony (*event*) diǎnlǐ 典礼;
    (*ritual*) yíshì 仪式

certain (*sure*) kěndìng 肯定;
    (*particular*) mǒuzhǒng 某种; *it's ~
    that ...* kěndìng ... 肯定 ...; *a ~
    Mr S.* yígè jiào S xiānsheng de rén
    一个叫 S 先生的人; *make ~*
    quèdìng 确定; *know / say for ~*
    kěyǐ kěndìng 可以肯定

certainly (*definitely*) yídìng 一定;

certainty

(*of course*) méi wèntí 没问题; ~ **not!** juéduì bùxíng! 绝对不行！

certainty (*confidence*) quèxìn 确信; (*inevitability*) bìrán xìng 必然性; **it's a ~** kěndìng 肯定

certificate (*qualification*) zhèngshū 证书; (*official paper*) zhèngmíng 证明

certified public accountant hégé kuàijì shī 合格会计师

certify zhèngmíng 证明

Cesarean n pōufù 剖腹

cessation xiūzhǐ 休止

c/f (= cost and freight) chéngběn jiā yùnfèi 成本加运费

CFC (= chlorofluorocarbon) hánlǜ fútīng 含氯氟烃

chain 1 n liàntiáo 链条; (*of stores, hotels*) liánsuǒ diàn 连锁店 2 v/t: **~ X to Y** bǎ X shuānzài Y shàng 把 X 拴在 Y 上

chain reaction liánsuǒ fǎnyìng 连锁反应; **chain smoke** yìzhī jiē yìzhī de chōuyān 一支接一支地抽烟; **chain smoker** yānbù líkǒu de rén yān bù lí kǒu 的人; **chain store** liánsuǒdiàn 连锁店

chair 1 n yǐzi 椅子; (*arm ~*) fúshǒu yǐ 扶手椅; (*at university*) jiàoshòu zhíwèi 教授职位; **the ~** (*electric ~*) diànyǐ 电椅; (*at meeting*) zhǔxí 主席; **go to the ~** zuò diànyǐ 坐电椅; **take the ~** zhǔchí huìyì 主持会议 2 v/t meeting zhǔchí 主持

chair lift shēngjiàng yǐ 升降椅

chairman zhǔxí 主席

Chairman Mao Máo Zhǔxí 毛主席

chairperson, chairwoman zhǔxí 主席

chalk (*for writing*) fěnbǐ 粉笔; (*in soil*) báihuī 白灰

challenge 1 n (*difficulty, in race, competition*) tiǎozhàn 挑战 2 v/t (*defy*) fǎnduì 反对; (*call into question*) zhìyí 质疑; **~ X to Y** tiǎozhàn X zuò Y 挑战 X 做 Y

challenger tiǎozhàn zhě 挑战者

challenging job, undertaking yǒu tiǎozhàn xìng 有挑战性

chambermaid nǚ fúwùyuán 女服务员

Chamber of Commerce shānghuì 商会

chamois (*leather*) jǐpí 麂皮

champagne xiāngbīn jiǔ 香槟酒

champion 1 n SP guànjūn 冠军; (*of cause*) hànwèi zhě 捍卫者 2 v/t (*cause*) zhīchí 支持

championship (*event*) jǐnbiāosài 锦标赛; (*title*) guànjūn 冠军

chance (*possibility*) kěnéng 可能; (*opportunity*) jīhuì 机会; (*risk*) fēngxiǎn 风险; (*luck*) jīyù 机遇; **by ~** yìwài 意外; **take a ~** màoxiǎn 冒险; **I'm not taking any ~s** wǒ bùcún jiǎoxìng zhīxīn 我不存侥幸之心

Chancellor (*in Germany*) Zǒnglǐ 总理; **~ of the Exchequer** (*in Britain*) Cáizhèngdàchén 财政大臣

chandelier diàodēng 吊灯

Changbai Mountain Chángbáishān 长白山

change 1 n (*alteration: to plan, idea, script*) gǎibiàn 改变; (*in society, climate, condition*) biànhuà 变化; (*small coins*) língqián 零钱; (*from purchase*) zhǎoqián 找钱; (*different situation etc*) gēnghuàn 更换; **for a ~** huàn kǒuwèi 换口味; **a ~ of clothes** tìhuàn yīfu 替换衣服 2 v/t (*alter*) gǎibiàn 改变; bankbill, trains, planes, one's clothes, (*replace*) huàn 换 3 v/i biàn 变; (*put on different clothes*) huàn yīfu 换衣服; (*take different train / bus*) huàn 换

channel (*on TV, radio*) píndào 频道; (*waterway*) hǎixiá 海峡

chant 1 n hǎnjiào 喊叫 2 v/i gāohū 高呼

chaos hùnluàn 混乱

chaotic hùnluàn 混乱

chapel xiǎo jiàotáng 小教堂

chapped gānliè 干裂

chapter (*of book*) zhāng 章; (*of organization*) zhībù 支部

character (*nature*) běnxìng 本性; (*person*) rén 人; (*in book, play*) rénwù 人物; (*personality*) xìnggé

性格; *(for writing Chinese etc)* zì zì; *he's a real ~* tā hěn yǒu gèxìng 他很有个性

characteristic 1 *n* tèdiǎn 特点 **2** *adj* diǎnxíng 典型

characterize *(be typical of)* diǎnfàn 典范; *(describe)* miáoshù 描述

charbroiled kǎo kǎo 烤烤

charcoal *(for barbecue)* mùtàn 木炭; *(for drawing)* tànbǐ 炭笔

charge 1 *n (fee)* fèiyòng 费用; LAW kònggào 控告; *free of ~* miǎnfèi 免费; *will that be cash or ~?* xiànjīn háishi jìzhàng? 现金还是记账？; *be in ~* fùzé 负责; *take ~* jiēguǎn 接管 **2** *v/t sum of money* shōufèi 收费; *(put on account)* jìzhàng 记账; LAW zhǐkòng 指控; *battery* chōngdiàn 充电 **3** *v/i (of troops)* chōngfēng 冲锋; *(of animal)* jìngōng 进攻

charge account shēzhàng hùkǒu 赊账户口

charge card jìzhàng kǎ 记账卡

charisma mèilì 魅力

charitable *institution, donation, person* císhàn 慈善

charity *(assistance)* zhènjì 赈济; *(organization)* císhàng jīgòu 慈善机构

charm 1 *n (appealing quality)* mèilì 魅力; *(on bracelet etc)* xiǎo zhuāngshì pǐn 小装饰品 **2** *v/t (delight)* xīyǐn 吸引

charming mírén 迷人; *idea* yǒu xīyǐn lì 有吸引力

charred shāojiāo 烧焦

chart *(diagram)* túbiǎo 图表; *(map: for sea)* hánghǎi tú 航海图; *(for airplane)* hángkōng tú 航空图; *the ~s* MUS liúxíng chàngpiān xuǎnmù 流行唱片选目

charter *v/t* bāozū 包租

charter flight bāojī 包机

chase 1 *n* zhuīzhú 追逐 **2** *v/t* zhuī 追

♦**chase away** gǎnzǒu 赶走

chaser *(drink)* suí lièjiǔ yǐhòu hēde dīdùjiǔ 随烈酒以后喝的低度酒

chassis *(of car)* dǐpán 底盘

chat 1 *n* liáotiān 聊天 **2** *v/i* liáo 聊

chatter 1 *n* diédie bùxiū 喋喋不休 **2** *v/i (talk)* xiánliáo 闲聊; *(of teeth)* dǎzhàn 打颤

chatterbox ráoshé zhě 饶舌者

chatty *person* jiàntán 健谈; *letter* jiācháng xiánhuà 家常闲话

chauffeur *n* sījī 司机

chauvinist *(male ~)* dà nánrén zhǔyì zhě 大男人主义者

cheap *adj (inexpensive)* piányi 便宜; *(nasty)* dījí 低级; *(mean)* xiǎoqì 小气

cheat 1 *n (person)* piànzi 骗子 **2** *v/t* piàn 骗; *X out of Y* cóng Y nǎli piànchū X 从 Y 那里骗出 X **3** *v/i (in exam)* zuòbì 作弊; *(in cards etc)* gǎoguǐ 搞鬼; *~ on one's husband* gěi zhàngfu dài lǜ màozi 给丈夫戴绿帽子

check¹ *n & adj (in pattern)* fānggé 方格

check² FIN zhīpiào 支票; *(in restaurant etc)* zhàngdān 账单; *the ~ please* zhàngdān 账单

check³ *n (to verify sth)* jiǎnchá 检查; *keep in ~, hold in ~* kòngzhì 控制; *keep a ~ on* héduì 核对 **2** *v/t (verify)* cháchá 查查; *(machinery)* jiǎnchá 检查; *(restrain)* yìzhì 抑制; *(stop)* kòngzhì zhù 控制住; *(with a ~mark)* dǎgōu 打勾; *(coat, package etc)* cúnfàng 存放 **3** *v/i* cháchá 查查; *~ for* jiǎnchá 检查

♦**check in** *(at airport)* lǐng dēngjī kǎ 领登机卡; *(at hotel)* dēngjì 登记

♦**check off** héduì 核对

♦**check on** chákàn 察看

♦**check out 1** *v/i (of hotel)* ⇩ jiézhàng 结账 **2** *v/t (look into)* diàochá 调查; *club, restaurant etc* shìshi 试试

♦**check up on** diàochá 调查

♦**check with** *(of person)* wèn 问; *(tally: of information, facts)* fúhé 符合

checkbook zhīpiào běn 支票本

checked *material* gézi 格子

checkerboard tiàoqí pán 跳棋盘

checkered *pattern* zònghéng-jiāocuò 纵横交错; *career* bǎojīng cāngsāng 饱经沧桑

checkers tiàoqí 跳棋

check-in (counter) lǐng dēngjī kǎ guìtái 领登机卡柜台

checking account zhīpiào zhànghù 支票帐户

check-in time lǐng dēngjī kǎ shíjiān 领登机卡时间

checklist qīngdān 清单; check mark gōuhào 勾号; checkmate *n* jiàngsǐ 将死; checkout (in supermarket) guìtái 柜台; check-out time (from hotel) ⇩ jiézhàng shíjiān 结账时间; checkpoint (military, police) guānqiǎ 关卡; checkroom (for coats) yīmào jiān 衣帽间; (for baggage) xínglǐ cúnfàng chù 行李存放处; checkup *medical* jiànkāng jiǎnchá 健康检查; *dental* yáchǐ jiǎnchá 牙齿检查

cheek miànjiá 面颊

cheekbone quángǔ 颧骨

cheer 1 *n* huānhū 欢呼; ~s! (toast) gānbēi! 干杯！2 *v/t* shòu huānyíng 受欢迎 3 *v/i* hècǎi 喝采

♦ cheer on hècǎi 喝采

♦ cheer up 1 *v/i* gāoxìng qǐlái 高兴起来; ~! gǔ qǐ jìnr lái! 鼓起劲儿来！2 *v/t*: cheer X up ràng X gāoxìng 让 X 高兴

cheerful kuàihuó 快活

cheering huānhū 欢呼

cheerleader lālāduì yuán 啦啦队员

cheese ⇩ nǎilào 奶酪

cheeseburger nǎilào hànbǎobāo 奶酪汉堡包

cheesecake ⇩ nǎilào dàngāo 奶酪蛋糕

chef chúshī 厨师

chemical 1 *adj* huàxué 化学 2 *n* huàxué zhìpǐn 化学制品

chemical warfare huàxué zhàn 化学战

chemist huàxué jiā 化学家

chemistry huàxué 化学; *fig* mòqì 默契

chemotherapy huàxué liáofǎ 化学疗法

cherish *memory, hope* zhēnxī 珍惜

cherry (fruit) yīngtáo 樱桃; (tree) yīnghuā shù 樱花树

chess xiàngqí 象棋

chessboard qípán 棋盘

chest (of person) xiōng 胸; (box) xiāngzi 箱子

chestnut lìzi 栗子; (tree) lìzi shù 栗子树

chest of drawers tì guì 屉柜

chew *v/t* jiáo 嚼; (of dog, rats) kěn 啃

♦ chew out F shǔluò 数落

chewing gum kǒuxiāng táng 口香糖

Chiang Kai-shek Jiǎng Jièshí 蒋介石

chick xiǎojī 小鸡; F (girl) niū妞

chicken 1 *n* jī 鸡; (food) jīròu 鸡肉; F dǎnxiǎo guǐ 胆小鬼 2 *adj* F (cowardly) dǎnxiǎo 胆小

♦ chicken out dǎ tuìtánggǔ 打退堂鼓

chickenfeed F méi yóushui 没油水

chicken pox shuǐdòu 水痘

chief 1 *n* (head) tóunǎo 头脑; (of tribe) zúzhǎng 族长 2 *adj* zhǔyào 主要

chiefly zhǔyào 主要

chilblain dòngchuāng 冻疮

child háizi 孩子; *pej* yòuzhì yòuzhì 幼稚

childbirth shēngchǎn 生产

childhood tóngnián 童年

childish *pej* yòuzhì yòuzhì 幼稚

childless wú zǐnǚ 无子女

childlike tiānzhēn wúxié 天真无邪

Children's Day Értóngjié 儿童节

chill 1 *n* (in air) lěngqì 冷气; (illness) gǎnmào 感冒 2 *v/t* (wine) lěngcáng 冷藏

chilli (pepper) làjiāo 辣椒

chilly *weather* hánlěng 寒冷; *welcome* lěngdàn 冷淡; I'm ~ wǒ yǒudiǎn lěng 我有点冷

chime *v/i* míng 鸣

chimney yāncōng 烟囱

chimpanzee hēi xīngxing 黑猩猩

chin xiàba 下巴

china cíqì 磁器; (*material*) cí 磁

China Zhōngguó 中国

China Central Television Zhōngyāng Diànshìtái 中央电视台; China Daily Zhōngguó Rìbào 中国日报; China International Travel Service Zhōngguó Guójì Lǚxíngshè 中国国际旅行社; China Travel Service Zhōngguó Lǚxíngshè 中国旅行社; Chinatown (*in other countries*) Tángrénjiē 唐人街

Chinese 1 *adj* Zhōngguó 中国; (*in Chinese*) Zhōngwén 中文 2 *n* (*written language*) Zhōngwén 中文; (*spoken language*) Zhōngguó huà 中国话; (*person*) Zhōngguó rén 中国人

Chinese character hànzì 汉字; Chinese checkers tiàoqí 跳棋; Chinese chess xiàngqí 象棋; Chinese doctor zhōngyī 中医; Chinese dumpling jiǎozi 饺子; Chinese foot (*measurement*) chǐ 尺; Chinese inch (*measurement*) cùn 寸; Chinese leaf / cabbage báicài 白菜; Chinese leek jiǔcài 韭菜; Chinese medicine zhōngyī 中医; (*herbs, drugs*) zhōngyào 中药; Chinese New Year Chūnjié 春节; Chinese New Year's Day Chūyī 初一; Chinese New Year's Eve Chúxī 除夕; Chinese onion cōng 葱; Chinese-style Zhōngshì 中式

chink (*gap*) fèng 缝; (*sound*) dīngdāng shēng 叮当声

chip 1 *n* (*fragment*) suìxiè 碎屑; (*damage*) liè kǒu 裂口; (*in gambling*) chóumǎ 筹码; in COMPUT xīnpiàn 芯片; *potato* ~s ⇩ shǔpiàn 薯片 2 *v/t* (*damage*) nòng pò yìdiǎn 弄破一点

♦ chip in (*interrupt*) chāzuǐ 插嘴; (*with money*) chūqián bō qián 出钱

chiropractor ànmójìshī 按摩技师

chirp *v/i* jījī jiào 唧唧叫

chisel *n* záozi 凿子

chivalrous xiáyì 侠义

chives jiǔcài 韭菜

chlorine lǜ 氯

chockfull yōngjǐ 拥挤

chocolate qiǎokèlì 巧克力; *hot* ~ rè qiǎokèlì 热巧克力

chocolate cake qiǎokèlì dàngāo 巧克力蛋糕

choice 1 *n* xuǎnzé 选择; (*selection*) gèsè gèyàng 各色各样; (*preference*) xuǎnzé 选择; *I had no* ~ wǒ méiyǒu xuǎnzé yúdì 我没有选择余地 2 *adj* (*top quality*) jīngxuǎn 精选

choir héchàngtuán 合唱团

choke 1 *n* MOT zǔfēngmén 阻风门 2 *v/i* qiǎ 卡; *he* ~*d on a bone* tā qiǎle gútou 他卡了骨头 3 *v/t* qiā bózi 掐脖子

cholesterol dǎngùchún 胆固醇

choose 1 *v/t* xuǎnzé 选择 2 *v/i* tiāoxuǎn 挑选

choosey F tiāotì 挑剔

chop 1 *n* kǎn 砍; (*meat*) páigǔ 排骨; (*seal*) túzhāng 图章 2 *v/t wood* kǎn 砍; *meat, vegetables* duò 跺

♦ chop down (*tree*) kǎndǎo 砍倒

chopper (*tool*) kǎndǎo dāo 砍刀; F (*helicopter*) zhíshēng fēijī 直升飞机

chopsticks kuàizi 筷子

chord MUS xián 弦

chore (*household task*) jiāwù 家务

choreographer wǔdǎo biāndǎo 舞蹈编导

choreography biān wǔ shù 编舞术

chorus (*singers*) héchàng tuán 合唱团; (*of song*) héchàng 合唱

Chou En-lai Zhōu Ēnlái 周恩来

Christ Jīdū 基督; ~*!* wǒde tiān ya! 我的天呀!

christen xǐlǐ 洗礼

Christian 1 *n* Jīdū tú 基督徒 2 *adj* Jīdū jiào 基督教; *attitude* Jīdū 基督

Christianity Jīdūjiào 基督教

Christian name míng 名

Christmas Shèngdànjié 圣诞节; *at* ~ Shèngdànjié qījiān 圣诞节期间; *Merry* ~*!* Shèngdàn kuàilè! 圣诞快乐!

Christmas card Shèngdàn kǎ 圣

诞卡；Christmas Day
Shèngdànjié 圣诞节；Christmas
Eve Shèngdàn yè 圣诞夜；
Christmas present Shèngdàn
lǐwù 圣诞礼物；Christmas tree
Shèngdàn shù 圣诞树

chrome, chromium gè 铬

chronic mànxìng 慢性

chronological shíjiān shùnxù 时
间顺序；in ~ order àn shíjiān
shùnxù 按时间顺序

chrysanthemum júhuā 菊花

chubby féipàng 肥胖

chuck v/t F rēng 扔

♦chuck out object rēngdiào 扔掉；
person hōng 轰

chuckle 1 n qīngxiào 轻笑 2 v/i
gēgē de xiào 咯咯地笑

chunk dàkuài 大块

church jiàotáng 教堂

chute xiécáo 斜槽；(for garbage)
lājī dào 垃圾道

CIA (= Central Intelligence
Agency) Zhōngyāng Qíngbào Jú
中央情报局

cider píngguǒ jiǔ 苹果酒

CIF (= cost insurance freight)
chéngběn jiā bǎoxiǎn fèi 成本加
保险费

cigar xuějiā 雪茄

cigarette xiāngyān 香烟

cinema (Br: building) diànyǐng
yuàn 电影院；(as institution)
diànyǐng 电影

cinnamon ròuguì 肉桂

circle 1 n yuánquān 圆圈；(group)
quānzi 圈子 2 v/t (draw circle
around) dǎquān 打圈 3 v/i (of
plane, bird) pánxuán 盘旋

circuit Elec xiànlù 线路；(lap) quān
圈

circuit board xiànlù bǎn 线路板

circuit breaker duànlù kāiguān 断
路开关

circular 1 n (giving information)
tōngzhī 通知 2 adj yuánxíng 圆形

circulate 1 v/i xúnhuán 循环 2 v/t
(memo) chuányuè 传阅

circulation BIO xúnhuán 循环；(of
newspaper, magazine) xiāolù 销路

circumference yuánzhōu 圆周

circumstances qíngkuàng 情况；
(financial) jīngjì qíngkuàng 经济
情况；under no ~ juébùnéng 决
不能；under the ~ zài zhèzhǒng
qíng kuàng xià 在这种情况下

circus mǎxìtuán 马戏团

cistern shuǐxiāng 水箱

citizen gōngmín 公民

citizenship guójí 国籍

CITS (= China International Travel
Service) Zhōngguó Guójì
Lǚxíngshè 中国国际旅行社

city chéngshì 城市；~ center
zhōngxīn 市中心；~ hall shìzhèng
tīng 市政厅

civic adj chéngshì 城市；pride,
responsibilities gōngmín 公民

civil (as opposed to military) mínjiān
民间；disobedience etc gōngmín 公
民；(polite) yǒu lǐmào 有礼貌

civil engineer tǔmù gōngchéngshī
土木工程师

civilian 1 n píngmín 平民 2 adj
clothes biànzhuāng 便装

civilization wénmíng 文明

civilize person jiàodǎo 教导

civil rights gōngmín quán 公民
权；civil servant gōngwùyuán 公
务员；civil service xíngzhèng
jīguān 行政机关；civil war
nèizhàn 内战

claim 1 n (request) suǒpéi 索赔；
(right) quánlì 权利；(assertion)
zhǔzhāng 主张 2 v/t (ask for as a
right) suǒqǔ 索取；(assert)
shēngchēng 声称；lost property
lǐng 领；they have ~ed responsibility for the attack tāmen duì
zhècì gōngjī biǎoshì fùzérèn 他们
对这次攻击表示负责任

claimant shēngqǐng rén 申请人；
LAW yuángào 原告

clam gélí 蛤蜊

♦clam up F sǐbù kāikǒu 死不开
口

clammy hands niánhūhu 黏糊糊；
weather mēnrè 闷热

clamor (noise) xuānhuáshēng 喧哗
声；(outcry) hūshēng 呼声

♦clamor for chǎozheyào 吵着要

clamp 1 n (fastener) jiāzi 夹子 2 v/t

(fasten) jiājǐn 夹紧

♦ **clamp down** yāzhì 压制

♦ **clamp down on** duì … jiāyǐ kòngzhì 对 … 加以控制

clan jiāzú 家族

clandestine mìmì 秘密

clang 1 n kēngqiāngshēng 铿锵声 **2** v/i yīshēng kēng'de yì xiǎng 铿锵地一响

clap 1 v/i (applaud) pāishǒu 拍手 **2** v/t pāi 拍

clarify chéngqīng 澄清

clarinet dānhuángguǎn 单簧管

clarity qīngxīdù 清晰度

clash 1 n chōngtú 冲突; (of personalities) bù xiétiáo 不协调 **2** v/i fāshēng chōngtú 发生冲突; (of opinions) bùyīzhì 不一致; ~ **with** … (of events) hé … fāshēng chōngtú 和 … 发生冲突; (of colors) hé … bù xiétiáo 和 … 不协调

clasp 1 n jiāzi 夹子 **2** v/t (in hand) jǐnwò 紧握

class 1 n (lesson) kè 课; (group of people) bān 班; (category) děngjí 等级; (social ~) jiēcéng 阶层 **2** v/t guīlèi 归类

classic 1 adj (typical) diǎnxíng 典型; (definitive) quánwēi xìng 权威性 **2** n jīngdiǎn zuòpǐn 经典作品

classical music gǔdiǎn 古典

classification (act) děngjí 等级; (category) fēnlèi 分类

classified information jīmì 机密

classified ad(vertisement) fēnlèi guǎnggào 分类广告

classify (categorize) fēnlèi 分类

classmate tóngxué 同学; **classroom** jiàoshì 教室; **class warfare** jiējí dòuzhēng 阶级斗争

classy F gāojí 高级

clatter 1 n huālā 哗啦 **2** v/i kuāngdāng kuāngdāng xiǎng 哐当哐当响

clause (in agreement) tiáokuǎn 条款; GRAM cóngjù 从句

claustrophobia yōubì kǒngbù zhèng 幽闭恐怖症

claw 1 n (of lobster, crab) qiánzi 钳子; (of cat, woman) zhuǎzi 爪子 **2** v/t (scratch) zhuā 抓

clay niántǔ 粘土

clean 1 adj gānjìng 干净 **2** adv F (completely) wánquán 完全 **3** v/t teeth, shoes shuā 刷; house, room dǎsǎo 打扫; car, hands, face, clothes xǐ 洗; **have … ~ed** bǎ … náqù xǐ 把 … 拿去洗

♦ **clean out** room, cupboard dǎsǎo gānjìng 打扫干净; fig bǎ X shū guāng le 把 X 输光了

♦ **clean up 1** v/t shōushí gānjìng 收拾干净 **2** v/i dǎsǎo 打扫; (wash) shūxǐ 梳洗; (on stock market etc) fācái 发财

cleaner (person) qīngjié gōng 清洁工; **dry ~** gānxǐ diàn 干洗店

cleaning woman qīngjié nǚgōng 清洁女工

cleanse (skin) qīngjié 清洁

cleanser (for skin) qīngjié jì 清洁剂

clear 1 adj explanation, photograph, voice qīngchu 清楚; (obvious) míngxiǎn 明显; weather, sky qínglǎng 晴朗; water, eyes qīngchè 清澈; skin guāngjié 光洁; conscience qīngbái 清白; **a ~ thinker** tóunǎo mǐnruì de rén 头脑敏锐的人; **I'm not ~ about it** wǒ bù dà míngbái 我不大明白; **I didn't make myself ~** wǒ méi jiǎng qīngchu 我没讲清楚 **2** adv: **stand ~ of** bùyào kàojìn 不要靠近; **steer ~ of** bǎochí jùlí 保持距离 **3** v/t roads etc qīngchú 清除; (acquit) chéngqīng 澄清; (authorize) yǔnxǔ 允许; (earn) zhèng 挣; **~ one's throat** qīng sǎngzi 清嗓子 **4** v/i (of sky, mist) qíngle 晴了; (of face) kāilǎng 开朗

♦ **clear away** v/t shōushí 收拾

♦ **clear off** v/i táopǎo 逃跑; **~!** gǔnkāi! 滚开!

♦ **clear out 1** v/t (cupboard) qīnglǐ 清理 **2** v/i táopǎo 逃跑

♦ **clear up 1** v/i (tidy up) shōushí 收拾; (of weather) zhuǎnqíng 转晴; (of illness, rash) xiāoshī 消失 **2** v/t (tidy) shōushí 收拾; mystery, problem jiějué 解决

clearance (*space*) kōngjiān 空间; (*authorization*) xǔkě 许可

clearance sale qīngcāng dà pāimài 清仓大拍卖

clearly (*with clarity*) qīngchu 清楚; (*evidently*) míngxiǎn 明显

clemency réncí 仁慈

clench *teeth* yǎojǐn 咬紧; *fist* wòjǐn 握紧

clergy shénzhí rényuán 神职人员

clergyman mùshī 牧师

clerk (*administrative*) zhíyuán 职员; (*in store*) fúwùyuán 服务员

clever *person, animal, idea* cōngmíng 聪明; *gadget, device* qiǎomiào 巧妙

click 1 *n* COMPUT diǎnjī 点击 2 *v/i* kādāshēngxiǎng 咔嗒声响

click on COMPUT àn 按

client gùkè 顾客

cliff xuányá 悬崖

climate qìhòu 气候; *economic ~* jīngjì qìhòu 经济气候

climax *n* gāocháo 高潮

climb 1 *n* (*up mountain*) pāndēng 攀登 2 *v/t* pá 爬 3 *v/i* (*in mountains etc*) pá 爬; *fig* (*inflation etc*) shàngshēng 上升

climb down pá xiàlái 爬下来; *fig* ràngbù 让步

climber (*person*) dēngshān zhě 登山者

clinch: *~ a deal* dáchéng jiāoyì 达成交易

cling (*of clothes*) tiēshēn 贴身

cling to (*of child*) zhānzhe 粘着; *ideas, tradition* gùshǒu 固守

clingfilm bǎoxiān zhǐ 保鲜纸

clingy *child, boyfriend* chánrén 缠人

clinic zhěnsuǒ 诊所

clinical línchuáng 临床

clink 1 *n* (*noise*) dīngdāngshēng 叮当声 2 *v/i* dīngdāng zuòxiǎng 叮当作响

clip¹ 1 *n* (*fastener*) jiāzi 夹子 2 *v/t* jiā 夹; *~ X to Y* bǎ X jiādào Y shàng 把 X 夹到 Y 上

clip² 1 *n* (*extract*) jiǎnjí 剪辑 2 *v/t* *hair, hedge, grass* jiǎn 剪

clipboard xiězì jiábǎn 写字夹板

COMPUT jiántiē bǎn 剪贴板

clippers (*for hair*) tuīzi 推子; (*for nails*) zhǐjiǎdāo 指甲刀; (*for gardening*) jiǎncǎo qián 剪草钳

clipping (*from newspaper*) jiǎnbào 剪报

cloak *n* dǒupeng 斗篷

clock zhōng 钟; (*speedometer*) jìchéng qì 记程器

clock radio shōuyīnjī nàozhōng 收音机闹钟

clockwise shùn shízhēn 顺时针

clockwork fātiáo 发条; *it went like ~* yíqiè shùnlì 一切顺利

clog up 1 *v/i* dǔzhù 堵住 2 *v/t* sāizhù 塞住

close¹ 1 *adj* *family, friend* qīnmì 亲密; *resemblance* xiāngjìn 相近 2 *adv* jìn 近; *~ at hand* zài shēnbiān 在身边; *~ by* fùjìn 附近; *it's ~ to the stores* lí shāngdiàn jìn, hěn fāngbiàn 离商店近, 很方便; *be ~ to X* (*as a friend etc*) hé X qīnjìn 和 X 亲近

close² 1 *v/t* guān 关; (*permanently: business*) guānbì 关闭 2 *v/i* (*of door, store*) guānmén 关门; (*of window*) guān 关; (*of eyes*) bìshàng 闭上; (*of store: permanently*) guānbì 关闭

close down *v/t & v/i* guānbì 关闭

close in *v/i* pòjìn 迫近

close up 1 *v/t* *building* fēngbì 封闭 2 *v/i* (*move closer*) kàolǒng 靠拢

closed *store* guānmén 关门; *eyes* bìshàng 闭上

closed-circuit television bìlù diànshì 闭路电视

closely *listen, watch* zǐxì 仔细; *cooperate* mìqiè 密切

closet yīguì 衣柜

close-up tèxiě jìngtóu 特写镜头

closing time guānmén shíjiān 关门时间

closure guānbì 关闭

clot 1 *n* (*of blood*) xuèkuài 血块 2 *v/i* (*of blood*) jiékuài 结块

cloth (*fabric*) bùliào 布料; (*for kitchen, cleaning*) mābù 抹布

clothes yīfu 衣服

clothes brush shuāzi 刷子

clothes hanger yījià 衣架

clothing yīfu 衣服

cloud n yún 云; *a ~ of smoke / dust* yízhèn yān / chéntǔ 一阵烟 / 尘土

♦cloud over (of sky) tiānyīnle 天阴了

cloudburst qīngpéndàyǔ 倾盆大雨

cloudy yīntiān 阴天

clout fig (influence) yǐngxiǎng 影响

clown n (in circus) xiǎochǒu 小丑; (joker) chǒujiǎo 丑角; pej chǔncái 蠢材

club n (weapon) mùgùn 木棍; (golf iron) qiúgān 球杆; (organization) jùlèbù 俱乐部

clue n xiànsuǒ 线索; *I haven't a ~* wǒ wánquán bù zhīdào 我完全不知道

clued-up zàiháng 在行

clump n (of earth) tǔkuài 土块; (group) cuō 撮

clumsiness bènzhuō 笨拙

clumsy person bènshǒu bènjiǎo 笨手笨脚

cluster 1 n (of people) qún qún 群群; (of houses) pái pái 排排 2 v/i (of people) jùjí 聚集; (of houses) jízhōng 集中

clutch 1 n MOT líhéqì 离合器 2 v/t jǐnwò 紧握

♦clutch at shìtú zhuāzhù 试图抓住

Co. (= *Company*) gōngsī 公司

c/o (= *care of*) fánjiāo 烦交

coach 1 n (trainer) jiàoliàn 教练 2 v/t zhǐdǎo 指导

coagulate (of blood) níngjié 凝结

coal méi 煤

coalition liánméng 联盟

coal-mine méikuàng 煤矿

coarse fabric cūcāo 粗糙; hair cūyìng 粗硬; (vulgar) cūsú 粗俗

coast n hǎibiān 海边; *at the ~* zài hǎibiān 在海边

coastal línhǎi 临海

coastguard hǎi'àn jǐngwèi duì 海岸警卫队; (person) hǎi'àn jǐngwèi 海岸警卫

coastline hǎi'àn xiàn 海岸线

coat 1 n wàiyī 外衣; (over~) dàyī 大衣; (of animal) máopí 毛皮; (of paint etc) céng 层 2 v/t (cover) jiāshàng yīcéng 加上一层

coathanger yījià 衣架

coating céng 层

coax hǒng 哄

cobweb zhīzhūwǎng 蜘蛛网

cocaine kěkǎyīn 可卡因

cock n (chicken) gōngjī 公鸡; (any male bird) gōngniǎo 公鸟

cockeyed idea etc huāngmiù 荒谬

cockpit (of plane) zuòcāng 座舱

cockroach zhāngláng 蟑螂

cocktail jīwěijiǔ 鸡尾酒

cocoa (plant) kěkě shù 可可树; (drink) kěkě 可可

coconut (to eat) yēzi 椰子

coconut milk yēzi nǎi 椰子奶

coconut palm yēzi shù 椰子树

COD (= *collect on delivery*) huòdào fùkuǎn 货到付款

coddle sick person zhàoliào 照料; child jiāoshēng guànyǎng 娇生惯养

code n mìmǎ 密码

co-educational nánnǚ héxiào 男女合校

coerce qiǎngpò 强迫

coexist gòngcún 共存

coexistence gòngchǔ 共处

coffee kāfēi 咖啡

coffee break xiǎoxī 小息; coffee maker kāfēi jī 咖啡机; coffee pot kāfēi hú 咖啡壶; coffee shop kāfēi diàn 咖啡店; coffee table chájī 茶几

coffin guāncai 棺材

cog lúnchǐ 轮齿

cognac báilándì 白兰地

cogwheel qiàn chǐlún 嵌齿轮

cohabit tóngjū 同居

coherent liánguàn 连贯

coil 1 n (of rope) juǎn 卷 2 v/t juǎn 卷; ~ (up) juǎn qǐlái 卷起来

coin n yìngbì 硬币

coincide qiǎohé 巧合

coincidence qiǎohé 巧合

coke F (cocaine) kěkǎyīn 可卡因

Coke® kěkǒu kělè 可口可乐

cold 1 adj lěng 冷; *I'm (feeling) ~*

wǒ juéde hěnlěng 我觉得很冷;
it's ~ tiānqì hěnlěng 天气很冷;
in ~ blood lěngkù 冷酷; **get ~
feet** dǎ tuìtánggǔ 打退堂鼓 **2** *n*
hánlěng 寒冷; **I have a ~** wǒ
gǎnmàole 我感冒了

cold boiled water liáng kāishuǐ
凉开水; **cold-blooded** lěngxuè 冷
血; *fig* lěngkù 冷酷; **cold cuts**
lěngpán 冷盘; **cold noodles**
lěngmiàn 冷面; **cold sore**
zuǐbiān pàozhěn 嘴边疱疹

coleslaw *(northern China)* liángbàn
yángbáicài 凉拌洋白菜;
(southern China) liángbàn
juǎnxīncài 凉拌卷心菜

colic jiǎotòng 绞痛

collaborate *(in research, etc)* hézuò
合作; *(with enemy)* gōujié 勾结

collaboration hézuò 合作; *(with
enemy)* gōujié 勾结

collaborator hézuò zhě 合作者;
(with enemy) gōujié zhě 勾结者

collapse dǎotā 倒塌; *(of person)*
bēngkuì 崩溃

collapsible zhédié 折迭

collar lǐngzi 领子; *(for dog, cat)*
xiàngquān 项圈

collarbone suǒgǔ 锁骨

colleague tóngshì 同事

collect 1 *v/t person* jiē 接; *tickets,
cleaning etc* ná 拿; *(gather, as
hobby)* shōují 收集 **2** *v/i (gather
together)* jízhōng 集中 **3** *adv:* **call
~** shòuhuàrén fùfèi 受话人付费

collect call shòuhuàrén fùfèi 受话
人付费

collected *works, poems etc* quánjí
全集; *person* zhènjìng 镇静

collection *(of art)* shōucángpǐn 收
藏品; *(fashions)* shízhuāng
zhǎnlǎn 时装展览; *(in church)*
mùjuān 募捐

collective 1 *adj* gòngtóng 共同;
POL jítǐ 集体 **2** *n* POL jítǐ 集体

collective bargaining jítǐ xiédìng
集体协定

collector shōucáng jiā 收藏家

college xuéyuàn 学院

college exam ⇩ gāokǎo 高考

collide pèngzhuàng 碰撞

collision xiāngzhuàng 相撞

colloquial kǒuyǔ 口语

colon *(punctuation)* màohào 冒号;
ANAT jiécháng 结肠

colonel shàngxiào 上校

colonial *adj* zhímíndì 殖民地

colonize *country* kāituò zhímíndì
开拓殖民地

colony zhímíndì 殖民地

color 1 *n* yánsè 颜色; *(in cheeks)*
liǎnsè 脸色; **in ~** *(movie etc)* cǎisè
彩色; **~s** MIL jūnqí 军旗 **2** *v/t
one's hair* rǎnsè 染色 **3** *v/i (blush)*
liǎnhóng 脸红

color-blind sèmáng 色盲

colored *adj person* hēi 黑

color fast bú tuìsè 不褪色

colorful xiānyàn 鲜艳; *account*
jīngcǎi 精彩

coloring yánsè 颜色; *(of the skin)*
fūsè 肤色

color photograph cǎisè zhàopiān
彩色照片; **color scheme** sècǎi
shèjì 色彩设计; **color TV** cǎisè
diànshì 彩色电视

colt xióngjū 雄驹

column liè 列; *(architectural)*
yuánzhù 圆柱; *(of text)* lánlán 栏栏;
(newspaper feature) zhuānlán 专栏

columnist zhuānlán zuòjiā 专栏
作家

coma hūnmí 昏迷

comb 1 *n* shūzi 梳子 **2** *v/t* shū 梳;
area sōuxún 搜寻

combat 1 *n* zhàndòu 战斗 **2** *v/t* yǔ
... zuò dòuzhēng 与 ... 做斗争

combination zǔhé 组合; *(of safe)*
mìmǎ 密码

combine 1 *v/t ingredients* hùnhé 混
合; **~ X with Y** jiāngù X hé Y jiān
gù X 和 Y **2** *v/i (of chemical
elements)* huàhé 化合

combine harvester liánhé
shōugējī 联合收割机

combustible yìrán 易燃

combustion ránshāo 燃烧

come *(toward speaker)* lái 来;
(toward listener) qù 去; *(of train,
bus)* láile 来了; **don't ~ too close**
bié tài kàojìn 别太靠近; **in the
years to ~** zài jīnhòu jǐnián 在今

后几年; **how ~?** F zěnme? 怎么?

♦ **come about** (*happen*) fāshēng 发生

♦ **come across 1** v/t *items* wúyì zhōng fāxiàn 无意中发现; *person* wúyì zhōng yùdào 无意中遇到 **2** v/i: *it didn't ~* (*of idea, humor*) méi rén míngbái 没人明白; *she comes across as ...* tā sìhū shì ... 她似乎是 ...

♦ **come along** (*come too*) yīdàolái 一道来; (*turn up*) láidào 来到; (*progress*) jìnzhǎn 进展

♦ **come apart** kě chāizhuāng 可拆装; (*break*) suìle 碎了

♦ **come around** (*to s.o.'s home*) lái lái 来; (*regain consciousness*) sūxǐng 苏醒

♦ **come away** (*leave*) líkāi 离开; (*of button etc*) diàole 掉了

♦ **come back** huílái 回来; *it came back to me* wǒ xiǎng qǐláile 我想起来了

♦ **come by 1** v/i bàifǎng 拜访 **2** v/t (*acquire*) dédào 得到

♦ **come down** xià lái 下来; (*in price, amount etc*) xiàjiàng 下降; (*of rain, snow*) xià 下; *he came down the stairs* tā zǒuxià lóutī 他走下楼梯

♦ **come for** (*attack*) gōngjī 攻击; (*collect: thing*) láiqǔ 来取; (*collect: person*) láijiē 来接

♦ **come forward** (*present oneself*) tǐngshēn érchū 挺身而出

♦ **come from** láizì 来自

♦ **come in** zǒu jìnlái 走进来; (*of train*) dàodá 到达; (*of tide*) zhǎngcháo 涨潮; *~!* qǐngjìn! 请进！; *the horse came in fourth* nà mǎ pǎole dìsì 那马跑了第四

♦ **come in for**: *~ criticism* shòudào pīpíng 受到批评

♦ **come in on**: *~ a deal* jiārù jiāoyì 加入交易

♦ **come off** (*of handle etc*) tuōluò 脱落

♦ **come on** (*progress*) jìnzhǎn 进展; *~!* kuàidiǎnr! 快点儿！; (*in disbelief*) bùkěnéng 不可能

♦ **come out** (*of person*) chū出; (*of sun, results, product*) chūlái 出来; (*of stain*) xiāoshī 消失; (*of book, record*) fāxíng 发行

♦ **come to 1** v/t *place* dàodá 到达; (*of hair, dress, water*) dádào 达到; *that comes to $70* zǒnggòng qīshí měiyuán 总共七十美元 **2** v/i (*regain consciousness*) sūxǐng 苏醒

♦ **come up** shàngqù 上去; (*of sun*) shēng qǐlái 升起来; *something has ~* yǒushì fāshēng 有事发生

♦ **come up with** *new idea etc* xiǎng qǐlái 想起来

comeback: *make a ~* dōngshān zàiqǐ 东山再起

comedian xǐjù yǎnyuán 喜剧演员; *pej* chǒujiǎo 丑角

comedown luòpò 落泊

comedy xǐjù 喜剧

comet huìxīng 彗星

comeuppance: *he'll get his ~* tā huì dédào bàoyìng 他会得到报应

comfort 1 n xiǎngshòu 享受; (*consolation*) ānwèi 安慰 **2** v/t ānwèi 安慰

comfortable *chair, house, room* shūfu 舒服; *be ~* (*of person*) shūfu 舒服; (*financially*) fùyù 富裕

comic 1 n (*to read*) mànhuà 漫画 **2** adj yǒuqù 有趣

comical huájī 滑稽

comic book mànhuà shū 漫画书

comics liánhuán mànhuà 连环漫画

comma dòuhào 逗号

command 1 n mìnglìng 命令 **2** v/t mìnglìng 命令

commander zhǐhuīguān 指挥官

commander-in-chief zǒngsīlìng 总司令

commemorate jìniàn 纪念

commemoration: *in ~ of ...* jìniàn ... 纪念 ...

commence v/t & v/i kāishǐ 开始

comment 1 n yìjiàn 意见; *no ~* wúkě fènggào 无可奉告 **2** v/i fābiǎo yìjiàn 发表意见

commentary pínglùn 评论

commentator pínglùn jiā 评论家

commerce shāngyè 商业

commercial 1 adj shāngyè 商业 **2** n (ad) guǎnggào 广告

commercial break guǎnggào 广告

commercialize v/t shāngyè huà 商业化

commercial traveler lǚxíng tuīxiāo yuán 旅行推销员

commiserate tóngqíng 同情

commission 1 n (payment) yòngjīn 佣金; (job) chéngbāo 承包; (committee) wěiyuánhuì 委员会 **2** v/t (for a job) wěituō 委托

commit money chéngnuò 承诺; ~ a crime fànzuì 犯罪; ~ oneself tóurù 投入

commitment zérèn 责任

committee wěiyuánhuì 委员会

commodity shāngpǐn 商品

common (not rare) píngcháng 平常; (shared) gòngtóng 共同; in ~ gòngtóng zhīchù 共同之处; have something in ~ with X hé X yǒu gòngtóng zhīchù 和 X 有共同之处

common law wife tóngjū qīzi 同居妻子; **commonplace** adj píngyōng 平庸; **common sense** chángshì 常识

commotion sāodòng 搔动

communal gōngyòng 公用

commune gōngshè 公社

communicate 1 v/i (have contact, make self understood) gōutōng 沟通 **2** v/t zhuǎndá 转达

communication gōutōng 沟通

communications tōngxùn yè 通讯业

communications satellite tōngxùn wèixīng 通讯卫星

communicative person ài shuōhuà 爱说话

Communism Gòngchǎnzhǔyì 共产主义

Communist 1 adj Gòngchǎnzhǔyì 共产主义 **2** n Gòngchǎndǎngyuán 共产党员

Communist China Zhōnggòng 中共

Communist Party Gòngchǎndǎng 共产党

community shèqū 社区

commute 1 v/i (to work) chéngchē shàngbān 乘车上班; he ~s to work in Tianjin tā chéngchē qù Tiānjīn shàngbān 他乘车去天津上班 **2** v/t LAW jiǎnxíng 减刑

commuter chéngchē shàngbān zhě 乘车上班者; the trains are packed with ~s huǒchē jǐmǎnle chéngchē shàngbān zhě 火车挤满了乘车上班者

commuter traffic shàngxiàbān jiāotōng 上下班交通

commuter train chéngchē shàngxià bān huǒchē 乘车上下班火车

compact 1 adj xiùzhēn 袖珍 **2** n MOT xiǎoxíng kèchē 小型客车

compact disc MUS jīguāng chàngpiàn 激光唱片; COMPUT guāngpán 光盘

companion bànlǚ 伴侣

companionship péibàn 陪伴

company COM gōngsī 公司; (companionship) péibàn 陪伴; (guests) kèrén 客人

company car gōngsī chē 公司车

company law gōngsī fǎ 公司法

comparable (which can be compared) kě bǐjiào 可比较; (similar) lèisì 类似

comparative 1 adj (relative) xiāngduì 相对; study bǐjiào 比较; ~ form GRAM bǐjiào jí 比较级 **2** n GRAM bǐjiào jí 比较级

comparatively xiāngduì éryán 相对而言

compare 1 v/t bǐjiào 比较; ~ X with Y jiāng X yǔ Y xiāng bǐjiào 将 X 与 Y 相比较; ~d with X yǔ X xiāngbǐ 与 X 相比 **2** v/i bǐjiào 比较

comparison bǐjiào 比较; there's no ~ méidebǐ 没的比

compartment (cupboard) chúguì 橱柜; (for credit cards etc) jiácéng 夹层

compass luópán yí 罗盘仪; (pair of) ~es yuánguī 园规

compassion tóngqíng 同情

compassionate yǒu tóngqíng xīn

有同情心

疾病

compatibility fúhé xìng 符合性

compatible *people* hédelái 合得来; *blood types, life styles* fúhé 符合; COMPUT xiāngróng 相容; *we're not ~* wǒmen hébùlái 我们合不来

compel *(force)* qiǎngpò 强迫; *I felt ~led to …* wǒ bùdébù … 我不得不 …

compelling *argument* lìngrén xìnfú 令人信服; *movie, book* yǐnrén rùshèng 引人入胜

compensate 1 *v/t (with money)* péicháng 赔偿 **2** *v/i: ~ for* bǔcháng 补偿

compensation *(money)* péicháng 赔偿; *(reward)* hǎochù 好处; *(comfort)* ānwèi 安慰

compete jìngzhēng 竞争; *(take part)* cānjiā 参加; *~ for* zhēngduó 争夺

competence, competency nénglì 能力

competent *person* chèngzhí 称职; *work* hégé 合格; *I'm not ~ to judge* wǒ bùgòu zīgé qù pànduàn 我不够资格去判断

competition *(contest, competing)* jìngzhēng 竞争; SP bǐsài 比赛; *(competitors)* duìshǒu 对手; *the government wants to encourage ~* zhèngfǔ yào gǔlì jìngzhēng 政府要鼓励竞争

competitive *(able to compete: price, offer)* yǒu jìngzhēng lì 有竞争力; *(liking to compete)* hào jìngzhēng 好竞争; *profession, sport* jìngzhēnglì hěnqiáng 竞争力很强

competitor *(in contest)* bǐsài zhě 比赛者; COM jìngzhēng duìshǒu 竞争对手

compile biānzhì 编制

complacency zìmǎn 自满

complacent zhānzhan zìxǐ 沾沾自喜

complain *v/i* bàoyuàn 抱怨; *(to store, manager)* tóusù 投诉; *~ of* MED zhǔsù 主诉; *~ about X* bàoyuàn X 抱怨 X

complaint tóusù 投诉; MED jíbìng

complement *v/t* xiāngpèi 相配; *they ~ each other* tāmén hěn xiāngchèn 他们很相衬

complementary hùwéi bǔchōng 互为补充

complete 1 *adj (total)* shízú 十足; *(full)* wánzhěng 完整; *(finished)* wángōng 完工 **2** *v/t building, course, task etc* wánchéng 完成; *form* tiánxiě 填写

completely wánquán 完全

completion wánchéng 完成

complex 1 *adj* fùzá 复杂 **2** *n* PSYCH bìngtài kǒngjù 病态恐惧; *(of buildings)* zhōngxīn 中心

complexion *(facial)* miànsè 面色

compliance zūncóng 遵从

complicate shǐ fùzá huà 使复杂化

complicated fùzá 复杂

complication kùnnan 困难; *~s* MED bìngfā zhèng 并发症

compliment 1 *n* zànměi 赞美 **2** *v/t* zànměi 赞美

complimentary *speech* zànměi 赞美; *(free)* miǎnfèi 免费; *(in restaurant, hotel)* zèngsòng 赠送; *be very ~ about* jíkǒu chēngzàn 极口称赞

compliments slip biàntiáo 便条

comply fúcóng 服从; *~ with …* zūnshǒu … 遵守 …

component bùfen 部分

compose *v/t* zǔchéng 组成; MUS chuàngzuò 创作; *be ~d of X* yóu X zǔchéng 由 X 组成; *~ oneself* shǐ zìjǐ píngjìng xiàlái 使自己平静下来

composed *(calm)* píngjìng 平静

composer MUS zuòqǔ jiā 作曲家

composition *(make-up)* zǔchéng chéngfèn 组成成分; MUS zuòpǐn 作品; *(essay)* zuòwén 作文

composure zhènjìng 镇静

compound *n* CHEM huàhé wù 化合物

compound interest fùlì 复利

comprehend *(understand)* lǐjiě 理解

comprehension lǐjiě 理解

comprehensive zōnghé xìng 综合性

comprehensive insurance zǒngkuò bǎoxiǎn 总括保险

compress 1 n MED fūbù 敷布 2 v/t air, gas, information yāsuō 压缩

comprise (consist of) bāohán 包含; (make up) gòuchéng 构成; be ~d of ... yóu ... zǔchéng 由 ... 组成

compromise 1 n tuǒxié 妥协 2 v/i tuǒxié 妥协 3 v/t principles fàngqì 放弃; reputation etc sǔnhài 损害; ~ oneself liánlèi zìjǐ 连累自己

compulsion PSYCH qiángpò xìng shénjīng zhì 强迫性神经质

compulsive behavior bùyóu zìzhǔ 不由自主; reading yùbà bùnéng 欲罢不能

compulsory yìwù 义务; class bìxiū 必修; ~ education yìwù jiàoyù 义务教育

computer diànnǎo 电脑; it's on ~ zài diànnǎo shang 在电脑上

computer-controlled diànnǎo kòngzhì 电脑控制

computer game diànzǐ yóuxì 电子游戏

computerize diànnǎo huà 电脑化

computer literate huìyòng diànnǎo 会用电脑; computer science jìsuànjì kēxué 计算机科学; computer scientist jìsuànjì kēxué jiā 计算机科学家

computing diànnǎo shíyòng 电脑使用

comrade (friend) péngyou 朋友; POL tóngzhì 同志

comradeship yǒuyì 友谊

con F 1 n piànjú 骗局 2 v/t piàn 骗

conceal fact, truth etc yǐnmán 隐瞒; object yǐncáng 隐藏

concede v/t (admit) chéngrèn 承认

conceit zìfù 自负

conceited zìgāo zìdà 自高自大

conceivable kě xiǎngxiàng 可想象

conceive v/i (of woman) huáiyùn 怀孕; ~ of (imagine) shèxiǎng 设想

concentrate 1 v/i (on task) jízhōng jīnglì 集中精力 2 v/t one's attention, energies jízhōng 集中

concentrated juice etc nóngsuō 浓缩

concentration zhuānxīn 专心

concept gàiniàn 概念

conception (of child) huáiyùn 怀孕

concern 1 n (anxiety) dānyōu 担忧; (care) guānxīn 关心; (business) shìwù 事务; (company) gōngsī 公司 2 v/t (involve) shèjí 涉及; (worry) dānyōu 担忧; ~ oneself with guǎn 管

concerned (anxious) gǎndào bù ān 感到不安; (caring) guānxīn 关心; (involved) yǒuguān 有关; as far as I'm ~ jiù wǒ ér yán 就我而言

concerning prep yǒuguān 有关

concert yīnyuè huì 音乐会

concerted (joint) liánhé 联合

concertmaster shǒuxí xiǎo tíqín yǎnzòu zhě 首席小提琴演奏者

concerto xiézòu qǔ 协奏曲

concession (giving in) ràngbù 让步

conciliatory ānfǔ 安抚

concise jiǎnmíng 简明

conclude 1 v/t (deduce) tuīduàn chū 推断出; (end) jiéshù 结束; ~ X from Y yóu Y tuīduàn chū X 由 Y 推断出 X 2 v/i jiéshù 结束

conclusion (deduction) jiélùn 结论; (end) jiéwěi 结尾; in ~ zuìhòu 最后

conclusive juédìng xìng 决定性

concoct meal, drink tiáozhì 调制; excuse, story biānzào 编造

concoction (food, drink) tiáozhì pǐn 调制品

concrete[1] adj (not abstract) jùtǐ 具体

concrete[2] n hùnníngtǔ 混凝土

concubine qiè 妾

concur v/i tóngyì 同意

concussion zhèndàng 震荡

condemn action qiǎnzé 谴责; building xuāngào ... bù shìyú 宣告 ... 不适于

jūzhù 宣告 ... 不适于居住; (doom) zhùdìng 注定; **~ to death** pàn sǐxíng 判死刑

condemnation (of action) qiǎnzé 谴责

condensation (on walls, windows) lěngníng wù 冷凝物

condense 1 v/t (make shorter) yāsuō 压缩 **2** v/i (of steam) shǐ lěngníng 使冷凝

condensed milk liànrǔ 炼乳

condescend: he ~ed to speak to me tā fàngxià jiàzi hé wǒ jiǎnghuà 他放下架子和我讲话

condescending (patronizing) bào cì'ēn tàidù 抱赐恩态度

condition 1 n (state, of health) zhuàngtài 状态; MED bìng bìng 病; (requirement, term) tiáojiàn 条件; **~s** (circumstances) tiáojiàn 条件; **on ~ that** ... zhǐyào ... 只要 ... **2** v/t PSYCH shǐ xíngchéng tiáojiàn fǎnshè 使形成条件反射

conditional 1 adj acceptance yǒu tiáojiàn 有条件; **~ on** ... shì ... érdìng shì ... 而定 **2** n GRAM tiáojiàn 条件

conditioner (for hair) hùfà jì 护发剂; (for fabric) qiānwēi bǎohù jì 纤维保护剂

conditioning PSYCH tiáojiàn fǎnshè 条件反射

condo → **condominium**

condolences diàoyàn 吊唁

condom ♀ bìyùn tào 避孕套

condominium = gòngxiáng gōnggòng shèshī de gōngyù 共享公共设施的公寓

condone actions kuānróng 宽容

conducive: ~ to yǒu zhùyú 有助于

conduct 1 n (behavior) jǔzhǐ 举止 **2** v/t (carry out) shíshī 实施; ELEC chuándǎo 传导; MUS zhǐhuī 指挥; **~ oneself** biǎoxiàn 表现

conducted tour dǎoyóu lǚyóu 导游旅游

conductor MUS zhǐhuī jiā 指挥家; (on train) lièchē zhǎng 列车长

cone (in geometry) yuánzhuī tǐ 圆锥体; (of pine tree) sōngtǎ 松塔;

(on highway) zhuīxíng lùbiāo 锥性路标; **an ice-cream ~** dànjuǎn bīngqílín 蛋卷冰淇淋

confectioner tiánpǐn shāng 甜品商

confectioners' sugar tángfěn 糖粉

confectionery (candy) tiánshí 甜食

confederation tóngméng 同盟

confer 1 v/t (bestow) shòuyǔ 授予 **2** v/i (discuss) jiāohuàn yìjiàn 交换意见

conference tǎolùn huì 讨论会

conference room huìyì tīng 会议厅

confess 1 v/t sin, guilt chéngrèn 承认; crime tǎnbái 坦白; REL chànhuǐ 忏悔; **I ~ I don't know** wǒ chéngrèn wǒ bù zhīdào 我承认我不知道 **2** v/i chéngrèn 承认; (to priest) chànhuǐ 忏悔; (to police) tǎnbái 坦白; **~ to a weakness for X** chéngrèn xǐ'ài X 承认喜爱 X

confession gòngrèn 供认; (to police) rènzuì shū 认罪书; REL chànhuǐ 忏悔

confessional REL gàojiě shì 告解室

confessor REL gàojiě shénfù 告解神父

confide 1 v/t tùlù 吐露 **2** v/i: **~ in** ... (trust) xìnrèn ... 信任 ...

confidence (assurance) xìnxīn 信心; (trust, secret) xìnrèn 信任; **in ~** zuòwéi mìmì 作为秘密

confident (self-assured) zìxìn 自信; (convinced) kěndìng 肯定

confidential jīmì 机密

confine (imprison) jiānjìn 监禁; (restrict) júxiàn yú 局限于; **be ~d to one's bed** wòbìng zàichuáng 卧病在床

confined space xiázhǎi 狭窄

confinement (imprisonment) jiānjìn 监禁; MED fēnmiǎn 分娩

confirm v/t quèdìng 确定; theory, statement, fears zhèngshí 证实

confirmation zhèngmíng 证明; (of theory statement, fears) zhèngshí 证实

confirmed (*inveterate*) jiāndìng 坚定

confiscate mòshōu 没收

conflict **1** *n* (*disagreement*) zhēngyì 争议; (*clash*) chōngtū 冲突; (*war*) zhànzhēng 战争 **2** *v/i* (*clash*) chōngtū 冲突

conform zūnshǒu guīzhāng 遵守规章; (*of product*) fúhé 符合; ~ **to government standards** fúhé zhèngfǔ biāozhǔn 符合政府标准

conformist *n* shùncóng de rén 顺从的人

confront (*face*) miànduì 面对; (*tackle*) shǐ duìzhì 使对质

confrontation chōngtū 冲突

Confucianism Rújiā 儒家

Confucius Kǒngzǐ 孔子

confuse hùnxiáo 混淆; ~ **X with Y** bǎ X dāngchéng Y 把X当成Y

confused kùnhuò 困惑

confusing lìngrén hútú 令人糊涂

confusion (*muddle, chaos*) hùnxiáo 混淆

congeal (*of blood, fat*) nínggù 凝固

congenial (*pleasant*) lìngrén yúkuài 令人愉快; **a ~ host** hàokè de zhǔrén 好客的主人

congenital MED xiāntiān xìng 先天性

congested *roads* dǔsè 堵塞

congestion (*on roads*) dǔsè 堵塞; (*in chest*) chōngxuè 充血; **traffic ~** jiāotōng dǔsè 交通堵塞

congratulate zhùhè 祝贺

congratulations zhùhè 祝贺; ~ **on ...** zhùhè ... 祝贺 ...

congregate (*gather*) jùjí 聚集

congregation REL jiàotáng jíhuì 教堂集会

congress (*conference*) dàibiǎo dàhuì 代表大会; **Congress** (*of US*) Guóhuì 国会

Congressional Guóhuì 国会

Congressman Guóhuì yìyuán 国会议员

conifer zhēnyè shù 针叶树

conjecture *n* (*speculation*) cāicè 猜测

conjugate *v/t* GRAM lièjǔ cíxíng biànhuà 列举词形变化

conjunction GRAM liánjiē cí 连接词; **in ~ with** liántóng 连同

conjunctivitis jiémó yán 结膜炎

♦ conjure up (*produce*) biàn móshù bān biànchū 变魔术般变出; (*evoke*) lìngrén xiǎngqǐ 令人想起

conjurer, conjuror (*magician*) móshù shī 魔术师

conjuring tricks móshù 魔术

con man piànzi 骗子

connect (*join*) liánjiē 连接; TELEC jiētōng 接通; (*link*) yǒu guānxì 有关系; (*to power supply*) jiētōng diànlù 接通电路

connected **be well-~** duō guànxì hù 多关系户; **be ~ with ...** yǔ ... yǒu guānxì 与 ... 有关系

connecting flight ⇩ liányùn fēijī 联运飞机

connection (*in wiring*) liánjiē 连接; (*link, personal contact*) guānxì 关系; (*when traveling*) liányùn 联运; **in ~ with ...** yǔ ... yǒuguānxì 与 ... 有关系

connector COMPUT liánjiē qì 连接器

connoisseur hángjiā 行家

conquer zhēngfú 征服; *fig* (*fear etc*) zhànshèng 战胜

conqueror zhēngfú zhě 征服者

conquest (*of territory*) zhēngfú 征服

conscience liángxīn 良心; **a guilty ~** nèijiù 内疚; **it has been on my ~** wǒ yīzhí gǎndào nèijiù 我一直感到内疚

conscientious rènzhēn 认真

conscientious objector jù fú bīngyì zhě 拒服兵役者

conscious *adj* (*aware*) zìjué 自觉; (*deliberate*) yǒuyì 有意; MED qīngxǐng 清醒; **be ~ of ...** yìshí dào ... 意识到 ...

consciousness (*awareness*) yìshí 意识; MED zhījué 知觉; **lose/regain ~** shīqù/huīfù zhījué 失去/恢复知觉

consecutive liánxù 连续

consensus yīzhì yìjiàn 一致意见

consent 1 n zànxǔ 赞许 2 v/i tóngyì 同意

consequence (result) hòuguǒ 后果

consequently (therefore) suǒyǐ 所以

conservation (preservation) bǎohù 保护

conservationist n tíchàng fánghù zhě 提倡防护者

conservative adj (conventional), estimate bǎoshǒu 保守; clothes lǎoqì 老气

conservatory (for plants) nuǎnfáng 暖房; MUS yīnyuè xuéyuàn 音乐学院

conserve 1 n (jelly) guǒjiàng 果酱 2 v/t energy, strength bǎocún 保存

consider (regard) rènwéi 认为; (show regard for, think about) kǎolǜ 考虑; it is ~ed to be … zhòngsuǒ zhōuzhī … 众所周知 …

considerable xiāngdāng dà 相当大

considerably zài hěndà chéngdù shàng 在很大程度上

considerate tǐtiē 体贴

consideration (thought) kǎolǜ 考虑; (thoughtfulness, concern) guānxīn 关心; (factor) yào kǎolǜ de shì 要考虑的事; take X into ~ kǎolǜ X 考虑 X

consignment COM huòwù 货物

♦consist of bāokuò 包括

consistency (texture) niánchóu dù 黏稠度; (unchangingness) yīzhì xìng 一致性

consistent (unchanging) yīguàn 一贯

consolation ānwèi 安慰

console v/t ānwèi 安慰

consonant n GRAM fǔyīn 辅音

consortium hézǔ 合组

conspicuous xiǎnyǎn 显眼

conspiracy yīnmóu 阴谋

conspire mìmóu 密谋

constant (continuous) bùduàn 不断

consternation jīngkǒng 惊恐

constipated biànmì 便秘

constipation biànmì 便秘

constituent n (component) zǔfēn 组分

constitute (account for) zhàn 占; (represent) gòuchéng 构成

constitution POL xiànfǎ 宪法; (of person) tǐzhì 体质

constitutional adj POL xiànfǎ 宪法

constraint (restriction) xiànzhì 限制

construct v/t building etc jiànzào 建造

construction (of building etc) jiànzào 建造; (building, trade etc) jiànzhù 建筑; under ~ zài jiànzào zhōng 在建造中

construction industry jiànzhù yè 建筑业; construction site shīgōng gōngdì 施工工地; construction worker jiànzhù gōngrén 建筑工人

constructive yǒu jiànshè xìng 有建设性

consul lǐngshì 领事

consulate lǐngshì guǎn 领事馆

consult (seek the advice of) hé … shāngliàng 和 … 商量

consultancy (company) zīxún gōngsī 咨询公司; (advice) zīxún 咨询

consultant (adviser) gùwèn 顾问

consultation cuōshāng 磋商

consume (eat, drink) shíyòng 食用; (use) hàoyòng 耗用

consumer (purchaser) gùkè 顾客

consumer confidence gùkè xìnxīn 顾客信心; consumer goods xiāofèi pǐn 消费品; consumer society xiāofèi zhě shèhuì 消费者社会

consumption (of energy) xiāohào 消耗; (quantity used) xiāohào liàng 消耗量

contact 1 n (person) shóurén 熟人; (communication, physical) jiēchù 接触; keep in ~ with X yǔ X bǎochí liánluò 与 X 保持联络 2 v/t liánluò 联络

contact lens yǐnxíng yǎnjìng 隐形眼镜

contact number liánxì diànhuà 联

系电话

contagious chuánrǎn 传染; *fig*
mànyán 蔓延

contain *tears, laughter* kòngzhì 控
制; *it ~ed my camera* wǒde
zhàoxiàngjī zài lǐmiàn 我的照像
机在里面; **~ oneself** kòngzhì zìjǐ
控制自己

container (*recipient*) róngqì 容器;
COM ⇩ jízhuāng xiāng 集装箱

container ship ⇩ jízhuāng xiāng
chuán 集装箱船

contaminate wūrǎn 污染

contamination wūrǎn 污染

contemplate *v/t* (*look at*) zhùshì 注
视; (*think about*) sīkǎo 思考

contemporary **1** *adj* dāngdài 当代
2 *n* tóngdài rén 同代人; (*at
school*) tóngjiè 同届

contempt qīngmiè 轻蔑; *be beneath ~* bùzhí yīgù 不值一顾

contemptible bēiliè 卑劣

contemptuous biǎoshì qīngmiè 表
示轻蔑

contend: *~ for ...* jìngzhēng ... 竞
争...; *~ with ...* yìngfu ... 应付...

contender (*in sport, competition*)
jìngzhēng zhě 竞争者; (*against
champion*) zhēngduó zhě 争夺者;
POL jìngxuǎn rén 竞选人

content[1] *n* nèiróng 内容

content[2] **1** *adj* mǎnzú 满足 **2** *v/t*: **~
oneself with ...** mǎnzú yú ... 满足
于...

contented mǎnzú 满足

contention (*assertion*) lùndiǎn 论
点; *be in ~ for ...* zhēngduó ... 争
夺...

contentment mǎnzú 满足

contents (*of house, letter, bag etc*)
nèiróng 内容

contest[1] (*competition*) bǐsài 比赛;
(*struggle, for power*) zhēngduó 争
夺

contest[2] *v/t leadership etc* jìngzhēng
竞争; (*oppose*) duì ... tíchū zhìyí
对...提出质疑

contestant cānsài zhě 参赛者

context shàngxià wén 上下文;
look at X in ~ gēnjù jùtǐ huánjìng
lái kǎolǜ X 根据具体环境来考

虑 X; *look at X out of ~* tuōlí jùtǐ
huánjìng lái kǎolǜ X 脱离具体
环境来考虑 X

continent *n* dàlù 大陆

contingency bùcè shìjiàn 不测事
件

continual bùduàn 不断

continuation xùjí 续集

continue **1** *v/t* jìxù 继续; *to be ~d*
wèiwán dàixù 未完待续 **2** *v/i*
jìxù 继续

continuity liánguàn xìng 连贯性

continuous bùtíng 不停

contort *face, body* niǔqū 扭曲

contour lúnkuò 轮廓

contraception bìyùn 避孕

contraceptive *n* (*device*) bìyùn qì
避孕器; (*pill*) bìyùn yào 避孕药

contract[1] *n* hétóng 合同

contract[2] **1** *v/i* (*shrink*) shōusuō 收
缩 **2** *v/t illness* gǎnrǎn 感染

contractor chéngbāo rén 承包人

contractual hétóng 合同

contradict *statement* yǔ ... yǒu
máodùn 与...有矛盾; *person*
fǎnbó 反驳

contradiction máodùn 矛盾

contradictory *account* xiānghù
duìlì 相互对立

contraption F qíyì jīqì 奇异机器

contrary[1] **1** *adj* duìlì 对立; *~ to ...*
yǔ ... xiāngfǎn 与...相反 **2** *n*: *on
the ~* zhèng xiāngfǎn 正相反

contrary[2] (*perverse*) hào yǔ rén
zuòduì 好与人作对

contrast **1** *n* duìzhào 对照 **2** *v/t*
duìzhào 对照 **3** *v/i* xíngchéng
duìbǐ 形成对比

contrasting jiérán xiāngfǎn 截然
相反

contravene wéifǎn 违反

contribute **1** *v/i* (*with money,
material*) juānxiàn 捐献; (*with
time*) gòngxiàn 贡献; (*to magazine,
paper*) tóugǎo 投稿; (*to discussion*)
fābiǎo yìjiàn 发表意见; *~ to
(help to cause*) cùchéng 促成 **2** *v/t
money* juānxiàn 捐献; *time,
suggestion* gòngxiàn 贡献

contribution (*money*) juānxiàn 捐
献; (*to political party, debate, of*

time, effort) gòngxiàn 贡献; (*to magazine*) tóugǎo 投稿

contributor (*of money*) juānkuǎn rén 捐款人; (*to magazine*) tóugǎo rén 投稿人

contrive cémóu 策谋

control 1 *n* (*of country, emotion etc*) kòngzhì 控制; be in ~ of ... kòngzhì zhe ... 控制着...; bring X under ~ déyǐ kòngzhì X 得以控制 X; get out of ~ shīqù kòngzhì 失去控制; lose ~ of X shīqù kòngzhì X de nénglì 失去控制 X 的能力; lose ~ of oneself shīqù zìkòng 失去自控; the situation is under ~ yīqiè zhèngcháng 一切正常; circumstances beyond our ~ wǒmen wúfǎ kòngzhì de yīnsù 我们无法控制的因素; ~s (*of aircraft, vehicle*) cāozòng zhuāngzhì 操纵装置; (*restrictions*) guǎnzhì cuòshī 管制措施 2 *v/t* (*govern*) kòngzhì 控制; (*restrict*) xiànzhì 限制; (*regulate*) guǎnlǐ 管理; ~ oneself (*not get angry, emotional*) zìkòng 自控; (*not overeat etc*) kèzhì zìjǐ 克制自己

control center kòngzhì zhōngxīn 控制中心; control freak F kòngzhì kuáng 控制狂; control key COMPUT kòngzhìjiàn 控制键

controlled substance shòu guǎnzhì yàowù 受管制药物

controlling interest FIN kònggǔ quányì 控股权益

control panel kòngzhì pán 控制盘

control tower zhǐhuī diàodù tái 指挥调度台

controversial yǒu zhēngyì 有争议

controversy zhēnglùn 争论

convalesce yǎngbìng 养病

convalescence liáoyǎng qī 疗养期

convene *v/t* zhàojí 召集

convenience (*of having sth, location*) fāngbiàn 方便; (*of arrangement, time*) shìyí 适宜; at your/my ~ zài nǐ/wǒ fāngbiàn de

shíhou zài nǐ/wǒ fāngbiàn de shíhou 在你/我方便的时候; all (*modern*) ~s suǒyǒu xiàndàihuà shèbèi 所有现代化设备

convenience food fāngbiàn shípǐn 方便食品

convenience store fāngbiàn xiǎo shāngdiàn 方便小商店

convenient location, device fāngbiàn 方便; time, arrangement héshì 合适

convent nǚ xiūdào yuàn 女修道院

convention (*tradition*) shèhuì xísú 社会习俗; (*conference*) dàhuì 大会

conventional person, ideas, method píngcháng 平常

convention center huìyì zhōngxīn 会议中心

conventioneer yǔhuì zhě 与会者

conversant: be ~ with ... shúxī ... 熟悉...

conversation jiāotán 交谈

conversational kǒuyǔ 口语

converse *n* (*opposite*) xiāngfǎn 相反

conversely lìngyī fāngmiàn 另一方面

conversion (*of figures, money*) zhésuàn 折算

conversion table huànsuàn biǎo 换算表

convert 1 *n* guīfù zhě 归附者 2 *v/t* house, room etc gǎijiàn 改建; unit of measurement zhéhé 折合; energy zhuǎnhuà 转化; person gǎibiàn xìnyǎng 改变信仰

convertible *n* (*car*) zhépéng chē 折蓬车

convey (*transmit*) chuándì 传递; (*give*) biǎoshì 表示; (*express*) biǎodá 表达; (*carry*) shūsòng 输送

conveyor belt chuánsòng dài 传送带

convict 1 *n* qiúfàn 囚犯 2 *v/t* LAW xuānpàn yǒuzuì 宣判有罪; ~ X of Y yǐ Y zuìxíng xuānpàn X 以 Y 罪行宣判 X

conviction LAW dìngzuì 定罪;

convince

(belief) quèxìn 确信

convince (persuade) shuōfú 说服; **I'm ~d that ...** wǒ kěndìng ... 我肯定 ...

convincing lìngrén xìnfú 令人信服

convivial (friendly) huānlè 欢乐

convoy (of ships) chuánduì 船队; (of vehicles) chēduì 车队

convulsion MED chōuchù 抽搐

cook 1 n chúshī 厨师 **2** v/t zuò 做; (roast, bake) kǎo 烤; (steam) zhēng 蒸; (stir fry) chǎo 炒 **a ~ed meal** xiànzuòde fàn 现做的饭 **3** v/i (of person) zuòfàn 做饭; (roast, bake) kǎo 烤; (steam) zhēng 蒸; (stir fry) chǎo 炒

cookbook pēngrèn shū 烹饪书

cookery pēngtiáo 烹调

cookie qǔqí 曲奇

cooking (food) fàncài 饭菜

cool 1 n: **keep one's ~** F bǎochí lěngjìng 保持冷静; **lose one's ~** F shīqù kòngzhì 失去控制 **2** adj weather, breeze liángshuǎng 凉爽; drink liáng 凉; (calm) lěngjìng 冷静; (unfriendly) lěngmò 冷漠; F (great) kù酷 **3** v/i (of food) tānliáng 摊凉; (of tempers) píngxī 平息; (of interest) shīqù rèqíng 失去热情 **4** v/t: **~ it** F lěngjìng xiàlái 冷静下来

♦**cool down** v/i (of food, stove) tānliáng 摊凉; (of weather) liángkuài qǐlái 凉快起来; (of person) liángkuài 凉快; fig (of tempers) píngxī 平息 ◆ v/t food shǐ biànliáng 使变凉; fig shǐ píngxī 使平息

cooperate hézuò 合作

cooperation hézuò 合作

cooperative 1 n COM hézuò shè 合作社 **2** adj COM hézuò 合作; (helpful) lèyì pèihé 乐意配合

coordinate activities xiétiáo 协调

coordination (of activities, body) xiétiáo 协调

cop F tiáozi 条子

cope yìngfu 应付; **~ with ...** yìngfu ... 应付 ...

copier (machine) fùyìn jī 复印机

copilot fù jiàshǐ yuán 副驾驶员

copious notes hěnduō 很多; amount of food fēngshèng 丰盛

copper n (metal) tóng 铜

copy 1 n (imitation) fùzhì pǐn 复制品; (duplicate) fùběn 副本; (photocopy) fùyìn jiàn 复印件; (of book) běn 本; (of record, CD) pán盘; (written material) gǎozi 稿子; **make a ~ of a file** COMPUT fùzhì yīfèn dǎng'àn 复制一份档案 **2** v/t (imitate) fǎngzào 仿造; (duplicate) fùxiě 复写; (photocopy) fùyìn 复印; COMPUT: file fùzhì 复制; (in writing) chāoxiě 抄写; (in order to cheat) chāoxí 抄袭; **~ a key** pèi yàoshi 配钥匙

copy cat F fǎngxiào zhě 仿效者; **copycat crime** fǎngzhì fànzuì 仿制犯罪; **copyright** n bǎnquán 版权; **copy-writer** (in advertising) guǎngào wénzì zhuàngǎo rén 广告文字撰稿人

coral shānhú 珊瑚

cord (string) shéng 绳; (cable) xiàn 线

cordial adj rèqíng 热情

cordless phone wúxiàn diànhuà 无线电话

cordon jǐngjiè xiàn 警戒线

♦**cordon off** fēngsuǒ 封锁

cords (pants) dēngxīnróng kù dēngxīnróng kù灯芯绒裤

corduroy dēngxīnróng 灯芯绒

core 1 n (of fruit) xīnr 心儿; (of problem) yàodiǎn 要点; (of organization, party) héxīn 核心 **2** v/t fruit wāxīn 挖心 **3** adj issue, meaning zuì zhòngyào 最重要

cork (in bottle) píngsāi 瓶塞; (material) ruǎnmù 软木

corkscrew ⇩ luósī qǐzi 螺丝起子

corn yùmǐ 玉米

corner 1 n (of page) jiǎo 角; (of room) jiǎoluò 角落; (of table) zhuōjiǎo 桌角; (of street) jiējiǎo 街角; (bend: on road) zhuǎnwān 转弯; (in soccer) jiǎoqiú 角球; **in the ~** zài jiǎoluò lǐ 在角落里; **on**

the ~ (of street) zài jiējiǎo 在街角 2 v/t person shǐ zǒutóu wúlù使走投无路; ~ the market lǒngduàn shìchǎng 垄断市场 3 v/i (of driver, car) guǎiwānr 拐弯儿

corner kick (in soccer) jiǎoqiú 角球

cornstarch diànfěn 淀粉

corny F joke sútào 俗套; F gesture duōchóu shàngǎn 多愁善感

coronary 1 adj guànzhuàng dòngmài 冠状动脉 2 n (coronary thrombosis) guànzhuàng dòngmài xuèshuān 冠状动脉血栓; (heart attack) guànxīnbìng 冠心病

coroner yànshī guān 验尸官

corporal n xiàshì 下士

corporal punishment tǐfá 体罚

corporate COM jítuán 集团; ~ image gōngsī xíngxiàng 公司形象; sense of ~ loyalty gōngsī guāngróng gǎn 公司光荣感

corporation (business) gǔfèn yǒuxiàn gōngsī 股份有限公司

corps bùduì 部队

corpse sīshī 死尸

corpulent féipàng 肥胖

corpuscle xuèqiú 血球

corral n chùlán 畜栏

correct 1 adj zhèngquè 正确 2 v/t jiūzhèng 纠正; proofs, homework xiūgǎi 修改

correction xiūgǎi 修改

correspond (match) xiāngfú 相符; (write letters) tōngxìn 通信; ~ to ... děngyú ... 等于 ...; ~ with ... (match) fúhé ... 符合 ...

correspondence (matching) yī zhìxìng 一致性; (letters) xìnjiàn 信件; (exchange of letters) tōngxìn liánluò 通信联络

correspondent (letter writer) tōngxìn zhě 通信者; (reporter) tōngxùn yuán 通讯员

corresponding (equivalent) duìděng 对等

corridor (in building) zǒuláng 走廊

corroborate zhèngshí 证实

corrode v/t & v/i fǔshí 腐蚀

corrosion fǔshí 腐蚀

corrugated cardboard wǎléng zhǐbǎn 瓦楞纸板

corrugated iron wǎléng tiě 瓦楞铁

corrupt 1 adj fǔbài 腐败; COMPUT pòhuài 破坏 2 v/t shǐ duòluò 使堕落; (bribe) huìlù 贿赂

corruption shòuhuì 受贿

cosmetic adj měiróng 美容; fig zhuāngshì xìng 装饰性

cosmetics huàzhuāng pǐn 化妆品

cosmetic surgeon zhěngróng wàikē yīshēng 整容外科医生

cosmetic surgery zhěngróng wàikē 整容外科

cosmonaut yǔháng yuán 宇航员

cosmopolitan city shìjiè xìng 世界性

cost 1 n (price) jiàgé 价格; (in finance) chéngběn 成本; fig dàijià 代价; ~s COM fèiyòng 费用 2 v/t $50 etc xūyào 需要; time shí sàngshī 使丧失; FIN: project gūjià 估价; how much does it ~? duōshao qián? 多少钱？; it ~ them $500 tāmen huāle wǔbǎi měijīn 他们花了五百美金; it ~ me my health wǒde jiànkāng yīncǐ ér shòusǔn 我的健康因此而受损

cost and freight COM huòjià jiā yùnjià 货价加运价; cost-conscious jiéyuē 节约; cost-effective huásuàn 划算; cost, insurance and freight COM huòjià, bǎoxiǎn jiā yùnjià 货价，保险加运价

costly mistake dàijià cǎnzhòng 代价惨重

cost of living shēnghuó fèiyòng 生活费用

cost price chéngběn jiàgé 成本价格

costume (for actor) xìzhuāng 戏装

costume jewelry jiǎ zhūbǎo 假珠宝

cot (camp-bed) xíngjūn chuáng 行军床

cottage cūnshè 村舍

cottage cheese nóngjiā xiān gānlào 农家鲜干酪

cotton 1 n miánhua 棉花 2 adj

miánbù 棉布

♦ **cotton on** F míngbái 明白

♦ **cotton on to** F duì … chǎnshēng hǎogǎn 对 … 产生好感

♦ **cotton to** F xǐhuān 喜欢

cotton candy miánhuā táng 棉花糖

couch n cháng shāfā 长沙发

couch potato pào diànshì de rén 泡电视的人

couchette zuòwò liǎngyòng chuáng 坐卧两用床

cough n & v/i késou 咳嗽

♦ **cough up** 1 v/t blood etc ké 咳; F money tāochū 掏出 2 v/i F (pay) tāoqián 掏钱

cough medicine, cough syrup zhǐké tángjiāng 止咳糖浆

could: ~ I have my key? kěyǐ gěiwǒ yàoshi ma? 可以给我钥匙吗？; ~ you help me? láojià bāngbang máng 劳驾帮帮忙; this ~ be the our bus yěxǔ shì wǒmén de gōnggòng qìchē 也许是我们的公共汽车; you ~ be right méizhǔn nǐshì duìde 没准儿你是对的; I ~n't say for sure wǒ bùnéng kěndìng 我不能肯定; he ~ have got lost tā kěnéng mílù le tā 他可能迷路了; you ~ have warned me! zǎo bù shuō! 早不说！

council (assembly) yìhuì 议会; (authority) zhèngfǔ 政府

councilman zhèngwùhuì wěiyuán 政务会委员

councilor zhèngwùhuì wěiyuán 政务会委员

counsel 1 n (advice) quàngào 劝告; (lawyer) lǜshī 律师 2 v/t course of action tíyì 提议; person fǔdǎo 辅导

counseling fǔdǎo 辅导

counselor (adviser) fǔdǎo yuán 辅导员; LAW lǜshī 律师

count 1 n (number arrived at) zǒngshù 总数; (action of ~ing) shùshù 数数; (in baseball, boxing) huījī cìshù 挥击次数; keep ~ of … shù … de quèqiè shùmù 数 … 的确切数目; lose ~ of …

shǔbùqīng … 数不清 …; at the last ~ zuìhòu yīcì shǔde shíhòu 最后一次数的时候 2 v/i (to ten etc) shǔ 数; (calculate) jìsuàn 计算; (be important) yǒu zhòngyào yìyì 有重要意义; (qualify) suàn 算 3 v/t (~ up) shǔ 数; (calculate) jìsuàn 计算; (include) bāokuò 包括

♦ **count on** yīkào 依靠

countdown dào shùshù 倒数数

countenance v/t zànchéng 赞成

counter[1] (in store, café) guìtái 柜台; (in game) chóumǎ 筹码

counter[2] 1 v/t fǎnjī 反击 2 v/i (retaliate) fǎnbó 反驳

counter[3]: **run ~ to …** yǔ … bùxiāng fúhé 与 … 不相符合

counteract v/t zhōnghé 中和

counter-attack 1 n fǎnjī 反击 2 v/i jìnxíng fǎnjī 进行反击

counterbalance pínghéng lì 平衡力; **counterclockwise** nì shízhēn 逆时针; **counterespionage** fǎn jiàndié huódòng 反间谍活动

counterfeit v/t & adj wěizào 伪造

counterpart (person) duìfāng 对方

counterproductive qǐ fǎn zuòyòng 起反作用

countersign v/t huìqiān 会签

countless shǔbù jìn 数不尽

country (nation) guójiā 国家; (as opposed to town) xiāngxià 乡下; in the ~ zài xiāngxià 在乡下

country and western MUS xiāngcūn yǔ xībù yīnyuè 乡村与西部音乐; **countryman** (fellow ~) tóngbāo 同胞; **countryside** nóngcūn 农村

county (in US & China) xiàn 县

coup POL zhèngbiàn 政变; fig piàoliàng de yìjǔ 漂亮的一举

couple (married) fūqī 夫妻; (man & woman) qínglǚ 情侣; (two people) yīduì 一对; just a ~ zhǐyǒu jǐge 只有几个; a ~ of (people) jǐge 几个; a ~ of days jītiān 几天; a ~ of matters jǐjiàn shì 几件事; a ~ of tickets jǐzhāng piào 几张票

coupon (form) suǒqǔ dān 索取

单; (voucher) zèngquàn 赠券

courage yǒngqì 勇气

courageous yǒnggǎn 勇敢

courier (messenger) xìnshǐ 信使; (with tourist party) dǎoyóu 导游

course n (series of lessons) kèchéng 课程; (part of meal) dàocài 道菜; (of ship, plane) hángxiàng 航向; (for horse race, golf) chǎng场; (for cross-country running, skiing) dào 道; (= certainly) dāngrán 当然; (naturally) zìrán 自然; **of ~ not** dāngrán bù 当然不; **~ of action** cǎiqǔ de xíngdòng 采取的行动; **~ of treatment** liáochéng 疗程; **in the ~ of ...** zài ... qījiān 在 ... 期间

court n LAW fǎtíng 法庭; (courthouse) fǎyuàn 法院; SP chǎng 场; **take X to ~** hé X dǎ guānsī 和X打官司

court case fǎtíng ànjiàn 法庭案件

courteous yǒu lǐmào 有礼貌

courtesy lǐmào 礼貌

courthouse fǎyuàn 法院; **court martial** 1 n jūnshì fǎtíng 军事法庭 2 v/t yǐ jūnfǎ shěnpàn 以军法审判; **court order** fǎtíng zhīlìng 法庭指令; **courtroom** shěnpàn shì 审判室; **courtyard** yuànzi 院子

cousin (older male on father's side) tángxiōng 堂兄; (younger male on father's side) tángdì 堂弟; (older female on father's side) tángjiě 堂姐; (younger female on father's side) tángmèi 堂妹; (older male on mother's side) biǎoxiōng 表兄; (younger male on mother's side) biǎodì 表弟; (older female on mother's side) biǎojiě 表姐; (younger female on mother's side) biǎomèi 表妹

cove (small bay) xiǎo hǎiwān 小海湾

cover 1 n (protective) zhào zhào 罩; (of book, magazine) fēngmiàn 封面; (for bed) bèizi 被子; (shelter) yǎnbì 掩蔽; (insurance) bǎoxiǎn 保险; **take ~ from the rain** bìyǔ 蔽雨 2 v/t fùgài 覆盖; (hide)

yǎngài 掩盖; (of insurance policy) bǎoxiǎn 保险; distance xíngshǐ 行驶; (of journalist) bàodào 报道; **with his hands ~ed in ...** mǎnshǒu dōushì ... 满手都是 ...

♦**cover up 1** v/t gàizhù 盖住; fig yǎngài 掩盖 2 v/i fig yǐnmán 隐瞒; **~ for X** tì X yǎnshì cuòwù 替X掩饰错误缺点

coverage (by media) bàodào 报道

covering letter fùxìn 附信

covert mìmì 秘密

coverup (concealment) yǎnshì 掩饰

cow n mǔniú 母牛

coward dǎnxiǎo guǐ 胆小鬼

cowardice dǎnxiǎo 胆小

cowardly dǎnxiǎo 胆小

cowboy niúzǎi 牛仔

cower quánsuō 蜷缩

coy (evasive) hánhu qící 含糊其辞; (flirtatiously) xiū dáda 羞答答

cozy shūshì 舒适

CPU (= central processing unit) zhōngyāng chǔlǐ jī 中央处理机

crab n pángxiè 螃蟹

crack 1 n lièfèng 裂缝; (joke) xiàohua 笑话 2 v/t cup, glass shǐ chǎnshēng lièfèng 使产生裂缝; nut zá 砸; code pòyì 破译; F (solve) zhēnpò 侦破; **~ a joke** shuō xiàohuà 说笑话 3 v/i liè 裂; **get ~ing** kāishǐ gàn 开始干

♦**crack down on** zhìcái 制裁

♦**crack up** (have breakdown) kuǎdiào 垮掉; F (laugh) pěngfù dàxiào 捧腹大笑

crackbrained yúchǔn 愚蠢

crackdown zhìcái 制裁

cracked cup, glass pòliè 破裂; F (crazy) fēngkuáng 疯狂

cracker (to eat) bócuì bǐnggān 薄脆饼干

crackle v/i (of fire) huālā 哗啦

cradle n (for baby) yáolán 摇篮

craft[1] NAUT chuán 船

craft[2] (skill) gōngyì 工艺; (trade) zhíyè 职业

craftsman shǒuyì rén 手艺人

crafty jiǎohuá 狡猾

crag (rocky) xiǎnyá 险崖

cram v/t sāi 塞

cramped *room, apartment* zhǎixiǎo 窄小

cramps chōujīn 抽筋

cranberry yuèjú 越橘

crane 1 *n* (*machine*) qǐzhòng jī 起重机 2 *v/t:* ~ **one's neck** shēncháng bózi 伸长脖子

crank *n* (*strange person*) guàirén 怪人

crankshaft qūzhóu 曲轴

cranky (*bad-tempered*) bàozào 暴躁

crap F shǐ 屎; (*bad quality goods*) pòlàn 破烂; (*nonsense*) húshuō 胡说

crash 1 *n* (*noise*) huālā shēng 哗啦声; (*of thunder*) pīlì pīléi 霹雳霹雷; (*accident*), COMPUT shìgù 事故; (*plane* ~) fēijī shīshì 飞机失事; COM dǎobì 倒闭 2 *v/i* (*of wave*) huālā yìshēng jī 哗啦一声击; (*of vase*) pādī yīshēng diào 啪地一声掉; (*of thunder*) tūrán fāchū jùxiǎng 突然发出巨响; (*of car*) zhuàng 撞; (*of airplane*) zhuìhuǐ 坠毁; (COM: *of market*) bàodiē bàodiē 暴跌; COMPUT chū shìgù 出事故; F (*sleep*) guòyè 过夜 3 *v/t car* zhuànghuǐ 撞毁

♦ **crash out** F (*fall asleep*) shuìzháo 睡着

crash course sùchéng kè 速成课

crash diet kuàisù jiǎnféi 快速减肥; **crash helmet** fángzhuàng tóukuī 防撞头盔; **crash landing** shuāijī zháolù 摔机着陆

crate (*packing case*) xiāngzi 箱子

crater (*of volcano*) huǒshān kǒu 火山口

crave kěwàng 渴望

craving kěwàng 渴望; **a ~ for ...** fēicháng xiǎngyào ... 非常想要 ...

crawl 1 *n* (*in swimming*) zìyóuyǒng 自由泳; **at a ~** (*very slowly*) fēicháng huǎnmàn 非常缓慢 2 *v/i* (*on floor*) pá 爬; (*move slowly*) huǎnmàn xíngjìn 缓慢行进

♦ **crawl with** jǐmǎn 挤满

crayon làbǐ 蜡笔

craze kuángrè 狂热; **the latest ~** zuì shímáo de kuángrè 最时髦的狂热

crazy *adj* fāfēng 发疯; **be ~ about ...** duì ... zháomí 对 ... 着迷

creak 1 *n* zhīgā zhīgā shēng 吱嘎吱嘎声 2 *v/i* zhīgā zhīgā zuòxiǎng 吱嘎吱嘎作响

cream 1 *n* (*for skin, coffee, cake*) rǔshuāng 乳霜; (*color*) mǐsè 米色 2 *adj* (*color*) mǐsè 米色

cream cheese nǎiyóu gānlào 奶油干酪

creamer (*jug*) nǎizhōng 奶盅; (*for coffee*) nǎifěn 奶粉

creamy (*with lots of cream*) duō nǎiyóu 多奶油

crease 1 *n* (*accidental*) zhòuwén 皱纹; (*deliberate*) kùxiàn 裤线 2 *v/t* (*accidentally*) nòngzhòu 弄皱

create 1 *v/t* (*make*) chuàngzào 创造; (*lead to*) yǐnqǐ 引起 2 *v/i* (*be creative*) chuàngxīn 创新

creation chuàngzào 创造; REL chuàngzào tiāndì 创造天地; (*something created*) chuàngzàode zuòpǐn 创造的作品

creative yǒu chuàngzào nénglì 有创造能力

creator chuàngzào zhě 创造者; (*author*) zuòzhě 作者; (*founder*) fāqǐ rén 发起人; **the Creator** REL Zàowù zhǔ 造物主

creature (*animal*) dòngwù 动物; (*person*) rén 人

credibility (*of person*) xìnyù 信誉; (*of story*) kěxìn xìng 可信性

credible (*believable*) kě xiāngxìn 可相信; *candidate etc* kě xìnrèn 可信任

credit 1 *n* FIN shēqiàn 赊欠; (*use of ~ cards*) xìnyòng 信用; (*honor*) zànyáng 赞扬; (*payment received*) dàifāng dàifāng 贷方; **be in ~** yǒu yú'é 有余额; **get the ~ for X** yóuyú X dédào zànyáng 由于 X 得到赞扬 2 *v/t* (*believe*) xiāngxìn 相信; **~ an amount to an account** cúnrù zhànghù 存入帐户

creditable zhíde zànyáng 值得赞扬

credit card xìnyòng kǎ 信用卡

credit limit (*of credit card*) xìndài xiàn'é 信贷限额

creditor zhàizhǔ 债主

creditworthy xìnyù zhuózhù 信誉卓著

credulous qīngxìn 轻信

creed (*beliefs*) xìntiáo 信条

creek (*stream*) xiǎohé 小河

creep 1 *n pej* tǎoyàn guǐ 讨厌鬼 **2** *v/i* nièshǒu nièjiǎo de zǒu 蹑手蹑脚地走

creeper BOT púfú zhíwù 匍匐植物

creeps: the house / he gives me the ~ zhè fángzi / tā shǐwǒ húnshēn qǐ jīpí gēda 这房子 / 他使我浑身起鸡皮疙瘩

creepy lìngrén máogǔ sǒngrán 令人毛骨悚然

cremate huǒhuà 火化

cremation huǒhuà 火化

crematorium huǒhuà chǎng 火化场

crescent *n* (*shape*) yuèyá xíng 月牙形

crest (*of hill*) dǐng 顶; (*of bird*) ròuguàn 肉冠

crestfallen jǔsàng 沮丧

crevice lièfèng 裂缝

crew *n* (*of ship, airplane*) quántǐ gōngzuò rényuán 全体工作人员; (*of repairmen etc*) zǔ 组; (*crowd, group*) yīhuǒ rén 一伙人

crew cut píngtóu 平头

crew neck shuǐshǒu lǐng 水手领

crib *n* (*for baby*) xiǎohái chuáng 小孩床

crick: ~ in the neck jǐngbù tòngxìng jìngluán 颈部痛性痉挛

cricket (*insect*) xīshuài 蟋蟀

crime (*offence*) zuìxíng 罪行; (*shameful act*) lìngrén yíhàn de shì 令人遗憾的事; **the ~ rate** fànzuì lǜ 犯罪率

criminal 1 *n* zuìfàn 罪犯 **2** *adj* xíngshì 刑事; (*shameful*) lìngrén yíhàn 令人遗憾

crimson *adj* shēnhóng sè 深红色

cringe xiàde wànghòu suō 吓得往后缩

cripple 1 *n* (*disabled person*) cánjí rénshì 残疾人士 **2** *v/t person* shòushāng zhì cán 受伤至残; *fig* shǐ xiànyú tānhuàn 使陷于瘫痪

crisis wēijī 危机

crisp *adj weather, air* liángshuǎng 凉爽; *lettuce, apple* xīnxiān ér cuìshēng 新鲜而脆生; *bacon, toast* cuì 脆; *new shirt, bills* tǐngkuò 挺括

criterion (*standard*) biāozhǔn 标准

critic pínglùn jiā 评论家

critical (*making criticisms*) tiāocì 挑刺儿; (*serious*) wēijī 危急; *moment etc* jǐnyào 紧要; MED yánzhòng 严重

critically *speak etc* yǒu pīpíng xìng 有批评性; **~ ill** bìngde hěn yánzhòng 病得很严重

criticism pīpíng 批评

criticize *v/t* pīpíng 批评

croak 1 *n* (*of frog*) guāguā jiàoshēng 呱呱叫声; (*of person*) dīyǎ de shuōhuà shēng 低哑的说话声 **2** *v/i* (*of frog*) guāguā jiào 呱呱叫; (*of person*) dīyǎ di shuōhuà 低哑地说话

crockery táoqì 陶器

crocodile èyú 鳄鱼

crony F mìyǒu 密友

crook *n* (*dishonest*) piànzi 骗子

crooked (*not straight*) wānqū 弯曲; (*dishonest*) bù lǎoshí 不老实

crop 1 *n* shōucheng 收成; *fig* pī批; **~s** zhuāngjia 庄稼 **2** *v/t hair, photo* xiūjiǎn 修剪

♦**crop up** (*be mentioned*) tídào 提到; (*happen unexpectedly*) yìwài de fāshēng 意外地发生

cross 1 *adj* (*angry*) shēngqì 生气 **2** *n* (*X*) chāzi 叉子; (*Christian symbol*) shízìjià 十字架 **3** *v/t* (*go across*) chuānguò 穿过; **~ oneself** REL yòng shǒu huà shízì 用手画十子; **~ one's legs** jiāochā shuāngtuǐ 交叉双腿; **keep one's fingers ~ed** qíqiú zǒuyùn 祈求走运; **it never ~ed my mind** wǒ gēnběn jiù méiyǒu xiǎng 我根本就没有想 **4** *v/i* (*go across the road*) guò mǎlù 过马路; (*of lines*) jiāochā 交叉

♦cross off, cross out qǔxiāo 取消

crossbar (of goal) héngmù 横木; (of bicycle) chējià héngliáng 车架横梁; (in high jump) hénggān 横杆

cross-country (skiing) yuèyě (huáxuě) 越野(滑雪)

crossed check huàxiàn zhīpiào 划线支票

cross-examine LAW fǎn jiéwèn 反诘问

cross-eyed nèi xiéshì 内斜视

crossing NAUT héngdù héngjiě

crossroads shízì lùkǒu 十字路口; cross-section (of people) jùyǒu dàibiǎo xìng de gèsè rénwù 具有代表性的各色人物; crosswalk ⇩ rénxíng héngdào 人行横道; crossword (puzzle) zònghéng tiánzì mí 纵横填字迷

crouch v/i dūn 蹲

crow n (bird) wūyā 乌鸦; as the ~ flies yán zhíxiàn 沿直线

crowd n rénqún 人群; (at sports event) guānzhòng 观众

crowded yōngjǐ 拥挤

crown 1 n (on tooth) chǐguān 齿冠 2 v/t tooth xiāng chǐguān 镶齿冠

crucial guānjiàn 关键

crude 1 adj (vulgar) cūlǔ 粗鲁; (unsophisticated) jiǎnlòu 简陋 2 n: ◊ (oil) yuányóu 原油

cruel cánrěn 残忍

cruelty cánrěn 残忍

cruise 1 n hángxíng 航行 2 v/i (in ship) hángxíng 航行; (of car) huǎnmàn xúnxíng 缓慢巡行; (of plane) yǐ jīngjì xúnxíng sùdù fēixíng 以经济巡行速度飞行

cruise liner dàxíng yóutǐng 大型游艇

cruising speed jūnsù 均速

crumb zhāzi 渣子

crumble 1 v/t nòngsuì 弄碎 2 v/i (of bread, stonework) suìluò 碎裂; fig (of opposition etc) bēngkuì 崩溃

crumple 1 v/t (crease) nòngzhòu 弄皱 2 v/i (collapse) dǎoxià 倒下

crunch 1 n: when it comes to the ~ F dāng guānjiàn shíkè dàolái shí 当关键时刻到来时 2 v/i (of snow, gravel) gāzhī zuòshēng 嘎吱作声

crusade n fig yùndòng 运动

crush 1 n (crowd) yōngjǐ de rénqún 拥挤的人群; have a ~ on rèliàn 热恋 2 v/t yā 压; (crease) nòngzhòu 弄皱; they were ~ed to death tāmén bèi yā sǐle 他们被压死了 3 v/i (crease) zhòu 皱

crust (on bread) miànbāo pí 面包皮

crutch (for injured person) T zì xíng guǎizhàng T字形拐杖

cry 1 n (call) hǎnjiào 喊叫; have a ~ kū yīchǎng 哭一场 2 v/t (call) hǎnjiào 喊叫 3 v/i (weep) kū 哭

♦cry out 1 v/t dàshēng shuōchū 大声说出 2 v/i hǎnjiào 喊叫

♦cry out for (need) pòqiè xūyào 迫切需要

crystal (mineral) shuǐjīng 水晶; (glass) jīngzhì bōlí 晶质玻璃

crystallize 1 v/t jiéjīng 结晶 2 v/i (of thoughts etc) jiéjīng 结晶

CTS (= China Travel Service) Zhōngguó Lǚxíngshè 中国旅行社

cub yòushòu 幼兽

Cuba Gǔbā 古巴

Cuban 1 adj Gǔbā 古巴 2 n Gǔbā rén 古巴人

cube (shape) lìfāng xíng 立方形

cubic lìfāng 立方

cubic capacity TECH róngjī liàng 容积量

cubicle (changing room) gēngyī shì 更衣室

cucumber huángguā 黄瓜

cuddle n & v/t yōngbào 拥抱

cuddly kitten etc dòurén lián'ài 逗人怜爱; (liking cuddles) xǐhuān lǒulou bàobào 喜欢搂搂抱抱

cue n (for actor etc) tíshì 提示; (for pool) qiúgān 球杆

cuff 1 n (of shirt) xiùkǒu 袖口; (of pants) kùjiǎo fānbiān 裤角翻边; (blow) zhǎngjī 掌击; off the ~ wèijīng zhǔnbèi 未经准备 2 v/t *(hit)* zhǎngjī 掌击

cuff link xiùkòu liànkòu 袖口链扣

culinary pēngtiáo 烹调

culminate: ~ in ... yǐ ... gàozhōng 以 ... 告终

culmination dǐngdiǎn 顶点

culprit zuìfàn 罪犯

cult *(sect)* zōngpài 宗派

cultivate *land* gēngzuò 耕作; *person* péiyǎng 培养

cultivated *person* yǒu xiūyǎng 有修养

cultivation *(of land)* gēngzuò 耕作

cultural *(relating to the arts)* yǒu xiūyǎng 有修养; *(relating a country's identity)* wénhuà 文化

Cultural Revolution Wénhuà Dàgémìng 文化大革命

culture *n (artistic)* wénmíng 文明; *(of a country)* wénhuà 文化

cultured *(cultivated)* yǒu xiūyǎng 有修养

culture shock wénhuà chōngjī 文化冲击

cumbersome léizhuì 累赘

cunning *n & adj* jiǎohuá 狡猾

cup *n* bēi 杯; *(trophy)* bēi 杯; *a ~ of tea* yìbēi chá 一杯茶

cupboard guìzi 柜子

curable kěyī 可医

curator guǎnzhǎng 馆长

curb **1** *n (of street)* lùyuán 路缘; *(on powers etc)* yuēshù 约束 **2** *v/t* kòngzhì 控制

curdle *v/i (of milk)* níngjié 凝结

cure **1** *n* MED liáofǎ 疗法 **2** *v/t* MED zhìhǎo 治好; *meat, fish* yān 腌

curfew xiāojìn lìng 宵禁令

curiosity *(inquisitiveness)* hàoqí xīn 好奇心

curious *(inquisitive)* hàoqí 好奇; *(strange)* qítè 奇特

curiously *(inquisitively)* hàoqí 好奇; *(strangely)* qíguài 奇怪; *~ enough* qíguàide shì qíguàide 奇怪的是

curl **1** *n (in hair)* quánfà 鬈发; *~ of smoke* yānquānr 烟圈儿 **2** *v/t hair* juǎn 卷; *(wind)* chánrào 缠绕 **3** *v/i (of hair)* juǎn 卷; *(of leaf, paper etc)* quánqū 蜷曲

◆**curl up** quánqū 蜷曲

curly *tail* quánqū 蜷曲; *~ hair* quánfà 鬈发

currant *(dried fruit)* xiǎo pútáo gān 小葡萄干

currency *(money)* huòbì 货币; *foreign ~* wàihuì 外汇

current **1** *n (in sea)* jīliú 激流; ELEC diànliú 电流; *(of opinions etc)* qīngxiàng 倾向 **2** *adj (present)* mùqián 目前

current affairs, current events shíshì 时事

current affairs program shíshì tǎolùn jiémù 时事讨论节目

currently mùqián 目前

curriculum kèchéng 课程

curse **1** *n (spell)* zǔzhòu 诅咒; *(swearword)* zǔzhòu 诅咒; *(swear at)* zhòumà 咒骂 **3** *v/i (swear)* màrén 骂人

cursor COMPUT ⇩ guāngbiāo 光标

cursory cūlüè 粗略

curt tángtū cǎoshuài 唐突草率

curtail jiéduǎn 截短

curtain chuānglián 窗帘; THEA wéimù 帷幕

curve **1** *n* qūxiàn 曲线 **2** *v/i (bend)* wānqū 弯曲

cushion **1** *n (for couch etc)* kàodiàn 靠垫 **2** *v/t blow, fall* huǎnhé ... de chōngjī 缓和 ... 的冲击

custard dànnǎi hù dàn nǎi hù 蛋奶糊

custody *(of children)* fúyǎng quán 扶养权; *in ~* LAW bèi jūliú 被拘留

custom *(tradition)* xíguàn 习惯; COM huìgù 惠顾; *as was his ~* àn tā píngcháng xíguàn 按他平常习惯

customary chángguī 常规; *it is ~ to ...* chángguī shàng ... 常规上 ...

customer gùkè 顾客

customer relations gùkè guānxi 顾客关系

customs hǎiguān 海关

customs clearance tōngguān 通关; **customs inspection** yànguān 验关; **customs officer** hǎiguān guānyuán 海关官员

cut 1 n (with knife, scissors) qiēkŏu 切口; (injury) shāngkŏu 伤口; (of garment, hair) kuǎnshì 款式; (reduction) xiāojiǎn 削减; **my hair needs a ~** wǒ gāi jiǎn tóufà le 我该剪头发了 **2** v/t qiē 切; (reduce) xiāojiǎn 削减; COMPUT: text jiǎnqiē 剪切; **get one's hair ~** jiǎn tóufà 剪头发

♦ **cut back 1** v/i (in costs) suōjiǎn 缩减 **2** v/t employees cáiyuán 裁员

♦ **cut down 1** v/t tree kǎndǎo 砍倒 **2** v/i (in smoking etc) jiǎnshǎo 减少

♦ **cut down on: ~ smoking/ drinking** shǎo chōuyān/hējiǔ 少抽烟/喝酒

♦ **cut off** (with knife, scissors etc) jiǎndiào 剪掉; (isolate) géjué 隔绝; TELEC duànxiàn 断线; **we were cut off** diànhuà duànxiàn le 电话断线了

♦ **cut out** (with scissors) jiǎnchū 剪出; alcohol, smoking jiè 戒; (eliminate) páichú 排除; **cut that out!** F gòule! 够了！; **be ~ for X** shìhé yú X 适合于 X

♦ **cut up** v/t meat etc qiēsuì 切碎

cutback xiāojiǎn 削减

cute (pretty) kě'ài 可爱; (sexually attractive, male) yīngjùn 英俊; (sexually attractive, female) piàoliàng 漂亮; (smart, clever) shuǎ xiǎo cōngmíng 耍小聪明

cuticle biǎopí 表皮

cut-price xiāojià 削价

cut-throat competition cánkù 残酷

cutting 1 n (from newspaper etc) jiǎnjí 剪辑 **2** adj remark shāngrén gǎnqíng 伤人感情

cyberspace diànnǎo kōngjiān 电脑空间

cycle 1 n (bicycle) zìxíngchē 自行车; (series of events) xúnhuán 循环 **2** v/i qí zìxíngchē 骑自行车

cycling qí zìxíngchē 骑自行车

cyclist qí zìxíngchē de rén 骑自行车的人

cylinder (container) yuántǒng róngqì 圆筒容器; (in engine) qìgāng 汽缸

cylindrical yuánzhù xíng 圆柱形

cynic fènshì jísú zhě 愤世嫉俗者

cynical fènshì jísú 愤世嫉俗

cynicism fènshì jísú 愤世嫉俗

cyst nángzhǒng 囊肿

Czech 1 adj Jiékè 捷克; **the ~ Republic** Jiékè Gònghéguó 捷克共和国 **2** n (person) Jiékè rén 捷克人; (language) Jiékè yǔ 捷克语

D

DA (= **district attorney**) dìfāng jiǎnchá guān 地方检查官

dab 1 n (*small amount*) shǎoliàng 少量 **2** v/t (*remove*) qīngcā 轻搽; (*apply*) cā 搽

♦ **dabble in** suíbiàn gǎogao 随便搞搞

dad bà ba 爸爸

dagger bǐshǒu 匕首

daily 1 n (*paper*) rìbào 日报 **2** adj měirì 每日

dainty yōuměi 优美

dairy products rǔzhì pǐn 乳制品

dais tái 台

dam 1 n (*for water*) shuǐbà 水坝 **2** v/t *river* zhùdībà 筑堤坝

damage 1 n sǔnshī 损失; *fig* (*to reputation etc*) sǔnhài 损害 **2** v/t sǔnhuài 损坏; *fig* (*reputation etc*) sǔnshāng 损伤

damages LAW péicháng 赔偿

damaging yǒu pòhuài xìng 有破坏性

dame F (*woman*) nǚrén 女人

damn 1 interj gāisǐ 该死 **2** n: **I don't give a ~!** wǒ cái bùguǎn ne! 我才不管呢！**3** adj gāisǐ 该死 **4** adv zhēn 真 **5** v/t (*condemn*) qiǎnzé 谴责; **~ it!** zhēn qìsǐ rén! 真气死人！; **I'm ~ed if ...** wǒ cái bù ... 我才不

damned → **damn**

damp *building, cloth* shī 湿

dampen nòng shī 弄湿

dance 1 n tiàowǔ 跳舞; (*social event*) wǔhuì 舞会 **2** v/i tiàowǔ 跳舞; **would you like to ~?** kěyǐ qǐngnǐ tiàowǔ ma? 可以请你跳舞吗？

dancer wǔdǎo jiā 舞蹈家; (*performer*) wǔdǎo yǎnyuán 舞蹈演员

dancing wǔdǎo 舞蹈

dandruff tóupíxiè 头皮屑

Dane Dānmài rén 丹麦人

danger wēixiǎn 危险; *out of ~* (*of patient*) tuōlí wēixiǎn 脱离危险

dangerous wēixiǎn 危险; *assumption* màoxiǎn 冒险

dangle 1 v/t yáohuang 摇晃 **2** v/i xuánchuí 悬垂

Danish 1 adj Dānmài 丹麦 **2** n (*language*) Dānmài yǔ 丹麦语

Danish (*pastry*) Dānmài dàngāo 丹麦蛋糕

dare 1 v/i gǎn 敢; **how ~ you!** nǐgǎn! 你敢！**2** v/t: **~ X to do Y** tiǎodòu X qù zuò Y 挑斗 X 去做 Y

daring adj dàdǎn 大胆

dark 1 n hēi'àn 黑暗; **after ~** tiānhēi yǐhòu 天黑以后; **keep X in the ~** *fig* bú gàosù X 不告诉 X **2** adj *room, night* hēi 黑; *hair, eyes* shēn yánsè 深颜色; **~ green/blue** shēn lǜ/lán 深绿/蓝

darken (*of sky*) biàn hēi 变黑

dark glasses hēi yǎnjìng 黑眼镜

darkness hēi'àn 黑暗

darling 1 n qīn'ài de 亲爱的 **2** adj qī'ài 亲爱

darn¹ 1 n (*mend*) bǔdīng 补丁 **2** v/t (*mend*) bǔ 补

darn², **darned** → **damn**

dart 1 n (*for throwing*) fēibiāo 飞标 **2** v/i měngchōng 猛冲

dash 1 n (*punctuation*) pòzhé hào 破折号; (*small amount*) shǎoliàng 少量; (MOT: *dashboard*) yíbiǎo bǎn 仪表板; **a ~ of brandy** shǎoliàng báilándì 少量白兰地; **make a ~ for** jíchōng 急冲 **2** v/i jíchōng 急冲 **3** v/t hopes pòmiè 破灭

♦ **dash off 1** v/i gǎnkuài líkāi 赶快离开 **2** v/t (*write quickly*) cōngmáng xiě 匆忙写

dashboard yíbiǎo bǎn 仪表板

data shùjù 数据

database shùjù kù 数据库;**data capture** shùjù fúhuò 数据俘获;**data processing** shùjù chǔlǐ 数据处理;**data protection** zīliào bǎomì 资料保密;**data storage** shùjù chǔcún 数据储存

date¹ (fruit) zǎo 枣

date² **1** n rìqī 日期;(meeting) yuēhuì 约会;(person) yuēhuì duìxiàng 约会对象;**what's the ~ today?** jīntiān jǐhào? 今天几号？;**out of ~** clothes guòshí 过时;passport guòqī 过期;**up to ~** zuìxīn 最新 **2** v/t letter, cheque zhùmíng rìqī 注明日期;(go out with) tán liàn'ài 谈恋爱;**that ~s you** (shows your age) xiǎnshì nǐde niánlíng 显示你的年龄

dated guòshí 过时

daub v/t luàntú 乱涂

daughter nǚ'ér 女儿

daughter-in-law érxífu 儿媳妇

daunt v/t shǐ qìněi 使气馁

dawdle màntūntun de zuò 慢吞吞地做

dawn **1** n pòxiǎo 破晓;fig (of new age) kāiduān 开端 **2** v/i: **it ~ed on me that ...** wǒ yìshí dào ... 我意识到 ...

day tiān 天;**what ~ is it today?** jīntiān xīngqī jǐ? 今天星期几？;**~ off** fàngjià 放假;**by ~** báitiān 白天;**by ~** yī tiāntiān dì yī tiān tiān de 一天天地;**the ~ after** dì'èr tiān 第二天;**the ~ after tomorrow** hòutiān 后天;**the ~ before** qián yī tiān 前一天;**the ~ before yesterday** qiántiān 前天;**~ in ~ out** měitiān 每天;**in those ~s** nà shíhòu 那时候;**one ~** yǒu yītiān 有一天;**the other ~** (recently) zuìjìn 最近;**let's call it a ~!** xiūxība! 休息吧!

daybreak pòxiǎo 破晓;**daydream 1** n báirì mèng 白日梦 **2** v/i báirì zuòmèng 白日做梦;**daylight** rìguāng 日光;**daytime:** **in the ~** báitiān 白天;**daytrip** yīrìyóu 一日游

daze: **in a ~** bùzhī suǒcuò 不知

所措 (by good/bad news) bùzhī suǒcuò 不知所措;(by a blow) fāhūn 发昏

dazed (by good/bad news) bùzhī suǒcuò 不知所措;(by a blow) fāhūn 发昏

dazzle v/t (of light) huǎng 晃;fig mízhù 迷住

dead 1 adj person, plant sǐ 死;battery, phone, bulb shīlíng 失灵;F (place) sǐqì chénchén 死气沉沉 **2** adv F (very) hěn 很;**~ beat**, **~ tired** jīnpí lìjìn 筋疲力尽;**that's ~ right** hěn zhèngquè 很正确 **3** n: **the ~** (dead people) sǐrén 死人;**in the ~ of night** shēnyè 深夜

deaden pain, sound shǐ jiǎnshǎo 使减少

dead end (street) sǐ hútòng 死胡同;**dead-end job** méi qiántú de gōngzuò 没前途的工作;**dead heat** tóngshí dàodá zhōngdiǎn 同时到达终点;**deadline** qīxiàn 期限;(for newspaper, magazine) zuìhòu qīxiàn 最后期限;**dead-lock** n (in talks) jiāngjú 僵局

deadly adj (fatal) zhìmìng 致命;F (boring) sǐqì chénchén 死气沉沉

deaf lóng 聋

deaf-and-dumb lóngyǎ 聋哑

deafen shǐ tīng bū jiàn 使听不见

deafening jí dàshēng 极大声

deafness lóng 聋

deal 1 n jiāoyì 交易;**it's a ~** (we have reached an agreement) chéngjiāo 成交;(it's a promise) méi wèntí 没问题;**a good ~** (bargain) hǎo jiàqián 好价钱;**a great ~** (a lot) hěnduō 很多;**a great ~ of** (lots) hěnduō 很多 **2** v/t cards fāpái 发牌;**a blow to** dǎjī 打击

◆**deal in:** **~ X** (trade in) zuò X mǎimài 做 X 买卖

◆**deal out** cards fāpái 发牌

◆**deal with** (handle) chǔlǐ 处理;(do business with) dǎ jiāodào 打交道

dealer (merchant) shāngrén 商人;(drug ~) fàndú zhě 贩毒者;(in card game) fāpái zhě 发牌者

dealing (drug ~) fàndú 贩毒

dealings (business) jiāowǎng 交往

dean (*of college*) yuànzhǎng 院长

dear *adj* qīn'ài 亲爱; (*expensive*) guì 贵; *Dear Sir* zūnjìngde xiānsheng 尊敬的先生; *Dear Wang Li* qīn'àide Wáng Lì 亲爱的王丽; (*oh*) ~!, ~ me! wǒde tiān'a! 我的天啊!

dearly *love* shēn 深

death sǐwáng 死亡

death penalty sǐxíng 死刑

death toll sǐwáng zǒngshù 死亡总数

debatable kě zhēnglùn 可争论

debate 1 *n* (*between opposing sides*) biànlùn 辩论; (*discussion*) tǎolùn 讨论 **2** *v/i* (*discuss*) tǎolùn 讨论; (*between opposing sides*) biànlùn 辩论 **3** *v/t* biànlùn 辩论

debauchery fàngdàng 放荡

debit 1 *n* jièfāng 借方 **2** *v/t account* jièfāng 借方; ~ *his account with $30* zài tāde jièfāng zhàngshang jì sānshí měiyuán 在他的借方帐上记三十美元

debris cánjì 残迹

debt zhài 债; *be in ~* (*financially*) qiànzhài 欠债

debtor jièfāng 借方

debug *room* chāichú qiètīngqì 拆除窃听器; COMPUT chúcuò 除错

début *n* shǒuyǎn 首演

decade shínián 十年

decadent tuífèi 颓废

decaffeinated wú kāfēiyīn 无咖啡因

decanter xì jǐng píng 细颈瓶

decapitate shīshǒu fēnlí 尸首分离

decay 1 *n* (*process, matter*) fǔlàn 腐烂; (*of civilization*) shuāituì 衰退; (*in teeth*) làn làn 2 *v/i* fǔlàn 腐烂; (*of civilization*) shuāituì 衰退; (*of teeth*) làn làn

deceased: *the ~* sǐzhě 死者

deceit qīpiàn 欺骗

deceitful bù lǎoshi 不老实

deceive qīpiàn 欺骗

December shí'èryuè 十二月

decency zhèngpài 正派; *he had the ~ to ...* tā qǐmǎ zhīdào qù ... 他起码知道去 ...

decent *person* zhèngpài 正派; *salary, price* gòudà 够大; *size* gòudà 够大; *meal, sleep* zúgòu 足够; *I'm not ~ yet!* (*adequately dressed*) wǒ hái méi chuānhǎo yīfu ne! 我还没穿好衣服呢!

decentralize *administration* shūsàn 疏散

deception qīpiàn 欺骗

deceptive kàobuzhù 靠不住

deceptively: *it looks ~ simple* kànqǐlái jiǎndān kàn qilái hěn jiǎndān 看起来简单

decibel fēnbèi 分贝

decide 1 *v/t* (*make up one's mind*) juédìng 决定; (*conclude*) xià juéxīn 下决心; (*settle*) pànjué 判决 **2** *v/i* juédìng 决定; *you ~* nǐ lái juédìng 你来决定

decided (*definite*) jiānjué 坚决; (*obvious*) míngxiǎn 明显

decider (*match etc*) juédìng sài 决定赛

decimal *n* xiǎoshù 小数

decimal point xiǎoshù diǎn 小数点

decimate èshā dà bùfen 扼杀大部分

decipher jiě mìmǎ 解密码

decision juédìng 决定; *come to a ~* xià juéxīn 下决心

decision-maker dāngquán zhě 当权者

decisive guǒduàn 果断; (*crucial*) juédìng xìng 决定性

deck (*of ship*) jiǎbǎn 甲板; (*of cards*) yīfù zhǐpái 一副纸牌

deckchair jiǎbǎn yòng yǐ 甲板用椅

declaration (*statement*) shēngmíng 声明; (*of independence*) xuānbù 宣布; *of war* xuānzhàn 宣战

declare (*state*) shēngmíng 声明; *independence* xuānbù 宣布; (*at customs*) chéngbào 呈报; *~ war* xuānzhàn 宣战

decline 1 *n* (*fall*) xiàjiàng 下降; (*in standards*) shuāituì 衰退; (*in health*) jiàngdī 降低; (*in health*) shuāituì 衰退 **2** *v/t invitation* xièjué 谢绝; *~ to comment / accept* xièjué fābiǎo yìjiàn / jiēshòu 谢绝发表意见 / 接

受 **3** *v/i* (*refuse*) xièjué 谢绝；
(*decrease*) jiǎnshǎo 减少；(*of
health*) shuāituì 衰退

declutch qǔxià líhéqì 取下离合
器

decode yìmǎ 译码

decompose fǔlàn 腐烂

décor zhuānghuáng 装潢

decorate (*with paint, paper*)
zhuāngxiū 装修；(*adorn*) zhuāngshì 装饰；*soldier* shòuxūn 授勋

decoration (*paint, paper*)
zhuānghuáng 装潢；(*ornament*)
zhuāngshì 装饰

decorative zhuāngshì 装饰

decorator (*interior ~*)
zhuānghuáng gōngrén 装潢工人

decoy *n* yòu'ěr 诱饵

decrease 1 *n* xiàjiàng 下降 **2** *v/t*
suōjiǎn 缩减 **3** *v/i* xiàjiàng 下降

dedicate *book etc* tíxiàn 题献；**~
oneself to ...** xiànshēn yú ... 献身
于 ...

dedication (*in book*) xiàntí 献题；
(*to cause, work*) zhìlì 致力

deduce tuīlǐ 推理

deduct: ~ X from Y cóng Y zhōng
jiǎnqù X 从 Y 中减去 X

deduction (*from salary*) kòuchú 扣
除；(*conclusion*) tuīlùn 推论

deed *n* (*act*) xíngwéi 行为；LAW
qìyuē 契约

deep *hole, water, color* shēn 深；
shelf zòngshēn 纵深；*voice*
shēnchén 深沉；*thinker* shēnrù 深
入；**~ trouble** shēnxiàn kùnjìng 身
陷困境

deepen 1 *v/t* bǎ ... jiāshēn 把 ... 加
深 **2** *v/i* biànshēn 变深；(*of crisis,
mystery*) jiāzhòng 加重

deep freeze *n* bīngxiāng 冰箱；
deep-frozen food lěngdòng
shípǐn 冷冻食品；**deep-fry**
yóuzhá 油炸

deer lù 鹿

deface sǔnhuài biǎomiàn 损坏表
面

defamation fěibàng 诽谤

defamatory fěibàng 诽谤

default *adj* COMPUT yuándìng 原定

defeat 1 *n* (*conquering ~*) jībài 击败；

(*losing*) shībài 失败 **2** *v/t* jībài 击
败；(*of task, problem*) cuòbài 锉败

defeatist *adj attitude* shībài zhǔyì
失败主义

defect *n* quēxiàn 缺陷

defective yǒu quēxiàn 有缺陷

defend bǎowèi 保卫；*cause* hànwèi
捍卫；(*stand by*) wéihù 维护；
(*justify*) biànhù 辩护；**~ X** LAW wèi
X biànhù 为 X 辩护

defendant bèigào 被告

defense *n* bǎowèi 保卫；SP
fángshǒu 防守；LAW bèigào 被
告；(*justification*) biànhù 辩护；(*of
cause*) hànwèi 捍卫；**come to X's
~** bāngzhù X 帮助 X

defense budget guófáng
kāizhī 国防开支

defense lawyer biànhù lǜshī 辩护
律师

defenseless gūlì wúyuán 孤立无
援

defense player SP shǒuwèi
duìyuán 守卫队员；**Defense
Secretary** POL guófáng bùzhǎng
国防部长；**defense witness**
LAW biànhù zhèngrén 辩护证人

defensive 1 *n*: **on the ~** cǎiqǔ
shǒushì 采取守势；**go on the ~**
cǎiqǔ shǒushì 采取守势 **2** *adj
weaponry* fángyù 防御；*person*
zìwǒ biànhù 自我辩护

defer *v/t* tuīchí 推迟

deference jìngyì 敬意

deferential biǎoshì jìngyì 表示敬
意

defiance duìkàng 对抗；**in ~ of**
wéikàng 违抗

defiant tiǎozhàn 挑战

deficiency (*lack*) quēfá 缺乏

deficient: be ~ in quēfá 缺乏

deficit kuīsǔn 亏损

define *word* xià dìngyì 下定义；
objective míngquè 明确

definite *date, answer, improvement*
míngquè 明确；(*certain*) kěndìng
肯定；**are you ~ about that?** nǐ
néngbùnéng kěndìng？你能不能
肯定？；**nothing ~ has been
arranged** zuìhòu ānpái hái méiyǒu quèdìng 最后安排还没有

确定

definite article dìngguàncí 定冠词

definitely kěndìng 肯定

definition (*of word*) dìngyì 定义; (*of objective*) chǎnshù 阐述

definitive quánwēi xìng 权威性

deflect *ball*, *blow* shǐ zhuǎnxiàng 使转向; *criticism* niǔzhuǎn 扭转; (*from course of action*) niǔzhuǎn fāngxiàng 扭转方向; *be ~ed from* shǐ cóng ... zhuǎnbiàn fāngxiàng 使从 ... 转变方向

deform shǐ chéng jīxíng 使成畸形

deformity jīxíng 畸形

defraud piànqǔ 骗取

defrost *v/t food* jiědòng 解冻; *fridge* huàbīng 化冰

deft língqiǎo 灵巧

defuse *bomb* chāichú yǐnxìn 拆除引信; *situation* tiáojiě 调解

defy wéikàng 违抗

degenerate *v/i* duòluò 堕落; *~ into* tuìhuà 退化

degrade shǐ diūliǎn 使丢脸

degrading *position*, *work* dījí 低级

degree (*from university*) xuéwèi 学位; (*of temperature*, *angle*, *latitude*) dù dù 度度; (*amount*) chéngdù 程度; *by ~s* zhújiàn 逐渐; *get one's ~* huòdé xuéwèi 获得学位

dehydrated tuōshuǐ 脱水

de-ice chúbīng 除冰

de-icer (*spray*) chúbīng qì 除冰器

deign: *~ to* ... qūzūn ... 屈尊 ...

deity shén 神

dejected jǔsàng 沮丧

delay 1 *n* yánchí 延迟 **2** *v/t* tuīchí 推迟; *be ~ed* bèi dāngē 被耽搁 **3** *v/i* tuīchí 推迟

delegate 1 *n* dàibiǎo 代表 **2** *v/t task*, *person* shòuquán 授权

delegation (*of task*, *people*) shòuquán 授权

delete shānqù 删去; COMPUT shānchú 删除; (*cross out*) huàdiào 划掉

deletion (*act*) xiāochú 消除; (*that deleted*) shānchú 删除

deli shóushí diàn 熟食店

deliberate 1 *adj* gùyì 故意 **2** *v/i*

zǐxì kǎolǜ 仔细考虑

deliberately gùyì 故意

delicacy (*of fabric*) jīngzhì 精致; (*of problem*) mǐngǎn 敏感; (*of health*) xūruò 虚弱; (*tact*) jǐnshèn 谨慎; (*food*) měishí 美食

delicate *fabric* jīngzhì 精致; *problem* mǐngǎn 敏感; *health* xūruò 虚弱

delicatessen shóushí diàn 熟食店

delicious hǎochī 好吃; *that was ~* zhēn hǎochī 真好吃

delight *n* xìngfèn 兴奋

delighted gāoxìng 高兴

delightful *evening* yúkuài 愉快; *person* kě'ài 可爱

delimit huàqīng jièxiàn 划清界线

delirious MED zhānwàng 谵妄; (*ecstatic*) jídù xīngfèn 极度兴奋

deliver sòng 送; *message* dìjiāo 递交; *baby* shēng 生; *~ a speech* jiǎnghuà 讲话

delivery (*of goods*, *mail*) sònghuò 送货; (*of baby*) fēnmiǎn 分娩

delivery date sònghuò rìqī 送货日期; **delivery note** sònghuò dān 送货单; **delivery van** sònghuò chē 送货车

delude qīpiàn 欺骗; *~ oneself* zìqī 自欺

deluge 1 *n* dàyǔ 大雨; *fig* fēngyōng érzhì 蜂拥而至 **2** *v/t fig* yānmò 淹没

delusion wàngxiǎng 妄想

de luxe *adj* háohuá 豪华

demand 1 *n* yāoqiú 要求; COM xūqiú 需求; *in ~* xūyào 需要 **2** *v/t* yāoqiú 要求

demanding *job* gāo yāoqiú 高要求; *person* kēkè 苛刻

demented jīngshén cuòluàn 精神错乱

demise qùshì 去世; *fig* mièwáng 灭亡

demitasse xiǎobēi 小杯

demo (*protest*) shìwēi 示威; (*of video etc*) shìfàn 示范

democracy mínzhǔ 民主

democrat mínzhǔ zhǔyì zhě 民主主义者; *Democrat* POL Mínzhǔ

dǎngrén 民主党人

democratic mínzhǔ 民主

demo disk shìfàn dié 示范碟

demolish *building* chāihuǐ 拆毁; *argument* cuīhuǐ 摧毁

demolition (*of building*) chāihuǐ 拆毁; (*of argument*) cuīhuǐ 摧毁

demon móguǐ 魔鬼

demonstrate 1 *v/t* (*prove*) zhèngmíng 证明; *machine* shìfàn 示范 **2** *v/i* (*politically*) shìwēi 示威

demonstration (*show*) xiǎnshì 显示; (*protest*) shìwēi 示威; (*of machine*) shìfàn 示范

demonstrative: *be* ~ gǎnqíng wàilù 感情外露

demonstrator (*protester*) shìwēi zhě 示威者

demoralized qìněi 气馁

demoralizing lìngrén xièqì 令人泄气

den (*study*) shūfáng 书房

Deng Xiaoping Dèng Xiǎopíng 邓小平

Deng Xiaoping theory Dèng Xiǎopíng lìlùn 邓小平理论

denial (*of rumour, accusation*) fǒurèn 否认; (*of request*) jùjué 拒绝

denim niúzǎi bù 牛仔布

denims (*jeans*) niúzǎikù 牛仔裤

Denmark Dānmài 丹麦

denomination (*of money*) miàn'é 面额; (*religious*) jiàopài 教派

dense (*thick*) nónghòu 浓厚; *foliage* chóumì 稠密; *crowd* mìjí 密集; (*stupid*) chídùn 迟钝

densely: ~ *populated* rénkǒu mìjí 人口密集

density (*of population*) chóumì dù 稠密度

dent 1 *n* āochù 凹处 **2** *v/t* shǐ āoxià 使凹下

dental *treatment* yáchǐ 牙齿; *hospital* yákē 牙科

dentist yáyī 牙医

dentures jiǎyá 假牙

deny *charge, rumour* fǒurèn 否认; *right, request* jùjué 拒绝

deodorant ⇩ chúxiù jì 除臭剂

depart líkāi 离开; ~ *from* (*deviate from*) wéibèi 违背

department (*of company, store*) bùmén 部门; (*of university*) xì 系; (*of government*) bù 部; *Department of Defense* Guófáng bù 国防部; *Department of the Interior* Nèizhèng bù 内政部; *Department of State* Guówùyuàn 国务院

department store bǎihuò shāngchǎng 百货商场

departure (*leaving*) dòngshēn 动身; (*of train, bus*) chūfā 出发; (*of person from job*) líkāi 离开; (*deviation*) piānlí 偏离; *a new* ~ (*for government, organization*) xīn qǐdiǎn 新起点; (*for company*) xīn fāzhǎn 新发展; (*for actor, artist, writer*) xīn fāngxiàng 新方向

departure lounge hòujī shì 候机室

departure time qǐchéng shíjiān 启程时间

depend: *that* ~*s* shì qíngxíng ér dìng 视情形而定; *it* ~*s on the weather* kàn tiānqì ba 看天气吧; *I* - *on you* wǒ kǎozhe nǐle 我靠着你了

dependable kěkào 可靠

dependence, dependency yīlài 依赖

dependent 1 *n* yīkào zhě 依靠者 **2** *adj* yīkào 依靠

depict (*in painting, writing*) miáoshù 描述

deplorable lìngrén yíhàn 令人遗憾

deplore tòngxī 痛惜

deport qūchú chūjìng 驱除出境

deportation qūchú chūjìng 驱除出境

deportation order qūchú lìng 驱除令

deposit 1 *n* (*in bank*) cúnchǔ 存储; (*of mineral*) chénjī 沉积; (*on purchase*) dìngjīn 定金 **2** *v/t money* cúnchǔ 存储; (*put down*) gē gē 搁; *silt, mud* yūjī 淤积

deposition LAW xuānshì zhèng 宣誓证

depot (*train station*) huǒchē zhàn 火车站

火车站; (*bus station*) qìchē zhàn 汽车站; (*for storage*) cāngkù 仓库

depreciate *v/i* FIN biǎnzhí 贬值

depreciation FIN biǎnzhí 贬值

depress *person* shǐ yōuyù 使忧郁

depressed *person* yōuyù 忧郁

depressing lìngrén shāngxīn 令人伤心

depression MED yōuyù zhèng 忧郁症; (*economic*) xiāotiáo 萧条; (*meteorological*) dīyā qū 低压区

deprive: **~** *X* **of** *Y* cóng X nàlǐ názǒu Y 从 X 那里拿走 Y

deprived pínkùn 贫困

depth (*of water, shelf, thought*) shēndù 深度; (*of voice*) dīchén dù 低沉度; (*of color*) nóngdù 浓度; **in ~** (*thoroughly*) shēnrù 深入; **in the ~s of winter** lóngdōng jìjié 隆冬季节; **be out of one's ~** (*in water*) zài shuǐ shēnde mòdīng chù 在水深得及顶处; *fig* (*in discussion etc*) wúfǎ lǐjiě 无法理解

deputation shòuquán 授权

♦ **deputize for** tìdài 替代

deputy dàilǐ 代理

deputy leader fù zǒngguǎn 副总管

derail: **be ~ed** (*of train*) tuōguǐ 脱轨

deranged fākuáng 发狂

derelict *adj* shīxiū 失修

deride qǔxiào 取笑

derision qǔxiào 取笑

derisive *remarks, laughter* cháonòng 嘲弄

derisory *amount, salary* wēibù zúdào 微不足道

derivative (*not original*) pàishēng 派生

derive *v/t* dédào 得到; **be ~d from** (*of word*) qǐyuán yú 起源于

derogatory biǎnyì 贬义

descend 1 *v/t* xiàlái 下来; **be ~ed from** shì … de hòuyì 是 … 的后裔

descend 2 *v/i* (*of airplane*) xiàjiàng 下降; (*of road*) xiàxié 下斜; (*of mood, darkness*) lǒngzhào 笼罩

descendant hòuyì 后裔

descent (*from mountain*) xiàlái 下来; (*of airplane*) xiàjiàng 下降; (*ancestry*) zǔxiān 祖先; **of Chinese ~** huáyì 华裔

describe miáoshù 描述; **~ X as Y** bǎ X xíngróng chéng Y 把 X 形容成 Y

description miáoxiě 描写; (*of criminal*) miáoshù 描述

desegregate qǔxiāo zhǒngzú gélí 取消种族隔离

desert[1] *n also fig* shāmò 沙漠

desert[2] **1** *v/t* (*abandon*) pāoqì 抛弃 **2** *v/i* (*of soldier*) kāi xiǎochāi 开小差

deserted huāngliáng 荒凉

deserter MIL táobīng 逃兵

desertion (*abandoning*) pāoqì 抛弃; MIL kāi xiǎochāi 开小差

deserve yīngdé 应得

design 1 *n* (*subject, of an object*) shèjì 设计; (*drawing*) shèjì túyàng tú 设计图; (*pattern*) túàn 图案 **2** *v/t building, car, machine* shèjì 设计; **not ~ed for heavy use** zhǐ xiàn qīngyòng 只限轻用

designate *v/t person* rènmìng 任命; *area* zhǐdìng 指定

designer (*of building, car, ship, audio*) shèjì shī 设计师

designer clothes míngpái fúzhuāng 名牌服装

design fault shèjì shīwù 设计失误

design school shèjì xuéyuàn 设计学院

desirable *residence* chèngxīn rúyì 称心如意; (*to be recommended*) zhíde zhídé 值得

desire *n* (*wish*) yuànwàng 愿望; (*sexual*) xìngyù 性欲

desk shūzhuō 书桌; (*in hotel*) wènxùn tái 问讯台

desk clerk jiēdàiyuán 接待员;

desktop computer COMPUT ⇩ táishìjī 台式机; **desktop publishing** zhuōmiàn páibǎn 桌面排版

desolate *adj place* huāngliáng 荒凉

despair 1 *n* juéwàng 绝望; **in ~**

juéwàng 绝望 **2** *v/i* juéwàng 绝望; ~ *of* duì ... búbào xīwàng 对 ... 不抱希望

desperate *person* zǒutóu wúlù 走投无路; *action* gūzhù yīzhì 孤注一掷; *situation* wēijí 危急; *be ~ for a drink / cigarette* pòqiè xūyào yǐnliào / xiāngyān 迫切需要饮料 / 香烟

desperation gūzhù yīzhì 孤注一掷; *an act of ~* gūzhù yīzhì zhījǔ 孤注一掷之举

despise kànbùqǐ 看不起

despite jǐnguǎn 尽管

despondent yìqì xiāochén 意气消沉

despot bàojūn 暴君

dessert tiánpǐn 甜品

destination mùdìdì 目的地

destiny yuánfèn 缘分

destitute pínkùn 贫困

destroy cuīhuǐ 摧毁

destroyer (*boat*) qūchú jiàn 驱除舰

destruction pòhuài 破坏

destructive *power* pòhuài xìng 破坏性; *criticism* xiāojí 消极; *child* táoqì 淘气

detach fēnkāi 分开

detachable kě fēnkāi 可分开

detached (*objective*) wú piānjiàn 无偏见

detachment (*objectivity*) bùpiān bùyǐ 不偏不倚

detail *n* (*small point*) zhījié 枝节; (*piece of information*) xìjié 细节; (*irrelevancy*) suǒsuì xiǎoshì 琐碎小事; *in ~* xiángxì 详细

detailed xiángxì 详细

detain (*hold back*) dāngé 耽搁; (*as prisoner*) jūliú 拘留

detainee: *political ~* zhèngzhì fàn 政治犯

detect chájué 察觉; (*of device*) jiàncè 检测

detection (*of criminal, crime*) zhēnchá 侦察; (*of smoke etc*) jiàncè 检测

detective (*policeman*) zhēntàn 侦探

detective novel zhēntàn xiǎoshuō

侦探小说

detector tàncè qì 探测器

détente POL huǎnhé 缓和

detention (*imprisonment*) jūliú 拘留

deter (*frighten*) wēishè 危慑; (*stop*) zhìzhǐ 制止; *~ X from doing Y* zǔzhǐ X zuò Y 阻止 X 做 Y

detergent xǐdí jì 洗涤剂

deteriorate èhuà 恶化

determination (*resolution*) juéxīn 决心

determine (*establish*) chámíng 查明

determined xià juéxīn 下决心; *effort* jiānjué 坚决

deterrent *n* wēishè yīnsù 危慑因素

detest tǎoyàn 讨厌

detonate **1** *v/t* shǐ bàozhà 使爆炸 **2** *v/i* bàozhà 爆炸

detour *n* yūhuí 迂回; (*diversion*) ràodào xíngshǐ 绕道行驶

♦detract from *achievement, enjoyment* yǒusǔn yú 有损于; *appearance of sth* shǐ jiǎnsè 使减色

detriment: *to the ~ of* duì ... búlì 对 ... 不利

detrimental búlì 不利

deuce (*in tennis*) píngjú 平局

devaluation (*of currency*) biǎnzhí 贬值

devalue *currency* biǎnzhí 贬值

devastate *also fig* cuīhuǐ 摧毁

devastating cuīhuǐ xìng 摧毁性

develop **1** *v/t film* chōngxǐ 冲洗; *land, site* jiànshè 建设; *activity, business* kuòdà 扩大; (*originate*) fāmíng 发明; (*improve on*) gǎijìn 改进; *illness, cold* kāishǐ 开始 **2** *v/i* (*grow*) fāzhǎn 发展; (*of person*) zhǎngdà 长大

developer (*of property*) búdòngchǎn shāng 不动产商

developing country fāzhǎn zhōng guójiā 发展中国家

development (*of film*) chōngxǐ 冲洗; (*of land, site*) jiànshè 建设; (*of business, country*) fāzhǎn 发展; (*event*) shìjiàn 事件; (*origination*) fāmíng 发明; (*improving*) gǎijìn 改进; **~ area** kāifāqū 开发区

device (*tool*) qìjù 器具

devil móguǐ 魔鬼

devious (*sly*) jiǎohuá 狡猾

devise fāmíng 发明

devoid: ~ of wánquán méiyǒu 完全没有

devote *time, effort* gòngxiàn 贡献

devoted *son etc* zhōngshí 忠实; **be ~ to X** (*to parents, grandparents*) xiàoshùn X 孝顺 X; (*to any other person*) zhōngshí yú X 忠实于 X

devotion zhuānxīn 专心

devour *food* lángtūn hǔyàn 狼吞虎咽; *book* zháomí 着迷

devout qiánchéng 虔诚

dew lùshuǐ 露水

dexterity shúliàn jìqiǎo 熟练技巧

diabetes tángniàobìng 糖尿病

diabetic 1 *n* tángniàobìng huànzhě 糖尿病患者 **2** *adj* tángniàobìng 糖尿病

diagonal *adj* xié 斜

diagram tú 图

dial 1 *n* (*of clock*) zhōngmiàn 钟面; (*of meter*) yíbiǎo 仪表; TELEC bōhào pán 拨号盘 **2** *v/i* TELEC bōhào 拨号 **3** *v/t* TELEC: *number* bō 拨

dialect fāngyán 方言

dialog duìhuà 对话

dial tone bōhàoyīn 拨号音

diameter zhíjìng 直径

diametrically: ~ opposed jiérán xiāngfǎn 截然相反

diamond (*jewel*) zuànshí 钻石; (*in cards*) fāngkuàir 方块儿; (*shape*) língxíng 菱形

diaper niàobù 尿布

diaphragm ANAT gémó 隔膜; (*contraceptive*) zǐgōng tuō 子宫托

diarrhea fùxiè 腹泻, lādùzi 拉肚子 F

diary rìjì 日记

dice 1 *n* tóuzi 骰子 **2** *v/t* (*cut*) qiē chéng dīng 切成丁

dichotomy liǎng duìlì 两对立

dictate *v/t letter, novel* kǒushòu 口授

dictation kǒushòu 口授

dictator POL dúcái zhě 独裁者

dictatorial *tone of voice* mìnglìng shì 命令式; *person, power* dúcái 独裁

dictatorship zhuānzhèng 专政

dictionary zìdiǎn 字典

die sǐ 死; **~ of cancer / AIDS** sǐyú áizhèng / àizībìng 死于癌症 / 艾滋病; **I'm dying to know / leave** wǒ jí xiǎng zhīdào / líkāi 我极想知道 / 离开

◆ **die away** (*of noise*) zhújiàn xiāoshī 逐渐消失

◆ **die down** (*of noise*) jiàngdī 降低; (*of storm*) jiǎnruò 减弱; (*of fire*) biànruò 变弱; (*of excitement*) píngxī 平息

◆ **die out** (*of custom, species*) mièjué 灭绝

diesel (*fuel*) cháiyóu 柴油

diet 1 *n* (*regular food*) shíwù 食物; (*for losing weight*) jiǎnféi shípǐn 减肥食品; (*for health reasons*) tèzhǒng yǐnshí 特种饮食 **2** *v/i* (*to lose weight*) jiǎnféi 减肥

differ (*be different*) bùtóng 不同; (*disagree*) yìjiàn xiāngzuǒ 意见相左

difference chābié 差别; (*disagreement*) fēnqí 分歧; **it doesn't make any ~** (*doesn't change anything*) méi shénme chābié 没什么差别; (*doesn't matter*) méi shénme guānxi 没什么关系

different bùtóng 不同

differentiate: ~ between qūfēn 区分

differently yǔzhòng bùtóng 与众不同

difficult bù róngyì 不容易

difficulty kùnnan 困难; **with ~** chīlì 吃力

dig 1 *v/t* wā 挖 **2** *v/i*: **it was ~ging into me** juérù wǒ juérù 掘入我

◆ **dig out** (*find*) zhǎochū 找出

◆ **dig up** juéqǐ 掘起; *information* cháchū 查出

digest *v/t* xiāohuà 消化; *information* lǐnghuì 领会

digestible *food* kě xiāohuà 可消化

digestion xiāohuà 消化

digit (number) shùzì 数字; **a four ~ number** sìwèi shùzì 四位数字

digital shùzì 数字

dignified yǒu zūnyán 有尊严

dignitary dáguān guìrén 达官贵人

dignity zūnyán 尊严

digress zànshí lítí 暂时离题

digression zànshí lítí 暂时离题

dike (wall) dī 堤

dilapidated tānhuǐ 坍毁

dilate (of pupils) kuòzhāng 扩张

dilemma jìntuì liǎngnán 进退两难; **be in a ~** chùyú jìntuì liǎngnán de jìngdì 处于进退两难的境地

diligent qínfèn 勤奋

dilute v/t xīshì 稀释

dim 1 adj room, light hūn'àn 昏暗; outline bù xiǎnzhù 不显著; (stupid) shǎ 傻; prospects bēiguān 悲观 2 v/t: **~ the headlights** shǐ chē qiándēng àndàn 使车前灯暗淡 3 v/i (of lights) biàn àndàn 变暗淡

dimension (measurement) chǐcun 尺寸

diminish 1 v/t value shǐ jiǎnshǎo 使减少; authority xiāoruò 削弱 2 v/i biànshǎo 变少

diminutive 1 n àichēng 爱称 2 adj xiǎo 小

dimple jiǔwō 酒窝

dim sum diǎnxīn 点心

din n xuānnào shēng 喧闹声

dine yòngcān 用餐

diner (person) yòngcān zhě 用餐者; (restaurant) xiǎo cānguǎn 小餐馆

dinghy xiǎochuán 小船

dingy atmosphere hūn'àn 昏暗; (dirty) zāng zāng 脏

dining car cānchē 餐车; **dining room** cānshì 餐室; **dining table** cānzhuō 餐桌

dinner (in the evening) wǎncān 晚餐; (at midday) wǔcān 午餐; (gathering) yànhuì 宴会

dinner guest yànhuì kèrén 宴会客人; **dinner jacket** xiǎo lǐfú 小礼服; **dinner party** yànhuì 宴会

dinosaur kǒnglóng 恐龙

dip 1 n (swim) yóuyǒng yóuyǒng 游泳; (for food) zhānliào 沾料; (in road) āoxiàn 凹陷 2 v/t zhān 沾; **~ the headlights** diǎn chē qiándēng àndàn 使车前灯暗淡 3 v/i (of road) qīngxié 倾斜

diploma wénpíng 文凭

diplomacy wàijiāo 外交; (tact) lǎoliàn 老练

diplomat wàijiāo guān 外交官

diplomatic wàijiāo 外交; (tactful) lǎoliàn 老练

dire (urgent) pòbù jídài 迫不及待

direct 1 adj zhíjiē 直接; flight, train zhídá 直达; person zhíshuǎng 直爽 2 v/t (to a place) zhǐyǐn 指引; play, movie dǎoyǎn 导演; attention zhíxiàng 指向

direct current ELEC zhíliú 直流

direction fāngxiàng 方向; (of movie, play) dǎoyǎn 导演; **~s** (instructions) zhǐshì 指示; (to a place) fāngwèi 方位; (for use) yòngfǎ 用法

direction indicator MOT fāngwèi zhǐshì 方位指示

directly 1 adv (straight) zhíjiē 直接; (soon) hěnkuài 很快; (immediately) lìjí 立即 2 conj yīdāng 一当

director (of company) zhǔguǎn 主管; (of play, movie) dǎoyǎn 导演

directory zhǐdǎo 指导; TELEC diànhuà bù 电话簿

dirt (grime) zāng dōngxī 脏东西

dirt cheap hěn piányi 很便宜

dirty 1 adj zāng 脏; (pornographic) huángsè 黄色 2 v/t nòngzāng 弄脏

dirty trick bēibǐ xíngwéi 卑鄙行为

disability cánjí 残疾

disabled 1 n cánjí rénshēn 残疾人士 2 adj cánjí 残疾

disadvantage (drawback) bùlì zhīchù 不利之处; **be at a ~** chīkuī 吃亏

disadvantaged shèhuì dìwèi dīxià

社会地位低下

disadvantageous búlì 不利

disagree (of person) bù tóngyì 不同意

♦**disagree with:** ~ **X** (of person) yǔ X yìjiàn bù yízhì 与X意见不一致; (of food) yǔ X bù xiāngyí 与X不相宜

disagreeable lìngrén bù yúkuài 令人不愉快

disagreement bùtóng yìjiàn 不同意见; (argument) zhēngzhí 争执

disappear xiāoshī 消失; (run away) pǎodiào 跑掉

disappearance (of item) xiāoshī 消失; (of person) shīzōng 失踪

disappoint shǐ shīwàng 使失望

disappointed shīwàng 失望

disappointing lìngrén shīwàng 令人失望

disappointment shīwàng 失望

disapproval zhǐzé 指责

disapprove bù zànchéng 不赞成; ~ **of** bù zànchéng 不赞成

disarm 1 v/t robber jiěchú wǔqì 解除武器; militia shǐ sàngshī shānghài nénglì 使丧失伤害能力 **2** v/i cáijūn 裁军

disarmament (of militia) jiěchú wǔzhuāng 解除武装; (of country) cáijūn 裁军

disarming shǐrén xiāochú huáiyí 使人消除怀疑

disaster zāinàn 灾难

disaster area shòuzāi dìqū 受灾地区; fig (person) mǎdàhā 马大哈

disastrous sǔnshī cǎnzhòng 损失惨重

disbelief: in ~ bùkě xiāngxìn 不可相信

disc (CD) guāngdié 光碟

discard old clothes etc rēngdiào 扔掉; boyfriend, theory pāoqì 抛弃

discern improvement chájué 察觉; (make out) biànchū 辨出

discernible kě biànrèn chū 可辨认出

discerning yǒu yǎnlì 有眼力

discharge 1 n (from hospital) chūyuàn 出院; (from army) tuìwǔ

退伍; (of waste) páichū 排出 **2** v/t (from hospital) yǔnxǔ chūyuàn 允许出院; (from army) qiǎnsàn 遣散; (from job) kāichú 开除; waste páichū 排出

disciple (religious) zǐdì 子弟

disciplinary chéngjiè xìng 惩戒性

discipline 1 n jìlǜ 纪律 **2** v/t child, dog, employee chéngfá 惩罚

disc jockey DJ DJ

disclaim fǒurèn 否认

disclose tòulù 透露

disclosure (of information, name) tòulù 透露; (about scandal etc) xièlòu 泄露

disco dísīkē 迪斯科; (place) ⇩ dítīng 迪厅

discolor shǐ biànsè 使变色

discomfort n (pain) tòngkǔ 痛苦; (embarrassment) bú zìzài 不自在

disconcert shǐ wéinán 使为难

disconcerted jiǒngpò 窘迫

disconnect (detach: hose, electrical/ gas appliance) shǐ bù jiētōng 使不接通; supply, telephones qiēduàn 切断; **I was ~ed** TELEC wǒ bèi qiēduàn le 我被切断了

disconsolate jǔsàng 沮丧

discontent bùmǎn 不满

discontented bú mǎnyì 不满意

discontinue product tíngzhǐ shēngchǎn 停止生产; bus, train service, magazine zhōngzhǐ 中止

discord MUS bù xiétiáo 不协调; (in relations) bù héxié 不和谐

discotheque dísīkē 迪斯科; (place) ⇩ dítīng 迪厅

discount 1 n zhékòu 折扣 **2** v/t goods dǎ zhékòu 打折扣; theory bù kǎolǜ 不考虑

discourage (dissuade) quànzǔ 劝阻; (dishearten) shǐ jǔsàng 使沮丧

discover fāxiàn 发现

discoverer fāxiàn zhě 发现明者

discovery fāxiàn 发现

discredit v/t person shǐ sàngshī míngyù 使丧失名誉; theory shǐrén bù xiāngxìn 使人不相信

discreet person jǐnshèn 谨慎; restaurant kǎolǜ zhōudào 考虑周到

discrepancy chācuò 差错

discretion pànduàn nénglì 判断能力; *at your ~* yóu nǐ zhuóqíng chǔlǐ 由你酌情处理

discriminate: ~ *against* qíshì 歧视; ~ *between* (*distinguish*) qūbié 区别

discriminating yǒu yǎnlì 有眼力

discrimination (*sexual, racial etc*) qíshì 歧视

discus SP tiěbǐng 铁饼

discuss tǎolùn 讨论; (*of article*) xiángshù 详述

discussion tǎolùn 讨论

disease jíbìng 疾病

disembark v/i (*from plane*) xià fēijī 下飞机; (*from ship*) xià chuán 下船

disenchanted: ~ *with* duì ... shīqù xìngqù 对 ... 失去兴趣

disengage fàngkāi 放开

disentangle jiětuō kāi 解脱开

disfigure shǐ huǐróng 使毁容

disgrace 1 n xiūchǐ 羞耻; *a ~* (*person*) bù guāngcǎi de rén 不光彩的人; *it's a ~* bùzhī hàisào 不知害臊; *in ~* diūliǎn 丢脸 2 v/t shǐ diūliǎn 使丢脸

disgraceful *behaviour, situation* yǒushī tǐmiàn 有失体面

disgruntled bùmǎn 不满

disguise 1 n wěizhuāng 伪装; (*costume, make-up*) jiǎ miànjù 假面具 2 v/t yǐnmán yǐncáng 隐瞒掩藏; *fear, anxiety* yǎncáng 掩藏; ~ *oneself as* zhuāngbàn chéng 装扮成; *he was ~d as* tā jiǎzhuāng shì tā 他假装是他假装

disgust 1 n jíwéi fǎngǎn 极为反感 2 v/t shǐ fǎngǎn 使反感

disgusting *habit, smell, food* lìngrén zuò'ǒu 令人作呕

dish (*part of meal*) càicài 菜菜; (*container*) diézi 碟子

dishcloth xǐwǎn bù 洗碗布

disheartened jǔsàng 沮丧

disheartening lìngrén shāngxīn 令人伤心

disheveled bù zhěngqí 不整齐

dishonest bù chéngshí 不诚实

dishonesty bù chéngshí 不诚实

dishonor n chǐrǔ 耻辱; *bring ~ on* dàilái chǐrǔ 带来耻辱

dishonorable kěchǐ 可耻

dishwasher (*machine*) xǐwǎn jī 洗碗机; (*person*) xǐwǎn gōng 洗碗工

dishwashing liquid xǐjiéjīng 洗洁精

dishwater xǐwǎn shuǐ 洗碗水

disillusion v/t shǐ huànxiǎng pòmiè 使幻想破灭

disillusionment huànmiè 幻灭

disinclined bú yuànyì 不愿意

disinfect xiāodú 消毒

disinfectant xiāodú jì 消毒剂

disinherit bōduó jìchéng quán 剥夺继承权

disintegrate lièkāi 裂开; (*of marriage, building*) wǎjiě 瓦解

disinterested (*unbiased*) zhōnglì 中立

disjointed tuōjié 脱节

disk (*shape*) yuánpán 圆盘; COMPUT cípán 磁盘; *on ~* chǔcún zài cípán shàng 储存在磁盘上

disk drive COMPUT cípán dàijī 磁盘带机

diskette ⇩ ruǎn cípán 软磁盘

dislike 1 n fǎngǎn 反感 2 v/t bù xǐhuān 不喜欢

dislocate *shoulder* tuōwèi 脱位

dislodge shǐ yídòng 使移动

disloyal bù zhōngchéng 不忠诚

disloyalty bùzhōng 不忠

dismal *weather* zāogāo 糟糕; *news, prospect* lìngrén jǔsàng 令人沮丧; *person* (*sad*) yōuxīn chōngchong 忧心忡忡; *person* (*negative*) xiāochén 消沉; *failure* bēicǎn 悲惨

dismantle *object* chāi 拆; *organization* shǐ jiětǐ 使解体

dismay 1 n (*alarm*) jīng'è 惊愕; (*disappointment*) shīwàng 失望 2 v/t shǐ huīxīn 使灰心

dismiss *employee* jiěgù 解雇; *suggestion, idea* kǎolǜ bù kǎolǜ 不考虑; *possibility* bú fàngzài xīnshàng 不放在心上

dismissal (*of employee*) jiěgù 解雇

disobedience bù fúcóng 不服从

disobedient juéjiàng 倔强

disobey wéibèi 违背

disorder (*untidiness*) záluàn 杂乱; (*unrest*) bàoluàn 暴乱; MED shītiáo 失调

disorderly *room, desk* záluàn 杂乱; *mob* bù shǒu zhìxù 不守秩序

disorganized wú zǔzhi 无组织

disoriented míhuo 迷惑

disown tuōlí guānxì 脱离关系

disparaging biǎnyì 贬抑

disparity xuánshū 悬殊

dispassionate (*objective*) bù piānxīn 不偏心

dispatch *v/t* (*send*) fāchū 发出

dispensary (*in pharmacy*) yàofáng 药房

dispense: ~ **with** shěngquè 省却

disperse **1** *v/t* qūsàn 驱散 (*of crowd*) shūsàn 疏散; (*of mist*) qūsàn 驱散

displace (*supplant*) páijǐ 排挤

display **1** *n* zhǎnlǎn 展览; (*of emotion*) biǎoshì 表示; (*in store window*) chénliè 陈列; COMPUT xiǎnshì 显示; **be on** ~ (*at exhibition*) zhǎnlǎn 展览; (*be for sale*) chénliè 陈列 **2** *v/t emotion* xiǎnshì 显示; (*at exhibition*) zhǎnlǎn 展览; (*for sale*) chénliè 陈列; COMPUT xiǎnshì 显示

display cabinet (*in museum, store*) zhǎnlǎn chúchuāng 展览橱窗

displease shǐ bù gāoxìng 使不高兴

displeasure bùmǎn 不满

disposable *diapers, contact lenses* yīcìxìng 一次性; ~ **income** shèngyú shōurù 剩余收入

disposal rēngdiào 扔掉; (*of pollutants, nuclear waste*) chǔlǐ 处理; **I am at your** ~ wǒ tīng nǐ zhǐhuī 我听你之指挥; **put X at Y's** ~ ràng Y zìyóu zhīpèi X 让Y自由支配X

dispose: ~ **of** rēngdiào 扔掉

disposed: **be** ~ **to do X** (*willing*) yuànyì zuò X 愿意做X; **be well** ~ **toward X** duì X yǒu hǎogǎn 对X有好感

disposition (*nature*) qīngxiàng 倾向

disproportionate bùchéng bǐlì 不成比例

disprove fǎnzhèng 反证

dispute **1** *n* zhēnglùn 争论; (*between the two countries*) zhēngbiàn 争辩; (*industrial*) zhēngzhí 争执 **2** *v/t* zhēnglùn 争论; (*fight over*) zhēngduó 争夺

disqualify qǔxiāo zīgé 取消资格

disregard *n & v/t* hūshì 忽视

disrepair: **in a state of** ~ shīxiū 失修

disreputable shēngmíng bàihuài 声名败坏; *area* shēngyù bùhǎo 声誉不好

disrespect bù zūnzhòng 不尊重

disrespectful bù lǐmào 不礼貌

disrupt *train service* shǐ tíngdùn 使停顿; (*intentionally*) rǎoluàn 扰乱

disruption (*of train service*) tíngdùn 停顿; (*of meeting, class*) pòhuài 破坏; (*intentional*) rǎoluàn 扰乱

disruptive pòhuài xìng 破坏性

dissatisfaction bùmǎn 不满

dissatisfied bù mǎnyì 不满意

dissension yìjiàn fēnqí 意见分歧

dissent **1** *n* chí yìyì 持异议 **2** *v/i*: ~ **from** chàng fǎndiào 唱反调

dissident *n* chí bùtóng zhèngjiàn zhě 持不同政见者

dissimilar bùtóng 不同

dissociate: ~ **oneself from X** fǒurèn zìjǐ hé X yǒu guānxi 否认自己和X有关系

dissolute fàngdàng 放荡

dissolve *v/t & v/i* róngjiě 溶解

dissuade quànzhǐ 劝止; ~ **X from Y** quànzǔ X bùyào qù zuò Y X bùyào qù zuò Y 劝阻X不要去做Y

distance **1** *n* jùlí 距离; **in the** ~ zài yuǎnchù 在远处 **2** *v/t*: ~ **oneself from X** shǐ zìjǐ yǔ X bǎochí jùlí 使自己和X保持距离

distant *place, time, relative* yuǎn 远; *fig* (*aloof*) bǎochí yīdìngde jùlí 保持一定的距离

distaste xiánwù 嫌恶

distasteful lìngrén yànwù 令人厌恶

distinct (*clear*) míngxiǎn 明显; (*different*) bùtóng 不同; **as ~ from X** yǔ X bùtóng 与 X 不同

distinction (*differentiation*) qūbié 区别; **hotel / product of ~** gāo zhìliàng lǚguǎn / chǎnpǐn 高质量旅馆 / 产品

distinctive tèyǒu 特有

distinctly qīngchǔ 清楚; (*decidedly*) míngxiǎn 明显

distinguish (*see*) biànbié 辨别; **~ between X and Y** qūfēn X hé Y 区分 X 和 Y

distinguished (*famous*) zhùmíng 著名; (*dignified*) yǔzhòng bùtóng 与众不同

distort wāiqū 歪曲

distract *person* shǐ fēnxīn 使分心; *attention* fēnsàn zhùyì lì 分散注意力

distracted (*worried*) yōulù 忧虑

distraction (*of attention*) fēnshén wù 分神物; (*amusement*) yúlè 娱乐; **drive X to ~** shǐ X fēnxīn 使 X 分心

distraught xīnshén bùdìng 心神不定

distress 1 *n* (*mental suffering*) kǔnǎo 苦恼; (*physical pain*) tòngkǔ 痛苦; **in ~** (*ship, aircraft*) wēinàn zhōng 危难中 2 *v/t* (*upset*) shāngxīn 伤心

distress signal qiújiù xìnhào 求救信号

distribute fēngěi 分给; *leaflets* sànfā 散发; *wealth* fēnpèi 分配; COM jīngxiāo 经销

distribution (*handing out*) fēnfā 分发; (*of wealth*) fēnpèi 分配; COM jīngxiāo 经销

distribution arrangement COM jīngxiāo hétóng 经销合同

distributor COM jīngxiāo shāng 经销商

district qū 区

district attorney dìfāng jiǎnchá guān 地方检察官

distrust *n & v/t* huáiyí 怀疑

disturb (*interrupt*) dǎjiǎo 打搅; (*upset*) dānyōu 担忧; **do not ~** qǐngwù dǎjiǎo 请勿打搅

disturbance (*interruption*) gānrǎo 干扰; **~s** sāoluàn 骚乱

disturbed (*concerned, worried*) dānxīn 担心; **mentally ~** jīngshén shīcháng 精神失常

disturbing lìngrén shāngxīn 令人伤心

disused fèiqì 废弃

ditch 1 *n* kēng 坑 2 *v/t* F (*get rid of*) pāoqì 抛弃

dive 1 *n* tiàoshuǐ 跳水; (*underwater*) qiánshuǐ 潜水; (*of plane*) fǔchōng 俯冲; (*bar etc*) xiàděng chǎngsuǒ 下等场所; **take a ~** (*of dollar etc*) tūrán xiàjiàng 突然下降 2 *v/i* tiàoshuǐ 跳水; (*underwater*) qiánshuǐ 潜水; (*of plane*) fǔchōng 俯冲

diver (*off board*) tiàoshuǐ zhě 跳水者; (*underwater*) qiánshuǐ zhě 潜水者

diverge chàkāi 岔开

diverse duōyàng huà 多样化

diversification COM duōzhǒng jīngyíng 多种经营

diversify *v/i* COM duōzhǒng jīngyíng 多种经营

diversion (*for traffic*) gǎixiàn 改线; (*to distract attention*) qiānzhì 牵制

diversity duōyàng huà 多样化

divert *traffic* gǎixiàn 改线; **~ attention** fēnsàn zhùyì lì 分散注意力

divest: **~ X of Y** gěi X bōduó Y 给剥夺 Y

divide fēn 分; *fig: country, family* fēnliè 分裂

dividend FIN gǔxī 股息; **pay ~s** *fig* lìng shòuyì 令受益

divine REL shén 神; F gài le mào le 盖了帽了

diving (*from board*) tiàoshuǐ 跳水; (*scuba ~*) qiánshuǐ 潜水

diving board tiàoshuǐ bǎn 跳水板

divisible kě chú jìn 可除尽

division MATH chúfǎ 除法; (*split: in party etc*) fēnliè 分裂; (*splitting into parts*) fēngē 分割; (*of company*) bùmén 部门

divorce 1 *n* líhūn 离婚; **get a ~**

líhūn 离婚 2 *v/t & v/i* líhūn 离婚

divorced líhūn 离婚; *get ~d* líhūn 离婚

divorcee líhūn zhě 离婚者

divulge tòulù 透露

DIY (= *do-it-yourself*) zìjǐ dòngshǒu 自己动手

DIY store zìjǐ dòngshǒu shāngdiàn 自己动手商店

dizzy: *feel ~* tóuyūn 头晕

DNA (= *deoxyribonucleic acid*) tuōyǎng hétáng hésuān 脱氧核糖核酸

do 1 *v/t* zuò 做; *one's hair* shū 梳; *the beds* pū 铺; *French, chemistry etc* xuéxí 学习; *100mph etc* xíngshǐ 行驶; *what are you ~ing tonight?* nǐ jīnwǎn gànshénme? 你今晚干什么?; *I don't know what to ~* wǒ bùzhī gāi zěnme bàn 我不知该怎么办; *no, I'll ~ it* bùyòng, wǒ lái ba 不用,我来吧; *~ it right now!* mǎshàng jiù gàn! 马上就干!; *have you done this before?* yǐqián gàn guò ma? 以前干过吗?; *have one's hair done* zuò tóufa shū 做头发 2 *v/i* (*be suitable, enough*) yě kěyǐ 也可以; *that will ~!* xíngle! 行了!; *~ well* (*of person*) chénggōng 成功; (*of business*) chāngshèng 昌盛; *well done!* (*congratulations!*) gōngxǐ! 恭喜!; *how ~ you ~?* nǐ hǎoma? 你好吗? 3 *auxiliary*: *~ you know him?* nǐ rènshì tā ma? 你认识他吗?; *I don't know* wǒ bù zhīdào 我不知道; *~ you like ...? – yes I ~* nǐ xǐhuan ... ma? – wǒ xǐhuan 你喜欢 ... 吗? –我喜欢; *he works hard, doesn't he?* tā gōngzuò hěn nǔlì, shìba? 他工作很努力,是吧?; *don't you believe me?* nǐ nándào bù xiāngxìn wǒ? 你难道不相信我?; *you ~ believe me, don't you?* nǐ quèshí xiāngxìn wǒ, shìba? 你确实相信我,是吧?; *you don't know the answer, ~ you? – no I don't* nǐ bù zhīdào dá'àn, shìba? – wǒ bù zhīdào 你不知道答案,是吧? –我不知道

♦ **do away with** fèichú 废除

♦ **do in**: *I'm done in* F wǒ lèisǐ le 我累死了

♦ **do out of**: *do X out of Y* piàn XY 骗 XY

♦ **do up** (*renovate*) gǎizhuāng 改装; (*fasten*) jìláo 系牢; *buttons* kòuhǎo 扣好; *laces* bǎng xiédài 绑鞋带

♦ **do with**: *I could ~ ...* wǒ xiǎngyào ... 我想要 ...; *he won't have anything to ~ it* (*won't get involved*) tā bùxiǎng jièrù 他不想介入

♦ **do without 1** *v/i* méiyǒu yěxíng 没有也行 2 *v/t* bù xūyào 不需要

docile *person* shùncóng 顺从; *animal* xùnfú 驯服

dock[1] **1** *n* NAUT chuánwù 船坞 **2** *v/i* (*of ship*) kào mǎtóu 靠码头; (*of spaceship*) duì jiē chù 对接处

dock[2] LAW bèigào xí 被告席

dockyard chuánchǎng 船厂

doctor *n* MED yīshēng 医生; (*form of address*) yīshēng 医生

doctorate bóshì 博士

doctrine jiàotiáo 教条

docudrama jìshí diànshì jù 记实电视剧

document *n* wénjiàn 文件

documentary (*program*) jìlù piān 纪录片

documentation wénjiàn 文件

dodge *v/t blow* shǎnkāi 闪开; *person, issue* duǒbì 躲避; *question* bìkāi 避开

doe (*deer*) mǔlù 母鹿

dog 1 *n* gǒu 狗 **2** *v/t* (*of bad luck*) bànsuí 伴随

dog catcher zhuā gǒu rén 抓狗人

dog-eared *book* juǎnjiǎo 卷角

dogged gùzhí 固执

doggie (*in children's language*) gǒugǒu 狗狗

doggy bag gǒu shí dài 狗食袋

doghouse: *be in the ~* shòu lěngyù 受冷遇

dogma jiàotiáo 教条

dogmatic jiàotiáo zhǔyì 教条主义

do-gooder Léi Fēng shūshu 雷锋叔叔

dog tag MIL shēnfèn shíbié pái 身份识别牌

dog-tired lèi sǐ le 累死了

do-it-yourself zìjǐ dòngshǒu 自己动手

doldrums: *be in the ~ (of economy)* wú shēngqì 无生气

♦**dole out** shǎoliàng pèijǐ 少量配给

doll *(toy)* wáwa 娃娃; F *(woman)* měimào shàonǚ 美貌少女

♦**doll up**: *get dolled up* dǎbàn dǎ扮

dollar měiyuán 美元

dollop *n* yīdìng liàng 一定量

dolphin hǎitún 海豚

dome *(of building)* yuándǐng 圆顶

domestic *adj* chores jiātíng 家庭; news, policy guónèi 国内; *(for agriculture)* jiāchù 家畜

domesticate animal xùnhuà 驯化; *be ~d (of person)* zuò jiāwù 做家务

domestic flight guónèi hángbān 国内航班

dominant zhǔyào 主要; member zhǔdǎo 主导; BIO zhàn yōushì 占优势

dominate kòngzhì 控制; landscape gāosǒng yú 高耸于

domination kòngzhì 控制

domineering bàdào 霸道

donate money juān 捐; toys, books, MED juānxiàn 捐献; time, energy fùchū 付出

donation *(of money, toys, books)*, MED juānxiàn 捐献; *(of time, energy)* fùchū 付出

donkey lǘ 驴

donor *(of money)*, MED juānxiàn zhě 捐献者

donut ⇩ zhá miànbǐngquān 炸面饼圈

doom *n (fate)* mìngyùn 命运; *(ruin)* zāinàn 灾难

doomed project zhùdìng shībài 注定失败; *we are ~ (bound to fail)* wǒmen sǐdìng le 我们死定了; *the ~ ship/plane* yùnàn

chuánzhī/fēijī 遇难船只/飞机

door mén 门; *(entrance)* dàmén 大门; *there's someone at the ~* yǒurén qiāomén 有人敲门

doorbell ménlíng 门铃; **door-knob** mén bǎshǒu 门把手; **doorman** shǒumén rén 守门人; **doormat** méndiàn 门垫; **door-step** ménjiē 门阶; **doorway** rùkǒu 入口

dope **1** *n (drugs)* dúpǐn 毒品; *(idiot)* shǎzi 傻子; *(information)* qíngbào 情报 **2** *v/t* shǐ mázuì 使麻醉

dormant plant xiūmián 休眠; *~ volcano* jìng huǒshān 静火山

dormitory sùshè 宿舍

dosage yòngliàng 用量

dose *n* yòngliàng 用量

dot *n (also in e-mail)* diǎn 点; *on the ~ (exactly)* zhǔnshí 准时

♦**dote on** chǒng'ài 宠爱

dotted line diǎnxiàn 点线

double **1** *n (amount)* shuāngbèi 双倍; *(person)* chóngyǐng 重影; *(of movie star)* tìdài yǎnyuán 替代演员; *(room)* shuāngrén fáng 双人房 **2** *adj (twice as much)* liǎngbèi 两倍; whisky jiābèi 加倍; sink, oven shuāng 双; doors liǎngchóng 两重; layer liǎngcéng 两层; *in ~ figures* liǎngwèi shù 两位数 **3** *adv* liǎngbèi 两倍; **4** *v/t* jiābèi 加倍; *(fold)* duìzhé 对折 **5** *v/i* fānyīfān 翻一番

♦**double back** *v/i (go back)* fǎnhuí 返回

♦**double up** *v/i (in pain)* wānshēn 弯身; *(share)* héyòng 合用

double-bass dīyīn tíqín 低音提琴; **double bed** shuāngrén chuáng 双人床; **double-breasted** shuāngpái kòushì 双排扣式; **doublecheck** *v/t & v/i* fùchá 复查; **double chin** shuāngxiàba 双下巴; **double click** COMPUT shuāngjī 双击; **doublecross** *v/t* qīpiàn 欺骗; **double glazing** shuāngcéng bōli 双层玻璃; **double-quick**: *in ~ time* jíkuài 极快; **double room**

shuāngrén fáng 双人房

doubles (*in tennis*) shuāngdǎ 双打

doubt 1 *n* yíwèn 疑问; (*uncertainty*) yóuyù 犹豫; **be in ~** nányǐ quèdìng 难以确定; **no ~** (*probably*) wúyí 无疑 **2** *v/t* huáiyí 怀疑

doubtful *remark, look* zhíde huáiyí 值得怀疑; **be ~** (*of person*) ná bùzhǔn 拿不准; **it is ~ whether** nányǐ yùliào 难以预料

doubtfully huáiyí 怀疑

doubtless wúyí 无疑

dough shēngmiàn tuán 生面团; F (*money*) qián 钱

dove gēzi 鸽子; *fig* zhǔhé pài rénwù 主和派人物

dowdy bù xiāosǎ 不潇洒

Dow Jones Average Dào Qióng píngjūn zhí 道琼平均值

down[1] *n* (*feathers*) róng róng 绒绒

down[2] **1** *adv* (*downward, onto the ground*) xià 下; **~ there** zài xiàbiān 在下边; *fall ~* shuāidǎo 摔倒; *$200 ~* (*as deposit*) xiānfù èrbǎi měiyuán 现付二百美元; **~ south** zài nánfāng 在南方; **be ~** (*of price, rate*) xiàjiàng 下降; (*of numbers, amount*) jiǎnshǎo 减少; (*not working*) shīling 失灵; F (*depressed*) qíngxù dīluò 情绪低落 **2** *prep* xiàngxià 向下; (*along*) yánzhe 沿着; *it fell ~ the hole* diào kūlonglǐ le 掉窟窿里了; *go ~ this street* yánzhe zhètiáo jì zǒu 沿着这条街走; *there are stores all ~ the street* mǎnjiē dōushì shāngdiàn 满街都是商店; *he walked ~ the hill* tā xià shān le 他下山了 **3** *v/t* (*swallow*) tūnxià 吞下; (*destroy*) jībài 击败

down-and-out *n* qióngkùn liáodǎo 穷困潦倒; **downcast** (*dejected*) jǔsàng 沮丧; **downfall** *n* kuǎtái 垮台; (*reason for ~*) kuǎtái de yuányīn 垮台的原因; (*of politician*) xiàtái 下台; **down-grade** *v/t* jiàngdī děngjí 降低等级; *employee* jiàngzhí 降职; **downhearted** jǔsàng 沮丧; **downhill** *adv* xiàpō 下坡; *go ~ fig*

zǒu xiàpō lù 走下坡路; **~ skiing** xiàpō huáxuě 下坡滑雪;

download COMPUT xiàzǎi 下载;

downmarket *adj* dījí 低级;

down payment dìngjīn 定金;

downplay *v/t* qīngmiáo dànxiě 轻描淡写; **downpour** qīngpén dàyǔ 倾盆大雨; **downright 1** *adj* *lie, idiot* shízài 十足 **2** *adv* *dangerous, stupid etc* shízài shì shízài shì 实在是; **downside** (*disadvantage*) quēxiàn 缺陷; **downsize 1** *v/t* car shēngchǎn xiǎoxíng 生产小型; *company* cáiyuán cáiyuán 裁员 **2** *v/i* (*of company*) cáiyuán cáiyuán 裁员; **downstairs** *adj & adv* lóuxià 楼下; **down-to-earth** *approach* jiǎotà shídì 脚踏实地; *person* shíshì qiúshì 实事求是; **down-town** *adj & adv* shì zhōngxīn 市中心; **downturn** (*in economy*) xiàjiàng qūshì 下降趋势

downward 1 *adj glance* xiàngxià 向下; *trend* xiàjiàng 下降 **2** *adv* wǎngxià 往下

doze *n & v/i* dǎdùnr 打盹儿

♦ **doze off** dǎ kēshuì 打瞌睡

dozen shí'èr 十二, dǎ dǎ 打; **~s of X** F jǐshíge X 几十个 X

drab dāndiào 单调

draft 1 *n* (*of air*) guòtáng fēng 过堂风; (*of document*) cǎogǎo 草稿; MIL zhēngbīng 征兵; **~** (*beer*), *beer on ~* shēng píjiǔ 生啤酒 **2** *v/t document* qǐ cǎogǎo 起草稿; MIL zhēngbīng 征兵

draft dodger táobì bīngyì zhě 逃避兵役者

draftee yìngzhēng rùwǔ zhě 应征入伍者

draftsman huìtú yuán 绘图员; (*of plan*) qǐcǎo rén 起草人

drafty tōngfēng 通风

drag 1 *n*: *it's a ~ having to ...* yào zuò ... shízài shì tài méijìnr le 要做 ... 实在是太没劲了; *he's a ~* tā méi shénme jìn 他没什么劲; *the main ~* jiēdào jiēxīn 街道中心; *in ~* nánbàn nǚzhuāng 男扮女装 **2** *v/t* (*pull*) lā 拉; *person, oneself* yìnglā 硬拉; (*search*) sǎo sǎo 扫扫;

COMPUT tuōdòng 拖动 3 v/i (of time) tuō tuō 拖拖; (of show, movie) méijìnr 没劲儿; ~ X into Y (involve) yìng bǎ X lāchě jìn Y 硬把X拉扯进Y; ~ X out of Y (get information from) cóng Y nàlǐ nádào X 从Y那里拿到X

♦ drag away : **drag oneself away from the TV** qiángpò zìjǐ bùkàn diànshì 强迫自己不看电视

♦ drag in (into conversation) yìngchě rù 硬扯入

♦ drag on (last long time) tuō tuō 拖拖

♦ drag out (prolong) tuōcháng 拖长

♦ drag up (mention) lǎotí 老提

dragon lóng 龙; fig pōfù 泼妇

Dragon Boat Festival Duānwǔjié 端午节

dragonfly qīngtíng 蜻蜓

drain 1 n (pipe) xiàshuǐ guǎndào 下水管道; (under street) xiàshuǐ dào 下水道; **a ~ on resources** hàofèi cáifù zhīwù 耗费财富之物 2 v/t water lù 滤; oil páigān 排干; vegetables páigān shuǐfèn 排干水分; land shǐ gānhé 使干涸; glass, tank dàoguāng 倒光; (exhaust: person) jīnpí lìjìn 筋疲力尽 3 v/i (of dishes) dīshuǐ 滴水

♦ drain away (of liquid) páiqù 排去

♦ drain off water páiqù 排去

drainage (drains) xiàshuǐ dào 下水道; (of water from soil) páishuǐ 排水

drainpipe páishuǐ guǎn 排水管

drama (art form, play in theater) xìjù 戏剧; (play on TV) jiémù 节目; (dramatic event) xìjùxìng shìjiàn 戏剧性事件; (excitement) xīngfèn 兴奋

dramatic xìjù 戏剧; (exciting) xìjù xìng 戏剧性; gesture zuòzuò 做作

dramatist jùzuò jiā 剧作家

dramatize (play) gǎibiān chéng xìjù 改编成戏剧

dramatize story gǎibiān chéng xìjù 改编成戏剧; fig zuòzuò 做作

drape v/t cloth, coat guà 挂; **~d in** (covered with) fùgài 覆盖

drapery bùshì 布饰

drapes chuānglián 窗帘

drastic (extreme) yánzhòng 严重; measures jíduān 极端; change jídà 极大

draw 1 n (in match, competition) píngjú 平局; (in lottery) kāijiǎng 开奖; (attraction) xīyǐn 吸引 2 v/t picture, map huà 画; cart, curtain lā 拉; lottery ticket chōu 抽; gun, knife chōuchū 抽出; (attract) xīyǐn 吸引; (lead) jiào 叫; (from bank account) tíkuǎn 提款 3 v/i huàhuà 画画; (in match, competition) dǎ píngjú 打平局; **~ near** (of person) zǒujìn 走近; (of date) línjìn 临近

♦ draw back 1 v/i (recoil) suōhuí 缩回 2 v/t (pull back) lākāi 拉开

♦ draw on 1 v/i (advance) línjìn 临近 2 v/t (make use of) lìyòng lìyòng 利用

♦ draw out billfold, money qǔchū 取出

♦ draw up 1 v/t document qǐcǎo 起草; chair lā guòlái 拉过来 2 v/i (of vehicle) tíng 停

drawback bìduān 弊端

drawer[1] (of desk etc) chōutì 抽屉

drawer[2]: **she is a good ~** tā hěnhuì huàhuàr 她很会画画儿

drawing (picture) huà 画; (skill) huìtú 绘图

drawing board túbǎn 图板; **go back to the ~** chóngxīn kāishǐ 重新开始

drawl n màn tūntun de jiǎnghuà 慢吞吞地讲话

dread v/t hàipà 害怕

dreadful zāogāo 糟糕

dreadfully (extremely) jíduān 极端; behave zāogāo 糟糕

dream 1 n mèng 梦 2 adj house etc mèngzhōng 梦中 3 v/t & v/i zuòmèng 做梦; (day~) mèngxiǎng 梦想

♦ dream up píngkōng xiǎngchū 凭空想出

dreamer (day~) mèngxiǎng jiā 梦想家

dreamy voice, look jīngshén huǎnghū 精神恍惚

dreary chénmèn 沉闷

dredge *harbour, canal* shūjùn 疏浚
♦ **dredge up** *fig* wāchū 挖出
dregs *(of coffee)* zhāzi 渣子; **the ~ of society** shèhuì zhāzǐ 社会渣滓
drench *v/t* shǐ shītòu 使湿透; **get ~ed** bèi yǔlín 被雨淋
dress 1 *n (for woman)* ⇩ liányīqún 连衣裙; *(clothing)* fúzhuāng 服装 **2** *v/t wound* fūguǒ 敷裹; **~ X person** gěi X chuān yīfu 给 X 穿衣服; **get ~ed** chuān yīfu 穿衣服 **3** *v/i (get ~ed)* chuān yīfu 穿衣服; *(well, in black etc)* chuānzhe 穿著
♦ **dress up** *v/i* dǎbàn 打扮; *(wear a disguise)* yǎnzhuāng 伪装; **~ as** zhuāngbàn chéng 装扮成
dress circle tèděng bāoxiāng 特等包厢
dresser *(dressing table)* shūzhuāng tái 梳妆台; *(in kitchen)* wǎndié guì 碗碟柜
dressing *(for salad)* tiáowèi zhī 调味汁儿; *(for wound)* fūliào 敷料
dressing room *(in theater)* huàzhuāng shì 化装室
dressing table shūzhuāng tái 梳妆台
dressmaker cáiféng 裁缝
dress rehearsal cǎipái 彩排
dressy jiǎngjiu 讲究
dribble *v/i (of person, baby)* liú kǒushuǐ 流口水; *(of water)* dī dī 滴; SP dàiqiú 带球
dried *fruit etc* gān 干; **~ bean curd** gāndòufu 干豆腐
drier *(machine)* shuǎigān jī 甩干机
drift 1 *n (of snow)* xuěduī 雪堆 **2** *v/i (of snow)* xuě chéngduī 雪成堆; *(of ship)* piāofú 漂浮; *(go off course)* piāobó 漂泊; *(of person)* liúdàng 流荡
♦ **drift apart** *(of couple)* shūyuǎn 疏远
drifter liúláng zhě 流浪者
drill 1 *n (tool)* zuàn 钻; *(exercise)* yǎnxí 演习; MIL cāoliàn 操练 **2** *v/t hole* zuàn 钻; *(for oil)* zuàn 钻; MIL cāoliàn 操练
drilling rig *(platform)* yóutái 油台
drily *remark* lěng bīngbīng 冷冰冰
drink 1 *n* yǐnliào 饮料; **a ~ of**

water yīdiǎn shuǐ 一点水; **go for a ~** qù hē diǎn dōngxi 去喝点东西 **2** *v/t* hē 喝 **3** *v/i* hē 喝; *(consume alcohol)* hējiǔ 喝酒; **I don't ~** wǒ bù hējiǔ 我不喝酒
♦ **drink up** *v/t & v/i* hēguāng 喝光
drinkable kěyǐ hē 可以喝
drinker yǐnjiǔ zhě 饮酒者
drinking *(of alcohol)* hējiǔ 喝酒
drinking water yǐnyòng shuǐ 饮用水
drip 1 *n (liquid)* dī 滴; MED diǎndī 点滴 **2** *v/i* dī 滴
dripdry dīgān 滴干
dripping: **~ (wet)** quánbù shītòu 全部湿透
drive 1 *n* lùtú 旅途; *(outing)* dōufēng 兜风; *(energy)* jīnglì 精力; COMPUT cípán dàijī 磁盘带机; *(campaign)* yùndòng 运动; **left-/right-hand ~** MOT zuǒ / yòu zuò jiàshǐ 左 / 右座驾驶 **2** *v/t vehicle* jiàshǐ 驾驶; *(own)* yōngyǒu 拥有; *(take in car)* yòng chē sòng 用车送; TECH qūdòng 驱动; **that noise / he is driving me mad** nàge zàoyīn / tā lìngwǒ fāfēng 那个噪音 / 他令我发疯 **3** *v/i* jiàshǐ 驾驶
♦ **drive at**: **what are you driving at?** nǐ shénme yìsi? 你什么意思？
♦ **drive away 1** *v/t* qūchē líkāi 驱车离开; *(chase off)* hōng hōng 哄哄 **2** *v/i* qūchē líkāi 驱车离开
♦ **drive in** *v/t nail* qiāojìn 敲进
♦ **drive off** *v/i* qūchē líkāi 驱车离开
driver sījī 司机
driver's license jiàshǐ zhízhào 驾驶执照
driveway qìchē dào 汽车道
driving 1 *n* jiàshǐ 驾驶 **2** *adj rain* měngliè 猛烈
driving force dònglì 动力; **driving instructor** jiàshǐ jiàoliàn 驾驶教练; **driving lesson** xuéchē kèchéng 学车课程; **driving school** ⇩ jiàshǐ xuéxiào 驾驶学校; **driving test** jiàzhǐ kǎoshì 驾驶考试

drizzle 1 *n* máomao yǔ 毛毛雨
2 *v/i* xià máomao yǔ 下毛毛雨

drone *n* (*noise*) wēngmíng shēng 嗡
鸣声

droop *v/i* xiàchuí 下垂; (*of plant*)
kūwěi 枯萎

drop 1 *n* (*of rain*) dī 滴; (*small
amount*) yìdiǎn 一点; (*in price,
temperature*) diē 跌; (*in number*)
xiàjiàng 下降 **2** *v/t* rēng 扔; (*and
lose*) diūshī 丢失; *person from car*
ràng ... xiàchē 让 ... 下车; *person
from team* chúqù 除去; (*stop
seeing*) duànjué guānxi 断绝关
系; *charges, demand etc* qǔxiāo 取
消; (*give up*) fàngqì 放弃; **~ a line
to** jì fēng duǎn xìn 寄封短信
3 *v/i* diēluò 跌落; (*decline*) xiàjiàng
下降; (*of wind*) jiǎnhuǎn 减缓

♦ **drop in** (*visit*) shùnbiàn láifǎng 顺
便来访

♦ **drop off 1** *v/t* person ràng ...
xiàchē 让 ... 下车; (*deliver*)
shùnbiàn sòng 顺便送 **2** *v/i* (*fall
asleep*) shuìzháo 睡着; (*decline*)
zhújiàn xiàjiàng 逐渐下降

♦ **drop out** (*withdraw*) tuìchū 退出;
(*of school*) zhōngtú tuìxué 中途
退学

dropout (*from school*) tuìxué
xuéshēng 退学学生; (*from
society*) tuìchū shìsú zhě 退出世
俗者

drops (*for eyes*) yǎn yàoshuǐ 眼药
水

drought gānhàn 干旱

drown 1 *v/i* yānsǐ 淹死 **2** *v/t person*
yānsǐ 淹死; *sound* yānmò 淹没;
be ~ed yānsǐ 淹死

drowsy fākùn 发困

drudgery dāndiào 单调

drug 1 *n* MED yào 药; (*illegal*) dúpín
毒品; **be on ~s** yǒu xīdú shìhào
有吸毒嗜好 **2** *v/t* xiàdú 下毒

drug addict xīdú chéngyǐn zhě 吸
毒成瘾者; **drug dealer** fàndú
zhě 贩毒者; **drug trafficking**
fàndú 贩毒

druggist yàojì shī 药剂师

drugstore yàofáng 药房

drum 1 *n* MUS gǔ 鼓; (*container*)

tǒng 桶

♦ **drum into**: **drum X into Y** xiàng
Y qiángdiào X 向Y强调X

♦ **drum up**: **~ support** zhāolǎn
zhīchí 招揽支持

drummer gǔshǒu 鼓手

drumstick MUS gǔchuí 鼓槌; (*of
poultry*) jītuǐ 鸡腿

drunk 1 *n* zuìguǐ 醉鬼 **2** *adj*
hēzuìle hēzuì 喝醉了; **get ~** hēzuì 喝醉

drunken *voices, laughter* hēzuì 喝
醉; **~ party** zuìjiǔ huì 醉酒会

drunk driving jiǔhòu kāichē 酒后
开车

dry 1 *adj* skin, clothes, weather, wine
gān 干; (*ironic*) wākǔ 挖苦;
(*alcohol banned*) jìnjiǔ 禁酒 **2** *v/t
dishes* cāgān 擦干 **3** *v/i* liànggān
晾干

♦ **dry out** (*of alcoholic*) jièjiǔ 戒酒

♦ **dry up** (*of river*) gānkū 干枯; (*be
quiet*) bìzuǐ 闭嘴

dry-clean *v/t* gānxǐ 干洗

dry cleaner gānxǐ diàn 干洗店

dry cleaning (*clothes*) gānxǐ yīwù
干洗衣物

dryer (*machine*) shuǎigān jī 甩干
机

DTP (= **desktop publishing**)
zhuōmiàn páibǎn 桌面排版

dual shuāng 双

dub *movie* pèiyīn 配音

dubious kào bùzhù 靠不住;
(*having doubts*) yǒu huáiyí 有怀疑

duck 1 *n* yā 鸭 **2** *v/i* duǒcáng 躲藏
3 *v/t one's head* dītóu 低头;
question huíbì 回避

dud *n* (*false bill*) jiǎ chāopiào 假钞
票

due (*owed*) qiàn 欠; (*proper*)
shìdàng 适当; **is there a train ~?**
huǒchē shìbùshì gāiláile? 火车是
不是该来了？; **when is the
baby ~?** háizi shénme shíhòu
chūshēng? 孩子什么时候出
生?; **~ to** (*because of*) yóuyú 由于;
be ~ to X (*be caused by*) yīn X ér
chǎnshēng 因X而产生; **in ~
course** zuìzhōng 最终

dull *weather* yīn chénchen 阴沉沉;
sound bù qīngcuì 不清脆; *pain*

dùn 钝; (boring) dāndiào 单调

duly (as expected) zhǔnshí 准时; (properly) shìdàng 适当

dumb (mute) yǎ 哑; (stupid) shǎ 傻

dump 1 n (for garbage) lājī zhàn 拉圾站; (unpleasant place) guǐdìfāng 鬼地方 2 v/t (deposit) qīngdào 倾倒; (dispose of) rēng 扔; toxic waste, nuclear waste diūqì 丢弃

dumpling tuánzi 团子

dune shāqiū 沙丘

dung fènbiàn 粪便

dungarees lián yīkù 连衣裤

dunk biscuit diǎn 点

duo MUS yīduì 一对

duplex (apartment) ⇩ èrliánshì gōngyù 二连式公寓

duplicate 1 n fùjiàn 复件; in ~ liǎngfèn 两份 2 v/t (copy) fùzhì 复制; (repeat) chóngfù 重复

duplicate key fùzhì yàoshi 复制钥匙

durable material láo 牢; relationship chíjiǔ 持久

duration qījiān 期间

duress: under ~ zài xiépò xià 在胁迫下

during: ~ X zài X qījiān 在 X 期间

dusk huánghūn 黄昏

dust 1 n chéntǔ 尘土 2 v/t: ~ X with Y (sprinkle) bǎ Y sǎzài X shàng 把 Y 洒在 X 上

dust cover (for furniture) jiājù zhào jiāsù 罩家具; (for book) shūpí 书皮

duster (cloth) mābù 抹布

dust jacket (of book) shūjí hùfēng 书籍护封

dustpan bòji 簸箕

dusty duō chéntǔ 多尘土

Dutch 1 adj Hélán 荷兰; go ~ gèzì fùkuǎn 各自付款 2 n (language) Hélán yǔ 荷兰语; the ~ Hélán rénmín 荷兰人民

duty zérèn 责任; (task) rènwù 任务; (on goods) shuì 税; be on ~ zhíbān 值班; be off ~ xiàbān 下班

duty-free 1 adj miǎnshuì 免税 2 n miǎnshuì wùpín 免税物品

duty-free store miǎnshuì shāngdiàn 免税商店

DVD COMPUT ⇩ shùzì shìpín guāngpán 数字视频光盘

dwarf 1 n zhūrú 侏儒 2 v/t shǐ xiǎnde ǎixiǎo 使显得矮小

♦ dwell on lǎoshì xiǎngzhe 老是想着

dwindle jiǎnshǎo 减少

dye 1 n rǎnliào 染料 2 v/t rǎnsè 染色

dying person chuísǐ 垂死; industry, tradition etc jíjiāng mièjué 即将灭绝

dynamic person jīnglì chōngpèi 精力充沛

dynamism (energy) dònglì 动力

dynamite n zhàyào 炸药

dynamo TECH diàndòng jī 电动机

dynasty cháodài 朝代; Ming Dynasty Míngcháo 明朝

dyslexia sòngdú kùnnán 诵读困难

dyslexic 1 adj sòngdú kùnnán 诵读困难 2 n sòngdú kùnnán bìng huànzhě 诵读困难病患者

E

each 1 *adj* měigè 每个 2 *adv* fēnbié 分别; *they're $1.50 ~* měigè yī měiyuán wǔshí měifēn 每个一美元五十美分 3 *pron* měigè 每个; *~ other* bǐcǐ 彼此

eager kěwàng 渴望; *be ~ to do X* rèzhōngyú zuò X 热衷于做 X

eager beaver rèxīnchángde rén 热心肠的人

eagerly rèqiè 热切

eagerness rèxīn 热心

eagle yīng 鹰

ear (*of person, animal*) ěrduǒ 耳朵; (*of corn*) suì 穗

earache ěrtòng 耳痛

eardrum gǔmó 鼓膜

early 1 *adj* (*not late*) zǎo 早; (*ahead of time*) tíqián 提前; (*farther back in time*) zǎoqī 早期; (*in the near future*) xùnsù 迅速 2 *adv* (*not late*) zǎo 早; (*ahead of time*) tíqián 提前

early bird (*in morning*) zǎochén 早晨; (*who arrives early*) xiānxíng zhě 先行者

earmark *money* bōchū 拨出; *~ X for Y* wèi Y ānpái X 为 Y 安排 X

earn zhèng 挣; *holiday, drink etc* yīngdé 应得; *respect* yíngdé 赢得

earnest rènzhēn 认真; *in ~* rènzhēn 认真

earnings zhuànde qián 赚的钱

earphones ěrjī 耳机; ear-piercing *adj* cì'ěr 刺耳; earring ěrhuán 耳环; earshot: *within ~* zài tīnglì fànwéi zhīnèi 在听力范围之内; *out of ~* bú zài tīnglì fànwéi zhīnèi 不在听力范围之内

earth (*soil*) tǔ 土; (*world, planet*) dìqiú 地球; *where on ~ ... ?* dàodǐ zài nǎr ... ? 到底在哪儿 ... ?

earthenware *n* táoqì 陶器

earthly xiànshì 现世; *it's no ~ use ... ...* wánquán wúyòng ... 完全无用

earthquake dìzhèn 地震

earth-shattering lìngrénzhènjīng 令人震惊

ease 1 *n* róngyì 容易; *be at (one's) ~, feel at ~* gǎndào shūfu 感到舒服; *be or feel ill at ~* gǎndào bù shūfu 感到不舒服 2 *v/t* (*relieve*) fàngsōng 放松 3 *v/i* (*of pain*) jiānqīng 减轻

♦ ease off 1 *v/t* (*remove*) xiǎoxīn yídiào 小心移掉 2 *v/i* (*of pain, rain*) jiānhuǎn 减缓

easel (*for blackboard*) hēibǎnjià 黑板架; (*for artist*) huàjià 画架

easily (*with ease*) róngyì 容易; (*by far*) wúyí 无疑

east 1 *n* dōngfāng 东方 2 *adj* dōng 东 3 *adv travel* xiàng dōngfāng 向东

East China Sea Dōnghǎi 东海

Easter Fùhuójié 复活节

Easter egg Fùhuójié cǎidàn 复活节彩蛋

easterly cóng dōng láide 从东来的

eastern dōngbù 东部; (*Oriental*) Dōngfāng 东方

easterner (*from the east coast*) dōnghǎi'àn de rén 东海岸的人

eastward(s) xiàngdōng 向东

easy (*not difficult*) róngyì 容易; (*relaxed*) fàngsōng 放松; *take things ~* (*slow down*) bùjǐnzhāng 不紧张; *take it ~!* (*calm down*) biéjǐnzhāng! 别紧张!

easy chair ānlèyǐ 安乐椅

easy-going suíhé 随和

eat *v/t & v/i* chī 吃

♦ eat out chūqù chī 出去吃

♦ eat up *food* chīguāng 吃光; *fig* hàojìn 耗尽

eatable kěchī 可吃

eaves wūyán 屋檐

eavesdrop tōutīng 偷听

ebb v/i (of tide) tuìluò 退落

♦**ebb away** fig (of courage, strength) jiǎnshǎo 减少

ebb tide tuìcháo 退潮

eccentric 1 adj gǔguài 古怪 **2** n gǔguài de rén 古怪的人

echo 1 n huíshēng 回声 **2** v/i huídàng 回荡 **3** v/t words chóngfù 重复; views chóngshēn 重申

eclipse 1 n (of sun) rìshí 日蚀; (of moon) yuèshí 月蚀 **2** v/t fig shèngguò 胜过

ecological shēngtài 生态

ecological balance shēngtài pínghéng 生态平衡

ecologically friendly lǜsè 绿色

ecologist shēngtàixuéjiā 生态学家

ecology shēngtàixué 生态学

economic jīngjì 经济

economical (cheap) jīngjì 经济; (thrifty) jiéshěng 节省

economically (in terms of economics) jīngjì shang 经济上; (thriftily) jiéjiǎn 节俭

economics (science) jīngjìxué 经济学; (financial aspects) jīngjì qíngkuàng 经济情况

economist jīngjìxuéjiā 经济学家

economize jǐnsuō kāizhī 紧缩开支

♦**economize on** jiéshěng 节省

economy (of a country) jīngjì 经济; (saving) jiéshěng 节省

economy class jīngjìcāng 经济舱; **economy drive** jiéyuē xíngdòng 节约行动; **economy size** jīngjìzhuāng 经济装

ecosystem shēngtài xìtǒng 生态系统

ecstasy kuángxǐ 狂喜; (drug) yáotóuwánr 摇头丸儿

ecstatic xīnxǐ ruò kuáng 欣喜若狂

eczema shīzhěn 湿疹

edge 1 n (of knife) fēng fēng 锋锋; (of table, road etc) biānyuán 边缘; (in voice) cì'ěr 刺耳; **on ~** jízào 急躁 **2** v/t xiāngbiān 镶边 **3** v/i (move slowly) huǎnmàn yídòng 缓慢移动

edgewise: I couldn't get a word in ~ wǒ chābúshàng huà 我插不上话

edgy jízào 急躁

edible kě shíyòng 可食用

edit text, file, book, newspaper biānjí 编辑; TV program jiǎnjí 剪辑; movie jiǎnjiē 剪接

edition bǎnběn 版本

editor (of text, book, newspaper, TV program, movie) biānjí 编辑; **sports/political ~** tǐyù/zhèngzhì lán biānjí 体育/政治栏编辑

editorial adj biānjí 编辑 **2** n shèlùn 社论

EDP (= electronic data processing) diànzǐ shùjù chǔlǐ 电子数据处理

educate child jiàoyù 教育; consumers yǐndǎo 引导

educated person shòuguò jiàoyù 受过教育

education jiàoyù 教育

educational jiàoyù 教育; informative yǒu jiàoyù yìyì 有教育意义

eel mán 鳗

eerie guàiyì 怪异

effect n xiàoguǒ 效果; negative hòuguǒ 后果; **take ~** (of medicine, drug) shēngxiào 生效; **come into ~** (of law) shíshí 实施

effective (efficient) yǒuxiào 有效; (striking) chǎnshēng shēnkè yìnxiàng 产生深刻印象; **~ May 1** cóng wǔyuè yīrì qǐ shēngxiào 从五月一日起生效

effeminate nǚrénqì 女人气

effervescent yǒu qìpào 有气泡; personality huóyuè 活跃

efficiency xiàolǜ 效率

efficient yǒu xiàolǜ 有效率

efficiently yǒu xiàolǜ 有效率

effort (struggle) fèilì 费力; (attempt) nǔlì 努力; **make an ~ to do X** nǔlì zuò X 努力做X

effortless róngyì 容易

effrontery wúchǐ 无耻

effusive guòyú jīdòng 过于激动

e.g. lìrú 例如

egalitarian adj píngděngzhǔyì 平等主义

egg (of hen) jīdàn 鸡蛋; (of bird) dàn 蛋

♦egg on sǒngyǒng 怂恿

eggcup jīdànbēi 鸡蛋杯; egg fried rice dànchǎofàn 蛋炒饭; egghead wénrén 文人; eggplant qiézi 茄子; eggshell dànké 蛋壳

ego PSYCH zìwǒ 自我; (self-esteem) zìzūn 自尊

egocentric yǐ zìwǒ wéi zhōngxīn 以自我为中心

Egypt Āijí 埃及

Egyptian 1 adj Āijí 埃及 2 n Āijí rén 埃及人

eiderdown (quilt) yǔróng 羽绒

eight bā 八

eighteen shíbā 十八

eighteenth dì shíbā 第十八

eighth dì bā 第八

eightieth dì bāshí 第八十

eighty bāshí 八十

either 1 adj rèn yīgè 任一个; (both) liǎng gè 两个 2 pron nǎge dōuxíng 哪个都行 3 adv: I won't go ~ wǒ yě bú qù 我也不去 4 conj: ~ ... or huòzhě ... huòzhě 或者 ... 或者

eject 1 v/t zhúchū 逐出 2 v/i (from plane) tánshè 弹射

eke out yányòng 延用

el (elevated railroad) gāojià tiělù 高架铁路

elaborate 1 adj jīngxīn zhìzuò 精心制作 2 v/i xiángjìn jiěshì 详尽解释

elapse liúshì 流逝

elastic 1 adj yǒu tánxìng 有弹性 2 n sōngjǐndài 松紧带

elastic band xiàngpíjīn 橡皮筋

elasticity tánxìng 弹性

elasticized dài sōngjǐn 带松紧

elated xìnggāocǎiliè 兴高采烈

elation xìnggāocǎiliè 兴高采烈

elbow 1 n zhǒu 肘 2 v/t: ~ out of the way yòng zhǒu jǐchū yìtiáo lù 用肘挤出一条路

elder 1 adj niánzhǎng 年长 2 n niánzhǎngzhě 年长者

elderly shàng niánjì 上年纪

eldest 1 adj: the ~ brother dàgē 大哥; the ~ sister dàjiě 大姐 2 n: the ~ zuìdà 最大

elect v/t xuǎn 选; ~ to do X xuǎnzé zuò X 选择做 X

elected xuǎnchū 选出

election xuǎnjǔ 选举

election campaign jìngxuǎn huódòng 竞选活动

election day xuǎnjǔrì 选举日

elective kěxuǎn 可选

elector xuǎnmín 选民

electoral system xuǎnjǔ zhìdù 选举制度

electorate quántǐ xuǎnmín 全体选民

electric diàn 电; fig shǐrén tūrán xīngfèn 使人突然兴奋

electrical diàn 电

electric blanket diànrètǎn 电热毯

electric chair diànyǐ 电椅

electrician diàngōng 电工

electricity diàn 电

electrify shǐ diànqìhuà 使电气化; fig cìjī 刺激

electrocute diànsǐ 电死

electrode diànjí 电级

electron diànzǐ 电子

electronic diànzǐ 电子

electronic data processing diànzǐ shùjù chǔlǐ 电子数据处理

electronic mail diànzǐ yóujiàn 电子邮件

electronics diànzǐxué 电子学

elegance gāoyǎ 高雅

elegant gāoyǎ 高雅

element CHEM yuánsù 元素

elementary (rudimentary) chūjí 初级

elementary school xiǎoxué 小学

elementary teacher xiǎoxué lǎoshī 小学老师

elephant dàxiàng 大象

elevate tígāo 提高

elevated railroad gāojià tiělù 高架铁路

elevation (altitude) hǎibá 海拔

elevator diàntī 电梯

eleven shíyī 十一

eleventh dì shíyī 第十一; *at the ~ hour* zuìhòu guāntóu 最后关头

eligible hégé 合格

eligible bachelor héyì nánshì 合意男士

eliminate (*get rid of*) chúdiào 除掉; (*rule out*) páichú 排除; (*kill*) gàndiào 干掉; *be ~d (from competition)* bèi táotài 被淘汰

elimination (*from competition*) táotài 淘汰; (*of poverty*) xiāochú 消除; (*murder*) gàndiào 干掉

elite **1** *n* jīngyīng 精英 **2** *adj* gāoděng 高等

elk túolù 驼鹿

ellipse tuǒyuán 椭圆

elm yúmù 榆木

elope sībēn 私奔

eloquence kǒucái 口才

eloquent xióngbiàn 雄辩

eloquently xióngbiàn 雄辩

else: *anything ~?* hái yào biéde ma? 还要别的吗？; *if you've got nothing ~ to do* rúguǒ nǐ méiyǒu biéde shì yào zuò 如果你没有别的事要做; *no one ~* méiyǒu biérén 没有别人; *every-one ~ is going* biérén dōu qù bié rén qù 别人都去; *who ~ was there?* hái yǒu shéi zài nàr? 还有谁在那儿？; *someone ~* biérén 别人; *something ~* biéde dōngxi 别的东西; *let's go somewhere ~* zánmen qù biéde dìfang ba 咱们去别的地方吧; *or ~ (otherwise)* fǒuzé 否则

elsewhere biéchù 别处

elude *escape from* táobì 逃避; *avoid* duǒbì 躲避

elusive nányǐ pǔzhuō 难以扑捉

emaciated xiāoshòu 消瘦

e-mail **1** *n* diànzǐ yóujiàn 电子邮件 **2** *v/t person* dǎ diànzǐ yóujiàn 打电子邮件; *text* yòng diànzǐ yóujiàn jì 用电子邮件寄

e-mail address diànzǐ xìnxiāng 电子信箱

emancipated *woman* jiěfàng 解放

emancipation jiěfàng 解放

embalm bǎocún 保存

embankment *of river* dī'àn 堤岸; RAIL lùdī 路堤

embargo *n* jìnyùn 禁运

embark *v/i* shàngchuán 上船 ♦*embark on* kāishǐ 开始

embarrass shǐ gāngà 使 ... 尴尬

embarrassed gāngà 尴尬

embarrassing lìngrén gāngà 令人尴尬

embarrassment gāngà 尴尬

embassy dàshǐguǎn 大使馆

embellish zhuāngshì 装饰; *story* jiāgōng 加工

embers yújìn 余烬

embezzle dàoyòng 盗用

embezzlement dàoyòng 盗用

embitter shǐkǔnǎo 使苦恼

emblem xiàngzhēng 象征

embodiment huàshēn 化身

embody tǐxiàn 体现

embolism shuānsè 栓塞

emboss *metal* fútú 浮凸; *paper, fabric* tūyìn 凸印

embrace **1** *n* yōngbào 拥抱 **2** *v/t* (*hug*) yōngbào 拥抱; (*take in*) bāokuò 包括 **3** *v/i* (*of two people*) yōngbào 拥抱

embroider cìxiù 刺绣; *fig* xūgòu qíngjié 虚构情节

embroidery cìxiù 刺绣

embryo pēitāi 胚胎

emerald (*precious stone*) lǜbǎoshí 绿宝石; (*color*) zǔmǔlǜ 祖母绿

emerge (*appear*) chūxiàn 出现; *it has ~d that ...* jùxī ... 据悉 ...

emergency jǐnjí qíngkuàng 紧急情况; *in an ~* yùdào jǐnjí qíngkuàng 遇到紧急情况

emergency exit jǐnjí chūkǒu 紧急出口

emergency landing jǐnjí zhuóluò 紧急着落

emigrant *n* yímín 移民

emigrate yíjū guówài 移居国外

emigration yíjū guówài 移居国外

eminent jiéchū 杰出

eminently fēicháng 非常

emission (*of gases*) páifàng 排放

emotion qínggǎn 情感

emotional *problems, development*

qínggǎn 情感; *(full of emotion)* fùyú qínggǎn 富于情感

empathize: ~ **with** tóngqíng 同情

emperor huángdì 皇帝

emphasis zhòngdiào 重调

emphasize qiángdiào 强调

emphatic kěndìng 肯定

empire dìguó 帝国

employ gùyòng 雇佣; *(use)* shǐyòng 使用; *he's ~ed as a ...* tā bèi gù zuò ... 他被雇作 ...

employee gùyuán 雇员

employer gùzhǔ 雇主

employment zhíyè 职业; *(work)* gōngzuò 工作; *be seeking ~* zài qiúzhí 在求职

employment agency zhíyè jièshàosuǒ 职业介绍所

empress huánghòu 皇后

emptiness kōngxū 空虚

empty 1 *adj* kōng 空; *promises* kōngdòng 空洞 **2** *v/t pockets* tāokōng 掏空; *drawer* dàokōng 倒 空; *glass, bottle* dào 倒 **3** *v/i (of room, street)* biànkōng 变空

emulate gǎnchāo 赶超

enable shǐde néngzuò 使得能做

enact *law* zhìdìng 制定; THEA yǎnchū 演出

enamel *n* tángcí 搪瓷; *(on tooth)* fàlángzhì 珐琅质; *(paint)* cíqī 瓷漆

enchanting *smile, village, person* mírén 迷人

encircle bāowéi 包围

enclose *(in letter)* fùjiàn 附件; *area* wéizhù 围住; *please find ~d ...* zífùshàng ... 兹附上 ...

enclosure *(with letter)* fùjiàn 附件

encore *n* zàilái yígè 再来一个

encounter 1 *n* xièhòu 邂逅 **2** *v/t person* jiēchù 接触; *problem, resistance* yùdào 遇到

encourage gǔlì 鼓励

encouragement gǔlì 鼓励

encouraging lìngrén gǔwǔ 令人鼓舞

♦**encroach on** *land* qīnzhàn 侵占; *rights* qīnfàn 侵犯; *time* zhànyòng 占用

encyclopedia bǎikēquánshū 百科

全书

end 1 *n (extremity)* jìntóu 尽头; *(conclusion)* jiéwěi 结尾; *(purpose)* mùdì 目的; *in the ~* zuìhòu 最后; *for hours on ~* chíxùbúduàn 持续不断; *stand X on ~* zhílì X 直立 X; *at the ~ of July* qīyuèmò 七月末; *put an ~ to* jiéshù 结束 **2** *v/t & v/i* jiéshù 结束

♦**end up** jiéguǒ 结果

endanger wēijí 危及

endangered species bīnlín mièjuéde wùzhǒng 濒临灭绝的物种

endearing tǎorén xǐhuān 讨人喜欢

endeavor 1 *n* nǔlì 努力 **2** *v/t* jìnlì 尽力

ending jiéjú 结局; GRAM cíwěi 词尾

endless wúzhǐjìng 无止境

endorse *check* bèishū 背书; *candidacy* zhīchí 支持; *product* cùxiāo 促销

endorsement *(of check)* bèiqiān 背签; *(of candidacy)* zhīchí 支持; *(of product)* cùxiāo 促销

end product zhōngduān chǎnpǐn 终端产品

end result zuìzhōng jiéguǒ 最终结果

endurance rěnnàilì 忍耐力

endure 1 *v/t* rěnnài 忍耐 **2** *v/i (last)* chíxù 持续

enduring chíjiǔ 持久

end-user zhōngduān yònghù 终端用户

enemy dírén 敌人

energetic jùliè 剧烈; *person* yǒu jīngshen 有精神; *fig: measures* jījí 积极

energy *(gas, electricity etc)* néngyuán 能源; *(of person)* jīnglì 精力

energy-saving *device* jiénéng 节能

enforce shíshī 实施

engage 1 *v/t (hire)* pìnyòng 聘用 **2** *v/i* TECH niéhé 啮合

♦**engage in** cóngshì 从事

engaged *(to be married)* dìnghūn 订婚; *get ~* dìnghūn 订婚

engagement (*appointment*) yuēhuì 约会; (*to be married*) dìnghūn 订婚; MIL jiāozhàn 交战

engagement ring dìnghūn jièzhǐ 订婚戒指

engaging *smile, person* xīyǐnrén 吸引人

engine yǐnqíng 引擎

engineer 1 *n* gōngchéngshī 工程师; NAUT lúnjīzhǎng 轮机长; RAIL gōngchéngshī 工程师 2 *v/t* *fig* (*meeting etc*) qiǎomiàode ānpái 巧妙地安排

engineering gōngchéng 工程

England Yīnggélán 英格兰

English 1 *adj* Yīngguó 英国 2 *n* (*language*) Yīngyǔ 英语; *the ~* Yīnggélán rén 英格兰人

Englishman Yīnggélán nánzǐ 英格兰男子

Englishwoman Yīnggélán nǚzǐ 英格兰女子

engrave diāokè 雕刻

engraving (*drawing*) bǎnhuà 版画; (*design*) diāokè 雕刻

engrossed: *~ in* quánshén guànzhùyú 全神贯注于

engulf tūnmò 吞没

enhance zēngqiáng 增强

enigma mí 谜

enigmatic shénmì 神秘

enjoy xǐhuan 喜欢; *~ oneself* guòde kuàilè 过得快乐; *~!* (*said to somebody eating*) chīhǎo! 吃好!

enjoyable lìngrén yúkuài 令人愉快

enjoyment lèqù 乐趣

enlarge kuòdà 扩大

enlargement kuòdà 扩大

enlighten qǐdí 启迪

enlist 1 *v/i* MIL bàomíng cānjūn 报名参军 2 *v/t* zhāomù 召募; *~ the help of X* jiào X bāngmáng 叫 X 帮忙

enliven shǐhuóyuè 使活跃

enormity (*size*) pángdà 庞大; (*wickedness*) qióngxiōngjí'è 穷凶极恶

enormous jùdà 巨大; *satisfaction, patience* jídà 极大

enormously fēicháng 非常

enough 1 *adj* zúgòu 足够 2 *pron* zúgòu 足够; *will $50 be ~?* wǔshí měiyuán gòu le ma? 五十美元够了吗?; *I've had ~!* wǒ shòugòu le 我受够了!; *that's ~, calm down!* xíngle, lěngjìngdiǎn 行了, 冷静点儿! 3 *adv* zúgòu 足够; *strangely ~* qíguài 奇怪的是

enquire, enquiry → *inquire, inquiry*

enraged jīnù 激怒

enrich *vocabulary* kuòdà 扩大; *somebody's life* fēngfù 丰富

enroll *v/i* zhùcè 注册

enrolment zhùcè 注册

ensure bǎozhèng 保证

entail qiānshè 牵涉

entangle: *become ~d in* (*in rope*) chánràozài 缠绕在; (*in love affair*) xiànrù 陷入

enter 1 *v/t* *room, house* jìnrù 进入; *competition* cānjiā 参加; *person, horse in race* bàomíng 报名; *write down* xiěxià 写下; COMPUT jiànrù 键入 2 *v/i* jìnrù 进入; THEA shàngchǎng 上场; (*in competition*) bàomíng 报名 3 *n* COMPUT huíchējiàn 回车健

enterprise (*initiative*) jìnqǔxīn 进取心; (*venture*) qǐyè 企业

enterprising yǒu jìnqǔxīn 有进取心

entertain 1 *v/t* (*amuse*) shǐrén kuàilè 使人快乐; (*consider: idea*) yuànyì kǎolǜ 愿意考虑 2 *v/i* (*have guests*) zhāodài 招待

entertainer biǎoyǎnzhě 表演者

entertaining *adj* yǒuqù 有趣

entertainment yúlè 娱乐

enthrall mízhù 迷住

enthusiasm rèqíng 热情

enthusiast rèzhōngzhě 热中者

enthusiastic rèxīn 热心

entice yòuhuò 诱惑

entire zhěngzǔ 整个

entirely wánquán 完全

entitle fùyǔ quánlì 赋予权利

entitled *book* dìngmíng 定名

entrance *n* (*doorway*) rùkǒu 入口;

(fact of entering) jìnrù 进入; THEA chūchǎng 出场; *(admission)* zhǔnyǔ jìnrù 准予进入

entranced zháomí 着迷

entrance fee rùchǎngfèi 入场费

entrant cānjiā zhě 参加者

entrenched *attitudes* gēnshēndìgù 根深蒂固

entrepreneur qǐyèjiā 企业家

entrepreneurial yǒu chuàngyè cáinéng 有创业才能

entrust: ~ *X with Y*, ~ *Y to X* bǎ Y wěituōgěi X 把 Y 委托给 X

entry *(way in)* rùkǒu 入口; *(admission)* jìnrù 进入; *(for competition)* cānjiāzhě 参加者; *(in diary, accounts)* xiàngmù 项目

entry form cānsàibiǎo 参赛表

entry visa rùjìng qiānzhèng 入境签证

envelop bāozhù 包住

envelope xìnfēng 信封

enviable zhídé xiànmù 值得羡慕

envious mǎnhuái jídù 满怀嫉妒; *be ~ of X* xiànmù X 羡慕 X

environment *(nature)* zìrán huánjìng 自然环境; *(surroundings)* huánjìng 环境

environmental yǒuguān huánjìng 有关环境

environmentalist huánjìng bǎohùlùn zhě 环境保护论者

environmentally friendly lǜsè 绿色

environmental pollution huánjìng wūrǎn 环境污染

environmental protection huánjìng bǎohù 环境保护

environs jìnjiāo 近郊

envisage xiǎngxiàng 想象

envoy shǐzhě 使者

envy 1 *n* jídù 嫉妒; *be the ~ of X* lìng X jídù 令 X 羡慕 **2** *v/t*: dùxiàn 妒羡; ~ *X Y* xiànmù X de Y 羡慕 X 的 Y

epic 1 *n* shǐshī 史诗 **2** *adj journey* shǐshībān 史诗般; *a task of ~ proportions* zhòngdà rènwù 重大任务

epicenter ⇩ zhènzhōng 震中

epidemic liúxíngxìng 流行性

epilepsy diānxiánzhèng 癫痫症

epileptic *n* diānxián 癫痫

epileptic fit diānxián fāzuò 癫痫发作

epilog jiéwěi bùfen 结尾部分

episode *(of story, soap opera)* yìjí 一集; *(happening)* shíjiàn 事件

epitaph mùzhìmíng 墓志铭

epoch jìyuán 纪元

epoch-making huàshídài 划时代

equal 1 *adj* xiāngtóng 相同; *be ~ to (a task)* néngshèngrèn 能胜任 **2** *n* děngtóng 等同 **3** *v/t (with numbers)* děngyú 等于; *(be as good as)* búxùnsè 不逊色

equality píngděng 平等

equalize 1 *v/t* jūnhéng 均衡 **2** *v/i* SP bānpíng bǐfēn 扳平比分

equalizer SP píngfēnqiú 平分球

equally tóngděng 同等; *~, ...* cǐwài, ... 此外 ...

equate: ~ *X with Y* děngtóng X hé Y 等同 X 和 Y

equation MATH děngshì 等式

equator chìdào 赤道

equilibrium pínghéng 平衡

equinox: *Spring ~* Chūnfēn 春分; *Autumn ~* Qiūfēn 秋分

equip: ~ *X* zhuāngbèi X 装备 X; *he's not ~ped to handle it fig* tā wúlì chǔlǐ cǐshí 他无力处理此事

equipment zhuāngbèi 装备

equity COM pǔtōnggǔ 普通股

equivalent 1 *adj* xiāngtóng 相同; *be ~ to* xiāngdāngyú 相当于 **2** *n*: *X is the ~ of Y* X xiāngdāngyú Y X 相当于 Y

era jìyuán 纪元

eradicate gēnchú 根除

erase *(with eraser)* cādiào 擦掉; *tape* xǐdiào 洗掉; COMPUT shānchú 删除

eraser *(for blackboard)* hēibǎncā 黑板擦; *(for pencil)* xiàngpí 橡皮

erect 1 *adj* zhílì 直立 **2** *v/t* shùqǐ 竖起

erection *(of building etc)* shùqǐ 竖起; *(of penis)* bóqǐ 勃起

erode qīnshí 侵蚀; *fig: rights, power* qīnfàn 侵犯

erosion qīnshí 侵蚀; *fig* qīnfàn 侵犯

erotic sèqíng 色情

eroticism xìngyù 性欲

errand chāishǐ 差使; ***run ~s*** pǎotuǐ 跑腿

erratic wúcháng 无常

error cuòwù 错误

error message COMPUT cuòwù xìnxī 错误信息

erupt (*of volcano*) bàofā 爆发; (*of violence*) tūrán fāshēng 突然发生; (*of person*) fāhuǒ 发火

eruption (*of volcano*) bàofā 爆发; (*of violence*) tūrán fāshēng 突然发生

escalate zhúbù shēngjí 逐步升级

escalation shēngjí 升级

escalator zìdòngfútī 自动扶梯

escape **1** *n* (*of prisoner, animal*) táotuō 逃脱; (*of gas*) lòuchū 漏出; ***have a narrow ~*** jiǔsǐyìshēng 九死一生 **2** *v/i* (*of prisoner, animal*) táotuō 逃脱; (*of gas*) lòuchū 漏出 **3** *v/t*: ***the word ~s me*** wǒ xiǎngbùqǐlái zhèigè cí le 我想不起来这个词了

escape chute tuōxiǎn huátī 脱险滑梯

escort **1** *n* péitóng 陪同; (*guard*) hùwèi 护卫 **2** *v/t* (*socially*) péi péi 陪; (*act as guard to*) hùwèi 护卫

especially yóuqí 尤其

espionage jiàndié huódòng 间谍活动

essay *n* duǎnwén 短文

essential *adj* bìyào 必要

essentially jīběnshàng 基本上

establish *company* chénglì 成立; (*create*) chuàngzào 创造; (*determine*) quèdìng 确定; ***~ oneself as*** wèi zìjǐ yíngdé 为自己赢得

establishment (*firm, store etc*) jīgòu jīgòu 机构; ***the Establishment*** dāngquánpài 当权派

estate (*area of land*) dìchǎn 地产; (*possessions of dead person*) yíchǎn 遗产

esthetic měiguān 美观

estimate *n & v/t* gūjì 估计

estimation: ***he has gone up / down in my ~*** zēngjiā / jiàngdī duì tā de zūnjìng zēngjiā / jiàngdī duì tā de zūnjìng 增加 / 降低对他的尊敬; ***in my ~*** (*opinion*) zhào wǒ kànlái 照我看来

estranged *wife, husband* shūyuǎn 疏远

estuary hékǒuwān 河口湾

ETA (= ***estimated time of arrival***) yùjì dàodá shíjiān 预计到达时间

etching shíkèshù 蚀刻术

eternal yǒnghéng 永恒

eternity yǒnghéng 永恒

ethical dàodé 道德

ethics lúnlǐxué 伦理学

ethnic zhǒngzú 种族

ethnic group zhǒngzú shèqū 种族社区

ethnic minority shǎoshù mínzú 少数民族

euphemism wěiwǎn shuōfǎ 委婉说法

euphoria xīnkuàigǎn 欣快感

Europe Ōuzhōu 欧洲

European **1** *adj* Ōuzhōu 欧洲 **2** *n* Ōuzhōu rén 欧洲人

euthanasia ānlèsǐ 安乐死

evacuate (*clear people from*) chèkōng 撤空; (*leave*) chèlí 撤离

evade bìkāi 避开

evaluate pínggū 评估

evaluation pínggū 评估

evangelist fúyīn chuándào zhě 福音传道者

evaporate (*of water*) zhēngfā 蒸发; (*of confidence*) xiāoshī 消失

evasion táobì 逃避

evasive bùtǎnshuài 不坦率

eve chúxī 前夕

even **1** *adj* (*regular*) jūnyún 均匀; (*level*) píng píng 平; (*number*) ǒushù 偶数; ***get ~ with X*** bàofù X 报复 X **2** *adv* shènzhì 甚至; ~ ***bigger / better*** gèngdà / hǎo 更大 / 好; ***not*** ~ lián ... yěbù 连 ... 也不; ~ ***so*** jǐnguǎn rúcǐ 尽管如此; ~ ***if*** jíshǐ 即使 **3** *v/t*: ~ ***the score*** lāpíng bǐfēn 拉平比分

evening wǎnshang 晚上; ***in the ~*** wǎnshang 晚上; ***this ~*** jīntiān wǎnshang 今天晚上; *good ~* wǎnshang 好晚上好

evening class yèxiào 夜校; **evening dress** (*for man, woman*) wǎnlǐfú 晚礼服; **evening paper** wǎnbào 晚报

evenly (*regularly*) jūnyún 均匀

event shìjiàn 事件; SP bǐsài xiàngmù 比赛项目; *at all ~s* wúlùn rúhé 无论如何

eventful yǒu xǔduō dàshì 有许多大事

eventual zuìzhōng 最终

eventually zhōngyú 终于

ever *adv* (*with past or perfect tense questions*) céngjīng 曾经; (*with past or perfect tense negative*) cónglái 从来; (*with conditionals*) yídàn 一旦; (*for emphasis*) dàodǐ 到底; *did you ~ go abroad before you were 15?* shíwǔ suì yǐqián nǐ céngjīng chūguò guó ma? 十五岁以前你曾经出过国吗?; *have you ~ been to … ?* nǐ céng dàoguo … ma? 你曾到过 … 玛 ?; *he hasn't ~ been there* tā cónglái méi qùguò nàr 他从来没去过那儿; *if you ~ come to China, give me a call* nǐ yàoshì yídàn lái Zhōngguó, gěi wǒ dǎge diànhuà 你要是一旦来中国, 给我打个电话; *for ~* yǒngyuǎn 永远; *~ since* céng nà yǐhòu 从那以后; *~ since he came to China …* cóng tā lái Zhōngguó yǐhòu … 从他来中国以后 …

Everest: *Mount ~* ⇩ Zhūmùlǎngmǎfēng 珠穆朗玛峰

evergreen *n* chángqīng 常青

everlasting yǒngjiǔ 永久

every měiyī 每一; *~ other day* měigéyītiān 每隔一天; *~ now and then* ǒu'ěr 偶尔

everybody měigèrén 每个人

everyday měitiān 每天

everyone měigèrén 每个人

everything yíqiè 一切

everywhere gèchù 各处; (*wherever*) dàochù 到处

evict zhúchū 逐出

evidence hénjì 痕迹; LAW zhèngjù 证据; *give ~* chūzhèng 出证

evident míngxiǎn 明显

evidently (*clearly*) míngxiǎn 明显; (*apparently*) xiǎnrán 显然

evil *1 adj* xié'è 邪恶 *2 n* è 恶

evoke *image* huànqǐ 唤起

evolution jìnhuà 进化

evolve *v/i* (*of animals*) jìnhuà 进化; (*develop*) zhújiàn xíngchéng 逐渐形成

ewe mǔyáng 母羊

ex- qián 前

ex *n* ⊢ (*former wife*) qiánqī 前妻; (*former husband*) qiánfū 前夫

exact *adj* quèqiè 确切

exactly qiàqià 恰恰; *~!* jiùshì! 就是!; *not ~* bù quánshì 不全是

exaggerate *1 v/i* kuādà 夸大 *2 v/i* kuāzhāng 夸张

exaggeration yán guò qí shí 言过其实

exam kǎoshì 考试; *take an ~* cānjiā kǎoshì 参加考试; *pass/ fail an ~* tōngguò/bùtōngguò kǎoshì 通过/不通过考试

examination (*of facts etc*) diàochá 调查; (*of patient*) jiǎnchá 检查; EDU kǎoshì 考试

examine *study* diàochá 调查; *patient* jiǎnchá 检查; EDU kǎo 考

examiner EDU zhǔkǎorén 主考人

example lìzi 例子; *for ~* bǐrú 比如; *set a good/bad ~* shùlì hǎo/bùhǎo bǎngyàng 树立好/不好榜样

exasperate rěnǎo 惹恼

excavate *v/t* (*dig*) wājué 挖掘; (*archeologist*) fājué 发掘

excavation wājué 挖掘

excavator wājuéjī 挖掘机

exceed (*be more than*) chāoguò 超过; (*go beyond*) chāochū 超出

exceedingly jíduān 极端

excel *1 v/i* shàncháng 擅长; *~ at X* shàncháng X 擅长 X *2 v/t: ~ oneself* shèngguò guòqù 胜过过去

excellence yōuxiù 优秀

excellent hěn hǎo 很好

except chúle 除了; *~ for* chúle X yǐwài 除了 X 以外; *~ that …*

zhǐshì ... 只是 ...

exception lìwài 例外; **with the ~ of** chúle 除了; **take ~ to** fǎndù 反对

exceptional (*very good*) jiéchū 杰出; (*special*) tèshū 特殊

exceptionally (*extremely*) yìcháng 异常

excerpt jiélù 节录

excess 1 n guòdù 过度; **eat / drink to ~** chī / hē wúdù 吃 / 喝无度; **in ~ of** duōyú 多于 2 adj duōyú 多余

excess baggage chāozhòngde xíngli 超重的行李

excess fare bǔpiàofèi 补票费

excessive guòfèn 过分

exchange 1 n (*of views, information*) jiāohuàn 交换; (*between schools*) jiāoliú 交流; **in ~** zuòwéi jiāohuàn 作为交换; **in ~ for** yòngláai huànqǔ 用来换取 2 v/t (*in store*) gēnghuàn 更换; *addresses* hùhuàn 互换; *currency* duìhuàn 兑换; **~ X for Y** yòng X huàn Y 用 X 换 Y

exchange rate FIN duìhuànlǜ 兑换率

excitable yìxīngfèn 易兴奋

excite (*make enthusiastic*) jīdòng 激动

excited xīngfèn 兴奋; **get ~** xīngfèn 兴奋; **get ~ about X** wèi X gǎndào xīngfèn 为 X 感到兴奋

excitement xīngfèn 兴奋

exciting lìngrén xīngfèn 令人兴奋

exclaim jīngjiào 惊叫

exclamation gǎntàn 感叹

exclamation point gǎntànhào 感叹号

exclude (*not include*) páichú zàiwài 排除在外; *possibility* páichú 排除; (*bar: from club etc*) páichì 排斥

excluding chúle 除了

exclusive *hotel, restaurant* dútè 独特; *rights* dúyǒu 独有; *interview* dújiā 独家

excruciating *pain* jùliè 剧烈

excursion yuǎnzú 远足

excuse 1 n jièkǒu 借口 2 v/t

(*forgive*) yuánliàng 原谅; **please ~ me** (*allow to leave*) shīpéi 失陪; **~ X from Y** miǎnchú X zuò Y 免除 X 做 Y; **~ me** (*to get attention*) qǐngwèn 请问; (*to get past*) láojià 劳驾; (*interrupting somebody*) hěn bàoqiàn 很抱歉

execute *criminal* chǔjué 处决; *plan* shíshī 实施

execution (*of criminal*) sǐxíng 死刑; (*of plan*) shíshī 实施

executioner xíngxíngrén 行刑人

executive n zhǔguǎn rényuán 主管人员

executive briefcase zhǔguǎn rényuán gōngshìbāo 主管人员公事包

executive washroom zhǔguǎn guànxǐshì 主管盥洗室

exemplary mófàn 模范

exempt: **be ~ from** miǎnchú 免除

exercise 1 n (*physical*) duànliàn 锻炼; EDU liànxí 练习; MIL yǎnxí 演习; **take ~** zuò yùndòng 作运动 2 v/t *muscle* duànliàn 锻炼; *dog* liù 遛; *caution, restraint* yìngyòng 应用 3 v/i duànliàn 锻炼

exercise book EDU liànxíběn 练习本

exert *authority* xíngshǐ 行使; **~ oneself** yònglì 用力

exertion fèilì 费力

exhale hūchū 呼出

exhaust 1 n (*fumes*) fèiqì 废气; (*pipe*) páiqìguǎn 排气管 2 v/t (*tire*) shǐpíjuàn 使疲倦; (*use up*) yòngjìn 用尽

exhaust fumes páichūde fèiqì 排出的废气

exhausted (*tired*) jīnpílijìn 筋疲力尽

exhausting lìngrénpíjuàn 令人疲倦

exhaustion láolèi guòdù 劳累过度

exhaustive chèdǐ 彻底

exhaust pipe páiqìguǎn 排气管

exhibit 1 n (*in exhibition*) zhǎnpǐn 展品 2 v/t (*of gallery*) zhǎnlǎn 展览; (*of artist*) zhǎnchū 展出; (*give evidence of*) xiǎnchū 显出

exhibition zhǎnlǎnhuì 展览会; (of bad behavior) chūchǒu 出丑; (of skill) biǎoyǎn 表演

exhibitionist fēngtóu zhǔyì zhě 风头主义者

exhilarating lìngrén yúkuài 令人愉快

exile 1 n liúwáng 流亡; (person) qùguó zhě 去国者 2 v/t liúfàng 流放

exist cúnzài 存在; ~ on X kào X shēngcún 靠 X 生存

existence cúnzài 存在; (life) shēngcún 生存; in ~ xiàncún 现存; come into ~ xíngchéng 形成

existing xiàncún 现存

exit 1 n (way out) chūkǒu 出口; (from highway) chūlù 出路; THEA tuìchǎng 退场 2 v/i COMPUT tuìchū 退出

exonerate xuānbù wúzuì 宣布无罪

exorbitant guògāo 过高

exotic fùyǒu yìguó qíngdiào 富有异国情调

expand 1 v/t kuòdà 扩大 2 v/i zēngzhǎng 增长; (of metal) péngzhàng 膨胀

♦expand on xiángshù 详述

expanse guǎngkuò 广阔

expansion zēngzhǎng 增长; (of metal) péngzhàng 膨胀

expect 1 v/t qīdài 期待; baby huáiyùn 怀孕; (suppose) rènwéi 认为; (demand) yāoqiú 要求 2 v/i: be ~ing yǒule 有了; I ~ so wǒ xiǎng huì de 我想会的

expectant huáiyǒu xīwàng 怀有希望

expectant mother zhǔn mǔqīn 准母亲

expectation qīwàng 期望; ~s (demands) zhīwàng 指望

expedient n yǒuyì 有益

expedition tànxiǎn 探险; (group) tuán 团; (to do shopping, sightseeing) xíng 行

expel person kāichú 开除

expend energy huāfèi 花费

expendable person kě xiāofèi 可消耗

expenditure huāfèi 花费

expense xiāofèi 消费; at the company's ~ yóu gōngsī fùfèi 由公司付费; a joke at my ~ kāi wǒde wánxiào 开我的玩笑; at the ~ of his health zài sǔnhài tā shēntǐ de qíngkuàng xià 在损害他身体的情况下

expense account bàoxiāo zhànghù 报销帐户

expenses yòngfèi 用费

expensive ángguì 昂贵

experience 1 n (event) jīnglì 经历; (in life) tǐyàn 体验; (in particular field) jīngyàn 经验 2 v/t pain, pleasure gǎnjué 感受; problem, difficulty yùdào 遇到

experienced yǒujīngyàn 有经验

experiment 1 n shìyàn 试验 2 v/i shíyàn 实验; ~ on X (on animals etc) yòng X zuò shíyàn 用 X 做实验; ~ with (try out) shìyàn 试验

experimental yòngyú shíyàn 用于实验

expert 1 adj shúliàn 熟练 2 n zhuānjiā 专家

expert advice zhuānjiā jiànyì 专家建议

expertise zhuānmén zhīshi 专门知识

expire dàoqī 到期

expiry qīmǎn 期满

expiry date zhōngzhǐ rìqī 终止日期

explain 1 v/t shuōmíng 说明 2 v/i jiěshì 解释

explanation jiěshì 解释

explicit instructions míngquè 明确

explicitly state, forbid míngquè 明确

explode v/i & v/t bomb bàozhà 爆炸

exploit[1] n yīngyǒng shìjì 英勇事迹

exploit[2] v/t person bōxuē 剥削; resources lìyòng 利用

exploitation (of person) bōxuē 剥削

exploration tànsuǒ 探索

exploratory surgery tànsuǒxìng 探索性

explore country etc kǎochá 考察;

possibility tàntǎo 探讨

explorer tànsuǒ zhě 探索者

explosion bàozhà 爆炸; (*in population*) jīzēng 激增

explosive *n* zhàyào 炸药

export 1 *n* (*action*) chūkǒu 出口; (*item*) chūkǒuwù 出口物 **2** *v/t goods* chūkǒu 出口; COMPUT dǎochū 导出

export campaign chūkǒu xuānchuán 出口宣传

exporter chūkǒushāng 出口商

expose (*uncover*) lùchū 露出; *scandal* jiēlù 揭露; *person* jiēchuān 揭穿; **~ X to Y** ràng X shòudào Y 让 X 受到 Y

exposure bàolù 暴露; MED tǐwēn guòdī 体温过低; (*of dishonest behavior*) jiēchuān 揭穿; (*part of film*) bàoguāng 曝光

express 1 *adj* (*fast*) xùnsù 迅速; (*explicit*) míngquè 明确 **2** *n* (*train*) tèkuài 特快; (*bus*) kuàisù 快速 **3** *v/t* (*speak of, voice*) biǎoshì 表示; *feelings* biǎodá 表达; **~ oneself well** qīngchǔ biǎodá zìjǐde yìsi 清楚表达自己的意思; **~ oneself** (*emotionally*) zìwǒ biǎodá 自我表达

express elevator tèkuài diàntī 特快电梯

expression (*voiced*) biǎoshì 表示; (*on face*) biǎoqíng 表情; (*phrase*) biǎodáfǎ 表达法; (*expressiveness*) gǎnqíng 感情

expressive fùyǒu biǎoqíng 富有表情

expressly (*explicitly*) qīngchǔ biǎomíng 清楚表明; (*deliberately*) tèdì 特地

expressway gāosù gōnglù 高速公路

expulsion (*from school*) kāichú 开除; (*of diplomat*) qūzhú 驱逐

exquisite (*beautiful*) jīngměi 精美

extend 1 *v/t* kuòdà 扩大; *runway, path* yáncháng 延长; *contract, visa* yánqī 延期; *thanks, congratulations* biǎoshì 表示 **2** *v/i* (*of garden etc*) shēnzhǎn 伸展

extension (*to house*) kuòjiàn 扩建;

(*of contract, visa*) yánqī 延期; TELEC fēnjī 分机

extension cable dǎoxiàn 导线

extensive guǎngfàn 广泛

extent chéngdù 程度; **to such an ~ that** dàodá rúcǐ chéngdù yǐzhìyú 到达如此程度以致于; **to a certain ~** zài yídìng chéngdù shang 在一定程度上

exterior 1 *adj* wàibù 外部 **2** *n* (*of building*) wàiguān 外观; (*of person*) wàibiǎo 外表

exterminate *vermin* xiāomiè 消灭; *race* mièjué 灭绝

external (*outside*) wàimiàn 外面

extinct *species* xīmiè 熄灭

extinction juézhǒng 绝种

extinguish *fire* pūmiè 扑灭; *cigarette* xīmiè 熄灭

extinguisher mièhuǒqì 灭火器

extort **~ money from X** lèsuǒ X de jīnqián 勒索 X 的金钱

extortion lèsuǒ 勒索

extortionate guògāo 过高

extra 1 *n* (*sth ~*) éwàide shìwù 额外的事物 **2** *adj* éwài 额外; **be ~** (*cost more*) lìngwài shōufèi 另外收费 **3** *adv* géwài 格外

extra charge fùjiāfèi 附加费

extract 1 *n* xuǎnlù 选录 **2** *v/t* qǔchū 取出; *oil, juice* zhàchū 榨出; *coal* wā 挖; *tooth* báchū 拔出; *information* huòqǔ 获取

extraction (*process*) zhàchū 榨出; (*of tooth*) báchū 拔出

extradite yǐndù 引渡

extradition yǐndù 引渡

extradition treaty yǐndù gōngyuē 引渡公约

extramarital hūnwài 婚外

extraordinarily yìcháng 异常

extraordinary bùpíngcháng 不平常

extravagance shēchǐ 奢侈

extravagant (*with money*) huīhuò 挥霍

extreme 1 *n* jíduān 极端 **2** *adj* jídù 极度; *views* piānjī 偏激

extremely jíqí 极其

extremist *n* jíduānzhǔyì zhě 极端主义者

extricate jiějiù 解救
extrovert *n* xìnggé wàixiàng de rén 性格外向的人
exuberant xìnggāocáiliè 兴高采烈
exult kuángxǐ 狂喜
eye 1 *n* yǎnjīng 眼睛; (*of needle*) zhēnbír 针鼻儿; **keep an ~ on** (*look after*) zhàokàn 照看; (*monitor*) guānchá 观察 **2** *v/t* qiáo 瞧

eyeball yǎnqiú 眼球; **eyebrow** méimao 眉毛; **eyeglasses** yǎnjìng 眼镜; **eyelash** jiémáo 睫毛; **eyelid** yǎnjiǎn 眼睑; **eyeliner** yǎnxiànyè 眼线液; **eyeshadow** yǎnyǐnggāo 眼影膏; **eyesight** shìlì 视力; **eyesore** bú shùnyǎn 不顺眼; **eye strain** yǎnjīng píláo 眼睛疲劳; **eyewitness** mùjīzhě 目击者

F

F (= *Fahrenheit*) Huáshì 华氏
fabric bùliào 布料
fabulous jí hǎo 极好
façade (*of building*) zhèngmiàn 正面; (*of person*) wàibiǎo 外表
face **1** *n* liǎn 脸; **to ~** miàn duì miàn 面对面; **lose ~** diūliǎn 丢脸 **2** *v/t person, the sea* miànduì 面对
facelift miànbù lāpí shǒushù 面部拉皮手术
face value piàomiàn jiàzhí 票面价值; **take X at ~** cóng biǎomiàn shang kàn X 从表面上看 X
facilitate shǐ ... biànlì 使 ... 便利
facilities shèshī 设施
fact shìshí 事实; **in ~, as a matter of ~** shíjì shang 实际上
factor yīnsù 因素
factory gōngchǎng 工厂
faculty (*hearing etc*) nénglì 能力; (*at university*) xì 系
fade *v/i* (*of colors*) xiāotuì 消退
faded *color, jeans* tuìsè 退色
fag F (*homosexual*) tóngxìngliàn 同性恋
Fahrenheit Huáshì 华氏
fail **1** *v/i* shībài 失败 **2** *v/t*: **~ an exam** kǎoshì bù jígé 考试不及格
failure shībài 失败
faint **1** *adj* bù míngxiǎn 不明显 **2** *v/i* hūndǎo 昏倒
fair¹ *n* COM jiāoyìhuì 交易会
fair² *adj hair* qiǎnsè 浅色; *complexion* báixī 白皙; (*just*) gōngzhèng 公正; **it's not ~** zhè bù gōngpíng 这不公平
fairly *treat* gōngzhèng 公正; (*quite*) xiāngdāng 相当
fairness (*of treatment*) gōngzhèng 公正
fairy xiānzǐ 仙子
fairy tale shénhuà gùshì 神话故事

faith xìnxīn 信心; REL xìnyǎng 信仰
faithful zhōngchéng 忠诚; **be ~ to one's partner** duì pèiǒu zhōngchéng 对配偶忠诚
fake **1** *n* yànpǐn 赝品 **2** *adj* fǎngzhì 仿制
fall¹ (*autumn*) qiūtiān 秋天
fall² **1** *v/i* (*of person*) shuāidǎo 摔倒; (*of government*) kuǎtái 垮台; (*of prices, temperature, exchange rate*) xiàjiàng 下降; (*of night*) láilín 来临; **it ~s on a Tuesday** nà tiān shì xīngqī'èr 那天是星期二; **~ ill** shēngbìng 生病 **2** *n* (*of person*) shuāijiāo 摔跤; (*of government, minister*) dǎotái 倒台; (*in price, temperature*) xiàjiàng 下降
♦ **fall back on** yǐkào 依靠
♦ **fall down** dǎoxià 倒下
♦ **fall for** *person* àishang 爱上; (*be deceived by*) xìnyǐwéizhēn 信以为真
♦ **fall out** (*of hair*) diàoluò 掉落; (*argue*) nào bièniu 闹别扭
♦ **fall over** dǎoxià 倒下
♦ **fall through** (*of plans*) luòkōng 落空
fallout fàngshèchén 放射尘
false cuòwù 错误
false teeth jiǎyá 假牙
falsify wěizào 伪造
fame míngyù 名誉
familiar *adj* (*intimate*) qīnjìn 亲近; *form of address* qīnqiè 亲切; **be ~ with X** shúxī X 熟悉 X
familiarity (*with subject etc*) tóngxiǎo 通晓
familiarize shǐ shúxī 使熟悉; **~ oneself with X** shǐ zìjǐ shúxī yíxià X 使自己熟悉一下 X
family jiātíng 家庭
family doctor jiātíng yīshēng 家庭医生; family name xìng 姓;

family planning jìhuà shēngyù 计划生育

famine jīhuang 饥荒

famous zhùmíng 著名; **be ~ for X** yǐ X zhùmíng 以 X 著名

fan[1] n (supporter) mí 迷

fan[2] n (for cooling, electric) diànshàn 电扇; (handheld) shànzi 扇子 2 v/t: ~ **oneself** gěi zìjǐ shānfēng 给自己扇风

fanatic kuángrè zhě 狂热者

fanatical kuángrè 狂热

fan belt MOT fēngshàn pídài 风扇皮带

fancy adj design jīngzhì 精致

fancy dress qítè fúzhuāng 奇特服装

fancy-dress party huàzhuāng wǎnhuì 化妆晚会

fang jiānyá 尖牙

fanny pack yāobāo 腰包

fantastic (very good) bàngjíle 棒极了; (very big) jùdà 巨大

fantasy huànxiǎng 幻想

far adv yuǎn 远; (much) fēicháng 非常; ~ **away** yáoyuǎn 遥远; **how ~ is it to X?** dào X qù duōyuǎn? 到 X 去有多远？; **as ~ as the corner/hotel** dào jiǎoluò/bīnguǎn nàme yuǎn 到角落/宾馆那么远; **as ~ as I can see** yī wǒ kàn 依我看; **as ~ as I know** jùwǒsuǒzhī 据我所知; **you've gone too ~** (in behavior) nǐzuòde guòfèn 你做得过分; **so ~ so good** dào mùqián wéizhǐ, yíqiè dōu hěn shùnlì 到目前为止，一切都很顺利

farce (ridiculous goings-on) nàojù 闹剧

fare n (for travel) piàojià 票价

Far East Yuǎndōng 远东

farewell n cíbié 辞别

farewell party sòngbié yànhuì 送别宴会

farfetched qiānqiáng 牵强

farm n nóngchǎng 农场

farmer nóngfū 农夫

farmhouse nóngshè 农舍

farmworker nóngchǎng gōngrén 农场工人

farsighted yǒu yuǎnjiàn 有远见; (optically) yuǎnshì 远视

fart F 1 n pì 屁 2 v/i fàngpì 放屁

farther adv gèngyuǎn 更远

farthest travel etc zuìyuǎn 最远

fascinate v/t shǐ zháomí 使着迷; **be ~d by X** bèi X xīyǐnzhù 被 X 吸引住

fascinating mírén 迷人

fascination (with subject) chīmí 痴迷

fascism fǎxīsī zhǔyì 法西斯主义

fascist 1 n fǎxīsī zhǔyì zhě 法西斯主义者 2 adj fǎxīsī 法西斯

fashion n shíshàng 时尚; (manner) fāngshì 方式; **in ~** liúxíng 流行; **out of ~** guòshí 过时

fashionable clothes, person, idea shímáo 时髦

fashion-conscious yǒu shíshàng yìshí 有时尚意识

fashion designer shízhuāng shèjìshī 时装设计师

fast[1] 1 adj kuài 快; **be ~** (of clock) kuài 快 2 adv kuài 快; **stuck ~** dǔzhùle 堵住了; ~ **asleep** shúshuì 熟睡

fast[2] n (not eating) jìnshí 禁食

fasten 1 v/t shǐ gùdìng 使固定; ~ **X onto Y** bǎ X gùdìng zài Y shang 把 X 固定在 Y 上 2 v/i (of dress etc) jì xì 系

fastener (for dress) lāliàn 拉链; (for lid) jīngqìqì 紧器

fast food kuàicān 快餐; **fast-food restaurant** kuàicāndiàn 快餐店; **fast forward** 1 n (on video etc) kuàijìnjiàn 快进健 2 v/i kuàijìn 快进; **fastlane** kuàisù chēdào 快速车道; **fast train** kuàichē 快车

fat 1 adj pàng 胖 2 n (on meat) zhīfáng 脂肪

fatal zhìmìng 致命; error wúkě wǎnjiù 无可挽救

fatality sǐwáng 死亡

fatally: **be ~ injured** shòu zhìmìng shāng 受致著伤

fate mìngyùn 命运

father n fùqīn 父亲

fatherhood shēnwéirénfù 身为人父

father-in-law (*woman's*) gōnggong 公公; (*man's*) yuèfù 岳父

fatherly sì fùqīn 似父亲

fathom *n* NAUT yīngxún 英寻

fatigue *n* píjuàn 疲倦

fatso F pàngzi 胖子

fatty 1 *adj* hán zhīfáng duo 含脂肪 多 **2** *n* F (*person*) pàngzi 胖子

faucet lóngtóu 龙头

fault *n* (*defect*) máobìng 毛病; *it's your* / *my* ~ shì nǐde / wǒde cuò 是 你的 / 我的错; *find* ~ *with X* zhǎo X de cuò 找 X 的错

faultless wánměi 完美

faulty *products* yǒu máobìng 有毛病

favor *n* xǐ'ài 喜爱; *in* ~ *of X* (*resign, withdraw*) duì X yǒulì 对 X 有利; *be in* ~ *of* ... zhīchí ... 支持 ...; *do X a* ~ bāng X ge máng 帮 X 个忙; *do me a* ~! (*don't be stupid*) bàituō! 拜托！

favorable *reply etc* zànchéng 赞成

favorite 1 *n* zuì xǐhuān 最喜欢; (*food*) piān'ài 偏爱 **2** *adj* zuì xǐhuān 最喜欢

fax 1 *n* chuánzhēn 传真; *send X by* ~ bǎ X yòng chuánzhēn chuánsòng 把 X 用传真传送 **2** *v/t* yòng chuánzhēn chuán 用传 真传; ~ *X to Y* bǎ X chuánzhēn gěi Y 把 X 传真给 Y

FBI (= *Federal Bureau of Investigation*) Liánbāng Diàochájú 联邦 调查局

fear 1 *n* kǒngjù 恐惧 **2** *v/t* hàipà 害怕

fearless wúwèi 无畏

feasibility study kěxíngxìng yánjiū 可行性研究

feasible qièshí kěxíng 切实可行

feast *n* shèngyàn 盛宴

feat jìyì 技艺

feather yǔmáo 羽毛

feature 1 *n* (*on face*) róngmào 容貌; (*of city, building, plan, style*) tèsè 特色; (*article in paper*) zhuāntí 专题; (*movie*) zhèngpiān 正片; *make a* ~ *of X* qiángdiào X 强调 X **2** *v/t* (*of movie*) yóu ... zhǔyǎn 由 ... 主演

February èryuè 二月

federal liánbāngzhì 联邦制

federation liánbāng 联邦

fed up *adj* F yànfán 厌烦; *be* ~ *with X* yīn X ér yànfán 因 X 而厌 烦

fee fèiyòng 费用; (*of lawyer, doctor, consultant*) chóujīn 酬金; (*for entrance*) fèi 费; (*for membership*) huìfèi 会费

feeble *person* xūruò 虚弱; *attempt* wúlì 无力; *laugh* wēiruò 微弱

feed *v/t* gōngyǎng 供养; *animal* wèi 喂

feedback ⇩ fǎnkuì xìnxī 反馈信息

feel 1 *v/t* (*touch*) chùmō 触摸; (*sense*) gǎndào 感到; *pain, pleasure, sensation* gǎnzhī 感知; (*think*) rènwéi 认为 **2** *v/i* (*of cloth etc*) gěirén gǎnjué 给人感觉; *it* ~*s like silk* / *cotton* mōqǐlái xiàng sī / miánhuā 摸起来像丝 / 棉花; *your hand* ~*s hot* / *cold* nǐde shǒu mōqǐlái rè / liáng 你的手摸起来 热 / 凉; *I* ~ *hungry* / *tired* wǒ gǎnjué è / lèi le 我觉得饿 / 累了; *how are you* ~*ing today?* nǐ jīntiān gǎnjué zěnmeyàng? 你今 天感觉怎么样？; *how does it* ~ *to be rich?* fùyǒu shì shénme gǎnjué? 富有是什么感觉？; *do you* ~ *like a drink* / *meal?* xiǎng bù xiǎng hē / chīdiǎnr shénme? 想 不想喝 / 吃点儿什么？; *I* ~ *like going* / *staying* wǒ xiǎng zǒu / dāi zài zhèr 我想走 / 呆在这儿; *I don't* ~ *like it* wǒ bù xiǎngyào wǒ 不想要

◆**feel up to** rènwéi yǒu nénglì zuò 认为有能力做

feeler (*of insect*) chùjiǎo 触角

feelgood factor lèiguān xīnlǐ 乐观心理

feeling (*of happiness*) gǎnjué 感觉; (*emotion*) gǎnqíng 感情; (*sensation*) zhījué 知觉; *what are your* ~*s about it?* nǐ shì zěnme xiǎng de? 你是怎么想的？; *I have mixed* ~*s about him* wǒ duì tā yǒu hěn máodùnde gǎnqíng 我

对他有很矛盾的感情
fellow (*man*) jiāhuo 家伙
fellow citizen tóngbāo 同胞;
fellow countryman tóngbāo 同
胞; **fellow man** quánrénlèi 全人
类
felony zhòngzuì 重罪
felt *n* máozhān 毛毡
felt tip, felt-tip(ped) pen
zhāntóubǐ 毡头笔
female 1 *adj animal, plant* cíxìng 雌
性; (*referring to people*) nǚxìng 女
性; **2** *n* (*of animals, plants*) cíxìng
dòngzhíwù 雌性动植物;
(*person*) nǚxìng 女性; *pej* (*woman*)
nǚrén 女人
feminine 1 *adj qualities* yǒu nǚxìng
qìzhì 有女性气质; GRAM yīnxìng
阴性; *she's very ~* tā hěn yǒu
nǚrén wèidào 她很有女人味道
2 *n* GRAM yīnxìng 阴性
feminism ⇩ nǚquán zhǔyì 女权
主义
feminist ⇩ **1** *n* nǚquán zhǔyì zhě
女权主义者 **2** *adj* nǚquán zhǔyì
fen (*Chinese money*) fēn 分
fence *n* zhàlán 栅栏
♦ **fence in** *land* yòng zhàlán wéiqǐ
用栅栏围起
fencing SP jíjiàn 击剑
fend: *~ for oneself* dúlì shēnghuó
独立生活
fender MOT yìzǐbǎn 翼子板
ferment[1] *v/i* (*of liquid*) fājiào 发酵
ferment[2] *n* (*unrest*) dòngdàng bù'ān
动荡不安
fermentation fājiào 发酵
fern jué 蕨
ferocious cánrěn 残忍
ferry *n* dùchuán 渡船
fertile *soil* féiwò 肥沃; *woman,
animal* néng shēngyù 能生育
fertility (*of soil*) féiwò 肥沃; (*of
woman, animal*) fányù 繁育
fertility drug cùyùnyào 促孕药
fertilize *v/t ovum* shǐ shòujīng 使受
精
fertilizer (*for soil*) féiliào 肥料
fervent *admirer* rèchéng 热诚
fester *v/i* (*of wound*) huànnóng 化脓
festival jiérì 节日

festive jiérì 节日
festivities huānqìng 欢庆
fetch *person* jiē jiē 接; *thing* ná 拿;
price màidé 卖得
fetus tāi'ér 胎儿
feud *n* shìchóu 世仇
fever fāshāo 发烧
feverish fāshāo 发烧; *fig:
excitement* jīdòng 激动
few 1 *adj* (*not many*) hěnshǎo 很少;
a ~ (*things*) jǐgè 几个; *quite a ~, a
good ~* (*a lot*) xiāngdāngduō 相当
多 **2** *pron* (*not many*) jǐgè
少数几个; *a ~* (*some*) yìxiē 一些;
quite a ~, a good ~ (*a lot*) xǔduō
许多
fewer *adj* gèngshǎo 更少; *~ than
...* shǎoyú ... 少于...
fiancé wèihūnfū 未婚夫
fiancée wèihūnqī 未婚妻
fiasco chèdǐde shībài 彻底的失
败
fib *n* xiǎohuǎng 小谎
fiber *n* xiānwéi 纤维
fiberglass bōlí xiānwéi 玻璃纤维
fiber optic guāng xiān 光纤; **fiber optics** guāngdǎo xiānwéi 光
导纤维
fickle biànhuà wúcháng 变化无常
fiction (*novels*) xiǎoshuō 小说;
(*made-up story*) biānzàode shì 编
造的事
fictitious xūgòu 虚构
fiddle 1 *n* F (*violin*) xiǎotíqín 小提
琴 **2** *v/i*: *~ with* bǎinòng 摆弄; *~
around with* húluàn bǎinòng 胡
乱摆弄 **3** *v/t accounts, results*
cuàngǎi 篡改
fidelity zhōngzhēn 忠贞
fidget *v/i* fánzào bù'ān 烦躁不安
field *n* tiándì 田地; (*for sport*)
chǎng 场; (*competitors in race*)
cānsài zhě 参赛者; (*of research,
knowledge etc*) lǐngyù 领域; *that's
not my ~* nà búzài wǒde fànwéi
zhīnèi 那不在我的范围之内
field events tiánsài 田赛
fierce *animal* xiōngměng 凶猛;
wind, storm qiángliè 强烈
fiery *personality* yìnù 易怒; *temper*
bàozào 暴躁

fifteen shíwǔ 十五

fifteenth dìshíwǔ 第十五

fifth dìwǔ 第五

fiftieth dì wǔshí 第五十

fifty wǔshí 五十

fifty-fifty adv duìbàn 对半

fig wúhuāguǒ 无花果

fight 1 n zhàndòu 战斗; fig (for survival, championship) zhēngdòu 争斗; (in boxing) quánjī 拳击 **2** v/t enemy, person yǔ ... dǎzhàng 与 ... 打仗; (in boxing) jiāofēng 交锋; a disease, injustice zuò dòuzhēng 作斗争 **3** v/i dǎjià 打架

♦**fight for** one's rights, cause zhēngqǔ 争取

fighter zhànshì 战士; (airplane) zhàndòujī 战斗机; (boxer) quánjīshǒu 拳击手; she's a ~ tāshìge fèndòu zhě 她是个奋斗者

figurative use of word bǐyù 比喻; art yòng túxíng biǎoxiàn 用图形表现

figure 1 n (digit) shùzì 数字; (of person) xíngtǐ 形体; (form, shape) túxíng 图形 **2** v/t F (think) rènwéi 认为

♦**figure on** F (plan) jìhuà 计划

♦**figure out** (understand) lǐjiě 理解; calculation jìsuànchū 计算出

figure skating huāyàng huábīng 花样滑冰

file[1] n (of documents) dàng'àn 档案; COMPUT wénjiàn 文件 **2** v/t documents zhěnglǐ 整理

♦**file away** documents jiāng ... guīdàng 将 ... 归档

file[2] n (for wood, fingernails) cuòdāo 锉刀

file cabinet dàng'ànxiāng 档案箱

file manager COMPUT wénjiàn guǎnlǐ chéngxù 文件管理程序

Filipino 1 adj Fēilǜbīn 菲律宾 **2** n (person) Fēilǜbīn rén 菲律宾人

fill 1 v/t zhùmǎn 注满 **2** n: eat one's ~ chīgebǎo 吃个饱

♦**fill in** form tiánxiě 填写; hole tiánmǎn 填满

♦**fill in for** línshí tìdài 临时替代

♦**fill out 1** v/t form tiánxiě 填写

2 v/i (get fatter) zhǎngpàng 长胖

♦**fill up 1** v/t zhuāngmǎn 装满 **2** v/i (of stadium, theater) chōngmǎn 充满

fillet n lǐjī 里脊

fillet steak lǐjī niúpái 里脊牛排

filling 1 n (in sandwich) xiàn 馅; (in tooth) bǔyá 补牙 **2** adj food róngyi bǎorén 容易饱人

filling station jiāyóuzhàn 加油站

film 1 n (for camera) jiāojuǎn 胶卷; (movie) diànyǐng 电影 **2** v/t person, event pāishè 拍摄

film-maker zhìpiàn rén 制片人

film star diànyǐng míngxīng 电影明星

filter 1 n guòlùqì 过滤器 **2** v/t coffee, liquid guòlù 过滤

♦**filter through** (of news reports) mànmàn chuánkāi 慢慢传开

filter tip (cigarette) guòlùzuǐ 过滤嘴

filth huìwù 污物

filthy āngzāng 肮脏; language etc wěixiè 猥亵

fin (of fish) qí 鳍

final 1 adj (last) zuìhòu 最后; decision quèdìng 确定 **2** n SP juésài 决赛

finalist cānjiā juésài zhě 参加决赛者

finalize plans, design quèdìng 确定

finally zuìhòu 最后; (at last) zhōngyú 终于

finance 1 n jīnróng 金融 **2** v/t tígōng zījīn 提供资金

financial jīnróng 金融

financier jīnróngjiā 金融家

find v/t zhǎodào 找到; if you ~ it too hot / cold rúguǒ nǐ juédé tài rè/lěng 如果你觉得太热/冷; ~ X innocent / guilty LAW cáidìng X wúzuì/yǒuzuì 裁定 X 无罪/有罪

♦**find out 1** v/t huòzhī 获知 **2** v/i (inquire) cháxún 查询; (discover) liǎojiědào 了解到

fine[1] adj day, weather qínglǎng 晴朗; wine, performance, city hǎo 好; distinction xìwēi 细微; line xì 细; how's that? – that's ~ nǐ kàn zěnmeyàng? – hǎo 你看怎么样？－

好; *that's ~ by me* wǒ juédé kěyǐ
我觉得可以; *how are you? - ~*
nǐ hǎo ma? – hěn hǎo 你好吗？
–很好
fine² 1 n (*penalty*) fájīn 罚金 2 v/t
fákuǎn 罚款
finger n shǒuzhǐ 手指
fingernail shǒuzhǐjiǎ 手指甲
fingerprint shǒuyìn 手印; fingertip zhǐjiān 指尖; *have X at
one's ~s* duì X liǎo rú zhǐzhǎng 对
X 了如指掌
finicky *person* guòfèn tiāotì 过分
挑剔; *design, pattern* guòfèn
jiǎngjiū xìjié 过分讲究细节
finish 1 v/t jiéshù 结束; *~ doing X*
zuòwán X 做完 X 2 v/i jiéshù 结
束 3 n (*of product*) zuìhòu bùfen
最后部分; (*of race*) zhōngdiǎn 终
点
♦finish off v/t: *~ a drink / meal /
one's work* bǎ shèngxiàde hē /
chī / zuòwán 把剩下的喝/吃/
做完
♦finish up v/t *food* chīwán 吃完;
*he finished up liking it / living
there* tā hòulái xǐhuān tā le / zhù
zài nàr le 他后来喜欢它了/住
在那儿了
♦finish with: *~ X with boyfriend etc*
yǔ X duànjué guānxi 与X断绝关
系
finishing line zhōngdiǎnxiàn 终点
线
Finland Fēnlán 芬兰
Finn Fēnlán rén 芬兰人
Finnish 1 adj Fēnlán 芬兰 2 n
(*language*) Fēnlán yǔ 芬兰语
fir lěngshān 冷杉
fire 1 n huǒ 火; (*electric, gas*) nuǎnlú
暖炉; (*blaze*) shīhuǒ 失火;
(*bonfire, campfire etc*) gōuhuǒ 篝
火; *be on ~* zháohuǒ 着火; *catch
~* shāozháo 烧着; *set X on ~, set
~ to X* gěi X fànghuǒ 给 X 放火
2 v/i (*shoot*) shèjī 射击 3 v/t F
(*dismiss*) jiěgù 解雇; *be ~d* bèi
chǎo yóuyú le 被炒鱿鱼了
fire alarm huǒjǐng jǐngbào 火警
警报; firearm qiāngzhī 枪支;
firecracker biānpào 鞭炮; fire

department xiāofángduì 消防
队; fire escape ānquán chūkǒu
安全出口; fire extinguisher
mièhuǒqì 灭火器; firefighter
xiāofángduìyuán 消防队员;
fireplace bìlú 壁炉; fire truck
xiāofángchē 消防车; firewood
mùchái 木柴; fireworks yānhuǒ
烟火; (*display*) yānhuǒ biǎoyǎn 烟
火表演
firm¹ adj grip, handshake wěn ér
yǒulì 稳而有力; flesh, muscles
jiēshi jiēshí 结实; voice, decision jiāndìng
坚定; *a ~ deal* yíxiàng kěndìng de
xiéyì 一项肯定的协议
firm² n COM gōngsī 公司
first 1 adj dìyī 第一; *who's ~
please?* shéi shì dìyīge? 谁是第
一个？ 2 n dìyīge 第一个 3 adv
arrive, finish dìyī 第一;
(*beforehand*) xiān 先; *~ of all* (*for
one reason*) shǒuxiān 首先; *at ~*
qǐchū 起初
first aid jíjiù 急救; first-aid box,
first-aid kit jíjiùxiāng 急救箱;
first-born adj zhǎngzǐ(nǚ) 长子
(女); first class 1 adj ticket,
compartment tóuděng 头等; (*very
good*) yīliú 一流 2 adv travel
tóuděng jīcāng 头等舱; first floor yīlóu 一
楼; first-hand adj qīnshēn 亲身
firstly shǒuxiān 首先; first name míngzi 名字
first-rate yīliú 一流
fiscal cáizhèng 财政
fiscal year cáizhèng niándù 财政
年度
fish 1 n yú 鱼 2 v/i diàoyú 钓鱼
fishbone yúcì 鱼刺
fisherman yúfū 渔夫
fishing bǔyú 捕鱼
fishing boat yúchuán 鱼船; fishing line diàosī 钓丝; fishing rod
diàoyúgān 钓鱼竿
fish stick yútiáo 鱼条
fishy F (*suspicious*) kěyí 可疑
fist quán 拳
fit¹ n MED hūnjué 昏厥; *a ~ of
rage / jealousy* yígǔ nùhuǒ / jídù
qíngxù 一股怒火/嫉妒情绪
fit² adj (*physically*) jiànkāng 健康;

(morally) qiàdàng 恰当; **keep ~** jiànshēn 健身

fit³ 1 *v/t (of clothes)* héshì 合适; *(attach)* ānzhuāng 安装 2 *v/i (of clothes)* héshì 合适; *(of piece of furniture etc)* róngdexià 容得下 3 *n: it is a good ~* hěn héshì 很合适; *it's a tight ~* yǒudiǎnr jǐn 有点儿紧

♦**fit in** *(of person in group)* héqún 合群; *it fits in with our plans* zhè yǔ wǒmende jìhuà yízhì 这与我们的计划一致

fitful *sleep* bù wěndìng 不稳定

fitness *(physical)* jiànkāng 健康

fitness center jiànshēn zhōngxīn 健身中心

fitted carpet gùdìnghǎode dìtǎn 固定好的地毯

fitted kitchen yǒu gùdìng shèbèi de chúfáng 有固定设备的厨房

fitter *n* zhuāngpèigōng 装配工

fitting *adj* qiàdàng 恰当

fittings zhuāngzhì 装置

five wǔ 五

Five Year Plan Wǔnián Jìhuà 五年计划

fix 1 *n (solution)* jiějué 解决; *be in a ~* F xiànrù kùnjìng 陷入困境 2 *v/t (attach)* dìngláo 钉牢; *(repair)* xiūlǐ 修理; *(arrange: meeting etc)* ānpái 安排; *lunch* zhǔnbèi 准备; *(dishonestly: match etc)* zuòbì 作弊; *~ X onto Y* bǎ X gùdìng zài Y shang 把 X 固定在 Y 上; *I'll ~ you a drink* wǒ gěi nǐ nòng diǎn yǐnliào 我给你弄点饮料

♦**fix up** *meeting* ānpái 安排; *it's all fixed up* dōu shì ānpái hǎode dōu 是安排好的

fixed *(in one position)* gùdìng 固定; *timescale, exchange rate* quèdìng bùbiàn 确定不变

fixture *(in room)* gùdìng zhuāngzhì 固定装置

flab *(on body)* sōngchíde jīròu 松弛的肌肉

flabbergast: be ~ed F dàchīyìjīng 大吃一惊

flabby *muscles, stomach* sōngchí 松弛

flag¹ *n* qí 旗

flag² *v/i (tire)* píjuàn 疲倦

flair *(talent)* tiānfèn 天份; **have a natural ~ for X** duì X yǒu tiānfèn 对 X 有天份

flake *n* suìpiàn 碎片

♦**flake off** *v/i* bōluò 剥落

flaky yì bōluò 易剥落

flaky pastry sūbǐng 酥饼

flamboyant *personality* ài xuànyào 爱炫耀

flame *n* huǒyàn 火焰

flammable yì ránshāo 易燃烧

flan guǒxiànbǐng 果馅饼

flank 1 *n (of horse etc)* lèibù 肋部; MIL cèyì 侧翼; **be ~ed by X** liǎngcè yǒu X 两侧有 X

flap 1 *n (of envelope, pocket)* kǒugài 口盖; *(of table)* huódòngbiān 活动边; **be in a ~** F jǐnzhāng huāngluàn 紧张慌乱 2 *v/t wings* jīnyì 襟翼 3 *v/i (of flag etc)* yáodòng 摇动

flare 1 *n (distress signal)* shǎnguāng zhuāngzhì 闪光装置; *(in dress)* lǎbazhuàng 喇叭状 2 *v/t nostrils* gǔqǐ 鼓起

♦**flare up** *(of violence)* tūqǐ 突起; *(of illness, rash)* fùfā 复发; *(of fire)* biànwàng 变旺; *(get very angry)* fānù 发怒

flash 1 *n (of light)* shǎnshuò 闪烁; PHOT shǎnguāngdēng 闪光灯; *in a ~* F shǎndiànbān 闪电般; *have a ~ of inspiration* língjīyídòng 灵机一动; *~ of lightning* shǎndiàn 闪电 2 *v/i (of light)* shǎnliàng 闪亮 3 *v/t headlights* yòng guāng liánluò 用光联络

flashback *(in movie)* shǎnhuí 闪回

flashbulb shǎnguāng dēngpào 闪光灯泡

flasher MOT shǎnguāng zhǐshìdēng 闪光指示灯

flashlight shǒudiàntǒng 手电筒; PHOT shǎnguāngdēng 闪光灯

flashy *pej* huāshao 花哨

flask nuǎnpíng 暖瓶

flat 1 *adj surface, land* píngtǎn 平坦; *beer* pǎoqì 跑气; *battery* yòngwán diàn 用完电; *tire* qì bùzú 气不足; *shoes* píngdǐ 平底; *sound, tone* píngdàn 平淡; *and that's ~* F shuōdìngle 说定了 **2** *adv* MUS yǐ dīdiào 以低调; *~ out work, run, drive* jiéjìnquánlì 竭尽全力

flat-chested píngxiōng 平胸

flat rate tǒngyī shōufèilǜ 统一收费率

flatten *v/t land, road* biànpíng 变平; *(by bombing, demolition)* jīdǎo 击倒

flatter *v/t* fèngcheng 奉承

flattering *comments* tǎohǎo 讨好; *color, clothes* shǐrén gèng piàoliàng 使人更漂亮

flattery fèngcheng 奉承

flavor 1 *n* wèidao 味道 **2** *v/t: ~ X food* gěi X tiáowèi 给 X 调味

flavoring tiáowèipǐn 调味品

flaw *n* xiácī 瑕疵

flawless wánměi 完美

flea tiàozao 跳蚤

flee *v/i* táopǎo 逃跑

fleet *n* NAUT jiànduì 舰队; *(of taxis, trucks)* chēduì 车队

fleeting *visit etc* duǎnzàn 短暂; *catch a ~ glimpse of* piējiàn 瞥见

flesh ròutǐ 肉体; *(of fruit)* guǒròu 果肉; *meet/see X in the ~* jiàndào X běnrén 见到 X 本人

flex *v/t muscles* huódòng 活动

flexible línghuó 灵活; *I'm quite ~ (about arrangements, timing)* wǒ kěyǐ jīdòng 我可以机动

flick *v/t tail* qīngtán 轻弹; *he ~ed a fly off his hand* tā gǎndiàole shǒushangde cángyíng 他赶掉了手上的苍蝇; *she ~ed her hair out of her eyes* tā bōkāi le yǎnqiánde tóufa 她拨开了眼前的头发

♦ **flick through** *book, magazine* liúlǎn 浏览

flicker *v/i (of light, candle, computer screen)* shǎndòng 闪动

flies *(on pants: zipper)* lāliànr 拉链儿; *(buttons)* kāikòu 开扣

flight *(in airplane)* hángbān 航班; *(flying)* fēixíng 飞行; *(fleeing)* táopǎo 逃跑; *~ (of stairs)* lóutīde

yíduàn 楼梯的一段

flight crew jīzǔ rényuán 机组人员; **flight deck** fēixíng jiǎbǎn 飞行甲板; **flight number** hángbānhào 航班号; **flight path** fēixíng lùxiàn 飞行路线; **flight recorder** fēixíng jìlùyí 飞行记录仪; **flight time** *(departure)* qǐfēi shíjiān 起飞时间; *(duration)* fēixíng shíjiān 飞行时间

flighty qīngfú 轻浮

flimsy *structure, furniture* bù jiēshi 不结实; *dress, material* qīng'érbó 轻而薄; *excuse* bù zúxìn 不足信

flinch tuìsuō 退缩

fling *v/t* rēng 扔; *~ oneself into a chair* zāidào yǐzi shang 栽到椅子上

♦ **flip through** *book, magazine* liúlǎn 浏览

flipper *(for swimming)* jiǎopǔ 脚蹼

flirt 1 *v/i* tiáoqíng 调情 **2** *n* tiáoqíng zhě 调情者

flirtatious ài tiáoqíng 爱挑情

float *v/i* piāofú 漂浮; FIN fúdòng 浮动

flock *n (of sheep)* yìqún 一群

flog *v/t (whip)* biāndǎ 鞭打

flood 1 *n* hóngshuǐ 洪水 **2** *v/t (of river)* yānmò淹没; *~ its banks (of river)* yānmò tī'àn 淹没堤岸

flooding hóngshuǐ fànlàn 洪水泛滥

floodlight *n* fànguāngdēng 泛光灯

floor *n* dìbǎn 地板; *(story)* lóucéng 楼层

floorboard yíkuài dìbǎn 一块地板; **floor cloth** pū dìbǎn de hòubù r] 铺地板的厚布; **floor lamp** luòdìdēng 落地灯

flop 1 *v/i* měngrán tǎngxià 猛然躺下; F *(fail)* chèdǐ shībài 彻底失败 **2** *n* F *(failure)* chèdǐ shībài 彻底失败

floppy *adj (not stiff)* sōngruǎn 松软; *(weak)* xūruò 虚弱

floppy *(disk)* ⇩ ruǎnpán 软盘

floppy drive COMPUT ruǎnqū 软驱

florist huāshāng 花商

flour miànfěn 面粉

flourish *v/i* fánróng 繁荣

flourishing *trade* xīngwàng 兴旺

flow 1 *v/i* (*of river, electric current, traffic*) liúdòng 流动; (*of work*) jìnxíng 进行 **2** *n* (*of river*) liúdòng 流动; (*of information, ideas*) jiāoliú 交流

flowchart liúchéngtú 流程图

flower 1 *n* huā 花 **2** *v/i* kāihuā 开花

flowerbed huātán 花坛

flowerpot huāpén 花盆

flowery *pattern* duōhuā 多花; *style of writing* cízǎo huálì 词藻华丽

flu liúgǎn 流感

fluctuate *v/i* bōdòng 波动

fluctuation bōdòng 波动

fluency (*in a language*) liúlì 流利

fluent *adj* liúlì 流利; **he speaks ~ Chinese** tā jiǎng yīkǒu liúlìde Hànyǔ 他讲一口流利的汉语

fluently *speak, write* liúlì 流利

fluff: a bit of ~ (*material*) yìdiǎn róngmáo 一点绒毛

fluffy *adj material, hair* péngsōng 蓬松; *clouds* sōngruǎn 松软; **~ toy** sōngruǎnde wánjù 松软的玩具

fluid *n* liútǐ 流体

flunk *v/t* F *subject* bù jígé 不及格

fluorescent *light* fā yíngguāng 发荧光

flush 1 *v/t toilet* chōngxǐ 冲洗; **~ X down the toilet** bǎ X chōngjìn cèsuǒ 把 X 冲进厕所 (*of toilet*) chōngxǐ 冲洗; (*go red in the face*) biànhóng 变红 **3** *adj* (*level*) qípíng 齐平; **be ~ with X** yǔ X wángquán qípíng 与 X 完全齐平

♦ **flush away** (*down toilet*) chōngdiào 冲掉

♦ **flush out** *rebels etc* gǎnchū 赶出

fluster *v/t* shǐ jǐnzhāng 使紧张; **get ~ed** jǐnzhāng 紧张

flute chángdí 长笛

flutter *v/i* (*of bird, wings*) bǎichì bǎichì 摆翅; (*of flag*) piāodòng 飘动; (*of heart*) pūdòng 扑动

fly[1] *n* (*insect*) cāngyíng 苍蝇

fly[2] *n* (*on pants: zipper*) lāliàn 拉链儿; (*buttons*) kāikòu 开扣

fly[3] **1** *v/i* (*of bird, airplane*) fēixíng 飞行; (*in airplane*) chéngjī 乘机; (*of flag*) piāoyáng 飘扬; (*rush*) fēipǎo 飞跑; **~ into a rage** bórán dànù 勃然大怒 **2** *v/t airplane* jiàshǐ 驾驶; *airline* dāchéng 搭乘; (*transport by air*) kōngyùn 空运

♦ **fly away** (*of bird, airplane*) fēizǒu 飞走

♦ **fly back** *v/i* (*travel back*) fēihuí 飞回

♦ **fly in 1** *v/i* (*of airplane, passengers*) fēidào 飞到 **2** *v/t supplies etc* kōngyùn 空运

♦ **fly off** (*of hat etc*) fēituō 飞脱

♦ **fly out** *v/i* chéng jī qù chéngjī qù 乘机去

♦ **fly past** (*in formation*) biānduì fēixíng biānduì fēixíng 编队飞行; (*of time*) fēishì 飞逝

flying *n* fēixíng 飞行

foam *n* (*on liquid*) pàomò 泡沫

foam rubber pàomò xiàngjiāo 泡沫橡胶

FOB (= *free on board*) lí'àn jiàgé 离岸价格

focus *n* (*of attention*) jízhōng 集中; PHOT jiāojù 焦距; **be in ~ / out of ~** PHOT zài / búzài jiāodiǎn shang 在 / 不在焦点上

♦ **focus on** *problem, issue* jízhōng yú 集中于; PHOT jùjiāo yú 聚焦于

fodder sìliào 饲料

fog wù 雾

foggy duōwù 多雾

foil[1] *n* (*silver ~ etc*) xīzhǐ 锡纸

foil[2] *v/t* (*thwart*) cuòbài 挫败

fold[1] **1** *v/t paper etc* zhédié 折叠; **~ one's arms** hébào shuāngbì 合抱双臂 **2** *v/i* (*of business*) tíngyè 停业 **3** *n* (*in cloth etc*) zhě 褶

♦ **fold up 1** *v/t* zhé qǐlái 折起来 **2** *v/i* (*of chair, table*) néng zhédié 能折叠

fold[2] *n* (*for sheep etc*) yánglán 羊栏

folder *also* COMPUT wénjiànjiá 文件夹

folding zhédié 折叠; **~ chair** zhédiéyǐ 折叠椅

foliage yèzi 叶子

folk (*people*) rénmen 人们; **my ~** (*family*) wǒde jiārén 我的家人; **come in, ~s** F dàjiā qǐngjìn 大家

请进

folk dance ⇩ mínjiānwǔ 民间舞;
folk music mínyuè 民乐; **folk
singer** míngēshǒu 民歌手; **folk
song** míngē 民歌

follow gēnsuí 跟随; *road* yánzhe ... qiánjìn 沿着 ... 前
进; *guidelines, instructions* zūnxún
遵循; *TV series, news* liánxù kàn
连续看; *(understand)* míngbái 明
白; **~ me** gēn wǒ lái 跟我来 **2** v/i
gēnzhe 跟着; *(logically)* bìrán
fāshēng 必然发生; **it ~s from
this that ...** yóucǐ fāshēng ... 由此
发生 ...; **as ~s** rúxià 如下

♦**follow up** v/t *letter, inquiry* hòuxù
后续

follower *(of politician etc)* zhuīsuí
zhě 追随者; *(of football team)*
zhīchí zhě 支持者; *(of TV
program)* zhōngshí guānzhòng 忠
实观众

following 1 *adj day, night* jiēzhe 接
着; *points* xiàshù 下述; *pages* yǐxià
以下 **2** n *(people)* yìpī zhīchí zhě
一批支持者; **the ~** rúxià 如下

follow-up meeting gēnzōng huìyì
跟踪会议

follow-up visit *(to doctor etc)*
liánxùde bàifǎng 连续的拜访

folly *(madness)* yúchǔn 愚蠢

fond *(loving)* xǐ'ài 喜爱; *memory*
zhēn'ài 珍爱; **be ~ of** xǐhuan 喜
欢

fondle àifǔ 爱抚

fondness xǐ'ài 喜爱

font *(for printing)* zìtǐ 字体

food *(formal word)* shíwù 食物;
(informal word) chīde 吃的

food freak F dàchī 大吃; **food
mixer** shíwù jiǎobànqì 食物搅拌
器; **food poisoning** shíwù
zhòngdú 食物中毒

fool n chǔnrén 蠢人; **make a ~ of
oneself** shǐ zìjǐ chūchǒu 使自己
出丑

♦**fool around** húnào 胡闹;
(sexually) yǒu wàiyù 有外遇

♦**fool around with** *knife, drill etc*
bǎinòng 摆弄

foolish yúchǔn 愚蠢

foolproof búhuì chūcuò 不会出
错

foot jiǎo 脚; *(measurement)* yīngchǐ
英尺; **on ~** bùxíng 步行; **at the ~
of the page / hill** zài yè / shān jiǎo
xià 在页 / 山角下; **put one's ~ in
it** F *(by saying sth)* lìngrénnánkān
说错话; *(by doing sth)* zuò cuòshì
做错事

football měishì zúqiú 美式足球;
(soccer) zúqiú 足球; *(ball)* zúqiú
足球; **football player** měishì
zúqiú duìyuán 美式足球队员;
(soccer) qiúyuán 球员; **foot-
bridge** bùxíngqiáo 步行桥

footer COMPUT jiǎozhù 脚注

foothills shānlù xiǎoqiū 山麓小丘

footing *(basis)* jīchǔ 基础; **lose
one's ~** shīzú diēdǎo 失足跌倒;
be on the same / a different ~
píngděng / bù píngděng de dìwèi
平等 / 不平等的地位; **be on a
friendly ~ with X** yǔ X guānxi
róngqià 与X关系融洽

footlights jiǎodēng 脚灯; **footnote** jiǎozhù 脚注; **footpath**
xiǎolù 小路; **footprint** jiǎoyìn 脚
印; **footstep** jiǎobù 脚步; **follow
in X's ~s** xiàofǎng X xiàofǎng X;
footwear xié 鞋

for ◇ *(purpose, destination etc)* wèile
为了; **save up ~ a vacation** wèile
dùjià zǎnqián 为了度假攒钱;
study ~ an exam wèile kǎoshì
xuéxí 了为了考试学习; **a train ~ X**
qù X de huǒchē 去X的火车;
clothes ~ children tóngzhuāng tóng
zhuāng; **it's too big / small ~ you** nǐ
chuān tài dà / xiǎo 你穿太大 / 小;
here's a letter ~ you zhè shì nǐde
xìn 这是你的信; **this is ~ you**
zhè shì gěi nǐde 这是给你的;
what is there ~ lunch? wǔcān chī
shénme? 午餐吃什么? **the
steak is ~ me** niúpái shì wǒde 牛
排是我的; **what is this ~?** zhè
shì gàn shénme yòngde? 这是干
什么用的? **~ what?**
wèishénme? 为什么? ◇ *(time)*:
three days / two hours sān
tiān / liǎnggè xiǎoshí 三天 / 两个

小时; *please get it done ~ Monday* qǐng zài xīngqīyī yǐqián zuòwán 请在星期一以前做完 ◊ *(distance)*: *I walked ~ a mile* wǒ zǒule yìyīnglǐ 我走了一英里; *it stretches ~ 100 miles* liánmián yìbǎi yīnglǐ 连绵一百英里 ◊ *(in favor of)*: *I am ~ the idea* wǒ tóngyì zhège xiǎngfǎ 我同意这个想法 ◊ *(instead of, in behalf of)*: *let me do that ~ you* wǒ gěi nǐ zuò ba 我给你做吧; *we are agents ~* wǒmen shì X de dàilǐrén 我们是 X 的代理人 ◊ *(in exchange for)*: *I bought it ~ $25* wǒ huāle èrshíwǔ měiyuán mǎide 我花了二十五美元买的; *how much did you sell it ~?* nǐ duōshao qián màide? 你多少钱卖的？

forbid jìnzhǐ 禁止; *~ X to do Y* jìnzhǐ X zuò Y 禁止 X 做 Y

forbidden yánjìn 严禁; *smoking / parking* = jìnzhǐ xīyān / tíngchē 禁止吸烟 / 停车

Forbidden City Zǐjìnchéng 紫禁城

forbidding yánjùn 严峻

force 1 *n (violence)* wǔlì 武力; *(of explosion, wind, punch)* lìliàng 力量; *come into ~ (of law etc)* shēngxiào 生效; *the ~s* MIL bùduì 部队 2 *v/t door, lock* yònglì dǎkāi 用力打开; *~ X to do Y* qiǎngpò X zuò Y 强迫 X 做 Y; *~ X open* qiángxíng dǎkāi X 强行打开 X

forced *laugh, smile* miǎnqiǎng 勉强; *confession* bèipò 被迫

forced landing pòjiàng 迫降

forceful *argument* qiángyǒulì 强有力; *speaker* yǒu shuōfúlì 有说服力; *character* jiānqiáng 坚强

forceps qiánzi 钳子

forcible *entry* yòng qiánglì 用强力; *argument* yǒu shuōfúlì 有说服力

ford *n* héliú qiǎnchù 河流浅处

fore: *come to the ~* tuō yǐng ér chū 脱颖而出

foreboding bùxiángde yùgǎn 不祥的预感; forecast 1 *n* yùcè 预测;

(of weather) yùbào 预报 2 *v/t* yùbào 预报; forecourt *(of garage)* jiāyóuchù 加油处; forefathers zǔxiān 祖先; forefinger shízhǐ 食指; foregone *that's a ~ conclusion* nà shì bìránde 那是必然的; foreground qiánbù 前部; forehand *(in tennis)* zhèngshǒu dǎo 正手打; forehead é 额

foreign wàiguó 外国

foreign affairs wàijiāo shìwù 外交事务

foreign currency wàibì 外币

foreigner wàiguórén 外国人

foreign exchange wàihuì 外汇; foreign language wàiyǔ 外语; Foreign Office *Br* Wàijiāobù 外交部; foreign policy wàijiāo zhèngcè 外交政策; Foreign Secretary *Br* Wàijiāobùzhǎng 外交部长

foreman lǐngbān 领班; foremost zuì zhòngyào 最重要; forerunner xiānqū 先驱; foresee yùjiàn 预见; foreseeable kě yùjiàn 可预见; *in the ~ future* zài kě yùjiànde wèilái 在可预见的未来; foresight xiānjiàn zhī míng 先见之明

forest sēnlín 森林

forestry sēnlínxué 森林学

foretaste qiǎncháng 浅尝

foretell yùliào 预料

forever *adv* yǒngyuǎn 永远

foreword qiányán 前言

forfeit *v/t right, privilege etc* sàngshī 丧失

forge *v/t (counterfeit)* wěizào 伪造; *signature* mófǎng 模仿

forger wěizàorén 伪造人

forgery *(bank bill)* jiǎ chāopiào 假钞票; *(document)* wěizàopǐn 伪造品

forget wàngjì 忘记

forgetful jiànwàng 健忘

forget-me-not *(flower)* wùwàngwǒ 勿忘我

forgive 1 *v/t* yuánliàng 原谅 2 *v/i* liàngjiě 谅解

forgiveness yuánliàng 原谅

fork n chāzi 叉子; (in road) fēnchàchù 分岔处

♦**fork out** v/i F (pay) chūqián 出钱

forklift (truck) chāchē 叉车

form 1 n (shape) xíngzhuàng 形状; (document) biǎogé 表格 **2** v/t (in clay etc) sùzào 塑造; friendship jiànlì 建立; opinion xíngchéng 形成; past tense etc xíngshì 形式 **3** v/i (take shape, develop) xíngchéng 形成

formal zhèngshì 正式; recognition etc guānfāng 官方

formality guīfàn 规范; it's just a ~ zhè zhǐshì yìzhǒng xíngshì 这只是一种形式

formally adv speak, behave zhèngshì 正式; recognized guānfāng 官方

format 1 v/t diskette shǐ géshìhuà 使格式化; document ānpái ... bǎnshì 安排... 版式 **2** n (size: of magazine, paper etc) kāibèn 开本; (make-up: of program) fēnggé 风格

formation (act of forming) xíngchéng 形成; (of airplanes) biānduì 编队

formative lìyú chéngzhǎng 利于成长; in his ~ years zài tā xìnggé xíngchéng de shíqí 在他性格形成的时期

former yǐqián 以前; the ~ qiánzhě 前者

formerly yǐqián 以前

formidable kěpà 可怕

formula MATH gōngshì 公式; CHEM fēnzǐshì 分子式; (for success etc) mìjué 秘诀

formulate (express) biǎodá 表达

fort MIL yàosài 要塞

forth: back and ~ láihuí 来回; and so ~ děngděng 等等

forthcoming (future) jíjiāng fāshēng 即将发生; personality rèxīn 热心

fortieth dìsìshí 第四十

fortnight Br bàngèyuè 半个月

fortress MIL chéngbǎo 城堡

fortunate xìngyùn 幸运

fortunately xìngkuī 幸亏

fortune yùnqì 运气; (lot of money)

dàbǐde qián 大笔的钱

fortune-teller suànmìng zhě 算命者

forty sìshí 四十

forward 1 adv xiàngqián 向前 **2** adj pej zhíjiéliǎodàng 直截了当 **3** n SP qiánfēng 前锋 **4** v/t letter zhuǎndì 转递

forwarding agent COM zhuǎnyùnshāng 转运商

fossil huàshí 化石

foster child lǐngyǎngde háizi 领养的孩子

foster parents yǎngfùmǔ 养父母

foul 1 n SP fànguī xíngwéi 犯规行为 **2** adj smell, taste nánwén 难闻; weather èliè 恶劣 **3** v/t SP fànguī 犯规

found v/t school etc chuàngbàn 创办

foundation (of theory etc) jīchǔ 基础; (of organization) chénglì 成立; (organization) jījīnhuì 基金会

foundations (of building) dìjī 地基

founder n chuàngjiànrén 创建人

foundry zhùzàochǎng 铸造厂

fountain pēnquán 喷泉

four sì 四

four-star hotel etc sìxīngjí 四星级

fourteen shísì 十四

fourteenth dìshísì 第十四

fourth dìsì 第四

fowl qín 禽

fox n húli 狐狸

fraction xiǎobùfen 小部分; (decimal) fēnshù 分数

fracture 1 n gǔzhé 骨折 **2** v/t zhéduàn 折断

fragile yìsuì 易碎

fragment n yíbùfen 一部分

fragmentary zhīlípòsuì 支离破碎

fragrance fāngxiāng 芳香

fragrant yǒu xiāngwèi 有香味

Fragrant Hills Xiāngshān 香山

frail xūruò 虚弱

frame 1 n kuàng 框; ~ of mind xīnqíng 心情 **2** v/t picture gěi ... xiāngkuàng 给... 镶框; F person xiànhài 陷害

framework kuàngjià 框架

France Fǎguó 法国

frank tǎnshuài 坦率

frankly tǎnbái 坦白; ~, *it's not worth it* tǎnbáide shuō, bù zhídé 坦白地说，不值得

frantic fāfēng 发疯

fraternal xiōngdìbān 兄弟般; ~ *love* shǒuzú zhī qíng 手足之情

fraud qīpiàn 欺骗; (*person*) piànzi 骗子

fraudulent qīpiànxìng 欺骗性

frayed *cuffs* mósǔn 磨损

freak **1** n (*unusual event*) fǎncháng xiànxiàng 反常现象; (*two-headed person, animal etc*) jīxíng chùxíng 畸形; F (*strange person*) guàirén 怪人; *movie / jazz ~* F diànyǐng / juéshìyuè mí 电影 / 爵士乐迷 **2** *adj wind, storm etc* yìcháng qiángliè 异常强烈

freckle quèbān 雀斑

free **1** *adj* (*at liberty*) zìyóu 自由; (*no cost*) miǎnfèi 免费; *room, table* kòngyú 空余; *are you ~ this afternoon?* nǐ jīntiān xiàwǔ yǒukòng ma? 你今天下午有空吗？; *~ and easy* bùjū xíngshì 不拘形式; *for ~* (*travel, get something*) miǎnfèi 免费 **2** *v/t prisoners* shìfàng 释放

freebie F zèngpǐn 赠品

freedom zìyóu 自由

freedom of the press xīnwén zìyóu 新闻自由

free kick (*in soccer*) rènyì qiú 任意球; freelance **1** *adj* gètǐ 个体 **2** *adv: I work ~* wǒ shì gètǐhù 我是个体户; freelancer gètǐhù 个体户; free market economy zìyóu shìchǎng jīngjì 自由市场经济; free sample miǎnfèi yàngpǐn 免费样品; free speech yánlùn zìyóu 言论自由; freeway gāosù gōnglù 高速公路; freewheel v/i (*on bicycle*) guànxìng huáxíng 惯性滑行

freeze **1** *v/t food, river* lěngdòng 冷冻; *wages, bank account* dòngjié 冻结; *video* zàntíng 暂停 **2** *v/i* (*of water*) nínggù 凝固

♦ **freeze over** (*of river*) quánmiàn jiébīng 全面结冰

freezer lěngdòngshì 冷冻室

freezing **1** *adj* jílěng 冷冷; *it's ~ out here* dòngsǐ rén le 冻死人了; *it's ~* (*cold*) (*of weather, water*) lěngjíle 冷极了; *I'm ~* (*cold*) wǒ dòngsǐle 我冻死了 **2** n língdù 度; *10 below ~* língxià shídù 零下十度

freezing compartment lěngdòngxiāng 冷冻箱

freezing point bīngdiǎn 冰点

freight n huòwù 货物; (*costs*) yùnfèi 运费

freight car (*on train*) huòchēxiāng 货车厢

freighter (*ship*) huòchuán 货船; (*airplane*) yùnshūjī 运输机

freight train huòyùn lièchē 货运列车

French **1** *adj* Fǎguó 法国 **2** n (*language*) Fǎyǔ 法语; *the ~* Fǎguó rén 法国人

French doors luòdìchuāng 落地窗; French fries shǔtiáo 薯条; Frenchman Fǎguó nánrén 法国男人; Frenchwoman Fǎguó nǚrén 法国女人

frequency pínlǜ 频率; (*of radiowave*) bōduàn 波段

frequent[1] *adj* jīngcháng 经常

frequent[2] *v/t bar* chángqù 常去

frequently shícháng 时常

fresh *fruit, meat etc* xīnxiān 新鲜; (*cold*) liángshuǎng 凉爽; xīn 新; (*impertinent*) cūlǔ 粗鲁 ~ *start* chóngxīn kāishǐ 重新开始

♦ **freshen up** **1** *v/i* shūxǐ 梳洗 **2** *v/t room, paintwork* shǐ … huànrán yì xīn 使…焕然一新

freshman xīnshēng 新生

freshness (*of fruit, meat*) xīnxiān 新鲜; (*of style, approach*) xīnyíng 新颖; (*of weather*) liángshuǎng 凉爽

fresh orange (*juice*) xīnxiānde júzizhī 新鲜的橘子汁

freshwater *adj* dànshuǐ 淡水

fret v/i fánzào 烦躁

friction PHYS mócā 摩擦; (*between people*) chōngtū 冲突

friction tape juéyuán jiāobù 绝缘

胶布

Friday xīngqīwǔ 星期五

fridge bīngxiāng 冰箱

fried egg jiāndàn 煎蛋; **fried noodles** chǎomiàn 炒面; **fried potatoes** shǔtiáo 薯条; **fried rice** chǎofàn 炒饭

friend péngyou 朋友; **make ~s** (of one person) jiāo péngyou 交朋友; (of two people) chéngwéi péngyou 成为朋友; **make ~s with X** yǔ X jiāo péngyou 与 X 交朋友

friendly adj atmosphere yǒuhǎo 友好; person héshàn 和善; (easy to use) qīnhéxìng 亲和性; **be ~ with X** (be friends) yǔ X guānxi róngqià 与 X 关系融洽

friendship yǒuyì 友谊

Friendship Store Yǒuyì Shāngdiàn 友谊商店

fries shǔtiáo 薯条

fright jīngxià 惊吓; **give X a ~** xià le X yítiào 吓了 X 一跳

frighten v/t jīngxià 惊吓; **be ~ed** hàipà 害怕; **don't be ~ed** bié hàipà 别害怕; **be ~ed of X** hàipà X 害怕 X

frightening xiàrén 吓人

frigid (sexually) lěngdàn 冷淡

frill (on dress etc) shìbiān 饰边; (fancy extra) fùjiāwù 附加物

fringe (on dress, curtains etc) shìbiān 饰边; (in hair) liúhǎi 刘海儿; (edge) biānyuán 边缘

frisk v/t sōuchá 搜查

frisky puppy etc huópo yǒulì 活泼有力

♦ **fritter away** time, fortune xiāohào 消耗

frivolous person, pleasures fūqiǎn 肤浅

frizzy hair juǎn 卷

frog wā 蛙

frogman wārén 蛙人

from 1 (in time): **~ 9 to 5** (o'clock) cóng jiǔdiǎn dào wǔdiǎn 从九点到五点; **~ the 18th century** cóng shíbā shìjì qǐ 从十八世纪起; **~ today on** cóng jīntiān qǐ 从今天起; **~ next Tuesday** cóng xiàge xīngqī èr qǐ 从下个星期二起

◊ (in space): **~ here to there** cóng zhèr dào nàr 从这儿到那儿; **we drove here ~ Shanghai** wǒmen cóng Shànghǎi kāichē láide 我们从上海开车来的 ◊ (origin): **a letter ~ Jo** Qiáo de láixìn 乔的来信; **a gift ~ the management** guǎnlǐ bùmén sòngde lǐwù 管理部门送的礼物; **it doesn't say who it's ~** méiyǒu shǔmíng 没有署名; **I am ~ New Jersey** wǒ láizì Xīn Zéxī zhōu 我来自新泽西州; **made ~ bananas** yòng xiāngjiāo zuòde 用香蕉做的 ◊ (because of): **tired ~ the journey** yīn lǚxíng ér píláo 因旅行而疲劳; **it's ~ overeating** shì yóu dàliàng jìnshí yǐnqǐde 是由大量进食引起的

front 1 n (of building, book) zhèngmiàn 正面; (cover organization) huǎngzi 幌子; MIL qiánxiàn 前线; (of weather) fēngfēng 锋; **in ~** zài qiánmian 在前面; (in a race) lǐngxiān 领先; **in ~ of X** zài X de qiánmian 在 X 的前面; **at the ~ of X** zài X de qiánbù 在 X 的前部 **2** adj wheel, seat qiánmian 前面 **3** v/t TV program zhǔchí 主持

front cover fēngmiàn 封面; **front door** qiánmén 前门; **front entrance** zhèngmén 正门

frontier biānjiāng 边疆; fig (of knowledge, science) jíxiàn 极限

front page (of newspaper) tóubǎn 头版; **front page news** tóubǎn xīnwén 头版新闻; **front row** qiánpái 前排; **front seat passenger** (in car) qiánpáizuò chéngkè 前排座乘客; **front-wheel drive** qiánlún qūdòng 前轮驱动

frost n shuāng 霜

frostbite dòngshāng 冻伤

frostbitten dòngshāng 冻伤

frosted glass móshā bōlí 磨砂玻璃

frosting (on cake) tángshuāng 糖霜

frosty weather yánhán 严寒; fig: welcome lěngdàn 冷淡

froth *n* pàomò 泡沫

frothy *cream etc* qǐ pàomò 起泡沫

frown *n & v/i* zhòuméi 皱眉

frozen *feet etc* bīngliáng 冰凉; *landscape* bīngfēng 冰封; *food* lěngdòng 冷冻; *I'm ~* F wǒ dònghuài le 我冻坏了

frozen food lěngdòng shípǐn 冷冻食品

fruit shuǐguǒ 水果

fruitful *talks etc* chénggōng 成功

fruit juice guǒzhī 果汁

fruit salad shuǐguǒ sèlā 水果色拉

frustrate *v/t person* shǐ ... jǔsàng 使 ... 沮丧; *plans* zǔ'ài 阻碍

frustrated *look, sigh* jǔsàng 沮丧

frustrating shǐrén xīnfán 使人心烦

frustratingly *slow, hard* lìngrén huīxīn 令人灰心

frustration huīxīn 灰心; *sexual ~* xìng shēnghuó shīyì 性生活失意; *the ~s of modern life* xiàndài shēnghuó de bújìnrényì 现代生活的不尽人意

fry *v/t* (*stir-~*) chǎo 炒; (*deep-~*) yóuzhá yóuzhá 油炸

fuck *v/t* V (*screw*) cào 操; *~!* māde! 妈的 !; *~ him/that!* qù tāmāde! 去他妈的 !

◆fuck off V: *~!* gǔnkāi! 滚开 !

fucking V tāmāde 他妈的

fuel *n* ránliào 燃料

fugitive táofàn 逃犯

fulfill *v/t* shíxiàn 实现; *feel ~ed* gǎndào mǎnzú 感到满足

fulfilling *job* lìngrén mǎnyì 令人满意

fulfillment (*of contract etc*) lǚxíng 履行; (*moral, spiritual*) mǎnzú 满足

full *bottle* zhuāngmǎn 装满; *hotel, bus* mǎnyuán 满员; *diskette* mǎn 满; *account, report* xiángxì 详细; *life* chōngshí 充实; *schedule, day* fánmáng 繁忙; *~ of X* (*of water etc*) chōngmǎn X 充满 X; (*of tourists etc*) dàochù shì 到处是; (*of errors*) quánshì 全是; *~ up* *hotel etc* kèmǎn 客满; (*with food*) chī bǎo le 吃饱了; *pay in ~*

quánbù fùqīng 全部付清

full coverage (*insurance*) zǒngkuò bǎoxiǎn 总括保险; full-grown chéngshú 成熟; full-length *dress* quáncháng 全长; *movie* wèi shānjié未删节; full moon mǎnyuè 满月; full stop jùhào 句号; full-time **1** *adj worker, job* quánrìzhì 全日制 **2** *adv work* quánrì 全日

fully *booked* quánbù 全部; *recovered* wánquán 完全; *understand, explain* quánmiàn 全面; *describe* xiángxì 详细

fumble *v/t catch, job* bènzhuóde chǔlǐ 笨拙地处理

◆fumble around mōsuǒde zhǎo 摸索地找

fume: *be fuming* F (*be very angry*) dànù 大怒

fumes fèiqì 废气

fun lèqù 乐趣; *it was great ~* hěn kāixīn 很开心; *bye, have ~* zàijiàn, jìnqíng wánr ba! 再见, 尽情玩儿吧 !; *for ~* wèile wán 为了玩; *make ~ of X* qǔxiào X 取笑 X

function **1** *n* zuòyòng 作用; (*reception etc*) jíhuì 集会 **2** *v/i* yùnzhuàn 运转; *~ as X* qǐ X de zuòyòng 起 X 的作用

fund **1** *n* jījīn 基金 **2** *v/t project etc* bōkuǎn 拨款

fundamental (*basic*) jīběn 基本; (*substantial*) běnzhì 本质; (*crucial*) shífēn zhòngyào 十分重要

fundamentally *different, altered* cóng gēnběn shang 从根本上

funeral zànglǐ 葬礼

funeral home bìnyíguǎn 殡仪馆

funicular (*railway*) lǎnsuǒ tiědào 缆索铁道

funnel *n* (*of ship*) yāncōng 烟囱

funnily (*oddly*) qíguài 奇怪; (*comically*) huájī 滑稽; *~ enough* qíguàide shì 奇怪的是

funny (*comical*) kěxiào 可笑; (*odd*) gǔguài 古怪

fur máopí 毛皮

furious (*angry*) fènnù 愤怒; *at a ~ pace* fēikuàide 飞快地

furnace lúzi 炉子

furnish *room* zhuāngbèi 装备; (*supply*) tígōng 提供

furniture jiāju 家具; *a piece of ~* yíjiàn jiāju 一件家具

furry *animal* máopí fùgài 毛皮覆盖

further **1** *adj* (*additional*) jìnyíbù 进一步; (*more distant*) gèngyuǎn 更远; *until ~ notice* lìngxíng tōngzhī 另行通知; *have you anything ~ to say?* nǐ hái yǒu shénme yào shuō de ma? 你还有什么要说的吗？ **2** *adv walk, drive* gèngyuǎn 更远; *~, I want to say …* cǐwài, wǒ yào shuō … 此外，我要说 …; *2 miles ~ (on)* zài zǒu liǎng yīnglǐ 再走两英里 **3** *v/t cause etc* cùjìn 促进

furthest *adj & adv* zuìyuǎn 最远

furtive *glance* tōutōu 偷偷

fury (*anger*) bàonù 暴怒

fuse ELEC **1** *n* bǎoxiǎnsī 保险丝 **2** *v/i* bǎoxiǎnsī shǎoduàn 保险丝烧断 **3** *v/t* shǎoduàn bǎoxiǎnsī 烧断保险丝

fusebox bǎoxiǎnsī hé 保险丝盒

fuselage jīshēn 机身

fuse wire bǎoxiǎnsī xiàn 保险丝线

fusion rónghé 熔合

fuss *n* dàjīng xiǎoguài 大惊小怪; *make a ~* (*complain*) tóusù 投诉; (*behave in exaggerated way*) xiǎotí dàzuò 小题大做; *make a ~ of* (*be very attentive to*) guòyú guānzhù 过于关注

fussy *person* tiāotì 挑剔; *design etc* tài duō zhuāngshì 太多装饰; *a ~ eater* tiāotì shíwù de rén 挑剔食物的人

futile wúxiào 无效

future *n* (*of person, company*) qiántú 前途; (*of humanity, earth*) wèilái 未来; GRAM jiāngláishí 将来时; *in ~* yǐhòu 以后

futures FIN qīhuò 期货

futures market FIN qīhuò shìchǎng 期货市场

futuristic *design* wèiláishì 未来式

fuzzy *hair* juǎn 卷; (*out of focus*) móhu 模糊

G

gadget xiǎozhuāngzhì 小装置

gag 1 n dǔ zuǐ bù 堵嘴布; (joke) xiàohuà 笑话 2 v/t person sāizhù ... de zuǐ 塞住 ... 的 嘴; the press yāzhì 压制

gain v/t (acquire) yíngdé 赢得; ~ speed jiāsù 加速; ~ 10 pounds tǐzhòng zēngjiā shí bàng 体重 增加了十磅

gale dàfēng 大风

gallant yǒu shēnshì fēngdù 有绅士风度

gall bladder dǎnnáng 胆囊

gallery (for art) huàláng 画廊; (in theater) dǐngcéng lóuzuò 顶层楼座

galley (on ship) chuán shàng chúfáng 船上厨房

gallon jiālún 加仑; ~s of tea dàliàng de chá 大量的茶

gallop v/i fēipǎo 飞跑

gallows jiǎoxíngjià 绞刑架

gallstone dǎnjiéshí 胆结石

gamble dǔbó 赌博

gambler dǔtú 赌徒

gambling dǔbó 赌博

game n (match) bǐsài 比赛; (sport) yùndòng 运动; (children's) yóuxì 游戏; (in tennis) yìjú 一局

gang yìbāng 一帮

♦gang up on héhuǒ gōngjī 合伙攻击

Gang of Four Sìrénbāng 四人帮

gangster dǎitú 歹徒

gangway tiàobǎn 跳板

gap (in wall) lièfèng 裂缝; (for parking) kòngr 空儿; (in figures) chājù 差距; (in time, conversation) jiànxì 间隙; (between two people's characters) chāyì 差异

gape v/i (person) zhāngkǒu 张口; (hole) lièkāi 裂开

♦gape at mùdèng kǒudāi de níngshì 目瞪口呆地凝视

gaping adj hole lièkāi 裂开

garage for parking chēkù 车库; for gas jiāyóuzhàn 加油站; for repairs qìchē xiūlǐzhàn 汽车修理站

garbage ⇩ lājī 垃圾; fig (nonsense) fèihuà 废话

garbage can lājīxiāng 垃圾箱; garbage collection shōu lājī 收垃圾; garbage dump lājī zhàn 垃圾站

garden huāyuán 花园

gardener yuándīng 园丁; (professional) yuánlínshī 园林师

gardening yuányì 园艺

gargle v/i shùkǒu 漱口

garish súbùkěnài 俗不可耐

garland n huāhuán 花环

garlic dàsuàn 大蒜

garment fúzhuāng 服装

garnish v/t diǎnzhuì 点缀

garrison n (place) zhùdì 驻地; (troops) wèishù bùduì 卫戍部队

garter diàowàdài 吊袜带

gas n qìtǐ 气体; (gasoline) qìyóu 汽油

gash n qièkǒu 切口

gasket diànpiàn 垫片

gasoline qìyóu 汽油

gasp 1 n chuǎnxī 喘息 2 v/i qìchuǎn 气喘; ~ for breath chuǎnqì 喘气

gas pedal yóuménr 油门儿; gas pump yóubèng 油泵; gas station jiāyóuzhàn 加油站; gas works méiqìchǎng 煤气厂

gate (of house, castle) dàmén 大门; (at airport) dēngjīkǒu 登机口

gatecrash bùqǐngzìdào 不请自到

gateway ménkǒu 门口; fig tújìng 途径

gather 1 v/t facts, information sōují 搜集; am I to ~ that ... ? wǒ yīnggāi lǐjiě wéi ... ? 我应该理解为 ... ?; ~ speed jiāsù 加速

2 v/i (*understand*) tuīxiǎng 推想

♦ **gather up** *possessions* jīlěi 积累

gathering (*group of people*) jùhuì 聚会

gaudy huāshao 花哨

gauge 1 n jìliángqì 计量器 **2** v/t cèdìng 测定

gaunt qiáocuì 憔悴

gauze bóshā 薄纱

gay n & adj (*homosexual*) tóngxìngliàn 同性恋

gaze 1 n zhùshì 注视 **2** v/i níngshì 凝视

♦ **gaze at** níngshì 凝视

GB (= *Great Britain*) Dà Bùlièdiān 大不列颠

GDP (= *gross domestic product*) guónèi shēngchǎn zǒngzhí 国内生产总值

gear n equipment yòngjù 用具; in vehicles chílún 齿轮; ~ *lever*, ~*shift* biànsùgǎnr 变速杆

gel (*for hair*) rǔ yǎn 乳液; (*for shower*) yè yè 液

gem zhēnbǎo 珍宝; fig (*book etc*) zhēnpǐn 珍品; you're a ~ (*person*) nǐ zhēn hǎo 你真好

gender xìngbié 性别

gene jīyīn 基因; it's in his ~s tā shēnglái rúcǐ 他生来如此

general 1 n (*in army*) jiāngjūn 将军; in ~ dàtǐshang 大体上 **2** adj (*overall, miscellaneous*) zǒngde 总的; (*widespread*) pǔbiàn 普遍

general election pǔxuǎn 普选

generalization gàikuò 概括; that's a ~ nà shì gè gàikuò 那是个概括

generalize gàikuò 概括

generally yìbānde 一般地

generate (*create*) chǎnshēng 产生; (*in linguistics*) shēngchéng 生成; ~ *electricity* fādiàn 发电

generation dài dài 代; ~ *gap* dàigōu 代沟

generator fādiànjī 发电机

generosity dàfang 大方

generous (*with money*) dàfang 大方; (*not too critical*) kuānhóng dàliàng 宽宏大量; portion etc dàliàng 大量

genetic yíchuán 遗传

genetically yíchuán yīnzi shang 遗传因子上

genetic engineering yíchuán gōngchéng 遗传工程

genetic fingerprint gètǐ yíchuán xìngzhēng 个体遗传性征

geneticist yíchuánxuéjiā 遗传学家

genetics yíchuánxué 遗传学

Genghis Khan Chéngjísīhàn 成吉思汗

genial person, company qīnqiè 亲切

genitals shēngzhíqì 生殖器

genius tiāncái 天才

gentle wēnróu 温柔

gentleman shēnshì 绅士

gents (*toilet*) nányòngwèishēngjiān 男用卫生间

genuine zhēnpǐn 真品; (*sincere*) zhēnchéng 真诚

geographical features dìlǐ 地理

geography (*of area*) dìxíng 地形; (*subject*) dìlǐxué 地理学

geological dìzhì 地质

geologist dìzhìxué zhě 地质学者

geology (*of area*) dìzhì 地质; (*subject*) dìzhìxué 地质学

geometric(al) jīhéxué 几何学

geometry jǐhé 几何

geriatric 1 adj lǎonián 老年 **2** n lǎoniánbìngxué 老年病学

germ bìngjūn 病菌; of idea etc méngyá 萌芽

germ warfare xìjūn zhànzhēng 细菌战争

German 1 adj Déguó 德国 **2** n (*person*) Déguó rén 德国人; (*language*) Déyǔ 德语

Germany Déguó 德国

gesticulate zuò shǒushì 做手势

gesture n (*with hand*) shǒushì 手势; fig (*of friendship*) biǎoshì 表示

get (*obtain*) dédào 得到; (*fetch*) gěi ... ná gěi ... 拿; (*receive: letter*) shōudào 收到; (*receive: knowledge, respect etc*) huòdé 获得; (*catch: bus, train etc*) zuò 坐; (*arrive*) dào 到; (*understand*) míngbái 明白; can I ~ you a *drink?* nǐ xiǎng hē shénme? 你想喝什么?; **~ going** (*leave*) zǒu zǒu ◊ (*become, grow*): **~ tired** (*become, grow*): **~ tired** lèi le/lǎo lē 累了/老了 ◊ (*causative*) bǎ … bǎ …;; **~ one's hair cut** bǎ tóufa jiǎn le 把头发剪了; **~ the car fixed** bǎ chē xiūle 把车修了; **~ X ready** bǎ X zhǔnbèi hǎo 把X 准备好; **~ X to do Y** jiào X zuò Y 叫X做Y ◊ (*have opportunity*): **I got to meet him** wǒ yǒu jīhuì jiàndào tā 我有机会见到他; **did you ~ to go there?** nǐ yǒu jīhuì qù nàr le ma? 你有机会去那儿了吗? ◊: **~ to know** rènshi 认识 ◊: **have got** yǒu 有: **have you got any children?** nǐ yǒu háizi ma? 你有孩子吗?; **I've got three tickets** wǒ yǒu sānzhāng piào 我有三张票; **I've got a headache** wǒ tóutòng 我头痛; **have you got time?** nǐ yǒu shíjiān ma? 你有时间吗? ◊: **have got to** (*must*) bìxū 必须; **I have got to study** wǒ bìxū xuéxí/kàn tā 我必须学习/看他; **I don't want to, but I've got to** wǒ bùdébù 我不得不

♦ **get around** (*travel*) lǚxíng 旅行; (*be mobile*) zǒudòng 走动

♦ **get along** (*progress*) jìnzhǎn 进展; (*come to party etc*) dào 到; (*with somebody*) yú … chùdelái 与 … 处得来

♦ **get at** (*criticize*) pīpíng 批评; (*imply, mean*) yìzhǐ 意指

♦ **get away 1** v/i (*leave*) líkāi 离开 **2** v/t: **get X away from Y** bǎ X cóng Y názǒu 把X从Y拿走

♦ **get away with** táozuì 逃罪

♦ **get back 1** v/i (*return*) huídào 回到; **I'll ~ to you on that** wǒ yíhuìr zài huídá nǐde wèití 我一会儿再回答你的问题 **2** v/t (*obtain again*) chóngxīn dédào 重新得到

♦ **get by** (*pass*) tōngguò 通过; (*financially*) wéichí 维持

♦ **get down 1** v/i (*from ladder etc*) xiàlái 下来; (*duck*) wān yāo 弯腰 **2** v/t (*depress*) jiào rén jǔsàng 叫人沮丧

♦ **get down to** (*start: work*) kāishǐ rènzhēn duìdài 开始认真对待; (*reach: real facts*) zhuījiū 追究

♦ **get in 1** v/i (*arrive: of train, plane*) dàodá 到达; (*come home*) dàojiā 到家; (*to car*) jìnrù 进入; **how did they ~?** tāmen zěnme jìnlaide? 他们怎麼进来的？ **2** v/t (*to suitcase etc*) fàngjìnqù 放进去

♦ **get off 1** v/i (*from bus etc*) cóng … xiàlái 从 … 下来; (*finish work*) xià bān 下班; (*not be punished*) táotuō chǔfèn 逃脱处分 **2** v/t (*remove*) nádiào 拿掉; **top, boots, clothes** tuō 脱; **~ the grass!** wùtà cǎopíng! 勿踏草坪！

♦ **get off with** (*Br: sexually*) yǔ … jiéshí 与 … 结识; **~ a small fine** jiāo diǎnr fájīn jiù liǎoshì le 交点儿罚金就了事

♦ **get on 1** v/i (*be friendly*) chùdelái 处得来; (*advance: of time*) bù zǎo le 不早了; (*become old*) lǎo le 老了; (*make progress*) jìnzhǎn 进展; **~ to the train/bus/one's bike** shàng chē 上车; **~ to the airplane** shàng fēijī 上飞机; **it's getting on** tiānwǎn le 天晚了; **he's getting on** tā shàngle niánjì 他上了年纪; **he's getting on for 50** tā kuài wǔshí le 他快五十了 **2** v/t: **~ the bus/one's bike** shàng chē 上车; **get one's hat on** dài shàng màozi 戴上帽子; **I can't get these pants on** wǒ chuān bú shàng kùzi 我穿不上裤子

♦ **get out 1** v/i (*of car etc*) chūlái 出来; **~ of prison** chūyù 出狱; **~!** gǔnchūqù! 滚出去！; **let's ~ of here** zánmen kuài zǒu ba 咱们快走吧; **I don't ~ much these days** jìnlái wǒ bú tài chūqù 近来我不太出去 **2** v/t **nail, something jammed** nòngchū 弄出; **stain** chúqù 除去; **gun, pen** tāochū 掏出

♦ **get over fence** yuèguò 越过; **lover etc** wàngquè 忘却; **disappointment** kèfú 克服

♦ **get over with: let's get it over**

with zánmen kuàidiǎnr bǎ tā nòngwán ba 咱们快点儿把它弄完吧

♦ **get through** (*on telephone*) dǎtōng 打通; (*make self understood*) ràng rén tīng dǒng 让人听懂

♦ **get up 1** *v/i* (*in morning*) qǐchuáng 起床; (*from chair etc*) zhànqǐlái 站起来; (*of wind*) dà qǐlái 大起来 **2** *v/t* (*climb: hill*) pá 爬

♦ **get up to**: ***what have you been getting up to?*** nǐ zuìjìn gànshénme? 你最近干什么?

getaway (*from robbery*) táopǎo 逃跑; **~ car** qiántáochē 潜逃车

get-together jùhuì 聚会

ghastly (*horrible*) kěpà 可怕

gherkin xiǎohuángguā 小黄瓜

ghetto shǎoshùmínzú jūzhùqū 少数民族居住区

ghost guǐ 鬼

ghostly guǐyíyàng 鬼一样

giant 1 *n* jùrén 巨人 **2** *adj* pángdà 庞大

gibberish fèihuà 废话

giblets nèizàng 内脏

giddiness xuànyūn 眩晕

giddy tóuyūn 头晕

gift lǐwù 礼物

gifted yǒu tiānfù 有天赋

giftwrap bāozhuāng shāngpǐn 包装商品

gigabyte COMPUT qiānzhào zìjié 千兆字节

gigantic jùdà 巨大

giggle 1 *v/i* gēgē de xiào 咯咯地笑 **2** *n* shǎxiào 傻笑

gill (*of fish*) sāi sāi 鳃

gilt *n* dùjīn cáiliào 镀金材料; **~s** FIN jīnbiānr gǔpiào 金边儿股票

gimmick guībǎxì 鬼把戏

gin dùsōngzǐjiǔ 杜松子酒; **~ and tonic** ⇩ kuíníng dùsōngzǐjiǔ 奎宁杜松子酒

ginger *n* (*spice*) jiāng 姜

gingerbread jiāngbǐng 姜饼

ginseng rénshēn 人参

gipsy jípǔsàirén 吉普赛人

giraffe chángjǐnglù 长颈鹿

girder *n* dàliáng 大梁

girl nǚhái 女孩

girlfriend (*of boy*) nǚ péngyou 女朋友; (*of girl*) nǚxìng péngyou 女性朋友

girlie magazine huángsè zázhì 黄色杂志

girl scout nǚ tóngzǐjūn 女童子军

gist yàozhǐ 要旨

give gěi 给; (*supply: electricity etc*) gōngjǐ 供给; **~ a talk** zuò jiǎngzuò 作讲座; **~ a lecture** jiǎngkè 讲课; **~ a cry** dàshēng hūhǎn 大声呼喊; **~ her my love** xiàng tā wènhǎo 向她问好

♦ **give away** (*as present*) sòng 送; (*betray*) xièlòu 泄漏; **give oneself away** bàolù zìjǐ 暴露自己

♦ **give back** huán 还

♦ **give in 1** *v/i surrender* qūfú 屈服 **2** *v/t* (*hand in*) jiāochū 交出

♦ **give off** *smell, fumes* fāchū 发出

♦ **give onto** (*open onto*) tōngxiàng 通向

♦ **give out 1** *v/t leaflets etc* fēnfā 分发; **~ a groan** shēnyín 呻吟 **2** *v/i* (*of supplies, strength*) yòngwán 用完

♦ **give up 1** *v/t smoking etc* jiè 戒; **give oneself up** (*to police etc*) tóu'àn 投案 **2** *v/i* (*cease habit*) jiè 戒; (*stop making effort*) fàngqì 放弃

♦ **give way** (*of bridge etc*) bēngkuì 崩溃

given name míngzi 名字

glacier bīngchuān 冰川

glad gāoxìng 高兴

gladly yúkuài 愉快

glamor mèilì 魅力

glamorous yǒu mèilì 有魅力

glance 1 *n* yìpiē 一瞥 **2** *v/i* sǎoshì 扫视

♦ **glance at** sǎoshì 扫视

gland xiàn 腺

glandular fever línbāxiàn rè 淋巴腺炎

glare 1 *n* (*of sun, headlights*) qiángliède guāng 强烈的光 **2** *v/i* (*of sun, headlights*) shǎnyào 闪耀

♦ **glare at** nùmù ér shì 怒目而视

glaring *adj mistake* tūchū 突出

glass (*material*) bōli 玻璃; (*for drink*) bōlibēi 玻璃杯

glasses (*eye~*) yǎnjìng 眼镜

glasshouse nuǎnfáng 暖房

glaze n guānghuámiàn 光滑面

♦glaze over (*of eyes*) biànde móhu 变得模糊

glazed expression dāizhì 呆滞

glazier zhuāng bōli gōngrén 装玻璃工人

glazing chuāngyòngbōli 窗用玻璃

gleam 1 n wēiguāng 微光 2 v/i shǎnshuò 闪烁

glee kuàilè 快乐

gleeful lìngrén xīngfèn 令人兴奋

glib yóuzuǐhuáshé 油嘴滑舌

glide huáxiáng 滑行

glider huáxiáng jī 滑翔机

gliding n (*sport*) huáxiáng yùndòng 滑翔运动

glimmer 1 n (*of light*) wēiguāng 微光; a ~ of hope yíxiàn xīwàng 一线希望 2 v/i fāwēiguāng 发微光

glimpse 1 n yìpiē 一瞥; catch a ~ of piējiàn 瞥见 2 v/t piējiàn 瞥见

glint 1 n shǎnshuò 闪烁 2 v/i (*of light*) fāwēiguāng 发微光; (*of eyes*) shǎnxiàn mǒuzhǒng shénsè 闪现某种神色

glisten v/i shǎnguāng 闪光

glitter v/i shǎnshǎn fāguāng 闪闪发光

glitterati yǒu míngqì de ren 有名气的人

gloat v/i zhānzhānzìxǐ 沾沾自喜; ~ over xìngzāilèhuò de kǎolǜ ... 幸灾乐祸地考虑

global (*worldwide*) quánqiú 全球; (*without exceptions*) pǔbiàn 普遍

global economy quánqiú jīngjì 全球经济; global market quánqiú shìchǎng 全球市场; global warming quánqiú qìwēn shēnggāo 全球气温升高

globe (*the earth*) dìqiú 地球; (*model of earth*) dìqiúyí 地球仪

gloom (*darkness*) yīn'àn 阴暗; (*mood*) yōuyù 忧郁

gloomy room yīn'àn 阴暗; mood, person yōuchóu 忧愁

glorious weather, day qínglǎng 晴朗; victory guāngróng 光荣

glory n róngyù 荣誉

gloss n (*shine*) guāngzé 光泽; (*general explanation*) zhùshì 注释

glossary cíhuìbiǎo 词汇表

gloss paint yǒuguāng túliào 有光涂料

glossy 1 adj paper guānghuá 光滑 2 n (*magazine*) guāngmiàn 光面

glove shǒutào 手套

glow 1 n (*of light, fire*) guānghuī 光辉; (*in cheeks*) hóngrùn 红润 2 v/i (*of light, fire*) fāguāng 发光; (*of cheeks*) xiànchū hóngrùn 现出红润

glowing description rèqíng 热情

glue 1 n jiāo 胶 2 v/t zhān 粘; ~ X to Y bǎ X zhānzài Y shàng 把X粘在Y上

glum yōuyù 忧郁

glutinous rice nuòmǐ 糯米

glutton tānshí zhě 贪食者

gluttony tānshí 贪食

GMT (= Greenwich Mean Time) Gélínwēizhì biāozhǔn shíjiān 格林威治标准时间

gnarled branch niǔqū 扭曲; hands gǔjié línxún 骨节嶙峋

gnat ruì méng 蚋

gnaw v/t bone kěn 啃

GNP (= gross national product) guómín shēngchǎn zǒngzhí 国民生产总值

Go (*game*) wéiqí 围棋

go 1 n: on the ~ mánglù 忙碌 2 v/i qù 去; (*leave: of train, plane, of people*) líkāi 离开; (*work, function*) yùnzhuǎn 运转; (*become*) biànde 变得; (*come out: of stain etc*) diào 掉; (*cease: of pain etc*) méile 没了; (*match: of colors etc*) pèi 配; ~ shopping / jogging qù mǎi dōngxi / mànpǎo 去买东西 / 慢跑; I must be ~ing wǒ děi zǒule 我得走了; let's ~ zǒuba 走吧; ~ for a walk qù sànbù 去散步; ~ to bed shàngchuáng 上床; ~ to school shàngxué 上学; how's the work ~ing? gōngzuò jìnzhǎn rúhé? 工作进展如何？;

they're ~ing for $50 (being sold at) yǐ wǔshí měiyuán chūshòu 以五十美元出售; **hamburger to ~** hànbǎobāo, dàizǒu 汉堡包、带走; **be all gone** (finished) yòngwánle 用完了; **be ~ing to do X** yàozuò X 要做X

♦**go ahead** (and do something) gàn(shuō)ba 干 (说) 吧; (on you go) qùba 去吧

♦**go ahead with** plans etc àn … jìnxíng 按 … 进行

♦**go along with** suggestion zàntóng 赞同

♦**go at** (attack) gōngjī 攻击

♦**go away** (of person) líkāi 离开; (of rain) tíng 停; (of pain, clouds) xiāoshī 消失

♦**go back** (return) huíqù 回去; (date back) zhuīsù 追溯; ~ **to sleep** zài shuì 再睡; **we ~ a long way** wǒmen xiāngshí duōnián le 我们相识多年了

♦**go by** (of car, people) guòqù 过去; (of time) tuīyí 推移

♦**go down** xiàqù 下去; (of sun, ship) luòxià 落下; (of swelling) xiāoqù 消去; ~ **well / badly** (of suggestion etc) shòu / búshòu huānyíng 受 / 不受欢迎

♦**go for** (attack) xíjī 袭击; (like) xǐhuān 喜欢

♦**go in** (to room, house) jìnqù 进去; (of sun) yǐnmò 隐没; (fit: of part etc) ān ǎn 安

♦**go in for** competition, race cānjiā 参加; (like, take part in) kù'ài 酷爱

♦**go off 1** v/i (leave) líkāi 离开; (of bomb) bàozhà 爆炸; (of gun) zǒuhuǒ 走火; (of alarm) xiǎngqǐ 响起; (of milk etc) huàile 坏了 **2** v/t (stop liking) bú zài xǐhuān 不再喜欢

♦**go on** (continue) jìxù 继续; (happen) fāshēng 发生; **what's going on?** fāshēng shénme shì le? 发生什么事了?; ~, **do it!** (encouraging) zuò ba! 做吧!

♦**go on at** (nag) láodao 唠叨

♦**go out** (of person) chūqù 出去;

(of light, fire) xīmiè 熄灭

♦**go over** v/t (check) zǐxì jiǎnchá 仔细检查; (do again) zài guò yíbiàn 再过一遍

♦**go through** v/t illness, hard times jīnglì 经历; (check) jiǎnchá 检查; (read through) liúlǎn 浏览

♦**go under** (sink) chénmò 沉没; (of company) pòchǎn 破产

♦**go up** (climb) shàngqù 上去; mountain pāndēng 攀登; (of prices) shàngzhǎng 上涨

♦**go without 1** v/t food etc méiyǒu yě xíng 没有也行 **2** v/i rěnshòu méiyǒu 忍受没有

goad v/t cìjī 刺激

go-ahead 1 n xǔkě 许可; **get the ~** dédào xǔkě 得到许可 **2** adj (enterprising, dynamic) yǒujìnqǔxīn 有进取心

goal (sport: target) mùbiāo 目标; (sport: point) bǐfēn 比分; (objective) mùbiāo 目标

goalkeeper shǒuményuán 守门员

goalpost ménzhù 门柱

goat shānyáng 山羊

♦**gobble up** lángtūnhǔyàn 狼吞虎咽

go-between zhōngjiānrén 中间人

Gobi Desert ⇩ Gēbìtān 戈壁滩

god shén 神; **thank God!** xiètiānxièdì! 谢天谢地!; **oh God!** tiānna! 天哪!

goddess nǚshén 女神

godfather (in mafia) bāngtóu 帮头

godforsaken place, town dǎoméi dǎoméi 倒霉

goggles hùmùjìng 护目镜

going adj price etc xiànxíng 现行; ~ **concern** xīngwàng de qǐyè 兴旺的企业

goings-on fāshēng de shìqíng 发生的事情

gold 1 n huángjīn 黄金; (~ medal) jīnpái 金牌 **2** adj jīn 金

golden sky, hair jīnsè 金色; ~ **handshake** wèiláojīn 慰劳金; ~ **wedding anniversary** jīnhūn jìniàn 金婚纪念

goldfish jīnyú 金鱼

goldsmith jīnshǒushìshāng 金首

饰商

golf gāo'ěrfū 高尔夫
golf club (organization) gāo'ěrfū jùlèbù 高尔夫俱乐部; (stick) gāo'ěrfū qiúgùn 高尔夫球棍
golf course gāo'ěrfū qiúchǎng 高尔夫球场
golfer dǎ gāo'ěrfūqiúde ren 打高尔夫球的人
gong luó luó 锣; (in wrestling) míngluó lìng 鸣锣令
good person, weather, movie, news, child hǎo 好; food hǎochī 好吃; a ~ many xǔduō 许多; be ~ at ... shànyú ... 善于...; be ~ for X duì X yǒuyòng 对X有用
goodbye zàijiàn 再见; say ~ to X, wish X ~ gàobié X 告别X
good-for-nothing n méiyòng de rén 没用的人; Good Friday Fùhuójié Xīngqīwǔ 复活节星期五; good-humored xīnqínghǎo 心情好; good-looking woman, man hǎokàn 好看; good-natured píqi hǎo 脾气好
goodness (moral) shànxíng 善行; (of fruit etc) jīnghuá 精华; thank ~! xiètiānxièdì! 谢天谢地!
goods COM shāngpǐn 商品
goodwill yǒuhǎo 友好
goody-goody n chǎnmèi zhě 谄媚者
gooey nián 粘
goof v/i F nòngzāole 弄糟了
goose é 鹅
gooseberry cùlì 醋栗
gooseflesh jīpí gēda 鸡皮疙瘩
gorge 1 n xiágǔ 峡谷 2 v/t: ~ oneself on ... dàchī ... 大吃...
gorgeous weather fēnghé rìlì 风和日丽; dress, woman, hair piàoliang 漂亮; smell hěn xiāng 很香
gorilla dàxīngxing 大猩猩
go-slow dàigōng 怠工
Gospel (in Bible) Fúyīn 福音
gossip 1 n liúyán fēiyǔ 流言蜚语; (person) chángshé 长舌 2 v/i xiánliáo 闲聊
govern zhìlǐ 治理
government zhèngfǔ 政府
governor zhōuzhǎng 州长

gown (long dress) chángfú 长服; (wedding dress) jiéhūn lǐfú 结婚礼服; (of academic, judge, priest) lǐfúshì chángpáo 礼服式长袍; (of surgeon) dàguà 大褂
grab v/t zhuāzhù 抓住; ~ some food suíbiàn chīxiē kuàicān 随便吃些快餐; ~ some sleep xiǎoshuì 小睡
grace yōuměi 优美
graceful yōuyǎ 优雅
gracious person réncí 仁慈; style, living yǎzhì 雅致
grade 1 n (quality) děngjí 等级; EDU niánjí 年级 2 v/t gěi ... fēnlèi 给...分类
grade crossing píngmiàn jiāochā 平面交叉
gradient xiépō 斜坡
gradual zhújiàn 逐渐
gradually zhújiàn 逐渐
graduate n bìyèshēng 毕业生
graduation bìyè 毕业
graffiti húluàn túmǒ 胡乱涂抹
graft n BOT jiàjiē 嫁接; MED yízhí 移植; F (hard work) xīnkǔ de huór 辛苦的活儿
grain lì 粒; (in wood) mùwén 木纹; go against the ~ gégé bú rù 格格不入
gram kè 克
grammar yǔfǎ 语法
grammatical héhū yǔfǎ 合乎语法
grand 1 adj zhuàngguān 壮观; F (very good) hǎojíle 好极了 2 n F ($1000) yìqiān 一千
grandad (paternal) yéye 爷爷; (maternal) wàigōng 外公
grandchild (son's son) sūnzi 孙子; (son's daughter) sūnnǚ 孙女; (daughter's son) wàisūnzi 外孙子; (daughter's daughter) wàisūnnǚ 外孙女
Grand Canal Dàyùnhé 大运河
granddaughter (son's daughter) sūnnǚ 孙女; (daughter's daughter) wàisūnnǚ 外孙女
grandeur hóngwěi 宏伟
grandfather (paternal) zǔfù 祖父; (maternal) wàizǔfù 外祖父;

grandma (*paternal*) nǎinai 奶奶;
(*maternal*) lǎolao 姥姥; grandmother (*paternal*) zǔmǔ 祖母;
(*maternal*) wàizǔmǔ 外祖母;
grandpa (*paternal*) yéye 爷爷;
(*maternal*) wàigōng 外公; grandparents (*paternal*) zǔfùmǔ 祖父
母; (*maternal*) wàizǔfùmǔ 外祖父
母; grand piano dàgāngqín 大钢
琴; grandson (*son's son*) sūnzi 孙
子; (*daughter's son*) wàisūnzi 外孙
子; grandstand zhèngmiàn
kàntái 正面看台

granite huāgǎngshí 花岗石

granny (*paternal*) nǎinai 奶奶;
(*maternal*) wàipó 外婆

grant 1 n money bōkuǎn 拨款;
(*money: for university, school*)
zhùxuéjīn 助学金 2 v/t wish,
peace shòuyǔ 授予; visa zhǔnyǔ
准予; request tóngyì 同意; take X
for ~ed (*assume to be true*) rènwéi
X lǐ suǒ dāngrán 认为X理所当
然; (*not appreciate fully*) bú gòu
zhēnshì X 不够珍视 X

granulated sugar shātáng 砂糖

granule xìlì 细粒

grape pútao 葡萄

grapefruit pútaoyòu 葡萄柚;
grapefruit juice pútaoyòuzhī 葡
萄柚汁; grapevine: hear X
through the ~ xiǎodào tīngláide
X 小道听来的X

graph túbiǎo 图表

graphic 1 adj description etc
shēngdòng 生动 2 n COMPUT
túxíng 图形

graphics COMPUT túxíngxué 图形
学

graphics card COMPUT túxíngkǎ
图形卡

graphics controller COMPUT
túxíng kòngzhìqì 图形控制器

♦grapple with attacker yǔ ...
gédòu 与 ... 格斗; problem etc
jìnlì jiějué 尽力解决

grasp 1 n (*physical*) zhuā 抓;
(*mental*) zhǎngwò 掌握 2 v/t
(*physically*) zhuāzhù 抓住;
(*understand*) lǐjiě 理解

grass cǎo 草

grasshopper zhàměng 蚱蜢;
grasslands cǎoyuán 草原;
grass widow yǔ zhàngfu chángqī
fēnjū de nǚzǐ 与丈夫长期分居
的女子

grassy duōcǎo 多草

grate¹ n (*metal*) lúgé 炉格

grate² 1 v/t (*in cooking*) mósuì 磨碎
2 v/i (*of sounds*) cāxiǎng 擦响

grateful gǎnjī 感激; be ~ to X duì
X xīncún gǎnjī 对X心存感激

grater cāzi 擦子

gratification mǎnzú 满足

gratify shǐmǎnzú 使满足

grating 1 n (*on drain etc*) gé gé 格
格 2 adj sound, voice cì'ěr 刺耳

gratitude gǎn'ēn 感恩

gratuity xiǎofèi 小费

grave¹ n fénmù 坟墓

grave² adj error yánzhòng 严重;
face, voice zhuāngzhòng 庄重

gravel n lìshí 砾石

gravestone mùbēi 墓碑

graveyard mùdì 墓地

gravity PHYS zhònglì 重力

gravy ròuzhī 肉汁

gray adj huīsè 灰色; he/his hair is
going ~ tóufa báile 头发白了

gray-haired tóufa huābái 头发花
白

graze¹ v/i (*of cow, horse*) chīcǎo 吃
草

graze² 1 v/t arm etc cāshāng 擦伤
2 n mùcǎo 牧草

grease yóu 油

greasy food yóuzhī guòduō 油脂
过多; hair, skin, hands, plate yóunì
油腻

great mistake, misunderstanding,
disappointment hěndà 很大; open
space guǎngkuò 广阔; sum of
money dàliàng 大量; (*major:
composer, writer*) wěidà 伟大;
(*very good*) hěnbàng 很棒; ~ to
see you! jiàndào nǐ zhēn gāoxìng!
见到你真高兴!

great-grandfather (*paternal*)
zēngzǔfù 曾祖父; (*maternal*)
zēngwàizǔfù 曾外祖父; great-
grandmother (*paternal*)
zēngzǔmǔ 曾祖母; (*maternal*)

zēngwàizǔmǔ 曾外祖母; **Great Hall of the People** Rénmín Dàhuìtáng 人民大会堂; **Great Leap Forward** Dàyuèjìn 大跃进

greatly fēicháng 非常

greatness wěidà 伟大

Great Wall (of China) (Wànlǐ) Chángchéng (万里)长城

greed tānxīn 贪心

greedy tānlán 贪婪

green lǜsè 绿色; (*environmentally*) lǜsè 绿色

greengrocer shūcài shuǐguǒ shāng 蔬菜水果商; **greenhorn** shēngshǒu 生手; **greenhouse** wēnshì 温室; **greenhouse effect** wēnshì xiàoyìng 温室效应; **greenhouse gas** wēnshì qìtǐ 温室气体; **green tea** lùchá 绿茶

greet yíngjiē 迎接

greeting wènhòu 问候

grenade shǒuliúdàn 手榴弹

grid wǎng 网

gridiron SP měishì zúqiúchǎng 美式足球场

gridlock (*in traffic*) jiāotōng dǔsè 交通堵塞

grief bēishāng 悲伤

grievance láosāo 牢骚

grieve bēitòng 悲痛; ~ **for X** āidào X 哀悼 X

grill 1 n (*for cooking*) kǎojià 烤架; (*window*) gézi 格子 **2** v/t food kǎo 烤; (*interrogate*) yánlì pánwèn 严厉盘问

grille gézi 格子

grim kěbù 可怖

grimace n guàixiàng 怪相

grime chéngòu 尘垢

grimy āngzāng 肮脏

grin 1 n liězuǐ 咧嘴 **2** v/i lòuchǐ'érxiào 露齿而笑

grind v/t coffee, meat niǎnsuì 碾碎

grip 1 n (*on rope etc*) jǐnwò 紧握; **be losing one's ~** (*losing one's skills*) sàngshī nénglì 丧失能力 **2** v/t zhuāzhù 抓住

gristle ruǎngǔ 软骨

grit n (*dirt*) cūshā 粗砂; (*for roads*) shālì 砂砾

groan 1 n shēnyínshēng 呻吟声 **2** v/i shēnyín 呻吟

grocer záhuòshāng 杂货商

groceries záhuò 杂货

grocery store záhuòdiàn 杂货店

groin fùgǔgōu 腹股沟

groom 1 n (*for bride*) xīnláng 新郎; (*for horse*) mǎfu 马夫 **2** v/t horse shuā 刷; (*train, prepare*) péixùn 培训; **well ~ed** (*in appearance*) xiūshì de hǎo 修饰得好

groove cáo 槽

grope 1 v/i (*in the dark*) ànzhōng mōsuǒ 暗中摸索 **2** v/t (*sexually*) mōsuǒ 摸索
♦ **grope for** door handle, the right word xúnzhǎo 寻找

gross adj (*coarse, vulgar*) cūsú 粗俗; (*exaggeration*) shízú 十足; FIN zǒng 总; ~ **domestic product** guónèi shēngchǎn zǒngzhí 国内生产总值; ~ **national product** guómín shēngchǎn zǒngzhí 国民生产总值

ground 1 n dìmiàn 地面; (*reason*) lǐyóu 理由; ELEC diànbù 电步; **on the** ~ zài dìshang 在地上 **2** v/t ELEC shǐjiēdì 使接地

ground control dìmiàn kòngzhì 地面控制

ground crew dìqín rényuán 地勤人员

groundless wúgēnjù 无根据

ground meat suìròu 碎肉

groundnut luòhuāshēng 落花生; **ground plan** píngmiàntú 平面图; **ground staff** SP qiúchǎng guǎnlǐyuán 球场管理员; (*at airport*) dìqín rényuán 地勤人员; **groundwork** jīchǔ gōngzuò 基础工作

group 1 n zǔ 组; **divide ... into ~s** bǎ ... fēnzǔ 把...分组 **2** v/t (*put together*) zǔhé 组合; (*classify*) fēnlèi 分类

grow 1 v/i (*of child, animal*) chéngzhǎng 成长; (*of plants*) shēngzhǎng 生长; (*of hair, beard*) liú 留; (*of number, amount*) zēngzhǎng 增长; (*of business*) fāzhǎn 发展; **~ old / ~ tired** (become) lǎo le / lèi le 老了 / 累了 **2** v/t flowers zhòngzhí 种植

♦ **grow up** (of person) zhǎngdà 长大; (of city etc) kuòdà 扩大; **~!** bié xiàng háizi sìde! 别象孩子似的!

growl 1 n páoxiàoshēng 咆哮声 **2** v/i páoxiào 咆哮

grown-up 1 n chéngrén 成人 **2** adj chéngshú 成熟

growth (of person) chéngzhǎng 成长; (of company) fāzhǎn 发展; (increase) zēngzhǎng 增长; MED liú liú 瘤

grub (of insect) qícáo 蛴螬

grubby wūhuì 污秽

grudge 1 n yuànhèn 怨恨; **bear a ~** jìhèn 记恨 **2** v/t: **~ a person …** dùjì mǒurén de … 妒忌某人的 …

grudging miǎnqiǎng 勉强

grueling climb, task shǐ rén jīnpílìjìn 使人筋疲力尽

gruff cūbào 粗暴

grumble bàoyuàn 抱怨

grumbler ài fā láosāo de rén 爱发牢骚的人

grunt 1 n hūlushēng 呼噜声 **2** v/i zuò hūlushēng 作呼噜声

guarantee 1 n bǎozhèng 保证; **~ period** bǎozhèngqī 保证期 **2** v/t dānbǎo 担保

guarantor dānbǎorén 担保人

guard 1 n (security) jǐngwèi 警卫; MIL wèibīng 卫兵; (in prison) kānshǒu 看守; **be on one's ~ against** dīfang tífáng 提防 **2** v/t shǒuwèi 守卫

♦ **guard against** fángzhǐ 防止

guarded reply xiǎoxīn jǐnshèn 小心谨慎

guardian LAW jiānhùrén 监护人

guerrilla yóujīduì 游击队

guess 1 n cāicè 猜测 **2** v/t answer cāixiǎng 猜想; **I ~ so / not** kěnéng 可能 **3** v/i cāi 猜

guesswork tuīcè 推测

guest n kèrén 客人

guesthouse zhāodàisuǒ 招待所

guestroom kèfáng 客房

guffaw n & v/i kuángxiào 狂笑

guidance zhǐdǎo 指导

guide 1 n (person) dǎoyóu 导游; (book) zhǐnán 指南 **2** v/t xiàngdǎo 向导

guidebook zhǐnán 指南

guided missile dǎodàn 导弹

guided tour (in museum, art gallery) yǒu dǎoyóu de cānguān 有导游的参观

guidelines fāngzhēn 方针

guilt (legal, moral) yǒukuì 有愧; (guilty feeling) nèijiù 内疚

guilty LAW yǒuzuì 有罪; (responsible) chéngdān zérèn 承担责任; smile nèijiù 内疚; **have a ~ conscience** wèn xīn yǒu kuì 问心有愧

guinea pig túnshǔ 豚鼠; fig gòng shìyàn yòng de rén 供试验用的人

guitar jítā 吉他

guitarist tán jítā de rén 弹吉他的人

gulf hǎiwān 海湾; fig fēnqí 分歧

gull ōu 鸥

gullet yānhóu 咽喉

gullible yì shòupiàn 易受骗

gulp 1 n (of water etc) tūnyàn 吞咽 **2** v/i (in surprise) chījīng 吃惊

♦ **gulp down** yìyǐn ér jìn 一饮而尽; breakfast, food lángtūnhǔyàn 狼吞虎咽

gum¹ (in mouth) chíyín 齿龈

gum² (of glue) shùjiāo 树胶; (chewing ~) kǒuxiāngtáng 口香糖

gun qiāng 枪

♦ **gun down** qiāngdǎ 枪打

gun fire pàohuǒ 炮火; **gunman** (robber) chíqiāng dǎitú 持枪歹徒; **gunshot** shèjī 射击; **gunshot wound** qiāngshāng 枪伤

gurgle v/i (of baby) gēgē de xiào lo lo de xiào 咯咯地笑; (of drain) gǔgǔ de liú lo lo de 汩汩地流

gush v/i (of liquid) yǒngchū 涌出

gushy F (very enthusiastic) guòfèn duōqíng 过分多情

gust zhènfēng 阵风

gusty weather fēngdà 风大; **~ wind** dàfēng 大风

gut **1** *n* nèizàng 内脏; F (*stomach*)
dùzi 肚子; **~s** F (*courage*)
dǎnliàng 胆量 **2** *v/t* (*of fire*)
huǐhuài ... de nèibù 毁坏 ... 的内
部

gutter (*on sidewalk*) yáncáo 檐槽;
(*on roof*) tiāngōu 天沟

guy F jiāhuo 家伙; *hey, you ~s*
hèi, nǐmen 嘿，你们

gym (*sports club*) tǐyùguǎn 体育
馆; (*in school*) yùndòngshì 运动
室

gym shoes yùndòngxié 运动鞋
gymnasium tǐyùguǎn 体育馆; (*in
school*) yùndòngshì 运动室
gymnast tǐcāojiā 体操家
gymnastics tǐcāo 体操
gynecologist fùkē yīshēng 妇科医
生
gypsy jípǔsàiren 吉普赛人

H

habit xíguàn 习惯
habitable shìyú jūzhù 适于居住
habitat qīxīdì 栖息地
habitual guàncháng 惯常; *smoker, drinker* jīngcháng 经常
hack *n poor writer* wénqǐ 文乞
hacker COMPUT hēikè 黑客
hackneyed chénfǔ 陈腐
haddock hēixiànxuě 黑线鳕
haggard qiáocuì 憔悴
haggle tǎojià huánjià 讨价还价
hail *n* bīngbáo 冰雹
hailstorm báobào 雹暴
Hainan Island Hǎinán Dǎo 海南岛
hair tóufa 头发; (*on body, animal*) máo 毛
hairbrush shūzi 梳子; haircut lǐfà 理发; hairdo fàshì 发式; hairdresser lǐfàshī 理发师; *at the ~* zài lǐfàdiàn 在理发店; hairdryer, hairdryer chuīfēngqì 吹风器
hairless wúmáo 无毛
hairpin fàjiā 发夹; hairpin curve jízhuǎnwān 急转弯; hair-raising máogǔ sǒngrán 毛骨悚然; hair-splitting *n* wúyì ěr suǒsuì de fēnxī 无益而琐碎的分析; hairstyle fàxíng 发型
hairy *arm, animal* duōmáo 多毛; F (*frightening*) jí rén 急人
half 1 *n* yībàn 一半; *~ past ten, ~ after ten* shídiǎnbàn 十点半; *~ an hour* bàngè xiǎoshí 半个小时; *a pound* bànbàng 半磅 2 *adj* bàn 半 3 *adv* yíbàn 一半
half-hearted sānxīn'èryì 三心二意; half term xuéqí zhōngxiū 学期中休; half time 1 *n* SP bànchǎng 半场 2 *adj*: *~ job* bànrì gōngzuò 半日工作; halfway 1 *adj* *stage, point* bàntú 半途 2 *adv* zhōngjiān 中间; *the bookstore is*

~ down Zhongshan Avenue
shūdiàn zài Zhōngshān dàjì de zhōngjiān 书店在中山大街的中间;
hall (*large room*) dàtīng 大厅; (*hallway in house*) zǒuláng 走廊
halo guānghuán 光环
halt 1 *v/i* tíngzhǐ 停止 2 *v/t* zhìzhù 止住 3 *n*: *come to a ~* tíngzhì bùqián 停滞不前
halve *v/t* fēnchéng liǎngbàn 分成两半
ham huǒtuǐ 火腿
hamburger ⇩ hànbǎobāo 汉堡包
hammer 1 *n* chuízi 锤子 2 *v/i* chuídǎ 锤打; *~ at the door* zámén 砸门
hammock diàochuáng 吊床
hamper¹ *n* (*for food*) fànkuāng 饭筐
hamper² *v/t* (*obstruct*) zǔ'ài 阻碍
hamster cāngshǔ 仓鼠
Han Hàn 汉; (*nationality*) Hànzú 汉族
Han Dynasty Hàncháo 汉朝
hand 1 *n* shǒu 手; (*of clock*) zhēn 针; (*worker*) gōngrén 工人; *at ~, to* = zài shēnbiān 在身边; *at first ~* dìyīshǒu 第一手; *by ~* write yòngshǒu 用手; *deliver* zhuānrén 专人; *on the one ~ …, on the other ~ …* yīfāngmiàn … lìngyìfāngmiàn … 一方面 … 另一方面 …; *in ~* (*being done*) zài chǔlǐ zhōng 在处理中; *on your right ~* yòumiàn 右面; *~s off!* bié pèng! 别碰!; *~s up!* jǔqǐshǒulái! 举起手来!; *change ~s* zhuǎnshǒu 转手
♦ hand down chuánxiàlái 传下来
♦ hand in jiāochū 交出
♦ hand on chuánxiàqù 传下去
♦ hand out fēnfā 分发
♦ hand over yíjiāo 移交; *to*

authorities shàngjiāo 上交

handbag *Br* shǒutíbāo 手提包;
handbook shǒucè 手册; **hand-
brake** *Br* shǒuzhá 手轧; **handcuffs** shǒukào 手铐

handicap *n* zhàng'ài zhàng'ài 障碍

handicapped (*physically*) cánjí shōu
jí; *~ by lack of funds* yóuyú zìjīn
ér shòuxiàn 由于资金
而受阻

handicraft shǒugōngyì 手工艺

handiwork shǒugōng 手工

handkerchief shǒujuàn 手绢

handle 1 *n* bǎshou 把手 2 *v/t goods*
bānyùn 搬运; *case, deal* chǔlǐ 处
理; *difficult person* duìfu 对付; *let
me ~ this* wǒ lái chǔlǐ ba 我来处
理吧

handlebars chēbǎ 车把

hand luggage shǒutí xínglí 手提
行李; **handmade** shǒugōng zhìzuò 手工制作; **handrail** fúshǒu
扶手; **handshake** wòshǒu 握手

hands-off bùgānshè 不干涉

handsome shuài 帅

hands-on qīnzì dòngshǒu 亲自动
手

handwriting zì zì 字字

handwritten shǒuxiě 手写

handy *tool, device* fāngbiàn 方便; *it
might come in ~* yěxǔ huì
yǒuyòng 也许会有用

hang 1 *v/t picture* guà 挂; *person*
diàosǐ 吊死 2 *v/i* (*of dress, hair*)
chuíxià 垂下 3 *n*: *get the ~ of X*
zhǎodào X de qiàomén 找到 X 的
窍门

◆**hang around** xiánguàng 闲逛

◆**hang on** (*wait*) děngdeng 等等

◆**hang on to** (*keep*) bǎoliú 保留

◆**hang up** TELEC guàduàn 挂断

hangar fēijīkù 飞机库

hanger *for clothes* yīfújià 衣服架

hang glider (*person*) xuánguà shì
huáxiáng zhě 悬挂式滑翔者;
(*device*) xuánguà shì huáxiángjī 悬
挂式滑翔机

hang gliding xuánguà shì
huáxiáng yùndòng 悬挂式滑翔
运动

hangover (*jiǔhòu*) tóutòng (酒后)
头痛

◆**hanker after** kěwàngyǒu 渴望
有

hankie, hanky F shǒujuàn 手绢

haphazard ǒuránxìng 偶然性

happen fāshēng 发生; *if you ~ to
see him* rúguǒ nǐ pèngqiǎo
jiàndào tā 如果你碰巧见到他;
what has ~ed to you? nǐ zěnme
le? 你怎么了？

◆**happen across** ǒurán fāxiàn 偶
然发现

happening shìjiàn 事件

happily gāoxìng 高兴; (*luckily*)
xìngyùn 幸运

happiness xìngfú 幸福

happy kuàilè 快乐

happy-go-lucky wúyōuwúlǜ 无忧
无虑

happy hour kuàilè shíjiān 快乐时
间

harass sāorǎo 骚扰

harassed jiāozào 焦躁

harassment sāorǎo 骚扰; *sexual
~* xìngsāorǎo 性骚扰

harbor 1 *n* gǎngwān 港湾 2 *v/t
criminal* bāobì 包庇; *grudge*
huáiyǒu 怀有

hard yìng 硬; (*difficult*) nán 难;
facts, evidence bùrónghuáiyí 不容
怀疑; *~ of hearing* zhòngtīng 重
听

hardback yìngpíshū 硬皮书;
hard-boiled *egg* zhǔ de lǎo 煮得
老; **hard copy** yìn wénběn 打
印文本; **hard core** POL
zhōngjiān fènzi 中坚分子; **hard
currency** ↓ yìngtōnghuò 硬通
货; **hard disk** ↓ yìngpán 硬盘

harden 1 *v/t* shǐbiànyìng 使变硬
2 *v/i* (*glue*) biànyìng 变硬;
(*attitude*) mánhèng 蛮横

hardheaded jiǎng shíjì 讲实际

hardliner qiángyìng lùxiàn zhě 强
硬路线者

hardly jīhūbù 几乎不

hardness yìngdù 硬度; (*difficulty*)
nándù 难度

hard seat (*on train*) yìngzuò 硬座

hardsell yìngxíng tuīxiāo 硬行推
销

hardship jiānnán 艰难

hard sleeper (*on train*) yìngwò 硬卧; **hard up** quēqián 缺钱; **hardware** jīnshǔ qìjù 金属器具; COMPUT yìngjiàn 硬件; **hardware store** wǔjīn shāngdiàn 五金商店; **hard-working** qínmiǎn 勤勉

hardy qiángzhuàng 强壮

hare yětù 野兔

harm 1 *n* sǔnhài 损害; *it wouldn't do any ~ to ...* ... méi shénme huàichù ... 没什么坏处 **2** *v/t* sǔnhài 损害

harmful yǒuhài 有害

harmless wúhài 无害

harmonious héxié 和谐

harmonize shǐ héxié 使和谐

harmony MUS héshēng 和声; (*in relationship etc*) xiétiáo 协调

harp shùqín 竖琴

♦ **harp on about** F xùdao 絮叨

harpoon *n* yúchā 鱼叉

harsh jiānkè 尖刻

harvest *n* shōuhuò 收获

hash: *make a ~ of X* F bǎ X nòngzāo 把 X 弄糟

hash browns shǔtiáo 薯条

hashish dàmá 大麻

haste cāngcù 仓促

hasty cǎoshuài 草率

hat màozi 帽子

hatch *n* (*for serving food*) chuāngkǒu 窗口; (*on ship*) cāngkǒu 舱口

♦ **hatch out** (*of eggs*) fūchū 孵出

hatchet duǎnbǐng xiǎofǔ 短柄小斧

hate *n* & *v/t* zēnghèn 憎恨

hatred zēnghèn 憎恨

haughty àomàn 傲慢

haul 1 *n*: *a ~ of fish* yīwǎngyú 一网鱼 **2** *v/t* (*pull*) tuōyè 托曳

haulage tuōyùn 托运

haulage company tuōyùn gōngsī 托运公司

haulier tuōyùn gōngsī 托运公司

haunch tuìtúnbù 腿臀部

haunt 1 *v/t* chángdào 常到; *this place is ~ed* zhè dìfang nàoguǐ 这地方闹鬼 **2** *n* cháng qù de dìfang 常去的地方

haunting *tune* yíngrào yú xīn 萦绕

have ◊ (*own*) yǒu 有; *I ~ three tickets* wǒ yǒu sānzhāng piào 我有三张票 ◊ *breakfast, lunch* chī 吃 ◊: *can I ~ a cup of coffee?* qǐng gěiwǒ yìbēi kāfēi? 请给我一杯咖啡?; *can I ~ more time?* qǐng zài gěiwǒ yìxiē shíjiān? 请再给我一些时间?; *do you ~ ... ?* nǐ yǒu ... ma? 你有 ... 吗 ? ◊ (*must*): *~ (got) to* bìxū 必须 *I have to study* / *see him* wǒ bìxū xuéxí/kàn tā 我必须学习/看他; ◊ (*causative*): *I had my hair cut* wǒ bǎ tóufa jiǎnle 我把头发剪了; *I'll ~ the car repaired* wǒ yào bǎ chē xiūle 我要把车修了 ◊ (*past tense*): *I ~ eaten* wǒ chīguò le 我吃过了; *~ you seen her?* nǐ jiàndào tā le ma? 你见到她了吗?

♦ **have back**: *when can I have it back?* shénme shíhou huángěi wǒ? 什么时候还给我 ?; *it's good to have you back* nǐ huíláile zhēnhǎo 你回来了真好

♦ **have on** (*wear*) chuān 穿; (*have planned*) yǒu shì hé zuò; *do you have anything on for tonight?* nǐ jīnwǎn yǒushì ma? 你今晚有事吗?

haven *fig* bìnànsuǒ 避难所

havoc hàojié 浩劫; *play ~ with X* jiāng X gǎode yītuán zāo 将 X 搞得一团糟

haw (*berry*) shānzhā 山楂

hawk yīngsǔn 鹰隼; *fig* qiángyìng pài rénwù 强硬派人物

hay gāncǎo 干草

hay fever huāfěnrè 花粉热

hazard *n* wēixiǎn 危险

hazard lights MOT xiǎnqíng zhìshìdēng 险情指示灯

hazardous màoxiǎn 冒险

haze bówù 薄雾

hazel (*tree*) zhēn 榛

hazelnut zhēnzi 榛子

hazy *view, image* wùméngméng 雾蒙蒙; *memories* mōhu 模糊; *I'm a bit ~ about it* wǒ duìcǐ bú tài qīngchǔ 我对此不太清楚

he tā 他

head 1 n tóu 头; (boss, leader) lǐng-dǎo 领导; (of school) xiàozhǎng 校长; (on beer) pàomò 泡沫; (of nail) dīngmào 钉帽; (of queue, line) qiánmiàn 前面; $15 a ~ měikè shíwǔ měiyuán 每客十五美元; ~s or tails? zhèngmiàn hái-shì fǎnmiàn? 正面还是反面？; at the ~ of the list míngdān shang dìyīwèi 名单上第一位; ~ over heels fall tóu cháoxià 头朝下; fall in love shēnshēn 深深; lose one's ~ (go crazy) fāfēng 发疯 2 v/t (lead) lǐngdǎo 领导; ball yòng tóu dǐng 用头顶

headache tóutòng 头痛

header (in soccer) dǐngqiú 顶球; (in document) tóulán 头栏

headhunter COM wùsè réncái de rén 物色人才的人

heading (in list) biāotí 标题

headlamp qiándēng 前灯; head-light qiándēng 前灯; headline (in newspaper) dàzì biāotí 大字标题; make the ~s chéngwéi tóutiáo xīnwén 成为头条新闻; head-long adv fall tóu xiàng qián 头向前; headmaster xiàozhǎng 校长; headmistress xiàozhǎng 校长; head office (of company) zǒngbù 总部; head-on adv & adj crash tóupéng tóu 头碰头; head-phones ěrjī 耳机; headquarters zǒng zhǐhuībù 总指挥部; headrest tóukào 头靠; head-room for vehicle under bridge jìngkōng gāodù 净空高度; in car tóushang kōngjiān 头上空间; headscarf tóujīn 头巾; head-strong rènxìng 任性; head teacher xiàozhǎng 校长; head waiter fúwùyuán zhǎng 服务员长; headwind nìfēng 逆风

heady drink, wine etc yìzuì 易醉

heal v/t & v/i yùhé 愈合

health jiànkāng 健康; your ~! zhù nǐ jiànkāng! 祝你健康！

health club jiànshēn jùlèbù 健身俱乐部; health food jiànkāng shípǐn 健康食品; ~ store

jiànkāng shípǐndiàn 健康食品店; health insurance jiànkāng bǎoxiǎn 健康保险; health re-sort liáoyǎngdì 疗养地

healthy person jiànkāng 健康; food, lifestyle yǒuyì jiànkāng 有益健康; economy zhuàngdà 壮大

heap n duī 堆

♦heap up v/t duījī 堆积

hear tīngjiàn 听见

♦hear about tīngdào 听到

♦hear from (have news from) dédào xiāoxī 得到消息

hearing tīnglì 听力; LAW shěnxùn 审讯; within ~ tīngjù 听距; out of ~ tīngbúdào 听不到

hearing aid zhùtīngqì 助听器

hearsay: by ~ chuánwén 传闻

hearse língchē 灵车

heart xīn 心; (of problem) shízhì 实质; (of city, organization) zhōngxīn 中心; know X by ~ shóujì X 熟记 X

heart attack xīnzàngbìng 心脏病; heartbeat xīntiào 心跳; heart-breaking lìngrén xīnsuì 令人心碎; heartburn fǎnxīn zhuórè 心口灼热; heart failure xīnlì shuāijié 心力衰竭; heartfelt sympathy fāzì nèixīn 发自内心

hearth bìlú 壁炉

heartless wúqíng 无情

heartrending plea, sight shāngxīn 伤心

hearts (in cards) hóngtáo 红桃

heart throb F ǒuxiàng 偶像

heart transplant xīnzàng yízhí 心脏移植

hearty meal fēngshèng 丰盛; person rèchén 热忱; ~ appetite hǎo wèikǒu 好胃口

heat rè 热

♦heat up jiārè 加热

heated swimming pool jiā le rè 加了热; discussion rèliè 热烈

heater fārèqì 发热器

heath huāngdì 荒地

heathen n yìjiàotú 异教徒

heating nuǎnqì 暖气

heat-resistant kàngrè 抗热; heatstroke zhòngshǔ 中暑;

heatwave rèlàng 热浪

heave v/t (lift) yònglì jǔqǐ 用力举起

heaven tiāntáng 天堂; **good ~s!** tiānna! 天哪！

heavy zhòng 重; *rain* dà 大; *traffic* yōngjǐ 拥挤; *accent* zhòng 重; *food* yóunì 油腻; *financial loss* chénzhòng 沉重; *loss of life, bleeding* dàliàng 大量; **~ smoker** yān chōu de duō de rén 烟抽得多的人; **~ drinker** jiǔ hē de duō de rén 酒喝得多的人

heavy-duty jìnyòng 禁用

heavyweight SP zhòngliàngjí 重量极

heckle v/t jiéwèn 诘问

hectic mánglù 忙碌

hedge n shùlí 树篱

hedgehog cìwei 刺猬

heed: **pay ~ to** zhùyì 注意

heel (of foot) jiǎohòugēn 脚后跟; (of shoe) xiégēn 鞋跟

heel bar xiūxiébù 修鞋部

hefty zhòng 重

height gāodù 高度; (of season) shèng 盛

heighten effect, tension zēngdà 增大

heir jìchéngrén 继承人

heiress nǚ jìchéngrén 女继承人

helicopter zhíshēngfēijī 直升飞机

hell dìyù 地狱; **what the ~ are you doing / do you want?** F nǐ jiūjìng zài gàn shénme / yào shénme? 你究竟在干什么 / 要什么？; **go to ~!** F qùnǐde! 去你的！; **a ~ of a lot** F duōde bùdéliǎo 多得不得了; **he's one ~ of a nice guy** F zhèi jiāhuo zhēn búcuò 这家伙真不错

hello nǐ hǎo 你好; TELEC wéi 喂

helm NAUT duò 舵

helmet tóukuī 头盔

help n & v/t bāngzhù 帮助; **~!** jiùmìng! 救命！; **can you ~ me?** jiègè shǒu, xíngma? 借个手，行吗？; **~ oneself** (to food) suíbiàn chī 随便吃; **I can't ~ it** wǒ rěnbúzhù 我忍不住; **I couldn't ~**

laughing wǒ jīnbúzhù xiàole 我禁不住笑了

helper zhùshǒu 助手

helpful yǒu bāngzhù 有帮助

helping (of food) yífèn 一份

helpless (unable to cope) bùnéng zìzhù 不能自助; (powerless) wúzhù 无助

help screen COMPUT jiěyí píngmù 解疑屏幕

hem n (of dress etc) zhébiān 折边

hemisphere bànqiú 半球

hemorrhage n & v/i chūxiè 出血

hemp dàmá 大麻

hen mǔjī 母鸡

henchman pej qīguǎnyán 妻管严; **~ husband** yǒu qīguǎnyán de zhàngfu 有妻管严的丈夫

hepatitis gānyán 肝炎

her 1 adj tāde 她的; **~ ticket** tāde piào 她的票 2 pron tā 她; **I know ~** wǒ rènshi tā 我认识她; **this is for ~** zhè shì gěi tā de 这是给她的

herb yàocǎo 药草

herb(al) tea yàocǎochá 药草茶

herbal medicine cǎoyào 草药

herd n shòuqún 兽群

here zhèr 这儿; **~'s to you!** (toast) wèi nǐ gānbēi! 为你干杯！; **~ you are** (giving sth) gěi nǐ 给你; **~ we are!** (finding sth) zài zhèr! 在这儿！

hereditary disease yíchuán 遗传

heritage shìxí yíchǎn 世袭遗产

hermit jūshì 居士

hernia MED shàn 疝

hero yīngxióng 英雄

heroic yīngyǒng 英勇

heroin hǎiluòyīn 海洛因

heroine nǚyīngxióng 女英雄

heron cānglù 苍鹭

herpes MED pàozhěn 疱疹

herring fēiyú 鲱鱼

hers tāde 她的; **a friend of ~** tāde péngyǒu 她的朋友

herself tā zìjǐ 她自己; **she hurt ~** tā nòngshāngle zìjǐ 她弄伤了自己; **by ~** tā dúzì 她独自

hesitate yóuyù 犹豫

hesitation yóuyù 犹豫

heterosexual *adj* yìxìng'ài 异性爱

heyday quánshèngqī 全盛期

hi nǐ hǎo 你好

hibernate dōngmián 冬眠

hiccup *n* dǎgér 嗝儿; (*minor problem*) xiǎowèntí 小问题; **have the ~s** dǎgér 打嗝儿

hick *pej* F xiāngxiàlǎo 乡下佬

hick town *pej* F qióngxiāng pìrǎng 穷乡僻壤

hidden *meaning* nèihán 内涵; *treasure* yǐncáng 隐藏

hide¹ *v/t & v/i* cáng 藏

hide² *n* (*of animal*) duǒcángchù 躲藏处

hide-and-seek zhuōmícáng 捉迷藏

hideaway pìjìngchù 僻静处

hideous kěpà 可怕; *crime* hài rén tīngwén 骇人听闻; *face* chǒulòu 丑陋

hiding¹ (*beating*) tòngdǎ 痛打

hiding²: **be in ~** duǒcángzhe 躲藏着; **go into ~** duǒcáng qǐlái 躲藏起来

hiding place duǒcángchù 躲藏处

hierarchy děngjí zhìdù 等级制度

hi-fi gāo bǎozhēn diànqì 高保真电器

high **1** *adj building, mountain, temperature, price, note, salary, speed* gāo 高; *quality* gāojí 高级; *society* shàngliú 上流; (*on drugs*) táozuì 陶醉; **~ wind** jìnfēng 劲风; **have a very ~ opinion of** duì ... yǒu hěn gāo píngjià 对 ... 有很高评价; **it is ~ time ...** gāi shì ... de shíhou le 该是 ... 的时候了 **2** *n* MOT gāofēng 高峰; (*in statistics*) gāofēng 高峰; EDU zhōngxué 中学 **3** *adv* gāo 高; **~ in the sky** gāogāo zài kōng 高高在空; **that's as ~ as we can go** (*in offer*) zhè shì wǒmen chū de zuìgāo jià 这是我们出的最高价

highbrow *adj* gāodiào 高调

highchair gāojiǎoyǐ 高脚椅

highclass gāojí 高级; **high diving** gāokōng tiàoshuǐ 高空跳水; **high-frequency** gāopín 高频;

high-grade yōuzhì 优质; **high-handed** zhuānhèng 专横; **high-heeled** gāogēn 高跟; **high jump** tiàogāo 跳高; **high-level** gāo jiēcéng 高阶层; **high life** háohuádé shēnghuó fāngshì 豪华的生活方式

highlight **1** *n* (*main event*) zuìjīngcǎi chǎngmiàn 最精采场面; (*in hair*) rǎnsè 染色 **2** *v/t* (*with pen*) yòng sèbǐ huà 用色笔划; COMPUT xuǎn 选

highlighter (*pen*) cǎibǐ 彩笔

highly *desirable, likely* fēicháng 非常; **be ~ paid** xīnshuǐ gāo 薪水高; **think ~ of X** duì X píngjià hěn gāo 对X评价很高

high performance *drill* dàgōnglǜ 高效率; *battery* gāonéng 高能; **high-pitched** gāoyīndiào 高音调; **high point** (*of life, career*) dǐngfēng 顶峰; **high-powered** *engine* dàgōnglǜ 大功率; *intellectual* yuānbó 渊博; *salesman* chíyǒu yàozhí 持有要职; **high pressure 1** *n* (*weather*) gāoyā 高压 **2** *adj* TECH gāoyā 高压; *salesman* qiángxìng tuīxiāo 强行推销; *job, lifestyle* yǒu hě ndà yālì 有很大压力; **high priest** dà jìsī 大祭司; **high school** zhōngxué 中学; **high society** shàngliú shèhuì 上流社会; **high-speed train** gāosù huǒchē 高速火车; **high-strung** shífēn mǐngǎn 十分敏感; **high tech** *n & adj* gāoxīn jìshù 高新技术; **high technology** gāoxīn jìshù 高新技术; **high-tension** *cable* gāoyā 高压; **high tide** gāocháo 高潮; **high water** gāocháo 高潮; **highway** gōnglù 公路; **high wire** (*in circus*) gāngsīshéng 钢丝绳

hijack *v/t* jiéchí 劫持; **~ a plane** jiéjī 劫机; **~ a bus** jiéchē 劫车

hijacker (*of plane*) jiéjī zhě 劫机者; (*of bus*) jiéchē zhě 劫车者

hike¹ **1** *n* yuǎnzú 远足 **2** *v/i* bùxíng 步行

hike² *n* (*in prices*) jígǔ táigāo 急遽抬高

hiker túbù lǚxíng zhě 徒步旅行者

hilarious fēicháng huájī 非常滑稽

hill xiǎoshānpō 小山坡; (*slope*) shānpō 山坡

hillbilly *pej* F xiāngxiàrén 乡下人

hillside shānpō 山坡

hilltop xiǎoshān shāndǐng 小山山顶

hilly yǒu pō 有坡

hilt jiànbǐng 剑柄

him tā 他

Himalayas Xīmǎlāyǎshān 喜马拉雅山

himself tā zìjǐ 他自己; *he hurt ~* tā nòngshāngle zìjǐ 他弄伤了自己; *by ~* tā dúzì 他独自

hinder zǔzhǐ 阻止

hindrance zhàng'ài 障碍

hindsight *with ~* shìhòude rènshi 事后的认识

hinge zhéyè 折页

hint (*clue*) tíshì 提示; (*piece of advice*) tíyì 提议; (*implied suggestion*) ànshì 暗示; (*of red, sadness etc*) lüèwēi 略微

hip túnbù 臀部

hip pocket pìdōur 屁兜儿

hippopotamus hémǎ 河马

hire *v/t* zū 租

his **1** *adj* tāde 他的; *a friend of ~* tāde péngyǒu 他的朋友

Hispanic **1** *adj* Lādīng Měizhōu 拉丁美洲 **2** *n* Lādīng Měizhōu rén 拉丁美洲人

hiss *v/i* (*of snake*) fā sīsī shēng 发嘶嘶声; (*of audience*) fā xūshēng 发嘘声

historian lìshǐxuéjiā 历史学家

historic yǒu lìshǐ yìyì 有历史意义

historical yǒuguān lìshǐ 有关历史

history lìshǐ 历史

hit **1** *v/t person, ball* dǎ 打; (*collide with*) zhuàng 撞; *he was ~ by a bullet* tā bèi zǐdàn dǎzhòng le 他被子弹打中了; *it suddenly ~ me* (*I realized*) wǒ tūrán yìshí dào 我突然意识到 **2** *n* (*blow*) dǎjī 打击; MUS liúxíng chàngpiàn 流行唱片; (*success*) jùdà chénggōng 巨大成功

♦ hit back fǎnjī 反击

♦ hit on *idea* pèngqiǎo zhǎodào 碰巧找到

♦ hit out at (*criticize*) pēngjī 抨击

hit-and-run: *~ accident* zhàoshì zhě táopǎo shìgù 肇事者逃跑事故; *~ driver* zhàoshì zhě táopǎo sījī 肇事者逃跑司机

hitch **1** *n* (*problem*) wèntí 问题; *without a ~* méiyǒu wèntí 没有问题 **2** *v/t* shuānzhù 拴住; *~ X to Y* bǎ X shuān zài Y shang 把X拴在Y上; *~ a ride* dā biànchē 搭便车 **3** *v/i* (*hitchhike*) miǎnfèi dāchē 免费搭车

♦ hitch up *wagon, trailer* lā 拉

hitchhike miǎnfèi dāchē 免费搭车; hitchhiker miǎnfèi dāchē de rén 免费搭车的人; hitchhiking miǎnfèi dāchē 免费搭车

hi-tech *n & adj* gāoxīn jìshù 高新技术

hitlist hēimíngdān 黑名单; hitman zhíyè shāshǒu 职业杀手; hit-or-miss pèng yùnqì 碰运气; hit squad tèshū rènwù zǔzhī 特殊任务组织

HIV rénlèi sàngshī miǎnyìlì bìngdú 人类丧失免疫力病毒

hive (*for bees*) fēngfáng 蜂房

♦ hive off *v/t* (COM: *separate off*) chéngwéi dāndúde tuántǐ 成为单独的团体

HIV-positive dàiyǒu rénlèi sàngshī miǎnyìlì bìngdú 带有人类丧失免疫力病毒

hoard **1** *n* mìcángde qiáncái 密藏的钱财 **2** *v/t* jiàocáng 窖藏

hoarse sīyǎ 嘶哑

hoax *n* qīpiàn 欺骗

hobble *v/i* pánshān 蹒跚

hobby shìhào 嗜好

hobo liúlànghàn 流浪汉

hockey (*ice ~*) bīngqiú 冰球

hog *n* (*pig*) zhū 猪

hoist **1** *n* qǐzhòngjī 起重机 **2** *v/t* (*lift*) shēngqǐ 举起; *flag* shēng shēng 升

hokum (*nonsense*) fèihuà 废话; (*sentimental stuff*) sútào qíngjié 俗

套情节

hold 1 *v/t* (*in hands*) ná 拿; (*support, keep in place*) zhīchí 支持; *passport, license* chíyǒu 持有; *prisoner, suspect* guānyā 关押; (*contain*) chéngyǒu 盛有; *job, post* rèn 任; *course* bǎochí 保持; **~ one's breath** bǐngzhù hūxī 屏住呼吸; **he can ~ his drink** tā hěn néng hē 他很能喝; **X respon- sible** shǐ X fùzé 使 X 负责; **~ that ...** (*believe, maintain*) rènwéi ... 认为 ...; **~ the line** TELEC qīng bié guàduàn 请别挂断 **2** *n* (*in ship, plane*) huòcāng 货舱; **catch or take ~ of X** zhuāzhù X 抓住 X; **lose one's ~ on X** (*on rope*) zhuābùzhù X 抓不住 X

♦ **hold against**: **hold X against Y** yīn X jìhèn Y 因 X 记恨 Y

♦ **hold back 1** *v/t crowds* lánzhù 拦住; *facts, information* yǐnmán 隐瞒 **2** *v/i* (*not tell all*) yǐnmán 隐瞒

♦ **hold on** *v/i* (*wait*, TELEC) děngyíxià 等一下; **now ~ a minute!** biézháojí! 别着急！

♦ **hold on to** (*keep*) bǎoliú 保留; *belief* jiānchí 坚持

♦ **hold out 1** *v/t hand* shēnchū 伸出; *prospect* jùyǒu 具有 **2** *v/i* (*of supplies*) wéichí 维持; (*trapped miners etc*) zhīchengzhù 支撑住

♦ **hold up** *v/t hand* shēnchū 伸出; *bank etc* qiǎngjié 抢劫; (*make late*) dāngē 耽搁; **hold X up as an ex- ample** bǎ X zuò lìzi 把 X 做例子

♦ **hold with** (*approve of*) zànchéng 赞成

holder (*container*) hé hé 盒; (*of passport, ticket, record etc*) chíyǒu zhě 持有者

holding company gǔdōng gōngsī 股东公司

holdup (*robbery*) qiǎngjié 抢劫; (*delay*) yánwù 延误

hole dòng 洞

holiday (*single day*) xiūxīrì 休息日; (*period*) jiàqī 假期; **take a ~** xiūjià 休假

holidaymaker dùjiàde rén 度假的人

Holland Hélán 荷兰

hollow *object* zhōngkōng 中空; *cheeks* āoxiàn 凹陷; *promise* xūjiǎ 虚假

holly dōngqīng 冬青

holocaust dà pòhuài 大破坏

hologram quánxītú 全息图

holster yāodài tào 腰带套

holy shénshèng 神圣

Holy Spirit Shènglíng 圣灵

Holy Week Fùhuójié qián yìzhōu 复活节前一周

home 1 *n* jiā 家; (*native country*) zǔguó 祖国; (*town, part of country*) jiāxiāng 家乡; (*for old people*) lǎorényuàn 老人院; **at ~** (*in my house*) zài jiā 在家; (*in my country*) zài guónèi 在国内; SP běnyíng 本营; **make yourself at ~** bié jūshù 别拘束; **at ~ and abroad** guónèiwài 国内外; **work from ~** zài jiā gōngzuò 在家工作 **2** *adv* jiā 家; **go ~** huíjiā 回家; (*to own country*) huíguó 回国

home address jiātíng zhùzhǐ 家庭住址; **homecoming** guījiā 归家; **home computer** jiāyòng diànnǎo 家用电脑

homeless *adj* wújiā 无家; **the ~** wújiāde rén 无家的人

homeloving liànjiā 恋家

homepage COMPUT zhǔyè 主页

homely (*homeloving*) yǒu jiā de qìfēn 有家的气氛; (*not good- looking*) bù piàoliang 不漂亮

homemade zìzhì 自制; **home match** zài běndì dǎ de bǐsài 在本地打的比赛; **home movie** jiātíng lùxiàng 家庭录像

homeopathy shùnshì liáofǎ 顺势疗法

homesick: **be ~** xiǎngjiā 想家

home town jiāxiāng 家乡

homeward *adv* (*to own house*) xiàng jiā zǒu 向家走; (*to own country*) xiàng běnguó zǒu 向本国走

homework EDU zuòyè 作业

homeworking COM zài jiā gōngzuò 在家工作

homicide (*crime*) móushā 谋杀;

(*police department*) mìng'ànbù 命
案部

homograph tóngxíngyìyìcí 同形
异义词

homophobia tóngxìngliàn zèngwù
gǎn 同性恋憎恶感

homosexual *n & adj* tóngxìngliàn
同性恋

honest chéngshí 诚实

honestly shuōzhēnde 说真的; ~!
zhēnshìde! 真的是！

honesty chéngshí 诚实

honey fēngmì 蜂蜜; F (*darling*)
qīn'àide 亲爱的

honeycomb cháopí 巢脾

honeymoon *n* mìyuè 蜜月

Hong Kong Xiānggǎng 香港; ~
handover Xiānggǎng huíguī 香港
回归

honk *v/t* horn àn lǎba 按喇叭

honor 1 *n* róngyù 荣誉 **2** *v/t* gěiyǐ
róngyù 给以荣誉

honorable guāngróng 光荣

hood (*over head*) dōumào 兜帽;
(*over cooker*) chōu yóuyán jī 抽油
烟机; MOT qìchē yǐnqíng gàizi 汽
车引擎盖子; F (*gangster*)
huàidàn 坏蛋

hoodlum èogùn 恶棍

hoof tí 蹄

hook (*to hang clothes on*) guàgōu 挂
钩; (*for fishing*) yúgōu 鱼钩; *off
the* ~ TELEC bú guà diànhuà 不挂
电话

hooked: *be* ~ *on X* bèi X mízhù 被
X 迷住; *be* ~ *on drugs* xīdú
chéngyǐn 吸毒成瘾

hooker F jìnǔ 妓女

hookey: *play* ~ táoxué 逃学

hooligan liúmáng 流氓

hooliganism liúmáng xíngwéi 流
氓行为

hoop gū 箍

hoot *v/t & v/i* (*of car horn*) àn lǎba
àn lǎba 按喇叭; (*of owl*) māotóuyīngjiào
猫头鹰叫

hop[1] *n* (*plant*) shémácǎo 蛇麻草

hop[2] *v/i* (*of people*) dānjiǎotiào 单
脚跳; (*of animals*) shuāngjiǎotiào
双脚跳

hope 1 *n* xīwàng 希望; *there's no
~ of that* nà shì bùkěnéng de 那
是不可能的 **2** *v/t* xīwàng 希望; *I
~ you like it* wǒ xīwàng nǐ xǐhuān
tā 我希望你喜欢它; *- for X*
qīwàng X 期望 X; *I - so* xīwàng
rúcǐ 希望如此; *I - not* wǒ bù
xīwàng zhèyàng 我不希望这样

hopeful (*optimistic*) lèguān 乐观;
(*promising*) yǒu xīwàng 有希望

hopefully *say* bàoyǒu xīwàng 抱有
希望; (*I/ we hope*) dànyuàn 但愿

hopeless *position, project* méiyǒu
xīwàng 没有希望; (*useless:
person*) méi qiántú 没前途

horizon dìpíngxiàn 地平线

horizontal shuǐpíng 水平

hormone hé'ěrméng 荷尔蒙

horn (*of animal*) jiǎo 角; MOT qìchē
lǎba 汽车喇叭

hornet dàhuángfēng 大黄蜂

horn-rimmed spectacles yǒu
jiǎozhījià de yǎnjìng 有角质架
的眼镜

horny F yǒu xìng chōngdòng 有性
冲动

horoscope xīngzhàn 星占

horrible zāogāo 糟糕

horrify: *I was horrified* wǒ bèi
xiàhuàile 我被吓坏了

horrifying *experience* kěpà 可怕;
idea, prices lìngrén zhènjīng 令人
震惊

horror kǒngbù 恐怖; *the -s of
war* zhànzhēngde kǒngbù 战争
的恐怖

horror movie kǒngbù diànyǐng 恐
怖电影

hors d'œuvre cānqiánde xiǎochī
餐前的小吃

horse mǎ 马

horseback: *on* ~ qímǎ 骑马;
horse chestnut qīyèshùshù
zhíwù 七叶树属植物; **horse-
power** mǎlì 马力; **horse race**
sàimǎ 赛马; **horseshoe** mǎtítiě
马蹄铁

horticulture yuányì 园艺

hose ruǎnguǎn 软管

hospice jiùjìyuàn 救济院

hospitable hàokè 好客

hospital yīyuàn 医院; *go into the*

~ zhùyuàn 住院

hospitality rèqíng zhāodài 热情招待

host *n (at party, reception)* zhǔrén 主人; *(of TV program)* zhǔchírén 主持人

hostage rénzhì 人质; *be taken* ~ bèi kòuzuò rénzhì 被扣作人质

hostage taker kòuyā rénzhì de rén 扣押人质的人

hostel *(for students)* xiàowài jìsùshè 校外寄宿舍; *(youth* ~*)* lǚdiàn 旅店

hostess *(at party, reception)* nǚzhǔrén 女主人; *(on airplane)* kōngjiě 空姐; *(in bar)* nǚzhāodài 女招待

hostile díduì 敌对

hostility *(of attitude)* díyì 敌意; **hostilities** zhànzhēng 战争

hot *weather, water, object, food* rè 热; *(spicy)* là 辣; *I'm* ~ wǒ hěn rè 我很热; F *(good)* jíhǎo 极好

hot dog hóngcháng miànbāo 红肠面包

hotel bīnguǎn 宾馆

hot key COMPUT kuàijiéjiàn 快捷键; **hotplate** diànlú 电炉; **hot spot** *(military, political)* rèdiǎn 热点

hour xiǎoshí 小时

hourly *adj* měixiǎoshí 每小时

house *n* fángzi 房子; *at your* ~ zài nǐjiā 在你家

houseboat chuánwū 船屋; **housebreaking** rùshì qiǎngjié 入室抢劫; **household** jiāshù 家属; **household name** jiāyùhùxiǎo 家喻户晓; **house husband** jiātíng zhǔnán 家庭主男; **housekeeper** guǎnjiā 管家; **housekeeping** *(activity)* jiāwù guǎnlǐ 家务管理; *(money)* jiāwù kāixiāo 家务开消; **House of Representatives** Zhòngyìyuàn 众议院; **housewarming (party)** qìngzhù qiānjū de jùhuì 庆祝迁居的聚会; **housewife** jiātíng zhǔfù 家庭主妇; **housework** jiāwù 家务

housing zhùfáng 住房; TECH xiāngxiāng 箱

housing conditions zhùfáng tiáojiàn 住房条件

hovel máoshè 茅舍

hover áoxiáng 翱翔

hovercraft qìdiànchuán 气垫船

how zěnme 怎么; ~ *are you?* nǐ hǎo ma? 你好吗？; ~ *about ... ?* ... zěnmeyàng? ... 怎么样？; ~ *much?* duōshao? 多少？; ~ *much is it?* *(cost)* duōshao qián? 多少钱？; ~ *many?* jǐge? 几个？; ~ *often?* duō jīngcháng? 多经常？; ~ *funny / sad!* duō huáji / bēiāi! 多滑稽 / 悲哀！

however bùguò 不过; ~ *big / rich / small they are* bùguǎn tāmen duō dà / fù / xiǎo 不管他们多大 / 富 / 小

howl *v/i (of dog)* háojiào 嚎叫; *(of person in pain)* āiháo 哀嚎; *(with laughter)* kuángxiào 狂笑

hub *(of wheel)* lúngǔ 轮毂; COMPUT jíxiànqì 集线器

hubcap gǔgài 毂盖

♦ **huddle together** quánsuō zài yìqǐ 蜷缩在一起

hue yánsè 颜色

huff: *be in a* ~ fā píqì 发脾气

hug *v/t* yōngbào 拥抱

huge jùdà 巨大

hull wàiké 外壳

hullabaloo xuānxiāo 喧嚣

hum 1 *v/t song, tune* hēngchàng 哼唱 **2** *v/i (of person)* fā hēnghēngshēng 发哼哼声; *(of machine)* fā wēngwēngshēng 发嗡嗡声

human 1 *n* rén 人 **2** *adj* rénlèi 人类; *strengths, weaknesses etc* rénxìng 人性; ~ *error* rénwéide cuòwù 人为的错误

human being rén 人

humane réndào 人道

humanitarian réndàozhǔyì zhě 人道主义者

humanity *(human beings)* rénxìng 人性; *(of attitude etc)* réncí 仁慈

human race rénlèi 人类

human resources *(department)* rénlèi zīyuán 人类资源

humble *attitude, person* qiānbēi 谦

卑; *origins* dīwēi 低微; *meal* jiǎndān 简单; *house* jiǎnlòu 简陋

humdrum dāndiào 单调

humid shīrè 湿热

humidifier zēngshīqì 增湿器

humidity shīdù 湿度

humiliate xiūrǔ 羞辱

humiliating diūliǎn 丢脸

humiliation xiūrǔ 羞辱

humility qiāngōng 谦恭

humor (*comical*) yōumò 幽默; (*mood*) qíngxù 情绪; *sense of ~* yōumògǎn 幽默感

humorous huīxié 诙谐

hump 1 *n* (*of camel*) tuófēng 驼峰; (*of person*) tuóbèi 驼背; (*on road*) xiépō 斜坡 **2** *v/t* (*carry*) bēizhe 背着

hunch (*idea*) yùgǎn 预感

hundred bǎi 百

hundredth dì yìbǎi 第一百

hundredweight yīngdàn 英担

Hungarian 1 *adj* Xiōngyálì 匈牙利 **2** *n* (*person*) Xiōngyálì rén 匈牙利人; (*language*) Xiōngyálì yǔ 匈牙利语

Hungary Xiōngyálì 匈牙利

hunger jī'è 饥饿

hung-over jiǔhòu tóutòng 酒后头痛

hungry jī'è 饥饿; *I'm ~* wǒ è le 我饿了

hunk: *great ~* F (*man*) kuíwú 魁梧

hunky-dory F rúyì 如意

hunt 1 *n* (*for animals*) shòuliè 狩猎; (*for a new leader, actor*) wùsè 物色; (*for criminal, missing child*) xúnzhǎo 寻找 **2** *v/t animal* lièqǔ 猎取

♦ **hunt for** sōuxún 搜寻

hunter (*as sport*) lièshǒu 猎手; (*for living*) lièrén 猎人

hunting dǎliè 打猎

hurdle SP tiàolán 跳栏; *fig* (*obstacle*) zhàng'ài 障碍

hurdler SP tiàolán yùndòngyuán 跳栏运动员

hurdles SP tiàolán 跳栏

hurl měngzhì 猛掷

hurray! hǎowa! 好哇!

hurricane jùfēng 飓风

hurried cōngcōng 匆匆

hurry 1 *n* cōngmáng 匆忙; *be in a ~* jímáng 急忙 **2** *v/i* kuàidiǎnr 快点儿

♦ **hurry up 1** *v/i* kuàidiǎnr 快点儿; *~!* gǎnjǐn! 赶紧! **2** *v/t* cuīcù 催促

hurt 1 *v/i* tòng 痛; *does it ~?* tòng bútòng? 痛不痛? **2** *v/t* shāng 伤; (*emotionally*) shānggǎnqíng 伤感情

husband zhàngfu 丈夫

hush *n* chénmò 沉默; *~!* biéchūshēng! 别出声!

♦ **hush up** *scandal etc* zhēyǎn 遮掩

husk (*of peanuts etc*) wàikè 外壳

husky *adj* shāyǎ 沙哑

hustle 1 *n* jǐ挤; *~ and bustle* rènao 热闹 **2** *v/t person* yìngjǐ 硬挤

hut péngwū 棚屋

hyacinth fēngxìnzǐ 风信子

hybrid *n* (*plant, animal*) zájiāo 杂交

hydrant xiāofáng lóngtóu 消防龙头

hydraulic yèyā 液压

hydro ... shuǐ 水

hydroelectric shuǐlì fādiàn 水力发电

hydrofoil (*boat*) shuǐyìtǐng 水翼艇

hydrogen qīng 氢; *~ bomb* qīngdàn 氢弹

hygiene wèishēng 卫生

hygienic wèishēng 卫生

hymn zànměishī 赞美诗

hype *n* dàchuī dàlèi 大吹大擂

hyperactive huódòng guòdù 活动过度; **hypermarket** dà xíng chāojí shìchǎng 大型超级市场; **hypersensitive** guòmǐn 过敏; **hypertension** guòdù jǐnzhāng 过度紧张; MED gāoxuèyā 高血压; **hypertext** COMPUT chāowénběn 超文本

hyphen liánzìhào 连字号

hyphenate cuīmiánshù 催眠术

hypnosis cuīmiánshù 催眠术

hypnotherapy cuīmián liáofǎ 催眠疗法

hypnotize: *~ X* shǐ X jìnrù cuīmián zhuàngtài 使 X 进入催眠状态

hypochondriac *n* yíbìngzhèng huàn zhě 疑病症患者

hypocrisy xūwěi 虚伪

hypocrite wěijūnzǐ 伪君子
hypocritical xūwěi 虚伪
hypothermia tǐwēn guòdī 体温过低
hypothesis jiǎshè 假设
hypothetical jiǎshè 假设
hysterectomy zǐgōng qiēchúshù 子宫切除术

hysteria xiēsīdǐlǐ 歇斯底里
hysterical *person, laugh* xiēsīdǐlǐ 歇斯底里; (*very funny*) huájī kěxiào 滑稽可笑; ***become** ~* biànde xiēsīdǐlǐ 变得歇斯底里
hysterics xiēsīdǐlǐde fāzuò 歇斯底里的发作; (*laughter*) kuángxiào 狂笑

I

I wǒ 我

ice bīng 冰; **break the ~** fig dǎpò chénmò 打破沉默

♦ice up (*of engine, wings*) jiébīng 结冰

iceberg bīngshān 冰山

icebox bīngxiāng 冰箱; ice-breaker (*ship*) pòbīngchuán 破冰船; ice cream bīngqílín 冰淇淋; ice-cream parlor bīngqílín diàn 冰淇淋店; ice cube bīngkuài 冰块

iced *drink* jiābīng 加冰

iced coffee bīngkāfēi 冰咖啡

ice hockey bīngqiú 冰球

ice rink bīngchǎng 冰场

I-Ching Yìjīng 易经

icicle bīngzhù 冰柱

icon (*cultural*) shèngxiàng 圣像; COMPUT túbiāo 图标

icy *road, surface* huá 滑; *welcome* lěngdàn 冷淡

idea zhǔyì 主意; **good ~!** hǎo zhǔyì! 好主意！; **I have no ~** wǒ bù zhīdào 我不知道; **it's not a good ~ to do X** zuò X bú tài shìhé 做X不太适合

ideal (*perfect*) lǐxiǎng 理想

idealistic lǐxiǎnghuà 理想化

identical yìmúyíyàng 一模一样; **~ twins** tóngluǎn shuāngtāi 同卵双胎

identification yànzhèng 验证; (*papers etc*) shēnfen zhèngmíng 身分证明

identify jiànbié 鉴别

identity shēnfen 身分; **~ card** shēnfenzhèng 身分证

ideology sīxiǎng 思想

ideological yìshíxíngtài 意识形态

idiom (*saying*) xíyǔ 习语

idiomatic (*natural*) dìdào 地道; **she speaks quite ~ English** tā néng jiǎng yìkǒu dìdào de yīngwén 她能讲一口地道的英文

idiosyncrasy píxìng 癖性

idiot báichī 白痴

idiotic yúchǔn 愚蠢

idle 1 *adj person* lǎnguǐ 懒鬼; *threat* shuōshuō ér yǐ 说说而已; *machinery* xiánzhì 闲置; **in an ~ moment** xiánxiáshí 闲暇时 2 *v/i* (*engine*) kōngzhuàn 空转

♦idle away *the time etc* dǎfa 打发

idol ǒuxiàng 偶像

idolize chóngbài 崇拜

idyllic tiányuánshì 田园式

if rúguǒ 如果

igloo xuěwū 雪屋

ignite 1 *v/t* diǎnrán 点燃 2 *v/i* zháo着着

ignition (*in car*) fādòng zhuāngzhì 发动装置; **~ key** dǎhuǒ yàoshi 打火钥匙

ignorance wúzhī 无知

ignorant wúzhī 无知; (*rude*) cūlǔ 粗鲁

ignore hūlüè 忽略

ill yǒubìng 有病; **fall ~, be taken ~** shēngbìng 生病; **feel ~ at ease** júcùbù'ān 局促不安

illegal fēifǎ 非法

illegible biànrèn bùqīng 辨认不清

illegitimate *child* sīshēng 私生

ill-fated búxìng 不幸

illicit wéifǎ 违法

illiterate wénmáng 文盲

ill-mannered jǔzhǐ cūlǔ 举止粗鲁

ill-natured píqì huài 脾气坏

illness jíbìng 疾病

illogical bù hé luójí 不合逻辑

ill-tempered píqì huài 脾气坏

ill-treat nüèdài 虐待

illuminate *building etc* zhàomíng 照明

illuminating *remarks etc* qǐfāxìng 启

发性

illusion huànxiàng 幻象

illustrate *book* chātú 插图; (*with examples*) shuōmíng 说明

illustration (*picture*) chātú 插图; (*with examples*) lìzhèng 例证

illustrator huìtúrén 绘图人

ill will èyì 恶意

image (*picture*) huàmiàn 画面; (*exact likeness*) xiàngxiàng 相象; (*of politician, company*) xíngxiàng 形象

image-conscious zhùyì xíngxiàng 注意形象

imaginable kěyǐ xiǎngxiàng 可以想象; *the biggest / smallest size* ~ kěyǐ xiǎngxiàngchū de zuìdà / zuìxiǎo chǐcùn 可以想象出的最大 / 最小尺寸

imaginary jiǎxiǎng 假想

imagination xiǎngxiàng 想象; *it's all in your* ~ dōu shì nǐ xiǎngxiàng de 都是你想象的

imaginative jùyǒu xiǎngxiànglì 具有想象力

imagine xiǎngxiàng 想象; *I can just* ~ *it* wǒ néng xiǎngxiàng chūlái 我能想象出来; *you're imagining things* nǐ shì zài húsīluànxiǎng 你是在胡思乱想

imbecile dīnéng'ér 低能儿

IMF (= *International Monetary Fund*) Guójì Huòbì Jījīn 国际货币基金

imitate mófǎng 模仿

imitation (*copying*) mófǎng 模仿; (*something copied*) fǎngzào 仿造

immaculate chúnjié 纯洁

immaterial (*not relevant*) wúguān jǐnyào 无关紧要

immature bù chéngshú 不成熟

immediate jíkè 即刻; *the* ~ *family* zhíxì qīnshǔ 直系亲属; *in the* ~ *neighborhood* jǐnlín 紧邻

immediately lìjí 立即; ~ *after the bank / church* yí guò yínháng / jiàotáng 一过银行 / 教堂

immense jùdà 巨大

immerse jìnpào 浸泡; ~ *oneself in studies etc* chénjìn 沉浸

immersion heater diàn rèshuǐqì

电热水器

immigrant *n* yímín 移民

immigrate yíjū 移居

immigration (*act*) yímín 移民; *Immigration* (*government office*) yímínjú 移民局

imminent pòjìn 迫近

immobilize *factory, person* shǐ ... tānhuàn shǐ ... 瘫痪; *car* suǒzhù 锁住

immoderate wú jiézhì 无节制

immoral bú dàodé 不道德

immorality bú dàodé 不道德

immortal bùxiǔ 不朽

immortality bùxiǔ 不朽

immune (*to illness, infection*) miǎnyì 免疫; (*from ruling, requirement*) miǎnchú 免除

immune system MED miǎnyì xìtǒng 免疫系统

immunity (*to infection*) miǎnyì 免疫; (*from ruling*) tèmiǎn 特免; *diplomatic* ~ wàijiāo miǎnyì lì 外交免疫力

impact *n* (*of meteorite, vehicle*) zhuàngjī 撞击; (*of new manager etc*) yǐngxiǎng lì 影响力; (*effect*) yǐngxiǎng 影响

impair sǔnhài 损害

impaired xuēruò 削弱

impartial gōngzhèng 公正

impassable *road* bùtōng 不通

impasse (*in negotiations etc*) jiāngjú 僵局

impassioned *speech, plea* jīdòng 激动

impassive lěngdàn 冷淡

impatience bú nàixīn 不耐心

impatient bú nàixīn 不耐心

impatiently bú nàixīn 不耐心

impeccable *turnout* wúxiēkějī 无懈可击; *English, Chinese* jīngtōng 精通

impeccably *dressed* wánměi 完美; *pronounce, speak* wánměi 完美

impede zǔ'ài 阻碍

impediment (*in speech*) kǒuchī 口吃

impending pò zài méijié 迫在眉睫

impenetrable cì bù chuān 刺不穿

imperative 1 *adj* jǐnjí 紧急 **2** *n* GRAM qíshǐ 祈使

imperceptible nányǐ chájué 难以察觉

imperfect 1 *adj* bù wánměi 不完美 **2** *n* GRAM bù wánzhěng 不完整

imperial huángdì 皇帝

imperialism dìguó zhǔyì 帝国主义

impersonal bú jù réngéxìng 不具人格性

impersonate (*as a joke*) jiǎbàn 假扮; (*illegally*) màochōng 冒充

impertinence wúlǐ 无礼

impertinent wúlǐ 无礼

imperturbable chéngzhuó lěngjìng 沉着冷静

impervious: ~ *to X* duì X wúdòngyúzhōng 对 X 无动于衷

impetuous qīngshuài 轻率

impetus (*of campaign etc*) tuīdònglì 推动力

implement 1 *n* gōngjù 工具 **2** *v/t measures etc* shíshī 实施

implicate: ~ *X in Y* xiǎnshì X shèjí Y 显示 X 涉及 Y

implication ànshì 暗示

implicit hánxù 含蓄; *trust* juéduì 绝对

implore kěnqiú 恳求

imply ànzhǐ 暗指

impolite bù lǐmào 不礼貌

import *n & v/i* jìnkǒu 进口

importance zhòngyàoxìng 重要性

important zhòngyào 重要

importer jìnkǒushāng 进口商

impose *tax* zhēngshōu 征收; ~ **oneself on X** yìng chánzhe X 硬缠着 X

imposing tūchū 突出

impossibility bù kěnéngxìng 不可能性

impossible bù kěnéng 不可能

impostor màomíng dǐngtì de rén 冒名顶替的人

impotence yángwěi 阳萎

impotent yángwěi 阳萎

impoverished pínkùn 贫困

impractical *person* bú xiànshí 不现实; *suggestion* bù shíjì 不实际

impress: ~ *X* (*impress another person*) gěi X liúxià shēnkè yìnxiàng 给 X 留下深刻印象; *be ~ed by X* X gěi rén liúxià shēnkè yìnxiàng X 给人留下深刻印象; *I'm not ~ed* wǒ bù mǎnyì 我不满意

impression yìnxiàng 印象; (*impersonation*) huájì de mófǎng 滑稽的模仿; *make a good / bad ~ on X* gěi X liúxià hǎo / huài yìnxiàng 给 X 留下好 / 坏印象; *I get the ~ that ...* wǒ juéde ... 我觉得 ...

impressionable yì shòu yǐngxiǎng 易受影响

impressive gěi rén yǐ shēnkè yìnxiàng 给人以深刻印象

imprint *n* (*of credit card*) yāyìn 压印

imprison jiānjìn 监禁

imprisonment jiānjìn 监禁

improbable bú dà kěnéng 不大可能

improper *behavior* bú qiàdàng 不恰当

improve 1 *v/t* gǎijìn 改进; *skills, Chinese* tígāo 提高; *relations* gǎishàn 改善 **2** *v/i* (*of health*) hǎozhuǎn 好转; (*of Chinese skills, life*) tígāo 提高

improvement gǎijìn 改进

improvize *v/i* jíxìng 即兴

impudent cūlǔ 粗鲁

impulse chōngdòng 冲动; *do X on an ~* yìshí chōngdòng zuò X 一时冲动做 X; ~ *buy* chōngdòng gòuwù 冲动购物

impulsive yì chōngdòng 易冲动

impunity: *with ~* bú shòu chěngfá 不受惩罚

impure *thoughts* āngzāng 肮脏; *substance* bùchún 不纯

in 1 *prep* ◊ zài lǐmiàn 在里面; ~ *Washington / China* zài Huáshèngdùn / Zhōngguó 在华盛顿 / 中国; ~ *the street* zài jiēshang 在街上; ~ *the box* zài hézi lǐ 在盒子里; *put it ~ your pocket* bǎ tā fàng zài nǐde dōulǐ

把它放在你的兜里；**~ed** 受伤
~ the leg / arm tuǐ / gēbo shòu
shāng 腿 / 胳膊受伤◊：**1999**
yījiǔjiǔjiǔ nián 19 99 年；**~ two
hours** (*from now*) liǎng ge xiǎoshí
yǐhòu 两个小时以后；(*over
period of*) liǎng ge xiǎoshí 两个小
时；**I haven't seen him ~ three
years** wǒ sānnián méi kànjiàn tāle
我三年没看见他了；**~ the
morning** zǎoshang 早上；**~ the
summer** xiàtiān 夏天；**~ August**
bāyuè 八月◊：**~ English / Chinese**
yòng Yīngyǔ / Hànyǔ 用英语 / 汉
语；**a loud voice** dàshēng 大声；
~ his style yǐ tāde fāngshì 以他的
方式；**dressed ~ yellow** chuān
huángsè yīfu 穿黄色衣服◊：**~
crossing the road** (*while*) guò
mǎlù shí 过马路时；**~ agreeing
to this** (*by virtue of*) yídàn tóngyì
zhège 一旦同意这个◊：**~ his
novel** zài tāde xiǎoshuō lǐ 在他的
小说里；**~ Confucius** zài
Kǒngzǐde zhùzuò lǐ 在孔子的著
作里◊：**three ~ all** yígòng sān gè
一共三个；**one ~ ten** shífēnzhīyī
十分之一 **2** *adv* (*at home, in the
building etc*) zài lǐmian 在里面；
(*arrived: train*) dàodá 到达；(*in its
position*) zài lǐtou 在里头；**~ here**
zài zhèr 在这儿 **3** *adj*
(*fashionable, popular*) liúxíng 流行
inability wúnéng 无能
inaccessible nán jiējìn 难接近
inaccurate bù jīngquè 不精确
inactive bù huóyuè 不活跃
inadequate bùshì dàng 不适当
inadvisable bù míngzhì 不明智
inanimate wú shēngmìng 无生命
inapplicable bú shìyòng 不适用
inappropriate bú shìdàng 不适当
inarticulate kǒuchǐ bùqīng 口齿
不清
inattentive bù jīngxīn 不经心
inaudible tīngbújiàn 听不见
inaugural *speech* jiùzhí 就职
inaugurate kāimù 开幕
inborn shēnglái 生来
inbreeding jìnqīn fánzhí 近亲繁
殖

inc. (= *incorporated*) gōngsī 公司
incalculable *damage* shǔbuqīng 数
不清
incapable wú nénglì 无能力；**be ~
of doing X** bùnéng zuò X 不能做
X
incendiary device ránshāodàn 燃
烧弹
incense[1] *n* xiāng 香
incense[2] *v/t* jīnù 激怒
incentive dònglì 动力
incessant liánxù 连续
incessantly bùtíng 不停
incest luànlún 乱伦
inch *n* yīngcùn 英寸
incident shìjiàn 事件
incidental bǔchōng 补充；**~ expenses** záfèi 杂费
incidentally shùnbiàn shuō yíxià
顺便说一下
incinerator fénhuàlú 焚化炉
incision qiēkāi 切开
incisive *mind, analysis* jiānruì 尖锐
incite shāndòng 煽动；**~ X to do Y**
shāndòng X zuò Y 煽动 X 做 Y
inclement *weather* èliè 恶劣
inclination *tendency, liking* yìyuàn
意愿
incline: be ~d to do X yǒu zuò X
de qīngxiàng 有做 X 的倾向
inclose → **enclose**
include bāokuò 包括
including *prep* bāokuò 包括
inclusive *adj & prep price* bāokuò
zàinèi 包括在内；**~ of X** bāokuò
X zàinèi 包括 X 在内 **3** *adv* yíqiè
bāokuò zàinèi 一切包括在内；
from Monday to Thursday ~ cóng
zhōuyī dào zhōusì 从周一到周
四
incoherent bù liánguàn 不连贯
income shōurù 收入
income tax suǒdéshuì 所得税
incoming *flight* jídá 到达；
phonecall, mail shōudào 收到；
president xīnrèn 新任；**~ tide**
zhǎngcháo 涨潮
incomparable bùkě bǐnǐ 不可比
拟
incompatibility bù xiāngfú 不相
符

incompatible bù xiāngfú 不相符

incompetence bú chènzhí 不称职

incompetent bú chènzhí 不称职

incomplete bù wánzhěng 不完整

incomprehensible bùkě lǐjiě 不可理解

inconceivable wúfǎ xiǎngxiàng 无法想象

inconclusive fēi jiélùnxìng 非结论性

incongruous bù xiétiáo 不协调

inconsiderate kǎolǜ bùzhōu 考虑不周

inconsistent bù yízhì 不一致

inconsolable wúfǎ wèijiè 无法慰藉

inconspicuous bù xiǎnyǎn 不显眼

inconvenience n bù fāngbiàn 不方便

inconvenient bù fāngbiàn 不方便

incorporate bāohán 包含

incorporated COM gōngsī 公司

incorrect bú zhèngquè 不正确

incorrectly bú zhèngquè 不正确

incorrigible bùkě jiùyào 不可救药

increase 1 v/t zēngjiā 增加 2 v/i tígāo 提高 3 n zēngjiā 增加

increasing zēngjiā 增加

increasingly yuèláiyuè 越来越

incredible (amazing, very good) lìngrén nányǐ zhìxìn 令人难以置信

incriminate xiànde yǒuzuì 显得有罪; ~ oneself shòuliánlèi 受连累

incubator (for chicks) fūhuàqì 孵化器; (for babies) héngwēn yùyīng xiāng 恒温育婴箱

incur zhāozhì 招致

incurable bùkě zhìyù 不可治愈

indebted: be ~ to X qiàn X zhài 欠 X 债

indecent xiàliú 下流

indecisive yóuyù bù jué 犹豫不决

indecisiveness yóuyùbùjué 犹豫不决

indeed (in fact) shìshí shàng 事实上; (yes, agreeing) díquèshì 的确

是; very much ~ fēicháng 非常

indefinable nányǐ miáoshù 难以描述

indefinite bú quèdìng 不确定; ~ article GRAM búdìngguàncí 不定冠词

indefinitely wú xiànqī 无限期

indelicate bù jīngxì 不精细

indent 1 n (in text) suǒjìn páiyìn 进排印 2 v/t line suōgé shūxiě 缩格书写

independence dúlì 独立

Independence Day Dúlìrì 独立日

independent dúlì 独立

independently deal with dúlì 独立; ~ of dāndú 单独

indescribable nányǐ xíngróng 难以形容; (very bad) zāo de wúfǎ xíngróng 糟得无法形容

indescribably wúfǎ xíngróng 无法形容; ~ bad zāo de wúfǎ xíngróng 糟得无法形容; ~ beautiful měi de wúfǎ xíngróng 美得无法形容

indestructible bùnéng sǔnhuài 不能损坏

indeterminate bú quèdìng 不确定

index (for book) suǒyǐn 索引

index card suǒyǐnkǎ 索引卡; index finger shízhǐ 食指; index-linked àn shēnghuó zhǐshù tiáozhěng 按生活指数调整

India Yìndù 印度

Indian 1 adj Yìndù 印度 2 n Yìndù rén 印度人; (American) Yìndì'ān rén 印第安人

Indian summer xiǎoyángchūn 小阳春

indicate 1 v/t biǎomíng 表明 2 v/i (when driving) zhǐshì 指示

indication zhǐshì 指示

indicator (on car) fāngxiàng zhǐshìqì 方向指示器

indict kònggào 控告

indifference mò bù guānxīn 漠不关心

indifferent mò bù guānxīn 漠不关心; (mediocre) yìbān 一般

indigestible bùnéng xiāohuà 不能

消化

indigestion xiāohuà bùliáng 消化
不良

indignant fènkǎi 愤慨

indignation fènkǎi 愤慨

indirect jiànjiē 间接

indirectly jiànjiē 间接

indiscreet qīngshuài 轻率

indiscretion (act) qīngshuài 轻率

indiscriminate rènyì ér wéi 任意
而为

indispensable bùkě quēshǎo 不可
缺少

indisposed (not well) xiǎobìng 小
病

indisputable bùróng zhìyí 不容置
疑

indisputably bùróng zhìyí 不容置
疑

indistinct móhu 模糊

indistinguishable wúfǎ qūbié 无
法区别

individual 1 n gèrén 个人 2 adj
(separate) dāndú 单独; (personal)
gèrén 个人

individualist gèrénzhǔyǐ zhě 个人
主义者

individually gèzì 各自

indivisible bùkě fēngē 不可分割

indoctrinate guànshū 灌输

indolence lǎnduò 懒惰

indolent lǎnduò 懒惰

Indochina Yìndùzhīnà 印度支那

Indochinese adj Yìndùzhīnà 印度
支那

Indonesia Yìndùníxīyà 印度尼西
亚

Indonesian 1 adj Yìndùníxīyà 印
度尼西亚 2 n (person)
Yìndùníxīyà rén 印度尼西亚人

indoor shìnèi 室内

indoors zài shìnèi 在室内

indorse → endorse

induction ceremony jiùzhí yíshì
就职仪式

indulge 1 v/t (oneself, one's tastes)
fàngzòng zìjǐ 放纵自己 2 v/i: ~ in
X jìnqíng xiǎngshòu X 尽情享受
X

indulgence (of tastes, appetite etc)
fàngzòng 放纵; (lax attitude)

shūhū 疏忽

indulgent (not strict enough) bù
yángé 不严格

industrial gōngyè 工业

industrial action gōngyè xíngdòng
工业行动

industrial dispute láozī jiūfēn 劳
资纠纷

industrialist shíyèjiā 实业家

industrialize 1 v/t shǐ gōngyèhuà
使工业化 2 v/i gōngyèhuà 工业
化

industrial waste gōngyè fèiliào 工
业废料

industrious qínmiǎn 勤勉

industry gōngyè 工业

ineffective xiàoguǒ bùjiā 效果不
佳

ineffectual person dīnéng 低能

inefficient wúxiàolǜ 无效率

ineligible wúzīgé 无资格

inept bùshúliàn 不熟练

inequality bùpíngděng 不平等

inescapable nánmiǎn 难免

inestimable nányǐ gūliàng 难以估
量

inevitable xiǎn ér yìjiàn 显而易见

inevitably bùkě bìmiǎn 不可避免

inexcusable bùkě yuánliàng 不可
原谅

inexhaustible person jīnglì
chōngpèi 精力充沛; supply
yuányuán búduàn 源源不断

inexpensive piányí 便宜

inexperienced méi jīngyàn 没经
验

inexplicable fèijiě 费解

inexpressible joy nán yǐ biǎoshù
难以表述

infallible juéduì kěkào 绝对可靠

infamous chòumíng yuǎnyáng 臭
名远扬

infancy (of person) yīng'érqī 婴儿
期; (of state, institution) chūjí
jiēduàn 初级阶段

infant yīng'ér 婴儿

infantile pej háiziqì 孩子气

infantry bùbīng 步兵

infantry soldier bùbīng 步兵

infatuated: be ~ with X mílìàn X
迷恋 X

infect (*of person*) yǐngxiǎng 影响; *food, water* wūrǎn 污染; **become ~ed** gǎnrǎn 感染

infected *wound* gǎnrǎn 感染

infection chuánrǎn 传染

infectious *disease* chuánrǎn 传染; *fig: laughter* gǎnrǎn 感染

infer: **~ X from Y** cóng Y tuīduànchū X 从 Y 推断出 X

inferior *quality* lièzhì 劣质; (*in rank, military*) dìwèidī 地位低; (*in company, workmanship*) zhíwèidī 职位低

inferiority (*in quality*) lièzhì 劣质

inferiority complex zìbēigǎn 自卑感

infertile bùnéng fányù 不能繁育

infertility wú shēngzhí nénglì 无生殖能力

infidelity bùzhōng 不忠

infiltrate *v/t* dǎrù 打入

infinite wúxiàn 无限

infinitive búdìngshì 不定式

infinity wúqióng 无穷

infirm tǐruò 体弱

infirmary yīyuàn 医院

infirmity tǐruò 体弱

inflame jīdòng 激动

inflammable yìrán 易燃

inflammation MED fāyán 发炎

inflatable *dinghy* kě chōngqì 可充气

inflate *v/t tire, dinghy* chōngqì 充气; *economy* péngzhàng 膨胀

inflation tōnghuò péngzhàng 通货膨胀

inflationary (*of inflation*) wùjià shàngzhǎng 物价上涨; (*causing inflation*) dǎozhì tōnghuò péngzhàng 导致通货膨胀

inflection (*of voice*) biànyīn 变音

inflexible *attitude, person* gùzhí 固执

inflict: **~ X on Y** shǐ Y zāoshòu X 使 Y 遭受 X

in-flight fēixíngzhōng 飞行中; **~ entertainment** fēixíngzhōng tígōng de yúlè huódòng 飞行中提供的娱乐活动

influence **1** *n* yǐngxiǎng 影响; (*power to influence*) yǐngxiǎnglì 影响力; **be a good/bad ~ on X** duì X yǒu hǎo/huài yǐngxiǎng 对 X 有好/坏影响 **2** *v/t* yǐngxiǎng 影响

influential yǒu yǐngxiǎng 有影响

influenza liúxíngxìng gǎnmào 流行性感冒

inform **1** *v/t* tōngzhī 通知; **~ X of Y** bǎ Y tōngzhī gěi X 把 Y 通知给 X; **please keep me ~ed** qǐng chuándá gěi wǒ 请传达给我 **2** *v/i* gàofā 告发; **~ on X** gàofā X 告发 X

informal fēi zhèngshì 非正式

informality fēi zhèngshì 非正式

informant tígōng xiāoxirén 提供消息人

information xìnxī 信息

information science xìnxīxué 信息学; information scientist xìnxīxuéjiā 信息学家; information technology xìnxī jìshù 信息技术

informative tígōng xìnxī 提供信息

informer gàofārén 告发人

infra-red *adj* hóngwàixiàn 红外线

infrastructure jīchǔ jiégòu 基础结构

infrequent shǎoyǒu 少有

infuriate jīnù 激怒

infuriating lìngrén shēngqì 令人生气

infuse *v/i* (*of tea*) pào 泡

infusion (*herb tea*) jìnpào 浸泡

ingenious jīngmíng 精明

ingenuity jīngmíng 精明

ingot dìng dìng 锭

ingratiate: **~ oneself with X** qǔyuè X 取悦 X

ingratitude wàng'ēnfùyì 忘恩负义

ingredient (*for cooking*) yuánliào 原料; *fig (for success)* yīnsù 因素

in-group xiǎoquānzi 小圈子

inhabit jūzhù 居住

inhabitable shìyú jūzhù 适于居住

inhabitant jūmín 居民

inhale **1** *v/t* xīrù 吸入 **2** *v/i* (*when smoking*) xīqì 吸气

inhaler xīrùqì 吸入器

inherit jìchéng 继承

inheritance jìchéng 继承

inhibit *growth, conversation etc* zǔzhǐ 阻止

inhibited yàyì 压抑

inhibition yāyì 压抑

inhospitable *(of people)* lěngdàn 冷淡; *(of place)* huāngliáng 荒凉

in-house *adj & adv* zài gōngsī nèi 在公司内

inhuman yěmán 野蛮

initial **1** *adj* zuìchū 最初 **2** *n* xìngmíng shǒu zìmǔ 姓名首字母 **3** *v/t (write initials on)* qiān xìngmíng shǒu zìmǔ 签姓名首字母

initially kāishǐ 开始

initiate *v/t* zhuóshǒu 着手

initiation kāichuàng 开创

initiative zhǔdòngxìng 主动性; *do X on one's own* ~ zhǔdòng zuò X 主动做X

inject *medicine, drug* zhùshè 注射; *fuel* shūsòng 输送; *capital* tóurù 投入

injection MED zhùshè 注射; *(of fuel)* shūsòng 输送; *(of capital)* tóurù 投入

injure shānghài 伤害

injured **1** *adj leg* shòushāng 受伤; *feelings* shòushānghài 受伤害 **2** *n: the* ~ shòushāng zhě 受伤者

injury shānghài 伤害

injustice fēizhèngyì 非正义

ink mòshuǐ 墨水

inkjet (printer) pēnmò (dǎyìnjī) 喷墨 (打印机)

inland nèilù 内陆

in-laws yīnqīn 姻亲

inlay *n* xiāngqiàn 镶嵌

inlet *(of sea)* hǎiwān 海湾; *(in machine)* rùkǒu 入口

inmate *(of prison)* fànrén 犯人; *(of mental hospital)* bìngyǒu 病友

inn xiǎolǚguǎn 小旅馆

innate tiānshēng 天生

inner nèibù 内部

inner city jiùchéngqū 旧城区

Inner Mongolia Nèi Ménggǔ 内蒙古

Inner Mongolian Grasslands Nèi Ménggǔ Dà Cǎo Yuán 内蒙古大草原

innermost zuìshēn 最深

inner tube nèitāi 内胎

innocence *(of child)* tiānzhēn 天真; LAW wúzuì 无罪

innocent *child* tiānzhēn 天真; LAW wúzuì 无罪

innovation géxīn 革新

innovative géxīn 革新

innovator géxīn zhě 革新者

innumerable shǔbuqīng 数不清

inoculate jiēzhǒng 接种

inoculation jiēzhǒng 接种

inoffensive bù chùfàn rén 不触犯人

inorganic wújī 无机

input *n & v/t (into project etc)* tóurù 投入; COMPUT shūrù 输入

input port COMPUT shūrù duānkǒu 输入端口

inquest shěnxùn 审讯

inquire xúnwèn 询问; ~ *into X* diàochá X 调查 X

inquiry xúnwèn 询问

inquisitive hàoqí 好奇

insane fēngkuáng 疯狂

insanitary bù wèishēng 不卫生

insanity fēngkuáng 疯狂

insatiable bùnéng mǎnzú 不能满足

inscription míngwén 铭文

inscrutable shénmì 神秘

insect kūnchóng 昆虫

insecticide shāchóngjì 杀虫剂

insect repellent fángchóngyào 防虫药

insecure bù ānquán 不安全

insecurity bù ānquángǎn 不安全感

insensitive bù mǐngǎn 不敏感

insensitivity bù língmǐnxìng 不灵敏性

inseparable *two issues* bùkě fēngē 不可分割; *two people* fēnbùkāi 分不开

insert **1** *n (in magazine etc)* fùjiāwù 附加物 **2** *v/t* chārù 插入; ~ *X into Y* bǎ X chārù Y 把X插入Y

insertion *(act)* chārù 插入

inside **1** *n (of house, box)* nèibù 内部; *(of road)* lǐcè 里侧; *somebody*

on the ~ nèibùrén 内部人; **~ out** lǐmiàn fāndào wàimiàn 里面翻到外面; **turn X ~ out** bǎ X lǐ fān wài 把 X 里翻外; **know X ~ out** chèdǐ liǎojiě X 彻底了解 X **2** prep zài ... lǐ 在 ... 里; **~ the house** zài wūlǐ 在屋里; **~ of 2 hours** bú dào liǎng xiǎoshí 不到两小时 **3** adv stay, remain zài lǐmiàn 在里面; go, carry lǐmiàn 里面; we went **~** wǒmen jìn lǐmiàn le 我们进里面了 **4** adj nèibù 内部; **~ information** nèibù xiāoxi 内部消息; **~ lane** SP lǐquān pǎodào 里圈跑道; (on road) lǐdào 里道; **~ pocket** lǐbiāndōu 里边兜

insider nèibùrén 内部人

insider trading FIN nèimù jiāoyì 内幕交易

insides lǐmiàn 里面

insidious yīnfú 隐伏

insight dòngchá 洞察

insignificant wú jiàzhí 无价值

insincere bù zhēnchéng 不真诚

insincerity xūwěi 虚伪

insinuate (imply) ànshì 暗示

insist jiānchí 坚持; please keep it, I **~** nǐ yídìng yào liúzhe 你一定要留着

♦insist on jiānjué yāoqiú 坚决要求

insistent jiānchí 坚持

insolent mánhèng 蛮横

insoluble problem bùnéng jiějué 不能解决; substance bù róngjiě 不溶解

insolvent wú chángzhài nénglì 无偿债能力

insomnia shīmián 失眠

inspect work, tickets, baggage jiǎnchá 检查; building, factory, school shìchá 视察

inspection (of work, tickets, baggage) jiǎnchá 检查; (of building, factory, school) shìchá 视察

inspector (in factory) jiǎncháyuán 检查员; (on buses) chápiàoyuán 查票员; (of police) xúnguān 巡官

inspiration línggǎn 灵感; (very good idea) hǎo zhǔyì 好主意

inspire (cause: respect etc) yǐnqǐ 引起; be **~d by X** cóng X dédào línggǎn 从 X 得到灵感

instability (of character, economy) bù wěndìng 不稳定

install computer, telephone, software ānzhuāng 安装

installation (of new equipment, software etc) ānzhuāng 安装; **military ~** jūnshì zhuāngbèi 军事装备

installment (of story, TV drama etc) jí 集; (payment) yīqī fùkuǎn 一期付款

installment plan fēnqī fùkuǎn 分期付款

instance (example) lìzi 例子; **for ~** lìrú 例如

instant 1 adj lìjí 立即 **2** n shànà 刹那; **in an ~** yíhuìr 一会儿

instantaneous jíkè 即刻

instant coffee sùróng kāfēi 速溶咖啡

instantly jíkè 即刻

instant noodles ⇩ fāngbiànmiàn 方便面

instead dàitì 代替; I'll take that one **~** nà wǒ ná nèige ba 那我拿那个吧; I haven't got tea, would you like coffee **~?** wǒ méiyǒu chá, nǐ hē kāfēi xíng ma? 我没有茶, 你喝咖啡行吗?; he didn't go home, he went to the bar **~** tā méi huíjiā, tā qù jiǔbā le 他没回家, 他去酒吧了; **~ of** ér búshì 而不是

instep jiǎobèi 脚背

instinct běnnéng 本能

instinctive běnnéng 本能

institute 1 n xiéhuì 协会; (special home) yuàn 院 **2** v/t new law, inquiry zhìdìng 制定

institution (governmental) jīgòu 机构; (something traditional) fēngsú xíguàn 风俗习惯; (setting up) jiànlì 建立

instruct (order) zhǐshì 指示; (teach) zhǐdǎo 指导; **~ X to do Y** (order) zhǐshì X zuò Y 指示 X 做 Y

instruction shuōmíng 说明; **~s for use** shǐyòng shuōmíngshū 使用

说明书

instruction manual shuōmíngshū
说明书

instructive yǒu zhǐdǎo yìyì 有指
导意义

instructor zhǐdǎoyuán 指导员

instrument MUS yuèqì 乐器;
(*gadget, tool*) qìjù 器具

insubordinate bùfúcóng 不服从

insufficient bùgòu 不够

insulate ELEC shǐ juéyuán 使绝缘;
(*against cold*) shǐ gérè 使隔热

insulation ELEC juéyuán cáiliào 绝
缘材料; (*against cold*) gérè 隔热

insulin yídǎosù 胰岛素

insult n & v/t wǔrǔ 侮辱

insurance bǎoxiǎn 保险

insurance company bǎoxiǎn
gōngsī 保险公司

insurance policy bǎoxiǎndān 保
险单

insure v/t gěi ... bǎoxiǎn 给 ... 保
险

insured: **be ~ed** cānjiā bǎoxiǎn 参
加保险

insurmountable wúfǎ chāoyuè 无
法超越

intact (*not damaged*) wèishòusǔn 未
受损

intake (*of college etc*) zhāoshōu 招
收

integrate v/t róngwéiyìtǐ 融为一
体

integrated circuit jíchéng diànlù
集成电路

integrity (*honesty*) chéngshí 诚实

intellect zhìlì 智力

intellectual 1 adj zhìlì 智力 **2** n
zhīshífènzǐ 知识分子

intelligence zhìlì 智力; (*news*)
qíngbào 情报

intelligence service qíngbàojú 情
报局

intelligent cōngmíng 聪明

intelligible kě lǐjiě 可理解

intend dǎsuàn 打算; **~ to do X** (*do
on purpose*) zhìzài zuò X 旨在做
X; (*plan to do*) dǎsuàn zuò X 打算
做 X; **that's not what I ~ed** nà bù
shì wǒde yìtú 那不是我的意图

intense *sensation, pleasure, heat,*

pressure jùliè 剧烈; *personality*
rèqíng 热情; *concentration* gāodù
高度

intensify 1 v/t *effect, pressure*
jiāqiáng 加强 **2** v/i (*pain*) jiājù 加
剧; (*fighting*) biànjiānglıè 变强烈

intensity (*of sensation, heat, pain*)
qiánglıè 强烈; (*of fighting*) jīliè 激
烈

intensive *study, training, treatment*
qiánghuà 强化

intensive care (**unit**) tèhù (bù) 特
护 (部)

intensive course (*of language
study*) jīngdúkè 精读课

intent: **be ~ on doing X** (*determined
to do*) jiānjué zuò X 坚决做 X;
(*concentrating on*) jízhōng jīnglì
zuò X 集中精力做 X

intention yìtú 意图; **I have no ~ of
...** (*refuse to*) wǒ gēnběn bù xiǎng
... 我根本不想...

intentional yǒuyì 有意

intentionally yǒuyì 有意

interaction xiānghù zuòyòng 相互
作用

interactive jiāohùshì 交互式

intercede tiáotíng 调停

intercept *ball* lánjié 拦截; *message*
jiéchá 截查; *missile* jiéjī 截击

interchange n (*of highways*)
jiāochādào 交叉道

interchangeable kěhùhuàn 可互
换

intercom duìjiǎngjī 对讲机

intercourse (*sexual*) xìngjiāo 性交

interdependent xiānghù yīlài 相
互依赖

interest 1 n xìngqù 兴趣; FIN lìxī
利息; **take an ~ in X** duì X yǒu
xìngqù 对 X 有兴趣 **2** v/t: **~ X**
yǐnqǐ X de xìngqù 引起 X 的兴
趣; **does that offer ~ you?** nǐ duì
zhèige tiáojiàn gǎn xìngqù ma? 你
对这个条件感兴趣吗？

interested yǒu xìngqù 有兴趣; **be
~ in X** duì X yǒu xìngqù 对 X 有兴
趣; **thanks, but I'm not ~** xièxie,
dàn wǒ bù gǎn xìngqù 谢谢，但
我不感兴趣

interesting yǒuqù 有趣

interest rate lìxīlǜ 利息率
interface 1 n jièmiàn 界面 2 v/i xiāngjiē 相接
interfere gānshè 干涉
♦ interfere with controls nònghuài 弄坏; plans gānrǎo 干扰
interference gānshè 干涉; (on radio) gānrǎo 干扰
interior 1 adj nèibù 内部 2 n (of house) nèibù 内部; (of country) nèilù 内陆; Department of the Interior Nèizhèngbù 内政部
interior decoration nèibù zhuāngxiū 内部装修; interior design shìnèi shèjì 室内设计; interior designer shìnèi shèjì zhě 室内设计者
interlude (at theater, concert) mùjiān 幕间; (period) shíjiān 时间
intermediary n zhōngrén 中人
intermediate adj zhōngjí 中级
intermission (in theater, movie theater) mùjiān xiūxī 幕间休息
intern v/t jūliú 拘留
internal nèibù 内部; trade guónèi 国内
internal combustion engine nèiránjī 内燃机
internally (in body) tǐnèi 体内; (within organization) nèibù 内部
Internal Revenue (Service) Guónèi Shuìshōu (bù) 国内税收 (部)
international 1 adj guójì 国际 2 n (match) guójì bǐsài 国际比赛; (player) guójì bǐsài xuǎnshǒu 国际比赛选手
International Court of Justice Guójì Fǎtíng 国际法庭
International Labor Day Guójì Láodòngjié 国际劳动节
internationally guójì 国际
International Monetary Fund Guójì Huòbì Jījīn Zǔzhí 国际货币基金组织
Internet yīntèwǎng 因特网, wǎngluò 网络; on the ~ zài wǎngluò shàng 在网络上
Internet café wǎngbā 网吧
internist nèikē yīshēng 内科医生

interpret 1 v/t (linguistically) kǒuyì 口译; piece of music, comment etc jiěshì 解释 2 v/i zuò fānyì 作翻译
interpretation (linguistic) kǒuyì 口译; (of piece of music, of meaning) lǐjiě 理解
interpreter kǒuyì zhě 口译者
interrelated facts xiānghù guānlián 相互关联
interrogate xúnwèn 询问
interrogation xúnwèn 询问
interrogative n GRAM yíwèn 疑问
interrogator shěnwèn zhě 审问者
interrupt 1 v/t speaker dǎduàn 打断 2 v/i chāhuà 插话
interruption zhōngduàn 中断
intersect v/t & v/i jiāochā 交叉
intersection (crossroads) shízì lùkǒu 十字路口
interstate n zhōujìjiān 州际间
interval jiàngé 间隔; (in theater, at concert) jiànxiē 间歇
intervene (of person, police etc) jièrù 介入
intervention jièrù 介入
interview 1 n (on TV, in paper) cǎifǎng 采访; (for job) miànshì 面试 2 v/t (on TV, for paper) cǎifǎng 采访; (for job) miànshì 面试
interviewee (on TV) bèi cǎifǎng zhě 被采访者; (for job) yìngshì zhě 应试者
interviewer (on TV, for paper) cǎifǎng zhě 采访者; (for job) miànshì zhě 面试者
intestine chángzi 肠子
intimacy (of friendship) qīnmì 亲密; (sexual) qīnnì 亲昵
intimate friend qīnmì 亲密; (sexually) qīnnì 亲昵; thoughts sīrén 私人
intimidate wēixié 威胁
intimidation wēixié 威胁
into dào ... lǐ 到 ... 里; he walked ~ the store tā zǒu dào diànlǐ 他走到店里; he put it ~ his suitcase tā bǎ tā fàngzài tāde yīxiāng lǐ 他把它放在他的衣箱里; translate ~ English fānyì chéng Yīngyǔ 翻译成英语; turn ~ biànchéng

变成; **be ~ X** F (*like*) xǐhuān X 喜欢 X; (*be involved with*) chīmí X 痴迷 X; **when you're ~ the job** dāng nǐ shúxī zhè gōngzuò de shíhòu 当你熟悉这工作的时候
intolerable bùnéng rěnshòu 不能忍受
intolerant bù róngrěn 不容忍
intoxicated táozuì 陶醉
intransitive bù jíwù 不及物
intravenous jìngmàinèi 静脉内
intrepid wúwèi 无畏
intricate fùzá 复杂
intrigue 1 n cèhuà 策划 **2** v/t yǐnqǐ hàoqíxīn 引起好奇心; **I would be ~d to know ...** wǒ huì yǒu xìngqù dézhī ... 我会有兴趣得知 ...
intriguing yǒu yìsi 有意思
introduce jièshào 介绍; *new technique etc* yǐnjìn 引进; **may I ~ ...?** wǒ lai jièshào yíxià ...... 我来介绍一下 ...
introduction (*to person, new food, sport etc*) jièshào 介绍; (*in book*) xùyán 序言; (*of new techniques etc*) yǐnjìn 引进
introvert n nèixiàng xìnggé de rén 内向性格的人
intrude v/i qīnfàn 侵犯
intruder qīnfàn zhě 侵犯者
intrusion qīnfàn 侵犯
intuition zhíjué 直觉
invade qīnlüè 侵略
invalid[1] *adj* wúxiào 无效
invalid[2] n MED bìngruò 病弱
invalidate *claim, theory* shǐ wúxiào 使无效
invaluable *help, contributor* wújià 无价
invariably (*always*) búbiàn 不变
invasion qīnlüè 侵略
invent fāmíng 发明
invention fāmíng 发明
inventive yǒu fāmíng cáinéng 有发明才能
inventor fāmíng zhě 发明者
inventory mùlù 目录
inverse *adj order* xiāngfǎn 相反
invert dàozhì 倒置
inverted commas yǐnhào 引号

invertebrate n wú jízhuī dòngwù 无脊椎动物
invest v/t & v/i tóuzī 投资
investigate diàochá 调查
investigation diàochá 调查
investigative journalism diàochá bàodào 调查报道
investment tóuzī 投资
investor tóuzī zhě 投资者
invigorating *climate* shǐrén shuǎngkuài 使人爽快
invincible wúdí 无敌
invisible bùkějiàn 不可见
invitation yāoqǐng 邀请
invite yāoqǐng 邀请; **can I ~ you for a meal?** wǒ kěyǐ qǐng nǐ chī dùn fàn ma? 我可以请你吃顿饭吗？
invoice 1 n zhàngdān 帐单 **2** v/t *customer* kāi zhàngdān 开帐单
involuntary fēiběnyì 非本意
involve *hard work, expense* xūyào 需要; (*concern*) shèjí 涉及; **what does it ~?** nà xūyào shénme? 那需要什么？; **get ~d with X** juǎnrù X 卷入 X; (*emotionally, romantically*) yǔ X yǒu gǎnqíng 与 X 有感情
involved (*complex*) fùzá 复杂
involvement (*in a project etc*) chāshǒu 插手; (*in a crime, accident*) juǎnrù 卷入
invulnerable búyì shòushāng 不易受伤
inward 1 *adj* nèibù 内部 **2** *adv* xiàngnèi 向内
inwardly nèixīn 内心
iodine diǎn 碘
IOU (= **I owe you**) jièjù 借据
IQ (= **intelligence quotient**) zhìshāng 智商
Iran Yīlǎng 伊朗
Iranian 1 *adj* Yīlǎng 伊朗 **2** n (*person*) Yīlǎng rén 伊朗人; (*language*) Yīlǎng yǔ 伊朗语
Iraq Yīlākè 伊拉克
Iraqi 1 *adj* Yīlākè 伊拉克 **2** n (*person*) Yīlākè rén 伊拉克人
Ireland Ài'ěrlán 爱尔兰
iris (*of eye*) hóngmó 虹膜; (*flower*) yuānwěishǔ zhíwù 鸢尾属植物

Irish Ài'ěrlán 爱尔兰

Irishman Ài'ěrlán nánzǐ 爱尔兰
男子

Irishwoman Ài'ěrlán nǚzǐ 爱尔兰
女子

iron 1 n (substance) tiě 铁; (for
clothes) yùndǒu 熨斗 **2** v/t shirts
etc yùn 熨

ironic(al) fěngcì 讽刺

ironing yùn 熨; **do the ~** yùn yīfu
熨衣服

ironing board yùnyībǎn 熨衣板

ironworks gāngtiěchǎng 钢铁厂

iron rice bowl (job for life) tiě
fànwǎn 铁饭碗

irony fěngcì 讽刺

irrational wúlǐxìng 无理性

irreconcilable wúfǎ héjiě 无法和
解

irrecoverable wúfǎ wǎnhuí 无法
挽回

irregular intervals bùguīlǜ 不规律;
sizes bùguīzé 不规则; behavior
bùguīfàn 不规范

irrelevant bùxiānggān 不相干

irreparable wúfǎ míbǔ 无法弥补

irreplaceable object, person bùkě
tìdài 不可替代

irrepressible sense of humor
bùnéng yìzhì 不能抑制; person
bùjūshù 不拘束

irreproachable wúkě zhǐzé 无可
指责

irresistible wúfǎ kàngjù 无法抗
拒

irrespective: **~ of X** búgù X 不顾 X

irresponsible búfùzérèn 不负责
任

irretrievable bùkě wǎnhuí 不可挽
回

irreverent bùqiánchéng 不虔诚

irrevocable bùkě qǔxiāo 不可取
消

irrigate guàngài 灌溉

irrigation guàngài 灌溉

irrigation canal guàngàiqú 灌溉
渠

irritable fánzào 烦躁

irritate rěnù 惹怒

irritating fánrén 烦人

irritation fánzào 烦燥

Islam Yīsīlánjiào 伊斯兰教

Islamic Yīsīlánjiào 伊斯兰教

island dǎo 岛; (traffic) ~
ānquándǎo 安全岛

islander dǎoyǔrén 岛屿人

isolate (separate) gélí 隔离; (cut
off) gūlì 孤立; (identify) fēngé 分
隔

isolated house gūlì 孤立;
occurrence dānyī 单一

isolation (of a region) gélí 隔离; **in
~** dāndú 单独

isolation ward gélíjiān 隔离间

Israel Yǐsèliè 以色列

Israeli 1 adj Yǐsèliè 以色列 **2** n
(person) Yǐsèliè rén 以色列人

issue 1 n (matter) shìqíng 事情;
(result) jiéguǒ 结果; (of magazine)
qī 期; **the point at ~** zhēnglùnde
wèntí 争论的问题; **take ~ with
X** yǔ X zhēngbiàn 与 X 争辩 **2** v/t
supplies, coins, passports, visa
fāxíng 发行; warning fābiǎo 发表

IT (= information technology) xìnxī
jìshù 信息技术

it tā 它 (not translated): **~'s on the
table** zài zhuōzi shang 在桌子上;
~'s raining xiàyǔ le 下雨了; **~'s
me/him** shì wǒ/tā 是我/他; **~'s
yellow** shì huángde 是黄的; **~'s
Charlie here** TELEC wǒ shì Chálí
我是查理; **~'s your turn** gāi nǐ
de le 该你的了; **that's ~!** (that's
right) duìle! 对了！; (finished)
wánle! 完了！

Italian 1 adj Yìdàlì 意大利 **2** n
(person) Yìdàlì rén 意大利人;
(language) Yìdàlì yǔ 意大利语

italic xiétǐ 斜体

Italy Yìdàlì 意大利

itch 1 n yǎng 痒 **2** v/i fāyǎng 发痒

item tiáo 条

itemize invoice fēnxiàng lièjǔ 分项
列举

itinerary lǚxíng jìhuà 旅行计划

its tāde 它的

itself tā zìjǐ 它自己; **by ~** (alone)
dúzì 独自; (automatically) zìdòng
自动

ivory (substance) xiàngyá 象牙

ivy chángchūnténg 常春藤

J

jab v/t chuō 戳

jack MOT qiānjīndǐng 千斤顶; (in cards) gōu 钩
♦jack up MOT yòng qiānjīndǐng dǐng 用千斤顶顶

jacket (coat) jiákè 茄克; (of book) hùfēng 护封

jacket potato MOT kǎo tǔdòu 烤土豆

jack-knife v/i wānchéng V zì xíng 弯成V字形

jackpot lěijì de dǔzhù 累积的赌注; hit the ~ fā dàcái 发大财

jade n yù 玉

jagged cēncī bùqí 参差不齐

jail n jiānyù 监狱

jam¹ guǒjiàng 果酱

jam² 1 n MOT shīlíng 失灵; F (difficulty) kùnjìng 困境; be in a ~ xiànrù kùnjìng 陷入困境 2 v/t (ram) bǎ ... sāijìn 把 ... 塞进; (cause to stick) qiǎzhù 卡住; broadcast gānrǎo 干扰; be ~med (of roads) dǔsè 堵塞; (of door, window) qiǎzhù 卡住 3 v/i (stick) qiǎzhù 卡住; (squeeze) jǐjìn 挤进

jam-packed yōngjǐ 拥挤

janitor kānménrén 看门人

January yīyuè 一月

Japan Rìběn 日本

Japanese 1 adj Rìběn 日本 2 n (person) Rìběn rén 日本人; (language) Rìyǔ 日语

jar¹ n (container) guàn 罐

jar² v/i (of noise) cì'ěr 刺耳; ~ on cìjī 刺激

jargon hánghuà 行话

jasmine tea mòlìhuāchá 茉莉花茶

jaundice huángdǎn 黄疸

jaw n hé 颌

jaywalker luànchuǎng mǎlù de rén 乱闯马路的人

jaywalking luànchuǎng mǎlù 乱闯马路

jazz juéshìyuè 爵士乐
♦jazz up F diǎnzhuì 点缀

jealous dùjì 妒忌; be ~ of ... dùjì ... 妒忌 ...

jealousy dùjì 妒忌

jeans niúzǎikù 牛仔裤

jeep jípǔchē 吉普车

jeer 1 n cháonòng 嘲弄 2 v/i qǐhòng 起哄; ~ at cháoxiào 嘲笑

jelly guǒdòng 果冻

jelly bean ruǎntáng 软糖

jellyfish hǎizhé 海蜇

jeopardize shǐ xiànyú kùnjìng 使陷于困境

jeopardy: be in ~ chǔyú wēixiǎn jìngdì 处于危险地地

jerk¹ 1 n měngrán yídòng 猛然一动 2 v/t měnglā 猛拉

jerk² F chǔnrén 蠢人

jerky movement hūdònghūtíng 忽动忽停

jersey (sweater) jǐnshēn tàoshān 紧身套衫; (fabric) yōují xìmáoshā 优级细毛纱

jest 1 n xiàohuà 笑话; in ~ kāi wánxiào 开玩笑 2 v/i kāi wánxiào 开玩笑

Jesus Yēsū 耶稣

jet 1 n (of water) pēnshèlìú 喷射流; (nozzle) guǎnzuǐ 管嘴; (airplane) pēnqìshì 喷气式 2 v/i (travel) fēi 飞

jet-black hēi yòu liàng 黑又亮; jet engine pēnqì fādòngjī 喷气发动机; jetlag shíchā fǎnyìng 时差反应

jettison tóuqì 投弃; fig fàngqì 放弃

jetty fángbōdī 防波堤

Jew Yóutàirén 犹太人

jewel zhūbǎo 珠宝; fig (person) shòu zhēnshì de rén 受珍视的人

jeweler zhūbǎoshāng 珠宝商

jewelry zhūbǎo 珠宝

Jewish Yóutài 犹太

jiao (*Chinese money*) jiǎo 角

jiffy: *in a ~* F yíhuìr 一会儿

jigsaw (*puzzle*) pīntú yóuxì 拼图游戏

jilt yíqì 遗弃

jingle 1 *n* (*song*) shùnkǒuliū 顺口溜 **2** *v/i* (*of keys, coins*) fā dīngdāngshēng 发叮当声

jinx (*person*) zāixīng 灾星; (*bad luck*) èyùn 厄运; *there's a ~ on this project* zhèige xiàngmù yǒu fáng'rén de dōngxi 这个项目有妨人的东西

jitters: *get the ~* F gǎndào jǐnzhāng 感到紧张

jittery jǐnzhāng 紧张

job (*employment*) gōngzuò 工作; (*task*) rènwù 任务; *out of a ~* shīyè 失业; *it's a good ~ you ...* xìngkuī nǐ ... 幸亏你 ...; *you'll have a ~* (*it'll be difficult*) nǐ yǒu huór gànle 你有活儿干了

job description gōngzuò zhízé shuōmíng 工作职责说明; **job satisfaction** gōngzuò de mǎnzúgǎn 工作的满足感; **job hunt**: *be ~ing* zhǎo gōngzuò 找工作

jobless méi gōngzuò 没工作

jockey *n* qíshī 骑师

jog 1 *n* mànpǎo 慢跑; *go for a ~* qù mànpǎo 去慢跑 **2** *v/i* (*as exercise*) mànpǎo 慢跑 **3** *v/t* elbow *etc* qīngtuī 轻推; *~ X's memory* yǐnqǐ X de huíyì 引起X的回忆

jogger (*person*) mànpǎo de rén 慢跑的人; (*shoe*) yùndòngxié 运动鞋

jogging mànpǎo 慢跑; *go ~* qù mànpǎo 去慢跑

jogging suit yùndòngyī 运动衣

john F (*toilet*) cèsuǒ 厕所

join 1 *v/i* liánjiēchù 联结处 **2** *v/i* (*of roads, rivers*) huìhé 汇合; (*become a member*) cānjiā 参加 **3** *v/t* (*connect*) liánjiē 连接; *person yǔ ... huìmiàn* 与 ... 会面; *club* cānjiā 参加; (*go to work for*) jiārù 加入; (*of road*) huìhé 汇合

♦**join in** cānjiā 参加

♦**join up** MIL cānjūn 参军

joiner mùgōng 木工

joint 1 *n* ANAT guānjié 关节; (*in woodwork*) liánjiēchù 连接处; (*of meat*) dàkuài ròu 大块肉; (*place*) dìfang 地方; (*of cannabis*) dàmáyān 大麻烟 **2** *adj* (*shared*) gòngtóng 共同

joint account liánhé zhànghù 联合帐户; **joint-stock company** gǔfèn gōngsī 股份公司; **joint venture** hézī qǐyè 合资企业

joke 1 *n* (*story*) gùshì 故事; (*practical ~*) xiàohua 笑话; *play a ~ on X* kāi X de wánxiào 开X的玩笑; *it's no ~* bùshì nàozhe wánr de 不是闹着玩儿的 **2** *v/i* (*pretend*) shuō xiàohuà 说笑话; (*having a ~*) yīqǐ shuōxiào 一起说笑

joker (*person*) xiàoxīng 笑星; *pej* shǎguā 傻瓜; (*in cards*) bǎidā 百搭

joking: *~ apart* shuō zhèngjing de 说正经的

jokingly kāi wánxiào 开玩笑

jolly yúkuài 愉快

jolt 1 *n* (*jerk*) diānbǒ 颠簸 **2** *v/t* (*push*) tuī 推

jostle *v/t* tuījǐ 推挤

♦**jot down** cōngcōng jìxià 匆匆记下

journal (*magazine*) zázhì 杂志; (*diary*) rìjì 日记

journalism (*writing*) xīnwén xiězuò 新闻写作; (*trade*) xīnwényè 新闻业

journalist xīnwén gōngzuò zhě 新闻工作者

journey *n* lǚxíng 旅行

joy kuàilè 快乐

jubilant xīnxǐ 欣喜

jubilation huānxīn 欢欣

judge 1 *n* LAW fǎguān 法官; (*in competition*) píngwěi 评委 **2** *v/t* pànduàn 判断; *competition* zuò píngwěi 作评委

judgment LAW cáijué 裁决; (*opinion*) kànfǎ 看法; (*good sense*) juéduànlì 决断力

judicial sīfǎ 司法

judicious míngzhì 明智

judo róudào 柔道

jug hú 壶

juggle wán záshuǎ 玩杂耍；*fig* bēnbō 奔波

juggler wán záshuǎ de rén 玩杂耍的人

juice zhī 汁

juicy duōzhī 多汁；*news, gossip* yǒuqù 有趣

jukebox zìdòng diǎnchàngjī 自动点唱机

July qīyuè 七月

jumble *n* yìtuán 一团

jumble up húluànde hùnzài yìqǐ 胡乱地混在一起

jump 1 *n* tiào 跳；(*increase*) tūzēng 突增；**give a ~** (*of surprise*) xiàrényìtiào 吓人一跳 2 *v/i* tiào 跳；(*in surprise*) jīngtiào 惊跳；(*increase*) měngzēng 猛增；**~ to one's feet** zhàn qǐlái zhàn qǐlái 站起来；**~ to conclusions** cōngcōng zuò juédìng 匆匆做决定 3 *v/t fence etc* tiàoyuè 跳跃；F (*attack*) tūrán gōngjī 突然攻击

♦ **jump at** *opportunity* pòbùjídài de zhuāzhù 迫不急待地抓住

jumper (SP: *person*) tiàoyuè de rén 跳跃的人

jumpy jǐnzhāng 紧张

junction (*of roads*) jiāochā lùkǒu 交叉路口

June liùyuè 六月

jungle cónglín 丛林

junior 1 *adj* (*subordinate*) dìwèi dī 地位低；(*younger*) dī 低 2 *n* (*in rank*) dìwèi jiào dī zhě 地位较低者；**she is ten years my ~** tā bǐ wǒ xiǎo shísuì 她比我小十岁

junk fèipǐn 废品；(*boat*) fānchuán 帆船

junk food ⇩ kuàicān 快餐

junkie yǒu dúyǐn zhě 有毒瘾者

junk mail lājī yóujiàn 垃圾邮件

junkyard fèipǐnzhàn 废品站

jurisdiction LAW sīfǎquán 司法权

juror péishěnyuán 陪审员

jury péishěntuán 陪审团

just 1 *adj law* gōngzhèng 公正；*war, cause* zhèngyì 正义 2 *adv* (*barely*) gānggāng 刚刚；(*exactly*) qiàhǎo 恰好；(*only*) zhǐshì 只是；**I've ~ seen her** wǒ gānggāng kàndào tā 我刚刚看到她；**~ about** (*almost*) jīhū 几乎；**I was ~ about to leave when ...** wǒ zhèngyào líkāi, zhèshí ... 我正要离开，这时 ...；**~ like that** (*abruptly*) mòmíng qí miào 莫名其妙；(*exactly like that*) jiù nèiyàng 就那样；**~ now** (*a few moments ago*) gānggāi cáng 刚才；(*at the moment*) xiànzài 现在；**~ you wait!** nǐ děngzhe ba! 你等着吧！；**~ be quiet!** bié chūshēng! 别出声！

justice gōngpíng 公平；(*of cause*) zhèngyì 正义

justifiable kě zhèngmíng wéi zhèngdāng 可证明为正当

justifiably yǒu lǐyóu 有理由

justification zhèngdāng lǐyóu 正当理由

justify zhèngmíng ... shì zhèngdāng 证明 ... 是正当；*text* shēnmíng yuányóu 申明缘由

justly (*fairly*) gōngzhèng 公正；(*rightly*) zhèngquè 正确

♦ **jut out** *v/i* shēnchū 伸出

juvenile 1 *adj* wèi chéngnián 未成年；*pej* yòuzhì 幼稚 2 *n fml* wèi chéngnián zhě 未成年者

juvenile delinquency shàonián fànzuì 少年犯罪

juvenile delinquent shàoniánfàn 少年犯

K

k (= **kilobyte**) qiānzìjié 千字节; (= **thousand**) qiān 千

karaoke kǎlā O K 卡拉 OK

karate kōngshǒudào 空手道

karate chop zhǎngcèpī 空手道的掌侧劈

Kazakh 1 *adj* Hāsàkèsītǎn 哈萨克斯坦 2 *n* (*person*) Hāsàkèsītǎn rén 哈萨克斯坦人

Kazakhstan Hāsàkèsītǎn 哈萨克斯坦

keel *n* NAUT lónggǔ 龙骨

keen rèqiè 热切; (*intense*) qiángliè 强烈

keep 1 *n* (*maintenance*) shēngjì 生计; *for ~s* F yǒngyuǎn 永远 2 *v/t* bǎoliú 保留; (*not give back*) yǒngyǒu 拥有; (*not lose*) bǎozhù 保住; (*detain*) zǔdǎng 阻挡; (*in specific place*) cúnfàng 存放; *family* gōngyǎng 供养; *animals* yǎng 养; *~ a promise* bǎoshǒu chéngnuò 保守承诺; *~ ... company* péibàn ... 陪伴 ...; *~ X waiting* ràng X děng 让 X 等; *~ ... to oneself* (*not tell*) bǎ ... bǎozhù mìmì 把 ... 保住秘密; *~ X from Y* bùràng Y zhīdào X 不让 Y 知道 X; *~ on trying* jìxù chángshì 继续尝试; *~ on interrupting* zǒngshì gānrǎo 总是干扰 3 *v/i* (*remain*) bǎochí 保持; (*of food, milk*) bǎozhì 保质

♦ keep away 1 *v/i* bú kàojìn 不靠近; *~ from X* bié kàojìn X 别靠近 X 2 *v/t* shǐ rén bú kàojìn 使人不靠近

♦ keep back *v/t* (*hold in check*) zǔzhǐ 阻止; *information* yǐnmán 隐瞒

♦ keep down *v/t* *voice, noise* yādī 压低; *costs, inflation etc* bǎochí dīshuǐpíng 保持低水平; *food* tūnxià 吞下

♦ keep in (*in hospital*) liúzài 留在; (*in school*) fá xuéshēng liúxiào 罚学生留校

♦ keep off 1 *v/t* (*avoid*) bìmiǎn 避免; *~ the grass!* wùtà cǎopíng! 勿踏草坪! 2 *v/i* (*of rain*) wèixià wèixià 未下

♦ keep out *v/i* bìkāi 避开; *~!* (*as sign*) xiánrén miǎnjìn! 闲人免进!

♦ keep to *path, rules* zūnxún 遵循

♦ keep up *v/i* (*when walking, running etc*) gēnshàng 跟上 2 *v/t* *pace, payments* gēnshang 跟上; *bridge* zhīchēng 支撑; *pants* tí提

♦ keep up with *tóngsù shàngshēng* 同速上升; (*stay in touch with*) yǔ X bǎochí liánxì 与 X 保持联系

keeping: *in ~ with* yízhì 一致

keg xiǎotǒng 小桶

kennel gǒuwō 狗窝

kennels yǎnggǒuchǎng 养狗场

kernel héxīn 核心

kerosene méiyóu 煤油

ketchup fānqiéjiàng 番茄酱

kettle hú壶

key 1 *n* (*to door, drawer*) yàoshi 钥匙; COMPUT, MUS jiàn 键 2 *adj* (*vital*) guānjiàn 关键 3 *v/t* COMPUT jiànrù 键入

♦ key in *data* yòng jiànpán shūrù 用键盘输入

keyboard COMPUT, MUS jiànpán 键盘; keyboarder COMPUT cāozuò jiànpán de rén 操作键盘的人; keycard yàoshi kǎ 钥匙卡; keyed-up jǐnzhāng 紧张; keyhole suǒkǒng 锁孔; keynote speech dìng jīdiào de yǎnshuō 定基调的演说; keyring yàoshiquān 钥匙圈

kick 1 *n* tī踢; F (*thrill*) kuàigǎn 快感; (*just*) *for ~s* F wèile qǔlè 为了取乐 2 *v/t* tī踢; F *habit* jièchú 戒

除 3 v/i tī 踢

♦ **kick around** v/t ball tīzhewánr 踢着玩儿；(treat harshly) shuānnòng 耍弄；F (discuss) shāngtán 商谈

♦ **kick in** v/t F money gòngxiàn 贡献 2 v/i (of boiler etc) qǐdòng 开始启动

♦ **kick off** v/i kāiqiú 开球；F (start) kāishǐ 开始

♦ **kick out** qūzhú 驱逐；**be kicked out of the company / army** bèi qūzhúchū gōngsī / bùduì 被驱逐出公司 / 部队

♦ **kick up**: ~ **a fuss** nàoshì 闹事
kickback F (bribe) huíkòu 回扣
kickoff F kāiqiú 开球
kid 1 n (child) xiǎoháir 小孩儿；~ **brother / sister** dìdi / mèimei 弟弟 / 妹妹 2 v/t kāi wánxiào 开玩笑 3 v/i kāi wánxiào 开玩笑；**I was only ~ding** wǒ zhǐshì zài kāi wánxiào 我只是在开玩笑
kidder F huì kāi wánxiào de rén 会开玩笑的人
kidnap bǎngjià 绑架
kidnap(p)er bǎngjià zhě 绑架者
kidnap(p)ing bǎngjià 绑架
kidney ANAT shèn 肾；(food) yāozi 腰子
kill v/t shāsǐ 杀死；plant nòngsǐ 弄死；time xiāomó 消磨；**be ~ed in an accident** zài shìgù zhōng sàngshēng 在事故中丧生；~ **oneself** zìshā 自杀
killer (murderer) xiōngshǒu 凶手；(cause of death) zhìmìngde dōngxi 致命的东西
killing móushā 谋杀；**make a ~** (lots of money) dàzǒucáiyùn 大走财运
killingly: ~ **funny** F jíwéiyǒuqù 极为有趣
kiln yáo 窑
kilo gōngjīn 公斤
kilobyte qiānzìjié 千字节；**kilogram** gōngjīn 公斤；**kilometer** gōnglǐ 公里
kimono héfú 和服
kind¹ adj yǒuhǎo 友好
kind² n zhǒnglèi 种类；(make) pǐnpái 品牌；**what ~ of ...?** shén-

meyàngde ...？什么样的 ...？；**all ~s of people** gèzhǒnggèyàngde rén 各种各样的人；**nothing of the ~** háowú xiāngsì zhīchù 毫无相似之处；~ **of sad / strange** F yǒudiǎnr nánguò / qíguài 有点儿难过 / 奇怪
kindergarten yòu'éryuán 幼儿园
kind-hearted hǎoxīn de rén 好心
kindly 1 adj yǒuhǎo 友好 2 adv réncí 仁慈；(please) qǐng qǐng 请请
kindness hǎoyì 好意
king guówáng 国王
kingdom wángguó 王国
king-size(d) F tèdà 特大
kink (in hose etc) niǔjié 扭结
kinky F biàntài 变态
kiosk shòuhuòtíng 售货亭
Kirg(h)iz 1 adj Jíěrjísī 吉尔吉斯 **2** n (person) Jíěrjísī rén 吉尔吉斯人；(language) Jíěrjísī yǔ 吉尔吉斯语
kiss 1 n wěn 吻 **2** v/t wěn 吻 **3** v/i qīnwěn 亲吻
kit (equipment) chéngtào yòngpǐn 成套用品；(for assembly) zǔzhuāngjiàn 组装件
kitchen chúfáng 厨房
kitchenette xiǎochúfáng 小厨房
kitchen sink: **everything but the ~** F chúle guōtái 除了锅台
kite fēngzheng 风筝；**fly a ~** fàng fēngzheng 放风筝
kitten xiǎomāo 小猫
kitty (fund) gòngtóngde zījīn 共同的资金
klutz F (clumsy person) bènzhuóde rén 笨拙的人
KMT Guómíndǎng 国民党
knack juéqiào 诀窍
knead dough róu 揉
knee n xī 膝
kneecap n xīgàigǔ 膝盖骨
kneel guìxià 跪下
knick-knacks xiǎoshìwù 小饰物
knife 1 n dāo 刀 **2** v/t yòngdāocì 用刀刺
knit 1 v/t zhī 织 **2** v/i biānzhī 编织
♦ **knit together** (of broken bone) láogùde zhǎngzài yìqǐ 牢固地长在一起

knitting (*something being knitted*) biānzhīwù 编织物; (*activity*) biānzhī 编织

knitwear zhēnzhī yīfú 针织衣服

knob (*on door*) lāshǒu 拉手

knock 1 n (*on door*) qiāo 敲; (*blow*) zhuàngjī 撞击 **2** v/t (*hit*) jī 击; F (*criticize*) pīpíng 批评 **3** v/i (*on the door*) qiāo 敲

♦**knock around 1** v/t (*beat*) cūbàode dǎ 粗暴地打 **2** v/i F (*travel*) mànyóu 漫游

♦**knock down** (*of car*) zhuàngdǎo zài dìshang 撞倒在地上; *object, building etc* chāichú 拆除; F (*reduce the price of*) jiàngjià 降价

♦**knock out** (*make unconscious*) shǐ hūnmí 使昏迷; (*of medicine*) mázuì 麻醉; *power lines etc* jīdǎo 击倒

♦**knock over** bàndǎo 绊倒; (*of car*) zhuàngdǎo 撞倒

knockdown: *a ~ price* dīlián 低廉

knockout n (*in boxing*) jīdǎo 击倒; (*competition*) táotàisài 淘汰赛

knot 1 n jié 结 **2** v/t dǎjié 打结

knotty *problem* jíshǒu 棘手

know zhīdao 知道; *person* rènshi 认识; *place* shúxī 熟悉; *language* dǒng 懂; (*recognize*) rènchū 认出 **2** v/i: *I don't ~* wǒ bù zhīdào 我不知道; *yes, I ~* shì, wǒ zhīdào 是,我知道 **3** n: *be in the ~* xiāoxī

língtōng 消息灵通

knowhow jìnéng 技能

knowing xīnzhào bù xuān 心照不宣

knowingly (*wittingly*) zhīxī 知悉; *smile etc* xīnzhào bù xuān 心照不宣

know-it-all F zì yǐwéi wúsuǒbùzhī de rén 自以为无所不知的人

knowledge zhīshí 知识; *to the best of my ~* jùwǒsuǒzhī 据我所知; *have a good ~ of X* jīngtōng X 精通 X

knowledgeable zàiháng 在行

knuckle zhǐguānjié 指关节

♦**knuckle down** káishǐ rènzhēn gōngzuò 开始认真工作

♦**knuckle under** qūfú 屈服

KO jīdǎo 击倒

Korea (*South*) Nán Hán 南韩; (*North*) Běi Cháoxiǎn 北朝鲜

Korean 1 *adj* (*South*) Nán Hán 南韩; (*North*) Běi Cháoxiǎn 北朝鲜 **2** n (*South*) Nán Hán rén 南韩人; (*North*) Běi Cháoxiǎn rén 北朝鲜人; (*language*) Cháoxiǎn yǔ 朝鲜语

kosher REL hélí 合礼; F zhèngdāng 正当

Kowloon Jiǔlóng 九龙

kudos róngyù 荣誉

kung-fu gōngfu 功夫

Kyrgyzstan Jíěrjísī 吉尔吉斯

L

lab shíyàn shì 实验室
label 1 n biāoqiān 标签 **2** v/t baggage tiē biāoqiān 贴标签
labor n (work) láodòng 劳动; (workers) gōngrén 工人; (in pregnancy) fēnmiǎn 分娩; **be in ~** zài fēnmiǎn zhōng 在分娩中
laboratory shíyàn shì 实验室
laboratory technician shíyàn shì jìshī 实验室技师
Labor Day Láodòngjié 劳动节
labored style, speech bú zìrán 不自然
laborer láodòng zhě 劳动者
laborious (difficult) fèilì 费力
labor union gōnghuì 工会
labor ward chǎnfáng 产房
lace 1 n (material) huābiān 花边; (for shoe) xiédài 鞋带
♦ **lace up** shoes gēdài 绑带
lack 1 n quēshǎo 缺少 **2** v/t quēfá 缺乏 **3** v/i quēfá 缺乏; **be -ing** quēfá quēfá 缺乏
lacquer n (for hair) dìng fàjiāo 定发胶
lacquerware qīqì 漆器
lad xiǎo huǒzi 小伙子
ladder tīzi 梯子
laden zhuāngmǎnle 装满了
ladies room nǚcè 女厕
ladle n cháng bǐngsháo 长柄勺
lady nǚshì 女士
ladybug piáochóng 瓢虫
lag v/t pipes zhuāng wàitào 装外套
♦ **lag behind** luòhòu 落后
lager chénzhǔ píjiǔ 陈贮啤酒
lagoon huánjiāo hú 环礁湖
laidback yōuxián 悠闲
lake hú 湖
lamb (animal) gāoyáng 羔羊; (meat) gāoyáng ròu 羔羊肉
lame person qué 瘸; excuse zhàn búzhù jiǎo 站不住脚
lament 1 n (speech) dàocí 悼词; (song) wǎngē 挽歌; (music) āiyuè 哀乐 **2** v/t wèi ... ér bēitòng 为 ... 而悲痛
lamentable lìngrén wǎnxī 令人惋惜
laminated yóu bópiàn diéchéng 由薄片迭成; **~ glass** céngyā bōli 层压玻璃
lamp dēng 灯
lamppost lùdēng zhù 路灯柱
lampshade dēngzhào 灯罩
land 1 n tǔdì 土地; (shore) lùdì 陆地; (country) guójiā 国家; **by ~** yóu lùlù 由陆路; **on ~** zài lùdì 在陆地; **work on the ~** (as farmer) gàn nónghuó 干农活 **2** v/t airplane zhuólù 着陆; job dédào 得到 **3** v/i (airplane) zhuólù 着陆; (ball, something thrown) luò luò 落落
landing (of airplane) zhuólù 着陆; (top of staircase) (lóutī) píngtái (楼梯) 平台
landing field fēijī qǐjiàng chǎng 飞机起降场; **landing gear** qǐluò zhuāngzhì 起落装置; **landing strip** jiǎnbiàn jīchǎng 简便机场
landlady (of bar) lǎobǎnniáng 老板娘; (of apartment etc) fángdōng 房东; **landlord** (of bar) lǎobǎn 老板; (of apartment etc) fángdōng 房东; **landmark** lùbiāo 路标; fig lǐchéng bēi 里程碑; **land owner** dìzhǔ 地主; **landscape 1** n fēngjǐng 风景; (painting) fēngjǐng huà 风景画 **2** adv print héngpái 横排; **landslide** níshí liú 泥石流; **landslide victory** yādào duōshù de xuǎnpiào 压倒多数的选票
lane (in country) xiǎoxiàng 小巷; (alley) hútòng 胡同; (on freeway) hángdào 行道
language yǔyán 语言
lank hair píngzhí 平直

lanky

lanky *person* yòushòu yòugāo 又瘦又高

lantern dēnglóng 灯笼

Lantern Festival Yuánxiāojié 元宵节

Lao Lǎowō yǔ 老挝语

Laos ⇩ Lǎowō 老挝

Laotian 1 *adj* Lǎowō 老挝 **2** *n* (*person*) Lǎowō rén 老挝人

lap[1] *n* (*of track*) quān 圈

lap[2] *n* (*of water*) pōlàng pāidǎ shēng 波浪拍打声

♦ **lap up** *drink, milk* tiǎn 舔; *flattery* xīnrán jiēshòu 欣然接受

lap[3] *n* (*of person*) dàtuǐ 大腿

lapel fānlǐng 翻领

laptop COMPUT ⇩ xiédài shì diànnǎo 携带式电脑

larceny tōuqiè 偷窃

lard zhūyóu 猪油

larder shípǐn chǔcáng shì 食品储藏室

large *building, country, hands, head* dà 大; *sum of money* duō 多; **at ~** (*of criminal*) xiāoyáo fǎwài 逍遥法外; (*of wild animal*) wèi bèibǔ 未被捕

largely (*mainly*) zhǔyào 主要

lark (*bird*) yúnquè 云雀

larva yòuchóng 幼虫

laryngitis hóuyán 喉炎

larynx yānhóu 咽喉

laser jīguāng 激光

laser beam jīguāng guāngshù 激光光束

laser printer jīguāng dǎyìn jī 激光打印机

lash[1] *v/t* (*with whip*) biāndǎ 鞭打

♦ **lash down** (*with rope*) bǎngzhù 绑住

lash[2] *n* (*eyelash*) yǎn jiémáo 眼睫毛

last[1] *adj* (*in series*) zuìhòu 最后; (*preceding*) shàng yīcì 上一次; **~ but one** dàoshǔ dì'èrgè 倒数第二个; **~ night** zuówǎn 昨晚; **~ but not least** zuìhòu dàn bìngfēi zuì bú zhòngyàode 最后但并非最不重要的; **at ~** zhōngyú 终于; **Last Emperor** Mòdài Huángdì 末代皇帝

last[2] *v/i* chíxù 持续

lastly zuìhòu 最后

latch *n* ménshuān 门闩

late (*behind time*) chídào 迟到; (*in day*) wǎn 晚; **it's getting ~** yǐjīng wǎn le 已经晚了; **of ~** zuìjìn 最近; **the ~ 19th/20th century** shíjiǔ/èrshí shìjì mòqī 十九/二十世纪末期

lately zuìjìn 最近

later *adv* hòulái 后来; **see you ~!** yìhuǐr jiàn! 一会儿见！; **~ on** yǐhòu 以后, hòulái 后来

latest *news, girlfriend* zuìxīn 最新

lathe chēchuáng 车床

lather (*from soap*) pàomòr 泡沫儿; (*sweat*) hànmòr 汗沫儿

Latin America Lādīng Měizhōu 拉丁美洲

Latin American 1 *adj* Lādīng Měizhōu 拉丁美洲 **2** *n* Lādīng Měizhōu rén 拉丁美洲人

latitude (*geographical*) wěidù 纬度; (*freedom to maneuver*) kuānróng dù 宽容度

latter hòuzhě 后者

laugh 1 *n* xiàoshēng 笑声; **it was a ~** kāiwánxiào 开玩笑 **2** *v/i* xiào 笑

♦ **laugh at** cháoxiào 嘲笑

laughing stock: make oneself a ~ shǐ zìjǐ chéngwéi xiàobǐng 使自己成为笑柄; **become a ~** biànchéng xiàobǐng 变成笑柄

laughter xiàoshēng 笑声

launch 1 *n* (*boat, without engine*) xiǎochuán 小船; (*with engine*) xiǎotǐng 小艇; (*of rocket*) fāshè 发射; (*of ship*) xiàshuǐ 下水; (*of product*) fāxíng 发行 **2** *v/t rocket* fāshè 发射; *ship* shǐchuán xiàshuǐ 使船下水; *new product* fāxíng 发行

launch(ing) ceremony (*for new product*) fāxíng qìngzhù 发行庆祝

launch(ing) pad fāshè tái 发射台

launder xǐ 洗

laundromat zìzhù xǐyī diàn 自助洗衣店

laundry (*place*) xǐyī diàn 洗衣店;

(*clothes*) yīwù 衣物; **get one's ~ done** xǐ yīfu 洗衣服

laurel yuèguì 月桂

lavatory (*place*) cèsuǒ 厕所; (*equipment*) mǎtǒng 马桶

lavender xūnyīcǎo 熏衣草

lavish *adj* huīhuò 挥霍

law fǎlìng 法令; (*as subject*) fǎlǜ 法律; **against the ~** fànfǎ 犯法; **forbidden by ~** fǎlǜ bùzhǔn 法律不准

law court fǎtíng 法庭

lawful héfǎ 合法

lawless méiyǒu fǎjì 没有法纪

lawn cǎopíng 草坪

lawn mower gēcǎo jī 割草机

lawsuit sùsòng 诉讼

lawyer lǜshī 律师

lax sōngkuǎ 松垮

laxative *n* tōngxiè yào 通泄药

lay *v/t* (*put down*) fàngxià 放下; *eggs* xià 下; V (*sexually*) shuì 睡

♦ **lay into** (*attack*) tòngdǎ 痛打

♦ **lay off** *workers* jiěgù 解雇

♦ **lay on** (*provide*) zhǔnbèi 准备

♦ **lay out** *objects* ānpái 安排; *page* zhǎnkāi 展开

lay-by (*on road*) lùpáng tíngchē chù 路旁停车处

layer *n* céng 层

layman fēi zhuānyè rényuán 非专业人员

layout *n* bùjú 布局; COMPUT géshì 格式

♦ **laze around** lǎnsǎn 懒散

lazy *person* lǎn 懒; *day* lǎnsǎn 令人懒散

lb (= **pound**(*s*)) bàng 磅

LCD (= **liquid crystal display**) yèjīngtǐ xiǎnshìqì 液晶体显示器

lead¹ 1 *v/t procession, race* lǐngtóu 领头; *company, team* lǐngdǎo 领导; (*guide, take*) dàilǐng 带领 **2** *v/i* (*in race, competition*) lǐngxiān 领先; (*provide leadership*) lǐngdǎo 领导; *a street ~ing off the square* cóng guǎngchǎng fāchū de yìtiáo jiē 从广场发出的一条街; **where is this ~ing?** zhè yǐndào nǎr? 这引到哪儿? **3** *n* (*in race*)

lǐngxiān 领先; **be in the ~** lǐngxiān 领先; **take the ~** jū shǒuwèi 居首位; **lose the ~** luòhòu 落后

♦ **lead on** (*go in front*) zǒuzài qiánmiàn 走在前面

♦ **lead up to** yǐndào 引到

lead² *n* (*for dog*) jiāngshéng 缰绳

lead³ *n* (*substance*) qiān 铅

leader lǐngxiù 领袖

leadership (*of party etc*) lǐngdǎo dìwèi 领导地位; **under his ~** zài tāde lǐngdǎo xià 在他的领导下; **skills of ~** lǐngdǎo jìqiǎo 领导技巧

leadership contest lǐngdǎo dìwèi jìngzhēng 领导地位竞争

lead-free *gas* bù hán qiān 不含铅

leading *adj runner* dìyī 第一; *company, product* lǐngxiān 领先

leading-edge *adj technology* lǐngxiān 领先

leaf yèzi 叶子

♦ **leaf through** fānyuè 翻阅

leaflet dānzhāng 单张

league (*group*) liánméng 联盟; (*in sport*) liánsài 联赛

leak 1 *n* lòulòu 漏; (*of information*) xièlòu 泄漏 **2** *v/i* lòulòu 漏

♦ **leak out** (*of air, gas*) lòuqì 漏气; (*of news*) xièlòu 泄漏

leaky *pipe, boat* lòulòu 漏

lean¹ 1 *v/i* (*be at an angle*) wāi 歪; **~ against X** kàozhe X 靠着 X **2** *v/t* kàozhe kào X 靠 X kàozài Y shàng 把 X 靠在 Y 上

lean² *adj meat* shòu 瘦; *style, prose* jiǎnjié 简洁

leap 1 *n* tiào 跳; **a great ~ forward** jìnle yī dàbù 进了一大步 **2** *v/i* tiào 跳

leap year rùnnián 闰年

learn xuéxí 学习; **~ how to do X** xuéxí zuò X 学习做 X

learner xuéshēng 学生

learning *n* (*knowledge*) zhīshì 知识; (*act*) xuéxí 学习

learning curve xuéxí qūxiàn 学习曲线; **be on the ~** zài xuéxí qūxiàn shàng 在学习曲线上

lease 1 *n* zūqì 租契 **2** *v/t apartment, equipment* zū 租

♦lease out zūchū 租出

lease purchase zūjiè gòumǎi 租借购买

leash n (for dog) jiāngsheng 缰绳

least 1 adj movement zuì qīngwēi 最轻微; reason zuìxiǎo 最小; amount zuìshǎo 最少 2 adv zuìbù 最不 3 n zuìshào 最少; not in the ~ surprised / disappointed yìbù yěbù qíguài / shīwàng 一点也不奇怪 / 失望; at ~ zhìshǎo 至少

leather n & adj pí pí

leave 1 n (vacation) jiàqī 假期; on ~ fàngjià 放假 2 v/t city, place líkāi 离开; person yǔ … fēnshǒu 与 … 分手; husband, wife pāoqì 抛弃; food on plate shèngxia 剩下; scar, memory liúxià 留下; (forget, leave behind) wàngjì 忘记; let's ~ things as they are xiànzài jiù zhèyàng ba 现在就这样吧; how did you ~ things with him? nǐ zěnme hé tā jiāodài de nǐ zěnme hé tā jiāodài de 你怎么和他交待的 ？; ~ X alone (not touch) biépèng X bié pèng X; (not interfere with) bù dǎjiǎo 不打搅; (not damage) bié nònghuài le bié nònghuài le 别弄坏了; be left shèngxia 剩下; there is nothing left méishèng shénme 没剩什么 2 v/i (of person) líkāi 离开; (of airplane) qǐfēi 起飞; (of train, bus) chūfā 出发; (of ship) qǐháng 启航

♦leave behind (intentionally) yíliú 遗留; (forget) yíwàng 遗忘

♦leave on hat dàizhe 带着; coat chuānzhe 穿着; TV, computer biéguān 别关

♦leave out word, figure shěnglüè 省略; (not put away) liúzhe 留着; leave me out of this bié suànwǒ 别算我

leaving party gàobié huì 告别会

lecture 1 n jiǎngzuò 讲座 2 v/i (at university) jiāo 教

lecture hall jiǎngyǎn tīng 讲演厅

lecturer jiǎngshī 讲师

LED (= light-emitting diode) fāguāng èrjí guǎn 发光二极管

ledge (on rock face) yánjiāo 岩礁; (of window) chuāngtái 窗台

ledger COM zǒngzhàng 总帐

leek jiǔcōng 韭葱

leer n (sexual) xiéshì 邪视; (evil) hán èyìde yìpiē 含恶意的一瞥

left 1 adj zuǒ 左 2 n zuǒbiān 左边; POL zuǒpài 左派; on the ~ zài zuǒbiān 在左边; on the ~ of … zài … de zuǒbiān 在 … 的左边; to the ~ turn, look zài zuǒcè 在左侧 3 adv turn, look zài zuǒcè 在左侧

left-hand zài zuǒbiān 在左边; bend zài zuǒbiān 左边; left-hand drive zuǒbiān jiàshǐ chē 左边驾驶车; left-handed guànyòng zuǒshǒu de 惯用左手的; left-overs (food) shèngcài 剩菜; left-wing POL zuǒyì 左翼

leg tuǐ 腿; pull X's ~ gēn X kāi wánxiào 跟 X 开玩笑

legacy yíchǎn 遗产

legal (allowed) héfǎ 合法; (relating to the law) fǎlǜ 法律

legal adviser fǎlǜ zīxún yuán 法律咨询员

legalism (philosophy) fǎjiā 法家

legalist philosophy fǎjiā 法家

legality héfǎ xìng 合法性

legalize shǐhéfǎ 使合法

legend chuánshuō 传说

legendary chūmíng 出名

legible yìbiànrèn 易辨认

legislate lìfǎ 立法

legislation (laws) fǎguī 法规; (passing of laws) lìfǎ guòchéng 立法过程

legislative powers lìfǎ 立法; assembly yǒu lìfǎ quán 有立法权

legislature POL lìfǎ jīgòu 立法机构

legitimate héfǎ 合法

leg room shēnjiǎo kōngjiān 伸脚空间

leisure kòngxián 空闲; at your ~ yǒu kòng shí 有空时

leisure center yúlè zhōngxīn 娱乐中心

leisurely pace cóngróng 从容

leisure time kòngyú shíjiān 空余时间

lemon níngméng 柠檬

lemonade níngméng shuǐ 柠檬水

lemon juice níngméng zhīr 柠檬汁儿

lemon tea níngméng chá 柠檬茶

lend: ~ *X to Y* jiègěi Y X 借给 Y X

length chángdù 长度; (*piece: of material etc*) yíduàn 一段; *at ~ describe, explain* xiángxì de 详细地; (*eventually*) zuìzhōng 最终

lengthen shǐ biàncháng 使变长

lengthy *speech* rōngcháng 冗长; *stay* mànchángs 漫长

lenient kuāndà 宽大

Lenin Lièníng 列宁

lens (*of camera*) jìngtóu jìngtóu 镜头; (*contact lens, of eyeglasses, of eye*) yǎnjìng 眼镜

lens cover (*of camera*) jìngtóu gài 镜头盖

Lent Dàzhāijié 大斋节

lentil bīngdòu 兵豆

lentil soup bīngdòutāng 兵豆汤

leopard bào 豹

leotard jǐnshēnyī 紧身衣

lesbian *n* nǚtóng xìngliàn zhě 女同性恋者

less: *eat* / *talk* ~ shǎo chī / shuō 少吃 / 说; ~ *interesting* / *serious* méi nàme yǒuqù / rènzhēn 没那么有趣 / 认真; *it cost* ~ bǐjiào piányi 比较便宜; ~ *than $200* shǎoyú liǎngbǎi měiyuán 少于两百美元

lesson kè 课

let *v/t* (*allow*) ràng 让; ~ *X do Y* ràng X zuò Y 让 X 做 Y; ~ *me go!* ràng wǒ zǒu! 让我走!; ~ *him come in* ràng tā jìnlái 让他进来; ~*'s go* / *stay* wǒmén zǒu ba / bùzǒu ba 我们走吧 / 不走吧; ~*'s not argue* wǒmén bié cháole 我们别吵了; ~ *alone* gèng bù yòng shuō 更不用说; ~ *go of* (*of rope, handle*) fàngkāi 放开
♦ **let down** *hair* fàngsōng 放松; *blinds* fàngxià 放下; *skirt, pants* fànchángs 放长; *let X down* (*disappoint*) ràng X shīwàng 让 X 失望
♦ **let in:** *let X in* (*to house*) ràng X jìnlái 让 X 进来
♦ **let off** (*not punish*) fàngguò 放过;

(*from car*) xiàchē 下车
♦ **let out** (*of room, building*) chūzū 出租; *jacket etc* fàngdà 放大; ~ *a cry* shīshēng 失声
♦ **let up** *v/i* (*stop*) tíngzhǐ 停止

lethal zhìmìng 致命

lethargic lǎnsàn 懒散

letter (*of alphabet*) zìmǔ 字母; (*in mail*) xìnjiàn 信件

letterhead (*heading*) xìnzhǐ táitóu 信纸台头; (*headed paper*) táitóu xìnzhǐ 台头信纸

letter of credit COM shāngyè xìnyòng shū 商业信用书

lettuce shēngcài yè 生菜叶

letup: *without a* ~ méiyǒu zhōngzhǐ 没有中止

leukemia báixuè bìng 白血病

level *1 adj field, surface* píngtǎn 平坦; (*in competition, scores*) bìngjìn 并进; *draw* ~ *with* ... hé ... lāpíng hé ... lāpíng 和 ... 拉平 *2 n* (*on scale*) shuǐpíng 水平; (*in hierarchy*) jíbié 级别; (*amount, quantity*) lǜ lǜ 率; (*of alcohol in blood etc*) nóngdù 浓度; *on the* ~ (*on level ground*) zài píngmiàn shàng 在平面上; (*honest*) tǎnshuài 坦率

level-headed tóunǎo lěngjìng 头脑冷静

lever *1 n* gànggǎn 杠杆 *2 v/t* yòng gànggǎn yídòng 用杠杆儿移动; ~ *X open* bǎ X qiàokāi 把 X 撬开

leverage gànggǎn lìliàng 杠杆儿力量; (*influence*) yǐngxiǎng 影响

levy *v/t taxes* zhēngshōu 征收

lewd yínwěi 淫猥

Lhasa Lāsà 拉萨

liability (*responsibility*) zérèn 责任; (*likeliness*) kěnéng xìng 可能性

liability insurance dìsān fāng bǎoxiǎn 第三方保险

liable (*answerable*) fùzé 负责; *be* ~ *to* (*likely*) yǒu kěnéng 有可能
♦ **liaise with** yǔ ... jiànlì liánxì 与 ... 建立联系

liaison (*contacts*) liánluò 联络

liar shuōhuǎng zhě 说谎者

libel *n & v/t* fěibàng 诽谤

liberal *adj* (*broad-minded*) dàfāng 大方

liberate 大方; (*generous: portion etc*) kāngkǎi 慷慨; POL zìyóu 自由

liberate jiěfàng 解放

liberated *woman* bèi jiěfàng 被解放

liberty zìyóu 自由; *at ~* (*prisoner etc*) huòdé zìyóu 获得自由; *be at ~ to do X* yǒu quánlìzuò X 有权利做 X

librarian túshū guǎnyuán 图书馆员

library túshūguǎn 图书馆

Libya Lìbǐyà 利比亚

Libyan 1 *adj* Lìbǐyà 利比亚 **2** *n* Lìbǐyà rén 利比亚人

license 1 *n* zhízhào 执照 **2** *v/t bar* xǔkě 许可; *a company to produce ...* xǔkě gōngsī shēngchǎn ... 许可公司生产...

license number zhízhào hàomǎ 执照号码

license plate (*of car*) chēpái 车牌

lick 1 *n* shétiǎn 舌舔 **2** *v/t* tiǎn 舔; *~ one's lips* chuíxián 垂涎

licking: *get a ~* F (*defeat*) bèi dǎbài 被打败

lid gàizi 盖子

lie[1] *n* (*untruth*) huǎnghuà 谎话 **2** *v/i* shuō huǎnghuà 说谎话

lie[2] *v/i* (*of person: on back*) tǎng 躺; (*on stomach*) pā 趴; (*of object*) píng fàngzhe 平放着; (*be situated*) wèiyú 位于

♦ **lie down** tǎngxià 躺下

lie-in: *have a ~ Br* shuì lǎnjiào 睡懒觉

lieutenant zhōngwèi 中尉

life shēngmìng 生命; (*of machine*) shòumìng 寿命; *all her ~* tā yī bèizi shēn ... 她一辈子; *that's ~!* zhè jiùshì rénshēng! 这就是人生！

life belt jiùshēng quān 救生圈;
lifeboat jiùshēng tǐng 救生艇;
life expectancy yùqī shòumìng 预期寿命; **lifeguard** jiùshēng yuán 救生员; **life history** shēnghuó shǐ 生活史; **life insurance** rénshòu bǎoxiǎn 人寿保险; **life jacket** jiùshēng yī 救生衣

lifeless wú shēngmìng 无生命

lifelike shēngdòng 生动; **lifelong** zhōngshēn 终身; **life preserver** (*for swimmer*) shuǐshàng jiùshēng gōngjù 水上救生工具; **life-saving** *adj medical equipment, drug* jiùshēng 救生; **lifesized** yǔ yuánwù yībān dàxiǎo 与原物一般大小; **life-threatening** yǒu shēngmìng wēixiǎn 有生命危险; **lifetime** shòumìng 寿命; *in my ~* zài wǒ yìshēng zhōng 在我一生中

lift 1 *v/t* jǔqǐ 举起 **2** *v/i* (*fog*) xiāosàn 消散 **3** *n* (*Br: elevator*) diàntī 电梯; (*in car*) dā biànchē 搭便车; *give X a ~* ràng X dāchē 让 X 搭车

♦ **lift off** *v/i* (*of rocket*) fāshè 发射

ligament rèndài 韧带

light[1] **1** *n* guāngxiàn 光线; (*lamp*) dēng 灯; *in the ~ of* jiànyú 鉴于; *have you got a ~?* kěyǐ jiègè huǒ ma? 可以借个火吗？**2** *v/t fire, cigarette* diǎnhuǒ 点火; (*illuminate*) zhàomíng 照明 **3** *adj* (*not dark*) míngliàng 明亮

♦ **light up 1** *v/t* (*illuminate*) zhàoliàng 照亮 **2** *v/i* (*start to smoke*) diǎnyān 点烟

light[2] **1** *adj* (*not heavy*) qīngqīng 轻 **2** *adv:* *travel ~* méi shénme xíngli 没什么行李

light bulb diàndēng pào 电灯泡

lighten[1] *v/t color* huǎnhé 缓和

lighten[2] *v/t load* shǐ biànqīng 使变轻

♦ **lighten up** (*of person*) fàngsōng 放松

lighter (*for cigarettes*) dǎhuǒ jī 打火机

light-headed (*dizzy*) yūnxuàn 晕眩; **light-hearted** xiǎngdekāi 想得开; **lighthouse** dēngtǎ 灯塔

lighting zhàomíng 照明

lightly *touch* qīngqīng 轻轻; *get off ~* táotuō chéngfá 轻易逃脱惩罚

lightness[1] (*of room, color*) yōuyǎ 优雅

lightness[2] (*in weight*) qīngqīng 轻

lightning shǎndiàn 闪电

lightning conductor bìléi dǎoxiàn 避雷导线

light pen guāngbǐ 光笔

lightweight (*in boxing*) qīngliàng jí 轻量级

light year guāngnián 光年

likable kě'ài 可爱

like[1] **1** *prep* xiàng 象; *be ~ X* (*in looks, character*) xiàng X 象 x; *what is she ~?* (*in looks, character*) tā zhǎngde shénmeyàng? 她长得什么样？; *it's not ~ him* (*not his character*) bú xiàng tā 不象他 **2** *conj* X (*as*) rú 如; *~ I said* zhèngrú wǒyán 正如我言

like[2] *v/t* xǐhuān 喜欢; *I ~ it* wǒ xǐhuan 我喜欢; *I ~ her* wǒ xǐhuan tā 我喜欢她; *I would ~ ...* wǒ xiǎngyào ... 我想要 ...; *I would ~ to ...* wǒ xīwàng ... 我希望 ...; *would you ~ ... ?* nǐyào ma? 你要 ... 吗？; *would you ~ to ... ?* nǐyào ... ma? 你要 ... 吗？; *~ to do X* xǐhào X 喜好 x; *if you ~* suíbiàn nǐ 随便你

likeable kě'ài 可爱

likelihood kěnéng xìng 可能性; *in all ~* duōbànr 多半儿

likely (*probable*) kěnéng 可能; *not ~!* méiménr! 没门儿！

likeness (*resemblance*) lèisì 类似

liking: to your ~ hé nǐ kǒuwèir 合你口味儿; *take a ~ to X* kāishǐ xǐhuān X 开始喜欢 X

lilac (*flower*) dīngxiāng huā 丁香花; (*color*) dàn zǐsè 淡紫色

lily bǎihé huā 百合花

lily of the valley línglán 铃兰

limbs sìzhī 四肢

lime[1] (*fruit, tree*) suānchéng 酸橙

lime[2] (*substance*) shíhuī 石灰

limegreen lǜhuáng sè 绿黄色

limelight: be in the ~ yǐnrén zhùmù 引人注目

limit 1 *n* xiàndù 限度; *within ~s* zài yídìng fànwéi nèi 在一定范围内; *off ~s* jìnzhǐ rùnèi 禁止入内; *that's the ~!* shízài tài guòfèn le! 实在太过分了！ **2** *v/t* xiànzhì 限制

limitation júxiàn 局限

limited company yǒuxiàn gōngsī 有限公司

limo, limousine gāojí jiàochē 高级轿车

limp[1] *adj material* róuruǎn 柔软; *body* ruò 弱

limp[2] *n* bǒxíng 跛行; *he has a ~* tā bǒxíng 他跛行

line[1] *n* (*on paper, road*) xiàntiáo 线条; TELEC diànhuà xiàn 电话线; (*of people, trees*) pái 排; (*of text*) háng 行; (*of business*) zhíyè 职业; *the ~ is busy* zhànxiàn 占线; *hold the ~* qǐng shāoděng yìhuǐr 请稍等一会儿; *draw the ~ at X* xiànzhì X 限制 X; *~ of inquiry* diàochá fāngfǎ 调查方法; *~ of reasoning* sīlù 思路; *stand in ~* páiduì 排队; *in ~ with ...* (*conforming with*) fúhé ... 符合 ...; *he's out of ~* (*not doing the proper thing*) tā tài guòfènle 他太过分了

line[2] *v/t* (*with material*) ānchènlǐ 安衬里

♦ **line up** *v/i* páiduì 排队

linen (*material*) yàmá bù 亚麻布; (*sheets etc*) chuángshàng yòngpǐn 床上用品

liner (*ship*) bānchuán 班船

linesman SP xúnbiān yuán 巡边员

linger (*of person*) dòuliú 逗留; (*of pain*) áizhe 挨着

lingerie nǚ nèiyī 女内衣

linguist yǔyán xuéjiā 语言学家

linguistic yǔyán 语言

lining (*of clothes*) chènlǐ 衬里; (*of pipe*) chènliào 衬料; (*of brakes*) chèndiàn 衬垫

link 1 *n* (*connection*) liánjiē 连接; (*in chain*) yìjié 一节 **2** *v/t* liánjiē 连接

♦ **link up** *v/i* huìhé 会合; TV liánjiē 联接

lion shīzi 狮子

lip zuǐchún 嘴唇

lipread *v/i* chúndú 唇读

lipstick kǒuhóng 口红

liqueur lìkǒu jiǔ 利口酒

liquid 1 *n* yètǐ 液体 **2** *adj* yèzhuàng 液状

liquidation qīngsuàn 清算; *go into*

~ **pòchǎn** 破产

liquidity liúdòng chǎn liúdòng chǎn 流动产

liquor jiǔjīng yǐnliào 酒精饮料

liquorice gāncǎo 甘草

liquor store mài jiǔdiàn 卖酒店

lisp 1 n kǒuchī bùqīng 口齿不清 **2** v/i kǒuchī bùqīng de shuōhuà 口齿不清地说话

list 1 n yìlán biǎo 一览表 **2** v/t biānliè 编列

listen tīng 听

◆ **listen in** pángtīng 旁听

◆ **listen to** radio, person tīng 听

listener (to radio) tīngzhòng 听众; **he's a good ~** tā hěn liúxīn tīng tā 他很留心听

listings magazine jiémù biǎo 节目表

listless wújīng dǎcǎi 无精打采

liter gōngshēng 公升

literal wánquán yīzhào yuánwén 完全依照原文; **~ translation** zhíyì 直译

literary wénxué 文学

literate: **be ~** yǒu wénhuà 有文化

literature wénxué 文学

litter lājī 垃圾; (of animal) yīwō 一窝

little 1 adj xiǎo 小; **the ~ ones** xiǎo péngyǒu 小朋友 **2** n shǎoxǔ 少许; **the ~ I know** wǒ suǒ zhīdào de nà yī diǎndian 我所知道的那一点点; **a ~** yīdiǎn 一点; **a ~ bread** yīdiǎn miànbāo/jiǔ 一点面包/酒; **a ~ is better than nothing** zǒng bǐ méiyǒu yào qiáng 总比没有要强 **3** adv shāoxǔ 稍许; **a ~ better/bigger** hǎo/dà yīdiǎn 好/大一点; **a ~ before 6** bǐ liùdiǎn zǎo yīdiǎn 比六点早一点

Little Red Book Máo Zhǔxí Yǔlù 毛主席语录

live[1] v/i (reside) zhùzài 住在; (be alive) shēnghuó 生活

◆ **live on 1** v/t rice, bread kào … shēnghuó 靠…生活 **2** v/i (continue living) huó xiàqù 活下去

◆ **live up**: **live it up** kuánghuān 狂欢

◆ **live up to** bú kuìyú 不愧于

◆ **live with**: **~ X** (with a person) hé X tóngjū 和X同居

live[2] adj broadcast shíkuàng 实况; **~ ammunition** shídàn 实弹

livelihood shēngjì 生计

lively huópo 活泼

liver MED gānzàng 肝藏; (food) gān 肝

livestock shēngchù 牲畜

livid (angry) fēicháng shēngqì 非常生气

living 1 adj huóde 活的 **2** n móushēng 谋生; **earn one's ~** móushēng 谋生; **standard of ~** shēnghuó shuǐpíng 生活水平

living room kètīng 客厅

lizard xīyì 蜥蜴

load 1 n fùdān 负担; ELEC fùzài 负载; **~s of** dàliàng 大量, truck zhuāng 装; camera zhuāng jiāojuǎn 装胶卷; gun zhuāng dànyào 装弹药; COMPUT: software zhuāng ruǎnjiàn 装软件; **~ X onto Y** bǎ X zhuāngdào Y shàng 把X装到Y上

loaded F (very rich) hěn yǒuqián 很有钱; (drunk) hēzuì le 喝醉了

loaf cháng miànbāo 长面包; **a ~ of bread** yīgè miànbāo 一个面包

◆ **loaf around** yóushǒu hàoxián 游手好闲

loafer (shoe) píngdǐ píbiànxié 平底皮便鞋

loan 1 n dàikuǎn 贷款; **on ~** jièyòng 借用 **2** v/t jiè qián 借; **~ X Y** jiègěi X Y 借给X Y

loathe tǎoyàn 讨厌

lobby (in hotel, theater) méntīng 门厅; POL yuànwài huódòng jítuán 院外活动集团

lobster lóngxiā 龙虾

local 1 adj dìfang 地方; **I'm not ~** wǒ bùshì běndìde 我不是本地的 **2** n (person) běndì rén 本地人

local anesthetic júmá 局麻; **local call** TELEC qūnèi diànhuà 区内电话; **local government** dìfang zhèngfǔ 地方政府

locality suǒzàiqū 所在区

locally live, work zài dāngdì 在当

地

local produce dāngdì tèchǎn 当地特产

local time dāngdì shíjiān 当地时间

locate *new factory etc* shèzhì 设置; (*identify position of*) zhǎochū 找出; **be ~d** zài mǒuchù 在某处

location (*siting*) dìngwèi 定位; (*identifying position of*) wèizhì 位置; **on ~** *movie* wàijǐng 外景

lock¹ (*of hair*) lǚ 缕

lock² **1** *n* (*on door*) suǒ 锁 **2** *v/t door* suǒ 锁; **~ X in position** bǎ X gùdìng 把 X 固定

♦**lock away** suǒ qǐlái 锁起来

♦**lock in** *person* suǒ zài lǐmiàn 锁在里面

♦**lock out** (*of house*) suǒzài wàimiàn 锁在外面; **I've locked myself out** wǒ bǎ zìjǐ suǒ zài ménwài le 我把自己锁在门外了

♦**lock up** (*in prison*) jūjìn 拘禁

locker yǒu suǒguì 有锁柜

locket xiǎo hé 小盒

locksmith suǒjiàng 锁匠

locust huángchóng 蝗虫

lodge 1 *v/t complaint* shēnsù 申诉 **2** *v/i* (*of bullet, ball*) qiǎzhù 卡住

lodger fángkè 房客

loft gélóu 阁楼

lofty *heights* wēi'é 巍峨; *ideals* gāo'ào 高傲

log (*wood*) yuánmù 圆木; (*written record*) jìlù 记录

♦**log off** (*from computer system*) xiàjī 下机; (*from network, database*) xiàwǎng 下网

♦**log on** (*to computer system*) shàngjī 上机; (*to network, database*) shàngwǎng 上网

♦**log on to** *computer system* shàngjī 上机; *network, database* shàngwǎng 上网

logbook rìzhì 日志

log cabin mùwū 木屋

logic luóji 逻辑

logical yǒu luóji 有逻辑

logistics hòuqín xué 后勤学

logo biāozhì 标志

loiter xiánguàng 闲逛

London Lúndūn 伦敦

loneliness (*of person*) gūdú gǎn 孤独感; (*of place*) jìmò gǎn 寂寞感

lonely *person* gūdú 孤独; *place* jìmò 寂寞

loner bù héqún de rén 不合群的人

long¹ **1** *adj road, leg time, wait* cháng 长; *journey* yuǎnde 远的; **it's a ~ way** hěnyuǎn a 很远啊 **2** *adv* chángjiǔ 长久; **don't be ~** kuàidiǎn huílái 快点儿回来; **5 weeks is too ~** wǔge xīngqī tàicháng le 五个星期太长了; **will it take ~?** shìbùshì yào hěn cháng shíjiān? 是不是要很长时间?; **that was ~ ago** nàshì hěnjiǔ yǐqián le 那是很久以前了; **~ before then** lǎozǎo 老早; **before ~** bùjiǔ 不久; **we can't wait any ~er** wǒmén bùnéng zài děng le 我们不能再等了; **he no ~er works here** tā búzài zhèlǐ gōngzuò le 他不在这里工作了; **so ~ as** (*provided*) zhǐyào 只要; **so ~!** mànzǒu! 慢走!

long² *v/i*: **~ for X** pànwàng X 盼望 X; **be ~ing to do X** kěwàng zuò X 渴望做 X

long-distance *adj phonecall* chángtú 长途; *race, flight* yuǎn jùlí 远距离

longing *n* kěwàng 渴望

longitude jīngdù 经度

long jump tiàoyuǎn 跳远; **Long March** Chángzhēng 长征; **long-range** *missile* yuǎnchéng 远程; *forecast* chángyuǎn 长远; **long-sighted** yuǎnshì 远视; **long-sleeved** chángxiù 长袖; **long-standing** chángjiǔ chíxù 长久持续; **long-term** *adj* chángqī 长期; **long wave** chángpō 长波

loo *Br* cèsuǒ 厕所

look 1 *n* (*appearance*) wàiguān 外观; (*glance*) kàn kàn 看看; **give X a ~** kàn X yíyǎn 看 X 一眼; **have a ~ at X** (*examine*) kànyíkàn X 看一看 X; **can I have a ~?** wǒ néng kàn yíxià ma? 我能看一下吗?; **can I**

have a ~ around? wǒ néng kànkan ma? 我能看看吗？；*~s (beauty)* měimào 美貌 2 *v/i* kàn 看；*(search)* xúnzhǎo 寻找；*(seem)* sìhū 似乎；*you ~ tired / different* nǐ kànqǐlái hěn lèi / bù yíyàng 你看起来很累 / 不一样

♦**look after** zhàogù 照顾

♦**look around** *museum, city* guānguāng 观光

♦**look at** kàn 看；*(examine)* jiǎnchá 检查；*(consider)* kàn 看

♦**look back** huígù 回顾

♦**look down on** kànbùqǐ 看不起

♦**look for** zhǎo 找

♦**look forward to** qīdài 期待

♦**look in on** *(visit)* shùnbiàn kànwàng 顺便看望

♦**look into** *(investigate)* diàochá 调查

♦**look on 1** *v/i (watch)* pángguān 旁观 **2** *v/t: ~ X as (consider)* bǎ X kànzuò 把 X 看作

♦**look onto** *garden, street* cháoxiàng 朝向

♦**look out** *v/i (of window etc)* cháo wàikàn 朝外看；*(pay attention)* liúshén 留神；*~!* xiǎoxīn! 小心！

♦**look out for** xúnzhǎo 寻找；*(be on guard against)* dāngxīn 当心

♦**look out of** *window* cháo wàikàn 朝外看

♦**look over** *house, translation* zǐxì jiǎnchá 仔细检查

♦**look through** *magazine, notes* liúlǎn 浏览

♦**look to** *(rely on)* yīkào 依靠

♦**look up 1** *v/i (from paper etc)* xiàng shàngkàn 向上看；*(improve)* hǎozhuǎn 好转；*things are looking up* yǒu hǎozhuǎn 有好转 **2** *v/t* *word, phone number* chákàn 查看；*(visit)* bàifǎng 拜访

♦**look up to** *(respect)* zūnjìng 尊敬

♦**lookout** *(person)* kānshǒu zhě 看守；*be on the ~ for* xúnzhǎo 寻找

♦**loom up** yǐnyuē di chūxiàn 隐约地出现

loony F **1** *n* fēngzi 疯子 **2** *adj* fēngkuáng 疯狂

loop *n* quān 圈

loophole *(in law etc)* lòudòng 漏洞

loose *connection, wire, button* sōng 松；*clothes* kuānsōng 宽松；*morals* fàngdàng 放荡；*wording* bù yángé 不严格；*~ change* língqián 零钱；*~ ends (of problem, discussion)* shìqíng shàngwèi wánchéng de xìjié 事情尚未完成的细节

loosely *tied* sōngsōng 松松；*worded* bù yángé 不严格

loosen *collar, knot* jiěkāi 解开

loot 1 *n* zāngwù 赃物 **2** *v/i* luèduó 掠夺

looter luèduó zhě 掠夺者

♦**lop off** kǎndiào 砍掉

lop-sided bù pínghéng 不平衡

Lord *(God)* Shàngdì 上帝；*~'s Prayer* Zhǔdǎo Wén 主祷文

lorry *Br* huòchē 货车

lose *v/t object* diūshī 丢失；*match* shū 输；*I'm lost* wǒ mílù le 我迷路了；*get lost!* gǔndàn! 滚蛋！**2** *v/i* SP shūdiào 输掉；*(of clock)* zǒumàn 走慢

♦**lose out** shīlì 失利

loser SP shūzhě 输者；*(in life)* shībài zhě 失败者

loss *(of object)* sǔnshī 损失；*(of loved one)* sàngshī 丧失；*(in business)* kuīsǔn 亏损；*make a ~* kuīsǔn 亏损；*be at a ~* bù zhī suǒcuò 不知所措

lost shīqù 失去

lost-and-found *(office)* shīwù zhāolǐng chù 失物招领处

lot: *a ~, ~s* hěnduō 很多；*a ~ of, ~s of* hěnduō 很多；*a ~ better / a ~ easier* hǎo de duō / róngyì de duō 好得多 / 容易得多

lotion xǐjì 洗剂

loud *music, voice, noise* xiǎng 响；*color* súyàn 俗艳

loudspeaker yángshēng qì 扬声器

♦**lounge around** xiánguàng 闲逛

lounge suit xīzhuāng 西装

louse shīzi 虱子

lousy *meal, weather, vacation* bù zěnme yàng 不怎么样；*thing to do* tǎoyàn 讨厌；*I feel ~* wǒ bù shūfú 我不舒服

lout liúmáng 流氓

lovable kě'ài 可爱

love 1 n ài 爱; (in tennis) língfēn 零分; be in ~ zài liàn'ài zhīzhōng 在恋爱之中; fall in ~ with àishàng 爱上; make ~ zuò'ài 作爱; yes, my ~ hǎode, wǒ qīn àide 好的，我亲爱的 2 v/t person, country, wine ài 爱; ~ to do X xǐ ài zuò X 喜欢作 X

love affair fēngliú yùnshì 风流韵事; lovelife àiqíng shēnghuó 爱情生活; love letter qíngshū 情书

lovely face, hair měilì 美丽; color piàoliang 漂亮; tune yōuměi 优美; person, meal hěn hǎo 很好; vacation, weather lìngrén yúkuài 令人愉快; we had a ~ time wǒmen kě kāixīn le 我们可开心了

lover qíngrén 情人

loving adj zhōngqíng 钟情

low 1 adj bridge, wall ǎi 矮; salary, price, voice dī 低; quality chà 差; be feeling ~ gǎndào qíngxù bùhǎo 感到情绪不好; be ~ on gas/tea méi duōshǎo méiqì/cháyè 没多少煤气/茶叶 2 n (in weather) dīqìyā qū 低气压区; (in sales, statistics) zuì dīdiǎn 最低点

lowbrow adj quēfá wénhuà sùyǎng 缺乏文化素养; low-calorie dī kǎlùlǐ 低卡路里; low-cut dress dī língkǒu 低领口

lower boat, something to the ground fàngxià 放下; flag jiàng 降; hemline fàng 放; pressure, price jiàngdī 降低

low-fat dīzhīfáng 低脂肪; lowkey dīdiào 低调; lowlands dīdì 低地; low-pressure area dīyā dìqū 低压地区; low season dànjì 淡季; low tide dīcháo 低潮

loyal zhōngxīn 忠心

lozenge (shape) língxíng 菱形; (tablet) zhǐké táng 止咳糖

Ltd (= limited) yǒuxiàn gōngsī 有限公司

lubricant rùnhuá jì 润滑剂

lubricate rùnhuá 润滑

lubrication rùnhuá 润滑

lucid (clear) míngliǎo 明了; (sane) shénzhì qīngxǐng 神志清醒

luck yùnqì 运气; bad ~ èyùn 恶运; hard ~! dǎoméi! 倒霉！; good ~ xìngyùn 幸运; good ~! zhùnǐ zǒuyùn! 祝你走运！

◆luck out F jiǎoxìng chénggōng 侥幸成功

luckily xìngyùnde 幸运地

lucky person xìngyùn 幸运; day, number jíxiáng 吉祥; coincidence jiǎoxìng 侥幸; you were ~ nǐ zhēn zǒuyùn 你真走运; he's ~ to be alive tā jiǎoxìng déyǐ táoshēng 他侥幸得以逃生; that's ~! zhēn zǒuyùn! 真走运！

ludicrous huāngtáng 荒唐

luggage xíngli 行李

lukewarm water wēiwēn 微温; reception bú rèqíng 不热情

lull 1 n (in storm, fighting) zànshí píngxī 暂时平息; (in conversation) jiànxiē 间歇; ~ X into a false sense of security shǐ X chǎnshēng bù zhēnshíde ānquán gǎn 使 X 产生不真实的安全感

lullaby cuīmián qǔ 催眠曲

lumbago yāoténg 腰疼

lumber n (timber) mùcái 木材

luminous guāngmíng 光明

lump (of sugar) kuài 块; (swelling) zhǒngkuài 肿块

◆lump together bǎ … guībìng zài yìqǐ 把 … 归并在一起

lump sum zǒng'é 总额

lumpy āotū bùpíng 凹凸不平

lunacy jíduān yúchǔn 极端愚蠢

lunar yuèliang 月亮

lunatic n fēngzi 疯子

lunch wǔcān 午餐; have ~ chī wǔcān 吃午餐

lunch box ⇩ wǔcān hé 午餐盒; lunch break wǔxiū 午休; lunch hour wǔxiū 午休; lunchtime wǔcān shíjiān 午餐时间

lung fèi 肺

lung cancer fèi'ái 肺癌

◆lunge at chōngjī 冲击

lurch v/i (of person) pánshān 蹒跚; (of ship) qīngxié 倾斜

lure *n* & *v/t* yòuhuò 诱惑
lurid *color* huǒhóng 火红; *details* sòngrén tīngwén 耸人听闻
lurk (*of person*) qiáncáng 潜藏; (*of doubt*) qiánzài 潜在
luscious *fruit, dessert* gānměi 甘美; *woman, man* xìnggǎn 性感
lust *n* xìngyù 性欲

luxurious háohuá 豪华
luxury *n* & *adj* háohuá 豪华
lychee lìzhī 荔枝
lymph gland línbājié 淋巴结
lynch sīxíng chùsǐ 私刑处死
lynx shānmāo 山猫
lyricist cí zuòzhě 词作者
lyrics gēcí 歌词

M

MA (= *Master of Arts*) wénkē shuòshì 文科硕士
ma'am nǚshì 女士
Macanese 1 *adj* Àomén 澳门 2 *n* (*person*) Àomén rén 澳门人
Macao Àomén 澳门
machine 1 *n* jīqì 机器 2 *v/t* (*on sewing machine*) féngrènjī 缝纫机; TECH jīzhì 机制
machine gun *n* jīqiāng 机枪
machine-readable kě jídú 可机读
machinery (*machines*) jīqì 机器
machismo nánzǐ qìgài 男子气概
macho dànánzǐqì 大男子气
mackintosh yǔyī 雨衣
macro COMPUT hóng huìbiān 宏汇编
mad (*insane*) fēng 疯; (*angry*) nǎohuǒ 恼火; be ~ about X (*keen on*) duì X zháomí 对X着迷; drive X ~ shǐ X fāfēng 使X发疯; go ~ (*become insane*) fāfēng 发疯; (*with enthusiasm*) kuángrèqǐlái 狂热起来; like ~ run, work pīnmìng 拼命
madden (*infuriate*) shǐrén nǎohuǒ 使人恼火
maddening shǐrén nǎohuǒ 使人恼火
made-to-measure dìngzuò 定做
madhouse *fig* yí piàn hùnluàn 一片混乱
madly fēngkuáng 疯狂; ~ in love rèliàn 热恋
madman fēngrén 疯人
madness jīngshén shīcháng 精神失常
Mafia: the ~ hēishǒudǎng 黑手党
magazine (*printed*) zázhì 杂志
maggot qū 蛆
magic 1 *n* mófǎ 魔法; (*tricks*) móshù 魔术; like ~ móshùbān 魔术般 2 *adj* juémiào 绝妙
magical *powers* mófǎ 魔法;

moment miàobùkěyán 妙不可言
magician (*performer*) móshùshī 魔术师
magic spell fúzhòu 符咒
magic trick móshù 魔术
magnanimous kāngkǎi 慷慨
magnet císhí 磁石
magnetic yǒucíxìng 有磁性; *fig*: *personality* yǒumèilì 有魅力
magnetism (*of person*) mèilì 魅力
magnificence zhuànglì 壮丽
magnificent zhuàngguān 壮观
magnify fàngdà 放大; *difficulties* kuādà 夸大
magnifying glass fàngdàjìng 放大镜
magnitude dàxiǎo 大小
magpie xǐquè 喜鹊
mah-jong májiàng 麻将
maid nǚpú 女仆; (*in hotel*) fúwùyuán 服务员
maiden name niángjiāxìng 娘家姓
maiden voyage shǒuháng 首航
mail 1 *n* yóuzhèng 邮政; put X in the ~ yóujì X 邮寄X 2 *v/t letter* yóujì 邮寄; *person* yóudìyuán 邮递员
mailbox (*in street*) yóutǒng 邮筒; (*for house, e-mail*) xìnxiāng 信箱
mailman yóudìyuán 邮递员
mail-order catalog yóugòu mùlù 邮购目录; mail-order firm yóugòu shāngpǐn gōngsī 邮购商品公司
maim zhìcán 致残
main *adj* zhǔyào 主要
mainboard COMPUT zhǔbǎn 主板; mainframe COMPUT zhǔjītǐ 主机体; mainland dàlù 大陆; on the ~ zài dàlù shang 在大陆上; mainland China Zhōngguó dàlù 中国大陆
mainly zhǔyào 主要

main road dàlù 大路

main street zhǔjiē 主街

maintain *peace, law and order* wéichí 维持; *pace, speed, ship* bǎochí 保持; *machine, house* bǎoyǎng 保养; *family* gōngyǎng 供养; *innocence, guilt* jiānchí 坚持; **~ that** duànyán 断言

maintenance *(of machine, house)* bǎoyǎng 保养; *(money)* fǔyǎngfèi 抚养费; *(of law and order)* wéihù 维护

majestic wēiyán 威严

major 1 *adj (significant)* zhǔyào 主要; *in C ~* MUS C dàdiào C 大调 **2** *n* MIL shàoxiào 少校

♦**major in** zhǔxiū 主修

majority dàduōshù 大多数; POL duōdéde piàoshù 多得的票数; **be in the ~** zhàn duōshù 占多数

make 1 *n (brand)* páizi 牌子 **2** *v/t* zuò 做; *(earn)* zhèng 挣; MATH děngyú 等于; **~ X do Y** *(force to)* pòshǐ X zuò Y 迫使 X 做 Y; *(cause to)* cùshǐ X zuò Y 促使 X 做 Y; **you can't ~ me do it** nǐ bùnéng pòshǐ wǒ zuò zhèijiànshì 你不能迫使我做这件事; **~ X happy / angry** shǐ X gāoxìng / shēngqì 使 X 高兴 / 生气; **~ a decision** zuò juédìng 做决定; **~ a telephone call** dǎ ge diànhuà 打个电话; **made in China** Zhōngguó zhìzào 中国制造; **~ it** *(catch bus, train)* gǎnshàng 赶上; *(succeed)* huòdé chénggōng 获得成功; *(survive)* cúnhuó 存活; **sorry, I can't ~ it tomorrow** *(come)* duìbùqǐ, wǒ míngr qùbùliǎo 对不起，我明儿去不了; **what time do you ~ it?** nǐ biǎo jǐdiǎnle? 你表几点了？; **~ believe** jiǎzhuāng 假装; **~ do with X** yòng X jiāngjiù 用 X 将就; **what do you ~ of it?** nǐ juédé zěnmeyàng? 你觉得怎么样？

♦**make for: ~ X** *(go toward)* cháo X yídòng 朝 X 移动

♦**make off** táozǒu 逃走

♦**make off with** *(steal)* tōuzǒu 偷走

♦**make out** *list* xiěchū 写出; *check*

kāichū 开出; *(see)* biànrèn 辨认; *(imply)* ànshì 暗示

♦**make over: make X over to Y** bǎ X zhuǎnràng gěi Y 把 X 转让给 Y

♦**make up 1** *v/i (of woman, actor)* huàzhuāng 化妆; *(after quarrel)* héjiě 和解 **2** *v/t story, excuse* biānzào 编造; *face* huàzhuāng 化妆; *(constitute)* zhàn 占; **be made up of X** yóu X zǔchéng 由 X 组成; **~ one's mind** xià juéxīn 下决心; **make it up** *(after quarrel)* héhǎo 和好

♦**make up for** míbǔ 弥补

♦**make-believe** *n* jiǎxiǎng 假想

maker zhìzào zhě 制造者

makeshift dàiyòngpǐn 代用品

make-up *(cosmetics)* huàzhuāngpǐn 化妆品

maladjusted xīnlǐ shītiáo 心理失调

malaria nüèjí 疟疾

Malay *(person)* Mǎláixīyà rén 马来西亚人; *(language)* Mǎlái yǔ 马来语

Malaysia Mǎláixīyà 马来西亚

Malaysian Mǎláixīyà 马来西亚

male 1 *adj (masculine)* nánxìng 男性; *animal, bird, fish* xióng, gōng 雄, 公 **2** *n (man)* nánrén 男人; *(animal, bird, fish)* xióngxìng 雄性

male chauvinist *(pig)* dànánzǐ zhǔyì zhě 大男子主义者

male nurse nán hùshi 男护士

malevolent èdú 恶毒

malfunction 1 *n* shīlíng 失灵 **2** *v/i* fāshēng gùzhàng 发生故障

malice èyì 恶意

malicious èyì 恶意

malignant *tumor* èxìng 恶性

mall *(shopping ~)* gòuwù zhōngxīn 购物中心

malnutrition yíngyǎng bùliáng 营养不良

malpractice wánhūzhíshǒu 玩忽职守

maltreat nüèdài 虐待

maltreatment nüèdài 虐待

mammal bǔrǔ dòngwù 哺乳动物

mammoth *adj (enormous)* jùdà 巨大

man n nánrén 男人; (*human being*) rén 人; (*humanity*) rénlèi 人类; (*in checkers*) qízǐ 棋子

manage 1 v/t *business* jīngyíng 经营; *money* guǎn 管; *suitcase* nádòng ná拿动; **~ to ...** zuòchéng ... 做成... **2** v/i (*cope*) yìngfù 应付; (*financially*) wéichí shēnghuó 维持生活; **can you ~?** nǐ néngxíng ma? 你能行吗？

manageable yì chǔlǐ 易处理

management (*managing*) guǎnlǐ 管理; (*managers*) zhǔguǎn rényuán 主管人员; **under his ~** zài tāde guǎnlǐ xià 在他的管理下

management buyout guǎnlǐ rényuán shōumǎi guǎnlǐ rényuán 管理人员收买; **management consultant** jīngyíng gùwèn 经营顾问; **management studies** guǎnlǐxué 管理学; **management team** guǎnlǐ rényuán 管理人员

manager jīnglǐ 经理

managerial jīngyíng 经营

managing director zǒngjīnglǐ 总经理

Manchu (*nationality*) Mǎnzú 满族

Manchuria Mǎnzhōu 满洲

Mandarin (*language*) ⇩ Pǔtōnghuà 普通话

mandarin (*in China*) guānlì 官吏

mandarin orange júzi 橘子

mandate (*authority*) shòuquán 授权; (*task*) shǐmìng 使命

mandatory qiángzhì 强制

mane (*of horse*) zōng 鬃

maneuver 1 n xíngdòng 行动 **2** v/t *vehicle* dǎfǎ yídòng 设法移动

mangle v/t (*crush*) huǐhuài 毁坏

manhandle *person* cūbàode duìdài 粗暴地对待; *object* yònglì yídòng 用力移动

manhood (*maturity*) chéngnián 成年; (*virility*) nánzǐhànqì 男子汉气

man-hour gōngzuò shí 工作时

mania (*craze*) pǐhào 癖好

maniac kuángrén 狂人

manicure n xiūjiǎn zhǐjiǎ 修剪指甲

manifest 1 adj míngxiǎn 明显

2 v/t xuānyán 宣言; **~ itself** xiǎnlù 显露

manipulate *person* bǎibù 摆布; *bones* jiǎozhèng 矫正; *equipment* cāozòng 操纵

manipulation (*of person*) bǎibù 摆布; (*of bones*) jiǎozhèng 矫正

manipulative ài cāozòng rén 爱操纵人

mankind rénlèi 人类

manly yǒu nánzǐqì 有男子气

man-made rénzào 人造

mannequin (*for clothes*) réntǐ móxíng 人体模型

manner (*of doing sth*) fāngshì 方式; (*attitude*) tàidù 态度

manners: **good/bad ~** yǒu/méiyǒu lǐmào 有/没有礼貌; **have no ~** méilǐmào 没礼貌

manpower láodònglì 劳动力

mansion zháidì 宅第

mantelpiece, mantelshelf bìlútái 壁炉台

manual 1 adj shǒugōng 手工 **2** n zhǐnán 指南

manufacture 1 n zhìzào 制造 **2** v/t *equipment* zhìzào 制造

manufacturer zhìzàoshāng 制造商

manufacturing (*industry*) zhìzào 制造

manure féiliào 肥料

manuscript shǒugǎo 手稿

many 1 adj xǔduō 许多; **~ times** xǔduō cì 许多次; **not ~ people/taxis** méiyǒu duōshao rén/chūzūchē 没有多少人/出租车; **too ~ problems/beers** tàiduō wèntí/píjiǔ 太多问题/啤酒 **2** pron xǔduō rén 许多人; **a great ~, a good ~** xiāngdāng duō 相当多; **how ~ do you need?** nǐ xūyào duōshao? 你需要多少？

mao (*Chinese money*) máo 毛

Mao badge Máo Zhǔxí xiàngzhāng 毛主席像章; **Mao jacket** Zhōngshānfú 中山服; **Mao Tse-tung, Mao Zedong** Máo Zédōng 毛泽东; **Mao Zedong thought** Máo Zédōng sīxiǎng 毛泽东思想

map 504

map *n* dìtú 地图
♦map out chóuhuà 筹划
maple fēng 枫
mar pòhuài 破坏
marathon (*race*) mǎlāsōng 马拉松
marble (*material*) dàlǐshí 大理石
March sānyuè 三月
march 1 *n* xíngjūn 行军;
(*demonstration*) yóuxíng 游行
2 *v/i* (*in protest*) yóuxíng 游行
mare mǔmǎ 母马
margarine rénzào huángyóu 人造
黄油
margin (*of page*) kòngbái 空白;
(COM: *profit margin*) yínglì 盈利;
by a narrow ~ hěnxiǎode chāshù
很小的差数
marginal (*slight*) hěnxiǎo 很小
marginally (*slightly*) shāowēi 稍微
marihuana, marijuana dàmá 大
麻
marina yóutǐng tíngbó gǎng 游艇
停泊港
marinade *n* yānpàozhī 腌泡汁
marinate yānpào 腌泡
marine 1 *adj* hǎiyáng 海洋 2 *n* MIL
hǎilùbīng 海陆兵
marital hūnyīn 婚姻
maritime hǎishàng 海上
mark 1 *n* (*stain*) wūdiǎn 污点;
(*sign, token*) biāozhì 标志; (*trace*)
jìxiàng 迹象; EDU fēnshù 分数;
leave one's ~ liúxià chíjiǔ yìnxiàng 留下持久印象 2 *v/t* (*stain*)
liú hénjī yú liú hénjī 留下痕迹于; EDU pīgǎi
批改; (*indicate*) biāomíng 标明;
(*commemorate*) jìniàn 纪念 3 *v/i*
(*of fabric*) liúyóu wūjì 留有污迹
♦mark down *goods* jiàngdī biāojià
降低标价
♦mark out (*with a line etc*) huàxiàn
biāochū 划线标出; *mark X out*
fig (*set apart*) shǐ X yǔ zhòng
bùtóng 使X与众不同
♦mark up *price* tígāo biāojià 提高
标价; *goods* zài chéngběn shang
jiājià 在成本上加价
marked (*definite*) míngquè 明确
marker (*highlighter*) biāojìbǐ 标记
笔
market 1 *n* jíshì 集市; (*for*

particular commodity) shìchǎng 市
场; (*outlet*) xíngxiāo dìqū 行销地
区; (*stock ~*) zhèngquàn shìchǎng
证券市场; *on the ~* shàngshì 上
市 2 *v/t* xiāoshòu 销售
market economy shìchǎng jīngjì
市场经济
market forces shìchǎng lìliàng 市
场力量
marketing tuīxiāo 推销
market leader shìchǎng zhǔdǎo 市
场主导; market-place shìchǎng
市场; market research shìchǎng
diàochá 市场调查; market
share shìchǎng zhànyǒulǜ 市场
占有率
mark-up jiàgé tígāo 价格提高
marmalade chéngzijiàng 橙子酱
marquee dàzhàngpéng 大帐篷
marriage (*institution*) hūnyīnzhì 婚
姻制; (*state of being married*)
hūnyīn 婚姻; (*event*) hūnlǐ 婚礼
marriage certificate jiéhūn
zhèngshū 结婚证书
marriage counselor hūnyīn
gùwèn 婚姻顾问
married yǐhūn 已婚; *be ~ to X* yǔ
X jiéhūn 与X结婚
marry jiéhūn 结婚; (*of priest*)
zhǔchí hūnlǐ 主持婚礼; *get
married* jiéhūn 结婚
marsh zhǎozé 沼泽
marshal *n* (*police officer*) jǐngchá
警察; (*official*) sīyí 司仪
marshmallow miánhuātáng 棉花
糖
martial arts wǔshù 武术
martial law jièyánlìng 戒严令
martyr *n* xùndào zhě 殉道者
martyred miǎnqiǎng 勉强
marvel *n* qíyìde shìwù 奇异的事
物
♦marvel at dàwéijīngyà 大为惊
讶
marvelous jíhǎo 极好
Marx Mǎkèsī 马克思
Marxism Mǎkèsīzhǔyì 马克思主
义
Marxist 1 *adj* Mǎkèsīzhǔyì 马克
思主义 2 *n* Mǎkèsīzhǔyì zhě 马

克思主义者
Marxism-Leninism Mǎlièzhǔyì 马列主义
Marxist-Leninist Mǎlièzhǔyì zhě 马列主义者
mascara jiémáogāo 睫毛膏
mascot jíxiángde rénwù 吉祥的人物
masculine *also* GRAM nánzǐqì 男子气
masculinity (*virility*) yángxìng 阳性
mash v/t dǎochénghúzhuàng 捣成糊状
mashed potatoes tǔdòuní 土豆泥
mask **1** n miànjù 面具 **2** v/t *feelings* yǎngài 掩盖
masochism shòunüèkuáng 受虐狂
masochist shòunüèkuáng zhě 受虐狂者
mason níwǎjiàng 泥瓦匠
masonry (*stonework*) zhuānshí jiégòu 砖石结构; (*skill*) shígōng jìqiǎo 石工技巧
masquerade **1** n fig jiǎzhuāng 假装 **2** v/i: ~ **as X** wěizhuāng wéi X 伪装为 X
mass[1] **1** n (*great amount*) zhòngduō 众多; (*body*) tuán 团; **the ~es** qúnzhòng 群众; **~es of** hěnduō 很多 **2** v/i jíjié 集结
mass[2] REL zuò mísa 作弥撒
massacre **1** n dàtúshā 大屠杀; F (*in sport*) cǎnbài 惨败 **2** v/t túshā 屠杀; F (*in sport*) yǐ xuánshū bǐfēn zhànshèng 以悬殊比分战胜
massage **1** n ànmó 按摩 **2** v/t zuò ànmó 作按摩; *figures* tiáozhěng 调整
massage parlor ànmóyuàn 按摩院
masseur nán ànmóshī 男按摩师
masseuse nán xiǎojiě 男小姐
massive jùdà 巨大
mass media dàzhòng chuánméi 大众传媒; mass-produce dàliàng shēngchǎn 大量生产; mass production dàliàng

shèngchǎn dàliàng shēngchǎn 大量生产
mast (*of ship*) chuánwéi 船桅; (*for radio signal*) tiānxiàntǎ 天线塔
master **1** n (*of dog*) zhǔrén 主人; (*of ship*) chuánzhǎng 船长; **be a ~ of X** zhǎngwò X 掌握 X **2** v/t *skill, language* jīngtōng 精通; *situation* kòngzhì 控制
master bedroom zhǔwòshì 主卧室
master key wànnéng yàoshi 万能钥匙
masterly gāomíng 高明
mastermind **1** n juécè zhě 决策者 **2** v/t mùhòu cèhuà 幕后策划; **Master of Arts** wénkē shuòshì 文科硕士; **master of ceremonies** sīyí 司仪; **masterpiece** jiézuò 杰作; **master's (degree)** shuòshì 硕士
mastery jīngtōng 精通
masturbate shǒuyín 手淫
mat n (*for floor*) diàn diàn 垫; (*for table*) gérèdiàn 隔热垫
match[1] (*for cigarette*) huǒchái 火柴
match[2] **1** n (*competition*) bǐsài 比赛; **be no ~ for X** bùnéng yǔ X pǐdí 不能与 X 匹敌; **meet one's ~** qígǔ xiāngdāng qígǔ 旗鼓相当 **2** v/t (*be the same as*) yǔ ... yīyàng 与 ... 一样; X (*equal*) yǔ X pǐdí yǔ X 匹敌 **3** v/i (*of colors, patterns*) xiāngpèi xiāngpèi 相配
matchbox huǒcháihé 火柴盒
matching adj xiétiáo 协调
mate **1** n (*of animal*) ǒu ǒu 偶; NAUT fùshǒu 副手 **2** v/i jiāopèi 交配
material **1** n (*fabric*) bùliào 布料; (*substance*) cáiliào 材料 **2** adj wùzhì 物质
materialism wéiwù zhǔyì 唯物主义
materialist wéiwù zhǔyì zhě 唯物主义者
materialistic wéiwùlùn 唯物论
materialize chéngxiàn 呈现
materials yuánliào 原料
maternal mǔqīn fāngmiàn 母亲方面
maternity mǔxìng 母性
maternity dress yùnfù fúzhuāng

孕妇服装; **maternity leave**
chǎnjià 产假; **maternity ward**
chǎnkē bìngfáng 产科病房
math shùxué 数学
mathematical *calculations, formula*
shùxué 数学; *mind, person* luóji
逻辑
mathematician shùxuéjiā 数学家
mathematics shùxué 数学
matinée xiàwǔchǎng 下午场
matriarch nǚzúzhǎng 女族长
matrimony hūnyīn 婚姻
matt cūmiàn 粗面
matter (*affair*) shìqíng 事情; PHYS
wùzhì 物质; *as a ~ of course*
lǐsuǒdāngrán 理所当然; *as a ~*
of fact shíshí shang 事实上;
what's the ~? zěnmele? 怎么
了?; *no – what she says* bùguǎn
tā shuō shénme 不管她说什么
2 *v/i* yàojǐn 要紧; *it doesn't ~*
méiguānxi 没关系
matter-of-fact búdònggǎnqíng 不
动感情
mattress chuángdiàn 床垫
mature 1 *adj* chéngshú 成熟 **2** *v/i*
(*of person*) chéngshú 成熟; (*of*
insurance policy etc) dàoqī 到期
maturity chéngshú 成熟
maximize zēngzhì zuìdà xiàndù zēng
至 最大限度
maximum 1 *adj* zuìgāo 最高 /
大 **2** *n* zuìduō 最多
May wǔyuè 五月
may ◇ (*possibility*) yěxǔ 也许; *it ~*
rain kěnéng huì xiàyǔ 可能会下
雨; *you ~ be right* nǐ yěxǔ duì 你
也许对; *it ~ not happen* zhèshìr
kěnéng búhuì fāshēng 这事儿可
能不会发生 ◇ (*permission*) kěyǐ
可以; *~ I help / smoke?* wǒ kěyǐ
bāngmáng / xīyān ma? 我可以帮
忙 / 吸烟吗?; *you ~ if you like*
nǐ yuànyì de huà, kěyǐ 你愿意的
话, 可以
maybe kěnéng 可能
May Day Wǔyī Jié 五一节
mayo, mayonnaise ◇
dànhuángjiàng 蛋黄酱
mayor shìzhǎng 市长
maze mígōng 迷宫; *fig* qūjìng 曲

径
MB (= *megabyte*) zhàozìjié 兆字
节
MBA (= *Master of Business Ad-*
ministration) ◇ gōngshāng
guǎnlǐxué shuòshì 工商管理学
硕士
MBO (= *management buyout*)
guǎnlǐ rényuán shōumǎi 管理人
员收买
MD (= *Doctor of Medicine*) dàifu
大夫
me wǒ 我; *it's ~* shì wǒ 是我
meadow cǎopíng 草坪
meager shǎoliàng 少量
meal cān 餐
mealtime jìncān shíjiān 进餐时间
mean[1] (*with money*) lìnsè 吝啬;
(*nasty*) bēibǐ 卑鄙
mean[2] **1** *v/t* (*intend*) yìzhǐ 意指;
(*signify*) biǎoshì 表示; *~ to do X*
dǎsuàn zuò X 打算做 X; *be ~t for*
(*of remark*) zhǐdìng 指定; *be ~t*
for X yǒuyì wèi X zhǔnbèi 有意
为 X 准备; *doesn't it ~ anything*
to you? (*doesn't it matter?*) zhè
nándào yǔ nǐ wúguān ma? 这难
道与你无关吗? **2** *v/i*: *~ well*
huái hǎoyì 怀好意
meaning (*of word*) hányì 含义
meaningful (*comprehensible*) yǒu
yìyì 有意义; (*constructive*) jījí积
极; *glance* yìwèi shēncháng 意味
深长
meaningless *sentence etc* wúyìyì 无
意义; *gesture* kōngdòng 空洞
means (*financial*) cáiyuán 财源;
(*way*) fāngfǎ 方法; *~ of transport*
jiāotōng gōngjù 交通工具; *by all*
~ (*certainly*) dāngrán kěyǐ 当然可
以; *by no ~ rich / poor* gēnběn bù
fù / qióng 根本不富 / 穷; *by ~ of*
yòng 用
meantime: *in the ~* tóngshí 同时
measles mázhěn 麻疹
measure 1 *n* (*step*) cuòshī 措施;
(*certain amount*) chéngdù 程度
2 *v/t* cèliáng 测量 **3** *v/i* (*of*
length etc) ... cháng / kuān 长 / 宽; *it ~s 15*
yards by 5 yards cháng shíwǔ mǎ,
kuān wǔ mǎ 长十五码, 宽五码

♦measure out liángchū 量出

♦measure up to: ~ **X** dádào X de biāozhǔn 达到 X 的标准

measurement (action) cèliáng 测量; (dimension) chǐcun 尺寸; **system of ~** dùliánghéng 度量衡

meat ròu 肉

meatball ròuwánzi 肉丸子

meatloaf ròugāo 肉糕

mechanic jìgōng 技工

mechanical device jīxiè 机械; gesture dāibǎn 呆板

mechanically jīxiè 机械; do sth dāibǎn 呆板

mechanism jīxiè zhuāngzhì 机械装置

mechanize shǐ jīxièhuà 使机械化

medal jiǎngzhāng 奖章

medalist jiǎngzhāng huòdé zhě 奖章获得者

meddle gānshè 干涉

media: **the ~** dàzhòng chuánméi 大众传媒

media hype méitǐ xuànrǎn 媒体渲染

median strip zhōngyāng fēnchēdài 中央分车带

mediate tiáojiě 调解

mediation tiáojiě 调解

mediator tiáojiěrén 调解人

medical 1 adj yīliáo 医疗 2 n tǐgé jiǎnchá 体格检查

medical certificate jiànkāng zhèngshū 健康证书

Medicare yīliáo bǎozhàng fāng'àn 医疗保障方案

medicated hán yàowù 含药物

medication yào 药

medicinal yǒu yàoxìng 有药性

medicine (science) yīxué 医学; (medication) yào 药

medieval zhōngshìjì 中世纪

mediocre píngyōng 平庸

mediocrity (of work etc) píngyōng 平庸; (person) píngyōngde rén 平庸的人

meditate dǎzuò 打坐

meditation dǎzuò 打坐

medium 1 adj (average) zhōngděng 中等; steak bāfēnshóu 八分熟 2 n (in size) zhōnghào 中号;

(vehicle) méijiè 媒介; (spiritualist) língméi 灵媒

medium-sized zhōnghào 中号

medium wave RAD zhōngbō 中波

medley (assortment) hùnhé 混合

meek wēnshùn 温顺

meet 1 v/t jiàn 见; (collect) jiē 接; (of eyes) xiāngyù 相遇; (satisfy) dádào 达到; ~ **X** (in competition) yǔ X bǐsài 与 X 比赛 2 v/i jiànmiàn 见面; (in competition) bǐsài 比赛; (of eyes) xiāngyù 相遇; (of committee etc) jùhé 聚合 3 n SP yùndònghuì 运动会

♦meet with person huìwù 会晤; opposition, approval etc zāodào 遭到

meeting huìyì 会议; **he's in a ~** tā zài kāihuì 他在开会

meeting place huìchǎng 会场

Mekong River Méigōnghé 湄公河

melancholy adj yōuyù 忧郁

mellow 1 adj róuhé 柔和 2 v/i (of person) wēnhé 温和

melodious yuè'ěr 悦耳

melodramatic gǎnqíng kuāzhāng 感情夸张

melody xuánlù 旋律

melon guā 瓜

melt v/t & v/i rónghuà 融化

♦melt away fig xiāoshī 消失

♦melt down v/t metal rónghuǐ 熔毁

melting pot fig rónglú 熔炉

member chéngyuán 成员; **~ of Congress** guóhuì yìyuán 国会议员

membership chéngyuán zīgé 成员资格; (number of members) chéngyuán rénshù 成员人数

membership card chéngyuánzhèng 成员证

membrane mó 膜

memento jìniànpǐn 纪念品

memo bèiwànglù 备忘录

memoirs huíyìlù 回忆录

memorable zhídé jìniàn 值得纪念

memorial 1 adj jìniàn 纪念 2 n

jìniànbēi 纪念碑

Memorial Day Zhènwáng Jiàngshì jìniànrì 阵亡将士纪念日

memorize jìzhù 记住

memory (*recollection*) jìyì 记忆; (*power of recollection*) jìyìlì 记忆力; (COMPUT: *device*) cúnchǔqì 存储器; (COMPUT: *capacity*) cúnchǔlì 存储力; **have a good / bad ~** jìyìlì hǎo / huài 记忆力好 / 坏; **in ~ of X** zuòwéi duì X de jìniàn 作为对X的纪念

menace 1 n (*threat*) wēixié 威胁; (*person*) wēixiǎn zhě 危险者 **2** v/t wēixié 威胁

menacing wēixié 威胁

mend v/t xiūlǐ 修理 **2** n xiūlǐ 修理; **be on the ~** (*after illness*) zài hǎozhuǎn zhōng 在好转中

menial adj dīxià 低下

meningitis nǎomóyán 脑膜炎

menopause juéjīngqī 绝经期

men's room náncè 男厕

menstruate xíngjīng 行经

menstruation xíngjīngqī 行经期

mental jīngshén 精神; F (*crazy*) fēng 疯

mental arithmetic xīnsuàn 心算; **mental cruelty** jīngshén nüèdài 精神虐待; **mental hospital** jīngshénbìngyuàn 精神病院; **mental illness** jīngshénbìng 精神病

mentality xīnlǐ zhuàngtài 心理状态

mentally (*inwardly*) zài nè xīn 在内心; *calculate etc* xīnlǐ jì 心里; **~ handicapped** dīnéng 低能; **~ ill** xīnlǐ jíbìng 心理疾病

mention 1 n tíjí 提及 **2** v/t tídào 提到; **don't ~ it** búyòng kèqì 不用客气

mentor liángshīyìyǒu 良师益友

menu (*for food*, COMPUT) càidān 菜单

mercenary 1 adj túlì 图利 **2** n MIL gùyōngbīng 雇佣兵

merchandise huòpǐn 货品

merchant shāngrén 商人

merciful réncí 仁慈

mercifully (*thankfully*) xìng'ér 幸而

merciless wúqíng 无情

mercury shuǐyín 水银

mercy réncí 仁慈; **be at X's ~** rènyóu X bǎibù 任由X摆布

mere adj zhǐbúguò 只不过

merely jǐnjǐn 仅仅

merge v/i (*of two lines etc*) héwéiyītǐ 合为一体; (*of companies*) hébìng 合并

merger COM hébìng 合并

merit 1 n (*worth*) jiàzhí 价值; (*advantage*) yōudiǎn 优点 **2** v/t zhíde 值得

merry yúkuài 愉快; **Merry Christmas!** Shèngdàn kuàilè! 圣诞快乐！

merry-go-round xuánzhuàn mùmǎ 旋转木马

mesh n wǎngyǎn 网眼

mess n (*untidiness*) zāngluàn zāngluàn 脏乱; (*trouble*) kùnjìng 困境; **be a ~** (*of room, desk, hair*) záluàn 杂乱; (*of situation, life*) yītuánzāo 一团糟

♦**mess around 1** v/i xiánxiao 瞎闹 **2** v/t person hùnong 糊弄

♦**mess around with** bǎinòng 摆弄; *s.o.'s wife* sītōng 私通

♦**mess up** room, papers nònglluàn 弄乱; *task* gǎozāo 搞糟; *plans, marriage* gǎohuài 搞坏

message (*of movie, book*) qǐshì 启示; **can I leave a ~?** wǒ kěyǐ liúyán ma? 我可以留言吗？

messenger (*courier*) tōngxìnyuán 通信员

messy room língluàn 凌乱; *person* lātà邋遢; *job* zāng 脏; *divorce, situation* fùzá 复杂

metabolism xīnchéndàixiè 新陈代谢

metal n & adj jīnshǔ 金属

metallic (sì) jīnshǔ (似) 金属

meteor liúxīng 流星

meteoric fig fēisù 飞速

meteorite yǔnxīng 陨星

meteorological qìxiàng 气象

meteorologist qìxiàngxuéjiā 气象学家

meteorology qìxiàngxué 气象学

meter[1] (*for measuring*) biǎo 表; (*parking ~*) qì器

meter[2] (*unit of length*) mǐ米

method fāngfǎ 方法

methodical yǒutiáolǐ 有条理

methodically yǒutiáobùwěn 有条不紊

meticulous jíjīngxì 极精细

metric gōngzhì 公制

metropolis dà dūshì 大都市

metropolitan *adj* dà dūshì 大都市

mew → *miaow*

Mexican 1 *adj* Mòxīgē 墨西哥 **2** *n* Mòxīgē rén 墨西哥人

Mexico Mòxīgē 墨西哥

mezzanine (**floor**) zhōngjiān lóucéng 中间楼层

miaow 1 *n* miāo 喵 **2** *v/i* zuò miāomiāo shēng 作喵喵声

mickey mouse *adj* F *course, qualification* yějī 野鸡

microchip wēijīngpiàn 微晶片; **microcosm** wēiguān shìjiè 微观世界; **microelectronics** wēidiànzǐxué 微电子学; **microfilm** suōwēi jiāojuǎn 缩微胶卷; **microphone** màikèfēng 麦克风; **microprocessor** wēichǔlǐjī 微处理机; **microscope** xiǎnwēijìng 显微镜; **microscopic** jíwēixiǎo 极微小; **microwave** (*oven*) wēibōlú 微波炉

midair: *in ~* zài bànkōngzhōng 在半空中

midday zhōngwǔ 中午

middle 1 *adj* zhōngjiān 中间 **2** *n* zhōngyāng 中央; *in the ~ of X* (*floor, room*) zài X zhōngyāng de X 中央; *in the ~ of* (*period of time*) zài ... zhōng 在 ... 中; *be in the ~ of doing X* zhèngzài zuò X 正在做 X 当中

middle-aged zhōngnián 中年; **Middle Ages** Zhōngshìjì 中世纪; **middle-class** *adj* zhōngchǎn jiējí 中产阶级; **middle classes** zhōngchǎn jiējí 中产阶级; **Middle East** Zhōngdōng 中东; **Middle Kingdom** Zhōngguó 中国; **middleman** jīngjìrén 经纪人; **middle name** zhōngjiānmíng 中

间名; **middleweight** *n* (*boxer*) zhōngliàngjí 中量级

middling zhōngděng 中等

midget *adj* xiùzhēn 袖珍

midnight wǔyè 午夜; *at ~* wǔyèshí 午夜时; **midsummer** zhòngxià 仲夏; **midway** zhōngtú 中途; **midweek** *adv* lǐbài zhōng 礼拜中; **Midwest** Zhōngxībù 中西部; **midwife** zhùchǎnshì 助产士; **midwinter** zhòngdōng 仲冬

might[1] yěxǔ 也许; *I ~ be late* wǒ yěxǔ chídào 我也许迟到; *it ~ rain* tiān yěxǔ yào xiàyǔ 天也许要下雨; *it ~ never happen* zhè yěxǔ yǒngyuǎn búhuì fāshēng 这也许永远不会发生; *I ~ have lost it* wǒ yěxǔ bǎ tā gěi diūle 我也许把它给丢了; *he ~ have left* tā yěxǔ yǐjīng zǒule 他也许已经走了; *you ~ as well spend the night here* nǐ háibùrú jiù zài zhèr guòyè 你还不如就在这儿过夜; *you ~ have told me!* nǐ zá méi gàosu wǒ! 你咋没告诉我!

might[2] *n* (*power*) lìliàng 力量

mighty 1 *adj* qiángyǒulì 强有力 **2** *adv* F (*extremely*) jíqí 极其

migraine piàntóutòng 偏头痛

migrant worker liúdòng gōngrén 流动工人

migrate qiānyí 迁移

migration qiānjū 迁居

mike màikèfēng 麦克风

mild wēnhé 温和

mildew méi 霉

mildly shìdù 适度

mildness wēnhé 温和

mile yīnglǐ 英里; *~s better/easier* hǎo/róngyì déduō 好/容易得多

mileage lǐchéng 里程

milestone *fig* lǐchéngbēi 里程碑

militant 1 *adj* yǒu zhàndòuxìng 有战斗性 **2** *n* jījí fènzǐ 积极分子

military 1 *adj* jūnshì 军事 **2** *n*: *the ~* jūnduì 军队

military academy jūnshì xuéyuàn 军事学院

militia mínbīng 民兵

milk 1 *n* nǎi 奶 **2** *v/t* jǐnǎi 挤奶

milk chocolate niúnǎi qiǎokèlì 牛

奶巧克力

milk shake nǎixī 奶昔

mill n (for grain) mòfáng 磨坊; (for textiles) máofǎngchǎng 毛纺厂

♦ **mill around** luànzhuàn 乱转

millennium yīqiānnián 一千年

milligram(me) háokè 毫克

millimeter háomǐ 毫米

million bǎiwàn 百万; **hundred ~** yì yì 一亿

millionaire bǎiwànfùwēng 百万富翁

mime v/t dǎ yǎyǔ 打哑语

mimic 1 n hào xuéyàng zhě 好学样者 **2** v/t mófǎng 模仿

mince v/t qiēsuì 切碎

mincemeat ròuxiàn 肉馅

mind 1 n tóunǎo 头脑; **it's all in your ~** dōu zài nǐde nǎohǎilǐ 都在你的脑海里; **be out of one's ~** fāfēng 发疯; **bear** or **keep X in ~** jìzhù X 记住X; **I've a good ~ to ...** wǒ zhēn xiǎng ... 我真想...; **change one's ~** gǎibiàn zhǔyi 改变主意; **it didn't enter my ~** gēnběn méi xiǎngdào 根本没想到; **give X a piece of one's ~** zébèi X 责备X; **make up one's ~** juédìng 决定; **have X on one's ~** guàlǜ X 挂虑X; **keep one's ~ on X** zhuānxīnyú X 专心于X **1** v/t (look after) zhàokàn 照看; (object to) jièyì 介意; (heed) liúxīn 留心; **I don't ~ what we do** wǒ bú zàihu zánmen zuò shénme 我不在乎咱们做什么; **do you ~ if I smoke?, do you ~ my smoking?** wǒ chōuyān nǐ bù fǎnduì ma? 我抽烟你不反对吗? **would you ~ opening the window?** qǐng bǎ chuāngzi dǎkāi hǎoma? 请把窗子打开好吗? **~ the step!** zhùyì jiǎoxià! 注意脚下! **~ your own business!** bùguǎn nǐde shì! 不关你的事! **3** v/i: **(be careful)** dāngxīn 当心; **never ~!** méiguānxi! 没关系! **I don't ~** wǒ wúsuǒwèi 我无所谓

mind-boggling jīngrén 惊人

mindless violence wútóunǎo 无头脑

mine¹ pron wǒde 我的; **a friend of ~** wǒde péngyǒu 我的朋友

mine² v/i (for coal etc) kuàng 矿 **2** v/i (for coal etc) kāicǎi 开采; **~ for** kāicǎi 开采

mine³ 1 n (explosive) dìléi 地雷 **2** v/t pūléi 铺雷

minefield MIL bùléiqū 布雷区; fig qiánzài kùnnánqū 潜在困难区

miner kuànggōng 矿工

mineral n kuàngwù 矿物

mineral water kuàngquánshuǐ 矿泉水

minesweeper NAUT sǎoléi tǐng 扫雷艇

Ming Dynasty Míngcháo 明朝

mingle v/i (of sounds, smells) hùnhé 混合; (at party) jiāowǎng 交往

mini (skirt) chāoduǎnqún 超短裙

minibus xiǎoxíng gōnggòngqìchē 小型公共汽车

miniature adj xiùzhēnxíng 袖珍型

minimal zuìxiǎo 最小

minimize jiǎnzhì zuìxiǎo 减至最小; (downplay) jìnkěnéng jiǎnshǎo 尽可能减少

minimum 1 adj zuìshǎo 最少 **2** n zuìdī xiàndù 最低限度

minimum wage zuìdī gōngzī 最低工资

mining kuàngyè 矿业

miniskirt chāoduǎnqún 超短裙

minister POL bùzhǎng 部长; REL mùshī 牧师

ministerial bùzhǎng 部长

ministry POL bù 部

mink (fur) diāopí 貂皮; (coat) diāopí dàyī 貂皮大衣

minor 1 adj cìyào 次要; **in D ~** MUS D xiǎodiào D小调 **2** n LAW wèichéngniánrén 未成年人

minority shǎoshù 少数; **be in the ~** zhànshǎoshù 占少数

mint n (herb) bòhe 薄荷; (chocolate) bòhexīn 薄荷点心; (hard candy) bòhe táng 薄荷糖

minus 1 n (~ sign) jiǎnhào 减号 **2** prep jiǎnqù 减去

minuscule wēixiǎo 微小

minute¹ n (of time) fēnzhōng 分钟;

in a ~ (soon) yíhuìr 一会儿; *just a ~* děngyíxià 等一下

minute² *adj (tiny)* wēixiǎo 微小; *(detailed)* xiángxì 详细; *in ~ detail* jùtǐ xìzhì 具体细致

minutely *(in detail)* xiángxì 详细

minutes *(of meeting)* jìlù 记录

miracle qíjī 奇迹

miraculous qíjībān 奇迹般

miraculously qíjī 奇迹

mirage hǎishì shènlóu 海市蜃楼

mirror 1 *n* jìngzi 镜子; MOT *(rearview)* hòushìjìng 后视镜; *(wing)* dàoguāngjìng 到光镜 **2** *v/t* fǎnshè 反射

misanthropist yànwù rénlèi zhě 厌恶人类者

misapprehension: *be under a ~* zài wùjiě de qíngkuàng xià 在误解的情况下

misbehave jǔzhǐbúdàng 举止不当

misbehavior búdàngde jǔzhǐ 不当的举止

miscalculate *v/t & v/i* wùsuàn 误算

miscalculation wùsuàn 误算

miscarriage MED liúchǎn 流产; *~ of justice* wùpàn 误判

miscarry *(of plan)* shībài 失败

miscellaneous gèzhǒng gèyàng 各种各样

mischief *(naughtiness)* èzuòjù 恶作剧

mischievous *(naughty)* wánpí 顽皮; *(malicious)* yǒuhài 有害

misconception wùjiě 误解

misconduct wánhū zhíshǒu 玩忽职守

misconstrue wùhuì 误会

misdemeanor qīngzuì 轻罪

miser shǒucáinú 守财奴

miserable *(unhappy)* nánguò 难过; *weather, performance* lìngrén búkuài 令人不快

miserly *amount* shǎodékělián 少得可怜

misery *(unhappiness)* tòngkǔ 痛苦; *(wretchedness)* bēicǎn 悲惨

misfire *(of joke, scheme)* wèidé yùqīxiàoguǒ 未得预期效果

misfit *(in society)* yǔ shèhuì gégébúrù de rén 与社会格格不入的人

misfortune búxìng 不幸

misgivings gùlǜ 顾虑

misguided wùdǎo 误导

mishandle chǔlǐbúdàng 处理不当

mishap búxìng shìgù 不幸事故

misinterpret qūjiě 曲解

misinterpretation qūjiě 曲解

misjudge *person, situation* cuòwù gūjì 错误估计

mislay yíshī 遗失

mislead yǐndǎocuò 引导错

misleading shǐrén wùjiě 使人误解

mismanage guǎnlǐ búshàn 管理不善

mismanagement búdàngde guǎnlǐ 不当的管理

mismatch pèihé búdàng 配合不当

misplaced *loyalty, enthusiasm* cuòwùde fùchū 错误地付出

misprint *n* cuòyìn 错印

mispronounce fācuò 发错

mispronunciation fāyīn cuòwù 发音错误

misread *word, figures* dúcuò 读错; *situation* wùjiě 误解

misrepresent wāiqū 歪曲

miss¹: *Miss Wang* Wáng xiǎojiě 王小姐

miss² **1** *n* SP wèijīzhòng 未击中; *give X a ~ meeting, party etc* búqù X 不去 X **2** *v/t (not hit)* wèijīzhòng 未击中; *(emotionally)* xiǎngniàn 想念; *bus, train, plane* méigǎnshàng 没赶上; *(not notice, fail to take)* cuòguò 错过; *(not be present at)* bùchūxí 不出席; *you've just ~ed him (not met)* tā gāng zǒule 他刚走了 **3** *v/i* wèijīzhòng 未击中

misshapen jīxíng 畸形

missile *(guided)* dǎodàn 导弹

missing diūshī 丢失; *be ~* xiàluò-bùmíng 下落不明

mission *(task)* rènwù 任务; *(people)* shǐmìngtuán 使命团

missionary REL chuánjiàoshì 传教士

misspell pīnxiěcuò 拼写错

mist bówù 薄雾

♦ **mist over** (of eyes) móhu 模糊

♦ **mist up** (of window etc) méngshàng shuǐqì 蒙上水汽

mistake 1 n cuòwù 错误; **make a ~** fàn cuòwù 犯错误; **by ~** cuòwùde 错误地; **mix X up with Y** hùnxiáo X hé Y 混淆 X 和 Y 误错; **~ X for Y** wùjiāng X rènzuò Y 误将 X 认作 Y

mistaken: be ~ nòngcuò 弄错

mister xiānsheng 先生

mistress (lover) qíngfù 情妇; (of servant, dog) nǚzhǔrén 女主人

mistrust 1 n búxìnrèn 不信任 **2** v/t huáiyí 怀疑

misty weather bówù lǒngzhào 薄雾笼罩; eyes móhu 模糊; color méngménglónglóng 朦朦胧胧

misunderstand wùjiě 误解

misunderstanding (mistake) wùjiě 误解; (argument) zhēngzhí 争执

misuse 1 n wùyòng 误用 **2** v/t yòngcuò 用错

mitigating circumstances jiǎnqīngde qíngjié 减轻的情节

mitt (in baseball) bàngqiú shǒutào 棒球手套

mitten liánzhǐ shǒutào 连指手套

mix 1 n (mixture) hùnhé 混合; (in cooking) hùnhéwù 混合物; (cooking: ready to use) hùnhé pèiliào 混合配料 **2** v/t hùnhé 混合; cement jiǎohuo 搅和 **3** v/i (socially) xiāngchǔ 相处

♦ **mix up** gǎoluàn 搞乱; **mix X up with Y** hùnxiáo X hé Y 混淆 X 和 Y; **be mixed up** (emotionally) míwǎng 迷惘; (of figures, papers) nòngluàn 弄乱; **be mixed up in X** yǔ X yǒu qiānlián 与 X 有牵连; **get mixed up with X** yǔ X sīhùn 与 X 厮混

♦ **mix with** (associate with) jiāowǎng 交往

mixed feelings fùzá 复杂; reactions, reviews gèzhǒng gèyàng 各种各样

mixed marriage yìzú tōnghūn 异族通婚

mixer (for food) jiǎobànqì 搅拌器; (drink) tiáopèi yǐnliào 调配饮料; **she's a good ~** tā hěn héqún 她很合群

mixture hùnhé(wù) 混合 (物); (medicine) fùfāngyào 复方药

mix-up hùnluàn 混乱

moan 1 n (of pain) shēnyín 呻吟; (complaint) láosao 牢骚 **2** v/i (in pain) shēnyín 呻吟; (complain) bàoyuàn 抱怨

mob 1 n bàomín 暴民 **2** v/t bāowéi 包围

mobile 1 adj person kě línghuó zǒudòng 可灵活走动; (that can be moved) kěyídòng 可移动 **2** n (for decoration) fēngdòng shìwù 风动饰物; Br (phone) yídòng 移动, dàgēdà 大哥大

mobile home huódòng zhùfáng 活动住房

mobile phone Br yídòng 移动, (formal use) shǒutí diànhuà 手提电话

mobility yídòngxìng 移动性

mobster dàitú 歹徒

mock 1 adj mónǐ 摹拟 **2** v/t qǔxiào 取笑

mockery (derision) cháonòng 嘲弄; (travesty) duì zhèngyì de wāiqū 对正义的歪曲

mock-up (model) dàmóxíng 大模型

mode (form) fāngshì 方式; COMPUT cāozuò fāngfǎ 操作方法

model 1 adj employee, husband mófàn 模范; boat, plane móxíng 模型 **2** n (miniature) chúxíng 雏型; (pattern) móshì 模式; (fashion ~) mótèr 模特儿; **male ~** nán mótèr 男模特儿 **3** v/t zhǎnshì 展示 **4** v/i (for designer, artist) zuò mótèr 作模特儿

modem tiáozhì jiětiáoqì 调制解调器

moderate 1 adj shìdù 适度; POL wēnhé 温和 **2** n POL wēnhépài 温和派 **3** v/t biànhéhuǎn 变和缓 **4** v/i jiǎnruò 减弱

moderately shìdù 适度

moderation (*restraint*) jiézhì 节制；*in* ~ shìdù 适度

modern xiàndài 现代

modernization xiàndàihuà 现代化

modernize **1** *v/t* shǐxiàndàihuà 使现代化 **2** *v/i* (*of business, country*) xiàndàihuà 现代化

modest *house, apartment* pǔsù 朴素；(*small*) búdà 不大；(*not conceited*) qiānxùn 谦逊

modesty (*of house, apartment*) pǔsù 朴素；(*of wage, improvement*) shìdù 适度；(*lack of conceit*) qiānxùn 谦逊

modification xiūgǎi 修改

modify xiūgǎi 修改

modular *furniture* dāntǐ shèjì 单体设计

module dāntǐ 单体；(*space ~*) cāng 舱

moist cháoshī 潮湿

moisten nòngshī 弄湿

moisture shīrùn 湿润

moisturizer (*for skin*) rùnfūshuāng 润肤霜

molar móyá 磨牙

molasses tángjiāng 糖浆

mold[1] *n* (*on food*) méi 霉

mold[2] **1** *n* múzi 模子 **2** *v/t clay etc* jiāozhù 浇铸；*character, person* lèixíng 类型

moldy *food* fāméi 发霉

mole (*on skin*) zhì 痣

molecular fēnzǐ 分子

molecule fēnzǐ 分子

molest *child, woman* sāorǎo 骚扰

mollycoddle nì'ài 溺爱

molten rónghuà 熔化

mom F mā 妈

moment piànkè 片刻；*at the* ~ xiànzài 现在；*for the* ~ zànshí 暂时

momentarily (*for a moment*) shùnjiān 瞬间；(*in a moment*) jíkè 即刻

momentary duǎnzàn 短暂

momentous jízhòngyào 极重要

momentum dònglì 动力

monarch jūnzhǔ 君主

monastery xiūdàoyuàn 修道院

monastic xiūdào 修道

Monday xīngqīyī 星期一

monetary huòbì 货币

money qián 钱

money-lender fàngzhài zhě 放债者；**money market** jīnróng shìchǎng 金融市场；**money order** huìkuǎndān 汇款单

Mongolia Měnggǔ 蒙古

Mongolian **1** *adj* Měnggǔ 蒙古 **2** *n* (*person*) Měnggǔ rén 蒙古人

mongrel zázhǒnggǒu 杂种狗

monitor **1** *n* COMPUT jiānshìqì 监视器 **2** *v/t* chíxù guānchá 持续观察

monk héshàng 和尚；*become a* ~ chūjiā 出家

monkey hóu 猴，F (*child*) tiáopíguǐ 调皮鬼

♦**monkey around with** F bǎinòng 摆弄

monkey wrench huódòng bānshǒu 活动扳手

monogram *n* zìshǒu 字首

monogrammed zìshǒu 字首

monolog dúbái 独白

monopolize lǒngduàn 垄断

monopoly dúzhàn 独占

monosodium glutamate wèijīng 味精

monotonous dāndiào fáwèi 单调乏味

monotony wúliáo 无聊

monsoon jìfēng 季风

monsoon season jìfēng yǔjì 季风雨季

monster *n* yāoguài 妖怪

monstrosity jīxíng 畸形

monstrous jīxíng 畸形

month yuè 月

monthly **1** *adj* měiyuè 每月 **2** *adv* měiyuè yícì 每月一次 **3** *n* (*magazine*) yuèkān 月刊

monument jìniànbēi 纪念碑

mood (*frame of mind*) xīnqíng 心情；(*bad* ~) huàiqíngxù 坏情绪；(*of meeting, country*) qìfēn 气氛；*be in a good / bad* ~ qíngxù hǎo / huài 情绪好 / 坏；*be in the* ~ *for* yǒu xìngzhì 有兴致

moody xǐnùwúcháng 喜怒无常

moon *n* yuèliang 月亮

moonlight **1** *n* yuèguāng 月光

moonlit

2 v/i F jiānzhí 兼职
moonlit yǒu yuèguāng 有月光
moor v/t boat tíngpō 停泊
moorings tíngbó qū 停泊区
moose tuólù 驼鹿
mop 1 n tuōbù 拖布 2 v/t floor tuōdì 拖地; eyes, face cā 擦
♦ **mop up** cājìng 擦净; MIL sùqīng 肃清
mope yùyùbùlè 郁郁不乐
moral 1 adj dàodé 道德; person, behavior jiǎngdàodé 讲道德 2 n (of story) yùyì 寓意; ~s xíngwéide biāozhǔn 行为的标准
morale shìqì 士气
morality měidé 美德
morbid bìngtài 病态
more 1 adj gèngduō 更多; we need ~ time wǒmen xūyào gèng-duo de shíjiān 我门需要更多的时间; some ~ tea? zài láidiǎnr chá ma? 再来点儿茶吗?; ~ and ~ students / time yuèláiyuè-duōde xuésheng / shíjiān 越来越多的学生 / 时间 2 adv gèng(duō) 更 (多); ~ important gèng zhòngyào 更重要; ~ often gèng pínfán 更频繁; ~ and ~ yuèfā(duō) 越发 (多); ~ or less dàzhì 大致; once ~ zàiyícì 再一次; ~ than duōyú 多于; I don't live there any ~ wǒ búzài zhù nàrle 我不再住那儿了 3 pron gèngduōde shùliàng 更多的数量; do you want some ~? nǐ hái yàodiǎn ma? 你还要点儿吗?; a little ~ zài lái yìdiǎndiǎn 再来一点点
moreover érqiě 而且
morgue tíngshīfáng 停尸房
morning (before 10am) zǎochén 早晨; (between 10am and 12pm) shàngwǔ 上午; in the ~ (before 10am) zǎochén zǎochén 早晨; (between 10am and 12pm) shàngwǔ 上午; (tomorrow: before 10am) míngtiān zǎochén 明天早晨; (tomorrow: between 10am and 12pm) míngtiān shàngwǔ 明天上午; this ~ (before 10am) jīntiān zǎochén 今天早晨; (usually between 10am

and 12pm) jīntiān shàngwǔ 今天上午; tomorrow ~ (before 10am) míngtiān zǎochén 明天早晨; (between 10am and 12pm) míngtiān shàngwǔ 明天上午; good ~ (before 10am) zǎochén hǎo 早晨好; (between 10am and 12pm) shàngwǔ hǎo 上午好
moron shǎguā 傻瓜
morose guāipì 乖僻
morphine mǎfēi 吗啡
morsel: a ~ of yīxiǎopiàn 一小片
mortal 1 adj bìsǐ 必死; blow zhìmìng 致命; enemy búgòngdài-tiān 不共戴天 2 n rén 人
mortality bùmiǎnyīsǐ 不免一死, sǐwáng lǜ 死亡率
mortar[1] MIL pǎijīpào 迫击炮
mortar[2] (cement) shājiāng 砂浆
mortgage 1 n dǐyā 抵押 2 v/t dǐyā jièkuǎn 抵押借款
mortician bìnyíyè zhě殡仪业者
mortuary tàipíngjiān 太平间
mosaic mǎsàikè 马赛克
Moscow Mòsīkē 莫斯科
mosquito wénzi 蚊子
mosquito coil wénxiāng 蚊香
mosquito net wénzhàng 蚊帐
moss tái 苔
mossy zhǎngmǎn qīngtái 长满青苔
most 1 adj duōshù 多数 2 adv (very) hěn 很; the ~ beauti-ful / interesting zuì piàoliàng / yǒuqù 最漂亮 / 有趣; that's the one I like ~ nàge shì wǒ zuì xǐhuān de 那个是我最喜欢的; ~ of all zuì zhòngyào 最重要 3 pron dàduōshù 大多数; at (the) ~ zhìduō 至多; make the ~ of jǐnliàng lìyòng 尽量利用
mostly zhǔyào 主要
motel qìchē lǚguǎn 汽车旅馆
moth é 蛾
mother 1 n mǔqīn 母亲 2 v/t xiàng mǔqīnbān zhàogù 像母亲般照顾
motherboard COMPUT mǔbǎn 母板; **motherhood** mǔqīn shēnfèn 母亲身份; **mother-in-law** (of man) yuèmǔ 岳母; (of woman)

pópó 婆婆

motherly mǔxìng 母性

mother-of-pearl zhēnzhūmǔ 珍珠母; **Mother's Day** Mǔqīnjié 母亲节; **mother tongue** mǔyǔ 母语

motif zhuāngshì shìyàng 装饰式样

motion **1** n (*movement*) yùndòng 运动; (*proposal*) tíyì 提议; **put** or **set things in** ~ zuò bìyào de ānpái 作必要的安排 **2** v/t: **he** ~**ed me forward** tā shìyì wǒ qiánxíng 他示意我前行

motionless búdòng 不动

motivate *person* cùdòng 促动

motivation dònglì 动力

motive dòngjī 动机

motor fādòngjī 发动机

motorbike mótuōchē 摩托车; **motorboat** qìchuán 汽船; **motorcade** qìchē chángliè 汽车长列; **motorcycle** mótuōchē 摩托车; **motorcyclist** qí mótuōchē de rén 骑摩托车的人; **motor home** zhùfáng qìchē 住房汽车

motorist sījī 司机

motor rickshaw bèngbèngchē 蹦蹦车; **motorscooter** xiǎoxíng mótuōchē 小型摩托车; **motor vehicle** jīdòngchē 机动车

motto zuòyòumíng 座右铭

mound (*hillock*) tǔqiū 土丘; (*in baseball*) tóushǒu chǎngdì 投手场地; (*pile*) duī 堆

mount **1** n (*mountain*) shān 山; (*horse*) zuòqí 坐骑 **2** v/t steps pá 爬; *horse, bicycle* qíshàng 骑上; *campaign* fāqǐ 发起; *photo, painting* biǎotiē 裱贴 **3** v/i zēngzhǎng 增长

♦ **mount up** jījù 积聚

mountain shān 山

mountain bike shāndìchē 山地车

mountaineer dēngshānjiā 登山家

mountaineering dēngshān yùndòng 登山运动

mountainous duōshān 多山

mourn **1** v/t dàoniàn 悼念 **2** v/i āidào 哀悼; ~ **for X** dàoniàn X 悼念 X

mourner āidào zhě 哀悼者

mournful bēi'āi 悲哀

mourning fúsāng 服丧; **be in** ~ zài fúsāng 在服丧; **wear** ~ chuān sāngfú 穿丧服

mouse shǔ 鼠; COMPUT ⇩ shǔbiāo 鼠标

mouse mat COMPUT shǔbiāodiàn 鼠标垫

mouth n (*of person*) zuǐ 嘴; (*of river*) hékǒu 河口

mouthful (*of food, drink*) yīkǒu 一口

mouthorgan kǒuqín 口琴; **mouthpiece** (*of instrument*) chuīkǒu 吹口; (*spokesperson*) hóushé hóuzé 喉舌; **mouthwash** shùkǒujì 漱口剂; **mouthwatering** lìngrén chuíxián 令人垂涎

move **1** n (*in chess, checkers*) yībù 一步; (*step, action*) jǔcuò 举措; (*change of house*) bānjiā 搬家; **get a** ~ **on!** gǎnkuài! 赶快！; **don't make a** ~! bùxǔdòng! 不许动！ **2** v/t object yídòng 移动; (*transfer*) zhuǎnyí 转移; (*emotionally*) gǎndòng 感动 **3** v/i dòng 动; (*transfer*) zhuǎn 转; ~ **house** bānjiā 搬家

♦ **move around** (*in room*) zǒudòng 走动; (*from place to place*) qiānyí 迁移

♦ **move away** yíkāi 移开; (*move house*) bānzǒu 搬走

♦ **move in** bānjìn 搬进

♦ **move on** (*to another town*) jìxù xíngjìn 继续行进; (*to another job*) diào tiáo 调调; (*to another subject*) zhuǎnxiàng 转向

♦ **move out** (*of house*) bānchū 搬出; (*of area*) chèlí 撤离

♦ **move up** (*in league*) tíshēng 提升; (*make room*) nuódòng 挪动

movement dòngzuò 动作; (*organization*) yùndòng 运动; MUS yuèzhāng 乐章

movers bānyùn gōngrén 搬运工人

movie diànyǐng 电影; **go to a** ~ / **the** ~**s** qù kàn diànyǐng 去看电影

moviegoer guānzhòng 观众

movie theater diànyǐngyuàn 电影院

moving (*which can move*) huódòng 活动; (*emotionally*) gǎnrén 感人

mow grass gē 割

♦**mow down** sǎomiè 扫灭

mower yìcǎojī 刈草机

moxibustion jiǔshù 灸术

MP (= *Military Policeman*) jūnjǐng 军警

mph (= *miles per hour*) yīnglǐ shísù 英里时速

Mr xiānsheng 先生; *~ Wang* Wáng xiānsheng 王先生

Mrs tàitai 太太; *~ Wang* Wáng tàitai 王太太

Ms nǚshì 女士; *~ Wang* Wáng nǚshì 王女士

much 1 *adj* xǔduō 许多; *~ money* xǔduō qián 许多钱; *there's not ~ difference* méiyǒu duōshao chābié 没有多少差别; *as ~ X as Y* (*same amount as*) hé Y yíyàng duō de X 和 Y 一样多的 X **2** *adv* hěn 很; *he is ~ admired* tā hěn lìngrén xiànmù 他很令人羡慕; *I don't like him ~* wǒ bútài xǐhuan tā 我不太喜欢他; *~ better* hǎo de duō 好得多; *~ cheaper* piányi de duō 便宜得多; *~ very ~* fēicháng 非常; *thank you very ~* fēicháng gǎnxiè 非常感谢; *too ~* guòduō 过多; *you talk too ~* nǐ shuōde guòduō 你说得过多 **3** *pron* duōshǎo 多少; *nothing ~* méi shénme 没什么; *as ~ as ...* gēn ... yíyàng (duō) 跟 ... 一样 (多); *I lost as ~ as you did* wǒ shūde yíyàng duō wǒ gēn nǐ shūde yíyàng duō 我跟你输的一样多; *do as ~ as you can* jìnliàng zuò ba 尽量做吧; *take as ~ as you want* suíbiàn ná 随便拿; *as ~ as ten thousand dollars* duōdá yíwàn měiyuán 多达一万美元; *I thought as ~* wǒ jiùshì zhènme xiǎngde 我就是这么想的

muck (*dirt*) zāngwù 脏物

mucus niányè 粘液

mud ní 泥

muddle 1 *n* hùnluàn 混乱 **2** *v/t*

muddle up gǎoluàn 搞乱

muddy *adj* nínìng 泥泞

muffin sōngbǐng 松饼

muffle yāyì 压抑

♦**muffle up** *v/i* chuān hòu yīdiǎn 穿厚一点

muffler MOT páiqì xiāoshēngqì 排气消声器

mug[1] *n* (*for tea, coffee*) dàbēi 大杯; F (*face*) liǎndànr 脸蛋儿

mug[2] *v/t* (*attack*) xíngxiōng qiǎngjié 行凶抢劫

mugger xíngxiōng qiǎngjié zhě 行凶抢劫者

mugging xíngxiōng qiǎngjié 行凶抢劫

muggy mēnrè 闷热

♦**mull over** zǐxì kǎolǜ 仔细考虑

multilingual shǐyòng duōzhǒng yǔyán 使用多种语言

multimedia *n* duōméitǐ 多媒体

multinational 1 *adj* guójì 国际 **2** *n* COM duōguó 多国

multiple *adj* duōgè 多个

multiplication zēngduō 增多

multiply 1 *v/t* chéng 乘 **2** *v/i* zēngjiā 增加

mumble 1 *n* gūnong 咕哝 **2** *v/t* gūnong 咕哝 **3** *v/i* hánhude shuō 含糊地说

mumps sāixiànyán 腮腺炎

munch 1 *v/t* yònglì jǔjué 用力咀嚼 **2** *v/i* dàjǔdàjué 大咀大嚼

municipal shìzhèng 市政

mural *n* bìhuà 壁画

murder 1 *n* móushā 谋杀 **2** *v/t person* móushā 谋杀; *song* zāotà 糟蹋

murderer xiōngshǒu 凶手

murderous *rage, look* shāqì téngténg 杀气腾腾

murmur 1 *n* dīyǔshēng 低语声 **2** *v/t* dīyǔ 低语

muscle jīròu 肌肉

muscular *pain, strain* jīròu 肌肉; *person* jīròu fādá 肌肉发达

muse *v/i* chénsī 沉思

museum bówùguǎn 博物馆

mushroom 1 *n* mógū 蘑菇 **2** *v/i* xùnsù zēngzhǎng 迅速增长

music yīnyuè 音乐; (*in written form*) yuèpǔ 乐谱

musical 1 *adj* yīnyuè 音乐; *person* yǒu yuègǎn 有乐感; *voice* yuè'ěr 悦耳 **2** *n* (*movie*) yīnyuèpiān 音乐片; (*on stage*) gēwǔjù 歌舞剧

musical instrument yuèqì 乐器

musician yīnyuèjiā 音乐家

mussel yíbèi 贻贝

must ◊ (*necessity*): *I ~ be on time* wǒ bìxū zhǔnshí 我必须准时; *I ~* wǒ bìxūděi … 我必须得 …; *I ~n't be late* wǒ bùnéng chídào 我不能迟到 ◊ (*probability*): *it ~ be about 6 o'clock* dàgài liùdiǎnzhōng le 大概六点钟了; *they ~ have arrived by now* tāmen xiànzài kěndìng dàole 他们现在肯定到了

mustache bāzì hú 八字胡

mustard jièmò 芥末

musty yǒu méiwèir 有霉味儿

mute *adj animal* wúshēng 无声

muted jiǎnruò 减弱

mutilate sǔnshāng 损伤

mutiny 1 *n* pànluàn 叛乱 **2** *v/i* fǎnpàn 反叛

mutter 1 *v/i* gūnong 咕哝 **2** *v/t* dīshēng shuō 低声说

mutton yángròu 羊肉

mutual xiānghù 相互

muzzle 1 *n* (*of animal*) bíkǒu bùfen 鼻口部分; (*for dog*) kǒutào 口套 **2** *v/t*: *~ the press* qiánzhì xīnwén 钳制新闻

my wǒde 我的

myopic jìnshì 近视

myself wǒzìjǐ 我自己; *by ~* dúzì 独自

mysterious shénmì 神秘

mysteriously bùkě sīyì 不可思议

mystery mí 谜

mystify míhuo 迷惑

myth shénhuà 神话; *fig* xūhuà 虚话

mythical cúnzài yú shénhuà zhōng 存在于神话中

mythology shénhuàxué 神话学

N

nab (*take for oneself*) qiǎng qiǎng 抢

nag **1** *v/i (of person)* láodao bùtíng 唠叨不停 **2** *v/t* fán fàn 烦饭; **~ X to do Y** méiwán méiliǎo de yào X qùzuò Y 没完没了地要 X 去做 Y

nagging *person* hào láodao 好唠叨; *doubt* kùnrǎo 困扰; *pain* lìngrén fánnǎo 令人烦恼

nail (*for wood*) dīng 钉; (*on finger, toe*) zhǐjia 指甲

nail clippers zhǐjia dāo 指甲刀; nail file zhǐjia cuò 指甲锉; nail polish zhǐjia yóu 指甲油; nail polish remover zhǐjia yóu qùchú jì 指甲油去除剂; nail scissors zhǐjia jiǎn 指甲剪; nail varnish zhǐjia yóu 指甲油

naïve tiānzhēn 天真

naked luǒtǐ 裸体; **to the ~ eye** yòng ròuyǎn láikàn 用肉眼来看

name **1** *n* míngzi 名字; **what's your ~?** nǐ jiào shénme míngzi? 你叫什么名字? ; (*formal use*) qǐngwèn guìxìng? 请问贵姓? ; **call X ~s** jiào X wàihào 叫 X 外号; **make a ~ for oneself** chéngmíng 成名 **2** *v/t* qǐmíng 起名

♦ name for: **name X for Y** yǐ Y de míngzi wèi X qǐmíng 以 Y 的名字为 X 起名

namely jí 即

namesake tóngmíng rén 同名人

nametag (*on clothing etc*) biāoqiān 标签

nanny *n* bǎomǔ 保姆

nap *n* xiǎoshuì 小睡; **have a ~** dǎdǔnr 打盹儿

nape: **~ of the neck** hòu bójǐng 后脖颈

napkin (*table ~*) cānjīn 餐巾; (*sanitary*) wèishēngjīn 卫生巾

narcotic *n* mázuì pǐn 麻醉品

narcotics agent fǎndú jǐng 反毒警

narrate xùshù 叙述

narration (*telling*) xùshù 叙述

narrative **1** *n* (*story*) gùshì 故事 **2** *adj poem, style* xùshì tǐ 叙事体

narrator xùshì zhě 叙事者

narrow *street, bed etc* xiázhǎi 狭窄; *views, mind* xiáyì 狭隘; *victory* miǎnqiáng 勉强

narrowly *win* miǎnqiángde 勉强地; **~ escape X** miǎnqiǎng de táotuō X 勉强地逃脱 X

narrow-minded xīnxiōng xiázǎi 心胸狭窄

nasal *voice* bíyīn zhòng 鼻音重

nasty *person, thing to say* bēibǐ 卑鄙; *smell, weather* èliè 恶劣; *cut, wound, disease* yánzhòng 严重

nation guójiā 国家

national **1** *adj currency, identity, issues* guójiā 国家; *newspaper, security* guójiā 国家; *economic indicators* guómín 国民; *pride* àiguó 爱国 **2** *n* guómín 国民

national anthem guógē 国歌

National Day Guóqìngjié 国庆节

national debt guózhài 国债

nationalism mínzú zhǔyì 民族主义

Nationalist Party (*KMT*) Guómíndǎng 国民党

nationality guójí 国籍

nationalize *industry etc* shǐ guóyǒu huà 使国有化

national park guójiā gōngyuán 国家公园

National People's Congress Quánguó Rénmín Dàibiǎo Dàhuì 全国人民代表大会

native **1** *adj* (*of a country*) běnguó 本国; (*of a place*) běndì 本地; **~ language** (*of a country*) běnguó yǔ 本国语; (*mother tongue*) mǔyǔ 母语 **2** *n* dāngdì rén 当地人; (*tribesman*) tǔrén 土人

native country zǔguó 祖国

native speaker jiǎng běnguóyǔ de rén 讲本国语的人
NATO (= *North Atlantic Treaty Organization*) Běiyuē 北约
natural zìrán 自然; *resources, forces* zìrán jiè 自然界; *death* zìrán 自然; *flavor* fēi rénzào 非人造; *a ~ blonde* tiānshēng jīn tóufà rén 天生金头发人
natural gas tiānrán qì 天然气
naturalist bówù xuéjiā 博物学家
naturalize: *become ~d* jiārù guójí 加入国籍
naturally (*of course*) dāngrán 当然; *behave, speak* zìrán de 自然地; (*by nature*) tiānshēng 天生
natural science zìrán kēxué 自然科学
natural scientist zìrán kēxué jiā 自然科学家
nature zìrán 自然; (*of person*) xìnggé 性格; (*of problem*) běnzhì 本质
nature reserve zìrán bǎohùqū 自然保护区
naughty táoqì 淘气; *photograph, word etc* bùdétǐ 不得体
nausea ěxin 恶心
nauseate *fig* (*disgust*) shǐ ěxin 使恶心
nauseating *smell, taste* lìngrén zuò'ǒu 令人作呕; *person* ròumá 肉麻
nauseous: *feel ~* juéde ěxin 觉得恶心
nautical hánghǎi 航海
nautical mile hǎilǐ 海里
naval hǎijūn 海军
naval base hǎijūn jīdì 海军基地
navel dùqí 肚脐
navigable *river* kě tōngháng 可通航
navigate *v/i* (*in ship, airplane*) cèháng 测航; (*in car*) zhǐlù 指路; COMPUT zǒu 走
navigation (*nautical, in airplane*) hángxíngxué 航行学; (*in car*) lǐnglù 领路; (*skills*) yǐndǎo 引导
navigator (*on ship*) hánghǎi jiā 航海家; (*in airplane*) jiàshǐ yuán 驾驶员; (*in car*) zhǐlùrén 指路人

navy hǎijūn 海军
navy blue *n & adj* hǎijūn lán 海军兰
near 1 *adv* jìn 近 **2** *prep* jiējìn 接近; *~ the bank* jìn yínháng 近银行; *do you go ~ the bank?* nǐ huìbúhuì zǒu yínháng nàbiān? 你会不会走银行那边？ **3** *adj* jìn 近; *the ~est bus stop* zuìjìnde gōnggòng qìchē zhàn 最近的公共汽车站; *in the ~ future* bùyuǎnde jiānglái 不远的将来
nearby *adv* live zài fùjìn 在附近
nearly jīhū 几乎
near-sighted jìnshì 近视
neat *room, desk* zhěngjié 整洁; *person* zhěngqí 整齐; *whiskey* chún 纯; *solution* qiǎomiào 巧妙; F (*terrific*) tǐnghǎo 挺好
necessarily yídìng 一定
necessary bìbù kěshǎo 必不可少; *it is ~ to X* yǒu bìyào zuò X 有必要做X
necessitate xūyào 需要
necessity (*being necessary*) bìyào xìng 必要性; (*sth necessary*) bìxū pǐn 必需品
neck bózi 脖子
necklace xiàngliàn 项链; **neckline** (*of dress*) lǐngkǒu 领口; **necktie** lǐngdài 领带
née mǔjiā xìng 母家姓
need 1 *n* xūyào 需要; *if ~ be* rúguǒ yǒu xūyào dehuà 如果有需要的话; *in ~* yǒu kùnnán 有困难; *be in ~ of X* xūyào X 需要X; *there's no ~ to be rude / upset* méi bìyào zhème cūlǔ / shāngxīn 没必要这么粗鲁／伤心 **2** *v/t* xūyào 需要; *you'll ~ to buy one* nǐ yǒu bìyào mǎi yíge 你有必要买一个; *you don't ~ to wait* nǐ bùbì děngzhe 你不必等着; *I ~ to talk to you* wǒ yào hé nǐ tánhuà 我要和你谈话; *~ I say more?* wǒ háiyǒu shénme kěshuōde? 我还有什么可说的？
needle (*for sewing*) zhēn 针; (*for injection*) zhēntóu 针头; (*on dial*) zhǐzhēn 指针
needlework zhēnxiàn huór 针线

活儿

needy qióng 穷

negative 1 adj verb, sentence fǒudìng 否定; attitude, person xiāojí 消极; ELEC fùdiàn 负电 **2** n: answer in the ~ jǐyǔ fǒudìngde huídá 给予否定的回答

neglect 1 n hūlüè 忽略 **2** v/t garden, one's health zhàogù bùzhōu 照顾不周; ~ to do X méiyǒu zuò X 没有做 X

neglected gardens, author bùshòu zhòngshì 不受重视; feel ~ gǎndào bùshòu zhòngshì 感到不受重视

negligence wánhū zhíshǒu 玩忽职守

negligent cūxīn dàyì 粗心大意

negligible quantity, amount kěyǐ hūlüè 可以忽略

negotiable salary, contract kě xiéshāng 可协商

negotiate 1 v/i xiéshāng 协商 **2** v/t deal, settlement xiéshāng 协商; obstacles jiějué 解决; bend in road tōngguò 通过

negotiation xiéshāng 协商

negotiator tánpàn yuán 谈判员

Negro (person) Hēi rén 黑人

neigh v/i sī 嘶

neighbor línjū 邻居

neighborhood (in town) dìqū 地区; in the ~ of ... fig dàyuē ... 大约

neighboring house, state fùjìn 附近

neighborly yǒuhǎo 友好

neither 1 adj liǎngzhě dōubù 两者都不; ~ answer was correct liǎng ge dá'àn dōu búduì 两个答案都不对 **2** pron něige dōu bù 哪个都不 **3** adv: ~ ... nor ... jìbù ... yěbù ... 既不 ... 也不 ... **4** conj yěbù 也不; ~ do I wǒ yě bù 我也不

neon light níhóng dēng 霓虹灯

Nepal Níbó'ěr 尼泊尔

Nepalese 1 adj Níbó'ěr 尼泊尔 **2** n (person) Níbó'ěr rén 尼泊尔人; (language) Níbó'ěr yǔ 尼泊尔语

nephew (brother's son) zhízi 侄子; (sister's son) wàisheng 外甥

nerd F guàirén 怪人

nerve shénjīng 神经; (courage) yǒngqì 勇气; (impudence) dàliàng dǎnliàng 胆量; it's bad for my ~s duì wǒde shénjīng bùhǎo 对我的神经不好; get on X's ~s shǐ X xīnfán yíluàn 使 X 心烦意乱

nerve-racking shǐrén xīnfán 使人心烦

nervous person jǐnzhāng 紧张; twitch shénjīng xìng 神经性; be ~ about doing X hàipà zuò X 害怕做 X

nervous breakdown jīngshén bēngkuì 精神崩溃

nervous energy jīnglì chōngpèi 精力充沛

nervousness jǐnzhāng 紧张

nervous wreck hěn jǐnzhāng derén 很紧张的人

nervy (fresh) dàdǎn 大胆

nest n cháo 巢

nestle shūshìde āndūn xiàlái 舒适地安顿下来

net¹ (for fishing) yúwǎng 鱼网; (for tennis) wǎngqiú wǎng 网球网

net² adj price, amount chún 纯; weight jìng 净

net curtain shā chuānglián 纱窗帘

net profit jìnglì 净利

nettle xúnmá 荨麻

network (of contacts, cells) liánluò wǎng 联络网; COMPUT wǎngluò 网络

neurologist shénjīngbìng xuéjiā 神经病学家

neurosis shénjīng jīnéng bìng 神经机能病

neurotic adj shénjīng zhì 神经质

neuter v/t animal yāngē 阉割

neutral 1 adj country zhōnglì 中立; color fēi cǎisè 非彩色 **2** n (gear) kōngdǎng 空档; in ~ zài kōngdǎng 在空档

neutrality zhōnglì dìwèi 中立地位

neutralize *effect of drug etc* shǐ zhōnghé 使中和; *argument* shǐ wúxiào 使无效

never ◊ *(in past)* cónglái méi 从来没; *I've ~ eaten this* wǒ cónglái méi chīguo zhèige 我从来没吃过这个◊ *(in present)* cónglái bù 从来不; *she ~ goes to the movies* tā cónglái búqù kàn diànyǐng 她从来不去看电影◊ *(in future tenses)* juébúhuì 绝不会; *she will ~ marry him* tā juébúhuì gēn tā jiéhūn 她绝不会跟他结婚◊ *(in disbelief)* bùkěnéng 不可能; *you're ~ going to believe this* nǐ búhuì xiāngxìn zhè jiàn shì 你不会相信这件事; *you ~ promised, did you?* nǐ cónglái méiyǒu xǔnuòguò, shìba? 你从来没有许诺过, 是吧？

never-ending méiwán 没完

nevertheless dànshì 但是

new xīn 新; *this system is still ~ to me* wǒ duì zhège xìtǒng háishì bù shúxī 我对这个系统还是不熟悉; *I'm ~ to the job* wǒ shì xīnlái de 我是新来的; *that's nothing ~* méiyǒu shénme kě qíguàide 没有什么可奇怪的

newborn *adj* xīnshēng 新生

newcomer xīnlái de rén 新来的人

newly *(recently)* zuìjìn 最近

newly-weds xīnhūn rén 新婚人

new moon xīnyuè 新月

news xīnwén 新闻; *(on TV, radio)* xīnwén bàodǎo 新闻报导; *that's ~ to me* wǒ méi tīngshuō guo zhèjiànshì 我没听说过这件事

news agency tōngxùnshè 通讯社; **newscast** TV xīnwén guǎngbō 新闻广播; **newscaster** TV xīnwén guǎngbōyuán 新闻广播员; **newsdealer** bàokān jīngshòu rén 报刊经售人; **news flash** jǐnjí xīnwén bàodào 紧急新闻报道; **newspaper** bàozhǐ 报纸; **newsreader** TV *etc* xīnwén bōyīn yuán 新闻播音员; **news report**

newsstand bàotān 报摊儿; **newsvendor** bàofàn 报贩

New Territories *(in Hong Kong)* Xīnjiè 新界

New Year Xīnnián 新年; *(Chinese)* Chūnjié 春节; *Happy ~!* Xīnnián kuàilè! 新年快乐！

New Year's Day *(Jan 1)* Yuándàn 元旦; *(Chinese)* Chūyī 初一

New Year's Eve *(Dec 31)* Yuándàn Qiányè 元旦前夜; *(Chinese)* Chúxī 除夕

New York Niǔyuē 纽约

New Zealand ⇩ Xīnxīlán 新西兰

New Zealander ⇩ Xīnxīlán rén 新西兰人

next 1 *adj (in time, space)* xià yīgè 下一个; *the ~ week / month he came back again* xiàgè xīngqī / xiàgè yuè tā zàilái 下个星期 / 下个月他再来; *who's ~?* shuí shì xià yīgè? 谁是下一个？

2 *adv* xià yībù 下一步; *~ to X (beside)* zài X de pángbiān 在 X 的旁边; *(in comparison with)* yǔ X xiāngbǐ 与 X 相比

next door *adj & adv* gébì 隔壁

next of kin zuìjìnde qīnshǔ 最近的亲属

nibble *v/t* kěn 啃

nice *person* tǐtiē 体贴; *day, weather, meal, food, party, trip, vacation* lìngrén yúkuài 令人愉快; *house, hair* piàoliang 漂亮; *be ~ to your sisters* duì nǐ jiěmèi hǎodiǎnr 对你姐妹好点儿; *that's very ~ of you* nǐ tàihǎole 你太好了

nicely *presented etc* jīngxīn de 精心地; *(pleasantly)* héyí di 合宜地

niceties: *social ~* shèjiāo lǐjié 社交礼节

niche *(in market)* quēkǒu 缺口; *(special position)* héshìde wèizhí 合适的位置

nick *n (cut)* kěhén 刻痕; *in the ~ of time* qiàhǎo 恰好

nickel niè 镍

nickname *n* wàihào 外号

niece *(brother's daughter)* zhínǚ 侄女; *(sister's daughter)* wài shengnǚ

外甥女
niggardly *adj amount, person* xiǎoqì 小气

night yè 夜; **tomorrow ~** míngyè 明 夜; (*evening*) míngwǎn 明晚; **11 o'clock at ~** wǎnshàng shíyī diǎn 晚上十一点; **travel by ~** yèjiān lǚxíng 夜间旅行; **during the ~** yèjiān 夜间; **stay the ~** guòyè 过 夜; **a room for 2/3 ~s** yīgè fángjiān, liǎngsān yè 一个房间, 两三夜; **work ~s** shàng yèbān 上 夜班; **good ~** wǎn'ān 晚安; **in the middle of the ~** bànyè sāngēng 半夜三更

nightcap (*drink*) shuìqián jiǔ 睡前 酒; **nightclub** yèzǒnghuì 夜总 会; **nightdress** shuìyī 睡衣; **nightfall**: **at ~** huánghūn 黄昏; **night flight** yèjiān fēixíng 夜间 飞行; **nightgown** shuìyī 睡衣
nightingale yèyīng 夜莺
nightlife yè shēnghuó 夜生活
nightly 1 *adj* yèjiān 夜间 **2** *adv* zài yèjiān 在夜间
nightmare èmèng 恶梦; *fig* kěpà de jīngyàn 可怕的经验; **night-market** yèshì 夜市; **night porter** yèbān fúwùyuán 夜班服 务员; **night school** yèxiào 夜校; **night shift** yèbān 夜班; **night-shirt** shuìyī 睡衣; **nightspot** yèzǒnghuì 夜总会; **nighttime**: **at ~, in the ~** zài yèjiān 在夜间
nil líng 零
nimble jīling 机灵
nine jiǔ 九
nineteen shíjiǔ 十九
nineteenth dìshíjiǔ 第十九
ninetieth dìjiǔshí 第九十
ninety jiǔshí 九十
ninth dìjiǔ 第九
nip *n* (*pinch*) qiā 掐; (*bite*) yǎo 咬
nipple rǔtóu 乳头
nitrogen dàn 氮
no 1 *adv* bù 不; **do you understand? – ~** nǐ dǒng ma? – bùdǒng 你懂吗? – 不懂; **does he agree? – ~** tā tóngyì ma? – bù tóngyì 他同意吗? – 不同意 **2** *adj* méiyǒu 没有; **there's ~**

coffee / tea left méiyǒu kāfēi / chá le 没有咖啡 / 茶了; **I have ~ family / money** wǒ méiyǒu jiātíng / qián 我没有家庭 / 钱; **I'm ~ linguist / expert** wǒ bùshì yǔyán xuéjiā / zhuānjiā 我不是语 言学家 / 专家; **~ smoking / parking** jìnzhǐ xīyān / tíngchē 禁 止吸烟 / 停车
nobility guìzú 贵族
noble *adj* gāoguì 高贵
nobody méirén 没人; **~ knows** méirén zhīdào 没人知道; **there was ~ at home** méirén zàijiā 没人 在家
nod *n* & *v/i* diǎntóu 点头
♦**nod off** (*fall asleep*) dǎ kēshuì 打 瞌睡
no-hoper bù zhōngyòng derén 不 中用的人
noise shēngyīn 声音; (*loud, unpleasant*) zàoyīn 噪音
noisy xuānhuá 喧哗
nominal *amount* míngyì shàng de 名 义上
nominate (*appoint*) tímíng 提名; **~ X for a post** (*propose*) tuījiàn X rèn mǒuzhí zhíwèi 推荐 X 任某个 职位
nomination (*appointment*) rènmìng 任命; (*proposal*) tímíng 提名; (*person proposed*) bèi tímíng rén 被提名人
nominee bèi tímíng rén 被提名人
non ... bù ... 不 ...
nonalcoholic bù hán jiǔjīng 不含 酒精
nonaligned bù jiéméng 不结盟
nonchalant mòbù guānxīn 漠不 关心
noncommissioned officer fēi shòumìng guānyuán 非受命官 员
noncommittal *person, response* bù mínglǎng 不明朗
nondescript méiyǒu tèzhēng 没有 特征
none méi yīgè 没一个; **~ of the students** méi yīgè xuéshēng 没一 个学生; **~ of the chocolate** méi yìzhǒng qiǎokèlì 没一种巧克

力; **there is / are ~ left** méishèngde 没剩的

nonentity wúzú qīngzhòng 无足轻重

nonetheless rán'ér 然而

nonexistent bù cúnzài 不存在;
nonfiction fēi xiǎoshuō 非小说;
non(in)flammable bùrán 不燃;
noninterference, nonintervention bù gānyù 不干预; **non-iron** *shirt* miǎnyùntàng 免熨烫

no-no: *that's a ~* bùxíngde 不行的

no-nonsense *approach* rènzhēn 认真

nonpayment wèifù 未付; **nonpolluting** fēi wūrǎn 非污染;
nonresident *n* kèrén 客人; **nonreturnable** bù kětuì 不可退

nonsense húshuō 胡说; *don't talk ~* bié húshuō 别胡说; *~, it's easy!* húshuō, zhèhěn róngyì! 胡说,这很容易!

nonskid *tires* fánghuá 防滑; **nonslip** *surface* bùhuá 不滑; **nonsmoker** *(person)* bù xīyān zhě 不吸烟者; **nonstandard** fēi chánggù 非常规; **nonstick** *pan* bùzhān 不粘; **nonstop 1** *adj* *flight, train* zhídá 直达; *chatter* bùtíng 不停 **2** *adv* *fly, travel* zhídá 直达; *chatter, argue* bùtíng 不停; **nonswimmer** búhuì yóuyǒng zhě 不会游泳者; **nonunion** *adj* bùshǔ gōnghuì 不属工会; **nonviolence** fēi bàolì 非暴力; **nonviolent** fēi bàolì 非暴力

noodles miàntiáo 面条
noodle soup tāngmiàn 汤面
nook jiǎoluò 角落
noon zhōngwǔ 中午; *at ~* zài zhōngwǔ 在中午
noose quāntào 圈套
nor yòubù 又不; *~ do I* wǒ yěbù 我也不
norm zhǔnzé 准则
normal zhèngcháng 正常
normality zhèngcháng 正常
normalize *relationships* zhèngcháng huà 正常化
normally *(usually)* yībān de 一般

地; *(in a normal way)* zhèngcháng de 正常地

north 1 *n* běibù 北部; *to the ~ of X* X yǐběi X 以北 **2** *adj* běibù 北部 **3** *adv* *travel* xiàngběi 向北; *~ of X* X běibù X 北部

North America Běiměi 北美
North American 1 *adj* Běiměizhōu de 北美洲 **2** *n* Běiměizhōu rén 北美洲人

northeast *n* dōngběi bù 东北部
northerly yǐběi 以北
northern běifāng 北方
northerner běifāng rén 北方人
North Korea ⇩ Běicháoxiǎn 北朝鲜

North Korean ⇩ **1** *adj* Běicháoxiǎn 北朝鲜 **2** *n* Běicháoxiǎn rén 北朝鲜人

North Pole Běijí 北极
northward *travel* xiàngběi 向北
northwest *n* xīběi bù 西北部
Norway Nuówēi 挪威
Norwegian 1 *adj* Nuówēi 挪威 **2** *n* *(person)* Nuówēi rén 挪威人; *(language)* Nuówēi yǔ 挪威语
nose bízi 鼻子; *it was right under my ~* jiù zài wǒ yǎnqián 就在我眼前

♦**nose around** tàntīng 探听
nosebleed liú bíxuè 流鼻血
nostalgia huáijiù 怀旧
nostalgic huáijiù 怀旧
nostril bíkǒng 鼻孔
nosy hàoguǎn xiánshì 好管闲事
not ◊ *(present and future)* bù 不; *~ this one, that one* búshì zhèige, shì nèige 不是这个,是那个; *~ now* xiànzài bùxíng 现在不行; *~ there* nàr bùxíng 那儿不行; *~ like that* bùnéng nàyàng 不能那样; *~ before Tuesday / next week* xīngqī èr / xià xīngqī qián bùxíng 星期二/下星期前不行; *~ for me, thanks* wǒ bùyào, xièxiè 我不要,谢谢; *~ a lot* yīdiǎndian 一点点; *it's ~ allowed* méi chéng bù yǔnxǔ 没成吧 不允许; *I don't know* wǒ bù zhīdào 我不知道; *I am ~ American* wǒ búshì Měiguó rén 我不是美国人; *I'm ~ going* wǒ

búqù 我不去; *it won't be cold tomorrow* míngtiān bùnéng lěng 明天不能冷◊ (*past tense, and with* you) méi méi 没; *he didn't help* tā méi bāngmáng 他没帮忙; *he wasn't there* tā méi zài chū méi zài 他没在; *I haven't told him yet* wǒ hái méi gàosu ta 我还没告诉他; *I don't have that book* wǒ méiyǒu nèi běn shū 我没有那本书; *we don't have a car* wǒmen méiyǒu chē 我们没有车

notable zhùyuè 卓越

notary gōngzhèng rén 公证人

notch āokǒu 凹口

note *n* (*short letter*) biàntiáo 便条; MUS yīndiào 音调; (*memo to self*) jìlù 记录; (*comment on text*) zhùshì 注释; *take ~s* jì bǐjì 记笔记; *take ~ of X* zhùyì dào X 注意到 X

♦**note down** jìlù xiàlái 记录下来

notebook *also* COMPUT bǐjì běn 笔记本

noted zhùmíng 著名

notepad biàntiáo běn 便条本

notepaper biàntiáo zhǐ 便条纸

nothing méiyǒu shénme 没有什么; *~ for me thanks* wǒ shénme yě búyào xièxie 我什么也不要谢谢; *there was ~ to eat* méiyǒu shénme chīde 没有什么吃的; *there's ~ left* méiyǒu shénme le 没有什么了; *~ works in this office* bàngōngshì lǐ shénme dōu huài le 办公室里什么都坏了; *~ but* zhǐ 只; *there's ~ but work in his life* tā shēnghuó zhōng zhǐyǒu gōngzuò 他生活中只有工作; *he wants ~ but the best* tā zhǐ yào zuìhǎo de 他只要最好的; *~ much* duōshǎo 多少; *for ~* (*for free*) miǎnfèi 免费; (*for no reason*) wúyuán wúgù 无缘无故; *I'd like ~ better* zuì hǎole 最好了

notice **1** *n* (*on bulletin board, in street, in newspaper*) tōnggào 通告; (*advance warning*) yùxiān tōngzhī 预先通知; (*to leave job*) cízhí tōngzhī 辞职通知; (*to leave house*) zūpíng tōngzhī 租凭通知;

at short ~ tūrán 突然; *until further ~* zài lìngxíng tōngzhī zhīqián 在另行通知之前; *give X his/her ~* (*to quit job*) xiàng X tíchū cízhí tōngzhī 向 X 提出辞职通知; (*to leave house*) xiàng X tíchū tuìfáng tōngzhī 向 X 提出退房通知; *hand in one's ~* (*to employer*) tíchū cízhí tōngzhī 提出辞职通知; *four weeks' ~* sìgè xīngqī de yùxiān tōngzhī 四个星期的预先通知; *take ~ of X* zhùyì X 注意 X; *take no ~ of X* bùyào guǎn X 不要管 X **2** *v/t* zhùyì 注意

noticeable míngxiǎn 明显

notify tōngzhī 通知

notion kànfǎ 看法

notions zhēnxiàn 针线

notorious shēngmíng lángjí 声名狼籍

nougat jiá jiānguǒ táng 夹坚果糖

nought *Br* líng 零

noun míngcí 名词

nourishing yǒu yíngyǎng 有营养

nourishment yíngyǎng 营养

novel *n* xiǎoshuō 小说

novelist xiǎoshuō jiā 小说家

novelty (*being novel*) xīnyíng 新颖; (*sth novel*) xīnyíng shìwù 新颖事物

November shíyī yuè 十一月

novice xuétú 学徒

now xiànzài 现在; *~ and again, and then* yǒushí 有时; *by ~* zhèshí 这时; *from ~ on* cóng xiànzài kāishǐ 从现在开始; *right ~* cǐkè 此刻; *just ~* (*at this moment*) xiànzài 现在; (*a little while ago*) gāngcái 刚才; *~, ~!* déla 得啦! 得啦! ; *~, where did I put it?* nàme, wǒ bǎ tā fàng zài nǎrle? 那么, 我把它放在哪儿了?

nowadays xiànjīn 现今

nowhere wúchù 无处; *it's ~ near finished* lí wánchéng hái zǎozhe ne 离完成还早着呢

nozzle pēnzuǐ 喷嘴

nuclear yuánzǐhé 原子核

nuclear energy hénéng 核能;

nuclear fission hé lièbiàn 核裂变; **nuclear-free** wúhé 无核; **nuclear physics** yuánzǐhé wùlǐ 原子核物理; **nuclear power** hénéng 核能; **nuclear power station** hénéng zhàn 核能站; **nuclear reactor** hé fǎnyìng duī 核反应堆; **nuclear waste** hé fèiwù 核废物; **nuclear weapons** hé wǔqì 核武器

nude 1 adj luǒtǐ 裸体 **2** n (painting) luǒtǐ huà 裸体画; **in the ~** chì luǒluo 赤裸裸

nudge v/t qīngtuī 轻推

nudist n luǒtǐ zhǔyì zhě 裸体主义者

nuisance fánrén 烦人; **make a ~ of oneself** lìngrén tǎoyàn 令人讨厌; **what a ~!** tǎoyàn! 讨厌!

nuke v/t yòng hé wǔqì gōngjī 用核武器攻击

null and void wúxiào 无效

numb mámù 麻木; (emotionally) chídùn 迟钝

number 1 n (figure) shùmù 数目; (quantity) ruògān 若干; (of hotel room, house, phone number etc) shùzì 数字 **2** v/t (put a number on) biānhào 编号

numeral shùmù 数目

numerate jìshù nénglì qiáng 计数能力强

numerous xǔduō 许多

nun nígū 尼姑; **become a ~** chūjiā 出家

nurse hùshì 护士

nursery tuō'érsuǒ 托儿所; (for plants) miáopǔ 苗圃

nursery rhyme tóngyáo 童谣; **nursery school** yòu'éryuán 幼儿园; **nursery school teacher** yòu'éryuán lǎoshī 幼儿园老师

nursing hùlǐ 护理

nursing home (for old people) lǎorén yuàn 老人院

nut jiānguǒ 坚果; (for bolt) luómǔ 螺母; **~s** F (testicles) dàn dàn 蛋蛋

nutcrackers jiānguǒ qián 坚果钳

nutrient n yíngyǎng pǐn 营养品

nutrition yíngyǎng 营养

nutritious yǒu yíngyǎng 有营养

nuts adj F (crazy) fēng 疯; **be ~ about X** míliàn X 迷恋 X

nutshell: **in a ~** yíyàn yǐ bìzhī 一言以蔽之

nutty taste jiānguǒ wèir 坚果味儿; F (crazy) fēngkuáng 疯狂

nylon nílóng 尼龙

O

oak (*tree*) xiàngshù 橡树; (*wood*) xiàngmù 橡木
oar jiǎng 桨
oasis lǜzhōu 绿洲; *fig* shìwài táoyuán 世外桃源
oath LAW shìyán 誓言; (*swearword*) zǔzhòu 诅咒; **on ~** zài shìyán de yuēshù xià 在誓言的约束下
oatmeal yànmàipiàn 燕麦片
oats yànmàipiàn 燕麦片
obedience fúcóng 服从
obedient fúcóng 服从
obey fúcóng 服从
obituary *n* fùgào 讣告
object¹ *n* (*thing*) wùtǐ 物体; (*aim*) mùdì 目的; GRAM bīnyǔ 宾语
object² *v/i* fǎnduì 反对
♦object to fǎnduì 反对
objection fǎnduì 反对
objectionable (*unpleasant*) tǎoyàn 讨厌
objective **1** *adj* kèguān 客观 **2** *n* mùbiāo 目标
obligation yìwù 义务; **be under an ~ to X** duì X yǒu yìwù 对 X 有义务
obligatory bìxū 必须
oblige: **much ~d!** duōxièle! 多谢了!
obliging lèyú zhùrén 乐于助人
oblique **1** *adj* reference hánhu qící 含糊其辞 **2** *n* (*in punctuation*) xiéxiàn 斜线
obliterate *city* huǐmiè 毁灭; *memory* chúqù 除去
oblivion (*being forgotten*) yíwàng 遗忘; **fall into ~** jiànbèi wàngquè 渐被忘却
oblivious: **be ~ of ...** yìshí búdào ... 意识不到 ...
oblong *adj* chángfāngxíng 长方形
obnoxious yīnrén fǎngǎn 引人反感
obscene yínhuì 淫秽; *salary, poverty* guòfèn 过分

obscure (*hard to see*) hūn'àn 昏暗; (*hard to understand*) nánjiě 难解; (*little known*) wúmíng 无名
observance (*of festival*) zūnshǒu 遵守
observant liúxīn 留心
observation (*of nature, stars*) guānchá 观察; (*comment*) yìjiàn 意见
observatory tiānwén tái 天文台
observe *behavior* zhùyì 注意; *people* kàndào kàn到; *nature* guāncè 观测
observer (*of human nature etc*) guānchá zhě 观察者; (*at conference, elections*) guāncháyuán 观察员
obsess: **be ~ed with X** duì X zháomí 对 X 着迷
obsession pǐ'ǎi 癖; (*with a person, hobby*) zháomí 著迷
obsessive *behavior* guòfèn 过分
obsolete yǐ fèiqì 已废弃
obstacle (*physical*) zhàng'ài wù 障碍物; (*to progress etc*) zhàng'ài 障碍
obstetrician chǎnkē yīshī 产科医师
obstinacy wángù 顽固
obstinate wángù 顽固
obstruct *road, passage* zǔsè 阻塞; *investigation, police* zǔdǎng 阻挡
obstruction (*on road etc*) zhàng'ài wù 障碍物
obstructive *behavior* fáng'ài 妨碍
obtain dédào 得到
obtainable *products* kě huòdé 可获得
obvious (*evident, not subtle*) míngxiǎn 明显
obviously míngxiǎnde 明显地; **~!** dāngránle! 当然了!
occasion jīhuì 机会
occasional ǒu'ěr 偶尔

occasionally ǒurán 偶然

occult 1 adj shénmì 神秘 2 n: the ~ mìshù 秘术

occupant (of vehicle) chéngkè 乘客; (of house) jūzhù zhě 居住者

occupation (job) zhíyè 职业; (of country) zhànlǐng 占领

occupy one's time, mind zhànyòng 占用; position in company chōngrèn 充任; country zhànlǐng 占领

occur fāshēng 发生; it ~red to me that ... wǒ xiǎngdào ... 我想到...

occurrence chūxiàn 出现

ocean hǎiyáng 海洋

o'clock: at five/six ~ wǔ/liù diǎnzhōng 五／六点钟

October shíyuè 十月

octopus zhāngyú 章鱼

odd (strange) qíguài 奇怪; (not even) jīshù 奇数; the ~ one out yúzhòng bùtóng 与众不同; 50 ~ dàgài wǔshí 大概五十

odds: be at ~ with X yǔ X duìlì 与 X 对立

odds and ends (objects) língxīng cánwù 零星残物; (things to do) suǒsuì shì 琐碎事

odometer lǐchéng biǎo 里程表

odor qìwèi 气味

of: the name ~ the street/hotel jiē/lǚguǎn de míngzi 街／旅馆的名字; the color ~ the car qìchē yánsè 汽车颜色; the works ~ Dickens Díkèngsī zhùzuò 狄更斯著作; five/ten minutes ~ twelve shí'èr diǎn chà wǔ/shí fēn 十二点差五／十分; die ~ cancer/a stroke sǐyú áizhèng/zhòngfēng 死于癌症／中风; love ~ money/adventure duì qián/màoxiǎn de xǐ'ài 对钱／冒险的喜爱; ~ the three this is ... sāngè zhīzhōng zhèshì ... 三个之中这是...

off 1 prep: ~ the main road (away from) líkāi dà mǎlù 离开大马路; (leading from) cóng dà mǎlù fēnchà chūlái 从大马路分岔出来; $20 ~ the price jiǎnjià èrshí měiyuán 减价二十美元; he's ~ his food tā bùchī dōngxi 他不吃东西

2 adv: be ~ (of light) méi kāidēng 没开灯; (of TV, machine) méikāi 没开; (of brake) méi shàng zhá 没上闸; (of lid, top) méi gàizhe gàir 没盖着盖儿; (not at work) méi shàngbān 没上班; (canceled) qǔxiāo 取消; we're ~ tomorrow (leaving) wǒmén míngtiān líkāi 我们明天离开; I'm ~ to New York wǒ qù Niǔyuē 我去纽约; with his pants ~ tā bù chuān kùzi 他不穿裤子; with his hat ~ tā bù dài màozi 他不戴帽子; take a day ~ xiūjià yītiān 休假一天; it's 3 miles ~ sān yīnglǐ yuǎn 三英里远; it's a long way ~ (in the distance) hái yuǎn zhene 还远着呢; (in future) hái qiě zhene 还且着呢; drive/walk ~ kāizǒu/zǒukāi 开走／走开 3 adj: the ~ switch guānbì jiàn 关闭键

offend v/t (insult) màofàn 冒犯

offender LAW zuìfàn 罪犯

offense LAW zuìxíng 罪行

offensive 1 adj behavior, remark, smell tǎoyàn 讨厌 2 n MIL (attack) gōngjī 攻击; go onto the ~ cǎiqǔ gōngjī 采取攻击

offer 1 n tígōng 提供 2 v/t tígōng 提供; ~ X Y gěi X Y 给 X Y

offhand adj attitude bùjū lǐjié 不拘礼节

office (building) bàngōnglóu 办公楼; (room) bàngōngshì 办公室; (position) zhíwèi 职位

office block bàngōng dàlóu 办公大楼

office hours bàngōng shíjiān 办公时间

officer MIL jūnguān 军官; (in police) jǐngguān 警官

official 1 adj organization, statement view, theory guānfāng 官方; (confirmed) zhèngshì 正式 2 n guānyuán 官员

officially (strictly speaking) zhèngguī láishuō 正规来说

off-line adj working, input xiàwǎng 下网; go ~ líxiàn 离线; off-peak rates, season dīfēng shíjiān 低峰时间; ~ electricity dīfēng shíjiān gōngdiàn 低峰时间供电; **off-season 1** *adj rates, vacation* dànjì 淡季 **2** *n* dànjì 淡季; **offset** *v/t losses, disadvantage* díxiāo 抵消; **offside 1** *adj wheel etc* wàibiān 外边 **2** *adv* sp yuèwèi 越位; **off-spring** hòudài 后代; **off-white** *adj* huībáisè 灰白色

often jīngcháng 经常

oil 1 *n* (*for machine, food, skin*) yóu 油; (*as resource*) shíyóu 石油 **2** *v/t hinges, bearings* jiāyóu 加油

oil company shíyóu gōngsī 石油公司; **oil painting** yóuhuà 油画; **oil rig** yóujǐng 油井; **oil tanker** yóuchuán 油船; **oil well** yóujǐng 油井

oily yǒuyóu 有油; *food* yóunì 油腻

ointment ruǎngāo 软膏

ok kěyǐ 可以; *can I?* - ~ kěyǐ ma? - kěyǐ 可以吗? - 可以; *is it with you if ... ?* ... nǐ bù jièyì ba? ... 你不介意吧?; *that's ~ by me* wǒ tóngyì 我同意; *are you ~?* (*well, not hurt*) nǐ méishìr ba? 你没事儿吧?; *are you ~ for Friday?* xīngqī wǔ xíngma? 星期五行吗?; *he's ~* (*is a good guy*) tā tǐnghǎo 他挺好; *is this bus ~ for ... ?* zhè gōnggòng qìchē qù ... ma? 这公共汽车去 ... 吗?

old lǎo 老; (*previous*) jiù 旧; *how ~ are you/is he?* nǐ/tā duōdà niánji le? 你/他多大年纪了?; *he's getting ~* tā shàng niánji le 他上年纪了

old age lǎonián 老年

old-fashioned guòshí 过时

Old Summer Palace Yuánmíng-yuán 圆明园

olive gǎnlǎn 橄榄

olive oil gǎnlǎn yóu 橄榄油

Olympic Games Àoyùnhuì 奥运会

omelet jiān dànjuǎn 煎蛋卷

ominous yùzhào 预兆

omission yílòu 遗漏

omit yílòu 遗漏; ~ *to do X* wàngjì zuò X 忘记做 X

on 1 *prep*: ~ *the table/wall* zài zhuō/qiáng shàng 在桌/墙上; ~ *the bus/train* gōnggòng qìchē/huǒchē lǐ 公共汽车/火车里; ~ *TV/the radio* diànshì shàng/guǎngbō lǐ 电视上/广播里; *Sunday* xīngqī tiān 星期天; ~ *the 1st of ...* ... dìyī hào ... 第一大号; *this is ~ me* (*I'm paying*) wǒ lái fùqián 我来付钱; ~ *his arrival/departure* tā dàodá/líkāi shí 他到达/离开时 **2** *adv*: *be ~* (*of light*) kāidēng 开灯; (*of TV, computer etc*) kāi 开; (*of brake*) shàngzhá 上闸; (*of lid, top*) gàizhe gàir 盖着盖儿; (*of program: being broadcast*) kāiyǎn 开演; (*of meeting etc: be scheduled to happen*) jìnxíng 进行; *what's ~ tonight?* (*on TV etc*) jīnwǎn yǒu shénme jiémù? 今晚有什么节目?; (*what's planned?*) jīnwǎn gàn shénme? 今晚干什么?; *with his jacket ~* tā chuānzhe wàiyī 他穿着外衣; *with his hat ~* tā dàizhe màozi 他戴着帽子; *you're ~* (*I accept your offer etc*) xíng 行; ~ *you go* (*go ahead*) nǐ gànba 你干吧; *walk/talk ~* zǒu/tán xiàqù 走/谈下去; *and so ~* děngděng 等等; ~ *and talk etc* méiwán méiliǎo 没完没了 **3** *adj*: *the ~ switch* kāiqǐ jiàn 开启键

once 1 *adv* (*one time*) yīcì 一次; (*formerly*) céngjīng 曾经; ~ *again*, ~ *more* yòu yīcì 又一次; *at ~* (*immediately*) lìjí 立即; *all at ~* (*suddenly*) tūrán 突然; (*all*) *at ~* (*together*) yīqǐ 一起; ~ *upon a time there was ...* cóngqián yǒu ... 从前有 ... **2** *conj*: ~ *you have finished* nǐ yī wánle yǐhòu 你一完了以后

one 1 *n* (*number*) yī 一; (*in phone numbers*) yāo 幺 **2** *adj* yīgè 一个; ~ *day* yītiān 一天; ~ *country, two systems* yīguó liǎngzhì 一国两制 **3** *pron* yīgè 一个; *which ~?* nǎ yīgè? 哪一个?; ~ *by ~ enter, deal with* yīyī 一一; ~ *another* hùxiāng 互相; *the little ~s* xiǎo péngyǒu mén 小朋友们 **4** *personal pron*: *what can ~ say?*

háiyǒu shénme kě shuō de? 还有什么可说的？

one child policy jìhuà shēngyù 计划生育; **one-off** n (unique event, person) yīcì xìng 一次性; (exception) tèshū qíngkuàng 特殊情况; **one-parent family** dānshēn fùmǔ jiātíng 单身父母家庭

oneself zìjǐ 自己; **do X by ~** zìjǐ zuò X 自己做 X

one-sided discussion, fight yībiān dǎo 一边倒; **one-way street** dānxíng dào 单行道; **one-way ticket** dānchéng piào 单程票

onion yángcōng 洋葱

on-line adj shàngwǎng 上网; **be ~** zài wǎngshang 在网上; **go ~ (to)** shàngwǎng 上网

on-line service COMPUT wǎngluò fúwù 网络服务

onlooker pángguān zhě 旁观者

only 1 adv zhǐ 只; **not ~ X but also Y** bù jǐnjǐn X, Y yěshì 不仅仅 X, Y 也是; **~ just** gānggang 刚刚 **2** adj wéiyī 唯一; **~ son/daughter** dúzǐ/nǚ 独子/女

onset jiànglín 降临

onside adv SP wèi yuèwèi 未越位

onto: **put X → Y** bǎ X fàngdào Y shàng 把 X 放到 Y 上

onward xiàngqián 向前; **from ... ~** ... zhīhòu ... 之后

oolong tea wūlóngchá 乌龙茶

ooze 1 v/i (of liquid, mud) shènchū 渗出 **2** v/t: **he ~s charm** tā xiǎnde hěnyǒu mèilì 他显得很有魅力

opaque glass bù tòumíng 不透明

OPEC (= *Organization of Petroleum Exporting Countries*) Shíyóu Shūchūguó Zǔzhī 石油输出国组织

open 1 adj door, store, file kāizhe 开着; (honest, frank) tǎnbái 坦白; relationship wú zhàng'ài 无障碍; countryside kōngkuàng 空旷; **in the ~ air** lùtiān 露天 **2** v/t door, store, window, bottle kāi 开; book, paper tānkāi 摊开; COMPUT: file dǎkāi 打开; meeting kāishǐ 开始; **~ a bank account** kāi hù 开户 **3** v/i (of door, store, flower) kāi 开

♦**open up** v/i (of person) fàngkāi 放开

open-air adj meeting, concert lùtiān 露天; **~ pool** shìwài yóuyǒng chí 室外游泳池; **open-door policy** kāifàng zhèngcè 开放政策; **open-ended** contract etc bú gùdìng 不固定

opening (in wall etc) kòngxì 空隙; (beginning of movie, novel etc) kāishǐ 开始; (job going) kòngquē 空缺

openly (honestly, frankly) tǎnshuài 坦率

open-minded xūxīn 虚心; **open plan office** tǒngyī bàngōngshì 统一办公室; **open ticket** fēi gùdìng piào 非固定票

opera gējù 歌剧; **Peking Opera** Jīngjù 京剧

opera glasses xiǎo wàngyuǎnjìng 小望远镜; **opera house** gējù yuàn 歌剧院; **Peking Opera House** Jīngjù Yuàn 京剧院; **opera singer** gējù jiā 歌剧家

operate 1 v/i (of company) jīngyíng 经营; (of airline, bus service) guǎnlǐ 管理; (of machine) yùnzhuǎn 运转; MED dòng shǒushù 动手术 **2** v/t machine cāozuò 操作

♦**operate on** MED gěi ... kāidāo 给 ... 开刀

operating instructions cāozuò shǒuzé 操作手则; **operating room** MED shǒushù shì 手术室; **operating system** COMPUT cāozuò xìtǒng 操作系统

operation MED shǒushù 手术; (of machine) cāozuò 操作; **~s** (of company) jīngyíng 经营; **have an ~** MED zuò shǒushù 做手术

operator TELEC jiēxiàn shēng 接线生; (of machine) cāozuò zhě 操作者; (tour) lǚxíng dàiyíng zhě 旅行代营者

ophthalmologist yǎnkē yīshēng 眼科医生

opinion (view) kànfǎ 看法; **what's your ~?** nǐ yǒu shénme yìjiàn? 你有什么意见？; **in my ~** zài wǒ

kànlái 在我看来
opium yāpiàn 鸦片
Opium War Yāpiàn Zhànzhēng 鸦片战争
opponent duìshǒu 对手
opportunity jīhuì 机会
oppose fǎnduì 反对; **be ~d to ...** fǎnduì ... 反对 ...; **as ~d to X** yǔ X xiāngfǎn 与 X 相反
opposite 1 *adj side of road, end of town* duìmiàn 对面; *direction, meaning* xiāngfǎn 相反; *views, characters* duìkàng 对抗; **the ~ sex** yìxìng 异性 **2** *n* fǎnmiàn 反面
opposition *(to plan)* fǎnduì 反对; *Br* POL zàiyědǎng 在野党
oppress *the people* yāpò 压迫
oppressive *rule, dictator* bàonüè 暴虐; *weather* chénzhòng 沉重
optical illusion cuòshì 错视
optician yǎnjìng diàn 眼镜店
optimism lèguān 乐观
optimist lèguān zhě 乐观者
optimistic lèguān 乐观
optimum 1 *adj* zuì shìyí 最适宜 **2** *n* zuìjiā tiáojiàn 最佳条件
option xuǎnzé 选择, xuǎnxiàng 选项
optional kě xuǎnzé 可选择
optional extras kě xuǎnzé de fùjiā jiàn 可选择的附加件
or huò 或; **~ else!** bùrán dehuà děngzhe qiáo! 不然的话等着瞧!
oral exam kǒushì 口试; **oral hygiene** kǒuqiāng wèishēng 口腔卫生; **oral sex** kǒuyín 口淫
orange 1 *adj (color)* chéng 橙 **2** *n (fruit)* chéng 橙; *(color)* chéngsè 橙色
orangeade chéngzhīr 橙汁儿
orange juice ⇩ chéngzhīr 橙汁儿
orator yǎnshuōjiā 演说家
orbit 1 *n (of earth)* tiāntǐ yùnxíng guǐdào 天体运行轨道; **send X into ~** jiāng X sòngrù guǐdào 将 X 送入轨道 **2** *v/t the earth* rào guǐdào yùnxíng 绕轨道运行
orchard guǒyuán 果园

orchestra guǎnxián yuèduì 管弦乐队
orchid lánhuā 兰花
ordeal kǔnàde jīnglì 苦难的经历
order 1 *n (command)* mìnglìng 命令; *(sequence)* cìxù 次序; *(being well arranged)* zhìxù 秩序; *(for goods)* dìnggòu 定购; *(in restaurant)* dìng càidān 定菜单; **in ~ to** wèile ... 为了...; **out of ~** *(not functioning)* shīlíng 失灵; *(not in sequence)* cìxù diāndǎo 次序颠倒 **2** *v/t (put in sequence etc)* ānpái 安排; *goods* dìnghuò 定货; *meal* jiàocài 叫菜; **~ X to do Y** mìnglìng X qù zuò Y 命令 X 去做 Y **3** *v/i (in restaurant)* diǎncài 点菜
orderly 1 *adj* yǒu zhìxù 有秩序 **2** *n (in hospital)* qínzá gōng 勤杂工
ordinary pǔtōng 普通
ore kuàngshí 矿石
organ ANAT qìguān 器官; MUS fēngqín 风琴
organic *food, fertilizer* zìrán 自然
organism shēngwù 生物
organization jīgòu 机构; *(organizing)* zǔzhī 组织
organize zǔzhī 组织
organizer *(person)* zǔzhī zhě 组织者
orgasm xìngyù gāocháo 性欲高潮
Orient Dōngfāng 东方
orient *v/t (direct)* cháo X de fāngxiàng 朝 X 的方向; **~ oneself** *(get bearings)* rènqīng xíngshì 认清形势
Oriental 1 *adj* Dōngfāng 东方 **2** *n* Dōngfāng rén 东方人
origin qǐyuán 起源; **person of Chinese ~** Huáyì 华裔; **idea of Chinese ~** qǐyuán yú Zhōngguóde sīxiǎng 起源于中国的思想
original 1 *adj (not copied)* yuánzuò 原作; *(first)* zuìchū 最初 **2** *n (painting etc)* yuán zuòpǐn 原作品
originality dúchuànglì 独创力
originally yuánxiān 原先
originate 1 *v/t scheme, idea* fāmíng

发明 2 v/i (of idea, belief) fāqǐ 发起; (of family) láizì yú 来自于

originator (of scheme etc) fāqǐrén 发起人; **he's not an ~** tā bùshì gè fāmíngjiā 他不是个发明家

ornament zhuāngshì wù 装饰物

ornamental zhuāngshì 装饰

ornate style huá ér bùshí 华而不实

orphan gū'ér 孤儿

orphanage gū'ér yuàn 孤儿院

orthopedic adj jiǎoxíng wàikē 矫形外科

ostentatious style, behavior zìgāo zìdà 自高自大; clothes kuāzhāng 夸张

other 1 adj (referring to people) qítā 其他; (referring to things, animals) qítā 其它; **the ~ day** (recently) nàtiān 那天; **every ~ day / person** měi liángtiān / gèrén zhōng de yīgè 每两天 / 个人中的一个 2 n líng yīgè 另一个; **the ~s** (people) qítāde 其他的; (things, animals) qítāde 其它的

otherwise (differently) bùtóng 不同

otter shuǐtǎ 水獭

ought: **I / you ~ to know** wǒ / nǐ yīnggāi zhīdào 我 / 你应该知道; **you ~ to have done it** nǐ zǎo yīnggāi zuòle 你早应该做了

ounce àngsī 盎司

our wǒmen 我们

ours wǒménde 我们的; **a friend of ~** wǒménde péngyǒu 我们的朋友

ourselves wǒmén zìjǐ 我们自己; **by ~** wǒmén zìjǐ 我们自己

oust (from office) miǎnzhí 免职

out: **be ~** (of light) guāndiào 关掉; (of fire) xīmiè 熄灭; (of flower) shèngkāi 盛开; (of sun) chūlái 出来; (not at home, not in building) búzài 不在; (of calculations) cuò 错; (be published) chūbǎn 出版; (of secret) xiǎnlòu 显露; (no longer in competition) táotài 淘汰; (no longer in fashion) guòshí 过时; **~ here in Dallas** zài zhèlǐ Dálāsī 在这里达拉斯; **he's ~ in the gar-**

den tā zài huāyuán lǐ tā在花园里; (get) **~! chūqù!** 出去！; (get) **~ of my room!** gǔnchū wǒ fāngjiān! 滚出我房间！; **that's ~** (out of the question) bùxíng 不行; **he's ~ to win** (fully intending to) tā fēi yíng bùkě 他非赢不可

outboard motor chuánwěi diàndòngjī 船尾电动机

outbreak (of violence, war) bàofā 爆发

outburst (emotional) bèngfā 迸发

outcast n bèi yíqì zhě 被遗弃者

outcome jiéguǒ 结果

outcry qiángliè kàngyì 强烈抗议

outdated guòshí 过时

outdo shèngguò 胜过

outdoor toilet, activities, life shìwài 室外

outdoors adv shìwài 室外

outer wall etc wàibù 外部

outer space tàikōng 太空

outfit (clothes) tàozhuāng 套装; (company, organization) zǔzhí 组织

outgoing flight chūháng 出航; personality kāilǎng 开朗

outgrow old ideas chāoguò 超过

outing (trip) chūyóu 出游

outlet (of pipe) chūkǒu 出口; (for sales) xiāoshòu diǎn 销售点; ELEC chāzuò 插座

outline 1 n (of person, building etc) lúnkuò 轮廓; (of plan, novel) cǎotú 草图 2 v/t plans etc dǎ cǎotú 打草图

outlive huóde bǐ ... gèngjiǔ 活得比 ... 更长

outlook (prospects) zhǎnwàng 展望

outlying areas biānyuǎn 边远

outnumber: **X ~s Y by ... times** X bǐ Y dà ... bèi X比Y大 ... 倍

out of ◊ (motion): **run ~ the house** pǎochū wūwài 跑出屋外 ◊ (position): **20 miles ~ Nanjing** Nánjīng yǐwài èrshí yīnglǐ 南京以外二十英里 ◊ (cause): **jealousy / curiosity** yóuyú jídù / hàoqí 由于 嫉妒 / 好奇 ◊ (without): **we're ~ gas** wǒmén chē méi yóu le 我们车没油了◊ (from a group): **5 ~ 10** shífen zhīwǔ 十分之五

out-of-date guòshí 过时

out-of-the-way huāngpì 荒僻

outperform bǐ ... hǎo bǐ ... 好

output 1 n (of factory) chǎnliàng 产量; COMPUT shūchū 输出 **2** v/t (produce) shēngchǎn 生产; COMPUT: signal fāchū 发出

outrage 1 n (feeling) gōngfèn 公愤; (act) bàoxíng 暴行 **2** v/t yǐnqǐ fènkǎi 引起愤慨; **I was ~d to hear X** dāng wǒ tīngdào X shí gǎndào shífèn fènnù 当我听到X时感到十分愤怒

outrageous acts wúchǐ 无耻; prices guòfèn 过分

outright 1 adj winner chèdǐ 彻底 **2** adv win chèdǐ 彻底; kill ~ jísǐ 即死

outrun (run faster than) pǎode gèngkuài 跑得更快; (run for longer than) pǎode gèngjiǔ 跑得更久

outset kāishǐ 开始; **from the ~** yī kāitóu 一开头

outside 1 adj surface, wall, lane wàibù 外部 **2** adv sit, go wàimiàn 外面 **3** prep zài ... yǐwài 在 ... 以外; (apart from) chúle 除了 **4** n (of building, case etc) wàimiàn 外面; **at the ~** zuìduō 最多

outside broadcast lùyīn shìwài bōyīn 录音室外播音

outsider lěngmén 冷门

outsize adj clothing tè dàhào 特大号

outskirts jiāoqū 郊区

outspoken zhíyán búhuì 直言不讳

outstanding success, quality xiǎnzhù 显著; writer, athlete jiéchū 杰出; FIN: invoice, sums wèifù 未付

outward adj appearance wàibiǎo 外表; **~ journey** wàichū lǚchéng 外出旅程

outward-going kāilǎng 开朗

outwardly xiàngwàide 向外地

outweigh bǐ ... zhòngyào 比 ... 重要

outwit zhìshèng 智胜

oval adj tuǒyuán tuǒyuán 椭圆

ovary luǎncháo 卵巢

oven kǎoxiāng 烤箱

over 1 prep (across) guò qù; (more than) chāoguò 超过; (above) zài ... shàngfāng 在 ... 上方; (during) zài ... qījiān 在 ... 期间; **travel all ~ China** yóulǎn quán Zhōngguó 游览全中国; **you find them all ~ China** tāmen biànbù Zhōngguó 它们遍布中国; **let's talk ~ a drink / meal** wǒmen biān hē / chī biān tán 我们边喝 / 吃边谈; **we're ~ the worst** wǒmen yǐjīng dùguòle zuì kùnnán de shíkè 我们已经渡过了最困难的时刻 **2** adv: **be ~** (finished) wánjié 完结; (left) shèngyú 剩余; **~ to you** (your turn) gāi nǐ le 该你了; **~ in Europe** zài Ōuzhōu 在欧洲; **~ here** zài zhèlǐ 在这里; **~ there** zài nàlǐ 在那里; **it hurts all ~** húnshēn dōu téng wǒ húnshēn dōu téng 我浑身都疼; **painted white all ~** quánbù shuā báisè 全部刷白色; **it's all ~** quánwánle 全完了; **~ and again** lǚcì 屡次; **do X ~** (again) zàicì zuò X 再次做X

overall 1 adj length zǒngtǐ 总体 **2** adv cóng tóu zhì wěi 从头至尾

overawe: **be ~d by X** bèi X xiàzhù 被X吓住

overboard: **man ~!** yǒurén luòshuǐ! 有人落水！; **go ~ for X** duì X kuángrè zhuīqiú 对X狂热追求

overcast day, sky duōyún 多云

overcharge v/t customer guògāo yàojià 过高要价

overcoat dàyī 大衣

overcome difficulties, shyness zhēngfú 征服; **be ~ by emotion** bùnéng zìzhì 不能自制

overcrowded yōngjǐ 拥挤

overdo (exaggerate) kuāzhāng 夸张; (in cooking) zhǔ guòhuǒr 煮过火儿; **you're ~ing things** guòyú láolèi 过于劳累

overdone meat guòhuǒ 过火

overdose n guòliàng 过量

overdraft chāozhī 超支; **have an ~** yǒu chāozhī 有超支

overdraw *account* chāozhī 超支; **be $800 ~**n chāozhī bābǎi měiyuán 超支八百美元

overdrive MOT chāosù 超速

overdue *apology, alteration* qīdài yǐjiǔ 期待以久

overestimate *abilities, value* guògāo gūjì 过高估计

overexpose *photograph* guòdù gǎnguāng 过度感光

overflow **1** n (*pipe*) fànlàn 泛滥 **2** v/i (*of water*) shǐ yìchū 使溢出

overgrown *garden* cùyè cóngshēng 簇叶丛生; **he's an ~ baby** tā shuǎ xiǎohái píqí 他耍小孩脾气

overhaul v/t *engine* dàxiū 大修; *plans* chèdǐ jiǎnchá 彻底检查

overhead **1** adj *lights* tóudǐng shàng 头顶上; *railroad* jiàkōng 架空 **2** n FIN tōngcháng kāizhī 通常开支

overhear tōutīng 偷听

overjoyed kuángxǐ 狂喜

overland adj & adv jīngguò lùdì 经过陆地

overlap v/i (*of tiles, periods of time etc*) chóngdié 重迭; (*of theories*) fùhé 复合; ELEC fùhé guòzhòng 负荷过重

overlook (*of tall building etc*) fǔshì 俯视; (*not see*) hūlüè 忽略

overly guòdù de 过度地; **not ~ ...** méi guòdù de ... 没过度地 ...

overnight adv yèjiān 夜间

overnight bag guòyè dài 过夜袋

overpaid fùqián guòduō 付钱过多

overpass lìtǐ jiāochā 立体交叉

overpower v/t (*physically*) jībài 击败

overpowering *smell* nóngliè 浓裂; *sense of guilt* qiángliè 强烈

overpriced yàojià guògāo 要价高

overrated guògāo gūjì 过高估计

overrule *decision* fǒujué 否决

overrun *country* qīnzhàn 侵占; *time* chāoshí 超时; **be ~ with** mànyán 蔓延

overseas adj & adv hǎiwài 海外

overseas Chinese Huáqiáo 华侨

oversee jiānshì 监视

oversight shūhū 疏忽

oversleep shuì guòtóu 睡过头

overtake (*in work, development*) chāoguò 超过; *Br* MOT chāochē 超车

overthrow tuīfān 推翻

overtime *work* jiābān 加班

overture MUS xùqǔ 序曲; **make ~s to** tíchū jiànyì 提出建议

overturn **1** v/t *vehicle, object* fānzhuàn 翻转; *government* tuīfān 推翻 **2** v/i (*of vehicle*) fān fān 翻翻

overweight chāozhòng 超重

overwhelm (*with work*) bèi gōngzuò yàde chuǎnbù guòqì 被工作压得喘不过气; (*with emotion*) bùzhī suǒcuò 不知所措; **be ~ed by** (*by response*) jīngxǐ jiāojí 惊喜交集

overwork **1** n guòdù gōngzuò 过度工作 **2** v/i gōngzuò guòdù 工作过度 **3** v/t: **~ X** shǐ X píláo guòdù 使 X 疲劳过度

owe v/t qiàn 欠; **~ X $500** qiàn X wǔbǎi měiyuán 欠 X 五百美元; **~ X an apology** yīng xiàng dàoqiàn 应向 X 道歉; **how much do I ~ you?** wǒ qiàn nǐ duōshǎo? 我欠你多少？

owing to yóuyú 由于

owl māotóuyīng 猫头鹰

own[1] v/t yōngyǒu 拥有

own[2] **1** adj zìjǐ 自己 **2** pron: **an apartment of my ~** wǒ zìjǐde gōngyù 我自己的公寓; **on my / his ~** wǒ / tā zìjǐ 我 / 他自己

♦ **own up** tǎnbái de chéngrèn 坦白地承认

owner yōngyǒu zhě 拥有者

ownership suǒyǒu quán 所有权

ox niú 牛

oxide yǎnghuà wù 氧化物

oxygen yǎngqì 氧气

oyster háo 蚝

oyster sauce háoyóu 蚝油

ozone chòuyǎng 臭氧

ozone layer chòuyǎng céng 臭氧层

P

pace 1 n (step) bù 步; (speed) sùdù 速度 2 v/i: ~ up and down duóbù 踱步

pacemaker MED qǐbóqì 起搏器; SP dìng sùdù zhě 定速度者

Pacific: the ~ (Ocean) Tàipíngyáng 太平洋

Pacific Rim: the ~ Tàipíngyáng àn 太平洋岸; ~ countries Tàipíngyáng guójiā 太平洋岸国家

pacifier (for baby) xiàngpí nǎitóu 橡皮奶头

pacifism hépíng zhǔyì 和平主义

pacifist n hépíng zhǔyì zhě 和平主义者

pacify ānfǔ 安抚

pack 1 n (back~) bēibāo 背包; (of cereal, food) dài 袋; (of cigarettes) bāo 包; (of cards) fù 副 2 v/t bag jiāng dōngxi zhuāngrù 将东西装入; item of clothing etc fàngrù xínglǐ 放入行李; goods bāozhuāng 包装; groceries zhuāngrù kǒudài 装入口袋 3 v/i zhěnglǐ xíngzhuāng 整理行装

package 1 n (parcel) bāoguǒ bāo 裹; (of offers etc) zhěngdài cáiliào 整袋材料 2 v/t (in packs) dǎbāo 打包; (for promotion) bāozhuāng 包装

package deal (for vacation) bāobàn lǚxíng 包办旅行

package tour bāobàn lǚxíng 包办旅行

packaging (of product) bāozhuāng 包装; (of rock star etc) xíngxiàng bāozhuāng 形象包装

packed (crowded) mǎnyuán 满员

packet bāo 包

pact xiéyì 协议

pad¹ 1 n (piece of cloth etc) diànliào 垫片; (for writing) biànjiānběn 便笺本 2 v/t (with material) diànchèn 垫衬; speech, report pīncòu 拼凑

pad² v/i (move quietly) qīngqīng zǒu 轻轻走

padded jacket, shoulders dài chèndiàn 带衬垫

padding (material) chènliào 衬料; (in speech etc) fèihuà 废话

paddle¹ 1 n (for canoe) lǚ 橹 2 v/i (in canoe) yáolǔ yáolǔ 摇橹

paddle² v/i (in water) tāngshuǐ tāngshuǐ 趟水

paddock xiǎowéichǎng 小围场

paddy dàozi 稻子

paddy field dàotián 稻田

padlock 1 n guàsuǒ 挂锁 2 v/t gate yòng guàsuǒ suǒ 用挂锁锁; ~ X to Y yòng guàsuǒ bǎ X suǒ zài Y shàng 用挂锁把 X 锁在 Y 上

page¹ n (of book etc) yè 页; ~ number yèmǎ 页码

page² v/t (call) ⇩ chuánhū 传呼

pager ⇩ chuánhūjī 传呼机

pagoda bǎotǎ 宝塔

paid employment yǒucháng gùyòng 有偿雇佣

pail tǒng 桶

pain téngtòng 疼痛; be in ~ tòngtòng 痛痛; take ~s to ... fèi kǔxīn ... 费苦心...; X is a ~ in the neck F X zhēn fánrén X 真烦人

painful arm, leg etc téngtòng 疼痛; (distressing) lìngrén tòngkǔ 令人痛苦; (laborious) fèishì 费事

painfully (extremely, acutely) tèbié 特别

painkiller zhǐtòngpiàn 止痛片

painless wútòng 无痛

painstaking zǐxì zǐxì 仔细仔细

paint 1 n (for wall, car) túliào 涂料; (for artist) yánliào 颜料 2 v/t wall etc shàng túliào 上涂料; picture yòng yánliào huà 用颜料画 3 v/i (as art form) huìhuà 绘画

paintbrush (for wall, ceiling) qīshuā 漆刷; (of artist) huàbǐ 画笔

painter (*decorator*) fěnshuāgōng 粉刷工; (*artist*) huàjiā 画家

painting (*activity*) huìhuà 绘画; (*picture*) túhuà 图画

paintwork (*in room*) fěnshuā 粉刷; (*of car*) qī 漆

pair duì 对; *a ~ of shoes / sandals* yìshuāng xié / liángxié 一双鞋 / 凉鞋

pajama jacket shuìyī 睡衣

pajama pants shuìkù 睡裤

pajamas shuìyīkù 睡衣裤

Pakistan Bājīsītǎn 巴基斯坦

Pakistani 1 *adj* Bājīsītǎn 巴基斯坦 2 *n* Bājīsītǎn rén 巴基斯坦人

pal F (*friend*) gēmenr 哥们儿; *hey ~, got a light?* lǎoxiōng, jiè ge huǒr? 老兄, 借个火儿?

palace gōngdiàn 宫殿

palate è 腭

palatial fùlì 富丽

pale *person* cāngbái 苍白; *~ pink / blue* dànfěn / lánsè 淡粉 / 蓝色

pallet huòbǎn 货板

pallor liǎnsè cāngbái 脸色苍白

palm[1] (*of hand*) shǒuzhǎng 手掌

palm[2] (*tree*) zōnglǘshù 棕榈树

palpitations MED xīnjì 心悸

paltry wēibùzúdào 微不足道

pamper fàngzòng 放纵

pamphlet xiǎocèzi 小册子

pan 1 *n* (*for cooking*) guō 锅 2 *v/t* F (*criticize severely*) yánlì pīpíng 严厉批评

♦ pan out (*develop*) fāzhǎn 发展

pancake bóbǐng 薄饼

panda xióngmāo 熊猫

pandemonium dà hùnluàn 大混乱

pane (*of glass*) kuài 块

panel (*section*) xiāngbǎn 镶板; (*people*) xiǎozǔ 小组

paneling xiāngqiàn 镶嵌

panhandle *v/i* F xíngqǐ 行乞

panic 1 *n* kǒnghuāng 恐慌 2 *v/i* shòujīng 受惊; *don't ~* biéhuāng 别慌

panic buying FIN kǒnghuāng gòumǎi 恐慌购买; panic selling FIN kǒnghuāng pāoshòu 恐慌抛售; panic-stricken jīnghuāng

shīcuò 惊惶失措

panorama quánjǐng 全景

panoramic *view* quánjǐng 全景

pansy (*flower*) sānsèjǐn 三色堇; F jiǎxiǎozi 假小子

pant *v/i* chuǎnxī 喘息

panties nèikù 内裤

pants kùzi 裤子

pantyhose liánkùwà 连裤袜

paper 1 *n* (*material*) zhǐ 纸; (*news~*) bàozhǐ 报纸; (*wall~*) bìzhǐ 壁纸; (*academic*) lùnwén 论文; (*examination*) kǎoshìjuàn 考试卷; *~s* (*documents*) wénjiàn 文件; (*identity ~s*) zhèngjiàn 证件; *a piece of ~* yìzhāng zhǐ 一张纸 2 *adj* zhǐzhì 纸制 3 *v/t room, walls* biǎohú 裱糊

paperback píngzhuāngshū 平装书; paper bag zhǐdài 纸袋; paper clip huíxíngzhēn 回形针; paper cup zhǐ bēizi 纸杯子; paperwork wénshū gōngzuò 文书工作

par (*in golf*) biāozhǔn gānshù 标准杆数; *be on a ~ with X* yǔ X tóngděng zhòngyào 与 X 同等重要; *feel below ~* gǎnjué bú tài hǎo 感觉不太好

parachute 1 *n* jiàngluòsǎn 降落伞 2 *v/i* tiàosǎn 跳伞 3 *v/t troops, supplies* (yòng jiàngluòsǎn) kōngtóu (用降落伞) 空投

parachutist tiàosǎn zhě 跳伞者

parade 1 *n* (*procession*) yuèbīng 阅兵 2 *v/i* xíngzǒu 行走 3 *v/t knowledge, new car* xuànyào 炫耀

paradise *Biblical* lèyuán 乐园; *fig* tiāntáng 天堂

paradox zìxiāng máodùn 自相矛盾

paradoxical sì fēi ér shì 似非而是

paradoxically sì fēi ér shì 似非而是

paragraph duànluò 段落

parallel *n* (*line*) píngxíngxiàn 平行线; (*of latitude*) wěidùxiàn 纬度线; *fig* xiāngsì zhī chù 相似之处; *do two things in ~* tóngshí zuò liǎngjiàn shì 同时做两件事

2 adj line píngxíng 平行; fig tóngshí fāshēng 同时发生 **3** v/t (match) xiāngdāng 相当

paralysis tānhuàn 瘫痪

paralyze tānhuàn 瘫痪; fig bù zhī suǒ cuò 不知所措

paramedic hùlǐ rényuán 护理人员

parameter jièxiàn 界限

paramilitary 1 adj zhǔn jūnshì 准军事 **2** n zhǔn jūnshì bùduì chéngyuán 准军事部队成员

paramount zuì zhòngyào 最重要; be ~ tóudēng dàshì 头等大事

paranoia wàngxiǎngkuáng 妄想狂

paranoid adj duōyí 多疑

paraphernalia záqīzábāde dōngxi 杂七杂八的东西

paraphrase shìyì 释义

paraplegic n xiàshēn tānhuàn de rén 下身瘫痪的人

parasite jìshēngchóng 寄生虫; fig kào jiùjì wéishēng 靠救济为生

parasol yángsǎn 阳伞

paratrooper sǎnbīng 伞兵

parcel n bāoguǒ 包裹

♦**parcel up** bāoqǐ 包起

parch v/t shǐ jiāogān 使焦干; be ~ed (of person) kě jíle 渴极了

pardon 1 n LAW shèmiǎn 赦免; I beg your ~? (what did you say) nǐ shuō shénme? 你说什么？; I beg your ~ (I'm sorry) qǐng yuánliàng 请原谅 qǐng yuánliàng yuánliàng 原谅; LAW shèmiǎn 赦免; ~ me? nǐ shuō shénme? 你说什么？

pare (peel) xiāopí 削皮

parent jiāzhǎng 家长

parental fùmǔ 父母

parent company zǒnggōngsī 总公司

parent-teacher association jiāzhǎng jiàoshī liányìhuì 家长教师联谊会

park[1] (area) gōngyuán 公园

park[2] MOT **1** v/t tíngfàng 停放 **2** v/i tíngchē 停车

parka fēngxuě dàyī 风雪大衣

parking MOT tíngchē 停车; no ~ jìnzhǐ tíngchē 禁止停车

parking brake shǒuzhá 手扎;

parking garage shìnèi tíngchēchǎng 室内停车场; **parking lot** tíngchēchǎng 停车场; **parking meter** tíngchē jìshí shōufèiqì 停车计时收费器; **parking place** tíngchēchù 停车处; **parking ticket** wéizhāng tíngchē fákuǎndān 违章停车罚款单

parliament yìhuì 议会

parliamentary yìhuì 议会

parole 1 n jiǎshì 假释; be on ~ huòdé jiǎshì 获得假释 **2** v/t zhǔnxǔ jiǎshì 准许假释

parrot yīngwǔ 鹦鹉

parsley ōuqín 欧芹

part 1 n yíbùfen 一部分; (section, area) bùfen 部分; (of machine) língjiàn 零件; (in play, movie) juésè 角色; MUS shēngbù 声部; (in hair) fèng 缝; take ~ in cānjiā 参加 **2** adv (partly) bùfen 部分 **3** v/i fēnkāi 分开 **4** v/t: ~ one's hair jiāng tóufà fēnkāi 将头发分开

♦**part with** things chūràng 出让

part exchange bùfen dǐjià jiāoyìfǎ 部分抵价交易法; take X in ~ yǐ bùfen dǐjià jiāoyìfǎ gòumǎi X 以部分抵价交易法购买X

partial (incomplete) bù wánquán 不完全; be ~ to piān'ài 偏爱

partially bùfen 部分

participant cānjiā zhě 参加者

participate cānjiā 参加; ~ in X cānjiā X 参加X

participation cānjiā 参加

particle PHYS lìzǐ 粒子; (small amount) yìdiǎnr 一点儿

particular (specific) tèbié 特别; (special) tèshū 特殊; (fussy) tiāotì 挑剔; in ~ yóuqí 尤其

particularly tèbié 特别

parting 1 n (of people) líbié 离别

partition 1 n (screen) píngfēng 屏风; (of country) fēnliè 分裂 **2** v/t country fēnliè 分裂

♦**partition off** gékāi 隔开

partly bùfen 部分

partner COM héhuǒrén 合伙人; (in relationship) tóngbàn 同伴; (in particular activity) dādàng 搭档

partnership COM héhuǒ jīngyíng 合伙经营; (*in particular activity*) dādàng guānxi 搭档关系

part of speech cíxìng 词性; **part owner** gòngyǒu zhě 共有者; **part-time 1** *adj* jiānzhí 兼职 **2** *adv* work jiānzhí 兼职

party 1 *n* (*celebration*) qìngzhùhuì 庆祝会; POL dǎng 党; (*group of people*) zǔ组; **be a ~ to** cānyù 参与 **2** *v/i* F wánr 玩儿

party member dǎngyuán 党员

pass 1 *n* (*for getting into a place*) tōngxíngzhèng 通行证; SP chuánqiú 传球; (*in mountains*) guān'ài 关隘; **make a ~ at X** xiàng X tiáoqíng 向 X 调情 **2** *v/t* (*hand*) dì 递; (*go past*) jīngguò 经过; (*overtake*) yuèguò 越过; (*go beyond*) chāoguò 超过; (*approve*) biǎojué tōngguò 表决通过; SP chuánqiú 传球; **~ an exam** tōngguò kǎoshì 通过考试; **~ sentence** LAW pànxíng 判刑; **~ the time** xiāomó shíjiān 消磨时间 **3** *v/i* (*of time*) tuīyí 推移; (*in exam*) jígé 及格; SP chuándì 传递; (*go away*) xiāoshī 消失

♦**pass around** hùxiāng chuán 互相传

♦**pass away** (*die*) qùshì 去世

♦**pass by** *v/t & v/i* (*go past*) jīngguò 经过

♦**pass on 1** *v/t* information, book chuándì 传递 **2** *v/i* (*die*) qùshì 去世

♦**pass out** (*faint*) hūnjué 昏厥

♦**pass through** *town* tújīng 途经

♦**pass up** opportunity fàngguò 放过

passable *road* kě tōngguò 可通过; (*acceptable*) guòdéqù 过得去

passage (*corridor*) tōngdào 通道; (*from poem, book*) yīduàn 一段; (*of time*) tuīyí 推移

passageway zǒuláng 走廊

passenger chéngkè 乘客

passenger seat chéngkè zuòwèi 乘客座位

passer-by guòlùrén 过路人

passion (*emotion*) qínggǎn 情感; (*sexual desire*) xìng'ài 性爱; (*fervor*) rèqíng 热情

passionate *lover* rèliàn 热恋; (*fervent*) rèqíng 热情

passive 1 *adj* bèidòng 被动 **2** *n* GRAM bèidòng yǔtài 被动语态; **in the ~** bèidòng xíngshi 被动形式

pass mark jígéfēn 及格分

passport hùzhào 护照

passport control hùzhào jiǎnchá-chù 护照检查处

password kǒulìng 口令

past 1 *adj* (*former*) yǐqián 以前; **the ~ few days** jìnjǐtiān 近几天; **that's all ~ now** nà dōu yǐjing guòqù le 那都已经过去了 **2** *n* guòqù 过去; **in the ~** zài guòqù 在过去 **3** *prep* (*in time*) chíyú 迟于; (*in position*) jīngguò 经过; **it's half ~ two** xiànzài liǎngdiǎnbàn 现在两点半 **4** *adv*: **run / walk ~** pǎo / zǒuguò 跑 / 走过

paste 1 *n* (*adhesive*) jiānghu 糨糊 **2** *v/t* (*stick*), COMPUT zhāntiē 粘贴

pastel 1 *n* (*color*) qīngdànsè 清淡色 **2** *adj* qīngdàn 清淡

pastime xiāoqiǎn 消遣

pastor jiàoqū mùshī 教区牧师

past participle guòqù fēncí 过去分词

pastrami wǔxiāng xūnniúròu 五香熏牛肉

pastry (*for pie*) yóusū miàntuán 油酥面团; (*small cake*) sūpí gāodiǎn 酥皮糕点

past tense guòqùshí 过去时

pasty *adj* complexion cāngbái 苍白

pat 1 *n* qīngpāi 轻拍; **give X a ~ on the back** *fig* xiàng X biǎoshì zhùhè 向 X 表示祝贺 **2** *v/t* pāipāi 拍拍

patch 1 *n* (*on clothing*) bǔdīng 补丁; (*period of time*) yīduàn shíqī 一段时期; (*area*) bùfen 部分; **be not a ~ on** F yuǎnyuǎn bùrú 远远不如 **2** *v/t* clothing dǎ bǔdīng 打补丁

♦**patch up** (*repair temporarily*) línshí xiūlǐ 临时修理; *quarrel* jiějué 解决

patchwork 1 n (needlework) zápǐn huābù 杂拼花布; 杂拼花布 **2** adj quilt zápǐn huābù miánbèi 杂拼花布棉被

patchy quality bùyízhì 不一致; work, performance xiáyúhùjiàn 瑕瑜互见

patent 1 adj míngxiǎn 明显 **2** n (for invention) zhuānlì 专利 **3** v/t invention qǔdé zhuānlìquán 取得专利权

patent leather qīpí 漆皮

patently (clearly) míngxiǎn 明显

paternal relative fùxì 父系; pride, love fùqīnbān 父亲般

paternalism jiāzhǎng zhǔyì 家长主义

paternalistic jiāzhǎng zuòfēng 家长作风

paternity fùqīn shēnfen 父亲身分

path xiǎolù 小路; fig tújìng 途径, lùjìng 路径

pathetic (invoking pity) zhāorén liánmǐn 招人怜悯; F (very bad) kěbēi 可悲

pathological bìngtài 病态

pathologist bìnglǐxuéjiā 病理学家

pathology bìnglǐxué 病理学

patience nàixīn 耐心

patient 1 n bìngrén 病人 **2** adj yǒu nàixīn 有耐心; just be ~! nàixīn diǎnr! 耐心点儿！

patiently nàixīn 耐心

patio píngtái 平台

patriot àiguó zhě 爱国者

patriotic àiguó 爱国

patriotism àiguó zhǔyì 爱国主义

patrol 1 n xúnluóduì 巡逻队; be on ~ zài xúnluó zhōng 在巡逻中 **2** v/t streets, border xúnluó 巡逻

patrol car xúnluóchē 巡逻车; **patrolman** xúnjǐng 巡警; **patrol wagon** qiúchē 囚车

patron (of store, movie house) gùkè 顾客; (of artist, charity etc) zànzhùrén 赞助人

patronage (of artist, charity etc) zànzhù 赞助

patronize person gāorén yīdǎngde duìdài 高人一等地对待

patronizing gāorén yīdǎng 高人一等

patter 1 n (of rain etc) pādāshēng 啪嗒声; F (of salesman) xuétóu 噱头 **2** v/i pāidǎ 拍打

pattern n (on wallpaper, fabric) tú'àn 图案; (for knitting, sewing) yàngshì 样式; (model) móxíng 模型; (in behavior, events) fāngshì 方式

patterned yǒu tú'àn 有图案

paunch dà dùzi 大肚子

pause 1 n tíngdùn 停顿 **2** v/i tíngdùn 停顿 **3** v/t tape zàntíng 暂停

pave pū 铺; ~ the way for X fig wèi X chuàngzào tiáojiàn 为X创造条件

pavement (roadway) lùmiàn 路面

paving stone pùlù shíbǎn 铺路石板

paw 1 n (of animal) zhuǎzi 爪子; (hand) shǒuzhuǎzi 手爪子 **2** v/t yòng shǒu luànmō 用手乱摸

pawn[1] n (in chess) zú 卒; fig xiǎozú 小卒

pawn[2] v/t diàndàng 典当

pawnbroker dàngpù lǎobǎn 当铺老板

pawnshop dàngpù 当铺

pay 1 n xīnjīn 薪金; in the ~ of X shǔgù yú X 受雇于X **2** v/t employee fùqián gěi付钱给; sum, bill fù 付; ~ attention zhùyì 注意; ~ X a compliment biǎoyáng X 表扬X **3** v/i fùzhàng 付帐; (be profitable) yǒu lìrùn 有利润; it doesn't ~ to do X zuò X débùchángshī 做X得不偿失; ~ for X (purchase) fù X fèi 付X费; you'll ~ for this! fig nǐ děngzhe qiáoba! 你等着瞧吧！

♦**pay back** person huánqián 还钱; loan chánghuán 偿还; (get revenge on) bàofù 报复

♦**pay in** (to bank) cúnrù 存入

♦**pay off 1** v/t debt chángqīng 偿清; corrupt official huìlù 贿赂 **2** v/i (be profitable) yǒu bàocháng 有报偿

♦**pay up** quánbù fùqīng 全部付清

payable yīng zhīfù 应支付

pay check xīnjīn zhīpiào 薪金支票

payday fāxīnrì 发薪日

payee shōukuǎnrén 收款人

pay envelope gōngzīdài 工资袋

payer fùkuǎnrén 付款人

payment (of bill) fùkuǎn 付款; (money) fùchūde kuǎnxiàng 付出的款项

pay phone gōngyòng diànhuà 公用电话

payroll (money) xīnshuǐ zǒng'é 薪水总额; (employees) xīnshuǐ míngcè 薪水名册; **be on the ~** shì gùyuán 是雇员

PC (= **personal computer**) gèrén diànnǎo 个人电脑; (= **politically correct**) wú zhèngzhì cuòwù 无政治错误

pea wāndòu 豌豆

peace (as opposed to war) hépíng 和平; (quietness) níngjìng 宁静

peaceable person héqì 和气

Peace Corps Hépíngduì 和平队

peaceful píngjìng 平静

peacefully ānjìng 安静

peach táozi 桃子

peacock kǒngquè 孔雀

pee v/i F sāniào 撒尿

peak 1 n (of mountain) shāndǐng 山顶; (mountain) shānfēng 山峰; fig dǐngfēng 顶峰 2 v/i dádào dǐngfēng 达到顶峰

peak consumption gāofēng xiāohào 高峰消耗

peak hours gāofēng shíjiān 高峰时间

peanut huāshēng 花生; **get paid ~s** F zhèng bù liǎo jǐfēn qián zhèng bù liǎo jǐfēn qián 挣不了几分钱; **that's ~s to him** F nà duì tā láishuō búsuàn shénme 那对他来说不算什么

peanut butter huāshēngjiàng 花生酱

pear lí 梨

pearl zhēnzhū 珍珠

Pearl River Zhūjiāng 珠江

Pearl River Delta Zhūjiāng sānjiǎozhōu 珠江三角洲

peasant nóngmín 农民

pebble luǎnshí 卵石

pecan měizhōu shānhétáo 美洲山核桃

peck 1 n (bite) zhuó 啄; (kiss) cōngcōngyīwěn 匆匆一吻 2 v/t (bite) zhuó 啄; (kiss) cōngcōngde wěn 匆匆地吻

peculiar (strange) qíguài 奇怪; **~ to** (special) tèyǒu 特有

peculiarity (strangeness) guàiyì 怪异; (special feature) dútèxìng 独特性

pedal 1 n (of bike) tàbǎn 踏板 2 v/i (turn ~s) cǎi tàbǎn 踩踏板; (cycle) qí shào

pedal rickshaw dàoqílǘ 倒骑驴

pedantic shūdāizìqì 书呆子气

pedestal (for statue) jīzuò 基座

pedestrian n xíngrén 行人

pedestrian crosswalk rénxíng héngdào 人行横道

pedestrian precinct xíngrénqū 行人区

pediatrician érkēxuéjiā 儿科学家

pediatrics érkēxué 儿科学

pedicab sānlúnchē 三轮车

pedigree 1 n (of dog, racehorse) chúnzhǒng 纯种; (of person) xuètǒng 血统 2 adj chúnzhǒng 纯种

pee v/i F sāniào 撒尿

peek 1 n yìyǎn 一眼 2 v/i piējiàn 瞥见

peel 1 n guǒpí 果皮 2 v/t fruit, vegetables xiāopí 削皮 3 v/i (of nose, shoulders) tuōluò 脱落; (of paint) bōluò 剥落

peep → **peek**

peephole kuīkǒng 窥孔

peer[1] n (equal) tóngděngrén 同等人

peer[2] v/i níngshì 凝视; **~ through the mist** xiàng wùzhōng zhāngwàng 向雾中张望; **~ at** zǐxìkàn 仔细看

peeved F nǎonù 恼怒

peg n (for hat, coat) guàgōu 挂钩; (for tent) zhuāng 桩; **off the ~** xiànchéng 现成

pejorative biǎnyì 贬抑

Peking Běijīng 北京

Peking duck Běijīng kǎoyā 北京烤鸭

Peking Opera Jīngjù 京剧

pellet xiǎotuán 小团; (bullet) zǐdàn 子弹

pelt 1 v/t: ~ X with Y jiāng Y tóuxiàng X 将 Y 投向 X 2 v/i: they ~ed along the road tāmen yánlù xùnsù qiánjìn 他们沿路迅速前进; it's ~ing down dàyǔ piáopō 大雨瓢泼

pelvis gǔpén 骨盆

pen¹ n (ballpoint) yuánzhūbǐ 圆珠笔; (fountain ~) zìláishuǐbǐ 自来水笔

pen² (enclosure) juàn quān 圈

pen³ F (penitentiary) láo 牢

penalize bùlìyú 不利于

penalty chéngfá 惩罚; SP fáqiú 罚球

penalty area SP fáqiúqū 罚球区

penalty clause wéiyuē fákuǎn de guīdìng 违约罚款的规定

pencil qiānbǐ 铅笔

pencil sharpener xiāoqiānbǐ dāo 削铅笔刀

pendant (necklace) chuíshì 垂饰

pending 1 prep zhídào 直到 2 adj: be ~ (awaiting a decision) xuán ér wèi jué 悬而未决; (about to happen) pòjìn 迫近

penetrate chuāntòu 穿透; market dǎrù 打入

penetrating stare shēnmíng zhēnxiàng 深明真相; scream jiānruì 尖锐; analysis yǒu dòngcháli 有洞察力

penetration tūpò 突破

pen friend bǐyǒu 笔友

penicillin qīngméisù 青霉素

peninsula bàndǎo 半岛

penis yīnjīng 阴茎

penitence chànhuǐ 忏悔

penitent adj hòuhuǐ 后悔

penitentiary jiānyù 监狱

pen name bǐmíng 笔名

pennant jǐnbiāoqí 锦标旗

penniless yīwénbùmíng 一文不名

penpal bǐyǒu 笔友

pension yǎnglǎojīn 养老金

♦pension off bèipò tuìxiū 被迫退休

pension fund yǎnglǎo jījīn 养老基金

pension scheme yǎnglǎojīn fāng'àn 养老金方案

pensive chénsī 沉思

Pentagon: the ~ Wǔjiǎo Dàlóu 五角大楼

penthouse dǐngcéng gōngyù 顶层公寓

pent-up yāyì 压抑

penultimate dàoshǔ dì'èr 倒数第二

peony mǔdān 牡丹

people rén 人; (race, tribe) mínzú 民族; the ~ rénmín 人民; the American ~ Měiguó rénmín 美国人民; ~ say that ... tīngshuō ... 听说...

People's Commune Rénmín Gōngshè 人民公社; People's Congress Rénmín Dàibiǎo Dàhuì 人民代表大会; People's Daily Rénmín Rìbào 人民日报; People's Liberation Army Jiěfàngjūn 解放军; People's Republic of China Zhōnghuá Rénmín Gònghéguó 中华人民共和国

pepper (spice) hújiāofěn 胡椒粉; (vegetable) làjiāo 辣椒

peppermint (candy) bòhétáng 薄荷糖; (flavoring) hújiāo bòhe 胡椒薄荷

pep talk gǔlìde huà 鼓励的话

per měi 每

per annum měinián 每年

perceive (with senses) juéchá 觉察; (view, interpret) lǐjiě 理解

percent bǎifēnzhī 百分之; one hundred ~ bǎifēnzhī bǎi 百分之百

percentage bǎifēnbǐ 百分比

perceptible kě juéchá 可觉察

perceptibly kàndechū 看得出

perception (through senses) gǎnzhī nénglì 感知能力; (of situation) kànfǎ 看法; (insight) dòngcháli 洞察力

perceptive person, remark yǒu dòngcháli 有洞察力

perch 1 n (for bird) qīxīchù 栖息处 2 v/i (of bird) qīxī 栖息; (of *person)* dāzuò 搭坐

percolate *v/i (of coffee)* guòlǜ 过滤

percolator guòlǜshì kāfēihú 过滤式咖啡壶

percussion dǎjīyuè 打击乐

percussion instrument dǎjī yuèqì 打击乐器

perfect 1 *n* GRAM wánchéngshì 完成式 2 *adj* wánměi 完美 3 *v/t* wánshàn 完善

perfection wánměi 完美; **to ~** qiàdào hǎochù 恰到好处

perfectionist wánměi zhǔyì zhě 完美主义者

perfectly jíjiā 极佳; *(totally)* wánquán 完全

perforated dǎkǒng 打孔

perforated line xūxiàn 虚线

perforations chǐkǒng 齿孔

perform 1 *v/t (carry out)* zuò 做; *(of actor, musician etc)* biǎoyǎn 表演 2 *v/i (of actor, musician, dancer)* biǎoyǎn 表演; *(of machine)* yùnzhuǎn 运转

performance *(by actor, musician etc)* biǎoyǎn 表演; *(of employee, company etc)* biǎoxiàn 表现; *(by machine)* xìngnéng 性能

performance car gāonéng qìchē 高能汽车

performer biǎoyǎn zhě 表演者

perfume *(for woman)* xiāngshuǐ 香水; *(of flower)* xiāngwèi 香味

perfunctory fūyǎn 敷衍

perhaps yěxǔ 也许

peril wēixiǎn 危险

perilous duōxiǎn 多险

perimeter zhōubiān 周边

perimeter fence zhōubiān zhàlan 周边栅栏

period *(time)* yíduàn 一段; *(menstruation)* yuèjīng 月经; *(punctuation mark)* jùhào 句号; *I don't want to, ~!* wǒ bùxiǎng zuò, jiù zhèiyàng! 我不想做，就这样！

periodic zhōuqīxìng 周期性

periodical *n* qīkān 期刊

periodically dìngqī 定期

peripheral 1 *adj (not crucial)* cìyào 次要 2 *n* COMPUT wàiwéi zhuāngzhì 外围装置

periphery biānyuán 边缘

perish *(of rubber)* fǔlàn 腐烂; *(of person)* mò méi 殁殁

perishable *adj food* yìhuài 易坏

perjure: **~ oneself** zuò wěizhèng 作伪证

perjury zuò wěizhèng 作伪证

perk *n (of job)* dàiyù 待遇

♦perk up 1 *v/t shì ... kuàihuó qǐlai ... 快起 2 *v/i huóyuè qǐlái 活跃起来

perky *(cheerful)* yǒu huólì 有活力

perm *n & v/t* tàngfà 烫发

permanent *adj* yǒngjiǔ 永久

permanently chángqī 长期

permissible róngxǔ 容许

permission xǔkě 许可

permissive fàngrèn 放任

permit 1 *n* xǔkězhèng 许可证 2 *v/t* róngxǔ 容许; **~ X to do Y** zhǔnxǔ X zuò Y 准许X做Y

perpendicular *adj* chuízhí 垂直

perpetual chíxù 持续

perpetually búduàn 不断

perpetuate shǐ yǒngcún 使永存

perplex shǐ kùnhuò 使困惑

perplexed kùnhuò 困惑

perplexity kùnhuò 困惑

persecute *oppress* pòhài 迫害

persecution pòhài 迫害

perseverance jiānchíbúxiè 坚持不懈

persevere jiānchí zuò 坚持做

persist chíxù 持续; **~ in** zhíyì zuò 执意做

persistence *(perseverance)* jiānchíbúxiè 坚持不懈; *(continuation)* jìxù cúnzài 继续存在

persistent *person* gùzhí 固执; *questions, rain, unemployment etc* chíxù búduàn 持续不断

persistently *(continually)* liánxù búduàn 连续不断

person rén 人; **in ~** qīnzì 亲自

personal *(private)* sīrén 私人; *(relating to a particular individual)* gèrén 个人; ***don't make ~ remarks*** bié tánlùn biérén 别谈论别人

personal assistant sīrén zhùlǐ 私人助理; **personal computer**

gèrén diànnǎo 个人电脑; **personal hygiene** gèrén wèishēng 个人卫生

personality gèxìng 个性; (*celebrity*) míngrén 名人

personally (*for my part*) jiù wǒ láishuō 就我来说; (*in person*) qīnzì 亲自; **don't take it ~** bié wèicǐ fánnǎo 别为此烦恼

personal pronoun rénchēng dàicí 人称代词

personal stereo suíshēntīng 随身听

personnel (*employees*) zhíyuán 职员; (*department*) rénshì bùmén 人事部门

personnel manager rénshìbù zhǔrèn 人事部主任

perspiration hànshuǐ 汗水

perspire chūhàn 出汗

persuade *person* shuōfú 说服; **~ X to do Y** shuōfú X zuò Y 说服X做Y

persuasion quànshuō 劝说

persuasive yǒu shuōfúlì 有说服力

pertinent yǒuguān 有关

perturb shǐ bù'ān 使不安

perturbing lìngrén bù'ān 令人不安

pervasive *influence, ideas* pǔbiàn cúnzài 普遍存在

perverse (*awkward*) bèilǐ 背理

perversion (*sexual*) biàntài xīnlǐ 变态心理

pervert *n* (*sexual*) xìngbiàntài 性变态

pessimism bēiguān 悲观

pessimist bēiguān zhě 悲观者

pessimistic bēiguān 悲观

pest (*bird*) hàiniǎo 害鸟; (*insect*) hàichóng 害虫; (*animal*) hàishòu 害兽; F tǎoyànguǐ 讨厌鬼

pest control xiāomiè yǒuhài dòngwù 消灭有害动物

pester jiūchán 纠缠; **~ X to do Y** chánzhe X zuò Y 缠着X做Y

pesticide shāchóngjì 杀虫剂

pet 1 *n* (*animal*) chǒngwù 宠物; (*favorite*) chǒng'ér 宠儿 **2** *adj* (*favorite*) zuì xǐhuān 最喜欢 **3** *v/t*

animal fǔmō 抚摸 **4** *v/i* (*of couple*) àifǔ 爱抚

petal huābàn 花瓣

♦**peter out** jiànjiàn xiāoshī 渐渐消失

petite jiāoxiǎo 娇小

petition *n* qīngyuànshū 请愿书

petrified shòujīngxià 受惊吓

petrify xiàdāi 吓呆

petrochemical shíyóu huàxué chǎnpǐn 石油化学产品

petroleum shíyóu 石油

petty *person, behavior* xiǎoqì 小气; *details, problem* suǒsuì 琐碎

petty cash língyòng xiànjīn 零用现金

petulant xìngjí 性急

pew jiàotáng chángyǐ 教堂长椅

pewter xīqiān héjīn 锡铅合金

pharmaceutical zhìyào 制药

pharmaceuticals zhìyào gōngsī 制药公司

pharmacist (*in store*) yàoshāng 药商

pharmacy (*store*) yàofáng 药房

phase jiēduàn 阶段

♦**phase in** zhúbù yǐnjìn 逐步引进

♦**phase out** zhúbù zhōngzhǐ 逐步中止

PhD (= *Doctor of Philosophy*) bóshì 博士

phenomenal fēifán 非凡

phenomenally jīngrén 惊人

phenomenon xiànxiàng 现象

philanthropic réncí 仁慈

philanthropist císhànjiā 慈善家

philanthropy réncí 仁慈

Philippines: the ~ Fēilǜbīn 菲律宾

philistine *n* yìmáng 艺盲

philosopher zhéxuéjiā 哲学家

philosophical yǒu zhélǐ 有哲理

philosophy zhéxué 哲学

phobia kǒngbùzhèng 恐怖症

phoenix fènghuáng 凤凰

phone 1 *n* diànhuàjī 电话机 **2** *v/t & v/i* dǎ diànhuà 打电话

phone book diànhuàbù 电话簿; **phone booth** diànhuàtíng 电话亭; **phonecall** diànhuà 电话; **phone number** diànhuà hàomǎ 电话号码

phon(e)y *adj* wěizhuāng 伪装

photo *n* xiàngpiàn 相片

photo album xiàngcè 相册;
photocopier yǐngyìnjī 影印机;
photocopy 1 *n* yǐngyìnběn 影印
本 2 *v/t* yǐngyìn 影印

photogenic shàngxiàng 上相

photograph 1 *n* zhàopiàn 照片
2 *v/t* pāishè 拍摄

photographer shèyǐngshī 摄影师

photography shèyǐng 摄影

phrase 1 *n* piànyǔ 片语 2 *v/t*
cuòcí 措词

phrasebook duǎnyǔ shǒucè 短语
手册

physical 1 *adj* (*relating to the body*)
shēntǐ 身体 2 *n* MED tǐgé jiǎnchá
体格检查

physical handicap cánjí 残疾

physically shēntǐ shang shen 身体上

physician yīshēng 医生

physicist wùlǐxuéjiā 物理学家

physics wùlǐ 物理

physiotherapist lǐliáo yīshēng 理
疗医生

physiotherapy lǐliáo 理疗

physique tǐgé tǐzhì 体格体质

pianist gāngqínjiā 钢琴家

piano gāngqín 钢琴

pick 1 *n*: *take your ~* xuǎnba 选吧
2 *v/t* (*choose*) xuǎn 选; *flowers,
fruit* cǎi 采; *~ one's nose* wā bíkǒng 挖鼻孔 3 *v/i*: *~ and choose*
tiāotiāojiǎnjiǎn 挑挑拣拣

♦ pick at: *~ one's food* xiǎokǒu chī
dōngxi 小口吃东西

♦ pick on (*treat unfairly*) qīfu 欺负;
(*select*) xuǎn 选

♦ pick out (*identify*) rènchū 认出

♦ pick up 1 *v/t* náqǐ 拿起; (*from
ground*) jiǎnqǐ 拣起; (*collect*)
qǔhuí 取回; (*from airport etc*) jiē-
jiē 接; (*in car*) ràngrén dā biànchē 让
人搭便车; (*in sexual sense*)
gōuyǐn 勾引; *language, skill*
xuéhuì 学会; *habit* yǎngchéng 养
成; *illness* gǎnrǎn 感染; (*buy*) mǎi
买; *criminal* dàibǔ 逮捕; *~ the tab*
mǎidān 买单 2 *v/i* (*improve*)
hǎozhuǎn 好转

picket 1 *n* (*of strikers*) jiūcháduì 纠

察队 2 *v/t* shèzhì jiūchá 设置纠
察

picket fence jiānbǎntiáo zhàlan 尖
板条栅栏

picket line jiūcháxiàn 纠察线

pickle *v/t* yānzì 腌渍

pickles pàocài 泡菜

pickpocket páshǒu 扒手

pick-up (truck) qīngxíng xiǎohuòchē 轻型小货车

picky F tiāoti 挑剔

picnic *n & v/i* yěcān 野餐

picture 1 *n* (*photo*) zhàopiàn 照
片; (*painting*) huìhuà 绘画;
(*illustration*) chātú 插图; (*movie*)
diànyǐng 电影; *keep X in the ~*
shǐ X liǎojiě shíqíng 使 X 了解实
情 2 *v/t* xiǎngxiàng 想象

picture book túhuàshū 图画书

picture postcard míngxìnpiàn 明
信片

picturesque rúhuà 如画

pie pài 派

piece (*fragment*) suìpiàn 碎片;
(*component*) bùfen 部分; (*in board
game*) zǐr 子儿; *a ~ of pie / bread*
yíkuài pài / miànbāo 一块派/面
包; *a ~ of advice* yíxiàng jiànyì 一
项建议; *go to ~s* jīngshén bēngkuì 精神崩溃; *take to ~s* chāikāi
拆开

♦ piece together *broken plate*
zǔzhuāng 组装; *facts, evidence*
pīncòu pīncòu 拼凑

piecemeal *adv* yíbùfen yíbùfen 一
部分一部分

piecework *n* jìjiàn gōngzuò 计件
工作

pierce (*penetrate*) cìtòu 刺透; *ears*
zhāyǎn 扎眼

piercing *noise* jiānlì 尖利; *eyes* ruìlì
锐利; *wind* cìgǔ 刺骨

pig zhū 猪; (*unpleasant person*) húndàn 混蛋

pigeon gēzi 鸽子

pigheaded wángù 顽固

pigpen (*also fig*) zhūjuàn 猪圈

pigskin zhūpí 猪皮

pigtail mǎwěibiàn 马尾辫

pile duī 堆; *a ~ of work* xǔduō 许
多

♦ **pile up 1** v/i (of work, bills) jījù 积聚 **2** v/t duīchéngduī 堆成堆

piles MED zhìchuāng 痔疮

pile-up MOT liánhuán pèngzhuàng 连环碰撞

pilfering xiǎotōu xiǎomō 小偷小摸

pilgrim cháoshèng zhě 朝圣者

pilgrimage cháoshèng zhī xíng 朝圣之行

pill yào 药; **the ~** kǒufú bìyùnyào 口服避孕药; **be on the ~** chī bìyùnyào 吃避孕药

pillar zhùzi 柱子

pillion (of motor bike) mótuōchē hòuzuò 摩托车后座

pillow n zhěntou 枕头

pillowcase, pillowslip zhěntào 枕套

pilot 1 n (of airplane) fēixíngyuán 飞行员 **2** v/t airplane jiàshǐ 驾驶

pilot plant shìyàn qū 试验区

pilot scheme shìyàn fāng'àn 试验方案

pimp n lāpítiáode nánrén 拉皮条的男人

pimple fěncì 粉刺

PIN (= **personal identification number**) mìmǎ 密码

pin 1 n (for sewing) dàtóuzhēn 大头针; (in bowling) mùzhù 木柱; (badge) huīzhāng 徽章; ELEC chātóu 插头 **2** v/t (hold down) ànzhù 按住; (attach) yòng zhēn gùdìng 用针固定

♦ **pin down: pin X down to a date** jiào X dìngge shíjiān 叫 X 定个时间

♦ **pin up** notice zhāngtiē 张贴

pincers áo áo 螯 螯; **a pair of ~** yìbǎ qiánzi 一把钳子

pinch 1 n niē 捏; (of salt, sugar etc) yìniē 一捏; **at a ~** bìyàoshí 必要时 **2** v/t niē 捏 **3** v/i (of shoes) jiājiǎo 夹脚

pine n (tree) sōngshù 松树; (wood) sōngmù 松木

♦ **pine for** sīniàn 思念

pineapple ⇩ bōluó 菠萝

ping 1 n pēngde yìshēng 砰的一声 **2** v/i fāchū pēngde yìshēng 发

出砰的一声

ping-pong pīngpāngqiú 乒乓球

pink (color) fěnhóngsè 粉红色

pinnacle fig dǐngfēng 顶峰

pinpoint míngquè zhǐchū 明确指出

pins and needles fāmá 发麻

pinstripe adj xìtiáowén 细条纹

pint píntuō 品脱

pin-up (girl) měinǚ 美女

pinyin pīnyīn 拼音

pioneer 1 n fig chuàngshǐrén 创始人 **2** v/t shǒuchàng fāqǐ 首倡

pioneering adj work kāituò 开拓

pious qiánchéng 虔诚

pip n (of fruit) zhǒngzi 种子

pipe 1 n (for smoking) yāndǒu 烟斗; (for water, gas, sewage) guǎnzi 管子 **2** v/t yòng guǎndào shūsòng 用管道输送

♦ **pipe down** ānjìng 安静

piped music bèijǐng yīnyuè 背景音乐

pipeline guǎndào 管道; **in the ~** jíjiāng fāshēng 即将发生

piping hot gǔntàng 滚烫

pirate v/t software etc dàobǎn 盗版

piss 1 v/i F (urinate) sāniào 撒尿 **2** n F niào 尿

pissed F (annoyed) nǎonù nǎonù 恼怒; Br (drunk) hēzuìle 喝醉了

pistol shǒuqiāng 手枪

piston huósāi 活塞

pit n (hole) kēng 坑; (coal mine) kuàngkēng 矿坑

pitch[1] n MUS yīndiào 音调

pitch[2] **1** v/i (in baseball) tóuqiú 投球 **2** v/t tent dā dā 搭搭; ball tóu tóu 投投

pitch black qīhēi 漆黑

pitcher[1] (baseball player) tóushǒu 投手

pitcher[2] (container) guàn 罐

piteous kělián 可怜

pitfall xiànjǐng 陷阱

pith (of citrus fruit) suǐ 髓

pitiful sight lìngrén liánmǐn 令人怜悯; excuse, attempt kěbǐ 可鄙

pitiless wúqíng 无情

pittance wēibóde gōngzī 微薄的工资

pity 1 n tóngqíng 同情; **it's a ~**

that ... yíhàn ... 遗憾...; **what a ~!** zhēn yíhàn! 真遗憾！; **take ~ on** chūyú tóngqíng ér bāngzhù 出于同情而帮助 **2** *v/t person* tóngqíng 同情

pivot 1 *v/i* zài zhīdiǎn shang zhuàndòng 在支点上转动 **2** *n* zhīdiǎn 支点

pizza bǐsà 比萨

PLA (= People's Liberation Army) Jiěfàngjūn 解放军

PLA soldier Jiěfàngjūn 解放军

placard biāoyǔpái 标语牌

place 1 *n* dìfang 地方; *(bar, restaurant)* cānyǐnchù 餐饮处; *(apartment, house)* jiā 家; *(in book)* yè 页; *(in race, competition)* míngcì 名次; *(seat)* zuòwèi 座位; **at my / his ~** zài wǒ / tā nàr 在我 / 他那儿; **in ~ of** dàitì 代替; **feel out of ~** gǎndào bù xiāngchèn 感到不相称; **take ~** fāshēng 发生; **in the first ~** *(firstly)* shǒuxiān 首先; *(in the beginning)* kāishǐ 开始 **2** *v/t (put)* fàng 放; *(identify)* rèndìng 认定; **~ an order** dìnghuò 订货

place mat cānjù diàn 餐具垫

placid ānjìng 安静

plague 1 *n* wēnyì 瘟疫 **2** *v/t (bother)* fánrǎo 烦扰

plain¹ *n* píngyuán 平原

plain² *adj (clear, obvious)* qīngchǔ 清楚; *(not fancy)* qīngdàn 清淡; *(not pretty)* pǔtōng 普通; *(not patterned)* méiyǒu tú'àn 没有图案; *(blunt)* shuàizhí 率直; **~ chocolate** chún qiǎokèlì 纯巧克力 **2** *adv* xiǎnrán 显然; **it's ~ crazy** zhēnshì fēngkuáng 真是疯狂

plain clothes: in ~ chuān biànyī 穿便衣

plainly *(clearly)* qīngchǔ 清楚; *(bluntly)* zhíshuài 直率; *(simply)* pǔsù 朴素

plain-spoken zhíyánbúhuì 直言不讳

plaintiff yuángào 原告

plaintive āishāng 哀伤

plait 1 *n (in hair)* biànzi 辫子 **2** *v/t hair* biān biànzi 编辫子

plan 1 *n (project, intention)* jìhuà 计划; *(drawing)* shèjìtú 设计图 **2** *v/t (prepare)* zhǔnbèi 准备; *(design)* shèjì 设计; **~ to do X, ~ on doing X** dǎsuàn zuò X 打算做 X **3** *v/i* dìng jìhuà 订计划

plane¹ *(airplane)* fēijī 飞机

plane² *(tool)* bàozi 刨子

planet xíngxīng 行星

plank *(of wood)* mùbǎn 木板; *fig (of policy)* zhèngcè zhǔnzé 政策准则

planning jìhuà 计划; **at the ~ stage** zài chóuhuà zhōng 在筹划中

plant¹ *n* zhíwù 植物 **2** *v/t* zhòng 种

plant² *n (factory)* chǎng 厂; *(equipment)* shèbèi 设备

plantation dà zhòngzhíyuán 大种植园

plaque *(on wall)* shìbǎn 饰板; *(on teeth)* yábān 牙斑

plaster 1 *n (on wall, ceiling)* huīní 灰泥 **2** *v/t wall, ceiling* yòng huīní túmǒ 用灰泥涂抹; **be ~ed with** túmǎn 涂满

plaster cast shígāo bēngdài 石膏绷带

plastic 1 *n* sùliào 塑料 **2** *adj (made of ~)* sùliào 塑料

plastic bag sùliàodài 塑料袋

plastic money xìnyòngkǎ 信用卡; **plastic surgeon** zhěngxíng wàikē yīshēng 整形外科医生; **plastic surgery** zhěngxíng wàikē 整形外科

plate *n (for food)* pánzi 盘子; *(sheet of metal)* bóbǎncái 薄板材

plateau gāoyuán 高原

platform *(stage)* wǔtái 舞台; *(of railroad station)* ⇩ zhàntái 站台; *fig (political)* zhènggāng 政纲

platinum *n & adj* bó 铂

platitude chéncí làndiào 陈词滥调

platonic *relationship* chún yǒuyì 纯友谊

platoon *(of soldiers)* pái 排

platter *(for meat, fish)* dà qiǎnpán 大浅盘

plausible sìhū yǒu dàolǐ 似乎有道理

play 1 n (in theater, on TV) jù jù 剧; (of children) yóuxì 游戏; TECH huódòng 活动; SP bǐsàide biǎoxiàn 比赛的表现 **2** v/i (of children) wánr 玩儿; (of musician) tánzòu 弹奏; (SP: perform) dǎ dǎ 打; (SP: take part) cānsài 参赛 **3** v/t musical instrument tán 弹; piece of music yǎnzòu 演奏; game wánr 玩儿; opponent yǔ ... bǐsài 与 ... 比赛; (perform: Macbeth etc) biǎoyǎn 表演; ~ **a joke on X** kāi X de wánxiào 开 X 的玩笑

play around (be unfaithful) sīhùn 斯混

♦**play down** dànhuà 淡化

♦**play up** (of machine) chū gùzhàng 出故障; (of child) rě máfan rěmáfan 惹麻烦; (of tooth, back etc) gěi rén tòngkǔ 给人痛苦

playact (pretend) jiǎzhuāng 假装

playback huífàng 回放

playboy huāhuāgōngzǐ 花花公子

player SP yùndòng yuán 运动员; (musician) yǎnzòu zhě 演奏者; (actor) yǎnyuán 演员

playful punch etc nàozhe wánr 闹着玩儿

playground yóuxìchǎng 游戏场

playing card zhǐpái 纸牌

playing field yùndòngchǎng 运动场

playmate yóuxìde huǒbàn 游戏的伙伴

playwright jùzuòjiā 剧作家

plaza (for shopping) gòuwù zhōngxīn 购物中心

plea n kěnqiú 恳求

plead v/i qǐngqiú 请求; ~ **for** kěnqiú 恳求; ~ **guilty / not guilty** fú / bùfú zuì 服 / 不服罪; ~ **with X** qǐngqiú X 请求 X

pleasant lìngrén yúkuài 令人愉快

please 1 adv qǐng 请; **more tea? ~ yes, ~** hái yào chá ma? – hǎode, xièxiè 还要茶吗？– 好的，谢谢; ~ **do** méiwèntí 没问题 **2** v/t shǐ gāoxìng 使高兴; ~ **yourself**

qǐngbiàn 请便

pleased gāoxìng 高兴; ~ **to meet you** hěn gāoxìng rènshí nǐ 很高兴认识你

pleasing shǐrén yúkuài 使人愉快

pleasure (happiness, satisfaction) kuàilè 快乐; (as opposed to work) yúlè 娱乐; (delight) lèqù 乐趣; **it's a ~** (you're welcome) méiguānxi 没关系; **with ~** dāngrán 当然

pleat n (in skirt) zhě 褶

pledge 1 n (promise) bǎozhèng 保证; **Pledge of Allegiance** Zhōngchéng Xuānshì 忠诚宣誓 **2** v/t (promise) chéngnuò 承诺

plentiful dàliàng 大量

plenty (abundance) fùzú 富足; ~ **of** xǔduō 许多; **that's ~** zúgòu duō le 足够多了; **there's ~ for everyone** yǒudeshì gěi dàjiā 有的是给大家

pliable kěsù 可塑

pliers qiánzi 钳子; **a pair of ~** yìbǎ qiánzi 一把钳子

plight kùnjìng 困境

plod v/i (walk) jiānnán xíngzǒu 艰难行走

♦**plod along** (with a job) huǎnmàn jìnxíng 缓慢进行

plodder (at work, school) chénmèn kǔgàn de rén 沉闷苦干的人

plot[1] n (land) xiǎokuài tǔdì 小块土地

plot[2] 1 n (conspiracy) yīnmóu 阴谋; (of novel) qíngjié 情节 **2** v/t mìmóu 密谋 **3** v/i mìmóu 密谋

plotter yīnmóu zhě 阴谋者; COMPUT huìtúyí 绘图仪

plow 1 n lí 犁 **2** v/t & v/i gēngdì 耕地

♦**plow back** profits fǎn tóuzī 反投资

pluck v/t eyebrows zhāichú 摘除; chicken bámáo 拔毛

♦**pluck up** ~ **courage** gǔqǐ yǒngqì 鼓起勇气

plug 1 n (for sink, bath) sāizi 塞子; (electrical) chātóu 插头; (spark ~) huǒhuāsāi 火花塞; (for new book etc) xuānchuán 宣传 **2** v/t hole yòng sāizi dǔ 用塞子堵; *new book etc* tuīxiāo 推销

♦**plug away** F nǔlì búxiè 努力不懈

♦**plug in** *v/t* jiētōng diànyuán 接通电源

plum 1 *n* lǐzi 李子 **2** *adj job* yōuyuè 优越

plumage yǔyī 羽衣

plumb *adj* chuízhí 垂直

plumber shuǐnuǎngōng 水暖工

plumbing (*pipes*) guǎndào zhuāngzhì 管道装置

plume *n* yǔmáo 羽毛

plummet (*of airplane*) kuàisù luòxià 快速落下; (*of share prices*) dàdiē 大跌

plump *adj* féipàng 肥胖

♦**plump for** xuǎnzé 选择

plunge 1 *n* měngrán diēluò 猛然跌落; (*in prices*) xiàdiē 下跌; *take the ~* cǎiqǔ dàdǎn cuòshī 采取大胆措施 **2** *v/i* tūrán diēluò 突然跌落; (*of prices*) xiàdiē 下跌 **3** *v/t* tóurù 投入; *the city was ~d into darkness* zhèi chéngshì xiànrù yípiàn hēi'àn zhōng 这城市陷入一片黑暗中; *the news ~d him into despair* tā tīngdào nà xiāoxi jiù xiànrùle juéwàng 他听到那消息就陷入了绝望

plunging: *~ neckline* shēn V zì lǐng 深V字领

plural 1 *adj* fùshù xíngshì 复数形式 **2** *n* fùshù 复数

plus 1 *prep* jiāshàng 加上 **2** *adj* duō 多; *$500 ~* wǔbǎiduō měiyuán 五百多美元 **3** *n* (*symbol*) jiāhào 加号; (*advantage*) hǎochù 好处 **4** *conj* (*moreover, in addition*) érqiě 而且

plush háohuá 豪华

plywood jiāohébǎn 胶合板

p.m. xiàwǔ 下午

pneumatic chōngqì 充气

pneumatic drill fēngzuàn 风钻

pneumonia fèiyán 肺炎

poach[1] (*cook*) wēi huǒ mèn

poach[2] **1** *v/i* tōubǔ 偷捕 **2** *v/t* salmon etc tōubǔ 偷捕

poached egg wò jīdàn 卧鸡蛋

P.O. Box yóuzhèng xìnxiāng 邮政信箱

pocket 1 *n* kǒudài 口袋; *line one's own ~s* fā wāicái 发歪财; *be out of ~* péiqián 赔钱 **2** *adj* (*miniature*) wēixíng 微型 **3** *v/t* jùwéijǐyǒu 据为己有

pocketbook (*woman's*) xiǎo shǒutíbāo 小手提包; (*wallet*) qiánbāo 钱包; (*book*) píngzhuāngshū 平装书; **pocket calculator** xiǎo jìsuànqì 小计算器; **pocketknife** xiǎo zhédāo 小折刀

podium zhǐhuītái 指挥台

poem shī 诗

poet shīrén 诗人

poetic person, description yǒu shīyì 有诗意

poetic justice yīngdéde jiǎngchéng 应得的奖惩

poetry shīgē 诗歌

poignant tòngqiè 痛切

point 1 *n* (*of pencil, knife*) jiānduān 尖端; (*in competition, exam*) fēn 分; (*purpose*) yìyì 意义; (*moment*) shíkè 时刻; (*in argument, discussion*) guāndiǎn 观点; (*in decimals*) diǎn 点; *beside the ~* lítí 离题; *be on the ~ of* zhèngyào … 正要 …; *get to the ~* shuō zhèngshì 说正事; *the ~ is ...* wèntí shì … 问题是 …; *there's no ~ in waiting / trying* děng / shì gēnběn méiyòng 等 / 试根本没用 **2** *v/i* zhǐ 指 **3** *v/t gun* duìzhǔn 对准

♦**point at** (*with finger*) zhǐxiàng 指向

♦**point out** sights shǐ zhùyì 使注意; advantages etc zhǐchū 指出

♦**point to** (*with finger*) yòngshǒu zhǐ 用手指; *fig* (*indicate*) ànshì 暗示

point-blank 1 *adj refusal, denial* zhíjiéliǎodàng 直截了当; *at ~ range* zài jìnjùlí nèi 在近距离内 **2** *adv refuse, deny* duànrán 断然

pointed jiānruì 尖锐

pointer (*for teacher*) jiàobiān 教鞭; (*hint*) diǎnzi 点子; (*sign, indication*) jìxiàng 迹象

pointless wúyìyì 无意义; *it's ~*

trying to do X chángshì zuò X 尝试做 X
gēnběn méiyòng 根本没用

point of sale (*place*) xiāohòudiǎn
销货点; (*promotional material*)
cùxiāo zīliào 促销资料

point of view guāndiǎn 观点

poise zìzhì 自制

poised *person* tàiránzìruò 泰然自
若

poison 1 *n* dúyào 毒药 **2** *v/t* dúhài
毒害

poisonous yǒudú 有毒

poke 1 *n* tǒng tǒng 捅 **2** *v/t* (*prod*) tǒng
捅; (*stick*) shēnchū 伸出; **~ fun at**
cháoxiào 嘲笑; **~ one's nose into**
gānyù 干预

♦**poke around** xúnzhǎo 寻找

poker (*card game*) pūkèpái 扑克牌

poky (*cramped*) xiáxiǎo 狭小

Poland Bōlán 波兰

polar dìjí 地极

polar bear běijíxióng 北极熊

polarize *v/t* liǎngjí fēnhuà 两极分
化

Pole Bōlán rén 波兰人

pole¹ (*of wood, metal*) gān gǎn 杆杆

pole² (*of earth*) dìjí 地极

polevault chēnggān tiàogāo 撑竿
跳高

police *n* jǐngfāng 警方

policeman jǐngchá 警察; **police
state** jǐngchá guójiā 警察国家;
police station jǐngcháiǔ 警察局;
policewoman nǚjǐngchá 女警察

policy¹ zhèngcè 政策

policy²: **insurance ~** bǎoxiǎndān 保
险单

polio xiǎo'ér mábìzhèng 小儿麻
痹症

Polish 1 *adj* Bōlán 波兰 **2** *n*
(*language*) Bōlán yǔ 波兰语

polish 1 *n* (*product*) cāguāngjì 擦
光剂 **2** *v/t* cāliàng 擦亮; *speech*
rùnsè 润色

♦**polish off** *food* chīguāng 吃光

♦**polish up** *skill* tígāo 提高

polished *performance* xùnliàn-
yǒusù 训练有素

Politburo Zhèngzhìjú 政治局

polite yǒu lǐmào 有礼貌

politely lǐmào 礼貌

politeness lǐmào 礼貌

political zhèngzhì 政治

politically correct wú zhèngzhì
cuòwù 无政治错误

politician zhèngzhìjiā 政治家

politics zhèngzhì 政治; ***what are
his ~?*** tā yǒu shénme zhèngzhì
xìnyǎng? 他有什么政治信仰?

poll 1 *n* (*survey*) mínyì cèyàn 民意
验; **the ~s** (*election*) xuǎnjǔ 选
举; **go to the ~s** (*vote*) xuǎnjǔ
tóupiào 选举投票 **2** *v/t people*
diàochá 调查; *votes* huòdé 获得

pollen huāfěn 花粉

pollen count huāfěn jìshù 花粉计
数

polling booth tóupiàozhàn 投票
站

pollster mínyì cèyàn zhě 民意测
验者

pollutant wūrǎn wùzhì 污染物质

pollute wūrǎn 污染

pollution wūrǎn 污染

polo neck (*sweater*) yuán gāo fānlǐng 圆高翻领

polo shirt gāolǐngshān 高领衫

polyethylene jùyǐxī 聚乙烯

polyester jùzhǐxiānwéi 聚酯纤维

polystyrene jùběnyǐxī 聚苯乙烯

polyunsaturated hányòu duō-
chóng bùbǎohé huàhéwù 含有多
重不饱和化合物

pompous zìfù gāorù 自负

pond chítáng 池塘

ponder *v/i* shēnsī 深思

pony xiǎomǎ 小马

ponytail mǎwěifà 马尾发

poodle juǎnmáo xiǎogǒu 卷毛小
狗

pool¹ (*swimming ~*) chí池 chí; (*of
water, blood*) tān 摊

pool² (*game*) ⇩ pǔ'ěrdànzǐxì 普尔
弹子戏

pool³ 1 *n* (*common fund*) gòngtóng
chǔjīn 共同储金 **2** *v/t resources*
jíhé 集合

pool hall pǔ'ěrdànzǐxì tīng 普尔弹
子戏厅

pool table pǔ'ěrdànzǐxì zhuō 普尔
弹子戏桌

pooped F jīnpílìjìn 筋疲力尽

poor 1 *adj* (*not wealthy*) pínqióng 贫穷; (*not good*) bùhǎo 不好; (*unfortunate*) búxìng 不幸; *be in ~ health* shēntǐ bùhǎo 身体不好; *~ old Tony!* kěliánde Tuōní! 可怜 的托尼！2 *n*: *the ~* qióngrén 穷 人

poorly 1 *adv* hěnzāo 很糟 2 *adj* (*unwell*) bùshūfu 不舒服

pop[1] 1 *n* (*noise*) pēngde yīshēng 砰 的一声 2 *v/i* (*of balloon etc*) fāchū pēngde yīshēng 发出砰的一声 3 *v/t cork* báchū 拔出; *balloon* bàopò 爆破

pop[2] 1 *n* MUS liúxíng yīnyuè 流行 音乐 2 *adj* liúxíng 流行

pop[3] (*father*) bà ba 爸爸

pop[4] *v/t* (*put*) fàng 放

♦ **pop up** *v/i* (*appear suddenly*) tūrán chūxiàn 突然出现

popcorn yùmǐhuā 玉米花

pope jiàohuáng 教皇

poplar yángshù 杨树

poppy yīngsù 罂粟

Popsicle® bàngbàngbīng 棒棒冰

pop song liúxíng gēqǔ 流行歌曲

popular shòu huānyíng 受欢迎; *belief, support* pǔbiàn 普遍

popularity (*of person*) shēngwàng 声望

populate jūzhù 居住

population rénkǒu 人口

porcelain *n & adj* cí 瓷

porch ménláng 门廊

porcupine háozhū 豪猪

pore *n* (*of skin*) máokǒng 毛孔

♦ **pore over** xìkàn 细看

pork zhūròu 猪肉

porn *n* huángsè zuòpǐn 黄色作品

porn(o) *adj* huángsè 黄色

pornographic huángsè 黄色

pornography sèqíng zuòpǐn 色情 作品

porous tòu shuǐqì 透水汽

port[1] *n* (*town*) gǎngshì 港市; (*area*) gǎngkǒu 港口; COMPUT duānkǒu 端口

port[2] *adj* (*left-hand*) zuǒxián 左舷

portable 1 *adj* shǒutíshì 手提式 2 *n* COMPUT bǐjìběn 笔记本; *~ TV*

wēixíng diànshì 微型电视

porter (*at railroad station*) bān-yùngōng bānyùngōng 搬运工; (*doorman in hotel*) ménwèi 门卫

porthole NAUT xiánchuāng 舷窗

portion *n* yíbùfen 一部分; (*of food*) fèn 份

portrait 1 *n* (*painting, photograph*) xiàoxiàng 肖像; (*depiction*) miáoxiě 描写 2 *adv print* shùpái 竖排

portray (*of artist*) huà 画; (*of photographer*) pāi 拍; (*of actor*) bànyǎn 扮演; (*of author*) miáoshù 描述

portrayal (*by actor*) bànyǎn 扮演; (*by author*) miáoshù 描述

Portugal Pútáoyá 葡萄牙

Portuguese 1 *adj* Pútáoyá 葡萄 牙 2 *n* (*person*) Pútáoyá rén 葡萄 牙人; (*language*) Pútáoyá yǔ 葡萄 牙语

pose 1 *n* (*pretense*) zhuāngqiāng zuòshì 装腔作势 2 *v/i* (*for artist, photographer*) bǎi zīshì 摆姿势; *~ as* zhuāngzuò 装作 3 *v/t*: *~ a problem / a threat* zàochéng kùn-nán / wēixié 造成困难 / 威胁

position 1 *n* (*location*) wèizhi 位 置; (*stance*) zīshì 姿态; (*in race, competition*) wèi 位; (*occupied by soldiers*) zhèndì 阵地; (*point of view*) lìchǎng 立场; (*situation*) chǔjìng 处境; (*job*) zhíwèi 职位; (*status*) dìwèi 地位 2 *v/t* ānfàng 安 放

positive *attitude* lèguān 乐观; *response* biǎoshì tóngyì 表示同 意; *medical test* yángxìng 阳性; GRAM kěndìng 肯定; ELEC zhèngjí 正极; *be ~ (sure)* quèdìng 确定

positively (*decidedly*) shífēn kěn-dìng 十分肯定; (*definitely*) juéduì 绝对

possess chíyǒu 持有

possession (*ownership*) chíyǒu 持 有; (*thing owned*) cáichǎn 财产; *~s* suǒyǒuwù 所有物

possessive *person* xiǎnshì zhàn-yǒuyù 显示占有欲

possessive pronoun GRAM wùzhǔ dàicí 物主代词

possibility kěnéng xìng 可能性

possible kěnéng 可能; **the short-est / quickest ~ ...** jìn kěnéng zuì-duǎn / zuìkuài ...尽可能最短/最快...; **the best ~ ...** jìn kěnéng zuìhǎo ...尽可能最好...

possibly yóudǐ (perhaps) yěxǔ 也许; **that can't ~ be right** nà bù kěnéng duì 那不可能对; **could you ~ tell me ... ?** nǐ néng-bùnéng gàosù wǒ ... ? 你能不能告诉我 ... ?

post[1] n (of wood, metal) gānzi 杆子了 n zhāngtiē 张贴; profits gōngbù 公布; **keep X ~ed** ràng X zhīdào 让X知道

post[2] n (place of duty) zhíwèi 职位 2 v/t soldier, employee pàiwǎng 派往; guards bùzhì 布置

postage yóuzī 邮资

postal yóudì 邮递

postcard míngxìnpiàn 明信片

postdate tiánwǎn rìqī 填晚日期

poster hǎibào 海报

posterior n hum (buttocks) pìgu 屁股

posterity hòudài 后代

postgraduate 1 n yánjiūshēng 研究生 2 adj dàxué bìyèhòu 大学毕业后

posthumous novel zuòzhě sǐhòu chūbǎn 作者死后出版; award sǐhòu huòdé 死后获得; baby yífù 遗腹

posthumously sǐhòu fāshēng 死后发生

posting (assignment) wěipài 委派

postmark yóuchuō 邮戳

postmortem yànshī 验尸

post office yóujú 邮局

postpone tuīchí 推迟

postponement yánqī 延期

posture zīshì 姿势

postwar zhànhòu 战后

pot[1] (for cooking in) guō 锅; (for coffee, tea) hú 壶; (for plant) pén 盆

pot[2] F (marijuana) dàmá 大麻

potato tǔdòu 土豆

potato chips ⇩ zháshǔpiàn 炸薯片

potent drug, medicine xiàolì dà 效力大; ruler qiángyǒulì 强有力

potential 1 adj kěnéng chūxiàn 可能出现 2 n qiánlì 潜力

potentially yǒu kěnéng 有可能

pothole (in road) kēngwā 坑洼

potter n táogōng 陶工

pottery (activity) zhìtáoshù 制陶术; (items) táoqì 陶器; (place) táoqì zuòfang 陶器作坊

potty n (for baby) biànpén 便盆

pouch (bag) xiǎodài 小袋

poultry (birds) jiāqín 家禽; (meat) jiāqínròu 家禽肉

pounce v/i (of animal) měngpū 猛扑; fig túrán xíjī 突然袭击

pound[1] (weight) bàng 磅

pound[2] (for strays) wéichǎng 围场; (for cars) mòshōu chēliàng chù 没收车辆处

pound[3] v/i (of heart) jùliè tiàodòng 剧烈跳动; **~ on** (hammer on) zhòngjī 重击

pound sterling yīngbàng 英镑

pour 1 v/t liquid dào 倒 2 v/i yǒngchū 涌出; **it's ~ing (with rain)** dàyǔqīngpén 大雨倾盆

♦ **pour out** liquid dàochū 倒出; troubles qīngsù 倾诉

pout v/i juēzuǐ 撅嘴

poverty pínkùn 贫困

poverty-stricken pínkùn bùkān 贫困不堪

powder 1 n fěnmò 粉末; (for face) fěn fěn 粉 2 v/t face chāfěn 搽粉

powder room nǚcèsuǒ 女厕所

power 1 n (strength) lì 力; (author-ity) quánlì 权力; (energy) néng-liàng 能量; (electricity) diàn 电; **in ~** POL zhízhèng 执政; **fall from ~** POL shīshì 失势 2 v/t be ~ed by X yóu X zuò dònglì 由X作动力

power-assisted yǒu dònglì yuán-zhù 有动力援助; power cable diànyuán diànlǎn 电源电缆; power cut tíngdiàn 停电

powerful qiángyǒulì 强有力

powerless wúlìliàng 无力量; **be ~ to ...** wúnéngwéilì ... 无能为力 ...

power line diànxiàn 电线; power outage tíngdiàn 停电; power

station fādiànzhàn 发电站;
power steering gāonéng zhuǎnxiàng 高能转向; power unit
néngliàng dānwèi 能量单位
PR (= public relations) gōngguān
公关
practical experience shíjì 实际;
person xiànshí 现实; (functional)
shíyòng 实用
practical joke èzuòjù 恶作剧
practically behave, think shíshìqiú-
shì 实事求是; (almost) jīhū 几乎
practice 1 n shíjiàn 实践, liànxí
练习; (rehearsal) páiliàn 排练;
(custom) chángguī 常规; in ~ (in
reality) shíjì shang shíjì 实际上; be out
of ~ shūyúliànxí 疏于练习 2 v/i
xùnliàn 训练 3 v/t liànxí 练习;
law, medicine zhíyè 执业
pragmatic wùshí 务实
pragmatism shíyòngzhǔyì 实用主
义
prairie dàcǎoyuán 大草原
praise 1 n zànyù 赞誉 2 v/t
chēngzàn 称赞
praiseworthy zhídé chēngzàn 值
得称赞
prank n èzuòjù 恶作剧
prattle v/i xiánliáo 闲聊
pray qídǎo 祈祷
prayer dǎogào 祷告
PRC (= People's Republic of
China) Zhōnghuá Rénmín Gònghéguó 中华人民共和国
preach 1 v/i (in church) bùdào 布
道; (moralize) shuōjiào 说教 2 v/t:
~ a sermon bùdào 布道
preacher chuándàorén 传道人
precarious bù wěndìng 不稳定
precariously bù wěngù 不稳固
precaution yùfáng cuòshī 预防措
施
precautionary measure yùfáng 预
防
precede v/t (in time) xiānyú 先于;
(walk in front of) lǐngxiān zǒu 领
先走
precedence: take ~ yōuxiān 优
先; take ~ over ... lǐngxiānyú ...
领先于 ...
precedent n xiānlì 先例

preceding week qiányī 前一;
chapter shàngyī 上一
precinct (district) qūyù 区域
precious bǎoguì 宝贵
precipitate v/t crisis jiāsù 加速
précis n zhāiyào 摘要
precise zhǔnquè 准确
precisely jīngquè 精确
precision jīngquè 精确
precocious child zǎoshú 早熟
preconceived idea shìxiān xíngchéng 事先形成
precondition bìbèi 必备
predator (animal) shíròu dòngwù
食肉动物
predecessor (in job) qiánrènzhě
前任者; (machine) qiányī xínghào
前一型号
predestination sùmìng 宿命
predicament jiǒngkuàng 窘况
predict yùyán 预言
predictable kě yùyán 可预言
prediction yùyán 预言
predominant zhàn yōushì 占优势
predominantly zhǔyào 主要
predominate zhàn yōushì 占优势
prefabricated yùzhì 预制
preface n qiányán 前言
prefecture (in ancient China) zhōu
州
prefer gèng xǐhuān 更喜欢; ~ X to
Y yǔ Y xiāngbǐ gèng xǐhuān X 与
Y 相比更喜欢 X; ~ to do
nìngyuàn zuò 宁愿做
preferable gèng chènxīn 更称心;
be ~ to gèng shìyí 更适宜
preferably gèng kěqǔ 更可取
preference piān'ài 偏爱
preferential yōuxiān 优先
prefix qiánzhuì 前缀
pregnancy yùnqī 孕期
pregnant huáiyùn 怀孕
prehistoric shǐqián 史前
prejudice 1 n piānjiàn 偏见 2 v/t
person yǐngxiǎng 影响; chances
xuēruò 削弱
prejudiced piānxīn 偏心
preliminary adj yùbèixìng 预备性
premarital hūnqián 婚前
premature: ~ birth zǎochǎn 早产
premeditated yùmóu 预谋

premier n (prime minister) zǒnglǐ 总理

première n shǒucì gōngyǎn 首次公演

premises dìfang 地方

premium n (in insurance) bǎoxiǎnfèi 保险费

premonition yùgǎn 预感

prenatal chǎnqián 产前

preoccupied xīnbúzàiyān 心不在焉

preparation (act) zhǔnbèi 准备; **in ~ for X** wèi X zuòhǎo zhǔnbèi 为 X 作好准备; **~s** zhǔnbèi gōngzuò 准备工作

prepare 1 v/t zhǔnbèi 准备; **be ~d to do X** (willing) yuànyì zuò X 愿意做 X 2 v/i zhǔnbèi 准备

preposition jiècí 介词

preposterous huāngmiù 荒谬

prerequisite bìbèi 必备

prescribe (of doctor) kāi yàofāng 开药方

prescription MED yàofāng 药方

presence zàichǎng 在场; **in the ~ of X** zài X miànqián 在 X 面前

presence of mind yùshì bùhuāng 遇事不慌

present[1] 1 adj (current) mùqián 目前; **be ~** zàichǎng 在场 2 n dāngqián 当前; **the ~** xiànzài 现在; GRAM xiànzàishí 现在时; **at ~** cǐkè 此刻

present[2] 1 n (gift) lǐwù 礼物 2 v/t award, bouquet shòuyǔ 授予; program zhǔchí 主持; **~ X with Y**, **~ Y to X** bǎ Y zèngsònggěi X 把 Y 赠送给 X

presentation (to audience) bàogào 报告

present-day dāngjīn 当今

presently (at the moment) xiànzài 现在; (soon) bùjiǔ 不久

preservation bǎochí 保持

preservative n fángfǔjì 防腐剂

preserve 1 n (domain) lǐngyù 领域 2 v/t standards, peace etc wéihù 维护; wood etc bǎohù 保护; food bǎocún 保存

preside v/i (at meeting) zhǔchí 主持

presidency zǒngtǒng zhíwèi 总统职位

president POL zǒngtǒng 总统; (of company) dǒngshìzhǎng 董事长

presidential zǒngtǒng 总统

press 1 n: **the ~** xīnwénjiè 新闻界 2 v/t button àn 按; (urge) dūncù 敦促; (squeeze) jǐyā 挤压; clothes yùn 熨 3 v/i: **~ for** cuīcù 催促

press conference jìzhě zhāodàihuì 记者招待会

pressing adj pòqiè 迫切

pressure 1 n yālì 压力; **be under ~** chéngshòu yālì 承受压力; **be under ~ to do X** pòyú yālì zuò X 迫于压力做 X 2 v/t qiǎngpò 强迫

prestige wēiwàng 威望

prestigious yǒu wēiwàng 有威望

presumably dàgài 大概

presume tuīcè 推测; **~ to do** màomèi zuò 冒昧做

presumption (of innocence, guilt) tuīdìng 推定

presumptuous màoshī 冒失

pre-tax nàshuì qián 纳税前

pretend 1 v/t zhuāngzuò 装作 2 v/i jiǎzhuāng 假装

pretense xūjiǎ 虚假

pretentious xuànyào 炫耀

pretext jièkǒu 借口

pretty 1 adj piàoliang 漂亮 2 adv (quite) xiāngdāng 相当

prevail (triumph) zhànshèng 战胜

prevailing shèngxíng 盛行

prevent fángzhǐ 防止; **~ X (from) doing Y** zǔzhǐ X zuò Y 阻止 X 做 Y

prevention yùfáng 预防

preventive yùfángxìng 预防性

preview n (of movie, exhibition) yùzhǎn 预展

previous qiányī 前一

previously yǐqián 以前

prewar zhànqián 战前

prey n lièwù 猎物

♦ **prey on** bǔshí 捕食; fig (of conman etc) lièqǔ 猎取

price 1 n jiàgé 价格 2 v/t COM dìngjià 定价

priceless wújià 无价

price war jiàgézhàn 价格战

pricey ángguì 昂贵

prick **1** n (*pain*) cì chuō 刺 戳 **2** v/t (*jab*) chuō 戳

prick² n V (*penis*) jībā 鸡巴; (*person*) chǔnrén 蠢人

♦ prick up: ~ one's ears (*of dog*) shùqǐ ěrduo 竖起耳朵; (*of person*) tūrán kāishǐ zhùyì tīng 突然开始注意听

prickle (*on plant*) cì 刺

prickly *beard, plant* duōcì 多刺; (*irritable*) yìnù 易怒

prickly heat fèizi pàizi 痱子疿子

pride **1** n (*in person, achievement*) zìháo 自豪; (*self-respect*) zìzūn 自尊 **2** v/t: ~ oneself on X yǐ X wéi zìháo 以 X 为自豪

priest mùshi 牧师

primarily zhǔyào 主要

primary **1** adj zhǔyào 主要 **2** n POL chūxuǎn 初选

prime **1** n: be in one's ~ zhèngzhí shèngnián 正值盛年 **2** adj *example, reason* zhǔyào 主要; of ~ importance zhìguān zhòngyào 至关重要

prime minister shǒuxiàng 首相

prime time TV huángjīn shíjiān 黄金时间

primitive yuánshǐ 原始; *conditions* jiǎnlòu 简陋

prince wángzǐ 王子

princess gōngzhǔ 公主

principal **1** adj zhǔyào 主要 **2** n (*of school*) xiàozhǎng 校长

principally zhǔyào 主要

principle (*in moral sense*) zhǔnzé 准则; (*rule*) yuánzé 原则; on ~ yījù zìjǐ de yuánzé 依据自己的原则; in ~ yuánzé shang 原则上

print **1** n (*in book etc*) yìnshuā zìtǐ 印刷字体; PHOT zhàopiàn 照片; out of ~ juébǎn 绝版 **2** v/t yìnshuā 印刷; COMPUT dǎyìn 打印; (*in block capitals*) dàxiě 大写

♦ print out yìnchū 印出

printed matter yìnshuāpǐn 印刷品

printer (*person*) yìnshuāshāng 印刷商; (*machine*) ⇩ dǎyìnjī 打印机

printing press yìnshuājī 印刷机

printout dǎyìnchū de zīliào 打印出的资料

prior **1** adj xiānshí 事先 **2** prep: ~ to zài ...yǐqián 在 … 以前

prioritize (*put in order of priority*) huàfēn qīngzhòng huǎnjí 划分轻重缓急; (*give priority to*) jǐyǔ yōuxiān 给予优先

priority yàowèi 要位; have ~ yǒu yōuxiānquán 有优先权

prison jiānyù 监狱

prisoner qiúfàn 囚犯; take X ~ fúlǔ X 俘虏 X

prisoner of war zhànfú 战俘

privacy sīrén kōngjiān 私人空间

private **1** adj sīrén 私人 **2** n MIL shìbīng 士兵; in ~ sīxià 私下

privately (*in private*) sīxià 私下; *funded, owned* gèrén 个人; (*inwardly*) nèixīn 内心

private sector mínyíng qǐyè 民营企业

privilege (*special treatment*) tèquán 特权; (*honor*) róngxìng 荣幸

privileged xiǎngyǒu tèquán 享有特权; (*honored*) róngxìng 荣幸

prize **1** n jiǎngshǎng 奖赏 **2** v/t zhēnshì 珍视

prizewinner huòjiǎng zhě 获奖者

prizewinning huòjiǎng 获奖

pro¹ n: the ~s and cons yōushì hé lièshì 优势和劣势

pro² → professional

pro³: be ~ ... (*in favor of*) zànchéng ... 赞成 ...

probability kěnéng xìng 可能性

probable hěn kěnéng 很可能

probably yěxǔ 也许

probation (*in job*) shìyòng shìyòng 试用; LAW huǎnxíng 缓刑

probation officer huǎnxíng jiāndūguān 缓刑监督官

probation period (*in job*) shìyòngqī 试用期

probe **1** n (*investigation*) diàochá 调查; (*scientific*) tàncè 探测 **2** v/t tànchá 探查; (*investigate*) diàochá 调查

problem wèntí 问题; no ~ méi

wèntí 没问题

procedure bùzhòu 步骤

proceed 1 v/i (go: of people) qiánxíng 前行; (of work etc) jìnzhǎn 进展 **2** v/t: **~ to do X** jìxù zuò X 继续做 X

proceedings (events) jìnchéng 进程

proceeds shōurù 收入

process 1 n guòchéng 过程; **in the ~** (while doing it) zài … de guòchéng zhōng 在 … 的过程中 **2** v/t food, raw materials jiāgōng 加工; data chǔlǐ 处理; application etc shěnchá 审查

procession hángliè 行列

processor COMPUT chǔlǐqì 处理器

proclaim xuānbù 宣布

prod n & v/t tǒng 捅

prodigy: (**infant**) ~ shéntóng 神童

produce 1 n chǎnpǐn 产品 **2** v/t commodity shēngchǎn 生产; (bring about) yǐnqǐ 引起; (bring out) náchū 拿出; play, movie, TV program zhìzuò 制作

producer (of commodity) zhìzào chǎngjiā 制造厂家; (of play, movie, TV program) zhìpiānrén 制片人

product chǎnpǐn 产品; (result) jiéguǒ 结果

production chǎnliàng 产量; (of play, movie, TV program) zhìzuò 制作; (play, movie, TV program) zuòpǐn 作品

production capacity shēngchǎn nénglì 生产能力

production costs shēngchǎn chéngběn 生产成本

productive duōchǎn 多产; meeting yǒu chéngxiào 有成效

productivity shēngchǎnlì 生产力

profane language xiàliú 下流

profess shēngchēng 声称

profession zhíyè 职业

professional 1 adj (not amateur), advice, help zhuānyè 专业; piece of work yǒu jiqiǎo 有技巧; **turn ~** biànchéng zhuānyè 变成专业 **2** n (doctor, lawyer etc, expert) zhuānyè rénshì 专业人士; (not

an amateur) zhíyè rényuán 职业人员

professionally play sport zuòwéi zhuānyè 作为专业; (well, skillfully) zhuānyè 专业

professor jiàoshòu 教授

proficiency jīngtōng 精通

proficient jīngtōng 精通

profile (of face) cèmiàn 侧面; (description) jièshào 介绍

profit 1 n lìrùn 利润 **2** v/i: **~ by,** **~ from** cóngzhōng xīqǔ yìchù 从中吸取益处

profitability yǒulìkětú 有利可图

profitable kěhuò lìrùn 可获利润

profit margin lìrùnlǜ 利润率

profound shēnqiè 深切

profoundly shēnshēn 深深

prognosis yùhòu 预后

program 1 n jìhuà 计划; (on radio, TV) jiémù 节目; COMPUT chéngxù 程序; (in theater) jiémùdān 节目单 **2** v/t COMPUT biān chéngxù 编程序

programmer COMPUT chéngxùyuán 程序员

progress 1 n jìnbù 进步; **make ~** yǒu jìnbù 有进步; **in ~** jìnxíngzhōng 进行中 **2** v/i (advance in time) jìnzhǎn 进展; (move on) jìnxíng 进行; (make progress) qǔdé jìnbù 取得进步; **how is the work ~ing?** gōngzuò jìnzhǎnde zěnmeyàng? 工作进展得怎么样？

progressive adj (enlightened) kāimíng 开明; (which progresses) zhúbù fāzhǎn 逐步发展

progressively zhúbù 逐步

prohibit jìnzhǐ 禁止

prohibition jìnzhǐ 禁止; **Prohibition** jìnjiǔ shíqí 禁酒时期

prohibitive prices gāode mǎibùqǐ 高得买不起

project¹ n (plan) jìhuà 计划; (undertaking) xiàngmù 项目; EDU kètí 课题; (housing area) ⇩ tǒngjiàn zhùzháiqū 统建住宅区

project² v/t figures, sales jìhuà 计划; movie fàngyìng 放映 **2** v/i (stick out) tūchū 突出

projection (forecast) yùcè 预测

projector (*for slides*) fàngyìngjī 放映机

proletariat wúchǎn jiējí 无产阶级

prolific *writer, artist* duōchǎn 多产

prolong yáncháng 延长

prom (*school dance*) wǔhuì 舞会

prominent *nose, chin* tūchū 突出; (*significant*) xiǎnzhù 显著

promiscuity xìng luànjiāo 性乱交

promiscuous xìngluàn 性乱

promise 1 *n* chéngnuò 承诺 **2** *v/t* xǔnuò 许诺; ~ **to ...** xǔnuò zuò ... 许诺做...; ~ **X to Y** X xǔnuò gěi Y 许诺给 Y X **3** *v/i* bǎozhèng 保证

promising yǒu qiántú 有前途

promote *employee* jìnshēng 晋升; (*encourage, foster*) zēngjìn 增进; COM xuānchuán 宣传

promoter (*of sports event*) chuàngbànrén 创办人

promotion (*of employee*) jìnjí 晋级; (*of scheme, idea*) xuānchuán 宣传; COM cùxiāo 促销

prompt 1 *adj* (*on time*) zhǔnshí 准时; (*speedy*) jíshí 及时 **2** *adv:* **at two o'clock** ~ liǎngdiǎnzhěng 两点正 **3** *v/t* (*cause*) jīqǐ 激起; *actor* tící 提词 **4** *n* COMPUT tíshìfú 提示符

promptly (*on time*) jíshí 及时; (*immediately*) lìjí 立即

prone: *be* ~ *to* yìyú zuò 易于做

pronoun dàicí 代词

pronounce *word* fāyīn 发音; (*declare*) xuānbù 宣布

pronounced *accent* míngxiǎn 明显; *views* míngquè 明确

pronunciation fāyīn 发音

proof *n* zhèngjù 证据; (*of book*) jiàoyàng 校样

prop 1 *v/t* xiékào 斜靠 **2** *n* (*in theater*) dàojù 道具
♦ **prop up** zhīchēngqǐ 支撑起; *regime* zhīchí 支持

propaganda xuānchuán 宣传

propel tuījìn 推进

propellant (*in aerosol*) qǐ tuījìn zuòyòng 起推进作用

propeller (*of boat*) luóxuánjiǎng 螺旋桨

proper (*real*) zhēnzhèng 真正; (*correct*) qiàdàng 恰当; (*fitting*) shìdàng 适当

properly (*correctly*) zhèngquè 正确; (*fittingly*) shìdàng 适当

property cáichǎn 财产; (*land*) fángdìchǎn 房地产

property developer fángdìchǎn kāifārén 房地产开发人

prophecy yùyán 预言

prophesy zuò yùyán 作预言

proportion bǐlì 比例，bùfen 部分; ~**s** (*dimensions*) miànjī 面积

proportional chéng bǐlì 成比例

proposal (*suggestion*) tíyì 提议; (*of marriage*) qiúhūn 求婚

propose 1 *v/t* (*suggest*) jiànyì 建议; (*plan*) jìhuà 计划 **2** *v/i* (*make offer of marriage*) qiúhūn 求婚

proposition 1 *n* jiànyì 建议 **2** *v/t* *woman* tíchū xìngyàoqiú 提出性要求

proprietor yèzhǔ 业主

proprietress nǚ yèzhǔ 女业主

prose sǎnwén 散文

prosecute *v/t* LAW tíqǐ gōngsù 提起公诉

prosecution LAW qǐsù 起诉; (*lawyers*) yuángàofāng 原告方

prosecutor gōngsùrén 公诉人

prospect 1 *n* (*chance, likelihood*) kěnéng 可能; (*thought of sth in the future*) qīwàng 期望; ~**s** qiánjǐng 前景 **2** *v/i:* ~ *for gold* kāntàn 勘探

prospective kěnéng 可能

prosper chénggōng 成功

prosperity xīngshèng 兴盛

prosperous xīngwàng 兴旺

prostitute *n* jìnǚ 妓女; *male* ~ nánjì 男妓

prostitution màiyín 卖淫

prostrate: *be* ~ *with grief* bēitòngyùjué 悲痛欲绝

protect *v/t* bǎohù 保护

protection bǎohù 保护

protection money bǎohùfèi 保护费

protective yǒu bǎohùxìng 有保护性

protector bǎohù zhě 保护者

protein dànbáizhì 蛋白质

protest 1 *n* kàngyì 抗议; (*demonstration*) shìwēi 示威 **2** *v/t* shēnmíng 申明; (*object to*) fǎnduì 反对 **3** *v/i* shēngbiàn 声辩; (*demonstrate*) shìwēi 示威

Protestant 1 *n* Xīnjiàotú 新教徒 **2** *adj* Xīnjiào 新教

protester shìwēi zhě 示威者

protocol lǐyí 礼仪

prototype móxíng 模型

protracted yáncháng 延长

protrude *v/i* tūchū 凸出

proud jiāo'ào 骄傲; (*independent*) zìzūn 自尊; *be ~ of* yǐ ... wéi zìháo 以 ... 为自豪

proudly zìháo 自豪

prove zhèngmíng 证明

proverb yànyǔ 谚语

provide tígōng 提供; *~ Y to X*, *~ X with Y* wèi X tígōng Y 为 X 提供 Y; *~d (that)* (*on condition that*) zhǐyào 只要

♦**provide for** *family* gōngyǎng 供养; *~ X* (*of law etc*) guīdìng X 规定 X

province shěng 省

provincial *city* shěng 省; *pej* (*attitude*) shǒujiù 守旧

provision (*supply*) gōngyìng 供应; (*of law, contract*) tiáokuǎn 条款

provisional línshí 临时

proviso fùdài tiáojiàn 附带条件

provocation tiǎoxìn 挑衅

provocative tiǎoxìn 挑衅; (*sexually*) tiǎodòu 挑逗

provoke (*cause*) yǐnqǐ 引起; (*annoy*) jīnù 激怒

prow NAUT chuánshǒu 船首

prowess zhuāncháng 专长

prowl *v/i* (*of tiger etc*) qīngqīng yídòng 轻轻移动; (*of burglar*) qiánxíng 潜行

prowler guǐguǐsuìsuìde rén 鬼鬼祟祟的人

proximity línjìn 邻近

proxy (*authority*) dàilǐ quán 代理权; (*person*) dàilǐ rén 代理人

prude jiǎzhèngjīng 假正经

prudence shènshèn 审慎

prudent shènshèn 审慎

prudish jiǎzhèngjīng 假正经

prune[1] *n* xīméifú 西梅脯

prune[2] *v/t plant* xiūjiǎn 修剪; *fig* xuējiǎn 削减

pry dǎtīng 打听

♦**pry into** cìtàn 刺探

PS (= *postscript*) dùjí 又及

PSB (= *Public Security Bureau*) Gōng'ān Jú 公安局

pseudonym huàmíng 化名

psychiatric jīngshénbìng 精神病

psychiatrist jīngshénkē yīshēng 精神科医生

psychiatry jīngshénbìngxué 精神病学

psychic *adj* yǒu tèyì gōngnéng 有特异功能

psychoanalysis jīngshén fēnxī 精神分析

psychoanalyst jīngshén fēnxīxuéjiā 精神分析学家

psychoanalyze zuò jīngshén fēnxī 作精神分析

psychological xīnlǐ 心理

psychologically xīnlǐ 心理

psychologist xīnlǐxuéjiā 心理学家

psychology xīnlǐxué 心理学

psychopath jīngshén biàntài zhě 精神变态者

puberty qīngchūnqī 青春期

pubic hair yīnmáo 阴毛

public 1 *adj* gōngzhòng 公众 **2** *n*: *the ~* mínzhòng 民众; *in ~* dāngzhòng 当众

publication (*of book, report*) chūbǎn 出版; (*by newspaper*) kāntóu 刊出; (*book, newspaper*) chūbǎnwù 出版物

publicity xuānchuán 宣传

publicize (*make known*) xuānchuán 宣传; COM zuò guǎnggào 作广告

publicly dāngzhòng 当众

public minibus xiǎo gōnggòng 小公共; **public prosecutor** gōngsùrén 公诉人; **public relations** gōngguān 公关; **public school** gōngxué 公学; **public sector** zhèngfǔ jīgòu 政府机构; **Public Security Bureau** Gōng'ān Jú 公安局

publish chūbǎn 出版

557 **purpose**

publisher chūbǎnshè 出版社

publishing chūbǎnyè 出版业

publishing company chūbǎn gōngsī 出版公司

puddle n shuǐkēng 水坑

puff 1 n (of wind, smoke) yīgǔ 一股 2 v/i (pant) chuǎnxī 喘息; ~ on a cigarette yīkǒuyīkǒude chōuyān 一口一口地抽烟

puffy eyes, face péngzhàng 膨胀

pull 1 n (on rope) lā 拉; F (appeal) xīyǐnlì 吸引力; F (influence) yǐngxiǎnglì 影响力 2 v/t (drag) lā 拉; (tug) chě 扯; tooth bá 拔; muscle lāshāng 拉伤 3 v/i zhuāi 拽
♦ pull apart (separate) lākāi 拉开
♦ pull away v/t chōukāi 抽开
♦ pull down (lower) lāxià 拉下; (demolish) chāihuǐ 拆毁
♦ pull in v/i (of bus, train) jìn zhàn 进站
♦ pull off leaves etc lādiào 拉掉; F deal zuòchéng shì 做成事
♦ pull out 1 v/t chōuchū 抽出; troops chèlí 撤离 2 v/i (of an agreement, a competition) tuìchū 退出; (of troops) chèlí 撤离; (of ship) shǐchū 驶出
♦ pull through (from an illness) kāngfù 康复
♦ pull together 1 v/i (cooperate) tōnglìhézuò 通力合作 2 v/t: pull oneself together kòngzhì zìjǐ 控制自己
♦ pull up 1 v/t (raise) tíqǐ 提起; plant, weeds báqǐ 拔起 2 v/i (of car etc) tíng 停

pulley huálún 滑轮

pullover jǐnshēn tàoshān 紧身套衫

pulp guǒròu 果肉; (for papermaking) zhǐjiāng 纸浆

pulpit bùdàotán 布道坛

pulsate (of heart, blood) bódòng 搏动; (of rhythm) chàndòng 颤动

pulse màibó 脉搏

pump 1 n (machine) ⇩ bèng pù 泵; (gas ~) qìyóubèng 汽油泵 2 v/t yòng bèng chōuyā 用泵抽压
♦ pump up gěi ... chōngqì 给 ... 充气

pumpkin nánguā 南瓜

pun shuāngguānyǔ 双关语

punch 1 n (blow) jīdǎ 击打; (implement) dǎkǒngjī 打孔机 2 v/t (with fist) yòng quán jī 用拳击; hole, ticket dǎ kǒng 打孔

punch line miàoyǔ 妙语

punctual zhǔnshí 准时

punctuality shǒushí 守时

punctually zhǔnshí 准时

punctuate jiā biāodiǎn 加标点

punctuation biāodiǎn fúhào yòngfǎ 标点符号用法

punctuation mark biāodiǎn fúhào 标点符号

puncture 1 n xiǎokǒng 小孔 2 v/t chuān kǒng 穿孔

pungent cìbí 刺鼻

punish person chéngfá 惩罚

punishing pace, schedule chīlì 吃力

punishment chéngfá 惩罚

puny person ruòxiǎo 弱小

pup yòuxiǎo dòngwù 幼小动物

pupil[1] (of eye) tóngkǒng 瞳孔

pupil[2] (student) xuésheng 学生

puppet mù'ǒu 木偶

puppet government kuǐlěi zhèngfǔ 傀儡政府

puppet show mù'ǒuxì 木偶戏

puppy xiǎogǒu 小狗

purchase[1] n & v/t gòumǎi 购买

purchase[2] (grip) jǐnwò 紧握

purchaser mǎizhǔ 买主

pure silk, wool chún 纯; air, water jiéjìng 洁净; white etc chúncuì 纯粹; sound chúnzhèng 纯正; (morally) chúnjié 纯洁

purely wánquán 完全

purge 1 n (of political party) zhěngsù 整肃 2 v/t qīngchú 清除

purify water jìnghuà 净化

puritan qīngjiàotú 清教徒

puritanical qīngjiàotúshì 清教徒式

purity chúndù 纯度; (moral) chúnjié 纯洁

purple adj zǐsè 紫色

Purple Heart MIL Zǐxīn Xúnzhāng 紫心勋章

purpose (aim, object) mùdì 目的;

on ~ gùyì 故意
purposeful jiāndìng 坚定
purposely yǒuyì 有意
purr v/i (of cat) hūlūshēng 呼噜声
purse n (pocketbook) shǒudài 手袋
pursue v/t person zhuīzhú 追逐;
career zhuīqiú 追求; course of
action jìxù jìnxíng 继续进行
pursuer zhuīgǎn zhě 追赶者
pursuit (chase) zhuīgǎn 追赶; (of
happiness etc) zhuīqiú 追求;
(activity) huódòng 活动; those in
~ nàxiē zhuībǔ de rén 那些追捕
的人
pus nóng 脓
push 1 n (shove) tuī 推; (of button)
àn 按 **2** v/t (shove) tuī 推; button
àn 按; (pressurize) bīpò 逼迫;
drugs fàndú 贩毒; be ~ed for X
(be short of) X jǐn X 紧; be ~ing 40
kuài sìshí le 快四十了 **3** v/i tuī
推
♦ **push along** cart etc xiàng qián tuī
向前推
♦ **push away** tuīkāi 推开
♦ **push off 1** v/t lid tuīdiào 推掉
2 v/i (leave) líkāi 离开; ~! zǒukāi!
走开!
♦ **push on** v/i (continue) jìxù qiánjìn
继续前进
♦ **push up** prices shàngtiáo 上调
push-button yòng ànniǔ cāozòng
用按纽操纵
pusher (of drugs) dúpǐn fànzi 毒品
贩子
push-up fǔ wòchēng 俯卧撑
pushy kèqiú 苛求
puss, pussy (cat) māomī 猫咪
put fàng 放; question wèn 问; ~ the
cost at ... gūjià ... 估价 ...
♦ **put aside** money chǔcún 储存;
work fàngzài yìbiān 放在一边
♦ **put away** (in closet etc) shōuqǐlái
收起来; (in institution) guānjìn 关
进; (consume) hē 喝; money chǔcún 储存; animal jiéguǒ 结果
♦ **put back** (replace) fànghuí yuánchù 放回原处
♦ **put by** money chǔcún 储存
♦ **put down** fàngxià 放下; deposit
fù dìngjīn 付定金; rebellion

zhènyā 镇压; (belittle: person)
qīngshì 轻视; (in writing) xiěxià 写
下; put one's foot down (in car)
cǎi yóuménr 踩油门儿; (be firm)
jiāndìng 坚定; put X down to Y
(attribute) bǎ X guīyīn yú Y 把 X
归因于 Y
♦ **put forward** idea etc jiànyì 建议
♦ **put in** fàngjìnqù 放进去; time
fúchū 付出; request, claim
chéngjiāo 呈交
♦ **put in for** shēnqǐng 申请
♦ **put off** light, radio, TV guāndiào
关掉; (postpone) tuīchí 推迟;
(deter) shǐ rén búzuò 使人不做;
(repel) gǎndào fǎngǎn 感到反感;
put X off Y shǐ X bù xǐhuān Y 使 X
不喜欢 Y
♦ **put on** light, radio, TV dǎkāi 打
开; tape, music fàng 放; jacket,
shoes chuān 穿; make-up cháyòng
搽用; brake shā 刹; (perform)
yǎnchū 演出; (assume) jiǎzhuāng
假装; ~ weight zēngjiā tǐzhòng 增
加体重; she's just putting it on
tā zhǐshì zhuāng de 她只是装底
♦ **put out** hand shēnchū 伸出; fire
xīmiè 熄灭; light guāndiào 关掉
♦ **put through** (on phone) jiētōng
接通
♦ **put together** (assemble) zǔhéchéng yītǐ 组合成一体;
(organize) zǔzhī 组织
♦ **put up** v/t hand jǔqǐ 举起; (give a
bed to) gōngyìng shísù chù 供应食宿
(erect) shùqǐ 竖起; prices tígāo 提
高; poster, notice zhāngtiē 张贴;
money tígōng 提供; ~ for sale
chūshòu 出售
♦ **put up with** (tolerate) rěnshòu 忍
受
putty yóuhuī 油灰
puzzle 1 n (mystery) mí mèi 谜;
(game) zhìlì yóuxì 智力游戏; (jigsaw ~)
pīntú wánjù 拼图玩具;
(crossword ~) zònghéng zìmí 纵横
字谜 **2** v/t shǐkùnhuò 使困惑
puzzling lìngrén fèijiě 令人费解
PVC jùlǜyǐxī jùyǐxī 聚氯乙烯
pylon diànlǎntǎ 电缆塔
pyramid selling chuánxiāo 传销

Q

Qin Dynasty Qín Cháo 秦朝
Qing Dynasty Qīng Cháo 清朝
quack[1] n (of duck) guāguā yīshēng 呱呱一声 2 v/i guāguā jiào 呱呱叫
quack[2] F (bad doctor) jiānghú yīshēng 江湖医生
quadrangle (figure) sìbiān xíng 四边形; (courtyard) sìfāng yuàn 四方院
quadruped sìzú dòngwù 四足动物
quadruple v/i chéng sìbèi 成四倍
quadruplets sì bāotāi 四胞胎
quaint little cottage gǔyǎ xiǎoqiǎo 古雅小巧; (slightly eccentric: ideas etc) gǔguài 古怪
quake 1 n (earthquake) dìzhèn 地震 2 v/i (of earth) dìzhèn 地震; (with fear) duōsuo 哆嗦
qualification (from university etc) wénpíng 文凭; (of remark etc) xiānjué tiáojiàn 先决条件; have the right ~s for a job yǒu zuò yīfèn gōngzuò de zīgé 有做一份工作的资格
qualified doctor, engineer etc hégé 合格; (restricted) yǒu xiàndù 有限度; I am not ~ to judge wǒ bùgòu zīgé lái juédìng 我不够资格来决定
qualify 1 v/t (of degree, course etc) shǐ jùyǒu zīgé 使具有资格; remark etc xiànzhì 限制 2 v/i (get degree etc) qǔde zīgé 取得资格; (in competition) qǔde bǐsài zīgé 取得比赛资格; our team has qualified for the semi-final wǒmen duì huòdé cānjiā bànjuésài de zīgé 我们队获得参加半决赛的资格; that doesn't ~ as ... nà bùsuàn ... 那不算 ...
quality zhìliàng 质量; (characteristic) tèxìng 特性

quality control (activity) zhìliàng kòngzhì 质量控制; (department) zhìliàng guǎnlǐ 质量管理
qualm dānyōu 担忧; have no ~s about ... bù dānyōu ... 不担忧 ...
quantify yòng shùliàng biǎoshì 用数量表示
quantity liàng 量
quarantine gélí 隔离
quarrel n & v/i chǎozuǐ 吵嘴
quarrelsome ài chǎojià 爱吵架
quarry (for mining) cǎishíchǎng 采石场
quart kuātuō 夸脱
quarter 1 n sìfēn zhīyī 四分之一; (part of town) dìqū 地区; a ~ of an hour yīkèzhōng 一刻钟; a ~ to 5 chà yīkè wǔdiǎn 差一刻五点; ~ past 5 wǔdiǎn yīkè 五点一刻 2 v/t fēnchéng sìfēn 分成四份
quarterback SP sìfēnwèi 四分卫; quarterfinal sìfēn zhīyī juésài 四分之一决赛; quarterfinalist jìnrù sìfēn zhīyī juésài zhě 进入四分之一决赛者
quarterly adj & adv jìdù 季度
quarternote MUS sìfēn yīnfú 四分音符
quarters MIL yíngfáng 营房
quartet (instrumentalists) sì chóngzòu 四重奏; (singers) sì chóngchàng 四重唱
quartz shíyīng 石英
quaver 1 n (in voice) chàndǒu 颤抖 2 v/i (of voice) chàndǒu 颤抖
queen nǚwáng 女王; (monarch's wife) wánghòu 王后
queen bee fēngwáng 蜂王
queer (peculiar) gǔguài 古怪
quench flames xīmiè 熄灭; ~ one's thirst zhǐkě 止渴
query 1 n yíwèn 疑问 2 v/t (express doubt about) duì ... biǎoshì yíwèn 对 ... 表示疑问;

(*check*) wèn 问; ~ **X** *with* **Y** wèn Y yǒuguān X 问 Y 有关 X

question 1 *n* wèntí 问题; *in* ~ (*being talked about*) suǒtán 所谈; (*in doubt*) bèi huáiyí 被 怀疑; *it's a* ~ *of money* / *time* shì qián / shíjiān de wèntí 是 钱 / 时间 的 问 题; *that's out of the* ~ bù kěnéng 不 可能 **2** *v/t person* wèn 问; LAW shěnwèn 审问; (*doubt*) huáiyí 怀疑

questionable *honesty* kě huáiyí 可 怀疑; *figures, statement* bù kěxìn 不 可信

questioning *look, tone* cháwèn 查 问

question mark yídiǎn 疑点

questionnaire wèndá juàn 问答卷

quick kuài 快; *be* ~! kuàidiǎnr! 快 点 儿!; *let's have a* ~ *drink* wǒmen kuàizhe hē diǎnr ba 我们 快 着 喝 点 儿 吧; *can I have a* ~ *look?* wǒ néngbúnéng kàn yīyǎn? 我 能 不 能 看 一 眼? ; *that was* ~! zhème kuài! 这么快!

quicksand liúshā 流沙; **quicksilver** shuǐyín 水银; **quickwitted** jīmǐn 机敏

quiet *voice, music* xiǎoshēng 小声; *engine* dī zàoyīn 低 噪音; *street* ānjìng 安静; *life, town* píngjìng 平静; *keep ~ about* **X** bù tí X de shì 不 提 X 的 事; ~! bìzuǐ! 闭嘴!

♦**quieten down 1** *v/t children, class* shǐ ānjìng 使 安静 **2** *v/i* (*of children*) ānjìng xiàlái 安静 下来; (*of political situation*) píngjìng xiàlái 平 静 下 来

quilt (*on bed*) bèizi 被子

quinine kuíníng 奎宁

quip 1 *n* qiàopí huà 俏皮话 **2** *v/i* shuō qiàopí huà 说 俏皮话

quirky gǔguài 古怪; *machine* bù wěndìng 不 稳定

quit 1 *v/t job* cízhí 辞职; ~ *doing* **X** fàngqì zuò X 放弃 做 X **2** *v/i* (*leave job*) cízhí 辞职; COMPUT tuìchū 退出

quite (*fairly*) xiāngdāng 相当; (*completely*) wánquán 完全; *not* ~ *ready* méi wánquán zhǔnbèi hǎo 没 完全 准备 好; *I didn't* ~ *understand* wǒ bù tài míngbái 我 不 太 明 白; *is that right?* – *not* ~ duìma? – bù wánquán 对 吗? – 不 完全; ~! zhèngshì zhèyàng! 正 是 这样!; ~ *a lot* hěn duō 很 多; *it was* ~ *a surprise* / *change* zhēn jīngrén / biànhuà xiāngdāng dà 真 惊人 / 变化 相当 大

quits: *be* ~ *with* **X** (*person*) yǔ X liǎngqīng 与 X 两清

quiver *v/i* chàndǒu 颤抖

quiz 1 *n* wèndá bǐsài 问答比赛 **2** *v/t* pánwèn 盘问

quiz program wèndá bǐsài jiémù 问答比赛节目

quota dìngliàng 定量

quotation (*from author*) yǐnwén 引文; (*price*) bàojià 报价; *give* **X** *a* ~ *for* **Y** gěi X tígōng yīgè Y de bàojià 给 X 提供 一个 Y 的 报价

quotation marks yǐnhào 引号

quote 1 *n* (*from author*) yǐnwén 引文; (*price*) bàojià 报价; (*quotation mark*) yǐnhào 引号 **2** *v/t text* yǐnyòng 引用; *price* bàojià 报价 **3** *v/i*: ~ *from an author* yǐnyòng yīgè zuòjiā de zuòpǐn 引用 一个 作家 的 作品

R

rabbit tùzi 兔子

rabies kuángquǎn bìng 狂犬病

raccoon huànxióng 浣熊

race¹ 1 *n* (*of people*) zhǒngzú 种族

race² 2 *n* SP jìngsài 竞赛; *the ~s* (*horse ~s*) pǎomǎ 跑马 2 *v/i* (*run fast*) jíxíng 疾行; SP cānjiā jìngsài 参加竞赛; *he ~d through his meal / work* tā xùnsù chīwánle fàn / zuòwánle gōngzuò 他迅速吃完了饭 / 做完了工作 3 *v/t*: *I'll ~ you* wǒ hé nǐ bǐsài 我和你比赛

racecourse pǎomǎ dào 跑马道; **racehorse** bǐsài yòng mǎ 比赛用马; **racetrack** pǎodào 跑道

racial zhǒngzú 种族; *~ equality* zhǒngzú píngděng 种族平等

racing jìngsài 竞赛

racing car sàichē 赛车

racing driver sàichē yùndòngyuán 赛车运动员

racism zhǒngzú qíshì 种族歧视

racist 1 *n* zhǒngzú qíshì zhě 种族歧视者 2 *adj* zhǒngzú qíshì 种族歧视

rack 1 *n* (*for parking bikes*) zìxíngchē jià 自行车架; (*for bags on train*) xínglǐ jià 行李架; (*for CDs*) chàngpiān jià 唱片架 2 *v/t*: *~ one's brains* jiǎojìn nǎozhī 绞尽脑汁

racket¹ SP qiúpāi 球拍

racket² (*noise*) xuānnào 喧闹; (*criminal activity*) piànjú 骗局

radar léidá 雷达

radiant *smile, appearance* hóngguāng mǎnmiàn 红光满面

radiate *v/i* (*of heat, light*) guāngmáng sìshè 光芒四射

radiation PHYS fàngshè 放射

radiator (*in room*) nuǎnqì 暖气; (*in car*) qǔnuǎn qì 取暖器

radical 1 *adj* chèdǐ 彻底; POL *views*

jījìn 激进 2 *n* POL jījìn zhǔyì zhě 激进主义者

radicalism POL jījìn zhǔyì 激进主义

radically chèdǐ 彻底

radio shōuyīnjī 收音机; *on the ~* shōuyīnjī lǐ 收音机里; *by ~* yòng wúxiàndiàn 用无线电

radioactive fàngshè xìng 放射性; **radio alarm** shōuyīnjī nàozhōng 收音机闹钟; **radio station** guǎngbō diàntái 广播电台; **radio taxi** wúxiàn chūzūchē 无线出租车; **radio telephone** wúxiàn diànhuà 无线电话; **radiotherapy** fàngshè liáofǎ 放射疗法

radish xiǎoluóbo 小萝卜

radius bànjìng 半径

raffle *n* chōujiǎng 抽奖

raft mùpái 木排

rafter chuánzi 椽子

rag (*for cleaning etc*) mābù 抹布

rage 1 *n* kuángnù 狂怒; *be in a ~* fānù 发怒; *all the ~* fēngxíng yīshí 风行一时 2 *v/i* (*of person*) fānù 发怒; (*of storm*) kuángbào 狂暴

ragged *edge* pòlàn 破烂; *appearance* luàn péngpéng 乱蓬蓬; *clothes* lánlǚ 褴褛

raid 1 *n* (*by troops, police*) tūxí 突袭; (*by robbers*) qiǎngjié 抢劫; FIN jítǐ pāoshòu 集体抛售 2 *v/t* (*of troops, police*) tūrán sōuchá 突然搜查; (*of robbers*) tūrán xíjī 突然袭击

raider (*on bank etc*) qiǎngjié fàn 抢劫犯

rail (*on track*) tiěguǐ 铁轨; (*hand-*) fúshǒu 扶手; (*for towel*) máojīn jià 毛巾架; *by ~* (*of people*) zuò huǒchē 坐火车; (*of goods*) yòng tiělù 用铁路

railings (*around park etc*) lángān 栏杆

railroad tiělù 铁路

railroad station huǒchē zhàn 火车站

rain 1 *n* yǔ 雨; *in the ~* yǔzhōng 雨中; *the ~s* yǔjì 雨季 2 *v/i* xiàyǔ 下雨; *it's ~ing* xià zhe yǔ ne 下着雨呢

rainbow cǎihóng 彩虹; **rain-check: can I take a ~ on that?** (*take up offer later*) shìfǒu kěyǐ tuīchí? 是否可以推迟？; **rain-coat** yǔyī 雨衣; **raindrop** yǔdiǎnr 雨点儿; **rainfall** jiàngyǔ liàng 降雨量; **rain forest** yǔlín 雨林; **rainstorm** bàofēngyǔ 暴风雨

rainy duōyǔ 多雨; *it's ~* lǎo xiàyǔ 老下雨

rainy season yǔjì 雨季

raise 1 *n* (*in salary*) zēngjiā 增加 2 *v/t shelf etc* shēnggāo 升高; *offer* tígāo 提高; *children* fǔyǎng 抚养; *question* tíchū 提出; *money* chóují 筹集

raisin pútáo gān 葡萄干

rake *n* (*for garden*) pázi 耙子

rally *n* (*meeting, reunion*) jíhuì 集会; MOT gōnglù sàichē 公路赛车; (*in tennis*) liánxù duìdǎ 连续对打

♦ **rally round** 1 *v/i* jíhé qǐlái 集合起来 2 *v/t*: ~ **X** tuánjié zài X de zhōuwéi 团结在X的周围

RAM (= *random access memory*) nèicún 内存

ram 1 *n* gōngyáng 公羊 2 *v/t ship, car* zhuàng 撞

ramble 1 *n* (*walk*) mànbù 漫步 2 *v/i* (*walk*) mànbù 漫步; (*when speaking*) dōnglā xīchě 东拉西扯; (*talk incoherently*) màntán 漫谈

rambler (*walker*) mànbù zhě 漫步者

rambling 1 *n* (*walking*) mànbù 漫步; (*in speech*) dōnglā xīchě 东拉西扯 2 *adj speech* màntán 漫谈

ramp pōdào 坡道; (*for raising vehicle*) xiépō 斜坡; (*unevenness in*

road) qīngxié lùmiàn 倾斜路面

rampage 1 *v/i* héngchōng zhízhuàng 横冲直撞 2 *n*: **go on the ~** bàotiào rúléi 暴跳如雷

rampart bìlěi 壁垒

ramshackle yáoyao yùzhuì 摇摇欲坠

ranch dà mùchǎng 大牧场

rancher mùchǎng zhǔ 牧场主

rancid hāla 哈喇

rancor jīyuàn 积怨

R & D (= *research and development*) yánfā 研发

random 1 *adj* suíjī 随机; *~ sample* suíjī chōuyàng 随机抽样 2 *n*: *at ~* suíbiàn 随便

range 1 *n* (*of products*) xìliè 系列; (*of gun*) shèchéng 射程; (*of airplane*) zuìdà xíngchéng 最大行程; (*of voice*) yīnyù 音域; (*of mountains*) shānmài 山脉 2 *v/i*: *~ from X to Y* zài X yǔ Y zhījiān 在X与Y之间

ranger (*for park and forest*) hùlínyuán 护林员; (*police in thinly populated area*) qíjǐng 骑警

rank 1 *n* MIL jūnxián 军衔; (*in society*) děngjí 等级; *the ~s* MIL shìbīng 士兵 2 *v/t* pái 排

♦ **rank among** zài ... zhī liè 在 ... 之列

ransack xǐjié 洗劫

ransom shújīn 赎金; *hold X to ~* bǎngpiào 绑票

rant *v/i*: *~ and rave* kǒutǔ kuángyán 口吐狂言

rap 1 *n* (*at door etc*) kòujī shēng 叩击声; MUS shuōchàng yīnyuè 说唱音乐 2 *v/t table etc* kòujī 叩击

♦ **rap** *at window etc* qiāo 敲

rape *n* & *v/t* qiángjiān 强奸

rape victim qiángjiān shòuhài zhě 强奸受害者

rapid kuài 快

rapidity kuàisù 快速

rapids jíliú 急流

rapist qiángjiān fàn 强奸犯

rapture xīnxǐ ruòkuáng 欣喜若狂

rapturous huānxǐ 欢喜

rare hǎnjiàn 罕见; *steak* chūshú 初熟

rarely hěnshǎo 很少

rarity xīshǎo 稀少

rascal xiǎo táoqì 小淘气

rash[1] MED pízhěn 皮疹

rash[2] *action, behavior* lǔmǎng 鲁莽

raspberry xuángōuzi 悬钩子

rat lǎoshǔ 老鼠

rate 1 *n* (*of exchange*) bǐlǜ 比率; (*of pay*) lǜ 率; (*price*) jiàgé 价格; (*speed*) sùdù 速度; *~ of interest* FIN lìxī lǜ 利息率; *at this ~* (*at this speed*) zhào zhèyàng de sùdù 照这样的速度; (*carrying on like this*) zhào zhèyàng 照这样 2 *v/t* (*consider, rank*) rènwéi 认为

rather xiāngdāng 相当; *I would stay here* wǒ qíngyuàn zài zhèr zhù 我情愿在这儿住; *or would you ~ …* ? nǐ shìfǒu gèng xǐhuān …? 你是否更喜欢…?

ration 1 *n* pèijǐ liàng 配给量 2 *v/t supplies* dìngliàng gōngyìng 定量供应

rational hélǐ 合理

rationality hélǐ xìng 合理性

rationalization (*of production etc*) hélǐ huà 合理化

rationalize 1 *v/t production etc* shǐ hélǐ huà 使合理化; *emotions, one's actions etc* jiěshì jiěshì 解释 2 *v/i* zhǎo jièkǒu 找借口

rat race shǔpīn 鼠拼

rattle 1 *n* (*noise*) gāga shēng 嘎嘎声; (*toy*) bōlànggǔ 拨浪鼓 2 *v/t chains etc* shǐ fāchū gāga shēng 使发出嘎嘎声 3 *v/i* (*of chains etc*) fāchū gāga shēng 发出嘎嘎声; (*of crates*) fāchū gāla galā shēng 发出嘎拉galā声

♦**rattle off** *poem, list of names* yìkǒuqìde shuō 一口气地说

rattlesnake xiǎngwěishé 响尾蛇

ravage: *~d by war* shòudào zhànzhēng de chuàngshāng 受到战争的创伤

rave *v/i* (*talk deliriously*) jiǎng húhuà 讲胡话; (*talk wildly*) húchě 胡扯; *~ about X* (*be very enthusiastic*) kuángrè de tánlùn X 狂热地谈论 X

raven dà wūyā 大乌鸦

ravenous *appetite* èhuàile 饿坏了

rave review jiāokǒu chēngzàn 交口称赞

ravine shēngǔ 深谷

raving: *~ mad* fēngle 疯了

ravishing mírén 迷人

raw *meat, vegetable* shēng 生; *sugar, iron* wèijīng jiāgōng 未经加工

raw materials yuán cáiliào 原材料

ray guāngxiàn 光线; *a ~ of hope* yīxiàn xīwàng 一线希望

razor tìxū dāo 剃须刀

razor blade tìxū dāo dāopiàn 剃须刀刀片

re COM yǒuguān 有关

reach 1 *n*: *within ~* zài fùjìn 在附近; *out of ~* ná búdào 拿不到 2 *v/t city etc* dàodá dì dá 到达; (*go as far as*) dào 到; *decision, agreement, conclusion* dédào 得到

♦**reach out** shēnchū shǒu 伸出手

react fǎnyìng 反应

reaction fǎnyìng 反应

reactionary *n & adj* POL fǎndòng pài 反动派

reactor (*nuclear*) fǎnyìng duī 反应堆

read 1 *v/t book. disk* dú 读; *Chinese* rènshi 认识 2 *v/i* yuèdú 阅读; *~ to X* dúgěi X tīng 读给 X 听

♦**read out** (*aloud*) lǎngsòng 朗诵

♦**read up on** yuèdú xuéxí 阅读学习

readable *handwriting* yìdú 易读

reader (*person*) dúzhě 读者

readily *admit, agree* xīnrán xīnrán 欣然

readiness (*for action*) zhǔnbèi jiùxù 准备就绪; (*to agree*) yuànyì 愿意

reading (*activity*) yuèdú 阅读; (*from meter etc*) dúshù 读数

reading matter yuèdú cáiliào 阅读材料

readjust 1 *v/t equipment, controls* tiáozhěng 调整 2 *v/i* (*to conditions*) shìyìng 适应

read-only file COMPUT zhǐdú dǎng'àn 只读档案

read-only memory COMPUT zhǐdú cúnchǔ qì 只读存储器

ready (*prepared*) zhǔnbèi hǎo 准备好; (*willing*) yuànyì 愿意; **get** (*oneself*) ~ zhǔnbèi hǎo 准备好; **get X** ~ bǎ X zhǔnbèi hǎo 把X准备好

ready-made *stew, solution etc* xiànchéng 现成

ready-to-wear xiànchéng yīfu 现成衣服

real *adj* zhēn 真

real estate fángdì chǎn 房地产

realism xiànshí zhǔyì 现实主义

realist xiànshí zhǔyì zhě 现实主义者

realistic xiànshí 现实

reality xiànshí 现实

realization (*of ideal, hope*) shíxiàn 实现

realize *v/t truth, importance* yìshí dào 意识到; *ideal, hope* shíxiàn 实现; FIN zhuànde 赚得; *I ~ now that …* wǒ xiànzài cái yìshí dào … 我现在才意识到 …

really zhēnzhèng 真正; (*very*) hěn 很; *~?* zhēnde ma? 真的吗？; *not* ~ (*not much*) bù zěnme yàng 不怎么样

real time COMPUT shíshí 实时

realtor búdòng chǎn zhōngjiān shāng 不动产中间商

reap shōugē 收割

reappear chóngxiàn 重现

rear **1** *n* hòumian 后面 **2** *adj legs* hòu 后; *seats, wheels, lights* hòumian 后面

rearm *v/t & v/i* chóngxīn wǔzhuāng 重新武装

rearmost zuìhòu 最后

rearrange *flowers, furniture* chóngxīn bǎifàng 重新摆放; *schedule, meetings* chóngxīn ānpái 重新安排

rear-view mirror hòushì jìng 后视镜

reason **1** *n* (*faculty*) lǐzhì 理智; (*cause*) yuányīn 原因 **2** *v/i*: *~ with* hé … jiǎnglǐ 和 … 讲理

reasonable *person, behavior* hélǐ 合理; *price* gōngpíng 公平; *a ~ number of people* bùshǎo rén 不少人

reasonably *act, behave* hélǐ de 合理地; (*quite*) jīhū 几乎

reassure dǎxiāo yílǜ dǎxiāo yílǜ 打消疑虑

reassuring lìngrén yǒu xìnxīn 令人有信心

rebate (*money back*) zhékòu 折扣

rebel *n* fǎnpàn zhě 反叛者; *~ troops* fǎnpàn jūnduì 反叛军队

rebellion fǎnpàn 反叛

rebellious bù fúguǎn 不服管

rebound *v/i* (*of ball etc*) tán huílái 弹回来

rebuff *n* cuòzhé 挫折

rebuild chóngjiàn 重建

rebuke *v/t* zhízé 指责

recall *v/t ambassador* zhāohuí 召回; (*remember*) jìqǐ 记起

recapture MIL duóhuí 夺回; *criminal* zàicì zhuāhuò 再次抓获

receding: *~ hair* kāishǐ tūtóu 开始秃头

receipt shōujù 收据; *acknowledge ~ of X* quèrèn shōudào X 确认收到X; *~s* FIN shōurù 收入

receive shōudào 收到

receiver (*of letter*) shōuxìn rén 收信人; TELEC tīngtǒng 听筒; (*for radio*) shōuyīnjī 收音机

receivership: *be in* ~ pòchǎn 破产

recent zuìjìn 最近

recently zuìjìn 最近

reception (*in hotel, company*) jiēdài chù 接待处; (*formal party*) zhāodài huì 招待会; (*welcome*) huānyíng 欢迎; (*for radio, mobile phone*) jiēshōu lì 接收力

reception desk jiēdài chù 接待处

receptionist jiēdài yuán 接待员

receptive: *be ~ to X* yì jiēshòu X 易接受X

recess (*in wall etc*) āochù 凹处; EDU xiūxi 休息; (*of parliament*) xiūjià 休假

recession (*economic*) bù jǐngqì 不景气

recharge *battery* chōngdiàn 充电

recipe càipǔ 菜谱

recipient (*of parcel etc*) jiēshōu rén 接收人; (*of payment*) shōukuǎn rén 收款人

reciprocal hùhuì 互惠

recital MUS yǎnzòu huì 演奏会

recite *poem* bèisòng 背诵; *details, facts* xùshù 叙述

reckless búgù hòuguǒ 不顾后果

reckon (*think, consider*) rènwéi 认为

♦ **reckon with**: *have X to ~* duìfu X 对付X

reclaim *land from sea* shōuhuí 收回

recline v/i xiéyǐ 斜倚

recluse yǐnshì 隐士

recognition (*of state, achievements*) chéngrèn 承认; *changed beyond ~* biànde rènbùchū 变得认不出

recognizable rèndechū 认得出

recognize *person, voice, tune* rènde 认得; *symptoms* biànrèn chū 辨认出; POL: *state* chéngrèn 承认; *it can be ~d by ...* píng ... biànrèn chū 凭 ... 辨认出

recollect huíyì 回忆

recollection huíyì 回忆

recommend tuījiàn 推荐

recommendation tuījiàn 推荐

recompense *n* bǔcháng 补偿; LAW péicháng 赔偿

reconcile *people, differences* tiáojiě 调解; *facts* shǐ yīzhì 使一致; *~ oneself to ...* gānxīn yú ... 甘心于 ...; *be ~d* (*of two people*) héhǎo 和好

reconciliation (*of people, differences*) tiáojiě 调解; (*of facts*) yīzhì 一致

recondition xiūfù 修复

reconnaissance MIL zhēnchá 侦察

reconsider 1 v/t *offer, one's position* chóngxīn kǎolǜ 重新考虑 **2** v/i chóngxīn kǎolǜ 重新考虑

reconstruct *city, one's life* chóngjiàn 重建; *crime* xiànchǎng shìfàn 现场示范

record 1 *n* MUS chàngpiàn 唱片; SP jìlù 纪录; (*written document, in database*) jìlù 记录; *~s* dǎngàn 档案; *say sth off the ~* fēi guānfāng de shuō 非官方地说; *have a criminal ~* yǒu xíngshì jìlù 有刑事记录; *have a good ~ for punctuality* yíxiàng zhǔnshí 一向

准时 **2** v/t (*on tape etc*) lù 录

record-breaking dǎpò jìlù 打破纪录

recorder MUS shùdí 竖笛

record holder jìlù bǎochí zhě 纪录保持者

recording lùyīn 录音

recording studio lùyīn shì 录音室

record player diànchàngjī 电唱机

recoup *financial losses* míbǔ 弥补

recover 1 v/t *sth lost, stolen goods* zhǎohuí 找回; *composure* huīfù 恢复 **2** v/i (*from illness*) huīfù 恢复

recovery (*of sth lost, stolen goods*) zhǎohuí 找回; (*from illness*) huīfù 恢复; *he has made a good ~* tā huīfù de hěnhǎo 他恢复得很好

recreation yúlè 娱乐

recruit 1 *n* MIL xīnbīng 新兵; (*to company*) xīnlái de 新来的 **2** v/t *new staff* zhāopìn 招聘; MIL zhēngmù 征募

recruitment zhāopìn 招聘

recruitment drive dà guīmó zhāopìn 大规模招聘

rectangle chángfāng xíng 长方形

rectangular chángfāng xíng 长方形

recuperate huīfù yuánqì 恢复元气

recur zàicì chūxiàn 再次出现

recurrent zàifā 再发

recycle huíshōu 回收

recycling huíshōu 回收

red hóng 红; *in the ~* yǒu chìzì 有赤字

Red Army Hóngjūn 红军; **Red China** Hóngsè Zhōngguó 红色中国; **Red Cross** Hóngshízì 红十字

redden v/i (*blush*) biànhóng 变红

redecorate v/t chóngxīn zhuāngxiū 重新装修

redeem *debt* fùqīng 付清; *sinners* miǎnzuì 免罪

redeeming *adj*: *~ feature* wéiyī kěqǔ zhīchù 唯一可取之处

redevelop *part of town* chóngxīn fāzhǎn 重新发展

Red Guard Hóngwèibīng 红卫兵;

red-handed: *catch X ~* dāngchǎng bǔhuò X 当场捕获X;
redhead yǒu hóng tóufà de rén 有红头发的人;**red-hot** rè téngteng 热腾腾;**red light** (*at traffic light*) hóngdēng 红灯;**red light district** hóngdēng qū 红灯区;**red meat** niú yáng ròu 牛羊肉;**redneck** xiāngbālǎo 乡巴佬;**red pepper** làjiāo 辣椒;**red tape** guānliáo chéngxù 官僚程序

reduce jiàngdī 降低

reduction jiǎnshǎo 减少

redundant (*unnecessary*) duōyú 多余

reed BOT lúwěi 芦苇

reef (*in sea*) jiāo 礁

reef knot suōfān jié 缩帆结

reek v/i fā chòuqì 发臭气; *~ of ...* yǒu ... wèir 有 ... 味儿

reel n (*of film, thread*) juǎn 卷

refer 1 v/t: *~ a decision / problem to s.o.* bǎ juédìng / wèntì jiāogěi mǒurén 把决定/问题交给某人 **2** v/i: *~ to ...* (*allude to*) tídào ... 提到 ...; (*to dictionary etc*) cānkǎo ... 参考

referee SP cáipàn 裁判;(*for job*) tuījiàn rén 推荐人

reference (*allusion*) shèjí 涉及; (*for job*) tuījiàn 推荐;(*~ number*) cānkǎo hàomǎ 参考号码;*with ~ to* guānyú 关于

reference book cānkǎo shū 参考书

referendum gōngmín tóupiào 公民投票

refill v/t tank, glass zài zhuāngmǎn 再装满

refine oil, sugar tíliàn 提炼; *technique* shǐ jīngměi 使精美

refined manners, language wényǎ 文雅

refinery tíliàn chǎng 提炼厂

reflation tōnghuò zài péngzhàng 通货再膨胀

reflect 1 v/t light fǎnshè 反射; *be ~ed in ...* fǎnshè zài ... zhīzhōng 反射在 ... 之中 **2** v/i (*think*) fǎnxǐng 反省

reflection (*in water, glass etc*) fǎnshè 反射;(*consideration*) fǎnxǐng 反省

reflex (*in body*) fǎnyìng nénglì 反应能力

reflex reaction zìdòng fǎnyìng 自动反应

reform n & v/t gǎigé 改革

refrain[1] v/i yìzhì 抑制;*please ~ from smoking* qǐngwù xīyān 请勿吸烟

refrain[2] n (*in song*) fùgē 副歌;(*in poem*) diéjù 迭句

refresh person shǐ jīngshén zhènzuò 使精神振作;*feel ~ed* gǎndào jīngshén zhènzuò 感到精神振作

refresher course fùxí kèchéng 复习课程

refreshing drink qīngshuǎng 清爽; *experience* qīngxīn yuèmù 清新悦目

refreshments chádiǎn 茶点

refrigerate lěngcáng 冷藏

refrigerator bīngxiāng 冰箱

refuel v/t & v/i jiā ránliào 加燃料

refuge bìhù 庇护;*take ~* (*from storm etc*) duǒbì 躲避

refugee nànmín 难民

refund n & v/t tuìkuǎn 退款

refusal jùjué 拒绝

refuse: *~ to do X* jùjué zuò X 拒绝做 X

regain control, lost territory, the lead chónghuò 重获

regard 1 n: *have great ~ for* zūnzhòng 尊重;*in this* zài zhèi fāngmiàn 在这方面;*with ~ to* guānyú 关于;(*kind*) *~s* wènhòu 问候;*give my ~s to X* dài wǒ wènhòu X 代我问候X;*with no ~ for ...* bù kǎolǜ ... 不考虑 ... **2** v/t: *regard X as Y* bǎ X kànzuò Y 把 X 看作 Y;*as ~s X* guānyú X 关于 X

regarding guānyú 关于

regardless háowú gùjì 毫无顾忌; *~ of* bùgù 不顾

regime (*government*) zhèngquán 政权

regiment n tuán 团

region dìqū 地区;*in the ~ of* dàyuē

大约

regional dìqū 地区

register 1 n dēngjì bù 登记簿
2 v/t birth, death dēngjì 登记;
vehicle shàngpái 上牌; letter
guàhào 挂号; emotion xiǎnshì 显
示; **send a ~ed letter** jì guàhào
xìn 寄挂号信 3 v/i (for a course,
with police) dēngjì 登记

registered letter guàhào xìn 挂号
信

registrar (of births etc) dēngjì rén
登记人

registration (for a course) zhùcè 注
册; (with police) dēngjì 登记

regret 1 v/t hòuhuǐ 后悔 2 n yíhàn
遗憾

regrettable búxìng 不幸

regrettably búxìng 不幸

regular 1 adj flights dìngqī 定期;
intervals, habits yǒu guīlǜ 有规律;
pattern, shape yúnchèn 匀称;
(normal, ordinary) pǔtōng 普通
2 n (at bar etc) chángkè 常客

regulate kòngzhì 控制

regulation (rule) guīzhāng 规章

rehabilitate ex-criminal gǎixiéguīzhèng 改邪归正

rehearsal páiyǎn 排演

rehearse v/t & v/i páiyǎn 排演

reign n & v/i tǒngzhì 统治

reimburse bǔcháng 补偿

rein jiāngsheng 缰绳

reincarnation línghún zhuǎnshì 灵
魂转世

reinforce structure xiūbǔ 修补;
beliefs jiāqiáng 加强

reinforced concrete gāngjīn hùnníng tǔ 钢筋混凝土

reinforcements MIL yuánjūn 援军

reinstate person in office shǐ fùzhí
使复职; paragraph in text chóngxīn bǔshàng 重新补上

reject v/t jùjué 拒绝

rejection jùjué 拒绝

relapse MED jiùbìng fùfā 旧病复
发; **have a ~** jiùbìng fùfā 旧病复
发

relate 1 v/t story xùshù 叙述; **~ X
to Y** jiāng X yǔ Y liánxì qǐlái 将X
与Y联系起来 2 v/i: **to ...** (be

connected with) yǔ ... yǒu guānlián
与 ... 有关联; **he doesn't ~ to
people** tā hé rén xiāngchǔ bùhǎo
他和人相处不好

related (by family) yǒu qīnshǔ
guānxì 有亲属关系; events, ideas
etc xiāngguān 相关

relation (in family) qīnshǔ 亲属;
(connection) guānxì 关系; **business / diplomatic ~s** shāngyè /
wàijiāo guānxì 商业/外交关系

relationship guānxì 关系; **have a
~** (sexual) fāshēng guānxì 发生关
系

relative 1 n qīnqi 亲戚 2 adj
xiāngduì 相对; **X is ~ to Y** X yǔ Y
yǒuguān X与Y有关

relatively xiāngduì 相对

relax 1 v/i fàngsōng 放松; **~!,
don't get angry** xiǎng kāi diǎnr,
bié shēngqì! 想开点儿，别生
气！2 v/t muscle fàngsōng 放松;
pace of work sōngxiè 松懈

relaxation fàngsōng 放松

relay 1 v/t message zhuǎngào 转告;
radio, TV signals zhuǎnbō 转播
2 n: **~ (race)** jiēlì sài 接力赛

release 1 n (from prison) shìfàng
释放; (of CD etc) fāxíng 发行
2 v/t prisoner shìfàng 释放;
parking brake sōngkāi 松开;
information gōngbù 公布

relent ràngbù 让步

relentless (determined) búxiè 不
懈; rain etc wúqíng 无情

relevance guānlián 关联

relevant yǒuguān 有关

reliability kěkào xìng 可靠性

reliable kěkào 可靠

reliably kěndìng 肯定; **I am ~
informed that ...** wǒ dédào kěkào
xiāoxi shuō ... 我得到可靠消息
说 ...

reliance yīkào 依靠; **~ on ...** yīkào
... 依靠 ...

relic (object) yíwù 遗物; (of tradition) yísú 遗俗

relief kuānwèi 宽慰; **that's a ~**
tàihǎole 太好了; **in ~** (in art)
fúdiāo 浮雕

relieve pressure, pain jiǎnqīng 减

轻; (take over from) jiētì 接替; **be ~d** (at news etc) kuānwèi 宽慰

religion zōngjiào 宗教

religious zōngjiào 宗教

religiously (conscientiously) rènzhēn 认真

relish 1 n (sauce) bàncài zhīr 伴菜汁儿 **2** v/t idea, prospect xǐhuan 喜欢

relive the past, an event zài tǐyàn 再体验

relocate v/i (of business, employee) bānqiān 搬迁

reluctance miǎnqiáng 勉强

reluctant miǎnqiáng 勉强; **be ~ to do X** bù qíngyuàn zuò X 不情愿做 X

reluctantly miǎnqiáng 勉强

♦**rely on** yīkào 依靠; **~ X to do Y** yīkào X zuò Y 依靠 X 去做 Y

remain (be left) shèngxia 剩下; (stay) dāizài 呆在; (continue) réngrán 仍然; **~ silent / loyal** bǎochí chénmò / zhōngchéng 保持沉默 / 忠诚

remainder (rest) yúxià 余下; MATH yúshù 余数

remains (of body) yítǐ 遗体

remand 1 v/t: **~ X in custody** jūliú X 拘留 X **2** n: **be on ~** huányā 还押

remark 1 n huà 话 **2** v/t pínglùn 评论

remarkable fēifán 非凡

remarkably fēifán 非凡

remarry v/i zàihūn 再婚

remedy n MED liáofǎ 疗法; fig bǔjiù 补救

remember 1 v/t s.o., sth jìde 记得; **~ to lock the door** jìzhù suǒmén 记住锁门; **~ me to her** tì wǒ wèn tā hǎo 替我问她好 **2** v/i jìde 记得; **I don't ~** wǒ bú jìde 我不记得

remind v/t: **~ X to do Y** tíxǐng X zuò Y 提醒 X 做 Y; **~ X of Y** (call to mind) shǐ X xiǎngqǐ Y 使 X 想起 Y

reminder tíxǐng wù 提醒物; (COM: for payment) cuīzhàng dān 催账单

reminisce huáijiù 怀旧

reminiscent: be ~ of X huíyì qǐ X 回忆起 X

remnant cánjì 残迹

remorse àohuǐ 懊悔

remorseless person, pace, demands wúqíng 无情

remote village piānpì 偏僻; possibility, connection jíxiǎo 极小; (aloof) lěngmò 冷漠; ancestor jiǔyuǎn 久远

remote access COMPUT yuǎnchéng tōnglù 远程通路

remote control yáokòng 遥控

remotely related, connected shūyuǎn 疏远; **just ~ possible** yǒu jíxiǎo kěnéng xìng 有极小可能性

removal (of garbage, demonstrators) yídòng 移动; (of doubt) páichú 排除; (from home) qiānjū 迁居

remove yídòng 移动; top, lid nákāi 拿开; growth, tumor qùchú 去除; coat etc tuō 脱; doubt, suspicion jiēchú 解除

remuneration bàochóu 报酬

remunerative yǒu lìrùn 有利润

rename chóngxīn mìngmíng 重新命名

render service jǐyǔ 给予; **~ X helpless / unconscious** shǐ X gūlì wúyuán / hūnmí 使 X 孤立无援 / 昏迷

rendering (of piece of music) yǎnzòu 演奏

rendez-vous (romantic) yuēhuì 约会; MIL zhǐdìng jíhé diǎn 指定集合点

renew contract, license zhǎnqī 展期; discussions chóngxīn kāishǐ 重新开始; **feel ~ed** gǎndào jīnglì chōngpèi 感到精力充沛

renewal (of contract etc) zhǎnqī 展期; (of discussions) chóngxīn kāishǐ 重新开始

renminbi FIN rénmínbì 人民币

renounce v/t title, rights xuānbù fàngqì 宣布放弃

renovate zhěngxiū 整修

renovation zhěngxiū 整修

renown shēngyù 声誉

renowned zhùmíng 著名

rent 1 n zūjīn 租金; *for ~* chūzū 出租 2 v/t *apartment, car, equipment* zū 租; (*~ out*) chūzū 出租

rental (*for apartment, for TV etc*) zūjīn 租金

rental agreement zūyuē 租约

rental car zūyòng chē 租用车

rent-free adv miǎnzū 免租

reopen 1 v/t *business, store* chóngxīn kāizhāng 重新开张; *negotiations* zài jìnxíng 再进行; LAW: *case* chóngshěn 重审 2 v/i (*of theater etc*) chóngxīn kāizhāng 重新开张

reorganization (*of business*) gǎizǔ 改组; (*of room, schedule*) chóngxīn ānpái 重新安排

reorganize *business* gǎizǔ 改组; *room, schedule* chóngxīn ānpái 重新安排; *chapter* gǎibiān 改编

rep COM dàilǐ shāng 代理商

repaint chóngxīn shuā yóuqī 重新刷油漆

repair 1 v/t xiūlǐ 修理 2 n xiūlǐ 修理; *in a good / bad state of ~* wánhǎo wúsǔn / pòsǔn 完好无损 / 破损

repairman xiūlǐ gōng 修理工

repatriate sòng huíguó 送回国

repay *money* chánghuán 偿还; *person* bàodá 报答

repayment fùhuíkuǎn 付回款

repeal v/t *law* fèichú 废除

repeat 1 v/t *sth said, performance, experience* chóngfù 重复; *am I ~ing myself?* wǒ shìbúshì chóngfù le? 我是不是重复了? 2 v/i chóngfù 重复; *I ~, do not touch it* wǒ zàishuō yīcì, biépèng wǒ zài shuō yícì, biépèng wǒ zài shuō yīcì, biépèng 我再说一次, 别碰 3 n (*TV program etc*) chóngbō 重播

repeat business COM huítóu shēngyì 回头生意

repeated fǎnfù 反复

repeat order COM chóngfù dìnghuò 重复定货

repel v/t *invaders, attack* jītuì 击退; *insects* qūgǎn 驱赶; (*disgust*) shǐ yànwù 使厌恶

repellent 1 n (*insect ~*) qūchóng jì 驱虫剂 2 adj lìngrén yànwù 令人厌恶

repent v/i hòuhuǐ 后悔

repercussions yǐngxiǎng 影响

repetition chóngfù 重复

repetitive chóngfù 重复

replace (*put back*) fànghuí 放回; (*take the place of*) tìdài 替代

replacement (*person*) dàitì rén 代替人; (*thing*) dàitì wù 代替物

replacement part tìjiàn 替件

replay 1 n (*recording*) chóngfàng zhòng 重放; (*match*) chóngsài zhòng 重赛 2 v/t *match* chóngsài 重赛

replica fùzhì pǐn 复制品

reply n, v/t & v/i huídá 回答

report 1 n (*account*) bàogào 报告; (*by journalist*) bàodào 报道 2 v/t *facts* bàodào 报道; (*to authorities*) tōngzhī 通知; *~ one's findings to X* jiāng diàochá jiéguǒ huìbào gěi X 将调查结果汇报给 X; *~ X to the police* xiàng jǐngfāng gàofā X 向警方告发 X; *he is ~ed to be in Hong Kong* jù shuō tā zài Xiānggǎng jùshuō 据说他在香港 3 v/i (*of journalist*) bàodào 报道; (*present oneself*) bàodào 报到; *who do you ~ to?* (*in business*) shuí shì nǐde shàngjí? 谁是你的上级?

report card huìbào 汇报

reporter jìzhě 记者

repossess COM shōuhuí 收回

reprehensible yīngshòu zhǐzhāi 应受指摘

represent (*act for*) dàibiǎo 代表; (*stand for*) zhǔzhāng 主张; (*of images in painting etc*) miáohuì 描绘

representative 1 n dàibiǎo rén 代表人; COM dàilǐ shāng 代理商; POL zhòngyìyuán 众议员 2 adj (*typical*) diǎnxíng 典型

repress *revolt* zhènyā 镇压; *feelings, natural urges* yāyì 压抑; *laugh* rěnzhe 忍着

repression POL zhènyā 镇压

repressive POL yāzhì 压制

reprieve n & v/t *also fig* huǎnxíng 缓刑

reprimand v/t shēnchì 申斥

reprint 1 n zàibǎn 再版 2 v/t chóngyìn 重印

reprisal bàofù xíngwéi 报复行为; **take ~s** jìnxíng bàofù xíngwéi 进行报复行为

reproach 1 n zébèi 责备; **be beyond ~** wúkě zhǐzé 无可指责 2 v/t zhǐzé 指责

reproachful zhǐzé 指责

reproduce 1 v/t atmosphere, mood zàixiàn 再现 2 v/i BIO fánzhí 繁殖

reproduction BIO fánzhí 繁殖; (of sound, images) fùzhì 复制; (piece of furniture) fùzhì pǐn 复制品

reproductive BIO fánzhí 繁殖

reptile páxíng dòngwù 爬行动物

republic gònghé guó 共和国

republican 1 n gònghé zhǔyì zhě 共和主义者; POL **Republican** Gònghé dàngrén 共和党人 2 adj gònghé zhǔyì 共和主义

Republic of China Zhōnghuá Mínguó 中华民国

repudiate (deny) fǒudìng 否定

repulsive lìngrén yànwù 令人厌恶

reputable yǒu míngshēng 有名声

reputation míngyù 名誉; **have a good/bad ~** yǒuhǎo/huài míngshēng 有好/坏名声

request 1 n yāoqiú 要求; **on ~** yījīng yāoqiú 一经要求 2 v/t yāoqiú 要求

require (need) xūyào 需要; **it ~s great care** yào hěn xiǎoxīn 要很小心; **as ~d by law** àn fǎlǜ guīdìng 按法律规定; **guests are ~d to ...** kèrénmen bìxū ... 客人们必须 ...

required (necessary) bìyào 必要

requirement (need) xūyào 需要; (condition) tiáojiàn 条件

reroute airplane etc gēnggǎi xiànlù 更改线路

rerun tape fùyìng 复映

rescue 1 n yuánjiù 援救; **come to X's ~** yuánjiù X 援救 X 2 v/t yuánjiù 援救

rescue party yuánjiù duì 援救队

research n yánjiū 研究

♦**research into** yánjiū 研究

research and development yánjiū yǔ fāzhǎn 研究与发展

research assistant zhùlǐ yánjiū yuán 助理研究员

researcher yánjiū yuán 研究员

research project yánjiū kètí 研究课题

resemblance xiāngsì chù 相似处

resemble xiàng 像

resent bùmǎn 不满

resentful bùmǎn 不满

resentment bùmǎn 不满

reservation (of room, table) yùdìng 预定; (mental) bǎoliú 保留; (special area) bǎohù qū 保护区; **I have a ~** wǒ yǒugè yùdìng 我有个预定

reserve 1 n (store) chǔbèi 储备; (aloofness) hánxù 含蓄; SP yùbèi duìyuán 预备队员; **~s** FIN chǔbèi jīn 储备金; **keep X in ~** chǔbèi X dàiyòng 储备 X 待用 2 v/t seat, table yùdìng 预定; judgment bǎoliú 保留

reserved person, manner nèixiàng 内向; table, seat bèi yùdìng 被预定

reservoir (for water) shuǐkù 水库

reside zhù 住

residence (house etc) zhùsuǒ 住所; (stay) jūzhù 居住

residence permit jūliúzhèng 居留证

resident 1 n jūmín 居民 2 adj (living in a building) zhùdì 驻地

residential district zhùzhái qū 住宅区

residue cánzhā 残渣

resign 1 v/t position cízhí zìrán 辞职; **~ oneself to** tīngqí zìrán 听其自然 2 v/i (from job) cízhí 辞职

resignation (from job) cízhí 辞职; (mental) wúkě nàihé 无可奈何

resigned tīngtiān yóumìng 听天由命; **we have become ~ to the fact that ...** wǒmen yǐjīng jiēshòu ... 我们已经接受 ...

resilient personality dáguān 达观; material nàiyòng 耐用

resin sōngxiāng 松香

resist 1 v/t *enemy, s.o.'s advances* dǐkàng 抵抗; *new measures* dǐzhì 抵制; **~ temptation** bùshòu yòuhuò 不受诱惑 **2** v/i dǐkàng 抵抗

resistance (*to enemy, advances*) dǐkàng 抵抗; (*to new measures*) zǔlù 阻力; (*to disease, heat etc*) dǐkàng lì 抵抗力

resistant *material* jiāngù 坚固; **~ to heat / rust** fángrè / xiù 防热/锈

resolute jiānjué 坚决

resolution (*decision*) juéyì 决议; (*made at New Year etc*) juédìng 决定; (*determination*) juéxīn 决心; (*of problem*) jiějué fāngfǎ 解决方法; (*of image*) qīngxī dù 清晰度

resolve *problem, mystery* jiějué 解决; **~ to do X** juédìng zuò X 决定做 X

resort 1 n (*place*) dùjià shèngdì 度假胜地; **as a last ~** zuòwéi zuìhòu yīzhāo 作为最后一招

resounding *success, victory* chèdǐ 彻底

resource zīyuán 资源; **we don't have the ~s for such a big contract** wǒmen méiyǒu zuò zhème dà hétong de zīyuán 我们没有做这么大合同的资源

resourceful zúzhì duōmóu 足智多谋

respect 1 n zūnjìng 尊敬; (*consideration*) zūnzhòng 尊重; **show ~ to** duì ... biǎoshì zūnzhòng 对 ... 表示尊重; **with ~ to** guānyú 关于; **in this / that ~** zài zhèi / nà fāngmiàn 在这/那方面; **in many ~s** zài xǔduō fāngmiàn 在许多方面; **pay one's last ~s to s.o.** xiàng sǐzhě gàobié 向死者告别 **2** v/t *person, s.o.'s opinion, privacy* zūnzhòng 尊重; *law* zūnshǒu 遵守

respectable *person* tǐmiàn 体面; *bar* xiàngyàng 象样

respectful yǒu lǐmào 有礼貌

respectfully yǒu lǐmào 有礼貌

respective gèzì 各自

respectively fēnbié 分别

respiration hūxī 呼吸

respirator MED réngōng hūxī qì 人工呼吸器

respite huǎnhé 缓和; **without ~** bùtíng 不停

respond (*answer*) dáfù 答复; (*react*) zuòchū fǎnyìng 做出反应; (*to treatment*) fǎnyìng 反应

response (*answer*) dáfù 答复; (*reaction*) fǎnyìng 反应

responsibility zérèn 责任; **accept ~ for** fù zé fùzé 负责; (*duty*) zérèn 责任; **a job with more ~** yǒu gèngduō zérèn de gōngzuò 有更多责任的工作

responsible (*to blame*) fùzé 负责; (*liable, for children, production etc*) fùzé 负责; (*trustworthy, showing seriousness*) kěkào 可靠; (*involving responsibility: job*) xūyào fùzé 需要负责

responsive *audience* yì shòu gǎndòng 易受感动; *brakes* mǐngǎn 敏感

rest¹ 1 n xiūxi 休息 **2** v/i xiūxi 休息; **~ on ...** (*be based on*) yǐ ... wéi jīchǔ 以 ... 为基础; (*lean against*) gē zài ... shàng 搁在 ... 上; **it all ~s with him** dōu zàiyú tāle 都在于他了 **3** v/t (*lean, balance etc*) kào kào 靠

rest² n: **the ~** yúxià 余下

restaurant cānguǎn 餐馆

restaurant car cānchē 餐车

rest cure xiūyǎng liáofǎ 休养疗法

rest home yǎnglǎo yuàn 养老院

restless bù ānfèn 不安分; **have a ~ night** méi shuì hǎo jiào 睡好

restoration xiūfù 修复

restore *building etc* xiūfù 修复

restrain *dog, troops* yuēshù 约束; *emotions* yìzhì 抑制; **~ oneself** kòngzhì zìjǐ 控制自己

restraint (*moderation*) jiézhì 节制

restrict xiànzhì 限制; **I'll ~ myself to ...** (*in speech, book*) wǒ jǐn tán ... 我仅谈 ...

restricted *view* shòu xiànzhì 受限制

restricted area MIL jìndì 禁地

restriction xiànzhì 限制

rest room wèishēngjiān 卫生间

result n jiéguǒ 结果; *as a ~ of this* yīncǐ 因此

♦**result from** qǐyú 起于

♦**result in** dǎozhì 导致

resume v/t huīfù 恢复

résumé lǚlì 履历

resurface 1 v/t roads lìng pū lùmiàn 另铺路面 2 v/i (reappear) chóngxīn chūxiàn 重新出现

resurrection REL fùhuó 复活

resuscitate shǐ sūxǐng 使苏醒

retail 1 adv yǐ língshòu fāngshì 以零售方式 2 v/i: ~ *at ...* língshòu jià wéi ... 零售价为...

retail price língshòu jià 零售价

retailer língshòu shāng 零售商

retain bǎoliú 保留

retainer FIN pìnjīn 聘金

retaliate bàofù 报复

retaliation bàofù 报复

retarded (mentally) zhìlì chídùn 智力迟钝

retire v/i (from work) tuìxiū 退休

retired tuìxiū 退休

retirement tuìxiū 退休

retirement age tuìxiū niánlíng 退休年龄

retiring miǎntiǎn 腼腆

retort n & v/i fǎnbó 反驳

retrace footsteps shùn yuánlù fǎnhuí 顺原路返回

retract v/t claws suōjìn 缩进; undercarriage shōusuō 收缩; statement shōuhuí 收回

retreat 1 v/i MIL chètuì 撤退; (in discussion etc) tuìràng 让 2 n MIL chètuì 撤退; (place) yǐnjū chù 隐居处

retrieve wǎnjiù 挽救

retriever (dog) lièquǎn 猎犬

retroactive law etc zhuīsù 追溯

retrograde move, decision hòutuì 后退

retrospect n: *in ~* xiànzài kànlái 现在看来

retrospective huígù 回顾

return 1 n (coming back, going back) fǎnhuí 返回; (giving back) tuìhuán 退还; COMPUT fǎnhuí 回; (in tennis) huíqiú 回球; *by ~*

(of post) lìjí huífù 立即回复; ~*s* (profit) lìrùn 利润; *many happy ~s (of the day)* zhù nǐ chángshòu 祝你长寿 2 v/t (give back) tuìhuán 退还; (put back) fànghuí 放回; favor, invitation huíbào 回报 3 v/i (go back, come back) fǎnhuí 返回; (of good times, doubts etc) huífù 回复

return flight huíchéng fēijī 回程飞机

return journey huíchéng 回程

reunification tǒngyī 统一

reunion tuánjù 团聚

reunite v/t tǒngyī 统一

reusable kě zài yòng 可再用

reuse zàiyòng 再用

rev n huízhuǎn 回转; ~*s per minute* měi fēnzhōng huízhuǎn cìshù 每分钟回转次数

♦**rev up** v/t engine cǎi yóuménr 踩油门儿

revaluation chóngxīn píngjià 重新评价

reveal (make visible) xiǎnshì 显示; secret, truth jiēlù 揭露; feelings lùchū 露出

revealing remark tòulù zhēnxiàng 透露真相; dress lùtǐ 露体

revelation xièlù 泄露

revenge n bàofù 报复; *take one's ~* wèi zìjǐ bàochóu 为自己报仇

revenue shōurù 收入

reverberate (of sound) huíxiǎng 回响

revere chóngjìng 崇敬

Reverend mùshī 牧师

reverent qiánchéng 虔诚

reverse 1 adj sequence diāndǎo 颠倒 2 n (opposite) xiāngfǎn 相反; (back) bèimiàn 背面; MOT dàodǎng 倒档 3 v/t sequence diāndǎo 颠倒; vehicle dàochē 倒车 4 v/i MOT dàochē 倒车

review 1 n (of book, movie) pínglùn 评论; (of troops) jiǎnyuè 检阅; (of situation etc) shěnchá 审查 2 v/t book, movie pínglùn 评论; troops jiǎnyuè 检阅; situation etc shěnchá 审查; EDU fùxí 复习

reviewer (of book, movie) pínglùn

jiā 评论家

revise *v/t opinion* xiūzhèng 修正; *text* jiàozhèng 校正

revision (*of opinion*) xiūzhèng 修正; (*of text*) jiàozhèng 校正

revisionism POL xiūzhèng zhǔyì 修正主义

revival (*of custom, old style etc*) fùxīng 复兴; (*of patient*) sūxíng 苏醒

revive 1 *v/t custom, old style etc* fùxīng 复兴; *patient* shǐ sūxíng 使苏醒 **2** *v/i* (*of business, exchange rate etc*) shǐ shàngshēng 使上升

revoke law fèichú 废除; *license* qǔxiāo 取消

revolt 1 *n* fǎnkàng 反抗 **2** *v/i* zàofǎn 造反

revolting (*disgusting*) ěxin 恶心

revolution POL *etc* gémìng 革命; (*turn*) xuánzhuǎn 旋转; *1911 Revolution* Xīnhāi Gémìng 辛亥革命; *1949 Revolution* Jiěfàng jiěfàng

revolutionary 1 *n* POL gémìng jiā 革命家 **2** *adj spirit, forces* gémìng 革命; *new ideas* chuàngxīn 创新

revolutionize chèdǐ biàngé 彻底变革

revolve *v/i* xuánzhuǎn 旋转

revolver zuǒlún shǒuqiāng 左轮手枪

revolving door xuánzhuǎn mén 旋转门

revue THEA shíshì fěngcì jù 时事讽刺剧

revulsion fǎngǎn 反感

reward 1 *n* (*financial*) shǎngjīn 赏金; (*benefit derived*) bàochóu 报酬 **2** *v/t* (*financially*) jiǎnglì 奖励

rewarding *experience* zhíde zuò 值得做

rewind *v/t film, tape* dǎo 倒

rewrite *v/t* chóngxiě 重写

rhetoric huálìde cízǎo 华丽的词藻

rhetorical question fǎnwèn 反问

rheumatism fēngshī bìng 风湿病

rhinoceros xīniú 犀牛

rhubarb cài yòng dàhuáng 菜用大黄

rhyme 1 *n* yùn 韵 **2** *v/i* yāyùn 压韵; *~ with …* yǐ … yāyùn 以 … 压韵

rhythm jiézòu 节奏

rib lèigǔ 肋骨

ribbon sīdài 丝带

rice mǐ 米

rice bowl fànwǎn 饭碗; **rice cooker** diànfànguō 电饭锅; **ricefield** dàotián 稻田; **rice noodles** mǐfěn 米粉; **rice porridge** zhōu 粥; **rice wine** mǐjiǔ 米酒

rich 1 *adj* (*wealthy*) yǒuqián 有钱; *food* yóunì 油腻 **2** *n: the ~* fùrén 富人

rickshaw rénlìchē 人力车

rid: *get ~ of garbage, unwanted furniture* rēngdiào 扔掉; *foreign accent, excess weight, illusions* bǎituō 摆脱

riddle míyǔ 谜语

ride 1 *n* (*on horse*) qímǎ 骑马; (*in vehicle*) chèngchē jīhuì 乘车机会; (*journey*) lǚtú 旅途; *do you want a ~ into town?* xiǎng dāchē jìnchéng ma? 想搭车进城吗？; *thanks for the ~* xièxie nǐ jiào wǒ dāchē 谢谢你叫我搭车 **2** *v/t horse, bike* qí mǎ 骑马 **3** *v/i* (*on horse*) qímǎ 骑马; (*on bike*) qí zìxíngchē 骑自行车; (*in vehicle*) chèngchē 乘车

rider (*on horse*) qímǎ rén 骑马人; (*on bike*) qí zìxíngchē rén 骑自行车人

ridge (*raised strip*) jǐ 脊; (*of mountain*) shānjǐ 山脊; (*of roof*) wūjǐ 屋脊

ridicule 1 *n* xīluò 奚落 **2** *v/t* fěngcì 讽刺

ridiculous huāngmiù 荒谬

ridiculously huāngmiù 荒谬

riding (*on horseback*) qímǎ 骑马

rifle *n* láifù qiāng 来复枪

rift (*in earth*) lièxì 裂隙; (*in party etc*) fēnliè 分裂

rig 1 *n* (*oil ~*) yóujǐng 油井; (*truck*) qiānyǐn tuōchē 牵引拖车 **2** *v/t elections* cāozòng 操纵

right 1 *n* (*correct*) zhèngquè 正

确; (*proper, just*) zhèngdāng 正当; (*suitable*) héshì 合适; (*not left*) yòu 右; (*of answer*) zhèngquè 正确; (*of person*) zhèngzhí 正直; (*of clock*) zhǔnquè 准确; **that's ~!** duì a! 对啊！; **put things ~** jiūzhèng cuòwù 纠正错误; **that's not ~** (*not allowed, not fair*) nà bùxíng 那不行; **~ alright 2** adv (*directly*) jiù 就; (*correctly*) zhèngquè 正确; (*completely*) chèdǐ 彻底; (*not left*) yòu 右; **~ now** (*immediately*) mǎshàng 马上; (*at the moment*) xiànzài 现在 **3** n (*civil, legal etc*) quánlì 权利; (*not left*) yòu 右; POL yòupài 右派; **on the ~** = zài yòubiān 在右边, POL zài yòuyì nàbiān 在右翼那边; **turn to the ~, take a ~** xiàng yòu guǎi 向右拐; **be in the ~** yǒulǐ 有理; **know ~ from wrong** qūbié hǎo-huài 区别好坏

right-angle zhíjiǎo 直角; **at ~s to ... chéng zhíjiǎo ... 成直角 ...**

rightful *heir, owner etc* héfǎ 合法

right-hand adj yòubiān 右边; **on the ~ side** zài yòubiān 在右边

right-hand drive MOT yòuzuǒ fāngxiàngpán 右座方向盘

right-handed yòu piě zi 右撇子

right-hand man délì zhùshǒu 得力助手; **right of way** (*in traffic*) yōuxiān xíngshǐ quán 优先行驶权; (*across land*) tōngxíng quán 通行权; **right wing** n POL, SP yòuyì 右翼; **right-wing** adj POL yòuyì 右翼; **~ extremism** POL jíyòu zhǔyì 极右主义; **right-winger** POL yòupài 右派

rigid *material* jiānyìng 坚硬; *principles* wěngù 稳固; *attitude* kèbǎn 刻板

rigor (*of discipline*) yángé 严格; **the ~s of the winter** dōngrì de jiānxīn 冬日的艰辛

rigorous *discipline* yángé 严格; *tests, analysis* jīngquè 精确

rim (*of wheel*) lúnyuán 轮缘; (*of cup*) biān 边; (*of eyeglasses*) jìngkuàng 镜框

ring¹ (*circle*) yuánquān 圆圈; (*on

finger*) jièzhi 戒指; (*in boxing*) quánjī chǎng 拳击场; (*at circus*) mǎxì quān 马戏圈

ring² **1** n (*of bell*) zhōngshēng 钟声; (*of voice*) shēngdiào 声调 **2** v/t bell qiāozhōng 敲钟 **3** v/i (*of bell*) míng 鸣; **please ~ for attention** ànlíng zhāohuàn fúwù 按铃召唤服务

ringleader tóumù 头目

ring-pull lāhuán 拉环

rink liūbīng chǎng 溜冰场

rinse 1 n (*for hair color*) rǎnsè 染色 **2** v/t clothes, dishes, hair piǎoxǐ 漂洗

riot 1 n bàoluàn 暴乱 **2** v/i nàoshì 闹事

rioter nàoshì zhě 闹事者

riot police píngluàn jīngchá 平乱警察

rip 1 n (*in cloth etc*) sīliè 撕裂 **2** v/t cloth etc sīliè 撕裂; **~ X open** sīkāi X 撕开 X

♦**rip off** F *customers* shōufèi guògāo 收费过高; (*cheat*) qiāo zhúgàng 敲竹杠

ripe fruit shóu 熟

ripen v/i (*of fruit*) chéngshóu 成熟

ripeness (*of fruit*) shóu 熟

rip-off n F bōxuē 剥削

ripple (*on water*) xìlàng 细浪

rise 1 v/i (*from chair etc*) qǐlái 起来; (*of sun*) shēngqǐ 升起; (*of rocket*) fāshè 发射; (*of price, temperature*) shàngzhǎng 上涨; (*of water level*) shàngshēng 上升 **2** n (*in price, temperature*) shàngzhǎng 上涨; (*in water level*) shàngshēng 上升; (*in salary*) tígāo 提高

risk 1 n fēngxiǎn 风险; **take a ~** màoxiǎn 冒险 **2** v/i màoxiǎn fēngxiǎn 冒 ... 风险; **let's ~ it** wǒmen shìshìba 我们试试吧

risky màoxiǎn 冒险

ritual n & adj yíshì 仪式

rival 1 n duìshǒu 对手 **2** v/t yǔ ... jìngzhēng 与 ... 竞争; **I can't ~ that** wǒ bǐ bú guò 我比不过

rivalry jìngzhēng 竞争

river héliú 河流

riverbed héchuáng 河床

riverside hébiān 河边

rivet 1 n mǎodīng 铆钉 2 v/t mǎojiē 铆接; ~ X to Y bǎ X dīngláo dào Y shàng 把X钉牢到Y上

RMB (= **renminbi**) rénmínbì 人民币

road lù 路; **it's just down the ~** jiù zài nàbiān 就在那边

roadblock lùzhàng 路障; **road hog** kāichē zài lù zhōngjiān 开车在路中间; **road holding** (of vehicle) gāosù jiàshǐ néngli 高速驾驶能力; **road map** xiànlù tú 线路图; **roadside: at the ~** zài lùbiān 在路边; **roadsign** lùbiāo 路标; **roadway** gōnglù 公路; **roadworthy** shìyú gōnglù xíngshǐ 适于公路行驶

roam mànyóu 漫游

roar 1 n (of traffic, engine) hōngmíng shēng 轰鸣声; (of lion) páoxiào 咆哮; (of person) dàshēng chǎo 大声吵 2 v/i (of engine) hōngmíng 轰鸣; (of lion) páoxiào 咆哮; (of person) dàshēng chǎo 大声吵; **~ with laughter** dàshēng xiào 大声笑

roast 1 n (of beef etc) kǎoròu 烤肉 2 v/t kǎo 烤 3 v/i (of food) kǎo 烤; **we're ~ing** F wǒmen rèsǐle 我们热死了

roast beef kǎo niúròu 烤牛肉

roast pork kǎo zhūròu 烤猪肉

rob person, bank qiǎngjié 抢劫; **I've been ~bed** wǒ bèi qiǎngjié le 我被抢劫了

robber qiǎngjié zhě 抢劫者

robbery qiǎngjié 抢劫

robe (of judge) guānfú 官服; (of priest) fǎyī 法衣; (bath~) yùyī 浴衣

robin dōng 䳆

robot jīqìrén 机器人

robust person, health jiànzhuàng 健壮; material, structure jiāngù 坚固

ROC (= **Republic of China**) Zhōnghuá Mínguó 中华民国

rock 1 n yánshí 岩石; MUS yáogǔn yuè 摇滚乐; **on the ~s** drink chānbīng 掺冰; marriage jíjiāng pòliè 即将破裂 2 v/t baby, cradle

qīngyáo 轻摇; (surprise) shǐ zhènjīng 使震惊 3 v/i (on chair) yáodòng 摇动; (of boat) yáohuang 摇晃

rock bottom: **reach ~** zǒurù zuìdīdiǎn 走入最低点

rock-bottom adj prices zuìdī 最低

rocket 1 n huǒjiàn 火箭 2 v/i (of prices etc) jùzēng 剧增

rocking chair yáoyǐ 摇椅

rock'n'roll yáogǔn yuè 摇滚乐

rock star yáogǔn yuè gēxīng 摇滚乐歌星

rocky beach, path duō yánshí 多岩石

rod gùn 棍; (for fishing) gān 竿

rodent nièchǐmù dòngwù 啮齿目动物

rogue táoqìbāo 淘气包

role juésè 角色

role model bǎngyàng 榜样

roll 1 n (bread) xiǎo yuán miànbāo 小圆面包; (of film) juǎn 卷; (of thunder) lónglong shēng 隆隆声; (list, register) míngcè 名册 2 v/i (of ball etc) gǔn 滚; (of boat) yáobǎi 摇摆 3 v/t: **~ X into a ball** bǎ X juǎn chéngqiú 把X卷成球

♦roll over 1 v/i fānshēn 翻身 2 v/t person, object fān 翻; (renew, extend) yánxù 延续

♦roll up 1 v/t sleeves juǎnqǐ 卷起 2 v/i (arrive) chūxiàn 出现

roll call diǎnmíng 点名

roller (for hair) juǎnfà juǎn 卷发卷

roller blade n sìlún huáxíng xié 四轮旱冰鞋; **roller blind** juǎnlián 卷帘; **roller coaster** guò shān chē 过山车; **roller skate** n hànbīng xié 旱冰鞋

rolling pin gǎnmiànzhàng 擀面杖

ROM (= **read only memory**) zhǐ dú cúnchǔ qì 只读存储器

Roman Catholic 1 n Tiānzhǔjiào tú 天主教徒 2 adj Tiānzhǔjiào 天主教

romance (affair) fēngliú yùnshì 风流韵事; (novel, movie) chuánqí 传奇

romantic làngmàn 浪漫

roof wūdǐng 屋顶

roof rack MOT chēdǐng jià 车顶架

room fángjiān 房间; (space) kōngjiān 空间; **there's no ~ for X** méi yǒu X de dìfang 没有 X 的地方

room clerk jiēdài yuán 接待员;
roommate shìyǒu 室友; **room service** fángjiān fúwù 房间服务

roomy house etc dàchǎng kuānchǎng 大敞宽敞; clothes dà 大

root gēn 根; (of word) cígēn 词根; **~s** (of person) gēnjī 根基
♦ **root out** (get rid of) sǎochú 扫除; (find) zhǎodào 找到

rope shéng 绳
♦ **rope off** yòng shéngzi gékāi 用绳子隔开

rose BOT méigui 玫瑰

rostrum jiǎngtái 讲台

rosy cheeks hóngrùn 红润; future guāngmíng 光明

rot 1 n (in wood, teeth) fǔlàn 腐烂 **2** v/i (of food, wood, teeth) fǔlàn 腐烂

rota lúnzhí biǎo 轮值表

rotate v/i (of blades, earth) xuánzhuǎn 旋转

rotation (around the sun etc) xuánzhuǎn 旋转; **do in ~** lúnliú zuò 轮流做

rotten food, wood etc fǔlàn 腐烂; trick, thing to do lìngrén tǎoyàn 令人讨厌; weather, luck jíhuài 极坏

rough 1 adj surface bùpíng 不平; hands, skin cūcāo 粗糙; voice shāyǎ 沙哑; (violent) cūbào 粗暴; crossing, seas jiānnán 艰难; (approximate) dàgài 大概; **~ draft** cǎogǎo 草稿 **2** adv: **sleep ~** lùsù 露宿 **3** n (in golf) zhàng'ài qūyù 障碍区域 **4** v/t: **~ it** còuhe 凑合

roughage (in food) cū sìliào 粗饲料

roughly (approximately) dàyuē 大约

roulette lúnpán dǔ 轮盘赌

round 1 adj yuán 圆; **in ~ figures** zhěngshù 整数 **2** n (of postman, doctor) xúnhuí 巡回; (of toast) piàn 片; (of drinks) lún 轮; (of competition) chǎng 场; (in boxing match) huíhé 回合 **3** v/t corner ràoxíng 绕行 **4** adv & prep → **around**
♦ **round off** edges bǎ ... xiūyuán 把 ... 修圆; meeting, night out jiéshù 结束
♦ **round up** figure bǎ ... tiáogāo chéng zhěngshù 把 ... 调高成整数; suspects, criminals dōubǔ 兜捕

roundabout adj route, way of saying sth jiànjiē 间接

round trip láihuí lǚxíng 来回旅行

round trip ticket láihuí piào 来回票

round-up (of cattle) gǎnlǒng 赶拢; (of suspects, criminals) dōubǔ 兜捕; (of news) zōnghé bàodào 综合报道

rouse (from sleep) xǐng 醒; interest, emotions shāndòng 煽动

rousing speech, finale lìngrén zhènfèn 令人振奋

route lùxiàn 路线

routine 1 adj chángguī 常规 **2** n chángguī 常规; **as a matter of ~** zuòwéi chángguī 作为常规

row[1] (line) pái 排; (in spreadsheet etc) háng 行; **5 days in a ~** jiēlián wǔ tiān jiē lián 连五天

row[2] **1** v/t boat huá 划 **2** v/i huáchuán 划船

rowboat huátǐng 划艇

rowdy hào chǎonào 好吵闹

row house páifáng 排房

royal adj huángjiā 皇家

royalty (royal persons) huángzú 皇族; (on book, recording) chōubǎn fèi 筹办费

rub v/t cuō 搓
♦ **rub down** (to clean) cāshuā 擦刷
♦ **rub off 1** v/t dirt cādiào 擦掉; paint etc módiào 磨掉 **2** v/i: **it rubs off on you** duì nǐ yǒu yǐngxiǎng 对你有影响
♦ **rub out** (with eraser) móqù 磨去

rubber 1 n (material) xiàngpí 橡皮 **2** adj xiàngjiāo 橡胶

rubbish Br lājī 垃圾; (poor quality item) pòlàn 破烂; (nonsense) húshuō 胡说

rubble cūshí 粗石
ruby (*jewel*) hóng bǎoshí 红宝石
rucksack bèibāo 背包
rudder duò 舵
ruddy *complexion* hóngrùn 红润
rude cūlǔ 粗鲁; *it is ~ to ...* shì cūlǔ de ... 是粗鲁的; *I didn't mean to be ~* wǒ bìngbùshì gùyì wúlǐ 我并不是故意无礼
rudeness wúlǐ 无礼
rudimentary jīběn 基本
rudiments jīběn yuánlǐ 基本原理
ruffian ègùn 恶棍
ruffle 1 *n* (*on dress*) zhě 褶 **2** *v/t hair* nòngluàn 弄乱; *clothes* nòngzhòu 弄皱; *person* shǐ xīnfán yìluàn 使心烦意乱; *get ~d* xīnfán yìluàn 心烦意乱
rug xiǎo dìtǎn 小地毯; (*blanket*) tǎnzi 毯子
rugged *scenery, cliffs* qíqū 崎岖; *face* cūguǎng 粗犷; *resistance* jiānqiáng 坚强
ruin 1 *n:* *~s* fèixū 废墟; *in ~s* (*of city, building*) chéng fèixū 成废墟; (*of marriage*) pòliè 破裂; (*of plans*) pòchǎn 破产 **2** *v/t party, birthday, vacation, plans* pòhuài 破坏; *reputation* huǐhuài 毁坏; *be ~ed* (*financially*) pòchǎn 破产
rule 1 *n* (*of club, game*) guīzé 规则; (*of monarch*) tǒngzhì 统治; (*for measuring*) chǐdù 尺度; *as a ~* tōngcháng 通常 **2** *v/t country* tǒngzhì 统治; *the judge ~d that ...* fǎguān pàndìng ... 法官判定 ... **3** *v/i* (*of monarch*) tǒngzhì 统治
◆**rule out** páichú 排除
ruler (*for measuring*) chǐzi 尺子; (*of state*) tǒngzhì zhě 统治者
ruling 1 *n* cáijué 裁决 **2** *adj party* dāngquán 当权
rum (*drink*) lǎngmǔ jiǔ 朗姆酒
rumble *v/i* (*of stomach*) lónglóng zuòxiǎng 隆隆作响; (*of train in tunnel*) lùlù shǐguò 辘辘驶过
◆**rummage around** fānxún 翻寻
rummage sale jiùwù chūshòu 旧物出售
rumor 1 *n* yáoyán 谣言 **2** *v/t: it is ~ed that ...* yǒu yáoyán shuō ...

有谣言说 ...
rump (*of animal*) túnbù 臀部
rumple *clothes, paper* nòngzhòu 弄皱
rumpsteak túnbù niúpái 臀部牛排
run 1 *n* (*on foot*) pǎobù 跑步; (*in car*) xíngchéng 行程; (*in tights*) chōusī 抽丝; (THEA: *of play*) liánxù yǎnchū 连续演出; *go for a ~* pǎobù 跑步; *go for a ~ in the car* zuòchē qù dōu gè quān 坐车去兜个圈; *make a ~ for it* táopǎo 逃跑; *a criminal on the ~* zàitáo zuìfàn 在逃罪犯; *in the short/long ~* cóng duǎnqī/chángyuǎn láikàn 从短期/长远来看; *a ~ on the dollar* měiyuán jǐduì 美元挤兑 **2** *v/i* (*of person, animal*) pǎo pǎo 跑跑; (*of river*) liú liú 流流; (*of trains etc*) xíngshǐ 行驶; (*of paint, makeup*) tǎngliú 淌流; (*of nose, eyes*) tǎng 淌; (*of tap*) kāi 开; (*of play*) liánxù yǎnchū 连续演出; (*of engine, machine, software*) yùnzhuǎn 运转; (*in election*) jìngxuǎn 竞选; *~ for President* jìngxuǎn zǒngtǒng 竞选总统 **3** *v/t race* jìngsài 竞赛; *3 miles etc* pǎo 跑; *business, hotel, project etc* guǎnlǐ 管理; *software* yùnzhuǎn 运转; *car* yōngyǒu 拥有; *can I you to the station?* wǒ kěyǐ kāichē sòng nǐ qù chēzhàn ma? 我可以开车送你去车站吗？; *he ran his eye down the page* tā liúlǎn le zhè yīyè 他浏览了这一页
◆**run across** (*meet*) pèngjiàn 碰见; (*find*) zhǎodào 找到
◆**run away** táopǎo 逃跑
◆**run down 1** *v/t* (*knock down*) zhuàngdǎo 撞倒; (*criticize*) biǎndī 贬低; *stocks* jiǎnshǎo 减少 **2** *v/i* (*of battery*) hàojìn 耗尽
◆**run into** (*meet*) pèngjiàn 碰见; *difficulties* yùdào 遇到
◆**run off 1** *v/i* táopǎo 逃跑 **2** *v/t* (*print off*) dǎyìn 打印
◆**run out** (*of contract*) qīmǎn 期满; (*of time*) yòngwán 用完; (*of*

supplies) hàojìn 耗尽

♦**run out of** *time* yòngwán 用完; *patience* shīqù 失去; *supplies* yòngguāng 用光; *I ran out of gas* wǒ chē méi yóu le 我车没油了

♦**run over 1** *v/t (knock down)* zhuàngdǎo 撞倒; *can we ~ the details again?* wǒmén zàikàn yíbiàn xiángqíng hǎoma? 我们再看一遍详情好吗? **2** *v/i (of water etc)* yìchū 溢出

♦**run through** *(rehearse)* páiliàn 排练; *(go over)* liúlǎn 浏览

♦**run up** *v/t debts, large bill* lěijī 累积; *clothes* gǎnzhì 赶制

run-down *person* píjuàn 疲倦; *part of town* pòjiù 破旧; *building* shīxiū 失修

rung *(of ladder)* tījí 梯级

runner *(athlete)* sàipǎo zhě 赛跑者

runner-up yàjūn 亚军

running 1 *n* SP sàipǎo 赛跑; *(of business)* jīngyíng 经营 **2** *adj: for two days ~* liánxù liǎngtiān 连续两天

running dog *pej* zǒugǒu 走狗

running water *(from tap)* zìláishuǐ 自来水; *(flowing)* liúshuǐ 流水

runny *liquid* liúdòng 流动; *~ nose* liú bítì 流鼻涕

run-up SP yùbèi jiēduàn 预备阶段; *in the ~ to* zài yùbèi jiēduàn qījiān 在预备阶段期间

runway pǎodào 跑道

rupture 1 *n* pòliè 破裂 **2** *v/i (of pipe etc)* pòliè 破裂

rural nóngcūn 农村

rush 1 *n* tūjī 突击; *do ... in a ~* cōngmáng zuò ... 匆忙做...; *be in a ~* máng 忙; *what's the big ~?* máng shénme? 忙什么? **2** *v/t person* cuī 催; *meal* kuàichī 快吃; *~ X to the hospital* bǎ X huǒsù sòngjìn yīyuàn 把X火速送进医院 **3** *v/i* gǎn 赶

rush hour gāofēng shíjiān 高峰时间

Russia Éluósī 俄罗斯

Russian 1 *adj* Éluósī 俄罗斯 **2** *n (person)* Éluósī rén 俄罗斯人; *(language)* Éyǔ 俄语

rust 1 *n* xiù 锈 **2** *v/i* shēngxiù 生锈

rustle 1 *n (of silk, leaves)* shāshashēng 沙沙声 **2** *v/i (of silk, leaves)* shāsha zuòxiǎng 沙沙作响

♦**rustle up** F *meal* cōngcōng zuò 匆匆做

rust-proof *adj* fángxiù 防锈

rust remover chúxiùjì 除锈剂

rusty shēngxiù 生锈; *French, math etc* shēngshū 生疏; *I'm a little ~* wǒ yǒudiǎnr shēng le 我有点儿生了

rut *(in road)* chēzhé 车辙; *fig* chángguī 常规; *be in a ~* guò kèbǎnde shēnghuó 过刻板的生活

ruthless wúqíng 无情

ruthlessness wúqíng 无情

rye hēimài 黑麦

rye bread hēimài miànbāo 黑麦面包

S

sabbatical n (of academic) xiūjiànián 休假年

sabotage n & v/t pòhuài 破坏

saccharin n tángjīng 糖精

sachet (of shampoo, cream etc) yīxiǎodài 一小袋

sack 1 n (bag) dà kǒudài 大口袋 2 v/t jiěgù 解雇

sacred shénshèng 神圣

sacrifice 1 n (act) xīshēng 牺牲; (person, animal sacrificed) jìpǐn 祭品; make ~s fig zuòchū xīshēng 作出牺牲 2 v/t xiànjì 献祭; one's freedom etc xīshēng 牺牲

sad person, face, song bēishāng 悲伤; state of affairs yíhàn 遗憾

saddle n ānzi 鞍子

sadism shīnüèkuáng 施虐狂

sadist nüèdàikuáng zhě 虐待狂者

sadistic yǒu shīnüèkuáng 有施虐狂

sadly look, sing etc yōuchóu 忧愁; (regrettably) lìngrén yíhàn 令人遗憾

sadness yōuchóu 忧愁

safe 1 adj (not dangerous) ānquán 安全; (not in danger) wúwēixiǎn 无危险; investment, prediction wúfēngxiǎn 无风险 2 n bǎoxiǎnguì 保险柜

safeguard 1 n ānquán zhuāngzhì 安全装置; as a ~ against X zuòwéi fángzhǐ X de bǎohù cuòshī 作为防止X的保护措施 2 v/t bǎohù 保护

safekeeping: give X to Y for ~ bǎ X gěi Y tuǒshàn bǎoguǎn 把X给Y妥善保管

safely arrive píng'ān 平安; complete tests etc yǒu bǎwò 有把握; drive ānquán 安全; assume kěndìng 肯定

safety ānquán 安全; (of investment, prediction) bǎoxiǎn 保险; be in ~ chùyú ānquán zhuàngtài 处于安全状态

safety belt ānquándài 安全带; safety-conscious yǒu ānquán yìshí 有安全意识; safety first ānquán dìyī 安全第一; safety pin biézhēn 别针

sag 1 n (in ceiling etc) xiàchuí 下垂 2 v/i (of ceiling, rope) xiàchuí 下垂; (of output, tempo) xiàjiàng 下降

sage (herb) shǔwěicǎo 鼠尾草

sail 1 n fān 帆; (trip) hángchéng 航程; go for a ~ chéngchuán yóulǎn 乘船游览 2 v/t yacht jiàshǐ 驾驶 3 v/i jiàshǐchuán 驾驶船; (depart) qǐháng 启航

sailboard 1 n fānbǎn 帆板 2 v/i zuò fānbǎn yùndòng 作帆板运动

sailboarding fānbǎn yùndòng 帆板运动

sailboat fānchuán 帆船

sailing SP fānchuán yùndòng 帆船运动

sailing ship fānchuán 帆船

sailor (in the navy) hǎiyuán 海员; SP shuǐshǒu 水手; be a good / bad ~ bùcháng / chángcháng yùnchuán de rén 不常 / 常常晕船的人

saint shèngtú 圣徒

sake: for my / your ~ wèile wǒ / nǐ 为了我 / 你; for the ~ of X wèile X 为了X

salad ⇩ sèlā 色拉

salad dressing ⇩ sèlā tiáowèizhī 色拉调味汁

salary xīnshuǐ 薪水

salary scale xīnshuǐ jíbié 薪水级别

sale xiāoshòu 销售; (reduced prices) liánshòu 廉售; for ~ (sign) dàishòu 待售; be on ~ yǒushòu 有售; (at reduced prices) liánjià

chūshòu 廉价出售
sales (*department*) xiāoshòu 销售
sales clerk (*in store*) shòuhuòyuán 售货员; **sales figures** xiāoshòu'é 销售额; **salesman** tuīxiāoyuán 推销员; **sales manager** yíngyè jīnglǐ 营业经理; **sales meeting** xiāoshòu huìyì 销售会议
saliva tuòyè 唾液
salmon dàmǎhāyú 大马哈鱼
saloon MOT xiǎojiàochē 小轿车; (*bar*) jiǔbā 酒吧
salt yán 盐
saltcellar yánpíng 盐瓶
salty xián 咸
salutary *experience* yǒuyì 有益
salute 1 *n* MIL jìnglǐ 敬礼 **2** *v/t & v/i* zhìjìng 致敬
salvage *v/t* (*from wreck*) qiǎngjiù 抢救
salvation zhěngjiù 拯救
Salvation Army Jiùshìjūn 救世军
same 1 *adj* tóngyàng 同样 **2** *pron*: **I'll have the ~ as you** hé nǐ yīyàng 和你一样; **Happy New Year – the ~ to you** Xīnnián kuàilè – Xīnnián kuàilè 新年快乐–新年快乐; **he's not the ~ any more** tā búzài hé yǐqián yíyàng le 他不再和以前一样了; **all the ~** jǐnguǎn rúcǐ 尽管如此; **men are all the ~** nánrén dōu yíyàng 男人都一样; **it's all the ~ to me** duì wǒ láishuō dōu yíyàng 对我来说都一样 **3** *adv*: **look / sound the ~** kànqǐlái / tīngqǐlái yíyàng 看起来/听起来一样
sample *n* yàngběn 样本
sanatorium liáoyǎngyuàn 疗养院
sanction 1 *n* (*approval*) pīzhǔn 批准; (*penalty*) zhìcái 制裁 **2** *v/t* (*approve*) tóngyì 同意
sanctity shénshèng 神圣
sanctuary REL shèngdì 圣地; (*for wild animals*) yěshēng dòngwù bǎohù qū 野生动物保护区
sand 1 *n* shā 沙 **2** *v/t* (*with paper*) yòng shāzhǐ móguāng 用砂纸磨光
sandal liángxié 凉鞋

sandbag shādài 沙袋; **sandblast** pēnshā qīngxǐ 喷沙清洗; **sand dune** shāqiū 沙丘
sander (*tool*) dǎmójī 打磨机
sandpaper 1 *n* shāzhǐ 砂纸 **2** *v/t* yòng shāzhǐ móguāng 用砂纸磨光; **sandpit** shākēng 沙坑; **sandstone** shāyán 沙岩
sandwich 1 *n* sānmíngzhì 三明治 **2** *v/t*: **be ~ed between two ...** shòujiáyú liǎng ... zhījiān 受夹于两 ... 之间
sandy *beach*, *soil* duōshā 多沙; *hair* shāsè 沙色
sane shénzhì zhèngcháng 神志正常
sanitarium liáoyǎngyuàn 疗养院
sanitary *conditions* wèishēng 卫生; *installations* qīngjié 清洁
sanitary napkin wèishēngjīn 卫生巾
sanitation (*sanitary installations*) wèishēng shèbèi 卫生设备; (*removal of waste*) xiàshuǐ xìtǒng 下水系统
sanitation department huánjìng wèishēng bùmén 环境卫生部门
sanity shénzhì zhèngcháng 神志正常
Santa Claus Shèngdàn Lǎorén 圣诞老人
sap 1 *n* (*in tree*) shùyè 树液 **2** *v/t s.o.'s energy* xuēruò 削弱
sapphire *n* (*jewel*) lánbǎoshí 蓝宝石
sarcasm jīfěng 讥讽
sarcastic jīfěng 讥讽
sardine shādīngyú 沙丁鱼
sash (*on dress*, *uniform*) jiāndài 肩带; (*in window*) chuāngkuàng 窗框
Satan Sādàn 撒旦
satellite wèixīng 卫星
satellite dish wèixīng diànshì pán 卫星电视盘
satellite TV wèixīng diànshì 卫星电视
satin duànzi 缎子
satire fěngcì 讽刺
satirical hán fěngcì yìwèi 含讽刺意味
satirist fěngcì zhě 讽刺者

satisfaction mǎnzú 满足; *get ~ out of X* cóng X zhōng dédào mǎnzú 从 X 中得到满足; *a feeling of ~* mǎnyìde gǎnjué 满意的感觉; *is that to your ~?* nǐ duìcǐ mǎnyì ma? 你对此满意吗？

satisfactory lìngrén mǎnyì 令人满意; *(just good enough)* fúhé yāoqiú 符合要求; *this is not ~* zhè hái búgòu hǎo 这还不够好

satisfy *customers* shǐ mǎnyì 使满意; *needs, hunger, sexual desires* mǎnzú 满足; *conditions* fúhé 符合; *I am satisfied that he ...* *(convinced)* wǒ xiāngxìn tā ... 我相信他 ...; *I hope you're satisfied!* wǒ xiǎng nǐ gāi mǎnyì le ba! 我想你该满意了吧！

Saturday xīngqīliù 星期六

sauce jiàng jiàng 酱

saucepan píngdǐguō 平底锅

saucer chábēidié 茶杯碟

saucy *person* wúlǐ 无礼; *dress* tòuguāng 透光

Saudi (Arabia) Shātè Ālābó 沙特阿拉伯

Saudi (Arabian) 1 *adj* Shātè Ālābó 沙特阿拉伯 **2** *n (person)* Shātè Ālābó rén 沙特阿拉伯人

sauna zhēngqìyù 蒸汽浴

saunter mànbù 漫步

sausage xiāngcháng 香肠

savage 1 *adj animal* yěxìng 野性; *attack* cánkù 残酷; *criticism* èdú 恶毒 **2** *n* yěrén 野人

save 1 *v/t (rescue)* jiù 救; *money* chǔcún 储存; *time* jiéshěng 节省; *(collect)* sōují 搜集; COMPUT cúnpán 存盘; *goal* jiùqiú 救球; *~ as* COMPUT cúnwéi 存为; *you could ~ yourself a lot of effort* nǐ kěyǐ jiéshěng hěnduō jīnglì 你可以节省很多精力 **2** *v/i (put money aside)* zǎnqián 攒钱; SP jiùqiú 救球 **3** *n* SP jiùqiú 救球

♦**save up for** wèi ... zǎnqián 为 ... 攒钱

saving *(amount saved)* jiéshěng 节省; *(activity)* cúnqián 存钱

savings cúnkuǎn 存款

savings account chǔxù zhànghù

储蓄帐户

savings bank chǔxū yínháng 储蓄银行

savior REL jiùshìzhǔ 救世主

savor 1 *n* fēngwèi 风味 **2** *v/t* pǐncháng pǐnshǎng 品尝

savory *adj (not sweet)* xián 咸

saw 1 *n (tool)* jù 锯 **2** *v/t* jùkāi 锯开

♦**saw off** jùdiào 锯掉

sawdust jùmò 锯末

saxophone sàkèsīguǎn 萨克斯管

say *v/t* shuō 说; *can I ~ something?* wǒ kěyǐ fābiǎo yīxià wǒde yìjiàn ma? 我可以发表一下我的意见吗？; *that is to ~* nà jiùshì shuō 那就是说; *what do you ~ to that?* nǐ juédé nàyàng rúhé? 你觉得那样如何？ **2** *n:* *have one's ~* biǎodá yìjiàn 表达意见

saying yànyǔ 谚语

scab jiǎ jiā 痂

scaffold(ing) jiǎoshǒujià 脚手架

scald *v/t* tàngshāng 烫伤

scale^1 *(on fish)* línpiàn 鳞片

scale^2 *n (size)* guīmó 规模; *(on thermometer etc)* kèdù 刻度; *(of map)* bǐlì 比例; MUS yīnjiē 音阶; *on a larger / smaller ~* gèngdà / gèngxiǎo guīmó 更大／更小规模 **2** *v/t cliffs etc* pāndēng 攀登

scale drawing bǐlì huìtú 比例绘图

scales *(for weighing)* tiānpíng 天平

scalp *n* tóupí 头皮

scalpel shǒushùdāo 手术刀

scalper ♦ piàofànzi 票贩子

scan 1 *v/t horizon, page* sǎoshì 扫视; MED sǎomiáo 扫描; COMPUT sōusuǒ 搜索 **2** *n* MED sǎomiáo 扫描

♦**scan in** COMPUT sōusuǒ jìnrù 搜索进入

scandal liúyán fēiyǔ 流言蜚语

scandalous *affair* diūliǎn 丢脸; *prices* lìngrén zhènjīng 令人震惊

scanner MED sǎomiáoqì 扫描器; COMPUT sǎomiáoyí 扫描仪

scantily *adv:* *~ clad* chuānzhuó dānbó 穿着单薄

scanty *clothes* dānbó 单薄

scapegoat tìzuìyáng 替罪羊

scar **1** *n* shāngbā 伤疤 **2** *v/t* liúxià shānghén 留下伤痕

scarce (*in short supply*) duǎnquē 短缺; *make oneself ~* bìkāi 避开

scarcely jīhūbù 几乎不

scarcity quēfá 缺乏

scare **1** *v/t* jīngxià 惊吓; *be ~d of X* hàipà X 害怕 X **2** *n* (*panic, alarm*) jīngkǒng 惊恐; *give X a ~* gěi X xiàle yī tiào 给 X 吓了一跳
♦ **scare away** xiàpǎo 吓跑

scarecrow dàocǎorén 稻草人

scarf (*around neck*) wéijīn 围巾; (*over head*) tóujīn 头巾

scarlet xiānhóng 鲜红

scarlet fever xīnghóngrè 猩红热

scary *music, movie* hěn kǒngbù 很恐怖

scathing kèbó 刻薄

scatter **1** *v/t leaflets, seeds* sǎ 撒; *be ~ed all over the room* fángjiānlǐ dàochù dōushì 房间里到处都是 **2** *v/i* (*of crowd etc*) sànkāi 散开

scatterbrained jiànwàng 健忘

scattered *showers* língxīng 零星; *family, villages* fēnsàn 分散

scenario qíngkuàng 情况

scene THEA chǎng 场; (*view, sight*) qíngjǐng 情景; (*of accident, crime etc*) shìfā dìdiǎn 事发地点; (*of novel, movie*) chǎngjǐng 场景; (*argument*) chǎonào 吵闹; *make a ~* dàchǎo dànào 大吵大闹; *~s* THEA bùjǐng 布景; *jazz / rock ~* juéshìyuè / yáogǔnyuè lǐngyù 爵士乐/摇滚乐领域; *behind the ~s* zài mùhòu 在幕后

scenery jǐngsè 景色; THEA wǔtái bùjǐng 舞台布景

scent *n* (*smell*) xiāngwèi 香味; (*perfume*) xiāngjīng 香精; (*of animal*) xiùjī 臭迹

schedule **1** *n* (*of events*) chéngxùbiǎo 程序表; (*of work*) jìhuàbiǎo 计划表; (*for trains*) shíkèbiǎo 时刻表; (*of lessons*) kèchéngbiǎo 课程表; *be on ~* (*work, of workers, of train etc*) àn yùdìng shíjiān 按预定时间; *be*

behind ~ (*of work, of workers, of train etc*) luòhòuyú yùdìng jìhuà 落后于预定计划 **2** *v/t* (*put on schedule*) lièrù jìhuà 列入计划; *it's ~d for completion next month* dìngyú xiàgèyuè wánchéng 定于下个月完成

scheduled flight dìngqī hángbān 定期航班

scheme **1** *n* (*plan*) jìhuà 计划; (*plot*) yīnmóu 阴谋 **2** *v/i* (*plot*) túmóu 图谋

scheming *adj* guǐjì duōduān 诡计多端

schizophrenia jīngshén fēnlièzhèng 精神分裂症

schizophrenic **1** *n* jīngshén fēnlièzhèng huànzhě 精神分裂症患者 **2** *adj* jīngshén fēnliè zhèng 精神分裂症

scholar xuézhě 学者

scholarship (*work*) xuéshù chéngjiù 学术成就; (*financial award*) jiǎngxuéjīn 奖学金

school xuéxiào 学校; (*university*) xuéyuàn 学院

schoolbag xiǎoshūbāo 小书包; schoolboy zhōngxiǎoxué nánshēng 中小学男生; schoolchildren zhōngxiǎoxué xuéshēng 中小学生; school days xuésheng shídài 学生时代; schoolgirl zhōngxiǎoxué nǚ xuésheng 中小学女生; schoolmate xiàoyǒu 校友; schoolteacher zhōngxiǎoxué jiàoshī 中小学教师

sciatica zuògǔ shénjīngtòng 坐骨神经痛

science kēxué 科学

science fiction kēhuàn 科幻

scientific kēxué 科学

scientist kēxuéjiā 科学家

scissors jiǎnzi 剪子

scoff[1] *v/t* (*eat fast*) tānlánde chī 贪婪地吃; (*eat whole lot*) chīguāng 吃光

scoff[2] *v/i* jīxiào 讥笑
♦ **scoff at** cháoxiào 嘲笑

scold *v/t child, husband* zémà 责骂

scoop **1** *n* (*implement*) chǎnzi 铲子; (*story*) qiǎngxiān bàodào 抢先

报道 2 *v/t* (*pick up*) yǎochū 咬出
♦ **scoop up** pěngqǐ 捧起

scooter (*with motor*) xiǎoxíng
mótuōchē 小型摩托车; (*child's*)
tàbǎnchē 踏板车

scope fànwéi 范围; (*freedom,
opportunity*) jīhuì 机会

scorch *v/t* tàngjiāo 烫焦

scorching hot rèsǐle 热死了

score 1 *n* SP bǐfēn 比分; (*written
music*) yuèpǔ 乐谱; (*of movie etc*)
pèiyuè 配乐; **what's the ~?** bǐfēn
shì duōshǎo? 比分是多少?;
have a ~ to settle with X gēn X
suàn jiùzhàng 跟 X 算旧帐 2 *v/t
goal, point* défēn 得分; (*cut: line*)
huàhénr 划痕 3 *v/i* défēn 得分;
(*keep the score*) jìfēn 记分; **that's
where he ~s** nà shì tāde
qiángxiàng 那是他的强项

scorer (*of goal, point*) défēn yùndòngyuán 得分运动员; (*score-
keeper*) jìfēnyuán 记分员

scorn 1 *n* bǐshì 鄙视; **pour ~ on X**
yòng qīngmiède kǒuwěn tán X 用
轻蔑的口吻谈 X 2 *v/t idea,
suggestion* àomànde jùjué 傲慢地
拒绝

scornful qīngmiè 轻蔑

Scot Sūgélán rén 苏格兰人

Scotch (*whiskey*) wēishìjì 威士忌

Scotland Sūgélán 苏格兰

Scottish Sūgélán 苏格兰

scot-free: **get off ~** xiāoyáo fǎwài
逍遥法外

scoundrel wúlài 无赖

scour[1] (*search*) sōuxún 搜寻

scour[2] *pans* shuājìng 刷净

scout *n* (*boy ~*) tóngzǐjūn 童子军

scowl 1 *n* nùróng 怒容 2 *v/i* nùshì
怒视

scram F pǎo 跑

scramble 1 *n* (*rush*) mángluàn 忙
乱 2 *v/t message* rǎopín 扰频 3 *v/i*
(*climb*) pāndēng 攀登; **he ~d to
his feet** tā téngde zhàn qǐlái 他腾
地站起来

scrap 1 *n* (*metal*) fèijīnshǔ 废金
属; (*fight*) dǎjià 打架; (*little bit*)
shǎoliàng 少量 2 *v/t plan, project,
paragraph etc* fèidiào 废掉

scrapbook jiǎntiēbù 剪贴簿

scrape 1 *n* (*on paintwork etc*) guācā
刮擦 2 *v/t paintwork* guādiào 刮
掉; **one's arm** cāshāng 擦伤;
vegetables yòng dāo xiāojìng 用刀
削净; **~ a living** miǎnqiǎng wéichí
shēnghuó 勉强维持生活

♦ **scrape through** (*in exam etc*)
miǎnqiǎng jígé 勉强及格

scrap heap fèiliàoduī 废料堆;
good for the ~ háowúyòngchù 毫
无用处

scrap metal fèijīnshǔ 废金属

scrappy *work* záluànwúzhāng 杂
乱无章

scratch 1 *n* (*mark*) huàhén 划痕;
have a ~ (*to stop itching*) sāoyǎng
搔痒; **start from ~** cónglíng
kāishǐ 从零开始; **not up to ~**
búgòuhǎo 不够好

scratch 2 *v/t* (*mark: skin, paint*)
zhuāshāng 抓伤; (*because of itch*)
sāoyǎng sāoyǎng 搔痒 3 *v/i* (*of cat, nails*)
zhuā 抓

scrawl 1 *n* liáocǎode zìjì 潦草的
字迹 2 *v/t* luànxiě 乱写

scream 1 *n* jiānjiàoshēng 尖叫声
2 *v/i* jiānjiào 尖叫

screech 1 *n* (*of tires*) jiānlìshēng
尖利声; (*scream*) jiānjiàoshēng 尖
叫声 2 *v/i* (*of tires*) fāchū
jiānlìshēng 发出尖利声;
(*scream*) fāchū jiānjiàoshēng 发出
尖叫声

screen 1 *n* (*in room, hospital*)
gélián 隔帘; (*protective*) yǎnbìwù
掩避物; (*in movie theater*) yínmù
银幕; COMPUT píngmù 屏幕; **on
the ~** (*in movie theater*) zài
yínmùshang 在银幕上; **on (the)
~** COMPUT zài píngmùshang 在屏
幕上 2 *v/t* (*protect, hide*) zhēbì 遮
蔽; *movie* fàngyìng 放映; (*for
security reasons*) shěnchá 审查

screenplay diànyǐng jùbě 电影
剧本; **screen saver** COMPUT
píngmù bǎohùqì 屏幕保护器;
screen test shìjìng 试镜

screw 1 *n* luósīdīng 螺丝钉; ∨
(*sex*) xìngjiāo 性交 2 *v/t* ∨ gèn ...
shuìjiào 跟 ... 睡觉; F (*cheat*)

qīpiàn 欺骗; ~ *X to Y* yòng luósīdīng bǎ X nǐngzǎi Y shàng 用螺丝钉把X拧在Y上

♦ **screw up 1** *v/t* eyes niǔqū 扭曲; *piece of paper* róuchéntuán 揉成团; F (*make a mess of*) dǎluàn 打乱 **2** *v/i* F (*make a bad mistake*) nòngzāo 弄糟

screwdriver luósīdāo 螺丝刀

screwed up F (*psychologically*) shénjīng 神经

screw top (*on bottle*) xuángài 旋盖

scribble 1 *n* liáocǎode zìjì 潦草的字迹 **2** *v/t* (*write quickly*) cǎocǎo shūxiě 草草书写 **3** *v/i* luànxiě 乱写

script (*for play etc*) jiǎoběn 脚本; (*form of writing*) shūxiětǐ 书写体

scripture: the (*Holy*) **Scriptures** Shèngjīng 圣经

scriptwriter zhuàngǎorén 撰稿人

scroll *n* (*manuscript*) zhǐjuǎn 纸卷

♦ **scroll down** *v/i* COMPUT chuízhí xiàyí 垂直下移

♦ **scroll up** *v/i* COMPUT chuízhí shàngyí 垂直上移

scrounger wúlài 无赖

scrub *v/t* floors, hands cāxǐ 擦洗

scrubbing brush (*for floor*) yìngshuāzi 硬刷子; (*for hands*) xǐshǒushuā 洗手刷

scruffy lātà 邋遢

♦ **scrunch up** plastic cup etc niǎnsuì 捻碎

scruples gùlǜ 顾虑; **have no ~ about doing X** duì zuò X wúsuǒ gùjì 对做X无所顾忌

scrupulous (*with moral principles*) shènshèn 审慎; (*thorough*) zìxì chèdǐ 仔细彻底; attention to detail yìsībùgǒu 一丝不苟

scrutinize (*examine closely*) xìchá 细察

scrutiny (*examine closely*) xìchá 细察; **come under ~** bèishěnchá 被审查

scuba diving dài shuǐfèi qiánshuǐ 戴水肺潜水

scuffle *n* niǔdǎ 扭打

sculptor diāokè (sù) jiā 雕刻 (塑) 家

sculpture *n* (*art*) diāokè (sù) kè 雕刻 (塑); (*sth sculpted*) diāosù 雕塑

scum (*on liquid*) fúgòu 浮垢; pej (*people*) zhāzi 渣子

scythe *n* chángbǐng dàiliándāo 长柄大廉刀

sea dàhǎi 大海; **by the ~** zài hǎibiān 在海边

seafaring nation hǎishàng 海上; **seafood** hǎiwèi 海味; **seafront** bīnhǎiqū 滨海区; **seagoing** vessel shìyú yuǎnháng 适于远航; **seagull** hǎiʾōu 海鸥

seal [1] *n* (*animal*) hǎibào 海豹

seal [2] *n* (*on document*) yìnzhāng 印章; TECH mìfēng 密封 **2** *v/t* container mìfēng 密封

♦ **seal off** area fēngsuǒ 封锁

sea level: above / below ~ hǎibá / dìyú hǎipíngmiàn 海拔 / 低于海平面

seam *n* (*on garment*) fèng 缝; (*of ore*) kuàngcéng 矿层

seaman shuǐshǒu 水手

seamstress nǚcáiféng 女裁缝

seaport hǎigǎng 海港

sea power (*nation*) hǎijūn qiángguó 海军强国

search 1 *n* sōuxún 搜寻 **2** *v/t* city, files sōuchá 搜查

♦ **search for** xúnzhǎo 寻找

searching adj look, question jiānruì ér shēnkè 尖锐而深刻

searchlight tànzhàodēng 探照灯; **search party** sōusuǒduì 搜索队; **search warrant** sōucházhèng 搜查证

seasick yùnchuán yūnchuán 晕船; **get ~** yùnchuán 晕船; **seaside** hǎibīn 海滨; **at the ~** zài hǎibīn 在海滨; **go to the ~** qù hǎibīn 去海滨; **seaside resort** hǎibīn shèngdì 海滨胜地

season *n* (*winter etc*) jìjié 季节; (*for tourism etc*) wàngjì 旺季

seasoned wood fēnggān 风干; traveler etc yǒu jīngyàn 有经验

seasoning zuóliào 作料

season ticket chángqīpiào 长期票

seat 1 *n* zuòwèi 座位; (*of pants*) túnbù 臀部; POL xíwèi 席位;

please take a ~ qǐng luòzuò 请落坐 **2** v/t (have seating for) zuòdexià 坐得下; ***please remain ~ed*** jiùzuò wùdòng 就座勿动

seat belt ānquándài 安全带

sea urchin hǎidǎn 海胆

seaweed hǎidài 海带

secluded rénjīhǎnzhì 人际罕至

seclusion yúshìgéjué 与世隔绝

second 1 n (of time) yī miǎozhōng 一秒钟; ***just a ~*** děngyíxià 等一下 **2** adj dì'èr 第二 **3** adv come in yǐ dì'èrwèi 以第二位 **4** v/t motion fùyì 附议

secondary cìyào 次要; ***of ~ importance*** cìyào 次要

secondary education zhōngděng jiàoyù 中等教育

second best adj dì'èr hǎo 第二好; **second biggest** dì'èr dà 第二大; **second class** adj ticket èrděng 二等; **second gear** MOT èrdàng 二档; **second hand** (on clock) miǎozhēn 秒针 **second-hand** èrshǒu 二手

secondly qícì 其次

second-rate èrliú 二流

second thoughts *I've had* ~ wǒ gǎibiàn zhǔyì le 我改变主意了

secrecy bǎomì 保密

secret 1 n mìmì 秘密; ***do X in ~*** mìmì zuò X 秘密做 X **2** adj garden, passage mìmì 秘密; work, department bǎomì 保密

secret agent tègōng rényuán 特工人员

secretarial tasks, job mìshū 秘书

secretary mìshū 秘书; POL bùzhǎng 部长

Secretary of State Guówùqīng 国务卿

secrete (give off) fēnmì 分泌; (hide away) yǐncáng 隐藏

secretion (of liquid) fēnmì 分泌; (liquid secreted) fēnmìwù 分泌物; (hiding) cángnì 藏匿

secretive àibǎomì 爱保密

secretly mìmì 秘密

secret police mìmì jǐngchá 秘密警察

secret service tèwù jīguān 特务机关

sect pàibié 派别

section bùfen 部份

sector bùmén 部门

secular shìsú 世俗

secure 1 adj shelf etc láogù 牢固; feeling wú yōulù 无忧虑; job, contract yǒu bǎozhèng 有保证 **2** v/t shelf etc gùdìngzhù 固定住; s.o.'s help, finances dédào 得到

security (in job) bǎozhàng 保障; (for investment) bǎozhèng 保证; (at airport etc) ānquán 安全; (department responsible for ~) bǎo'ānbù 保安部; (of beliefs etc) wěngù 稳固; **securities** FIN zhèngquàn 证券; ***securities market*** FIN zhèngquàn shìchǎng 证券市场

security alert ānquán jǐngtì 安全警惕; **security check** ānquán jiǎnchá 安全检查; **security-conscious** yǒu ānquán yìshí de 有安全意识; **security forces** bǎo'ān bùduì 保安部队; **security guard** bǎo'ān rényuán 保安人员; **security risk** (person) wēixiǎn rénwù 危险人物

sedan xiǎo jiàochē 小轿车

sedative n zhènjìngyào 镇静药

sediment chéndiànwù 沉淀物

seduce (sexually) gōuyǐn 勾引

seduction (sexual) yǐnyòu 引诱

seductive dress yòurén 诱人; offer yǒu xīyǐnlì 有吸引力

see kànjiàn 看见; (understand) míngbái 明白; ***I ~*** wǒ míngbái le 我明白了; ***can I ~ the manager?*** wǒ kěyǐ jiàn jīnglǐ ma? 我可以见经理吗？; ***you should ~ a doctor*** nǐ yīnggāi qù kàn yīshēng 你应该去看医生; ***~ X home*** sòng X huíjiā 送 X 回家; ***I'll ~ you to the door*** wǒ sòng nǐ dào ménkǒu 我送你到门口; ***~ you!*** zàijiàn! 再见！

♦ **see about** (look into) chǔlǐ 处理

♦ **see off** (at airport etc) sòngxíng 送行; (chase away) gǎnpǎo 赶跑

♦ **see out** *see X out* (to the door) sòngsòng X 送送 X

♦ **see to** (*deal with*) chǔlǐ 处理; ~ *it that X gets done* wùbì bǎozhèng zuòwán X 务必保证做完X

seed zhǒngzi 种子; (*in tennis*) zhǒngzi xuǎnshǒu 种子选手; *go to* ~ (*of person, district*) shuāibài 衰败

seedling yòumiáo 幼苗

seedy *bar, district* pòjiù 破旧

seeing (*that*) jìrán 既然

seek 1 *v/t employment* xúnzhǎo 寻找; *truth* zhuīqiú 追求 **2** *v/i* tànsuǒ 探索

seem kànqǐlái 看起来; *it ~s that ...* kànqǐlái sìhū ... 看起来似乎 ...

seemingly kànshàngqu 看上去

seep (*of liquid*) lòuchū 漏出

♦ **seep out** (*of liquid*) shènlòu 渗漏

seesaw qiāoqiāobǎn 跷跷板

see-through *dress, material* tòumíng 透明

segment bàn 瓣

segmented língsuì 零碎

segregate gélí 隔离

segregation gélí 隔离

seismology dìzhènxué 地震学

seize *person, arm* zhuāzhù 抓住; *opportunity* bǎwò 把握; (*of customs, police etc*) kòuyā 扣押

♦ **seize up** (*of engine*) qiǎzhù 卡住

seizure MED fāzuò 发作; (*of drugs etc*) kòuyā 扣押

seldom hǎnjiàn 罕见

select 1 *v/t* xuǎnzé 选择 **2** *adj* (*exclusive*) gāojí 高级

selection (*choosing*) xuǎnzé 选择; (*that / those chosen*) xuǎnchūde 选出的; (*assortment*) kě gōng tiāoxuǎn 可供挑选

selection process xuǎnzé guòchéng 选择过程

selective tiāojiǎn 挑拣

self zìjǐ 自己

self-addressed envelope xiě yǒu zìjǐ dìzhǐ de xìnfēng 写有自己地址的信封; **self-assured** yǒu bǎwò 有把握; **self-catering apartment** zìchuī gōngyù 自炊公寓; **self-centered** yǐ zìwǒ wéi zhōngxīn 以自我为中心; **self-**

confessed zìjǐ tǎnbái 自己坦白; **self-confidence** zìxìn 自信; **self-confident** zìxìn 自信; **self-conscious** búzìrán 不自然; **self-contained** *apartment* shèbèi qíquán 设备齐全; **self control** zìzhìlì 自制力; **self-criticism** zìwǒ pīpíng 自我批评; **self-defense** zìwǒ 自卫; **self-discipline** zìwǒ yuēshù 自我约束; **self-doubt** zìwǒ kùnhuò 自我困惑; **self-employed** gètǐ 个体; **self-evident** bùyán'éryù 不言而喻; **self-interest** sīlì 私利

selfish zìsī 自私

selfless wúsī 无私

self-made man báishǒuqǐjiāde rén 白手起家的人; **self-possessed** chénzhuó 沉着; **self-reliant** yīkào zìjǐ 依靠自己; **self-respect** zìzūn 自尊; **self-righteous** *pej* zìyǐwéishì 自以为是; **self-satisfied** *pej* zìmíngdéyì 自鸣得意; **self-service** *adj* zìzhùshì 自助式; **self-service restaurant** zìzhù cānguǎn 自助餐馆; **self-study** zìxué 自学

sell 1 *v/t* mài 卖; *you have to ~ yourself* nǐ děi tuīxiāo zìjǐ 你得推销自己 **2** *v/i* (*of products*) xiāoshòu 销售

seller màifāng 卖方

selling *n* COM xiāoshòu 销售

selling point COM shāngpǐn tèsè 商品特色

semen jīngyè 精液

semester xuéqī 学期

semi (*truck*) jiǎojiēchē 铰接车

semicircle bànyuánxíng 半圆形

semicircular bànyuánxíng 半圆形; **semiconductor** ELEC bàndǎotǐ 半导体; **semifinal** bànjuésài 半决赛

seminar yántǎohuì 研讨会

semiskilled bànshúliàn 半熟练

senate cānyìyuàn 参议院

senator cānyìyuán 参议员

send *v/t* (*by mail*) yóujì 邮寄; (*by mail, e-mail, fax etc*) fā 发; ~ *X to Y* bǎ X yóu fāgěi Y 把X邮发给Y; ~ *X to see Y* jiào X qù jiàn Y 叫X

去见 Y; **~ her my best wishes** xiàng tā wènhǎo 向她问好

♦ **send back** sònghuí 送回; *food in restaurant* tuìhuán 退还

♦ **send for** *doctor, help* pàirén qùzhǎo 派人去找

♦ **send in** *troops* pàiqiǎn 派遣; *next interviewee* jiào … jìnqù lái … jìn qù 叫 … 进去; *application form* jìqù 寄去

♦ **send off** *letter, fax etc* fāchū 发出

♦ **send up** (*mock*) qǔxiào 取笑

sender (*of letter*) yóujìrén 邮寄人

senile shuāilǎo 衰老

senility shuāilǎo zhuàngtài 衰老状态

senior (*older*) niánzhǎng 年长; (*in rank*) gāojí 高级; **be ~ to X** (*in rank*) bǐ X zīgé lǎo 比 X 资格老

senior citizen lǎorén 老人

sensation (*feeling*) gǎnjué 感觉; (*surprise event*) hōngdòng 轰动; **be a ~** (*very good*) hěn bàng 很棒

sensational *news, discovery* hōngdòng 轰动; (*very good*) juémiào 绝妙

sense 1 *n* (*meaning*) yìyì 意义; (*purpose, point*) yìsi 意思; (*common ~*) jiànshi 见识; (*of sight, smell etc*) guānnéng 官能; (*feeling*) gǎnjué 感觉; **in a ~** zài mǒuzhǒng yìyì shang 在某种意义上; **talk ~, man!** hēi, shuōdiǎnr yǒu dàolǐ de huà! 嘿，说点儿有道理的话！; **it doesn't make ~** zhè méi dàolǐ 这没道理; **there's no ~ in trying / waiting** chángshì / děngdài méiyǒu yòng 尝试 / 等待没有用 **2** *v/t* *s.o.'s presence* yìshídào 意识到

senseless (*pointless*) wú yìyì 无意义

sensible *person, decision* míngzhì 明智; *advice* hélǐ 合理

sensitive *skin* jiāonèn 娇嫩; *person* mǐngǎn 敏感

sensitivity (*of skin, person*) mǐngǎnxìng 敏感性

sensual xìnggǎn 性感

sensuality ròuyù 肉欲

sensuous cìjī gǎnguān 刺激感官

sentence 1 *n* GRAM jùzi 句子;

LAW túxíng 徒刑 **2** *v/t* LAW pànxíng 判刑

sentiment (*sentimentality*) róunuò qínggǎn 柔懦情感; (*opinion*) yìjiàn 意见

sentimental shānggǎn 伤感

sentimentality róunuò qíngdiào 柔懦情调

sentry shàobīng 哨兵

separate 1 *adj* dúlì 独立; **keep X ~ from Y** fēnkāi X hé Y 分开 X 和 Y **2** *v/t* fēnkāi 分开; **~ X from Y** bǎ X yǔ Y fēnkāi 把 X 与 Y 分开 **3** *v/i* (*of couple*) fēnjū 分居

separated *couple* fēnshǒu 分手

separately *pay* fēnzhe 分着; *treat, deal with* fēnbié 分别

separation fēnlí 分离; (*of couple*) fēnshǒu 分手

September jiǔyuè 九月

septic gǎnrǎn 感染; **go ~** (*of wound*) shòu gǎnrǎn 受感染

sequel xùjí 续集

sequence *n* shùnxù 顺序; **in ~** àn shùnxù 按顺序; **out of ~** bú àn shùnxù 不按顺序; **the ~ of events** shìqíng fāshēng de xiānhòu shùnxù 事情发生的先后顺序

serene níngjìng 宁静

sergeant zhōngshì 中士

serial *n* liánxù gùshì 连续故事

serialize *novel on TV* liánbō 连播

serial killer liánxù shārénfàn 连续杀人犯; **serial number** (*of product*) biānhào 编号; **serial port** COMPUT chuànxíng duānkǒu 串行端口

series (*of numbers, events, errors*) xìliè 系列

serious *illness, situation, damage* yánzhòng 严重; (*person: earnest*) rènzhēn 认真; *company* zhèngshì 正式; **I'm ~** wǒ zài shuō zhèngjīngde 我在说正经的; **listen, this is ~** tīngzhe, zhè shì zhèngshìr 听着，这是正事儿; **we'd better take a ~ look at it** wǒmen zuì hǎo hǎohǎo kànyíxià 我们最好好好看一下

seriously *injured, understaffed*

yánzhòng 严重; **~ intend to ...**
zhēnde xiǎng 真的想...; **~?**
shuōzhēnde ma? 说真的吗？;
take X ~ rènzhēn duìdài X 认真
对待 X

sermon jiǎngdào 讲道

servant púrén 仆人

serve 1 n (in tennis) fāqiú 发球
2 v/t food, meal duānshang 端上；
customer in store zhāodài 招待；
one's country, the people fúwù 服
务；**it ~s you / him right** nǐ / tā zuì
yǒu yīngdé 你 / 他罪有应得
3 v/i (give out food) shàng cài 上
菜；(as politician etc) gòngzhí 供
职；(in tennis) fāqiú 发球

♦**serve up** meal tígōng 提供

server (in tennis) fāqiúrén 发球人；
COMPUT fúwùqì 服务器

service 1 n (to customers, community) fúwù 服务；(for vehicle,
machine) wéixiū 维修；(in tennis)
fāqiú 发球；**the ~s** jūnduì 军队
2 v/t vehicle, machine wéixiū 维修

service area fúwùqū 服务区；
service charge (in restaurant,
club) fúwùfèi 服务费；**service
industry** fúwù hángyè 服务行
业；**serviceman** MIL jūnrén 军人；
service provider COMPUT fúwù
tígōng zhě 服务提供者；**service
sector** fúwù hángyè 服务行业；
service station jiāyóuzhàn 加油
站

sesame oil xiāngyóu 香油

session (of Congress etc) huìyì 会
议；(with psychiatrist, consultant etc)
yíduàn shíjiān 一段时间

set 1 n (of tools, books etc) tào 套；
(group of people) yìhuǒrén 一伙
人；MATH jíhé 集合；THEA: scenery
bùjǐng 布景；(where a movie is
made) pāishè chǎngdì 拍摄场地；
(in tennis) pán 盘；**television ~**
diànshì jī 电视机 **2** v/t (place)
fàng 放；movie, novel etc yǐ ... wéi
bèijǐng 以 ... 为背景；date, time,
limit dìng 定；mechanism tiáozhěng
调整；alarm clock tiáohé 调合；
broken limb jiēhǎo 接好；jewel
xiāngqiàn 镶嵌；(type~) páibǎn 排

版；**~ the table** bǎifàng cānjù 摆
放餐具；**~ a task for X** gěi X yígè
rènwù 给 X 一个任务 **3** v/i (of
sun) luò 落；(of glue) níngjié 凝结
4 adj views, ideas wángù 顽固；**be
dead ~ on X** jiānjué zuò X 坚决
做 X；**be very ~ in one's ways** yì
chéng búbiàn 一成不变；**~
book / reading** (in course) zhǐdìng
jiàocái / yuèdú cáiliào 指定教材 /
阅读材料；**~ meal** dìngcān 定餐

♦**set apart**: **set X apart from Y** shǐ
X yǔ Y bùtóng qǐlái 使 X 与 Y 不同

♦**set aside** (for future use) bōchū
拨出

♦**set back** (in plans etc) zǔ'ài
jìnchéng 阻碍进程；**it set me
back $400** huāle wǒ sìbǎi
měiyuán 花了我四百美元

♦**set off 1** v/i (on journey) chūfā 出
发 **2** v/t explosion, chain reaction
dǎozhì 导致

♦**set out 1** v/i (on journey) chūfā
出发；**~ to do X** (intend) yǒu mùdì
de zuò X 有目的地做 X **2** v/t
ideas, proposal chénshù 陈述；
goods bǎifàng 摆放

♦**set to** (start on a task) kāishǐ gàn
开始干

♦**set up 1** v/t new company chénglì
成立；system jiànlì 建立；
equipment, machine zhuāngpèi 装
配；market stall shèlì 设立；F
(frame) shè quāntào 设圈套 **2** v/i
(in business) chénglì 成立

setback zǔ'ài 阻碍

setting (of novel etc) bèijǐng 背景；
(of house) huánjìng 环境

settle 1 v/i (of liquid) chéngqīng 澄
清；(of dust) xiàchén 下沉；(to
live) dìngjū 定居；(of bird) tíngxiē
停歇 **2** v/t dispute, issue jiějué 解
决；s.o.'s debts chánghuán 偿还；
check jiésuàn 结算；**that ~s it!** nà
jiù dìng le! 那就定了！

♦**settle down** v/i (stop being noisy)
ānjìng 安静；(stop wild living)
āndìng xiàlái 安定下来；(in an
area) dìngjū 定居

♦**settle for** (take, accept) miǎnqiǎng
rènkě 勉强认可

shape

settlement (of claim, debt) qīngcháng 清偿; (of dispute) jiějué 解决; (payment) chángfù 偿付

settler (in new country) zhímín zhě 殖民者

set-up (structure) xìtǒng 系统; (relationship) guānxi 关系; F (frameup) kēnghài 坑害

seven qī 七

seventeen shíqī 十七

seventeenth dìshíqī 第十七

seventh dìqī 第七

seventieth dìqīshí 第七十

seventy qīshí 七十

sever v/t arm, cable etc qiēduàn 切断; relations zhōngduàn 中断

several adj & pron jǐge 几个

severe illness, penalty yánzhòng 严重; teacher, face yánlì 严厉; winter, weather èliè 恶劣

severely punish yánlì 严厉; speak, stare kēkè 苛刻; injured, disrupted yánzhòng 严重

severity (of illness, penalty) yánzhòng 严重; (of look etc) yánsù 严肃

sew 1 v/t féng 缝 2 v/i féngrèn 缝纫

♦ sew on button féngshang 缝上

sewage wūwù 污物

sewage plant wūwù chǔlǐchǎng 污物处理场

sewer wūshuǐguǎn 污水管

sewing (skill) féngrèn 缝纫; (that being sewn) xiànhuózhēni 针线活

sewing machine féngrènjī 缝纫机

sex (act) xìngjiāo 性交; (gender) xìngbié 性别; have ~ with X yǔ X xìngjiāo 与 X 性交

sexual xìng fāngmiàn 性方面

sexual intercourse xìngjiāo 性交

sexually transmitted disease xìng chuánbō jíbìng 性传播疾病

sexy xìnggǎn 性感

SEZ (= special economic zone) jīngjì tèqū 经济特区

shabby coat etc hánsuān 寒酸; treatment bù gōngpíng 不公平

shack péngzi 棚子

shade 1 n (for lamp) dēngzhào 灯罩; (of color) sèdù 色度; (on window) liánzi 帘子; in the ~ yīnliángchù 阴凉处 2 v/t (from sun, light) zhēbì 遮蔽

shadow n yǐngzi 影子

shady spot yīnliáng 阴凉; character, dealings kàobúzhù 靠不住

shaft (of axle) zhóu 轴; (of mine) kuàngjǐng 矿井

shaggy hair, dog cūnóng péngsōng 粗浓蓬松

shake 1 n: give X a good ~ bǎ X hǎohǎo yáohuàng yíxià 把 X 好好摇晃一下 2 v/t yáo 摇; ~ hands wòshǒu 握手; ~ hands with X yǔ X wòshǒu 与 X 握手; ~ one's head yáotóu 摇头 3 v/i (of hands, voice) chàndǒu 颤抖; (of building) huàngdòng 晃动

shaken (emotionally) fādǒu 发抖

shake-up chóngzǔ 重组

shaky table etc yáohuàng 摇晃; (after illness, shock) ruò 弱; grasp of sth, grammar etc bù zhāshí 不扎实

shall I ~ do my best wǒ jiāng jìnwǒsuǒnéng 我将尽我所能; ~ we go now? wǒmen xiànzài zǒuba? 我们现在走吧?

shallow water qiǎn 浅; person qiǎnbó 浅薄

shallow fry jiān 煎

shame 1 n xiūchǐ 羞耻; bring ~ on X gěi X dàilái chǐrǔ 给 X 带来耻辱; what a ~! zhēn yíhàn! 真遗憾!; ~ on you! zhēn kěchǐ! 真可耻! 2 v/t diūliǎn 使丢脸; X into doing Y shǐ X gǎndào xiūkuì ér zuò Y 使 X 感到羞愧而做 Y

shameful bù tǐmiàn 不体面

shameless bú yào liǎn 不要脸

shampoo 1 n xǐfàjīng 洗发精; a ~ and set xǐ tóufa bìng zuò tóufa 洗头发并做头发 2 v/t gěirén xǐtóufa 给人洗头发

Shandong Peninsula Shāndōng Bàndǎo 山东半岛

Shanghai Shànghǎi 上海

shape 1 n xíngzhuàng 形状 2 v/t clay, s.o.'s life sùzào 塑造; the *future* cùchéng 促成

shapeless *dress etc* wú dìngxíng 无定形

shapely *figure* yúnchèn 匀称

share 1 *n* yífèn 一份；FIN gǔfèn 股份；*do one's ~ of the work* zuò yīngzuòde gōngzuò 做应做的工作 **2** *v/t* fēnxiǎng 分享；*s.o.'s feelings, opinions* gòngtóng jùyǒu 共同具有 **3** *v/i* fēnxiǎng 分享；*do you mind sharing with Patrick?* (*bed, room, table*) nǐ yǔ Pàtèlǐkè gòngyòng hǎoma? 你与帕特里克共用好吗？

♦ **share out** píngfēn 平分

shareholder gǔdōng 股东

shark shā 鲨

sharp 1 *adj knife* fēnglì 锋利；*mind* língmǐn 灵敏；*pain* jùliè 剧烈；*taste* xīnlà 辛辣 **2** *adv* MUS piāngāo 偏高；*at 3 o'clock ~* sāndiǎn zhěng 三点整

sharpen *knife* shǐ fēnglì 使锋利；*skills* tígāo 提高

sharp practise bēibǐ jiāoyì 卑鄙交易

shatter 1 *v/t glass* fěnsuì 粉碎；*illusions* pòmiè 破灭 **2** *v/i* (*of glass*) dǎsuì 打碎

shattered F (*exhausted*) jīnpílìjìn 筋疲力尽；(*very upset*) fēicháng nánguò 非常难过

shattering *news, experience* lìngrén zhènjīng 令人震惊；*effect* lìngrén jīngtàn 令人惊叹

shave 1 *v/t* guā 刮 **2** *v/i* guālián 刮脸 **3** *n*: *have a ~* guālián 刮脸；*that was a close ~* nà zhēnshì jiāoxìng tuōxiǎn 那真是侥幸脱险

♦ **shave off** *beard* guādiào 刮掉；(*from piece of wood*) bàoqù yìcéng 刨去一层

shaven *head* tìguāng 剃光

shaver (*electric*) tìdāo 剃刀

shaving brush húshuā 胡刷

shaving soap tìxūgāo 剃须膏

shawl pījiān 披肩

she tā 她

shears dàjiǎndāo 大剪刀

sheath *n* (*for knife*) qiào 鞘；

(*contraceptive*) bìyùntào 避孕套

shed[1] *v/t blood, tears* liú 流；*leaves* tuōluò 脱落；*light on X* fig shǐ X gèng qīngchǔ xiē 使X更清楚些

shed[2] *n* péng 棚

sheep miányáng 绵羊

sheepdog mùyángquǎn 牧羊犬

sheepish xiūqiè 羞怯

sheepskin *adj lining* yángpí 羊皮

sheer *adj madness, luxury* shízú 十足；*drop, cliffs* jìnhū chuízhí 近乎垂直

sheet (*for bed*) chuángdān 床单；(*of paper*) zhāng 张；(*of metal, glass*) bǎn 板

shelf jià 架；*shelves* jià 架

shell 1 *n* (*of mussel, egg, tortoise etc*) ké 壳；MIL pàodàn 炮弹；*come out of one's ~* fig búzài xiūqiè 不再羞怯 **2** *v/t peas* bāoké 剥壳；MIL pàojī 炮击

shellfire pàohuǒ 炮火；*come under ~* zāodào pàohuǒ xíjī 遭到炮火袭击

shellfish bèilèi 贝类

shelter 1 *n* (*refuge*) bìhù 庇护；(*construction*) yǎnbìwù 掩蔽物 **2** *v/i* (*from rain, bombing etc*) duǒbì 躲避 **3** *v/t* (*protect*) bǎohù 保护

sheltered *place* kě bì fēngyǔ 可避风雨；*lead a ~ life* guòzhe wúyōuwúlǜde shēnghuó 过着无忧无虑的生活

shepherd *n* mùyángrén 牧羊人

sherry xuělìjiǔ 雪利酒

shield 1 *n* dùn 盾；(*sports trophy*) dùnxíng jǐnbiāo 盾形锦标；TECH hùbǎn 护板 **2** *v/t* (*protect*) bǎohù 保护

shift 1 *n* (*in attitude, thinking*) gǎibiàn 改变；(*switchover*) zhuǎnbiàn 转变；(*in direction of wind etc*) zhuǎnxiàng 转向；(*period of work*) bān 班 **2** *v/t* (*move*) yídòng 移动；*stains etc* nòngdiào 弄掉；*~ the emphasis onto* bǎ zhòngdiǎn zhuǎnyídào 把重点转移到 **3** *v/i* (*move*) nuódòng 挪动；(*in attitude, opinion*) gǎibiàn 改变；(*of wind*) zhuǎnbiàn 转变；*that's ~ing!* F tàikuàile! 太快了！

shift key COMPUT huàndǎngjiàn 换档键

shift work lúnbānde gōngzuò 轮班的工作

shifty pej bū duì jìnr 不对劲儿

shifty-looking pej guǐgui suìsuì 鬼祟祟

shimmer v/i fā shǎnshuò de wēiguāng 发闪烁的微光

shin n jìngbù 胫部

shine 1 v/i (of sun, moon) zhàoyào 照耀; (of shoes, polish) fāguāng 发光; fig (of student etc) chūzhòng 出众 2 v/t flashlight etc zhàoyìzhào 照一照 3 n (on shoes etc) guāngzé 光泽

shingle (on beach) hǎibīn shāshí 海滨砂石

shingles MED dàizhuàng pàozhěn 带状疱疹

shiny surface fāliàng 发亮

ship 1 n chuán 船 2 v/t (send) yùnsòng 运送; (send by sea) hǎiyùn 海运

shipment (consignment) huòwù 货物

shipowner chuánzhǔ 船主

shipping (sea traffic) chuánbó 船舶; (sending) yùnsòng 运送; (sending by sea) hǎiyùn 海运

shipping company yùnshū gōngsī 运输公司

shipshape adj zhěngqí 整齐

shipwreck 1 n hǎinàn 海难 2 v/t shǐ rén zāoyù hǎinàn 使人遭遇海难; be ~ed yù hǎinàn 遇海难; shipyard zàochuánchǎng 造船厂

shirk táobì 逃避

shirt chènshān 衬衫; in his ~ sleeves tā chuānzhe chènshān, méi chuān wàiyī 他穿着衬衫, 没穿外衣

shit F 1 n shǐ 屎; (bad quality goods, work) gǒushǐ bùrú 狗屎不如; I need a ~ wǒ děi qù lāshǐ 我得去拉屎 2 v/i lāshǐ 拉屎 3 interj māde 妈的

shitty F zāogāo 糟糕

shiver v/i chàndǒu 颤抖

shock 1 n zhènjīng 震惊; ELEC chùdiàn 触电; be in ~ MED chǔyú xiūkè zhuàngtài 处于休克状态 2 v/t shǐrén zhènjīng 使人震惊; be ~ed by X bèi X xià le yítiào 被X吓了一跳

shock absorber MOT jiǎnzhènqì 减震器

shocking behavior, poverty lìngrén zhènjīng 令人震惊; F (very bad) hěn zāo 很糟

shoddy goods lièzhì 劣质; behavior bēiliè 卑劣

shoe xié 鞋

shoelace xiédài 鞋带; shoestore xiédiàn 鞋店; shoestring: do X on a ~ yòng jíshǎo de qián zuò X 用极少的钱做X

◆ shoo away children, chicken fā xūshēng gǎnzǒu 发嘘声赶走

shoot 1 n BOT nènyá 嫩芽 2 v/t shèzhòng shè zhòng; (and kill) qiāngbì 枪毙; movie pāishè 拍摄; ~ X in the leg X tuǐshang zhòngle yídàn X 腿上中了一弹

◆ shoot down airplane jīluò 击落; suggestion bódǎo 驳倒

◆ shoot off (rush off) pǎodiào 跑掉

◆ shoot up (of prices) xùnsù shàngshēng 迅速上升; (of children) zhǎnggāo 长高; (of new suburbs, buildings etc) xùnsù jiànqǐ 迅速建起

shooting star liúxīng 流星

shop 1 n shāngdiàn 商店; talk ~ shuō hánghuà 说行话 2 v/i mǎi dōngxi 买东西; go ~ping qù mǎi dōngxi 去买东西

shopkeeper diànzhǔ 店主

shoplifter rùdiàn xíngqiè 入店行窃

shopper gòuwùrén 购物人

shopping (activity) gòuwù 购物; (items) mǎidào de dōngxi 买到的东西; do one's ~ gòuwù 购物

shopping mall gòuwù zhōngxīn 购物中心

shop steward gōnghuì fāyánrén 工会发言人

shore àn àn; on ~ (not at sea) ànshang 岸上

short 1 adj (in height) ǎi 矮; road,

distance, time duǎn 短; **be ~ of** quēfá 缺乏 **2** *adv*: **cut a vacation/meeting ~** suōduǎn jiàqī/huìyì 缩短假期/会议; **stop a person ~** shǐrén de tánhuà gāran ér zhǐ shǐ rén使人的谈话 尴尬而止使人的谈话嘎然而止; **go ~ of** qiànquē 欠缺; **in ~** jiǎn ér yánzhī 简而言之

shortage quēfá 缺乏

short circuit *n* duǎnlù 短路; **shortcoming** quēdiǎn 缺点; **short cut** jiéjìng 捷径

shorten *v/t dress, hair etc* nòngduǎn 弄短; *chapter, article* biànduǎn 变短; *vacation, work day* suōduǎn 缩短

shortfall chìzì 赤字; **shorthand** *n* sùjì 速记; **shortlist** *n* (*of candidates*) juéxuǎn 决选; **short-lived** duǎnzàn 短暂

shortly (*soon*) bùjiǔ 不久; **~ before that** jiù zài nà yǐqián 就在那以前

shorts duǎnkù 短裤; (*underwear for men*) sānjiǎo kù 三角裤

shortsighted jìnshì 近视; *fig* wú yuǎnjiàn 无远见; **short-sleeved** duǎnxiù 短袖; **short-staffed** rényuán bùzú 人员不足; **short story** duǎnpiān xiǎoshuō 短篇小说; **short-tempered** ài fā píqì 爱发脾气; **short-term** duǎnqī 短期; **short time**: **be on ~** (*of workers*) chǔyú duǎngōng shíqī 处于短工时期; **short wave** duǎnbō 短波

shot (*from gun*) shèjīshēng 射击声; (*photograph*) jìngtóu 镜头; (*injection*) zhùshè 注射; **be a good/poor ~** hǎo/chàjìn de shèshǒu 好/差劲的射手; **like a ~** *accept, run off* háobùyóuyù 毫不犹豫; **in one ~** *drink, write etc* yíxiàzi 一下子

shotgun lièqiāng 猎枪

should yīnggāi 应该; **what ~ I do?** wǒ gāi zuò shénme? 我该做什么? ; **you ~n't do that** nǐ bù yīnggāi nàme zuò 你不应该那么做; **that ~ be long enough** nà yīnggāi gòucháng le 那应该够长

了; **you ~ have heard him!** nǐ zhēn yīnggāi tīngtīng tā shuōde! 你真应该听听他说的!

shoulder *n* jiānbǎng 肩膀

shoulder blade jiānjiǎgǔ 肩胛骨

shout 1 *n* hǎnshēng 喊声 **2** *v/i* jiàohǎn 叫喊 **3** *v/t order* mìnglìng 命令

♦ **shout at** duì … hǎn 对 … 喊

shouting *n* hǎnjiào 喊叫

shove 1 *n* zhuàng 撞 **2** *v/t* bān 搬 **3** *v/i* jǐ 挤

♦ **shove in** *v/i* (*in line-up*) jiāxiēr 加楔儿

♦ **shove off** *v/i* F (*go away*) zǒukāi 走开

shovel *n* tiěqiāo 铁锹

show 1 *n* THEA, TV jiémù 节目; (*display*) biǎolù 表露; **on ~** (*at exhibition*) zài zhǎnlǎn 在展览; **it's all done for ~** *pej* dōu shì wèi gěi biérén kàn de 都是为给别人看的 **2** *v/t passport, ticket* chūshì 出示; *interest, emotion* biǎodá 表达; (*at exhibition*) zhǎnshì 展示; *movie* diànyǐng 电影; **~ X to Y** bǎ X gěi Y kàn 把X给Y看 *v/i* (*be visible*) kàndéjiàn 看得见; (*of movie*) shàngyìng 上映; **does it ~?** néng kànchūlái ma? 能看出来吗?

♦ **show off 1** *v/t skills* zhǎnshì 展示 **2** *v/i pej* xuányào 炫耀

♦ **show up 1** *v/t s.o.'s shortcomings etc* xiǎnxiànchū 显现出; **don't show me up in public** (*embarrass*) bié dāngzhòng ràng wǒ chūchǒu 别当众让我出丑 **2** *v/i* (*arrive, turn up*) dàolái 到来; (*be visible*) kàndéjiàn 看得见

show business yányìjiè 演艺界

showdown zuìhòu jiàoliàng 最后较量

shower 1 *n* (*of rain*) zhènyǔ 阵雨; (*to wash*) línyù 淋; **take a ~** línyù 淋浴 **2** *v/i* línyù 淋浴 **3** *v/t*: **~ X with compliments/praise** jiélì zànshǎng/biǎoyáng X 竭力赞赏/表扬X

shower bath línyù 淋浴; **shower cap** yùmào 浴帽; **shower**

curtainlínyùlián 淋浴帘;
showerproofadj fángyǔ 防雨
show jumpingmǎpī zhàng'ài
yùndòng 马匹障碍运动
show-offài xuányào de rén 爱炫
耀的人
showroomshāngpǐn chénlièshì 商
品陈列室
showyjacket, behavior kuāyào 夸
耀
shred 1 n (of paper etc) suìpiàn 碎
片; (of evidence etc) sīháo 丝毫
2 v/t paper sīchéng suìpiàn 撕成
碎片; (in cooking) qiēchéng
xiǎotiáo 切成小条
shredder (for documents) qiēsuìjī
切碎机
shrewdjīngmíng 精明
shriek 1 n jiānjiào 尖叫 **2** v/i
jiānshēng shuōchū 尖声说出
shrimpxiǎoxiā 小虾
shrineshénkān 神龛
shrinkv/i (of material) suōshuǐ 缩
水; (of level of support etc) jiǎnruò
减弱
shrink-wrapsùmó bāozhuāng 塑
膜包装
shrink-wrapping (process) sùmó
bāozhuāng 塑膜包装; (material)
sùmó 塑膜
shrivelwěisuō 萎缩
shrubguànmù 灌木
shrubberyguànmùcóng 灌木丛
shrug 1 n sōngjiān 耸肩; he gave
a ~ and left tā sōnglesǒng jiān jiù
zǒule 他耸了耸肩就走了 **2** v/i
sōngjiān 耸肩 **3** v/t: ~ one's
shoulders sōngjiān 耸肩
shudder 1 n (of fear, disgust) fādǒu
发抖; (of earth etc) zhèndòng 震
动 **2** v/i (with fear, disgust) fādǒu
发抖; (of earth, building)
zhèndòng 震动
shuffle v/t cards xǐ 洗 **2** v/i (in
walking) jiǎo cèng dì 脚蹭地
shunduǒbì 躲避
shutv/t guān 关 v/i guān 关;
they were ~ tāmen yǐjīng guānle
他们已经关了
♦**shut down 1** v/t business tíngyè
停业; computer guānjī 关机 **2** v/i

(of business) guānbì 关闭; (of
computer) guānjī 关机
♦**shut up**v/i (be quiet) ānjìng 安
静; ~ zhùzuǐ! 住嘴！
shutter (on window) chuāngbǎn 窗
板; PHOT kuàiménr 快门儿
shuttlev/i chuānsuō 穿梭
shuttlebus (at airport) chuānsuō
yíngyùn 穿梭营运; **shuttlecock**
SP yǔmáo qiú 羽毛球; **shuttle
service**chuānsuō yèwù 穿梭业
务
shyhàixiū 害羞
shynessmiǎntiǎn 腼腆
Siamese twinsliántǐ shuāngbāotāi 连体双胞胎
Sichuan BasinSìchuān Péndì 四
川盆地
sickshēngbìng 生病; sense of
humor cánkù 残酷; society bìngtài
病态; I feel ~ (about to vomit) wǒ
gǎndào ěxīn 我感到恶心; I'm
going to be ~ (vomit) wǒ yào tù wǒ
要吐; be ~ of (fed up with)
gǎndào yànwù 感到厌恶
sicken 1 v/t (disgust) shǐrén gǎndào
yànwù 使人感到厌恶 **2** v/i be
~ing for déle ... bìng 得了 ... 病
sickeningadj lìngrén yànwù 令人
厌恶
sickleliándāo 镰刀
sick leavebìngjià 病假; be on ~
xiū bìngjià 休病假
sicklyperson duōbìng 多病; color
bú jiànkāng 不健康
sicknessjíbìng 疾病; (vomiting)
ǒutù 呕吐
side n (of box, house) cèmiàn 侧面;
(of room, field) biān 边; (of
mountain) miàn 面; (of person) lèi
肋; SP yìfāng 一方; (favor
one side) piānxiàng 偏向; take ~s
with zhīchí 支持; I'm on your ~
wǒ zhīchí nǐ 我支持你; ~ by ~
bìngpái 并排; at the ~ of the
road zài lùbiān 在路边; on the
big / small ~ piān dà / xiǎo 偏大 /
小
♦**side with**zhīchí 支持
sideboard (furniture) cānjùguì 餐
具柜; **sideburns**liánbìn húzi 连

鬓胡子；**side dish** xiǎocài 小菜；

side effect fùzuòyòng 副作用；

sidelight MOT cèdēng 侧灯；

sideline 1 n fùyè 副业 **2** v/t: **feel ~d** gǎndào bèi hūshì 感到被忽视；

sidetrack v/t chàkāi 岔开；**get ~ed** bèi chàkāi 被岔开；**sidewalk** xíngréndào 人行道；**side street** xiǎoxiàng 小巷；

sidewalk café lùbiān kāfēiguǎn 路边咖啡馆；**sideways** adv xiézhe 斜着

siege wéikùn 围困；**lay ~ to** bāowéi 包围

sieve n shāizi 筛子

sift v/t corn, ore shāi 筛

♦ **sift through** details, data xìshěn 细审

sigh 1 n tànxī 叹息；**heave a ~ of relief** sōng yìkǒu qì 松一口气 **2** v/i tànqì 叹气

sight n qíngjǐng 情景；(power of seeing) shìlì 视力；**~s** (of city) míngshèng 名胜；**catch ~ of** kànjiàn 看见；**know by ~** miànshú 面熟；**within ~ of X** zài X shìyě zhī nèi 在 X 视野之内；**out of ~** zài shìchéng zhī wài 在视程之外；fig F gàilemàole 盖了帽了；**what a ~ you are!** kàn nǐ shì shénme xíngxiàng！看你是什么形象！；**lose ~ of** objective etc hūlüè 忽略

sightseeing guānguāng 观光；**go ~** qù guānguāng 去观光

sightseeing tour guānguāng lǚyóu 观光旅游

sightseer n guānguāngkè 观光客

sign 1 n (indication) jìxiàng 迹象；(road ~) zhǐshìpái 指示牌；(outside store, on building) zhāopai 招牌；**it's a ~ of the times** shídàide biāozhì 时代的标志 **2** v/t & v/i qiānzì 签字

♦ **sign up** v/i (join the army) yìngzhēng 应征

signal 1 n xìnhào 信号；**be sending out all the right / wrong ~s** fāchū zhèngquè / cuòwù de ànshì 发出正确／错误的暗示 **2** v/i (of driver) zhǐshì 指示

signatory qiānyuēfāng 签约方

signature qiānmíng 签名

signature tune kāishǐqǔ 开始曲

significance (importance) zhòngyàoxìng 重要性；(meaning) yìyì 意义

significant event etc zhòngyào 重要；(quite large) dàliàng 大量

signify yìwèi 意味

sign language shǒushì yǔyán 手势语言

signpost lùbiāo 路标

silence 1 n chénmò 沉默；**in ~** work, march ānjìng 安静；**~!** sùjìng! 肃静！ **2** v/t yāzhì 压制

silencer (on gun) xiāoyīnqì 消音器

silent ānjìng 安静；movie wúshēng 无声；**stay ~** (not comment) yīshēng bùkēng 一声不吭

silent partner búrù shíyè de gǔdōng 不入实业的股东

silhouette n lúnkuò 轮廓

silicon ⇩ guī 硅

silicon chip ⇩ guīpiàn 硅片

silk 1 n sīchóu 丝绸 **2** adj shirt etc sīzhì 丝制

Silk Road Sīchóu zhī lù 丝绸之路

silly shǎ 傻

silver 1 n yín 银；(~ medal) yínpái 银牌 **2** adj ring yínzhì 银制；hair huībái 灰白

silver-plated dùyín dèyín 镀银

similar xiāngsì 相似

similarity xiāngsì 相似

simmer v/i (in cooking) dùn 炖；(with rage) yíchùjífā 一触即发

♦ **simmer down** ānjìngxiàlái 安静下来

simple (easy) jiǎndān 简单；person tóunǎo jiǎndān 头脑简单

simplicity jiǎndān 简单

simplified characters jiǎntǐzì 简体字

simplify shǐ jiǎndān 使简单

simplistic guòyú jiǎndānhuà 过于简单化

simply (absolutely) juéduì 绝对；(in a simple way) jiǎndān 简单；**it is ~ the best** jiǎnzhí shì zuìhǎode 简直是最好的

simulate móní 摹拟

simultaneous tóngshí 同时

simultaneously tóngshí 同时

sin 1 n zuì'è 罪恶 2 v/i fànyǒu zuì'è 犯有罪恶

since 1 prep zìcóng 自从; ~ *last week* zìcóng shàngzhōu yǐlái 从上周以来 2 adv zìnà yǐhòu 自那以后; *I haven't seen him ~* zìnà yǐhòu, wǒ zài méi jiànguò tā 自那以后，我再没见过他 3 conj (expressions of time) cóng ... yǐlái 从 ... 以来; (seeing that) jìrán 既然; ~ *you left* zìcóng nǐ zǒu yǐhòu 自从你走以后; ~ *you don't like it* jìrán nǐ bù xǐhuān 既然你不喜欢

sincere chéngzhì 诚挚

sincerely chéngzhì 诚挚; hope zhēnchéng 真诚; *Yours ~* jǐnqǐ 谨启

sincerity zhēnchéng 真诚

sinful xié'è 邪恶

sing chàng 唱

Singapore Xīnjiāpō 新加坡

Singaporean 1 adj Xīnjiāpō 新加坡 2 n (person) Xīnjiāpō rén 新加坡人

singe v/t shāojiāo 烧焦

singer gēshǒu 歌手

single 1 n (sole) wéiyī 唯一; (not double) yígè 一个; (not married) dúshēn 独身; *there wasn't a ~ ...* yígè ... dōu méiyǒu 一个 ... 都没有; *in ~ file* chéngdānháng 成单行 2 n MUS dānqǔ chàngpiàn 单曲唱片; ~s (in tennis) dāndǎ 单打

♦ single out (choose) tiāochū 挑出; (distinguish) shǐrén chūzhòng 使人出众

single-breasted dānpáikòu 单排扣; single-handed 1 adj dāngqiāng pǐmǎ 单枪匹马 2 adv dúzì 独自; single-minded zhuānxīnzhìzhì 专心致志; single mother dānshēn mǔqīn 单身母亲; single parent dānqīn 单亲; single parent family dānqīn jiātíng 单亲家庭

singular GRAM 1 adj dānshù 单数 2 n dānshù xíngshì 单数形式; *in

the ~ dānshù xíngshì 单数形式

sinister xié'è 邪恶

sink 1 n xǐdícáo 洗涤槽 2 v/i (of ship, object) chénmò 沉没; (of sun) luòxià 落下; (of interest rates, pressure etc) xiàjiàng 下降; *he sank onto the bed* tā zāidǎo zài chuáng shàng 他栽倒在床上 3 v/t ship chénmò 沉没; funds xiàjiàng 下降

♦ sink in v/i (of liquid) shènrù 渗入; *it still hasn't really sunk in* (of realization) háishì méiyǒu zhēnzhèng yìshí dào 还是没有真正意识到

sinner zuìrén 罪人

Sino- Zhōng- 中

Sino-Japanese war Zhōng Rì Zhànzhēng 中日战争

sinologist Hànxuéjiā 汉学家

sinology Hànxué 汉学

Sino-Tibetan Hàn Zàng 汉藏

sinusitis MED dòuyán 窦炎

sip 1 n yìxiǎokǒu 一小口 2 v/t xiǎokǒu hē 小口喝

sir xiānsheng 先生

siren bàojǐngqì 报警器

sirloin niúyāoròu 牛腰肉

sister (older) jiějie 姐姐; (younger) mèimei 妹妹

sister-in-law (wife's elder sister) qīzǐ 妻姊; (wife's younger sister) qīmèi 妻妹; (husband's elder sister) dàgūjiě 大姑姐; (husband's younger sister) xiǎogū 小姑; (younger brother's wife) dìmèi 弟妹; (older brother's wife) sǎozi 嫂子

sit v/i zuò 坐

♦ sit down zuòxia 坐下

♦ sit up (in bed) zuòqǐlái 坐起来; (straighten back) zuòzhí 坐直; (wait up at night) áoyè 熬夜

sitcom TV qíngjǐng xǐjù 情景喜剧

site 1 n chǎngdì 场地 2 v/t new offices etc zédìng wèizhi 择定位置

sitting (of committee, court) kāitíng 开庭; (for artist) gōngrén huàxiàng huò pāizhào de shíjiān 供人

画像或拍照的时间; (*for meals*) shíjiānduàn 时间段

sitting room kètīng 客厅

situated *be* ~ zuòluòzài 坐落在

situation xíngshì 形势; (*of building etc*) wèizhi 位置

six liù 六

sixteen shíliù 十六

sixteenth dìshíliù 第十六

sixth dìliù 第六

sixtieth dìliùshí 第六十

sixty liùshí 六十

size dàxiǎo 大小; (*of jacket, shoes*) hàomǎ 号码

♦**size up** gūliáng 估量

sizeable xiāngdāng dà 相当大

sizzle fā sīsī shēng 发嘶嘶声

skate 1 *n* (*for ice*) huábīng 滑冰; (*roller skate*) huá hànbīng 滑旱冰 **2** *v/i* (*on ice*) huábīng 滑冰; (*roller skating*) huá hànbīng 滑旱冰

skateboard *n* huábǎn 滑板

skater huábīngrén 滑冰人

skating huábīng 滑冰

skeleton kūlóu 骷髅

skeleton key wànnéng yàoshi 万能钥匙

skeptic huáiyílùn zhě 怀疑论者

skeptical huáiyí 怀疑

skepticism huáiyí tàidù 怀疑态度

sketch 1 *n* cǎotú 草图; THEA huájī duǎnjù 滑稽短剧 **2** *v/t* xiěshēng 写生

sketchbook sùmiáobù 素描簿

sketchy *knowledge etc* fúqiǎn 肤浅

ski *n & v/i* huáxuě 滑雪

skid 1 *n* shāchē 刹车 **2** *v/i* dǎhuá 打滑

skier huáxuě zhě 滑雪者

skiing huáxuě 滑雪

ski lift diàosuǒ yùnshūchē 吊索运输车

skill jìqiǎo 技巧

skilled yǒujìnéng 有技能

skilled worker jìgōng 技工

skillful shúliàn 熟练

skim *surface* lüèguò 掠过; *milk* piēqù 撇去

♦**skim off** *the best* tíqǔ 提取

♦**skim through** *text* liúlǎn 浏览

skimmed milk tuōzhīrǔ 脱脂乳

skimpy *account etc* qùfá quēfá 缺乏; *little dress* bàolù 暴露

skin 1 *n* pífū 皮肤 **2** *v/t* qùpí 去皮

skin diving qiányóu yùndòng 潜游运动

skinny píbāogǔ 皮包骨

skin-tight jǐnshēn 紧身

skip 1 *n* (*little jump*) bèng 蹦 **2** *v/t* (*omit*) lüèguò 略过

ski pole huáxuězhàng 滑雪杖

skipper NAUT chuánzhǎng 船长; (*of team*) duìzhǎng 队长

skirt *n* qúnzi 裙子

ski run huáxuědào 滑雪道

ski tow diàosuǒ yùnshūchē 吊索运输车

skull tóulúgǔ 头颅骨

sky tiānkōng 天空

skylight tiānchuāng 天窗; **skyline** kōngzhōng lúnkuò xiàn 空中轮廓线; **skyscraper** mótiāndàlóu 摩天大楼

slab (*of stone*) hòubǎn 厚板; (*of cake etc*) yídàkuài 一大块

slack *rope* sōngchí 松弛; *discipline* xièdài 懈怠; *person* bùrènzhēn 不认真; *work* cūxīn 粗心; *period* qīngdàn 清谈

slacken *v/t rope* sōngchí 松弛; *pace* fàngmàn 放慢

♦**slacken off** *v/i* (*of trading*) jiǎnhuǎn 减缓; (*of pace*) fàngmàn 放慢

slacks kuānsōng kù 宽松裤

slam 1 *v/t door* pēngde guānshang 砰地关上 **2** *v/i* (*of door etc*) fāchū pēngshēng 发出砰声

♦**slam down** shuāi 摔

slander *n & v/t* fěibàng 诽谤

slang líyǔ 俚语; (*of a specific group*) hánghuà 行话

slant 1 *v/i* qīngxié 倾斜 **2** *n* xiépō 斜坡; (*given to a story*) guāndiǎn 观点

slanting qīngxié 倾斜

slap *n & v/t* zhǎngjī 掌击

slash 1 *n* (*cut*) kǎnhén 砍痕; (*in punctuation*) xiéxiàn 斜线 **2** *v/t skin etc* luànkǎn 乱砍; *prices, costs* dà xùjiǎn 大削减; ~ **one's wrists**

gēwàn 割腕

slate **1** n (type of rock) bǎnyán 板岩; (for writing on) shíbǎn 石板

slaughter **1** n (of animals) túshā 屠杀; (of people, troops) shālù 杀戮 **2** v/t animals túshā 屠杀; people, troops shālù 杀戮

slave n núlì 奴隶

slay shā 杀

slaying (murder) móushā 谋杀

sleazy bar, characters xiàliú 下流

sled(ge) n xuěqiāo 雪橇

sledge hammer dàchuí 大锤

sleep **1** n shuìjiào 睡觉; go to ~ qù shuìjiào 去睡觉; I need a good ~ wǒ xūyào hǎohǎo shuìyíjiào 我需要好好睡一觉; I couldn't get to ~ wǒ shuìbùzháo 我睡不着 **2** v/i shuì 睡
♦ sleep in (sleep late) shuìgè lǎnjiào 睡个懒觉
♦ sleep on v/t proposal, decision dàicì rì juédìng 待次日再定
♦ sleep with (have sex with) yǔ ... shuìjiào 与 ... 睡觉

sleeping bag shuìdài 睡袋; sleeping car wòchē 卧车; sleeping pill ānmiányào 安眠药

sleepless night bùmián 不眠

sleep walker mèngyóu zhě 梦游者

sleepy yawn kùnjuàn 困倦; town yōujìng 幽静; I'm ~ wǒ kùn le 我困了

sleet n yǔjiáxuě 雨夹雪

sleeve (of jacket etc) xiùzi 袖子

sleeveless wúxiù 无袖

sleigh n xuěqiāo 雪橇

sleight of hand qiǎomiàode shǒufǎ 巧妙的手法

slender figure, arms xiānxì 纤细; chance wēixiǎo 微小; income, margin wēibó 微薄

slice **1** n (of bread, tart) piàn piàn 片片; fig (of profits etc) fènr 份儿 **2** v/t loaf etc qiēchéng báopiàn 切成薄片

sliced bread qiēpiàn miànbāo 切片面包

slick **1** adj performance búfèilì 不费力; pej (cunning) yuánhuá 圆滑 **2** n (of oil) fúyóu 浮油

slide **1** n (for kids) huátī 滑梯; PHOT huàndēngpiàn 幻灯片 **2** v/i huá 滑; (drop: of exchange rate etc) xiàjiàng 下降 **3** v/t nuó 挪

sliding door lāmén 拉门

slight **1** adj person, figure miáotiáo 苗条; (small) xiǎo 小; no, not in the ~est bù, yìdiǎnr yě bù 不，一点儿也不 **2** n (insult) wǔrǔ 侮辱

slightly shāowēi 稍微

slim **1** adj miáotiáo 苗条; chance wēixiǎo 微小 **2** v/i jiǎnféi 减肥

slime níjiāng 泥浆

slimy liquid yǒu níjiāng 有泥浆

sling **1** n (for arm) xuándài 悬带 **2** v/t (throw) rēng 扔

slip **1** n (on ice etc) shuāijiāo 摔跤; (mistake) cuòwù 错误; a ~ of paper yīxiǎokuài zhǐ 一小块纸; a ~ of the tongue zǒuzuǐ 走嘴; give X the ~ bǎituō X 摆脱 X **2** v/i (on ice etc) huá 滑; (decline: of quality etc) xiàjiàng 下降; he ~ped out of the room tā liūchūle fángjiān 他溜出了房间 **3** v/t (put) qīngfàng 轻放; he ~ped it into his brief-case tā qīngqīngde bǎ tā fàng jìng wénjiànbāo lǐ 他轻轻地把它放进文件包里
♦ slip away (of time) liúshì 流逝; (of opportunity) shīqù 逝去; (die quietly) qiǎorán qùshì 悄然去世
♦ slip off v/t jacket etc tuōdiào 脱掉
♦ slip out v/i (go out) liūchūqù 溜出去
♦ slip up (make mistake) chū chācuò 出差错

slipped disc tūchùde zhuījiānpán 突出的椎间盘

slipper tuōxié 拖鞋

slippery slippery huá 滑

slipshod cūxīn 粗心

slit **1** n (tear) kǒuzi 口子; (hole) lièfèng 裂缝; (in skirt) kāichà 开叉 **2** v/t sīkāi 撕开

slither v/i huálái huáqù 滑来滑去

slobber v/i liú kǒushuǐ 流口水

slogan kǒuhào 口号

slop v/t yìchū 溢出

slope **1** n pō 坡; (of mountain) xiépō 斜坡; built on a ~ zài pōshang jiàn de 在坡上建的 2 v/i qīngxié 倾斜; *the road ~s down to the sea* dàolù xiàng hǎimiàn qīngxié 道路向海面倾斜

sloppy *work* cǎoshuài 草率; (*in dress*) yīzhuó bùzhěng 衣着不整; (*too sentimental*) yōngsú shānggǎn 庸俗伤感

slot n fèngxì 缝隙; (*in schedule*) ānpáide shíjiān 安排的时间
♦ **slot in** 1 v/t shǐ chārù 使插入 2 v/i chārù 插入

slot machine (*for vending*) ⇩ tóubìshòuhuòjī 投币售货机

slouch v/i lǎnsǎn 懒散

slovenly lātā 邋遢

slow màn 慢; *be ~* (*of clock*) mànle 慢了
♦ **slow down** 1 v/t gǎnsuàn jiǎnmàn 减慢 2 v/i mànxiàlái 慢下来

slowdown (*in production*) xiàjiàng 下降

slow motion: *in ~* màndòngzuò 慢动作

slug n (*animal*) kuòyú gūyú 蛞蝓

sluggish xíngdòng chíhuǎn 行动迟缓

slum n pínmínkū 贫民窟

slump 1 n (*in trade*) xiāotiáoqī 萧条期 2 v/i (*economically*) zhòurán xiàdiē 骤然下跌; (*collapse: of person*) chénzhòngde dǎoxià 沉重地倒下

slur 1 n (*on s.o.'s character*) dǐhuǐ 诋毁 2 v/t *words* hánhúbùqīngde shuōhuà 含糊不清地说话

slurred *speech* hánhúbùqīng 含糊不清

slush bànróngxuě 半融雪; *pej* (*sentimental stuff*) gǎnshāngde dōngxi 感伤的东西

slush fund hēiqián 黑钱

slut fàngdàng nǚzǐ 放荡女子

sly jiǎohuá 狡猾; *on the ~* mìmì 秘密

smack 1 n zhǎngjī 掌击 2 v/t *child* zhǎngjī 掌击; *bottom* pāidǎ 拍打

small 1 adj xiǎo 小 2 n: *the ~ of the back* hòuyāo 后腰

small change língqián 零钱

small hours língchén shífēn 凌晨时分; smallpox tiānhuā 天花; small print xiǎozì 小字; small talk liáotiān 聊天

smart 1 adj (*elegant*) piàoliang 漂亮; (*intelligent*) cōngmín 聪敏; *pace* mǐnjié 敏捷; *get ~ with X* gēn X shuǎ huátóu 跟 X 耍滑头 2 v/i (*hurt*) cìtòng 刺痛

smart card ⇩ shuǎkǎ 刷卡
♦ **smarten up** v/t shǐ gèng yǒu tiáolǐ 使更有条理

smash 1 n (*noise*) huālā yīshēng 哗啦一声; (*car crash*) zhuàngsuì 撞碎; (*in tennis*) kòuqiú 扣球 2 v/t (*break*) dǎsuì 打碎; (*hit hard*) zhàngjī zhuàngjī 撞击; *~ X to pieces* bǎ X zhuàngsuì 把 X 撞碎 3 v/i (*break*) pòsuì 破碎; *the driver ~ed into ...* sījī bǎ chē zhuàngdào ... 司机把车撞到 ...

smash hit F jíwéi hōngdòng 极为轰动

smattering (*of a language*) yīzhībànjiě 一知半解

smear 1 n (*of ink etc*) wūjì 污迹; MED túpiàn 涂片; (*on character*) wūmiè 污蔑 2 v/t *paint etc* túmǒ 涂抹; *character* fěibàng 诽谤

smear campaign fěibàng huódòng 诽谤活动

smell 1 n qìwèi 气味; *it has no ~* tā méiyǒu qìwèi 它没有气味; *sense of ~* xiùjué嗅觉 2 v/t wénchū 闻出 3 v/i (*unpleasantly*) yǒu chòuwèi 有臭味; (*sniff*) wén 闻; *what does it ~ of?* tā yǒu shénme wèir? 它有什么味儿？; *you ~ of beer* nǐ yǒu píjiǔwèi 你有啤酒味

smelly yǒu chòuwèi 有臭味

smile n & v/i wēixiào 微笑
♦ **smile at** duì ... wēixiào 对 ... 微笑

smirk n & v/i jiānxiào 尖笑

smog yānwù 烟雾

smoke 1 n yān 烟; *have a ~* xīyān 吸烟 2 v/t *cigarettes* xī 吸; *bacon* yòng yānxūn 用烟熏 3 v/i xīyān 吸烟; *I don't ~* wǒ bù xīyān 我不吸烟

smoker (*person*) xīyānde rén 吸烟
的人

smoking xīyān 吸烟; *no ~* jìnzhǐ
xīyān 禁止吸烟

smoking compartment RAIL xīyān chēxiāng 吸烟车厢

smoky *room, air* duōyān 多烟

smolder (*of fire*) huǎnmàn ránshāo
缓慢燃烧; *fig* (*with anger*) yùjí yùjī 郁积; (*with desire*) yùhuǒzhōngshāo
欲火中烧

smooth **1** *adj surface, skin, sea*
guānghuá 光滑; *ride* píngwěn 平
稳; *transition* shùnlì 顺利; *pej*
(*person*) yuánhuá 圆滑 **2** *v/t hair*
shǐ guānghuá 使光滑

♦smooth down (*with sandpaper
etc*) móguāng 磨光

♦smooth out *paper, cloth* lāpíng 拉
平

♦smooth over: *smooth things
over* shǐ shìqíng huǎnjiě 使事情
缓解

smother *flames* mēnzhù 闷住;
person shǐ zhìxī 使窒息; *~ X with
kisses* bùtíngde qīnwěn X 不停
地亲吻 X; *~ bread with jam* bǎ
guǒjiàng hòuhòude fàngzài miànbāo shang 把果酱厚厚地放在
面包上

smudge **1** *n* wūjì 污迹 **2** *v/t* nòngzāng 弄脏

smug zìmǎn 自满

smuggle *v/t* zǒusī 走私

smuggler zǒusī zhě 走私者

smuggling zǒusī 走私

smutty *joke, sense of humor* xiàliú
下流

snack *n* xiǎochī 小吃

snack bar xiǎochīdiàn 小吃店

snag (*problem*) xiǎo wèntí 小问题

snail wōniú 蜗牛

snake *n* shé 蛇

snap **1** *n* kāchāshēng 喀嚓声;
PHOT zhàopiàn 照片 **2** *v/t* (*break*)
duànliè 断裂; (*say sharply*)
lìshēng shuō 厉声说 **3** *v/i* (*break*)
pāde zhéduàn 啪地折断 **4** *adj
decision, judgment* kuàisù 快速

♦snap up *bargains* qiǎnggòu 抢购

snappy *person, mood* yìnù 易怒;

decision, response lìluò 利落;
(*elegant*) shímáo 时髦

snapshot zhàopiàn 照片

snarl **1** *n* (*of dog*) nùhǒu 怒吼 **2** *v/i*
chánjié 缠结

snatch **1** *v/t* duódé 夺得; (*steal*)
tōuzǒu 偷走; (*kidnap*) bǎngjià 绑
架 **2** *v/t* zhuāqǔ 抓取

snazzy shuài 帅

sneak **1** *v/t* (*remove, steal*) tōuná 偷
拿; *~ a glance at* tōukàn yīyǎn 偷
看一眼 **2** *v/i*: *~ into the room /
out of the room* tōutōu liūjìn /
liūchū fángjiān 偷偷溜进 / 溜出
房间

sneakers fānbùxié 帆布鞋

sneaking *adj*: *have a ~ suspicion
that ...* xīnzhōng yǒu nányí
xiāochú de cāiyí ... 心中有难以
消除的猜疑 ...

sneaky F (*crafty*) guǐguǐsuìsuì 鬼鬼
祟祟

sneer *n & v/i* lěngxiào 冷笑

sneeze **1** *n* pēntì 喷嚏 **2** *v/i* dǎ
pēntì 打喷嚏

sniff **1** *v/i* (*to clear nose*) yòng bí
xīqì 用鼻吸气; (*of dog*) xiù 嗅
2 *v/t* (*smell*) wén 闻

sniper jūjīshǒu 狙击手

snitch F (*telltale*) bānnòngshìfēi
de rén 搬弄是非的人 **2** *v/i* (*tell
tales*) gàomì 告密

snob shìlìyǎn 势利眼

snobbish shìlì 势利

snooker ⇩ táiqiú 台球

♦snoop around kuīchá 窥察

snooty mùzhōngwúrén 目中无人

snooze **1** *n* kēshuì 瞌睡 **2** *v/i* dǎ
xiǎoshuì 小睡 **2** *v/i* dǎ kēshuì 打
瞌睡

snore *v/i* dǎ hān 打鼾

snoring *n* hānshēng 鼾声

snorkel *n* tōngqìguǎn 通气管

snort *v/i* (*of bull, horse*) pēnbíxī 喷
鼻息; (*of person: disdainfully*)
fāhēngshēng 发哼声

snout (*of pig, dog*) kǒubíbù 口鼻
部

snow **1** *n* xuě 雪 **2** *v/i* xià xuě 下雪

♦snow under: *be snowed under
with work* gōngzuò mángbúguòlái

工作忙不过来

snowball n xuěqiú 雪球; **snow-bound** bèi xuě kùnzhù 被雪困住; **snow chains** MOT fáng huá liàn 防滑链; **snowdrift** xuěduī 雪堆; **snowdrop** xuělián 雪莲; **snowflake** xuěhuā 雪花; **snowman** xuěrén 雪人; **snowplow** xuělí 雪犁; **snowstorm** bàofēngxuě 暴风雪

snowy weather duōxuě 多雪; roads, hills jīxuě 积雪

snub n & v/t dàimàn 怠慢

snub-nosed tābí 塌鼻

snug nuǎnhuo 暖和; (tight-fitting) jǐnshēn 紧身

♦ **snuggle down** quánfú 蜷伏

♦ **snuggle up to** wēiyīzhe 偎依着

so 1 adv: ~ hot/cold tàirè/lěng 太热/冷; not ~ much búnàme 不那么; ~ much better/easier hǎo/róngyì duōle 好/容易多了; eat/drink ~ much chī/hē hěnduō 吃/喝很多; I miss you ~ wǒ hěn xiǎng nǐ 我很想你; ~ am I/do I wǒ yě shì 我也是; ~ is she/does she tā yě shì 她也是; and ~ on děngděng 等等 2 pron: I hope/think ~ wǒ xīwàng rúcǐ/rènwéi shì zhèiyàng 我希望如此/我认为是这样; you didn't tell me – I did ~ nǐ méi gàosù wǒ – wǒ gàosù nǐ le 你没告诉我 – 我告诉你了; 50 or ~ dàyuē wǔshí 大约五十 3 conj (for that reason) yīncǐ 因此; (in order that) shǐde 使得; and ~ I missed the train jiùzhèiyàng wǒ méi gǎnshang huǒchē 就这样我没赶上火车; ~ (that) I could come too to jiùshì shuō wǒ yě néng qù 那就是说我也能去; ~ what? nà yòu zěnmeyàng? 那又怎么样？

soak v/t (steep) pào 泡; (of water, rain) jìnshī 浸湿

♦ **soak up** liquid xīshōu 吸收

soaked shītòu 湿透

so-and-so F (unknown person) mǒumǒu rén 某某人; (annoying person) tǎoyànguǐ 讨厌鬼

soap n (for washing) féizào 肥皂

soap (opera) féizào jù 肥皂剧

soapy water hán féizào 含肥皂

soar (of rocket) shēngrù 升入; (of bird, plane) áoxiáng 翱翔; (of prices) měngzēng 猛增

sob 1 n wūyān 呜咽 2 v/i chōuqì 抽泣

sober (not drunk) qīngxǐng 清醒; (serious) yánsù 严肃

♦ **sober up** xǐngjiǔ 醒酒

so-called suǒwèi 所谓

soccer zúqiú 足球

sociable héqún 合群

social adj shèhuì 社会; (recreational) shèjiāo 社交

socialism shèhuì zhǔyì 社会主义

socialist 1 adj shèhuì zhǔyì 社会主义 2 n shèhuì zhǔyì zhě 社会主义者

socialize shèjiāo 社交

social work shèhuì gōngzuò 社会工作

social worker shègōng 社工

society shèhuì 社会; (organization) shètuán 社团

sociology shèhuì xué 社会学

sock¹ (for wearing) wàzi 袜子

sock² 1 n (punch) quán 拳 2 v/t (punch) zòu 揍

socket (electrical) chāzuò 插座; (of arm, eye) wō 窝

soda (~ water) sūdá 苏打; (ice-cream ~) bīngqílíng sūdá shuǐ 冰淇淋苏打水; (soft drink) ruǎnxìng yǐnliào 软性饮料

sofa shāfā 沙发

sofa bed shāfā chuáng 沙发床

soft pillow, chair ruǎn 软; voice wēnróu 温柔; music yuè'ěr 悦耳; light, color róuhé 柔和; skin róuhuá 柔滑; (lenient) kuānhòu 宽厚; have a ~ spot for X piān'ài X 偏爱 X

soft drink ruǎnxìng yǐnliào 软性饮料

soften 1 v/t position huǎnhé 缓和; impact, blow jiǎnqīng 减轻 2 v/i (of butter, ice cream) biànruǎn 变软

softly (quietly) dīshēng 低声

soft seat (*on train*) ruǎnzuò 软座

soft sleeper (*on train*) ruǎnwò 软卧

software ruǎnjiàn 软件

soggy shīrùn 湿润

soil 1 *n* (*earth*) tǔrǎng 土壤 **2** *v/t* nòngzāng 弄脏

solar energy tàiyáng néng 太阳能

solar panel tàiyáng diànchí bǎn 太阳电池板

soldier shìbīng 士兵

sole[1] *n* (*of foot*) jiǎodǐ bǎn 脚底板; (*of shoe*) xiédǐ 鞋底

sole[2] *adj* wéiyī 唯一; **~ responsibility** dāndú fùzé 单独负责

solely jǐnjǐn 仅仅

solemn (*serious*) yánsù 严肃; *promise* zhèngzhòng 郑重

solid *adj* (*hard*) yìng bāngbāng 硬梆梆; (*without holes*) wú kòngxì 无空隙; *gold, silver* chún 纯; (*sturdy*) láogù 牢固; *evidence* chōngfèn 充分; *support* chèdǐ 彻底

solidarity tuánjié yīzhì 团结一致

solidify *v/i* gùhuà 固化

solitaire (*card game*) ⇩ dānrén zhǐpái xì 单人纸牌戏

solitary *life, activity* gūdú 孤独; (*single*) gū línglíng 孤零零

solitude dúzì yīrén 独自一人

solo 1 *n* (*of instrumentalist*) dúzòu qǔ 独奏曲; (*of singer*) dúchàng qǔ 独唱曲 **2** *adj* dānrén 单人

soloist (*instrumentalist*) dúzòu yǎnyuán 独奏演员; (*singer*) dúchàng yǎnyuán 独唱演员

soluble *substance* kěróng 可溶; *problem* kě jiějué 可解决

solution jiědá 解答; (*mixture*) róngyè 溶液

solve jiějué 解决

solvent *adj* (*financially*) wú zhàiwù 无债务

somber *dark* huī'àn 灰暗; (*serious*) yánjùn 严峻

some 1 *adj* yīxiē 一些; **~ people say that ...** yǒuxiē rén shuō ... 有些人说...; **would you like ~ water/cookies?** nǐ yào diǎn shuǐ/

qǔqíbǐng ma? 你要点水/曲奇饼吗？ **2** *pron* yīxiē 一些; **~ of the group** zǔlǐ de yīxiē rén 组里的一些人; **would you like ~?** nǐ yào diǎnrma? 你要点儿吗？; **give me ~** gěiwǒ diǎnr 给我点儿 **3** *adv* (*a bit*) shāowēi 稍微; **we'll have to wait ~** wǒmen yào děnghuìr 我们要等会儿

somebody yǒurén 有人

someday yǒuzhāo yīrì 有朝一日

somehow (*by some means*) xiǎng bànfa 想办法; (*for some unknown reason*) bùzhī zěnde 不知怎的

someone yǒurén 有人

someplace → **somewhere**

somersault 1 *n* jīndǒu 筋斗 **2** *v/i* fān jīndǒu 翻筋斗

something dōngxi 东西; **would you like ~ to drink/eat?** nǐ yàobùyào hē/chī diǎnr dōngxi? 你要不要喝/吃点儿东西？; **is ~ wrong?** zěnme le? 怎么了？

sometime gǎirì 改日; **~ last year** qùnián mǒugè shíhòu 去年某个时候

sometimes yǒushí 有时

somewhere 1 *adv* mǒugè dìfang 某个地方 **2** *pron* mǒuchù 某处

son érzi 儿子

song gēqǔ 歌曲

Song Dynasty Sòng Cháo 宋朝

Song Dynasty lyrics Sòngcí 宋词

songwriter cíqǔ zuòjiā 词曲作者

son-in-law nǚxù 女婿

son of a bitch *n* F húndàn 混蛋

soon (*in no time*) hěnkuài 很快; (*early*) zǎo 早; **soon after** bùjiǔ zhīhòu 不久之后; **as ~ as ...** yī ... jiù ... 一...就...; **as ~ as possible** jǐnkuài jìnkuài 尽快; **~er or later** chízǎo 迟早; **the ~er the better** yuèkuài yuèhǎo 越快越好

soot yóuyān 油烟

soothe *pain* jiǎnqīng 减轻; *person* ānwèi 安慰

sophisticated *person* jīngtōng shìgù 精通世故; *tastes, lifestyle* búluò sútào 不落俗套; *machine* jīngmì 精密

sophomore èrniánjí 二年级

soprano n gāoyīn 高音

sordid affair, business bēibì 卑鄙

sore 1 adj (painful) téng téng 疼疼; F (angry) nǎohuǒ 恼火; **is it ~?** téng bùténg? 疼不疼？ 2 n chuāng chuāng 疮

sorghum gāoliáng 高粱

sorrow n (sad things) shāngxīn shì 伤心事; (sadness) yōushāng 忧伤

sorry (regretful) hòuhuǐ 后悔; (sad) nánguò nánguò 难过; **I'm ~ that** (apology) duìbuqǐ ... 对不起...; (expressing sympathy) hěn yíhàn ... 很遗憾...; (I'm) ~! duìbuqǐ! 对不起！; **I feel ~ for her** wǒ wèi tā gǎndào nánguò 我为她感到难过

sort 1 n zhǒng zhǒng 种; ~ **of ...** F yǒu nàme diǎnr ... 有那么点儿...; **is it finished? – ~ of** F wánle ma? – chàbùdō 完了吗？ – 差不多 2 v/t fēnlèi 分类; COMPUT páiliè 排列

♦ **sort out** papers zhěnglǐ 整理; problem jiějué 解决

so-so adv còuhe 凑和

soul REL línghún 灵魂; fig (of a nation etc) jīngshén 精神; (character) shēngqì 生气; (person) rén 人

sound[1] adj (sensible) hélǐ 合理; (healthy) jiànkāng 健康; business qiángzhuàng 强壮; (strong, not damaged) wánhǎo wúsǔn 完好无损; **a ~ sleep** hānshuì 酣睡

sound[2] 1 n shēngyīn 声音; (noise) shēng 声 2 v/t (pronounce) fāyīn 发音; MED tīngzhěn 听诊; ~ **one's horn** àn lǎba 按喇叭 3 v/i: **that ~s interesting** tīngqǐlái hěn yǒuqù 听起来很有趣; **that ~s like a good idea** tīngqǐlái xiàng hǎo zhǔyi 听起来象好主意; **she ~ed unhappy** tā hǎoxiàng bù gāoxìng 她好像不高兴

sound card COMPUT shēngkǎ 声卡

soundly sleep shóu shú 熟; beaten chèdǐ 彻底

soundproof adj géyīn 隔音

soundtrack pèiyuè 配乐

soup tāng 汤

soup bowl tāngwǎn 汤碗

sour adj apple, orange suān 酸; milk sōu 馊; expression, comment jiānsuān kèbó 尖酸刻薄

source n láiyuán 来源; (of river) yuántóu 源头; (person) xiāoxirén 消息人

south 1 adj nán 南 2 n nánbù 南部; **to the ~ of X** zài X de nánbiān 在X的南边 3 adv wǎngnán 往南

South Africa Nánfēi 南非; **South African** 1 adj Nánfēi 南非 2 n Nánfēi rén 南非人; **South America** Nánměi 南美; **South American** 1 adj Nánměi 南美 2 n Nánměi rén 南美人; **South China Sea** Nánhǎi 南海; **South Korea** Nánhán 南韩; **South Korean** 1 adj Nánhán 南韩 2 n Nánhán rén 南韩人; **southeast** 1 n dōngnán bù 东南部 2 adj dōngnán 东南 3 adv wǎng dōngnán 往东南; **it's ~ of X** zài X de dōngnán fāng 在X的东南方; **Southeast Asia** Dōngnán yà 东南亚; **Southeast Asian** adj Dōngnán yà 东南亚; **southeastern** dōngnán 东南

southerly adj nán 南

southern nán 南

southward adv xiàng nán 向南

southwest 1 n xīnán bù 西南部 2 adj xīnán 西南 3 adv wǎng xīnán 往西南; **it's ~ of X** zài X de xīnán fāng 在X的西南方

southwestern xīnán 西南

souvenir jìniàn pǐn 纪念品

sovereign adj state zhǔquán 主权

sovereignty (of state) zhǔquán 主权

Soviet Union Sūlián 苏联

sow[1] n (female pig) mǔzhū 母猪

sow[2] v/t seeds bōzhòng 播种

soy bean huángdòu 黄豆; **soy bean oil** dòu yóu 豆油; **soy milk** dòujiāng 豆浆; **soy sauce** jiàngyóu 酱油

space n (beyond earth) tàikōng 太空; (area) kòngbái 空白; (room) kōngjiān 空间

♦ **space out** bǎ ... jiàngé kāi 把 ... 间隔开

space bar COMPUT kònggé jiàn 空隔键; spacecraft yǔzhòu fēichuán 宇宙飞船; spaceship yǔzhòu fēichuán 宇宙飞船; space shuttle ⇩ hángtiān fēijī 航天飞机; space station yǔzhòu kōngjiān zhàn 宇宙空间站; spacesuit yǔháng fú 宇航服

spacious kuānchang 宽敞

spade (for digging) qiāo xiān 锹; ~s (in card game) hēitáo 黑桃

Spain Xībānyá 西班牙

span v/t kuà kǒng 跨; (of bridge) héngkuà 横跨

Spaniard Xībānyá rén 西班牙人

Spanish 1 adj Xībānyá 西班牙 2 n (language) Xībānyá yǔ 西班牙语

spank dǎ pìgù 打屁股

spare 1 v/t time, money yúnchū 匀出; (do without) shěngdiào 省掉; can you ~ the time? yǒukōngma? 有空吗？; there were five to ~ (left over, in excess) yǒu wǔgè shèngxià 有五个剩下 2 adj money duōyú 多余; (extra) bèiyòng 备用 3 n (part) língjiàn 零件

spare ribs páigǔ 排骨; spare room kèfáng 客房; spare time yèyú shíjiān 业余时间; spare tire MOT bèiyòng lúntāi 备用轮胎; spare wheel bèiyòng chēlún 备用车轮

spark n huǒxīng 火星

sparkle v/i shǎnyào 闪耀

sparkling wine qìjiǔ 汽酒

spark plug huǒhuāsāi 火花塞

sparrow máquè 麻雀

sparse vegetation xīshū 稀疏

sparsely: ~ populated rényān xīshǎo 人烟稀少

spatter v/t mud, paint jiàn 溅

speak 1 v/i shuōhuà 说话; we're not ~ing (to each other) (we've quarreled) wǒmen nào bièniu 我们闹别扭; ~ing TELEC wǒshì 我是 2 v/t foreign language huìjiǎng 会讲; ~ one's mind zhíshuō 直说

♦ speak to yǔ ... tánhuà 与 ... 谈话; (make a speech) fāyán 发言

♦ speak for dàibiǎo ... jiǎnghuà 代表 ... 讲话; speaking for myself jù wǒ lái kàn 据我来看

♦ speak out dàdǎn di shuō 大胆地说

♦ speak up (speak louder) dàshēng diǎn 大声点

♦ speak with yǔ ... tánhuà 与 ... 谈话

speaker (at conference) yǎnjiǎng zhě 演讲者; (orator) yǎnshuō jiā 演说家; (of sound system) yīnxiǎng 音箱

spearmint bòhe 薄荷

special tèshū 特殊; (particular) tèbié 特别

special economic zone jīngjì tèqū 经济特区

specialist zhuānjiā 专家

specialize zhuānmén cóngshì 专门从事; ~ in ... zhuānmén cóngshì ... 专门从事 ...

specially tèbié 特别

specialty (of company etc) zhuāncháng 专长; (of restaurant) náshǒu hǎocài 拿手好菜

species zhǒnglèi 种类

specific tèbié 特别

specifically tèbié 特别

specifications (of machine etc) guīgé 规格

specify zhǐdìng 指定

specimen yàngpǐn 样品

speck (of dust, soot) lì 粒

spectacle (impressive sight) zhuàngguān 壮观; (a pair of) ~s (yīfú) yǎnjìng (一副) 眼镜

spectacular adj (stunning) zhuàngguān 壮观; (impressive) yǐnrén zhùmù 引人注目

spectator guānzhòng 观众

spectrum fig fànwéi 范围

speculate v/i cāicè 猜测; FIN zuò tóujī mǎimài 做投机买卖

speculation cāicè 猜测; FIN tóujī mǎimài 投机买卖

speculator FIN tóujī shāng 投机商

speech (address) jiǎnghuà 讲话; (in play) táicí 台词; (ability to speak) shuōhuà nénglì 说话能力; (way of speaking) shuōhuà fāngshì

说话方式

speechless (with shock, surprise) yīshí jiǎng bùchū huà lái 一时讲不出话来

speech defect yányǔ quēxiàn 言语缺陷; speech therapist yányǔ jiǎozhì shī 言语矫治师; speech writer yǎnjiǎnggǎo zhuànxiě rén 演讲稿撰写人

speed 1 n sùdù 速度; at a ~ of 150 mph sùdù měi xiǎoshí yībǎi wǔshí yīnglǐ 速度每小时一百五十英里 2 v/i (walk quickly) kuàizǒu 快走; (drive too quickly) chāosù 超速

♦ speed by fēiguò 飞过
♦ speed up v/t & v/i jiākuài sùdù 加快速度

speedboat kuàitǐng 快艇

speedily xùnsù 迅速

speeding n (when driving) chāosù 超速

speeding fine chāosù xíngshǐ fákuǎn 超速行驶罚款

speed limit ↓ sùdù jíxiàn 速度极限

speedometer lǐchéng jì 里程计

speedy xùnsù 迅速

spell[1] v/t & v/i pīn 拼

spell[2] n (period of time) yīduàn shíjiān 一段时间

spellbound rùmí 入迷; spell-check COMPUT cháců 查错写; do a ~ on ... jiǎnchá ... de pīnxiě 检查 ... 的拼写; spellchecker COMPUT pīnxiě cháců chéngxù 拼查错程序

spelling pīnxiě 拼写

spend money huāqián 花钱; time dùguò 度过

spendthrift n pej dàshǒu dàjiǎo de rén 大手大脚的人

sperm jīngzǐ 精子; (semen) jīngyè 精液

sperm bank jīngzǐ kù 精子库

sphere qiútǐ 球体; fig lǐngyù 领域; ~ of influence shìlì fànwéi 势力范围

spice n (seasoning) xiāngliào 香料

spicy food duō xiāngliào 多香料

spider zhīzhū 蜘蛛

spiderweb zhīzhū wǎng 蜘蛛网

spike n jiāntóu 尖头; (on shoes) xiédīng 鞋钉

spill v/t & v/i sǎ 洒

spin[1] 1 n (turn) xuánzhuǎn 旋转 2 v/t xuánzhuǎn 旋转 3 v/i (of wheel) xuánzhuǎn 旋转; my head is ~ning wǒ tóuhūn nǎozhàng 我头昏脑胀

spin[2] v/t wool, cotton fǎng 纺; web jiéwǎng 结网

♦ spin around (of person) zhuǎnshēn 转身
♦ spin out tuōcháng 拖长

spinach bōcài 菠菜

spinal jǐzhù 脊柱

spinal column jǐzhù 脊柱

spin doctor xuānchuán jiā 宣传家; spin-dry v/t shuǎigān 甩干; spin-dryer shuǎigān jī 甩干机

spine (of person, animal) jǐzhù 脊柱; (of book) shūjí 书脊; (on plant, hedgehog) cì 刺

spineless (cowardly) méi gǔqì 没骨气

spin-off pàishēng chǎnpǐn 派生产品

spiral 1 n luóxuán 螺旋 2 v/i (rise quickly) jùjù shàngshēng 急剧上升

spiral staircase luóxuán shì lóutī 螺旋式楼梯

spire jiāntǎ 尖塔

spirit n (as opposed to body) jīngshén 精神; (of dead person) línghún 灵魂; (energy) huólì 活力; (courage) yǒngqì 勇气; (attitude) tàidù 态度; we did it in a ~ of cooperation / friendliness wǒmen yǐ hézuò / yǒuhǎo de jīngshén chūfā 我们以合作/友好的精神出发

spirited (energetic) shēngqì bóbo 生气勃勃

spirit level shuǐzhǔn yí 水准仪

spirits[1] (alcohol) lièjiǔ 烈酒

spirits[2] (morale) qíngxù 情绪; be in good / poor ~ jīngshén hǎo / huài 精神好/坏

spiritual adj shén 神

spiritualism wéilíng lùn 唯灵论

spiritualist *n* zhāohúnshù zhě 招魂术者

spit *v/i (of person)* tǔtán 吐痰; *it's ~ting with rain* xià xiǎoyǔ 下小雨

♦ **spit out** *food, liquid* tǔchū 吐出

spite *n* èyì 恶意; *in ~ of* jǐnguǎn 尽管

spiteful huáiyǒu èyì 怀有恶意

spitting image: be the ~ of X hé X jiǎnzhí yīmó yīyàng 和X简直一模一样

splash 1 *n (noise)* pūtōng 扑通; *(small amount of liquid)* yīdiǎnr 一点儿; *(of color)* bāndiǎn 斑点 **2** *v/t person* jiàn pō 溅; *water, mud* pō pō 泼 **3** *v/i* xǐshuǐ 嬉水; *(of water)* fēijiàn 飞溅

♦ **splash down** *(of spacecraft)* jiànluò 溅落

♦ **splash out** *(in spending)* dàshǒu dàjiǎo de huāqián 大手大脚地花钱; *I splashed out on a round the world trip* wǒ dàshǒu dàjiǎo de huāqián zài yīgè huánqiú lǚxíng shàng wǒ 大手大脚地花钱在一个环球旅行上

splendid jíhǎo 极好

splendor *(of achievement)* guānghuī cànlàn 光辉灿烂; *(of building, ceremony)* zhuàngguān 壮观

splint *n* MED jiábǎn 夹板

splinter 1 *n* cì 刺 **2** *v/i* fēnliè 分裂

splinter group xiǎo pàibié 小派别

split 1 *n (damage)* lièkǒu 裂口; *(disagreement)* fēnliè 分裂; *(division, share)* fēngè 分割 **2** *v/t (damage)* lièkāi 裂开; *logs* pī 劈; *(cause disagreement in)* fēnliè 分裂; *(divide)* fēn 分 **3** *v/i (tear)* lièkāi 裂开; *(disagree)* fēnliè 分裂

♦ **split up** *v/i (of couple)* fēnshǒu 分手

split personality PSYCH fēnliè rénge 分裂人格

splitting headache jùliè de tóutòng 剧烈的头痛

spoil *v/t child* chǒnghuài 宠坏; *party, fun* pòhuài ... de xìngzhì pòhuài ... 的兴致; *cooking, essay etc* nòngzāo 弄糟

spoilsport F bàixìng zhě 败兴者

spoilt *adj child* chǒnghuài 宠坏; *be ~ for choice* tàiduō xuǎnzé le 太多选择了

spoke *(of wheel)* chētiáo 车条

spokesman fāyánrén 发言人

spokesperson fāyánrén 发言人

spokeswoman fāyánrén 发言人

sponge *n* hǎimián 海绵

♦ **sponge off, sponge on** F kào ... báichī shí 靠 ... 白吃食

sponger F jìshēng chóng 寄生虫

sponsor 1 *n* dānbǎo rén 担保人 **2** *v/t* dānbǎo 担保

sponsorship dānbǎo 担保

spontaneous zìfā 自发; *person* zìrán 自然

spooky F yīn sēnsēn 阴森森

spool *n (for film)* juǎnpán 卷盘; *(for thread)* xiànzhóu 线轴

spoon *n* sháo 勺

spoonfeed *fig* tiányā shì guànshū 填鸭式灌输

spoonful: two ~s of sugar liǎng sháo táng 两勺糖

sporadic língsǎn 零散

sport *n* tǐyù yùndòng 体育运动

sporting *event* tǐyù yùndòng 体育运动; *(fair, generous)* dàfang 大方; *a ~ gesture* dàfang de jǔdòng 大方的举动

sportscar pǎochē 跑车; **sports-coat** yùndòng shàngyī 运动上衣; **sports journalist** tǐyù jìzhě 体育记者; **sportsman** yùndòng yuán 运动员; **sports news** tǐyù xīnwén 体育新闻; **sports page** tǐyù bǎn 体育版; **sportswoman** yùndòng yuán 运动员

sporty *person* àihào yùndòng 爱好运动; *clothes* huāshao 花哨

spot[1] *(pimple)* fěncì 粉刺; *(caused by measles etc)* qiūzhěn 丘疹; *(part of pattern)* bāndiǎn 斑点儿

spot[2] *(place)* dìdiǎn 地点; *on the ~ (in the place in question)* zài xiànchǎng 在现场; *(immediately)* dāngchǎng 当场; *put X on the ~* shǐ X nánkān 使X难堪

spot[3] *v/t (notice)* zhǎodào 找到; *(identify)* biànrèn 辨认

spot check chōuyàng jiǎnchá 抽样检查; **carry out spot checks** jìnxíng chōuyàng jiǎnchá 进行抽样检查

spotless yīchén bùrǎn 一尘不染

spotlight *n* jùguāng dēng 聚光灯

spotted *fabric* huādiǎn 花点

spotty (*with pimples*) duō fěncì 多粉刺

spouse *fml* pèi'ǒu 配偶

spout 1 *n* zuǐ zuǐ 嘴嘴 **2** *v/i* (*of liquid*) pēnchū 喷出

sprain *n & v/t* niǔshāng 扭伤

Spratley Islands Nánshā Qúndǎo 南沙群岛

sprawl *v/i* shēnkāi sìzhī 伸开四肢; (*of city*) mànyán 蔓延; **send X ~ing** (*of punch*) bǎ X shuāi pā zài dìshàng 把 X 摔趴在地上

sprawling *city, suburbs* mànyán 蔓延

spray 1 *n* (*of sea water*) lànghuā 浪花; (*from fountain*) shuǐhuā 水花; (*paint*) pēnqī 喷漆; (*for hair*) pēnfà jiāo 喷发胶; (*container*) pēnwù qì 喷雾器 **2** *v/t* pēn 喷; **~ X with Y** gěi X pēn Y 给 X 喷 Y

spraygun pēnqiāng 喷枪

spread 1 *n* (*of disease, religion etc*) mànyán mànyán 蔓延; F (*big meal*) shèngyàn 盛宴 **2** *v/t* (*lay*) tānkāi 摊开; *butter* mǒ 抹; *news, rumor, disease* chuánbō 传播; *arms, legs* shēnzhǎn 伸展 **3** *v/i* (*of fire*) mànyán 蔓延; (*of rumor, news, disease*) chuánbō 传播; (*of butter*) mǒ 抹

spreadsheet COMPUT biǎogé 表格

spree: **go (out) on a ~** F tòngkuài yīfān 痛快一番; **go on a shopping ~** dàmǎi tèmǎi yīfān 大买特买一番

sprightly huópo 活泼

spring[1] *n* (*season*) chūntiān 春天

spring[2] *n* (*device*) tánhuáng 弹簧

spring[3] *n* (*stream*) quán yuán 泉

spring[4] *n & v/i* (*jump*) tiàoyuè 跳跃
♦ **spring from** láizì 来自

springboard tiàobǎn 跳板;
  spring chicken: she's no ~ hum tā shàngle niánjì 她上了年纪;
  spring-cleaning dà sǎochú 大扫

除; **Spring Festival** Chūnjié 春节; **springtime** chūntiān 春天

springy *mattress, ground* yǒu tánxìng 有弹性; *walk* qīngkuài 轻快

sprinkle *v/t* sǎ 撒; **~ X with Y** jiāng X sǎzài Y shàng 将 X 撒在 Y 上

sprinkler (*for garden*) pēnsǎ qì 喷撒器; (*in ceiling*) pēnshuǐ zhuāngzhì 喷水装置

sprint *n & v/i* bēnpǎo 奔跑

sprinter SP duǎnpǎo yùndòng yuán 短跑运动员

sprout 1 *v/i* (*of seed*) fāyá 发芽 **2** *n* xīnyá 新芽; (*Brussels*) **~s** qiúzhuàng gānlán 球状甘蓝

spruce *adj* zhěngjié piàoliàng 整洁漂亮

spur *n* fig jīlì 激励; **on the ~ of the moment** píng yīshíde chōngdòng 凭一时的冲动
♦ **spur on** (*encourage*) jīlì … qiánjìn 激励 … 前进

spurt 1 *v/i* (*in race*) chōngcì 冲刺; **put on a ~** jiāsù fēibēn 加速飞奔 **2** *v/i* (*of liquid*) pēnshè 喷射

spy 1 *n* jiàndié jiàndié 间谍 **2** *v/i* (*of spy*) cóngshì jiàndié huódòng 从事间谍活动 **3** *v/t* F fāxiàn 发现
♦ **spy on** ànzhōng jiānshì 暗中监视

squabble *n & v/i* zhēngchǎo 争吵

squalid āngzāng 肮脏

squalor wūhuì wūhuì 污秽

squander *money* huīhuò 挥霍

square 1 *adj* (*in shape*) fāng 方; **~ mile/yard** píngfāng yīnglǐ/mǎ píng 平方英里/码 **2** *n* (*shape*) sìfāng xíng 四方形; (*in town*) guǎngchǎng 广场; (*in board game*) gé 格; MATH píngfāng 平方; **we're back to ~ one** wǒmen yòu huídào qǐdiǎn le 我们又回到起点了

square root píngfāng gēn 平方根

squash[1] *n* (*vegetable*) nánguā 南瓜

squash[2] *n* (*game*) bìqiú 壁球

squash[3] *v/t* (*crush*) yālàn 压烂

squat 1 *adj* (*in shape*) ǎi ǎi 矮 **2** *v/i* (*sit*) dūn 蹲; (*illegally*) shànzì zhànyòng 擅自占用

squatter shànzì zhàndì zhě 擅自占地者

squeak 1 n (of mouse) zhīzhi shēng 吱吱声; (of hinge) zhīgā shēng 吱嘎声 **2** v/i (of mouse) zhīzhi jiào 吱吱叫; (of hinge, shoes) zhīgā zuòxiǎng 吱嘎作响

squeal 1 n cháng ér jiān de jiàoshēng 长而尖的叫声 **2** v/i fāchū cháng ér jiān de jiàoshēng 发出长而尖的叫声

squeamish jiāoqì 娇气

squeeze 1 n (of hand, shoulder) jǐnwò 紧握 **2** v/t (press) jǐ 挤; package etc yònglì niē 用力捏; shoulder, hand jǐnwò 紧握; (remove juice from) zhà 榨

♦**squeeze in** v/i (to a car etc) jǐ jìn 挤进 **2** v/t sāi jìn 塞进

♦**squeeze up** v/i (to make space) jǐjīn 挤紧

squid yóuyú 鱿鱼

squint n xiéyǎn 斜眼

squirm (wriggle) niǔdòng 扭动; (in embarrassment) júcù bù'ān 局促不安

squirrel n sōngshǔ 松鼠

squirt 1 v/t pēnshè 喷射 **2** n pej wàngzì zūndà de rén 妄自尊大的人

stab 1 n F chángshì 尝试 **2** v/t person cì 刺

stability wěndìng 稳定

stabilize 1 v/t prices, currency wěndìng 稳定; boat pínghéng 平衡 **2** v/i (of prices etc) wěndìng 稳定

stable¹ n (for horses) mǎjiù 马厩

stable² adj wěndìng 稳定

stack 1 n (pile) dié dié 叠叠; (smokestack) dà yāncōng 大烟囱 **2** v/t bǎ ... diéchéng duī 把 ... 叠成堆

stadium tǐyùchǎng 体育场

staff n (employees) gùyuán 雇员; (teachers) jiàoyuán 教员

staffroom (in school) jiàoyuán shì 教员室

stage¹ (in life, project etc) jiēduàn 阶段; (of journey) duàn lù 段路

stage² **1** n THEA wǔtái 舞台; go on the ~ dāng yǎnyuán 当演员 **2** v/t play biǎoyǎn 表演; demonstration, strike jǔxíng 举行

stage door jùchǎng hòumén 剧场后门

stagger 1 v/i diēdie zhuàngzhuang 跌跌撞撞 **2** v/t (amaze) shǐ chījīng 使吃惊; coffee breaks etc cuòkāi 错开

staggering lìngrén chījīng 令人吃惊

stagnant water bù liúdòng 不流动; economy tíngzhì 停滞

stagnate fig (of person, mind) bù fāzhǎn 不发展

stag party hūnqián nánzi jùhuì 婚前男子聚会

stain 1 n (dirty mark) wūjì 污迹; (for wood) rǎnsè jì 染色剂 **2** v/t (dirty) zhānwū 沾污; wood rǎnsè 染色 **3** v/i (of wine etc) chǎnshēng wūjì 产生污迹; (of fabric) yìcún wūjì 易存污迹

stained-glass window cǎisè bōli chuāng 彩色玻璃窗

stainless steel n búxiùgāng 不锈钢

stain remover qùwū jì 去污剂

stair tǐjī 梯级; the ~s lóutī 楼梯

staircase lóutī 楼梯

stake 1 n (of wood) zhuāng 桩; (when gambling) dǔzhù 赌注; (investment) gǔfèn 股份; be at ~ zài wēixiǎn zhōng 在危险中 **2** v/t tree yòng zhuāng zhīchēng 用桩支撑; money xià dǔzhù 下赌注; person zīzhù 资助

stale bread zǒuwèir 走味儿; air mēn 闷; fig: news guòshí 过时

stalemate (in chess) jiāngjú 僵局; fig jiāngjú 僵局

Stalin Sīdàlín 斯大林

stalk¹ n (of fruit, plant) gěng 梗

stalk² v/t (follow) gēnzōng 跟踪

stalker (of person) gēnzōng zhě 跟踪者

stall¹ n (at market) tānzi 摊子; (for cow, horse) péng 棚

stall² **1** v/i (of engine) xīhuǒ 熄火; (of vehicle, plane) pāomáo 抛锚; (play for time) tuōyán 拖延 **2** v/t engine xīhuǒ 熄火; people fūyǎn 敷衍

stallion mǔmǎ 牡马

stalwart *adj support, supporter* jiāndìng 坚定

stamina nàilì 耐力

stammer n & v/i jiēba 结巴

stamp[1] 1 n (for letter) yóupiào 邮票; (device) yìnchuō 印戳; (mark made with device) yìn 印 2 v/t letter tiē yóupiào 贴邮票; document, passport gàizhāng 盖章

stamp[2] v/t: ~ one's feet duòjiǎo 跺脚

♦ **stamp out** (eradicate) xiāomiè 消灭

stampede n (of cattle etc) jīngpǎo 惊跑; (of people) fēngyōng 蜂拥

stance (position) tàidù 态度

stand 1 n (at exhibition) tānzi 摊子; (witness ~) zhèngrén xí 证人席; (support, base) zuò 座; take the ~ LAW zuòchéng 作证 2 v/i (be situated: of person) zhànlì 站立; (of object) bèi fàngzhì 被放置; (of building) sōnglì 耸立; (as opposed to sit) zhànzhe 站着; (rise) qǐlì 起立; ~ still yídòng bùdòng 一动不动; where do I ~ with you? wǒmen jiūjìng shì shénme guānxi? 我们究竟是什么关系? 3 v/t (tolerate) rěnshòu 忍受; (put) shùfàng 竖放; you don't ~ a chance nǐ gēnběn méi jīhuì 你根本没机会; ~ one's ground jiānchí zìjǐ de lìchǎng 坚持自己的立场

♦ **stand back** hòutuì 后退

♦ **stand by** 1 v/i (not take action) xiùshǒu pángguān 袖手旁观; (be ready) zuò hǎo zhǔnbèi 作好准备 2 v/t person zhīchí 支持; decision jiānchí 坚持

♦ **stand down** (withdraw) tuìchū 退出

♦ **stand for** (tolerate) róngrěn 容忍; (represent) dàibiǎo 代表

♦ **stand in for** dàitì 代替

♦ **stand out** yǐnrén zhùmù 引人注目

♦ **stand up** 1 v/i zhàn qǐlái 站起来 2 v/t: stand X up F (on date) ràng X báiděng 让X白等

♦ **stand up for** wéihù 维护

♦ **stand up to** miànduì 面对

standard 1 adj (usual) chángguī 常规 2 n (level of excellence) shuǐzhǔn 水准; (expectation), TECH biāozhǔn 标准; be up to ~ fúhé biāozhǔn 符合标准; not be up to ~ bù fúhé biāozhǔn 不符合标准

standard of living shēnghuó shuǐzhǔn 生活水准

standardize v/t shǐ biāozhǔn huà 使标准化

standby: on ~ (for flight) hòubǔ 候补

standby passenger hòubǔ lǚkè 候补旅客

standing n (in society etc) dìwèi 地位; (repute) shēngyù 声誉; a musician / politician of some ~ zhuóyuè de yīnyuèjiā / zhèngzhìjiā 卓越的音乐家 / 政治家

standing room zhànlì kōngjiān 站立空间

standoffish lěngmò 冷漠; **standpoint** guāndiǎn 观点; **standstill**: be at a ~ tíngdùn tíngdùn 停顿; bring ... to a ~ shǐ ... tíngdùn tíng ... 停顿

staple[1] n (foodstuff) zhǔshí 主食

staple[2] 1 n (fastener) dìngshūdīng 订书钉 2 v/t dìng 钉

staple diet zhǔshí 主食

staple gun tiěsī dìngshūjī 铁丝订书机

stapler dìngshūjī 订书机

star 1 n (in sky) xīng 星; fig míngxīng 明星 2 v/t (of movie) zhǔyǎn 主演 3 v/i (in movie) zhǔyǎn 主演

starboard adj yòuxián 右舷

stare 1 n níngshì 凝视 2 v/i mùbù zhuǎnjīng de kàn 目不转睛地看; ~ at dīngzhe 盯着

starfish hǎixīng 海星

stark 1 adj landscape huāngliáng 荒凉; room, surroundings kōng luòluo 空落落; reminder, etc yánkù 严酷; contrast xiānmíng 鲜明 2 adv: ~ naked yīsī bùguà 一丝不挂

starling liángniǎo 椋鸟

Stars and Stripes Xīngtiáo qí 星条旗

条旗

start 1 n (*beginning*) kāitóu 开头 ; **get off to a good / bad ~** (*in race, marriage, career*) yīkāishǐ hěnhǎo / zāo 一 开始很好 / 糟 ; **from the ~** yīkāishǐ 一 开始 ; **well, it's a ~!** qǐmǎ kāigètóu! 起码开个头 ! **2** v/i kāishǐ 开始 ; (*of engine, car*) fādòng 发动 ; **~ing from tomorrow** cóng míngtiān kāishǐ 从明天开始 **3** v/t kāishǐ 开始 ; *engine, car* fādòng 发动 ; *business* chuàngbàn 创办 ; **~ to do X, ~ doing X** kāishǐ zuò X 开始做 X

starter (*part of meal*) tóupán 头盘 ; (*of car*) qǐdòng zhuāngzhì 起动装置

starting point (*for walk, discussion, thesis*) chūfā diǎn 出发点

starting salary qǐshǐ gōngzī 起始工资

startle: ~ X shǐ X xià yītiào 使 X 吓一跳

startling jīngrén 惊人

starvation jī'è 饥饿

starve v/i ái'è 挨饿 ; **~ to death** èsǐ 饿死 ; **I'm starving** F wǒ èsǐ le 我饿死了

state¹ 1 n (*of car, house etc*) zhuàngkuàng 状况 ; (*part of country*) zhōu 州 ; (*country*) guójiā 国家 ; **the States** Měiguó 美国 **2** adj *capital etc* zhōu 州 ; (*ceremonial*) zhèngshì 正式 ; **~ banquet** guóyàn 国宴

state² v/t shēngmíng 声明

State Department Guówù Yuàn 国务院

statement (*to police*) kǒugòng 口供 ; (*announcement*) shēngmíng 声明 ; (*bank ~*) jiésuàn dān 结算单

state of emergency jǐnjí zhuàngtài 紧急状态

state-of-the-art adj zuì yōuliáng 最优良

statesman zhèngzhì jiā 政治家

state trooper zhōu jǐngchá 州警察

state visit guówù fǎngwèn 国务访问

static (electricity) jìngdiàn 静电

station 1 n RAIL huǒchē zhàn 火车站 ; RADIO, TV diàntái 电台 **2** v/t *guard etc* zhùzhā 驻扎 ; **be ~ed at** (*of soldier*) zhùzhā zài 驻扎在

stationary jìngzhǐ 静止

stationery wénjù 文具

station wagon kèhuò liǎngyòng jiàochē 客货两用轿车

statistical tǒngjì 统计

statistically cóng tǒngjìxué jiǎodù láishuō 从统计学角度来说

statistics (*science*) tǒngjì xué 统计学 ; (*figures*) tǒngjì zīliào 统计资料

statue sùxiàng 塑像

Statue of Liberty Zìyóu Nǚshén Xiàng 自由女神像

status dìwèi 地位

status symbol shēnfènde xiàngzhēng 身份的象征

statute fǎlìng 法令

staunch adj jiāndìng 坚定

stay 1 n dòuliú 逗留 **2** v/i (*in a place*) dòuliú 逗留 ; (*in a condition*) bǎochí 保持 ; **~ at home** dāi zài jiā lǐ 呆在家里 ; **~ in a hotel** dāi zài lǚguǎn 呆在旅馆 ; **~ right there!** biédòng! 别动 ! ; **~ put** (*don't move*) bié zǒukāi 别走开 ; **~ put in** (*in job, city*) yǒngyuǎn dāizài 永远呆在

♦ **stay away** líkāi 离开

♦ **stay away from** bù jiējìn 不接近

♦ **stay behind** wǎnzǒu 晚走

♦ **stay up** (*not go to bed*) bù qùshuì 不去睡

steadily *improve etc* zhújiàn 逐渐

steady 1 adj (*not shaking*) píngwěn 平稳 ; (*regular*) yǒu guīlǜ 有规律 ; (*continuous*) chíxù 持续 **2** adv: **be going ~** zuò qínglǚ 做情侣 ; **~ on!** yōu zhe diǎn! 悠着点儿 ! **3** v/t wěnzhù 稳住

steak niúpái 牛排

steal 1 v/t *money etc* tōu 偷 **2** v/i (*be a thief*) tōu dōngxi 偷东西 ; (*move quietly*) qiāoqiāode xíngzǒu 悄悄地行走

stealthy qiāoqiāo 悄悄

steam 1 n zhēngqì 蒸汽 **2** v/t *food*

zhēng 蒸

◆ **steam up 1** *v/i* (*of window etc*) méngshàng shuǐqì 蒙上水汽

2 *v/t*: **be steamed up** F nǎohuǒ 恼火

steamed bread mántou 馒头

steamer (*for cooking*) zhēngguō 蒸锅

steam iron zhēngqì diàn yùndǒu 蒸汽电熨斗

steel *n* & *adj* gāng 钢

steep¹ *adj hill etc* dǒu 陡; F *prices* guì 贵

steep² *v/t* (*soak*) pào 泡

steeple jiāntǎ 尖塔

steeplechase (*in athletics*) yuèyě sài 越野赛

steer¹ *n* (*animal*) yān gōngniú 阉公牛

steer² *v/t car, boat* jiàshǐ 驾驶; *person* yǐndǎo 引导; *conversation* diàozhuǎn 掉转

steering (*of motor vehicle*) jiàshǐ jīgòu 驾驶机构

steering wheel fāngxiàng pán 方向盘

stem¹ *n* (*of plant*) gàn 干; (*of glass*) jīng 茎; (*of pipe*) bǐng 柄; (*of word*) cígàn 词干

◆ **stem from** qǐyuán yú 起源于

stem² *v/t* (*block*) zhìzhǐ 制止

stemware bōli qìmǐn 玻璃器皿

stench èchòu 恶臭

step 1 *n* (*pace*) bù 步; (*stair*) jiētī 阶梯; (*measure*) cuòshī 措施; (*decision*) juédìng 决定; **~ by ~** zhúbùde 逐步地 **2** *v/i* (*put feet in/on sth*) cǎi 踩; (*walk forward*) zǒu 走

◆ **step down** (*from post etc*) ràngwèi 让位

◆ **step out** (*go out for a short time*) chūqù yīhuìr 出去一会儿

◆ **step up** *v/t* (*increase*) jiākuài 加快

stepbrother jìxiōngdì 继兄弟; **stepdaughter** jìnǚ 继女; **stepfather** jìfù 继父; **stepladder** zhétī 折梯; **stepmother** jìmǔ 继母

stepping stone tàijiǎo shí 踏脚石; *fig* jìnshēn zhījiē 进身之阶

stepsister (*same father different mother*) tóngfù yìmǔ jiěmèi 同父异母姐妹; (*same mother different father*) tóngmǔ yìfù jiěmèi 同母异父姐妹

stepson jìzǐ 继子

stereo *n* (*sound system*) yīnxiǎng 音响

stereotype *n* chéngjiàn 成见

sterile *woman, man* bùyù 不育; MED xiāodú 消毒

sterilize *woman* jiézhá 结扎; *equipment* xiāodú 消毒

sterling *n* FIN yīngbàng 英镑

stern *adj* yánsù 严肃

steroids jīsù 激素

stethoscope tīngzhěnqì 听诊器

Stetson® Sītàisēn Zhānmào 斯泰森毡帽

stevedore zhuāngxiè gōng 装卸工

stew *n* dùn shípǐn 炖食品

steward (*on plane, ship*) chéngwùyuán 乘务员

stewardess (*on plane, ship*) chéngwùyuán 乘务员

stick¹ *n* (*wood*) mùgùn 木棍; (*of policeman*) jǐnggùn 警棍; (*walking ~*) guǎizhàng 拐杖; **the ~s** F xiāngxià 乡下

stick² **1** *v/t* (*with adhesive*) niánzhù 粘住; F (*put*) fàng 放 **2** *v/i* (*jam*) qiǎ zhù le 卡住了; (*adhere*) niánzhù 粘住

◆ **stick around** F dāi yīhuìr 呆一会儿

◆ **stick by**: **~ X** F zhōngyú X 忠于 X

◆ **stick out** *v/i* (*protrude*) tūchū 突出; (*be noticeable*) xiǎnyǎn 显眼

◆ **stick to** (*adhere to*) niánzài ... shàngmiàn 粘在 ... 上面; F (*keep to*) jiānchí 坚持; *path, road* yánzhe 沿着; F (*follow*) jǐnsuí 紧随

◆ **stick together** F dāi zài yīqǐ 呆在一起

◆ **stick up** *poster, leaflet* shùqǐ 竖起

◆ **stick up for** F wèi ... biànhù 为 ... 辩护

◆ **stick with** F jiānchí 坚持

sticker biāoqiān 标签

sticking plaster hùchuānggāo 护

创膏
stick-in-the-mud mòshǒu chéng-guī zhě 墨守成规者
sticky hands, surface nián hūhu 黏糊糊; a ~ label tiēqiān 贴签
stiff 1 adj brush, cardboard, leather yìng bāngbang 硬邦邦; muscle, body jiāngyìng 僵硬; mixture, paste chóu mǐ; (in manner) jūjǐn 拘谨; drink nóngliè 浓裂; fine, penalty yánlì 严厉; competition jīliè 激烈 2 adv: be scared ~ hěn hàipà 很害怕; be bored ~ mènsǐle 闷死了
stiffen v/i biànde jǐnzhāng 变得紧张
♦ stiffen up (of muscle) biàn jiāngyìng 变僵硬
stifle v/t yawn, laugh rěnzhe 忍着; criticism, debate èshā 扼杀
stifling lìngrén zhìxī 令人窒息
stigma chǐrǔ 耻辱
stilettos (shoes) xì gāo gēnxié 细高跟鞋
still¹ 1 adj píngjìng 平静 2 adv: keep ~! bié dònglái dòngqù! 别动来动去！; stand ~! biédòng! 别动！
still² adv (yet) hái 还; (nevertheless) wúlùn rúhé 无论如何; do you ~ want it? nǐ háiyào ma? 你还要吗？; she ~ hasn't finished tā hái méiwán ne 她还没完呢; she might ~ come tā kěnéng réngrán huìlái 她可能仍然会来; they are ~ my parents tāmen zǒng háishì wǒde fùmǔ a 他们总还是我的父母啊; ~ more (even more) gèngduō 更多
stillborn: be ~ sǐchǎn 死产
stilted bú zìrán 不自然
stilts (under house) chēngzhù 撑柱
stimulant xīngfèn jì 兴奋剂
stimulate person cìjī 刺激; growth, demand cùjìn 促进
stimulating zhènfèn rénxīn 振奋人心
stimulation jīlì 激励
stimulus (incentive) dònglì 动力
sting 1 n (from bee, jellyfish) zhēcì 螫刺 2 v/t (of bee, jellyfish) zhē 螫

3 v/i (of eyes) fātòng 发痛; (of scratch) gǎndào cìtòng 感到刺痛
stinging remark, criticism kèbó 刻薄
stingy F kōuménr 抠门儿
stink 1 n (bad smell) chòuwèir 臭味儿; F (fuss) xuānrán dàbō 轩然大波; make a ~ F dànào yīchǎng 大闹一场 2 v/i (smell bad) dài chòuwèir 带臭味儿; F (be very bad) zāoitòule 精透了
stint n guīdìng de rènqī 规定的任期; do a ~ in the army fú bīngyì 服兵役
♦ stint on jiéshěng 节省
stipulate guīdìng 规定
stipulation tiáojiàn 条件
stir 1 n: give the soup a ~ jiǎo yī jiǎo tāng 搅一搅汤; cause a ~ fig yǐnqǐ yīchǎng fēngbō 引起一场风波 2 v/t jiǎobàn 搅拌 3 v/i (of sleeping person) nuódòng 挪动
♦ stir up crowd shāndòng 煽动; bad memories huíyì qǐ 回忆起
stir-crazy: be ~ F juànhuàile 圈坏了
stir-fry v/t wànghuǒ biānchǎo 旺火煸炒
stirring music, speech jīdòng rénxīn 激动人心
stitch 1 n (in sewing) zhēnjiǎo 针脚; (in knitting) yīzhēn 一针; ~es MED féngzhēn 缝针; have a ~ tūrán jùtòng 突然剧痛 2 v/t sew féng 缝
♦ stitch up wound féng qǐlái 缝起来
stitching (stitches) xiàn线
stock 1 n (reserves) chǔcún 储存; (COM: of store) huò 货; (animals) shēngchù 牲畜; FIN gǔpiào 股票; (food) tāng 汤; in / out of ~ yǒu / wúhuò 有 / 无货; take ~ píngjū评估 2 v/t COM bèiyǒu 备有
♦ stock up on chǔbèi 储备
stockbroker gǔpiào jīngjìrén 股票经纪人
stock exchange gǔpiào jiāoyìsuǒ 股票交易所; stockholder gǔdōng 股东
stocking chángtǒngwà 长统袜

stock market gǔpiào shìchǎng 股票市场; **stockmarket crash** gǔpiào shìchǎng bàodiē 股票市场暴跌; **stockpile 1** n (of food, weapons) chǔbèi wùzī 储备物资 **2** v/t chǔbèi 储备; **stockroom** cāngkù 仓库; **stocktaking** pándiǎn 盘点

stocky ǎizhuàng 矮壮

stock-still: *stand ~* yīdòng búdòng 一动不动

stodgy food yìbǎo 易饱

stomach 1 n (insides) dùzi 肚子; (abdomen) fùbù 腹部 **2** v/t (tolerate) rěnshòu 忍受

stomach-ache dùzi téng 肚子疼

stone n (material, pebble) shítou 石头; (precious ~) bǎoshí 宝石

stoned F (on drugs) mázuì 麻醉

stone-deaf wánquán lóng 完全聋

stonewall v/i F tángsè 搪塞

stony ground, path duōshí 多石

stool (seat) dèngzi 凳子

stoop[1] 1 n wānyāo qūbèi 弯腰曲背 **2** v/i (bend down) wānyāo 弯腰; (have bent back) hāyāo 哈腰

stoop[2] n (porch) ménláng 门廊

stop 1 n (for train, bus) zhàn 站; *come to a ~* tíngle 停了; *put a ~ to* tíngzhǐ 停止 **2** v/t (put an end to, cease) zhǐzhǐ 阻止; person in street lánzhù 拦住; car, bus, train, etc: of driver tíng 停; of pedestrian lánzhù 拦住; *~ talking immediately!* mǎshàng zhùzuǐ! 马上住嘴！; *I ~ped her from leaving* wǒ búràng tā ǒzu 我不让她走; *it has ~ped raining* yǔtíngle 雨停了; *~ a check* tíngzhǐ duìfù zhīpiào 停止兑付支票 **3** v/i tíng 停
- **stop by** (visit) shùnbiàn guòfǎng 顺便过访
♦ **stop off** zhōngtú tíngliú 中途停留
♦ **stop over** zhōngtú tíngliú 中途停留
♦ **stop up** sink dǔsāi 堵塞

stopgap línshí tìdài 临时替代; **stoplight** (traffic light) hónglǜdēng 红绿灯; (brake light) shāchē

dēng 刹车灯; **stopover** dòuliú 逗留; (in air travel) zhōngtú tíngliú 中途停留

stopper (for bath, basin) sāizi 塞子; (for bottle) píngsāi 瓶塞

stopping: *no ~* (sign) bùzhǔn tíngchē 不准停车

stop sign tíngchē biāozhì 停车标志

stopwatch miǎobiǎo 秒表

storage zhùcáng 贮藏; *put X in ~* bǎ X zhùcáng qǐlái 把X贮藏起来; *be in ~* zài zhùcáng kù 在贮藏库

storage capacity COMPUT cúnchǔ róngliàng 存储容量

storage space zhùcún kōngjiān 贮存空间

store 1 n shāngdiàn 商店; (stock) chǔbèi 储备; (storehouse) cāngkù 仓库 **2** v/t cúnfàng 存放; COMPUT chǔcún 储存

storefront línjiē diànpù 临街店铺; **storehouse** cāngkù 仓库; **storekeeper** diànzhǔ 店主; **storeroom** cāngkù 仓库; **store window** shāngdiàn chúchuāng 商店橱窗

storm n bàofēngyǔ 暴风雨

storm drain yǔshuǐ dào 雨水道; **storm window** wàichóng chuāng 外重窗; **storm warning** fēngbào jǐngbào 风暴警报

stormy weather yǒu bàofēngyǔ 有暴风雨; relationship yībō sānzhé 一波三折

story[1] (tale) gùshì 故事; (account) xùshù 叙述; (newspaper article) bàodào bàodào 报道; F (lie) huǎnghuà 谎话

story[2] (of building) céng 层

stout adj person féipàng 肥胖; boots nàichuān 耐穿

stove (for cooking) lúzi lúzi 炉子; (for heating) jiārè qì 加热器

stow chǔcáng 储藏
♦ **stow away** v/i (on ship) wúpiào tōuchéng 无票偷乘

stowaway wúpiào tōuchéng zhě 无票偷乘者

straight 1 adj line, hair zhí 直; back

bǐzhí 笔直; (*honest, direct*) tǎnshuài 坦率; (*not criminal*) zhèngpài 正派; (*whiskey etc*) chún纯; (*tidy*) zhěngqí 整齐; (*conservative*) bǎoshǒu 保守; (*not homosexual*) fēi tóngxìngliàn 非同性恋; **be a ~ A student** chéngjì yōuxiùde xuésheng 成绩优秀的学生 **2** *adv* (*in a straight line*) jìngzhí 径直; (*directly, immediately*) zhíjiē 直接; (*clearly*) zhèngquè 正确; **stand up ~!** zhànzhíle! 站直了!; **look X ~ in the eye** dīngzhe X de yǎnjing 盯着 X 的眼睛; **go ~** F (*of criminal*) gǎixié guīzhèng 改邪归正; **give it to me ~** F tǎnbái gàosù wǒ 坦白告诉我; **~ ahead be situated** jiùzài qiánmiàn 就在前面; **walk, drive** zhízhe zǒu 直着走; **look** xiàngqián kàn 向前看; **carry ~ on** (*of driver etc*) zhízhe zǒu 直着走; **~away, ~ off** mǎshàng 马上; **~ out** zhíjiēliǎodàng 直截了当; **~ up** (*without ice*) bù jiābīng 不加冰

straighten *v/t* nòngzhí 弄直

♦ **straighten out 1** *v/t situation* jiěshì qīng 解释清 **2** *v/i* (*of road*) biànzhí 变直

♦ **straighten up** tǐngzhí 挺直

straightforward (*honest, direct*) zhíjiéle liǎodàng 直截了当; (*simple*) jiǎndān 简单

strain[1] *n* (*on rope, engine, heart*) zuòyòng lì 作用力; (*on person*) zhòngfù 重负 **2** *v/t* (*injure*) shāng 伤; *fig: finances, budget* shíjiā yālì 施加压力

strain[2] *v/t vegetables* lǜgān 滤干; *oil, fat etc* guòlǜ 过滤

strainer (*for vegetables etc*) guòlǜ qì 过滤器

strait hǎixiá 海峡

straitlaced gǔbǎn 古板

strand[1] *n* (*of hair, wool, thread*) lǚlǚ 缕缕

strand[2] *v/t* shǐ chǔyú kùnjìng 使处于困境; **be ~ed** chǔyú kùnjìng 处于困境

strange (*odd, curious*) qíguài 奇怪; (*unknown, foreign*) mòshēng 陌生

strangely (*oddly*) qíguài 奇怪; **~ enough** chūhū yìliào外 出乎意料

stranger (*person you don't know*) mòshēng rén 陌生人; **I'm a ~ here myself** wǒ duì zhèlǐ yě hěn mòshēng 我对这里也很陌生

strangle *person* èsǐ 扼死

strap *n* (*of schoolbag*) shūbāo dài 书包带; (*of bra, dress*) jiāndài 肩带; (*of watch*) biǎodài 表带; (*of shoe*) xiédài 鞋带

♦ **strap in** jìhǎo ānquándài 系好安全带

strapless wúdài 无带

strategic zhànlüè 战略

strategy zhànlüè 战略

straw[1] cǎo 草; **that's the last ~!** zuìzhōng shǐrén wúfǎ rěnshòu! 最终使人无法忍受!

straw[2] (*for drink*) xīguǎn 吸管

strawberry cǎoméi 草莓

stray 1 *adj animal* shīsàn 失散; *bullet* liúdàn 流弹 **2** *n* (*dog*) zǒushī de gǒu 走失的狗; (*cat*) zǒushī de māo 走失的猫 **3** *v/i* (*of animal, child*) zǒushī 走失; *fig* (*of eyes, thoughts*) bùyóu zìzhǔ 不由自主

streak (*of dirt, paint*) tiáowén 条纹; *fig* (*of nastiness etc*) gèxìngde yímiàn 个性的一面; **he's got a cruel ~** tā yǒudiǎn cánrěn 他有点儿残忍 *v/i* (*move quickly*) fēibēn 飞奔 **3** *v/t*: **be ~ed with ...** yǒu ... de hénjì 有 ... 的痕迹

stream 1 *n fig* (*of people, complaints*) yìliánchuàn 一连串; **come on ~** kāishǐ shēngchǎn 开始生产 **2** *v/i* yuányuán búduàn 源源不断; **sunlight ~ed into the room** yángguāng zhàoshè rù fángjiān 阳光照射入房间

streamer héngfú 横幅

streamline *v/t fig* tígāo xiàolǜ 提高效率

streamlined *car, plane* liúxiànxíng 流线型; *fig: organization* gāo xiàolǜ 高效率

street jiēdào 街道

streetcar yǒuguǐ diànchē 有轨电车; **streetlight** jiēdēng 街灯;

streetpeople piāobó jiētóu rénshì 漂泊街头人士；**streetwalker** jìnǚ 妓女；**streetwise** adj yǒu chéngshì shēnghuó nénglì 有城市生活能力

strength (of person: physical) lìqì 力气；fig (strong point) yōudiǎn 优点；(of wind, current) qiángdù 强度；(of emotion, friendship etc) lìliàng 力量；(of organization, country, currency) shílì 实力

strengthen 1 v/t jiāqiáng 加强 **2** v/i biànqiáng 变强

strenuous jiānkǔ 艰苦

stress 1 n (emphasis) zhòngdiǎn 重点；(tension) yālì 压力；**be under ~** shòudào yālì 受到压力 **2** v/t syllable zhòngdú 重读；importance etc qiángdiào 强调；**I must ~ that ...** wǒ bìxū qiángdiào ... 我必须强调...

stressed out F jiāotóulàn'é 焦头烂额

stressful jǐnzhāng 紧张

stretch 1 n (of land, water) piàn piàn 片片；**at a ~** (non-stop) liánxù 连续 **2** adj fabric kě shēnsuō 可伸缩 **3** v/t material shēnzhǎn 伸展；small income jiéyuē 节约；F rules hūlüè 忽略；**he ~ed out his hand** tā shēnchū shǒu lái tā shēnchū shǒu lái tā shēnchū shǒu lái tā shēnchū shǒu lái tā shēnchū shǒu lái 他伸出手来；**a job that ~es me** yīfèn yǒu tiǎozhàn xìng de gōngzuò 一份有挑战性的工作 **4** v/i (to relax muscles) shēn lǎnyāo 伸懒腰；(to reach sth) shēnshǒu 伸手；(spread) yánshēn 延伸；(of fabric: give) shēnsuō 伸缩；(of fabric: sag) chēngcháng 撑长；**~ from X to Y** (extend) cóng X yánshēn zhì Y 从 X 延伸至 Y

stretcher dānjià 担架

strict person, instructions, rules yángé 严格

strictly yángé 严格；**it is ~ forbidden** juéduì bù yǔnxǔ 绝对不允许

stride 1 n dàbù 大步；**take ... in one's ~** cóngróngzìrúde chǔlǐ ... 从容自如地处理 ... **2** v/i dàbù zǒu 大步走

strident jiānruì cì'ěr 尖锐刺耳；fig: demands shēngsīlìjié 声嘶力竭

strike 1 n (of workers) bàgōng 罢工；(in baseball) hǎoqiú 好球；(of oil) fāxiàn 发现；**be on ~** zài bàgōng 在罢工；**go on ~** jǔxíng bàgōng 举行罢工 **2** v/i (of workers) bàgōng 罢工；(attack) xíjī 袭击；(of disaster) jiànglín 降临；(of clock) qiāoxiǎng 敲响 **3** v/t (hit) zhuàng chuàng 撞撞；fig (of disaster, illness) qīnxí 侵袭；match huá huá 划划；(of idea, thought) chūxiànyú nǎozhōng chūxiàn yú 出现于脑中；oil fāxiàn 发现；**she struck me as being ...** tā gěi wǒde yìnxiàng shì ... 她给我的印象是 ...

♦ **strike out** v/t huàdiào 划掉

strikebreaker pòhuài bàgōng zhě 破坏罢工者

striker (person on strike) bàgōng zhě 罢工者

striking (marked) xiǎnzhù 显著；(eye-catching) yǐnrén zhùmù 引人注目

string n (cord) xìshéng 细绳；(of violin, cello etc) xián xián 弦弦；(of tennis racket) bēngshéng 绷绳；**~s** (musicians) xiányuèqì yǎnzòu zhě 弦乐器演奏者；**pull ~s** lā guānxi 拉关系；**a ~ of** (series) yīliánchuàn 一连串

♦ **string along 1** v/i gēnsuí 跟随 **2** v/t: **string X along** yǒuyì wùdǎo X 有意误导 X

♦ **string up** F diàosǐ 吊死

stringed instrument xiányuèqì 弦乐器

stringent yángé 严格

string player xiányuèqì yǎnzòu zhě 弦乐器演奏者

strip 1 n chángtiáo 长条；(comic ~) liánhuánhuà 连环画 **2** v/t (remove) chúqù 除去；(undress) bōguāng yīfu 剥光衣服；**~ X of Y** bōduó X de Y 剥夺 X 的 Y **3** v/i (undress) tuōqù yīfu 脱去衣服；(of stripper) tuōguāng yīfu 脱光衣服

strip club tuōyīwǔ yèzǒnghuì 脱

衣舞夜总会

stripe tiáowén 条纹; (*indicating rank*) jíbié tiáowén 级别条纹

striped yǒu tiáowén 有条纹

stripper tuōyīwǔ biǎoyǎn zhě 脱衣舞表演者

strip show tuōyīwǔ biǎoyǎn 脱衣舞表演

striptease tuōyīwǔ 脱衣舞

strive 1 *v/t*: ~ **to do X** nǔlì zuò X 努力做 X 2 *v/i* fèndòu 奋斗; ~ **for** lǐzhēng 力争

stroke 1 *n* MED zhòngfēng 中风; (*when writing*) bǐhuà 笔画; (*when painting*) yìbǐ 一笔; (*style of swimming*) yóufǎ 游法; ~ **of luck** zǒuyùn 走运; **she never does a ~** (*of work*) tā cónglái bù gōngzuò 她从来不工作 2 *v/t* fǔmō 抚摸

stroll 1 *n* sànbù 散步 2 *v/i* xiánzǒu 闲走

stroller (*for baby*) yīng'érchē 婴儿车

strong *person* qiángzhuàng 强壮; *structure* jiāngù 坚固; *candidate* qiáng 强; *support, supporter* jiāndìng 坚定; *wind* qiángjìn 强劲; *drink* lièxìng 烈性; *tea, coffee* nóng 浓; *taste, smell* wèinóng 味浓; *views, objections* jiānjué 坚决; *currency* jiāntǐng 坚挺

stronghold *fig* gēnjùdì 根据地

strongly qiángliè 强烈

strong-minded yìzhì jiānqiáng 意志坚强

strong-willed yìzhì jiānjué 意志坚决

structural gòujià 构架

structure 1 *n* (*sth built*) jiànzhùwù 建筑物; (*way in which sth has been put together*) jiégòu 结构 2 *v/t* jìhuà 计划

struggle 1 *n* (*fight*) zhēngdòu 争斗; (*hard time*) jiānnán 艰难 2 *v/i* (*with a person*) gédòu 格斗; (*have a hard time*) nǔlì 努力 3 *v/t*: ~ **to do X** zhēngzhá zuò X 挣扎做 X

strum luàntán 乱弹

strut *v/i* dàyáodàbǎide zǒu 大摇大摆地走

stub 1 *n* (*of cigarette*) yāndì 烟蒂;

(*of check, ticket*) cúngēn 存根 2 *v/t*: **I ~bed my toe** wǒ cǎidào wǒde jiǎozhǐ 我踩到我的脚趾

♦**stub out** niǎnmiè 碾灭

stubble (*on man's face*) húcházi 胡茬子

stubborn gùzhí 固执; *defense* wánqiáng 顽强

stubby cū'ér duǎn 粗而短

stuck: **be ~ on X** duì X yǒu xìngqu 对 X 有兴趣

stuck-up *F* jiàzi bǎi jiàzi 摆架子

student xuésheng 学生; (*at college, university*) dàxuéshēng 大学生

student nurse shíxí hùshì 实习护士

student teacher shíxí jiàoshī 实习教师

studio (*of artist, sculptor*) gōngzuòshì 工作室; (*recording* ~) lùyīnpéng 录音棚; (*film* ~) shèyǐngpéng 摄影棚; (*TV* ~) yǎnbōshì 演播室

studious hàoxué 好学

study 1 *n* (*room*) shūfáng 书房; (*learning*) xuéxí 学习; (*investigation*) yánjiū 研究 2 *v/t* (*at school, university*) gōngdú 攻读; (*examine*) zǐxì chákàn 仔细看看 3 *v/i* xuéxí 学习

stuff 1 *n* (*objects, things*) dōngxi 东西; (*belongings*) suǒyǒuwù 所有物 2 *v/t turkey* tiánchōng 填充; ~ **X into Y** bǎ X sāijìn Y 把 X 塞进 Y

stuffed toy tiánliào wánjù 填料玩具

stuffing (*for turkey, in chair etc*) tiánliào 填料

stuffy *room* mèn 闷; *person* gǔbǎn 古板

stumble *v/i* bànjiǎo 绊脚

stumble across *v/t* yìwài fāxiàn 意外发现

stumble over *v/t* bàndǎo 绊到; *words* chūcuò 出错

stumbling block zhàng'ài 障碍

stump 1 *n* (*of tree*) shùzhuāng 树桩 2 *v/t* (*of question, questioner*) nánzhù 难住

♦**stump up** *F* fùchū 付出

stun (*of blow*) dǎhūn 打昏; (*of

news) dàchīyìjīng 大吃一惊

stunning (*amazing*) lìngrén jīngyì 令人惊异; (*very beautiful*) jí piàoliàng 极漂亮

stunt *n* (*for publicity*) xuétóu 噱头; (*in movie*) tèjì 特技

stuntman (*in movie*) tìshēn yǎnyuán 替身演员

stupefy mùdèngkǒudāi 目瞪口呆

stupendous jíhǎo 极好

stupid yúchǔn 愚蠢

stupidity yúchǔn 愚蠢

stupor shénzhì bùqīng 神志不清

sturdy jiēshí 结实

stutter *v/i* jiēba 结巴

sty (*for pig*) zhūjuàn 猪圈

style *n* (*method, manner*) fēnggé 风格; (*fashion*) liúxíng kuǎnshì 流行款式; (*fashionable elegance*) gédiào 格调; **go out of ~** búzài liúxíng 不再流行

stylish yǒu gédiào 有格调

subcommittee xiǎozǔ wěiyuánhuì 小组委员会

subcompact (*car*) chāoxiǎoxíng qìchē 超小型汽车

subconscious the ~ (*mind*) qiányìshí 潜意识

subcontract *v/t* fēnbāo hétóng 分包合同

subcontractor fēnbāorén 分包人

subdivide *v/t* xìfēn 细分

subdued *lighting* róuhé 柔和; *voice* dīluò 低落

subheading fùbiāotí 副标题

subject 1 *n* (*of country*) gōngmín 公民; (*topic*) zhǔtí 主题; (*branch of learning*) kēmù 科目; GRAM zhǔyǔ 主语; **change the ~** gǎibiàn huàtí 改变话题 **2** *adj*: **be ~ to X** yǒu X de qīngxiàng 有 X 的倾向; **~ to availability** shòuwán wéizhǐ 售完为止 **3** *v/t* shǐ ... zāoshòu 使 ... 遭受

subjective zhǔguān 主观

sublet *v/t* zhuǎnzū 转租

submachine gun chōngfēngqiāng 冲锋枪

submarine qiántǐng 潜艇

submerge 1 *v/t* yānmò 淹没 **2** *v/i* (*of submarine*) qiánrù 潜入

submission (*surrender*) tóuxiáng 投降; (*to committee etc*) chéngwén 呈文

submissive shùncóng 顺从

submit *v/t plan, proposal* chéngjiāo 呈交

subordinate 1 *adj employee, role etc* xiàjí 下级 **2** *n* xiàshǔ 下属

subpoena 1 *n* chuánpiào 传票 **2** *v/t person* chuánhuàn 传唤

♦ **subscribe to** *magazine etc* dìngyuè 订阅; *theory* zànchéng 赞成

subscriber (*to magazine*) dìngyuè zhě 订阅者

subscription dìng dìng 订订

subsequent suíhòu 随后

subsequently hòulái 后来

subside (*of flood waters*) tuìqù 退去; (*of high winds*) píngxī 平息; (*of building*) xiàxiàn 下陷; (*of fears, panic*) jiǎnruò 减弱

subsidiary *n* fùshǔ gōngsī 附属公司

subsidize zīzhù 资助

subsidy bǔzhù 补助

♦ **subsist on** kào ... shēnghuó 靠 ... 生活

subsistence farmer zìjǐ nóngchǎngzhǔ 自给农场主

subsistence level pínkùn shuǐzhǔn 贫困水准

substance (*matter*) wùzhì 物质

substandard dīyú biāozhǔn 低于标准

substantial xiāngdāng dà 相当大

substantially (*considerably*) kěguān 可观; (*in essence*) shízhì shang 实质上

substantiate *adj* zhèngmíng 证明

substantive *adj* shíjì 实际

substitute 1 *n* dàitìpǐn 代替品; SP tìhuàn zhě 替换者 **2** *v/t*: **X for Y** yòng X qǔdài Y 用 X 取代 Y **3** *v/i*: **~ for X** dàitì X 代替 X

substitution (*act*) qǔdài 取代; **make a ~** SP tìhuàn duìyuán 替换队员

subtitle 1 *n* zìmù 字幕 **2** *v/t movie* gěi ... jiā zìmù 给 ... 加字幕

subtle qiǎomiào 巧妙

subtract *v/t number* jiǎnqù 减去; **~**

X from Y cóng Y zhōng jiǎnqù X 从 Y 中减去 X

suburb jiāoqū 郊区; **the ~s** shìjiāo 市郊

suburban jiāoqū 郊区

subversive 1 adj yǒu diānfùxìng 有颠覆性 **2** n diānfù fènzǐ 颠覆分子

subway dìtiě 地铁

subzero adj xiàlíng 零下

succeed 1 v/i (be successful) chénggōng 成功; (to throne) jíwèi 即位; **~ in doing X** chénggōngde zuò X 成功地做 X **2** v/t (come after, monarch) jìrèn 继任

succeeding jiēxiàlái 接下来

success chénggōng 成功; **be a ~** chénggōng 成功

successful chénggōng 成功

successfully chénggōng 成功

succession (sequence) yíxìliè 一系列; (to the throne) jíwèi 即位; **in ~** yígè jiē yígè 一个接一个

successive jiēlián búduàn 接连不断

successor jìrènrén 继任人

succinct jiǎnyào 简要

succulent meat, fruit xiānměi 鲜美

succumb (give in) qūfú 屈服; **~ to temptation** qūcóngyú yòuhuò 屈从于诱惑

such 1 adj (of that kind) zhèyàng 这样; **~ a** (so much of a) nàme duō 那么多; **~ as** xiàng … yíyàng 像 … 一样; **there is no ~ word as …** méiyǒu rú … zhème yígè cí 没有如 … 这么个词 **2** adv zhème 这么; **as ~** qí běnshēn yìyì 按其本身意义

suck lollipop, hard candy shǔnxī 吮吸; **~ one's thumb** shǔnxī mǔzhǐ 吮吸拇指; **~ X from Y** cóng Y xīchū X 从 Y 吸出 X

♦ **suck up** moisture xīshōu 吸收

♦ **suck up to** F fèngcheng 奉承

sucker F (person) qīngxìn zhě 轻信者; F (lollipop) bàngbàngtáng 棒棒糖

sucking pig rǔzhū 乳猪

suction chōuxī 抽吸

sudden yìwài 意外; **all of a ~** tūrán 突然

suddenly tūrán 突然

suds (soap ~) pàomò 泡沫

sue v/t kònggào 控告

suede n róngmiàngé 绒面革

suffer 1 v/i (be in great pain) shòukǔ 受苦; (deteriorate) biànchà 变差; **be ~ing from** huànyǒu 患有 **2** v/t loss zāoshòu 遭受; setback jīngshòu 经受

suffering n tòngkǔ 痛苦

sufficient zúgòu 足够

sufficiently chōngzú 充足

suffocate v/i zhìxī ér sǐ 窒息而死 v/t shǐ … zhìxī 使 … 窒息

suffocation zhìxī 窒息

sugar 1 n shítáng 食糖 **2** v/t jiātáng 加糖

sugar bowl tángguàn 糖罐

sugar cane gānzhe 甘蔗

suggest v/t jiànyì 建议; **I ~ that we stop now** wǒ jiànyì wǒmen xiànzài tíngxià 我建议我们现在停下

suggestion jiànyì 建议

suicide zìshā 自杀; **commit ~** zìshā 自杀

suit 1 n xīzhuāng 西装; (in cards) huāsè pái 花色牌 **2** v/t (of clothes, color) shìhé 适合; **~ yourself!** suí nǐde biàn! 随你的便！; **be ~ed for X** shìhé X 适合 X

suitable shìyí 适宜

suitcase shǒutí yīxiāng 手提衣箱

suite (of rooms) tàojiān 套间; (furniture) yītào jiājù 一套家具; MUS zǔqǔ 组曲

sulfur liúhuáng 硫磺

sulk v/i shēng mènqì 生闷气

sulky shēng mènqì 生闷气

sullen mènmènbúlè 闷闷不乐

sultry climate mēnrè 闷热; (sexually) xìnggǎn 性感

sum (total) zǒngshù 总数; (amount) shùmù 数目; (in arithmetic) suànshù 算术; **a large ~ of money** amount yí dà bǐ qián 一大笔钱; **~ insured** amount bǎoxiǎn jīn'é 保险金额; **the ~ total of his efforts** tā yíqiè nǔlìde jiéguǒ 他一切努力的结果

♦ **sum up 1** v/t (summarize) gàikuò

概括; (*assess*) píngjià 评价 **2** *v/i* LAW gàishù 概述

summarize *v/t* gàikuò 概括

summary *n* zǒngjié 总结

summer xiàtiān 夏天

Summer Palace Yíhéyuán 颐和园

summit (*of mountain*) shāndǐng 山顶; *fig* zhìgāodiǎn 至高点; POL zuì gāojí huìyì 最高级会议

summon *staff, ministers* zhàojí 召集; *meeting* zhàokāi 召开

♦summon up *strength* fāhuī 发挥

summons LAW chuánpiào 传票

sump (*for oil*) rùnhuáyóuxiāng 润滑油箱

sun tàiyáng 太阳; *in the ~* zài yángguāng xià 在阳光下; *out of the ~* zài bèiyīnchù 在背阴处; *he has had too much ~* tā zhòngshǔ le 他中暑了

sunbathe shài tàiyáng 晒太阳; sunblock fángshàigāo 防晒膏; sunburn shàibān 晒斑; sunburnt shàishāng 晒伤

Sunday xīngqīrì 星期日

sundial rìguī 日晷

sundries záxiàng 杂项

sunglasses mòjìng 墨镜

sunken *cheeks* āoxiàn 凹陷

sunny *day* yángguāng chōngzú 阳光充足; *disposition* kāilǎng 开朗; *it is ~* tiānqì qínglǎng 天气晴朗

sunrise rìchū 日出; sunset rìluò 日落; sunshade yángsǎn 阳伞; sunshine yángguāng 阳光; sunstroke zhòngshǔ 中暑; suntan shàihēi 晒黑; *get a ~* shàichéng gǔtóngsè 晒成古铜色

Sun Yat-sen Sūn Zhōngshān 孙中山

super **1** *adj* F jíhǎo 极好 **2** *n* (*janitor*) guǎnlǐyuán 管理员

superb bàngjíle 棒极了

superficial *comments, analysis* fúqiǎn 肤浅; *person* qiǎnbó 浅薄; *wounds* biǎopí 表皮

superfluous duōyú 多余

superhuman *efforts* chāohūchángrén 超乎常人

superintendent (*of apartment block*) guǎnlǐyuán 管理员

superior **1** *adj* (*better*) gènghǎo 更好; *pej* (*attitude*) yǒu yōuyuègǎn 有优越感 **2** *n* (*in organization, society*) shàngjí 上级

supermarket chāojí shìchǎng 超级市场

supernatural **1** *adj powers* chāozìrán 超自然 **2** *n*: *the ~* chāozìrán de shìwù 超自然的事物

superpower POL chāojí dàguó 超级大国

supersonic *flight, aircraft* chāoyīnsù 超音速

superstition míxìn sīxiǎng 迷信思想

superstitious *person* míxìn 迷信

supervise jiāndū 监督

supervisor (*at work*) zhǐdǎo zhě 指导者

supper wǎnfàn 晚饭

supple róuruǎn 柔软

supplement (*extra payment*) fùjiāfèi 附加费

supplier COM gōngyìngshāng 供应商

supply **1** *n* gōngyìng 供应; *~ and demand* gōngyìng yǔ xūqiú 供应与需求; *supplies* gōngyìngpǐn 供应品 **2** *v/t goods* tígōng 提供; *~ X with Y* xiàng X tígōng Y 向 X 提供 Y; *be supplied with ...* zhuāngyǒu ... 装有 ...

support **1** *n* (*for structure*) zhīzhù 支柱; (*backing*) zhīchí 支持 **2** *v/t building, structure* zhīchéng 支撑; (*financially*) yuánzhù 援助; (*back*) zhīchí 支持

supporter yōnghù zhě 拥护者; (*of football team etc*) zhīchí zhě 支持者

supportive zhīchí 支持

suppose (*imagine*) liàoxiǎng 料想; *I ~ so* wǒ kàn shì zhèyàng 我看是这样; *be ~d to ...* (*be meant to*) yīnggāi ... 应该 ...; (*be said to be*) jùshuō ... 据说 ...; *you are not ~d to ...* (*not allowed to*) nǐ bùgāi ... 你不该 ...

suppository MED shuānjì 栓剂

suppress *rebellion etc* zhènyā 镇压

suppression zhènyā 镇压

supremacy zuìgāo quánwēi 最高权威

supreme *being, commander* zhìgāo-wúshàng 至高无上; *effort, courage, delight* jídà 极大

Supreme Court Gāojí Fǎtíng 高级法庭

surcharge fùjiāfèi 附加费

sure 1 *adj*: **I'm ~** wǒ néng quèdìng 我能确定; **I'm not ~** wǒ bú quèdìng 我不确定; **be ~ about X** duì X néng quèdìng 对 X 能确定; **make ~ that ...** cháming ... 查明 ... **2** *adv*: **~ enough** guǒrán rúcǐ 果然如此; **it ~ is hot today** F jīntiān quèshí rè 今天确实热; **~!** dāngrán! 当然！

surely yídìng 一定; (*gladly*) dāng-rán 当然

surf 1 *n* (*on sea*) jīlàng 激浪 **2** *v/t* *the Net* sōuxún 搜寻

surface 1 *n* (*of table, object*) biǎo-miàn 表面; (*of water*) shuǐmiàn 水面; **on the ~** *fig* biǎomiàn shang 表面上 **2** *v/i* (*of swimmer, submarine*) fúdào shuǐmiàn 浮到水面; (*appear*) chóngxīn chūxiàn 重新出现

surface mail pǔtōng yóujiàn 普通邮件

surfboard chōnglàngbǎn 冲浪板

surfer (*on sea*) chōnglàng zhě 冲浪者

surfing chōnglàng yùndòng 冲浪运动; **go ~** zuò chōnglàng yùn-dòng 作冲浪运动

surge *n* (*in electric current*) diànliú jíchōng 电流急冲; (*in demand, interest, growth etc*) jīzēng 激增

♦ **surge forward** (*of crowd*) yǒngjìn chōngjìn 涌进

surgeon wàikē yīshī 外科医师

surgery shǒushù 手术; **undergo ~** jiēshòu shǒushù zhìliáo 接受手术治疗

surgical wàikē 外科

surly guāilì 乖戾

surmount *difficulties* kèfú 克服

surname xìng 姓

surpass chāoguò 超过

surplus 1 *n* guòshèng 过剩 **2** *adj* shèngyú 剩余

surprise 1 *n* jīngqí 惊奇; **it'll come as no ~ to hear that ...** tīngdào ... bùzú wéiqí 听到 ... 不足为奇 **2** *v/t* shǐ ... chījīng 使 ... 吃惊; **be/look ~d** chīle yìjīng/kànqǐlái chīle yìjīng 吃了一惊／看起来吃了一惊

surprising lìngrén jīngyà 令人惊讶

surprisingly chūrényìwài 出人意外

surrender 1 *v/i* (*of army*) tóuxiáng 投降 **2** *v/t* (*hand in: weapons etc*) jiāochū 交出 **3** *n* tóuxiáng 投降; (*handing in*) jiāochū 交出

surrogate mother dàimǔ 代母

surround 1 *v/t* bāowéi 包围; **be ~ed by X** bèi X bāowéi 被 X 包围 **2** *n* (*of picture etc*) biānyuán 边缘

surrounding *adj* zhōuwéi 周围

surroundings huánjìng 环境

survey 1 *n* (*of modern literature etc*) gàikuàng 概况; (*of consumer habits*) diàochá 调查; (*of building*) jiàndìng 鉴定 **2** *v/t* (*look at*) shěnshì 审视; *building* jiàndìng 鉴定

surveyor jiàndìngrén 鉴定人

survival xìngcún 幸存

survive 1 *v/i* (*of species*) cúnhuó 存活; (*of patient*) yōuxìng cúnhuó 有幸存活; **how are you? – I'm sur-viving** nǐ hǎo ma?- wǒ miǎnqiǎng huózhe 你好吗？- 我勉强活着; **his two surviving daughters** tāde liǎnggè huózhede nǚ'ér 他的两个活着的女儿 **2** *v/t* *accident, operation* xìngcún 幸存; (*outlive*) bǐ ... chángmìng 比 ... 长命

survivor xìngcún zhě 幸存者; **he's a ~** *fig* tā shì yígè jīngdéqǐ fēngshuāng de rén 他是一个经得起风霜的人

susceptible (*emotionally*) yìshòu gǎndòng 易受感动; **be ~ to the cold/heat** duì lěng/rè mǐngǎn 对冷／热敏感

suspect 1 *n* xiányífàn 嫌疑犯

2 v/t person huáiyí 怀疑; (suppose) juéde 觉得

suspected murderer xiányí 嫌疑; the ~ cause bèi huáiyí de yuányīn 被怀疑的原因

suspend (hang) xuánguà 悬挂; (from office, duties) lèlìng tíngzhí 勒令停职

suspenders (for pants) diàokùdài 吊裤带

suspense jǐnzhānggǎn 紧张感

suspension (in vehicle) jiǎnzhèn zhuāngzhì 减震装置; (from duty) tíngzhí 停职

suspension bridge diàoqiáo 吊桥

suspicion huáiyí 怀疑

suspicious (causing suspicion) kěyí 可疑; (feeling suspicion) yǒu yíxīn 有疑心; be ~ of X duì X yǒu yíxīn 对 X 有疑心

sustain zhīcheng 支撑

swab 1 n yàoqiān 药签 **2** v/t yòng yàoqiān cā 用药签擦

swagger n zhǐgāoqìyáng 趾高气扬

swallow[1] **1** v/t liquid, food yàn 咽 **2** v/i yànshí 咽食

swallow[2] (bird) yànzi 燕子

swamp 1 n zhǎozé 沼泽 **2** v/t yānmò 淹没; be ~ed with X X yìngjiēbùxiá X 应接不暇

swampy ground shīruǎn 湿软

swan tiān'é 天鹅

swap 1 n jiāohuàn 交换; ~ X for Y yòng X huàn Y 用 X 换 Y **2** v/i huàn 换

swarm 1 n (of bees) dàqún 大群 **2** v/i (of ants, tourists etc) mìjí 密集; the town was ~ing with X chéngshìlǐ dàochù dōu shì X 城市里到处都是 X

swarthy face, complexion yǒuhēi 黝黑

swat v/t insect, fly zhòngpāi 重拍

sway 1 n (influence, power) yǐngxiǎng 影响 **2** v/i yáobǎi 摇摆

swear v/i (use swearword) zhòumà 咒骂; (promise) fāshì 发誓; LAW xuānshì 宣誓; ~ at X zhòumà X 咒骂 X

♦ **swear in** witness shì ... xuānshì 使 ... 宣誓

swearword màrénhuà 骂人话

sweat 1 n hànshuǐ 汗水; covered in ~ dàhànlínlí 大汗淋漓 **2** v/i chūhàn 出汗

sweater máoyī 毛衣

sweatshirt wúlǐng chángxiùshān 无领长袖衫

sweaty hands, smell hànlínlín 汗淋淋

Swede Ruìdiǎn rén 瑞典人

Sweden Ruìdiǎn 瑞典

Swedish 1 adj Ruìdiǎn 瑞典 **2** n (language) Ruìdiǎn yǔ 瑞典语

sweep 1 v/t floor, leaves sǎo 扫 **2** n (long curve) wānyán 蜿蜒

♦ **sweep up** v/t mess, crumbs sǎolǒng 扫拢

sweeping adj generalization, statement lǒngtǒng 笼统; changes yǒu guǎngfàn yǐngxiǎng 有广泛影响

sweet adj taste, tea tián 甜; F (kind) hǎoxīn 好心; F (cute) rěrén xǐ'ài 惹人喜爱

sweet and sour adj tángcù 糖醋

sweetcorn tián yùmǐ 甜玉米

sweeten v/t drink, food shǐ ... biàntián 使 ... 变甜

sweetener (for drink) tiánwèijì 甜味剂

sweetheart xīnshàng rén 心上人

swell 1 v/i (of limb etc) zhǒngzhàng 肿胀 **2** adj F (good) jíhǎo 极好 **3** n (of the sea) qǐfú 起伏

swelling n MED zhǒngkuài 肿块

sweltering heat, day kùrè 酷热

swerve v/i (of driver, car) tūrán zhuǎnxiàng 突然转向

swift adj xùnsù 迅速

swim 1 v/i yóuyǒng 游泳; go ~ming qù yóuyǒng 去游泳; my head is ~ming wǒ tóuyūnmùxuàn 我头晕目眩 **2** n yóuyǒng 游泳; go for a ~ qù yóuyǒng 去游泳

swimmer yóuyǒng zhě 游泳者

swimming yóuyǒng 游泳

swimming pool yóuyǒngchí 游泳池

swimsuit yóuyǒngyī 游泳衣

swindle 1 n piànjú 骗计 **2** v/t: ~ X

out of Y cóng Y piànde X 从 Y 骗得 X

swine F (*person*) xiàliúpǐ 下流坯

swing 1 *n* zhuǎnbiàn 转变; (*for child*) qiūqiān 秋千; **~ to the Democrats** zhuǎn ér zhīchí Mínzhǔdǎng 转而支持民主党 **2** *v/t* huīdòng 挥动; *hips* yáobǎi 摇摆 **3** *v/i* bǎidòng 摆动; (*turn*) zhuàndòng 转动; (*of public opinion etc*) biàndòng 变动

swing-door tuīhémén 推合门

Swiss 1 *adj* Ruìshì 瑞士 **2** *n* (*person*) Ruìshì rén 瑞士人

switch 1 *n* (*for light*) kāiguān 开关; (*change*) biànhuà 变化 **2** *v/t* (*change*) huàn 换 **3** *v/i* (*change*) gǎihuàn 改换

♦ **switch off** *v/t & v/i lights, engine, PC, TV* guāndiào 关掉

♦ **switch on 1** *v/t lights, engine, PC, TV* kāi 开 **2** *v/i* kāijī 开机

switchboard diànhuà jiāohuàntái 电话交换台

switchover (*to new system*) zhuǎnbiàn 转变

Switzerland Ruìshì 瑞士

swivel *v/i* (*of chair, monitor etc*) xuánzhuàn 旋转

swollen zhǒngzhàng 肿胀

swoop *v/i* (*of bird*) měngpū 猛扑

♦ **swoop down on** *prey* měngpū xiàng 猛扑向

♦ **swoop on** (*of police etc*) tūrán sōuchá 突然搜查

sword jiàn 剑

sycamore xīkèmò shù 西克莫树

syllable yīnjié 音节

syllabus dàgāng 大纲

symbol (*character*) fúhào 符号; (*in poetry etc*) xiàngzhēng 象征

symbolic yǒu xiàngzhēngxìng 有象征性

symbolism (*in poetry, art*) xiàngzhēng shǒufǎ 象征手法

symbolize xiàngzhēng 象征

symmetric(al) duìchèn 对称

symmetry duìchèn 对称

sympathetic (*showing pity*) biǎoshì tóngqíng 表示同情; (*understanding*) lǐjiě rén 理解人; **be ~ toward a person / an idea** duì rén / xiǎngfǎ biǎoshì tóngqíng, zhīchí 对人 / 想法表示同情、支持

♦ **sympathize with** *person, views* tóngqíng 同情

sympathizer POL yōnghù zhě 拥护者

sympathy (*pity*) tóngqíngxīn 同情心; (*understanding*) lǐjiě 理解; **don't expect any ~ from me!** bié zhǐwàng wǒ kělián nǐ! 别指望我可怜你!

symphony jiāoxiǎngyuè 交响乐

symptom MED zhèngzhuàng 症状; *fig* zhēngzhào 征兆

symptomatic: be ~ of X MED shì Xde zhèngzhuàng 是 X 的症状; *fig* shì Xde zhēngzhào 是 X 的征兆

synchronize *watches* shǐ ... tóngshí 使 ... 同时; *operations* shǐ ... tóngbù 使 ... 同步

synonym tóngyìcí 同义词

syntax jùfǎ 句法

synthetic rénzào 人造

syphilis méidú 梅毒

syringe zhùshèqì 注射器

syrup tángjiāng 糖浆

system (*method*) xìtǒng 系统; (*orderliness*) chéngxù 程序; (*computer*) zǔhé zhuāngzhì 组合装置; **the braking / fuel injection / digestive ~** shāchē / ránliào shūrù / xiāohuà xìtǒng 刹车 / 燃料输入 / 消化系统

systematic *approach, person* yǒu tiáolǐ 有条理

systematically *analyze, study* yǒu tiáolǐ 有条理; *destroy* xùyì 蓄意

system crash xìtǒng bēngkuì 系统崩溃

systems analyst COMPUT xìtǒng fēnxī zhě 系统分析者

Szechuan Sìchuān 四川

T

tab n lāshé 拉舌; (*in text*) fáng-mǒshé 防抹舌
table n zhuōzi 桌子; (*of figures*) biǎo 表
tablecloth zhuōbù 桌布
tablespoon cānsháor 餐勺儿
tablet yàopiànr 药片儿
table tennis pīngpāngqiú 乒乓球
tabloid n (*newspaper*) xiǎobào 小报
taboo adj bìhuì 避讳
tacit xīnzhào bù xuān 心照不宣
tack 1 n (*nail*) píngtóudīng 平头钉 2 v/t (*sew*) bēng 绷 3 v/i (*of yacht*) zhuǎnháng 转航
tackle 1 n (*equipment*) yòngjù 用具; SP zǔdǎng 阻挡 2 v/t SP jiéqiú 截球; *problem* chǔlǐ 处理; *intruder* zhuāzhù 抓住
tacky *paint, glue* nián 粘; (*cheap, poor quality*) súqi 俗气; *behavior* bù yǎguān 不雅观
tact jīzhì 机智
tactful détǐ 得体
tactical zhànshù 战术
tactics cèlüè 策略
tactless bù détǐ 不得体
tadpole kēdǒu 蝌蚪
tag (*label*) biāoqiān 标签
Tai: *Mount* ~ Tàishān 泰山
tai chi tàijíquán 太极拳
tail n wěiba 尾巴
tail coat yànwěifú 燕尾服
tail light wěidēng 尾灯
tailor cáifeng 裁缝
tailor-made *suit* dìngzuò 定做; *solution* shìdàng 适当
tail wind shùnfēng 顺风
tainted *food* wūrǎn 污染
Taipei Táiběi 台北
Taiwan Táiwān 台湾
Taiwanese 1 adj Táiwān 台湾 2 n (*person*) Táiwān rén 台湾人; (*dialect*) Táiwān huà 台湾话

Taiwan Straits Táiwān Hǎixiá 台湾海峡
Tajik Tǎjíkè rén 塔吉克人
Tajiki 1 adj Tǎjíkè 塔吉克 2 n (*language*) Tǎjíkè yǔ 塔吉克语
Tajikistan Tǎjíkè 塔吉克
take v/t (*remove*) ná 拿; (*steal*) tōu 偷; (*transport*) sòng 送; (*accompany*) péi 陪; (*accept: money, gift, credit cards*) jiēshòu 接受; (*study: math, French*) xué 学; *photograph* zhàoxiàng 照相; *exam, degree* kǎo 考; *shower* línyù 淋浴; *stroll* sànbù 散步; *s.o.'s temperature* liáng 量; (*endure*) rěnshòu 忍受; (*require*) xūyào 需要; *how long does it ~?* yào duōcháng shíjiān? 要多长时间？; *I'll ~ it* (*when shopping*) wǒ mǎi le 我买了
♦ **take after** xiàng 像
♦ **take away** *pain* jiěchú 解除; *object* názǒu 拿走; MATH jiǎn 减; *take X away from Y* cóng Y nàli názǒu X 从 Y 那里拿走 X
♦ **take back** (*return: object*) tuìdiào 退掉; *person* sòng 送; (*accept back: husband etc*) jiēshòu 接受; *that takes me back* (*of music, thought etc*) shǐ wǒ huíyìqǐ 使我回忆起
♦ **take down** (*from shelf*) qǔxià 取下; *scaffolding* chāidiào 拆掉; *pants* tuō 脱; (*write down*) xiěxià 写下
♦ **take in** (*take indoors*) ná jìnlái 拿进来; (*give accommodation*) shōuliú 收留; (*make narrower*) gǎixiǎo 改小; (*deceive*) qīpiàn 欺骗; (*include*) bāokuò 包括
♦ **take off** 1 v/t *clothes, hat* qǔxià 取下; *10% etc* jiàngjià 降价; (*mimic*) mófǎng 模仿; *can you take a bit off here?* (*to barber*) néngbùnéng zài zhèlǐ jiǎn yìdiǎnr? 能不能在

这里剪一点儿？；*take a day /
week off* fàngjià yītiān / yīxīngqī
放假一天 / 一星期 **2** *v/i (of
airplane)* qǐfēi 起飞；*(become
popular)* fēiyuè 飞跃

♦**take on** *job* dānrèn 担任；*staff*
pìnyòng 聘用

♦**take out** *(from bag, pocket)* náchū
拿出；*stain* qùdiào 去掉；*tooth*
qǔchū 取出；*appendix, word from
text* shānchú 删除；*money from
bank* qǔ 取；*(to dinner etc)* dài ...
chūqù 带 ... 出去；*insurance policy*
bànlǐ 办理；*take it out on X (s.o.)*
zài X de shēnshàng bàofù 在 X 的
身上报复

♦**take over 1** *v/t company etc*
jiānbìng 兼并；*tourists ~ the
town* mǎn zhèn dōushì lǚkè 满镇
都是旅客 **2** *v/i (of new
management etc)* jiēguǎn 接管；*(do
sth in s.o.'s place)* jiēshǒu 接手

♦**take to** *(like)* xǐhuan 喜欢；*(form
habit etc)* yǎngchéng ... xíguàn 养
成 ... 习惯

♦**take up** *carpet etc* jiēqǐ 揭起；
(carry up) ná shàngqù 拿上去；
(shorten: dress etc) shōuduǎn 收短；
hobby kāishǐ 开始；*judo, new
language* kāishǐ xuéxí 开始学习；
offer jiēshòu 接受；*new job* kāishǐ
cóngshì 开始从事；*space, time*
zhànqù 占去；*I'll take you up on
your offer* wǒ jiēshòu nǐde tíyì 我
接受你的提议

take-home pay shídé gōngzī 实得
工资

takeoff *(of airplane)* qǐfēi 起飞；
(impersonation) mófǎng 模仿；

takeover COM jiānbìng 兼并；
takeover bid jiānbìng tóubiāo 兼
并投标

takings shōurù 收入

talcum powder shuǎngshēnfěn 爽
身粉

tale gùshì 故事

talent tiāncái 天才

talented yǒu tiāncái 有天才

talk 1 *v/i* tánhuà 谈话；*can I ~
with ...?* qǐngzhǎo ...? 请找 ... ？；
I'll ~ to him about it wǒ huì hé tā

tán wǒ huì hé tā tán 我会和他谈 **2** *v/t English etc*
shuō 说；*business, politics* tán 谈；
X into doing Y shuōfú X zuò Y 说
服 X 做 Y **3** *n (conversation)* jiāotán
交谈；*(lecture)* yǎnjiǎng 演讲；
he's all ~ pej tā zhǐshì kōngtán 他
只是空谈

♦**talk over** tǎolùn 讨论

talkative jiàntán 健谈

talk show tánhuà jiémù 谈话节
目

tall gāo 高

tall order gāo yāoqiú 高要求

tall story kuādàde gùshì 夸大的
故事

tame *animal* xùnfú 驯服；*joke etc*
píngdàn 平淡

♦**tamper with** sǔnhuài 损坏

tampon ⇩ yuèjīng shuān 月经栓

tan 1 *n (from sun)* rì shài fūsè 日晒
肤色；*(color)* zōnghè sè 棕褐色
2 *v/i (in sun)* shài hēi 晒黑 **3** *v/t
leather* róu 鞣

tandem *(bike)* qiánhòu shuāngzuò
zìxíngchē 前后双座自行车

Tang Dynasty Táng Cháo 唐朝

tangerine gānjú 柑桔

tangle *n* yītuánzāo 一团糟

♦**tangle up: get tangled up** *(of
string etc)* chán zài yìqǐ 缠在一起

tango *n* tāngē wǔ 探戈舞

Tang poetry Tángshī 唐诗

tank chúshuǐ chí 储水池；MOT
xiāng 箱；MIL tǎnkè 坦克；*(for
skin diver)* shuǐfèi 水肺

tanker *(ship)* yóuchuán 油船；
(truck) guànchē 罐车

tanned shài hēi 晒黑

tantalizing yòurén 诱人

tantamount: be ~ to xiāngdāngyú
相当于

tantrum fā píqì 发脾气

Tao Dào 道

Taoism *(philosophy)* Dàojiā 道家；
(religion) Dàojiào 道教

Taoist priest Dàoshi 道士

tap 1 *n* lóngtóu 龙头 **2** *v/t (knock)*
qīngqiāo 轻敲；*phone* qiètīng 窃
听

♦**tap into** *resources* lìyòng 利用

tap dance *n* tīda wǔ 踢踏舞

tape 1 n (for recording) cídài 磁带; (sticky) jiāodài 胶带 **2** v/t conversation etc lùyīn 录音; (with sticky tape) zhān 粘

tape deck lùyīnzuò 录音座; **tape drive** COMPUT cídài qūdòngqì 磁带驱动器; **tape measure** juǎnchǐ 卷尺

taper v/i jiǎnxiǎo 减小

♦ **taper off** (of production) zhújiàn tíngzhǐ 逐渐停止; (of figures) zhújiàn jiǎnshǎo 逐渐减少

tape recorder lùyīnjī 录音机

tape recording lùyīn 录音

tapestry zhījǐn 织锦

tapeworm tāochóng 绦虫

tar n bǎiyóu 柏油

tardy huǎnmàn 缓慢

target 1 n (in shooting, for sales, production) mùbiāo 目标 **2** v/t market bǎ ... zuòwéi mùbiāo 把 ... 作为目标

target date mùbiāo rìqí 目标日期; **target group** COM duìxiàng zǔ 对象组; **target market** duìxiàng shìchǎng 对象市场

tariff (price) jiàmùbiǎo 价目表; (tax) shuì 税

tarmac (at airport) pǎodào 跑道

tarnish v/t metal shǐ ... shīqù guāngzé 使 ... 失去光泽; reputation sǔnhuài 损坏

tarpaulin yóubù 油布

tart n guǒxiànr bǐng 果馅儿饼

task rènwù 任务

task button rènwùniǔ 任务钮

task force tèbié gōngzuòzǔ 特别工作组

tassel liúsū 流苏

taste 1 n (sense, of food etc) wèidao 味道; (in clothes, art etc) pǐnwèi 品味; **he has no ~** tā méiyǒu shěnměi yǎnguāng 他没有审美眼光 **2** v/t food cháng 尝; (experience: freedom etc) chángshì 尝试

tasteful yǒu shěnměi yǎnguāng 有审美眼光

tasteless food méiwèir 没味儿; remark, person cūsú 粗俗

tasty xiāng 香

tattered clothes, book pòlàn 破烂

tatters: in ~ (of clothes) pòpo lànlàn 破破烂烂; (of reputation, career) chèdǐ cuīhuǐ 彻底摧毁

tattoo wénshēn 纹身

taunt n & v/t cháoxiào 嘲笑

taut jǐn 紧

tax 1 n shuì 税; **before / after ~** shuì qián / hòu 税前 / 后 **2** v/t people, product chōushuì 抽税

taxation (act of taxing) zhēngshuì 征税; (taxes) shuìshōu 税收

tax code shuìwù hàomǎ 税务号码; **tax-deductible** kě jiǎnshuì 可减税; **tax-free** miǎnshuì 免税

taxi ⇩ chūzūchē 出租车

taxidriver chūzūchē sījī 出租车司机

taxi rank, taxi stand chūzūchē tíngchēchù 出租车停车处; **tax inspector** shuìwù diàocháyuán 税务调查员; **tax payer** nàshuì rén 纳税人; **tax return** (form) nàshuì dān 纳税单

tea (drink) chá 茶; (meal) chádiǎn 茶点; **black ~** hóngchá 红茶; **green ~** lǜchá 绿茶

teabag chábāo 茶包

teach 1 v/t person, subject jiāo 教; **~ X to do Y** jiāo X zuò Y 教 X 做 Y **2** v/i jiāoshū 教书

teacher lǎoshī 老师

teacher training jiàoshī péixùn 教师培训

teaching (profession) jiāoxué 教学

teaching aid jiàojù 教具

teaching assistant zhùjiào 助教

tea cloth chájīn 茶巾; **teacup** chábēi 茶杯; **tea drinker** hēchárén 喝茶人; **tea house** cháguǎnr 茶馆儿

teak yòumù 柚木

tea leaf cháyè 茶叶

team zǔ 组

team spirit jítǐ jīngshén 集体精神

teamster kǎchē sījī 卡车司机

teamwork ⇩ pèihé 配合

teapot cháhú 茶壶

tear[1] **1** n (in clothes) lièkǒu 裂口 **2** v/t paper, cloth sī 撕; **be torn between two alternatives** yóuyù bùjué 犹豫不决 **3** v/i (run fast, *drive fast*) jí bēn 急奔

♦ **tear up** *paper* sī 撕; *agreement* sīhuǐ 撕毁

tear² *(in eye)* lèi 泪; **burst into ~s** fàngshēng dàkū 放声大哭; **be in ~s** kū 哭

teardrop yǎnlèi 眼泪

tearful yǎnlèi wāngwang 眼泪汪汪

tear gas cuīlèi qì 催泪气

tearoom cháshì 茶室

tease *v/t* dòunòng 逗弄

tea service, tea set chájù 茶具

teaspoon cháchí 茶匙

teat rǔtóu 乳头

tea towel cā wǎn bù 擦碗布

technical jìshù xìng 技术性

technicality *(technical nature)* zhuānmén xìng 专门性; LAW sùsòng xìjié 诉讼细节; *that's just a ~* nà zhǐshì xìjié éryǐ 那只是细节而已

technically *(strictly speaking)* yángé láishuō 严格来说

technician jìshùyuán 技术员

technique fāngfǎ 方法

technological jìshù 技术

technology jìshù 技术

technophobia kǒng jìshù bìng 恐技术病

tedious shǐrén yànfán 使人厌烦

tee *n (in golf)* qiúzuò 球座

teem: be ~ing with rain qīngpén dàyǔ 倾盆大雨; *be ~ing with tourists / ants* chōngmǎn yóukè / mǎyǐ 充满游客/蚂蚁

teenage *fashions* qīngshàonián 青少年; *~ boy / girl* shàonán / nǚ 少男/女

teenager qīngshàonián 青少年

teens: be in one's ~ shíjǐsuì 十几岁; *reach one's ~* jìnrù qīngshàonián shíqī 进入青少年时期

telecommunications diànxìn 电信

telegram diànbào 电报

telegraph pole diànxiàn gān 电线杆

telepathic xīnlíng gǎnyìng 心灵感应; *you must be ~!* nǐ kěndìng shì

xīnlíng gǎnyìng! 你肯定是心灵感应!

telepathy xīnlíng gǎnyìng 心灵感应

telephone 1 *n* diànhuà 电话; *be on the ~ (be speaking)* jiǎng diànhuà 讲电话; *(possess a phone)* yǒu diànhuà 有电话 **2** *v/t & v/i* dǎ diànhuà 打电话

telephone booth diànhuà tíng 电话亭; **telephone call** diànhuà 电话; **telephone directory** diànhuà běn 电话本; **telephone exchange** zǒngjī 总机; **telephone number** diànhuà hàomǎ 电话号码

telephoto lens shèyuǎn jìngtóu 摄远镜头

telesales diànhuà tuīxiāo 电话推销

telescope wàngyuǎnjìng 望远镜

televise diànshì bōfàng 电视播放

television diànshì 电视; *(set)* diànshì jī 电视机; *on ~* diànshì shang 电视上; *watch ~* kàn diànshì 看电视

television program diànshì jiémù 电视节目; **television set** diànshì jī 电视机; **television studio** diànshì shèyǐng shì 电视摄影室

tell 1 *v/t story, lie* jiǎng 讲; *the difference* qūfēn 区分; *~ X Y* gàosù X Y 告诉 X Y; *don't ~ Mom* bié gàosù māma 别告诉妈妈; *could you ~ me the way to ...?* qǐng gàosù wǒ zěnme qù ...? 请告诉我怎么去...?; *~ X to do Y* jiào X zuò Y 叫 X 做 Y; *you're ~ing me!* háiyòng nǐ shuō! 还用你说!; *the heat is ~ing on him* qìwēn duì tā chǎnshēng yǐngxiǎng 气温对他产生影响; *time will ~* shíjiān zì huì dìnglùn 时间自会定论

♦ **tell off** *(reprimand)* shǔluò 数落

teller *(in bank)* chūnàyuán 出纳员

telltale 1 *adj signs* xièlòu 泄露 **2** *n* xièmìzhě 泄密者

temp 1 *n (employee)* línshígōng 临

时工 **2** *v/i* dǎ línshígōng 打临时
工

temper (*bad ~*) píqi 脾气; *be in a*
~ fā píqi 发脾气; *keep one's ~*
nàzhe xìngzi 捺着性子; *lose*
one's ~ fā píqi 发脾气

temperament xìnggé 性格

temperamental (*moody*) yì jīdòng
易激动

temperature wēndù 温度; (*fever*)
fāshāo 发烧; *have a ~* fāshāo 发
烧

temple[1] REL miàoyǔ 庙宇

temple[2] ANAT tàiyángxué 太阳穴

Temple of Heaven Tiāntán 天坛

tempo sùdù 速度

temporarily zànshí 暂时

temporary zànshí 暂时

tempt xīyǐn 吸引

temptation yòuhuò 诱惑

tempting yǒu xīyǐnlì 有吸引力

ten shí 十

tenacious jiānrèn 坚韧

tenant (*of building*) fángkè 房客;
(*of farm, land*) diànhù 佃户

tend[1] *v/t* (*look after*) zhàogù 照顾

tend[2]: *- to do ...* qīngxiàng yú zuò
... 倾向于做 ...; *~ toward ...*
qīngxiàng yú ... 倾向于 ...

tendency qīngxiàng 倾向

tender[1] *adj* (*sore*) xūruò 虚弱;
(*affectionate*) wēnróu 温柔; *steak*
ruǎn 软

tender[2] *n* COM tóubiāo 投标

tenderness (*soreness*) xūruò 虚弱;
(*of kiss etc*) wēnróu gǎn 温柔感;
(*of steak*) ruǎn 软

tendon jiàn 腱

tennis wǎngqiú 网球

tennis ball wǎngqiú 网球; **tennis**
court wǎngqiú chǎng 网球场;
tennis player wǎngqiú shǒu 网
球手; **tennis racket** wǎngqiú pāi
网球拍

tenor *n* MUS nángāoyīn 男高音

tense[1] *n* GRAM shítài 时态

tense[2] *adj* *muscle* jǐn 紧; *voice,*
person, moment jǐnzhāng 紧张

♦ **tense up** *v/i* (*of muscles*) bēngjǐn
绷紧; (*of person*) jǐnzhāng 紧张

tension (*of rope*) lālì 拉力; (*in*

atmosphere, voice) jǐnzhāng 紧张;
(*in movie, novel*) jǐnyào guāntóu
紧要关头

tent zhàngpeng 帐篷

tentacle chùshǒu 触手

tentative yóuyù 犹豫

tenterhooks: *be on ~* tíxīn diàodǎn 提心吊胆

tenth dìshí 第十

tepid *water, reaction* wēiwēn 微温

term (*period of time*) shíqí 时期;
EDU xuéqí 学期; (*condition*) tiáojiàn 条件; (*word*) cí 词; *be on*
good/bad ~s with X yú X guānxi
hǎo/huài 与X关系好/坏; *in the*
long/short ~ cháng/duǎnqí 长/
短期; *come to ~s with X* duì X
cǎiqǔ jiāngjiù tàidù 对X采取将
就态度

terminal 1 *n* (*at airport*) chūrùjìng
kǒu 出入境口; (*for buses*) zhōngdiǎnzhàn 终点站; (*for containers*)
yùnshū zhōngdiǎnzhàn 运输终
点站; ELEC xiàn jiētóu 线接头;
COMPUT diànnǎo zhàn 电脑站
2 *adj illness* wǎnqī 晚期

terminally *adv* wǎnqī 晚期; *~ ill*
bìngzhèng wǎnqī 病症晚期

terminate 1 *v/t* *contract* zhōngzhǐ
终止; *pregnancy* liúchǎn 流产
2 *v/i* zhōngzhǐ 终止

termination (*of contract*) zhōngzhǐ
终止; (*of pregnancy*) réngōng
liúchǎn 人工流产

terminology shùyǔ 术语

terminus (*for buses, trains*) zhōngdiǎn zhàn 终点站

terrace (*of houses*) páifáng 排房;
(*on hillside*) tītián 梯田; (*patio*)
yángtái 阳台

terracotta chìtáo 赤陶

terracotta warriors bīngmǎyǒng
兵马俑

terrain dìshì 地势

terrestrial 1 *n* dìqiú jūmín 地球居
民 **2** *adj television* wúxiàn diànshì
无线电视; (*of the earth*) lùdì 陆
地

terrible kěpà 可怕

terribly (*very*) hěn 很

terrific liǎobuqǐ 了不起

terrifically (*very*) hěn 很

terrify kǒnghè 恐吓; *be terrified* hàipà 害怕

terrifying kěpà 可怕

territorial lǐngtǔ 领土

territorial waters lǐnghǎi 领海

territory lǐngtǔ 领土; *fig* lǐngyù 领域

terror kǒngjù 恐惧

terrorism kǒngbù zhǔyì 恐怖主义

terrorist kǒngbù fènzi 恐怖分子

terrorist organization kǒngbù jīgòu 恐怖机构

terrorize kǒnghè 恐吓

test 1 *n* (*of equipment, scientific*) cèyàn 测验; (*exam*) kǎoyàn 考验 2 *v/t machine, theory* cèyàn 测验; *student* kǎo 考

testament (*to s.o.*) shízhèng 实证; *Old / New Testament* REL Jiù / Xīnyù Quánshū 旧 / 新约全书

testicle gāowán 睾丸

testify *v/i* LAW zuòzhèng 作证

testimonial jièshào xìn 介绍信

test tube shìguǎn 试管

test-tube baby shìguǎn yīng'ér 试管婴儿

testy bàozào 暴躁

tetanus pòshāngfēng 破伤风

tether 1 *v/t horse* shuān 拴 2 *n* xìshéng 系绳; *be at the end of one's* ~ shānqióng shuǐjìn 山穷水尽

text yuánwén 原文

textbook kèběn 课本

textile fǎngzhī 纺织

texture zhìdì 质地

Thai 1 *adj* Tàiguó 泰国 2 *n* (*person*) Tàiguó rén 泰国人; (*language*) Tàiguó yǔ 泰国语

Thailand Tàiguó 泰国

than bǐ 比; *bigger / faster ~ me* bǐ wǒ dà / kuài 比我大 / 快

thank *v/t* xiè 谢; *~ you* xièxie 谢谢; *no ~ you* búyòng, xièxie 不用, 谢谢

thanks gǎnxiè 感谢; *~!* xièxie 谢谢; *~ to* guīgōng yú 归功于

thankful gǎnjī 感激

thankfully gǎnjī 感激; (*luckily*)

xìngkuī 幸亏

thankless *task* túláo 徒劳

Thanksgiving (Day) Gǎn'ēn jié 感恩节

that 1 *adj* nàge 那个; *~ one* nàge 那个 2 *pron* nà 那; *what's ~?* nàshì shénme? 那是什么？; *who's ~?* nàshì shuí? 那是谁？; *~'s mine* nàshì wǒde 那是我的; *~'s tea* nàshì chá 那是茶; *~'s very kind* nǐ tài hǎo le 你太好了; *I think ~ ...* wǒ xiǎng ... 我想...; *the person / car ~ you see* nǐ kànjiàndé nàge rén / nà liàng chē 你看见的那个人 / 那辆车 4 *adv* (*so*) nàme 那么; *~ big / expensive* nàme dà / guì 那么大 / 贵

thaw *v/i* huà 化

the ◊ (*no translation*): *~ border* biānjiè 边界; *~ embassy* dàshǐguǎn 大使馆; *is that ~ ring he gave you?* nà shì tā gěi nǐ de jièzhi ma? 那是他给你的戒指吗？; *~ capital of France* Fǎguó de shǒudū 法国的首都 ◊ (*when previous reference has been made*) zhè 这, nèi 那; *~ old man* nèige lǎotóu 那个老头; *~ blue bag is mine* zhè lánsè de bāo shì wǒde 这蓝色的包是我的 ◊ ~ *sooner ~ better* yuèkuài yuèhǎo 越快越好

theater jùchǎng 剧场

theatrical xìjù 戏剧; (*overdone*) zuòzuò 做作

theft tōuqiè 偷窃

their tāmende 他们的; (*his or her*) tā / tāde 他 / 她的

theirs tāmende 他们的; *a friend of ~* tāmende péngyǒu 他们的朋友

them tāmen 他们; (*him or her*) tā / tā 他 / 她

theme zhǔtí 主题

theme park yóulè yuán 游乐园

theme song zhǔtí gē 主题歌

themselves: *by ~* (*alone*) tāmen zìjǐ 他们自己

then (*at that time*) nàshí 那时; (*after that*) érhòu 而后; (*deducing*) nàme

那么; **by ~** dào nàshí 到那时

theology shénxué 神学

theoretical lǐlùn 理论

theory lǐlùn 理论; **in ~** lǐlùn shàng láishuō 理论上来说

therapeutic yīliáo 医疗

therapist zhìliáo xuéjiā 治疗学家

therapy liáofǎ 疗法

there nàr 那儿; **over ~ / down ~** zài nàr / xiàmiàn nàr 在那儿 / 下面那儿; **~ is / are ...** yǒu ... 有 ...; **is / are ~ ...?** yǒu ... ma? 有 ... 吗? ; **~ is / are not ...** méiyǒu ... 没有 ...; **~ you are** (*giving sth*) gěinǐ 给你; (*finding sth*) yuánlái nǐ zài zhèr 原来你在这儿; (*completing sth*) wánle 完了; **~ and back** láihuí 来回; **~ he is!** tā zài nàr! 他在那儿! ; **~, ~!** hǎole, hǎole! 好了, 好了!

thereabouts dàyū 大约

therefore yīncǐ 因此

thermometer wēndùjì 温度计

thermos flask bǎowēnpíng 保温瓶

thermostat héngwēnqì 恒温器

these zhèxiē 这些

thesis lùnwén 论文

they tāmen 他们; (*he or she*) tā 他 / 她; **~ say that ...** tīngshuō ... 听说 ...; **~ are going to change the law** tāmen yào xiūgǎi fǎlù 他们要修改法律

thick *hair* mì 密; *soup* chóu 稠; *crowd* chóumì 稠密; *fog* duō 多; *wall, book* hòu 厚; F (*stupid*) bèn 笨

thicken *sauce* shǐ biànchóu 使变稠

thickset ǎizhuàng 矮壮

thickskinned *fig* liǎnpí hòu 脸皮厚

thief xiǎotōu 小偷

thigh dàtuǐ 大腿

thimble dǐngzhēn 顶针

thin *hair, soup* xī 稀; *coat* báo 薄; *line* xì 细; *person* shòu 瘦

thing dōngxi 东西; **~s** (*belongings*) suǒyǒuwù 所有物; **how are ~s?** zuìjìn zěnyàng? 最近怎样? ; **good ~ you told me** xìngkuī nǐ gàosù wǒle 幸亏你告诉我了;

what a ~ to do / say! zěnme néng nàme zuò / shuō ne! 怎么能那么做 / 说呢!

thingumajig F (*item*) dōngxi 东西; (*person*) nèirén 那人

think xiǎng 想; **I ~ so** wǒ rènwéi rúcǐ 我认为如此; **I don't ~ so** wǒ bú rènwéi rúcǐ 我不认为如此; **I ~ so too** wǒ yě shì zhème xiǎng de 我也是这么想的; **what do you ~?** nǐ shuō ne? 你说呢? ; **what do you ~ of it?** nǐ duì cǐ yǒu hé xiǎngfǎ? 你对此有何想法? ; **I can't ~ of anything more** wǒ xiǎngbùchū qítādele 我想不出其它的了; **~ hard!** hǎohao xiǎngxiang! 好好想想! ; **I'm ~ing about emigrating** wǒ yǒuyì yímín 我有意移民

♦ **think over** kǎolǜ 考虑

♦ **think through** kǎolǜ 考虑

♦ **think up** *plan* xiǎngchū 想出

third **1** *adj* dìsān 第三 **2** *n* (*fraction*) sānfēnzhīyī 三分之一

thirdly dìsān 第三

third-party insurance dìsān fāng bǎoxiǎn 第三方保险; **third-rate** xiàděng 下等; **Third World** Dìsān Shìjiè 第三世界

thirst kě 渴

thirsty: be ~ kě 渴

thirteen shísān 十三

thirteenth dìshísān 第十三

thirtieth dìsānshí 第三十

thirty sānshí 三十

this **1** *adj* zhège 这个; **~ one** zhège 这个 **2** *pron* zhège 这个; **~ is good** zhè hǎo 这好; **~ is ...** (*introducing s.o.*) zhèshì ... 这是 ...; TELEC wǒshì ... 我是 ... **3** *adv* zhème 这么; **~ big / high** zhème dà / gāo 这么大 / 高

thorn cì 刺

thorough *search* chèdǐ 彻底; *knowledge* wánzhěng 完整; *person* búyànqífán 不厌其烦

thoroughbred (*horse*) chúnzhǒng 纯种

those *adj & pron* nàxiē 那些

though **1** *conj* (*although*) jǐnguǎn

尽管; **~ it might fail** jǐnguǎn kěnéng shībài 尽管可能失败; **as ~** hǎoxiàng hǎo duì 2 *adv* rán'ér 然而; **it's not finished ~** hái méi wánne 还没完呢

thought (*single*) xiǎngfa 想法; (*collective*) sīxiǎng 思想

thoughtful *look, face, person* chénsī 沉思; *book* jīng rènzhēn tuīqiāo 经认真推敲; (*considerate*) xìxīn 细心

thoughtless cūxīn 粗心

thousand qiān 千; **~s of** wúshù 无数; **ten ~** wàn 万

thousandth 1 *n* dì yī qiān gè 第一千个; (*fraction*) qiānfēnzhīyī 千分之一 2 *adj* dì yī qiān gè 第一千个

thrash *v/t* chōu 抽; sp dǎbài 打败
◆**thrash around** (*with arms etc*) fánzào bù'ān de dònglái dòngqù 烦躁不安地动来动去
◆**thrash out** *solution* jiějué wèntí 解决问题

thrashing tòngdǎ 痛打; sp cǎnbài 惨败

thread 1 *n* xiàn 线; (*of screw*) luówén 螺纹 2 *v/t* needle chuān-xiàn 穿线; *beads* chuān 穿

threadbare lánlǚ 褴褛

threat wēixié 威胁

threaten wēixié 威胁

threatening *gesture, tone* yǒu wēixié xìng 有威胁性; *sky* yīnchén 阴沉

three sān 三

Three Gorges Sānxiá 三峡; **Three Kingdoms** Sānguó 三国; **three-quarters** *n* sì fēn zhī sān 四分之三

thresh *v/t corn* tuōlì 脱粒

threshold (*of house*) ménkǎn 门槛; (*of new age*) kāiduān 开端; **on the ~ of** zài ... de kāiduān 在 ... 的开端

thrift jiéyuē 节约

thrifty jiéyuē 节约

thrill 1 *n* xìngfèn 兴奋 2 *v/t* shǐ ... xìngfèn 使 ... 兴奋; **be ~ed** gāoxìng 高兴

thriller (*movie*) jīngxiǎn diànyǐng 惊险电影; (*novel*) jīngxiǎn xiǎo-shuō 惊险小说

thrilling lìngrén máogǔ sǒngrán 令人毛骨悚然

thrive (*of plant*) zhuózhuàng shēng-zhǎng 茁壮生长; (*of business, economy*) fánróng 繁荣

throat hóulóng 喉咙

throat lozenges rùnhóu táng 润喉糖

throb 1 *n* (*of heart*) tiàodòng 跳动; (*of music*) zhènchàn 震颤 2 *v/i* (*of heart*) tiàodòng 跳动; (*of music*) zhènchàn 震颤

thrombosis xuèshuān xíngchéng 血栓形成

throne wángwèi 王位

throng *n* rénqún 人群

throttle 1 *n* (*on motorbike, boat*) jiéliú fá 节流阀 2 *v/t* (*strangle*) qiā zhù bózi 掐住脖子
◆**throttle back** *v/i* guānxiǎo yóumén jiǎnsù 关小油门减速

through 1 *prep* (*across*) chuānguò 穿过; (*during*) zài ... qījiān 在 ... 期间; (*thanks to*) yóuyú 由于; **go ~ the city** shìqū 穿过市区; **~ the winter / summer** dōng / xiàjì qījiān 冬 / 夏季期间; **Monday – Friday** xīngqī yī zhì wǔ 星期一至五; **arranged ~ him** tōngguò tā ānpái 通过他安排 2 *adv*: **wet ~** shī tòule 湿透了; **watch a movie ~** cóngtóu dàowěi kànwán yìchǎng diànyǐng 从头到尾看完一场电影; **read a book ~** cóngtóu dàowěi dúwán yìběn shū 从头到尾读完一本书 3 *adj*: **be ~** (*of couple*) wánle 完了; (*have arrived: of news etc*) dào-dá 到达; **you're ~** TELEC tōngle 通了; **I'm ~ with X** (*finished with a person*) wǒ yǔ X juéjiāo 我与X绝交; (*finished with a task*) wǒ wánchéng le X 我完成了X

through flight zhíháng fēijī 直航飞机

throughout 1 *prep* guànchuān 贯穿 2 *adv* (*in all parts*) dàochù 到处

through train zhítōng huǒchē 直通火车

throw 1 *v/t* rēng 扔; *(of horse)* shuāidǎo 摔倒; *(disconcert)* shǐ ... cānghuáng shīcuò shǐ ... 仓皇失措; *party* jǔxíng 举行 **2** *n* tóuzhì 投掷

♦**throw away** rēngdiào 扔掉
♦**throw out** *old things* rēngdiào 扔掉; *husband, drunk etc* niǎnzǒu 撵走; *plan* fǒujué 否决
♦**throw up 1** *v/t ball* pāoqǐ 抛起 **2** *v/i (vomit)* ǒutù 呕吐

throw-away *remark* suíyì 随意; *(disposable)* yīcì xìng 一次性
throw-in SP zhì jiè wài qiú 掷界外球

thru → **through**
thrush *(bird)* dōngniǎo 鸫鸟
thrust *v/t (push hard)* měngtuī 猛推; ~ **X into Y's hands** bǎ X sāirù Y shǒu zhōng 把 X 塞入 Y 手中; ~ **one's way through the crowd** chuǎngguò rénqún 闯过人群
thud *n* pēng de yìshēng 砰的一声
thug èguò 恶棍
thumb 1 *n* mǔzhǐ 拇指 **2** *v/t:* ~ **a ride** dāchē 搭车
thumbtack túdīng 图钉
thump 1 *n (blow)* zhòngjī 重击; *(noise)* pēng pēng 砰砰 **2** *v/t person* zhòngjī 重击; ~ **one's fist on the table** yòng quántóu chuí zhuōzi 用拳头捶桌子 **3** *v/i (of heart)* měngtiào 猛跳; ~ **on the door** pāimén 拍门
thunder *n* dǎléi 打雷
thunderstorm léiyǔ 雷雨
thundery *weather* yào dǎléi 要打雷
Thursday xīngqī sì 星期四
thus yīncǐ 因此
thwart *person, plans* héngxiàng 横向
thyroid (gland) jiǎzhuàngxiàn 甲状腺
Tiananmen *(incident)* liùsì 六四; *(square)* Tiān'ānmén 天安门
Tiananmen Square Tiān'ānmén Guǎngchǎng 天安门广场
Tibet Xīzàng 西藏
Tibetan 1 *adj* Xīzàng 西藏 **2** *n* *(person)* Xīzàng rén 西藏人;

(language) Xīzàng yǔ 西藏语
Tibetan Plateau Qīng Zàng Gāoyuán 青藏高原
tick 1 *n (of clock)* dīdā 滴答; *(checkmark)* dǎgōu 打勾 **2** *v/i (of clock)* dīdā dīdā xiǎng 滴答滴答响
♦**tick off** *(reprimand)* xùnchì 训斥
ticket piào 票
ticket collector shòupiào yuán 售票员; **ticket inspector** chápiào yuán 查票员; **ticket machine** shòupiàojī 售票机; **ticket office** *(at station, theater)* shòupiàochù 售票处
tickle 1 *v/t person* gēzhi gēzhi 胳肢 **2** *v/i (of material)* fāyǎng 发痒; *(of person)* shǐ fāyǎng 使发痒
ticklish *person* pàyǎng 怕痒
tidal wave làngcháo 浪潮
tide cháo 潮; **high** ~ gāocháo 高潮; **low** ~ dīcháo 低潮; **the** ~ **is in** / **out** zhǎngcháo / luòcháo 涨潮 / 落潮
tidy *person, habits* zhěngjié 整洁; *room, house* zhěngqí 整齐
♦**tidy up 1** *v/t room, shelves* shōushi 收拾; **tidy oneself up** bǎ zìjǐ shōushi yīxià 把自己收拾一下 **2** *v/i* shōushi 收拾
tie 1 *n (necktie)* lǐngdài 领带; (SP: *even result*) píngjú 平局; **he doesn't have any ~s** tā méiyǒu rènhé liánxì 他没有任何联系 **2** *v/t knot* dǎjié 打结; *hands* jì xì 系; ~ **two ropes together** bǎ liǎngtiáo shéngzi jì zài yìqǐ 把两条绳子系在一起 **3** *v/i* SP chéng píngjú 成平局
♦**tie down** *(with rope)* kǔnzhù 捆住; *(restrict)* yùshù yùshù 约束
♦**tie up** *person* bǎngzhù 绑住; *laces* jìzhù 系住; *boat* bó 泊; *hair* xì qǐlái 系起来; **I'm tied up tomorrow** *(busy)* míngtiān wǒ yǒushì 明天我有事
tier *(of hierarchy)* céng 层; *(in stadium)* pái 排
tiger lǎohǔ 老虎
tight 1 *adj clothes*, *(hard to move)* jǐn 紧; *security* yán 严; *(properly shut)*

yán 严; *(not leaving much time)*
jǐncòu 紧凑; F *(drunk)* zuì bèn
2 *adv* yán jǐn 紧; *shut* yán 严

tighten *screw* shǐ ... biànjǐn 使 ...
变紧; *control* shǐ ... yánggé 使 ...
严格; *security* shǐ ... yánjǐn 使 ...
严谨; **~ one's grip on ...** zhuā láo
... 抓牢 ...
♦ **tighten up** *v/i (in discipline,*
security) yánjǐn qǐlái 严谨起来
tight-fisted kōumēnr 抠门儿
tightrope bēngsuǒ 绷索
tile cízhuān 瓷砖
till¹ → **until**
till² *(cash register)* shōukuǎn tái 收
款台
till³ *v/t soil* gēngzhòng 耕种
tilt 1 *v/t* shǐ qīngxié 使倾斜 **2** *v/i*
qīngxié 倾斜
timber mùcái 木材
time shíjiān 时间; *(occasion)* cì cì 次次;
~ is up dào shíjiān le 到时间了;
for the ~ being zànshí 暂时; **have**
a good ~ kāixīn 开心; **have a**
good ~! wán kāixīn diǎnr! 玩儿
开心点儿！; **what's the ~?,**
what ~ is it? jǐdiǎnle? 几点了？;
the first ~ dìyīcì 第一次; **four ~s**
sìcì 四次; **~ and again** duōcì 多
次; **all the ~** yīzhí 一直; **two /**
three at a ~ yīcì liǎng / sāngè 一次
两 / 三个; **at the same ~** *speak,*
reply etc tóngshí 同时; *(however)*
dànshí 但是; **in ~** jíshí 及时; **on ~**
ànshí 按时; **in no ~** líkè 立刻
time bomb dìngshí zhàdàn 定时
炸弹; **time clock** *(in factory)*
jìshízhōng 计时钟; **time-**
consuming huā shíjiān 花时间;
time-lag shíjiān jiàngé 时间间
隔; **time limit** qīxiàn 期限
timely jíshí 及时
time out SP zàntíng 暂停
timer dìngshíqì 定时器
timesaving jiéshěng shíjiān 节省
时间; **timescale** *(of project)*
shíjiān fànwéi 时间范围; **time**
switch dìngshíqì 定时器; **time-**
table shíjiān biǎo 时间表;
timewarp (kēhuàn zhōng)
zhuǎnshì（科幻中）转时; **time**

zone shíqū 时区
timid miǎntiǎn 腼腆
timing *(choosing a time)* shíjiān
xuǎnzé 时间选择; *(of actor,*
dancer) shíjiān fēncùn 时间分寸
tin *(metal)* xī 锡
tinfoil xīpó 锡箔
tinge *n (of color)* wēirǎn 微染; *(of*
sadness) dài ... qìxī 带 ... 气息
tingle *v/i* yǒu cìtòng gǎn 有刺痛
感
♦ **tinker with** bǎinòng 摆弄
tinkle *n (of bell)* dīngdāng shēng 丁
当声
tinsel jīnyín sī 金银丝
tint 1 *n (of color)* dànsè 淡色; *(in*
hair) rǎnsè 染色 **2** *v/t hair* rǎnsè
染色
tinted *eyeglasses* fǎnguāng 反光;
paper zháosè 着色
tiny jíxiǎo 极小
tip¹ *n (of stick, finger)* jiān 尖; *(of*
mountain) shāntóu 山头; *(of*
cigarette) yānzuǐ 烟嘴
tip² *n (piece of advice)* quàngào 劝
告; *(money)* xiǎofèi 小费 **2** *v/t*
waiter etc gěi xiǎofèi 给小费
♦ **tip off** tōngfēng bàoxìn 通风报
信
♦ **tip over** *jug, liquid* dào 倒; **he**
tipped water all over me tā dào
de wǒ mǎn shēn dōu shì shuǐ 他
倒得我满身都是水
tipped *cigarettes* yǒu yānzuǐ 有烟
嘴
tippy-toe: on ~ yòng jiǎojiān 用脚
尖
tipsy shāozuì 稍醉
tire¹ *(on wheel)* chētāi 车胎
tire² **1** *v/t* láolèi 劳累 **2** *v/i* láolèi 劳
累; **he never ~s of it** tā yǒngyuǎn
bùhuì yànjuàn 他永远不会厌
倦
tired lèi 累; **be ~ of X** duì X
yànjuàn 对 X 厌倦
tireless *efforts* zīzī bùjuàn 孜孜不
倦
tiresome *(annoying)* tǎoyàn 讨厌
tiring pífá 疲乏
tissue ANAT zǔzhī 组织; *(hand-*
kerchief) zhǐjīn 纸巾

tissue paper ⇩ báozhǐ 薄纸

tit[1] (*bird*) shānquè 山雀

tit[2]: *for tat* yǐyá huányá 以牙还牙

tit[3] ∨ (*breast*) nǎizi 奶子

title (*of novel etc*) piānmíng 篇名; (*of person*) tóuxiánr 头衔儿; LAW suǒyǒu quán 所有权

titter v/i shǎxiào 傻笑

to 1 *prep* dào 到; ~ *China* dào Zhōngguó 到中国; ~ *Hangzhou* dào Hángzhōu 到杭州; *let's go ~ my place* zánmen dào wǒ nàr qù ba 咱们到我那儿去吧; *walk ~ the station* zǒu dào chēzhàn 走到车站; ~ *the north / south of X* dào X de běi / nánbiān 到X的北 / 南边; *give X ~ Y* jiāng X gěi Y 将X给Y; *from Monday ~ Wednesday* cóng xīngqīyī dào xīngqīsān 从星期一到星期三; *from 10 ~ 15 people* shí zhì shíwǔ rén 十至十五人 **2** *with verbs*: ~ *speak*, ~ *shout* jiǎnghuà, hǎnjiào 讲话，喊叫; *learn ~ drive* xuéxí jiàshǐ 学习驾驶; *nice ~ eat* hǎochī 好吃; *too heavy ~ carry* tàizhòng 太重; ~ *be honest with you* hé nǐ shíshuō le ba 和你实说了吧 **3** *adv*: ~ *and fro* láihuí 来回

toad làiháma 癞蛤蟆

toadstool sǎnjūn 伞菌

toast 1 *n* kǎo miànbāo 烤面包; (*drinking*) gānbēi 干杯; *propose a ~ to* wèi … gānbēi 为 … 干杯 **2** v/t (*when drinking*) wèi … gānbēi 为 … 干杯

tobacco yāncǎo 烟草

toboggan *n* píngdǐ xuěqiāo 平底雪橇

today jīntiān 今天

toddle (*of child*) xiǎoháir xíngzǒu 小孩儿行走

toddler xiǎoháir 小孩儿

toe 1 *n* jiǎozhǐ 脚指 **2** v/t: ~ *the line* fúcóng mìnglìng 服从命令

toffee tàifēi táng 太妃糖

tofu dòufu 豆腐

together yīqǐ 一起; (*at the same time*) tóngshí 同时

toil *n* kǔgàn 苦干

toilet cèsuǒ 厕所; *go to the* ~ qù cèsuǒ 去厕所

toilet paper cèzhǐ 厕纸

toiletries wèishēngjiān yòngpǐn 卫生间用品

token (*sign*) xiàngzhēng 象征; (*for gambling*) fúbì 辅币; (*gift* ~) shāngpǐn quàn 商品券

tolerable *pain etc* kěyǐ rěnshòu 可以忍受; (*quite good*) guòdéqù 过得去

tolerance kuānróng 宽容

tolerant kuānróng 宽容

tolerate *noise* róngxǔ 容许; *person* róngrěn 容忍; *I won't ~ it!* wǒ bùnéng róngrěn! 我不能容忍!

toll[1] v/i (*of bell*) míng 鸣

toll[2] (*deaths*) sǐwáng rénshù 死亡人数

toll[3] (*for bridge, road*) tōngxíng fèi 通行费; TELEC diànhuà fèi 电话费

toll booth shōufèichù 收费处; **toll-free** TELEC miǎnfèi diànhuà 免费电话; **toll road** shōufèi gōnglù 收费公路

tomato (*in northern China*) xīhóngshì 西红柿; (*in southern China*) fānqié 蕃茄

tomato ketchup fānqiéjiàng 蕃茄酱

tomb fénmù 坟墓

tomboy yěyātóu 野丫头

tombstone mùbēi 墓碑

tomcat gōngmāo 公猫

tomorrow míngtiān 明天; *the day after* ~ hòutiān 后天; ~ *morning* míngchén 明晨

ton dūn 吨

tone (*of color*) fēnggé 风格; (*of musical instrument*) yuèyīn 乐音; (*of conversation etc*) yǔqì 语气; (*of neighborhood*) qìfēn 气氛; ~ *of voice* shēngdiào 声调

♦ **tone down** *demands, criticism* huǎnhé 缓和

toner tiáosè jì 调色剂

tongs qiánzi 钳子; (*for hair*) juǎnfà qián 卷发钳

tongue *n* shétou 舌头

tonic MED yàoshuǐ 药水

tonic (water) ◊ tānglìshuǐ 汤力水

tonight jīnwǎn 今晚

tonsil biǎntáotǐ 扁桃体

tonsillitis biǎntáoxiàn yán 扁桃腺炎

too (also) yě 也; (excessively) tài 太; me ~ wǒ yě wǒ 也; ~ big/hot tài dà/rè 太大/热; ~ much rice tàiduō fàn 太多饭; eat ~ much chī tàiduō 吃太多

tool gōngjù 工具

toolbar COMPUT gōngjùgé 工具格

tooth yáchǐ 牙齿

toothache yáténg 牙疼

toothbrush yáshuā 牙刷

toothless méiyá 没牙

toothpaste yágāo 牙膏

toothpick yáqiān 牙签

top 1 n (of mountain, tree) dǐng 顶; (upper part) shàngbù 上部; (lid: of bottle etc, pen) gài gě 盖; (of the class, league) zuì yōuxiù 最优秀; (clothing) shàngyī 上衣; (MOT: gear) zuì gāodǎng 最高档; on ~ of zài ... zhī shàng 在 ... 之上; at the ~ of zài ... zuìshàng 在 ... 最上; at the ~ of the mountain zài shāndǐng 在山顶; get to the ~ (of company etc) shēng zhì zuìgāo zhíwèi 升至最高职位; be over the ~ (exaggerated) guòhuǒ 过火 2 adj branches zuìdǐng 最顶; floor zuìgāo yīcéng zuì gāo yī céng 最高一层; management, official gāojí 高级; player jiānzǐ 尖子; speed, note zuìgāo 最高 3 v/t: ~ped with cream shàng jiā nǎiyóu 上加奶油

top hat gāodǐngmào 高顶帽

topheavy tóuzhòng jiǎoqīng 头重脚轻

◆top up glass, tank zhuāng mǎn 装满

topic tímù 题目

topical zhǔtí 主题

topless adj luǒxiōng 裸胸

topmost branches, floor zuìgāo 最高

topping (on pizza) dǐngcéng fùjiā wù 顶层附加物

topple 1 v/i dǎo 倒 2 v/t government tuīfān 推翻

top secret adj juémì 绝密

topsy-turvy adj (in disorder) luànqī bāzāo 乱七八糟; world diāndǎo hēibái 颠倒黑白

torch (with flame) huǒbǎ 火把

torment 1 n zhémó 折磨 2 v/t person, animal zhémó 折磨; ~ed by doubt yílǜ chóngchong 疑虑重重

tornado lóngjuǎn fēng 龙卷风

torrent jīliú 激流; (of lava) róngliú 熔流; (of abuse, words) tāotao bùjué 滔滔不绝

torrential: ~ rain bàoyǔ 暴雨

tortoise wūguī 乌龟

torture n & v/t zhémó 折磨

toss 1 v/t ball jìn 掷; rider shuāidǎo 摔倒; salad bànyún 拌匀; ~ a coin zhìbì 掷币 2 v/i: ~ and turn zhǎnzhuǎn fǎncè 辗转反侧

total 1 n zǒngshù 总数 2 adj sum, amount zǒng 总; disaster, idiot juéduì 绝对; stranger wánquán 完全 3 v/t F car zálàn 砸烂

totalitarian jíquán zhǔyì 极权主义

totally wánquán 完全

tote bag dà shǒutí bāo 大手提包

totter (of person) pánshān 蹒跚

touch 1 n (act of touching) chùmō 触摸; (sense) chùjué 触觉; (little bit) shǎoxǔ 少许; SP biānxiàn wài 边线外; lose ~ with X (s.o.) yǔ X shīqù liánxì 与X失去联系; keep in ~ with X (s.o.) yǔ X bǎochí liánxì 与X保持联系; we kept in ~ wǒmén bǎochí liánxì 我们保持联系; be out of ~ tuōjié 脱节 2 v/t chùmō 触摸; (emotionally) shǐ gǎndòng 使感动 3 v/i mō 摸; (of two lines etc) jiēchù 接触

◆touch down v/i (of airplane) zháolù 着陆; SP chùdǐ 触地

◆touch on (mention) tídào 提到

◆touch up photo xiūshì 修饰; (sexually) dòngshǒu dòngjiǎo 动手动脚

touchdown (of airplane) zháolù 着陆; SP chùdì 触地

touching adj gănrén 感人

touch judge SP biānxiàn cáipànyuán 边线裁判员

touchline SP biānxiàn 边线

touchy person mǐngǎn 敏感

tough person jiānqiáng 坚强; meat bú yì jǔjiáo 不易咀嚼; question, exam nán 难; material jiānrèn 坚韧; punishment wúqíng 无情

tough guy yǒngshì 勇士

tour 1 n lǚyóu 旅游 2 v/t area cānguān 参观

tourism lǚyóu yè 旅游业

tourist lǚyóu zhě 旅游者

tourist (information) office lǚyóu zīliào chù 旅游资料处

tournament jǐnbiāo sài 锦标赛

tour operator lǚyóu gōngsī 旅游公司

tousled hair pénglùan 蓬乱

tow 1 v/t car, boat zhuāi 拽 2 n zhuāi 拽; **give X a** ~ bāng X zhuāi bāng X zhuāi 帮 X 拽

♦**tow away** car tuōzǒu 拖走

toward prep xiàng 向

towel máojīn 毛巾

tower n tǎ 塔

town zhèn 镇

town council zhèn zhèngfǔ 镇政府

town hall zhèn zhèngfǔ dàlóu 镇政府大楼

towrope tuōlǎn 拖缆

toxic yǒudú 有毒

toy wánjù 玩具

♦**toy with** object bǎinòng 摆弄; idea bú dà rènzhēnde kǎolǜ 不大认真地考虑

trace 1 n (of substance) wēiliàng 微量 2 v/t (find) xúnzhǎo 寻找; (follow: footsteps) gēnzōng 跟踪; (draw) miáohuì 描绘

track n (path) xiǎojìng 小径; (for racing) pǎodào 跑道; RAIL guǐdào 轨道; ~ **10** RAIL dì shí zhàntái 第十站台; **keep ~ of X** jìlù X 记录 X

♦**track down** criminal gēnzōng zhuībǔ 跟踪追捕; copy of a book cházhǎo dào 查找到

tracksuit chángxiù yùndòngfú 长袖运动服

tractor ⇩ tuōlājī 拖拉机

trade 1 n (commerce) màoyì 贸易; (profession, craft) hángyè 行业 2 v/i (do business) jīngyíng 经营; ~ **in X** zuò X de mǎimài 做 X 的买卖 3 v/t (exchange) jiāohuàn 交换; ~ **X for Y** yòng X huàn Y 用 X 换 Y

♦**trade in** v/t (when buying) yǐ jiù huàn xīn 以旧换新

trade fair màoyìhuì 贸易会;

trademark shāngbiāo 商标;

trade mission màoyì dàibiǎotuán 贸易代表团

trader shāngrén 商人

trade secret shāngyè mìmì 商业秘密

tradesman (plumber etc) shǒugōngyì zhě 手工艺者

trade(s) union gōnghuì 工会

tradition chuántǒng 传统

traditional chuántǒng 传统

traditional characters fántǐzì 繁体字

traditionally chuántǒng 传统

traffic n (on roads) jiāotōng 交通; (at airport) jiāoliú liàng 交流量; (in drugs) fànmài 贩卖

♦**traffic in** drugs fànmài 贩卖

traffic circle huánxíng jiāochā 环形交叉; **traffic cop** F jiāotōng jǐng 交通警; **traffic island** jiāotōng dǎo 交通岛; **traffic jam** jiāotōng dǔsè 交通堵塞; **traffic light** hónglǜdēng 红绿灯; **traffic police** jiāotōng jǐng 交通警; **traffic sign** jiāotōng biāozhì 交通标志

tragedy bēijù 悲剧

tragic búxìng 不幸

trail 1 n (path) xiǎojìng 小径; (of blood) hénjì 痕迹 2 v/t (follow) gēnzōng 跟踪; (tow) tuōlā 拖拉 3 v/i (lag behind) luòhòu 落后

trailer (pulled by vehicle) tuōchē 拖车; (mobile home) péngchē 篷车; (of movie) diànyǐng yùgào piān 电影预告片

train¹ n huǒchē 火车; **go by** ~ zuò huǒchē 坐火车

train² 1 v/t team, athlete, dog xùnliàn 训练

训练; *employee* péixùn 培训 2 *v/i* (*of team, athlete*) xùnliàn 训练; (*of teacher etc*) péixùn 培训

trainee shíxí shēng 实习生

trainer SP jiàoliàn yuán 教练员; (*of dog*) xùnshòu zhě 训兽者

trainers *Br* (*shoes*) yùndòng xié 运动鞋

training (*of new staff*) péixùn 培训; SP xùnliàn 训练; *be in* ~ xùnliàn zhōng 训练中; *be out of* ~ SP jìngjì zhuàngtài bùjiā 竞技状态不佳

training course péixùn kèchéng 培训课程

training scheme péixùn jìhuà 培训计划

train station huǒchē zhàn 火车站

trait tèxìng 特性

traitor pàntú 叛徒

tramp 1 *n* (*Br. hobo*) yóumín 游民 **2** *v/i* chénzhòng de zǒu 沉重地走

trample *v/t*: *be* ~*d to death* zhòng cǎi zhì sǐ 重踩至死; *be* ~*d underfoot* zhòngcǎi 重踩

♦ **trample on** *person, object* cǎi cǎi 踩踩

trampoline bēngchuáng 绷床

trance huǎnghū 恍惚; *go into a* ~ chūshénr 出神儿

tranquil níngjìng 宁静

tranquility níngjìng 宁静

tranquilizer zhènjìngjì 镇静剂

transact *deal, business* jiāoyì 交易

transaction jiāoyì 交易

transatlantic héngkuà Dàxīyáng 横跨大西洋

transcendental xiānyàn 先验

transcript jìlù 纪录

transfer 1 *v/t* diàodòng 调动; *passengers* zhuǎnjī 转机; *one's custom to another company etc* zhuǎnyí 转移 **2** *v/i* (*when traveling*) qiānyí 迁移; (*from one language to another*) zhuǎnhuàn 转换 **3** *n* (*move, of money*) diàodòng 调动; (*in travel*) diàohuàn 调换

transferable *ticket* kě diàohuàn 可调换

transform *v/t* gǎibiàn 改变

transformation gǎibiàn 改变

transformer ELEC biànyāqì 变压器

transfusion shūxuè 输血

transistor jīngtǐguǎn 晶体管; (*radio*) jīngtǐguǎn shōuyīnjī 晶体管收音机

transit: *in* ~ zài yùnshū zhōng 在运输中

transition guòdù 过渡

transitional guòdù 过渡

transit lounge (*at airport*) zhuǎnjī tīng 转机厅

translate fānyì 翻译

translation fānyì 翻译

translator fānyì 翻译

transliterate yīnyì 音译

transmission (*of news, program*) bōfàng 播放; (*of disease*) chuánrǎn 传染; MOT biànsùqì 变速器

transmit *news, program* bōfàng 播放; *disease* chuánrǎn 传染

transmitter (*for radio, TV*) chuándáqì 传达器

transpacific kuàyuè Tàipíngyáng 跨越太平洋

transparency PHOT huàndēngpiān 幻灯片

transparent tòumíng 透明; (*obvious*) míngxiǎn 明显

transplant *v/t & n* MED yízhí 遗植

transport *v/t & n* yùnshū 运输

transportation (*of goods, people*) yùnshū 运输; *means of* ~ jiāotōng gōngjù 交通工具; *public* ~ gōngzhòng jiāotōng yùnshū gōngjù 公众交通运输工具; *Department of Transportation* Jiāotōng Bù 交通部

transvestite yì zhuāng pì zhě 易装癖者

trap 1 *n* (*for animal*) bǔshòu jīguān 捕兽机关; (*question, set-up etc*) quāntào 圈套; *set a* ~ *for X* gěi X shè quāntào 给 X 设圈套 **2** *v/t animal* shèlì bǔshòu jīguān 设立捕兽机关; *person we* shèlì quāntào 设圈套; *be* ~*ped* (*by enemy, flames, landslide etc*) xiànrù quāntào 陷入圈套

trapdoor huóbǎnmén 活板门

trapeze diàojià 吊架

trappings (*of power*) wàizài

biāozhì 外在标志

trash (*garbage*) lājī 垃圾; (*poor product*) fèipǐn 废品; (*despicable person*) wúnéng de rén 无能的人

trashcan lājītǒng 垃圾桶

trashy *goods, novel* lièzhì 劣质

traumatic chuàngshāng xìng 创伤性

travel 1 *n* lǚxíng 旅行; ~**s** lǚtú 旅途 **2** *v/i & v/t* lǚxíng 旅行

travel agency lǚxíng shè 旅行社

travel bag lǚxíng dài 旅行袋

traveler lǚxíng zhě 旅行者

traveler's check lǚxíng zhīpiào 旅行支票

travel expenses jiāotōng fèiyòng 交通费用; **travel insurance** lǚxíng bǎoxiǎn 旅行保险; **travelsick** lǚxíng jíbìng 旅行疾病

trawler tuōwǎng yúchuán 拖网鱼船

tray tuōpán 拖盘

treacherous *person* bùzhōng 不忠; *currents, roads* àncáng wēixiǎn 暗藏危险

treachery pànnì 叛逆

tread 1 *n* zúyìn 足音; (*of staircase*) tīmiàn 梯面; (*of tire*) tāimiàn 胎面 **2** *v/i* zǒuguò 走过

♦**tread on** cǎi 踩

treason pànguó zuì 叛国罪

treasure 1 *n* cáifù 财富; (*person*) bùkě duōdé de réncái 不可多得的人材 **2** *v/t gift etc* zhēnxī 珍惜

treasurer sīkù 司库

Treasury Department Cáiwù Bù 财务部

treat 1 *n* kuǎndài 款待; *it was a real ~* fēicháng lìngrén mǎnyì 非常令人满意; *I have a ~ for you* wǒ yǒu yàng hǎo dōngxi gěi nǐ 我有样好东西给你; *it's my ~* (*I'm paying*) wǒ qīngkè wǒ 请客 **2** *v/t materials* chǔlǐ 处理; *illness* zhìliáo 治疗; (*behave toward*) duìdài 对待; *~ X to Y* yòng Y kuǎndài X 用Y款待X

treatment (*of materials*) chǔlǐ 处理; (*of illness*) zhìliáo 治疗; (*of people*) duìdài 对待

treaty tiáoyuē 条约

treble[1] MUS zuì gāoyīn bù 最高音部

treble[2] **1** *adv* sānbèi 三倍; ~ *the price* jiàgé zhǎng sānbèi 价格涨三倍 **2** *v/i* fānle sān fān 翻了三番

tree shù 树

tremble (*of person, hand, voice*) fādǒu 发抖; (*of building*) yáohuàng 摇晃

tremendous (*very good*) juémiào 绝妙; (*enormous*) jùdà 巨大

tremendously (*very*) hěn 很; (*a lot*) hěnduō 很多

tremor (*of earth*) zhèndòng 震动

trench gōu 沟

trend qūxiàng 趋向; (*fashion*) cháoliú 潮流

trendy xīncháo 新潮

trespass fēifǎ qīnrù 非法侵入; *no ~ing* bùdé rùnèi 不得入内

♦**trespass on** *land* fēifǎ qīnrù 非法侵入; *privacy* dǎrǎo 打扰

trespasser fēifǎ qīnrù zhě 非法侵入者

trial LAW shěnpàn 审判; (*of equipment*) shìyàn 试验; *on ~* LAW shòushěn 受审; *have X on ~ equipment etc* shìyàn X 试验X

trial period (*for employee*) shíxí qī 实习期; (*for equipment*) shìyàn qī 试验期

triangle sānjiǎo xíng 三角形

triangular sānjiǎo xíng 三角形

tribe bùluò 部落

tribunal cáipàn yuàn 裁判院

tributary zhīliú 支流

trick 1 *n* (*to deceive*) jìmóu zì móu 计谋; (*knack*) jìqiǎo 技巧; *play a ~ on X* zhuōnòng X 捉弄X **2** *v/t* qīpiàn 欺骗; *~ X into doing Y* piàn Y zuò Y 骗Y做Y

trickery qīpiàn 欺骗

trickle *n & v/i* dī 滴

trickster piànzi 骗子

tricky (*difficult*) jíshǒu 棘手

tricycle sānlúnchē 三轮车

trifle (*triviality*) suǒshì 琐事

trifling suǒsuì 琐碎

trigger *n* bānjī 扳机; (*on camcorder*) qǐdòng zhuāngzhì 起

动装置

♦**trigger off** chùfā 触发

trim 1 *adj* (*neat*) zhěngqí 整齐; *figure* miáotiáo 苗条 **2** *v/t hair, hedge* xiāo削; *budget, costs* xùjiǎn 削减; (*decorate: dress*) zhuāngshì 装饰 **3** *n* (*light cut*) xiāobiānr 削边儿; *just a ~, please* (*to hairdresser*) qǐng zhǐ xiāobiānr 请只削边儿; *in good ~* jīngjīng yǒutiáo 井井有条

trimming (*on clothes*) xiūshì pǐn 修饰品; *with all the ~s* yǒu suǒyǒu dāpèi 有所有搭配

trinket wányìr 玩意儿

trio MUS sānchóng chàng 三重唱

trip 1 *n* (*journey*) lǚxíng 旅行 **2** *v/t & v/i* (*~ up*) bàndǎo 绊倒

♦**trip up 1** *v/t* (*make fall*) bàndǎo 绊倒; (*cause to go wrong*) shǐ ... fàn cuòwù shǐ ... 犯错误 **2** *v/i* (*stumble*) bàndǎo 绊倒; (*make a mistake*) fàn cuòwù 犯错误

tripe (*food*) niúdǔ 牛肚

triple → **treble**

triplets sānbāotāi 三胞胎

tripod PHOT sānjiǎojià 三脚架

trite chénjiù 陈旧

triumph *n* shènglì de xǐyuè 胜利的喜悦

trivial suǒsuì 琐碎

triviality suǒshì 琐事

trombone chánghào 长号

troops jūnduì 军队

trophy jiǎngbēi 奖杯

tropic huíguīxiàn 回归线

tropical rèdài 热带

tropics rèdài dìqū 热带地区

trot *v/i* xiǎopǎo 小跑

trouble 1 *n* (*difficulties*) kùnnan 困难; (*illness*) bìngtòng 病痛; (*inconvenience*) máfan 麻烦; (*disturbance*) sāoluàn 骚乱; *go to a lot of ~ to do X* bùcí xīnkǔ qù zuò X 不辞辛苦去做 X; *no ~* méi wèntí 没问题; *get into ~* zhāozhì máfan 招致麻烦 **2** *v/t* (*worry*) dānyōu 担忧; (*bother, disturb*) máfan 麻烦; (*of back, liver etc*) shǐ bù shūfu 使不舒服

trouble-free wú gùzhàng 无故障

troublemaker dǎoluàn zhě 捣乱者

troubleshooter (*mediator*) tiáojiě-rén 调解人

troubleshooting páichú gùzhàng 排除故障

troublesome fánrén 烦人

trousers *Br* kùzi 裤子; *a pair of ~* yītiáo kùzi 一条裤子

trout zūnyú 鳟鱼

truce xiūzhàn 休战

truck kǎchē 卡车

truck driver kǎchē sījī 卡车司机; **truck farm** shūcài nóngchǎng 蔬菜农场; **truck farmer** càinóng 菜农; **truck stop** kǎchē sījī kuàicāndiàn 卡车司机快餐店

trudge *v/i & n* báshè 跋涉

true zhēn 真; *friend* gòu 够; *come ~* (*of hopes, dream*) shíxiàn 实现

truly zhēnde 真地; *Yours ~* cízhì cǐ zhì 此致

trumpet lǎba 喇叭

trunk (*of tree*) shùgàn 树干; (*of body*) qūgàn 躯干; (*of elephant*) xiàngbí 象鼻; (*large case*) dà píxiāng 大皮箱; (*of car*) xínglǐ xiāng 行李箱

trust 1 *n* xìnrèn 信任; FIN shòutuō jítuán 受托集团 **2** *v/t* xiāngxìn 相信; *I ~ you* wǒ xìnrèn nǐ 我信任你

trusted kěxìn 可信

trustee lǐshì 理事

trustful, trusting xìnrèn 信任

trustworthy zhíde xìnrèn 值得信任

truth shìshí 事实

truthful chéngshí 诚实

try 1 *v/t* chángshì 尝试; LAW shěn-pàn 审判; *~ to do X* qùzuò X 尝试去做 X **2** *v/i* shìshì 试试; *you must ~ harder* nǐ yīdìng yào gèngjiā nǔlì 你一定要更加努力 3 chángshì 尝试; *can I have a ~?* (*of food*) ràng wǒ shìshì 让我试试; (*at doing sth*) ràng wǒ shìshì 让我试试; *give X a ~* shìzuò X 试做 X

♦**try on** *clothes* shìchuān 试穿

♦**try out** *new machine, new method*

shìyòng 试用

trying (*annoying*) nányī róngrěn 难以容忍

T-shirt ⇩ yuánlǐng shān 圆领衫

tub (*bath*) yùgāng 浴缸; (*of liquid*) tǒng 桶; (*for yoghurt, ice cream*) hé 盒

tubby *adj* ǎipàng 矮胖

tube (*pipe*) guǎndào 管道; (*of toothpaste, ointment*) guǎn 管

tubeless *tire* wú nèitāi 无内胎

tuberculosis jiéhé bìng 结核病

tuck 1 *n* (*in dress*) zhě 褶 **2** *v/t* (*put*) sāijìn 塞进

♦**tuck away** (*put away*) shōucáng 收藏; (*eat quickly*) dàchī 大吃

♦**tuck in 1** *v/t children* gàihǎo bèizi 盖好被子; *sheets* sāihǎo guǒjǐn 塞好裹紧 **2** *v/i* (*start eating*) kāishǐ chī 开始吃

♦**tuck up** *sleeves etc* juǎnqǐ 卷起; **tuck X up in bed** gěi X gàihǎo bèizi ānshuì 给X盖好被子安睡

Tuesday xīngqī èr 星期二

tuft cóng 丛

tug 1 *n* (*pull*) lā 拉; NAUT tuōchuán 拖船 **2** *v/t* (*pull*) lā 拉

tuition fǔdǎo 辅导

tulip yùjīnxiāng 郁金香

tumble *v/i* dǎo 倒

tumbledown yáoyao yùzhuì 摇摇欲坠

tumble-dryer shuǎigān jī 甩干机

tumbler (*for drink*) wújiǎo bōlíbēi 无脚玻璃杯; (*in circus*) fān jīndǒu zhě 翻筋斗者

tummy dùzi 肚子

tummy ache dùzi téng 肚子疼

tumor zhǒngliú 肿瘤

tumult xuānnào 喧闹

tumultuous xuānnào 喧闹

tuna jīnqiāng yú 金枪鱼

tune 1 *n* qǔdiào 曲调; **in ~** hédiào 合调; **out of ~** zǒudiào 走调 **2** *v/t instrument* tiáo zhǔn yīndiào 调准音调

♦**tune in** *v/i* RAD shōutīng 收听; TV shōukàn 收看

♦**tune in to** RAD shōutīng 收听; TV shōukàn 收看

♦**tune up 1** *v/i* (*of orchestra,*

players) tiáoyīn 调音 **2** *v/t engine* tiáozhěng 调整

tuneful yīndiào yuè'ěr 音调悦耳

tuner (*hi-fi*) tiáoxié qì 调谐器

tunic EDU duǎnpáo 短袍

tunnel *n* suìdào 隧道

turbine (*operated by air*) qìlún jī 气轮机; (*operated by water*) wōlún jī 涡轮机; (*operated by steam*) yèlún jī 叶轮机

turbot dàlíngpíng 大菱鲆

turbulence (*in air travel*) tuānliú 湍流

turbulent *meeting, life, love affair* hǔnluàn 混乱; *weather* kuángbào 狂暴

turf cǎopí 草皮

Turk Tú'ěrqí rén 土耳其人

Turkey Tú'ěrqí 土耳其

turkey huǒjī 火鸡

Turkish 1 *adj* Tú'ěrqí 土耳其 **2** *n* (*language*) Tú'ěrqí yǔ 土耳其语

turmoil dòngluàn 动乱

turn 1 *n* (*rotation*) zhuǎndòng 转动; (*in road*) zhuàn 转; (*in vaudeville*) jiémù 节目; **take ~s doing X** lúnliú zuò X 轮流做 X; **it's my ~** gāi wǒ le 该我了; **it's not your ~ yet** méi dào nǐ ne 没到你呢; **take a ~ at the wheel** kāi yīhuìr chē 开一会儿车; **do X a good ~** wèi X zuò hǎoshì 为X做好事 **2** *v/t wheel* zhuàn 转; *corner* guǎiwānr 拐弯儿; **~ one's back on X** rēngxià X bùguǎn 扔下X不管 **3** *v/i* (*of driver, car, wheel*) zhuàn 转; **~ right / left here** zhuànyòu/zuò wánr 转右/左; **it has ~ed sour / cold** biànsuān/lěng le 变酸/冷了; **he has ~ed 40** tā sìshí le 他四十了

♦**turn around 1** *v/t object, company* niǔzhuǎn 扭转; (COM: *deal with*) wánchéng 完成 **2** *v/i* (*of person*) zhuǎnshēn 转身; (*of driver*) diàotóu 调头

♦**turn away 1** *v/t* (*send away*) jùjué 拒绝 **2** *v/i* (*walk away*) zǒule 走了; (*look away*) zhuǎnliǎn 转脸

♦**turn back 1** *v/t edges, sheets* fānhuí 翻回 **2** *v/i* (*of walkers, in* *course of action)* huítóu 回头

♦**turn down** *v/t offer, invitation* jùjué 拒绝; *volume, TV, heating* guānxiǎo 关小; *edge, collar* fānxià 翻下

♦**turn in 1** *v/i (go to bed)* shàngchuáng 上床 **2** *v/t (to police)* zìshǒu 自首

♦**turn off 1** *v/t TV, faucet, heater, engine* guān 关; F *(sexually)* shǐ shīqù xìngqù 使失去兴趣 **2** *v/i (of car, driver)* xià 下

♦**turn on 1** *v/t TV, faucet, heater, engine* kāi 开; F *(sexually)* cìjī 刺激 **2** *v/i (of machine)* kāi 开

♦**turn out 1** *v/t lights* guān 关 **2** *v/i: as it turned out* jiéguǒ shì 结果是

♦**turn over 1** *v/i (in bed)* fānshēn 翻身; *(of vehicle)* fān guòlái 翻过来 **2** *v/t (put upside down)* fān guòlái 翻过来; *page* fān piānr 翻篇儿; FIN zhōuzhuǎn 周转

♦**turn up 1** *v/t collar* fānqǐ 翻起; *volume, heating* kāidà 开大 **2** *v/i (arrive)* lòumiàn 露面

turning guǎijiǎo 拐角

turning point zhuǎnzhé diǎn 转折点

turnip luóbo 萝卜

turnout *(people)* cānjiā zhě 参加者

turnover FIN chéngjiāo liàng 成交量

turnpike gāosù gōnglù 高速公路

turnstile ràogān 绕杆

turntable *(of record player)* diànchàng pán 电唱盘

turquoise *adj* qīnglǜsè 青绿色

turret *(of castle)* jiǎolóu 角楼; *(of tank)* xuánzhuǎn pàotǎ 旋转炮塔

turtle wūguī 乌龟

turtleneck (sweater) gāolǐng tàoshān 高领套衫

tusk xiàngyá 象牙

tutor *(private)* ~ sīrén jiàoshī 私人教师

tuxedo lǐfú 礼服

TV diànshì 电视; *on* ~ diànshì shang 电视上

TV program diànshì jiémù 电视节目

twang 1 *n (in voice)* bíyīn 鼻音 **2** *v/t guitar string* shǐ fā xián shēng 使发弦声

tweezers nièzi 镊子

twelfth dìshí'èr 第十二

twelve shí'èr 十二

twentieth dìèrshí 第二十

twenty èrshí 二十

twice liǎngcì 两次; *~ as much* liǎngbèi nàme duō 两倍那么多

twiddle bǎinòng 摆弄; *~ one's thumbs* fig xiánzhe 闲着

twig *n* xìzhī 细枝

twilight huánghūn 黄昏

twin shuāng bāo tāi 双胞胎

twin beds liǎng zhāng chuáng 两张床

twinge *(of pain)* cìtòng 刺痛

twinkle *v/i (of stars)* shǎnyào 闪耀; *(of eyes)* fāguāng 发光

twin town yǒuyí shì 友谊市

twirl 1 *v/t* shǐ xuánzhuǎn 使旋转 **2** *n (of cream etc)* zhuāngshì 装饰

twist 1 *v/t* cuō 搓; *~ one's ankle* niǔle jiǎohuái 扭了脚踝 **2** *v/i (of road, river)* pánxuán 盘旋 **3** *n (in rope)* nǐng 拧; *(in road)* guǎiwānr 拐弯儿; *(in plot, story)* qūzhé 曲折

twisty *road* wānwan qūqu 弯弯曲曲

twit bèndàn 笨蛋

twitch 1 *n (nervous)* chōuchù 抽搐 **2** *v/i (jerk)* chōuchù 抽搐

twitter *v/i (of birds)* zhīzhī de jiào 吱吱地叫

two èr 二; *(with measure words)* liǎng 俩; *the ~ of them* tāmen liǎng 他们俩

two-faced liǎngmiànpài 两面派; **two-piece** *n (woman's suit)* tàofú tàofú 套服; **two-stroke** *adj engine* èrchōngchéng 二冲程; **two-way** *traffic* shuāngxiàng jiāotōng 双向交通

tycoon jùtóu 巨头

type 1 *n (sort)* zhǒnglèi 种类; *what ~ of ...?* nǎ yīzhǒng ...? 那一种 ... **2** *v/t & v/i (with a keyboard)* dǎzì 打字

typhoid (fever) shānghán 伤寒

typhoon táifēng 台风

typhus bānzhěn shānghán 斑疹伤寒

typical diǎnxíng 典型; *that's ~ of him* tā jiù shì nàyàng 他就是那样

typically diǎnxíng 典型; ~

American diǎnxíng Měiguórén 典型美国人

typist dǎzìyuán 打字员

tyrannical bàonüè 暴虐

tyrannize shī bàonüè 施暴虐

tyranny (*behavior*) bàonüè 暴虐; (*regime*) bàozhèng 暴政

tyrant bàojūn 暴君

U

ugly chǒulòu 丑陋

UK (= **United Kingdom**) Yīngguó 英国; (formal use) Liánhé Wángguó 联合王国

ulcer kuìyáng 溃疡

ultimate (best, definitive) zuìhǎo 最好; (final) zuìhòu 最后; (fundamental) gēnběn 根本

ultimately (in the end) zuìzhōng 最终

ultimatum zuìhòu tōngdié 最后通牒

ultrasound MED chāoshēngbō 超声波

ultraviolet adj zǐwài 紫外

umbilical cord qídài 脐带

umbrella sǎn 伞

umpire n cáipànyuán 裁判员

umpteen F wúshù 无数

UN (= **United Nations**) Liánhéguó 联合国

un ... (with adjs) bù, fēi (qiánzhuì) 不, 非 (前缀)

unable: be ~ to do X (not know how to) bùhuì zuò X 不会做 X; (not be in a position to) méiyǒu nénglì zuò X 没有能力做 X

unacceptable bùnéng jiēshòu 不能接受; it is ~ that ... ... shì lìngrén bùnéng jiēshòu de ... 是令人不能接受的

unaccountable wúfǎ jiěshì 无法解释

unaccustomed: be ~ to X bù xíguànyú X 不习惯于 X

unadulterated fig (absolute) shízú 十足

un-American (not fitting) fēi Měiguó 非美国

unanimous verdict yízhì tóngyì 一致 同意; be ~ on X duì X dáchéng yízhì 对 X 达成一致

unanimously vote, decide yízhì 一致

unapproachable person nányǐ jiējìn 难以接近

unarmed person wú wǔqì 无武器; ~ **combat** túshǒu gédòu 徒手格斗

unassuming qiānxùn 谦逊

unattached (without a partner) wú gùdìng bànlǚ 无固定伴侣

unattended wúzhǔ 无主; leave X ~ diūxià X bùguǎn 丢下 X 不管

unauthorized shànzì 擅自

unavoidable bùkě bìmiǎn 不可避免

unavoidably: be ~ detained chōu bù kāi shēn 抽不开身

unaware: be ~ of méiyǒu chájué dào 没有察觉到

unawares: catch X ~ shǐ X chījīng 使 X 吃惊

unbalanced bù pínghéng 不平衡; PSYCH shīcháng 失常

unbearable nányǐ rěnshòu 难以忍受

unbeatable team, quality bùkě zhànshèng 不可战胜

unbeaten team wèi bèi jībài 未被击败

unbeknownst: ~ to X X bù zhīdào X 不知道

unbelievable nányǐzhìxìn 难以置信; F heat, value jíduān 极端; he's ~ F (very good / bad) tā zhēn búshì yìbān rén 他真不是一般人

unbias(s)ed bù piāntǎn 不偏袒

unblock pipe qīngchú dǔsè 清除堵塞

unborn wèi chūshēng 未出生

unbreakable plate dǎbúpò 打不碎; world's record bùkě dǎpò 不可打破

unbutton jiěkāi niǔkòu 解开纽扣

uncalled-for wú lǐyóu 无理由

uncanny resemblance yìhūxúncháng 异乎寻常; skill bùkě sīyì

不可思议; (*worrying: feeling*) líqí
离奇

unceasing búduàn 不断

uncertain *future, weather* kěnéng
gǎibiàn 可能改变; *origins* bú
quèdìng 不确定; **be ~ about X**
duì X bú quèdìng 对 X 不确定

uncertainty (*of the future*) bú
quèdìng 不确定; **there is still ~
about X** háiyǒu bú
quèdìngxìng 对 X 还有不确定性

unchecked: **let X go** rèn X zìyóu
fāzhǎn 任 X 自由发展

uncle (*mother's brother*) jiùjiu 舅
舅; (*father's elder brother*) bóbo 伯
伯; (*father's younger brother*)
shūshu 叔叔; (*mother's sister's husband*) yífu 姨父; (*father's sister's
husband*) gūfu 姑父; (*to older non-
related men*) shūshu 叔叔

uncomfortable *chair* bù shūshì 不
舒适; *sitting position* bù shūfu 不
舒服; **feel ~ about X** (*about
decision etc*) duì X yǒu zhíyí 对 X
有质疑; **I feel ~ with him** wǒ gēn
tā zài yìqǐ gǎndào bú zìzài 我跟
他在一起感到不自在

uncommon bù xúncháng 不寻常;
it's not ~ zhè bù hǎnjiàn 这不罕
见

uncompromising bú ràngbù 不让
步

unconcerned lěngmò 冷漠; **be ~
about X** bù bǎ X fàngzài xīn
shang 不把 X 放在心上

unconditional wú tiáojiàn 无条件

unconscious MED shīqù zhíjué 失
去知觉; PSYCH xiàyìshí 下意识;
knock ~ dǎde X bùxǐngrénshì
打得 X 不醒人事; **be ~ of X** (*not
aware*) wèi chájué chū X 未察觉
出 X

uncontrollable *anger, desire,
children* kòngzhì bùliǎo 控制不
了

unconventional bùxún xísú 不循
习俗

uncooperative búyuàn hézuò 不
愿合作

uncork *bottle* báchū ... sāizi 拔出
... 塞子

uncover (*remove cover from*) jiēkāi
揭开; *plot* jiēlù zhēnbào 揭露; *ancient
remains* fājué 发掘

undamaged wèishòu sǔnshāng 未
受损伤

undaunted: **carry on ~** yǒng wǎng
zhí qián 勇往直前

undecided *question* xuán ér wèijué
悬而未决; **be ~ about X** duì X
yóuyù bú dìng 对 X 犹豫不定

undeniable bùkě fǒurèn 不可否
认

undeniably díquè 的确

under 1 *prep* (*beneath*) zài ...
xiàmian 在 ... 下面; (*less than*) bú
dào 不到 2 *adv* (*anesthetized*)
shīqù zhíjué 失去知觉

underage *drinking etc* wèi
chéngnián 未成年; **be ~** wèi dào
fǎdìng niánlíng 未到法定年龄

undercarriage qǐluòjià 起落架

undercover *adj agent* mìmì 秘密

undercut *v/t* COM xùjià qiǎng ...
shēngyì xiāo jìng 生意

underdog chǔyú lièshì de yìfāng
处于劣势的一方

underdone *meat* bù shútòu 不熟
透

underestimate *v/t person, skills,
task* guòfèn dīgū 过分低估

underexposed PHOT bàoguāng bù
zú 曝光不足

underfed yíngyǎng bùliáng 营养
不良

undergo *surgery, treatment* jiēshòu
接受; *experiences* jīngshòu 经受

underground 1 *adj also* POL dìxià
地下 2 *adv work* mìmì 秘密; **go ~**
POL zhuǎnrù dìxià 转入地下

undergrowth guànmùcóng 灌木
丛

underhand *adj* (*devious*) guǐzhà 诡
诈

underlie *v/t*: **~ the theory** gòuchéng zhè yī lǐlùn de jīchǔ 构成
这一理论的基础

underline *v/t text* xià huàxiàn 下划
线

underlying *causes, problems* gēnběn
根本

undermine *v/t s.o.'s position* xùruò

削弱; *theory* chèdǐ jīkuǎ 彻底击垮

underneath 1 *prep* zài ... dǐxià 在 ... 底下 **2** *adv* xiàngxià 向下

underpants nèikù 内裤

underpass (*for pedestrians*) dìxià tōngdào 地下通道

underprivileged dìwèi dīxià 地位低下

underrate *v/t* guòdī píngjià 过低评价

undershirt bèixīn 背心

undersized tàixiǎo 太小

underskirt chènqún 衬裙

understaffed rényuán bùzú 人员不足

understand 1 *v/t* lǐjiě 理解; *I ~ that you ...* wǒ tīngshuō nǐ ... 我听说你...; *they are understood to be in Canada* jù liǎojiě tāmen zài Jiānádà 据了解他们在加拿大 **2** *v/i* míngbái 明白

understandable kě lǐjiě 可理解

understandably kě lǐjiě 可理解

understanding 1 *adj person* tōngqíng dálǐ 通情达理 **2** *n* (*of problem, situation*) lǐjiě 理解; (*agreement*) xiéyì 协议; *on the ~ that ...* (*condition*) zài ... tiáojiàn xià 在 ... 条件下

understatement zhòngshì qīngshuō 重事轻说

undertake *task* chéngdān 承担; *~ to do X* (*agree to*) tóngyì zuò X 同意做X

undertaking (*enterprise*) shìyè 事业; (*promise*) xǔnuò 许诺

undervalue *v/t* dīgū 低估

underwear nèiyī 内衣

underweight *adj* biāozhǔn zhòngliàng yǐxià 标准重量以下

underworld (*criminal*) hēi shèhuì 黑社会; (*in mythology*) yīnjiān 阴间

underwrite *v/t* FIN tóngyì zīzhù 同意资助

undeserved bú qiàdàng 不恰当

undesirable *features, changes* búshòu huānyíng 不受欢迎; *person* tǎoyàn 讨厌; *~ element* (*person*) dǎoluàn fènzi 捣乱分子

undisputed *champion, leader* wúkě zhēngbiàn 无可争辩

undo *parcel, wrapping* dǎkāi 打开; *buttons, shirt, shoelaces* jiěkāi 解开; *s.o. else's work* fèichú 废除; COMPUT chèxiāo 撤销

undoubtedly wúyí 无疑

undreamt-of *riches* zuòmèng yě xiǎng bú dào 做梦也想不到

undress *v/t* ... tuō yīfu 给 ... 脱衣服; *get ~ed* tuō yīfu 脱衣服 **2** *v/i* tuō yīfu 脱衣服

undue (*excessive*) guòdù 过度

unduly *punished, blamed* bú shìdàng 不适当; (*excessively*) guòfèn 过分

unearth *ancient remains* fājué 发掘; *fig* (*find*) fāxiàn 发现; *secret* jiēkāi 揭开

unearthly: *at this ~ hour* zài zhè ge huāngmiù de shíhòu 在这个荒谬的时候

uneasy *relationship, peace* lìngrén bù'ān 令人不安; *feel ~ about X* wèi X gǎndào bù'ān 为X感到不安

uneatable bùnéng chī 不能吃

uneconomic bù jīngjì 不经济

uneducated wèi shòu liánghǎo jiàoyù 未受良好教育

unemployed shīyè 失业; (*laid off from state enterprise*) xiàgǎng 下岗; *the ~* shīyèzhě 失业者; (*from state enterprise*) xiàgǎng gōngrén 下岗工人

unemployment shīyè 失业

unending wú zhǐjìng 无止境

unequal bù píngděng 不平等; *be ~ to the task* nányǐ shèngrèn zhèi xiàng gōngzuò 难以胜任这项工作

unerring *judgment, instinct* wànwúyīshī 万无一失

uneven *quality* bù yízhì 不一致; *surface, ground* bù píng 不平

unevenly *distributed, applied* bù jūnyún 不均匀; *~ matched* (*of two contestants*) bú shìjūnlìdí 不势均力敌

uneventful *day, journey* píngdàn 平淡

unexpected chūhū yìliào 出乎意料

unexpectedly yìwài 意外

unfair bù gōngpíng 不公平

unfaithful *husband, wife* bù zhōng 不忠; *be ~ to X* duì X bù zhōng 对 X 不忠

unfamiliar bù shúxī 不熟悉; *be ~ with X* bù shúxī X 不熟悉 X

unfasten *belt* jiěkāi 解开

unfavorable *report, review* fùmiàn 负面; *weather conditions* búlì 不利

unfeeling *person* wúqíng 无情

unfinished wèi wánchéng 未完成; *leave X ~* bàntú rēngxià X 半途 扔下 X

unfit (*physically*) bú jiànkāng 不健康; (*not morally suited*) bú shìhé 不适合; *be ~ to eat / drink* bùyí shíyòng / yǐnyòng 不宜食用 / 饮用

unfix *part* chāixià 拆下; *screw* nǐngxià 拧下

unflappable zhèndìng zìruò 镇定自若

unfold 1 *v/t sheets, letter* tānkāi 摊开; *one's arms* zhāngkāi 张开 2 *v/i* (*of story etc*) zhǎnkāi 展开; (*of view*) xiǎnxiàn 显现

unforeseen wèi yùjiàn dào 未预见到

unforgettable nánwàng 难忘

unforgivable bù kě ráoshù 不可饶恕; *that was ~ of you* bùnéng yuánliàng nǐ 不能原谅你

unfortunate *people, event* búxìng 不幸; *choice of words* bú qiàdàng 不恰当; *that's ~ for you* nǐ bù zǒuyùn 你不走运

unfortunately búxìng de shì 不幸的是

unfounded wúduān 无端

unfriendly lěngmò 冷漠; *software* bú yì shǐyòng 不易使用

unfurnished wú jiājù shèbèi 无家具设备

ungodly: *at this ~ hour* zài zhème ge huāngmiù shíhòu 在这么个荒谬时候

ungrateful bù lǐngqíng 不领情

unhappiness bù yúkuài 不愉快

unhappy bù yúkuài 不愉快; (*not content: customers etc*) bù mǎnyì 不满意; *be ~ with X* duì X bù mǎnyì 对 X 不满意

unharmed píng'ān wúyàng 平安无恙

unhealthy *person* bú jiànkāng 不健康; *conditions, food, atmosphere* yǒuhài yú jiànkāng 有害于健康; *economy, balance sheet* bù jǐngqì 不景气

unheard-of qián suǒ wèi wén 前所未闻

unhurt wèi shòu shānghài 未受伤害

unhygienic bú wèishēng 不卫生

unification tǒngyī 统一

uniform 1 *n* zhìfú 制服 2 *adj* yízhì 一致

unify tǒngyī 统一

unilateral dān fāngmiàn 单方面

unimaginable nányǐ xiǎngxiàng 难以想象

unimaginative qùfá xiǎngxiànglì 缺乏想象力

unimportant bú zhòngyào 不重要

uninhabitable bú shìyú jūzhù 不适于居住

uninhabited *building, region* huāng wú rényān 荒无人烟

uninjured wèi shòu sǔnshāng 未受损伤

unintelligible nán lǐjiě 难理解

unintentional fēi gùyì 非故意

unintentionally wúxīn 无心

uninteresting wúliáo 无聊

uninterrupted *sleep, work* bù jiānduàn 不间断

union POL liánméng 联盟; (*labor ~*) gōnghuì 工会

unique dúyīwú'èr 独一无二; F (*very good*) biéjùyìgé 别具一格; *with his own ~ humor / style* yǐ tā dútè de yōumò / fēnggé 以他独特的幽默 / 风格

unit (*of measurement*) dānwèi 单位; (*section: of machine, structure*) bùjiàn 部件; (*part with separate function*) yuánjiàn 元件; (*department*) bù bù 部; MIL bùduì 部队; *work ~* dānwèi 单位; *we*

must work together as a ~ wǒmen bìxū zuòwéi yígè zhěngtǐ yìqǐ gōngzuò 我们必须作为一个整体一起工作

unit cost COM dānjià 单价

unite 1 *v/t* tǒngyī 统一; *family members* tuánjù 团聚 **2** *v/i* tuánjié 团结

united tuánjié 团结

United Kingdom Yīngguó 英国; (*formal use*) Liánhé Wángguó 联合王国

United Nations Liánhéguó 联合国

United States (of America) Měiguó 美国; (*formal use*) Měilìjiān Hézhòngguó 美利坚合众国

unity tǒngyī 统一

universal pǔbiàn 普遍

universally yízhì 一致

universe yǔzhòu 宇宙

university 1 *n* dàxué 大学; *he is at ~* tā zài dú dàxué 他在读大学 **2** *adj* dàxué 大学

unjust bù gōngzhèng 不公正

unkempt bù zhěngjié 不整洁

unkind kèbó 刻薄

unknown 1 *adj* wèizhī 未知 **2** *n*: *a journey into the ~* qiántú wèibǔ 前途未卜

unleaded *adj* wúqiān 无铅

unless chúfēi 除非

unlike *prep* búxiàng 不像; *it's ~ him to drink so much* tā hē zhèmeduō jiǔ búxiàng tā píngshí de yàngzi 他喝这么多酒不像他平时的样子; *the photograph was completely ~ her* zhàopiàn yìdiǎnr yě bú xiàng tā běnrén 照片一点儿也不像她本人

unlikely bù dà kěnéng 不大可能; *he is ~ to win* tā bú dà kěnéng yíng 他不大可能赢; *it is ~ that ... ...* bú dà kěnéng ... 不大可能

unlimited wúxiàn 无限

unload *truck, goods* xiè 卸

unlock dǎkāi 打开

unluckily yíhànde shì 遗憾的是

unlucky *day, choice* dǎoméi 倒霉; *person* búxìng 不幸; *that was so*

~ for you! nà nǐ tài dǎoméi le! 那你太倒霉了！

unmade-up *face* méi huàzhuāng 没化妆

unmanned *spacecraft* wúrén cāozòng 无人操纵

unmarried wèihūn 未婚

unmistakable juéwú jǐnyǒu 绝无仅有

unmoved (*emotionally*) wèi bèi gǎndòng 未被感动

unmusical *person* méiyǒu yīnyuè tiānfù 没有音乐天赋; *sounds* cì'ěr 刺耳

unnatural fǎncháng 反常; *it's not ~ to be annoyed* gǎndào fánnǎo shì zhèngcháng de 感到烦恼是正常的

unnecessary bú biyào 不必要

unnerving lìngrén qìněi 令人气馁

unnoticed: *it went ~* bèi hūlüè 被忽略

unobtainable *goods* mǎi bú dào 买不到; TELEC chábúdào 查不到

unobtrusive bù yǐnrén zhùmù 不引人注目

unoccupied *building, house* wúrén zhù 无人住; *room* kōngzhe 空着; *post* wúrén chéngdān 无人承担; *person* kòngxián 空闲

unofficial fēi zhèngshì 非正式

unofficially fēi zhèngshì 非正式

unpack 1 *v/t* dǎkāi 打开 **2** *v/i* dǎkāi bāoguǒ 打开包裹

unpaid *work* wúcháng 无偿

unpleasant shǐ rén bù yúkuài 使人不愉快; *he was very ~ to her* tā dài tā hěn cūlǔ 他待她很粗鲁

unplug *v/t* *TV, computer* báchū chātou 拔出插头

unpopular *person* bú shòu huānyíng 不受欢迎; *decision* bùdé rénxīn 不得人心

unprecedented kōngqián 空前; *it was ~ for a woman to X* dāngshí, nǚxìng X shì shǐwúqiánlì de 当时, 女性X是史无前例的

unpredictable *person, weather* fǎnfù wúcháng 反复无常

unprincipled *pej* bú dàodé 不道德

unpretentious *person, style, hotel* bù xuányào 不炫耀

unproductive *meeting, discussion* méiyǒu jiéguǒ 没有结果; *soil* bù féiwò 不肥沃

unprofessional *person, behavior* bú jìngyè 不敬业; *workmanship* zāogāo 糟糕

unprofitable bù yínglì 不盈利

unpronounceable nányǐ zhèngquè fāyīn 难以正确发音

unprotected *borders* wèi shèfáng 未设防; *machine* wèiyǒu ānquán zhuāngzhì 没有安全装置; **~ sex** wèi jīng bǎohù de xìng xíngwéi 未经保护的性行为

unprovoked *attack* wúduān 无端

unqualified *worker, doctor etc* bù hégé 不合格

unquestionably (*without doubt*) wúkě zhēngbiàn 无可争辩

unquestioning *attitude, loyalty* wú yìyì 无异议

unravel *v/t string, knitting* chāikāi 拆开; *mystery, complexities* chéngqīng 澄清

unreadable *book* bùzhíyìdú 不值一读

unreal bù zhēnshí 不真实; **this is ~!** F xiàng mèng yíyàng! 像梦一样!

unrealistic bú xiànshí 不现实

unreasonable *person* chāoyuè qínglǐ 超越情理; *demand, expectation* guòfèn 过分

unrelated *issues* bù xiāngguān 不相关; *people* wú qīnqī guānxi 无亲戚关系

unrelenting búxiè 不懈

unreliable bù kěkào 不可靠

unrest dòngluàn 动乱

unrestrained *emotions* wú jūshù 无拘束

unroadworthy búyí zài gōnglù shang xíngshǐ 不宜在公路上行使

unroll *v/t carpet, scroll* zhǎnkāi 展开

unruly bù guījǔ 不规矩

unsafe *bridge, vehicle, wiring* wēixiǎn 危险; *district, beach* bù ānquán 不安全; **~ to drink / eat** búyí hē / chī 不宜喝 / 吃; **it is ~ to X X** bù ānquán X 不安全

unsanitary *conditions, drains* bú wèishēng 不卫生

unsatisfactory bùnéng lìngrén mǎnyì 不能令人满意

unsavory *person, reputation* lìngrén tǎoyàn 令人讨厌; *district* lìngrén búkuài 令人不快

unscathed (*not injured*) wèi shòu sǔnshāng 未受损伤; (*not damaged*) wèi shòu sǔnhuài 未受损坏

unscrew *sth screwed on* xuánsōng 旋松; *top* nǐngkāi 拧开

unscrupulous bù jiǎng dàodé 不讲道德

unselfish wúsī 无私

unsettled *issue* wèi jiějué 未解决; *weather, stock market* yìbiàn 易变; *lifestyle* bù wěndìng 不稳定; *bills* wèi zhīfù 未支付

unshaven méi xiūmiàn 没修面

unsightly bù yǎguān 不雅观

unskilled wú tèshū jìnéng 无特殊技能

unsociable bù héqún 不合群

unsophisticated *person* zhìpǔ 质朴; *equipment* jiǎndān 简单

unstable *person* fǎnfù wúcháng 反复无常; *structure* bù jiāngù 不坚固; *area, economy* dòngdàng bù'ān 动荡不定

unsteady (*on one's feet*) bùwěn 不稳; *ladder* yáobǎi 摇摆

unstinting: be ~ in one's efforts búyíyúlì 不遗余力

unstuck: come ~ (*of notice etc*) méi zhānzhù 没粘住; (*of plan etc*) shībài 失败

unsuccessful *writer, party* bù chénggōng 不成功; *candidate, attempt* shībài 失败; **he tried but was ~** tā chángshìle kěshì méi chénggōng 他尝试了可是没成功

unsuccessfully *try, apply* shībài 失败

unsuitable bù héshì 不合适

unsuspecting wú jièxīn 无戒心

unswerving *loyalty, devotion* bú-biàn 不变

unthinkable bùkě sīyì 不可思议

untidy *room, desk, hair* língluàn 凌乱

untie *knot, laces, prisoner* jiěkāi 解开

until 1 *prep* zhídào 直到; *from Monday ~ Friday* cóng zhōuyī dào zhōuwǔ 从周一到周五; *I can wait ~ tomorrow* wǒ kěyǐ děng-dào míngtiān 我可以等到明天; *not ~ Friday* děi zhōuwǔ 得周五; *it won't be finished ~ July* qīyuè cái néng wánchéng 直到七月才能完成 **2** *conj: can you wait ~ I'm ready?* nǐ kěyǐ děng wǒ zhǔnbèi hǎo ma? 你可以等我准备好吗?; *they won't do any-thing ~ you say so* nǐ shuōle tāmen cái néng zuò 你说了他们才能做

untimely *death* guòzǎo 过早

untiring *efforts* bújuàn 不倦

untold *riches, suffering* wúxiàn 无限; *story* wèi tòulù 未透露

untranslatable bùnéng fānyì 不能翻译

untrue bù zhēnshí 不真实

unused[1] *goods* xīn 新

unused[2] *: be ~ to X* bù xíguàn X 不习惯 X; *be ~ to doing X* bù xíguàn zuò X 不习惯做 X

unusual bùtóng xúncháng 不同寻常

unusually yìcháng 异常

unveil *memorial, statue etc* jiēmù 揭幕

unwell bù shūfu 不舒服

unwilling: *be ~ to do X* búyuàn zuò X 不愿做 X

unwind 1 *v/t tape* jiěkāi 解开 **2** *v/i (of tape, story)* zhǎnkāi 展开; *(relax)* fàngsōng 放松

unwise bù míngzhì 不明智

unwrap *gift* dǎkāi 打开

unwritten *law, rule* wèi chéngwén 未成文

unzip *v/t dress etc* lākāi lāliàn 拉开拉链; COMPUT jiě yāsuō 解压缩

up 1 *adv* xiàngshàng 向上; *look ~*

xiàngshàng kàn 向上看; *~ in the sky / ~ on the roof* zài gāokōng / zài wūdǐng shang 在高空 / 在屋顶上; *~ here / there* zài zhè / nà shang 在这 / 那上; *be ~ (out of bed)* qǐchuáng 起床; *(of sun)* shēngqǐ 升起; *(be built)* jiànchéng 建成; *(of shelves)* ānhǎo 安好; *(of prices, temperature)* shàngshēng 上升; *(have expired)* dàoqī 到期; *what's ~?* zěnmele? 怎么了?; *~ to the year 1989* zhídào yījiǔbājiǔ nián zài 到 1989 年; *he came ~ to me* tā xiàng wǒ zǒuguòlái 他向我走过来; *what are you ~ to these days?* zuìjìn zài mángxiē shénme? 最近在忙些什么?; *what are those kids ~ to?* nàxiē háizimen zài gǎo shénme guǐ? 那些孩子们在搞什么鬼?; *be ~ to something (bad)* méi zuò shénme hǎoshì 没做什么好事; *I don't feel ~ to it* wǒ juédé zìjǐ bùnéng shèngrèn wǒ juédé zìjǐ bù néng shèngrèn 我觉得自己不能胜任; *it's ~ to you* nǐ lái juédìng 你来决定; *it is ~ to them to solve it (their duty)* jiějué zhèijiànshì shì tāmende zhízé 解决这件事是他们的职责; *be ~ and about (after illness)* qǐchuáng zǒudòng 起床走动 **2** *prep: further ~ the mountain* zài wǎng shānshàng yìxiē 再往山上一些; *he climbed ~ a tree* tā pádào shùshang qù le 他爬到树上去了; *they ran ~ the street* tāmen yánzhe jiē pǎo 他们沿着街跑; *the water goes ~ this pipe* shuǐ shùnzhe zhèitiáo guǎndào xiàngshàng xíng 水顺着这条管道上行; *we traveled ~ to Shanghai* wǒmen lǚxíng zhì Shànghǎi 我们旅行至上海 **3** *n: ~s and downs* gānkǔ 甘苦

upbringing jiàoyǎng 教养

upcoming *adj (forthcoming)* jíjiāng láilín 即将来临

update 1 *v/t file, records* xiūdìng 修订; *~ X on Y* xiàng X tígōng zuìxīn yǒuguān Y de xìnxī 向 X 提供最新有关 Y 的信息 **2** *n (of files,* *records*) xiūdìng 修订; (*software version*) zuìxīn bǎnběn 最新版本; *can you give me an ~ on the situation?* nǐ néng gàosù wǒ júshìde zuìxīn xìnxī ma? 你能告诉我局势的最新信息吗？

upgrade *v/t computers etc* gǎijìn 改进; (*replace with new versions*) gēngxīn 更新; *ticket* tígāo … děngjí 提高 … 等级

upheaval (*emotional*) jùbiàn 剧变; (*physical*) biàndòng 变动; (*political, social*) dòngluàn 动乱

uphill 1 *adv walk* shàngpō 上坡 **2** *adj struggle* jiānnán 艰难

uphold *traditions, rights* wéihù 维护; (*vindicate*) zhèngshí 证实

upholstery (*coverings*) jiājù zhuāngshì cáiliào 家具装饰材料; (*padding*) diànliào 垫料

upkeep *n* (*of old buildings, parks etc*) bǎoyǎng 保养

upload *v/t* COMPUT jiāzài 加载

upmarket *adj restaurant, hotel* gāojí 高级

upon → **on**

upper *part of sth* shàngbù 上部; *stretches of a river* shàngyóu 上游; *deck* shàngcéng 上层

upper atmosphere dàqì wàicéng 大气外层; **upper-class** *adj accent, family* shàngcéng shèhuì 上层社会; **upper classes** shàngděng jiēcéng 上等阶层

upright 1 *adj citizen* zhèngzhí 正直 **2** *adv sit* bǐzhí 笔直

upright (**piano**) shùshì (gāngqín) 竖式（钢琴）

uprising qǐyì 起义

uproar (*loud noise*) xuānxiāo 喧嚣; (*protest*) kàngyì 抗议

upset 1 *v/t drink, glass* nòngfān 弄翻; (*emotionally*) shǐrén nánguò 使人难过 **2** *adj* (*emotionally*) nánguò 难过; *get ~ about X* yīn X ér nánguò 因 X 而难过; *have an ~ stomach* gǎndào chángwèi búshì 感到肠胃不适

upsetting lìngrén nánguò 令人难过

upshot (*result, outcome*) zuìhòu

jiéguǒ 最后结果

upside down *adv* dǐ cháo shàng 底朝上; *turn X ~ box etc* bǎ X shàngxià diāndǎo guòlái 把 X 上下颠倒过来

upstairs 1 *adv* zài lóushàng 在楼上 **2** *adj room* lóushàng 楼上

upstart xīnguì 新贵

upstream *adv* xiàng shàngyóu 向上游

uptight F (*nervous*) jǐnzhāng 紧张; (*inhibited*) jūjǐn 拘谨

up-to-date *information* zuìxīn 最新; *fashions* xīnshì 新式

upturn (*in economy*) hǎozhuǎn 好转

upward *adv fly, move* xiàngshàng 向上; *~ of 10,000* yíwàn duō 一万多

uranium yóu 铀

urban dūshì 都市

urbanization chéngshìhuà 城市化

urchin wántóng 顽童

urge 1 *n* yùwàng 欲望 **2** *v/t*: *~ X to do Y* jiélì cuīcù X zuò Y 竭力催促 X 做 Y

♦**urge on** (*encourage*) gǔlì 鼓励

urgency (*of situation*) jǐnjí 紧急

urgent *job* jí 急; *letter* jǐnjí 紧急; *be in ~ need of X* jíxū X 急需 X; *is it ~?* shì jíshì ma? 是急事吗？

urinate páiniào 排尿

urine niào 尿

urn *n* (*for ashes*) gǔhuīwèng 骨灰瓮 **2** *n*

us wǒmen 我们

US(A) (= *United States* (*of America*)) Měiguó 美国; (*formal use*) Měilìjiān Hézhòngguó 美利坚合众国

usable kě shǐyòng 可使用

usage (*linguistic*) guànyòngfǎ 惯用法

use 1 *v/t shǐyòng* 使用; *skills, knowledge* yùnyòng 运用; *car* yòng 用; *a lot of gas* xiāohào 消耗; *pej: person* lìyòng 利用; *I could ~ a drink* F wǒ zhēn xiǎng hē dōngxi 我真想喝东西 **2** *n* shǐyòng 使用; *be of great ~ to X* duì X dàyǒu yòngchù 对 X 大有

用处; *be of no ~ to X* duì X méiyǒuyòng 对 X 没有用; *is that of any ~?* nà yǒuyòng ma? 那有用吗？; *it's no ~* méiyòng 没用; *it's no ~ trying / waiting* shì / děng yě méiyòng 试 / 等也没用

♦ **use up** yòngguāng 用光

used[1] *car etc* yòngguò 用过

used[2]: *be ~ to X* duì X xíguàn 对 X 习惯; *get ~ to X* duì X zhújiàn shìyìng 对 X 逐渐适应; *be ~ to doing X* xíguàn zuò X 习惯做 X; *get ~ to doing X* zhújiàn xíguàn zuò X 逐渐习惯做 X

used[3]: *I ~ to like him* wǒ céng xīhuānguò tā 我曾喜欢过他; *I don't work there now, but I ~ to* wǒ yǐqián zài nàlǐ gōngzuò, xiànzài bù le 我以前在那里工作，现在不了

useful *person, information, gadget* yǒuyòng 有用

usefulness yòngchù 用处

useless *information* méiyòng 没用; F *person* chàjìn 差劲; *machine, computer* bùnéng yòng 不能用; *it's ~ trying* shì yě méiyòng 试也

user (*of product*) yònghù 用户

user-friendly *software, device* yònghù yǒuhǎo 用户友好

usher *n* (*at wedding*) yíngbīnyuán 迎宾员

♦ **usher in** *new era* yùshì 预示

usherette nǚ yǐnzuòyuán 女引座员

usual tōngcháng 通常; *as ~* xiàng wǎngcháng yíyàng 像往常一样; *the ~, please* gēn píngcháng yíyàng 跟平常一样

usually tōngcháng 通常

utensil yòngjù 用具

uterus zǐgōng 子宫

utility (*usefulness*) shíyòngxìng 实用性; *public utilities* gōngyòng shíyè 公用实业

utilize yìngyòng 应用

utmost 1 *adj* jídù 极度 **2** *n*: *do one's ~* jiéjìn suǒnéng 竭尽所能

utter 1 *adj* wánquán 完全 **2** *v/t sound* fāchū 发出

utterly jiǎnzhí 简直

U-turn U xíngwān U 形弯; *fig* (*in policy*) zhuǎnxiàng 转向

V

vacant *building, position* kōng 空; *look, expression* mángrán 茫然

vacate *room* téngchū 腾出

vacation *n* xiūjià 休假; ***be on ~*** dùjià 度假; ***go to X on ~*** qù X dùjià 去 X 度假

vacationer dùjià zhě 度假者

vaccinate jiēzhòng yìmiáo 接种疫苗; ***be ~d against X*** jiēzhòng X yìmiáo 接种 X 疫苗

vaccination jiēzhòng yìmiáo 接种疫苗

vaccine yìmiáo 疫苗

vacuum 1 *n* PHYS zhēnkōng 真空; ***leave a ~ in one's life*** shǐ rénde shēnghuó biànde kōngxū 使人的生活变得空虚 **2** *v/t floors* xīchén 吸尘

vacuum cleaner xīchén qì 吸尘器; **vacuum flask** bǎowēn píng 保温瓶; **vacuum-packed** zhēnkōng bāozhuāng 真空包装

vagabond *n* liúlàng zhě 流浪者

vagina yīndào 阴道

vaginal yīndào 阴道

vague *answer, wording* bù mínglǎng 不明朗; *feeling, resemblance* móhu 模糊; *taste of sth* yīdiǎndian 一点点; ***he was very ~ about it*** tā hánhu qící 他含糊其辞

vaguely *answer* bù mínglǎng 不明朗; *(slightly)* yǒudiǎn yǒu diǎn 有点; ***~ possible*** bú tài kěnéng 不太可能

vain 1 *adj person* zìfù 自负; *hope* túláo 徒劳 **2** *n:* ***in ~*** bái fèilì 白费力; ***their efforts were in ~*** tāmen báigànle yīchǎng 他们白干了一场

valet *(person)* nán púcóng 男仆从

valet service *(for clothes)* xǐyī fúwù 洗衣服务; *(for cars)* xǐchē fúwù 洗车服务

valiant yǒnggǎn 勇敢

valid *passport, document* yǒuxiào 有效; *reason, argument* yǒu gēnjù 有根据

validate *(with official stamp)* shǐ shēngxiào 使生效; *(prove)* quèzhèng 确证

validity *(of reason, argument)* zhèngquè xìng 正确性

valley shāngǔ 山谷

valuable 1 *adj* yǒu jiàzhí 有价值 **2** *n:* ***~s*** guìzhòng wùpǐn 贵重物品

valuation gūjià 估价; ***at his ~*** jù tā gūjià 据他估价

value 1 *n* jiàzhí 价值; ***be good ~*** zhídàng 值当; ***~ for money*** qián huāde zhídé 钱花的值得; ***rise/fall in ~*** jiàzhí shàngshēng / xiàjiàng 价值上升/下降 **2** *v/t s.o.'s friendship, one's freedom* zhēnshì 珍视; ***I ~ your advice*** wǒ duì nǐde quàngào shífēn zhòngshì 我对你的劝告十分重视; ***have an object ~d*** jiào rén gūjià mǒuwù 叫人估价某物

valve fá 阀

van huòchē 货车

vandal pòhuài gōnggòng cáichǎn zhě 破坏公共财产者

vandalism pòhuài gōnggòng cáichǎn xíngwéi 破坏公共财产行为

vandalize sìyì pòhuài 肆意破坏

vanilla *n & adj* xiāngcǎo 香草

vanish xiāoshī 消失

vanity *(of person)* xūróng 虚荣; *(of hopes)* kōngxū 空虚

vanity case xiǎo shūzhuāng hé 小梳妆盒

vantage point *(on hill etc)* guānwàng diǎn 观望点

vapor qì 汽

vaporize *v/t* qìhuà 汽化

vapor trail *(of airplane)* wùhuà wěijī 雾化尾迹

variable 1 *adj amount* kěbiàn 可

变; *moods, weather* duōbiàn 多变
2 *n* MATH, COMPUT biànliàng 变量

variation biànhuà 变化

varicose vein jìngmài qūzhāng 静
脉曲张

varied *quality* bùtóng 不同; *range*
gèzhǒng gèyàng 各种各样; *diet*
fēngfù 丰富

variety duōyàng huà 多样化;
(*type*) zhǒnglèi 种类; *a ~ of
things to do* fēngfù duōcǎi de
huódòng 丰富多彩的活动

various (*several*) jǐge 几个;
(*different*) bùtóng 不同

varnish 1 *n* (*for wood*) qīngqī 清
漆; (*for fingernails*) zhǐjiǎ yóu 指
甲油 **2** *v/t* tú涂

vary 1 *v/i* biànhuà 变化; *it varies*
bù yīyàng 不一样 **2** *v/t* gǎibiàn 改
变

vase huāpíng 花瓶

vast *desert, city, subject* jùdà 巨大;
collection of books dàliàng 大量;
knowledge yuānbó 渊博

vaudeville záshuǎ 杂耍

vault[1] *n* (*in roof*) gǒngdǐng 拱顶;
~s (*cellar*) dìjiào 地窖

vault[2] **1** *n* (*in athletics*) chēnggān
tiào 撑杆跳 **2** *v/t beam etc*
yòngshǒu zhīchēng yuèguò 用手
支撑跃过

VCR (= *video cassette recorder*)
lùxiàng jī 录像机

veal xiǎo niúròu 小牛肉

vegan 1 *n* sùshí zhǔyì zhě 素食主
义者 **2** *adj* sùshí zhǔyì 素食主义

vegetable shūcài 蔬菜

vegetarian 1 *n* sùshí zhě 素食者
2 *adj* sùshí 素食

vehicle chēliàng 车辆; (*for
information etc*) gōngjù 工具

veil 1 *n* miànshā 面纱 **2** *v/t* yǐ
miànshā zhēyǎn 以面纱遮掩

vein (*in body*) jìngmài 静脉

Velcro® ® zhānkòu 粘扣

velocity sùdù 速度

velvet sīróng 丝绒

vending machine zìdòng shòuhuò
jī 自动售货机

vendor LAW màizhǔ 卖主

veneer (*on wood*) shìmiàn bóbǎn
饰面薄板; (*of politeness etc*)
wàibiǎo 外表

venereal disease xìngbìng 性病

venetian blind bǎiyè lián 百叶帘

vengeance bàofù 报复; *with a ~*
měngliè 猛烈; *raining with a ~*
dàyǔ pāngtuó 大雨滂沱

venison lùròu 鹿肉

venom (*of snake*) dúyè 毒液

vent *n* (*for air*) tōngfēng kǒng tōng fēng
孔; *give ~ to feelings, emotions*
fāxiè 发泄

ventilate *room, building* shǐ tōngfēng 使通风

ventilation tōngfēng 通风

ventilation shaft tōngfēng jǐng 通
风井

ventilator tōngfēng shèbèi 通风设
备

ventriloquist kǒujì yìrén 口技艺
人

venture 1 *n* (*undertaking*) màoxiǎn
冒险; COM tóujī huódòng 投机活
动 **2** *v/i* màoxiǎn 冒险

venture park chuàngyèyuán 创业
园

venue (*for meeting, concert etc*)
dìdiǎn 地点

veranda yóuláng 游廊

verb dòngcí 动词

verdict LAW cáijué 裁决; (*opinion,
judgment*) dìnglùn 定论

verge *n* (*of road*) lùbiān 路边; *be
on the ~ of ...* (*of ruin, collapse*)
bīnyú ... 濒于 ...; *be on the ~ of
tears* jīhū yào kūchūlái le 几乎要
哭出来了

♦**verge on** jiējìn 接近

♦**verification** héshí 核实;
(*confirmation*) zhèngmíng 证明

verify (*check out*) héshí 核实;
(*confirm*) zhèngmíng 证明

vermicelli mǐfěn 米粉

vermin hàichóng 害虫

vermouth wèiměisī jiǔ 味美思酒

vernacular *n* fāngyán 方言

versatile *person* duōcái duōyì 多才
多艺; *gadget* duō gōngnéng 多功
能; *mind* fǎnfù wúcháng 反复无
常

versatility (*of person*) duōcái duōyì

多才多艺; (of gadget) duō gōngnéng 多功能; (of mind) fǎnfù wúcháng 反复无常

verse (poetry) shī 诗; (part of poem, song) jié 节

versed: be well ~ in X jīngtōng X 精通 X

version (of book) bǎnběn 版本; (of song, story) gǎibiān běn 改编本; (of events) shuōfǎ 说法

versus: X ~ Y SP, LAW X duì Y X 对 Y

vertebra jǐzhuī 脊椎

vertebrate n yǒu jǐzhuī dòngwù 有 脊椎动物

vertical chuízhí 垂直

vertigo xuànyūn 眩晕

very 1 adv hěn 很; was it cold? – not ~ lěngbùlěng? – bù zěnme lěng 冷不冷？– 不怎么冷; the ~ best zuìhǎo 最好 2 adj: caught in the ~ act dāngchǎng zhuāhuò 当场抓获; that's the ~ thing I need zhèngshì wǒ suǒ xūyào de 正是我所需要的; the ~ thought (merely) yī xiǎngdào 一 想到; right at the ~ top / bottom zài zuì shàngmiàn / dǐxià 在最上 面 / 底下

vessel NAUT chuán 船

vest bèixīn 背心

vestige (of previous civilization etc) yíjì 遗迹; (of truth) sīháo 丝毫

vet² n shòuyī 兽医

vet² v/t applicants etc shěnchá 审查

veteran 1 n tuìwǔ jūnrén 退伍军 人 2 adj (old) lǎoshì 老式; (old and experienced) lǎoliàn 老练

veterinarian shòuyī 兽医

veto 1 n fǒujué quán 否决权 2 v/t fǒujué 否决

vex (concern, worry) shǐ shāng nǎojīn 使伤脑筋

vexed (worried) kǔnǎo 苦恼; the ~ question of ... zhēnglùn bùxiū de ... wèntí 争论不休的 ... 问题

via jīngguò 经过; (by means of) tōngguò 通过

viable life form néng yǎnghuó 能养 活; company néng dúlì shēngcún 能独立生存; alternative, plan

qièshí kěxíng 切实可行

vibrate v/i zhèndòng 振动

vibration zhèndòng 振动

vice èxí 恶习; the problem of ~ dàodé bàihuài de wèntí 道德败 坏的问题

vice president fù zǒngtǒng 副总 统

vice squad jǐngchá jiūbǔ duì 警察 纠捕队

vice versa fǎnzhī yìrán 反之亦然

vicinity dìdiǎn 地点; in the ~ of (the church etc) zài ... fùjìn 在 ... 附近; $500 etc ... zuǒyòu ... 左右

vicious dog xiōnghěn 凶狠; attack, temper, criticism èdú 恶毒

victim shòuhài zhě 受害者

victimize shǐ shòuhài 使受害

victor shènglì zhě 胜利者

victorious zhànshèng 战胜

victory shènglì 胜利; win a ~ over X zhànshèng X 战胜 X

video 1 n lùxiàng 录像; COMPUT shìpín 视频; in ~ lùle X dexiàng 录了 X 的像 2 v/t lùxiàng 录像

video camera shèxiàng jī 摄像机; **video cassette** lùxiàng dài 录像 带; **video conference** TELEC diànshì huìyì 电视会议; **video game** diànshì yóuxì 电视游戏; **videophone** kěshì diànhuà 可视 电话; **video recorder** lùxiàng jī 录像机; **video recording** lùxiàng lù 录像; **videotape** lùxiàng dài 录像带

Vietnam Yuènán 越南

Vietnamese 1 adj Yuènán 越南 2 n (person) Yuènán rén 越南人; (language) Yuènán yǔ 越南语

view 1 n fēngjǐng 风景; (of situation) guāndiǎn 观点; in ~ of jiànyú 鉴于; be on ~ (of paintings) zài zhǎnchū 在展出; with a ~ to X yǐ X wéi mùbiāo 以 X 为目标 2 v/t events, situation kàndài 看待; TV program, house for sale shōukàn 收 看 3 v/i (watch TV) kàn 看

viewer TV guānzhòng 观众

viewfinder PHOT qǔjǐng qì 取景器

viewpoint guāndiǎn 观点

vigor (*energy*) huólì 活力

vigorous *person* jīnglì chōngpèi 精力充沛; *shake* yònglì 用力; *denial* qiángliè 强烈

vile *thing to do* èluè 恶劣; *a ~ smell* èchòu 恶臭

village cūnzhuāng 村庄

villager cūnlǐ rén 村里人

villain huàidàn 坏蛋

vindicate (*prove correct*) zhèngmíng zhèngquè 证明正确; (*prove innocent*) zhèngmíng wúgū 证明无辜; *I feel ~d* wǒ gǎndào bèi zhèngshí le 我感到被证实了

vindictive yǒu bàofù xīn 有报复心

vine pútáo 葡萄

vinegar cù 醋

vineyard pútáo yuán 葡萄园

vintage 1 *n* (*of wine*) shēngchǎn niánfèn 生产年份 **2** *adj* (*classic*) jīngdiǎn 经典

violate *rules, sanctity of a place* wéifǎn 违犯; *treaty* wéibèi 违背

violation (*of rules, sanctity*) wéifǎn 违犯; (*of treaty*) wéibèi 违背; *traffic ~* wéifǎn jiāotōng fǎguī 违反交通法规

violence (*of person, movie*) bàolì 暴力; (*of emotion, reaction*) kuángrè 狂热; (*of gale*) měngliè 猛烈; *outbreak of ~* bàodòng bàofā 暴动暴发

violent *person, movie* bàolì 暴力; *emotion, reaction* kuángrè 狂热; *gale* měngliè 猛烈; *have a ~ temper* píqì bùhǎo 脾气不好

violently *react* qiángbào 强暴; *object* jīliè 激烈; *fall ~ in love with X* shēnshēn de àishàng X 深深地爱上 X

violet (*color*) zǐ luólán sè 紫罗兰色; (*plant*) zǐ luólán 紫罗兰

violin xiǎo tíqín 小提琴

violinist xiǎo tíqín jiā 小提琴家

VIP (= *very important person*) yàorén wùyù 要人

viral *infection* bìngdú bìngdú 病毒

virgin (*female*) chǔnǚ 处女; (*male*) chǔnán 处男

virginity zhēnjié 贞洁; *lose one's ~* shīshēn 失身

virile *man* qiángjìn 强劲; *prose*

virility nánzǐ qìgài 男子气概; (*sexual*) nánxìng shēngzhí lì 男性生殖力

virtual shízhì 实质

virtual reality xūnǐ xiànshí 虚拟现实

virtually (*almost*) jīhū 几乎

virtue pǐndé 品德; *in ~ of* yīnwèi 因为

virtuoso MUS yuèqì yǎnzòu míngshǒu 乐器演奏名手

virtuous dàodé gāoshàng 道德高尚

virulent *disease* èxìng 恶性

virus MED, COMPUT bìngdú 病毒

visa qiānzhèng 签证

visibility néngjiàn dù 能见度

visible *object* yìjiàn 易见; *difference* míngxiǎn 明显; *anger* yì chájué 易察觉; *not ~ to the naked eye* ròuyǎn kànbùjiàn 肉眼看不见

visibly *different* míngxiǎn 明显; *he was ~ moved* kěyǐ kànchū tā hěnshòu gǎndòng 可以看出他很受感动

vision (*eyesight*) shìlì 视力; REL *etc* yōulíng 幽灵

visit 1 *n* bàifǎng 拜访; (*to place, country*) yóulǎn 游览; *pay a ~ to the doctor / dentist* qù kàn yīshēng / yáyī 去看医生 / 牙医; *pay X a ~* bàifǎng X 拜访 X **2** *v/t person* bàifǎng 拜访; *place, country, city* yóulǎn 游览; *doctor, dentist* kàn kàn 看

visiting card míngpiàn 名片

visiting hours (*at hospital*) tànwàng shíjiān 探望时间

visitor (*guest*) kèrén 客人; (*to museum etc*) cānguān zhě 参观者; (*tourist*) yóukè 游客

visor màoshé 帽舌

visual shìjué 视觉; *arts* zhíguān 直观

visual aid zhíguān jiàojù 直观教具

visual display unit zhíguān xiǎnshì bùjiàn 直观显示部件

visualize xiǎngxiàng 想象; (*foresee*) shèxiǎng 设想

visually shìjué 视觉

visually impaired shìjué qùxiàn 视觉缺陷

vital (*essential*) bìbù kěshǎo 必不可少; *it is ~ that ...* .... shì hěn zhòngyào de ... 是很重要的 ...

vitality (*of person, city etc*) huólì 活力

vitally: *~ important* fēicháng zhòngyào 非常重要

vital organs wéichí shēngmìngde zhòngyào qìguān 维持生命的重要器官

vital statistics (*of woman*) nǚzǐ sānwéi 女子三围

vitamin wéitāmíng 维他命

vitamin pill wéitāmíng yàopiàn 维他命药片

vivacious huópo 活泼

vivacity huópo 活泼

vivid *color* xiānyàn 鲜艳; *memory* qīngxī 清晰; *imagination* huóyuè 活跃

V-neck jīxīn lǐng 鸡心领

vocabulary cíhuì 词汇; (*list of words*) cíhuì biǎo 词汇表

vocal (*to do with the voice*) sǎngyīn 嗓音; (*expressing opinions*) chàngsuǒ yùyán 畅所欲言

vocal cords shēngdài 声带

vocal group MUS gēchàng tuán 歌唱团

vocalist MUS gēchàng jiā 歌唱家

vocation (*calling*) shǐmìng 使命; (*profession*) zhíyè 职业

vocational *guidance* zhíyè 职业

vodka fútèjiā 伏特加

vogue liúxíng 流行; *be in ~* zhèngzài liúxíng 正在流行

voice 1 *n* shēngyīn 声音 2 *v/t* *opinions* biǎodá 表达

voicemail diànhuà dálù jī 电话答录机

void 1 *n* kōngjiān 空间 2 *adj:* *~ of* quēfá 缺乏

volatile *personality, moods* biànhuà wúcháng 变化无常

volcano huǒshān 火山

volley *n* (*of shots*) páiqiāng shèjī 排枪射击; (*in tennis*) jiéjī kōng-zhōng qiú 截击空中球

volleyball páiqiú 排球

volt fútè 伏特

voltage diànyā 电压

volume (*of container*) róngliàng 容量; (*of work, liquid etc*) liàng liàng; (*of business*) é'é; (*of book*) cè 册; (*of radio etc*) yīnliàng 音量

volume control yīnliàng tiáokòng 音量调控

voluntary *adj helper* zhìyuàn 志愿; *work* yìwù 义务

volunteer 1 *n* yìgōng 义工 2 *v/i* zhìyuàn 志愿

voluptuous *woman, figure* fēngmǎn 丰满

vomit 1 *n* ǒutù wù 呕吐物 2 *v/i* ǒutù 呕吐

◆**vomit up** ǒutù 呕吐

voracious *appetite* lángtūn hǔyàn 狼吞虎咽

vote 1 *n* xuǎnpiào 选票; *have the ~* (*be entitled to vote*) yǒu xuǎnjǔ quán 有选举权 2 *v/i* POL tóupiào 投票; *~ for / against ...* tóu zànchéng piào / fǎnduì piào 投赞成票 / 反对票 3 *v/t:* *they ~d him President* tāmen xuǎn tā dāng zǒngtǒng 他们选他当总统; *they ~d to stay behind* tāmen juédìng búqù 他们决定不去

◆**vote in** *new member* xuǎnrù 选入

◆**vote on** *issue* tóupiào juédìng 投票决定

◆**vote out** (*of office*) tóupiào shǐ luòxuǎn 投票使落选

voter POL yǒu tóupiào quán zhě 有投票权者

voting POL tóupiào 投票

voting booth tóupiào jiān 投票间

◆**vouch for** *truth of sth* bǎozhèng 保证; *person* dānbǎo 担保

voucher piàoquàn 票券

vow 1 *n* shìyuē 誓约 2 *v/t:* *~ to do X* lìshì yàozuò X 立誓要做 X

vowel yuányīn 元音

voyage (*by sea*) hánghǎi 航海; (*in space*) hángkōng 航空

vulgar *person, language* cūsú 粗俗

vulnerable (*to attack*) bóruò 薄弱; (*to criticism etc*) mǐngǎn 敏感

vulture měizhōu jiù 美洲鹫

W

wad n (of paper, absorbent wool etc) tuán 团; **a ~ of $100 bills** yìdá yìbǎiměiyuán de chāopiào 一沓一百美元的钞票

waddle v/i yáobǎide xíngzǒu 摇摆地行走

wade báshè 跋涉

♦ wade through book, documents fèilìde yuèdú 费力地阅读

wafer (cookie) wēifú bǐnggān 威佛饼干

waffle¹ n (to eat) wǎfūbǐng 瓦夫饼

waffle² v/i hánhude tánhuà 含糊地谈话

wag 1 v/t tail, finger yáodòng 摇动 2 v/i (of tail) bǎidòng 摆动

wage¹ v/t war zuòzhàn 作战

wage² n gōngzī 工资

wage earner yǐ gōngzī wéishēng de rén 以工资为生的人

waggle v/t hips, ears láihuí yáodòng 来回摇动; loose screw, tooth etc huàngdòng 晃动

wagon RAIL chǎngpéng huòchē 敞篷货车; **be on the ~** F jièjiǔ 戒酒

wail 1 n (of person, baby) tòngkūshēng 恸哭声; (of siren) jiānxiàoshēng 尖啸声 2 v/i (of person, baby) tòngkū 恸哭; (of siren) jiānxiào 尖啸

waist yāobù 腰部

waistline yāowéi 腰围

wait 1 n děngdài 等待 2 v/i děng 等; **we'll ~ until he's ready** wǒmen děng tā zhǔnbèihǎo 我们等他准备好 2 v/t meal zànhuǎn 暂缓; **~ table** zuò fúwùyuán 作服务员

♦ wait for děngdài 等待; **~ me!** děng wǒ! 等我!

♦ wait on person cìhou 伺候

♦ wait up děngzhe búshuì 等着不睡

waiter nán fúwùyuán 男服务员;

~! fúwùyuán! 服务员!

waiting n děngdài 等待; **no ~ sign** bùzhǔntíngchēde biāopái 不准停车的标牌

waiting list děnghòuzhě míngdān 等候者名单

waiting room děnghòushì 等候室

waitress nǚ fúwùyuán 女服务员

wake¹ 1 v/i: **~ (up)** xīnglái 醒来 2 v/t huànxǐng 唤醒

wake² (of ship) chuán hángguòhòu de bōlàng 船航过后的波浪; **in the ~ of** fig jǐnjiēzhe 紧接着; **follow in the ~ of X** zhuīsuí X yǐhòu 追随 X 以后

wake-up call huànxǐng diànhuà 唤醒电话

walk 1 n bùxíng 步行; (path) xiǎolù 小路; **it's a long / short ~ to the office** yào hěncháng / hěnduǎn shíjiān zǒu dào bàngōngshì 要很长/很短时间走到办公室; **go for a ~** qù sànbù 去散步 2 v/i zǒu 走; (as opposed to taking the car / bus etc) zǒulù 走路; (hike) chángtú túbù lǚxíng 长途徒步旅行 3 v/t dog liú zōu 遛; **~ the streets** (walk around) zài jiēshang zǒu 在街上走

♦ walk out (of spouse) zǒule 走了; (of room etc) tuìchǎng 退场; (go on strike) bàgōng 罢工

♦ walk out on spouse, family yíqì 遗弃

walker (hiker) túbù lǚxíngzhě 徒步旅行者; (for baby, old person) fúchē 扶车; **be a slow / fast ~** zǒulù màn / kuài de rén 走路慢/快的人

walkie-talkie bùhuàjī 步话机

walk-in closet dàxíng yīguì 大型衣柜

walking (as opposed to driving) zǒulù 走路; (hiking) chángtú

xíngzǒu 长途行走; **be within ~ distance** zài bùxíng jùlí zhīnèi 在步行距离之内

walking stick shǒuzhàng 手杖

walking tour túbù lǚxíng dùjià 徒步旅行度假

Walkman® suíshēntīng 随身听; **walkout** (*strike*) bàgōng 罢工; **walkover** (*easy win*) qīngyì huòdé de shènglì 轻易获得的胜利; **walk-up** n wú diàntī gōngyù 无电梯公寓

wall qiáng 墙; *fig* (*of silence etc*) sì qiángbì zhīwù 似墙壁之物; **go to the ~** (*of company*) pòchǎn 破产

wallet qiánbāo 钱包

wallop F **1** n (*blow*) zhòngjī 重击 **2** v/t měngdǎ 猛打; *opponent* dǎbài 打败

wallpaper 1 n bìzhǐ 壁纸 **2** v/t tiē bìzhǐ 贴壁纸

Wall Street Huá'ěrjiē 华尔街

walnut hétáo 核桃

waltz n huá'ěrzīwǔ 华尔兹舞

wan *face* cāngbái 苍白

wander v/i (*roam*) mànbù 漫步; (*stray*) zǒusàn 走散; (*of attention*) zǒushén 走神
♦ **wander around** mànyóu 漫游

wane (*of interest, enthusiasm*) jiǎnruò 减弱

wangle v/t yòng guǐjì huòdé 用诡计获得

want 1 n (*need*) xūyào 需要; **for ~ of** yīn quēfá 因缺乏 **2** v/t yào yào 要; (*need*) xūyào 需要; **~ to do X** xiǎngzuò X 想做 X; **I ~ to stay here** wǒ xiǎng dāi zài zhèr 我想待在这儿; **do you ~ to come too? – no, I don't ~ to** nǐ yě xiǎnglái ma? – bù, wǒ bù xiǎng 你也想来吗？- 不，我不想; **you can have whatever you ~** nǐ yào shénme dōu xíng 你要什么都行; **it's not what I ~ed** zhè búshì wǒ xiǎngyàode 这不是我想要的; **she ~s you to go back** tā yào nǐ huíqù 她要你回去; **he ~s a haircut** tā děi jiǎn tóufà 他得剪头发 **3** v/i: **~ for nothing** shénme

yě bùqù 什么也不缺

want ad suǒqiú guǎnggào 索求广告

wanted (*by police*) bèi tōngjī 被通缉

wanting: be ~ in qiànqù 欠缺

wanton adj zìyì 恣意

war n zhànzhēng 战争; **be at ~** chǔyú jiāozhàn zhuàngtài 处于交战状态

warble v/i (*of bird*) wǎnzhuǎnde jiào 婉转地叫

♦ **ward off** bìkāi 避开

warden (*of prison*) jiānguǎnrén 监管人

wardrobe (*for clothes*) yīguì 衣柜; (*clothes*) yīwù 衣物

warehouse cāngkù 仓库

warfare zhànzhēng 战争; **warhead** dàntóu 弹头; **warlord** jūnfá 军阀

warily jǐngtì 警惕

warm 1 adj nuǎnhuo 暖和; *welcome, smile* rèqíng 热情 **2** v/t shǐ nuǎnrè 使暖热
♦ **warm up 1** v/t rè 热 **2** v/i (*of person*) rèshēn 热身; (*of room, soup*) rèqǐlái 热起来; (*of athlete etc*) zhǔnbèi liànxí 准备练习

warmhearted rèxīncháng 热心肠

warmly *dressed* nuǎnhuo 暖和; *welcome, smile* rèqíng 热情

warmth wēnnuǎn 温暖; (*of welcome, smile*) rèqíng 热情

warn jǐnggào 警告

warning n jǐnggào 警告; **without ~** méiyǒu jǐnggào 没有警告

warp 1 v/t *wood* shǐ wānqū 使弯曲; *character* shǐ fáncháng 使反常 **2** v/i (*of wood*) qiáoleng 翘棱

warped *fig* fǎncháng 反常

warplane zhàndòujī 战斗机

warranty (*guarantee*) bǎodān 保单; **be under ~** zài bǎoxiūqī nèi 在保修期内

warrior wǔshì 武士

warship jūnjiàn 军舰

wart yóu 疣

wartime zhànshí 战时

wary jǐnshèn 谨慎;*be ~ of* jǐnfáng 谨防

wash 1 n xǐdí 洗涤;*have a ~* xǐyixǐ 洗一洗;*that jacket / shirt needs a ~* děi xǐyīxià nàjiàn jiákè / chènshān 得洗一下那件夹克 / 衬衫 2 v/t & v/i xǐ 洗

♦wash up (*wash one's hands and face*) xǐyīxǐ 洗一洗

washable kěxǐ 可洗

washbasin, washbowl liǎnpén 脸盆

washcloth máojīn 毛巾

washed out jīnpílìjìn 筋疲力尽

washer (*for faucet etc*) diànquān 垫圈; (*washing machine*) xǐyījī 洗衣机

washing xǐde yīwù 洗的衣物;*do the ~* xǐ yīfu 洗衣服

washing machine xǐyījī 洗衣机

Washington Huáshèngdùn 华盛顿

washroom guànxǐshì 盥洗室

wasp (*insect*) huángfēng 黄蜂

waste 1 n làngfèi 浪费; (*from industrial process*) fèiwù 废物;*it's a ~ of time / money* zhēnshì làngfèi shíjiān / jīnqián 真是浪费时间 / 金钱 2 adj fèiqì 废弃 3 v/t làngfèi 浪费

♦waste away shuāiruò 衰弱

wasteful huīhuò 挥霍

wasteland fèixū 废墟; wastepaper fèizhǐ 废纸; wastepaper basket fèizhǐlǒu 废纸篓; waste product fèipǐn 废品

watch 1 n (*timepiece*) shǒubiǎo 手表; *keep ~* fàngshào 放哨 2 v/t movie, TV kàn 看; (*spy on*) jiānshì 监视; (*look after*) zhàokàn 照看 3 v/i kàn 看

♦watch for shǒuhòu 守候

♦watch out xiǎoxīn 小心;*~!* xiǎoxīn! 小心!

♦watch out for (*be careful of*) dāngxīn 当心

watchful jǐngtì 警惕

watchmaker zhōngbiǎo jiàng 钟表匠

water 1 n shuǐ 水; *~s* NAUT lǐnghǎi 领海 2 v/t plant jiāo 浇 3 v/i (*of eyes*) liúlèi 流泪; *my mouth is ~ing* wǒ zài liú kǒushuǐ 我在流口水

♦water down drink xīshì 稀释

water chestnut gāncǎo lìzi 甘草栗子; watercolor shuǐcǎi 水彩; waterfall pùbù 瀑布

watering can jiāoshuǐtǒng 浇水筒

water level shuǐwèi 水位; waterlogged jìnmǎnshuǐ 浸满水; watermelon xīguā 西瓜; waterproof adj fángshuǐ 防水; waterside n shuǐbiān 水边; *at the ~* zài shuǐbiān 在水边; waterskiing huáshuǐ 滑水; watertight compartment búlòushuǐ 不漏水; waterway shuǐlù 水路

watery duōshuǐ 多水

watt wǎtè 瓦特

wave[1] n (*in sea*) bōlàng 波浪

wave[2] 1 n (*of hand*) zhìyì 致意 2 v/i (*with hand*) huīshǒu 挥手; *to X* xiàng X huīshǒu 向 X 挥手 3 v/t flag etc huīwǔ 挥舞

wavelength RAD bōcháng 波长; *be on the same ~* fig yìqù xiāng-tóu 意趣相投

waver dòngyáo 动摇

wavy hair, line bōfú 波状

wax n (*for floor, furniture*) là 蜡; (*in ear*) ěrgòu 耳垢

way 1 n (*method*) fāngfǎ 方法; (*of behaving etc*) fāngshì 方式; (*route*) lùxiàn 路线; *this ~* (*like this*) zhèyàng 这样; (*in this direction*) zhètiáolù 这条路; *by the ~* (*incidentally*) shùnbiàn wènyíxià 顺便问一下; *by ~ of* (*via*) jīngyóu 经由; (*in the form of*) zuòwéi 作为; *in a ~* (*in certain respects*) zài yìdìng chéngdùshang 在一定程度上; *be under ~* zài jìnxíngzhōng 在进行中; *give ~* MOT rànglù 让路; (*collapse*) tāntā 坍塌; *give ~ to X* (*be replaced by*) yóu X dàitì 由 X 代替; *have one's*

(*own*) ~ zìzhǔ xíngshì 自主行事;
OK, we'll do it your ~ hǎoba,
wǒmen àn nǐde fāngfǎ zuò 好吧，
我们按你的方法做; *lead the* ~
yǐnlù 引路; *lose one's* ~ mílù 迷
路; *be in the* ~ (*be an obstruction*)
dǎnglù 挡路; *it's on the* ~ *to the*
station tā jiù zài qù chēzhàn de
lùshang 它就在去车站的路上;
I was on my ~ *to the station* wǒ
zhèng zài qù chēzhàn de lù shang
我正在去车站的路上; *no* ~!
juéduì bù! 绝对不!; *there's no*
~ *he can do it* tā gēnběn bùnéng
zuò 他根本不能做 2 *adv* F
(*much*) yuǎnyuǎn 远远; *it's* ~ *too*
soon to decide xiànzài zuò
juédìng háishì tàizǎo 现在作决
定还是太早; *they are* ~ *behind*
with their work tāmende gōngzuò
yuǎnyuǎnde làzài hòumian 他们
的工作远远地落在后面

way in rùkǒu 入口; **way of life**
shēnghuó fāngshì 生活方式;
way out n chūkǒu 出口; *fig* (*from*
situation) chūlù 出路

we wǒmen 我们

weak tea, coffee dàn dàn 淡; *govern-*
ment, *currency* bóruò 薄弱;
(*physically*) xūruò 虚弱; (*morally*)
ruǎnruò 软弱

weaken 1 *v/t* xūruò 削弱 **2** *v/i*
biànruò 变弱

weakling (*morally*) ruòzhě 弱者;
(*physically*) tǐruò de rén 体弱的
人

weakness ruòdiǎn 弱点; *have a* ~
for X (*liking*) piān'ài X 偏爱 X

wealth cáifù 财富; *a* ~ *of* dàliàng
大量

wealthy fùyǒu 富有

weapon wǔqì 武器

wear 1 n: ~ (*and tear*) sǔnhào 损
耗; *clothes for everyday/evening*
~ rìjiān/wǎnyànfú 日间/晚宴服
2 *v/t* (*have on*) chuān 穿; (*damage*)
yònghuài 用坏 **3** *v/i* (*of carpet*,
fabric: *wear out*) mósǔn 磨损;
(*last*) nàiyòng 耐用

◆**wear away 1** *v/i* mósǔn 磨损
2 *v/t* chōngshí 冲蚀

◆**wear off** (*of effect*, *feeling*) xiāoshī
消失

◆**wear out 1** *v/t* (*tire*) shǐ pífá 使疲
乏; *shoes* yònghuài 用坏 **2** *v/i* (*of*
shoes, *carpet*) yòngjiù 用旧

wearing (*tiring*) shǐrén kùnfá 使人
困乏

weary kùnfá 困乏

weather 1 n tiānqì 天气; *be feel-*
ing under the ~ gǎndào bùshūfu
感到不舒服 **2** *v/t crisis* jīnglì 经
历

weather-beaten bǎo jīng fēngshuāng 饱经风霜; **weather**
forecast tiānqì yùbào 天气预
报; **weatherman** qìxiàng yùbàoyuán 气象预报员

weave 1 *v/t* biānzhī 编织 **2** *v/i*
(*move*) yūhuí xíngjìn 迂回行进

web (COMPUT, *of spider*) wǎng 网

webbed feet yǒu pǔ de jiǎo 有蹼
的脚

web page wǎngzhǐ 网址

web site wǎngzhǐ 网址, zhàndiǎn
站点

wedding hūnlǐ 婚礼

wedding anniversary jiéhūn
zhōunián 结婚周年; **wedding**
cake hūnlǐ dàngāo 婚礼蛋糕;
wedding day hūnlǐrì 婚礼日;
wedding dress hūnshā 婚纱;
wedding ring jiéhūn jièzhǐ 结婚
戒指

wedge n (*to hold sth in place*) xièzi
楔子; (*of cheese etc*) yījiǎo 一角

Wednesday xīngqīsān 星期三

weed 1 n zácǎo 杂草 **2** *v/t* chúqù
zácǎo 除去杂草

◆**weed out** (*remove*) táotài 淘汰

weedkiller chúcǎojì 除草剂

week xīngqī 星期; *a* ~ *tomorrow*
xiàyīzhōude míngtiān 下一周的
明天

weekday xīngqī yī dào wǔ 星期一
到五

weekend zhōumò 周末; *on the* ~
zhōumò 周末

weekly 1 adj měizhōu yīcì 每周一
次 **2** n (*magazine*) zhōukān 周刊
3 adv měizhōu yīcì 每周一次

weep kūqì 哭泣

weigh 1 *v/t* chēng ... de zhòngliàng 称 ... 的重量 **2** *v/i* cèchū zhòngliàng 测出重量

♦**weigh down: be weighed down with** (with bags) bèi ... yāwān 被 ... 压弯; (with worries) shǐrén jǔsàng 使人沮丧

♦**weigh up** (assess) gūliàng 估量

weight (of person, object) zhòngliàng 重量

weightlifter jǔzhòng yùndòngyuán 举重运动员

weightlifting jǔzhòng 举重

weir yàn 堰

weird guàiyì 怪异

weirdo *n* F gǔguàide rén 古怪的人

welcome 1 *adj* shòu huānyíng 受欢迎; **you're ~!** biékèqi! 别客气！; **you're ~ to try some** suíbiàn chángcháng 随便尝尝 **2** *n* (for guests etc) huānyíng 欢迎; *fig* (to news, proposal) yōnghù 拥护 **3** *v/t* guests etc yíngjiē 迎接; *fig: decision etc* duì ... gǎndào yúkuài 对 ... 感到愉快

weld *v/t* hànjiē 焊接

welder hànjiē gōngrén 焊接工人

welfare jiànkāng 健康; (financial assistance) fúlì jiùjì 福利救济; **be on** ~ jiēshòu fúlì jiùjìjīn 接收福利救济金

welfare check fúlì zhīpiào 福利支票; **welfare state** fúlì guójiā 福利国家; **welfare work** fúlì gōngzuò 福利工作; **welfare worker** fúlì gōngzuò zhě 福利工作者

well[1] *n* (for water, oil) jǐng 井

well[2] **1** *adv* hǎo 好; **as** ~ (too) yě 也; **as** ~ **as** (in addition to) hái 还; **it's just as** ~ **you told me** nǐ gàosu wǒ, shì jiàn hǎoshì 你告诉我，是件好事; **very** ~ (when acknowledging an order) shì shì; (signifying you don't agree with sth but are doing it anyway) hǎoba 好吧; ~, ~! (surprise) yōu, yōu! 呦，呦！; ~ ... (uncertainty, thinking) āi ... 哎 ... **2** *adj*: **be** ~ jiànkāng 健康; **feel** ~ gǎndào jiànkāng 感到

健康; **get** ~ **soon!** zǎorì kāngfù! 早日康复！

well-balanced *person* qíngxù wěndìng 情绪稳定; *meal, diet* yíngyǎng dāpèihǎo 营养搭配好; **well-behaved** xíngwéi guījù 行为规矩; **well-being** jiànkāng 健康; **well-done** *meat* shútòu 熟透; **well-dressed** yīzhuó zhěngjié 衣着整洁; **well-earned** yìngdé 应得; **well-known** zhòngsuǒ zhōuzhī 众所周知; **well-made** zuò-gōnghǎo 做工好; **well-mannered** bīnbīn yǒu lǐ 彬彬有礼; **well-off** fùyù 富裕; **well-read** bóxué 博学; **well-timed** shìshí 适时; **well-to-do** fùyòu 富有; **well-worn** yòngjiù 用旧

west 1 *n* xīmiàn 西面; **the West** (western nations) Xīfāng Guójiā 西方国家; (western part of a country) xībù 西部 **2** *adj* xī 西 **3** *adv* xiàngxī 向西; ~ **of X** X de xībù X 的西部

West Coast (of USA) Xī Hǎi'àn 西海岸

westerly xīfēng 西风

western 1 *adj* zài xībù 在西部; **Western** xīfāng guójiā 西方国家 **2** *n* (movie) xībùpiàn 西部片

Westerner Xīfāngrén 西方人

westernized xīfānghuà 西方化

Western medicine xīyī 西医; (drugs etc) xīyào 西药

West Lake Xīhú 西湖

westward xiàngxī 向西

wet *adj* shī 湿; (rainy) duōyǔ 多雨; "~ **paint**" "yóuqīwèigān" " 油漆未干 "; **be** ~ **through** shītòu 湿透

whack F **1** *n* (blow) zhòngjī 重击 **2** *v/t* jīdǎ 击打

whale jīng 鲸

whaling bǔjīng 捕鲸

wharf mǎtóu 码头

what 1 *pron* shénme 什么; ~ **is that?** nà shì shénme? 那是什么？; ~ **is it?** (what do you want?) zěnmele? 怎么了？; ~? (what do you want?) shénme shì? 什么事？; (what did you say?) shénme?

什么？; (*astonishment*) nǐ shuō shénme? 你说什么？; ~ *about some dinner?* chī diǎnr fàn zěnmeyàng? 吃点儿饭怎么样？; ~ *about heading home?* huíjiābā? 回家吧？; ~ *for?* (*why?*) wèishénme? 为什么？; *so* ~? nà yòu zěnmeyàng? 那又怎么样？ **2** *adj* shénme 什么; ~ *color is the car?* chē shì shénme yánsè? 车是什么颜色？; ~ *university are you at?* nǐ zài nǎge dàxué? 你在哪个大学？

whatever 1 *pron* búlùn shénme 不论什么; (*regardless of*) bùguǎn shénme 不管什么 **2** *adj* rènhé 任何; *you have no reason* ~ *to worry* nǐ gēnběn búyòng dānxīn 你根本不用担心

wheat xiǎomài 小麦

wheedle: ~ *X out of Y* hǒng Y yǐ dédào X 哄Y以得到X

wheel 1 *n* lúnzi 轮子; (*steering* ~) fāngxiàngpán 方向盘 **2** *v/t* bicycle tuī 推 **3** *v/i* (*of birds*) xuánzhuǎn 旋转

♦ **wheel around** zhuǎnshēn 转身

wheelbarrow shǒutuīchē 手推车; **wheelchair** lúnyǐ 轮椅; **wheel clamp** chēlún jiájù 车轮夹具

wheeze *v/i* hūxī yǒu shēngxiǎng 呼吸有声响

when 1 *adv* shénme shíhou 什么时候; ~ *do you go on vacation?* nǐ shénme shíhou qù dùjià? 你什么时候去度假？; *do you remember* ~ *you saw him last?* nǐ jì bu jìde shàngcì jiàndào tā shì shénme shíhou? 你记不记得上次见到他是什么时候？ **2** *conj* dāng ... de shíhou 当 ... 的时候; *I was a child* dāng wǒ shì ge háizi de shíhou 当我是个孩子的时候; *I'll tell her* ~ *I see her* wǒ kànjiàn tā jiù gàosu tā 我看见她就告诉她; *don't interrupt* ~ *I'm talking* wǒ shuōhuà de shíhou, bié dǎduàn wǒ 我说话的时候，别打断我

whenever wúlùn shénme shíhou 无论什么时候

where 1 *adv* nǎr 哪儿; ~ *should I put this?* wǒ bǎ zhèige fàng nǎr? 我把这个放哪儿？; *I can't remember* ~ *I put my glasses* wǒ bújìde bǎ yǎnjìng fàng nǎr le 我不记得把眼镜放哪儿了; *the hotel* ~ *Chairman Mao stayed* Máo Zhǔxí zhùguòde bīnguǎn 毛主席住过的宾馆; *this is* ~ *I used to live* zhè shì wǒ céngjīng zhùguò de dìfāng 这是我曾经住过的地方

whereabouts *adv* nǎli 哪里; ~ *in ... do you live?* nǐjiā zài ... nǎli? 你家在 ... 哪里？

wherever 1 *conj* wúlùn nǎli 无论哪里 **2** *adv* dàodǐ zài nǎli 到底在哪里

whet *appetite* yǐnqǐ 引起

whether shìfǒu 是否

which 1 *adj* nǎyíge 哪一个; ~ *one is yours?* nǎge shì nǐde? 哪个是你的？ **2** *pron* (*interrogative*) nǎge 哪个; (*relative*): *the book* ~ *I bought* wǒ mǎide nèibēn shū 我买的那本书; *the flight* ~ *I missed* wǒ méi gǎnshàng de fēijī 我没赶上的飞机; *take one, it doesn't matter* ~ ná yíge, nǎ yíge dōu kěyǐ 拿一个，哪一个都可以

whichever 1 *adj* rènhé 任何 **2** *pron* wúlùn nǎge 无论哪个

whiff (*smell*) yìgǔ qìwèi 一股气味

while 1 *conj*: ~ ... zài ... shíqí 在 ... 时期; (*although*) suīrán 虽然 **2** *n* shíjiān 时间; *a long* ~ hěncháng shíjiān 很长时间; *for a* ~ yíduàn shíjiān 一段时间; *I'll wait a longer* wǒ zài děng yíhuìr 我再等一会儿

♦ **while away** xiāoyáode dùguò 逍遥地度过

whim tūfā qíxiǎng 突发奇想

whimper 1 *n* wūyèshēng 呜咽声 **2** *v/i* wūyè 呜咽

whine *v/i* (*of dog*) fāchū chángjiàoshēng 发出长叫声; F (*complain*) bàoyuàn 抱怨

whip 1 *n* biānzi 鞭子 **2** *v/t* (*beat*) biāndǎ 鞭打; *cream* jiǎodǎ 搅打;

F (defeat) dǎbài 打败

♦ whip out F (take out) xùnsù náchū 迅速拿出

♦ whip up (arouse) huànqǐ 唤起

whipping (beating) biāndǎ 鞭打; F (defeat) dǎbài 打败

whirl 1 n: my mind is in a ~ wǒde sīxù yípiàn hùnluàn 我的思绪一片混乱 2 v/i xuánzhuǎn 旋转

whirlpool (in river) xuánwō 旋涡; (for relaxation) ànmó yùgāng 按摩浴缸

whirlwind xuànfēng 旋风

whir(r) v/i zuò hūhūshēng 作呼呼声

whisk 1 n (kitchen implement) jiǎodànqì 搅蛋器 2 v/t eggs jiǎobàn 搅拌

♦ whisk away chúqù 除去

whiskers (of man) húzi 胡子; (of animal) xū 须

whiskey, whisky wēishìjìjiǔ 威士忌酒

whisper 1 n ěryǔ 耳语 2 v/i qièqièsīyǔ 窃窃私语 3 v/t dīshēng shuō 低声说

whistle 1 n (sound) kǒushàoshēng 口哨声; (device) shàozi 哨子 2 v/i fā xūxūshēng 发嘘嘘声 3 v/t yòng kǒushào chuī 用口哨吹

white 1 n (color) báisè 白色; (of egg) dànbái 蛋白; (person) báirén 白人 2 adj cāngbái 苍白; person báirén 白人

white-collar worker báilǐng gōngrén 白领工人; White House Bái Gōng 白宫; white lie wú èyì de huǎngyán 无恶意的谎言; white meat báiròu 白肉; white-out (for text) túgǎiyè 涂改液; whitewash 1 n bái túliào 白涂料; fig yǎngài zhēnxiàng 掩盖真相 2 v/t fěnshuā 粉刷; white wine bái pútáojiǔ 白葡萄酒

whittle wood xùchéngxíng 削成形

♦ whittle down xùjiǎn 削减

whiz(z) n: be a ~ at .. F zài ... fāngmiàn chūsè 在 ... 方面出色

♦ whizz by, whizz past (of time, car) fēiguò 飞过

whizzkid F jiāozi 骄子

who ◊ (interrogative) shéi 谁; ~'s that? nà shì shéi? 那是谁？; ~ were you speaking to? nǐ gēn shéi shuōhuà? 你跟谁说话? ◊ (relative) shéi 谁; the man ~ taught me jiāoguò wǒ de nèige rén 教过我的那个人; those ~ can speak Chinese huì jiǎng Zhōngwén de rén 会讲中文的人

whoever wúlùn shì shéi 无论是谁

whole 1 adj zhěnggè 整个; the ~ town / country zhěnggè chéngshì / guójiā 整个城市 / 国家; it's a ~ lot easier / better zhèyàng róngyì / hǎo duō le 这样容易 / 好多了 2 n zhěngtǐ 整体; the ~ of the United States zhěnggè Měiguó 整个美国; on the ~ zǒngde kànlái 总的看来

whole-hearted quánxīn quányì 全心全意; wholesale 1 adj pīfā 批发; fig dàguīmó 大规模 2 adv yǐ pīfājià 以批发价; wholesaler pīfāshāng 批发商; wholesome cùjìn jiànkāng 促进健康

wholly wánquán 完全

whom: ~ did you see? fml nǐ jiànde shì nǎwèi? 你见的是哪位?

whooping cough bǎirìké 百日咳

whore n jìnǚ 妓女

whose 1 pron (interrogative) shéide 谁的; (relative): ~ is this? zhè shì shéide? 这是谁的? ; a country ~ economy is booming yígè jīngjì zhèngzài péngbó fāzhǎn de guójiā 一个经济正在蓬勃发展的国家 2 adj shéide 谁的; ~ bike is that? nà liàng zìxíngchē shì shéide? 那辆自行车是谁的?

why wèishénme 为什么; that's ~ nà jiùshì yuányīn 那就是原因; ~ not? wèishénme bù? 为什么不？; I don't know ~ I said that wǒ bù zhīdào wèishénme nàyàng shuō 我不知道为什么那样说

wicked xié'è 邪恶

wicker téngtiáo 藤条

wicker chair téngyǐ 藤椅

wicket (in station, bank etc) guìtái 柜台

柜台

wide *adj* kuānkuò 宽阔; *experience* fēngfù 丰富; *range* guǎngfàn 广泛; **be 12 yards ~** shí'èr mǎ kuān 十二码宽

wide awake wánquán qīngxǐng 完全清醒

widely *used, known* guǎngfàn 广泛

widen 1 *v/t* jiākuān 加宽 **2** *v/i* biànkuān 变宽

wide-open dàkāi 大开

widespread biànbù 遍布

widow guǎfu 寡妇

widower guānfū 鳏夫

width kuāndù 宽度

wield *weapon* huīdòng 挥动; *power* xíngshǐ 行使

wife ⇩ qīzi 妻子

wig jiǎfà 假发

wiggle *v/t hips* bǎidòng 摆动; *loose screw etc* niǔdòng 扭动

wild 1 *adj animal, flowers* yěshēng 野生; *teenager, party* yěxìng 野性; *(crazy: scheme)* mángmù 盲目; *applause* rèliè 热烈; **be ~ about** *(keen on)* rèzhōng yú 热衷于; **go ~** fēngkuáng huānhū 疯狂欢呼; *(become angry)* biàndé fènnù 变得愤怒; **run ~** *(of children)* zìyóu fàngdàng 自由放荡; *(of plants)* sìchù mànyán 四处蔓延 **2** *n:* **the ~s** huāngyě 荒野

wilderness *(empty place)* huāngyuán 荒原; *(garden)* zhīwù cóngshēng de dìfang 植物丛生的地方

wildfire: spread like ~ fēisù chuánkāi 飞速传开; **wildgoose chase** háowú xīwàng de zhuīxún 毫无希望的追寻; **wildlife** yěshēng niǎoshòu 野生鸟兽

willful *person* gùzhí 固执; *action* gùyì 故意

will¹ *n* LAW yízhǔ 遗嘱

will² *n* *(willpower)* yìzhì 意志

will³: *I ~ let you know tomorrow* míngtiān wǒ huì gàosù nǐ 明天我会告诉你; **~ you be there?** nǐ huì zài nàr ma? 你会在那儿吗？; *I won't be back until late* wǒ hěn wǎn cái néng huílái 我很

晚才能回来; **you ~ call me, won't you?** nǐ huì gěi wǒ dǎ diànhuà, shì ba? 你会给我打电话，是吧？; *I'll pay for this – no you won't* wǒ lái fùkuǎn – nǐ bú yòng fù 我来付款 – 你不用付; **the car won't start** chē qǐdòng bù liǎo 车启动不了; **~ you tell her that …?** nǐ kěyǐ gàosù tā … ma? 你可以告诉她 … 吗？; **~ you have some more tea?** nǐ yàobúyào zài hē yìdiǎn chá? 你要不要再喝一点茶？; **~ you stop that!** déleba! 得了吧！

willing lèyú 乐于

willingly gānxīn qíngyuàn 甘心情愿

willingness yuànyì 愿意

willow liǔshù 柳树

willpower yìzhì 意志力

wilt *v/i* *(of plant)* kūwěi 枯萎

wily jiǎohuá 狡猾

wimp F jiāoqìbāo 娇气包

win 1 *n* shènglì 胜利 **2** *v/t* huòshèng 获胜 **3** *v/i* yíngdé 赢得

wince *v/i* tuìsuō 退缩

wind¹ 1 *n* fēng 风; *(flatulence)* wèichángzhōng de qì 胃肠中的气; **get ~ of …** dédào … de fēngshēng 得到 … 的风声 **2** *v/t:* **be ~ed** qìchuǎnxūxū 气喘嘘嘘

wind² 1 *v/i* *(of path etc)* wānyán wānyán 蜿蜒蜿蜒 **2** *v/t cloth etc* chánrào 缠绕

♦ **wind down 1** *v/t* píngjìng 平静 **2** *v/t car window* yáoxià 摇下; *business* jiǎnchǎn 减产

♦ **wind up 1** *v/t clock* shàng fātiáo 上发条; *car window* yáoshàng 摇上; *speech, presentation, affairs* jiéshù 结束; *company* guānbì 关闭 **2** *v/i* *(finish)* jiéshù 结束; **~ in hospital** zuìzhōng zhùjìn yīyuàn 最终住进医院

windfall *fig* yìwài huòdé 意外获得

winding wānyán 蜿蜒

wind instrument guǎnyuèqì 管乐器

windmill fēngchē 风车

window chuānghu 窗户; COMPUT

shìchuāng 视窗; *in the* ~ (*of store*) chúchuāng 橱窗

windowpane chuāng bōli 窗玻璃; **window-shop**: **go ~ping** liúlǎn chúchuāng 浏览橱窗; **windowsill** chuāngtái 窗台

windshield dǎngfēng bōli 挡风玻璃; **windshield wiper** ⇩ guāshuǐqì 刮水器; **windsurfer** (*person*) fānbǎn yùndòngyuán 帆板运动员; (*board*) fānbǎn 帆板; **windsurfing** fānbǎn yùndòng 帆板运动

windy *weather*, *day* duōfēng 多风; *it's getting* ~ qǐ fēng le 起风了

wine pútaojiǔ 葡萄酒

wine list pútaojiǔ dān 葡萄酒单

wing *n* chìbǎng 翅膀; SP biāncè 边侧

wink 1 *n* zhǎyǎn 眨眼 **2** *v/i* (*of person*) shǐ yǎnsè 使眼色; ~ *at* xiàng ... zhǎyǎn 向 ... 眨眼

winner huòshèng zhě 获胜者

winning *adj* huòshèng 获胜

winning post zhōngdiǎn biāozhù 终点标柱

winnings yíngdéde qián 赢得的钱

winter *n* dōngtiān 冬天

winter sports dōngjì yùndòng 冬季运动

wintry hánlěng 寒冷

wipe *v/t* cā 擦; *tape* mǒdiào 抹掉
♦ **wipe out** (*kill, destroy*) cuīhuǐ 摧毁; *debt* huánqīng 还清

wire (*made of metal*) jīnshǔsī 金属丝; ELEC diànxiàn 电线

wire netting jīnshǔwǎng 金属网

wiring ELEC xiànlù 线路

wiry *person* shòu ér jiēshí 瘦而结实

wisdom zhìhuì 智慧

wisdom tooth zhìyá 智牙

wise yīngmíng 英明

wisecrack *n* fēngliánghuà 风凉话

wise guy *pej* néngnàigěng 能耐梗

wisely *act* míngzhì 明智

wish 1 *n* yuànwàng 愿望; *best ~es* zhùfú 祝福 **2** *v/t* xiǎngyào 想要; *I ~ that ...* yàoshì ... jiù hǎo le 要是 ... 就好了; ~ *X well* zhù

X zǒuyùn 祝 X 走运; *I ~ed him good luck* wǒ zhù tā hǎoyùn 我祝他好运 **3** *v/i*: ~ *for* qídǎo 祈祷

wishful thinking zhǔguān yuànwàng 主观愿望

wishy-washy *person* kōngdòng wúwù 空洞无物; *color* dàn ér wúwèi 淡而无味

wistful kěwàng 渴望

wit (*humor*) jīzhì yōumò 机智幽默; (*person*) jīzhì yōumò de rén 机智幽默的人; *be at one's ~s' end* zhìqióngjìjìn 智穷计尽

witch nǚwū 女巫

with ◊ (*accompanied by, proximity*) hé ... yìqǐ 和 ... 一起; *she came ~ her sister* tā hé tāde mèimei yìqǐ láide 她和她的妹妹一起来的; *I work ~ some very nice people* hé wǒ yìqǐ gōngzuò de rén dōu hěn hǎo 和我一起工作的人都很好; *I live ~ my daughter* wǒ hé wǒ nǚ'ér zhù zài yìqǐ 我和我女儿住在一起; *a meeting ~ the President* yǔ zǒngtǒng huìmiàn 与总统会面; ~ *no money* méiyǒu qián 没有钱; *are you ~ me?* (*do you understand?*) nǐ dǒng wǒde yìsi ma? 你懂我的意思吗? ◊ (*agency*) yòng 用; *decorated ~ flowers* yòng huā zhuāngshì 用花装饰; *write ~ a brush* yòng máobǐ xiězì 用毛笔写字 ◊ (*cause*) yóuyú 由于; *shivering ~ fear* yóuyú kǒngjù ér chàndǒu 由于恐惧而颤抖; ~ *a smile ~ a wave* wēixiàoshe/huīzheshǒu 微笑着/挥着手 ◊ (*possession*) yǒu 有; *the house ~ the red door* yǒu hóng mén de nèige fángzi 有红门的那个房子; *a girl ~ blue eyes* lán yǎnjīng de gūniang 蓝眼睛的姑娘; *we need someone ~ experience* wǒmen xūyào yǒu jīngyàn de rén 我们需要有经验的人

withdraw 1 *v/t* *complaint, application* chèxiāo 撤消; *money from bank* tíqǔ 提取; *troops* chèhuí 撤回 **2** *v/i* (*of competitor*) tuìchū 退出; (*of troops*) chètuì 撤退

withdrawal (*of complaint, application*) chèxiāo 撤消; (*of money*) tíkuǎn 提款; (*of troops*) chètuì 撤退; (*from drugs*) jièdú 戒毒

withdrawal symptoms jièdú shí de zhèngzhuàng 戒毒时的症状

withdrawn *adj person* gūpì 孤僻

wither diāoxiè 凋谢

withhold bù gěi 不给

within *prep* (*in expressions of distance*) bù chāoguò 不超过; (*inside*) zài ... lǐmiàn 在 ... 里面; (*in expressions of time*) zài ... zhīnèi 在 ... 之内; *we kept ~ the budget* wǒmen bǎochí zài yùsuàn zhīnèi 我们保持在预算之内; *~ my power* / *my capabilities* zài wǒde quánlì / nénglì zhīnèi 在我的权力/能力之内; *~ reach* zài shǒubiān 在手边

without méiyǒu 没有; *~ looking* / *asking* méi kàn / wèn 没看/问

withstand jīndézhù 禁得住

witness 1 *n* (*at trial*) zhèngrén 证人; (*of accident, crime*) mùjīzhě 目击者; (*to signature*) jiànzhèngrén 见证人 2 *v/t accident, crime* mùjī 目击; *signature* zuò liánshǔrén 作连署人

witness stand zhèngrénxí 证人席

witticism miàoyǔ 妙语

witty jīzhì 机智

wobble *v/i* yáohuàng 摇晃

wobbly bùwěn 不稳

wok guō 锅

wolf 1 *n* (*animal*) láng 狼; *fig* (*womanizer*) sèláng 色狼 2 *v/t*: *~ (down)* lángtūn hǔyàn 狼吞虎咽

wolf whistle *n* tiǎodòu hūshào 挑逗嘬哨

woman nǚrén 女人

woman doctor nǚ yīshēng 女医生

womanizer sèguǐ 色鬼

woman priest nǚ mùshī 女牧师

womb zǐgōng 子宫

Women's Day Sānbā Fùnǚjié 三八妇女节; **women's lib** fùnǚ jiěfàng 妇女解放; **women's libber** gǔchuī fùnǚ jiěfàng de rén 鼓吹妇女解放的人

wonder 1 *n* (*amazement*) jīngqí 惊奇; *no ~!* nánguài! 难怪！; *it's a ~ that ...* qíguàide shì ... 奇怪的是 ... 2 *v/i* gǎndào jīngyà 感到惊讶 3 *v/t* xiǎng zhīdào 想知道; *I - if you could help* wǒ xiǎng zhīdào nǐ néngbùnéng bāngmáng 我想知道你能不能帮忙

wonderful jíhǎo 极好

wood mù 木; (*forest*) shùlín 树林

wooded zhǎngmǎn shùmù 长满树木

wooden (*made of wood*) mùzhì 木制

woodwind MUS mùzhì guānyuèqì 木制管乐器

woodwork (*parts made of wood*) mùzhìpǐn 木制品; (*activity*) mùgōnghuó 木工活

wool yángmáo 羊毛

woolen 1 *adj* yángmáozhì 羊毛制 2 *n* yángmáo yīwù 羊毛衣物

word 1 *n* cí cí 词; (*news*) xiāoxi 消息; (*promise*) nuòyán 诺言; *is there any ~ from X?* yǒuméiyǒu X de xiāoxi? 有没有 X 的消息？; *you have my ~* wǒ xiàng nǐ bǎozhèng 我向你保证; *have ~s* (*argue*) zhēngchǎo 争吵; *have a ~ with X* yǔ X sīxià tántán 与 X 私下谈谈 2 *v/t article, letter* xuǎncí 选词

wording cuòcí 措辞

word processing wénzì chǔlǐ 文字处理

word processor (*software*) wénzì chǔlǐjī 文字处理机

work 1 *n* gōngzuò 工作; *out of ~* shīyè 失业; *be at ~* shàngbān 上班; *I go to ~ by bus* wǒ zuò gōngchē qù shàngbān 我坐公车去上班 2 *v/i* (*of person*) gōngzuò 工作; (*of machine*) yùnzhuǎn 运转; (*succeed*) zòuxiào 奏效; *I used to ~ with him* wǒ céng hé tā yìqǐ gōngzuò 我曾和他一起工作; *how does it ~?* (*of device*) zhèi dōngxi zěnme yùnzhuǎn? 这东西怎么运转？ 3 *v/t employee* shǐ gōngzuò 使工作; *machine* kāidòng 开动

♦ **work off** *bad mood, anger* xiāochú

消除; *f lab* chúqù 除去

♦ **work out 1** *v/t problem* nòng míngbái 弄明白; *solution* zhǎochū 找出 **2** *v/i (at gym)* dàliàng yùndòng 大量运动; *(of relationship etc)* qǔdé chénggōng 取得成功

♦ **work out to** *(add up to)* zǒngjìwéi 总计为

♦ **work up** *enthusiasm* jīqǐ 激起; *appetite* jīfā 激发; **get worked up** *(get angry)* shēngqì 生气; *(get nervous)* jīnghuāng 惊慌

workable *solution* kěxíng 可行

workaholic *n* F gōngzuòkuáng 工作狂

worker gōngrén 工人; **she's a good ~** *(of student)* tā hěn huì gōngzuò 她很会工作

work day *(hours of work)* gōngzuòrì 工作日; *(not a holiday)* fēi xiūxīrì 非休息日; **workforce** láodònglì 劳动力; **work hours** gōngzuò qíjiān 工作期间

working class *n* gōngrén jiējí 工人阶级

working-class *adj* gōngrén jiējí 工人阶级

working knowledge jīběn zhīshí 基本知识

workload gōngzuòliàng 工作量; **workman** gōngrén 工人; **workmanlike** jìshù xiánshú 技术娴熟; **workmanship** jìyì 技艺; **work of art** jīngzhìde wùpǐn 精致的物品; **workout** duànliàn 锻炼; **work permit** gōngzuò xǔkě 工作许可; **workshop** gōngchǎng 工场; *(seminar)* jiǎngxíbān 讲习班; **work station** gōngzuòzhàn 工作站; **work unit** (gōngzuò) dānwèi（工作）单位

world shìjiè 世界; **the ~ of computers / the theater** diànnǎo / xìjù lǐngyù 电脑 / 戏剧领域; **out of this ~** F hǎo dé bùdéliǎo 好得不得了

worldly shìsú 世俗; *person* lǎochéng liàndá 老成练达

world power shìjiè qiángguó 世界强国; **world war** shìjiè dàzhàn 世

界大战; **worldwide 1** *adj* biànjí shìjiè 遍及世界 **2** *adv* quánshìjiè 全世界

worm *n* chóngzi 虫子

worn-out *shoes, carpet, part* pòjiù 破旧; *person* jīnpílìjìn 筋疲力尽

worried dānyōu 担忧

worry 1 *n* dānyōu 担忧 **2** *v/t* dānxīn 担心; *(upset)* shǐrén yōuchóu 使人忧愁 **3** *v/i* dānyōu 担忧; *it will be alright, don't ~!* méiyǒushì, bié dānxīn! 没有事，别担心！

worrying lìngrén dānxīn 令人担心

worse 1 *adj* gènghuài 更坏 **2** *adv* gèng bùhǎo 更不好

worsen *v/i* biàndé gènghuài 变得更坏

worship 1 *n* chóngbài 崇拜 **2** *v/t* chóngbài 崇拜; *fig* àimù 爱慕

worst 1 *adj* zuìhuài 最坏 **2** *adv* zuìzāo 最糟 **3** *n: the ~* zuìhuài 最坏; *if the ~ comes to the ~* rúguǒ zuì zāogāo de shì fāshēng 如果最糟糕的事发生

worth *adj*: **$20 ~ of gas** jiàzhí wéi èrshí měiyuán de qìyóu 价值为二十美元的汽油; **be ~ ...** *(in monetary terms)* zhí ... zhí ...; **be ~ reading / seeing** zhídé dú / kàn 值得读 / 看; **be ~ it** hěn zhídé 很值得

worthless *object* wú jiàzhí 无价值; *person* méiyòng 没用

worthwhile *cause* zhídé zuò 值得做; **be ~** zhídé 值得

worthy kějìng 可敬; *cause* zhídé zhīchí 值得支持; **be ~ of** *(deserve)* zhídé 值得

would: **I ~ help if I could** rúguǒ wǒ néng de huà, wǒ huì bāngmángde 如果我能的话，我会帮忙的; **I said that I ~ go** wǒ shuōguò wǒ huì qù 我说过我会去; **I told him I ~ not leave unless ...** wǒ gàosù tā, chúfēi ... bùrán wǒ bùhuì zǒu 我告诉他，除非 ... 不然我不会走; **~ you like to go to the movies?** nǐ xiǎng qù kàn diànyǐng ma? 你想去看电影

吗 ？；~ *you mind if I smoked?*
wǒ chōuyān nǐ jièyì ma? 我抽烟
你介意吗？；~ *you tell her that
...?* qǐng nǐ gàosù tā ... hǎoma? 请
你告诉她 ... 好吗？；~ *you
close the door?* qǐng guānshang
mén, hǎoma? 请关上门，好
吗 ？；*I ~ have told you but ...* wǒ
běn yīnggāi gàosù nǐ, dànshì ... 我
本应该告诉你，但是 ...；*I ~
not have been so angry if ...* rúguǒ ... wǒ jiù búhuì nàme shēngqì
如果 ... 我就不会那么生气
wound 1 *n* shāng 伤 2 *v/t* (*with
weapon*) dǎshāng 打伤；(*with
remark*) shānghài 伤害
wow! *interj* āiya! 哎呀！
wrap *v/t parcel, gift* bāo 包；(*wind*)
chánrào 缠绕；(*cover*) bāozhù 包
住
♦ **wrap up** *v/i* (*against the cold*)
chuān nuǎnhuo de yīwù 穿暖和
的衣物
wrapper bāozhuāng zhǐdài 包装
纸袋
wrapping bāozhuāng cáiliào 包装
材料
wrapping paper bāozhuāngzhǐ 包
装纸
wreath huāquān 花圈
wreck 1 *n* cánhái 残骸；*be a
nervous ~* shìge shénjīngzhì 是个
神经质 2 *v/t* huǐhuài 毁坏；*plans,
career, marriage* huǐmiè 毁灭
wreckage (*of car, plane*) cánhái 残
骸；(*of marriage, career*) cánhuǐ
zhuàngtài 残毁状态
wrecker tuōchē 拖车
wrecking company gùzhàng qìchē fúwù gōngsī 故障汽车服务
公司
wrench 1 *n* (*tool*) bānzi 扳子；
(*injury*) niǔshāng 扭伤 2 *v/t*
(*injure*) niǔshāng 扭伤；(*pull*)
měnglā 猛拉
wrestle shuāijiāo 摔跤
♦ **wrestle with** *problems* nǔlì duìfù
努力对付
wrestler shuāijiāo yùndòngyuán
摔跤运动员

wrestling shuāijiāo yùndòng 摔跤
运动
wrestling match shuāijiāo bǐsài 摔
跤比赛
wriggle *v/i* (*squirm*) niǔdòng 扭动；
(*along the ground*) wānyán xíngjìn
蜿蜒行进
♦ **wriggle out of** zhǎo jièkǒu
bìmiǎn 找借口避免
♦ **wring out** *cloth* nínghǔ 拧出
wrinkle 1 *n* zhòuwén 皱纹 2 *v/t*
clothes shǐ qǐ zhòuzhě 使起皱褶
3 *v/i* (*of clothes*) chū zhòuzhě 出皱
褶
wrist shǒuwàn 手腕
wristwatch shǒubiǎo 手表
write *v/t* xiě 写；*check* kāi 开 2 *v/i*
xiě 写；(*of author*) xiězuò 写作；
(*send a letter*) xiěxìn 写信
♦ **write down** xiěxià 写下
♦ **write off** *debt* gōuxiāo 勾销；*car
in crash* shǐ chéng fèipǐn 使成废
品
writer zuòzhě 作者
write-up pínglùn 评论
writhe niǔdòng 扭动
writing (*as career*) xiězuò 写作；
(*hand-writing*) zìjì 字迹；(*words*)
wénzì 文字；(*script*) shūxiě tǐxì 书
写体系；*in ~* yǐ shūmiàn xíngshì
以书面形式
writing brush máobǐ 毛笔
writing paper xìnzhǐ 信纸
wrong 1 *adj* cuòwù 错误；*be ~* (*of
person*) cuòle 错了；(*morally*) bú
duì 不对；*what's ~?* zěnmele? 怎
么了？；*there is something ~
with the car* chē yǒu diǎn máobìng 车有点毛病 2 *adv* cuòwù
错误；*go ~* (*of person*) fàn cuòwù
犯错误；(*of marriage, plan etc*)
chūxiàn wèntí 出现问题 3 *n* bù
gōngzhèng de shì 不公正的事；
be in the ~ yīngshòu zébèi 应受
责备
wrongful bù héfǎ 不合法
wrongly cuòwù 错误
wrong number bōcuòle hàomǎ 拨
错了号码
wry: ~ *smile* kǔxiào 苦笑

XYZ

xenophobia kǒngwài zhèng 恐外症

X-ray 1 *n* X guāng zhàopiàn X 光照片 2 *v/t* zhào X guāng 照 X 光

yacht yóutǐng 游艇

yachting chèng yóutǐng 乘游艇

yachtsman yóutǐng jiàshǐ yuán 游艇驾驶员

yak máoniú 牦牛

Yangtze River Chángjiāng 长江

Yank F Měiguó Lǎo 美国佬

yank *v/t* měnglā 猛拉

yap *v/i* (*of small dog*) wāngwang jiào 汪汪叫; F (*talk a lot*) guālā guālā 呱啦呱啦

yard¹ (*of prison, institution etc*) fàngfēng chǎng 放风场; (*behind house*) yuànzi 院子; (*for storage*) duīchǎng 堆场

yard² (*measurement*) mǎ mǎ 码

yardstick *fig* héngliáng biāozhǔn 衡量标准

yarn *n* (*thread*) shāxiàn 纱线; F (*story*) qítán 奇谈

yawn *n* hēqiàn 呵欠 2 *v/i* dǎ hēqiàn 打呵欠

year nián 年; *for ~s* F xǔduō nián 许多年; *we were in the same ~* (*at school*) wǒmen shì tóngjí de wǒmen shì tóngjí de 我们是同级的; *~ of the tiger/dog* hǔ/gǒu nián 虎/狗年; *be born in the ~ of the ...* shǔ ... 属 ...; *I was born in the ~ of the dragon* wǒ shǔ lóng 我属龙

yearly *adj & adv* měinián 每年

yearn *v/i* kěwàng 渴望

♦yearn for kěwàng 渴望

yearning *n* xiàngwǎng 向往

yeast xiàomǔ 酵母

yell 1 *n* jiàohǎn 叫喊 2 *v/i* rāngrang 嚷嚷 3 *v/t* dàjiào 大叫

yellow 1 *n* huángsè 黄色 2 *adj* huáng 黄

Yellow Emperor Huángdì 黄帝; yellow pages huángyè 黄页; Yellow River Huánghé 黄河; Yellow Sea Huánghǎi 黄海

yelp *n & v/i* jiānjiào 尖叫

yen FIN rìyuán 日元

yes shìde 是的; *are you Mr Wang?* - ~ nín shì Wáng xiānsheng ma? - shìde 您是王先生吗？- 是的 ◊ (*repetition of verb etc*): *are you cold?* - ~ nǐ lěng bu lěng? - lěng 你冷不冷？- 冷; *do you like it here?* - ~ nǐ xǐhuan zhèr ma? - xǐhuan 你喜欢这儿吗？- 喜欢 ◊ (*showing agreement*) duì 对; *he should go* - ~ tā yīnggāi qù - duì 他应该去 - 对 ◊ (*accepting suggestion*) xíng 行; *let's go see a movie* - ~ zánmen qù kàn diànyǐng ba - xíng 咱们去看电影吧 - 行

yesman *pej* zǒugǒu 走狗

yesterday zuótiān 昨天; *the day before* ~ qiántiān 前天

yet 1 *adv* qìjīn 迄今; *as* ~ dàocǐ wéizhǐ 到此为止; *have you finished* ~? nǐ wánle méiyǒu? 你完了没有？; *he hasn't arrived* ~ tā hái méidào ne 他还没到呢; *is he here* ~? - *not* ~ tā láile ma? - méine 他来了吗？- 没呢 2 *conj*: ~ *I'm not sure* kěshì wǒ háishi bù kěndìng 可是我还是不肯定

yield 1 *n* (*from fields etc*) chǎnliàng 产量; (*from investment*) lìrùn 利润 2 *v/t fruit, good harvest* chūchǎn 出产; *interest* shēngxī 生息 3 *v/i* (*to enemy*) tóuxiáng 投降; (*to wish*) dāying 答应; (*of traffic*) rànglù 让路

yogurt suānnǎi 酸奶

yoke (*for carrying*) biǎndan 扁担; (*for oxen*) è 轭

yolk dànhuáng 蛋黄

you (*singular*) nǐ 你; (*plural*) nǐmen 你们; (*polite*) nín 您 (*polite plural, rare*) nínmen 您们; **~ never know** shéi zhīdào 谁知道; **it's good for ~** duì nǐ yǒu hǎochù 对你有好处

young *person* niánqīng 年青; *wine* wèi chéngsh óu 未成熟

youngster qīngshàonián 青少年

your (*singular*) nǐde 你的; (*plural*) nǐmende 你们的; (*polite singular*) nínde 您的; (*polite plural*) nínmende 您们的

yours (*singular*) nǐde 你的; (*plural*) nǐmende 你们的; (*polite singular*) nínde 您的; (*polite plural*) nínmende 您们的; yǒngyuǎn shì nǐde 永远是你的; **a friend of ~** nǐde péngyǒu 你的朋友

yourself nǐ zìjǐ 你自己; **by ~** nǐ zìjǐ dúzì 你自己独自

yourselves nǐmen zìjǐ 你们自己; **by ~** nǐmen zìjǐ 你们自己

youth (*age*) qīngchūn niándài 青春年代; (*young man*) xiǎo huǒzi 小伙子; (*young people*) qīngshào nián 青少年

youthful *fashion, ideas* shìyú qīngnián 适于青年; *person* zhāoqì péngbó 朝气蓬勃

youth hostel qīngnián zhāodàisuǒ 青年招待所

yuan (*Chinese money*) yuán 元

Yuan Dynasty Yuán Cháo 元朝

zap *v/t* COMPUT (*delete*) xiāochú 消除; F (*kill*) shāsǐ 杀死; F (*hit*) kuàijī 快击

♦**zap along** F (*move fast*) kuàisù jìnxíng 快速进行

zapped F (*exhausted*) jīngpí lìjìn 筋疲力尽

zappy F *car, pace* kuài 快; (*lively,*

energetic) jīnglì chōngpèi 精力充沛

zeal rèxīn 热心

zebra bānmǎ 斑马

Zen Chán 禅

Zen Buddhism Chánzōng Fójiào 禅宗佛教

zero líng 零; **10 below ~** língxià shídù 零下十度

zero growth wú zēngzhǎng 无增长

♦**zero in on** (*identify*) xiàng ... jízhōng zhùyì lì xiàng ... 集中注意力

zest rèqíng 热情

zigzag 1 *n* qūzhé xiàntiáo 曲折线条 **2** *v/i* qūzhé xíngjìn 曲折行进

zilch F yīwú suǒyǒu 一无所有

zinc xīn 锌

♦**zip up** *v/t dress, jacket* lā lālián 拉拉链; COMPUT yāsuō 压缩

zip code yóuzhèng biānmǎ 邮政编码

zip drive COMPUT yāsuō qūdòngqì 压缩驱动器

zipper lālián 拉链

zodiac huángdào dài 黄道带; **signs of the ~** huángdào shí'èr gōngtú 黄道十二宫图

zombie F (*idiot*) mùdāidai de rén 木呆呆的人; **feel like a ~** (*exhausted*) kuǎle kuǎ了

zone qū 区

zoo dòngwù yuán 动物园

zoological dòngwù xué 动物学

zoology dòngwù xué 动物学

zoom F (*move fast*) jísù xíngshǐ 急速行驶

♦**zoom in** COMPUT fàngdà 放大

♦**zoom in on** PHOT lājìn 拉近

♦**zoom out** COMPUT suōxiǎo 缩小

zoom lens kěbiàn jiāojù jìngtóu 可变焦距镜头

Taiwanese equivalents

This list contains a selection of mainland Chinese words in the first Chinese column and, in the second Chinese column, equivalents which are more likely to be used in Taiwan. The Taiwanese words are written in traditional characters. It should be said that there is a good deal of linguistic interaction between the two language groups.

ace (*in cards*)	jiānr 尖儿	A A
adhesive plaster	chuàngkětiē 创可贴	OK bèng OK绷
aerobics	zēng yǎng jiànshēn fǎ 增氧健身法	yǒuyǎng wǔdǎo 有氧舞蹈
afternoon: good afternoon	xiàwǔ hǎo 下午好	wǔ'ān 午安
air conditioning	kōngtiáo 空调	lěngqì 冷气
ankle	jiǎowàn 脚腕	jiǎohuái 脚踝
answerphone	lùyīn diànhuà 录音电话	diànhuà dálùjī 电话答录机
awesome F	gàilemàole 盖了帽了	kùbile 酷毙了
ballpoint (pen)	yuánzhū bǐ 圆珠笔	yuánzǐbǐ 原子笔
Band-Aid®	chuàngkětiē 创可贴	OK bèng OK绷
bar code	tiáoxíng mǎ 条形码	tiáomǎ 条码
barbecue *n*	shāokǎo huì 烧烤会	kǎoròu 烤肉
bicycle *n*	zìxíng chē 自行车	jiǎotàchē 脚踏车
blood donor	xiànxuè zhě 献血者	juānxiěrén 捐血人
burglar alarm	fángqiè jǐngbào qì 防窃警报器	fángdàoqì 防盗器 防窃警报器
butter *n*	huángyóu 黄油	nǎiyóu 奶油
cell phone	shǒutí diànhuà 手提电话	xíngdòng diànhuà 行动电话
check out (*of hotel*)	jiézhàng 结账	tuìfáng 退房
checkout time	jiézhàng shíjiān 结账时间	tuìfáng shíjiān 退房时间
cheese	nǎilào 奶酪	rǔluò 乳酪, qǐshì 黄鹑
cheesecake	nǎilào nàngāo 奶酪蛋糕	qǐshì dàngāo 起士蛋糕
chips	shǔpiàn 薯片	yángyùpiàn 洋芋片
college exam	gāokǎo 高考	liánkǎo 联考
condom	bìyùn tào 避孕套	bǎoxiǎntào 保险套
connecting flight	liányùn fēijī 联运飞机	zhuǎnjiē bānjī 转接班机
container COM	jízhuāng xiāng 集装箱	huòguì 货柜
container ship	jízhuāng xiāng chuán 集装箱船	huòguìchuán 货柜船
corkscrew	luósī qǐzi 螺丝起子	luósī kāijiǔqì 螺丝开酒器
crosswalk	rénxíng héngdào 人行横道	xíngrén chuānyuèdào 行人穿越道
cursor	guāngbiāo 光标	yóubiāo 游标

deodorant	chúxiù jì 除臭剂	fángchòujì 防臭剂
desktop	táishìjī 台式机	zhuōshàngxíng
computer		diànnǎo 桌上型电脑
disco(theque)	dítīng 迪厅	díshìkě 迪士可
(*place*)		
disk COMPUT	cípán 磁盘	cídiépiàn 磁碟片
disk drive	cípán dàijī 磁盘带机	cídiéjī 磁碟机
diskette	ruǎn cípán 软磁盘	cídiépiàn 磁碟片
donut	zhá miànbǐngquān 炸面饼圈	tiántiánquān 甜甜圈
dress *n*	liányīqún 连衣裙	yángzhuāng 洋装
(*for woman*)		
driving school	jiàshǐ xuéxiào 驾驶学校	jiàxùn zhōngxīn
		驾训中心
duplex	èrliánshì gōngyù	shuāngpīn gōngyù
(*apartment*)	二连式公寓	双拼公寓
DVD	shùzì shìpín guāngpán	shùwèi xiǎnshì guāngdié
	数字视频光盘	数位显示光碟
epicenter	zhènzhōng 震中	zhènyāng 震央
feedback	fǎnkuì xìnxī 反馈信息	huíkuì 回馈
feminism	nǚquán zhǔyì 女权主义	nǚxìngzhǔyì 女性主义
feminist	nǚquán zhǔyì zhě	nǚxìngzhǔyì zhě
	女权主义者	女性主义者
floppy (disk)	ruǎnpán 软盘	cídiépiàn 磁碟片
folk dance	mínjiānwǔ 民间舞	mínsú wǔdǎo 民俗舞蹈
garbage	lājī 垃圾	lèsè 垃圾
gin and tonic	kuíníng dùsōngzǐjiǔ	qínjiǔ jiā kuíníngshuǐ
	奎宁杜松子酒	琴酒加奎宁
Gobi Desert	Gēbìtān 戈壁滩	Gēbì dàshāmò
		戈壁大沙漠
hamburger	hànbǎobāo 汉堡包	hànbǎo 汉堡
hard currency	yìngtōnghuò 硬通货	qiángshì huòbì 强势货币
hard disk	yìngpán 硬盘	yìngdié 硬碟
highlighter (*pen*)	cǎibǐ 彩笔	yíngguāngbǐ 萤光笔
instant noodles	fāngbiànmiàn 方便面	pàomiàn 泡麵
junk food	kuàicān 快餐	lèsè shíwù 垃圾食物
Laos	Lǎowō 老挝	Liáoguó 寮国
laptop COMPUT	xiédài shì diànnǎo	bǐjìxíng diànnǎo
	携带式电脑	笔计型电脑
Mandarin	Pǔtōnghuà 普通话	Guóyǔ 国语
(*language*)		
mayo,	dànhuángjiàng 蛋黄酱	měinǎizī 美奶滋
mayonnaise		
MBA	gōngshāng guǎnlǐxué	qǐguǎn shuòshì
	shuòshì 工商管理学硕士	企管硕士
Mount Everest	Zhūmùlǎngmǎfēng	Shèngmǔfēng 圣母峰
	珠穆朗玛峰	
mouse COMPUT	shǔbiāo 鼠标	huáshǔ 滑鼠

New Zealand	Xīnxīlán 新西兰	Niǔxīlán 纽西兰
North Korea	Běicháoxiān 北朝鲜	Běi Hán 北韩
orange juice	chéngzhī 橙汁儿	liǔchéngzhī 柳橙汁
page (call)	chuánhū 传呼	dǎ hūjiàoqì 打呼叫器
pager	chuánhūjī 传呼机	hūjiàoqì 呼叫器
pineapple	bōluó 菠萝	fènglí 凤梨
platform RAIL	zhàntái 站台	yuètái 月台
pool (game)	pǔ'ěrdànzìxì 普尔弹子戏	zhuàngqiú 撞球
potato chips	zháshǔpiàn 炸薯片	yángyùpiàn 洋芋片
printer (machine)	dǎyìnjī 打印机	yìnbiǎojī 印表机
project (housing area)	tǒngjiàn zhùzháiqū 统建住宅区	guózhái 国宅
pump n	bèng 泵	(for water) chōushuǐjī 抽水机; (for air) dǎqìtǒng 打气筒
salad	sèlā 色拉	shālā 沙拉
salad dressing	sèlā tiáowèizhī 色拉调味汁	shālājiàng 沙拉酱
sauna	zhēngqìyù 蒸汽浴	sānwēnnuǎn 三温暖
scalper	piàofànzi 票贩子	mài huángniúpiàode rén 卖黄牛票的人
silicon	guī 硅	xì 矽
silicon chip	guīpiàn 硅片	xìpiàn 矽片
slot machine (for vending)	tóubìshòuhuòjī 投币售货机	zìdòng fànmàijī 自动贩卖机
smart card	shuākǎ 刷卡	cōngmíngkǎ 聪明卡
snooker	táiqiú 台球	sīnuòkè 斯诺克
solitaire (card game)	dānrén zhǐpái xì 单人纸牌戏	jiēlóng 接龙
space shuttle	hángtiān fēijī 航天飞机	tàikōngsuō 太空梭
speed limit	sùdù jíxiàn 速度极限	sùdù xiànzhì 速度限制
tampon	yuèjīng shuān 月经栓	wèishēngmiántiáo 卫生棉条
taxi	chūzūchē 出租车	jìchéngchē 计程车
teamwork	pèihé 配合	tuánduì jīngshén 团队精神
tissue paper	báozhǐ 薄纸	miànzhǐ 面纸
tonic (water)	tānglìshuǐ 汤力水	kuíníngshuǐ 奎宁水
tractor	tuōlājī 拖拉机	qiānyǐnjī 牵引机
T-shirt	yuánlǐng shān 圆领衫	T xuè T恤
Velcro®	zhānkòu 粘扣	móshùtiē 魔术贴
wife	qīzi 妻子	tàitai 太太, lǎopó 老婆
windshield wiper	guāshuǐqì 刮水器	yǔshuā 雨刷

Numbers

0	〇 líng
1	一 yī
2	二 èr *or* liǎng*
3	三 sān
4	四 sì
5	五 wǔ
6	六 liù
7	七 qī
8	八 bā
9	九 jiǔ
10	十 shí
11	十一 shíyī
12	十二 shí'ér
13	十三 shísān *etc*
20	二十 èrshì
30	三十 sānshí
40	四十 sìshí *etc*
21	二十一 èrshíyī
35	三十五 sānshíwǔ
99	九十九 jiǔshíjiǔ
100	百 bǎi
105	一百零五 yìbǎi líng wǔ
300	三百 sānbǎi
350	三百五十 sānbǎi wǔshí
356	三百五十六 sānbǎi wǔshíliù
1,000	千 qiān
1,005	一千零五 yìqiān líng wǔ
1,050	一千零五十 yìqiān líng wǔshí
5,300	五千三百 wǔqiān sānbǎi
10,000	万 wàn
65,300	六万五千三百 liùwàn wǔqiān sānbǎi
100,000	十万 shíwàn

1,000,000	百万 bǎiwàn
10,000,000	千万 qiānwàn
100,000,000	万万 wànwàn
100,000,000	亿 yì

The following more complex characters are also used on bills, checks etc.

0	零 líng
1	壹 yī
2	贰 èr
3	叁 sān
4	肆 sì
5	伍 wǔ
6	陆 liù
7	柒 qī
8	捌 bā
9	玖 jiǔ
10	拾 shí
100	佰 bǎi
1,000	仟 qiān

Ordinal numbers

Ordinal numbers are formed by putting **dì** in front of the cardinal numbers:

1	一 yī
1st	第一 dìyī
2	二 èr
2nd	第二 dì'èr
3	三 sān
3rd	第三 dìsān
	etc

* **liǎng** is used when the number two is used in combination with a measure word.